P9-BZG-329

Saint Joseph Pocket Edition of
THE
NEW TESTAMENT

Our Lord and Savior Jesus Christ

Saint Joseph Pocket Edition of the

NEW TESTAMENT

in the

NEW CATHOLIC VERSION

•

Illustrated

WITH HELPFUL FORMAT AND BIBLE AIDS

Dedicated to Saint Joseph
Patron of the Universal Church

CATHOLIC BOOK PUBLISHING CORP.
New Jersey

NIHIL OBSTAT: Fr. Oscar Alunday, SVD
Censor Librorum

IMPRIMATUR: ✣ Most Rev. Arturo M. Bastes, SVD, DD
*Chairman, Episcopal Commission on the
Biblical Apostolate*

RESCRIPT

In accord with Canon 825, par. 1 of the Code of Canon Law, the Catholic Bishops' Conference of the Philippines hereby approves for publication *The New Testament Books of the St. Joseph New Catholic Version*, published by Catholic Book Publishing Corporation. This translation of the New Testament is intended for private use and study only and may never be used for liturgical purposes.

_____

The text of *The New Testament, New Catholic Version* (NCV) may be quoted and/or reprinted up to and inclusive of two hundred (200) verses without express written permission of the publisher, provided that the verses quoted do not account for 50 percent or more of the total work in which they are quoted.

Notice of copyright must appear on the title or copyright page of the work as follows:

"Scripture taken from THE NEW TESTAMENT, NEW CATHOLIC VERSION®. Copyright © 2015 by Catholic Book Publishing Corp. Used by permission. All rights reserved."

When quotations from the NCV text are used in non-saleable media, such as church bulletins, orders of service, posters, transparencies or similar media, a complete copyright notice is not required, but the initials (NCV) must appear at the end of each quotation.

(T-630)

© 2016 CATHOLIC BOOK PUBLISHING CORP., N.J.

Printed in Korea

www.catholicbookpublishing.com

CONTENTS

5

ABBREVIATIONS OF BOOKS OF THE BIBLE

Acts—Acts of the Apostles
Am—Amos
Bar—Baruch
1 Chr—1 Chronicles
2 Chr—2 Chronicles
Col—Colossians
1 Cor—1 Corinthians
2 Cor—2 Corinthians
Dan—Daniel
Deut—Deuteronomy
Eccl—Ecclesiastes
Eph—Ephesians
Est—Esther
Ex—Exodus
Ezek—Ezekiel
Ezr—Ezra
Gal—Galatians
Gen—Genesis
Hab—Habakkuk
Hag—Haggai
Heb—Hebrews
Hos—Hosea
Isa—Isaiah
Jas—James
Jdg—Judges
Jer—Jeremiah
Jn—John
1 Jn—1 John
2 Jn—2 John
3 Jn—3 John
Job—Job
Joel—Joel
Jon—Jonah
Jos—Joshua
Jud—Judith
Jude—Jude
1 Ki—1 Kings

2 Ki—2 Kings
Lam—Lamentations
Lev—Leviticus
Lk—Luke
1 Mac—1 Maccabees
2 Mac—2 Maccabees
Mal—Malachi
Mic—Micah
Mk—Mark
Mt—Matthew
Nah—Nahum
Neh—Nehemiah
Num—Numbers
Ob—Obadiah
1 Pet—1 Peter
2 Pet—2 Peter
Phil—Philippians
Philem—Philemon
Prov—Proverbs
Ps(s)—Psalms
Rev—Revelation
Rom—Romans
Ru—Ruth
1 Sam—1 Samuel
2 Sam—2 Samuel
Sir—Wisdom of Ben Sira
Song—Song of Songs
1 Thes—1 Thessalonians
2 Thes—2 Thessalonians
1 Tim—1 Timothy
2 Tim—2 Timothy
Tit—Titus
Tob—Tobit
Wis—Wisdom
Zec—Zechariah
Zep—Zephaniah

PREFACE

In the words of the *Catechism of the Catholic Church*, "The Word of God, which is the power of God for salvation to everyone who has faith, is set forth and displays its power in a most wonderful way in the writings of the New Testament which hand on the ultimate truth of God's Revelation. Their central object is Jesus Christ, God's incarnate Son: his acts, teachings, Passion and glorification, and his Church's beginnings under the Spirit's guidance" (no. 124).

Hence, in the life of Christians there can never be too many translations of the New Testament. It is a well-known fact that different translations are able to bring out nuances of meaning specific to each one. The New Testament is so full of meaning that we can rightly say no single translation will do it justice.

Accordingly, it has become customary for Christians to make use of many translations of the sacred books in order to discover the riches of the New Testament and pray with its text. In doing so they are carrying out the recommendation of the Bishops of the United States:

"What is most necessary of all is that we begin . . . to meet with Christ as he speaks to us through the liturgical rites and the inspired word of Scripture. This should best start with the use of the primal form of 'mental prayer' or 'meditation,' traditionally known as . . . 'praying the Bible' " (*The Use of the Vernacular at Mass*, no. 1).

Following the highly acclaimed publication of the New Catholic Version of *The Psalms* in 2002, this translation of the New Catholic Version of *The New Testament* has been accomplished by the same board of highly qualified Scripture scholars under the direction of Rev. Jude Winkler, OFM Conv., S.S.L. They were committed to render as perfectly as possible a translation of literal or formal equivalence. Numerous translations were consulted

7

and decisions were made by consensus according to accepted principles of textual criticism.

With a deep desire to be faithful to God's inspired words, the translators used the best available Greek texts to achieve a dignified and accurate version of the sacred texts in language that is clear and meaningful to today's readers.

With extensive explanatory endnotes that reflect the most current consensus of Catholic scholarship, the New Catholic Version is a translation that can be trusted to provide the reader with a prayerful and fulfilling Bible experience suitable for private devotion and study.

A St. Joseph Edition

Therefore, we have thought it worthwhile to make available a Catholic Version of the New Testament in the renowned and exclusive format of our St. Joseph Editions of Bibles and Missals. The St. Joseph Edition is an editorial system developed over a span of fifty years. It consists in a series of features intended to ensure that a text (particularly a biblical or liturgical text) is user friendly, leading to greater readability and easier understanding.

The textual features or format in the present case are a readable typeface, additional headings and subheadings, and a full measure extension for long lines of poetry that clearly indicates when a line has a runover. It also includes a general introduction to the New Testament as well as introductions to each Book and pastoral notes. For easier reading, the notes have been grouped together at the end of the New Testament and are cross-referenced in the text itself. An asterisk (*) in the text indicates that there is a note to the text in question. Each note is in turn clearly marked with the number of the chapter and verse to which it pertains.

This particular edition also offers an Analytical Index as well as a Liturgical Index of Sunday Gospels.

How To Read the New Testament

We should read the New Testament with the mind of the Church who gave us the Bible and who interprets it for us. It will then become God's Word to us today.

The Catholic Church is the official interpreter of the Bible. As the people of God—both of the Old Covenant in figure and of the New Covenant in reality—she wrote the Sacred Scriptures. As the Church of Christ, she has interpreted them. And as the Church of Christians, she has always treasured them.

She encourages her members to study the Scriptures for she knows that they can discover nothing but what will make the Bible a greater force in her life and that of her members. And she knows that "ignorance of the Scriptures is ignorance of Christ."

"The Sacred Scriptures contain the Word of God and, since they are inspired, really are the Word of God. . . . This Sacred Council urges all the Christian faithful to learn by frequent reading of the divine Scriptures the 'excelling knowledge of Jesus Christ.' 'For ignorance of the Scriptures is ignorance of Christ' (St. Jerome). Therefore, they should gladly put themselves in touch with the sacred text. . . .

"And let them remember that prayer should accompany the reading of Sacred Scriptures, so that God and human beings may talk together; for 'we speak to Him when we pray; we hear Him when we read the divine saying.' " (Vatican II: *Dogmatic Constitution on Divine Revelation*, no. 25).

We trust that this new version of the New Testament will lead many into a better understanding of the Holy Books and a fuller knowledge of their principal author, the Triune God, and their primary protagonist, Jesus Christ, the incarnate Word.

Prayer before Reading Sacred Scripture

COME, Holy Spirit,
fill the hearts
of Your faithful
and enkindle in them
the fire of Your love.

℣. Send forth Your Spirit
and they shall be created.

℟. And You shall renew
the face of the earth.

Let us pray.

O God,
You instructed
the hearts of the faithful
by the light of the Holy Spirit.

Grant us by the same Spirit
to have a right judgment
in all things
and ever to rejoice
in His consolation.
Through Christ our Lord.
Amen.

Prayer after Reading Sacred Scripture

LET me not, O Lord,
be puffed up
with worldly wisdom,
which passes away.

Grant me that love
which never abates,
that I may not choose
to know anything
but Jesus,
and Him crucified.

I pray You, loving Jesus,
that as You have graciously given me
to drink in with delight
the words of Your knowledge,
so You would mercifully grant me
to attain one day to You,
the Fountain of all Wisdom,
and to appear forever
before Your face.
Amen.

GENERAL INTRODUCTION TO
THE NEW TESTAMENT

During the second century A.D. there were many writings in circulation that bore the name of Gospel, Acts, or Letter and claimed to be from the pen of an apostle, but only a few of these gained a place in the liturgy, catechesis, and preaching. Toward the end of that same century, it became customary to give the name "New Testament" to the collection of writings that had acquired authority everywhere in the Church as an important point of reference for the faith and that carried the guarantee of apostolic origin.

The first Christians did not immediately get the idea of connecting their writings with the Bible, Israel's book of revelation, which Christians were using in their liturgy and teaching. Gradually, however, the new writings acquired equal importance. To distinguish them from the Law and the Prophets or, in other words, the Bible, Christians spoke of a "New Testament," so that the other became in fact the "Old Testament."

The word "testament," in this context, is a translation of the Greek word used to convey the idea of a pact, that is, in this case, the Covenant that God had made with the people he had chosen. To speak of a "new covenant" was a bold step. It meant that the Covenant of Sinai, which was the foundation of the Jewish faith, had been completed and transcended by the coming of Christ. In the "passing over" of Jesus, God had established a new and definitive relationship with all human beings.

Henceforth, the Christian Bible had two parts: the Old and New Testaments. The Old was not rejected, but was interpreted as a prediction of the New and a way toward it. In reading the ancient texts, people now thought of the coming of Christ, which, for Christians, was the historical fulfillment of the hope of Israel.

The twenty-seven Books of the New Testament constitute the literature that is closest to Christian origins. Close in date, to be sure, but close, above all, by reason of the experience and faith to which they bear witness.

I. The Face of the New Testament
A Collection of Varied Writings

The New Testament writings are, then, close to Christ both in their date and in the experience they communicate. At the same time, however, even the writings that speak directly of him—the Gospels and Acts—are not in any sense a direct "news report"; they are testimonies and not reports. It is true that in one way or another all the New Testament writings communicate the essentials of a great event, but above all they are concerned with the meaning of that event. The Christ-event continues in the life of the community, and these writings are an expression of this continuity.

Texts Written at Various Periods

It must also be emphasized that the New Testament writings are not all from the same period. The earliest texts date from about twenty years after the death of Jesus. The earliest text is not one of the Gospels but the First Letter of Paul to the Christians of Thessalonica.

If we go through the Letters of the Apostle in their chronological order, we can discover evidence of a development of his thinking and see the series of problems that the communities of that particular period encountered.

The definitive form of the Synoptic Gospels points to a different period of writing, from about A.D. 65 to 80, the time when the need was felt to have available works covering the entire message and life of Christ.

The Church, which was widely scattered throughout the known world of the time, was gradually being separated from the period of her foundation, and no one wanted to lose the inspiration that came from it. The Church needed some essential points of reference, so that the person, message, and mystery of Christ would not be diluted or lost due to time, the movement away from the original geographical center, new currents of thought, and the problems raised by a different age. The idea was not that the Church should be fixated on the past but that she should preserve the memory of the living, concrete face of Jesus and the fervor of Pentecost.

We are, then, in the presence of a *new generation of believers*. The mother Church disappeared after the destruction of Jerusalem in A.D. 70.

The communities strengthened their bonds of union within the same region, since they had to face the same problems there. Given the ferment of new currents of religious thought, there was the need to know the essentials of the faith and catechesis, the true tradition. Christians were set apart, were regarded as suspect, and therefore needed to be encouraged. Some were overcome by nostalgia and mourned for the Jewish religion with its prestigious past, its highly developed body of law, its grandiose ceremonies, and its temple. Others looked with interest on new pagan religious trends.

Amid this jumble of cultures and religions it was necessary to determine the criteria of Christian authenticity and to organize the communities. The Catholic Letters, the Letter to the Hebrews, and the Pastoral Letters attributed to Paul, as well as the collection of works that go under the name of St. John, reflected comparable situations that had developed especially in Asia Minor.

When, subsequently, open persecution broke out and aimed to destroy Christianity in a systematic way, the Book of Revelation by its tone and its words encouraged Christians.

II. The Period
The Roman Empire

The Mediterranean was Roman. In all the lands that were in contact with its shores the Empire had established its legates, its procurators, its troops, and even its revenue agents. The great cities experienced notable growth. The most important ports, those in which Paul founded Christian communities, contained several hundred thousand inhabitants. Slaves made up about two-thirds of the population.

In philosophy, Epicureanism and Stoicism were the dominant schools. The latter managed to make its teaching popular because of its grand vision of the universe and of the human person and the earnestness of its moral demands.

Religions swarmed. Local divinities welcomed imported gods without showing any jealousy. During this period of uncertainty, more emotional kinds of cults were introduced from Asia: mystery cults with their secret initiations and ecstatic excitements. In their symbols and myths they succeeded in grasping the suffering and desire for rebirth that are innate in every soul.

In the more distant past Hellenistic rulers had imposed worship of the king, and the Jews had paid dearly for their rejection of this form of civic life and of submission. Rome had developed within a more republican tradition and was not quick to divinize its emperors, except verbally. But this cult seemed a means of more quickly unifying so many and such disparate peoples. Venerating the reigning emperor and bowing before his statue that had been turned into an idol—these became civic gestures, and Asia Minor was the soil most ready to spread this imperial cult.

However, for Christians Jesus alone is "Lord," that is, God; to proclaim the "emperor as lord," as they were asked to do, seemed an act of blasphemy and apostasy. Their refusal made them suspect and soon the object of persecution as well, as the Book of Revelation attests.

The Jews of the Diaspora enjoyed a special status that allowed them to remain faithful to their own religion and their own law; they were excused from worship of the emperor, on condition that they pray for him. For a long time the Christian communities, even though they admitted pagans into their midst, profited by that privilege. But soon the Jews, like the public authorities, could no longer tolerate this blurring of lines.

Judaism

The diversity within Judaism was a sign of a broad pluralism. In Judea, people were rather conservative and obsessed with the country's past; the temple, the Law, and the many observances derived from the Law were the focus of religious attention. The Bible was read in Hebrew, but there was freedom to paraphrase and interpret it in Aramaic, the then current language of the people.

In *Samaria*, the Law of Moses was observed, but a temple was built there to compete with the one in Jerusalem.

In *Galilee*, which was farther distant, the populace seemed dangerously mixed. The temple was far off, and for ordinary religious services Jews gathered in synagogues, which played a decisive role.

The Jews of the *Diaspora* were educated to a quite different mentality. In general, they were loyal to their faith and the Law, but they read the Bible in Greek, the usual language in the Mediterranean countries. These Jews, who were scattered almost everywhere and were called "Hellenists," often went on pilgrimage to Jerusalem. They were present in the city on Pentecost and some of them were baptized.

We must bear in mind that for internal affairs the Jews had their own tribunal, the *Great Sanhedrin*, composed of 71 members.

These included representatives of the lay aristocracy (the elders) and the principal priestly families (the chief priests, all of them Sadducees), as well as the scribes or interpreters of the Law, who were predominantly Pharisaic in outlook. The high priest currently in office presided over the Sanhedrin.

With the entry of Pompey into Jerusalem in 63 B.C. the country was subjected to Roman rule, which put an end to the last period of freedom that had been won by hard struggles in the time of the Maccabean wars.

The Herodian Rulers

At this time, then, the Jews were living in subjection to rulers imposed on them by the occupier. The *Herodians* were a dynasty of mixed blood; they earned the dislike of all by their cruelty, intrigues, and immorality. Herod the Great, who was married to a descendant of the Maccabees, reigned from 37 to 4 B.C.; this extraordinary builder began to rebuild a sumptuous temple, but he did not hesitate to rid himself without scruple of anyone who inconvenienced him, even his wives and his sons. The story of the slaughter of the innocents has kept alive over the centuries the impression of cruelty that he left behind him.

At his death, three of his sons divided the kingdom. *Antipas* governed Galilee and Perea from the city of Tiberias, which he built on the shore of Lake Gennesaret. He killed John the Baptist, who had become bothersome to him, and he hoped to meet Jesus. His half-brother, *Philip*, reigned over Ituraea and Trachonitis until A.D. 34. He beautified Panion and gave it the name Caesarea (known therefore as Caesarea Philippi, "Philip's Caesarea"). Finally, *Archelaus*, Antipas's brother, governed Judea, Samaria, and Idumea; but the Romans deposed him shortly afterward because of his arbitrary and unmeasured cruelty.

After the removal of Archelaus, Judea was united to the Province of Syria, and its government was entrusted to a procurator who was appointed directly by Rome and resided in Caesarea of Palestine. More than one of these men came to be hated by the populace for their detestable provocations; this was true especially of Pontius Pilate.

For a short period (A.D. 41–44), thanks to his friendship with the Emperor Claudius, *Agrippa* I, a nephew of Herod, was able to rule over a part of the Palestinian states, including Judea. In his desire to please the Jews, he launched the first persecution of Christians and had the Apostle James the Less executed. Agrippa was struck down by a sudden death.

His son, *Agrippa II*, did not receive the whole of his father's inheritance; he did have jurisdiction over the temple and obtained the government of the regions on the borders of Palestine. Like his sister Drusilla, he was pleased to listen to Paul, then a prisoner; this was on the occasion of a visit that he, along with his sister Berenice, paid to Festus, the procurator in Caesarea.

Jewish Uprisings

The period of Jesus' life and of the Church's beginnings was marked by serious upheavals. Repeated insurrections gave vent to the anger of many at the abuses of arbitrary and arrogant power, but they also expressed a refusal to accept with resignation the disappearance of Israel. The Jewish War, from A.D. 66 to 70, is one of the most tragic pages in the history of the Jewish people. The heroism of the rebels contrasted with the depth of their despair and the horror of the battle. The temple was destroyed in A.D. 70 and has remained in that condition to our day. Judaism, however, was reborn under the leadership of the Pharisees, with its center in the life of the synagogues, and, amid surprising ups and downs, it has survived until today. A second revolt in Palestine, from A.D. 132 to 135, was put down in a bloodbath.

The Pharisees

The *Pharisees* constituted the most important of the religious groups. They were not closed to new religious ideas, such as the resurrection, but they did have a scrupulous respect for the Law and were endlessly interpreting its details. They were "the pure"; they kept themselves free from political entanglements, detested the conceited power of the Sadducees and the arrogant intrigues of the Herodians, and accepted the Roman occupation.

Like Paul, who came from their ranks, they worked with their hands to earn their living. Despite their attitude of superiority, they became masters at teaching the people their religion and even domineered over consciences. They regarded it as inconceivable, however, that anyone should keep company with known sinners, and beyond imagining that tax collectors could be privileged recipients of God's mercy.

Jesus made some friends among them; one of them would provide him with a tomb. But he scandalized them deeply by his special attention to the poor and the outcasts of the Jewish religion and by his freedom in regard to legalistic and alienating observances. They were unable to share his joyous sense of God's mercy toward human beings and of the divine fatherhood that is so receptive of everyone.

According to the Gospels, Jesus regarded the Pharisees as hypocrites and faced up to them from the very beginning. They were the representatives of the traditional religion in the time of Jesus and were therefore, in the eyes of Christians, representatives of the synagogue's rejection of the Gospel. But we ought not generalize unduly: the Pharisees were often close to the Gospel. After the breakup of A.D. 70, they laid the moral and doctrinal foundations of future Judaism.

The Sadducees

The *Sadducees* were men of the temple. They linked themselves with the priestly line of Zadok. They represented official religious authority, the rich class, and the aristocracy of the rural areas. They were intriguers who collaborated with the occupying power and had nothing but contempt for the common people; in return, people hated them deeply. In religion they were conservatives and even ridiculed the resurrection so as to deny it more conspicuously. They were at home in Jerusalem; from the moment Jesus entered the city, he had to face this ruling class, which would decide on his death.

The Priests

What has been said of the Sadducees did not apply to the *priests*, who were divided into twenty-four classes and took turns officiating in the temple. Many of them were humble, devout, and faithful men, like Zechariah, father of John the Baptist. Some of them were among the first converts. The latter may have retained a nostalgia for the beautiful ceremonies of Jewish worship.

The Zealots

The *Zealots*, who arose at the beginning of the first century, were the sworn enemies of the Sadducees, the Herodians, and the occupying authorities. They were also called *sicarii*, from the Roman name for their weapon, a short dagger (*sica*) which they could easily hide and which they used in order to settle accounts secretly.

They were the leaders of the armed rebellions; they would be the great heroes but also, unfortunately, the victims of the Jewish War of A.D. 66–70 and later of the revolt of A.D. 135. Christ never tried to justify their actions, even though some of his disciples came from their circles.

The Herodians

The *Herodians* sided with the reigning dynasty and were quick to engage in denunciations and intrigues. For this reason they were distrusted.

The Essenes

The *Essenes*, finally, broke with the official religious institutions in order to recreate an Israel that awaited God. They lived in monastic austerity, without wives, without money, without violence, but they also seemed distrustful of joy. Christian religious circles shared several religious ideas with them. The monastery of Qumran, the life of which has become known to us through the famous Dead Sea Scrolls, may represent Essene spirituality.

The Scribes

The Gospels often speak of the *scribes* or *teachers* of the Law. Their official function was to interpret the Scriptures and religious teaching. We find them in the streets and synagogues; on the whole, they tended to be Pharisees.

III. Jesus of Nazareth
The Life of Jesus

This man, who was ignored by the age in which he lived, is unquestionably the most important figure in the history of humanity, due to the effect his name and his ideas have had down the centuries. Yet he is mentioned only on a couple of occasions, and then in vague terms, by historians of his time, specifically Tacitus and Suetonius at the beginning of the 2nd century.

He was sentenced and condemned to death by the Roman governor, Pontius Pilate, but the records of this trial have not been preserved. Nevertheless, of all the religious movements of that age, that of Jesus is the only one that has not disappeared.

The life of Jesus can be dated with some accuracy. We need only refer to the passages in which the Gospels mention personages and events that can be identified from other sources. Thus, we know that the first year of the Christian era was not accurately calculated: Jesus was born in the year 7 or 6 before the beginning of that era. He died on a Friday, the eve of Passover, between A.D. 28 and 33, perhaps on April 7, 30.

The Stages of Jesus' Preaching

The Galilean period began in a very promising way. There was a springtime atmosphere about it, a kind of explosion of joy at the proclamation that salvation had come. But the proclamation was not unambiguous. Jesus Christ spoke of the Kingdom of God; that is, in order to make himself understood, he used a word that was heavy with the hopes and expectations of the Jewish people. Consequently, the titles that others gave him—Son of David, Messiah, Son of God, or the title he gave himself: Son of Man—all had overtones of grandeur, but they also carried with them all too human hopes.

In fact, he was to carry out his vocation as Savior, the one who takes responsibility for the religious destiny of the world, in the form of the Suffering Servant, the unexpected figure described long before in the Book of Isaiah (42; 49; 50; 52:13—53:12). People refused to hear this, and understandably so. They were looking forward to a radical upheaval of the political situation, a glorious rehabilitation of Israel, and revenge on the pagan nations, for it was these that the Scriptures seemed to suggest.

Jesus, however, did not speak of this brutal turnaround, but of a new beginning, a change, a conversion, a new life. The lack of understanding between him and the crowd continued to grow. It reached its high point after the multiplication of the loaves, when he had to flee because some wanted to seize him and make him king.

When the misunderstanding reached the point of no return, Jesus changed his way of acting. He knew he would experience nothing but rejection, and he therefore devoted himself to the training of his disciples, the formation of the core group of individuals who would proclaim the kingdom once he was no longer there. He met with misunderstanding even among these men, but, more importantly, he won their unshakable affection. Through the experiences they shared with him, they learned his way of thinking and responding, and they would be able to pass this on later. The Kingdom of God was entrusted to a community, the Church.

The point came when the prospect of death became imminent; it was written in the foreseeable course of events. But Jesus did not change his program, even though he had to struggle with the instinctive horror of atrocious torment. Henceforth he clashed openly with entrenched positions, whether political or religious or social. The Gospel has preserved for us the tragic encounter of Jesus with the leaders of Judaism. He had to learn from experience that he would change the wills of human beings only by willingly making the supreme gift of his life.

IV. The Youthful Years of the Church

After the unforgettable experience of Pentecost, the group of disciples grew rapidly, as the disciples realized they were the agent of God's plan for the whole human race. The Spirit and events had given them this formidable mission. In the very beginning, indeed, the Church seemed desirous of falling back into the way of life and thinking of Judaism, but her destiny was to be one of continual and often difficult expansion, out to the ends of the then known world.

Believers of Palestinian origin were joined by others from the Diaspora: the Hellenists or Greek-speaking Jews. This was the first occasion for somewhat serious internal tensions and for the first efforts at organization; above all, however, it was the seed of development in new cultural areas. Various personages came to the fore in those early days: the Apostles Peter and John; the deacons Stephen and Philip, the former as the first martyr, the latter as one who overcame all difficulties in order to proclaim the Gospel. The first persecution, in A.D. 44—which claimed the Apostle James as a victim and would have claimed Peter, were it not for a miraculous deliverance—led to the dispersal of the community. From that point on, we know almost nothing about the majority of the Apostles.

Outside of Palestine, on the other hand, a dynamic enterprise, initially hidden, was brought fully into the open. Such men as Barnabas, John, Mark, and soon Paul, the converted persecutor who was aided by Timothy, began to establish one missionary center after another on the shores of the Mediterranean, moving finally into Europe; the Book of Acts creates for us a map of this expansion. Yet these men were certainly not the only missionaries.

We can only hint at the immense effort that the communities needed to set forth in order to give form to their experience and to express it. The Palestinian Jewish world was enmeshed in internal tensions, while the Christians affirmed that Jesus was the Christ, that is, the Messiah. They venerated him as the Son of God and celebrated him in the Liturgy, declaring his presence among them.

To affirm that Jesus was alive it was necessary to reinterpret his life and his work, the whole Old Testament and all the ideas of humanity concerning the meaning of life. These affirmations were not made in specialized schools but amid the demands of life, with its problems and its unforeseen questions, while seeking greater depth of understanding, which at times entailed tentative gropings.

The organization of the inner equilibrium of communities was also necessary. Jews and non-Jews, Greeks and barbarians, those privileged by culture or fortune and poor people, slaves and freemen had to acknowledge one another and express themselves as believers equally and entirely.

In a few years an unequaled transformation was worked in the name of a certitude: Jesus and his Spirit, and the salvation of all humanity. In a world turned upside down, a new seed was introduced. The little group had become a great community of believers, the Church; the first announcement had given rise to a magnificent Gospel. Without the Easter faith, which was at the origin of the movement and remained its core, none of this would have taken place. There would have been no Christianity, and the name of Jesus would forever be effaced from human memory.

THE GOSPELS

The Bible's table of contents (the "canon" of the Scriptures) gives the Gospels in the following order: Matthew, Mark, Luke, and John.

As a matter of fact, only the Book of Mark calls itself a "Gospel"; the others were given this title during the second century.

Alongside these officially recognized writings, a number of other gospels (known as the "apocrypha," that is, "secret" writings) circulated, but they were never accepted by the Church as inspired.

The Differences

The differences among the four Gospels are such that it is very difficult to combine their varied and often contrasting bits of information into a complete and solidly based biography of Jesus.

All four Gospels are very similar in their accounts of the Passion. But apart from that particular sequence, the difference between John and the other three is radical. When we read John, we are told that during his public life Jesus went up to Jerusalem three or four times for Passover and other feasts (Jn 2:13; 5:1; 7:10; 12:12); the other three Gospels report only one journey to the holy city, the one that ended in his arrest and death. According to the fourth Gospel, Jesus carried on a baptismal ministry at the same time as that of John the Baptist; the three Synoptic Gospels locate John's entire activity prior to that of Jesus (see Mt 4:12; Mk 1:14; Lk 3:1—4:15; and Jn 3:24).

Most importantly, the material in the majority of John's chapters is unknown to Matthew, Mark, and Luke, who nonetheless abound in sayings and stories; this cannot be explained as forgetfulness on either side. Finally, John's style has nothing in common with that of the other three. In the Synoptics, Jesus speaks in short, carefully wrought sentences that were easy to remember and to pass on orally; the Gospel of John, on the other hand, always starts with a solemn gesture of Jesus and follows with lengthy discourses that are marked by a careful and complex progression.

The Synoptic Problem

In contrast to John, the first three Gospels have much in common. They report the Christ-event according to the same pattern. In addition, the texts are similar, and each frequently follows the other two even in the details of images and sayings. This similarity makes it possible to read these three Gospels together, in parallel columns; we can read them "synoptically," that is, "seeing them together or at the same time" (Greek: *synopsis*), whence the name "Synoptic Gospels" or "Synoptics." In fact, of the 661 verses in Mark, 600 are found in Matthew and 350 in Luke.

At the same time, however, there are major differences. Matthew and Luke have many passages in common that are unknown to Mark. In addition, each Gospel has a sizable group of texts that are found only in it.

How are we to explain these surprising similarities and differences? This is the "Synoptic problem." The similarities are to be explained mainly by the development in the communities of a well structured oral tradition and by the formation of written collections organized according to genres or forms (parables, miracle stories, controversies, and so on). The kind of research known as the "study of forms" or literary genres endeavors to understand passages that had taken shape in the development of preaching.

But we have to go farther, because among the three Gospels there exist not only affinities due to tradition but also obvious editorial connections, so that it is also necessary to look into what is known as "redaction history." Different explanations of this history have been proposed, but scholars are generally in agreement on a hypothesis that includes the following points:

—The Synoptics use as their first source either the present Gospel of Mark (in the case of Matthew and Luke) or this same text but in an earlier editorial stage (all three evangelists).

—Matthew and Luke also use another source that had preserved chiefly the sayings of Jesus. This source could have been a single document or a family of similar documents.

—It can be presumed that prior to the composition of the Gospels there were contacts between the different sources at the various stages of their formation.

—Each Gospel also draws on sources of its own.

—Finally, each Gospel has its own point of view, its own way of proceeding, and its own visions of things, and all these are explained by the purpose the author set for himself, the setting in which he was living, and the readership he was addressing. We shall speak of these in the introduction to each Gospel.

The Purpose of the Gospels

These differences make clear the freedom that the communities and the authors had in adapting the Gospel story to the mentalities and problems of the communities. The purpose of the authors was not to present a detailed, structured story but rather a vision of what Jesus was and of what he presently is for the Church. A document that lacks all biographical detail is not a Gospel; on the other hand, a Gospel is always a theological discourse, a faith-inspired presentation, and not a simple historical description. The starting point of the Gospels is the Easter faith.

Consequently, before being a historical document and while having all the value of a historical document, a Gospel is an event. The Gospels preserve for us many biographical details about Jesus, but they are not primarily biographies, lives of Jesus. Their purpose is to bear witness to the Gospel, that is, the Good News of God's coming into the midst of humanity. In Jesus and by means of Jesus God speaks the final word about himself and about the destiny of humanity and the world.

THE GOSPEL ACCORDING TO MATTHEW

THE TEACHING OF JESUS FOR
THE LIFE OF THE COMMUNITIES

The form of the Our Father that we use in prayer and the formulation of the Beatitudes that we customarily follow are those that we read in the Gospel of Matthew; we also use this Gospel for most of the actions and words of Jesus. Since the very early centuries, Matthew's Gospel has stood at the head of the New Testament writings, thus earning it the name "the first Gospel."

Why has this Gospel enjoyed such success? It is pleasing for its literary qualities—its distinctive tone, its short, clear narratives, its well-organized text—but it is striking, above all, because the teaching of Jesus occupies such a very large place in it. Matthew's Gospel is par excellence the book of the Church and has rightly been called the "ecclesial Gospel," because as he reports what Jesus said, he has the life of the community constantly in mind.

What was the origin of this Gospel? The earliest tradition attributes it to the Apostle Matthew, also known as Levi, son of Alphaeus. Once this tax collector made the acquaintance of Jesus he was struck by his personality and immediately left his trade (a profitable one, even if at that time regarded as quite a reprehensible one) to join the group of disciples (Mt 9:9; Mk 2:14). Later on, according to this tradition, he gathered up his recollections in a book. Careful research has led to less simple conclusions. In its present form our first Gospel was written in Greek and completed in A.D. 70 or perhaps a little later. Other less fully developed collections preceded it. The first texts, written in Hebrew or Aramaic (the languages of Palestine at that time), date perhaps from the forties or fifties, a period still close to the death of Jesus.

The Book as we have it has drawn upon the Gospel of Mark and on another source on which Luke, too, draws. Despite these influences, Matthew reflects, better than the others, the early preaching to Christians of Jewish origin, and is perhaps the Book used for Christian preaching in Palestine. Rather than a simple biography, it is meant as God's word regarding our life and the world.

Each Gospel has its own way of highlighting the important moments in the activity of Jesus, culminating in the story of the Passion and Resurrection. Matthew has, then, his own characteristic traits. The "Good News" is proclaimed principally in Galilee: it is a joyous event, and Jesus immediately calls some disciples. But the drama of rejection soon begins; from that moment on, the tempo quickens, as Jesus remains apart from the crowds and trains his disciples, thus preparing for the coming Church. The clash with official Judaism at last becomes open and unrelenting. This tragic development ends in the Passion. Along the line of this general movement Matthew locates some key points: the discourses that are so characteristic of his Book. Each gathers together the sayings of Jesus about a theme, because Matthew is thinking primarily of forming the community, of "catechizing" it, as we might say today.

As a result, the five great discourses of Matthew's Gospel, separated from each other by sections of narrative, sum up the principal elements of a code of Christian life. The five are: the Sermon on the Mount, including the Beatitudes; the missionary discourse; the parables; the teaching on life in community; and perspectives on the end of the world. None of these discourses is developed like a fine lecture. Rather, the tradition Matthew follows gradually gathered sayings of Jesus on some central themes (the same sayings are often cited by the other evangelists in different contexts). In fact, as compositions, these discourses are quite unsuccessful. And yet what power flows from them to guide us in living a life worthy of the Christian name!

A Gospel is first and foremost the proclamation of Jesus as Savior of the human race. Matthew expresses this essential faith in words, ideas, and images that were accessible to the people of that time who were of Jewish origin. Therefore, he presents Jesus as the Messiah who had been promised and was long awaited, but then was rejected. And to give greater force to his arguments he heaps up citations from the Old Testament. More than once, this "proof" from Scripture seems artificial in its details, but the author is nonetheless able to explain the fate of Jesus in the light of the Bible as a whole.

Matthew's Gospel is the Gospel of the Church. And indeed it sets forth, for the community called together by Jesus, the main lines of a Christian life, and presents the life of the disciples as a model for all those who accept the mindset of the kingdom of God.

The Gospel of Matthew may be divided as follows:

Prologue: The Birth of the Messiah, Jesus of Nazareth (1:1—2:23)

  I: Jesus Inaugurates His Ministry as Savior (3:1—7:29)

 II: The Signs of the Kingdom of God (8:1—10:42)

III: Jesus Is the Expected Messiah (11:1—13:52)

IV: The Authentic Faith of Those Converted (13:53—18:35)

 V: The Coming of the Son of Man (19:1—25:46)

VI: The Passion and Resurrection (26:1—28:20)

PROLOGUE: THE BIRTH OF THE MESSIAH, JESUS OF NAZARETH*

1 The Genealogy of Jesus.* ¹ The account of the genealogy of Jesus Christ, * the son of David, the son of Abraham.

2   Abraham was the father of Isaac,
        Isaac the father of Jacob,
        Jacob the father of Judah and his brothers.
3   Judah was the father of Perez and Zerah, with Tamar* being their mother.
        Perez was the father of Hezron,
        Hezron the father of Ram,
4   Ram the father of Amminadab.
        Amminadab was the father of Nahshon,
        Nahshon the father of Salmon,
5   Salmon the father of Boaz, with Rahab being his mother.
        Boaz was the father of Obed, whose mother was Ruth.
        Obed was the father of Jesse,
6   and Jesse was the father of King David.

    David was the father of Solomon, whose mother had been the wife of Uriah.
7   Solomon was the father of Rehoboam,
        Rehoboam the father of Abijah,
        Abijah the father of Asa.
8   Asa was the father of Jehoshaphat,
        Jehoshaphat the father of Joram,
        Joram the father of Uzziah.
9   Uzziah was the father of Jotham,
        Jotham the father of Ahaz,
        Ahaz the father of Hezekiah.
10   Hezekiah was the father of Manasseh,
        Manasseh the father of Amos,
        Amos the father of Josiah.
11   Josiah was the father of Jechoniah and his brothers at the time of the deportation to Babylon.

12 After the deportation to Babylon,
   Jechoniah was the father of Shealtiel,
   Shealtiel the father of Zerubbabel,
13 Zerubabbel the father of Abiud.
   Abiud was the father of Eliakim,
   Eliakim the father of Azor,
14 Azor the father of Zadok.
   Zadok was the father of Achim,
   Achim the father of Eliud,
15 Eliud the father of Eleazar.
   Eleazar was the father of Matthan,
   Matthan the father of Jacob.
16 Jacob was the father of Joseph, the husband of Mary,
   who gave birth to Jesus who is called the Christ.*

¹⁷ Therefore, in total there were fourteen generations from Abraham to David, another fourteen generations from David to the deportation to Babylon, and another fourteen generations from the deportation to Babylon to the Christ.

The Birth of Jesus.* ¹⁸ The birth of Jesus Christ occurred in this way. When his mother Mary was engaged to Joseph, but before they came to live together, she was found to be with child through the Holy Spirit. ¹⁹ Her husband Joseph was a just man and did not wish to expose her to the ordeal of public disgrace; therefore, he resolved to divorce her quietly.

²⁰ After he had decided to follow this course of action, an angel of the Lord appeared to him in a dream and said, "Joseph, son of David, do not be afraid to receive Mary into your home as your wife. For this child has been conceived in her womb through the Holy Spirit. ²¹ She will give birth to a son, and you shall name him Jesus,* for he will save his people from their sins."

²² All this took place in order to fulfill what the Lord had announced through the prophet:

23 "Behold, the virgin shall conceive and give birth to a son,
   and they shall name him Emmanuel,"

a name that means "God is with us." *

[24] When Joseph rose from sleep, he did what the angel of the Lord had commanded him. He took Mary into his home as his wife, [25] but he engaged in no marital relations* with her until she gave birth to a son, whom he named Jesus.

2 **The Wise Men Render Homage to the Messiah.*** [1] After Jesus had been born in Bethlehem * of Judea during the reign of King Herod, wise men traveled from the east and arrived in Jerusalem, [2] inquiring, "Where is the newborn king of the Jews? We saw the rising of his star, and we have come to pay him homage."

[3] On hearing about their inquiry, King Herod was greatly troubled, as was true of the whole of Jerusalem. [4] Therefore, he summoned all the chief priests * and the scribes and questioned them about where the Christ was to be born. [5] They replied, "In Bethlehem of Judea, for thus has the prophet written:

[6]   'And you, Bethlehem, in the land of Judah,
        are by no means least among the rulers of Judah,
     for from you shall come a ruler
        who will shepherd my people Israel.' " *

[7] Then Herod secretly summoned the wise men, and he ascertained from them the exact time of the star's appearance, [8] after which he sent them on to Bethlehem, saying: "Go forth and search diligently for the child. When you have found him, bring me word, so that I can go and pay him homage."

[9] After receiving these instructions from the king, the wise men set out. And behold, the star that they had seen at its rising proceeded ahead of them until it stopped over the place where the child was. [10] The sight of the star filled them with great joy, [11] and when they entered the house they beheld the child with Mary his mother. Falling to their knees, they paid him homage. Then they opened their treasure chests and offered him gifts of gold, frankincense, and myrrh.* [12] And since they had been

warned in a dream not to return to Herod, they departed for their own country by another route.

The Flight into Egypt. ¹³ After the wise men had left, an
angel of the Lord appeared to Joseph in a dream and
instructed him, "Arise, take the child and his mother, and
flee to Egypt. Remain there until I tell you. Herod seeks
the child to kill him." ¹⁴ Therefore, he got up, took the
child and his mother, and departed that night for Egypt,
¹⁵ where they remained until the death of Herod. This was
to fulfill what the Lord had spoken through the prophet:
"Out of Egypt I called my son." *

The Slaughter of the Innocents at Bethlehem. ¹⁶ When
Herod realized that the wise men had deceived him, he
flew into a rage and issued an order to kill all the boys in
Bethlehem and the surrounding area who who were two
years old or less, in accordance with the information that
he had obtained from the wise men. ¹⁷ * Thus were fulfilled the words that had been spoken through the
prophet Jeremiah:

¹⁸   "A voice was heard in Ramah,
            lamenting and sobbing bitterly:
       Rachel weeping for her children,
            and refusing to be consoled,
            because they were no more."

The Return to the Land of Israel. * ¹⁹ After the death of
Herod, an angel of the Lord appeared in a dream to
Joseph in Egypt ²⁰ and said, "Arise, take the child and his
mother, and go to the land of Israel, for those who sought
to kill the child are dead." * ²¹ He got up, took the child
and his mother, and returned to the land of Israel.

²² But when Joseph learned that Archelaus * had succeeded his father Herod in Judea, he was afraid to go
there. After he had been warned in a dream concerning
this, he withdrew to the region of Galilee. ²³ He settled in
a town called Nazareth,* so that what had been spoken
through the Prophets might be fulfilled: "He shall be
called a Nazorean."

BETHLEHEM: TOWN OF CHRIST'S BIRTH—This is a view from the south of Bethlehem, the City of David, showing the belfry of the Church of the Nativity built on the site where Christ was born. (See Mt 2:1.)

CHURCH OF THE NATIVITY—Pictured above is the Basilica of the Church of the Nativity, showing the ancient columns and the arched door which leads down to the Grotto of the Nativity beneath the Church. (See Mt 2:1.)

JERUSALEM: RELIGIOUS CENTER OF ISRAEL—Air view of Jerusalem, showing the temple area from the north with the village of Siloam in the distance and the Galilee Gate on the left. (See Mt 2:1.)

DAMASCUS GATE AT JERUSALEM—Pictured above is the finest of the gates of the ancient walled city of Jerusalem, located approximately in the center of the third wall. Though it was not built when Jesus was born, it is suggestive of the gates that were. (See Mt 2:1.)

I: JESUS INAUGURATES HIS MINISTRY AS SAVIOR

3 **John the Baptist Preaches and Baptizes.** ¹ * In those days, John the Baptist* appeared in the desert of Judea, preaching: ² "Repent, * for the kingdom of heaven is close at hand." This was the man of whom the prophet Isaiah spoke when he said:

³   "The voice of one crying out in the wilderness:
     'Prepare the way of the Lord,
       make his paths straight.' " *

⁴ John's clothing was made of camel's hair, with a leather loincloth around his waist, and his food consisted of locusts and wild honey.* ⁵ The people of Jerusalem and the whole of Judea and the entire region along the Jordan went out to him, ⁶ and as they confessed their sins they were baptized by him in the Jordan River.

⁷ * But when he observed many of the Pharisees and Sadducees coming for baptism, he said to them, "You brood of vipers! Who warned you to flee from the wrath to come? ⁸ Produce good fruit as proof of your repentance. ⁹ Do not presume to say to yourselves: 'We have Abraham as our father.' For I tell you that God is able to raise up children for Abraham from these stones. ¹⁰ Even now the ax is laid to the root of the trees. Therefore, every tree that does not bear good fruit will be cut down and thrown into the fire.

¹¹ * "I baptize you with water for repentance, but the one who is coming after me is more powerful than I am. I am not worthy to carry his sandals. He will baptize you with the Holy Spirit and fire. ¹² His winnowing fan is in his hand. He will clear his threshing floor and gather his wheat into his barn, but the chaff he will burn with unquenchable fire." *

Jesus Is Baptized.* ¹³ Then Jesus arrived from Galilee and came to John at the Jordan to be baptized by him. ¹⁴ John tried to dissuade him, saying, "Why do you come to me? I am the one who needs to be baptized by you."

¹⁵ But Jesus said to him in reply, "For the present, let it be thus. It is proper for us to do this to fulfill all that righteousness demands." * Then he acquiesced.

¹⁶ After Jesus had been baptized, as he came up from the water, suddenly the heavens were opened and he beheld the Spirit of God descending like a dove and alighting on him. ¹⁷ And a voice came from heaven, saying, "This is my beloved Son, in whom I am well pleased." *

4 **Jesus Is Tempted by the Devil.** * ¹ Then Jesus was led by the Spirit into the desert to be tempted by the devil. ² He fasted for forty days and forty nights, after which he was famished.

³ Then the tempter approached him and said, "If you are the Son of God, * command these stones to be transformed into loaves of bread." ⁴ Jesus answered, "As it is written:

'Man does not live by bread alone,
     but by every word that comes forth from the
         mouth of God.' " *

⁵ Next the devil took him to the holy city and had him stand on the summit of the temple. * ⁶ * Then he said to him, "If you are the Son of God, throw yourself down. For it is written:

'He will command his angels concerning you,
     and with their hands they will raise you up
     lest you dash your foot against a stone.' "

⁷ Jesus said to him, "It is also written:

'You shall not put the Lord your God to the test.' "

⁸ Finally, the devil took him to an exceedingly high mountain and showed him all the kingdoms of the world in their splendor. ⁹ Then he said to him, "All these will I give you if you kneel down and worship me." ¹⁰ Jesus said to him in reply, "Depart from me, Satan! It is written:

'You shall worship the Lord your God,
     and him alone shall you serve.' " *

[11] Then the devil departed from him, and suddenly angels came and ministered to him.

Jesus Begins His Ministry in Galilee. [12]*When Jesus learned that John had been arrested,* he withdrew to Galilee.* [13] Departing from Nazareth, he settled in Capernaum* by the sea, in the region of Zebulun and Naphtali, [14] in order that what had been spoken through the prophet Isaiah might be fulfilled:

[15]   "Land of Zebulun and land of Naphtali,
         the passageway to the sea, beyond the Jordan,
         Galilee of the Gentiles:
[16]   The people who lived in darkness
         have seen a great light,
         and for those who dwell in a land darkened by the
           shadow of death
         light has dawned."

[17] From that day forward Jesus began to proclaim the message: "Repent, for the kingdom of heaven is close at hand."

Jesus Calls the First Disciples.* [18] As Jesus was walking by the Sea of Galilee, he saw two brothers, Simon who is called Peter, and his brother Andrew, casting a net into the water, for they were fishermen. [19] He said to them, "Come, follow me, and I will make you fishers of men." [20] Immediately, they abandoned their nets and followed him.

[21] As he proceeded farther, he saw two more brothers, James the son of Zebedee, and his brother John. They were in a boat with their father Zebedee, mending their nets, and he called them. [22] Immediately, they left their boat and their father and followed him.

Jesus Proclaims the Message and Heals the Sick.* [23] Jesus traveled all throughout Galilee, teaching in their synagogues, proclaiming the good news of the kingdom, and curing every type of disease and illness among the people. [24] His reputation spread throughout Syria,* and they brought to him all those who were sick, afflicted with various diseases, racked with pain, or possessed by demons, as well as those who were stricken with epilepsy or paralyzed, and he healed them. ²⁵ Great throngs from Galilee, the Decapolis, * Jerusalem, and Judea, and from beyond the Jordan, followed him.

A: The Sermon on the Mount—
Magna Carta of the Christian Life*

5 **The Beatitudes.*** ¹ When Jesus saw the crowds, he went up on the mountain. After he was seated, his disciples gathered around him. ² Then he began to teach them as follows:

³　　"Blessed are the poor in spirit,
　　　　for theirs is the kingdom of heaven.
⁴　　Blessed are those who mourn,
　　　　for they will be comforted.
⁵　　Blessed are the meek,
　　　　for they will inherit the earth.
⁶　　Blessed are those who hunger and thirst for justice,
　　　　for they will have their fill.
⁷　　Blessed are the merciful,
　　　　for they will obtain mercy.
⁸　　Blessed are the pure of heart,
　　　　for they will see God.
⁹　　Blessed are the peacemakers,
　　　　for they will be called children of God.
¹⁰　　Blessed are those who are persecuted in the cause of
　　　　justice,
　　　　for theirs is the kingdom of heaven.

¹¹ "Blessed are you when people insult you and persecute you and utter all kinds of calumnies against you for my sake. ¹² Rejoice and be glad, for your reward will be great in heaven. In the same manner, they persecuted the prophets who preceded you.

Salt of the Earth and Light of the World.* ¹³ "You are the salt of the earth. But if salt loses its taste, what can be done to make it salty once again? It is no longer good for anything, and thus it is cast out and trampled underfoot.

[14] "You are the light of the world. A city built upon a mountain cannot be hidden. [15] Nor would someone light a lamp and then put it under a basket; rather, it is placed upon a lampstand so that it may afford light to all in the house. [16] In the same way, your light must shine so that it can be seen by others; this will enable them to observe your good works and give praise to your Father in heaven.

B: The New Law*

The Fulfillment of the Law. [17] "Do not think that I have come to abolish the Law or the Prophets. I have come not to abolish but to fulfill them. [18] Amen, I say to you, until heaven and earth pass away, not a single letter,* not even a tiny portion of a letter, will disappear from the Law until all things have been accomplished. [19] Therefore, whoever breaks even one of the least of these commandments and teaches others to do the same will be considered least in the kingdom of heaven. But whoever observes these commandments and teaches them will be called great in the kingdom of heaven. [20] I tell you, if your righteousness does not exceed that of the scribes and Pharisees, you will never enter the kingdom of heaven.

Anger.* [21] "You have heard that your ancestors were told: 'You shall not kill, and anyone who kills will be subject to judgment.' [22] But I say this to you: Anyone who is angry with his brother will be subject to judgment, and whoever addresses his brother in an insulting way will answer for it before the Sanhedrin, and whoever calls his brother a fool will be liable to the fires of Gehenna.*

[23] "Therefore, when offering your gift at the altar, if you should remember that your brother has something against you, [24] leave your gift there at the altar and first go to be reconciled with your brother. Then return and offer your gift.

²⁵ "Come to terms quickly with your opponent while you are on the way to court with him. If you fail to do so, he may hand you over to the judge, and the judge will put you in the custody of the guard, and you will be thrown into prison. ²⁶ Believe the truth of what I tell you: you will not be given your freedom until you have paid your debt down to the last penny.*

Adultery. ²⁷ * "You have heard that it was said of old: 'You shall not commit adultery.' ²⁸ But I say to you that anyone who looks with lust at a woman has already committed adultery with her in his heart. ²⁹ If your right eye causes you to sin, tear it out and throw it away. It is preferable for you to lose one part of your body than to have your whole body thrown into Gehenna. ³⁰ And if your right hand causes you to sin, cut it off and throw it away. It is preferable for you to lose one of your limbs than to have your whole body thrown into Gehenna.

Divorce. ³¹ "It has also been said: 'Whoever divorces his wife shall give her a certificate of dismissal.' ³² But I say to you that anyone who divorces his wife, except if the marriage was unlawful, causes her to commit adultery, and whoever marries a divorced woman commits adultery.

Oaths.* ³³ "Again, you have heard that our ancestors were told: 'Do not swear falsely, but fulfill the vows you have made to the Lord.' ³⁴ But what I tell you is this: Do not swear at all, either by heaven, since it is God's throne, ³⁵ or by earth, since that is his footstool, or by Jerusalem, since that is the city of the great King. ³⁶ Nor should you swear by your head, for you cannot turn one hair of it white or black. ³⁷ All you need to do is to say 'Yes' if you mean 'Yes' and 'No' if you mean 'No.' Anything beyond this comes from the evil one.

Retaliation.* ³⁸ "You have heard that it was said: 'An eye for an eye and a tooth for a tooth.' ³⁹ But I say to you: Offer no resistance to someone who is wicked. If someone strikes you on your right cheek, turn and offer him the other cheek as well. ⁴⁰ If anyone wishes to sue you to

gain possession of your tunic, give him your cloak as well.
[41] If someone forces you to go one mile, go with him for a second mile. [42] Give to anyone who begs from you, and do not turn your back on anyone who wishes to borrow from you.

Love for Enemies.* [43] "You have heard that it was said: 'You shall love your neighbor and hate your enemy.' [44] But I say to you: Love your enemies and pray for those who persecute you. [45] This will make you children of your heavenly Father. For he causes his sun to rise on evil people as well as on those who are good, and his rain falls on both the righteous and the wicked. [46] If you love only those who love you, what reward will you receive? Do not even tax collectors* do the same? [47] And if you greet only your brethren, what about that is so extraordinary? Even the pagans do as much.

Perfection.* [48] "Therefore, strive to be perfect, just as your heavenly Father is perfect.

C: The True Practice of Religion*

6 **Giving Alms in Secret.** [1] "Beware of performing righteous deeds before others in order to impress them. If you do so, you will receive no reward from your Father in heaven. [2] Therefore, whenever you give alms, do not trumpet your generosity, as the hypocrites do in the synagogues and in the streets in order to win the praise of others. Amen, I say to you, they have already received their reward. [3] But when you give alms, do not let your left hand know what your right hand is doing. [4] Your almsgiving must be done in secret. And your Father who sees everything that is done in secret will reward you.

Praying in Secret. [5] "Whenever you pray, do not be like the hypocrites, who love to stand and pray in the synagogues and on street corners so that others may observe them doing so. Amen, I say to you, they have already received their reward. [6] But when you pray, go into your room, close the door, and pray to your Father in secret.

And your Father who sees everything that is done in secret will reward you.

The Lord's Prayer.* ⁷ "When you pray do not go on babbling endlessly as the pagans do, for they believe that they are more likely to be heard because of their many words. ⁸ Do not imitate them. Your Father knows what you need before you ask him.

⁹ "This is how you should pray:

'Our Father in heaven,
     hallowed be your name.
¹⁰   Your kingdom come.
     Your will be done
       on earth as it is in heaven.
¹¹   Give us this day our daily bread.
¹²   And forgive us our debts
     as we forgive our debtors.
¹³   And do not lead us into temptation,*
     but deliver us from the evil one.'

¹⁴ If you forgive others for the wrongs they have done, your heavenly Father will also forgive you. ¹⁵ But if you do not forgive others, then your Father will not forgive your transgressions.

Fasting in Secret.* ¹⁶ "Whenever you fast, do not assume a gloomy expression like the hypocrites who contort their faces so that others may realize that they are fasting. Amen, I say to you, they have received their reward. ¹⁷ But when you fast, put oil on your head and wash your face, ¹⁸ so that the fact that you are fasting will not be obvious to others but only to your Father who is hidden. And your Father who sees everything that is done in secret will reward you.

Treasures in Heaven.* ¹⁹ "Do not store up treasures for yourselves on earth, where they will be destroyed by moth and rust and where thieves break in and steal. ²⁰ Rather, store up treasure for yourselves in heaven, where neither moth nor rust destroys and where thieves cannot break in and steal. [21] For where your treasure is, there will your heart also be.

The Lamp of the Body.* [22] "The eyes are the lamp of the body. If your eyes are sound, your whole body will be filled with light. [23] However, if your eyes are diseased, your whole body will be in darkness. If then the light within you is darkness, how great will that darkness be!

God and Money. [24] "No one can serve two masters. For you will either hate the one and love the other or be devoted to the one and despise the other. You cannot serve both God and money.*

Seek First the Kingdom of God.* [25] "Therefore, heed my words. Do not be concerned about your life and what you will have to eat or drink, or about your body and what you will wear. Surely life is more than food, and the body is more than clothing.

[26] "Gaze upon the birds in the sky. They do not sow or reap or store in barns, and yet your heavenly Father feeds them. Are you not of far greater value than they? [27] Can any of you through worrying add a single moment to your span of life?

[28] "And why are you concerned about what you are to wear? Consider the lilies of the field and how they grow. They neither labor nor spin. [29] Yet I tell you that not even Solomon in all his royal splendor was clothed like one of these. [30] If God so clothes the grass of the field, which grows today and tomorrow is thrown into the furnace, will he not all the more clothe you, O you of little faith?

[31] "Therefore, stop being anxious about such things. Do not say: 'What shall we eat?' or 'What shall we drink?' or 'What shall we wear?' [32] These are things that are of concern to the Gentiles. Your heavenly Father is fully aware of all your needs. [33] Rather, seek the kingdom of God and his righteousness, and all these things will be given to you as well.

[34] "So do not worry about tomorrow, for tomorrow will take care of itself. Each day has enough troubles of its own.

7 Do Not Judge.* [1] "Do not judge, so that you in turn may not be judged. [2] For you will be judged in the same way that you judge others, and the measure that you use for others will be used to measure you.

[3] "Why do you take note of the splinter in your brother's eye but do not notice the wooden plank in your own eye? [4] How can you say to your brother, 'Let me remove that splinter from your eye,' while all the time the wooden plank remains in your own? [5] You hypocrite! First remove the wooden plank from your own eye, and then you will be able to see clearly enough to remove the splinter from your brother's eye.

Do Not Profane Sacred Things.* [6] "Do not give to dogs anything that is holy. And do not cast your pearls before swine, lest they trample them under their feet and then proceed to tear you to pieces.

Ask, Seek, Knock.* [7] "Ask, and it will be given to you; seek, and you will find; knock, and the door will be opened to you. [8] For everyone who asks will receive, and those who seek will find, and to those who knock the door will be opened.

[9] "Is there anyone among you who would give a stone to his son if he asks for bread, [10] or hand him a snake if he asks for a fish? [11] If you then, despite your evil nature, know how to give good gifts to your children, how much more will your Father in heaven give good things to those who ask him!

The Golden Rule of Love.* [12] "In everything, deal with others as you would like them to deal with you. This is the Law and the Prophets.

The Two Ways.* [13] "Enter through the narrow gate, for the gate is wide and the road broad that leads to destruction, and those who enter through it are many. [14] But

A TREE AND ITS FRUITS—"Thus, by their fruits you will know them. Not everyone who says to me, 'Lord, Lord,' will enter the kingdom of heaven, but only the one who does the will of my heavenly Father" (Mt 7:20-21).

THE STORM ON THE LAKE—With the boat in danger of being swamped by the waves, the disciples implored Jesus: " 'Lord, save us! We are going to die!' . . . Then he stood up and rebuked the winds and the sea, and there was a great calm" (Mt 8:25-26).

small is the gate and narrow the road that leads to life, and those who find it are few in number.

False Prophets and True Disciples.* [15] "Be on guard against false prophets who come to you disguised in sheep's clothing, but who inwardly are ravenous wolves. [16] By their fruits you will know them. Does one pick grapes from thornbushes or figs from thistles? [17] In the same way, every good tree bears good fruit, but a rotten tree produces bad fruit. [18] A good tree cannot bear bad fruit, nor can a bad tree bear good fruit. [19] Every tree that does not bear good fruit is cut down and thrown into the fire. [20] Thus, by their fruits you will know them.

[21] "Not everyone who says to me, 'Lord, Lord,' will enter the kingdom of heaven, but only the one who does the will of my heavenly Father. [22] Many will say to me on that day,* 'Lord, Lord, did we not prophesy in your name? Did we not drive out demons in your name? Did we not perform many miracles in your name?' [23] Then I will tell them plainly, 'I never knew you. Depart from me, you evildoers!'

The Wise and Foolish Builders.* [24] "Everyone who hears these words of mine and acts in accordance with them will be like a wise man who constructed his house on a rock foundation. [25] The rain came down, the flood waters rose, and fierce winds battered that house. However, it did not collapse, because it had its foundations on rock.

[26] "In contrast, everyone who hears these words of mine and does not act in accordance with them will be like a fool who constructed his house on a foundation of sand. [27] The rain came down, the flood waters rose, and the winds blew and buffeted that house. And it collapsed with a great crash."

The Authority of Jesus.* [28] When Jesus had finished this discourse, the crowds were astounded at his teaching, [29] because he taught them as one who had authority, and not as their scribes.

II. THE SIGNS OF THE KINGDOM OF GOD*

A: Ten Miracles*

8 **Jesus Heals a Man with Leprosy.*** [1] When he had come down from the mountain, large crowds followed him. [2] Suddenly, a man with leprosy approached, knelt before him, and said, "Lord, if you choose to do so, you can make me clean." [3] He stretched out his hand and touched him, saying, "I do choose. Be made clean." Immediately, his leprosy was cured. [4] Then Jesus said to him, "See that you tell no one, but go and show yourself to the priest and offer the gift that Moses prescribed. That will be proof for them."

Jesus Heals the Centurion's Servant.* [5] When Jesus entered Capernaum, a centurion approached him and pleaded for his help. [6] "Lord," he said, "my servant is lying at home paralyzed and enduring agonizing sufferings." [7] Jesus said to him, "I will come and cure him." [8] The centurion replied, "Lord, I am not worthy to have you come under my roof. But simply say the word and my servant will be healed.* [9] For I myself am a man subject to authority, with soldiers who are subject to me. I say to one 'Go,' and he goes, and to another, 'Come here,' and he comes, and to my servant, 'Do this,' and he does it."

[10] When Jesus heard this, he was amazed, and he said to those who were following him, "Amen, I say to you, in no one throughout Israel have I found faith as great as this. [11] Many, I tell you, will come from the east and the west to sit with Abraham and Isaac and Jacob at the banquet in the kingdom of heaven. [12] But the heirs of the kingdom will be thrown into the outer darkness, where there will be weeping and gnashing of teeth."

[13] Jesus then said to the centurion, "Return home. Your petition has been granted because of your faith." And at that very hour the servant was healed.

Jesus Heals Peter's Mother-in-Law. [14] Jesus then entered the house of Peter and found Peter's mother-in-law lying in bed with a fever. [15] He touched her hand and the fever left her, and she got up and began to serve him.

Jesus Drives Out the Evil Spirits. * [16] That evening they brought to him many who were possessed by demons. He cast out the spirits with a command and cured all who were sick. [17] This was to fulfill the words of the prophet Isaiah:

> "He took away our infirmities
> and bore our diseases."

The Cost of Following Jesus. * [18] When Jesus saw the great crowds around him, he gave orders to cross to the other side of the lake. [19] A scribe approached him and said, "Teacher, I will follow you wherever you go." [20] Jesus told him, "Foxes have holes and birds of the air have nests, but the Son of Man[+] has nowhere to lay his head." [21] Another man, one of the disciples, said, "Lord, allow me to go first and bury my father." [22] Jesus answered him, "Follow me, and let the dead bury their own dead."

Jesus Calms the Storm. * [23] He then got into the boat, followed by his disciples. [24] Suddenly, a great storm came up on the lake, so that the boat was being swamped by the waves. But he was asleep. [25] And so they went to him and awakened him, saying, "Lord, save us! We are going to die!" [26] He said to them in reply, "Why are you so frightened, O you of little faith?"

Then he stood up and rebuked the winds and the sea, and there was a great calm. [27] They were amazed and asked, "What sort of man is this, whom even the winds and the sea obey?"

Jesus Heals Two Demon-Possessed Men. * [28] When he reached the region of the Gadarenes * on the other side of the lake, two men who were possessed by demons came out of the tombs and approached him. They were so fiercely violent that no one dared to pass that way. [29] Suddenly, they shouted, "What do you want with us, Son of God? * Have you come here to torment us before the appointed time?"

[30] Some distance away a large herd of pigs was feeding. [31] The demons pleaded with him, "If you cast us out, send us into the herd of pigs." [32] He said to them, "Go, then!" They came out and entered the pigs. The entire herd rushed down the steep bank into the lake, and they perished in the water. [33] Those tending the pigs ran off, and when they reached the town, they related the whole story including what had happened to the men who had been possessed. [34] Then the whole town came out to meet Jesus, and when they saw him they begged him to leave their region.

9 The Healing of a Paralyzed Man.*

[1] Therefore, Jesus got into a boat and, crossing over the lake, arrived at his hometown.* [2] Some people then approached him, carrying a paralyzed man lying on a bed. On perceiving their faith, Jesus said to the man, "Take heart, son. Your sins are forgiven."

[3] On hearing this, some of the scribes said to themselves, "This man is blaspheming." * [4] Jesus perceived what they were thinking, and he said, "Why do you harbor evil thoughts in your hearts? [5] * Which is easier, to say: 'Your sins are forgiven,' or to say: 'Stand up and walk'? [6] But so that you may come to realize that the Son of Man has authority on earth to forgive sins"—he said to the paralyzed man—"Stand up, take your bed, and go to your home." [7] The man got up and returned to his home. [8] When the crowd saw this, they were filled with awe, and they glorified God for having given such authority to men.

Jesus Calls Matthew. [9] * As Jesus walked on from there, he noticed a man named Matthew sitting at the tax collector's booth. Jesus said to him, "Follow me," and he got up and followed him.

Jesus Dines with Sinners. [10] When he was sitting at dinner in the house, many tax collectors * and sinners were seated with Jesus and his disciples. [11] On seeing this, the

Pharisees said to his disciples, "Why does your teacher eat with tax collectors and sinners?" [12] When Jesus heard this, he said, "It is not the healthy who need a physician, but rather those who are sick. [13] Go and learn what this text means: 'I desire mercy, not sacrifice.' I have come to call not the righteous but sinners."

A Time of Joy and Grace. * [14] Then the disciples of John came to him and asked, "Why do we and the Pharisees fast but your disciples do not do so?" [15] Jesus answered, "How can the wedding guests mourn while the bridegroom is still with them? But the time will come when the bridegroom is taken away from them, and then they will fast.

[16] "No one sews a piece of unshrunken cloth on an old cloak, because the patch eventually pulls away from the cloak and a worse tear results. [17] Nor do people pour new wine into old wineskins, for if they do, the wineskins burst, the wine spills forth, and the skins are ruined. Rather, they pour new wine into fresh wineskins. In this way both are preserved."

Jesus Heals a Sick Woman and Raises a Dead Girl. * [18] While he was saying these things to them, an official * came forward. He knelt before him and said, "My daughter has just died. But if you come and lay your hand on her, she will live." [19] Jesus then rose and followed him, together with his disciples.

[20] Suddenly, a woman who had suffered from bleeding for twelve years came up behind him and touched the fringe of his cloak. [21] For she thought to herself, "If only I touch his cloak, I shall be healed." [22] Jesus turned and saw her, and he said, "Take heart, daughter! Your faith has healed you." And from that moment the woman was cured.

[23] When Jesus arrived at the official's house and saw the flute players * and the crowd making a commotion, [24] he said, "Go away! The girl is not dead; she is asleep," * but they laughed at him. [25] When the people had been sent

outside, he went in and took her by the hand, and the lit-tle girl stood up. [26] And the news of this spread through-out the entire district.

Jesus Heals Two Blind Men. [27] As Jesus proceeded from there, two blind men followed him, crying out loudly, "Son of David,* have pity on us." [28] When he had gone indoors, the blind men approached him. Jesus said to them, "Do you believe that I can do this?" They replied, "Yes, Lord, we do." [29] Then Jesus touched their eyes, say-ing, "Let it be done for you according to your faith." [30] And their sight was restored. Then Jesus sternly warned them, "See to it that no one learns about this." [31] But as soon as they had departed, they spread the news about him throughout that entire district.

Jesus Heals a Mute Demoniac. [32] As they left, a man who was possessed and unable to speak was brought to him. [33] When the demon had been driven out, the man who had been mute was able to speak. The crowds were amazed, and they said, "Nothing like this has ever been seen in Israel." [34] But the Pharisees responded, "He casts out demons by the prince of demons." *

The Harvest Is Abundant. * [35] Jesus traveled through all the towns and villages, teaching in their synagogues, pro-claiming the good news of the kingdom, and curing every kind of illness and disease. [36] When he saw the crowds, he had compassion on them because they were distressed and helpless like sheep without a shepherd. [37] Then he said to his disciples, "The harvest is abundant, but the laborers are few. [38] Therefore, ask the Lord of the harvest to send forth laborers for his harvest."

B: Instructions to the Apostles: The Charter of the Apostolate*

10 **Jesus Sends Out the Twelve Apostles.** * [1] Calling his twelve disciples together, he gave them authority over unclean spirits, with the power to drive them out and to cure every kind of disease and illness.

[2] These are the names of the twelve apostles: first, Simon, also called Peter, and his brother Andrew; James the son of Zebedee, and his brother John; [3] Philip and Bartholomew; Thomas and Matthew the tax collector; James the son of Alphaeus, and Thaddaeus; [4] Simon the Zealot, and Judas Iscariot,* the one who betrayed him.

[5] These twelve Jesus sent forth after giving them the following instructions: "Do not travel* to the territory of the Gentiles, and enter no Samaritan town. [6] Go rather to the lost sheep of Israel. [7] And as you go, proclaim: 'The kingdom of heaven is near.' [8] Cure the sick, raise the dead, cleanse those who have leprosy, drive out demons. You received without payment; give in the same way. [9] Take along no gold or silver or copper in your purses, [10] no sack for your journey, or an extra tunic, or sandals, or a staff. For the laborer deserves his keep.

[11] "Whatever town or village you enter, look for some honorable person who lives there, and stay with him until you leave. [12] As you enter a house, extend your blessing upon it. [13] If the house is worthy, let your peace come upon it, but if it is not worthy, let your peace return to you. [14] If anyone will not welcome you or listen to your message, shake the dust from your feet* as you leave that house or town. [15] Amen, I say to you, it will be more bearable for the land of Sodom and Gomorrah* on the day of judgment than for that town.

No Servant Is above His Master.* [16] "I am sending you out like sheep among wolves. Therefore, be as cunning as serpents and yet as innocent as doves. [17] Be on your guard, for people will hand you over to courts* and scourge you in their synagogues, [18] and you will be brought before governors and kings because of me to testify before them and the Gentiles.

[19] "When they hand you over, do not be concerned about how you are to speak or what you are to say. When the time comes, you will be given what you are to say. [20] For it will not be you who speak but the Spirit of your Father speaking through you.

²¹ "Brother will betray brother to death, and a father his child. Children will rise up against their parents and have them put to death. ²² You will be hated by all because of my name, but he who stands firm to the end will be saved. ²³ When you are persecuted in one town, flee to another. Amen, I say to you, you will not have finished traveling through all the towns of Israel before the Son of Man comes.*

²⁴ "No student is greater than his teacher, nor a servant greater than his master. ²⁵ It is enough for the student to be like his teacher and the servant like his master. If they have called the master of the house Beelzebul,* how much more those of his household?

The Conditions of Discipleship.* ²⁶ "Therefore, do not be afraid of them. There is nothing hidden that will not be disclosed, and nothing secret that will not become known. ²⁷ What I say to you in the dark, proclaim in the daylight, and what you hear whispered, shout from the housetops.

²⁸ "Have no fear of those who kill the body but cannot kill the soul. Rather, fear the one who can destroy both soul and body in Gehenna.*

²⁹ "Are not two sparrows sold for a penny? Yet not one of them can fall to the ground without your Father's knowledge. ³⁰ Even the hairs on your head have all been counted. ³¹ So do not be afraid; you are worth far more than any number of sparrows.

³² "Whoever acknowledges me before men, I will also acknowledge before my Father in heaven. ³³ But whoever denies me before men, I also will deny before my heavenly Father.

³⁴ "Do not think that I have come to bring peace to the earth. I have not come to bring peace but a sword.*

³⁵   For I have come to set a man against his father,
        a daughter against her mother,
        and a daughter-in-law against her mother-in-law;
³⁶   and one's enemies will be the members of his own
        household.

Whoever Receives You Receives Me. [37] "Anyone who loves his father or mother more than me is not worthy of me, and anyone who loves his son or daughter more than me is not worthy of me, [38] and anyone who does not take up his cross * and follow me is not worthy of me. [39] Whoever finds his life will lose it, and whoever loses his life for my sake will find it.*

[40] "Whoever receives you receives me; and whoever receives me receives the one who sent me. [41] Whoever receives a prophet * because he is a prophet will receive a prophet's reward, and whoever welcomes a righteous man because he is righteous will receive a righteous man's reward. [42] And whoever gives even a cup of cold water to one of these little ones because he is a disciple, amen, I say to you, he will not go unrewarded."

III: JESUS IS THE EXPECTED MESSIAH*

A: Jesus and John the Baptist*

11 **Report to John What You Hear and See.*** [1] When Jesus had finished giving these instructions to his twelve disciples, he moved on from there to teach and preach in their towns.

[2] When John who was in prison heard what Christ was doing, he sent his disciples [3] to ask him, "Are you the one who is to come,* or are we to wait for another?" [4] Jesus answered them, "Go back and tell John what you hear and see: [5] the blind receive their sight, the lame walk, those who have leprosy are cured, the deaf hear, the dead are raised to life, and the poor have the good news proclaimed to them. [6] And blessed is anyone who takes no offense at me." *

John Is the Elijah Who Was Destined To Return.* [7] As John's disciples were departing, Jesus spoke to the crowds about John: "What did you go out into the desert to see? A reed swaying in the wind? [8] Then what did you go out to see? Someone robed in fine clothing? Those who wear fine clothing are found in royal palaces. ⁹ What then did you go out to see? A prophet? Yes, I tell you, and far more than a prophet. ¹⁰ This is the one about whom it is written:

> 'Behold, I am sending my messenger ahead of you,
> who will prepare your way before you.'

¹¹ "Amen, I say to you, among those born of women, no one has been greater than John the Baptist, and yet the least in the kingdom of heaven is greater than he.* ¹² From the days of John the Baptist until now the kingdom of heaven has been subjected to violence, and the violent are taking it by force. ¹³ For all the Prophets and the Law prophesied until the arrival of John. ¹⁴ And if you are willing to accept it, John is the Elijah who was destined to return. ¹⁵ He who has ears to hear, let him hear!

Indecisive Children.* ¹⁶ "To what shall I compare this generation? It is like children who sit in the marketplace and call to one another:

¹⁷
> 'We played the flute for you,
>   but you would not dance;
> we sang a dirge,
>   and you refused to mourn.'

¹⁸ For John came neither eating nor drinking, and they said, 'He is possessed.' ¹⁹ The Son of Man came eating and drinking, and they say, 'Look at him! He is a glutton and a drunkard, a friend of tax collectors and sinners.' Yet wisdom is proved right by her actions."

Woe to the Cities of Galilee.* ²⁰ Then he began to reproach the cities in which most of his mighty deeds had been performed because they had refused to repent. ²¹ "Woe to you, Chorazin! Woe to you, Bethsaida! If the mighty deeds performed in your midst had been done in Tyre and Sidon, they would have repented long ago in sackcloth and ashes. ²² But I tell you, on the day of judgment it will be more tolerable for Tyre and Sidon than for you. ²³ And as for you, Capernaum:

'Will you be exalted to heaven?
    You will be cast down to the netherworld.'
For if the mighty deeds performed in your midst had been done in Sodom, it would be standing to this day. [24] But I tell you, on the day of judgment it will be more tolerable for the land of Sodom than for you."

The Self-Revelation of Jesus.* [25] At that time, Jesus said, "I thank you, Father, Lord of heaven and earth, because you have hidden these things from the wise and the learned and have revealed them to children. [26] Yes, Father, such has been your gracious will.

[27] "All things have been entrusted to me by my Father. No one knows the Son except the Father, and no one knows the Father except the Son and those to whom the Son wishes to reveal him.

The Gentle Mastery of Christ.* [28] "Come to me, all you who are weary and overburdened, and I will give you rest. [29] Take my yoke upon you and learn from me, for I am meek and humble of heart, and you will find rest for your souls. [30] For my yoke is easy and my burden is light."

B: Jesus Is the True Servant of God*

12 **Picking Grain on the Sabbath.** [1] * At that time, Jesus was walking through a field of grain on the Sabbath. His disciples were hungry, and they began to pick some heads of grain and eat them. [2] When the Pharisees saw this, they said to him, "Look at your disciples. They are doing what is forbidden on the Sabbath." *

[3] * He answered, "Have you not read what David did when he and his companions were hungry? [4] He entered the house of God and they ate the consecrated bread, which neither he nor his companions but only the priests were permitted to eat. [5] * Or have you not read in the Law that on the Sabbath the priests in the temple violate the Sabbath, but they are considered to be without guilt? [6] I tell you, one greater than the temple is here. [7] If you had truly understood what is meant by the words, 'I desire

mercy and not sacrifice,' you would not have condemned
these men who are without guilt. [8] For the Son of Man is
Lord of the Sabbath." *

The Man with a Withered Hand. * [9] Moving on from that
place, Jesus entered their synagogue. [10] A man was there
who had a withered hand, and hoping to find some
reason to accuse Jesus they asked him, "Is it lawful to heal
on the Sabbath?"

[11] He said to them, "Suppose you had only one sheep
and it fell into a pit on the Sabbath. Would you not lay
hold of it and lift it out? [12] How much more valuable a
man is than a sheep! Therefore, it is lawful to do good on
the Sabbath." [13] Then he said to the man, "Stretch out
your hand." He stretched it out, and it was restored, so
that it was as sound as the other one. [14] But the Pharisees
went out and began to plot how they might put him to
death. *

The Servant of the Lord. * [15] When Jesus became aware of
this, he departed from that place. Many people followed
him, and he healed all who were ill, [16] but he warned
them not to make him known. [17] This was to fulfill what
had been spoken through the prophet Isaiah:

[18]   "Behold, my servant, whom I have chosen,
        my beloved in whom I delight.
    I will place my spirit upon him,
        and he will proclaim justice to the Gentiles.
[19]   He will not cry out or shout,
        nor will anyone hear his voice in the streets.
[20]   A bruised reed he will not break,
        nor will he snuff out a smoldering wick,
    until he establishes justice as victorious;
[21]   and in his name the Gentiles will place their hope."

Whoever Is Not with Me Is against Me. * [22] Then they
brought to him a man who was unable to either see or
speak and who was possessed by a demon. He cured him,
so that the man who was mute both spoke and saw. [23] All
the people were astonished, and they said, "Is this not the

Son of David?" * ²⁴ But when the Pharisees heard this, they said, "It is only by Beelzebul,* the prince of demons, that this man casts out demons."

²⁵ He knew what they were thinking, and he said to them, "Every kingdom divided against itself is laid waste, and every city or household divided against itself cannot survive. ²⁶ If Satan drives out Satan, he is divided against himself. How then can his kingdom survive? ²⁷ If it is by Beelzebul that I cast out demons, by whom do your own children cast them out? Therefore, they will be your judges. ²⁸ But if it is by the Spirit of God that I cast out demons, then the kingdom of God has come to you.

²⁹ "Or again, how can anyone break into a strong man's house and steal his possessions unless he first ties up the strong man? Then indeed he can ransack the house.

³⁰ "Whoever is not with me is against me, and whoever does not gather with me scatters. ³¹ Therefore, I tell you that every sin and blasphemy will be forgiven but blasphemy against the Spirit will not be forgiven. ³² Whoever speaks a word against the Son of Man will be forgiven, but whoever speaks against the Holy Spirit will not be forgiven, either in this age or in the age to come.*

A Tree and Its Fruits. * ³³ "Make a tree good and its fruit will be good, or make a tree bad and its fruit will be bad. For a tree is known by its fruit. ³⁴ You brood of vipers! How can your speech be virtuous when you yourselves are evil? For the mouth speaks from the abundance of the heart. ³⁵ A good man brings forth good things from the good stored up within him, but an evil man brings forth evil things from his store of evil. ³⁶ I tell you that on the day of judgment people will have to render an account for every careless word they utter. ³⁷ For by your words you will be justified, and by your words you will be condemned."

The Sign of Jonah. * ³⁸ Then some of the scribes and Pharisees said to him, "Teacher, we would like you to show us a sign." ³⁹ He replied, "An evil and adulterous * generation asks for a sign, but the only sign it will be given is the sign of the prophet Jonah. [40] For just as Jonah spent three days and three nights in the belly of the whale, so will the Son of Man be in the heart of the earth for three days and three nights.*

[41] * "On the day of judgment the inhabitants of Nineveh will rise up with this generation and condemn it, for they repented at the preaching of Jonah, and now one greater than Jonah is here. [42] On the day of judgment the queen of the south will rise up with this generation and condemn it, because she came from the farthest reaches of the earth to hear the wisdom of Solomon, and now one greater than Solomon is here.

New Offensive from the Evil Spirit.* [43] "When an unclean spirit goes out of a person, it wanders through waterless regions seeking a place to rest, but it finds none. [44] Then it says, 'I will return to the home from which I departed.' And when it returns, it finds that home empty, swept clean, and put in order. [45] Then it goes off and brings back with it seven other spirits more wicked than itself, and they enter and settle there. As a result, the plight of that person is worse than before. So it will also be with this evil generation."

The True Family of Jesus.* [46] While he was still speaking to the crowds, his mother and his brethren* appeared. They were standing outside, wishing to speak with him. [[47] Someone told him, "Behold, your mother and your brothers are standing outside. They want to speak with you."] * [48] But Jesus replied to that man, "Who is my mother? Who are my brethren?" [49] Then, pointing to his disciples, he said, "Behold, my mother and my brethren. [50] Whoever does the will of my heavenly Father is my brother and sister and mother."

C: Jesus Teaches in Parables*

13 **The Day of Parables.** [1] That same day Jesus went out of the house and sat by the side of the lake. [2] However, such large crowds gathered around him that he got into a boat and sat down while all the people stood on the shore. ³ Then he told them many things in parables.*

The Parable of the Sower.* He said: "A sower went out to sow. ⁴ As he sowed, some seeds fell on the path, and the birds came and ate them up. ⁵ Other seeds fell on rocky ground, where there was little soil. They sprouted quickly, since the soil had very little depth, ⁶ but when the sun rose they were scorched, and since they lacked roots, they withered away. ⁷ Other seeds fell among thorns, and the thorns grew up and choked them. ⁸ But some seeds fell on rich soil and produced a crop—some a hundred, some sixty, and some thirty times what was sown. ⁹ He who has ears, let him hear!"

The Reason for Parables.* ¹⁰ Then his disciples approached and asked him, "Why do you speak to them in parables?" ¹¹ He replied, "To you has been granted knowledge of the mysteries * of the kingdom of heaven, but to them it has not been granted. ¹² To the one who has, more will be given, and he will have an abundance. As for the one who does not have, even what little he has will be taken away. ¹³ The reason I speak to them in parables is that they see but do not perceive and they listen but do not hear or understand. ¹⁴ In them is fulfilled the prophecy of Isaiah that says:

'You will indeed hear but not understand,
    you will indeed look but never see.
¹⁵ For this people's heart has become hardened;
        they have stopped up their ears
        and they have shut their eyes,
    so that they might not see with their eyes
        and hear with their ears
    and understand with their heart
        and then turn to me,
        and I would heal them.'

The Privilege of Discipleship.* ¹⁶ "But blessed are your eyes because they see, and your ears because they hear.

¹⁷ Amen, I say to you, many prophets and righteous people longed to see what you see but did not see it, and to hear what you hear but did not hear it.

The Explanation of the Parable of the Sower.* ¹⁸ "Therefore listen to the parable of the sower. ¹⁹ When anyone hears the word of the kingdom and does not understand it, the evil one comes and snatches away what has been sown in his heart; that is the seed sown on the path. ²⁰ As for the seed sown on rocky ground, this is the one who hears the word and immediately receives it with joy. ²¹ But such a person has no deep root, and he endures for only a short time. When some trouble or persecution arises on account of the word, he immediately falls away.

²² "The seed sown among thorns is the one who hears the word, but worldly cares and the lure of riches choke the word and it bears no fruit. ²³ However, the seed sown in rich soil is the one who hears the word and understands it; he indeed bears fruit and yields a hundred or sixty or thirty times what was sown."

The Parable of the Weeds.* ²⁴ He then proposed another parable to them: "The kingdom of heaven may be compared to a man who sowed good seed in his field. ²⁵ While everyone was asleep, his enemy came, sowed weeds* among the wheat, and then went away. ²⁶ When the wheat sprouted and ripened, the weeds also appeared.

²⁷ "The owner's servants came to him and asked, 'Master, did you not sow good seed in your field? Where then did these weeds come from?' ²⁸ He answered, 'One of my enemies has done this.' The servants then asked him, 'Do you want us to go and pull up the weeds?'

²⁹ "He replied, 'No, because in gathering the weeds you might uproot the wheat along with them. ³⁰ Let them both grow together until the harvest. At harvest time, I will tell the reapers, "Collect the weeds first and tie them in bundles to be burned. Then gather the wheat into my barn." ' "

The Parable of the Mustard Seed.* [31] He proposed still another parable: "The kingdom of heaven is like a mustard seed that a man took and sowed in his field. [32] It is the smallest of all the seeds, but when it has grown it is the greatest of plants and becomes a tree large enough for the birds to come and make nests in its branches." *

The Parable of the Yeast.* [33] And he offered them yet another parable: "The kingdom of heaven is like yeast that a woman took and mixed with three measures of flour until it was completely leavened."

The Use of Parables.* [34] Jesus told the crowds all these things in parables. Indeed he never spoke to them except in parables. [35] This was to fulfill what had been spoken through the prophet:

"I will open my mouth to speak in parables;
   I will proclaim what has been hidden since the
   foundation of the world."

Explanation of the Parable of the Weeds.* [36] Then he dismissed the crowds and went into the house. His disciples approached him and said, "Explain to us the parable of the weeds in the field." [37] He answered, "The one who sows good seed is the Son of Man. [38] The field is the world, and the good seed stands for the children of the kingdom. The weeds are the children of the evil one, [39] and the enemy who sowed them is the devil. The harvest is the end of the world, and the reapers are angels.

[40] "Just as the weeds are collected and burned in the fire, so will it be at the end of the world. [41] The Son of Man will send forth his angels, and they will gather out of his kingdom all who cause sin and all whose deeds are evil. [42] They will throw them into the fiery furnace, where there will be weeping and gnashing of teeth. [43] Then the righteous will shine like the sun in the kingdom of their Father. He who has ears to hear, let him hear!

The Parables of the Hidden Treasure and the Pearl.*
[44] "The kingdom of heaven is like treasure buried in a field, which a man found and buried again. Then in his

joy he went off and sold everything he had and bought that field.

⁴⁵ "Again, the kingdom of heaven is like a merchant searching for fine pearls. ⁴⁶ When he found one of great value, he went off and sold everything he had and bought it.

The Parable of the Net.* ⁴⁷ "Again, the kingdom of heaven is like a net cast into the sea where it caught fish of every kind. ⁴⁸ When it was full, they hauled it ashore. Then they sat down and collected the good fish into baskets but discarded those that were worthless. ⁴⁹ Thus will it be at the end of the world. The angels will go forth and separate the wicked from the righteous ⁵⁰ and throw them into the fiery furnace, where there will be weeping and gnashing of teeth.

Conclusion.* ⁵¹ "Have you understood all this?" he asked. They answered, "Yes." ⁵² Then he said to them, "Therefore, every teacher of the law who has been instructed about the kingdom of heaven is like the owner of a house who brings forth from his storeroom new treasures as well as old."

IV: THE AUTHENTIC FAITH OF THOSE CONVERTED*

A: Jesus Encounters Mixed Receptions*

Jesus Is Rejected at Nazareth.* ⁵³ When Jesus had finished these parables, he departed from that district.

⁵⁴ He came to his hometown, and he began to teach the people in the synagogue. They were astonished and wondered, "Where did this man get such wisdom and these mighty deeds? ⁵⁵ Is this not the carpenter's son? Is not his mother called Mary? Are not James and Joseph and Simon and Judas his brethren? ⁵⁶ And are not all his sisters here with us? Where then did this man get all this?" ⁵⁷ And so they took offense at him.

But Jesus said to them, "A prophet is always treated with honor except in his hometown and in his own house." [58] And he did not work many mighty deeds there because of their lack of faith.

14 John the Baptist, Herod, and Jesus.* [1] At that time Herod the tetrarch * heard reports about Jesus, [2] and he said to his servants, "This man is John the Baptist. He has risen from the dead. That is why such powers are at work in him."

[3] Now Herod had ordered the arrest of John, put him in chains, and imprisoned him on account of Herodias, his brother Philip's wife. [4] For John had told him, "It is against the law for you to have her." [5] Herod wanted to put John to death, but he was afraid of the people because they regarded John as a prophet. [6] But at a birthday celebration for Herod, the daughter of Herodias * danced in front of the guests, and she pleased Herod so much [7] that he promised with an oath to give her anything she asked for. [8] Prompted by her mother, she said, "Give me here the head of John the Baptist on a platter."

[9] The king was distressed, but because of his oaths and the guests present there, he ordered that her request be granted. [10] He had John beheaded in the prison.* [11] The head was brought in on a platter and given to the girl, who took it to her mother. [12] John's disciples came and removed the body and buried it. Then they went and told Jesus.

Jesus Feeds Five Thousand Men. [13] * When Jesus received this news, he withdrew from there in a boat by himself to a deserted place, but when the people learned of it, they followed him on foot from the towns.* [14] When he came ashore and saw the vast crowd, he had compassion on them and healed those who were sick.

[15] When evening approached, the disciples came up to him and said, "This is a deserted place and the hour is now late. Send the people away now so that they can go to the villages to buy some food for themselves."

¹⁶ Jesus replied, "There is no need for them to depart. Give them something to eat yourselves." ¹⁷ But they answered, "All we have here are five loaves of bread and two fish." ¹⁸ Jesus said, "Bring them here to me."

¹⁹ Then he ordered the people to sit down on the grass. Taking the five loaves and the two fish, he looked up to heaven, blessed and broke the loaves, and gave them to the disciples, and the disciples gave them to the crowds.* ²⁰ They all ate and were satisfied. Then they gathered up the fragments that were left over—twelve full baskets. ²¹ Those who had eaten numbered about five thousand men, in addition to women and children.*

Jesus Walks on the Water.* ²² Then Jesus instructed the disciples to get into the boat and go on ahead to the other side while he dismissed the crowds. ²³ After he sent them away, he went by himself up on the mountain to pray. When evening came, he was there alone. ²⁴ Meanwhile, the boat was already some distance from the shore, battered by waves and a strong wind.

²⁵ During the fourth watch* of the night, Jesus came toward them, walking on the water. ²⁶ When the disciples saw him walking on the water they were terrified, and they cried out in their fright, "It is a ghost!" ²⁷ But Jesus immediately spoke to them, saying, "Have courage! It is I. Do not be afraid."

²⁸ Peter answered, "Lord, if it is you, command me to come to you across the water." ²⁹ He said, "Come!" Then Peter got out of the boat and started walking on the water toward Jesus. ³⁰ But when he realized the force of the wind, he became frightened. As he began to sink, he cried out, "Lord, save me!" ³¹ Jesus immediately reached out his hand and caught hold of him, saying, "O you of little faith, why did you doubt?" ³² After they got into the boat, the wind died down. ³³ Those in the boat fell to their knees in worship, saying, "Truly you are the Son of God." *

Jesus Heals the Sick at Gennesaret. ³⁴ After they had completed the crossing, they landed at Gennesaret.* ³⁵ When

THE MIRACLES OF JESUS—". . . They also brought him all those who were sick and begged him to let them touch only the edge of his cloak. All who touched it were completely healed" (Mt 14:35-36).

JESUS TRANSFIGURED—"His face shone like the sun, and his clothes became dazzling white. Suddenly, there appeared to them Moses and Elijah, conversing with him" (Mt 17:2-3).

the people there recognized him, they sent word of his presence throughout the region. They also brought him all those who were sick [36] and begged him to let them touch only the edge of his cloak. All who touched it were completely healed.

15 Traditions That Falsify the Law of God.

[1] Then Pharisees and scribes came to Jesus from Jerusalem and asked, [2] * "Why do your disciples ignore the tradition of the elders? They do not wash their hands before eating." [3] He answered them, "And why do you break the commandment of God for the sake of your tradition? [4] For God said, 'Honor your father and your mother,' and 'Whoever curses his father or mother shall be put to death.' [5] But you say, 'If anyone says to his father or mother, "Anything I might have used for your support is dedicated to God," [6] then he is excused from his duty to honor his father or mother.' To uphold your tradition you have made God's word null and void. [7] You hypocrites! How rightly did Isaiah prophesy about you when he said:

[8]   'This people honors me with their lips,
       but their hearts are far from me;

[9]   in vain do they worship me,
       teaching as doctrines the commandments of men.'"

Clean and Unclean. * [10] Then he called the people to him and said to them, "Listen and understand. [11] It is not what goes into one's mouth that defiles a person; what comes out of the mouth is what defiles him."

[12] The disciples approached and said to him, "Do you realize that the Pharisees were greatly offended when they heard what you said?" [13] He answered, "Every plant that my Father has not planted will be uprooted. [14] Leave them alone. They are blind guides. And if one blind person guides another, they will both fall into a pit."

[15] Peter said to him, "Explain that parable to us." [16] Jesus replied, "Are even you still without understanding? [17] Do you not realize that whatever goes into the mouth passes through the stomach and is discharged into the sewer?

¹⁸ But what comes out of the mouth originates in the heart, and this is what defiles a person. ¹⁹ For from the heart come evil thoughts, murder, adultery, fornication, theft, perjury, slander. ²⁰ These are the things that defile a person, but to eat with unwashed hands does not make anyone unclean."

The Faith of a Pagan Woman.* ²¹ Jesus then left that place and withdrew to the region of Tyre and Sidon.* ²² And behold, a Canaanite woman from that region came out to meet him and cried out, "Have pity on me, Lord, Son of David. My daughter is sorely tormented by a demon." ²³ But he did not say a word to her in reply.

So his disciples came and urged him, "Send her away, for she keeps shouting after us." ²⁴ He answered, "I was sent only to the lost sheep of the house of Israel." ²⁵ But she came and knelt at his feet, saying, "Lord, help me!" ²⁶ He answered, "It is not right to take the children's bread and throw it to the dogs." ²⁷ She replied, "Yes, Lord, but even the dogs eat the scraps that fall from their masters' table." ²⁸ Then Jesus answered her, "Woman, you have great faith. Let it be done for you as you wish." And from that moment her daughter was healed.

Jesus Heals Many People. ²⁹ * After leaving that region, Jesus walked along the shores of the Sea of Galilee, and going up onto the mountain, he sat down. ³⁰ Large crowds flocked to him, bringing with them the lame, the blind, the deformed, the mute, and many others. They placed them at his feet, and he cured them. ³¹ The crowds were amazed when they observed the mute speaking, the crippled made whole, the lame walking, and the blind with their sight restored, and they gave praise to the God of Israel.

Jesus Feeds Four Thousand Men. ³² Jesus called his disciples to him and said, "I am moved with compassion for these people, because they have been with me now for three days and have nothing to eat. I do not want to send them away hungry, or they may collapse on the way."

[33] The disciples said to him, "Where can we ever get enough bread in this deserted place to feed such a great crowd?" [34] Jesus asked them, "How many loaves do you have?" "Seven," they replied, "and a few small fish."

[35] He ordered the crowd to sit down on the ground. [36] Then he took the seven loaves and the fish, and after giving thanks he broke them and gave them to the disciples, and the disciples gave them to the people. [37] They all ate and were satisfied. Afterward, they picked up seven baskets full of what remained. [38] Those who had eaten numbered four thousand men, not counting women and children. [39] And when he had sent away the crowds, he got into the boat and went to the region of Magadan.

16 The Demand for a Sign.*
[1] The Pharisees and Sadducees came, and to put him to the test they asked him to show them a sign from heaven. [2] He answered them, "When it is evening, you say, 'Tomorrow there will be fair weather, for the sky is red,' [3] and in the morning you say, 'It will be stormy today, for the sky is red and threatening.' You know how to interpret the appearance of the sky, but you cannot interpret the signs of the times. [4] An evil and adulterous * generation asks for a sign, but no sign will be given to it except the sign of Jonah." Then he left them and went away.

The Yeast of the Pharisees and Sadducees.* [5] In crossing to the other side of the lake, the disciples had forgotten to bring bread. [6] Jesus said to them, "Be careful, and beware of the yeast of the Pharisees and Sadducees." [7] They talked about this among themselves and concluded: "It is because we brought no bread."

[8] Aware of what they were saying, Jesus said, "O you of little faith, why are you talking about having no bread? [9] Do you still not understand? Do you not remember the five loaves for the five thousand and the number of baskets you collected? [10] Or the seven loaves for the four thousand and how many baskets you gathered? [11] How could you fail to see that I was not speaking about bread

when I said, 'Beware of the yeast of the Pharisees and Sadducees'?" ¹² Then they understood that he had not told them to beware of the yeast used in bread but of the teaching of the Pharisees and Sadducees.

Peter's Confession of Christ's Divinity. ¹³ * When Jesus came to the region of Caesarea Philippi,* he asked his disciples, "Who do people say that the Son of Man is?" ¹⁴ They replied, "Some say John the Baptist; others, Elijah; and still others, Jeremiah or one of the Prophets." ¹⁵ "But you," he said to them, "who do you say that I am?" ¹⁶ Simon Peter replied, "You are the Christ, the Son of the living God." *

¹⁷ Then Jesus said to him in reply, "Blessed are you, Simon son of Jonah. For flesh and blood * has not revealed this to you but my heavenly Father. ¹⁸ And I say to you: You are Peter, and on this rock I will build my Church,* and the gates of the netherworld will not prevail against it. ¹⁹ I will give you the keys of the kingdom of heaven. Whatever you bind on earth shall be bound in heaven, and whatever you loose on earth shall be loosed in heaven." * ²⁰ Then he gave the disciples strict orders not to tell * anyone that he was the Christ.

Jesus Predicts His Passion. ²¹ From then onward Jesus made it clear to his disciples that he must go to Jerusalem and endure great suffering at the hands of the elders, the chief priests, and the scribes, and be put to death, and be raised on the third day.*

²² * Peter took him aside and began to rebuke him, saying, "God forbid, Lord. Such a fate must never happen to you." ²³ He turned and said to Peter, "Get behind me, Satan! You are an obstacle to me. You are thinking not as God does, but as men do."

The Conditions of Discipleship. ²⁴ Jesus then said to his disciples, "Anyone who wishes to follow me must deny himself, take up his cross, and follow me. ²⁵ For whoever wishes to save his life will lose it, but whoever loses his life for my sake will find it.* ²⁶ What will it profit a man if he gains the whole world and forfeits his very life? Or what can he give in exchange for his life?

[27] "For the Son of Man will come with his angels in the glory of his Father, and then he will repay everyone according to what has been done. [28] Amen, I say to you, there are some standing here who will not taste death before they see the Son of Man coming in his kingdom." *

17 Jesus Is Transfigured.*

[1] Six days later, Jesus took Peter and James and his brother John and led them up a high mountain * by themselves. [2] And in their presence he was transfigured; his face shone like the sun, and his clothes became dazzling white. [3] Suddenly, there appeared to them Moses and Elijah, conversing with him. [4] Then Peter said to Jesus, "Lord, it is good for us to be here. If you wish, I will make three tents here—one for you, one for Moses, and one for Elijah."

[5] While he was still speaking, suddenly a bright cloud cast a shadow over them. Then a voice from the cloud said, "This is my beloved Son, with whom I am well pleased. Listen to him." [6] When the disciples heard this, they fell on their faces and were greatly frightened. [7] But Jesus came and touched them, saying, "Stand up, and do not be frightened." [8] And when they raised their eyes, they saw no one, but only Jesus.

Elijah Has Already Come.* [9] As they were coming down from the mountain, Jesus commanded them, "Tell no one about this vision until the Son of Man has been raised from the dead." [10] And the disciples asked him, "Why then do the scribes say that Elijah must come first?" [11] He said in reply, "Elijah will indeed come, and he will set everything right again. [12] However, I tell you that Elijah has already come, and they did not recognize him, but they did to him whatever they pleased. In the same way, the Son of Man will suffer at their hands." [13] Then the disciples understood that he was speaking to them about John the Baptist.

Jesus Heals a Boy with a Demon.* [14] When they returned to the crowd, a man came up to Jesus, fell to his knees before him, [15] and pleaded, "Lord, have pity on my son, for he is subject to epileptic seizures and endures great suffering. He falls often into fire and often into water. [16] I brought him to your disciples, but they could not cure him."

[17] Jesus said in reply, "O unbelieving and perverse generation, how much longer shall I remain with you? How much longer must I put up with you? Bring the boy here to me." [18] Then Jesus rebuked the demon, and it came out of the boy, and he was cured from that very moment.

[19] Then the disciples came to Jesus and asked him privately, "Why were we not able to cast it out?" [20] He answered, "Because you have such little faith. Amen, I say to you, if you have faith as tiny as a mustard seed, you will be able to say to this mountain: 'Move from here to there,' and it will move. Nothing will be impossible for you. [21 But this kind of demon does not come out except by prayer and fasting.]" *

Jesus Predicts His Passion a Second Time.* [22] When they were together in Galilee, Jesus said to them, "The Son of Man is going to be handed over into the power of men. [23] They will kill him, and on the third day he will be raised." And they were overwhelmed with grief.

Jesus Pays the Temple Tax.* [24] When they arrived at Capernaum, the collectors of the temple tax came up to Peter and asked, "Doesn't your teacher pay the temple tax?" [25] "Yes, he does," he replied.

When Peter went into the house, but before he had a chance to speak, Jesus asked him, "Simon, what is your opinion? From whom do the kings of the earth exact tolls and taxes—from their own sons or from others?" [26] And when he said, "From others," Jesus replied, "Then their sons are exempt. [27] However, lest we give offense to them, go to the lake and cast a hook. Take the first fish that you catch and open its mouth. There you will find a silver coin. Take it and give it to them for me and for yourself."

B: Instructions to the Disciples:
The Charter of the Community*

18 **Become Like Little Children.*** ¹ At that time, the disciples came to Jesus and asked, "Who is the greatest in the kingdom of heaven?" ² Then Jesus beckoned a child to come to him, placed it in their midst, ³ and said, "Amen, I say to you, unless you change and become like little children, you will never enter the kingdom of heaven. ⁴ Whoever humbles himself and becomes like this child is the greatest in the kingdom of heaven.

Woe to the World because of Scandals.* ⁵ "And whoever receives one such child in my name receives me. ⁶ But if anyone causes one of these little ones who believe in me to sin, it would be better for him to have a millstone fastened around his neck and to be drowned in the depths of the sea. ⁷ Woe to the world because of scandals. Such things are bound to occur, but woe to the one through whom they come.

⁸ * "If your hand or your foot is an occasion of sin for you, cut it off and throw it away. It is preferable for you to enter into life maimed or crippled than to have two hands or two feet and be cast into the eternal fire. ⁹ And if your eye causes you to sin, tear it out and throw it away. It is preferable for you to enter into life with one eye than to have two eyes and be cast into the fires of Gehenna.

¹⁰ "Take care that you do not despise one of these little ones, for I tell you that their angels in heaven gaze continually on the face of my heavenly Father. [¹¹ For the Son of Man has come to save what was lost.] *

The Parable of the Lost Sheep.* ¹² "Tell me your opinion. If a man owns a hundred sheep and one of them wanders away, will he not leave the other ninety-nine on the hillside and go off in search of the one who went astray? ¹³ And if he finds it, amen, I say to you, he is more filled with joy over it than over the ninety-nine who did not wander off. ¹⁴ In the same way, it is not the will of your

Father in heaven that a single one of these little ones should be lost.

The Church: Community of Love, Prayer, and Pardon.* [15] "If your brother wrongs you, go and take up the matter with him when the two of you are alone. If he listens to you, you have won your brother over. [16] But if he will not listen, take one or two others along with you, so that every detail may be confirmed by the testimony of two or three witnesses. [17] If he refuses to listen to them, report it to the Church. And if he refuses to listen to the Church, treat him as you would a Gentile or a tax collector.

[18] "Amen, I say to you, whatever you bind on earth shall be bound in heaven, and whatever you loose on earth shall be loosed in heaven. [19] [Amen,] I say to you, further, if two of you on earth agree about anything you ask for, it will be granted to you by my Father in heaven. [20] For where two or three are gathered together in my name, I am there in their midst."

[21] Then Peter came up to him and asked, "Lord, if my brother sins against me, how often must I forgive him? As many as seven times?" [22] Jesus answered, "I say to you, not seven times but seventy times seven.*

The Parable of the Unmerciful Servant.* [23] "For this reason, the kingdom of heaven may be compared to a king who decided to settle accounts with his servants. [24] When he began the accounting, a man was brought to him who owed him ten thousand talents.* [25] Since he had no possible way to repay what he owed, his master ordered him to be sold, together with his wife, his children, and all his property, to satisfy the debt. [26] At this, the servant fell to his knees, saying, 'Be patient with me, and I will repay you in full.' [27] Moved with compassion, the master of that servant let him go and canceled the debt.

[28] "However, when that servant left, he encountered one of his fellow servants who owed him one hundred denarii,* and, choking him, he demanded, 'Pay me back what you owe.' [29] His fellow servant fell to his knees and

pleaded with him, saying, 'Be patient with me and I will repay you.' [30] But he turned a deaf ear and had him thrown into prison until he had repaid the debt.

[31] "When his fellow servants observed what had happened, they were greatly upset, and, going to their master, they reported everything that had taken place. [32] Then his master sent for the man and said to him, 'You wicked servant! I forgave you for your complete debt because you begged me. [33] Should you not have had mercy on your fellow servant as I had mercy on you?' [34] And in his anger his master handed him over to be tortured until he repaid the entire debt. [35] In the same way, my heavenly Father will also deal with you unless each of you forgives his brother from the heart."

V: THE COMING OF THE SON OF MAN*

A: The Ministry in Judea and Jerusalem

19 **Marriage and Celibacy.*** [1] When Jesus had finished this discourse, he left Galilee and came into the region of Judea beyond the Jordan. [2] Large crowds followed him, and he healed them there.

[3] Some Pharisees came forward and tested him by asking, "Is it lawful for a man to divorce his wife for any reason whatsoever?" [4] He replied, "Have you not read that from the beginning the Creator 'made them male and female' [5] and said: 'That is why a man leaves his father and mother and is joined to his wife, and the two become one flesh'? [6] And so they are no longer two but one flesh. Therefore, what God has joined together, let no one separate."

[7] They said to him, "Why then did Moses command that a man give his wife a certificate of divorce and send her away?" [8] He replied, "It was because you were so hard-hearted that Moses allowed you to divorce your wives, but it was not like this from the beginning. [9] Now I say to you: if a man divorces his wife for any reason except if the marriage was unlawful and marries another, he commits adultery."

^{10} His disciples said to him, "If that is the situation between a husband and wife, it is better not to marry." ^{11} He replied, "Not everyone can accept this teaching, but only those to whom it has been given. ^{12} For there are eunuchs who have been made so from birth and eunuchs who were made so by others, and there are eunuchs who have made themselves eunuchs for the sake of the kingdom of heaven. Let those accept this who can do so." *

Jesus Receives Little Children. * ^{13} Then people brought children to him so that he might lay his hands on them and pray. The disciples rebuked them, ^{14} but Jesus said, "Let the little children come to me, and do not hinder them. For it is to such as these that the kingdom of heaven belongs." ^{15} And after he had laid his hands on them he proceeded on his way.

The Rich Young Man. * ^{16} Then a man came forward and asked him, "Teacher, what good thing must I do to achieve eternal life?" ^{17} He said to him, "Why do you ask me about what is good? There is only one who is good. But if you wish to enter into life, keep the commandments." ^{18} He said, "Which ones?" And Jesus answered, "You shall not kill. You shall not commit adultery. You shall not steal. You shall not bear false witness. ^{19} Honor your father and your mother. Love your neighbor as yourself." ^{20} The young man said to him, "I have observed all these. Is there anything more I must do?" ^{21} Jesus replied, "If you wish to be perfect, go, sell your possessions, and give the money to the poor, and you will have treasure in heaven. Then come, follow me." ^{22} When the young man heard this, he went away grieving, for he possessed great wealth.

^{23} Then Jesus said to his disciples, "Amen, I say to you, it will be difficult for a rich man to enter the kingdom of heaven. ^{24} Again I tell you, it is easier for a camel to pass through the eye of a needle than for someone who is rich to enter the kingdom of heaven." ^{25} When the disciples heard this, they were astonished, and they asked, "Who then can be saved?" ^{26} Jesus looked at them and said, "For men this is impossible, but for God all things are possible."

Reward for Following Jesus.* [27] Then Peter said in reply, "We have given up everything to follow you. What then will there be for us?" [28] Jesus replied, "Amen, I say to you, at the renewal of all things, when the Son of Man is seated on his glorious throne, you who have followed me will yourselves sit on twelve thrones, judging the twelve tribes of Israel. [29] And everyone who has left houses or brothers or sisters or father or mother or children or lands for the sake of my name will receive a hundred times more and will inherit eternal life. [30] But many who are first will be last, and the last will be first.

20 **The Parable of the Workers in the Vineyard.*** [1] "The kingdom of heaven is like a landowner who went out early in the morning to hire laborers for his vineyard. [2] After agreeing with the laborers for a denarius * a day, he sent them into his vineyard. [3] Going out about nine o'clock,* he saw some others standing idle in the marketplace. [4] He said to them, 'You also go into my vineyard and I will give you what is just.' [5] When he went out again around noon and at three in the afternoon,* he did the same. [6] Then, about five o'clock,* he went out and found others standing around, and he said to them, 'Why have you been standing here idle all day?' [7] They answered, 'Because no one has hired us.' He said to them, 'You too go into my vineyard.'

[8] "When evening came, the owner of the vineyard said to his foreman, 'Summon the workers and give them their pay, beginning with those who came last and ending with the first.' [9] When those who had started to labor at five o'clock came, each of them received a denarius. [10] Therefore, those who had come first thought that they would receive more, but they were paid a denarius, the same as the others. [11] And when they received it, they began to grumble against the landowner, [12] saying, 'These men who were hired last worked only one hour, and yet

you have rewarded them on the same level with us who have borne the greatest portion of the work and the heat of the day.'

¹³ "The owner replied to one of them, 'Friend, I am not treating you unfairly. Did you not agree with me to work for a denarius? ¹⁴ Take your pay and leave. I have chosen to pay the latecomers the same as I pay you. ¹⁵ Am I not free to do as I wish with my own money? Or are you envious because I am generous?' ¹⁶ Thus, the last will be first and the first will be last."

Jesus Predicts His Passion a Third Time.* ¹⁷ As Jesus was going up to Jerusalem, he took the twelve disciples aside by themselves and said to them, ¹⁸ "Behold, we are now going up to Jerusalem, and the Son of Man will be handed over to the chief priests and the scribes, and they will condemn him to death. ¹⁹ Then they will hand him over to the Gentiles to be mocked and scourged and crucified, and on the third day he will be raised to life."

The Son of Man Has Come To Serve.* ²⁰ Then the mother of the sons of Zebedee came to Jesus with her sons and made a request of him after kneeling before him. ²¹ "What do you wish?" he asked her. She said to him, "Promise that these two sons of mine may sit, one at your right hand and the other at your left, in your kingdom." ²² Jesus said in reply, "You do not know what you are asking. Can you drink the cup * I am going to drink?" They said to him, "We can."

²³ He then said to them, "You shall indeed drink my cup, but to sit at my right hand and at my left is not in my power to grant. Those places belong to those for whom they have been prepared by my Father."

²⁴ When the other ten disciples heard this, they were indignant at the two brothers. ²⁵ But Jesus called them over and said, "You know that the rulers of the Gentiles lord it over them, and their great ones make their authority over them felt. ²⁶ This must not be so with you. Instead, whoever wishes to be great among you must be your servant, ²⁷ and whoever wishes to be first among you

must be your servant. [28] In the same way, the Son of Man did not come to be served but rather to serve and to give his life as a ransom for many." *

Two Blind Men Receive Sight.* [29] As they were leaving Jericho, a large crowd followed Jesus. [30] Two blind men were sitting by the roadside, and when they learned that Jesus was passing by, they shouted, "Lord, Son of David, take pity on us." [31] The crowd rebuked them and told them to be silent, but they only shouted even more loudly, "Lord, Son of David, take pity on us."

[32] Jesus stopped and called them, saying, "What do you want me to do for you?" [33] They said to him, "Lord, grant that our eyes may be opened." [34] Jesus, moved with compassion, touched their eyes. Immediately, they received their sight and followed him.

B: Encounters at Jerusalem

21 **The Entry into Jerusalem.*** [1] When they drew near Jerusalem and had reached Bethphage on the Mount of Olives, Jesus sent off two disciples, [2] saying to them, "Go to the village directly ahead of you, and as soon as you enter you will find a tethered donkey and a colt with her. Untie them and bring them to me. [3] If anyone says anything to you, tell them, 'The Lord needs them.' Then he will let you have them at once." [4] This was to fulfill what had been spoken by the prophet:

[5]   "Say to the daughter of Zion: *
      'Behold, your king is coming to you,
      humble and riding on a donkey,
          and on a colt, the foal of a donkey.'"

[6] The disciples went off and did as Jesus had instructed them. [7] They brought the donkey and the colt, and laid their cloaks on their backs, and he sat on them.* [8] A very large crowd spread their cloaks on the road, while others cut branches from the trees and spread them on the road. [9] The crowds that preceded him and those that followed kept shouting:

"Hosanna to the Son of David!
Blessed is he who comes in the name of the Lord! *
Hosanna in the highest!"

¹⁰ And when he entered Jerusalem, the whole city was filled with excitement. "Who is this?" the people asked, ¹¹ and the crowds replied, "This is the prophet Jesus from Nazareth in Galilee."

Jesus Cleanses the Temple.* ¹² Then Jesus entered the temple and drove out all those whom he found buying and selling there. He overturned the tables of the money changers and the seats of those who were selling doves. ¹³ He said to them, "It is written:

'My house shall be called a house of prayer,'
but you are making it a den of thieves." *

¹⁴ The blind and the crippled came to him in the temple, and he cured them. ¹⁵ But when the chief priests and the scribes witnessed the wonderful things he was performing and heard the children crying out in the temple area, "Hosanna to the Son of David," they became infuriated ¹⁶ and said to him, "Do you hear what they are saying?" Jesus replied, "Yes. Have you never read the text:

'Out of the mouths of infants and babies who are nursing
you have received fitting praise'?"

¹⁷ Then he left them and went out of the city to Bethany, where he spent the night.

The Lesson of the Withered Fig Tree.* ¹⁸ Early the next morning, as he was returning to the city, he was hungry. ¹⁹ Noticing a fig tree by the side of the road, he went over to it but found nothing on its branches except leaves. Then he said to it, "May you never give forth fruit again!" And instantly the fig tree withered away.

²⁰ When the disciples witnessed this, they were stunned, and they asked, "How could that fig tree wither away in an instant?" ²¹ Jesus answered them, "Amen, I say to you, if you have faith and do not doubt, not only will

you do what has been done to this fig tree, but even if you say to this mountain, 'Be lifted up and thrown into the sea,' it will be accomplished. [22] Whatever you ask for in faith-filled prayer, you will receive."

The Authority of Jesus Questioned.* [23] When he entered the temple and began to teach, the chief priests and the elders of the people approached him and asked, "By what authority are you doing these things? And who gave you this authority?" [24] Jesus said to them in reply, "I will also ask you one question. If you give me an answer, then I will tell you by what authority I do these things. [25] Where did John's baptism originate? From heaven or from men?"

They argued among themselves, "If we say: 'From heaven,' he will say to us, 'Then why did you not believe him?' [26] But if we say, 'From men,' we are afraid of the people, for they all regard John as a prophet."

[27] Therefore, they answered Jesus, "We do not know." And Jesus said to them, "Then neither shall I tell you by what authority I do these things.*

The Parable of the Two Sons.* [28] "What is your opinion about this? A man had two sons. He went to the first and said, 'My son, go and work in the vineyard today.' [29] He answered, 'I will not,' but later he had a change of heart and went. [30] The father then gave the same instruction to the second son, who answered, 'Of course I will,' but then did not go. [31] Which of the two complied with his father's instruction?" They responded, "The first."

Then Jesus said to them, "Amen, I say to you, tax collectors and prostitutes are entering the kingdom of God ahead of you. [32] For John came to show you the path of righteousness, but you did not believe him, whereas the tax collectors and the prostitutes did. Yet even after you realized that, you still refused to change your minds and believe in him.

The Parable of the Tenants.* [33] "Listen to another parable. There was a landowner who planted a vineyard, fenced it in on all sides, dug a winepress in it, and built a watchtower. Then he leased it to tenants and went off on a journey.

³⁴ "When the time for harvest approached, he sent his servants to the tenants to collect his share of the produce. ³⁵ But the tenants seized his servants and beat one of them, killed another, and stoned a third. ³⁶ Again, he sent more servants, but they treated them in the same manner.

³⁷ "Finally, he sent his son to them, thinking, 'They will respect my son.' ³⁸ But when the tenants saw the son, they said to one another, 'This is the heir. Come, let us kill him and get his inheritance.' ³⁹ And so they seized him, threw him out of the vineyard, and killed him.

⁴⁰ "Now what do you think the owner of the vineyard will do to those tenants when he comes?" ⁴¹ They said to him, "He will kill those evil men, and then he will lease his vineyard to other tenants who will give him the produce at the harvest."

⁴² Jesus then said to them, "Have you never read in the Scriptures:

'The stone that the builders rejected
　　has become the cornerstone;
by the Lord has this been done,
　　and it is wonderful in our eyes'?

⁴³ Therefore, I tell you, the kingdom of God will be taken away from you and given to a people that will produce fruit in abundance. [⁴⁴ The one who falls on this stone will be broken into pieces, and the one on whom it falls will be crushed.]" *

⁴⁵ When the chief priests and the Pharisees heard his parables, they realized that he was speaking about them. ⁴⁶ They wanted to arrest him, but they were afraid of the crowds, who regarded him as a prophet.

22 The Parable of the Wedding Banquet.*

¹ Jesus spoke to them again in parables, saying, ² "The kingdom of heaven may be compared to a king who gave a wedding banquet for his son. ³ He sent forth his servants to summon those who had been invited to the banquet, but they

PAYING TAX TO THE EMPEROR—"When they brought him a denarius, he asked them, 'Whose image is this, and whose inscription?' . . . 'Give to Caesar what is due to Caesar, and to God what is due to God' " (Mt 22:19-21).

COMING OF THE SON OF MAN—"The sun will be darkened and the moon will not give forth its light; the stars will fall from the sky. . . . Then the sign of the Son of Man will appear in heaven" (Mt 24:29-30).

refused to come. [4] Then he sent other servants, saying, 'Tell those who have been invited, "Behold, my banquet has been prepared, my oxen and my fattened cattle have been slaughtered, and everything is ready. Come to the wedding banquet." '

[5] "But they ignored his invitation. One went off to his farm, another to his business, [6] while the rest seized his servants, mistreated them, and killed them.

[7] "The king was enraged, and he sent forth his troops who destroyed those murderers and burned their city to the ground. [8] Then he said to his servants, 'The wedding banquet is ready, but those who were invited were not worthy of that honor. [9] Go forth, therefore, to the main roads and invite everyone you can find to the wedding banquet.' [10] The servants went forth into the streets and gathered together everyone they could find, good and bad alike. And so the wedding hall was filled with guests.

[11] * "But when the king came in to greet the guests, he noticed one man who was not properly dressed for a wedding. [12] 'My friend,' he said to him, 'how did you gain entrance here without a wedding garment?' The man was speechless. [13] Then the king said to the attendants, 'Bind his hands and feet and cast him outside into the darkness, where there will be weeping and gnashing of teeth.' [14] For many are called, but few are chosen." *

God or Caesar. * [15] Then the Pharisees went off and made plans to trap him in what he said. [16] They sent some of their disciples to him, along with the Herodians,* and said, "Teacher, we know that you are truthful and that you teach the way of God in accordance with the truth. Nor are you concerned with anyone's opinion for you do not care about people's opinions. [17] Tell us then what you think about this: Is it lawful or not for us to pay taxes to Caesar?"

[18] Jesus was aware of their malicious intent, and he said, "You hypocrites! Why are you trying to trap me? [19] Show me the coin that is used for paying the tax." When they

brought him a denarius,* [20] he asked them, "Whose image is this, and whose inscription?" [21] They replied, "Caesar's." On hearing this, he said to them, "Give to Caesar what is due to Caesar, and to God what is due to God." * [22] Stunned on hearing this reply, they went away and left him alone.

Marriage and the Resurrection. * [23] On that same day, the Sadducees, who assert that there is no resurrection, approached him and posed this question, [24] "Teacher, Moses said that if a man dies without having children, his brother* is to marry his brother's wife and raise up children for his brother. [25] Now there were seven brothers who belonged to our group. The first one married and died without issue, and therefore left his wife to his brother. [26] The same result occurred with the second brother and the third, right down to the seventh. [27] Finally, the woman herself died. [28] Now at the resurrection, whose wife of the seven will she be, inasmuch as all of them had her?"

[29] Jesus answered them, "You are in error, for you do not understand the Scriptures or the power of God. [30] At the resurrection they will neither marry nor be given in marriage. They are like the angels in heaven.

[31] "And in regard to the resurrection of the dead, have you not read what God himself said to you: [32] 'I am the God of Abraham, the God of Isaac, and the God of Jacob'? He is not the God of the dead but of the living."

[33] When the crowds heard this, they were astonished at his teaching.

The Greatest Commandment. * [34] When the Pharisees learned that he had silenced the Sadducees, they gathered together, [35] and, to test him, one of them, a lawyer, asked this question, [36] "Teacher, which is the greatest commandment in the Law?"

[37] Jesus said to him, " 'You shall love the Lord your God with all your heart, and with all your soul, and with all your mind.' [38] This is the greatest and the first commandment. [39] The second is like it: 'You shall love your

neighbor as yourself.' ⁴⁰ Everything in the Law and the Prophets depends on these two commandments."

Jesus Is Lord.* ⁴¹ While the Pharisees were assembled together, Jesus asked them this question, ⁴² "What is your opinion about the Christ? Whose son is he?" They replied, "He is the son of David." ⁴³ He responded, "How is it then that David, under the inspiration of the Spirit, calls him 'Lord,' saying:

⁴⁴   'The Lord said to my Lord,
    "Sit at my right hand
      until I put your enemies under your feet"'?

⁴⁵ If David calls him 'Lord,' how can he be his son?" ⁴⁶ No one was able to give him an answer, and from that day onward no one dared to ask him any further questions.

23 **Portrait of the Scribes and Pharisees.*** ¹ Then Jesus addressed the crowds and his disciples: ² "The scribes and the Pharisees sit on Moses' seat. ³ Therefore, be careful to do whatever they tell you, but do not follow their example, for they do not practice what they preach. ⁴ They tie up heavy burdens that are difficult to bear and lay them on the shoulders of others, but they will not lift a finger to be of assistance.

⁵ "Everything they do is meant to attract the attention of others. They widen their phylacteries * and lengthen their tassels. ⁶ They love to have places of honor at banquets and the best seats in synagogues, ⁷ and to be greeted with respect in the marketplaces and to be addressed as 'Rabbi.'

Do Not Be Called Teacher.* ⁸ "But do not allow yourselves to be called 'Rabbi,' for you have only one Master, and you are all brethren. ⁹ Call no one on earth your father, for you have but one Father, and he is in heaven. ¹⁰ You must not be called 'teacher,' for you have only one Teacher, the Christ. ¹¹ The greatest among you must be your servant. ¹² All those who exalt themselves will be humbled, and all those who humble themselves will be exalted.

Woe to You, Teachers of the Law. * ¹³ "Woe to you, scribes and Pharisees, you hypocrites! You shut the entrance to the kingdom of heaven in people's faces. You yourselves do not enter, nor do you allow others to enter.

[¹⁴ "Woe to you, scribes and Pharisees, you hypocrites! For you devour the houses of widows, while for the sake of appearance you recite lengthy prayers. As a result, you will receive the severest possible condemnation.] *

¹⁵ "Woe to you, scribes and Pharisees, you hypocrites! You journey over sea and land to make a single convert,* and then you make that convert twice as worthy of Gehenna as you are.

¹⁶ * "Woe to you, blind guides! You say, 'If someone swears by the temple, that is not binding, but if someone swears by the gold of the temple, he is bound by his oath.' ¹⁷ You blind fools! Which is greater: the gold, or the temple that makes the gold sacred?

¹⁸ "And you say, 'If someone swears by the altar, that is not binding, but if someone swears by the offering that lies on the altar, he is bound by his oath.' ¹⁹ You blind fools! Which is of greater value—the offering, or the altar that makes the offering sacred?

²⁰ "The one who swears by the altar swears both by it and by everything that lies upon it. ²¹ The one who swears by the temple swears both by it and by the one who dwells within it. ²² And the one who swears by heaven swears both by the throne of God and by the One who is seated upon it.

²³ * "Woe to you, scribes and Pharisees, you hypocrites! You pay tithes of mint and dill and cumin, but you have neglected the more important aspects of the Law: justice, mercy, and faithfulness. You should have practiced these without neglecting the others. ²⁴ You blind guides! You strain out a gnat and then swallow a camel!

²⁵ "Woe to you, scribes and Pharisees, you hypocrites! You cleanse the outside of a cup and dish, but you leave the inside full of greed and self-indulgence. ²⁶ Blind

Pharisee! First cleanse the inside of the cup and dish so that the outside may also be clean.

²⁷ "Woe to you, scribes and Pharisees, you hypocrites! You are like whitewashed tombs * that look beautiful on the outside, but inside they are full of the bones of the dead and of all kinds of decay. ²⁸ In the same way, on the outside you appear to be righteous, but inside you are full of hypocrisy and wickedness.

The Judgment of God Has Already Come on This Generation.*
²⁹ "Woe to you, scribes and Pharisees, you hypocrites! You build the tombs of the Prophets and adorn the graves of the righteous, ³⁰ and you say, 'If we had lived in the time of our ancestors, we never would have collaborated with them in shedding the blood of the Prophets.' ³¹ Thus, you acknowledge that you are the descendants of those who murdered the Prophets. ³² Go and complete the work that your ancestors began.

³³ "You snakes! You brood of vipers! How can you escape being condemned to Gehenna? ³⁴ Behold, therefore, I am sending you prophets and wise men and teachers. Some of them you will kill and crucify, and some of them you will scourge in your synagogues and pursue from town to town. ³⁵ As a result, upon you will fall the guilt of all the innocent blood that has been shed upon the earth, from the blood of the righteous Abel to the blood of Zechariah son of Barachiah, whom you murdered between the sanctuary and the altar. ³⁶ Amen, I say to you, the guilt for all this will fall upon this generation.

The Lament over Jerusalem.* ³⁷ "Jerusalem, Jerusalem, you murder the Prophets and stone the messengers sent to you! How often have I longed to gather your children together as a hen gathers her chicks under her wings, but you would not allow it! ³⁸ Behold, your house has been abandoned and left desolate. ³⁹ I tell you, you will not see me again until you say: 'Blessed is he who comes in the name of the Lord.'"

C: Instructions for the Coming of the Kingdom*

The Time of the End*

24 **Jesus Announces the Destruction of the Temple.*** [1] As Jesus left the temple and was walking away, his disciples came up to him to call his attention to the buildings of the temple. [2] He thereupon said to them, "Do you see all these? Amen, I say to you, not one stone here will be left upon another; every one will be thrown down."

The End Has Not Yet Come.* [3] As he was sitting on the Mount of Olives, the disciples approached and spoke to him when they were alone. "Tell us," they said, "when will this happen, and what will be the sign of your coming and of the end of the age?"

[4] Jesus answered them, "Take care that no one deceives you. [5] For many will come in my name, saying, 'I am the Christ,' and they will lead many astray. [6] You will hear of wars and rumors of wars. Do not be alarmed, for those things are bound to happen, but the end is still to come. [7] For nation will rise against nation and kingdom against kingdom, and there will be famines and earthquakes in various places. [8] All these are only the beginning of the labor pains.

[9] "Then you will be handed over to be tortured and put to death, and you will be hated by all nations because of my name. [10] At that time, many will fall away from the faith; they will betray and hate one another. [11] Many false prophets will appear and lead many astray, [12] and with the increase of lawlessness, the love of many will grow cold. [13] But whoever endures to the end will be saved. [14] And the good news of the kingdom will be proclaimed throughout the entire world as a testimony offered to all the nations. And then the end will come.

The Great Trial.* [15] "Therefore, when you see the abomination of desolation, about which the prophet Daniel spoke, standing in the Holy Place (let the reader understand), [16] then those who are in Judea must flee to the mountains, [17] the one who is standing on the roof must not come down to collect what is in his house, [18] and someone who is in the field must not turn back to retrieve his coat.

[19] "Woe to those who are pregnant and to those who are nursing infants in those days! [20] Pray that you will not have to take flight in the winter or on a Sabbath. [21] For at that time there will be great suffering that has not been equaled since the beginning of the world until now, and will never again be duplicated. [22] And if those days had not been cut short, no one would be saved; but for the sake of the elect they will be shortened.

False Messiahs and False Prophets. [23] "Therefore, if anyone says to you, 'Look, here is the Christ,' or 'There he is,' do not believe it. [24] For false christs and false prophets will arise, and they will perform great signs and wonders that are impressive enough to deceive even the elect, if that were possible.

[25] "Remember, I have forewarned you about this. [26] So if anyone says to you, 'Behold, he is in the wilderness,' do not go out there. If they say, 'Behold, he is in the inner rooms,' do not believe it. [27] For just as lightning comes from the east and is visible even in the west, so will the coming of the Son of Man be. [28] Wherever the corpse is, there the vultures will gather.*

The Coming of the Son of Man.* [29] "Immediately after the distress of those days,

'the sun will be darkened
     and the moon will not give forth its light;
the stars will fall from the sky
     and the powers of the heavens will be shaken.'

[30] "Then the sign of the Son of Man will appear in heaven, and all the peoples of the earth will mourn, and they will see the Son of Man coming on the clouds of heaven with power and great glory. [31] And he will send forth his angels with a trumpet blast, and they will gather his elect from the four winds, from one end of the heavens to the other.

D: Be Vigilant in Expectation of the End*

The Parable of the Fig Tree.* ³² "Learn this lesson from the fig tree. As soon as its twigs become tender and its leaves begin to sprout, you know that summer is near. ³³ In the same way, when you see all these things take place, know that he is near, at the very gates. ³⁴ Amen, I say to you, this generation will not pass away until all these things have taken place. ³⁵ Heaven and earth will pass away, but my words will never pass away.

The Day and Hour Unknown.* ³⁶ "As for the exact day and hour, no one knows, neither the angels in heaven, nor the Son, but only the Father. ³⁷ For as it was in the days of Noah, so will it be at the coming of the Son of Man. ³⁸ In the days before the flood, people were eating and drinking, marrying and being given in marriage, up to the day that Noah entered the ark. ³⁹ They knew nothing about what would happen until the flood came and swept them all away.

"That is how it will be at the coming of the Son of Man. ⁴⁰ Two men will be out in the field; one will be taken and the other will be left. ⁴¹ Two women will be grinding at the mill; one will be taken and the other will be left. ⁴² Therefore, keep watch, for you do not know the day when your Lord is coming.

The Parable of the Owner of the House.* ⁴³ "But keep this in mind: if the owner of the house had known at what time of night the thief was coming, he would have stayed awake and not allowed his house to be broken into. ⁴⁴ Therefore, you must also be prepared, because the Son of Man will come at an hour when you do not expect him.

The Parable of the Faithful Servant.* ⁴⁵ "Who, then, is the faithful and wise servant whom his master has put in charge of his household to give its members their food at the proper time? ⁴⁶ Blessed is that servant if his master finds him doing so when he returns home. ⁴⁷ Amen, I say to you, he will put him in charge of all his property.

⁴⁸ "But if that servant is wicked and says to himself, 'My master is detained,' ⁴⁹ and he proceeds to beat his fellow servants and eats and drinks with drunkards, ⁵⁰ the master of that servant will return on a day when he does not expect him and at an hour he does not know. ⁵¹ He will punish him and assign him a place with the hypocrites, where there will be weeping and gnashing of teeth.

25 The Parable of the Ten Virgins.* ¹ "Then * the kingdom of heaven will be like ten virgins who took their lamps and went forth to meet the bridegroom. ² Five of them were foolish and five were wise. ³ When the foolish ones took their lamps, they neglected to take any oil with them, ⁴ whereas those who were wise took flasks of oil with their lamps. ⁵ Since the bridegroom was delayed in coming, they all became drowsy and fell asleep.

⁶ "At midnight, a shout was raised: 'Behold, the bridegroom! Come out to meet him!' ⁷ Then all the virgins got up and trimmed their lamps. ⁸ The foolish ones said to the wise, 'Give us some of your oil, for our lamps are going out.' ⁹ The wise ones replied, 'No, for there may not be enough for both us and you. You had better go to the merchants and buy some.'

¹⁰ "While they went off to purchase it, the bridegroom arrived, and those who were ready went in with him to the wedding banquet. Then the door was locked. ¹¹ Afterward, the other virgins returned, and they cried out, 'Lord! Lord! Open the door for us!' ¹² But he replied, 'Amen, I say to you, I do not know you.' ¹³ Therefore, stay awake, for you know neither the day nor the hour.

The Parable of the Talents.* ¹⁴ "Again, the kingdom of heaven will be like a man going on a journey who summoned his servants and entrusted his property to them. ¹⁵ To one he gave five talents,* to another two talents, to a third one talent—to each according to his ability. Then he set forth on his journey.

[16] "The servant who had received the five talents promptly went to invest them and gained five more. [17] In the same manner, the servant who had received the two talents gained two more. [18] But the servant who had received the one talent went off and dug a hole in the ground and hid his master's money.

[19] "After a long period of time, the master of those servants returned and settled accounts with them. [20] The one who had received the five talents came forward, bringing an additional five. 'Master,' he said, 'you gave me five talents. Behold, I have gained five more.' [21] His master said to him, 'Well done, good and faithful servant. Since you have been faithful in small matters, I will give you much greater responsibilities. Come and share your master's joy.'

[22] "Next, the one who had received the two talents also came forward and said, 'Master, you gave me two talents. Behold, I have gained two more.' [23] His master said to him, 'Well done, good and faithful servant. Since you have been faithful in small matters, I will give you much greater responsibilities. Come and share your master's joy.'

[24] "Then the one who had received the one talent came forward and said, 'Master, I knew that you were a hard man, reaping where you did not sow, and gathering where you did not scatter seed. [25] Therefore, out of fear I went off and hid your talent in the ground. Behold, I give it back to you.'

[26] "His master replied, 'You wicked and lazy servant. So you knew that I reap where I have not sown and gather where I have not scattered! [27] Then you should have deposited my money with the bankers, and on my return I would have gotten back my money with interest.

[28] " 'Therefore, take the talent from him and give it to the one with the ten talents. [29] For to everyone who has, more will be given, and he will have an abundance. But from the one who has not, even what he does have will be taken away. [30] As for this worthless servant, cast him out-

side into the darkness, where there will be weeping and gnashing of teeth.'

The Solemn Judgment at the End of Time.* [31] "When the Son of Man comes in his glory, and all the angels with him, then he will sit on the throne of his glory. [32] All the nations will be gathered before him, and he will separate people one from another as a shepherd separates the sheep from the goats. [33] He will place the sheep on his right and the goats on his left.

[34] "Then the King will say to those on his right, 'Come, you who are blessed by my Father, inherit the kingdom prepared for you from the foundation of the world. [35] For I was hungry and you gave me something to eat; I was thirsty and you gave me something to drink; I was a stranger and you welcomed me; [36] I was naked and you clothed me; I was ill and you took care of me; I was in prison and you came to visit me.'

[37] "Then the righteous will say to him, 'Lord, when did we see you hungry and give you something to eat, or thirsty and give you something to drink? [38] When did we see you a stranger and welcome you, or naked and clothe you? [39] When did we see you ill or in prison and come to visit you?' [40] And the King will answer, 'Amen, I say to you, whatever you did for one of the least of these brethren of mine, you did for me.'

[41] "Then he will say to those on his left, 'Depart from me, you accursed, into the eternal fire prepared for the devil and his angels. [42] For I was hungry and you did not give me anything to eat; I was thirsty and you did not give me anything to drink; [43] I was a stranger and you did not welcome me; I was naked and you did not give me any clothing; I was ill and in prison and you did not visit me.'

[44] "Then they will ask him, 'Lord, when did we see you hungry or thirsty or a stranger or naked or ill or in prison and not minister to you?' [45] He will answer them, 'Amen, I say to you, whatever you failed to do for one of the least of these brethren of mine, you failed to do for me.' [46] And

they will go away to eternal punishment, but the righteous will enter eternal life."

VI. THE PASSION AND RESURRECTION*

26 **The Plot against Jesus.*** [1] When Jesus had finished discoursing on all these subjects, he said to his disciples, [2] "In two days it will be Passover, at which time the Son of Man will be handed over to be crucified."

[3] Meanwhile, the chief priests and the elders of the people assembled together in the palace of the high priest, whose name was Caiaphas,* [4] and they made plans to arrest Jesus by deceit and have him put to death. [5] However, they said, "It must not occur during the feast, or the people may begin to riot."

A Woman of Bethany Anoints Jesus.* [6] Now when Jesus was in Bethany at the house of Simon the leper, [7] a woman came up to him with an alabaster jar of very expensive ointment and poured it over his head as he reclined at table. [8] When the disciples saw this, they became indignant, and they remarked, "Why this waste? [9] This ointment could have been sold for a considerable sum, with the money given to the poor."

[10] Jesus was aware of their attitude, and he said to them, "Why are you bothering this woman? She has performed a good deed for me. [11] The poor you will always have with you,* but you will not always have me. [12] In pouring this ointment on my body, she has prepared me for burial. [13] Amen, I say to you, wherever in the whole world this gospel is proclaimed, what she has done will be told in remembrance of her."

Judas Betrays Jesus.* [14] Then one of the Twelve, the man called Judas Iscariot, went to the chief priests [15] and asked, "What are you willing to give me if I hand him over to you?" They paid him thirty pieces of silver, [16] and from that moment he began to look for an opportunity to betray him.

The Preparations for the Passover Supper.* [17] On the first day of the feast of Unleavened Bread,* the disciples came to Jesus and asked, "Where do you want us to make the preparations for you to eat the Passover?" [18] He said: "Go to a certain man in the city and say to him, 'The Teacher says, "My appointed time is near. I intend to celebrate the Passover at your house with my disciples."'" [19] The disciples thereupon followed Jesus' instructions, and they prepared the Passover.

The Treachery of Judas Foretold.* [20] When evening came, he reclined at table with the Twelve. [21] And while they were eating, he said, "Amen, I say to you, one of you will betray me." [22] Greatly distressed on hearing this, they began to ask him, one after another, "Is it I, Lord?"

[23] He answered, "The one who has dipped his hand into the bowl with me is the one who will betray me. [24] The Son of Man indeed goes, as it is written of him, but woe to that man by whom the Son of Man is betrayed. It would be better for that man if he had never been born."

[25] Then Judas, the one who would betray him, said: "Is it I, Rabbi?" Jesus replied, "You have said so."

The Last Supper.* [26] While they were eating, Jesus took bread, and after he had pronounced the blessing, he broke it and gave it to his disciples, saying, "Take this and eat; this is my body." [27] Then he took a cup, and after offering thanks he gave it to them, saying, "Drink from this, all of you. [28] For this is my blood of the covenant, which will be shed on behalf of many for the forgiveness of sins. [29] And I tell you, from now on I shall not drink this fruit of the vine until the day when I shall drink it anew with you in the kingdom of my Father."

[30] And after singing a hymn, they went out to the Mount of Olives.

Jesus Predicts Peter's Denial.* [31] Then Jesus said to them, "This very night you will all be scandalized because of me, for it is written:

'I will strike the shepherd,
  and the sheep of the flock will be scattered.'

³² But after I have been raised up, I shall go ahead of you to Galilee."

³³ Peter said to him, "Even if all the others will be scandalized because of you, I will never be." ³⁴ Jesus replied, "Amen, I say to you, this very night, before the cock crows, you will deny me three times." * ³⁵ Peter said to him, "Even if I have to die with you, I will not deny you." And all the other disciples said the same thing.

The Agony in the Garden.* ³⁶ Then Jesus went with his disciples to a place called Gethsemane, and he said to them, "Sit here while I go over there to pray." ³⁷ He took Peter and the two sons of Zebedee, and he began to suffer grief and anguish.

³⁸ Then he said to them, "My soul is sorrowful, even to the point of death. Remain here and keep watch with me." ³⁹ Moving on a little farther, he threw himself prostrate on the ground in prayer, saying, "My Father, if it is possible, allow this cup to be taken from me. Yet let your will, not mine, be done."

⁴⁰ Returning to the disciples, he found them sleeping. He said to Peter, "Could you not keep watch with me for just one hour? ⁴¹ Stay awake and pray that you may not enter into temptation. The spirit is indeed willing, but the flesh is weak."

⁴² He went apart for a second time and prayed, "My Father, if it is not possible for this cup to be taken away unless I drink it, your will be done." ⁴³ Then he came back again and found them sleeping, for their eyes were heavy.

⁴⁴ He left them there and went away again, praying for the third time in the same words as before. ⁴⁵ Then he returned to the disciples and said to them, "Are you still sleeping and taking your rest? Behold, the hour has come for the Son of Man to be betrayed into the hands of sinners. ⁴⁶ Get up! Let us be going! Look, my betrayer is approaching."

JESUS IS BETRAYED BY JUDAS—"'The one I shall kiss is the man. Arrest him.' Proceeding directly to Jesus, he said, 'Greetings, Rabbi!' and kissed him" (Mt 26:48-49).

THE DEATH OF JESUS—"Two thieves were crucified with him. . . . Those people who passed by jeered at him. . . . Standing near the cross of Jesus [was] his mother. . . . Jesus again cried out in a loud voice and gave up his spirit" (Mt 27:38f; Jn 19:25; Mt 27:50).

Jesus Is Arrested.* [47]* While he was still speaking, Judas, one of the Twelve, arrived. With him there was a large crowd of men, armed with swords and clubs, who had been sent by the chief priests and the elders of the people. [48] Now his betrayer had agreed with them on a signal, saying, "The one I shall kiss is the man. Arrest him." [49] Proceeding directly to Jesus, he said, "Greetings, Rabbi!" and kissed him. [50] Jesus said to him, "Friend, do what you are here to do." Then they came forward, seized Jesus, and placed him under arrest.

[51] Suddenly, one of those who were accompanying Jesus reached for his sword, drew it, and struck a servant of the high priest, slicing off his ear. [52] Then Jesus said to him, "Put back your sword into its place. For all who take the sword shall die by the sword. [53] Do you suppose that I cannot appeal to my Father for help * and he will not immediately send me more than twelve legions of angels? [54] But then how would the Scriptures be fulfilled that say it must happen in this way?"

[55] At that hour, Jesus said to the crowd, "Why are you coming forth with swords and clubs to arrest me, as though I were a bandit? Day after day I sat teaching in the temple, and you did not arrest me. [56] But all this has taken place so that the writings of the Prophets might be fulfilled." Then all the disciples deserted him and fled.

Jesus Is Condemned by the Sanhedrin.* [57] Those who had arrested Jesus led him away to Caiaphas the high priest where the scribes and the elders had gathered. [58] Meanwhile, Peter followed him at a distance up to the courtyard of the high priest. Then, going inside, he sat down with the attendants to see what the outcome would be.

[59] The chief priests and the whole Sanhedrin tried to elicit some false testimony against Jesus so they could put him to death, [60] but they failed in their efforts, even though many witnesses came forward with perjured testimony. Finally, two men came forward [61] who stated, "This man said, 'I can destroy the temple of God and rebuild it within three days.'"

[62] The high priest then rose and said to him, "Have you no reply to counter the testimony that these witnesses have given?" [63] But Jesus remained silent. Then the high priest said to him, "I command you to tell us before the living God whether you are the Christ, the Son of God." [64] Jesus replied, "You have said it. But I tell you:

From now on you will see the Son of Man
    seated at the right hand of the Power
    and coming on the clouds of heaven."

[65] Then the high priest tore his robes and exclaimed, "He has blasphemed! What need do we have for any further witnesses? Behold, you have just heard the blasphemy. [66] What do you think?" They shouted in reply, "He deserves to die." [67] Then they spat in his face and struck him with their fists. Some taunted him as they beat him, [68] "Prophesy to us, Christ! Who hit you?"

Peter Denies Jesus. * [69] Meanwhile, Peter was sitting outside in the courtyard. One of the servant girls came over to him and said, "You too were with Jesus the Galilean." [70] But he denied it before all of them, saying, "I do not know what you are talking about." [71] When he walked out to the entrance gate, another servant girl caught sight of him and said to the people around her, "This man was with Jesus of Nazareth." [72] And again he denied it, this time with an oath: "I do not know the man."

[73] Shortly afterward, some bystanders came up to Peter and said to him, "You unquestionably are one of them. Even your accent gives you away." [74] Then he began to shout curses, and he swore an oath: "I do not know the man." At that very moment, a cock crowed, [75] and Peter remembered what Jesus had said: "Before the cock crows, you will deny me three times." And he went outside and began to weep uncontrollably.

27 Jesus Is Handed Over to Pilate.* [1] When morning came, all the chief priests and the elders of the people met together in council to decide how to put him to death.

[2] They bound him and led him away, and handed him over to Pilate, the governor.

Judas Hangs Himself.* [3] When Judas discovered that Jesus, whom he betrayed, had been condemned he was seized with a sense of remorse, and he brought back the thirty pieces of silver to the chief priests and the elders. [4] "I have sinned," he said, "for I have betrayed innocent blood." They replied, "Of what importance is that to us? That is your responsibility." [5] Flinging the silver pieces into the temple, he departed. Then he went off and hanged himself.

[6] The chief priests retrieved the silver coins and said, "It is not lawful for us to deposit this into the temple treasury, for it is blood money." [7] They conferred together, and then used it to purchase the potter's field as a burial place for foreigners. [8] This is the reason why that field to this very day is called the Field of Blood.

[9] Thus was fulfilled what had been spoken through the prophet Jeremiah: *

"And they took the thirty pieces of silver,
the price set on his head by the people of Israel,
[10] and they used them to purchase the potter's field
as the Lord had commanded me."

Jesus Is Questioned by Pilate. [11] * Meanwhile, Jesus was brought into the presence of the governor, who asked him, "Are you the king of the Jews?" Jesus replied, "You have said so." * [12] And when he was accused by the chief priests and the elders, he offered no reply. [13] Pilate then said to him, "Have you not heard how many charges they have brought against you?" [14] But he did not offer a single word in response, much to the governor's amazement.*

Jesus Is Sentenced to Death. [15] Now on the occasion of the feast, the governor's custom was to release to the people one prisoner whom they had designated. [16] At that particular time, they had in custody a notorious prisoner named Barabbas. [17] Therefore, after the people had gathered, Pilate asked them, "Which man do you want me to release to you: Barabbas, or Jesus who is called the Christ?" [18] For he knew that it was out of envy that they had handed him over.

[19] While he was still seated on the judge's bench, his wife sent him a message: "Have nothing to do with that innocent man. I have been greatly troubled today by a dream that I had about him." *

[20] Meanwhile, the chief priests and the elders had persuaded the crowd to ask for the release of Barabbas and to have Jesus executed. [21] Therefore, when the governor asked them, "Which of the two men do you want me to release to you?" they shouted, "Barabbas!" [22] Pilate asked them, "Then what shall I do with Jesus who is called the Messiah?" All of them shouted, "Let him be crucified!" [23] He asked, "Why? What evil has he done?" But they only screamed all the louder, "Let him be crucified!"

[24] When Pilate saw that he was getting nowhere and that a riot was about to occur, he took some water and washed his hands * in full view of the crowd, saying, "I am innocent of this man's blood. It is your responsibility." [25] With one voice the entire crowd cried out, "Let his blood be on us and on our children!" * [26] He then released Barabbas to them, and after Jesus had been scourged, he handed him over to be crucified.

Jesus Is Crowned with Thorns. * [27] Then the governor's soldiers took Jesus inside the praetorium and gathered the whole cohort around him. [28] They stripped him and put a scarlet robe on him, [29] and after twisting some thorns into a crown, they placed it on his head and put a reed in his right hand. Then, bending the knee before him, they mocked him, saying, "Hail, King of the Jews!" [30] They also spat upon him and, taking the reed, used it to strike him on the head. [31] And when they had finished mocking him, they stripped him of the robe, dressed him in his own clothes, and led him away to crucify him.

The Way of the Cross. [32] As they went out, they encountered a man from Cyrene* named Simon, and they forced him to carry the cross.

Jesus Is Crucified on Calvary. [33] When they came to a place called Golgotha, which means the Place of the Skull,* [34] they offered him some wine to drink that had been mixed with gall; but after tasting it, he refused to drink the mixture.* [35] And after they had crucified him,* they divided his garments among them by casting lots. [36] Then they sat down there to keep guard over him. [37] Above his head was inscribed the charge against him: "This is Jesus, the King of the Jews." [38] Two thieves were crucified with him, one on his right and the other on his left.*

[39] Those people who passed by jeered at him, shaking their heads [40] and saying, "You who claimed you could destroy the temple and rebuild it within three days, save yourself! If you truly are the Son of God, come down from the cross!"

[41] In much the same way, the chief priests, together with the scribes and the elders, joined in the mockery, saying, [42] "He saved others, but he cannot save himself. If he is the king of Israel, let him come down from the cross right now, and we will believe in him. [43] He trusted in God; now let God deliver him if he wants him, for he said, 'I am the Son of God.' " [44] The thieves who were crucified with him also taunted him in the same way.

Jesus Dies on the Cross.* [45] Beginning at midday, there was darkness over the whole land until three in the afternoon. [46] And about three o'clock* Jesus cried out in a loud voice, *"Eli, Eli, lema sabachthani?"*—that is, "My God, my God, why have you forsaken me?"

[47] On hearing this, some of the bystanders said, "This man is calling for Elijah." [48] One of them immediately ran off to get a sponge, which he soaked in vinegar, put on a stick, and gave to him to drink. [49] But the others said, "Wait! Let us see whether Elijah will come to save him." [50] Then Jesus again cried out in a loud voice and gave up his spirit.

[51] And behold, the veil of the sanctuary was torn in two from top to bottom. The earth quaked and rocks were split apart. [52] The tombs were opened, and the bodies of

many saints who had fallen asleep were raised. [53] And coming forth from their tombs after his resurrection, they entered the holy city and appeared to many.* [54] Now when the centurion and those who were keeping watch over Jesus with him witnessed the earthquake and all that was happening, they were terrified, and they said, "Truly, this man was the Son of God."

[55] Many women were also present, looking on from a distance. They had followed Jesus from Galilee and ministered to him. [56] Among these were Mary Magdalene,* Mary the mother of James and Joseph, and the mother of the sons of Zebedee.

Jesus Is Placed in the Tomb.* [57] When evening came, there arrived a rich man from Arimathea, named Joseph, who had himself become a disciple of Jesus. [58] He went to Pilate and requested the body of Jesus. So Pilate ordered that it be handed over to him.

[59] Joseph took the body, wrapped it in a clean linen shroud, [60] and laid it in his own new tomb that he had hewn out of the rock. He then rolled an immense stone against the entrance of the tomb and departed. [61] Mary Magdalene and the other Mary were there, sitting opposite the sepulcher.

The Guard at the Tomb. [62] The next day, on the morning after the preparation day,* the chief priests and the Pharisees came to Pilate in a group [63] and said to him, "Your Excellency, we recall that while he was still alive, this impostor said, 'After three days I will be raised up.' [64] Therefore, issue orders that the tomb be kept under surveillance until the third day. Otherwise, his disciples may go there and steal his body, and then tell the people, 'He has been raised from the dead.' This final deception would be worse than the first."

[65] Pilate said to them, "You have a guard. Go and make the grave as secure as you can." [66] And so they went forth and made the tomb secure by sealing the stone and posting a guard.

28 Jesus Is Raised from the Dead.* ¹After the Sabbath, at

dawn on the first day of the week, Mary Magdalene and the other Mary went to visit the sepulcher. ²And behold, there was a violent earthquake, for an angel of the Lord, descended from heaven, came and rolled back the stone and sat upon it. ³His face shone like lightning, and his garments were as white as snow. ⁴The guards were so paralyzed with fear of him that they became like dead men.

⁵But the angel said to the women, "Do not be afraid! I know that you are looking for Jesus who was crucified. ⁶He is not here, for he has been raised, as he promised he would be. Come and see the place where he lay. ⁷Then go quickly and tell his disciples: 'He has been raised from the dead and now he is going ahead of you to Galilee. There you will see him.' Behold, I have told you."

⁸They were filled with fear and great joy, and they ran from the tomb to inform his disciples. ⁹And behold, Jesus came to meet them, saying, "Greetings." They approached him, embraced his feet, and worshiped him. ¹⁰Then Jesus said to them, "Do not be fearful. Go and tell my brethren to go to Galilee. There they will see me." *

The Report of the Guard.* ¹¹While the women were on their way, some of the guards went into the city and reported to the chief priests everything that had happened. ¹²After the chief priests had conferred with the elders, they presented a large sum of money to the soldiers ¹³and gave them this order: "Say, 'His disciples came by night and stole the body while we were asleep.' ¹⁴And should the governor hear anything in this regard, we will explain the situation to him and you will be safe." ¹⁵The soldiers took the money and did as they had been instructed. And this story is still circulated among the Jews to this very day.

Jesus Gives the Great Commission.* ¹⁶Then the eleven disciples set out for Galilee, to the mountain where Jesus had told them to meet him. [17] When they saw him, they prostrated themselves before him, although some doubted. [18] Then Jesus approached them and said, "All authority in heaven and on earth has been given to me. [19] Go, therefore, and make disciples of all nations, baptizing them in the name of the Father and of the Son and of the Holy Spirit,* [20] and teaching them to observe all that I have commanded you. And behold, I am with you always, to the end of the world."

THE GOSPEL ACCORDING TO MARK

WHO IS JESUS?

Who is the author of this book? Ever since the 2nd century the tradition has held that the author was Mark, a personage known to us from the New Testament under the name of John, who was also called Mark (Acts 12:25). He accompanied his cousin Barnabas on a mission (Acts 13:5, 13; 15:39). He also became a companion of Paul for a time, but later separated from the latter, taking with him his cousin due to disagreement with Paul (Acts 13:13; 15:37-39). Toward the end, however, we find him once again a valuable helper of Paul (Col 4:10; Philem 24; 2 Tim 4:11). He must have had connections with Peter (Acts 12:12; 1 Pet 5:13), and it is thought that his Gospel reflects chiefly the preaching of the first apostle.

According to the majority of present-day scholars, this Gospel was written shortly before the destruction of Jerusalem in A.D. 70. It was written in Greek, perhaps at Rome, and is addressed to Christians of non-Jewish origin. By reason of its date, Mark's is the first Gospel known to history, the one that inaugurates this genre of writings that put us in touch with the actions and words of Jesus and with the mystery of his Death and Resurrection. And, in fact, both Matthew and Luke were familiar with the text of Mark when they wrote their own works; they complete or correct his Gospel in light of the information available to them and according to the needs of their readers. This explains why Mark was neglected by the Fathers and, until the recent reform, by the Liturgy. And yet what an extraordinary picture of Jesus he gives us!

Mark's language and talent are those of a popular story-teller. His work follows no particular order; its grammar is rudimentary, its vocabulary limited. In its expression it is often monotonous and schematic, but it can suddenly become animated, varied, and impressive; at such moments, its style is lively and picturesque.

Mark does not intend to paint a portrait or write a biography of Jesus, but rather to draw his readers' attention to the mystery of Christ's person. He also puts readers in the presence of the events, and forces them to participate in the action.

Unlike the other Gospels, Mark's begins abruptly with the preaching of John the Baptist and places us in the midst of the ongoing action.

This Gospel reports few of Jesus' discourses, but does like to tell the stories in detail. Rather than any teaching, it is the fate and work of Jesus that are meant to elicit the readers' response.

The Gospel of Mark may be divided as follows:

  I: Preparation for the Mission of Jesus (1:1-13)
  II: Is Jesus the Messiah? (1:14—8:30)
  III: The Mystery of Jesus Is Revealed (8:31—16:8)
  Appendix: The Longer Ending (16:9-20)

I. PREPARATION FOR THE MISSION OF JESUS*

1 **Beginning of the Good News.*** ¹ The beginning of the gospel of Jesus Christ, the Son of God.

² It is written in the prophet Isaiah: *

"Behold, I am sending my messenger ahead of you;
  he will prepare your way.

³   The voice of one crying out in the wilderness:
  'Prepare the way of the Lord,
    make his paths straight.'"

⁴ Hence, John the Baptist appeared in the desert, proclaiming a baptism of repentance for the forgiveness of sins. ⁵ People from the entire Judean countryside and all the inhabitants of Jerusalem went out to him, and as they confessed their sins they were baptized by him in the Jordan River.

⁶ John was clothed in a garment of camel's hair, with a leather belt around his waist, and his food consisted of locusts and wild honey. ⁷ And this was the message he proclaimed: "One who is far more powerful than I am is coming after me. I am not worthy even to stoop down

and loosen the straps of his sandals. [8] I have baptized you with water, but he will baptize you with the Holy Spirit."*

Jesus Is Baptized by John.* [9] At that time,* Jesus came from Nazareth in Galilee and was baptized by John in the Jordan. [10] * And as he was coming up out of the water, he beheld the heavens break open and the Spirit descending upon him like a dove. [11] And a voice came from heaven: "You are my beloved Son; in you I am well pleased."

Jesus Is Tempted in the Desert.* [12] The Spirit immediately drove him out into the desert. [13] He remained there for forty days, during which time he was tempted by Satan. He lived there among the wild beasts, while the angels ministered to him.

II. IS JESUS THE MESSIAH?*

A: First Testimonies of the Messiah's Mission

Jesus Inaugurates His Mission. [14] After John had been arrested,* Jesus came to Galilee proclaiming the gospel of God, and saying, [15] "The time of fulfillment has arrived, and the kingdom of God is close at hand. Repent, and believe in the gospel."

The First Disciples.* [16] As Jesus was walking along by the Sea of Galilee, he saw Simon and his brother Andrew casting their nets into the sea, for they were fishermen. [17] Jesus said to them, "Come, follow me, and I will make you fishers of men." [18] Immediately, they abandoned their nets and followed him.

[19] As he proceeded farther, he saw James, the son of Zebedee, and his brother John. They also were in a boat mending their nets. [20] Immediately, he called them, and they left their father Zebedee in the boat with the hired workers and followed him.

Jesus Heals a Man with a Demon.* [21] They journeyed to Capernaum, and on the Sabbath Jesus immediately entered the synagogue and began to instruct the people. [22] They were astounded at his teaching, for he taught them as one who had authority, and not as the scribes.

[23] In that synagogue there was a man with an unclean spirit, and he shrieked, [24] "What do you want with us, Jesus of Nazareth? Have you come to destroy us? I know who you are—the Holy One of God." * [25] But Jesus rebuked him, saying, "Be silent, and come out of him!"

[26] The unclean spirit threw the man into convulsions and with a loud cry emerged from him. [27] The people were all amazed, and they began to ask one another, "What is this? It must be a new kind of teaching! With authority he gives commands even to unclean spirits, and they obey him!" [28] His reputation quickly began to spread everywhere throughout the entire region of Galilee.

Jesus Heals Peter's Mother-in-Law. [29] Immediately on leaving the synagogue, he went with James and John into the house of Simon and Andrew. [30] Simon's mother-in-law* was lying in bed, sick with a fever, and they informed Jesus at once about her. [31] Jesus approached her, grasped her by the hand, and helped her up. Then the fever left her, and she began to serve them.

Other Healings. [32] That evening, after sunset, they brought to him all those who were sick or possessed by demons.* [33] The whole town was present, crowded around the door. [34] He cured many who were afflicted with various diseases, and he drove out many demons, although he would not permit them to speak because they knew who he was.

Jesus Proclaims the Message and Heals the Sick. [35] Early the next morning, long before dawn, he arose and went off to a secluded place, where he prayed. [36] Simon and his companions set forth in search of him, [37] and when they found him they said, "Everybody is looking for you." [38] He replied, "Let us move on to the neighboring towns so that I may proclaim the message there as well. For this is the reason why I came." [39] Then he traveled all throughout

Galilee, preaching in their synagogues and driving out
demons.

Jesus Heals a Man with Leprosy. [40] A man with leprosy *
approached and, kneeling before him, begged him, "If
you choose to do so, you can make me clean." [41] Moved
with pity, he stretched out his hand and touched him,*
saying, "I do choose. Be made clean!" [42] Immediately, the
leprosy left him and he was cured.

[43] Jesus then sent him away at once, after first sternly
warning him, [44] "See that you tell no one anything about
this. Just go and show yourself to the priest and offer for
your cleansing what Moses prescribed. That will be proof
for them." * [45] However, he went forth and began to proclaim the entire story, spreading the word far and wide.
As a result, Jesus could no longer go openly into any
town. Rather, he stayed outside in deserted places, and
people continued to come to him from every quarter.

B: First Oppositions*

2 **Jesus Heals a Paralyzed Man.** [1] When Jesus returned
some days later to Capernaum, the word quickly spread
that he was at home. [2] Such large multitudes gathered
there that no longer was any space available, even in front
of the door, and he was preaching the word to them.

[3] Some people arrived, bringing to him a man who was
paralyzed, carried by four men. [4] Since they were unable
to bring him near Jesus because of the crowd, they made
an opening in the roof above him and then lowered the
bed on which the paralyzed man was lying.

[5] On perceiving their faith, Jesus said to the paralyzed
man, "Son, your sins are forgiven." [6] Now some scribes *
were sitting there, thinking to themselves: [7] "How can this
man say such things? He is blaspheming! Who can forgive
sins but God alone?"

[8] Jesus was able immediately to discern in his spirit
what they were thinking, and he asked, "Why do you
entertain such thoughts in your hearts? [9] Which is easier:

to say to the paralyzed man, 'Your sins are forgiven,' or to say: 'Stand up, take your mat, and walk'? [10] But that you may come to realize that the Son of Man* has authority on earth to forgive sins"—he said to the paralyzed man— [11] "I say to you, stand up, take your bed, and go to your home." [12] The man stood up, immediately picked up his bed, and went off in full view of all of them. The onlookers were all astonished and they glorified God, saying, "We have never before witnessed anything like this."

Jesus Calls Levi (Matthew). [13] Once again Jesus went out to the shore of the lake,* and as a large crowd came to him, he taught them. [14] As he was walking along, he saw Levi* the son of Alphaeus sitting at the tax collector's booth. Jesus said to him, "Follow me," and he got up and followed him.

Jesus Eats with Sinners. [15] When he was sitting at dinner in his * house, many tax collectors and sinners were seated with him and his disciples, for there were many who followed Jesus. [16] Some scribes who were Pharisees noticed that Jesus was eating with sinners and tax collectors, and they asked his disciples, "Why does he eat with tax collectors and sinners?" [17] When Jesus overheard this remark, he said, "It is not the healthy who need a physician, but rather those who are sick. I have come to call not the righteous but sinners."

A Time of Joy and Grace. * [18] John's disciples and the Pharisees were observing a fast. Some people came to Jesus and asked, "Why do John's disciples and those of the Pharisees fast but your disciples do not do so?" [19] Jesus answered, "How can the wedding guests fast while the bridegroom is still with them? As long as they have the bridegroom with them, they cannot fast. [20] But the time will come when the bridegroom is taken away from them, and then on that day they will fast.*

[21] "No one sews a piece of unshrunken cloth on an old cloak. If he does, the patch tears away from it, the new from the old, and a worse tear results. [22] Nor does anyone

pour new wine* into old wineskins. If he does, the wine will burst the skins, and then the wine and the skins are both lost. Rather, new wine is poured into fresh wineskins."

Picking Grain on the Sabbath.* ²³ One day, as Jesus was passing through a field of grain on the Sabbath, his disciples began to pick some heads of grain as they walked along. ²⁴ The Pharisees said to him, "Behold, why are your disciples doing what is forbidden on the Sabbath?"

²⁵ He answered, "Have you never read what David did when he and his companions were hungry and in need of food? ²⁶ He entered the house of God when Abiathar* was high priest and ate the sacred bread that only the priests were permitted to eat, and he shared it with his companions." ²⁷ Then he said to them, "The Sabbath was made for man, not man for the Sabbath.* ²⁸ That is why the Son of Man is Lord even of the Sabbath."

3 **A Man with a Withered Hand.*** ¹ Again, Jesus entered the synagogue, and a man was there who had a withered hand. ² They watched him closely to see whether he would cure him on the Sabbath so that they might accuse him.

³ He said to the man with the withered hand, "Come here." ⁴ Then he said to the onlookers, "Is it lawful to do good or to do evil on the Sabbath, to save life or to kill?" But they offered no reply. ⁵ Looking at them with anger, he was saddened at the hardness of their hearts, and he said to the man, "Stretch out your hand." He stretched it out, and his hand was restored. ⁶ Then the Pharisees went out and immediately began to plot with the Herodians how they might put him to death.

C: The Disciples Bear Witness to the Kingdom of God*

Summary of the Activity of Jesus.* ⁷ Thereupon Jesus withdrew with his disciples to the lakeshore, and a great multitude of people from Galilee followed him. ⁸ In addition, having heard of all he was doing, large numbers also came to him from Judea, Jerusalem, Idumea, beyond the Jordan, and the region of Tyre and Sidon.*

⁹ He instructed his disciples to have a small boat ready for him so that he would not be crushed by the crowds. ¹⁰ For he had healed so many that all who were afflicted in any way came crowding around to touch him. ¹¹ And whenever unclean spirits saw him, they would fall at his feet and shout, "You are the Son of God." ¹² But he strictly ordered them not to make him known.

Jesus Establishes the Group of the Disciples.* ¹³ Jesus then went up onto the mountain and summoned those whom he wanted, and they came to him. ¹⁴ * He appointed twelve—whom he also named apostles— * that they might be his companions and that he might send them out to proclaim the message, ¹⁵ with the authority to drive out demons. ¹⁶ The twelve he appointed were: Simon, to whom he gave the name Peter; ¹⁷ James the son of Zebedee and John the brother of James, to whom he gave the name Boanerges, that is, "Sons of Thunder"; * ¹⁸ Andrew, Philip, Bartholomew, Matthew, Thomas, James the son of Alphaeus; Thaddaeus, Simon the Zealot, ¹⁹ and Judas Iscariot, who betrayed him.

D: Contrasting Reactions to the Person of Jesus*

The Concern of Jesus' Relatives.* ²⁰ Jesus then returned home,* and once again such a great crowd collected around them that they did not even find it possible to eat. ²¹ When his relatives heard about this, they went out to take charge of him, saying, "He has gone out of his mind."

The Blasphemy of the Scribes.* ²² Meanwhile, the scribes who had come down from Jerusalem said, "He is possessed by Beelzebul," and "He casts out demons by the prince of demons." ²³ Summoning them to him, he spoke to them in parables, "How can Satan drive out Satan? ²⁴ If a kingdom is divided against itself, that kingdom cannot survive. ²⁵ And if a household is divided against itself, that household will not be able to survive. ²⁶ If Satan has risen up against himself and is divided, he cannot survive; he is doomed.

²⁷ "But no one can break into a strong man's house and steal his possessions unless he first ties up the strong man; then he can ransack the house.

²⁸ "Amen, I say to you, all sins that people commit and whatever blasphemies they utter will be forgiven. ²⁹ But whoever blasphemes against the Holy Spirit will not be forgiven; he is guilty of an eternal sin." ³⁰ He said this because they had claimed he was possessed by an unclean spirit.

The True Family of Jesus.* ³¹ Then his mother and his brethren arrived, and, standing outside, they sent someone in to call him. ³² A crowd was sitting around him, and they said, "Behold, your mother and your brethren are outside asking for you." ³³ He replied, "Who are my mother and my brethren?" ³⁴ Then, looking around at those who were near him, he said: "Behold, my mother and my brethren. ³⁵ Whoever does the will of God is my brother and sister and mother."

E: The Parables—A Veiled Language*

4 **The Parable of the Sower.** ¹ On another occasion he began to teach by the side of the lake. However, such a large crowd gathered that he got into a boat and sat in it out on the lake, while the whole crowd gathered on the shore facing the lake. ² Then he taught them many things in parables.

In the course of his teaching, he said to them: ³ "Listen! A sower went out to sow. ⁴ As he sowed, some seed fell on the path, and the birds came and ate it up. ⁵ Other seed fell on rocky ground, where there was little soil. It sprouted quickly, since the soil had no depth, ⁶ but when the sun rose, it was scorched, and since it lacked roots, it withered away. ⁷ Other seed fell among thorns, and the thorns grew up and choked it, and it produced no crop. ⁸ But some seed fell onto rich soil and brought forth grain, increasing and yielding thirty, sixty, and a hundred times what was sown." ⁹ He then added, "He who has ears to hear, let him hear!"

The Reason for Parables. ¹⁰ When he was alone, the Twelve and his other companions asked him about the parables. ¹¹ He told them, "To you has been granted knowledge of the mysteries * of the kingdom of God, but to those outside, everything comes in parables, ¹² so that

'they may look and see but not perceive,
   and hear and listen but fail to understand,
      lest they be converted and be forgiven.' " *

The Explanation of the Parable of the Sower. * ¹³ He went on to say to them, "Do you not understand this parable? How then are you to understand any of the parables? ¹⁴ What the sower is sowing is the word.

¹⁵ "Some people are like seed that falls along the path where the word is sown. As soon as they hear it, Satan immediately comes and carries off the word that has been sown in them.

¹⁶ "Others are like the seed sown on rocky ground. As soon as they hear the word they immediately receive it with joy. ¹⁷ But they have no deep root and they endure for only a short time. When some trial or tribulation arises on account of the word, they immediately fall away.

¹⁸ "Those sown among thorns are the ones who hear the word, ¹⁹ but worldly cares, the lure of riches, and the desire for other things come in and choke the word, and it bears no fruit.

²⁰ "But those sown in rich soil are those who hear the word and accept it and bear fruit and yield thirty or sixty or a hundred times what was sown."

The Parable of the Lamp. * ²¹ He said to them, "Is a lamp brought in to be put under a basket or under a bed? To the contrary, it is placed on a lampstand. ²² For nothing is hidden that will not be disclosed, and nothing is secret that will not be brought to light. [23] If anyone has ears to hear, let him hear!"

The Parable of the Measure.* [24] He also told them, "Pay careful attention to what you hear. The measure you give will be the measure you will receive, and you will receive more in addition. [25] To the one who has, more will be given; from the one who does not have, even what little he has will be taken away." *

The Parable of the Secretly Growing Seed.* [26] He went on to say, "The kingdom of God is like this. A man scatters seed on the ground. [27] Night and day, while he sleeps and while he is awake, the seed sprouts and grows, though he does not understand how. [28] The ground produces fruit of its own accord—first the shoot, then the ear, then the full grain in the ear. [29] And when the crop is ripe, he immediately stretches out the sickle, because the time for harvest has come."

The Parable of the Mustard Seed.* [30] He then said, "With what shall we compare the kingdom of God, or what parable can we use to explain it? [31] It is like a mustard seed that, when it is sown in the ground, is the smallest of all the seeds on the earth. [32] But once it is sown, it springs up and becomes the greatest of all plants, and it puts forth large branches so that the birds of the air can make nests in its shade."

The Usefulness of Parables.* [33] With many such parables as these he spoke the word to them so far as they were able to comprehend it. [34] He never spoke to them except in parables, but he explained everything to his disciples when they were by themselves.

F: Jesus Overcomes Evil and Effects Salvation*

Jesus Calms the Storm.* [35] On that day, as evening approached, he said to them, "Let us cross over to the other side." [36] And so, leaving the crowd behind, they took him with them in the boat just as he was. Some other boats joined them.

³⁷ Suddenly, a great storm came up, and the waves were crashing over the boat so that it was almost swamped. ³⁸ Jesus was in the stern, asleep on a cushion. They awakened him and said, "Teacher do you not care that we are perishing?"

³⁹ Then he stood up and rebuked the wind, and he said to the sea, "Quiet! Be still!" The wind ceased, and there was a great calm. ⁴⁰ He said to them, "Why are you so frightened? Are you still without faith?" ⁴¹ They were filled with awe and said to one another, "Who can this be? Even the wind and the sea obey him."

5 **Jesus Heals the Gerasene Demoniac.*** ¹ They reached the region of the Gerasenes * on the other side of the lake. ² No sooner had he stepped out of the boat than a man with an unclean spirit came up to him from the tombs.* ³ The man had been living in the tombs, and no one could restrain him any longer, not even with chains. ⁴ For he had frequently been bound with shackles and chains, but he had snapped the chains and smashed the shackles to pieces, and no one had sufficient strength to subdue him. ⁵ Day and night among the tombs and on the mountains, he would howl and gash himself with stones.

⁶ When the man caught sight of Jesus from a distance, he ran up and prostrated himself before him, ⁷ as he shouted at the top of his voice, "What do you want with me, Jesus, Son of the Most High God? I implore you in God's name: do not torment me!" ⁸ For Jesus had said to him, "Unclean spirit, come out of the man!" ⁹ Then he asked him, "What is your name?" He replied, "My name is Legion, for there are many of us." * ¹⁰ And he begged him earnestly not to send them out of the country.

¹¹ Now on the mountainside a great herd of pigs was feeding. ¹² And they pleaded with him, "Send us into the pigs. Let us enter them." ¹³ He allowed this. With that, the unclean spirits came out and entered the pigs, and the herd, numbering about two thousand, charged down the steep bank into the lake and were drowned in the waters.

[14] Those tending the pigs ran off and reported the incident in the town and throughout the countryside. As a result, people came out to see what had happened. [15] When they came near Jesus, they saw the man who had been possessed by Legion sitting there fully clothed and in his right mind, and they were frightened. [16] Those who had been eyewitnesses to the incident confirmed what had happened to the demoniac and what had happened to the pigs. [17] Then they began to implore Jesus to leave their region.

[18] As Jesus was getting into the boat, the man who had been possessed with demons pleaded to be allowed to go with him. [19] However, Jesus would not permit him to do so, and instead told him, "Go home to your own people and tell them what the Lord has done for you, and how he has had mercy on you." [20] The man then departed and began to make known throughout the Decapolis what Jesus had done for him. And everyone was amazed.*

Jesus Heals a Woman and Raises a Child.* [21] When Jesus had crossed again in the boat to the other side, a large crowd gathered around him, and he stayed by the lake. [22] Then one of the leaders of the synagogue,* named Jairus, came forward, and when he saw Jesus he threw himself down at his feet [23] and pleaded with him, saying, "My little daughter is at the point of death. I beg you to come and lay your hands on her so that she may recover and live." [24] Jesus went with him, and a large number accompanied him and crowded around him.

[25] There was a woman who had suffered from bleeding for twelve years. [26] In spite of long and painful treatment at the hands of many doctors, her condition not only had failed to improve but had actually become worse, and she had spent everything she had. [27] Having heard about Jesus, she came up behind him in the crowd and touched his cloak, [28] for she thought, "If I simply touch his clothing, I shall be made well." [29] And immediately her bleeding dried up, and she felt in her body that she was healed of her affliction.

[30] Instantly aware that power had gone forth from him, Jesus turned around in the crowd and asked, "Who touched my clothing?" [31] His disciples said in reply, "You see this vast throng pressing upon you. How can you ask, 'Who touched me?'" [32] However, he continued to look around to determine who had done it. [33] Then the woman, knowing what had happened to her, approached in fear and trembling. She knelt before him and revealed to him the whole truth. [34] He said to her, "Daughter, your faith has healed you. Go in peace and be freed from your affliction."

[35] While he was still speaking, some people from the house of the synagogue leader arrived and said, "Your daughter has died. Why bother the Teacher any further?" [36] Jesus heard the message they had delivered, but he said to the leader of the synagogue, "Do not be afraid. Just have faith." [37] He allowed no one to accompany him except Peter, James, and John,* the brother of James.

[38] When they arrived at the house of the synagogue leader, he observed a great deal of commotion, with people weeping and wailing loudly. [39] When he entered, he said to them, "Why this commotion and weeping? The child is not dead; she is asleep." [40] In response, they laughed at him.

After sending them all outside, he took with him the child's father and mother and his own companions and entered the room where the child was. [41] He took the child by the hand and said to her, *"Talitha koum!"* which means: "Little girl, I say to you, arise!" [42] And immediately the girl, a child of twelve, got up and began to walk around.

On witnessing this, they were all overcome with amazement, [43] but he gave them strict instructions that no one should be told anything about this. Then he told them to give her something to eat.

6 Jesus Is Rejected at Nazareth.* [1] Departing from that district, Jesus went to his hometown accompanied by his

disciples. [2] On the Sabbath, he began to teach in the synagogue, and many of those who heard him asked in amazement, "Where did this man get all this? What is this wisdom that he has been granted? What mighty deeds he performs! [3] Is this not the carpenter, the son of Mary, and the brother* of James and Joses and Judas and Simon? Are not his sisters here with us?" And so they took offense at him.

[4] Then Jesus said to them, "A prophet is always treated with honor except in his hometown, and among relatives, and in his own house." [5] And he was unable to perform any mighty works there, aside from curing a few sick people by laying his hands on them. [6] He was amazed at their lack of faith.

G: Who Is Jesus?*

Jesus Sends Out the Twelve on Mission.* Jesus traveled through the villages teaching. [7] Calling the Twelve together, he began to send them out two by two, with authority over unclean spirits. [8] He instructed them to take nothing for their journey except a walking staff—no bread, no sack, no money in their purses. [9] They were to wear sandals but not to take along a second tunic.

[10] He said to them, "Whenever you enter a house, you are to stay there until you leave the area. [11] And if any will not welcome you and refuse to listen to you, leave them immediately and shake off the dust that is on your feet in testimony against them." [12] Then they set off and preached the need for repentance. [13] They cast out many demons, and they anointed with oil many people who were sick and cured them.*

The Name of Jesus Becomes Renowned.* [14] King Herod heard of it, for Jesus' name had become renowned, and some people were saying, "John the Baptist has been raised from the dead. That is why such powers are at work in him." [15] But others said, "He is Elijah," while still others proclaimed, "He is a prophet, like one of the prophets of old." [16] But when Herod heard of it, he said, "John, whom I beheaded, has been raised from the dead."

The Death of John the Baptist.* [17] It was this same Herod who had ordered John to be arrested and put in chains in prison on account of Herodias, his brother Philip's wife, because Herod had married her. [18] For John had told Herod, "It is unlawful for you to have your brother's wife."

[19] As for Herodias, she was filled with resentment against John and wanted to have him killed, but she was unable to do so, [20] because Herod was afraid of John, knowing him to be a holy and righteous man. Therefore, he protected him from harm. When he heard John speak, he was greatly perplexed by his words, but even so he liked to listen to him.

[21] Her opportunity came when Herod on his birthday gave a banquet for his court officials and military officers and the leaders of Galilee. [22] When the daughter of Herodias came in, she performed a dance that delighted Herod and his guests. The king said to the girl, "Ask me for whatever you wish, and I will give it to you." [23] And he solemnly swore to her, "Whatever you ask I will give you, even half of my kingdom."

[24] The girl went out and said to her mother, "What shall I ask for?" She replied, "The head of John the Baptist." [25] The girl then hurried back to the king and made her request, "I want you to give me at once the head of John the Baptist on a platter."

[26] The king was greatly distressed, but because of the oath he had sworn and the presence of the guests, he was unwilling to break his word to her. [27] Therefore, he immediately ordered an executioner to bring him John's head. The man went off and beheaded him in the prison. [28] Then he brought in the head on a platter and gave it to the girl, and the girl in turn gave it to her mother. [29] When John's disciples heard about this, they came and removed his body and laid it in a tomb.

The Return of the Twelve. [30] The apostles* returned to Jesus and reported to him all that they had done and taught. [31] He said to them, "Come away with me, by yourselves, to a deserted place and rest for a while." For people continued to come and go in great numbers, and they had no time even to eat.

[32] And so they went off by themselves in a boat to a deserted place. [33] Now many people saw them departing and recognized them, and they hurried there on foot from all the towns and arrived ahead of them. [34] As Jesus went ashore and beheld the vast crowd, he had compassion on them, for they were like sheep without a shepherd; and he began to teach them many things.

Jesus Feeds Five Thousand Men.* [35] When it began to be late in the day, his disciples came up to him and said, "This is a deserted place, and it is getting very late. [36] Send the people away now so that they can go to the farms and villages in the area and buy something for themselves to eat." [37] He replied, "Give them something to eat yourselves." They said to him, "Are we to go and spend two hundred denarii* on bread for them to eat?" [38] He asked, "How many loaves do you have? Go and see." When they found out, they reported: "Five loaves, and two fish."

[39] Then he ordered them to have all the people sit down on the green grass in groups. [40] They sat down in groups of hundreds and fifties. [41] Taking the five loaves and the two fish, he looked up to heaven, blessed and broke the loaves, and gave them to the disciples to distribute among the people. He also divided the two fish among them. [42] They all ate and were satisfied. [43] Then they gathered up the fragments of the bread and fish—twelve full baskets.* [44] Those who had eaten the loaves numbered five thousand men.

Jesus Walks on the Water.* [45] Immediately afterward, Jesus instructed his disciples to get into the boat and to go on ahead to Bethsaida on the other side of the lake while he dismissed the crowd. ⁴⁶ And when he had taken leave of them, he went up on the mountain to pray.

⁴⁷ When evening came, the boat was far out on the water while he was alone on the shore. ⁴⁸ He could see that the disciples were having difficulty in rowing the boat in the face of a headwind. Around the fourth watch of the night he came toward them, walking on the water. He was going to pass by them, ⁴⁹ but when the disciples saw him walking on the water they thought it was a ghost and they cried out, ⁵⁰ for they all had seen him and were terrified. But immediately he spoke to them, saying, "Have courage! It is I! * Do not be afraid!" ⁵¹ Then he got into the boat with them, and the wind died down. They were utterly astounded, ⁵² for they had not understood about the loaves. Their minds were closed.

Jesus Heals the Sick at Gennesaret.* ⁵³ After they had completed the crossing, they landed at Gennesaret and moored the boat. ⁵⁴ When they disembarked, the people recognized Jesus immediately. ⁵⁵ They rushed throughout the entire countryside, and began to bring the sick to him on pallets wherever they heard he was. ⁵⁶ Everywhere he went, whether to village or town or countryside, they laid the sick in the marketplaces and begged him to let them touch even the edge of his cloak. And all who touched it were completely healed.

7 **Traditions That Falsify the Law of God.*** ¹ When the Pharisees, along with some scribes who had come from Jerusalem, gathered around Jesus, ² they noted that some of his disciples were eating with defiled hands, that is, without washing them. ³ For the Pharisees, and in fact all Jews, do not eat without thoroughly washing their hands, thereby observing the tradition of the elders. ⁴ And on coming from the marketplace they do not eat without first washing. In addition, there are many other traditions that they observe, such as the washing of cups and jugs and bronze kettles and tables.*

⁵ Therefore, the Pharisees and the scribes asked him, "Why do your disciples not follow the tradition of the elders but eat with unclean hands?" ⁶ He answered, "How rightly Isaiah prophesied about you hypocrites, as it is written:

'This people honors me with their lips,
    but their hearts are far from me;
⁷   in vain do they worship me,
        teaching as doctrines the commandments of men.'

⁸ You thrust aside the commandment of God in order to preserve the traditions of men." *

⁹ Then he said to them, "How cleverly you have set aside the commandment of God to preserve your own tradition! ¹⁰ For Moses said, 'Honor your father and your mother,' and 'Whoever curses father or mother will be put to death.' ¹¹ But you say, 'If anyone tells his father or mother: "Anything I might have used for your support is *Corban*" ' * (that is, dedicated to God), ¹² then he is forbidden by you from that very moment to do anything for his father or mother. ¹³ You nullify the word of God for the sake of your tradition that you have handed down. And you do many other things just like that."

Clean and Unclean.* ¹⁴ Then he called the people to him and said to them: "Listen to me, all of you, and understand. ¹⁵ There is nothing that goes into a person from outside that can defile him. The things that come out of a person are what defile him. [¹⁶ If anyone has ears to hear, let him hear!]" *

¹⁷ When he had gone into the house, away from the crowds, his disciples questioned him about the parable. ¹⁸ He said to them, "Then are you also without understanding? Do you not realize that whatever goes into a person from outside cannot defile him, ¹⁹ since it enters not into the heart but into the stomach and is discharged into the sewer?" Thus, he pronounced all foods clean.

²⁰ Then he went on, "It is what comes out of a person that defiles. ²¹ For from within, from the human heart,

come evil thoughts, unchastity, theft, murder, [22] adultery, avarice, malice, deceit, indecency, envy, slander, arrogance, and folly. [23] All these evils come from within, and they defile a person."

The Faith of a Gentile Woman.* [24] He moved on from that place to the region of Tyre. He went into a house and did not want anyone to know he was there, but he was not able to avoid being recognized. [25] Almost immediately, a woman whose daughter was possessed by an unclean spirit heard about him and hastened to fall down at his feet. [26] The woman was a Gentile of Syrophoenician origin, and she begged him to drive the demon out of her daughter.

[27] Jesus said to her, "Let the children be fed first. For it is not right to take the children's bread and throw it to the dogs." [28] She replied, "Yes, Lord; but even the dogs under the table eat the scraps from the children." [29] Then Jesus said to her, "For saying this, you may go. The demon has gone out of your daughter." [30] And when she returned home, she found the child lying in bed and the demon gone.

Jesus Heals a Deaf Man.* [31] Returning from the region of Tyre, Jesus traveled by way of Sidon to the Sea of Galilee, and into the region of the Decapolis. [32] Thereupon people brought to him a deaf man who had a speech impediment and begged him to lay his hand on him. [33] He took him aside, away from the crowd, and put his fingers into the man's ears and, spitting, touched his tongue. [34] Then, looking up to heaven, he sighed and said to him, *"Ephphatha!"* which means, "Be opened!" [35] At once, the man's ears were opened, his tongue was loosened, and he spoke properly.

[36] Then he ordered them not to tell anyone, but the more he ordered them not to do so, the more widely they proclaimed it. [37] Their astonishment was beyond measure. "He has done all things well," they said. "He even makes the deaf able to hear and the mute able to speak."

JESUS HEALS A DEAF-MUTE—"[Jesus] put his fingers into the man's ears and, spitting, touched this tongue. . . . He sighed and said to him, *'Ephphatha!'* which means, 'Be opened!' At once, the man's ears were opened . . . and he spoke properly" (Mk 7:33-35).

JESUS FEEDS FOUR THOUSAND—"He took the seven loaves, and after giving thanks he broke them and gave them to his disciples to distribute. . . . There were also a few small fish, and after blessing them he commanded that these too should be distributed" (Mk 8:6-7).

8 **Jesus Feeds Four Thousand.*** [1] In those days, a great crowd had again assembled, and they had nothing to eat. Jesus called his disciples to him and said to them, [2] "I am moved with compassion for these people, because they have been with me now for three days and have nothing to eat. [3] If I send them away hungry to their homes, they will collapse on the way—and some of them have come from far off."

[4] His disciples replied, "How can anyone find enough bread here in this deserted place to feed these men?" [5] He asked them, "How many loaves do you have?" They replied, "Seven."

[6] Jesus ordered the crowd to sit down on the ground. Then he took the seven loaves, and after giving thanks he broke them and gave them to his disciples to distribute, and they distributed them to the people. [7] There were also a few small fish, and after blessing them he commanded that these too should be distributed. [8] They ate and were satisfied. Afterward, the disciples picked up the fragments left over—seven full baskets. [9] The people there numbered about four thousand. And when he had sent them away, [10] he immediately got into the boat with his disciples and went to the district of Dalmanutha.*

The Demand for a Sign.* [11] The Pharisees came forward and began to argue with him. To put him to the test they asked him to show them a sign from heaven. [12] Sighing from the depths of his spirit, he said, "Why does this generation ask for a sign? Amen, I say to you, no sign will be given to this generation." [13] Then he left them, got into the boat again, and sailed across to the other side.

The Yeast of the Pharisees.* [14] They had forgotten to bring any bread with them, and they had only one loaf in the boat. [15] Jesus then gave them this warning, "Be careful, and beware of the yeast of the Pharisees and the yeast of Herod." [16] They talked about this to one another and concluded: "It is because we have no bread."

[17] Becoming aware of what they were discussing, he said to them, "Why are you talking about having no bread? Do you still not understand or comprehend? Are your hearts hardened? [18] Do you have eyes and fail to see? Do you have ears and fail to hear?

"And do you not remember? [19] When I broke the five loaves for the five thousand, how many baskets filled with fragments did you collect?" They answered, "Twelve." [20] "When I broke the seven loaves for the four thousand, how many baskets filled with fragments did you collect?" They answered, "Seven." [21] He said to them, "Do you still not understand?"

Jesus Heals a Blind Man.* [22] They arrived at Bethsaida, and some people brought a blind man to Jesus and begged that he touch him. [23] He took the blind man by the hand and led him outside the village. Then, putting saliva on his eyes, he laid his hands on him and asked, "Can you see anything?" [24] Looking up, the man responded, "I can see people, but they look like trees walking around." [25] Jesus placed his hands on the man's eyes again, and the man looked around intently. His sight was restored, and he was able to see everything clearly. [26] Then he sent him away to his home, saying, "Do not even go into the village."

Peter's Confession That Jesus Is the Messiah.* [27] Then Jesus and his disciples set out for the villages of Caesarea Philippi. Along the way he asked his disciples, "Who do people say that I am?" [28] They responded, "[Some say] John the Baptist; others say Elijah; and still others, one of the prophets." [29] "But you," he asked, "who do you say that I am?" Peter answered him, "You are the Christ." [30] Then he gave them strict orders not to tell anyone about him.

III. THE MYSTERY OF JESUS IS REVEALED*

A: The Way of the Son of Man*

Jesus Predicts His Passion.* [31] After that, he began to teach them that the Son of Man must endure great suffering, be rejected by the elders, the chief priests, and the scribes,* and be put to death, and rise again after three days. ³² He told them these facts in plain words.

Then Peter took him aside and began to rebuke him. ³³ At this, Jesus turned and, looking at his disciples, rebuked Peter and said, "Get behind me, Satan! You are thinking not as God does, but as men do."

The Conditions of Discipleship.* ³⁴ He then called the people and his disciples to him and said to them, "Anyone who wishes to follow me must deny himself, take up his cross, and follow me. ³⁵ * For whoever wishes to save his life will lose it, but whoever loses his life for my sake and the sake of the gospel will save it. ³⁶ What does it profit a man to gain the whole world and forfeit his very life? ³⁷ Indeed, what can he give in exchange for his life?

³⁸ "If anyone in this adulterous and sinful generation is ashamed of me and of my words, the Son of Man will also be ashamed of him when he comes in the glory of his Father with the holy angels."

9 ¹ Then he said to them, "Amen, I say to you, there are some standing here who will not taste death before they see that the kingdom of God has come with power." *

Jesus Is Transfigured.* ² Six days later, Jesus took Peter, James, and John and led them up a high mountain apart by themselves. And in their presence he was transfigured; ³ his clothes became dazzling white—whiter than anyone on earth could bleach them. ⁴ And Elijah with Moses appeared, conversing with Jesus.

⁵ Then Peter said to Jesus, "Rabbi, it is good for us to be here. Let us make three tents—one for you, one for Moses, and one for Elijah." ⁶ He did not know what to say, for they were so frightened. ⁷ Then a cloud cast a shadow over them, and a voice came out of the cloud: "This is my beloved Son. Listen to him." ⁸ Suddenly, when they looked around, they saw no one with them anymore, but only Jesus.

Elijah Has Already Come.* [9] As they were coming down from the mountain, Jesus ordered them to tell no one what they had seen until the Son of Man had risen from the dead. [10] Therefore, they kept the matter to themselves, although they did argue about what rising from the dead could possibly mean.

[11] And they asked him, "Why do the scribes say that Elijah must come first?" [12] He said to them, "Elijah will indeed come first and restore all things. Yet how is it written about the Son of Man?—that he must endure great suffering and be treated with contempt! [13] However, I tell you that Elijah has come, and they did to him whatever they pleased, as it is written about him."

Jesus Heals a Boy Possessed by a Spirit.* [14] When they returned to the disciples, they saw a large crowd surrounding them, and some scribes were engaged in an argument with them. [15] As soon as the people saw Jesus, they were overcome with awe and ran forward to greet him. [16] He asked them, "What are you arguing about with them?"

[17] A man in the crowd answered him, "Teacher, I have brought you my son who is possessed by a spirit that makes him unable to speak. [18] Wherever it seizes him, it flings him to the ground, and he foams at the mouth, grinds his teeth, and becomes rigid. I asked your disciples to drive it out, but they were unable to do so."

[19] Jesus said to them in reply, "O unbelieving generation, how much longer shall I remain with you? How much longer must I put up with you? Bring the boy to me." [20] When they brought the boy to him, the spirit saw him and immediately threw the child into convulsions. He fell to the ground and rolled around, foaming at the mouth.

[21] Jesus asked the father, "How long has the boy been in this condition?" "From childhood," he replied. [22] "It has often tried to kill him by throwing him into a fire or into water. If it is possible for you to do anything, have pity on us and help us." [23] Jesus answered, "If it is possi-

ble! All things are possible for one who has faith."
[24] Immediately, the father of the child cried out, "I do
believe. Help my unbelief."

[25] When Jesus saw that a crowd was rapidly gathering
around them, he rebuked the unclean spirit, saying to it,
"Deaf and mute spirit, I command you: come out of him
and never enter him again!" [26] Shrieking and throwing the
boy into convulsions, it came out of him. He lay there like
a corpse, so that many remarked, "He is dead." [27] But
Jesus, taking him by the hand, raised him, and he stood
up.

[28] When he went indoors, his disciples asked him privately, "Why were we not able to cast it out?" [29] He
answered, "This kind cannot be driven out except by
prayer [and by fasting]." *

Jesus Predicts His Passion a Second Time. * [30] They proceeded from there and began to journey through Galilee,
but Jesus did not want anyone to know about it [31] because
he was teaching his disciples. He told them, "The Son of
Man * will be handed over into the power of men. They
will kill him, and three days after being killed he will rise."
[32] But they did not understand what he was saying, and
they were afraid to ask him about it.

The Greatest in the Kingdom. * [33] They came to Capernaum, and once they were in the house he asked them,
"What were you arguing about during the journey?"
[34] But they remained silent, for on the way they had been
arguing about which one of them was the greatest.

[35] Then he sat down, summoned the Twelve, and said
to them, "If anyone wishes to be first, he must become
the last of all and the servant of all." [36] He then took a
child, placed it in their midst, and put his arms around it
as he said, [37] "Whoever receives one such child in my
name receives me; and whoever receives me receives not
me but the one who sent me."

Whoever Is Not against Us Is for Us. [38] John said to him,
"Teacher, we observed someone expelling demons in

your name, and we forbade him because he was not one of us." * [39] Jesus replied, "Do not hinder him, for no one who performs a miracle in my name will be able soon afterward to speak evil of me. [40] Whoever is not against us is for us. [41] Amen, I say to you, whoever gives you a cup of water to drink because you bear the name of Christ will certainly not go unrewarded.

Woe to the World because of Scandals. * [42] "If anyone causes one of these little ones who believe in me to sin, it would be better for him if a great millstone were hung around his neck and he were thrown into the sea.

[43] "If your hand causes you to sin, cut it off.* It is preferable for you to enter life maimed than to have two hands and go into the unquenchable fire of Gehenna [[44] where the devouring worm never dies and the fire is never quenched].* [45] And if your foot causes you to sin, cut it off. It is better for you to enter life crippled than to have two feet and be thrown into Gehenna [[46] where the devouring worm never dies and the fire is never quenched]. [47] And if your eye causes you to sin, tear it out. It is preferable for you to enter into the kingdom of God with one eye than to have two eyes and be cast into Gehenna, [48] where the devouring worm never dies and the fire is never quenched.

The Simile of Salt. [49] "For everyone will be salted with fire.* [50] Salt is good, but if salt loses its saltiness, how can you revive its flavor? Have salt in yourselves, and be at peace with one another."

10 Marriage and Divorce.* [1] After departing from there, Jesus came into the region of Judea beyond the Jordan.* Again the crowds gathered around him, and, as was his custom, he began to teach them.

[2] Some Pharisees came forward and in order to test him asked, "Is it lawful for a man to divorce his wife?" [3] He replied, "What did Moses command you?" [4] They said, "Moses allowed a man to write a certificate of divorce and dismiss her." [5] But Jesus said to them, "It was

because of the hardness of your hearts that he wrote this commandment for you. [6] But from the very beginning of creation, 'God made them male and female.' [7] 'That is why a man leaves his father and mother and is joined to his wife, [8] and the two become one flesh.' And so they are no longer two but one flesh. [9] Therefore, what God has joined together, let no one separate."

[10] When they were again in the house, the disciples once more questioned Jesus about this. [11] He said to them, "If a man divorces his wife and marries another, he commits adultery against her. [12] In the same way, if a wife divorces her husband and marries another, she commits adultery."

Jesus Receives Little Children.* [13] People were bringing little children to him so that he might touch them, and the disciples sternly rebuked them. [14] But when Jesus became aware of this, he was indignant and said to them, "Let the little children come to me; do not hinder them. For it is to such as these that the kingdom of God belongs. [15] Amen, I say to you, whoever does not receive the kingdom of God like a little child will never enter it." [16] And he took them up into his arms, laid his hands on them, and blessed them.

The Rich Young Man.* [17] As Jesus was starting out on a journey, a man came running up to him, knelt down, and asked him, "Good teacher, what must I do to inherit eternal life?" [18] Jesus said to him, "Why do you call me good? No one is good but God alone. [19] You know the commandments: 'Do not kill. Do not commit adultery. Do not steal. Do not bear false witness. Do not defraud. Honor your father and your mother.'"

[20] The man said to him, "Teacher, I have observed all these since I was a child." [21] Looking at him, Jesus was moved with love and said, "You need to do one further thing. Go and sell what you own, and give to the poor, and you will have treasure in heaven. Then come, follow me." [22] When he heard these words, the man's face fell and he went away grieving, for he possessed great wealth.

^{23} Then Jesus looked around and said to his disciples, "How difficult it will be for those who are rich to enter the kingdom of God!" ^{24} The disciples were astounded on hearing his words, but Jesus insisted: "Children, how difficult it is to enter the kingdom of God! ^{25} It is easier for a camel to pass through the eye of a needle than for someone who is rich to enter the kingdom of God." ^{26} The disciples were even more greatly astonished, and they said to one another, "Then who can be saved?" ^{27} Jesus looked at them and said, "For men it is impossible, but not for God. For God all things are possible."

Reward for Following Jesus.* ^{28} Peter said to him, "We have given up everything to follow you." ^{29} Jesus answered, "Amen, I say to you, there is no one who has given up house or brothers or sisters or mother or father or children or lands for my sake and for the sake of the gospel ^{30} who will not receive in this age a hundred times more houses, brothers and sisters, mothers and children, and lands—as well as persecutions—and in the age to come, eternal life. ^{31} But many who are first will be last, and the last will be first."

Jesus Predicts His Passion a Third Time.* ^{32} As they were on the road going up to Jerusalem, Jesus walked ahead of them. The disciples were amazed, and those who followed were apprehensive. Once again, he took the Twelve aside and began to tell them what would happen to him. ^{33} "Behold, we are now going up to Jerusalem," he said, "and the Son of Man will be handed over to the chief priests and the scribes, and they will condemn him to death. Then they will hand him over to the Gentiles, ^{34} who will mock him, and spit upon him, and scourge him, and put him to death. And after three days he will rise again."

The Son of Man Has Come To Serve.* ^{35} Then James and John, the sons of Zebedee, came forward and said to him, "Teacher, we want you to do for us whatever we request." ^{36} He asked them, "What is it that you want me to do for you?" [37] They said to him, "Allow us to sit, one at your right hand and the other at your left, in your glory." [38] Jesus said to them, "You do not know what you are asking. Can you drink the cup that I drink,* or be baptized with the baptism with which I am baptized?" [39] They said to him, "We can."

Then Jesus said to them, "The cup that I drink you shall indeed drink, and with the baptism with which I am baptized you shall be baptized. [40] But to sit at my right hand or at my left is not in my power to grant. Those places belong to those for whom they have been prepared."

[41] When the other ten heard this, they began to be indignant at James and John. [42] Therefore, Jesus called them over and said, "You know that those considered to be rulers among the Gentiles lord it over them, and their great ones make their authority over them felt. [43] But this must not be so with you. Instead, whoever wishes to become great among you must be your servant, [44] and whoever wishes to be first among you must be the servant of all. [45] For even the Son of Man did not come to be served but to serve and to give his life as a ransom for many."

Jesus Heals a Blind Man.* [46] Then they came to Jericho. And as Jesus, his disciples, and a huge crowd were leaving Jericho, a blind man, Bartimaeus, the son of Timaeus,* was sitting by the roadside asking for alms. [47] When he heard that it was Jesus of Nazareth, he began to shout, "Jesus, Son of David, have pity on me!" [48] Many rebuked him and told him to be silent, but he only shouted all the louder, "Son of David, have pity on me!"

[49] Jesus stopped and said, "Call him." So they called the blind man, saying to him, "Take heart! Stand up! He is calling you!" [50] Casting aside his cloak, he jumped up and went to Jesus. [51] Then Jesus said to him, "What do you want me to do for you?" The blind man said to him, "Rabbi,* let me receive my sight." [52] Jesus said to him, "Go on your way! Your faith has made you well."

Immediately, he received his sight and followed him along the road.

B: Jesus at Jerusalem—The Break with Judaism*

11 **The Entry into Jerusalem.*** [1] When they drew near Jerusalem, to Bethphage and Bethany, near the Mount of Olives, he sent off two of his disciples, [2] saying to them, "Go into the village directly ahead of you, and as soon as you enter it you will find tied there a colt on which no one has ever ridden. Untie it and bring it here. [3] If anyone says to you, 'Why are you doing this?' say: 'The Lord needs it and will send it back immediately.'"

[4] The two went off and found a colt tied beside a door outside on the street. As they were untying it, [5] some of them said to them, "What are you doing, untying that colt?" [6] They answered as Jesus had instructed them, and they allowed them to take it. [7] Then they brought the colt to Jesus and spread their cloaks on its back. And he sat on it. [8] Many people spread their cloaks on the road, and others spread leafy branches that they had cut in the fields. [9] Those who went ahead and those who followed kept crying out:

> "Hosanna!*
> Blessed is he who comes in the name of the Lord!
> [10] Blessed is the coming kingdom of our father David.
> Hosanna in the highest heavens!"

[11] He entered Jerusalem and went into the temple, where he looked around at everything. Then, since the hour was already late, he went out to Bethany with the Twelve.

Jesus Curses a Sterile Fig Tree.* [12] On the next day, as they were leaving Bethany, he felt hungry. [13] Noticing in the distance a fig tree in leaf, he went to see if he could find any fruit on it. When he reached it, he found nothing except leaves, since it was not the season for figs. [14] Then he said to it, "May no one ever again eat fruit from your branches." And his disciples heard him say this.

Jesus Cleanses the Temple.* ¹⁵ Then they came to Jerusalem. He entered the temple and began to drive out those who were engaged there in buying and selling. He overturned the tables of the money changers and the seats of those who were selling doves. ¹⁶ Nor would he allow anyone to carry anything through the temple. ¹⁷ Then he taught them, saying: "Is it not written: *

> 'My house shall be called a house of prayer for all the nations'?
> But you have made it a den of thieves."

¹⁸ When the chief priests and the scribes heard about this, they plotted to do away with him. For they were afraid of him because the whole crowd was spellbound by his teaching. ¹⁹ And when evening came, they left the city.

The Lesson of the Withered Fig Tree.* ²⁰ Early the next morning, as they passed by, they saw the fig tree withered away to its roots. ²¹ Then Peter, recalling what had happened, said to Jesus: "Rabbi, look! The fig tree that you cursed has withered away."

²² Jesus said to them, "Have faith in God. ²³ Amen, I say to you, whoever says to this mountain, 'Be lifted up and thrown into the sea,' and does not doubt in his heart but believes that what he says will happen, it will be accomplished for him. ²⁴ So I tell you, whatever you ask for in prayer, believe that you have received it, and it will be yours.

²⁵ "And whenever you stand in prayer, forgive whatever grievance you have against anybody, so that your Father in heaven may forgive your wrongs too. [²⁶ But if you do not forgive others, then your Father in heaven will not forgive you your transgressions.]" *

The Authority of Jesus Questioned.* ²⁷ They returned once again to Jerusalem. As Jesus was walking in the temple, the chief priests, the scribes, and the elders approached him ²⁸ and asked, "By what authority are you doing these things? Or who gave you the authority to do them?" ²⁹ Jesus said to them, "I will ask you one question. Give me an answer, and I will tell you by what authority I do these things. ³⁰ Did John's baptism originate from heaven or from men? Tell me!"

³¹ They argued among themselves, "If we say: 'From heaven,' he will say, 'Then why did you not believe him?' ³² But how can we say, 'From men'?"—for they were afraid of the people, who all regarded John as a true prophet.

³³ Therefore, they answered Jesus, "We do not know." And Jesus said to them, "Then neither shall I tell you by what authority I do these things."

12 The Parable of the Tenants.*

¹ Then Jesus began to speak to them in parables: "A man planted a vineyard, put a fence around it, dug a pit for the winepress, and built a watchtower. Then he leased it to tenants and went off on a journey.

² "When the time arrived, he sent a servant to the tenants to collect from them his share of the produce of the vineyard. ³ But they seized the servant, beat him, and sent him away empty-handed. ⁴ Again, he sent them another servant, but they beat him over the head and treated him shamefully. ⁵ Then he sent another, and that one they killed. He also sent many others, some of whom they beat, and others of whom they killed.

⁶ "Finally, he had only one other to send—his beloved son. And so he sent him to them, thinking: 'They will respect my son.' ⁷ But those tenants said to one another, 'This is the heir. Come, let us kill him, and the inheritance will be ours!' ⁸ And so they seized him, killed him, and threw him out of the vineyard.

⁹ "What then will the owner of the vineyard do? He will come and put those tenants to death and give the vineyard to others. ¹⁰ Have you not read this Scripture:

'The stone that the builders rejected
    has become the cornerstone;
¹¹   by the Lord this has been done,
       and it is wonderful in our eyes'?"

[12] They wanted to arrest him because they realized that this parable was directed at them, but they were afraid of the crowd. Therefore, they left him and went away.

C: Controversies*

God or Caesar.* [13] Then they sent some Pharisees and Herodians to trap him in what he said. [14] They came and said to him, "Teacher, we know that you are truthful and are not concerned with anyone's opinion no matter what his station in life. Rather, you teach the way of God in accordance with the truth. Is it lawful or not for us to pay taxes to Caesar? Should we pay them or not?"

[15] He was aware of their hypocrisy and said to them, "Why are you trying to trap me? Bring me a denarius * and let me examine it." [16] When they brought one, he asked them, "Whose image is this, and whose inscription?" They replied and said to him, "Caesar's." [17] Jesus said to them, "Give to Caesar what is due to Caesar, and to God what is due to God." His reply left them completely amazed at him.

Marriage and the Resurrection.* [18] Then some Sadducees, who assert that there is no resurrection, approached him and posed this question, [19] "Teacher, Moses wrote down for us that if a man's brother dies, leaving a wife but no child, the man shall take his brother's wife and raise up children for his brother. [20] Now there were seven brothers. The first brother took a wife and died, leaving no children. [21] The second brother married the widow and died, leaving no children. The same was true of the third brother. [22] None of the seven left any children. Last of all, the woman herself died. [23] Now at the resurrection, when they rise up, whose wife will she be, inasmuch as all seven had her?"

[24] Jesus said to them, "Is not this the reason you are in error—namely, that you do not understand the Scriptures or the power of God? [25] For when they rise from the dead, they will neither marry nor be given in marriage. They are like angels in heaven.

²⁶ "And in regard to the dead being raised, have you not read in the book of Moses, in the account about the bush, how God said to him: 'I am the God of Abraham, the God of Isaac, and the God of Jacob'? ²⁷ He is not the God of the dead but of the living. You are very badly mistaken."

The Greatest Commandment.* ²⁸ Then one of the scribes who had listened to these discussions, and who had observed how well Jesus answered them, asked Jesus, "Which is the first of all the commandments?" *

²⁹ Jesus answered, "The first is: 'Hear, O Israel: the Lord our God, the Lord is one! ³⁰ You shall love the Lord your God with all your heart, and with all your soul, and with all your mind, and with all your strength.' ³¹ The second is this: 'You shall love your neighbor as yourself.' There is no other commandment greater than these."

³² Then the scribe said to him, "Well said, Teacher. You have truly said, 'He is one, and there is no other besides him.' ³³ And 'to love him with all your heart: and with all your understanding, and with all your strength, and to love your neighbor as yourself,' is worth more than any burnt offerings and sacrifices." ³⁴ And when Jesus saw with what great understanding he had spoken, he said to him, "You are not far from the kingdom of God." And after that no one dared to ask him any question.

Jesus Is Lord.* ³⁵ While Jesus was teaching in the temple area, he said, "How can the scribes say that the Christ is the Son of David? * ³⁶ David himself, inspired by the Holy Spirit, declared:

'The Lord said to my Lord:
"Sit at my right hand
    until I put your enemies under your feet." ' '

³⁷ David himself calls him 'Lord'; so how can he be his son?" And the large crowd listened to him with delight.

Denunciation of the Scribes.* ³⁸ In his teaching, he said, "Beware of the scribes, who like to walk around in long robes, to be greeted respectfully in the marketplace,

[39] and to have the best seats in the synagogues and the places of honor at banquets. [40] They devour the houses of widows, while for the sake of appearance they recite lengthy prayers. They will receive the severest possible condemnation."

The Poor Widow's Offering.* [41] As Jesus was sitting opposite the treasury,* he watched the crowd putting money into the treasury. Many wealthy people put in large sums. [42] A poor widow also came and put in two copper coins, that is, about a penny.* [43] Then he called his disciples to him and said, "Amen, I say to you, this poor widow has given more than all the other contributors to the treasury. [44] For the others have all contributed out of their abundance, but she out of her poverty has given everything she possessed, all that she had to live on."

D: When Will the End Come?*

13 **Jesus Announces the Destruction of the Temple.*** [1] As Jesus was making his departure from the temple, one of his disciples said to him, "Teacher, look at the size of these stones and buildings!" [2] Jesus said to him, "Do you see these great buildings? Not a single stone will be left upon another; every one will be thrown down."

The End Has Not Yet Come.* [3] As he was sitting on the Mount of Olives directly across from the temple, Peter,* James, John, and Andrew questioned him when they were alone. [4] "Tell us," they said, "when will this happen, and what will be the sign that all those things are about to be accomplished?"

[5] Jesus began to say to them, "Take care that no one deceives you. [6] Many will come in my name, saying, 'I am he,' and they will lead many astray. [7] And when you hear of wars and rumors of wars, do not be alarmed, for those things are bound to happen, but the end is still to come. [8] For nation will rise against nation and kingdom against kingdom. There will be earthquakes in various places, and there will be famine. These are only the beginning of the labor pangs.

The Coming Persecution. [9] * "Be on your guard. For they will hand you over to courts and beat you in synagogues. You will stand before governors and kings because of me to testify before them. [10] But first the gospel must be preached to all nations.

[11] "When they arrest you and bring you to trial, do not be concerned beforehand about what you are to say. Simply say whatever is given to you when that time comes, for it will not be you who speak but the Holy Spirit.

[12] "Brother will betray brother to death, and a father his child. Children will rebel against their parents and have them put to death. [13] You will be hated by all because of my name, but whoever stands firm to the end will be saved.

The Great Trial. [14] "Therefore, when you see the abomination of desolation* standing where it does not belong (let the reader understand), then those who are in Judea must flee to the mountains, [15] the one who is standing on the roof must not come down or go inside to take anything out of the house, [16] and someone who is in the field must not turn back to retrieve his coat.

[17] "Woe to those who are pregnant and those who are nursing infants in those days. [18] Pray that all this may not occur in winter. [19] For in those days there will be such suffering as has not been since the beginning of the creation that God made until now and will never be again. [20] And if the Lord had not cut short those days, no one would be saved; but for the sake of the elect whom he chose, he did cut short those days.

False Messiahs and False Prophets. * [21] "Therefore, if anyone says to you, 'Look, here is the Christ!' or 'Look, there he is!' do not believe it. [22] For false christs and false prophets will arise, and they will perform signs and wonders to lead astray God's chosen ones, if that were possible. [23] Be on your guard! I have forewarned you about everything.

The Coming of the Son of Man.* ²⁴ "But in those days, following that distress,

> the sun will be darkened
>> and the moon will not give forth its light,
²⁵ and the stars will be falling from the sky,
>> and the heavenly powers will be shaken.

²⁶ Then they will see 'the Son of Man coming in the clouds' with great power and glory. ²⁷ And he will send forth his angels and gather his elect from the four winds, from the ends of the earth to the ends of the heavens.

The Parable of the Fig Tree.* ²⁸ "Learn this lesson from the fig tree. As soon as its twigs become tender and its leaves begin to sprout, you know that summer is near. ²⁹ In the same way, when you see these things come to pass, know that he is near, at the very gates. ³⁰ Amen, I say to you, this generation will not pass away before all these things have taken place.* ³¹ Heaven and earth will pass away, but my words will never pass away.

The Day and Hour Unknown.* ³² "But as for that day or that hour, no one knows, neither the angels in heaven, nor the Son, but only the Father. ³³ Be on your guard and keep alert, because you do not know when the time will come.

³⁴ "It is like a man going on a journey. He leaves his house and puts his servants in charge, each with his own duties to perform, and he commands the doorkeeper to remain alert. ³⁵ Therefore, keep watch, for you do not know when the master of the house will return, whether in the evening, or at midnight, or at cockcrow, or at dawn, ³⁶ lest he arrive unexpectedly and find you asleep. ³⁷ What I say to you, I say to all: Keep awake!"

E: The Mystery Is Fully Manifested in the Passion and Resurrection*

14 **The Plot against Jesus.*** ¹ It was now two days before the Passover and the feast of Unleavened Bread, and the chief priests and the scribes were seeking to arrest Jesus by deceit and put him to death. [2] They said, "It must not occur during the feast, or the people may begin to riot."

A Woman of Bethany Anoints Jesus.* [3] When Jesus was in Bethany reclining at table in the house of Simon the leper, a woman came in with an alabaster jar of very costly ointment, made of pure nard. She broke open the jar and poured the ointment over his head. [4] Some of those present said to one another indignantly, "Why was this ointment wasted in such a manner? [5] It could have been sold for more than three hundred denarii,* with the money given to the poor." And they began to rebuke her sharply.

[6] However, Jesus said, "Let her alone! Why are you bothering her? She has performed a good action toward me. [7] The poor you will always have with you, and you can show kindness to them whenever you wish, but you will not always have me. [8] She has done what she could. She has anointed my body to prepare for my burial. [9] Amen, I say to you, wherever in the whole world this gospel is proclaimed, what she has done will be told in remembrance of her."

Judas Betrays Jesus.* [10] Then Judas Iscariot, who was one of the Twelve, went to the chief priests and offered to hand him over to them. [11] They were delighted when they heard his proposal, and they promised to give him money. Then he began to look for an opportunity to betray him.

The Preparations for the Passover.* [12] On the first day of the feast of Unleavened Bread, when it was customary to sacrifice the Passover lamb, the disciples said to Jesus, "Where do you want us to go and make the preparations for you to eat the Passover?"

[13] He sent forth two of his disciples, instructing them: "Go into the city, and a man carrying a jug of water will meet you. Follow him! [14] Wherever he enters, say to the master of the house, 'The Teacher asks: "Where is the

room where I can eat the Passover with my disciples?" ' ¹⁵ Then he will show you a large upper room furnished and ready. Make the preparations for us there." ¹⁶ The disciples went forth, entered the city, and found everything just as he had told them, and they prepared the Passover.

The Treachery of Judas Foretold.* ¹⁷ Now when evening came, he arrived with the Twelve. ¹⁸ And as they reclined at table and were eating, Jesus said, "Amen, I say to you, one of you will betray me, one who is eating with me." ¹⁹ On hearing this they began to be distressed and to say to him, one after another, "Is it I?"

²⁰ He said to them, "It is one of the Twelve, one who is dipping bread into the bowl with me. ²¹ For the Son of Man goes as it is written of him, but woe to that man by whom the Son of Man is betrayed! It would be better for that man if he had never been born."

The Last Supper.* ²² While they were eating he took bread, and after he had pronounced the blessing, he broke it and gave it to them, saying, "Take it; this is my body." ²³ Then he took a cup, and after offering thanks he gave it to them. After they all drank from it, ²⁴ he said to them, "This is my blood of the covenant, which will be shed on behalf of many. ²⁵ Amen, I say to you, from now on I shall not drink this fruit of the vine until the day when I shall drink it anew in the kingdom of God."

²⁶ And after singing a hymn, they went out to the Mount of Olives.

Jesus Predicts Peter's Denial.* ²⁷ Then Jesus said to them, "You will all be scandalized, for it is written:

'I will strike the shepherd,
    and the sheep will be scattered.'

²⁸ But after I have been raised up, I shall go ahead of you to Galilee." ²⁹ Peter said to him, "Even if all the others will be scandalized, I will never be." ³⁰ Jesus replied, "Amen, I say to you, this very night, before the cock crows twice,

you will deny me three times." [31] But Peter insisted, "If I have to die with you, I will not deny you." And they all said the same thing.

The Agony in the Garden.* [32] Then they went to a place that was called Gethsemane, and Jesus said to his disciples, "Sit here while I pray." [33] He took with him Peter and James and John, and he began to suffer distress and anguish. [34] And he said to them, "My soul is sorrowful, even to the point of death. Remain here and keep watch."

[35] Moving on a little farther, he threw himself on the ground and prayed that, if it were possible, the hour might pass him by, [36] saying, "Abba, Father, for you all things are possible. Take this cup from me. Yet not my will but yours be done."

[37] Returning to the disciples, he found them sleeping. He said to Peter, "Simon, are you asleep? Could you not keep watch for one hour? [38] Stay awake and pray that you may not enter into temptation. The spirit is indeed willing but the flesh is weak."

[39] Again, he went apart and prayed, saying the same words. [40] Then he came again and found them sleeping, for their eyes were very heavy, and they did not know what to say to him. [41] When he returned a third time, he said to them, "Are you still sleeping and taking your rest? Enough! The hour has come when the Son of Man is to be betrayed into the hands of sinners. [42] Get up! Let us go! Look, my betrayer is approaching."

Jesus Is Arrested.* [43] At once, while he was still speaking, Judas, one of the Twelve, arrived. With him there was a crowd of men, armed with swords and clubs, who had been sent by the chief priests, the scribes, and the elders. [44] Now his betrayer had agreed with them on a signal, saying, "The one I shall kiss is the man. Arrest him, and lead him away under guard!" [45] And so, when he came, he proceeded directly to Jesus and said "Rabbi!" and kissed him. [46] Then they seized him and placed him under arrest. [47] Meanwhile, one of the bystanders drew his sword and struck a servant of the high priest, slicing off his ear.

⁴⁸ Then Jesus said to them, "Why are you coming forth with swords and clubs to arrest me, as though I were a bandit? ⁴⁹ Day after day I was with you in the temple teaching, and you did not arrest me. But in this way the Scriptures must be fulfilled." ⁵⁰ Then everyone deserted him and fled. ⁵¹ * Among those who had followed Jesus was a young man wearing nothing but a linen cloth. They caught hold of him, ⁵² but he slipped out of the linen cloth and ran off naked.

Jesus Is Condemned by the Sanhedrin. * ⁵³ They led Jesus away to the high priest, where the chief priests, the elders, and the scribes were gathering. ⁵⁴ Meanwhile, Peter had followed him at a distance, right into the courtyard of the high priest, and he was sitting there with the attendants, warming himself at the fire.

⁵⁵ The chief priests and the entire Sanhedrin * tried to elicit testimony against Jesus so that they could put him to death, but they failed in their efforts. ⁵⁶ Many witnesses offered perjured testimony against him, but their statements did not agree. ⁵⁷ Then some stood up and gave this false witness against him: ⁵⁸ "We heard this man say, 'I will destroy this temple made with human hands, and in three days I will build another not made with hands.'" ⁵⁹ But even on this point their statements did not agree.

⁶⁰ The high priest then rose among them and asked Jesus, "Have you no reply to counter the testimony that these witnesses have given?" ⁶¹ * But he remained silent and offered no response. Again, the high priest questioned him, asking, "Are you the Christ, the Son of the Blessed One?" * ⁶² Jesus replied, "I am.

> And you will see the Son of Man
>   seated at the right hand of the Power
>   and coming with the clouds of heaven."

⁶³ Thereupon the high priest tore his garments and exclaimed, "What need do we have of any further wit-

nesses! [64] You have heard his blasphemy. What is your decision?" They all condemned him as guilty and deserving of death. [65] Some of them began to spit at him. They blindfolded him and struck him, taunting him as they said, "Prophesy!" And the guards also slapped him.

Peter Denies Jesus.* [66] While Peter was below in the courtyard, one of the high priest's servant girls came by. [67] When she noticed Peter warming himself, she stared at him and said, "You also were with Jesus, the man from Nazareth." [68] But he denied it, saying, "I neither know nor understand what you are talking about." Thereupon he went forth into the outer courtyard. Then the cock crowed.* [69] The servant girl saw him and again began to say to the bystanders: "This man is one of them." [70] But again he denied it.

Shortly afterward, some bystanders said to Peter, "You are unquestionably one of them, for you are a Galilean." [71] Then he began to shout curses, and he swore an oath: "I do not know this man you are talking about." [72] At that very moment, a cock crowed for a second time, and Peter remembered that Jesus had said to him, "Before the cock crows twice, you will deny me three times." And he broke down and wept.

15 Jesus before Pilate.*

[1] As soon as it was morning, the chief priests held a council with the elders and the scribes and the whole Sanhedrin. They bound Jesus and led him away, and handed him over to Pilate.

[2] Pilate asked him, "Are you the king of the Jews?" Jesus replied, "You have said so." [3] Then the chief priests brought many charges against him. [4] Again, Pilate questioned him, "Have you no answer to offer? Just consider how many charges they are leveling against you." [5] But Jesus offered no further reply, so that Pilate was amazed.

Jesus Is Sentenced to Death. [6] Now on the occasion of the feast, he released a prisoner to them, anyone for whom they asked.* [7] At the time, a man named Barabbas was in prison along with some rebels who had committed murder during an uprising. [8] When the crowd came forward and began to ask him to do the customary favor for them, [9] Pilate asked them, "Do you want me to release for you the king of the Jews?" * [10] For he realized that it was out of envy that the chief priests had handed him over.

[11] However, the chief priests incited the crowd to have him release Barabbas for them instead. [12] Pilate then asked, "And what shall I do with the man you call the king of the Jews?" [13] They shouted back, "Crucify him!" [14] Pilate asked them, "Why? What evil has he done?" But they only screamed all the louder, "Crucify him!" [15] And so Pilate, anxious to appease the crowd, released Barabbas to them, and after ordering Jesus to be scourged, he handed him over to be crucified.

Jesus Is Crowned with Thorns.* [16] Then the soldiers led Jesus away inside the palace, that is, the Praetorium, and they called the whole cohort together. [17] They dressed him in a purple robe and after twisting some thorns into a crown, they placed it on him. [18] Then they began to salute him with the words, "Hail, King of the Jews!" [19] They repeatedly struck his head with a reed, spat upon him, and knelt down before him in homage. [20] And when they had finished mocking him, they stripped him of his purple robe and dressed him in his own clothes. Then they led him out to crucify him.

The Way of the Cross.* [21] They compelled a passer-by who was returning from the country to carry his cross. The man was Simon of Cyrene, the father of Alexander and Rufus.

Jesus Is Crucified. [22] They brought him to the place called Golgotha, which means the place of the skull. [23] They offered him some wine that had been mixed with myrrh, but he refused to take it. [24] Then they crucified him and divided his garments among them, casting lots for them to see what each should take.*

[25] It was around nine o'clock in the morning when they crucified him.* [26] The inscription giving the charge

against him read, "The King of the Jews." [27] Along with him they crucified two thieves, one on his right and the other on his left. [[28] Thus was the Scripture fulfilled that says, "And he was counted among the wicked."] *

[29] Those people who passed by jeered at him, shaking their heads and saying, "Aha! You who claimed you could destroy the temple and rebuild it within three days, [30] save yourself and come down from the cross."

[31] In much the same way, the chief priests and the scribes joined in the mockery among themselves, saying, "He saved others, but he cannot save himself. [32] Let the Christ, the King of Israel, come down from the cross right now so that we may see it and come to believe." Those who were crucified with him also taunted him.

Jesus Dies on the Cross. * [33] Beginning at midday, there was darkness over the whole land until three in the afternoon. [34] At three o'clock, Jesus cried out in a loud voice, *"Eloi, Eloi, lema sabachthani?"* which means, "My God, my God, why have you forsaken me?"

[35] On hearing this, some of the bystanders said, "Listen! He is calling Elijah." [36] Someone ran off, soaked a sponge with sour wine, put it on a stick, and gave it to him to drink, saying, "Wait! Let us see whether Elijah will come to take him down."

[37] Then Jesus cried out in a loud voice and breathed his last. [38] And the veil of the sanctuary was torn in two, from top to bottom. [39] When the centurion who was standing facing him saw how Jesus had breathed his last, he said, "Truly this man was the Son of God."

[40] A number of women were also present, looking on from a distance. Among them were Mary Magdalene, Mary the mother of James the younger * and of Joses, and Salome. [41] These women used to follow Jesus when he was in Galilee and minister to his needs. And there were many other women there who had come up with him to Jerusalem.

THE WOMEN AT THE TOMB—"On entering the tomb, they saw a young man . . . sitting on the right hand side. . . . 'You are looking for Jesus of Nazareth, who was crucified. He has been raised. He is not here'" (Mk 16:5-6).

THE ASCENSION OF JESUS—"After he had spoken to them, the Lord Jesus was taken up into heaven, and there he took his place at the right hand of God" (Mk 16:19).

Jesus Is Placed in the Tomb.* ⁴²It was the Day of Preparation, that is, the day before the Sabbath. So when evening came, ⁴³Joseph of Arimathea, a respected member of the council, who was also awaiting the kingdom of God, boldly went to Pilate and requested the body of Jesus. ⁴⁴Pilate was surprised to hear that Jesus was already dead, and he summoned the centurion to ascertain that Jesus had indeed died. ⁴⁵When he learned from the centurion that such was the case, he turned over the body to Joseph.

⁴⁶Having purchased a linen shroud, he lowered Jesus from the cross, wrapped him in the shroud, and laid him in a tomb that had been hewn out of rock. He then rolled a stone against the entrance of the tomb. ⁴⁷Mary Magdalene and Mary the mother of Joses saw where the body was buried.

16 **Jesus Is Raised from the Dead.*** ¹When the Sabbath was over,* Mary Magdalene, Mary the mother of James, and Salome purchased aromatic spices so that they might go and anoint Jesus. ²And very early on the first day of the week, just after sunrise, they went to the tomb.

³They had been asking each other, "Who will roll back the stone for us from the entrance to the tomb?" ⁴But when they looked up, they observed that the stone, which was extremely large, had already been rolled back. ⁵On entering the tomb, they saw a young man arrayed in a white robe sitting on the right hand side, and they were stunned.

⁶He said to them, "Do not be alarmed. You are looking for Jesus of Nazareth, who was crucified. He has been raised. He is not here. See the place where they laid him. ⁷But go forth and tell his disciples and Peter: 'He is going ahead of you to Galilee. There you will see him just as he told you.'" ⁸Then the women emerged from the tomb and fled, overcome with trembling and amazement. They said nothing to anyone, for they were afraid.

APPENDIX

The Longer Ending*

Jesus Appears to Mary Magdalene. [9] After he had risen from the dead early on the first day of the week, Jesus appeared first to Mary Magdalene, from whom he had driven out seven demons. [10] She then went forth and related the story of his appearance to his mourning and weeping companions. [11] However, when they heard that he was alive and that she had seen him, they refused to believe it.

Jesus Appears to Two Disciples. [12] After this, Jesus appeared in a different form to two of them as they were on their way into the country. [13] They then returned and reported the news to the others, but they did not believe them either.

Jesus Appears to and Commissions the Eleven. [14] Still later, he appeared to the eleven while they were at table. He reproached them for their lack of faith and their hardness of heart because they refused to believe the witness of those who had seen him after he had risen.

[15] Then he said to them, "Go forth into the whole world and proclaim the gospel to all creation. [16] Whoever believes and is baptized will be saved; whoever does not believe will be condemned. [17] These are the signs that will mark those who believe: In my name they will cast out demons. They will be granted the gift of speaking in new languages. [18] If they pick up serpents in their hands or drink any deadly poison, they will remain unharmed. The sick on whom they lay their hands will recover."

Jesus Ascends to Heaven. [19] Then, after he had spoken to them, the Lord Jesus was taken up into heaven, and there he took his place at the right hand of God. [20] And they went forth to proclaim the gospel everywhere, while the Lord worked with them and confirmed the word by means of the signs that accompanied their preaching.

Noncanonical Endings

The Shorter Ending.* And they reported all the instructions briefly to Peter and his companions. Afterward, through them Jesus sent forth from east to west the sacred and perpetual proclamation of eternal salvation.

The Freer Logion.* And they excused themselves, saying, "This age of lawlessness and unbelief is under Satan, who does not allow the truth and power of God to prevail over the unclean things of the spirit. Therefore, reveal your righteousness now"—thus they spoke to Christ. And Christ replied to them, "The limit of the years of Satan's power has been reached, but other terrible things draw near. And for those who sinned I was handed over to death, that they might return to the truth and no longer sin, in order that they might inherit the spiritual and incorruptible glory of righteousness, which is in heaven."

THE GOSPEL ACCORDING TO LUKE

THE GOOD NEWS

Christian tradition has always identified Luke as the companion of Paul and his "beloved physician" (Col 4:14; Philem 24). In any case, the author of the third Gospel, who also wrote the Book of Acts, seems to be a conscientious historian.

As he himself says at the beginning of his work, he was very diligent in collecting testimonies and traditions, both oral and written, concerning the life of Jesus. He certainly knew the Gospel of Mark and, in addition, drew upon a source that Matthew likewise used. On the whole, the episodes and words found in the other Gospels are found also in Luke and in almost the same order. But many stories have reached us only through his Gospel. The book has its own style, its own way of presenting the material; from a literary point of view, it is more carefully written.

The work shows us, first and foremost, the author's deep faith in Jesus and his concern for the life of the Gospel. He contemplates the Lord with a special degree of sympathy, and an interiority and mysticism shine through his writing that make it far different from Mark's rough style. Jesus is Luke's Savior and Redeemer, his joy.

While writing at almost the same period as Matthew, Luke addresses his work to converts from the pagan world, men and women who must live in that world. He is therefore realistic in his teaching.

In addition, this Gospel will be continued in the Acts of the Apostles. In the latter work, Luke describes the beginnings of the young Christian Church, which had been charged by its Lord with proclaiming to all human beings that they have been saved, no matter what the culture was to which they belonged.

The Gospel is a personal and original work by a witness to the faith of the Church. Luke's primary desire is to present the mystery of Christ to us. Christ has brought to fulfillment the plan of God and therefore all the Old Testament promises.

The author does not multiply citations from the Bible, as Matthew does, but his continual, though unobtrusive, allusions to the Scriptures enable us to see in Jesus the new Moses and therefore the new head of the People of God, the new David, the new Solomon, the new Elijah, or, in short, the one who brings to fruition God's plan for the human race. It is to be observed that Luke calls Jesus "Lord" 16 times. This is the title that the Church immediately gave to the risen and glorified Christ, and it is the name given to God in the Old Testament.

More clearly than the other evangelists, Luke portrays the kindness of Jesus to sinners, showing him as the image of the limitless kindness of God. Jesus comes through as the Savior of sinners who seeks out the lost, the despised, and the outcasts and comforts them with the message of forgiveness. The motto of his ministry is found in the words of Jesus that occur only in Luke (19:10): "The Son of Man has come to seek out and to save what was lost." Luke's Book is the Gospel of mercy.

The evangelist emphasizes the universality of the message of Jesus (2:14; 2:32). In the genealogy, Jesus appears as the son of Adam, the father of all mankind (3:38); and the final command of the risen Lord is to proclaim the remission of sins to all nations (24:47).

Love of neighbor is another essential theme of Luke's Gospel. It is at the core of the Sermon on the Plain (6:20-49) and the teaching of the Parable of the Good Samaritan (10:29-37).

Luke is also the evangelist of the Holy Spirit. The latter breaks through from on high as a gift of God and acts with his divine power both in the life of Jesus and in his Messianic community (1:15; 3:22; 4:1; 10:21; 11:13; 12:12).

Another feature of this Gospel is its emphasis on prayer, which is connected with the action of the Holy Spirit. All the Gospels speak of the prayer of Jesus, but Luke alone shows Jesus praying at the most important stages of his ministry (3:21; 6:12; 9:18; 9:28; 11:1; 22:41; 23:46). The evangelist then goes on to stress the duty to pray on the part of all who follow Jesus. They must pray always, without ceasing (18:1ff).

This work has also been termed the Gospel of Women because of its domestic scenes (2:41-51; 10:38-42; 11:5-8) as well as other scenes in which women are mentioned (7:11-17; 8:2f; 23:17-31). From the account of Christ's birth in which Mary, Elizabeth, and Anna are prominent (1–2) to the events of the day of the Resurrection in which women have a large role (24:1-10), Luke brings out the major role that women played in the life and ministry of our Lord.

Finally, Luke calls for unconditional attachment to the things that can be truly good and the renunciation of material things (12:16-21; 16:19-31). Moreover, throughout his Gospel Luke stresses and exalts poverty (5:11; 5:28; 18:22). The evangelist also issues a series of warnings against the danger of riches (6:24; 12:13-21; 14:33, etc.).

The Gospel of Luke may be divided as follows:

Prologue: (11:-4)
  I: The Infancy Narrative (1:5—2:52)
 II: The Beginning of Jesus' Ministry (3:1—4:13)
III: The Ministry of Jesus in Galilee (4:14—9:50)
IV: The Journey to Jerusalem (9:51—19:27)
 V: The Activity of Jesus at Jerusalem (19:28—21:38)
VI: The Passion and Resurrection (22:1—24:53)

PROLOGUE*

1 ¹ Since many different individuals have undertaken the task to set down an account of the events that have been fulfilled among us, ² in accordance with their transmission to us by those who were eyewitnesses and ministers of the word from the beginning, ³ I too, after researching all the evidence anew with great care, have decided to write an orderly account for you, Theophilus, who are so greatly revered, ⁴ so that you may learn the unquestioned authenticity of the teachings you have received.

I. THE INFANCY NARRATIVE*

Announcement of the Birth of John.* ⁵ At the time of the reign of King Herod of Judea,* there was a priest named Zechariah, a member of the priestly order of Abijah. His wife Elizabeth was a descendant of Aaron. ⁶ Both of them were righteous in the eyes of God, observing blamelessly all the commandments and ordinances of the Lord. ⁷ But they had no children, because Elizabeth was barren and both were advanced in years.

⁸ On one occasion, when his division was on duty and he was exercising his priestly office before God, ⁹ he was designated by lot to enter the sanctuary of the Lord and offer incense.* ¹⁰ At the hour of the offering of incense, all the people were outside, praying. ¹¹ Then there appeared to him the angel of the Lord, standing to the right of the altar of incense.

¹² When Zechariah beheld him, he was terrified and overcome with fear. ¹³ But the angel said to him, "Do not be afraid, Zechariah, for your prayer has been heard. Your wife Elizabeth will bear for you a son, and you shall name him John. ¹⁴ He will be a source of joy and delight to you, and many will rejoice at his birth, ¹⁵ for he will be great in the sight of the Lord.

"He will never imbibe wine or any strong drink. Even when he is still in his mother's womb, he will be filled with the Holy Spirit, ¹⁶ and he will bring back many of the people of Israel to the Lord their God. ¹⁷ With the spirit and power of Elijah he will go before him, to reconcile fathers with their children and to convert the disobedient to the ways of the righteous, so that a prepared people might be made ready for the Lord."

¹⁸ Zechariah said to the angel, "How can I be assured of this? For I am an old man and my wife is well past the stage of giving birth." ¹⁹ The angel replied, "I am Gabriel. I stand in the presence of God, and I have been sent to speak to you and to convey to you this good news. ²⁰ But now, because you did not believe my words, which will be

fulfilled at their appointed time, you will lose your power of speech and will become mute until the day that these things take place."

[21] Meanwhile, the people were waiting for Zechariah and were surprised that he was delaying so long in the sanctuary. [22] When he did emerge, he could not speak to them, and they realized that he had seen a vision while he was in the sanctuary. He was only able to make signs to them, but he remained unable to speak.

[23] When his term of service was completed, he returned home. [24] Shortly thereafter his wife Elizabeth conceived, and she remained in seclusion for five months, saying, [25] "The Lord has granted me this blessing, looking favorably upon me and removing from me the humiliation I have endured among my people." *

Announcement of the Birth of Jesus. * [26] In the sixth month,* the angel Gabriel was sent by God to a town in Galilee called Nazareth, [27] to a virgin * betrothed to a man named Joseph, of the house of David. The virgin's name was Mary.

[28] The angel came to her and said, "Hail, full of grace! * The Lord is with you." [29] But she was greatly troubled by his words and wondered in her heart what this salutation could mean.

[30] Then the angel said to her, "Do not be afraid, Mary, for you have found favor with God. [31] Behold, you will conceive in your womb and bear a son, and you will name him Jesus. [32] He will be great and will be called Son of the Most High. The Lord God will give him the throne of his ancestor David. [33] He will rule over the house of Jacob forever, and of his kingdom there will be no end."

[34] Mary said to the angel, "How will this be, since I am a virgin?"* [35] The angel answered, "The Holy Spirit will come upon you, and the power of the Most High will overshadow you. Therefore, the child to be born will be holy, and he will be called the Son of God. [36] *And behold, your cousin Elizabeth in her old age has also con-

ceived a son, and she who was called barren is now in her sixth month, [37] for nothing will be impossible for God."

[38] Then Mary said, "Behold, I am the servant of the Lord. Let it be done to me according to your word." After this, the angel departed from her.

Mary Visits Elizabeth.* [39] In those days, Mary set out and journeyed in haste into the hill country to a town of Judah * [40] where she entered the house of Zechariah and greeted Elizabeth. [41] When Elizabeth heard Mary's greeting, the baby leaped in her womb.

Then Elizabeth was filled with the Holy Spirit, [42] and she exclaimed with a loud cry, "Blessed are you among women, and blessed is the fruit of your womb. [43] And why am I so greatly favored that the mother of my Lord should visit me? [44] For behold, the moment that the sound of your greeting reached my ears, the child in my womb leaped for joy. [45] And blessed is she who believed that what the Lord has said to her will be fulfilled."

The Canticle of Mary.* [46] And Mary said:

"My soul proclaims the greatness of the Lord
[47]   and my spirit rejoices in God my Savior.
[48] For he has looked with favor on the lowliness of his
         servant;
       henceforth all generations will call me blessed.
[49] The Mighty One has done great things for me,
       and holy is his name.
[50] His mercy is shown from age to age
       to those who fear him.
[51] He has shown the strength of his arm,
       he has routed those who are arrogant in the desires
         of their hearts.
[52] He has brought down the mighty from their thrones
       and lifted up the lowly.
[53] He has filled the hungry with good things
       and sent the rich away empty.
[54] He has come to the aid of Israel his servant,
       ever mindful of his merciful love,

⁵⁵   according to the promises he made to our ancestors,
       to Abraham and to his descendants forever."

⁵⁶ Mary remained with Elizabeth for about three months and then returned to her home.

The Birth of John. ⁵⁷ When the time came for Elizabeth to give birth, she bore a son. ⁵⁸ Her neighbors and relatives heard that the Lord had shown his great mercy to her, and they shared in her rejoicing.

⁵⁹ On the eighth day, when they came to circumcise the child, they were going to name him Zechariah after his father. ⁶⁰ However, his mother objected. "No," she said. "He is to be called John." ⁶¹ They said to her, "There is no one in your family who has this name." ⁶² They then made signs to his father to ask what name he wanted to be given to the child. ⁶³ He asked for a writing tablet, and he wrote: "His name is John." They were all filled with wonder.

⁶⁴ Immediately, his mouth was opened and his tongue was freed, and he began to speak, giving praise to God. ⁶⁵ All their neighbors were overcome with awe, and all these things were related throughout the entire hill country of Judea. ⁶⁶ All who heard them were deeply impressed, and they wondered, "What then is this child going to be?" For the hand of the Lord was with him.

The Canticle of Zechariah. * ⁶⁷ Then the child's father Zechariah was filled with the Holy Spirit and prophesied:

⁶⁸   "Blessed be the Lord, the God of Israel,
       for he has visited his people and redeemed them.
⁶⁹   He has raised up a horn of salvation for us
       from the house of his servant David,
⁷⁰   just as he proclaimed through the mouth of his holy
       prophets from age to age:
⁷¹   salvation from our enemies and from the hands of
       all who hate us,
⁷²   to show the mercy promised to our fathers
       and to remain mindful of his holy covenant,

THE BIRTH OF JESUS—"[Mary] gave birth to her firstborn son. She wrapped him in swaddling clothes and laid him in a manger, because there was no room for them in the inn" (Lk 2:7).

THE CIRCUMCISION OF JESUS—"On the eighth day, when the time for the child's circumcision had arrived, he was given the name Jesus, the name the angel had given him before he had been conceived in the womb" (Lk 2:21).

73   the oath that he swore to our father Abraham,
         and to grant us that, 74 delivered from the power of
            our enemies,
         without fear we might worship him 75 in holiness and
            righteousness
         in his presence all our days.

76   "And you, my child, will be called prophet of the
            Most High,
         for you will go before the Lord to prepare his ways,
77   to give his people knowledge of salvation
         through the forgiveness of their sins,
78   because of the tender mercy of our God
         by which the dawn from on high will break upon us
79   to shine on those who sit in darkness and in the
            shadow of death,
         to guide our feet along the path of peace."

The Son of the Wilderness. 80 The child grew and became strong in spirit. He lived in the wilderness until the day he appeared publicly to Israel.

2 The Birth of Jesus. 1 * In those days, a decree was issued by Caesar Augustus that a census should be taken throughout the entire world. 2 This was the first such registration, and it took place when Quirinius * was governor of Syria.

3 Everyone traveled to his own town to be enrolled. 4 Joseph therefore went from the town of Nazareth in Galilee to Judea, to the city of David called Bethlehem, because he was of the house and family of David. 5 He went to be registered together with Mary, his betrothed, who was expecting a child. 6 While they were there, the time came for her to have her child, 7 and she gave birth to her firstborn son. She wrapped him in swaddling clothes and laid him in a manger,* because there was no room for them in the inn.

8 In the nearby countryside there were shepherds living in the fields and keeping watch over their flock throughout the night. 9 Suddenly, an angel of the Lord

appeared to them, and the glory of the Lord shone around them. They were terror-stricken, [10] but the angel said to them, "Do not be afraid, for I bring you good news of great joy for all the people. [11] For this day in the city of David there has been born to you a Savior who is Christ, the Lord.

[12] "This will be a sign for you: you will find an infant wrapped in swaddling clothes and lying in a manger." [13] And suddenly there was with the angel a multitude of the heavenly host, praising God and saying,

[14]   "Glory to God in the highest heaven,
        and on earth peace to all those on whom his favor
        rests." *

The Visit of the Shepherds. [15] After the angels had departed from them to heaven, the shepherds said to one another, "Come, let us go to Bethlehem to see this thing that has taken place, which the Lord has made known to us." [16] And so they set off in haste and found Mary and Joseph, and the baby lying in a manger.

[17] When they saw the child, they recounted the message that had been told them about him. [18] All who heard it were amazed at what the shepherds said to them. [19] As for Mary, she treasured all these words and pondered them in her heart. [20] And the shepherds went back, glorifying and praising God for all they had heard and seen, just as they had been told.

The Circumcision and Naming of Jesus. [21] * On the eighth day, when the time for the child's circumcision had arrived, he was given the name Jesus, the name the angel had given him before he had been conceived in the womb.

Jesus Is Presented in the Temple. [22] When the days for their purification were completed according to the Law of Moses, they brought the child up to Jerusalem to present him to the Lord, [23] as it is prescribed in the Law of the Lord: "Every firstborn male shall be consecrated to the Lord," [24] and to offer a sacrifice in accordance with what is stated in the Law of the Lord, "a pair of turtledoves or two young pigeons."

The Prophecy of Simeon. ²⁵ At that time, there was a man in Jerusalem whose name was Simeon. This upright and devout man was awaiting the consolation of Israel, and the Holy Spirit rested on him. ²⁶ It had been revealed to him by the Holy Spirit that he would not experience death before he had seen the Christ of the Lord.

²⁷ Prompted by the Spirit, Simeon came into the temple. When the parents brought in the child Jesus to do for him what was required by the Law, ²⁸ he took him in his arms and praised God, saying:

²⁹   "Now, Lord, you may dismiss your servant in peace,
            according to your word;
³⁰   for my eyes have seen your salvation,
³¹   which you have prepared in the sight of all the peoples,
³²   a light of revelation to the Gentiles
            and glory for your people Israel."

³³ The child's father and mother marveled at what was being said about him. ³⁴ Then Simeon blessed them and said to Mary his mother: "This child is destined for the fall and rise of many in Israel, and to be a sign that will be opposed, ³⁵ so that the secret thoughts of many will be revealed, and you yourself a sword will pierce."

The Witness of Anna. ³⁶ There was also present a prophetess, Anna, the daughter of Phanuel, of the tribe of Asher. She was very advanced in years, having lived with her husband for seven years after their marriage, ³⁷ and then as a widow to the age of eighty-four. She never left the temple, but worshiped with fasting and prayer night and day. ³⁸ At that moment, she came forward and began to praise God, while she spoke about the child to all who were looking forward to the deliverance of Jerusalem.

The Return to Nazareth. ³⁹ When they had fulfilled everything required by the Law of the Lord, they returned to Galilee, to their own town of Nazareth. ⁴⁰ The child grew and became strong, filled with wisdom, and God's favor was upon him.

The Boy Jesus in the Temple.* [41] Every year his parents used to go to Jerusalem for the feast of Passover. [42] And when Jesus was twelve years old, they made the journey as usual for the feast. [43] When the days of the feast were over and they set off for home, the boy Jesus stayed behind in Jerusalem. His parents were not aware of this. [44] Assuming that he was somewhere in the group of travelers, they journeyed for a day. Then they started to look for him among their relatives and friends, [45] but when they failed to find him, they returned to Jerusalem to search for him.

[46] After three days they found him in the temple, where he was sitting among the teachers, listening to them and asking them questions. [47] And all who heard him were amazed at his intelligence and his answers. [48] When they saw him, they were astonished, and his mother said to him: "Son, why have you done this to us? Your father and I have been searching for you with great anxiety." [49] Jesus said to them, "Why were you searching for me? Did you not know that I must be in my Father's house?" [50] But they did not comprehend what he said to them.

Jesus Grows in Wisdom and Grace. [51] Then he went down with them and came to Nazareth, and he was obedient to them. His mother pondered all these things in her heart. [52] And Jesus increased in wisdom and in age and in grace with God and men.

II. THE BEGINNING OF JESUS' MINISTRY*

3 **The Ministry of John the Baptist.** [1] In the fifteenth year of the reign of Tiberius Caesar, when Pontius Pilate was governor of Judea, and Herod was tetrarch of Galilee, and his brother Philip was tetrarch of the region of Ituraea and Trachonitis, and Lysanias * was tetrarch of Abilene, [2] during the high priesthood of Annas and Caiaphas,* the word of God came to John the son of

Zechariah in the desert. ³ He journeyed throughout the entire region of the Jordan valley, proclaiming a baptism of repentance for the forgiveness of sins, ⁴ as it is written in the book of the words of the prophet Isaiah:

> "The voice of one crying out in the wilderness:
> 'Prepare the way of the Lord,
>   make straight his paths.
> ⁵ Every valley shall be filled in,
>   and every mountain and hill shall be leveled;
> the winding roads shall be straightened
>   and the rough paths made smooth,
> ⁶ and all mankind shall see the salvation of God.'"

⁷ He admonished the crowds who came out to be baptized by him: "You brood of vipers! Who warned you to flee from the wrath to come? ⁸ Produce good fruits as proof of your repentance. Do not begin to say to yourselves, 'We have Abraham as our father.' For I tell you, God is able to raise up children for Abraham from these stones. ⁹ Even now the ax is laid to the root of the trees. Therefore, every tree that does not bear good fruit will be cut down and thrown into the fire."

¹⁰ When the crowds asked him, "What then should we do?" ¹¹ he said to them in reply, "Anyone who has two coats must share with the person who has none, and whoever has food must do likewise." ¹² Even tax collectors were coming to him to be baptized, and they asked him, "Teacher, what should we do?" ¹³ He answered them, "Cease collecting more than the amount prescribed." ¹⁴ Some soldiers also asked him, "What about us? What should we do?" He replied, "Do not extort money from anyone, do not falsely accuse or threaten anyone, and be satisfied with your wages."

¹⁵ As the people began to experience a feeling of expectancy, they all wondered in their hearts whether John might be the Christ. ¹⁶ John answered, telling them all: "I baptize you with water, but there is one coming who is more powerful than I am. I am not worthy to

loosen the straps of his sandals. He will baptize you with the Holy Spirit and fire. ¹⁷ His winnowing fan is in his hand to clear his threshing floor and to gather the wheat into his barn, but the chaff he will burn with unquenchable fire." ¹⁸ And with many other exhortations, he proclaimed the good news to the people.

¹⁹ But Herod the tetrarch, after having been rebuked by John because of his affair with Herodias, his brother's wife, in addition to all the other evil deeds he had done, ²⁰ added still this, that he put John in prison.*

The Baptism of Jesus.* ²¹ After John had baptized all the people, and while Jesus was engaged in prayer after also having been baptized, heaven opened ²² and the Holy Spirit descended on him in bodily form like a dove. And a voice came from heaven: "You are my beloved Son; in you I am well pleased."

The Genealogy of Jesus.* ²³ When Jesus began his ministry, he was about thirty years old. He was the son, as it was thought, of Joseph,*

the son of Heli, ²⁴ the son of Matthat,
the son of Levi, the son of Melchi,
the son of Jannai, the son of Joseph,

²⁵   the son of Mattathias, the son of Amos,
the son of Nahum, the son of Esli,
the son of Naggai, ²⁶ the son of Maath,
the son of Mattathias,

the son of Semein, the son of Josech,
the son of Joda, ²⁷ the son of Joanan,
the son of Rhesa, the son of Zerubbabel,
the son of Shealtiel,

the son of Neri, ²⁸ the son of Melchi,
the son of Addi, the son of Cosam,
the son of Elmadam, the son of Er,

²⁹   the son of Joshua,

the son of Eliezer, the son of Jorim,
the son of Matthat, the son of Levi,

30   the son of Simeon, the son of Judah,
     the son of Joseph,

     the son of Jonam, the son of Eliakim,
31   the son of Melea, the son of Menna,
     the son of Mattatha, the son of Nathan,
     the son of David,

32   the son of Jesse, the son of Obed,
     the son of Boaz, the son of Sala,
     the son of Nahshon, 33 the son of Amminadab,
     the son of Admin,

     the son of Arni, the son of Hezron,
     the son of Perez, the son of Judah,
34   the son of Jacob, the son of Isaac,
     the son of Abraham,

     the son of Terah, the son of Nahor,
35   the son of Serug, the son of Reu,
     the son of Peleg, the son of Eber,
     the son of Shelah,

36   the son of Cainan, the son of Arphaxad,
     the son of Shem, the son of Noah,
     the son of Lamech, 37 the son of Methuselah, the
        son of Enoch,

     the son of Jared, the son of Mahalaleel,
     the son of Cainan, 38 the son of Enos,
     the son of Seth, the son of Adam,
     the son of God.

4 **Jesus Is Tempted by the Devil.*** ¹ Filled with the Holy
Spirit, Jesus returned from the Jordan and was led by the
Spirit into the desert ² for forty days, where he was tempted by the devil. During that time he ate nothing, and at
the end of it he was famished.

³ The devil said to him, "If you are the Son of God,
command this stone to be transformed into bread."
⁴ Jesus answered him: "As it states in Scripture:

   'Man does not live by bread alone.'"

⁵ Then the devil led him up and showed him in a single instant all the kingdoms of the world, ⁶ saying to him, "To you will I give all this dominion with its accompanying glory, for it has been delivered into my power, and I can bestow it on whomever I choose. ⁷ All this will be yours if you worship me." ⁸ Jesus answered him: "Scripture says:

'You shall worship the Lord your God,
    and him alone shall you serve.'"

⁹ Next the devil led him to Jerusalem and had him stand on the summit of the temple. Then he said to him, "If you are the Son of God, throw yourself down from here, ¹⁰ for according to Scripture:

'He will command his angels concerning you,
    to protect you,'

¹¹ and:

'With their hands they will raise you up
    lest you dash your foot against a stone.'"

¹² Jesus answered him, "Scripture says:

'You shall not put the Lord your God to the test.'"

¹³ When the devil had ended all his tempting, he departed from him until an opportune time.

III. THE MINISTRY OF JESUS IN GALILEE*

Jesus Is Accepted throughout Galilee. ¹⁴ Then Jesus, filled with the power of the Spirit, returned to Galilee, and reports about him began to spread throughout the surrounding region. ¹⁵ He taught in their synagogues and was praised by everyone.

Jesus at Nazareth. ¹⁶ * When he came to Nazareth, where he had been brought up, he went to the synagogue on the Sabbath day, as was his custom. He stood up to read, ¹⁷ and they handed him the scroll of the prophet Isaiah. Unrolling the scroll, he found the passage where it is written:

¹⁸   "The Spirit of the Lord is upon me,
        because he has anointed me
        to bring the good news to the poor.

He has sent me to proclaim release to prisoners
    and recovery of sight to the blind,
    to let the oppressed go free,
19   and to proclaim the year of the Lord's favor."

20 Then he rolled up the scroll, returned it to the attendant, and sat down. The eyes of all in the synagogue were fixed intently on him.

21 Then he began by saying to them, "Today this Scripture has been fulfilled in your hearing." 22 All present spoke highly of him and were amazed at the gracious words that flowed from his lips. They also asked, "Is this not the son of Joseph?"

23 He said to them, "Undoubtedly you will quote to me the proverb: 'Physician, heal yourself,' and say: 'Do here in your hometown* the deeds we have heard that you performed in Capernaum.' 24 Amen, I say to you," he went on, "no prophet is accepted in his own country.

25 * "I tell you in truth, there were many widows in Israel in the days of Elijah when the skies remained closed for three and a half years and there was a severe famine throughout the land. 26 Yet it was to none of them that Elijah was sent, but to a widow at Zarephath in the land of Sidon. 27 There were also many people with leprosy in Israel in the time of the prophet Elisha, but not one of these was cleansed except for Naaman the Syrian."

28 When they heard these words, all the people in the synagogue were roused to fury.* 29 They leapt up, drove him out of the town, and led him to the top of the hill upon which their town was built, intending to hurl him off the cliff. 30 However, he passed through the midst of the crowd and went on his way.

Jesus Heals a Man with a Demon. 31 * Jesus then went to Capernaum, a town in Galilee, and began to teach the people on the Sabbath. 32 They were astounded at his teaching because his message had authority.

33 In the synagogue there was a man possessed by the spirit of an unclean demon, and he shrieked loudly,

³⁴ "Leave us alone! What do you want with us, Jesus of Nazareth? Have you come to destroy us? I know who you are—the Holy One of God." * ³⁵ But Jesus rebuked him, saying, "Be silent and come out of him!"

Then the demon threw the man down in front of them and emerged from him without doing him any harm. ³⁶ The people were all amazed, and they said to one another: "What is this teaching? For with authority and power he gives commands to unclean spirits, and they come forth." ³⁷ And reports about him began to spread throughout the entire region.

Jesus Heals Peter's Mother-in-Law. ³⁸ On leaving the synagogue, he entered Simon's house. Simon's mother-in-law was suffering from a high fever, and they begged him to help her. ³⁹ Jesus stood over her and rebuked the fever, and it left her. She got up immediately and began to serve them.

Jesus Ministers throughout Galilee. ⁴⁰ At sunset they brought to him all those who were sick with various diseases. He laid his hands on each of them and healed them. ⁴¹ Demons also emerged from many people, shouting, "You are the Son of God!" But he rebuked them and would not allow them to speak because they knew that he was the Christ.

Jesus Is the Envoy of God for All Israel.* ⁴² At daybreak he departed and made his way to a secluded place. But the crowds went forth in search of him, and when they located him, they tried to prevent him from leaving there. ⁴³ However, he said to them, "I must preach the kingdom of God to the other towns as well, because this was the purpose for which I was sent." ⁴⁴ Thus, he continued to preach in the synagogues of Judea.

5 **Jesus Calls the First Disciples.*** ¹ One day, as Jesus was standing by the Lake of Gennesaret, with people crowding around him to hear the word of God, ² he caught sight of two boats at the water's edge. The fishermen had

THE CHILD JESUS IN THE TEMPLE—"After three days [his parents] found him in the temple, where he was sitting among the teachers, listening to them and asking him questions. And all who heard him were amazed at his intelligence and his answers" (Lk 2:46-47).

THE MIRACULOUS CATCH OF FISH—"They caught such a great number of fish that their nets were beginning to tear. . . . [Simon Peter] fell at the knees of Jesus, saying, 'Depart from me, Lord, for I am a sinful man.' . . . Jesus said to Simon, 'Do not be afraid. From now on you will be catching men' " (Lk 5:6-10).

gotten out of the boats and were washing their nets. [3] Getting into one of the boats, the one belonging to Simon, he asked him to put out a little way from the shore. Then he sat down and taught the crowds from the boat.

[4] When he had finished speaking, he said to Simon, "Put out into deep water and let down your nets for a catch." [5] Simon answered, "Master, we worked hard throughout the night and caught nothing; but if you say so, I will let down the nets." [6] When they had done this, they caught such a great number of fish that their nets were beginning to tear. [7] Therefore, they signaled to their companions in the other boat to come and help them. They came and filled both boats to the point that they were in danger of sinking.

[8] When Simon Peter saw what had happened, he fell at the knees of Jesus, saying, "Depart from me, Lord, for I am a sinful man." [9] For he and all of his companions were amazed at the catch they had made. [10] So too were Simon's partners James and John, the sons of Zebedee. Then Jesus said to Simon, "Do not be afraid. From now on you will be catching men." [11] When they brought their boats to the shore, they left everything and followed him.

Jesus Heals a Man with Leprosy.[*] [12] In one of the towns that he visited, a man appeared whose body was covered with leprosy. When he saw Jesus, he fell prostrate before him and pleaded for his help, saying, "Lord, if you choose to do so, you can make me clean." [13] He stretched out his hand and touched him, saying, "I do choose. Be made clean." Immediately, the leprosy left him.

[14] He then instructed him to tell no one. "Just go," he said, "and show yourself to the priest, and make an offering for your cleansing, as prescribed by Moses. That will be proof for them." [15] However, the reports about him continued to spread, so that large crowds assembled to listen to him and to be healed of their diseases. [16] But he would withdraw to deserted places to pray.

Jesus Pardons and Heals a Paralyzed Man.* [17] One day, as he was teaching, Pharisees and teachers of the law were sitting there. They had come from every village of Galilee and Judea, and from Jerusalem. And he possessed the power of the Lord to heal.

[18] Then some men appeared, carrying a paralyzed man on a bed. They tried to bring him in and set him down in front of Jesus. [19] However, finding no way to bring him in because of the crowd, they went up onto the roof and lowered him on the bed through the tiles into the middle of the crowd surrounding Jesus.

[20] On perceiving their faith, Jesus said, "Friend, your sins are forgiven you." [21] Then the scribes and the Pharisees began to ask each other, "Who is this man uttering blasphemies? Who can forgive sins but God alone?"

[22] Jesus discerned what they were thinking, and he said in reply, "Why do you entertain such thoughts in your hearts? [23] Which is easier—to say: 'Your sins are forgiven you,' or to say: 'Stand up and walk'? [24] But that you may come to realize that the Son of Man has authority on earth to forgive sins"—he said to the paralyzed man—"I say to you, stand up, and take your bed, and go to your home." [25] Immediately, the man stood up before them, picked up his bed, and went home glorifying God. [26] They were all overcome with amazement, and they praised God as, awestruck, they said, "We have witnessed unbelievable things today."

Jesus Calls Levi (Matthew).* [27] *After this, he went out and noticed a tax collector named Levi sitting at his customs post. Jesus said to him, "Follow me," [28] and, leaving everything behind, he got up and followed him.

Jesus Dines with Sinners. [29] Then Levi gave a great banquet in his house for him, and a large crowd of tax collectors and others were at table with them. [30] The Pharisees and their scribes complained to his disciples, saying, "Why do you eat and drink with tax collectors and sinners?" * ³¹ Jesus said to them in reply, "It is not the healthy who need a physician, but rather those who are sick. ³² I have not come to call the righteous but sinners to repentance."

A Time of Joy and Grace.* ³³ Then they said to him, "John's disciples fast frequently and pray often, and the disciples of the Pharisees do likewise, but your disciples eat and drink." ³⁴ Jesus said to them, "How can the wedding guests fast while the bridegroom is still with them? ³⁵ But the time will come when the bridegroom is taken away from them, and then, in those days, they will fast."

³⁶ He also told them this parable: "No one tears a piece from a new cloak and sews it on an old cloak. If he does, the new cloak will be torn, and the piece from it will not match that of the old. ³⁷ Nor does anyone pour new wine into old wineskins. If he does, the new wine will burst the skins and spill out, and the skins will be destroyed. ³⁸ Rather new wine must be put into fresh wineskins. ³⁹ And no one who has been drinking old wine will wish for new wine, for he says, 'The old is better.'"

6 **Picking Grain on the Sabbath.** ¹ * On one Sabbath, when Jesus was going through a field of grain, his disciples picked some heads of grain, rubbed them in their hands, and ate them. ² Some of the Pharisees said, "Why are you doing what is forbidden on the Sabbath?"

³ Jesus answered them, "Have you not read what David did when he and his companions were hungry? ⁴ He entered the house of God and took and ate the sacred bread that only the priests were permitted to eat, and he shared it with his companions." ⁵ Then he said to them, "The Son of Man * is lord of the Sabbath."

A Man with a Withered Hand. ⁶ On another Sabbath, Jesus entered the synagogue and began to teach. A man was there whose right hand was withered. ⁷ The scribes and the Pharisees watched him closely to see whether he would cure him on the Sabbath so that they would have a charge to bring against him.

⁸ But Jesus was fully aware of their thoughts, and he said to the man with the withered hand, "Come here and stand before us." The man got up and stood there. ⁹ Then Jesus said to them, "I put this question to you: Is it lawful to do good or to do evil on the Sabbath, to save life or to destroy it?" ¹⁰ After looking around at all of them, he said to the man, "Stretch out your hand." He did so, and his hand was restored. ¹¹ But they were filled with fury and discussed among themselves what they might do with Jesus.

Jesus Chooses the Twelve Apostles.* ¹² It was in those days that he went onto the mountain to pray, and he spent the entire night in prayer to God. ¹³ Then, when it was daylight, he summoned his disciples and chose twelve of them, whom he designated as apostles: ¹⁴ Simon, to whom he gave the name Peter, and his brother Andrew, James, John, Philip, Bartholomew, ¹⁵ Matthew, Thomas, James the son of Alphaeus, Simon called the Zealot, ¹⁶ Judas the son of James, and Judas Iscariot, who became a traitor.

The Crowds Seek Out Jesus.* ¹⁷ He then came down with them and stood on a spot of level ground, where there was a large crowd of his disciples and a great multitude of people from all sections of Judea and Jerusalem and the coastal region of Tyre and Sidon. ¹⁸ They had come there to listen to him and to be healed of their diseases. Those who were afflicted by unclean spirits were cured. ¹⁹ And everyone in the crowd was trying to touch him, because power came forth from him and healed them all.

A: The Sermon on the Plain*

The Beatitudes.* ²⁰ Then, turning to his disciples, he began to speak:

"Blessed are you who are poor,
for the kingdom of God is yours.
²¹   Blessed are you who hunger now,
for you will have your fill.

Blessed are you who weep now,
  for you will laugh.

[22] "Blessed are you when people hate you and ostracize you, when they insult you and denounce your name as evil on account of the Son of Man. [23] Rejoice on that day and dance for joy, for your reward will be great in heaven. This was the way their ancestors treated the Prophets.

[24]   "But woe to you who are rich,
    for you have received your consolation.
[25]   Woe to you who are well fed now,
    for you will go hungry.
  Woe to you who laugh now,
    for you will mourn and weep.
[26]   Woe to you when all speak well of you,
    for their ancestors treated the false prophets in the same fashion.

Love of Enemies.* [27] "But to those of you who are listening to me, I say: Love your enemies, do good to those who hate you, [28] bless those who curse you, pray for those who mistreat you. [29] If anyone strikes you on one cheek, offer him the other cheek as well, and should someone take your cloak, let him have your tunic as well. [30] Give to everyone who begs from you, and do not demand the return of what is yours from the one who has taken it.

[31] "Deal with others as you would like them to deal with you. [32] If you love only those who love you, what credit is that to you? Even sinners love those who love them. [33] And if you do good to those who do good to you, what credit is that to you? Even sinners do as much. [34] And if you lend only to those from whom you expect to be repaid, what credit is that to you? Even sinners lend to sinners, expecting to be repaid in full.

[35] "Rather, you must love your enemies and do good to them, and lend without expecting any repayment. In this way, you will receive a great reward. You will be sons of the Most High, for he himself is kind to the ungrateful and the wicked. [36] Be merciful, just as your Father is merciful.

Relations with Others. [37] * "Do not judge, and you will not be judged. Do not condemn, and you will not be condemned. Forgive, and you will be forgiven. [38] Give, and it will be given to you. A good measure, pressed down, shaken together, and running over, will be poured into your lap. The measure that you use for others will be used to measure you."

Parable of the Blind Leading the Blind. [39] He also told them a parable: "Can one blind man guide another who is also blind? Will not both of them fall into a pit? [40] No student is greater than his teacher, but a fully trained student will be like his teacher.

[41] "Why do you take note of the splinter in your brother's eye but do not notice the wooden plank in your own eye? [42] How can you say to your brother, 'Brother, let me remove the splinter that is in your eye,' while all the time you do not notice the wooden plank that is in your own eye? You hypocrite! First remove the wooden plank from your own eye, and then you will be able to see clearly enough to remove the splinter that is in your brother's eye.

A Tree Is Known by Its Fruit. [43] * "No healthy tree can bear rotten fruit, nor does a rotting tree bear healthy fruit. [44] Every tree is known by its own fruit. For people do not pick figs from thornbushes or grapes from brambles. [45] A good man produces good from the store of goodness in his heart, whereas an evil man produces evil from the store of evil within him. For the mouth speaks from the abundance of the heart.

Parable of the Two Foundations. [46] "Why do you call me, 'Lord, Lord,' but fail to do what I tell you? [47] I will show you what everyone is like who comes to me and hears my words and acts in accordance with them. [48] He is like a man who in building a house dug deeply and laid its foundations on rock. When the flood rose, it burst against that house but could not shake it because it had been solidly constructed. [49] In contrast, the one who hears and does not act in accordance with my words is like a man who built a house on the ground without a foundation. As soon as the river burst against it, the house collapsed and was completely destroyed."

B: From the Beatitudes to the Parables*

7 **Jesus Heals the Centurion's Servant.*** [1] After Jesus had finished speaking to the people, he entered Capernaum. [2] A centurion who dwelt there had a servant whom he regarded highly and who was ill and near death. [3] When he heard about Jesus, he sent some Jewish elders to ask him if he would come and heal his servant.

[4] When they came to Jesus, they pleaded earnestly with him, saying, "He deserves this favor from you, [5] for he loves our people, and he was the one who built our synagogue for us."

[6] Jesus went with them. When he drew near the house, the centurion sent friends to say to him, "Lord, do not trouble yourself, for I am not worthy to have you come under my roof. [7] That is the reason why I did not presume to approach you personally. But say the word and let my servant be healed. [8] For I also am a man subject to authority, with soldiers who are subject to me. I say to one: 'Go,' and he goes, and to another: 'Come here,' and he comes, and to my servant: 'Do this,' and he does it."

[9] When Jesus heard these words, he was amazed, and, turning to the crowd that was following him, he said, "I tell you, in no one throughout Israel have I found faith as great as this." [10] When the messengers returned to the house, they found the servant completely healthy.

Jesus Raises the Son of a Widow.* [11] Soon afterward, Jesus went to a town called Nain, accompanied by his disciples and a large crowd. [12] As he drew near to the gate of the town, a man who had died was being carried out, the only son of his widowed mother. A large group of people from the town accompanied her.

[13] When the Lord saw her, he was filled with compassion, and he said to her, "Do not weep." [14] After this, he

came forward and touched the bier, and the bearers halt-ed. Then he said, "Young man, I say to you, arise!" [15] The dead man sat up and began to speak, and Jesus gave him to his mother.

[16] Fear seized all who were present, and they glorified God, saying, "A great prophet has risen among us," and "God has visited his people." [17] The news of what he had done spread throughout Judea and the surrounding region.

Jesus Answers the Baptist's Question. * [18] When the disci-ples of John brought him reports about all these things, [19] John designated two of his disciples and sent them to the Lord to ask, "Are you the one who is to come, or are we to wait for another?" [20] When they came to him, they said, "John the Baptist has sent us to you to ask: 'Are you the one who is to come, or are we to wait for another?'"

[21] At that time, Jesus had just cured many people of dis-eases and afflictions and evil spirits, and had restored the sight of many who were blind. [22] And he gave them this reply: "Go back and tell John what you have seen and heard: the blind receive their sight, the lame walk, those who have leprosy are cleansed, the deaf hear, the dead are raised to life, the poor have the good news proclaimed to them. [23] And blessed is anyone who takes no offense at me."

Jesus Praises John the Baptist. [24] * When John's messen-gers had departed, Jesus spoke to the crowds about John: "What did you go out into the desert to see? A reed sway-ing in the wind? [25] What did you go out to see? Someone robed in fine clothing? Those who are robed in gorgeous clothing and live luxuriously are to be found in royal palaces. [26] Then what did you go out to see? A prophet? Yes, I tell you, and far more than a prophet. [27] This is the one about whom it is written:

> 'Behold, I am sending my messenger ahead of you,
> who will prepare your way before you.'

²⁸ "I tell you, among those born of women, no one is greater than John, and yet the least in the kingdom of God is greater than he."

²⁹ (All the people who heard him, including the tax collectors, acknowledged the saving justice of God, for they had received John's baptism. ³⁰ However, the Pharisees and the teachers of the Law who had refused his baptism rejected God's plan for them.)

Indecisive Children. ³¹ "Then to what shall I compare the people of this generation? What are they like? ³² They are like children sitting in the marketplace and calling to each other:

'We played the flute for you,
   but you would not dance;
we sang a dirge,
   and you refused to mourn.'

³³ "For John the Baptist has come, eating no bread and drinking no wine, and you say: 'He is possessed.' ³⁴ The Son of Man has come eating and drinking, and you say: 'Look at him! He is a glutton and a drunkard, a friend of tax collectors and sinners.' ³⁵ Yet wisdom is proved right by all her children."

Jesus Pardons a Sinful Woman.* ³⁶ One of the Pharisees invited Jesus to dine with him. When he arrived at the Pharisee's house, he took his place at table. ³⁷ A woman of that town, who was leading a sinful life, learned that Jesus was a dinner guest in the Pharisee's house. Carrying with her an alabaster jar of ointment,* ³⁸ she stood behind him at his feet, weeping, and began to bathe his feet with her tears and to dry them with her hair. Then she kissed his feet and anointed them with the ointment.

³⁹ When the Pharisee who had invited him saw this, he said to himself, "If this man were really a prophet, he would have known who and what kind of woman this is who is touching him—that she is a sinner." ⁴⁰ Jesus then said to the Pharisee, "Simon, I have something to say to you." He replied, "What is it, Teacher?"

[41] "There were two men who were in debt to a certain creditor. One owed him five hundred denarii, and the other owed fifty. [42] When they were unable to repay him, he canceled both debts. Now which one of them will love him more?" [43] Simon answered, "I would imagine that it would be the one who was forgiven the larger amount." Jesus replied, "You have judged rightly."

[44] Then, turning toward the woman, he said to Simon, "Do you see this woman? I entered your home, and you provided no water for my feet, but she has bathed them with her tears and wiped them with her hair. [45] You gave me no kiss, but she has not ceased to kiss my feet from the time I came in. [46] You did not anoint my head with oil, but she has anointed my feet with ointment. [47] Therefore, I tell you: her many sins have been forgiven her because she has shown great love. But the one who has been forgiven little has little love."

[48] Then Jesus said to her, "Your sins are forgiven." [49] Those who were at table began to say to themselves, "Who is this man who even forgives sins?" [50] But Jesus said to the woman, "Your faith has saved you. Go in peace."

C: Hearing the Word

8 **The Women Who Minister to Jesus.** [1] After that, Jesus journeyed through towns and villages preaching and proclaiming the kingdom of God. Traveling with him were the Twelve, [2]* as well as some women who had been cured of evil spirits and infirmities: Mary, called Magdalene, from whom seven demons had gone out; [3] Joanna, the wife of Herod's steward Chuza; Susanna; and many others. These women provided for them out of their own resources.

The Parable of the Sower.* [4] When a large crowd gathered together as people from every town flocked to him, he said in a parable: [5] "A sower went out to sow his seed. And as he sowed, some of the seed fell along the path and was trampled upon, and the birds of the sky ate it up. [6] Some fell on rock, and when it came up, it withered for lack of moisture. [7] Some seed fell among thorns, and the thorns grew with it and choked it. [8] And some fell onto good soil, and when it grew it produced a crop of a hundredfold."

After saying this, he cried out, "He who has ears to hear, let him hear."

The Purpose of Parables.* [9] Then his disciples asked him what the parable meant. [10] He said, "To you has been granted knowledge of the mysteries of the kingdom of God, but for others they are made known in parables, so that

'looking they may not see,
    and hearing they may not understand.'

The Explanation of the Parable of the Sower.* [11] "The meaning of the parable is this. The seed is the word of God. [12] The seed on the path represents those who hear, but then the devil comes and carries off the word from their hearts so that they may not come to believe and be saved. [13] Those on rock are the ones who, when they hear the word, receive it with joy. But these have no root; they believe for a short while, but in time of trial they fall away.

[14] "That which has fallen among thorns are the ones who have heard, but as they go along, they are choked by the concerns and riches and pleasures of life, and they fail to produce mature fruit. [15] But that which is on rich soil are the ones who, when they have heard the word with a good and upright heart, keep it and yield a harvest through their perseverance.

The Parable of the Lamp.* [16] "No one after lighting a lamp covers it with a pot or places it under a bed. Rather he places it on a lampstand so that those who enter may see the light. [17] For nothing is hidden that will not be disclosed, and nothing is concealed that will not be made known and brought to light. [18] Take great care, therefore, about how you listen. For to the one who has, more will be given; from the one who does not have, even what he thinks he has will be taken away."

The True Family of Jesus.* [19] Then his mother and his brethren arrived, looking for him, but they could not get near him because of the crowd. [20] He was told, "Your mother and your brethren* are standing outside, and they want to see you." [21] But he replied, "My mother and my brethren are those who hear the word of God and put it into practice."

D: The Progressive Revelation of the Mystery of Jesus

Jesus Calms the Storm.* [22] One day, Jesus got into a boat with his disciples and said to them, "Let us cross over to the other side of the lake." And so they set forth, [23] and as they sailed he fell asleep. Then a windstorm swept down on the lake. As a result, the boat was becoming filled with water, and they were in danger. [24] So they went to him and awakened him, saying, "Master! Master! We are perishing!"

Then he awakened and rebuked the wind and the turbulent waves. They subsided and there was calm. [25] He said to them, "Where is your faith?" They were filled with fear and a sense of awe, and they said to one another, "Who can this be? He gives orders to the winds and the water, and they obey him."

Jesus Casts Out a Legion of Demons.* [26] Then they sailed to the region of the Gerasenes, which is opposite Galilee. [27] As he stepped ashore, he was approached by a man from the town who was possessed by demons. For a long time he had worn no clothes. Moreover, he did not live in a house but among the tombs.

[28] When the man caught sight of Jesus, he cried out and fell at his feet, shouting at the top of his voice, "What do you want with me, Jesus, Son of the Most High God? I implore you, do not torment me!" [29] For he had ordered the unclean spirit to come out of the man. Many times in the past it had seized him, and on such occasions they used to restrain him with chains and shackles, but he would manage to break loose and be driven by the demon into the wilds.

30 Then Jesus asked him, "What is your name?" "Legion," he replied, for many demons had entered him. 31 And they begged him not to order them to go back into the abyss.

32 Now on the mountainside a large herd of pigs was feeding, and they pleaded with him to let them go into the pigs. He allowed this. 33 The demons then came out of the man and entered the pigs. Thereupon the herd charged down the steep bank into the lake and drowned.

34 When those tending the herd saw what had occurred, they ran off and reported the incident in the town and throughout the countryside. 35 As a result, people came out to see what had happened. When they came near Jesus, they found the man from whom the demons had gone out sitting at Jesus' feet, fully clothed and in his right mind, and they were frightened.

36 Those who had been eyewitnesses to the incident told how the one who had been possessed by demons had been healed. 37 Then all the people of the region of the Gerasenes asked Jesus to depart from them, for they were seized with great fear. So he got into the boat and went away.

38 The man from whom the demons had gone out pleaded that he be allowed to go with him, but Jesus sent him away, saying, 39 "Return to your home and give witness to what God has done for you." He then departed, proclaiming throughout the town what Jesus had done for him.

Jesus Heals a Woman and Raises a Child.* 40 When Jesus returned, the crowd welcomed him, for they had all been waiting for him. 41 Then a man named Jairus, a leader of the synagogue, came forward. Throwing himself at the feet of Jesus, he pleaded with him to come to his house, 42 because he had an only daughter, about twelve years old, who was dying. And as Jesus went forth, the crowds were pressing in on him.

⁴³ There was a woman who had been suffering from bleeding for twelve years, but no one had been able to cure her affliction. ⁴⁴ Coming up behind him, she touched the fringe of his cloak, and her bleeding stopped immediately.

⁴⁵ Jesus then asked, "Who was it who touched me?" When everyone denied doing so, Peter said, "Master, the crowds are surrounding you and pressing closely upon you." ⁴⁶ But Jesus said, "Someone touched me, for I could sense power going out from me."

⁴⁷ When the woman realized that she had not escaped notice, she came forward, trembling, and knelt down before him. In the presence of all the people, she related why she had touched him and how she had been healed immediately. ⁴⁸ Then Jesus said to her, "Daughter, your faith has healed you. Go in peace."

⁴⁹ While he was still speaking, someone came from the house of the synagogue leader and said, "Your daughter has died. Do not bother the Teacher any further." ⁵⁰ When Jesus heard this, he said, "Do not be afraid. Just have faith, and she will be saved."

⁵¹ When he arrived at the house, he permitted no one to go in with him except Peter, John, and James, and the child's father and mother. ⁵² Everyone was weeping and mourning for her, but he said, "Stop your weeping! She is not dead; she is asleep." ⁵³ They laughed at him because they knew that she had died.

⁵⁴ However, Jesus took her by the hand and called out to her, "Little child, arise." ⁵⁵ Her spirit returned, and she stood up at once. Then Jesus directed that she be given something to eat. ⁵⁶ Her parents were stunned, but he gave them strict instructions to tell no one what had happened.

9 **Jesus Sends Out the Twelve on Mission.*** ¹ Calling the Twelve together, Jesus gave them power and authority to cast out all demons and to cure diseases, ² and he sent them forth to proclaim the kingdom of God and to heal the sick.

³ He said to them, "Take nothing for the journey, neither walking staff, nor sack, nor bread, nor money. Nor are you to have a second tunic. ⁴ Whatever house you enter, stay there until you depart from that area. ⁵ As for those who do not welcome you, when you leave that town shake the dust from your feet in testimony against them." ⁶ Then they set forth and traveled from village to village, preaching the gospel and curing diseases everywhere.

John the Baptist, Herod, and Jesus.* ⁷ Now Herod the tetrarch heard about all that was taking place, and he was perplexed because some people were saying that John had been raised from the dead, ⁸ others that Elijah had appeared, and still others that one of the ancient prophets had come back to life. ⁹ But Herod said, "John I beheaded. Then who is this about whom I hear such things?" And he was anxious to see him.

Jesus Feeds Five Thousand Men.* ¹⁰ On their return, the apostles reported to Jesus what they had done. Then he took them along and withdrew privately to a town named Bethsaida. ¹¹ When the people learned of this, they followed him. Jesus welcomed them and spoke to them about the kingdom of God. He also cured those who were in need of healing.

¹² When evening was approaching, the Twelve came to Jesus and said, "Send the people away now so that they can go to the villages and farms in the area and obtain food and lodging, for we are in a deserted place." ¹³ He replied, "Give them something to eat yourselves." They said, "All we have are five loaves and two fish—unless we go and buy food for all these people." ¹⁴ For there were present about five thousand men.

Then he instructed his disciples, "Make them sit down in groups of about fifty." ¹⁵ They did so and made them sit down. ¹⁶ Taking the five loaves and the two fish, he looked up to heaven and blessed and broke them and gave them to the disciples to distribute among the people. [17] They all ate and were satisfied. Then they gathered up what was left over—twelve baskets of fragments.

Peter's Confession That Jesus Is the Christ. [18] * Once while Jesus was praying by himself, he asked his disciples who were standing close by, "Who do the people say that I am?" [19] They answered, "Some say John the Baptist; others say Elijah; and still others, that one of the ancient prophets has arisen." [20] "But you," he said to them, "who do you say that I am?" Peter answered him: "The Christ of God." [21] Thereupon he gave them strict orders and commanded them not to tell this to anyone.

Jesus Predicts His Passion. [22] He then went on to say, "The Son of Man must endure great suffering, be rejected by the elders, the chief priests, and the scribes, and be put to death, and on the third day be raised."

The Conditions of Discipleship.* [23] Then he said to all who were with him, "Anyone who wishes to follow me must deny himself, take up his cross daily, and follow me. [24] For whoever wishes to save his life will lose it, but whoever loses his life for my sake will save it. [25] What does it profit a man if he gains the whole world and loses or forfeits himself?

[26] "If anyone is ashamed of me and of my words, the Son of Man will be ashamed of him when he comes in his glory and in the glory of the Father and of the holy angels. [27] Truly I say to you, there are some standing here who will not taste death before they see the kingdom of God."

Jesus Is Transfigured.* [28] About eight days after he had said this, Jesus took Peter, John, and James and went up on a mountain to pray. [29] And while he was praying, the appearance of his face underwent a change, and his clothing became dazzling white. [30] Suddenly, there were two men talking with him, Moses and Elijah, [31] who appeared in glory and spoke of his departure, which would come to pass in Jerusalem. [32] Peter and his companions were very sleepy, but when they became fully awake they beheld his glory and the two men standing beside him.

[33] When they were ready to leave, Peter said to Jesus, "Master, it is good for us to be here. Let us make three tents—one for you, one for Moses, and one for Elijah." But he did not truly know what he was saying. [34] While he was speaking, a cloud came and cast its shadow over them, and the three disciples became frightened as they entered the cloud. [35] Then a voice came out of the cloud, saying, "This is my Son, my Chosen One.* Listen to him." [36] After the voice had spoken, they beheld only Jesus. They kept silent and at that time they did not tell anyone about what they had witnessed.

E: End of the Galilean Ministry

Jesus Heals a Boy with a Demon.* [37] On the following day, when they descended from the mountain, a large crowd came forth to meet him. [38] Then, suddenly, a man in the crowd cried out, "Teacher, I implore you to look at my son. He is my only child. [39] A spirit seizes him and with a shriek suddenly throws him into convulsions until he begins to foam at the mouth. It hardly ever leaves him, continuously torturing him. [40] I begged your disciples to drive it out, but they were unable to do so."

[41] Jesus said in reply, "O unbelieving and perverse generation! How much longer shall I remain with you and have to endure you? Bring your son here!" [42] As the boy was approaching him, the demon threw him into convulsions. But Jesus rebuked the unclean spirit, cured the boy, and gave him back to his father. [43] And all those present were awestruck at the greatness of God.

Jesus Predicts His Passion a Second Time.* Amid the astonishment of the crowds at everything he was doing, Jesus said to his disciples, [44] "Listen carefully to these words. The Son of Man is going to be handed over into the power of men." [45] But they did not understand what he was saying. Its meaning was hidden from them so that they could not comprehend his message, and they were afraid to ask him what he meant.

True Greatness.* [46] The disciples then began to argue about which of them was the greatest. [47] Jesus, aware of their inner thoughts, took a child, placed him by his side, [48] and said to them, "Whoever receives this child in my name receives me; and whoever receives me receives the one who sent me. For the one who is least among all of you is the one who is the greatest."

Whoever Is Not against You Is with You.* [49] John then said, "Master, we saw someone expelling demons in your name, and we forbade him because he is not with us." [50] Jesus replied, "Do not hinder him! For whoever is not against you is with you."

IV. THE JOURNEY TO JERUSALEM*

A: The Departure

Passing through Samaria.* [51] As the time drew near for him to be taken up, Jesus resolutely set his sights on Jerusalem, [52] and he sent messengers ahead of him. They entered a Samaritan village to make arrangements for his arrival, [53] but the people there would not receive him because his destination was Jerusalem. [54] When the disciples James and John saw this, they asked, "Lord, do you want us to call down fire from heaven to consume them?" * [55] But Jesus turned and rebuked them. [56] Then they journeyed forth to another village.

The Cost of Following Jesus.* [57] As they traveled along the road, a man said to him, "I will follow you wherever you go." [58] Jesus told him, "Foxes have holes, and birds of the air have nests, but the Son of Man has nowhere to lay his head."

[59] To another he said, "Follow me." The man replied, "Lord, allow me to go first and bury my father." [60] Jesus said to him, "Let the dead bury their own dead. You are to go and proclaim the kingdom of God."

[61] Another man said, "I will follow you, Lord, but allow me first to say farewell to my family at home." [62] Jesus said to him, "No one who puts his hand to the plow and then looks back is fit for the kingdom of God."

B: The Mission of All the Disciples

10 The Mission of the Seventy-Two. [1] * After this, the Lord appointed seventy-two others and sent them on ahead of him in pairs to every town and place he intended to visit. [2] He said to them: "The harvest is abundant, but the laborers are few. Therefore, ask the Lord of the harvest to send forth laborers for his harvest.

[3] "Go on your way. Behold, I am sending you out like lambs among wolves. [4] Carry no money bag or sack and wear no sandals. Greet no one on the road. [5] Whatever house you enter, let your first words be, 'Peace to this house!' [6] If a man of peace lives there, your peace will rest on him; if not, it will return to you.

[7] "Remain in the same house, and eat and drink whatever is offered to you, for the laborer deserves his wages. Do not move around from house to house. [8] Whenever you enter a town and its people welcome you, eat whatever is set before you. [9] Cure the sick who are there, and say, 'The kingdom of God has come unto you.'

[10] "But whenever you enter a town and the people do not welcome you, go out into the streets and say, [11] 'Even the dust of your town that clings to us we wipe off our feet as a sign against you. Yet know this: the kingdom of God is at hand.' [12] I tell you, on that day * it will be more bearable for Sodom than for that town.

Woe to the Cities of Galilee. [13] * "Woe to you, Chorazin! Woe to you, Bethsaida! If the mighty deeds performed in your midst had been done in Tyre and Sidon, they would have come to repentance long ago, sitting in sackcloth and ashes. [14] But at the judgment it will be more tolerable for Tyre and Sidon than for you. [15] And as for you, Capernaum:

Will you be exalted to heaven?

You will be brought down to the netherworld.*

[16] "Whoever listens to you listens to me, and whoever rejects you rejects me. And whoever rejects me rejects the one who sent me."

Joy of the Missionaries.* [17] The seventy-two returned rejoicing, and they said, "Lord, in your name even the demons are subject to us." [18] He said to them, "I watched Satan fall from heaven like lightning. [19] Behold, I have given you the power to tread upon snakes and scorpions and all the forces of the enemy, and nothing will ever harm you. [20] Nevertheless, do not rejoice in the knowledge that the spirits are subject to you. Rejoice rather that your names are inscribed in heaven."

Joy of Jesus. [21] * At that very hour, Jesus rejoiced in the Holy Spirit and said, "I thank you, Father, Lord of heaven and earth, because you have hidden these things from the wise and the learned and have revealed them to children. Yes, Father, such has been your gracious will.

[22] "All things have been entrusted to me by my Father. No one knows who the Son is except the Father, or who the Father is except the Son and those to whom the Son wishes to reveal him."

The Privilege of Discipleship. [23] Then he turned to his disciples and said privately, "Blessed are the eyes that see what you see. [24] I tell you, many prophets and kings desired to see what you see but did not see it, and to hear what you hear but did not hear it."

The Greatest Commandment. [25] * And behold, a lawyer came forward to test Jesus by asking, "Teacher, what must I do to gain eternal life?" [26] Jesus said to him, "What is written in the Law? How do you read it?" [27] He answered, "You shall love the Lord your God with all your heart, and with all your soul, and with all your strength, and with all your mind, and your neighbor as yourself." [28] Jesus then said to him, "You have answered correctly. Do this and you will live."

The Parable of the Good Samaritan. ²⁹ But because the man wished to justify himself, he asked, "And who is my neighbor?" ³⁰ Jesus replied, "A man was going down * from Jerusalem to Jericho, when he was attacked by robbers. They stripped him and beat him, and then went off leaving him half-dead. ³¹ A priest happened to be traveling along that same road, but when he saw him he passed by on the other side. ³² A Levite * likewise came to that spot and saw him, but he too passed by on the other side.

³³ "But a Samaritan who was traveling along that road came upon him, and when he saw him he was moved with compassion. ³⁴ He went up to him and bandaged his wounds after having poured oil and wine on them. Then he brought him upon his own animal to an inn and looked after him.

³⁵ "The next day, he took out two denarii * and gave them to the innkeeper, saying, 'Look after him, and when I return I will repay you for anything more you might spend.'

³⁶ "Which of those three, do you think, was a neighbor to the man who fell into the hands of the robbers?" ³⁷ He answered, "The one who showed him mercy." Jesus said to him, "Go and do likewise." *

Martha and Mary. * ³⁸ In the course of their journey, he came to a village where a woman named Martha welcomed him into her home. ³⁹ She had a sister named Mary who sat at the Lord's feet and listened to what he was saying.

⁴⁰ But Martha was distracted by her many tasks. So she came to him and said, "Lord, do you not care that my sister has left me to do all the work by myself? Tell her to come and help me." ⁴¹ The Lord answered her: "Martha, Martha, you are anxious and upset about many things, ⁴² when only one thing is necessary. Mary has chosen the better part, and it will not be taken away from her."

C: Prayer

11 The Lord's Prayer.* [1] One day, Jesus was praying in a certain place. When he finished, one of his disciples said to him, "Lord, teach us to pray, as John taught his disciples." [2] He said to them, "When you pray, say:

Father,
hallowed be your name.
Your kingdom come.
[3] Give us each day our daily bread.
[4] And forgive us our sins,
for we ourselves forgive everyone who is in debt to
us.
And do not lead us into temptation."

The Parable of the Persistent Friend. [5] * He also said to them, "Suppose one of you has a friend, and he goes to him at midnight and says: 'My friend, lend me three loaves of bread, [6] for a friend of mine has arrived at my house from a journey, and I have nothing to offer him,' [7] and the friend answers from inside: 'Do not bother me. The door is already locked, and my children and I are in bed; I cannot get up now to give you anything.' [8] I tell you: even though he will not get up and give it to him because of their friendship, he will get up and give him whatever he needs because of his persistence.

Ask, Seek, Knock. [9] "Therefore, I say to you: ask, and it will be given you; seek, and you will find; knock, and the door will be opened to you. [10] For everyone who asks will receive, and those who seek will find, and to those who knock the door will be opened.

The Parable of the Good Father. [11] "Is there any father among you who would hand his son a snake when he asks for a fish, [12] or hand him a scorpion when he asks for an egg? [13] If you, then, despite your evil nature, know how to give good gifts to your children, how much more will the heavenly Father give the Holy Spirit to those who ask him!"

D: For or against Jesus*

Jesus and Beelzebul.* [14] Jesus was driving out a demon that was mute, and when the demon had gone out, the man who was mute spoke, and the crowd was amazed. [15] But some of them said, "He casts out demons by Beelzebul, the prince of demons." [16] Others, to test him, demanded a sign from heaven.

[17] However, he knew what they were thinking, and he said to them, "Every kingdom divided against itself is laid waste, and a house divided against itself will collapse. [18] If Satan is divided against himself, how can his kingdom stand?

"For you say that I cast out demons by Beelzebul. [19] Now, if it is by Beelzebul that I cast out demons, by whom do your own children cast them out? Therefore, they will be your judges. [20] But if it is by the finger of God that I cast out demons, then the kingdom of God has come to you.

[21] "When a strong man is fully armed and guards his palace, his possessions are safe. [22] But when someone who is stronger than he is attacks and overpowers him, he carries off all the weapons upon which the owner relied and distributes the plunder.

No Compromise. [23] "Whoever is not with me is against me, and whoever does not gather with me scatters.

New Offensive from the Evil Spirit. [24] "When an unclean spirit goes out of a person, it wanders through waterless regions seeking a place to rest, and if it finds none it says, 'I will return to the home from which I departed.' [25] However, when it returns, it finds that home swept and put in order. [26] Then it goes off and brings back seven other spirits more wicked than itself, and they enter and settle there. As a result, the plight of that person is worse than before."

True Blessedness.* [27] While he was speaking, a woman in the crowd called out to him and said, "Blessed is the

womb that bore you and the breasts that nursed you!"
²⁸ Jesus replied, "Blessed, rather, are those who hear the
word of God and obey it!"

The Sign of Jonah.* ²⁹ As the crowd continued to increase
in number, Jesus said to them, "This is an evil generation.
It asks for a sign, but the only sign it will be given is the
sign of Jonah. ³⁰ For just as Jonah became a sign to the
inhabitants of Nineveh, so will the Son of Man be to this
generation.

³¹ "On the day of judgment the queen of the south will
rise up with the men of this generation and condemn
them, because she came from the farthest reaches of the
earth to hear the wisdom of Solomon, and now one
greater than Solomon is here. ³² On the day of judgment,
the men of Nineveh will rise up with this generation and
condemn it, because they repented at the preaching of
Jonah, and now one greater than Jonah is here.

The Parable of the Lighted Lamp. ³³ * "No one lights a
lamp and then puts it in a cellar or under a basket; rather,
he places it upon a lampstand so that people may see the
light when they come in.

The Lamp of the Body. ³⁴ "Your eyes are the lamp of your
body. If your eyes are sound, your whole body will be
filled with light. However, if your eyes are diseased, your
whole body will be in darkness. ³⁵ See to it then that the
light inside you is not darkness. ³⁶ Therefore, if your
whole body is full of light, with no part of it in darkness,
it will be as full of light as when a lamp illuminates you
with its rays."

Woe to the Scribes and Pharisees.* ³⁷ When he had finished speaking, a Pharisee invited him to dine at his
house. He went in and took his place at table. ³⁸ The
Pharisee was surprised to see that he had not first
washed * before the meal. ³⁹ But the Lord said to him,
"You Pharisees cleanse the outside of a cup and dish, but
you leave the inside full of greed and wickedness. ⁴⁰ You
fools! Did not the one who made the outside also make

the inside? [41] Let what is inside be given as alms to the poor, and everything will be clean for you.

[42] "Woe to you Pharisees! You pay tithes * of mint and rue and every garden herb, but you neglect justice and the love of God. You should have practiced these without neglecting the others.

[43] "Woe to you Pharisees! You love to have the best seats in synagogues and to be greeted with respect in the marketplaces.

[44] "Woe to you! For you are like unmarked graves * upon which people tread without realizing it."

[45] On hearing this, one of the lawyers said, "Teacher when you say such things you are insulting us too." [46] He replied, "Woe also to you lawyers! For you impose burdens on people that are difficult to bear, but you yourselves do not lift a finger to be of assistance.

[47] "Woe to you! For you build the tombs of the Prophets whom your ancestors murdered. [48] By acting in this way you bear witness to and approve of what your ancestors did. They killed the Prophets, and you build their tombs.

[49] "That is why the Wisdom of God said, 'I will send them Prophets and apostles, some of whom they will kill and persecute,' [50] so that this generation may be charged with the responsibility for the blood of all the Prophets shed since the foundation of the world, [51] from the blood of Abel to the blood of Zechariah * who perished between the altar and the sanctuary. Yes, I tell you, this generation will have to answer for it all.

[52] "Woe to you lawyers! For you have taken away the key of knowledge. You yourselves did not enter, and you blocked those from entering who were trying to go in."

[53] When he left the house, the scribes and the Pharisees were extremely hostile and they began to interrogate him about many things, [54] hoping to trap him in something he might say in reply.

12 The Yeast of the Pharisees.

¹ * Meanwhile a crowd of many thousands of people had gathered, and they were so tightly packed together that they were trampling on each other. Then Jesus began to speak, saying first to his disciples: "Beware of the yeast of the Pharisees—which is their hypocrisy. ² There is nothing hidden that will not be disclosed, and nothing secret that will not become known. ³ Therefore, whatever you have said in the dark will be heard in the daylight, and what you have whispered behind closed doors will be shouted from the housetops.

Courage in Time of Persecution. ⁴ "I tell you, my friends, have no fear of those who kill the body and after that can do nothing further. ⁵ But I will tell you whom to fear. Be afraid of the one who, after he has killed, has the authority to cast into Gehenna. I tell you, fear him!

⁶ "Are not five sparrows sold for two pennies? And yet not one of them is forgotten in God's sight. ⁷ Even the hairs on your head have all been counted. Do not be afraid. You are worth far more than any number of sparrows.

⁸ "I tell you this: whoever acknowledges me before men, the Son of Man will also acknowledge before the angels of God. ⁹ But whoever denies me before men, he will be denied before the angels of God.

Sayings about the Holy Spirit. ¹⁰ "Everyone who speaks a word against the Son of Man will be forgiven, but the person who blasphemes against the Holy Spirit will not be forgiven.* ¹¹ When you are brought before synagogues and rulers and authorities, do not be concerned about how or what you are to answer or what you are to say. ¹² When the time comes, the Holy Spirit will teach you what you are to say."

E: Be Poor in Order To Be Free

A Saying about Greed. ¹³ * Someone in the crowd said to him, "Teacher, tell my brother to share the family inheritance with me." ¹⁴ Jesus answered him, "Friend, who appointed me to be a judge and arbitrator in your regard?"

[15] * After this, he said to the crowd, "Take care to be on your guard against all kinds of greed. Life does not depend upon an abundance of one's possessions."

The Parable of the Rich Fool. [16] Then he told them a parable: "There was a wealthy man whose land yielded an abundant harvest. [17] He thought to himself, 'What shall I do, for I do not have sufficient space to store my crops?' [18] Then he said, 'This is what I will do. I will pull down my barns and build larger ones, where I will store my grain and other produce, [19] and I shall say to myself, "Now you have an abundance of goods stored up for many years to come. Relax, eat, drink, and be merry." '

[20] "But God said to him, 'You fool! This very night your life will be required of you. And who then will get to enjoy the fruit of your labors?' [21] That is how it will be for the one who stores up treasure for himself yet fails to become rich in the sight of God."

Trust in God. * [22] Then he said to his disciples, "Therefore, heed my words. Do not be concerned about your life and what you will have to eat, or about your body and what you will wear. [23] For life is more than food, and the body is more than clothing.

[24] "Consider the ravens. They do not sow or reap, they have no storehouse or barn, and yet God feeds them. You are of far greater importance than birds. [25] Can any of you through worrying add a single moment to your span of life? [26] If then such a small thing is beyond your power, why should you be concerned about the rest?

[27] "Consider the lilies and how they grow. They neither labor nor spin. Yet I tell you that not even Solomon in all his royal splendor was clothed like one of these. [28] If God so clothes the grass that grows today in the field and is thrown into the furnace tomorrow, how much more will he clothe you, O you of little faith!

²⁹ "Hence, do not be greatly concerned about what you are to eat and what you are to drink. Do not worry. ³⁰ The nations of the world are concerned for all these things. Your Father is aware of your needs. ³¹ Rather, seek his kingdom, and these things will be given to you as well.

Treasure in Heaven.* ³² "Fear not, little flock, for your Father has chosen to give you the kingdom. ³³ Sell your possessions and give to those in need. Provide money bags for yourselves that do not wear out, an inexhaustible treasure in heaven that no thief can come near and no moth can destroy. ³⁴ For where your treasure is, there will your heart also be.

F: Parables about Watchfulness*

The Parable of the Vigilant Steward* ³⁵ "Fasten your belts for service and have your lamps lit. ³⁶ Be like servants who are waiting for their master to return from a wedding banquet, so that they may open the door as soon as he comes and knocks. ³⁷ Blessed are those servants whom the master finds awake when he arrives. Amen, I say to you, he will fasten his belt, have them recline to eat, and proceed to wait on them himself. ³⁸ If he comes in the second watch,* or in the third and finds them still awake, blessed are those servants.

The Hour of the Son of Man.* ³⁹ "But keep this in mind: if the owner of the house had known at what hour the thief was coming, he would not have left his house to be broken into. ⁴⁰ So you must also be prepared, because the Son of Man will come at an hour when you do not expect him."

The Parable of the Faithful Servant.* ⁴¹ Then Peter asked, "Lord, are you directing this parable to us or do you mean it for everyone?" ⁴² The Lord replied, "Who then is the faithful and wise steward whom his master will put in charge of his household to give its members their allotment of food at the proper time? ⁴³ Blessed is that servant if his master finds him doing so when he arrives home.

[44] Truly I tell you, he will put him in charge of all his property.

[45] "But if that servant says to himself, 'My master is detained in arriving,' and he proceeds to beat the menservants and the maids, and to eat and drink and get drunk, [46] the master of that servant will return on a day when he does not expect him and at an hour he does not know. He will punish him and assign him a place with the unfaithful.

[47] "The servant who knew his master's wishes but did not get ready or do what his master wanted will receive a severe beating. [48] But the one who did not know those wishes, and who acted in such a manner as to deserve a beating, will be beaten less severely. Much will be demanded of a person to whom much has been given, and even more will be asked of a person to whom more has been entrusted.

G: The Urgency of Making the Decision

Jesus and His Passion. * [49] "I have come to spread fire on the earth, and how I wish it were already blazing! [50] I have a baptism with which to be baptized, and how great is my anguish until it has been completed!

Jesus, Cause of Dissensions. * [51] "Do you think that I have come to bring peace to the earth? No, I tell you, but rather division.

[52] "From now on a household of five will be divided, three against two and two against three; [53] they will be divided, father against son and son against father, mother against daughter and daughter against mother, mother-in-law against daughter-in-law and daughter-in-law against mother-in-law."

Discerning the Signs of the Times. * [54] He also said to the crowds, "When you see a cloud rising in the west, you immediately say, 'It is going to rain,' and so it happens. [55] And when you see the wind blowing from the south, you say, 'It is going to be hot,' and so it happens. [56] You hypocrites! You know how to interpret the appearance of

earth and sky. Why then do you not know how to interpret the present time?

Reconciling with Others before the Judgment.* [57] "And
why do you not judge for yourselves what is right?
[58] Thus, when you are going to court with your opponent,
make an effort to settle the matter with him on the way.
If you fail to do so, he may drag you before the judge, and
the judge will hand you over to the officer, and the officer
will throw you into prison. [59] I tell you, you will not be
given your freedom until you have paid your debt down
to the very last penny."

13 **Jesus Calls for Repentance.*** [1] At that time, some people who were present told Jesus about the Galileans
whose blood Pilate had mingled with the blood of their
sacrifices. [2] He asked them, "Do you think that because
the Galileans suffered in this way they were worse sinners
than all other Galileans? [3] No, I tell you. But unless you
repent, you will all perish as they did. [4] Or those eighteen
people who were killed when the tower fell on them at
Siloam—do you think that they were more guilty than all
the others living in Jerusalem? [5] No, I tell you—but unless
you repent, you will all perish as they did."

The Parable of the Barren Fig Tree.* [6] Then he told them
this parable: "A man had a fig tree planted in his vineyard, but whenever he came looking for fruit on it, he
found none. [7] Therefore, he said to his vinedresser, 'For
three years I have come looking for fruit on this fig tree
and have never found any. Cut it down! Why should it
continue to use up the soil?' [8] But the vinedresser replied,
'Sir, let it alone for one more year while I dig around it
and fertilize it. [9] Perhaps it will bear fruit next year. If so,
well and good. If not, then you can cut it down.'"

Jesus Heals a Woman on the Sabbath.* [10] On one Sabbath
as Jesus was teaching in the synagogue, [11] a woman was
present, possessed by a spirit that had crippled her for
eighteen years. She was bent over and completely unable
to stand up straight. [12] When Jesus saw her, he called her

forward and said, "Woman, you are freed from your infirmity." ¹³ Then he laid his hands on her, and immediately she stood up straight and began praising God.

¹⁴ But the leader of the synagogue was indignant because Jesus had effected a cure on the Sabbath, and he said to the assembled people, "There are six days when work is permitted. Come on those days and be cured, and not on the Sabbath." ¹⁵ The Lord said to him in reply, "You hypocrites! Is there a single one of you who does not untie his ox or his donkey and lead it from its stall to give it water on the Sabbath? ¹⁶ Should not this woman, a daughter of Abraham, whom Satan has held bound for eighteen long years, be set free from this bondage on the Sabbath?" ¹⁷ At these words, all his adversaries were put to shame, and the people rejoiced at all the wonderful things he was doing.

The Parable of the Mustard Seed. ¹⁸ * He went on to say, "What is the kingdom of God like? To what shall I compare it? ¹⁹ It is like a mustard seed that a man took and sowed in his garden. It grew and became a tree, and the birds of the air made nests in its branches."

The Parable of the Yeast. ²⁰ Again he said, "To what shall I compare the kingdom of God? ²¹ It is like yeast that a woman took and mixed with three measures of flour until it was completely leavened."

H: The Destiny of Israel

Who Will Enter into the Kingdom of God?* ²² Jesus continued journeying through towns and villages, teaching as he made his way to Jerusalem. ²³ Someone asked him, "Lord, will only a few be saved?" He answered, ²⁴ "Strive to enter through the narrow door, for many, I tell you, will try to enter but will not succeed in doing so.

²⁵ "When once the master of the house has gotten up and shut the door, you may find yourself standing outside knocking on the door and begging, 'Lord, open the door for us.' He will say in reply, 'I do not know where you

come from.' ²⁶ Then you will protest, 'We ate and drank with you, and you taught in our streets.' ²⁷ But he will say, 'I do not know where you come from. Depart from me, all you evildoers!'

²⁸ "There will be weeping and gnashing of teeth when you see Abraham and Isaac and Jacob and all the Prophets in the kingdom of God as you yourselves are being thrown out. ²⁹ Then from the east and the west, and from the north and the south, people will come and take their places at the banquet in the kingdom of God. ³⁰ Indeed some are last who will be first, and some are first who will be last."

Herod's Desire To Kill Jesus.* ³¹ At that time, some Pharisees came and said to him, "Leave this place and go somewhere else, for Herod wants to kill you." ³² He answered them, "Go and tell that fox: 'Behold, today and tomorrow I will be casting out demons and healing people, and on the third day I will finish my work. ³³ Yet I must continue to go on today and tomorrow and the next day, since it would not be right for a prophet to be killed outside Jerusalem.

The Lament over Jerusalem.* ³⁴ "Jerusalem, Jerusalem, you murder the Prophets and stone the messengers sent to you! How often have I longed to gather your children together as a hen gathers her chicks under her wings, but you would not allow it! ³⁵ Behold, your house has been abandoned. I tell you, you will not see me until you say: 'Blessed is he who comes in the name of the Lord.' "

I: A Dinner Given by a Pharisee*

14 **Jesus Heals a Man with Dropsy on the Sabbath.*** ¹ On one Sabbath, Jesus went to dine at the home of a prominent Pharisee, and the people were watching him closely. ² In front of him there was a man suffering from dropsy, ³ and Jesus asked the lawyers and the Pharisees, "Is it lawful to heal on the Sabbath or not?" ⁴ When they offered no reply, he took the man, healed him, and sent him on his way. [5] Then he said to them, "If one of you has a son or an ox that has fallen into a well, will you not immediately pull him out on the Sabbath day?" [6] And they were unable to give him any answer.

The Parable of the Ambitious Guest.* [7] When he noticed how the guests were securing places of honor, he told them a parable: [8] "When you have been invited by someone to attend a wedding banquet, do not sit down in the place of honor in case someone who is more distinguished than you may have been invited, [9] and then the host who invited both of you may approach you and say, 'Give this man your place.' Then you will be embarrassed as you proceed to sit in the lowest place.

[10] "Rather, when you are invited, proceed to sit in the lowest place, so that when your host arrives, he will say to you, 'My friend, move up to a higher place.' Then you will be honored in the presence of all your fellow guests. [11] For everyone who exalts himself will be humbled, and the one who humbles himself will be exalted."

Invite the Needy.* [12] Then he said to the one who had invited him, "When you host a luncheon or a dinner, do not invite your friends or your brothers or your relatives or your wealthy neighbors, lest they invite you back and thus repay you. [13] Rather, when you hold a banquet, invite the poor, the crippled, the lame, and the blind. [14] Then indeed will you be blessed because they have no way to repay you. But you will be repaid at the resurrection of the righteous."

The Parable of the Great Supper.* [15] On hearing this, one of the dinner guests said to him, "Blessed is the man who will dine in the kingdom of God." [16] Jesus said in reply, "A man gave a sumptuous banquet, to which he invited many. [17] When the hour for the banquet drew near, he sent his servant to say to those who had been invited: 'Come, for everything is now ready.'

[18] "But one after another they all began to make excuses. The first said, 'I have bought a parcel of land, and I

must go out to inspect it. Please accept my apologies.'
[19] Another said, 'I have purchased five yoke of oxen, and I am on my way to try them out. Please accept my regrets.' [20] Still another said, 'I have just gotten married, and therefore I am unable to come.'

[21] "When the servant returned, he reported all this to his master. Then the owner of the house became enraged, and he said to his servant, 'Go out quickly into the streets and alleys of the town and bring in here the poor, the crippled, the blind, and the lame.' [22] Shortly afterward, the servant told him, 'Sir, your orders have been carried out, and some room is still available.' [23] Then the master said to the servant, 'Go out to the open roads and along the hedgerows and compel people to come,* so that my house may be filled. [24] For I tell you, not one of those who were invited shall taste my banquet.' "

J: Conditions To Be a Disciple*

Renunciation of Everything for Jesus.* [25] Great crowds were accompanying Jesus on his journey, and he turned to them and said, [26] "If anyone comes to me and does not hate his father and mother,* wife and children, brothers and sisters, yes, and even his own life, he cannot be my disciple. [27] Whoever does not carry his own cross and follow me cannot be my disciple.

[28] * "Which one of you, intending to build a tower, would not first sit down and estimate the cost, to see whether he has sufficient funds for its completion? [29] Otherwise, if he has laid the foundation and then finds himself unable to finish the work, all who see it will ridicule him, saying, [30] 'There goes the man who started to build but was unable to complete the work.'

[31] "Or what king marching into battle against another king will not first sit down and consider whether with ten thousand soldiers he can defeat the enemy coming to oppose him with twenty thousand? [32] If he cannot, then, while the enemy is still a long distance away, he will send a delegation to ask for terms of peace. [33] In the same way,

any one of you who does not renounce all of his possessions cannot be my disciple.

The Simile of Salt.* ³⁴ "Salt is good. But if salt loses its taste, what can be done to make it salty once again? ³⁵ It is fit neither for the soil nor for the dungheap. Thus, it can only be thrown away. He who has ears to hear, let him hear!"

K: Salvation—Joy and Torment of God*

15 **This Man Receives Sinners.*** ¹ Now the tax collectors and sinners were all crowding around to listen to Jesus, ² and the Pharisees and the scribes began to complain, saying, "This man welcomes sinners and eats with them."

The Parable of the Lost Sheep.* ³ Therefore, he told them this parable: ⁴ "Which one of you, if you have a hundred sheep and lose one of them, will not leave the ninety-nine in the wilderness and go after the one that is lost until he finds it? ⁵ And when he does find it, he lays it on his shoulders joyfully. ⁶ Then, when he returns home, he calls together his friends and neighbors and says to them, 'Rejoice with me, because I have found my sheep that was lost.' ⁷ In the same way, I tell you, there will be more rejoicing in heaven over one sinner who repents than over ninety-nine righteous people who have no need of repentance.

The Parable of the Lost Coin.* ⁸ "Or again, what woman who has ten silver coins * and loses one will not light a lamp and sweep the house, searching thoroughly until she finds it? ⁹ And when she has found it, she calls together her friends and neighbors and says to them, 'Rejoice with me, for I have found the coin that I lost.' ¹⁰ In the same way, I tell you, there is rejoicing among the angels of God over one sinner who repents."

The Parable of the Lost (or Prodigal) Son.* ¹¹ Then he said: "There was a man who had two sons. ¹² The younger of them said to his father, 'Father, give me the share of your estate that I will inherit.' And so the father divided the property between them.

¹³ "A few days later the younger son gathered together everything he had and traveled to a distant country, where he squandered his inheritance on a life of dissolute living. ¹⁴ When he had spent it all, a severe famine afflicted that country, and he began to be in need. ¹⁵ So he went and hired himself out to one of the local inhabitants who sent him to his farm to feed the pigs.* ¹⁶ He would have willingly filled his stomach with the pods that the pigs were eating, but no one gave him anything.

¹⁷ "Then he came to his senses and said, 'How many of my father's hired workers have more food than they can consume, while here I am, dying of hunger. ¹⁸ I will depart from this place and go to my father, and I will say to him, "Father, I have sinned against heaven and against you. ¹⁹ I am no longer worthy to be called your son. Treat me like one of your hired workers." '

²⁰ "So he set out for his father's house. But while he was still a long way off, his father saw him and was filled with compassion. He ran to him, threw his arms around him, and kissed him. ²¹ Then the son said to him, 'Father, I have sinned against heaven and against you. I am no longer worthy to be called your son.'

²² "But the father said to his servants, 'Quickly bring out the finest robe we have and put it on him. Place a ring on his finger and sandals on his feet. ²³ Then bring the fatted calf and kill it, and let us celebrate with a feast. ²⁴ For this son of mine was dead and has come back to life. He was lost, and now he has been found.' And they began to celebrate.

²⁵ "Now the elder son had been out in the fields, and as he returned and drew near the house, he could hear the sounds of music and dancing. ²⁶ He summoned one of the servants and inquired what all this meant. ²⁷ The servant replied, 'Your brother has come home, and your father has killed the fatted calf because he has him back safe and sound.' ²⁸ The elder son then became angry and

refused to go in. His father came out and began to plead with him, [29] but he said to his father in reply, 'All these years I have worked like a slave for you, and I never once disobeyed your orders. Even so, you have never even given me a young goat so that I might celebrate with my friends. [30] But when this son of yours returns after wasting his inheritance from you on prostitutes, you kill the fatted calf for him.'

[31] "Then the father said to him, 'Son, you are with me always, and everything I have is yours. [32] But it was only right that we should celebrate and rejoice, because this brother of yours was dead and has come to life; he was lost and now he has been found.' "

L: Riches and Poverty*

16 **The Parable of the Crafty Steward.*** [1] Jesus also said to his disciples: "There was a rich man who had a steward, and he was informed that this steward was squandering his property. [2] Therefore, he summoned him and said, 'What are these reports that I hear about you? Give me an accounting of your stewardship, because you can no longer be my steward.'

[3] "Then the steward said to himself, 'What am I going to do, now that my master is dismissing me from being steward? I am not strong enough to dig, and I am too ashamed to beg. [4] What I must do is to make sure that people will welcome me into their homes once I am removed from being steward.'

[5] "Then he summoned his master's debtors one by one. He asked the first, 'How much do you owe my master?' [6] When he was told, 'One hundred jars of olive oil,' he said to the man, 'Take your bill, sit down quickly, and change the number to fifty.' [7] Then he asked another, 'And you, how much do you owe?' When he was told, 'One hundred measures of wheat,' he said to him, 'Take your bill and make it eighty.' [8] The master commended the crafty steward because he had acted shrewdly. For the

children of this world are more shrewd in dealing with their own kind than are the children of light.*

Application of the Parable.* ⁹ "And I tell you: use your worldly wealth to make friends for yourselves so that, when it has been exhausted, they will welcome you into eternal dwellings.

¹⁰ "Whoever can be trusted in small matters can also be trusted in great ones, but whoever is dishonest in small matters will also be dishonest in great ones. ¹¹ Therefore, if you have not been trustworthy in handling worldly wealth, who will entrust you with true riches? ¹² And if you have not shown yourself to be trustworthy with what belongs to another, who will give you anything of your own?

¹³ "No servant can serve two masters. For you will either hate the one and love the other or be devoted to the one and despise the other. You cannot serve both God and money."

M: Teachings concerning Justice and the Judaic Law

A Saying against the Pharisees.* ¹⁴ The Pharisees, who loved money, heard all this and they ridiculed him. ¹⁵ He said to them, "You people pretend to be upright when you wish to impress others, but God knows what is in your hearts. That which is highly esteemed in the eyes of men is detestable in the sight of God.

Sayings about the Law. ¹⁶ "The Law and the Prophets were in effect until John. From that time the kingdom of God has been proclaimed, and everyone is trying to force his way in.* ¹⁷ It is easier for heaven and earth to pass away than for one letter of the Law to be discarded.*

Sayings about Divorce.* ¹⁸ "Anyone who divorces his wife and marries another commits adultery, and anyone who marries a woman divorced from her husband commits adultery.

N: The Rich Man and Lazarus: A Warning

The Parable of the Rich Man and Lazarus.* ¹⁹ "There was a rich man who used to dress in purple garments and the finest linen and who feasted sumptuously every day. ²⁰ And at his gate lay a poor man named Lazarus, covered with sores, ²¹ who would have been grateful to be fed with the scraps that fell from the rich man's table. Even the dogs would come and lick his sores.

²² "Now the poor man died, and he was carried away by the angels to Abraham's side. The rich man also died and was buried. ²³ In the netherworld,* where he was in torment, he looked up and saw Abraham, far off, and Lazarus by his side. ²⁴ And he called out, 'Father Abraham, have pity on me. Send Lazarus to dip the tip of his finger in water and cool my tongue, for I am in agony in these flames.'

²⁵ "But Abraham replied, 'My child, remember that during your lifetime you received many good things, while Lazarus suffered greatly. Now he is being comforted while you are in agony. ²⁶ Moreover, between us and you a great chasm has been established, so that no one who wishes to do so can pass from our side to yours, nor can anyone pass from your side to ours.'

²⁷ "'Then I beg you, father,' he said, 'to send him to my father's house, ²⁸ to warn my five brothers, lest they too end up in this place of torment.' ²⁹ But Abraham responded, 'They have Moses and the Prophets. Let them listen to them.'

³⁰ "He said, 'No, father Abraham, but if someone from the dead goes to them, they will repent.' ³¹ Abraham answered, 'If they will not listen to Moses and the Prophets, they will not be persuaded even if someone should rise from the dead.' "

O: Various Episodes and Instructions

17 **Warning against Giving Scandal.*** ¹ Jesus said to his disciples, "Scandals are bound to occur, but woe to the man through whom they come! ²It would be better for him if a millstone were fastened around his neck and he were thrown into the sea than for him to cause one of these little ones to sin. ³Be on your guard!

The Need To Forgive.* "If your brother should sin, rebuke him, and if he repents, forgive him. ⁴Even if he wrongs you seven times a day, and comes back to you seven times to say, 'I am sorry,' you must forgive him."

Faith Knows How To Make Miracles.* ⁵The apostles said to the Lord, "Increase our faith." ⁶The Lord replied, "If you had faith as tiny as a mustard seed, you could say to this mulberry tree, 'Be uprooted and planted in the sea,' and it would obey you.

Unprofitable Servants.* ⁷"Which of you, when your servant returns from plowing or tending sheep in the fields, would say to him, 'Come right away and sit down to eat'? ⁸Would you not rather say, 'Prepare my dinner, put on your apron, and wait on me while I eat and drink, and then afterward you yourself may eat and drink'? ⁹Would you be grateful to that servant for doing what he was commanded? ¹⁰So should it be with you. When you have done all that you were ordered to do, say, 'We are unprofitable servants; we have only done our duty.' "

Jesus Heals Ten Men with Leprosy.* ¹¹As he continued on his journey to Jerusalem, he traveled along the border between Samaria and Galilee. ¹²When he entered a village, ten lepers approached him. Standing some distance away, ¹³they called out to him, "Jesus, Master, have pity on us." ¹⁴When he saw them, he said, "Go and show yourselves to the priests." And as they went, they were cleansed.

¹⁵One of them, when he realized that he had been cured, came back, praising God in a loud voice. ¹⁶He prostrated himself at the feet of Jesus and thanked him. This man was a Samaritan.

¹⁷Jesus asked, "Were not all ten made clean? Where are the other nine? ¹⁸Has no one except this foreigner

returned to give thanks to God?" [19] Then he said to him, "Stand up and go on your way. Your faith has made you well."

The Coming of the Kingdom of God.* [20] Once, the Pharisees asked him when the kingdom of God was coming. He answered, "The coming of the kingdom of God will not occur with signs that can be observed. [21] Nor will people say, 'Here it is,' or 'There it is.' For the kingdom of God is in your midst."

The Day of the Son of Man.* [22] Then he said to his disciples, "The time will come when you will long to see one of the days of the Son of Man, and you will not see it. [23] People will say to you, 'Look, there he is,' or 'Look, here he is.' Do not go running after them. [24] For just as lightning flashes and lights up the sky from one end to the other, so will the Son of Man be in his day. [25] But first he must endure great suffering and be rejected by this generation.

[26] "Just as it was in the days of Noah, so will it also be in the days of the Son of Man. [27] People were eating and drinking, marrying and being given in marriage, up to the day that Noah entered the ark. Then the flood came and destroyed all of them.

[28] "The same thing happened in the days of Lot. People were eating and drinking, buying and selling, planting and building. [29] But on the day that Lot left Sodom, fire and brimstone rained down from heaven and destroyed all of them.

[30] "It will be like that on the day that the Son of Man is revealed. [31] On that day, the one who is standing on the roof, with his possessions inside, must not come down to collect them, and someone who is in the field must not turn back. [32] Remember Lot's wife. [33] Whoever tries to preserve his life will lose it, and whoever loses his life will save it.

[34] "I tell you, on that night two people will be in one bed. One will be taken and the other will be left. [35] And

there will be two women grinding grain together. One will be taken and the other will be left. [³⁶ Two men will be out in the field. One will be taken and the other will be left.]" *

³⁷ They asked him, "Where, Lord?" He said in reply, "Where the corpse is, there the vultures will gather."

18 The Parable of the Importunate Widow.* ¹ Then Jesus told them a parable about the need for them to pray always and never to lose heart. ² He said, "In a certain town there was a judge who neither feared God nor had any respect for people. ³ In that same town there was a widow who kept coming to him and pleading, 'Grant me justice against my adversary.'

⁴ "For a long time he refused her request, but finally he said to himself, 'Even though I neither fear God nor have any respect for people, ⁵ yet because this widow keeps pestering me, I will see to it that she gets justice. Otherwise, she will keep coming and wear me out.'"

⁶ Then the Lord said, "You have heard what the unjust judge says. ⁷ Will not God, therefore, grant justice to his elect who cry out to him day and night? Will he delay in answering their pleas? ⁸ I tell you, he will grant them justice quickly. But when the Son of Man comes, will he find faith on the earth?"

The Parable of the Pharisee and the Tax Collector.* ⁹ He also told the following parable to some people who prided themselves about their own righteousness and regarded others with contempt: ¹⁰ "Two men went up to the temple to pray. One was a Pharisee and the other was a tax collector. ¹¹ The Pharisee stood up and said this prayer to himself: 'I thank you, God, that I am not like other people—greedy, dishonest, adulterous—or even like this tax collector. ¹² I fast twice a week and pay tithes on all my income.'

¹³ "The tax collector, however, stood some distance away and would not even raise his eyes to heaven. Rather,

he kept beating his breast as he said, 'God, be merciful to me, a sinner.' [14] This man, I tell you, returned to his home justified, whereas the other did not. For everyone who exalts himself will be humbled, but the one who humbles himself will be exalted."

Jesus Blesses the Children.* [15] People were bringing even infants to Jesus so that he might touch them. When the disciples observed this, they rebuked them. [16] However, Jesus called the children to him and said, "Let the little children come to me, and do not hinder them. For it is to such as these that the kingdom of God belongs. [17] Amen, I say to you, whoever does not receive the kingdom of God like a little child will never enter it."

The Rich Young Man. [18] * A certain ruler asked him, "Good Teacher, what must I do to inherit eternal life?" [19] Jesus said to him, "Why do you call me good? No one is good but God alone. [20] You know the commandments: 'Do not commit adultery. Do not kill. Do not steal. Do not bear false witness. Honor your father and your mother.'"

[21] The man replied, "I have kept all these since I was a child." [22] On hearing this, Jesus said to him, "You need to do one further thing. Sell everything you own and distribute the money to the poor, and you will have treasure in heaven. Then come, follow me." [23] But when he heard this, he became sad, because he was very rich.

Danger of Riches. [24] Jesus looked at him and said, "How difficult it is for those who are rich to enter the kingdom of God! [25] Indeed, it is easier for a camel to pass through the eye of a needle than for someone who is rich to enter the kingdom of God." [26] Those who heard this asked, "Then who can be saved?" [27] He replied, "What is impossible for men is possible for God."

The Reward of Renunciation. [28] Peter said to him, "We have given up our homes to follow you." [29] Jesus replied, "Amen, I say to you, there is no one who has given up house or wife or brothers or parents or children for the sake of the kingdom of God [30] who will not receive many times as much in this age, and eternal life in the age to come."

Jesus Predicts His Passion a Third Time.* ³¹ Then Jesus took the Twelve aside and said to them, "Behold, we are now going up to Jerusalem, and everything that has been written by the Prophets about the Son of Man will be fulfilled. ³² He will be handed over to the Gentiles, and he will be mocked and insulted and spat upon. ³³ After they have scourged him, they will put him to death, and on the third day he will rise again."

³⁴ But they understood nothing of this. Its meaning remained obscure to them, and they failed to comprehend what he was telling them.

Jesus Heals a Blind Man.* ³⁵ As Jesus approached Jericho, a blind man was sitting by the roadside begging. ³⁶ When he heard the crowd going past, he inquired what was happening. ³⁷ They told him, "Jesus of Nazareth is passing by." ³⁸ He shouted, "Jesus, Son of David, have pity on me!" ³⁹ The people in front rebuked him and ordered him to be silent, but he only shouted all the louder, "Son of David, have pity on me!"

⁴⁰ Jesus stopped and ordered that the man be brought to him. And when he had come near, Jesus asked him, ⁴¹ "What do you want me to do for you?" He answered, "Lord, let me receive my sight." ⁴² Jesus said to him, "Receive your sight. Your faith has made you well." ⁴³ Immediately, he received his sight and followed Jesus, praising God. And all the people who witnessed this also gave praise to God.

19 **Jesus and Zacchaeus, the Rich Tax Collector.*** ¹ Jesus entered Jericho and was passing through it. ² A man there, named Zacchaeus, was a chief tax collector and a rich man. ³ He wanted to see who Jesus was, but since he was short in stature, he could not see him because of the crowd. ⁴ Therefore, he ran ahead and climbed a sycamore tree in order to catch a glimpse of him for he was going to pass that way.

JESUS HEALS A BLIND BEGGAR—"Jesus asked him, 'What do you want me to do for you?' He answered, 'Lord, let me receive my sight.' Jesus said to him, 'Receive your sight. Your faith has made you well'" (Lk 18:40-42).

THE CLEANSING OF THE TEMPLE—"Then [Jesus] entered the temple and began to drive out those who were engaging in selling, saying to them, 'It is written, "My house shall be a house of prayer," but you have made it a den of thieves' " (Lk 19:45-46).

⁵ When he reached that spot, Jesus looked up and said to him, "Zacchaeus, hurry and come down, for I must stay at your house today." ⁶ Zacchaeus came down quickly and welcomed him joyfully.

⁷ When the people observed this, they began to complain, saying, "He has gone to be the guest of a man who is a sinner." ⁸ But Zacchaeus stood there and said to the Lord, "Behold, Lord, I intend to give half of everything I possess to the poor, and if I have defrauded someone of anything, I will repay that amount four times over."

⁹ Then Jesus said to him, "Today salvation has come to this house, because this man too is a son of Abraham. ¹⁰ For the Son of Man has come to seek out and to save what was lost."

The Parable of the Ten Gold Coins.* ¹¹ While the people were listening to him speak, Jesus went on to tell them a parable, because now he was near Jerusalem and because they thought that the kingdom of God might appear immediately. ¹² He said, "A man of noble birth was preparing to go to a distant country to receive a kingdom and then return. ¹³ So he summoned ten of his servants and gave them ten gold coins,* instructing them, 'Trade with the money I have given you until I return.' ¹⁴ But the citizens of his country hated him and sent a delegation after him to give this message, 'We do not want this man to be our king.'

¹⁵ "When he returned after having been made king, he sent for the servants to whom he had given the money to ascertain what profit they had made through their trading. ¹⁶ The first came forward and said, 'Sir, your money has increased tenfold in value.' ¹⁷ He said to him, 'Well done, my good servant. Because you have proved trustworthy in this very small matter, you shall be in charge of ten cities.'

¹⁸ "Next, the second servant came forward and said, 'Sir, your money has increased fivefold in value.' ¹⁹ He said to him, 'You shall be in charge of five cities.'

²⁰ "Then the third one came forward, saying, 'Sir, here is your money. I kept it wrapped up in a handkerchief. ²¹ For I was afraid of you, because you are a hard man. You take out what you did not put down, and you reap what you did not sow.'

²² "The master said to him, 'I will condemn you by your own words, you wicked servant. You knew I was a hard man, taking out what I did not put down, and reaping what I did not sow. ²³ Why then did you not deposit my money into a bank so that on my return I could have drawn it out with interest?'

²⁴ "Then he said to those standing by, 'Take the money from him and give it to the one with the ten gold coins.' ²⁵ They said to him, 'But sir, he already has ten gold coins.' ²⁶ He replied, 'I tell you, to everyone who has, more will be given, but from the one who has not, even what he does have will be taken away. ²⁷ But as for those enemies of mine who did not want me for their king, bring them here and put them to death in my presence.' "

V: THE ACTIVITY OF JESUS AT JERUSALEM*

Jesus Enters Jerusalem as the Messiah.* ²⁸ After he had said this, Jesus proceeded on his journey up to Jerusalem. ²⁹ As he drew near to Bethphage and Bethany at the place called the Mount of Olives, he sent off two of the disciples, saying, ³⁰ "Go into the village directly ahead, and upon entering it, you will find tied there a colt on which no one has ever ridden. Untie it and bring it here. ³¹ If anyone asks you, 'Why are you untying it?' simply say, 'The Lord needs it.' "

³² The two disciples who had been sent went off and found everything just as he had told them. ³³ As they were untying the colt, its owners asked them, "Why are you untying the colt?" ³⁴ They answered, "The Lord needs it."

³⁵ Then they brought the colt to Jesus, and after spreading their cloaks over the colt, they helped Jesus to mount it. ³⁶ As he rode along, people kept spreading their cloaks

on the road. ³⁷ And when he approached the downward path of the Mount of Olives, the entire multitude of his disciples began to praise God joyfully with a loud voice for all the mighty works they had seen him perform, ³⁸ proclaiming:

> "Blessed is the king
> who comes in the name of the Lord.
> Peace in heaven
> and glory in the highest heavens."

³⁹ Some of the Pharisees in the crowd said to him, "Teacher, rebuke your disciples." ⁴⁰ He answered, "I tell you, if they keep silent, the stones will cry out."

The Lament over Jerusalem.* ⁴¹ As Jesus drew near and beheld the city, he wept over it, ⁴² saying, "If only you had recognized on this day what would bring you peace! But now it is hidden from your sight. ⁴³ Indeed, the days will come upon you when your enemies will raise up fortifications all around you and hem you in on every side. ⁴⁴ They will smash you to the ground, you and your children with you, and they will not leave one stone upon another in you, because you did not recognize the time of your visitation."

Jesus Cleanses the Temple.* ⁴⁵ Then he entered the temple and began to drive out those who were engaging in selling, ⁴⁶ saying to them, "It is written,

> 'My house shall be a house of prayer,'
> but you have made it a den of thieves."

⁴⁷ Every day he was teaching in the temple. But the chief priests, the scribes, and the leaders of the people plotted to kill him. ⁴⁸ However, they were unable to do so because all the people hung on his every word.

A: Verbal Clashes*

20 The Authority of Jesus Questioned.*

¹ One day as Jesus was teaching in the temple and proclaiming the good news, the chief priests and scribes, accompanied by the

elders, approached and ² said to him, "Tell us by what authority you are doing these things. Or who is it that gave you this authority?" ³ He said to them in reply, "I will also ask you one question. Tell me: ⁴ Did John's baptism originate from heaven or from men?"

⁵ The question caused them to discuss it among themselves, saying, "If we say: 'From heaven,' he will say, 'Why did you not believe him?' ⁶ But if we say: 'From men,' all the people will stone us, for they are convinced that John was a prophet."

⁷ Therefore, they answered that they did not know where it came from. ⁸ And Jesus said to them, "Then neither shall I tell you by what authority I do these things."

The Parable of the Tenants.* ⁹ Then Jesus began to tell the people this parable: "A man planted a vineyard, leased it to tenants, and went off on a journey for a long period.

¹⁰ "When the time arrived, he sent a servant to the tenants to receive his share of the produce of the vineyard. But the tenants beat the servant and sent him away empty-handed. ¹¹ Again, he sent another servant, but him they also beat and treated shamefully and sent away empty-handed. ¹² Then he sent a third servant, but him too they wounded and cast out.

¹³ "Then the owner of the vineyard said, 'What shall I do? I will send my beloved son. Perhaps they will respect him.' ¹⁴ But when the tenants saw him, they said to one another, 'This is the heir. Let us kill him so that the inheritance will be ours.' ¹⁵ And so they threw him out of the vineyard and killed him.

"What then will the owner of the vineyard do to them? ¹⁶ He will come and put those tenants to death and give the vineyard to others."

When the people heard this, they said, "God forbid!" ¹⁷ But Jesus looked directly at them and said, "Then what is the meaning of that which is written:

'The stone that the builders rejected
    has become the cornerstone'?

¹⁸ Everyone who falls on that stone will be broken into pieces, and the one on whom it falls will be crushed."

¹⁹ The scribes and the chief priests realized that this parable was directed at them, and they wanted to seize him at that very hour, but they feared the people.

God or Caesar.* ²⁰ So they watched him closely and sent spies who pretended to be honorable men. They intended to trap Jesus in something he might say so that they could hand him over to the authority and jurisdiction of the governor.

²¹ They posed this question to him: "Teacher, we know that you say and teach what is right. Moreover, you show no partiality to anyone but teach the way of God in accordance with the truth. ²² Is it lawful or not for us to pay taxes to Caesar?"

²³ Jesus saw through their duplicity and said to them, ²⁴ "Show me a coin.* Whose image is this, and whose inscription?" They replied, "Caesar's." ²⁵ He said to them, "Give to Caesar what is due to Caesar, and to God what is due to God." ²⁶ They found they could not trap him by anything he said in the presence of the people, and, stunned at his reply, they fell silent.

Marriage and the Resurrection.* ²⁷ Then some Sadducees, who assert that there is no resurrection, approached him and posed this question: ²⁸ "Teacher, Moses wrote down for us that if a man's brother dies, having a wife but no children, the man must marry his brother's wife and raise up children for his brother. ²⁹ Now there were seven brothers. The first married a woman but died childless. ³⁰ Then the second ³¹ and the third married the widow, and it was the same with all seven: they all died leaving no children. ³² Last of all, the woman also died. ³³ Now at the resurrection, whose wife will the woman be, inasmuch as all seven had her?"

³⁴ Jesus said to them, "The children of this age marry and are given in marriage, ³⁵ but those who are judged worthy of taking part in the age to come and in the res-

urrection of the dead will neither marry nor be given in marriage. [36] They are no longer subject to death, for they are like angels; and they are the children of God because they are children of the resurrection.

[37] "That the dead are raised Moses himself showed in the account about the bush where he calls the Lord the God of Abraham, the God of Isaac, and the God of Jacob. [38] He is not the God of the dead, but of the living, for in his sight all are alive."

[39] Some of the scribes then said, "Teacher, you have answered well." [40] And they no longer dared to ask him anything.

Jesus Is Lord.* [41] Then Jesus said to them, "How can they say that the Christ is the Son of David? [42] For David himself says in the Book of Psalms:

'The Lord said to my Lord:
"Sit at my right hand
[43]   until I make your enemies your footstool." '

[44] David thus calls him 'Lord'; so how can he be his son?"

Denunciation of the Scribes.* [45] While all the people were listening, Jesus said to his disciples, [46] "Beware of the scribes who like to walk around in long robes and who love to be greeted respectfully in the marketplaces, and to have the best seats in the synagogues and the places of honor at banquets. [47] They devour the houses of widows, while for the sake of appearance they recite lengthy prayers. They will receive the severest possible condemnation."

21   The Poor Widow's Offering.*

[1] Looking up, Jesus saw wealthy people putting their offerings into the treasury, [2] and he also noticed a poor widow putting in two copper coins. [3] He said: "Truly I tell you, this poor widow has given more than all the rest. [4] For the others have all contributed out of their abundance, but she out of her poverty has given all that she had to live on."

B: The Destruction of the Temple and the Return of Christ*

Jesus Announces the Destruction of the Temple.* ⁵ When some people were talking about how the temple was adorned with beautiful stones and votive offerings, Jesus remarked, ⁶ "As for all these things that you are gazing at now, the time will come when not one stone here will be left upon another; everything will be thrown down."

The Signs of the End. ⁷ ᵐ They then asked him, "Teacher, when will this happen? And what will be the sign that it is about to take place?" ⁸ He answered, "Take care not to be deceived. For many will come in my name, saying, 'I am he,' and 'The time is near.' Do not follow them. ⁹ And when you hear of wars and insurrections, do not be terrified, for those things are bound to take place first, but the end will not follow immediately."

¹⁰ Then he added, "Nation will rise against nation and kingdom against kingdom. ¹¹ There will be tremendous earthquakes, famines, and plagues in various places, as well as dreadful portents and great signs from heaven.

The Coming Persecution. ¹² "But before all this happens, they will seize you and persecute you. You will be handed over to synagogues and imprisoned, and you will be brought before kings and governors because of my name. ¹³ This will give you an opportunity to bear witness to me. ¹⁴ But do not even consider preparing your defense beforehand, ¹⁵ for I myself will give you a depth of wisdom and eloquence that none of your adversaries will be able to resist or contradict.

¹⁶ "You will be betrayed even by parents and brothers, relatives and friends, and some of you will be put to death. ¹⁷ You will be hated by all because of my name, ¹⁸ but not a hair of your head will be lost. ¹⁹ By standing firm you will gain life.

The Great Trial.* ²⁰ "When you see Jerusalem surrounded by armies, you may be certain that her desolation is near. ²¹ Then those who are in Judea must flee to the mountains, and those who are within the city must escape from its boundaries, and those who are in country areas must not return. ²² For those will be days of retribution when all that is written will come to pass.

²³ "Woe to those who are pregnant and those who are nursing infants in those days. For there will be great distress on the earth, and terrible wrath shall afflict this people. ²⁴ They will fall by the sword and be carried away as captives among all the nations, and Jerusalem will be trampled underfoot by the Gentiles until the times of the Gentiles have been fulfilled.

The Coming of the Son of Man. ²⁵ * "There will be signs in the sun, the moon, and the stars, and on earth nations will be in great distress, bewildered at the roaring of the sea and its waves. ²⁶ Men will grow faint with terror and apprehension at what is coming upon the earth, for the powers of the heavens will be shaken. ²⁷ And then they will see the Son of Man coming in a cloud with power and great glory. ²⁸ When these things begin to take place, look up and hold your heads high, because the time of your redemption is drawing near."

The Parable of the Fig Tree. ²⁹ Then he told them this parable: "Look at the fig tree or indeed at any other tree. ³⁰ As soon as it begins to bud, you know that summer is already near. ³¹ In the same way, when you see these things come to pass, know that the kingdom of God is near. ³² Amen, I say to you, this generation will not pass away until all these things have taken place. * ³³ Heaven and earth will pass away, but my words will never pass away.

Exhortation To Be Vigilant. * ³⁴ "Be on your guard lest your hearts be weighed down by carousing and drunkenness and the anxieties of this life and that day will catch you unawares, ³⁵ like a trap. For that day will come upon everyone in the world. ³⁶ Be vigilant at all times, praying for the strength to survive all those things that will take place and to stand in the presence of the Son of Man."

Jesus' Last Days in Jerusalem. * ³⁷ Each day Jesus was teaching in the temple, but every evening he would go forth and spend the night on the hill called the Mount of Olives. [38] And all the people would rise early every morning to listen to him in the temple.

VI. THE PASSION AND RESURRECTION*

22 **The Conspiracy against Jesus.*** [1] Now the feast of Unleavened Bread, known as the Passover, was drawing near, [2] and the chief priests and the scribes were looking for some way to put Jesus to death, for they were afraid of the people.

Judas Betrays Jesus.* [3] Then Satan entered into Judas, called Iscariot, who was one of the Twelve. [4] And he went to the chief priests and temple guards to discuss how he might betray Jesus to them. [5] They were delighted and agreed to give him money. [6] He accepted their offer and began to look for an opportunity to betray him to them when no crowd was present.

A: The Last Supper*

Preparations for the Passover.* [7] When the day of the feast of Unleavened Bread arrived, on which the Passover lamb had to be sacrificed, [8] Jesus sent Peter and John, saying, "Go and make the preparations for us to eat the Passover." [9] They asked him, "Where do you want us to make the preparations?"

[10] He replied, "When you enter the city, a man will meet you carrying a jug of water. Follow him into the house that he enters [11] and say to the master of the house, 'The Teacher says this to you: "Where is the room where I can eat the Passover with my disciples?"'" [12] Then he will show you a large upper room that is furnished. Make the preparations there." [13] They went forth and found everything just as he had told them, and they prepared the Passover.

The Last Supper.* [14] When the hour came, Jesus took his place at table along with the apostles. [15] He said to them, "I have eagerly desired to eat this Passover with you before I suffer. [16] For I tell you that from this moment on I shall never eat it again until it is fulfilled in the kingdom of God."

[17] Then he took a cup, and after giving thanks he said, "Take this and share it among yourselves. [18] For I tell you that from this moment I will not drink of the fruit of the vine until the kingdom of God comes."

Jesus Gives His Body and His Blood.* [19] Then he took bread, and after giving thanks he broke it and gave it to them, saying, "This is my body, which will be given for you. Do this in memory of me." [20] And he did the same with the cup after supper, saying, "This cup is the new covenant in my blood, which will be poured out for you.

The Betrayer Foretold.* [21] "But behold, the hand of the one who will betray me is here with me on the table. [22] The Son of Man goes on his appointed path, but woe to that man by whom he is betrayed." [23] Then they began to question among themselves as to which one of them might do this.

The Disciples Are To Serve on Earth.* [24] Then a dispute also broke out among them as to which one of them should be considered the greatest. [25] Jesus said to them, "The kings of the Gentiles lord it over them, and those who exercise authority over them are given the title of 'Benefactor.' *

[26] "But it must not be so with you. Rather, the greatest among you should be like the youngest, and the leader must be like the one who serves. [27] For who is greater— the one seated at table or the one who serves? Surely, the one who sits at table. And yet I am in your midst as one who serves.

Judges of the Twelve Tribes.* [28] "You are the ones who have stood by my side in my trials, [29] and now I confer on you a kingdom just as my Father has conferred one on me. [30] In my kingdom, you will eat and drink at my table, and you will sit on thrones, judging the twelve tribes of Israel. *

THE UPPER ROOM—The room above is a medieval structure marking the traditional site in the southwest corner of the Upper City of Jerusalem where the Last Supper took place. (See Lk 22:7-13.)

MOUNT OF OLIVES—View of Mount of Olives showing the church built in the Garden of Gethsemane (foreground), looking from the Golden Gate and the Kidron Valley.

GARDEN OF GETHSEMANE—Close-up of the Garden of Gethsemane where Christ's Agony took place, showing part of the Basilica of All Nations on the left and the city wall with the Golden Gate on the hill beyond. (See Lk 22:41-45.)

Peter's Denial Foretold.* [31] "Simon, Simon, behold, Satan has desired to sift all of you like wheat. [32] But I have prayed that your own faith may not fail. And once you have turned back, you must strengthen your brethren." [33] Simon said to him, "Lord, I am ready to go with you to prison and to death." [34] Jesus replied, "I tell you, Peter, before the cock crows today, you will deny three times that you know me."

Instructions for the Time of Crisis.* [35] Then Jesus said to them, "When I sent you forth without a money bag or sack or sandals, were you ever in need of anything?" They answered, "No, not a thing." [36] He then remarked, "But now, the one who has a money bag should take it with him, as well as a sack. And if you do not have a sword, sell your cloak and purchase one.

[37] "For I tell you that this Scripture must be fulfilled in me: 'He was numbered with the wicked.' Indeed, everything written about me is being fulfilled." [38] They said, "See, Lord, here are two swords." He said to them, "That is enough."

B: The Passion

The Agony in the Garden.* [39] Jesus then went forth and made his way, as was his custom, to the Mount of Olives, and the disciples followed him. [40] When he reached the place, he said to them, "Pray that you may not enter into temptation." [41] After withdrawing from them about a stone's throw, he knelt down and prayed, [42] saying, "Father, if you are willing, take this cup from me. Yet not my will but yours be done."

[43] * Then an angel from heaven appeared to him and gave him strength. [44] In his anguish, he prayed so fervently that his sweat became like great drops of blood falling on the ground.

[45] When he rose from prayer and returned to the disciples, he found them sleeping, exhausted by grief. [46] He said to them, "Why are you sleeping? Get up and pray that you may not enter into temptation."

Jesus Is Betrayed and Arrested.* [47] While he was still speaking, a crowd of men suddenly approached, and the one called Judas, one of the Twelve, was leading them. He came up to Jesus to kiss him, [48] but Jesus said, "Judas, would you betray the Son of Man with a kiss?"

[49] When Jesus' disciples realized what was about to happen, they asked, "Lord, should we strike with our swords?" [50] And one of them struck a servant of the high priest, slicing off his right ear. [51] But Jesus said, "Stop! No more of this!" He then touched the servant's ear and healed him.

[52] Then Jesus said to the chief priests, the officers of the temple guard, and the elders who had come for him, "Why are you coming forth with swords and clubs as though I were a bandit? [53] When I was with you day after day in the temple, you did not raise a hand against me. But this is the hour for you and the power of darkness." *

Peter Denies Jesus.* [54] Then they arrested Jesus and led him away. They brought him into the house of the high priest, and Peter followed at a distance. [55] Lighting a fire in the middle of the courtyard, they sat around it, and Peter sat with them.

[56] A servant girl saw him sitting by the fire, looked closely at him, and said, "This man also was with him." [57] But he denied it, saying, "Woman, I do not know him." [58] A short time later, someone else saw him and said, "You too are one of them," but Peter replied, "No, I am not."

[59] About an hour later, another person strongly insisted, "This man was unquestionably with him, for he is a Galilean." [60] Peter said, "My friend, I do not know what you are talking about." At that very moment, while he was still speaking, a cock crowed, [61] and the Lord turned and looked at Peter. Then Peter recalled the word that the Lord had spoken to him: "Before the cock crows today, you will deny me three times." [62] And he went out and wept uncontrollably.

⁶³ The men who were guarding Jesus began to mock him and to beat him. ⁶⁴ They also blindfolded him and kept asking him, "Prophesy! Who hit you?" ⁶⁵ And they continued to taunt him with insult after insult.

Jesus before the Sanhedrin. * ⁶⁶ When the dawn came, the council of the elders of the people, both the chief priests and the scribes, assembled, and they brought him before their Sanhedrin.* ⁶⁷ Then they said, "If you are the Christ, tell us!" He replied, "If I tell you, you will not believe; ⁶⁸ and if I question you, you will not answer. ⁶⁹ But from now on, the Son of Man will be seated at the right hand of the power of God."

⁷⁰ All of them asked, "Are you then the Son of God?" He replied, "It is you who say that I am." ⁷¹ Then they said, "What need do we have for any further testimony? We have heard it ourselves from his own lips."

23 Jesus before Pilate.* ¹ Then the entire assembly rose and brought Jesus before Pilate. ² They began to accuse him, saying, "We charge this man with subverting our nation, opposing the payment of taxes to Caesar, and claiming that he is the Christ, a king." ³ Pilate asked him, "Are you the king of the Jews?" He replied, "You have said so."

⁴ Pilate then said to the chief priests and the crowds, "I find no evidence of a crime in this man." ⁵ But they continued to insist, saying, "He is stirring up the people by his teaching throughout all Judea, from Galilee, where he started, all the way to here."

⁶ When Pilate heard this, he asked if the man was a Galilean, ⁷ and upon learning that he came under Herod's jurisdiction, he sent him to Herod who was also in Jerusalem at that time.

Jesus before Herod. * ⁸ Herod was delighted when he saw Jesus, for he had heard about him and had been hoping for some time to see him and perhaps to witness him perform some sign. ⁹ He questioned him at length, but Jesus gave him no reply.

¹⁰ The chief priests and the scribes meanwhile were present, and they vehemently made accusations against him. ¹¹ Herod and his soldiers treated him with contempt and mocked him. Then Herod had him clothed in an elegant robe and sent him back to Pilate. ¹² That very day Herod and Pilate became friends, although previously they had been enemies.

Jesus before Pilate Again. ¹³ * Pilate then summoned the chief priests and the rulers and the people, ¹⁴ and said to them, "You brought this man before me and accused him of inciting the people to rebellion. I have examined him here in your presence and have not found him guilty of any of the charges you have brought against him. ¹⁵ Nor did Herod, for he has sent him back to us. It is clear that he has done nothing deserving of death. ¹⁶ Therefore, I will have him scourged and then release him."

Jesus Is Condemned to Death. [¹⁷ Now Pilate was obliged to release one man to them at the time of the festival.] * ¹⁸ And then the crowd all shouted in unison, "Away with this man! Release Barabbas to us!" ¹⁹ (He had been imprisoned for an insurrection that had occurred in the city as well as for murder.)

²⁰ In his desire to release Jesus, Pilate again pleaded with them, ²¹ but, they continued to shout, "Crucify him! Crucify him!" ²² A third time he addressed them: "Why? What evil has he done? I have not found in him any crime that deserves death. Therefore, I will have him scourged and let him go."

²³ However, with loud shouts they continued to insist that he should be crucified, and their voices prevailed. ²⁴ Pilate ordered that what they wanted was to be granted. ²⁵ He released the man they asked for, who had been thrown into prison for insurrection and murder, and he handed over Jesus to them to deal with as they wished.

The Way of the Cross. * ²⁶ As they led him away, they seized a man from Cyrene named Simon, who was returning from the country. They put the cross on his

THE WAY OF THE CROSS (VIA DOLOROSA)—The Sorrowful Way taken by Jesus on his journey to Calvary with his cross. In the distance is the 5th Station of the Cross, chapel of Simon the Cyrenian who helped Christ carry the cross. (See Lk 23:26.)

MOUNT OF THE ASCENSION—Presented above is an overall view of the Mount of Olives and surroundings where Jesus led his disciples before his Ascension. The Church of the Ascension rises in the background. (See Lk 24:50-51.)

ANCIENT JEWISH TOMB—The tomb pictured above is located a few miles west of Jerusalem. Note the large stone used to seal the entrance. The tomb in which Jesus was laid was probably similar to this one. (See Lk 24:2.)

back and forced him to carry it behind Jesus. ²⁷ A large number of people followed Jesus, among them many women who were mourning and lamenting over him.

²⁸ But he turned to them and said, "Daughters of Jerusalem, do not weep for me. Weep rather for yourselves and for your children. ²⁹ For behold, the days are coming when people will say, 'Blessed are the barren, the wombs that never bore children and the breasts that never nursed.' ³⁰ Then they will begin to say to the mountains, 'Fall on us!' and to the hills, 'Cover us!' ³¹ For if they do these things when the wood is green, what will happen when it is dry?"

Jesus Is Crucified.* ³² There were also two others, both criminals, who were led away to be executed with him. ³³ When they came to the place called The Skull, they crucified * Jesus there along with the two criminals, one on his right and the other on his left. ³⁴ Then Jesus said, "Father, forgive them, for they do not know what they are doing." * And they cast lots to divide his garments.

³⁵ The people stood there watching.* Meanwhile, the rulers jeered at him and said, "He saved others. Let him save himself if he is the Christ of God, the Chosen One." ³⁶ Even the soldiers mocked him. As they came forward to offer him sour wine, ³⁷ they said, "If you are the King of the Jews, save yourself!" ³⁸ There was also an inscription above his head that said, "This is the King of the Jews."

³⁹ One of the criminals hanging there taunted Jesus, saying, "Are you not the Christ? Save yourself and us!" ⁴⁰ But the other rebuked him, "Have you no fear of God, since you are under the same sentence? ⁴¹ In our case, we have been condemned justly, for we are getting what we deserve for our deeds. But this man has committed no wrong." ⁴² Then he said, "Jesus, remember me when you come into your kingdom." ⁴³ Jesus said to him, "Amen, I say to you, today you will be with me in Paradise." *

Jesus Dies on the Cross.* ⁴⁴ It was now about noon, and darkness came over the whole land until three in the afternoon, [45] for the sun was darkened. Then the veil of the temple was torn in two. [46] He cried out, "Father, into your hands I commend my spirit." And with these words he breathed his last.*

[47] On seeing what had taken place, the centurion praised God and said, "Surely, this man was innocent." [48] When all the people who had gathered there to witness the spectacle saw what had happened, they returned home beating their breasts.* [49] However, all his acquaintances, including the women who had followed him from Galilee, stood at a distance and watched all these events.

Jesus Is Buried.* [50] Now there was a good and upright man named Joseph * who was a member of the council. [51] However, he had not agreed to their plan and the action they had taken. He came from the Jewish town of Arimathea, and he was awaiting the kingdom of God. [52] This man went to Pilate and requested the body of Jesus. [53] Then he took it down, wrapped it in a linen shroud, and laid him in a tomb that had been hewn out of rock in which no one had ever been interred. [54] It was the Day of Preparation, and the Sabbath was about to begin.

[55] The women who had accompanied Jesus from Galilee followed Joseph. They saw the tomb and how his body was laid in it. [56] Then they returned and prepared spices and ointments. But on the Sabbath they rested in obedience to the commandment.

C. The Resurrection

24 **Jesus Rises from the Dead.*** [1] At daybreak on the first day of the week, the women came to the tomb with the spices they had prepared. [2] They found the stone rolled away from the tomb, [3] but when they went inside, they did not find the body of the Lord Jesus.

[4] While they stood there wondering about this, suddenly two men in dazzling clothes appeared at their side. [5] They were terrified and bowed their faces to the ground,

but the men said to them, "Why do you look among the dead for one who is alive? [6] He is not here. He has been raised. Remember what he told you while he was still in Galilee: [7] that the Son of Man must be handed over to sinners and be crucified and rise again on the third day." [8] Then they recalled his words.

[9] When they returned from the tomb, they reported all these things to the Eleven and to all the others. [10] It was Mary Magdalene, Joanna, Mary the mother of James, and the other women with them who told this to the apostles. [11] However, this story of theirs seemed to be nonsense, and the apostles did not believe them. [12] Nonetheless, Peter got up and ran to the tomb. Bending over, he looked inside and saw only the linen cloths. Then he returned home, wondering what had occurred.

Jesus Appears to Two Disciples at Emmaus.* [13] Now that same day two of them were on their way to a village called Emmaus, about seven miles from Jerusalem, [14] and they were talking with each other about all these things that had occurred. [15] While they were conversing and discussing these events, Jesus himself drew near and walked along with them, [16] but their eyes were prevented from recognizing him.

[17] He asked them, "What are you discussing with each other as you walk along?" They stood still, their faces filled with sadness. [18] Then one of them, whose name was Cleopas, answered him, "Are you the only stranger in Jerusalem who is not aware of all the things that have taken place there in these days?" [19] When he asked, "What things?" they replied, "The things that happened to Jesus of Nazareth, who was a prophet powerful in word and deed before God and all the people, [20] and how our chief priests and rulers handed him over to be sentenced to death and had him crucified.

[21] "We had been hoping that he would be the one who would redeem Israel. And what is more, this is the third day since all of this took place. [22] Some women from our

group have now given us astounding news. They went to the tomb early this morning, [23] but they failed to find his body. When they returned, they told us that they had seen a vision of angels who reported that he was alive. [24] Some of our companions went to the tomb and found everything exactly as the women had said, but they did not see him."

[25] Then he said to them, "How foolish you are, and how slow to believe all that the Prophets have spoken! [26] Was it not necessary that the Christ should suffer these things and enter into his glory?" [27] Then, beginning with Moses and going through all the Prophets, he interpreted for them all the passages from the Scriptures that pertained to him.

[28] As they approached the village to which they were going, he acted as though he would be going further. [29] However, they urged him strongly, "Stay with us, for it is nearly evening and the day is almost over." And so he went in to stay with them.

[30] When he was at table with them, he took bread, blessed and broke it, and gave it to them. [31] Then their eyes were opened and they recognized him, but he vanished from their sight. [32] They said to each other, "Were not our hearts burning within us while he spoke to us on the road and opened the Scriptures to us?"

[33] They set out immediately and returned to Jerusalem, where they found gathered together the Eleven and their companions [34] who were saying, "The Lord has truly been raised, and he has appeared to Simon!" * [35] Then the two described what had happened on their journey and how he had made himself known to them in the breaking of the bread.

Jesus Appears to the Disciples in Jerusalem. * [36] While they were still conversing about this, Jesus himself stood in their midst and said to them, "Peace be with you." [37] Startled and terrified, they thought that they were seeing a ghost.

[38] He said to them, "Why are you troubled, and why are doubts arising in your hearts? [39] Look at my hands and my feet. It is I myself. Touch me and see. For a ghost does not have flesh and bones as you can see that I have." [40] And when he had said this, he showed them his hands and his feet.

[41] In spite of their joy and amazement, they were still incredulous. So he said to them, "Do you have anything here to eat?" [42] They gave him a piece of fish, [43] and he took it and ate it in their presence.

[44] Then he said to them, "This is what I meant when I told you while I was still with you: Everything written about me in the Law of Moses, the Prophets, and the Psalms must be fulfilled." [45] Thereupon, he opened their minds to understand the Scriptures.

[46] And he said to them, "Thus it is written that the Christ would suffer and on the third day rise from the dead, [47] and that in his name repentance and forgiveness of sins are to be proclaimed to all nations, beginning from Jerusalem. [48] You are witnesses to all these things.

[49] "And behold, I am sending upon you the gift promised by my Father. Therefore, stay here in the city until you have been clothed with power from on high."

Jesus Ascends to Heaven.* [50] Then he led them out as far as Bethany, and lifting up his hands he blessed them. [51] While he was blessing them, he departed from them and was taken up to heaven. [52] They worshiped him and then returned to Jerusalem filled with great joy, [53] and they were continually in the temple praising God.

THE GOSPEL ACCORDING TO JOHN
THE WAY, THE TRUTH, AND THE LIFE

Who had the ability to compose a Gospel so different from the others? It took a remarkable personality to tackle such a work. On two occasions the Book itself specifically offers a guarantee provided by an eyewitness (Jn 1:14; 19:35). A disciple appears several times whose name is persistently omitted and who is called simply "the disciple whom Jesus loved" (Jn 13:23; 19:26, 27, 35; 21:7, 20, 24). There is nothing to prevent his being identified with the "other disciple" (Jn 18:15-16; see Jn 1:35-39), who appears with Peter but whose name is not given.

We have reason, then, to be somewhat puzzled. But think a bit. This Gospel cites the names of apostles (although it never gives a complete list); but it is a surprising fact that it never names John, although, according to all the other New Testament writings, he had a prominent place, alongside Peter, in the group of the Twelve. It is, then, a short, though not strictly demonstrable, step to identify the anonymous disciple of the fourth Gospel with John the apostle. And, in fact, since its early days, the Christian tradition has attributed the Gospel to John.

The fourth Gospel is written in Greek, in unaffected language and a style that is often solemn, sometimes monotonous. The work matured over a lengthy period, in a setting and an age in which many religious currents could have exerted an influence on it. Examples of such influences are an unusual vocabulary, distinctive symbols, and the very content of the themes developed. It is possible to identify Jewish and Christian motifs, an echo of the professions of faith and the Liturgy, perhaps a homiletic style, and even words that were in common usage at that time.

As we have it today, the fourth Gospel was, in all likelihood, published around the nineties of our era for the Christians of Asia Minor.

232

The fourth Gospel is rather different from the Synoptic Gospels. The latter pile up stories, miracles, and sayings of Jesus until they have made us familiar with that world which we all know. In the fourth Gospel, on the other hand, the selection of incidents is limited, and lengthy discourses are connected with them; almost everything takes place in Jerusalem and on the occasion of a feast; finally, the language is rather different. All this cannot be a matter of chance.

In fact, John seeks to express the message through especially significant incidents; these he calls "signs." These signs, seven in number, give the book its structure: seven sections, the last of which is in turn divided into seven parts. The discourses bring to light, and deepen our understanding of, the ideas that the signs suggest.

As a matter of fact, the incidents chosen by John do not follow in chronological order. Rather, they all contribute to highlighting the fundamental aspects of the mystery of Jesus. Despite this, the method of presentation chosen by the author does not detract from the historical truth of the facts reported. These incidents, which seem to be constructed with the same freedom as is shown in the discourses, have preserved many accurate details, and excavations in Palestine have confirmed some that are reported only in this Gospel.

John reaches his great insights into the life of Jesus in the light of Easter or, more accurately, in the light of the cross. It is in this perspective that he interprets the events and develops the discourses.

The life of Jesus is presented as an epiphany, the manifestation of the Word of God. The flesh is unable to hide the glory of the Son of God. This glory, almost in spite of itself, pierces through the veil of Christ's humanity. Thus when, during the Passion, Jesus presents himself to those who have come to arrest him, the latter draw back and fall on the ground. What is the reason if not that they have encountered the Lord in the person of Jesus.

In spite of this glorious aspect, John's Gospel is intensely dramatic. The life of Jesus is portrayed as a ruthless contest of cosmic proportions, a merciless duel between Light and Darkness, between Life and Death, between the Son of God and the Prince of this world. The conflict grows in intensity and culminates in the condemnation of Jesus. At that moment, darkness seems to have swallowed the Light. But it is precisely at that moment, at that "hour," that the perspectives are suddenly reversed. Paradoxically, the Condemned reveals himself as the Judge of the world, the Crucified as the Victor. The hour of death is precisely that of glory.

The Gospel according to John may be divided as follows:

I: *A New Creation (1:1—2:12)*

II: *Worship of the Father in Spirit and Truth (2:13—4:54)*

III: *Jesus Restores the Work of God (5:1-47)*

IV: *The Bread of Life (6:1-71)*

V: *The Light of the World (7:1—9:41)*

VI: *The Shepherd Who Gives Up His Life (10:1—11:54)*

VII: *The True Passover That Brings About the Salvation of Humankind (11:55—20:31)*

Epilogue: (21:1-25)

I. A NEW CREATION*

A: In the Beginning Was the Word*

1

The Word of God, Source of Life*

1   In the beginning was the Word,
and the Word was with God,
and the Word was God.

2   He was with God in the very beginning.

3   Through him all things came into existence,
and without him there was nothing.
That which came to be

4   found life in him,
and the life was the light of the human race.

5   The light shines in the darkness,
and the darkness has been unable to overcome it.

Faith Means Welcoming the Word of God Made Man.* [6] A man appeared, sent by God, whose name was John.* [7] He came as a witness to give testimony to the light, so that through him all might come to believe. [8] He himself was not the light; his role was to bear witness to the light.

[9]   The true light that enlightens everyone
      was coming into the world.
[10]   He was in the world,
      the world had come into existence through him,
      yet the world did not recognize him.
[11]   He came to his own,
      but his own did not accept him.
[12]   However, to those who did accept him
      and who believed in his name
      he granted the power to become children of God,
[13]   who were born not from blood
      or human desire or human will,
      but from God.
[14]   And the Word became flesh
      and dwelt among us.
      And we saw his glory,
      the glory as of the Father's only Son,
      full of grace and truth.

Jesus Christ, Fullness of Truth.* [15] John testified to him, proclaiming, "This is the one of whom I said, 'The one who comes after me ranks ahead of me because he existed before me.'"

[16]   From his fullness we have all received,
      grace upon grace.
[17]   For the Law was given through Moses,
      but grace and truth came through Jesus Christ.
[18]   No one has ever seen God.
      It is the only Son, God,
      who is at the Father's side,
      who has made him known.

B: Jesus Is the Expected Messiah*

John the Baptist Is Not the Messiah.* [19] This is the testimony offered by John when the Jews* sent priests and

Levites from Jerusalem to ask him, "Who are you?" [20] He confessed, he did not deny, but confessed, "I am not the Christ." * [21] Then they asked him, "Who then are you? Are you Elijah?" * He said, "I am not." "Are you the Prophet?" He answered, "No." [22] Therefore, they said to him, "Who are you, so we may have an answer to give to those who sent us? What do you have to say about yourself?" [23] He replied, in the words of the prophet Isaiah,

> "I am the voice of one crying out in the wilderness,
> 'Make straight the way of the Lord.'"

[24] Some Pharisees were present in this group, [25] and they asked him, "Why then are you baptizing if you are neither the Christ, nor Elijah, nor the Prophet?" [26] John answered them, "I baptize with water; but among you there is one whom you do not know, [27] the one who is coming after me. I am not worthy to loosen the strap of his sandal." [28] This took place in Bethany, beyond the Jordan, where John was baptizing.

Behold, the Lamb of God, Who Takes Away the Sin of the World. * [29] The next day John saw Jesus coming toward him, and he said,

> "Behold, the Lamb of God,
> who takes away the sin of the world
[30] This is the one of whom I said,
> 'After me is coming one
> who ranks ahead of me
> because he existed before me.'
[31] I myself did not know him,*
> but the reason I came to baptize with water
> was so that he might be revealed to Israel."

[32] John also gave this testimony, saying,

> "I saw the Spirit
> descending from heaven like a dove,
> and it came to rest on him.*
[33] I myself did not know him,
> but the one who sent me to baptize with water told
> me,

'The one on whom you see the Spirit descend and
  rest

is the one who is to baptize with the Holy Spirit.' *
34 And I myself have seen and have testified

that this is the Son of God."

We Have Found the Messiah. * [35] The next day John was
standing there with two of his disciples, [36] and as he
watched Jesus pass by, he said, "Behold, the Lamb of
God." [37] On hearing him say this, the two disciples began
to follow Jesus. [38] When Jesus turned and saw them following him, he asked them, "What are you looking for?"
They said to him, "Rabbi" (which, translated, is
"Teacher"), "where are you staying?" [39] He answered
them, "Come and see." So they went and saw where he
was staying, and they remained with him for the rest of
that day. It was about four o'clock in the afternoon.*

[40] One of the two who had heard John speak and had
followed Jesus was Andrew, the brother of Simon Peter.
[41] The first thing Andrew did was to seek out his brother
Simon and say to him, "We have found the Messiah" *
(which, translated, is "Christ"), [42] and he took him to
Jesus. Jesus gazed at him and said, "You are Simon son of
John. You will be called Cephas" * (which, translated, is
"Peter").

[43] The next day Jesus * decided to go to Galilee. Encountering Philip, he said to him, "Follow me." [44] Philip
came from the same town, Bethsaida,* as Andrew and
Peter. [45] Philip found Nathanael * and said to him, "We
have found the one about whom Moses in the Law and
also the Prophets wrote—Jesus the son of Joseph, from
Nazareth." [46] Nathanael said to him, "Can anything good
come from Nazareth?" Philip replied, "Come and see."

[47] When Jesus saw Nathanael coming toward him,
he said of him, "Behold, a true Israelite, in whom there is
no deception." * [48] Nathanael asked him, "How do you
know me?" Jesus answered him, "Before Philip summoned
you, when you were under the fig tree,* I saw you."

[49] Nathanael said to him, "Rabbi, you are the Son of God. You are the King of Israel." [50] Jesus responded, "Do you believe because I told you that I saw you under the fig tree? You will see greater things than that." [51] Then he added, "Amen, amen, I say to you, you will see the heavens opened and the angels of God ascending and descending upon the Son of Man." *

C: The First Sign Worked by Jesus

2 **The Wedding Feast at Cana.** * [1] On the third day, there was a wedding at Cana * in Galilee. The mother of Jesus was there, [2] and Jesus and his disciples had also been invited. [3] When the wine was exhausted, the mother of Jesus said to him, "They have no wine." [4] Jesus responded, "Woman,* what concern is this to us? My hour has not yet come." [5] His mother said to the servants, "Do whatever he tells you."

[6] Now standing nearby there were six stone water jars, of the type used for Jewish rites of purification, each holding twenty to thirty gallons. [7] Jesus instructed the servants, "Fill the jars with water." When they had filled them to the brim, [8] he ordered them, "Now draw some out and take it to the chief steward," and they did so.

[9] When the chief steward tasted the water that had become wine, he did not know where it came from, although the servants who had drawn the water knew. The chief steward called over the bridegroom [10] and said, "Everyone serves the choice wine first, and then an inferior vintage when the guests have been drinking for a while. However, you have saved the best wine until now." *

[11] Jesus performed this, the first of his signs,* at Cana in Galilee, thereby revealing his glory, and his disciples believed in him. [12] After this, he went down to Capernaum with his mother, his brethren,* and his disciples, and they remained there for a few days.

JESUS CHANGES WATER INTO WINE AT CANA—"When the wine was exhausted, the mother of Jesus said to him, 'They have no wine.'" Jesus told the servers to fill six stone water jars with water and take some to the man in charge of the feast who tasted it and found it to be very good wine. (See Jn 2:3-11.)

THE ROYAL OFFICIAL'S SON—"The royal official said to him, 'Sir, come down before my child dies.' Jesus replied, 'Return home. Your son will live' " (Jn 4:49-50).

II. WORSHIP OF THE FATHER IN SPIRIT AND TRUTH*

A: The Mystery of the New Temple

Jesus Casts the Merchants Out of the Temple.* ¹³When the time of the Passover of the Jews was near, Jesus went up to Jerusalem. ¹⁴In the temple he found people selling cattle, sheep, and doves, as well as money changers seated at their tables. ¹⁵Making a whip of cords, he drove them all out of the temple, including the sheep and the cattle. He also overturned the tables of the money changers, scattering their coins, ¹⁶and to those who were selling the doves he ordered, "Take them out of here! Stop turning my Father's house into a marketplace!" ¹⁷His disciples recalled the words of Scripture, "Zeal for your house will consume me."

¹⁸The Jews then challenged him, "What sign can you show us to justify your doing this?" ¹⁹Jesus answered, "Destroy this temple, and in three days I will raise it up." ²⁰The Jews responded, "This temple has taken forty-six years to build, and you are going to raise it up in three days!" ²¹But the temple he was talking about was the temple of his body. ²²After he had risen from the dead, his disciples remembered that he had said this, and they believed the Scripture and the words that Jesus had spoken.

B: The Mystery of the New Covenant

Jesus in Jerusalem. ²³* While Jesus was in Jerusalem for the feast of Passover, many people saw the signs he was performing and came to believe in his name. ²⁴However, Jesus would not entrust himself to them because he fully understood them all. ²⁵He did not need evidence from others about man, for he clearly understood men.

3 **Nicodemus Goes To Visit Jesus.** ¹There was a man from the Pharisees named Nicodemus,* a member of the Jewish ruling council, ²who came to Jesus at night. "Rabbi," he said, "we know that you are a teacher who has come from God, for no one would be able to perform the signs that you do unless God were with him." [3] Jesus replied,

> "Amen, amen, I say to you,
> no one can see the kingdom of God *
> without being born from above."

[4] Nicodemus asked, "How can a man be born again once he is old? Is it possible for him to enter a second time into his mother's womb and be born?" [5] Jesus said,

> "Amen, amen, I say to you,
> no one can enter the kingdom of God
> unless he is born of water and the Spirit.*

[6]   What is born of the flesh is flesh,
> and what is born of the Spirit is spirit.

[7]   "You should not be astonished when I say,
> 'You must be born from above.'

[8]   The wind blows where it chooses,
> and you hear the sound of it,
> but you do not know where it comes from
> or where it goes.
> So it is with everyone who is born of the Spirit."

[9] "How is this possible?" asked Nicodemus. [10] Jesus responded, "You are a teacher of Israel and you do not know these things?

[11]   "Amen, amen, I say to you,
> we speak of what we know
> and we testify to what we have seen,
> and yet you do not accept our testimony.

[12]   If I tell you about earthly things
> and you do not believe,
> how will you believe
> when I speak to you about heavenly things?

Jesus Christ, Savior and Judge*

[13]   "No one has gone up to heaven
> except the one who descended from heaven,
> the Son of Man.

14 And just as Moses lifted up the serpent in the desert,
    so must the Son of Man be lifted up,*
15 in order that everyone who believes in him
    may have eternal life.

16 "For God so loved the world
    that he gave his only Son,
    so that everyone who believes in him
    may not perish
    but may attain eternal life.

17 "For God did not send his Son into the world
    to condemn the world
    but in order that the world might be saved through
        him.
18 Whoever believes in him is not condemned,
    but whoever does not believe in him
    already stands condemned,
    because he has not believed in the name
    of the only-begotten Son of God.

19 "And the judgment is this:
    the light has come into the world,
    but people preferred darkness to light
    because their deeds were evil.
20 Everyone who does evil hates the light
    and avoids coming near the light
    so that his misdeeds may not be exposed.
21 However, whoever lives by the truth
    comes to the light
    so that it may be clearly seen
    that his deeds have been done
    in God."

Final Witness of John the Baptist.* 22 After this, Jesus went
with his disciples into the Judean countryside, where he
spent some time with them and baptized. 23 John was also
baptizing at Aenon * near Salem, because there was an
abundance of water there, and people were coming to be
baptized. 24 At that time, John had not yet been imprisoned.

²⁵ Now a dispute about ceremonial washings arose between a certain Jew and the disciples of John. ²⁶ Therefore, they came to John and said to him, "Rabbi, the one who was with you beyond the Jordan, to whom you bore witness, is baptizing, and everyone is flocking to him." ²⁷ John replied,

> "No one can receive anything
> except what has been given to him from heaven.

²⁸ You yourselves can testify that I said,
> 'I am not the Christ.
> I have been sent before him.'

²⁹ "It is the bridegroom who has the bride,
> but the friend of the bridegroom
> who stands by and listens for him
> rejoices greatly when he hears the bridegroom's
>   voice.
> This joy of mine
> is complete.

³⁰ He must increase;
> I must decrease.

He Who Comes from Above*

³¹ "The one who comes from above is above all.
> The one who is of the earth is earthly
> and speaks of earthly things.
> The one who comes from heaven is above all.

³² He bears witness to the things he has seen and heard,
> yet no one accepts his testimony.

³³ "Whoever accepts his testimony
> attests that God speaks the truth.

³⁴ For the one whom God has sent
> speaks the words of God,
> for God gives him the Spirit without measure.*

³⁵ The Father loves the Son,
> and he has entrusted everything into his hand.

³⁶ Whoever believes in the Son has eternal life;
> whoever does not believe in the Son will not see life,
> but the wrath of God rests upon him."

C: The Savior of the World and the New Worship

4 **Journeying to Galilee through Samaria.*** [1] Now when the Lord learned that the Pharisees had been informed that he had more disciples and was baptizing more people than John [2] (although actually it was not Jesus himself but his disciples who were baptizing), [3] he left Judea and set forth for Galilee.

Jesus and the Samaritan Woman.* [4] He had to pass through Samaria.* [5] So he came to a Samaritan town called Sychar,* near the plot of land that Jacob had given to his son Joseph. [6] Jacob's well was there, and Jesus, tired from his journey, sat down at the well. It was about noon.*

[7] When a Samaritan woman came to draw water, Jesus said to her, "Give me some water to drink." [8] His disciples had gone into the town to purchase food. [9] The Samaritan woman said to him, "You are a Jew. How can you ask me, a Samaritan woman,* for some water to drink?" (Jews do not share anything in common with Samaritans.) [10] Jesus replied,

> "If you recognized the gift of God
> and who it is that is asking you for something to drink,
> you would have asked him
> and he would have given you living water."

[11] "Sir," the woman said, "you do not have a bucket, and the well is deep.* Where can you get this living water? [12] Are you greater than our ancestor Jacob who gave us this well and drank from it himself along with his sons and his cattle?" [13] Jesus said to her,

> "Everyone who drinks this water
> will be thirsty again.
> [14] But whoever drinks the water that I will give him
> will never be thirsty.
> The water that I will give him
> will become a spring of water within him
> welling up to eternal life."

¹⁵ The woman said to him, "Sir, give me this water so that I may not be thirsty and have to come here to draw water."

¹⁶ Jesus told her, "Go, call your husband and come back here." ¹⁷ The woman answered him, "I have no husband." Jesus said to her, "You are right in saying, 'I have no husband'; ¹⁸ for you have had five husbands, and the man you have now is not your husband. What you have said is true."

¹⁹ The woman said to him, "Sir, I can see that you are a prophet. ²⁰ Our ancestors worshiped on this mountain,* but you say that the place where people must worship is in Jerusalem." ²¹ Jesus told her,

"Believe me, woman,
the hour is coming
when you will worship the Father
neither on this mountain
nor in Jerusalem.
²² You worship what you do not know;
we worship what we do know,
for salvation is from the Jews.

²³ "But the hour is coming,
indeed it is already here,
when the true worshipers
will worship the Father
in Spirit and truth.*
Indeed it is worshipers like these
that the Father seeks.
²⁴ God is Spirit,
and those who worship him
must worship in Spirit and truth."

²⁵ The woman said to him, "I know that the Messiah is coming, the one who is called Christ. When he comes, he will reveal everything to us." * ²⁶ Jesus said to her, "I am he,* the one who is speaking to you."

²⁷ At this point, his disciples returned, and they were astonished to find him speaking with a woman, but no one

asked, "What do you want from her?" or "Why are you conversing with her?" [28] The woman left behind her water jar and went off to the town, where she said to the people, [29] "Come and see a man who told me everything I have ever done. Could this be the Christ?" [30] And so they departed from the town and made their way to see him.

The Time of the Harvest.* [31] Meanwhile, the disciples urged him, "Rabbi, eat something." [32] But he told them,

> "I have food to eat
> about which you do not know."

[33] Then his disciples said to one another, "Could someone have brought him something to eat?" [34] Jesus said to them,

> "My food is to do the will
> of the one who sent me,
> and to accomplish his work.

[35]
> Do you not have a saying,
> 'Four months more,
> and then comes the harvest'?

> "I tell you,
> open your eyes and look at the fields;
> already they are white for the harvest.

[36]
> The reaper is even now receiving his pay;
> already he is gathering the crops for eternal life
> so that the sower and the reaper can rejoice together.

[37]
> "Thus, the saying holds true,
> 'One sows and another reaps.'

[38]
> I sent you to reap
> what you had not worked for.
> Others have performed the work,
> and you have reaped the benefits of their labor."

Jesus Is Truly the Savior of the World.* [39] Many Samaritans from that town came to believe in him because of the woman's testimony, "He told me everything I have ever done." [40] So when the Samaritans came to him, they pleaded with him to stay with them, and he remained there for two days. ⁴¹ And many more began to believe in him because of the words he spoke to them. ⁴² They said to the woman, "We no longer believe simply because of what you said, for we have heard him for ourselves, and we are convinced that this man is truly the Savior of the world."

Return to Galilee.* ⁴³ When the two days were over, Jesus departed for Galilee. ⁴⁴ He himself had declared that a prophet is not treated with honor in his own hometown. ⁴⁵ When he arrived in Galilee, the Galileans welcomed him, since they had seen all he had done in Jerusalem during the feast, having been at the feast themselves.

Jesus Heals the Official's Son.* ⁴⁶ He went again to Cana in Galilee where he had changed the water into wine. At Capernaum, there was a royal official whose son was ill. ⁴⁷ When this man heard that Jesus had come from Judea to Galilee, he went to him and pleaded that he come and heal his son who was near death.

⁴⁸ Jesus said to him, "Unless you witness signs and wonders, you will not believe." ⁴⁹ The royal official said to him, "Sir, come down before my child dies." ⁵⁰ Jesus replied, "Return home. Your son will live."

The man believed what Jesus said to him, and he departed. ⁵¹ While he was still on his way, his servants met him saying that his child was going to live. ⁵² He asked them at what time the boy had begun to recover, and they told him, "The fever left him yesterday at one o'clock in the afternoon." * ⁵³ Then the father realized that was the exact hour at which Jesus had assured him, "Your son will live," and he and his entire household came to believe.

⁵⁴ This was the second sign that Jesus performed after returning from Judea into Galilee.

III: JESUS RESTORES THE WORK OF GOD*

5 **The Sign Given on a Sabbath.*** ¹ Some time later, Jesus went up to Jerusalem for one of the Jewish feasts. ² Now in Jerusalem, by the Sheep Gate, there is a pool that in Hebrew is called Bethesda.* It has five porticos, ³ and in these a large number of invalids used to lie, people who were blind, lame, and paralyzed, waiting for the movement of the water.* [⁴ For occasionally an angel of the Lord would come down into the pool and stir up the water. The first one into the pool after each such disturbance would be cured of whatever disease he had.] *

⁵ A man who was there had been an invalid for thirty-eight years. ⁶ When Jesus saw him lying there and was aware that he had been ill for a long time, he said to him, "Do you want to get well?" ⁷ The invalid answered him, "Sir, I have no one to put me into the pool when the water is stirred up. While I am still on my way, someone else steps into the pool ahead of me." ⁸ Jesus said to him, "Rise! Take up your mat and walk!" ⁹ Immediately, the man was cured, and he took up his mat and began to walk.

Now that day was a Sabbath. ¹⁰ Therefore, the Jews said to the man who had been cured, "Today is the Sabbath. It is not lawful for you to carry your mat." ¹¹ He replied, "The man who cured me said to me, 'Take up your mat and walk!'" ¹² They asked him, "Who is the man who told you to take it up and walk?" ¹³ But the man who had been cured did not know who it was, for Jesus had disappeared into the crowd that was there.

¹⁴ Later, Jesus found him in the temple and said to him, "See, you have been made well. Do not sin anymore, so that nothing worse happens to you." ¹⁵ The man went away and told the Jews that Jesus was the man who had made him well. ¹⁶ Therefore, the Jews began to harass Jesus because he was doing such things on the Sabbath. ¹⁷ However, Jesus responded to them, saying,

> "My Father is still working,
> and I am at work as well."

¹⁸ For this reason, the Jews became even more determined to kill him, because he was not only breaking the

Sabbath but also calling God his own Father, making himself equal to God.

The Work of the Son.* ¹⁹ Jesus replied to them, saying,

"Amen, amen, I say to you,
the Son can do nothing by himself;
he can do only what he sees the Father doing.
For whatever the Father does,
the Son also does.

20 For the Father loves the Son
and shows him everything
that he himself is doing.
And he will show him
even greater works than these,
so that you might be astonished.

21 "Indeed, just as the Father raises the dead
and gives them life,
so does the Son give life
to anyone he chooses.

22 The Father judges no one,
for he has entrusted all judgment to the Son,

23 so that all may honor the Son
as they honor the Father.
Anyone who does not honor the Son
does not honor the Father who sent him.

24 "Amen, amen, I say to you,
whoever hears my words
and believes in the one who sent me
possesses eternal life.
He will not come to judgment
but has passed from death to life.

25 "Amen, amen, I say to you,
the hour is coming,
indeed it is already here,
when the dead will hear
the voice of the Son of God,
and all those who hear it will live.

26 For just as the Father has life in himself,
    so also he has granted the Son to have life in himself.
27 And he has also granted him
    the power to pass judgment,
    because he is the Son of Man.

28 "Do not be astonished at this,
    for the hour is coming
    when all those who are in their graves
    will hear his voice
29 and will come forth from their graves.
    Those who have done good deeds
    will rise to life,
    while those who have done evil
    will rise to judgment.

30 "I can do nothing on my own.
    As I hear, I judge,
    and my judgment is just,
    because I seek to do
    not my own will
    but the will of him who sent me.

A Witness to Jesus

31 * "If I were to testify about myself,
    my testimony would not be true.
32 However, there is another who testifies about me,
    and I know that his testimony is true,
    the testimony he bore concerning me.
33 You sent messengers to John,
    and he has testified to the truth.
34 Not that I accept such human testimony,
    but I say these things
    so that you may be saved.

35 "John was a burning and shining lamp,
    and for a time you were willing
    to exult in his light.
36 But I have testimony that is greater than John's.
    The works that my Father
    has given me to accomplish,

the very works that I am doing,
testify about me,
that the Father has sent me.

37 "And the Father who sent me
has himself testified about me.
You have not heard his voice
or seen his form,

38 and you do not have his word
abiding in you,
because you do not believe
him whom he has sent.

39 "Search the Scriptures carefully
because you believe that through them
you will gain eternal life.
Even they testify on my behalf.

40 Yet you refuse to come to me
to receive that life.

Unbelief of Jesus' Hearers

41 "I do not accept the praise of men.

42 Moreover, I know that you do not have
the love of God in your hearts.

43 I have come in the name of my Father,
yet you do not accept me.
But if another should come in his own name,
you will accept him.

44 How can you believe
when you accept praise from one another,
yet you do not seek
the praise that comes from
the only God?

45 "Do not think that I will accuse you
before the Father.
You have placed your hope in Moses,
and he is the one who will accuse you.

46 If you truly believed Moses,
you would have believed in me,
for it is about me that he wrote.

JESUS FEEDS FIVE THOUSAND—"Jesus took the loaves, and when he had given thanks, he distributed them to the people who were sitting there. He did the same with the fish, as much as they wanted" (Jn 6:11).

JESUS THE BREAD OF LIFE—"Whoever feeds upon my flesh and drinks my blood dwells in me and I dwell in him. . . . This is the bread that came down from heaven. . . . The one who feeds upon this bread will live forever" (Jn 6:56-58).

⁴⁷   But since you do not believe what he wrote, how will you believe what I say?"

IV: THE BREAD OF LIFE*

A: Signs of Salvation

6 **Jesus Feeds the Crowds.*** ¹ After this, Jesus crossed the Sea of Galilee, also called the Sea of Tiberias, ² and a large crowd of people followed him because they saw the signs he performed on the sick. ³ Jesus went up on a mountainside and sat down there with his disciples. ⁴ The Jewish feast of Passover was approaching.

⁵ When Jesus looked up and saw a large crowd coming toward him, he said to Philip, "Where are we to buy bread for them to eat?" ⁶ He said this to test him, because Jesus himself knew what he was going to do. ⁷ Philip answered him, "Two hundred days' wages * would not buy enough bread for each of them to have a small piece." ⁸ One of his disciples, Andrew, the brother of Simon Peter, said to him, ⁹ "There is a boy here who has five barley loaves and two fish. But what help will they be among so many?"

¹⁰ Jesus said, "Have the people sit down." Now there was plenty of grass in that place, so the men sat down, about five thousand of them. ¹¹ Then Jesus took the loaves, and when he had given thanks, he distributed them to the people who were sitting there. He did the same with the fish, as much as they wanted. ¹² When they all had eaten enough, he said to the disciples, "Gather up the fragments that are left over, so that nothing will be wasted." ¹³ So they gathered them up and filled twelve baskets with the fragments of the five barley loaves left by those who had eaten.

¹⁴ When the people saw the sign he had performed, they began to say, "This is indeed the Prophet who is to come into the world." ¹⁵ Then Jesus realized that they were going to come and carry him off to make him king, so he again withdrew to the mountain by himself.

Jesus Walks on the Water.* ¹⁶ When evening came, the disciples went down to the sea, ¹⁷ got into a boat, and set out across the sea to Capernaum. It was already dark, and Jesus had not yet joined them. ¹⁸ The sea then became rough because a strong wind had started to blow.

¹⁹ When they had rowed about three or four miles, they saw Jesus walking on the sea and approaching the boat, and they were terrified. ²⁰ But he said to them, "It is I.* Do not be afraid!" ²¹ They were ready to take him into the boat, but the boat immediately reached the shore toward which they were heading.

B: Jesus, the Bread of Life for Believers*

Earthly Food and Heavenly Bread.* ²² The next day, the crowd that had stayed on the other side of the sea realized that there had only been one boat there, and that Jesus had not gone along with his disciples; rather, the disciples had left by themselves. ²³ Then some boats from Tiberias came near the place where the people had eaten the bread after the Lord had given thanks. ²⁴ When the crowd saw that neither Jesus nor his disciples were there, they themselves got into the boats and came to Capernaum looking for Jesus.

²⁵ When the people found him on the other side of the sea, they said to him, "Rabbi, when did you come here?" ²⁶ Jesus answered them,

> "Amen, amen, I say to you,
> you came looking for me
> not because you have seen signs
> but because you ate the loaves
> and your hunger was satisfied.
> ²⁷ Do not work for food that perishes
> but for the food that endures for eternal life,
> which the Son of Man will give you.
> For it is on him
> that God the Father has set his seal."

²⁸ Then they asked him, "What must we do if we are to carry out the works of God?" ²⁹ Jesus replied,

"This is the work of God:
to believe in the one whom he has sent."

³⁰ They asked him further, "What sign can you give us that we can see and come to believe in you? What work will you do? ³¹ Our ancestors ate manna in the desert. As it is written, 'He gave them bread from heaven * to eat.' " ³² Jesus replied,

> "Amen, amen, I say to you,
> it was not Moses
> who gave you the bread from heaven.
> It is my Father
> who gives you the true bread from heaven.

33 For the bread of God is
    he who comes down from heaven
    and gives life to the world."

The Bread of Life.* ³⁴ "Sir," they begged him, "give us this bread always." ³⁵ Jesus answered them,

> "I am * the bread of life.
> Whoever comes to me will never be hungry,
> and whoever believes in me will never be thirsty.

36 But I said to you that you have seen me
    and yet you do not believe.

37 All that the Father gives me
    will come to me,
    and anyone who comes to me
    I will never turn away.

38 For I have come down from heaven
    not to do my own will
    but the will of him who sent me.

39 "And this is the will of him who sent me:
    that I should lose nothing
    of all that he has given me,
    but that I should raise it up
    on the last day.

40 This indeed is the will of my Father:
    that all who see the Son
    and believe in him

may have eternal life,
and I shall raise them up
on the last day."

Faith, a Gift of God.* [41] Then the Jews murmured about him because he said, "I am the bread that came down from heaven." [42] They said, "Is this not Jesus, the son of Joseph? We know his father and mother. How can he say, 'I have come down from heaven'?"

[43] "Stop murmuring among yourselves!" Jesus said.

[44]   "No one can come to me
unless he is drawn by the Father who sent me,
and I will raise up that person on the last day.

[45]   It is written in the Prophets,
'They will all be taught by God.'
Everyone who has listened to my Father
and learned from him
comes to me.

[46]   Not that anyone has seen the Father
except the one who is from God;
he has seen the Father.

[47]   "Amen, amen, I say to you,
whoever believes has eternal life.

My Flesh for the Life of the World*

[48]   "I am the bread of life.
[49]   Your ancestors ate the manna in the wilderness,
and yet they died.
[50]   This is the bread that comes down from heaven,
so that one may eat it and not die.
[51]   I am the living bread that came down from heaven.
Whoever eats this bread will live forever;
and the bread that I will give
is my flesh, for the life of the world."

[52] Then the Jews started to argue among themselves, saying, "How can this man give us his flesh to eat?" [53] Jesus said to them,

    "Amen, amen, I say to you,
unless you eat the flesh of the Son of Man

and drink his blood,
you do not have life within you.
54 Whoever feeds upon my flesh
and drinks my blood
has eternal life,
and I will raise him up on the last day.
55 For my flesh is real food,
and my blood is real drink.

56 "Whoever feeds upon my flesh and drinks my blood
dwells in me and I dwell in him.
57 Just as the living Father sent me
and I have life because of the Father,
so whoever feeds upon me will live because of me.
58 This is the bread that came down from heaven.
Unlike your ancestors who ate
and nevertheless died,
the one who feeds upon this bread
will live forever."

The Holy One of God.* 59 Jesus said these things while he
was teaching in the synagogue at Capernaum. 60 After
hearing his words, many of his disciples said, "This is a
hard saying. Who can accept it?" 61 Aware of the complaints of his disciples, Jesus said to them,

"Does this shock you?
62 What then if you were to behold the Son of Man
ascend to where he was before?
63 It is the spirit that gives life;
the flesh * can achieve nothing.
The words that I have spoken to you
are spirit and life.
64 But there are some among you
who do not believe."

For from the very beginning Jesus knew who did not
believe, and who would betray him. 65 He said,

"This is why I told you
that no one can come to me
unless it is granted to him by my Father."

⁶⁶ After this, many of his disciples turned away and no longer remained with him. ⁶⁷ Then Jesus said to the Twelve, "Do you also wish to leave?" ⁶⁸ Simon Peter answered him, "Lord, to whom shall we go? You have the words of eternal life. ⁶⁹ We have come to believe and know that you are the Holy One of God."

⁷⁰ Jesus replied, "Did I not choose you twelve? Yet one of you is a devil." ⁷¹ He was speaking of Judas, the son of Simon Iscariot. Although he was one of the Twelve, he would be the one who would betray him.

V: THE LIGHT OF THE WORLD*

A: Jesus, Sign of Contradiction

7 Jesus' Time Has Not Yet Been Fulfilled.* ¹ After this, Jesus resumed his travels throughout Galilee. He did not want to go about in Judea because the Jews were seeking to kill him.

² However, when the Jewish feast of Tabernacles was drawing near, ³ his brethren* said to him, "Depart from here and go into Judea so that your disciples can perceive the works you are doing. ⁴ No one who wishes to be publicly known acts in secret. Since you are doing these things, reveal yourself to the world." ⁵ For not even his brethren believed in him. ⁶ Jesus answered them,

> "My time has not yet come,
> but your time is always right.
> 7 The world cannot hate you,
> but it does hate me
> because I testify against it
> that its works are evil.
> 8 Go up to the feast yourselves.
> I am not going to this feast,
> because my time has not yet fully come."

⁹ After he had said this, he stayed behind in Galilee. ¹⁰ Later, however, after his brethren had gone up to the feast, he himself also went, not publicly, but in secret.

¹¹ During the feast the Jews were looking for him and asking, "Where is he?" ¹² There was widespread murmuring about him among the crowds. Some maintained, "He is a good man," but others insisted, "No, for he is leading the people astray." ¹³ However, no one spoke openly about him for fear of the Jews.

Do Not Judge by Appearances.* ¹⁴ When the feast was half over, Jesus went up into the temple and began to teach. ¹⁵ The Jews were astonished, and they wondered, "How has this man acquired such knowledge when he has never studied?" * ¹⁶ Jesus answered them,

"My teaching is not my own;
rather, it comes from him who sent me.

17   Anyone who resolves to do his will
will know whether my teaching comes from God
or whether I am speaking on my own authority.

18   Whoever speaks on his own authority
is simply seeking his own glory,
but whoever seeks the glory
of the one who sent him
is a truthful person,
and there is no dishonesty in him.

19   "Did not Moses give you the Law?
And not one of you keeps the Law.
Why are you trying to kill me?"

²⁰ The crowd shouted, "You are possessed! Who is trying to kill you?" ²¹ Jesus replied,

"I performed a single work,*
and all of you are astonished.

22   Moses gave you circumcision
—although it did not originate with Moses
but with the patriarchs—
and you circumcise a man on the Sabbath.

23   Now if a man can be circumcised on the Sabbath
so that the Law of Moses may not be broken,
why are you angry with me
for making a man's entire body

completely healthy on the Sabbath?
24 Do not base your judgment on appearances;
judge according to what is right."

Where Is Jesus from and Where Is He Going? * 25 Then
some of the inhabitants of Jerusalem said, "Is this not the
man they are trying to kill? 26 And yet he is speaking publicly, and they say nothing to him! Can it be that the
authorities realize that he is the Christ? 27 And yet we
know where this man is from. But when the Christ
appears, no one will know where he is from."

28 Then Jesus cried out as he was teaching in the
temple,

"You know me,
and you also know where I am from.
Yet I have not come of my own accord,
but he who sent me is true.
You do not know him,
29 but I know him
because I am from him
and it was he who sent me."

30 So they tried to arrest him, but no one laid a hand on
him because his hour had not yet come. 31 Yet many in
the crowd believed in him, and they said, "When the
Christ comes, will he perform more signs than this man
has accomplished?"

32 When the Pharisees overheard the crowd murmuring
about him, the chief priests and the Pharisees sent temple guards to arrest him. 33 Jesus then said,

"I will remain with you
only for a short time longer,
and then I shall return
to him who sent me.
34 You will search for me,
but you will not find me,
for where I am you cannot come."

35 The Jews said to one another, "Where does this man
intend to go that we will not be able to find him? Will he

go abroad to the people who are dispersed among the Greeks and teach the Greeks? [36] What does he mean when he says, 'You will search for me, but you will be unable to find me,' and 'Where I am you cannot come'?"

Streams of Living Water.* [37] * On the last and greatest day of the feast, Jesus stood up and cried out,

"If anyone is thirsty,
let him come to me and drink.
[38] Whoever believes in me,
as Scripture has said,
'Streams of living water
shall flow from within him.' "

[39] Now he was referring here to the Spirit whom those who believed in him were to receive. As yet the Spirit had not been bestowed because Jesus had not yet been glorified.

People Are Divided concerning Jesus.* [40] On hearing these words, some in the crowd said, "This must truly be the Prophet." [41] Others thought, "This is the Christ." But still others retorted, "How can the Christ come from Galilee? [42] Does not Scripture assert that the Christ will be of the seed of David and come from Bethlehem, the city where David lived?" [43] As a result, the crowd was sharply divided because of him. [44] Some of them even wanted to arrest him, but no one laid a hand on him.

[45] Then the temple guards went back to the chief priests and the Pharisees, who asked them, "Why did you not arrest him?" [46] The guards answered, "No one has ever spoken as this man has." [47] Then the Pharisees said, "Have you also been deceived? [48] Has any one of the authorities or of the Pharisees come to believe in him? [49] As for this crowd, they do not know the Law—they are cursed."

[50] One of them, Nicodemus, who had previously come to Jesus, said to them, [51] "Does our Law allow us to pass judgment on someone without first giving him a hearing to ascertain what he is doing?" [52] They replied, "Are you

too a Galilean? Look it up, and you will find that no
prophet is to arise from Galilee."

B: Jesus, Savior of Sinners

8 **A Woman Caught in Adultery.*** [⁵³ Then each of them
returned home. ¹ But Jesus went to the Mount of Olives.
² At daybreak he entered the temple courts, and all the
people gathered around him. He sat down and began to
teach them.

³ The scribes and the Pharisees brought in a woman
who had been caught in adultery. Forcing her to stand in
their midst, ⁴ they said to him, "Teacher, this woman was
caught in the very act of adultery.* ⁵ Now in the Law
Moses commanded us to stone such women.* What do
you have to say?"

⁶ They asked him this question as a test so that they
could bring a charge against him. Jesus bent down and
started to write on the ground with his finger. ⁷ When
they continued to persist in their question, he straightened up and said to them, "Let anyone among you who
is without sin be the first to throw a stone at her." *
⁸ Then he again bent down and wrote on the ground.

⁹ When they heard his response, they went away one by
one, beginning with the elders, until Jesus was left alone
with the woman standing before him. ¹⁰ Then Jesus
straightened up and said to her, "Woman, where are they?
Has no one condemned you?" ¹¹ She replied, "No one,
sir." "Neither do I condemn you," Jesus said. "Go on your
way, and sin no more."]

C: The Light Triumphs over Darkness

The Light of the World.* ¹² Jesus addressed them once
again, saying,

"I am * the light of the world.
The one who follows me

will never walk in darkness.
Rather, he will have the light of life."

¹³ On hearing this, the Pharisees said to him, "You are testifying on your own behalf. Your testimony is not true." ¹⁴ Jesus replied,

"Even though I testify on my own behalf,
my testimony is true,
because I know where I have come from
and where I am going,
whereas you do not know
where I have come from
or where I am going.
¹⁵ You judge by the flesh,
whereas I do not judge anyone.
¹⁶ Yet even if I do judge,
my judgment is true
because it is not I alone who judge,
but it is I and the Father who sent me.

¹⁷ "In your Law it is written
that the testimony of two witnesses is true.
¹⁸ I testify on my own behalf,
and the Father who sent me
also testifies on my behalf."

¹⁹ They continued to question him, saying, "Where is your Father?" Jesus answered,

"You know neither me nor my Father.
If you knew me,
you would know my Father also."

²⁰ He spoke these words while he was teaching at the treasury of the temple.* However, no one arrested him because his hour had not yet come.

I AM!* ²¹ Again he said to them,

"I am going away,
and you will search for me
but you will die in your sin.
Where I am going, you cannot come."

[22] Then the Jews wondered, "Is he planning to kill himself—because he was saying, 'Where I am going, you cannot come'?" [23] He continued,

> "You belong to what is below,
> whereas I belong to what is above.
> You belong to this world,
> but I am not of this world.
> [24] That is why I told you
> that you would die in your sins.
> For if you do not believe
> that I AM,
> you will die in your sins."

[25] "Who are you then?" they asked him. Jesus answered,

> "Just what I have been telling you
> from the beginning.
> [26] I have much to say about you,
> and much to condemn.
> But the one who sent me is true,
> and what I have heard from him
> I declare to the world."

[27] They did not understand that he was speaking to them about the Father. [28] Therefore, Jesus said,

> "When you have lifted up the Son of Man,
> then you will know
> that I AM,
> that I do nothing on my own authority
> and I say nothing except what
> the Father has taught me.
> [29] He who sent me is with me.
> He has not left me alone,
> for I always do what pleases him."

[30] On hearing these words, many came to believe in him.

Jesus and Abraham.* [31] Then Jesus said to those Jews who did believe in him,

> "If you remain faithful to my word,
> you will truly be my disciples.

32   You will know the truth,
       and the truth will set you free."

³³ They answered him, "We are descendants of
Abraham, and we have never been slaves to anyone. What
do you mean by saying, 'You will be set free'?" ³⁴ Jesus
replied,

       "Amen, amen, I say to you,
       everyone who sins
       is a slave of sin.
35   A slave does not remain in a household forever,
       but a son remains in it forever.
36   Therefore, if the Son sets you free,
       you then will truly be free.
37   "I know that you are descendants of Abraham,
       but you seek to kill me
       because my word has no place in your heart.
38   I speak of what I have seen
       in my Father's presence,
       whereas you do what you have heard
       from your father."

³⁹ The Jews said to him, "Abraham is our father." Jesus
said to them,

       "If you were Abraham's children,
       you would be doing the works that Abraham did.
40   But now you seek to kill me,
       a man who has told you the truth
       that I heard from God.
       This is not what Abraham did.
41   You are doing the works of your father!"

They retorted, "We are not illegitimate children. We
have one father—God." ⁴² Jesus said to them,

       "If God were your father,
       you would love me,
       for I came from God;
       neither did I come of my own will,
       but he was the one who sent me.

43 Why do you not understand
what I am saying?
It is because you cannot bear
to hear my words.

44 "You are from your father, the devil,
and you choose to carry out your father's desires.
He was a murderer from the beginning,
and he does not abide by the truth,
for there is no truth in him.
When he lies,
he speaks in accord with his own nature,
for he is a liar
and the father of lies.

45 But because I speak the truth
you refuse to believe me.

46 "Which of you can convict me of sin?
If I say what is true,
why do you not believe me?

47 Whoever comes from God
listens to the words of God.
The reason why you refuse to listen
is that you do not belong to God."

48 The Jews answered, "Are we not right in saying that
you are a Samaritan and are possessed?" 49 Jesus said,

"I am not possessed.
I honor my Father,
but you dishonor me.

50 I do not seek my own glory.
There is one who seeks it,
and he is the judge.

51 Amen, amen, I say to you,
whoever keeps my word
will never see death."

52 The Jews retorted, "Now we are positive that you are
possessed. Abraham died, and the Prophets are dead. Yet
you say, 'Whoever keeps my word will never taste death.'
53 Are you greater than our father Abraham? He is dead,

and the Prophets are also dead. Who do you claim to be?"
[54] Jesus answered,

> "If I glorify myself,
>   that glory is of no value.
> It is my Father who glorifies me,
>   the one about whom you say,
>   'He is our God,'
> [55] even though you do not know him.
>   However, I do know him.
> If I would say
>   that I do not know him,
> I would be a liar like you.
> But I do know him,
>   and I keep his word.
> [56] Your father Abraham rejoiced
>   that he would see my day.
> He saw it and was glad." *

[57] The Jews then said to him, "You are not yet fifty years old. How can you have seen Abraham?" [58] Jesus responded,

> "Amen, amen, I say to you,
> before Abraham was,
> I AM." *

[59] Then they picked up stones to throw at him, but he hid himself and left the temple.

D: A Sign of the Triumph of the Light*

9 **Jesus Cures a Man Born Blind.** * [1] As Jesus walked along, he saw a man who had been blind from birth. [2] His disciples asked him, "Rabbi, who sinned, this man or his parents, that he was born blind?" [3] Jesus answered,

> "Neither this man nor his parents sinned,
>   but it happened
> so that the works of God
>   might be revealed in him.
> [4] We must do
>   the works of him who sent me

while it is still day.
Night is coming when no one can work.
5 While I am in the world,
I am the light of the world."

[6] When he had said this, he spat on the ground, made a paste with the saliva, and smeared the paste on the eyes of the blind man. [7] Then he said to him, "Go and wash in the Pool of Siloam." * (The name means "Sent.") The man went forth and washed, and he returned seeing.

That Man Is a Prophet.* [8] His neighbors and those who had seen him begging asked, "Is this not the man who used to sit and beg?" [9] Some were saying, "Yes, this is the same man," but others insisted, "No. It simply is someone who looks like him." He said, "I am the man."

[10] Therefore, they asked him, "Then how were your eyes opened?" [11] He replied, "The man called Jesus made a paste and smeared it over my eyes. Then he said to me, 'Go to Siloam and wash.' So I went and washed, and then I was able to see." [12] They asked him, "Where is he?" He replied, "I do not know."

[13] They then brought the man who had formerly been blind to the Pharisees. [14] Now it was on a Sabbath day that Jesus had made the paste and opened his eyes.

[15] The Pharisees also asked him how he had gained his sight. He said to them, "He put a paste on my eyes. Then I washed, and now I can see."

[16] Some of the Pharisees said, "This man cannot be from God, for he does not observe the Sabbath." But others said, "How can a man who is a sinner perform such signs?" Thus, they were divided in their opinions. [17] And so they spoke again to the blind man, asking, "What do you have to say about him? It was your eyes that he opened." He replied, "He is a prophet."

[18] However, the Jews refused to believe that the man had been blind and had received his sight until they summoned the parents of the man who had received his sight [19] and asked them, "Is this your son who you say was born

blind? How then is he now able to see?" [20] His parents answered, "We know that this is our son and that he was born blind, [21] but we do not know how he is now able to see, nor do we know who opened his eyes. Ask him. He is of age. He can speak for himself."

[22] His parents responded in this way because they were afraid of the Jews. For the Jews had already agreed that anyone who acknowledged Jesus to be the Christ would be put out of the synagogue. [23] This is why his parents said, "He is of age. Ask him."

That Man Is from God.* [24] And so for a second time they summoned the man who had been blind and said to him, "Give glory to God. We know that this man is a sinner." [25] He answered, "I do not know whether he is a sinner. But one thing I do know: I was blind, and now I am able to see." [26] They then asked him, "What did he do to you? How did he open your eyes?" [27] He answered them, "I have told you already and you would not listen. Why do you want to hear it again? Do you also want to become his disciples?"

[28] Then they began to taunt him, saying, "It is you who are his disciple. We are disciples of Moses. [29] We know that God spoke to Moses, but as for this man, we do not know where he is from." [30] He answered, "That is what is so amazing. You do not know where he comes from, and yet he opened my eyes. [31] We know that God does not listen to sinners, but that he does listen to anyone who is devout and obeys his will.

[32] "Never since the world began has it been heard that anyone opened the eyes of a person born blind. [33] If this man were not from God, he could not have been able to accomplish anything." [34] They answered him, "You were born in sin and you would teach us?" Then they threw him out.

Do You Believe in the Son of Man?* [35] When Jesus heard that they had thrown him out, he found him and asked, "Do you believe in the Son of Man?" [36] He replied, "Who is he, sir, so that I may believe in him?" [37] "You have seen him," said Jesus, "and he is the one who is speaking to you." [38] He said, "I do believe, Lord," and he fell down in worship before him.

Spiritual Blindness.* [39] Then Jesus said,

> "It is for judgment
> that I have come into this world,
> so that those without sight may see
> and those who do see may become blind."

[40] On hearing this, some Pharisees who were present asked him, "Are we blind too?" [41] Jesus replied,

> "If you were blind,
> you would have no guilt;
> but since you claim, 'We see,'
> your guilt remains.

VI: THE SHEPHERD WHO GIVES UP HIS LIFE*

A: I Am the Good Shepherd*

10   **The Good Shepherd**

[1]
> "Amen, amen, I say to you,
> anyone who does not enter
> the sheepfold through the gate
> but climbs in some other way
> is a thief and a bandit.

[2]
> The one who enters through the gate
> is the shepherd of the flock.

[3]
> The gatekeeper opens for him,
> and the sheep hear his voice.
> He calls his own sheep by name
> and leads them out.

[4]
> "When he has brought out all his own,
> he goes on ahead of them,
> and the sheep follow him
> because they know his voice.

JESUS, THE GOOD SHEPHERD—"I am the good shepherd. The good shepherd lays down his life for the sheep. . . . There will only be one flock, one shepherd" (Jn 10:11-16).

THE SPIRIT OF TRUTH—"When the Advocate comes whom I will send you from the Father, the Spirit of truth who comes from the Father, he will testify on my behalf" (Jn 15:26).

5 However, they will never follow a stranger.
Rather, they will run away from him,
because they do not recognize
the voice of strangers."

⁶ Jesus used this parable to instruct them, but they did not understand what he was saying to them. ⁷ Therefore, Jesus spoke to them again,

"Amen, amen, I say to you,
I am the gate of the sheepfold.

8 All who came before me
were thieves and bandits,
but the sheep did not listen to them.

9 "I am the gate.
Anyone who enters through me
will be saved.
He will go in and out
and will find pasture.

10 "A thief comes only
to steal and kill and destroy.
I have come
that they may have life,
and have it in abundance.

11 "I am the good shepherd.
The good shepherd
lays down his life for the sheep.

12 The hired hand,
who is not the shepherd
nor the owner of the sheep,
sees the wolf approaching,
and he leaves the sheep and runs away,
while the wolf catches and scatters them.

13 He runs away
because he is only a hired hand
and he has no concern for the sheep.

14 "I am the good shepherd.
I know my own,
and my own know me,

¹⁵   just as the Father knows me
and I know the Father.
And I lay down my life for the sheep.

¹⁶   "I have other sheep too
that do not belong to this fold.
I must lead them as well,
and they will hear my voice.
Thus, there will only be one flock,
one shepherd.

¹⁷   "This is why the Father loves me,
because I lay down my life
in order to take it up again.

¹⁸   No one takes it away from me.
I lay it down of my own free will.
And as I have the power to lay it down,
I have the power to take it up again.
This command I have received from my Father."

¹⁹ Once again, these words provoked a division among the Jews. ²⁰ Many of them were saying, "He is possessed and out of his mind. Why should we listen to him?" ²¹ But others said, "No one possessed by a demon could speak like this. Can a demon open the eyes of the blind?" *

B: I and the Father Are One

Feast of the Dedication. * ²² At that time, the feast of the Dedication was taking place in Jerusalem. It was winter, ²³ and Jesus was walking in the temple along the Portico of Solomon.* ²⁴ The Jews gathered around him and asked, "How much longer will you keep us in suspense? If you are the Christ, tell us plainly." ²⁵ Jesus replied,

"I have told you,
but you do not believe.
The works that I do in my Father's name
bear witness to me,

²⁶   but you do not believe
because you are not my sheep.

²⁷ "My sheep listen to my voice.
 I know them, and they follow me.
²⁸ I give them eternal life,
 and they will never perish.
 No one will ever snatch them from my hand.
²⁹ My Father who has given them to me
 is greater than all,
 and no one can snatch them
 out of the Father's hand.
³⁰ I and the Father are one." *

³¹ Once again, the Jews picked up rocks to stone him,
³² but Jesus said to them, "I have performed in your presence many good works from my Father. For which of these works are you going to stone me?" ³³ The Jews answered, "We are not going to stone you for any good work you have done, but for blasphemy. Even though you are a man, you are claiming to be God." ³⁴ Jesus replied,

 "Is it not written in your Law,*
 'I said: You are gods'?
³⁵ If those to whom
 the word of God was addressed
 are called 'gods'
 —and Scripture cannot be set aside—
³⁶ how can you say, "You blaspheme,"
 to the one whom the Father has consecrated
 and sent into the world
 for saying, 'I am the Son of God'?

³⁷ "If I am not performing
 the works of my Father,
 then do not believe me.
³⁸ However, if I am doing them,
 then even if you do not believe me,
 at least believe my works,
 so that you may realize and understand
 that the Father is in me
 and I am in the Father."

³⁹ They again tried to seize him, but he escaped from their clutches.

The Testimony of John the Baptist.* [40] He went back across the Jordan to the place where John had first been baptizing, and he remained there. [41] Many people came to him, and they were saying, "John performed no sign, but everything that John said about this man was true." [42] And many there came to believe in him.

C: I Am the Resurrection*

11 **Death of Lazarus.*** [1] In Bethany, the village of Mary and her sister Martha, a certain man named Lazarus had fallen ill. [2] This Mary was the woman who had anointed the Lord with ointment and wiped his feet with her hair. It was her brother Lazarus who was ill. [3] And so the sisters sent this message to him, "Lord, the one you love is ill."

[4] When Jesus heard this, he said,

"This illness is not to end in death.
Rather, it is for God's glory,
so that by means of it
the Son of Man may be glorified."

[5] Jesus loved Martha and her sister and Lazarus. [6] So after learning that Lazarus was ill, he remained for two more days in the place where he was. [7] Then he said to his disciples, "Let us return to Judea." [8] His disciples said to him, "Rabbi, just a short time ago the Jews were trying to stone you. Why do you want to go back there?" [9] Jesus answered,

"Are there not twelve hours of daylight?
If someone walks in the daylight,
he does not stumble,
because he sees by the light of this world.

[10] But if he walks at night,
he stumbles,
because he does not have the light."

[11] After saying this, he went on to tell them, "Our friend Lazarus has fallen asleep, but I am going there to awaken him." [12] The disciples responded, "Lord, if he has fallen

asleep, he will recover." [13] Jesus, however, had been speaking about the death of Lazarus, but they thought that he was speaking of ordinary sleep.

[14] Finally, Jesus told them in plain words, "Lazarus is dead. [15] I am glad for your sake that I was not there, so that you may believe. Let us go to him." [16] Then Thomas (who was called "the Twin" *) said to his fellow disciples, "Let us also go so that we may die with him."

The Kingdom and the Promise of the Resurrection. * [17] When Jesus arrived, he learned that Lazarus had already been in the tomb for four days.* [18] Now Bethany was near Jerusalem, about two miles distant, [19] and many of the Jews had come to Martha and Mary to console them * for the loss of their brother.

[20] When Martha heard that Jesus was coming, she went forth to meet him, while Mary remained at home. [21] Martha said to Jesus, "Lord, if you had been here, my brother would not have died. [22] But even now I know that God will grant you whatever you ask of him." [23] Jesus said to her, "Your brother will rise again." [24] Martha replied, "I know that he will rise again in the resurrection on the last day." [25] Jesus then said to her,

"I am the resurrection and the life.
Whoever believes in me,
even though he dies, will live,
[26] and everyone who lives
and believes in me
will never die.
Do you believe this?"

[27] "Yes, Lord," she replied. "I believe that you are the Christ, the Son of God, the one who is to come into the world."

[28] When she had said this, she went back and took her sister Mary aside, telling her privately, "The Teacher is here and is asking for you." [29] As soon as she heard this, she got up quickly and went to him. [30] For Jesus had not yet come to the village, but was still at the place where

Martha had met him. [31] When the Jews who were in the house consoling her saw Mary get up quickly and go out, they followed her, assuming that she was going to the tomb to weep there.

[32] Mary came to the place where Jesus was, and as soon as she saw him, she fell at his feet and said to him, "Lord, if you had been here, my brother would not have died." [33] When Jesus saw her weeping, and beheld the Jews who were with her also weeping, he became deeply moved in spirit and angry. [34] He asked, "Where have you laid him?" They said to him, "Lord, come and see." [35] Jesus began to weep, [36] causing the Jews to say, "See how greatly he loved him!" [37] But some of them remarked, "He opened the eyes of the blind man. Why could he not have done something to prevent this man's death?"

[38] Again deeply moved, Jesus came to the tomb. It was a cave, with a stone closing the entrance. [39] Jesus said, "Take away the stone." Martha, the dead man's sister, said to him, "Lord, by now there will be a stench, for he has been dead for four days."

[40] Jesus replied, "Did I not tell you that if you have faith you will see the glory of God?" [41] And so they removed the stone. Then Jesus looked up and said,

> "Father, I thank you for hearing me.
[42] I know that you always hear me,
> but I have said this
> for the sake of the people standing here,
> so that they may believe
> that it was you who sent me."

[43] When he had said this, he cried out in a loud voice, "Lazarus, come out!" [44] The dead man came out, his hands and feet bound with linen bands, and his face wrapped in a cloth. Then Jesus said to them, "Untie him and let him go free."

One Man Must Die for the People. * [45] This caused many of the Jews who had come to visit Mary, and had seen what Jesus did, to believe in him. [46] However, some of them went to the Pharisees and reported to them what Jesus had done.

⁴⁷ As a result, the chief priests and the Pharisees summoned a meeting of the Sanhedrin and said, "What are we going to do? This man is performing many signs. ⁴⁸ If we let him go on like this, everyone will start to believe in him, and then the Romans will come and suppress both our temple and our nation."

⁴⁹ However, one of them, Caiaphas, who was high priest that year,* said to them, "You know nothing at all. ⁵⁰ You do not seem to realize that it is better for us that one man die for the people rather than the whole nation be destroyed."

⁵¹ He did not say this on his own, but as the high priest that year he was prophesying that Jesus was to die for the nation, ⁵² and not for the nation alone, but to gather into one the dispersed children of God. ⁵³ And so from that day on, they plotted to kill him.* ⁵⁴ As a result, Jesus no longer walked about openly among the Jews. He withdrew to a town called Ephraim* in the region bordering the desert, and he remained there with the disciples.

VII: THE TRUE PASSOVER THAT BRINGS ABOUT THE SALVATION OF HUMANKIND*

A: The Hour Has Come*

The Last Passover. ⁵⁵ * Now the Jewish Passover* was drawing near, and many people went up from the country to Jerusalem before the Passover in order to purify themselves. ⁵⁶ They kept looking for Jesus, and they asked one another as they stood in the temple, "What do you think? Will he come to the feast or not?" ⁵⁷ Meanwhile, the chief priests and the Pharisees had given orders that anyone who knew where he was should inform them so that they might arrest him.

12 **The Anointing at Bethany.** ¹ Six days before the Passover, Jesus came to Bethany, the hometown of Lazarus, whom he had raised from the dead. [2] They gave a dinner there for him. Martha served the meal, and Lazarus was among those at table with him.

[3] Mary brought in a pint* of very costly ointment, made from pure nard, anointed Jesus' feet, and dried them with her hair. The house was filled with the fragrance of the ointment. [4] Judas Iscariot, one of his disciples, the one who was about to betray him, said, [5] "Why was this ointment not sold for three hundred denarii* and the money given to the poor?" [6] He said this not because he had any concern for the poor but because he was a thief. He was in charge of the money bag, and he used to steal from it.

[7] Jesus said in response, "Leave her alone! Let her keep it for the day of my burial. [8] The poor you will always have with you, but you will not always have me."

[9] Meanwhile, a large number of Jews learned that he was there, and they came not only because of Jesus but also because they wanted to see Lazarus, whom he had raised from the dead. [10] The chief priests then decided to put Lazarus to death as well, [11] since it was because of him that many of the Jews were leaving and putting their faith in Jesus.

The Triumphal Entry into Jerusalem.* [12] The next day the great crowd of people who had come for the feast heard that Jesus was on his way to Jerusalem. [13] Thus, they went out to meet him, carrying branches of palm* and shouting,

"Hosanna!
Blessed is he who comes in the name of the Lord,
    the King of Israel."

[14] Jesus found a young donkey and rode it, as it is written,

[15]   "Do not be afraid, daughter of Zion.*
Behold, your King is coming,
    riding on a donkey's colt."

¹⁶ At first, his disciples did not understand this, but later, when Jesus had been glorified, they recalled that these things had been written about him and had happened to him.

¹⁷ Now the people who had been present when he called Lazarus out of the tomb and raised him from the dead continued to testify about this.* ¹⁸ Because the crowd had heard that he had performed this sign, they went out to meet him. ¹⁹ So the Pharisees said to one another, "As you see, we are getting nowhere. The entire world has gone after him."

The Glory of the Cross.* ²⁰ Among those who had come up to worship at the feast were some Greeks.* ²¹ They approached Philip, who was from Bethsaida in Galilee, and said to him, "Sir, we would like to see Jesus." ²² Philip went to tell Andrew of this, and Philip and Andrew informed Jesus. ²³ Jesus answered them,

"The hour has come
for the Son of Man to be glorified.
²⁴ Amen, amen, I say to you,
unless a grain of wheat
falls into the earth and dies,
it remains just a grain of wheat.
However, if it dies,
it bears much fruit.
²⁵ "Anyone who loves his life loses it,
but the one who hates his life in this world
will preserve it for eternal life.
²⁶ If anyone wishes to serve me,
he must follow me.
Where I am,
there also will my servant be.
If anyone serves me,
my Father will honor that person.
²⁷ "Now my soul is troubled.
Yet what should I say:
'Father, save me from this hour'?

No, it was for this
that I have come to this hour.
28   Father, glorify your name."

Then a voice came from heaven,

"I have glorified it,
and I will glorify it again."

²⁹ The crowd that was present heard this, and some of
them said that it was thunder, while others asserted, "An
angel has spoken to him." ³⁰ Jesus answered,

"This voice did not come for my sake
but for yours.
31   Now is the judgment on this world.
Now the prince of this world *
will be driven out.
32   And when I am lifted up from the earth,
I will draw all to myself."

³³ He said this to indicate the kind of death he was to
die.

³⁴ The crowd answered, "Our Law * teaches that the
Christ will remain forever. How then can you say that the
Son of Man must be lifted up? Who is this Son of Man?"
³⁵ Jesus replied,

"The light will be with you
for only a little longer.
Go on your way
while you still have the light,
so that the darkness
will not overtake you.

"Whoever walks in the darkness
does not know where he is going.
36   While you have the light,
believe in the light
so that you may become children of light."

After Jesus had said this, he departed and hid himself
from their sight.

The Choice To Believe in the Light. * ³⁷ Although he had performed so many signs in their presence, they did not believe in him. ³⁸ This was to fulfill the word of the prophet Isaiah,

> "Lord, who has believed our preaching?
>   To whom has the power of the Lord been revealed?"

³⁹ They therefore could not believe for as Isaiah said,

⁴⁰ "He has blinded their eyes
>   and hardened their hearts,
> lest they see with their eyes
>   and understand with their hearts,
> and thereby be converted,
>   so that I could heal them." *

⁴¹ Isaiah said this because he saw his glory, and his words referred to him.

⁴² Nevertheless, there were many, even among the authorities, who believed in him, but because of the Pharisees they did not confess their faith in him, for fear of being banned from the synagogue. * ⁴³ For they valued human glory more highly than the glory that comes from God.

The Choice To Believe in Jesus. * ⁴⁴ Then Jesus cried out,

> "Whoever believes in me
> believes not only in me
> but in him who sent me.
⁴⁵ And whoever sees me
> sees the one who sent me.
⁴⁶ I have come into the world as light
> so that everyone who believes in me
> may not have to remain in darkness.
⁴⁷ * "But if anyone listens to my words
> and fails to observe them,
> I will not pass judgment on him,
> for I did not come to judge the world
> but to save the world.
⁴⁸ Anyone who rejects me
> and does not accept my words

already has a judge.
On the last day,
   the word that I have spoken
   will serve as his judge.

49 "For I have not spoken on my own,
   but the Father who sent me
   has himself given me command
   about what I am to say
   and how I am to speak.

50 I know that his commandment
   is eternal life.
Therefore, what I speak
   is what the Father has told me to say."

B: The Testament of the Lord*

13 **Jesus Washes the Feet of the Disciples.*** [1] As the feast of Passover drew near, Jesus was aware that his hour had come to depart from this world and to go to the Father. He had loved his own who were in the world, and he loved them to the end.

[2] The devil had already put it into the mind of Judas, son of Simon Iscariot, to betray Jesus. During supper, [3] Jesus, fully aware that the Father had entrusted all things into his hands, and that he had come from God and was returning to God, [4] got up from the table, removed his outer garments, and took a towel that he tied around his waist. [5] Then he poured water into a basin and began to wash the disciples' feet and to wipe them with the towel wrapped around his waist.

[6] He came to Simon Peter, who said to him, "Lord, are you going to wash my feet?" [7] Jesus answered, "You do not understand now what I am doing, but later you will understand." [8] Peter said to him, "You shall never wash my feet." Jesus replied, "Unless I wash you, you will have no share with me." [9] Simon Peter said to him, "Lord, then wash not only my feet, but also my hands and my head."

¹⁰ Jesus then said, "Anyone who has bathed has no need to wash further, except for his feet, for he is clean all over. You also are clean, although not every one of you is clean." ¹¹ He knew the one who was going to betray him. That is why he added the words, "Not every one of you is clean."

¹² After he had finished washing their feet and had once again put on his outer garments, he reclined at table and said to them,

> "Do you understand
> what I have done for you?
13 You call me 'Teacher' and 'Lord,'
> and rightly so,
> for that is what I am.
14 So if I, your Lord and Teacher,
> have washed your feet,
> you also should wash one another's feet.

15 "I have given you an example.
> What I have done for you,
> you should also do.
16 Amen, amen I say to you,
> a servant is not greater than his master,
> nor is a messenger greater
> than the one who sent him.

17 "Now that you know these things,
> you will be blessed
> if you do them.

Jesus Predicts His Betrayal*

18 "I am not speaking about all of you.
> I know those whom I have chosen.
> However, what the Scripture says
> must be fulfilled,
> 'The one who ate bread with me
> has raised his heel against me.'
19 "I tell you this now,
> before it occurs,

so that when it does occur,
you may believe that I am. *
20 Amen, amen, I say to you,
whoever receives the one I send
receives me,
and whoever receives me
receives the one who sent me."

²¹ After saying this, Jesus was deeply distressed, and he declared,

"Amen, amen, I say to you,
one of you will betray me."

²² The disciples looked at one another, puzzled as to which one of them he meant. ²³ One of them, the disciple whom Jesus loved, was reclining at Jesus' side. ²⁴ Simon Peter signaled to him to ask Jesus which one he meant.

²⁵ Therefore, leaning back toward Jesus, he asked, "Lord, who is it?" ²⁶ Jesus answered, "It is the one to whom I give this piece of bread after I have dipped it into the dish." And when he had dipped the piece of bread, he gave it to Judas, son of Simon Iscariot.

²⁷ As soon as Judas had received the piece of bread, Satan entered into him. Jesus then said to him, "Do quickly what you are going to do." ²⁸ Now no one at the table knew why he had said this to him. ²⁹ Some thought that since Judas was in charge of the money bag, Jesus was telling him to purchase what was needed for the feast, or to give something to the poor. ³⁰ As soon as Judas had received the piece of bread, he immediately departed. It was night.

³¹ After Judas had departed, Jesus said,

"Now is the Son of Man glorified,
and God is glorified in him.
32   If God is glorified in him,
God will also glorify him in himself,
and he will glorify him at once.

A New Commandment*

33 "My children,
I will be with you
only a short time longer.
You will look for me,
and, as I told the Jews,
so I now say to you,
'Where I am going, you cannot come.'

34 "I give you a new commandment:
love one another.
Just as I have loved you,
so you should also love one another.

35 This is how everyone will know
that you are my disciples:
if you love one another."

Jesus Predicts Peter's Denial.* 36 Simon Peter said to him, "Lord, where are you going?" Jesus answered,

"Where I am going,
you cannot follow me now,
but you will follow me later on."

37 Peter said, "Lord, why can I not follow you now? I will lay down my life for you." 38 Jesus answered, "Will you really lay down your life for me? Amen, amen, I say to you, before the cock crows, you will have denied me three times.

C: The Way, the Truth, and the Life*

14 Jesus, the Way, Leads to the Father*

1 "Do not let your hearts be troubled.
You place your trust in God.*
Trust also in me.

2 In my Father's house
there are many dwelling places.
If there were not,
would I have told you
that I am going to prepare a place for you?

³ And if I go and prepare a place for you,
  I will come again
  and will take you to myself,
  so that where I am,
  you may also be.
⁴ You know the way
  to the place I am going."

⁵ Thomas said to him, "Lord, we do not know where you are going. How can we know the way?"

Jesus, the Truth, Reveals the Father*

⁶ Jesus replied,

  "I am the way, and the truth, and the life.
  No one comes to the Father
  except through me.
⁷ If you know me,
  then you will know my Father also.
  From now on you do know him.
  You have seen him."

⁸ Philip said to him, "Lord, show us the Father, it will be enough for us." ⁹ Jesus answered,

  "Have I been with you all this time, Philip,
  and you still do not know me?
  Whoever has seen me
  has seen the Father.
  How can you say,
  'Show us the Father'?
¹⁰ Do you not believe
  that I am in the Father
  and the Father is in me?

  "The words that I speak to you
  I do not speak on my own.
  The Father who dwells in me
  is doing his works.
¹¹ Believe me when I say
  that I am in the Father
  and the Father is in me.
  But if you do not,

then believe
because of the works themselves.

Jesus, the Life, Communicates the Spirit*

12   "Amen, amen, I say to you,
the one who believes in me
will also do the works that I do,
and indeed will do even greater ones than these,
because I am going to the Father.

13   Whatever you ask in my name I will do,
so that the Father may be glorified in the Son.

14   If you ask me for anything in my name,
I will do it.

15   "If you love me,
you will keep my commandments.

16   And I will ask the Father,
and he will give you another Advocate
to be with you forever,

17   the Spirit of Truth
whom the world cannot accept
because it neither sees him nor knows him.
But you know him,
because he dwells with you
and will be in you.

18   "I will not leave you orphans;
I will come to you.

19   In a little while,
the world will no longer see me,
but you will see me.
Because I live,
you also will live.

20   On that day, you will know
that I am in my Father,
and you in me, and I in you.

21   "Anyone who has received my commandments
and observes them
is the one who loves me.
And whoever loves me

will be loved by my Father,
and I will love him
and reveal myself to him."

²² Judas (not Judas Iscariot) * asked him, "Lord, why is
it that you are revealing yourself to us and not to the
world?" ²³ Jesus answered him,

"Whoever loves me will keep my word,
and my Father will love him,
and we will come to him
and make our abode with him.

²⁴ Whoever does not love me
does not keep my words.
And the word that you hear
is not my own,
but that of the Father who sent me.

²⁵ "I have told you these things
while I am still with you.

²⁶ However, the Advocate, the Holy Spirit,
whom the Father will send in my name,
will teach you everything
and remind you of all
that I have said to you.

The Peace of Jesus*

²⁷ "Peace I leave with you,
my peace I give to you.
Not as the world gives
do I give it to you.
Do not let your hearts be troubled;
be not afraid.

²⁸ "You have heard me say to you,
'I am going away,
and I will come back to you.'
If you loved me,
you would rejoice
that I am going to the Father,
for the Father is greater than I. *

29 And now I have told you this
    before it happens,
    so that when it does happen
    you may believe.

30 "I will no longer talk at length with you
    because the prince of the world is coming.
    He has no power over me,
31 but the world must come to understand
    that I love the Father
    and that I do
    just as the Father has commanded mc.
    Get up! Let us be on our way.

D: The Community of the Witnesses to Christ*

15   Union with Jesus*

1 "I am the true vine,
    and my Father is the vinegrower.
2 He removes every branch
    that does not bear fruit,
    and every branch that does
    he prunes to make it bear even more.
3 You have already been cleansed
    by the word I have spoken to you.

4 "Abide in me,
    as I abide in you.
    Just as a branch cannot bear fruit by itself
    unless it abides in the vine,
    so you cannot bear fruit
    unless you abide in me.

5 "I am the vine,
    you are the branches.
    Whoever abides in me, and I in him,
    will bear much fruit.
    Apart from me you can do nothing.
6 Whoever does not abide in me
    will be thrown away like a withered branch.

Such branches are gathered up,
thrown into the fire, and burned.

7 "If you abide in me
and my words abide in you,
you may ask for whatever you wish,
and it will be done for you.

8 By this is my Father glorified,
that you bear much fruit
and become my disciples.

9 "As the Father has loved me,
so have I loved you.
Remain in my love.

10 If you keep my commandments,
you will remain in my love,
just as I have kept my Father's commandments
and remain in his love.

11 "I have told you these things
so that my joy may be in you
and your joy may be complete.

Love as Jesus Does*

12 "This is my commandment:
love one another
as I have loved you.

13 No one can have greater love
than to lay down his life for his friends.

14 You are my friends
if you do what I command you.

15 "I shall no longer call you servants,
because a servant does not know
what his master is doing.
I have called you friends
because I have revealed to you
everything that I have heard from my Father.

16 "You did not choose me.
Rather, I chose you.
And I appointed you
to go out and bear fruit,

fruit that will remain,
so that the Father may give you
whatever you ask him in my name.

17 The command I give you is this:
love one another.

Witnesses to Jesus in the Face of the World's Hatred*

18 "If the world hates you,
be aware that it hated me
before it hated you.

19 If you belonged to the world,
the world would love you as its own.
But you do not belong to the world
because I have chosen you out of the world,
and therefore the world hates you.

20 "Remember the word that I said to you:
'a servant is not greater than his master.'
If they persecuted me,
they will persecute you.
If they kept my word,
they will keep yours as well.

21 But they will do all these things to you
on account of my name,
because they do not know the one who sent me.

22 "If I had not come
and spoken to them,
they would not be guilty of sin,
but now they have no excuse for their sin.

23 Whoever hates me
hates my Father also.

24 If I had not done works among them
that no one else had ever done,
they would not be guilty of sin.
But now they have seen and hated
both me and my Father.

25 All this was to fulfill the word
that is inscribed in their Law:
'They hated me without cause.'

26 "When the Advocate comes
whom I will send you from the Father,
the Spirit of truth who comes from the Father,
he will testify on my behalf.

27 And you also are my witnesses
because you have been with me from the beginning.

16

1 "I have told you this
to prevent you from falling away.

2 They will expel you from the synagogues.
Indeed the hour is coming
when anyone who kills you
will believe that by doing so
he is serving God.

3 And people will do such things
because they have not known the Father or me.

4 But I have told you this
so that when the hour arrives
you may remember that I forewarned you about
them.

The Spirit of Truth, Our Guide to All Truth*

"I did not tell you all this previously
because I was with you.

5 But now I am going away
to the one who sent me.
Not one of you asks me,
'Where are you going?'

6 However, because I have told you this,
you are overcome with grief.

7 "Nevertheless, I am telling you the truth:
it is better for you that I depart.
For if I do not go away,
the Advocate will not come to you,
whereas if I go,
I will send him to you.

8   "And when he comes,
he will prove the world wrong
about sin and righteousness and judgment:
9   about sin,
because they do not believe in me;
10   about righteousness,
because I am going to the Father
and you will see me no longer;
11   about judgment,
because the ruler of this world has been condemned.

12   "I have much more to tell you,
but you would not be able to bear it now.
13   But when the Spirit of truth comes,
he will guide you into all the truth.
He will not speak on his own authority,
but he will speak what he hears,
and he will declare to you
the things that are coming.
14   He will glorify me,
for he will take what is mine
and communicate it to you.
15   Everything that the Father has is mine.
That is why I said
that he will take what is mine
and communicate it to you.

Triumph of Jesus and the Joy of the Witnesses*

16   "In a little while
you will no longer see me,
and then a short time later
you will see me again."

[17] Then some of his disciples said to one another, "What does he mean by saying to us, 'In a little while you will no longer see me, and then a short time later you will see me again,' and 'Because I am going to the Father'? [18] What is this 'little while'? We do not know what he means."

[19] Jesus knew that they wanted to question him, so he said to them,

"You are asking one another
what I meant by saying,
'In a little while
you will no longer see me,
and then a short time later
you will see me again.'

20 Amen, amen, I say to you,
you will weep and mourn
while the world rejoices.
You will be sorrowful,
but your grief will turn into joy.

21 "A woman in labor suffers anguish
because her hour has come.
But when her baby is born,
she no longer recalls the suffering
because of her joy
that she has brought a child into the world.

22 In the same way,
you are now in anguish,
but I will see you again,
and your hearts will rejoice,
and no one shall deprive you of your joy.

23 "On that day,
you will not ask me anything further.
Amen, amen, I say to you,
if you ask the Father for anything in my name,
he will give it to you.

24 Until now, in my name,
you have not asked for anything.
Ask and you will receive,
so that your joy may be complete.

25 "I have used figures of speech
to explain these things to you.
The hour is coming
when I will no longer use figures,
but I will tell you about the Father in plain words.

26 When that day comes,
you will make requests in my name.

PRAYER IN JESUS' NAME—"Amen, amen, I say to you, if you ask the Father for anything in my name, he will give it to you. . . . Ask and you will receive, so that your joy may be complete" (Jn 16:23-24).

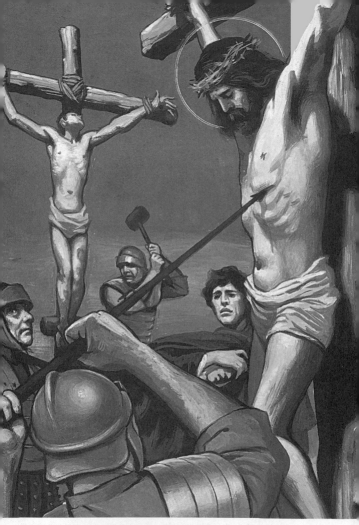

JESUS' SIDE IS PIERCED—"When they came to Jesus and saw that he was already dead, they did not break his legs, but one of the soldiers thrust a lance into his side, and immediately a flow of blood and water came forth" (Jn 19:33-34).

> I do not say
> that I will entreat the Father on your behalf.
>
> 27 For the Father himself loves you
> because you have loved me
> and have come to believe
> that I came from God.
>
> 28 I came from the Father
> and have come into the world.
> Now I am leaving the world
> and returning to the Father."

29 "At last you are speaking plainly," his disciples said, "and not using figures of speech. 30 Now we realize that you know everything and do not need to have anyone question you. Because of this, we believe that you came from God." 31 Jesus responded,

> "Have you finally come to believe?
>
> 32 I tell you, the hour is coming,
> indeed it has already come,
> when you will be scattered,
> each one going to his own home,
> and you will leave me alone.
> And yet I am not alone
> because the Father is with me.
>
> 33 "I have told you this
> so that in me you may be in peace.
> In the world
> you will endure suffering.
> But take courage!
> I have overcome the world."

E: The Priestly Prayer of Jesus*

17 Knowledge of the Father and the Son.* 1 After saying this, Jesus raised his eyes to heaven and said,

> "Father, the hour has come.
> Glorify your Son,
> so that your Son may glorify you,

² since you have given him authority
over all people,
so that he may give eternal life
to all those you have given him.

³ And eternal life is this:
to know you,
the only true God,
and the one you have sent,
Jesus Christ.

⁴ "I have glorified you on earth
by completing the work
that you entrusted to me.

⁵ So now, Father,
glorify me in your presence
with the glory I had with you
before the world began.

The Son and the Disciples*

⁶ "I have made your name known
to those whom you gave me from the world.
They were yours,
and you gave them to me,
and they have kept your word.

⁷ Now they have come to understand
that everything you gave me is from you.

⁸ For the words you gave to me
I have given to them,
and they have accepted them
and know with certainty
that I have come from you,
and they have believed that you sent me.

⁹ "It is for them that I pray.
I do not pray for the world,
but for those you gave me
because they are yours.

¹⁰ Everything I have is yours,
and everything you have is mine,
and through them I have been glorified.

11   I will remain no longer in the world,
      but they will still be in the world
      while I will be coming to you.

      "Holy Father,
      protect by the power of your name
      those you have given me,
      so that they may be one,
      even as we are one.

12   While I was with them
      I protected them by your name
      that you have given me,
      and I kept them safe.
      Not one of them was lost,
      except the one destined to be lost,*
      so that the Scripture might be fulfilled.

13   "Now I am coming to you,
      and I say these things
      while I am still in the world
      so that my joy may come
      to full measure in them.

14   I have given them your word,
      and the world has hated them
      because they do not belong to the world
      any more than I belong to the world.

15   I am not asking you
      to take them out of the world,
      but I do ask you
      to protect them from the evil one.

16   They do not belong to the world
      any more than I belong to the world.

17   "Consecrate them in the truth.
      Your word is truth.

18   As you sent me into the world,
      so have I sent them into the world.

19   And for their sakes I consecrate myself,
      so that they too may be consecrated in truth.

The Disciples and the Church To Come*

20 "I pray not only on behalf of these,
   but also for those who through their word
   will come to believe in me.
21 May they all be one.
   As you, Father, are in me
   and I in you,
   may they also be in us
   so that the world may believe
   that you have sent me.
22 "The glory that you have given me
   I have given to them,
   so that they may be one,
   as we are one,
23 I in them and you in me,
   that they may become completely one,
   and thus the world may know
   that you have sent me
   and that you have loved them
   even as you have loved me.
24 "Father, allow those you have given me
   to be with me where I am,
   so that they may behold my glory,
   which you have bestowed on me
   because you loved me
   before the foundation of the world.
25 "Righteous Father,
   the world has not known you;
   I have known you,
   and they have known that you have sent me.
26 I have made your name known to them,
   and I will make it known,
   so that the love with which you loved me
   may be in them, and I in them."

F: The Passion—The Supreme Testimony*

18 **Jesus Gives Himself Up Freely.** * ¹ After Jesus had spoken these words, he went out with his disciples and

crossed the Kidron * valley. He and his disciples entered
a garden there. [2] This place was known to Judas, his
betrayer, because Jesus had often met there with his disciples. [3] Therefore, Judas went to that garden with a
detachment of soldiers,* together with temple guards
provided by the chief priests and the Pharisees, equipped
with lanterns and torches and weapons.

[4] Then Jesus, fully aware of everything that was going
to happen to him, came forward and asked them,
"Whom are you looking for?" [5] They answered, "Jesus the
Nazorean." * Jesus replied, "I am." Judas who betrayed
him was standing with them.

[6] When Jesus said to them, "I am," they drew back and
fell to the ground. [7] Again, he asked them, "Whom are you
looking for?" And they said, "Jesus the Nazorean." [8] Jesus
answered, "I have told you that I am. If you are looking for
me, let these men go." [9] This was to fulfill the word he had
spoken, "I did not lose any of those you gave me." *

[10] Then Simon Peter, who had a sword, drew it and
struck the high priest's servant, slicing off his right ear.
The servant's name was Malchus. [11] Jesus said to Peter,
"Put your sword back into its scabbard! Am I not to drink
the cup * that the Father has given me?"

Jesus and Peter at the Hour of Bearing Witness. [12] * Then
the detachment of soldiers, their commander, and the
Jewish guards seized Jesus and bound him. [13] They took
him first to Annas, the father-in-law of Caiaphas who was
the high priest that year. [14] It was Caiaphas who had
advised the Jews that it was better for one man to die for
the people.

Peter's First Denial. [15] Simon Peter and another disciple
were following Jesus. That disciple was known to the high
priest, so he went with Jesus into the high priest's courtyard, [16] but Peter remained standing outside at the gate.
The other disciple who was known to the high priest went
out and spoke to the woman who was in charge of the
gate, and he brought Peter inside.

¹⁷ The woman said to Peter, "Are you not one of this man's disciples?" He replied, "I am not." ¹⁸ Since it was cold, the servants and the guards had made a charcoal fire, and they were standing around it, warming themselves. Peter was also standing there and warming himself.

The Inquiry before Annas. ¹⁹ * The high priest questioned Jesus about his disciples and about his teaching. ²⁰ Jesus answered,

> "I have spoken openly
> for the world to hear.
> I have always taught
> in synagogues and in the temple
> where all the Jews congregate.
> I have said nothing in secret.
> ²¹   Why do you ask me?
> Interrogate those who heard
> what I said to them.
> They know what I said."

²² * When he had said this, one of the temple guards standing there struck Jesus with his hand, saying, "Is that any way to answer the high priest?" ²³ Jesus replied, "If I have spoken wrongly, testify to my error. But if I have spoken rightly, why did you strike me?" ²⁴ Then Annas sent him bound to Caiaphas, the high priest.

Peter's Second and Third Denials. ²⁵ Meanwhile, as Simon Peter stood warming himself, he was asked, "Are you not also one of his disciples?" He denied it and said, "I am not." ²⁶ Then one of the servants of the high priest, a relative of the man whose ear Peter had sliced off, asked, "Did I not see you in the garden with him?" ²⁷ Again, Peter denied it. And at that very moment, a cock crowed.

Jesus Handed Over to Pilate. ²⁸ * Then they took Jesus from Caiaphas to the praetorium.* It was early in the morning, and they did not enter the praetorium in order to avoid becoming defiled and thus be able to eat the Passover meal.

²⁹ Therefore, Pilate went out to them and asked, "What charge do you bring against this man?" ³⁰ They answered, "If he were not a criminal, we would not have handed him over to you." ³¹ Pilate said to them, "Take him yourselves and judge him according to your law." The Jews replied, "We are not allowed to put anyone to death." ³² This was to fulfill what Jesus had said when he indicated the kind of death he was to die.

The First Hearing before Pilate. ³³ Then Pilate went back into the praetorium, and having summoned Jesus he asked him, "Are you the King of the Jews?" ³⁴ Jesus answered, "Are you saying this on your own, or have others told you about me?" ³⁵ Pilate said, "Am I a Jew? Your own people and the chief priests have handed you over to me. What have you done?" ³⁶ Jesus replied,

"My kingdom does not belong to this world.
If my kingdom did belong to this world,
my followers would have fought
to prevent me from being handed over to the Jews.
The fact is that my kingdom is not here."

³⁷ Pilate then said to him, "So you are a king!" Jesus answered,

"It is you who say
that I am a king.
For this was I born,
and for this I came into the world:
to testify to the truth.
Everyone who is of the truth
listens to my voice."

³⁸ Pilate responded, "What is truth?"

Barabbas Preferred to Jesus. Then, having said this, he went out again to the Jews and said, "I find no evidence of a crime in this man. ³⁹ But according to your custom, I release one prisoner to you at Passover. Do you want me to release to you the King of the Jews?" ⁴⁰ They shouted, "Not this man, but Barabbas!" Now Barabbas was a thief.*

19 Behold, the Man!

¹ Then Pilate ordered that Jesus be scourged.* ² The soldiers twisted together some thorns into a crown and placed it on his head, and they dressed him in a purple robe. ³ They kept going up to him, saying, "Hail, King of the Jews," while striking him on the face repeatedly.

⁴ Once again, Pilate went out and said to the Jews, "Look, I am bringing him out to you to let you know that I find no evidence of a crime in him." ⁵ Then Jesus came out, wearing the crown of thorns and the purple robe. Pilate said to them, "Behold, the man!"

⁶ When they saw him, the chief priests and the temple guards shouted, "Crucify him! Crucify him!" Pilate said to them, "Take him yourselves and crucify him. I find no evidence of a crime in him." ⁷ The Jews answered, "We have a Law, and according to that Law he ought to die because he has claimed to be the Son of God."

The Second Hearing before Pilate. ⁸ Now when Pilate heard this, he was more frightened than ever. ⁹ Returning to the praetorium, he asked Jesus, "Where are you from?" But Jesus offered no response. ¹⁰ Pilate then said to him, "Are you refusing to speak to me? Do you not realize that I have the power to release you and the power to crucify you?" ¹¹ Jesus answered him,

"You would have no authority over me at all
unless it had been given to you from above.
Therefore, the one who handed me over to you
is guilty of a greater sin."

Jesus Is Condemned to Death. ¹² From that moment on, Pilate sought to release him, but the Jews kept shouting, "If you release this man, you are no Friend of Caesar.* Everyone who claims to be a king opposes Caesar."

¹³ When Pilate heard these words, he brought Jesus out and seated him on the judge's bench at a place known as the Stone Pavement* (in Hebrew, "Gabbatha"). ¹⁴ It was the day of Preparation for the Passover, and it was about noon.* Pilate said to the Jews, "Behold, your King!"

[15] They shouted, "Away with him! Away with him! Crucify him!" "Am I to crucify your King?" Pilate asked them. The chief priests replied, "We have no king but Caesar." [16] Then he handed him over to them to be crucified.

Jesus Is Crucified. Then they took him away, [17] and, carrying the cross * by himself, he went out to what is called the Place of the Skull (in Hebrew, "Golgotha"). [18] There they crucified him * along with two others, one on either side, with Jesus in the middle.

[19] Pilate also had an inscription written and fastened to the cross. It read, "Jesus the Nazorean, King of the Jews." * [20] This inscription, in Hebrew, Latin, and Greek, was read by many Jews, because the place where Jesus was crucified was near the city. [21] Therefore, the chief priests of the Jews said to Pilate, "You should not write, 'The King of the Jews,' but rather, 'This man claimed to be the King of the Jews.'" [22] Pilate responded, "What I have written, I have written." *

[23] * When the soldiers had crucified Jesus, they took his clothes and divided them into four shares, one share for each soldier. They also took his tunic, which was woven seamless, top to bottom. [24] They said to one another, "Instead of tearing it, let us cast lots for it to see who is to get it." In this way, the Scripture was fulfilled that says,

> "They divided my garments among them,
> and for my clothing they cast lots."

And that is what the soldiers did.

Mary and John at the Cross. [25] Standing near the cross of Jesus were his mother and his mother's sister, Mary the wife of Clopas, and Mary Magdalene. [26] When Jesus saw his mother and the disciple whom he loved standing beside her, he said to his mother, "Woman, behold, your son." [27] Then he said to the disciple, "Behold, your mother." And from that hour the disciple took her into his home.

Jesus Dies on the Cross. [28] After this, aware that everything had now been completed, and in order that the Scripture might be fulfilled, Jesus said, "I thirst." [29] A jar filled with sour wine was standing nearby, so they soaked a sponge in the wine on a branch of hyssop and held it up to his lips. [30] When Jesus had taken the wine, he said, "It is finished." * Then he bowed his head and gave up his spirit.

The Blood and the Water. [31] It was the day of Preparation, and the Jews did not want to have the bodies remain on the cross on the Sabbath, especially since that Sabbath day was a great solemnity. Therefore, they requested Pilate to order that their legs be broken and the bodies taken down.

[32] So the soldiers came and broke the legs of the first man and then of the other who had been crucified with him. [33] However, when they came to Jesus and saw that he was already dead, they did not break his legs, [34] but one of the soldiers thrust a lance into his side, and immediately a flow of blood and water came forth. [35] An eyewitness has testified to this, and his testimony is true. He knows that what he says is true, so that you also may believe.

[36] This happened so that the Scripture might be fulfilled,

"Not one of his bones will be broken."

[37] And again, in another passage Scripture says,

"They shall look on the one
whom they have pierced."

Jesus Is Buried.* [38] Shortly thereafter, Joseph of Arimathea, who was a disciple of Jesus, but secretly, because of his fear of the Jews, asked Pilate for permission to remove the body of Jesus. Pilate granted him permission, and so he came and took his body away.

[39] Nicodemus, who had first come to Jesus at night, also came, bringing with him a mixture of myrrh and aloes

weighing about one hundred pounds.* [40] They took the body of Jesus and wrapped it with the spices in linen cloths, in accordance with the burial custom of the Jews.

[41] At the place where Jesus had been crucified there was a garden, and in that garden there was a new tomb in which no one had ever been buried. [42] And so, since it was the Jewish day of Preparation and the tomb was nearby, they laid Jesus there.

G: The Appearances of the Risen One*

20 **The Mystery of the Empty Tomb.*** [1] Early on the first day of the week, while it was still dark, Mary Magdalene came to the tomb and saw that the stone had been moved away from the tomb. [2] Therefore, she ran to Simon Peter and the other disciple, the one whom Jesus loved, and said to them, "They have taken the Lord out of the tomb, and we don't know where they have put him."

[3] Then Peter and the other disciple set out and made their way toward the tomb. [4] They both were running, but the other disciple outran Peter and reached the tomb first. [5] He bent down and saw the linen cloths lying there, but he did not go in.

[6] When Simon Peter caught up with him, he entered the tomb. He saw the linen cloths lying there, [7] and also the cloth that had covered his head not lying with the burial cloths but rolled up in a separate place. [8] Then the other disciple who had reached the tomb first also went inside, and he saw and believed. [9] They still did not understand the Scripture indicating that he must rise from the dead. [10] Then the disciples returned to their homes.

Mary Magdalene Recognizes Jesus.* [11] Mary Magdalene remained weeping outside the tomb. And as she wept, she bent down to look into the tomb, [12] and she saw two angels in white sitting there where the body of Jesus had been, one at the head and the other at the feet. [13] They asked her, "Woman, why are you weeping?" She answered, "They have taken my Lord away, and I do not know where they have put him."

[14] As she said this, she turned around and saw Jesus standing there, but she did not realize that it was Jesus. [15] Jesus said to her, "Woman, why are you weeping? Whom are you looking for?" Thinking he was the gardener, she said to him, "Sir, if you have removed him, tell me where you have put him, and I will take him away." [16] Jesus said to her, "Mary!" She turned and said to him in Hebrew, *"Rabbouni!"* * (which means "Teacher").

[17] Jesus then said to her, "Do not hold on to me, because I have not yet ascended to my Father. But go to my brethren and tell them, 'I am ascending to my Father and your Father, to my God and your God.' " * [18] Mary Magdalene then went and announced to the disciples, "I have seen the Lord," and repeated what he had said to her.

Jesus Appears to the Disciples. [19] * On the evening of that same day, the first day of the week, the doors of the house where the disciples had gathered were locked because of their fear of the Jews. Jesus then came and stood in their midst and said to them, "Peace be with you." [20] After saying this, he showed them his hands and his side.

The disciples were filled with joy when they saw the Lord. [21] "Peace be with you," Jesus said to them again.

> "As the Father has sent me,
>   so I send you."

[22] After saying this, he breathed on them and said,

> "Receive the Holy Spirit.
> [23] If you forgive anyone's sins,
>   they are forgiven.
>   If you retain anyone's sins,
>   they are retained."

Jesus Appears to Thomas. * [24] Now Thomas, called the Twin, who was one of the Twelve, was not with the rest when Jesus came. [25] When the other disciples told him, "We have seen the Lord," he replied, "Unless I see the

THE RESURRECTION OF JESUS—Jesus rose as he said he would. Then he appeared to Mary Magdalene and told her, "Go to my brethren and tell them, 'I am ascending to my Father and your Father, to my God and your God'" (Jn 20:17).

DOUBTING THOMAS—"[Jesus] said to Thomas, 'Put your finger here and see my hands. Reach out your hand and put it into my side. Do not doubt any longer, but believe' " (Jn 20:27).

mark of the nails on his hands and put my finger into the place where the nails pierced and insert my hand into his side, I will not believe."

²⁶ Eight days later, the disciples were again in the house, and on this occasion Thomas was with them. Although the doors were locked, Jesus came and stood in their midst, and he said, "Peace be with you." ²⁷ Then he said to Thomas, "Put your finger here and see my hands. Reach out your hand and put it into my side. Do not doubt any longer, but believe." ²⁸ Thomas exclaimed, "My Lord and my God!" ²⁹ Then Jesus said to him,

> "You have come to believe
> because you have seen me.
> Blessed are those who have not seen
> and yet have come to believe."

Believe in Order To Live.* ³⁰ Now Jesus performed many other signs in the presence of his disciples that are not recorded in this work. ³¹ But those written here have been recorded so that you may come to believe that Jesus is the Christ, the Son of God, and that through your belief you may have life in his name.

EPILOGUE

21 **Jesus Appears to Seven Disciples.*** ¹ Some time later, Jesus once again revealed himself to his disciples at the Sea of Tiberias, in the following manner. ² Simon Peter, Thomas called the Twin, Nathanael from Cana in Galilee, the sons of Zebedee, and two other disciples were gathered together. ³ Simon Peter said to them, "I am going out to fish." The others replied, "We will go with you." They set off and got into the boat, but that night they caught nothing.

⁴ Shortly after daybreak, Jesus was standing on the shore, but the disciples did not realize that it was Jesus. ⁵ Jesus called out, "Children, have you caught anything?" When they answered, "No," ⁶ he said to them, "Cast the net over the right side of the boat and you will find some-

thing." They did so, and they were unable to haul the net on board because of the great number of fish.

⁷ Then the disciple whom Jesus loved said to Peter, "It is the Lord." When Simon Peter heard him say that it was the Lord, he wrapped his outer garment around him, for he had taken it off, and jumped into the sea. ⁸ The other disciples came in the boat, towing the net full of fish, for they were not far from land, only about one hundred yards.

⁹ When they came ashore, they saw a charcoal fire there, with fish on it, and bread. ¹⁰ Jesus said to them, "Bring some of the fish you have just caught." ¹¹ Simon Peter went on board and dragged the net ashore, full of large fish, one hundred and fifty-three of them. Even though there were so many, the net was not torn.

¹² Jesus then said to them, "Come and have breakfast." None of the disciples dared to ask him, "Who are you?" because they knew that it was the Lord. ¹³ Jesus then came forward, took the bread, and gave it to them, and likewise the fish. ¹⁴ This was now the third time that Jesus revealed himself to his disciples after his resurrection from the dead.

Jesus and Peter.* ¹⁵ When they had finished breakfast, Jesus said to Simon Peter, "Simon, son of John, do you love me more than these?" He replied, "Yes, Lord, you know that I love you." Jesus said to him, "Feed my lambs."

¹⁶ Jesus said to him again, "Simon, son of John, do you love me?" He replied, "Yes, Lord, you know that I love you." Jesus said to him, "Tend my sheep."

¹⁷ Jesus said to him a third time, "Simon, son of John, do you love me?" Peter was hurt that Jesus had asked him a third time, "Do you love me?" "Lord," he said to him, "you know everything. You know that I love you." Jesus said to him, "Feed my sheep.

¹⁸   "Amen, amen, I say to you,
        when you were young

you used to fasten your own belt
and you would go wherever you wished.
But when you grow old,
you will stretch out your hands,
and someone else will put a belt around you
and take you where you do not wish to go."

¹⁹ He said this to indicate the kind of death by which Peter would glorify God. After this, he said to him, "Follow me."

The Beloved Disciple.* ²⁰ Peter looked around and saw the disciple whom Jesus loved following them—the one who had reclined next to Jesus at the supper and had asked, "Lord, who is it that will betray you?" ²¹ When Peter saw him, he said to Jesus, "Lord, what about him?" ²² Jesus replied, "If it should be my will that he remain until I come, how does that concern you? Follow me!"

²³ The saying then spread among the brethren that this disciple would not die. However, Jesus had not said to Peter, "He will not die," but, "If it should be my will that he remain until I come, how does that concern you?"

Signature of the Redactors.* ²⁴ This is the disciple who testifies to these things and has written them, and we know that his testimony is true. ²⁵ But there are also many other things that Jesus did; and if every one of them was recorded, I do not think the world itself could contain the books that would be written.

THE ACTS OF THE APOSTLES
THE POWER OF THE GOSPEL AND OF THE SPIRIT IN THE WORLD

Christ's work, which the Gospels showed us being carried on in Palestine, was then carried on, and is being carried on today, throughout the entire world.

Those desirous of learning about the first steps taken on that journey have the Book of the Acts of the Apostles, which bears witness to the presence of the good news and of the Spirit in the midst of the nations. It is a book that describes the Church's youth.

The title "Acts of the Apostles" was probably given to this book many years after the death of the author. In fact, the title corresponds only imperfectly to the contents of the work, since it follows in some detail the story of only two of the apostles: Peter and Paul. Nor does it intend to write their biographies, but simply to hand on to us recollections of the early events in the Church's life.

What it wants to tell us is, above all, the proclamation of a belief: A new age has begun in the history of mankind and the nations, the age of Easter, the age of the Church.

The author singles out the decisive turning points in this Spirit-sustained journey of the Gospel: Pentecost; the first martyrdom, that of Stephen the deacon; the conversion of Paul the persecutor; the acceptance of Gentiles into the Church through the intervention of Peter himself; the persecution in Jerusalem and the scattering of the apostles; and the establishment of Churches in the pagan world, at Antioch, Corinth, Ephesus, and finally Rome.

We must not expect the Book of Acts to tell us everything about the history of the very early Church. Events are reported in connection with some geographical points that mark the entrance of the Gospel into the world and its various cultures: Jerusalem, Antioch, Ephesus, Rome. Only a few of the principal figures appear. Peter and Paul share the pages of the work in almost equal measure, but we are not given their biogra-

phies. Both leave the scene of the story without our knowing anything of their further work or their martyrdom.

The Church is God's work, not a project of human beings, however great. There were other apostles, other communities; the author is well aware of this, but he does not mention them in his narrative. He has a different purpose.

In fact, he does not intend to serve as chronicler of the Church's beginnings; rather, as in the third Gospel, of which he is also the author, he intends to remain an evangelist. His guiding principle is to proclaim the great deeds of God that attest to the presence of salvation, to bear witness to the life of the communities, and to tell the signs of the conversion of the world.

Half of the Book is devoted to Paul, but we are told relatively little of the struggles and trials he had to face, or of the conflicts that shook the communities of Corinth and Galatia. Fortunately, Paul's own Letters have preserved lively traces of all these. The author sometimes refers to disagreements among the missionaries, but he does not regard these as important for the structure of his story.

Moreover, the Book ends too abruptly for our taste, when it has barely shown the way of the Gospel being opened throughout the world.

In this Book a lot of space is given to discourses. Ancient historians liked to put their own reflections and interpretations in the mouths of their heroes; by doing so they gave readers an opportunity to pause and reflect as the story moved on. It is not possible to say precisely the same of the author of Acts. Admittedly, he does not claim to be giving us a stenographic report of the discourses, but he does try to report, even if in concentrated form, the Christian preaching that was characteristic from the very beginning, and to show how sermons were developed.

The same author composed the third Gospel and the Book of Acts. There are no valid reasons for rejecting the tradition that this author was Luke.

These pages were composed around A.D. 80–90. Luke makes use of traditions preserved by various Churches that tell of their origin and the work of the first missionaries there, but he is also free to fill in the overall picture according to his own criteria. He recalls very early events, especially those that would inspire the Church of his own day; by the end of the first century, custom had already set a patina on the fervor of the early days.

The text of the Book of Acts has come down to us in two forms or redactions. Alongside the common redaction (the "Oriental" text) that is transmitted in the earliest manuscripts and versions, there existed as early as the second century a somewhat fuller redaction that added, not new events, but details that give the impression of coming from an eyewitness. This text (the "Western") is now regarded by the majority of scholars as an amplification of the first.

The Acts of the Apostles may be divided as follows:

   I: At Jerusalem (1:1—12:25)
  II: Antioch (13:1—18:22)
 III: Ephesus (18:23—20:38)
 IV: From Jerusalem to Rome (21:1—28:31)

I: AT JERUSALEM*

A: From Jesus to the Community of the Lord*

1 **Prologue.*** [1] In my previous book, Theophilus,* I wrote of everything that Jesus did and taught from the beginning [2] until the day he was taken up, after first giving instructions through the Holy Spirit to the apostles whom he had chosen.

The Promise of the Spirit.* [3] After his passion Jesus had presented himself alive to them by many proofs. He appeared to them during forty days and spoke to them about the kingdom of God. [4] When they were gathered together, he ordered them not to leave Jerusalem, saying, "Wait there for the promise of the Father about which you have heard me speak. [5] For John baptized with water, but within a few days you will be baptized with the Holy Spirit."

⁶ As they were all gathered together, they asked him, "Lord, is this the time when you are going to restore the kingdom to Israel?" ⁷ He replied, "It is not for you to know the dates or the times that the Father has designated by his own authority. ⁸ But you will receive power when the Holy Spirit comes upon you, and then you will be my witnesses not only in Jerusalem, but throughout Judea and Samaria, and indeed to the farthest ends of the earth."

The Ascension of Jesus.* ⁹ After he said this, he was lifted up as they looked on, and a cloud took him from their sight. ¹⁰ While he was departing as they gazed upward toward the sky, suddenly two men dressed in white robes stood beside them, ¹¹ and they said, "Men of Galilee, why are you standing there looking up into the sky? This Jesus who has been taken up from you into heaven will come back in the same way as you have seen him going into heaven."

The First Community Waiting for the Spirit. ¹² Then they returned to Jerusalem from the mount called Olivet, which is near Jerusalem, no farther distant than a Sabbath day's journey.* ¹³ When they arrived, they went to the upper room where they were staying: Peter and John and James and Andrew, Philip and Thomas, Bartholomew and Matthew, James son of Alphaeus and Simon the Zealot, and Judas son of James. ¹⁴ All of these were constantly engaged in prayer, together with the women and Mary the mother of Jesus, and with his brethren.*

The Choice of Judas's Successor.* ¹⁵ In those days, Peter stood up before the assembled brothers, numbering about one hundred and twenty, and said, ¹⁶ "Brethren, the Scripture had to be fulfilled that the Holy Spirit revealed through the mouth of David concerning Judas, who served as guide for those who arrested Jesus. ¹⁷ He was one of our number and was granted a share in this ministry.

[18] "With the money from his traitorous act, this man purchased a plot of land upon which he fell headlong, and he burst open, all of his entrails pouring out. [19] The news about this became known to all the people living in Jerusalem, so that in their own language that plot of land was called 'Hakeldama,' which means 'Field of Blood.' * [20] For it is written in the Book of Psalms,

'May his encampment become deserted,
    and may there be no one to dwell in it.'

And again,

'Let another take over his position.'

[21] "Therefore, it is necessary to choose one of the men who have accompanied us during the entire time that the Lord Jesus lived with us, [22] beginning from his baptism by John until the day when he was taken up from us. For he must become a witness with us of his resurrection."

[23] And so they nominated two candidates: Joseph called Barsabbas, who was also known as Justus, and Matthias. [24] Then they prayed, saying, "Lord, you know the hearts of everyone. Show us which one of these two you have chosen [25] to take the place in this apostolic ministry that Judas abandoned to go to his own place." [26] Then they cast lots for them, and the lot fell to Matthias, who was then added to the eleven apostles.

B: Pentecost*

2 **Descent of the Spirit and Birth of the Church.*** [1] When the day of Pentecost arrived, they were all assembled together in one place. [2] Suddenly, there came from heaven a sound similar to that of a violent wind, and it filled the entire house in which they were sitting. [3] Then there appeared to them tongues as of fire, which separated and came to rest on each one of them. [4] All of them were filled with the Holy Spirit and began to speak in different languages,* as the Spirit enabled them to do so.

[5] Now staying in Jerusalem there were devout Jews from every nation under heaven. [6] At this sound, a large

crowd of them gathered, and they were bewildered because each one heard them speaking in his own language.

⁷ They were astounded and asked in amazement, "Are not all these men who are speaking Galileans? ⁸ How is it then that each of us hears them in his own native language? ⁹ Parthians, Medes, and Elamites, residents of Mesopotamia, Judea, and Cappadocia, Pontus and Asia, ¹⁰ Phrygia and Pamphylia, Egypt and the districts of Libya around Cyrene, visitors from Rome, both Jews and proselytes,* ¹¹ Cretans and Arabs—we hear them speaking in our own languages about the mighty deeds of God."

¹² They were all astounded and perplexed, and they said to one another, "What does all this mean?" ¹³ However, others said mockingly, "They are filled with new wine."

Peter Preaches in the Name of the Twelve.* ¹⁴ Then Peter stood up with the Eleven and proclaimed to them in a loud voice, "Men of Judea and all you who live in Jerusalem, let this be known to you, and listen carefully to my words. ¹⁵ These men are not drunk, as you suppose. It is only nine o'clock in the morning.* ¹⁶ Rather, this is what was revealed through the prophet Joel:

17 'It will come to pass in the last days, God declares,
       that I will pour out my Spirit on all flesh.
    Your sons and your daughters shall prophesy;
       your young men shall see visions,
       and your old men shall dream dreams.
18 Indeed, even upon my servants and my handmaids
       I shall pour out my Spirit in those days,
       and they shall prophesy.
19 I will show portents in the sky above
       and signs on the earth below:
       blood and fire and billows of smoke.
20 The sun will be turned into darkness
       and the moon to blood

before the day of the Lord comes,
that great and glorious day.
21 Then it will come to pass
that everyone who calls on the name of the Lord
will be saved.'

22 "Men of Israel, hear these words. Jesus of Nazareth was a man commended to you by God by means of miracles and portents and signs that God worked through him, as you yourselves know. 23 By the set plan and foreknowledge of God, he was handed over into the hands of lawless men. Crucifying him, you killed him. 24 However, God raised him up, releasing him from the pangs of death, because it was impossible for him to be held in its power. 25 For David says of him:

'I saw the Lord always before me;
with him at my right hand I shall not be shaken.
26 Therefore, my heart rejoiced and my tongue exulted;
moreover, my flesh will live in hope.
27 For you will not abandon me to the netherworld
or allow your holy one to suffer corruption.
28 You have made known to me the way of life;
you will fill me with joy in your presence.'

29 "Brethren, I can say to you boldly that our ancestor David both died and was buried, and his tomb is in our midst to this very day. 30 But since he was a prophet and knew that God had sworn an oath to him that one of his descendants would sit on his throne, 31 he foresaw and spoke of the resurrection of the Christ, saying that he was not abandoned to the netherworld and that his flesh did not suffer corruption.

32 "God raised this Jesus to life. Of that we are all witnesses. 33 Exalted at God's right hand, he received from the Father the promise of the Holy Spirit and has poured out what you now see and hear. 34 For David did not ascend to heaven, and yet he said,

'The Lord said to my Lord,
"Sit at my right hand
35 until I make your enemies your footstool." '

³⁶ "Therefore, let the whole house of Israel know with complete certitude that God has made this Jesus whom you crucified both Lord and Christ."

³⁷ When they heard this, they were cut to the heart and said to Peter and to the other apostles, "What are we to do, brethren?" ³⁸ Peter answered, "Repent, and be baptized, every one of you, in the name of Jesus Christ so that your sins may be forgiven, and you will receive the gift of the Holy Spirit. ³⁹ For the promise that was made is for you, for your children, and for all those who are far away, for all those whom the Lord our God will call."

Life of the First Community—I.* ⁴⁰ He offered further testimony with many other arguments as he exhorted them, "Save yourselves from this corrupt generation." ⁴¹ Those who accepted his message were baptized, and on that day about three thousand people were added to their number. ⁴² They devoted themselves to the teaching of the apostles and to the communal fellowship, to the breaking of bread and to prayers.

⁴³ A sense of awe was felt by all for many wonders and signs were performed by the apostles. ⁴⁴ All the believers were together and owned everything in common. ⁴⁵ They would sell their property and possessions and distribute the proceeds to all according to what each one needed. ⁴⁶ Every day, united in spirit, they would assemble together in the temple. They would break bread in their homes and share their food with joyful and generous hearts ⁴⁷ as they praised God, and they were regarded with favor by all the people. And day by day the Lord added to those who were being saved.

C: First Encounter with the Authorities in Israel

3 **In the Name of Jesus Christ, Walk!*** ¹ One day, Peter and John were on their way to the temple for the hour of prayer at three o'clock in the afternoon.* ² A man who had been crippled from his birth was carried there every day and laid at the gate of the temple called the Beautiful

Gate * so that he could beg for alms from those who entered the temple.

³ When this man saw Peter and John about to enter into the temple, he asked them for alms. ⁴ Peter looked intently at him, as did John, and said to him, "Look at us!" ⁵ He looked at them attentively, expecting to receive something from them. ⁶ But Peter said, "I have neither silver nor gold, but what I have I give you. In the name of Jesus Christ of Nazareth, stand up and walk."

⁷ Then Peter grasped him by the right hand and helped him to get up. Immediately, his feet and ankles were strengthened. ⁸ He jumped up, stood straight, and began to walk, and he entered the temple with them, walking and leaping and praising God. ⁹ When all the people there saw him walking and praising God, ¹⁰ they recognized him as the man who used to sit and beg for alms at the Beautiful Gate of the temple, and they were filled with wonder and amazement at what had happened to him.

Peter Speaks to the People.* ¹¹ While he continued to cling to Peter and John, all the people came running in amazement toward them in Solomon's Portico, as it is called. ¹² When Peter saw the people assembling, he addressed them:

"Men of Israel, why are you so surprised at this? Why do you stare at us, as though we had enabled this man to walk by our own power or holiness? ¹³ The God of Abraham, and Isaac, and Jacob, the God of our ancestors, has glorified his servant * Jesus whom you handed over and disowned in the presence of Pilate after he had decided to release him. ¹⁴ You rejected the Holy and Righteous One and asked that a murderer be released to you. ¹⁵ The author of life * you put to death, but God raised him from the dead. Of this we are witnesses.

¹⁶ "By faith in his name, this man whom you see here and who is known to you has been made strong. Faith in him has made him completely well in the presence of all of you.

[17] "Now I am aware, brethren, that you acted out of ignorance as did your rulers. [18] God fulfilled what he had foretold through all the Prophets, revealing that his Christ would suffer. [19] Repent, therefore, and be converted so that your sins may be wiped away, [20] that a time of refreshment may come from the Lord, and that he may send the Christ appointed for you, that is, Jesus. [21] He must remain in heaven until the time comes for the universal restoration announced by God in ages past through his holy Prophets. [22] For Moses said,

'The Lord your God will raise up for you
a prophet like me
from among your own people.
To him shall you listen
in whatever he tells you.
[23] Everyone who refuses to listen to that prophet
will be cut off from the people.'

[24] "Furthermore, all the Prophets who have spoken, from Samuel onward, predicted these days.

[25] "You are the heirs of the Prophets and of the covenant that God made with your ancestors when he told Abraham, 'And in your descendants all the families of the earth shall be blessed.' [26] When God raised up his servant, he sent him first to you, to bless you by turning each one of you from your wicked ways."

4 First Phase of the Trial: A Warning.*

[1] While they were still speaking to the people, the priests, the captain of the temple guard,* and the Sadducees came over to them, [2] greatly annoyed that they were teaching and proclaiming to the people the resurrection of the dead through Jesus. [3] Therefore, they arrested them and placed them in custody until the next day, for it was already evening. [4] However, many of those who had listened to their message became believers, their total approaching five thousand.

[5] On the next day, their rulers, elders, and scribes assembled in Jerusalem, [6] with Annas the high priest,

Caiaphas, John, * Alexander, and all who belonged to the high priestly family. ⁷ They then brought the apostles before them and asked, "By what power or by what name have you done this?"

⁸ Then Peter, filled with the Holy Spirit, said to them, "Rulers of the people and elders, ⁹ if you are interrogating us today in regard to a good deed done to someone who was crippled and how he was healed, ¹⁰ let it be known to you and to all the people of Israel that it was in the name of Jesus Christ of Nazareth whom you crucified, and whom God raised from the dead, that this man standing before you was cured. ¹¹ This is

'the stone rejected by you, the builders,
    that has become the cornerstone.'

¹² There is no salvation in anyone else, nor is there any other name under heaven given to men by which we can be saved."

¹³ They were amazed to see the fearlessness shown by Peter and John and to discover that they were uneducated ordinary men. They recognized them as companions of Jesus, ¹⁴ but, when they saw the man who had been cured standing beside them, they could not say anything in reply. ¹⁵ They ordered them to stand outside while the Sanhedrin discussed the matter.

¹⁶ Then they said, "What are we going to do with these men? Everyone living in Jerusalem is aware that a notable sign has been worked through them, and we clearly cannot deny it. ¹⁷ But to stop the news from spreading any further among the people, let us issue them a warning never again to speak to anyone in his name."

¹⁸ Therefore, they summoned them back and ordered them not to speak or teach at all in the name of Jesus. ¹⁹ However, Peter and John answered them, "You be the judges about whether it is right in the sight of God to listen to you rather than to God. ²⁰ We cannot possibly refrain from speaking about what we have seen and heard."

²¹ After threatening them once again, they released them, for they could find no way to punish them inasmuch as the people were praising God for what had happened. ²² For the man who had been miraculously healed was over forty years old.

The Community's Prayer for the Apostles.* ²³ As soon as they were released, they went back* to the community and reported everything that the chief priests and the elders had said to them. ²⁴ When they heard it, they raised their voices to God with one accord and said, "Lord, maker of heaven and earth and the sea and of everything that is in them, ²⁵ you said by the Holy Spirit through the mouth of our ancestor David, your servant,

'Why do the Gentiles rage
  and the peoples devise futile plots?
²⁶   The kings of the earth take their stand,
    and the rulers gather together
    against the Lord and against his Anointed.'

²⁷ "Indeed, in this very city both Herod and Pontius Pilate along with the Gentiles and the peoples of Israel plotted against your holy servant Jesus, whom you anointed, ²⁸ to do whatever your hand and your decree had predestined to take place. ²⁹ And now, O Lord, be aware of their threats, and grant that your servants may proclaim your word with all boldness, ³⁰ as you stretch out your hand to heal and as signs and wonders are accomplished through the name of your holy servant Jesus."

³¹ When they had finished their prayer, the place where they were gathered together shook, and they were all filled with the Holy Spirit and proclaimed the word of God fearlessly.

Life of the First Community—II.* ³² The entire community of believers was united in heart and soul. No one claimed any of his possessions as his own, for everything was held in common. ³³ With great power, the apostles bore witness to the resurrection* of the Lord Jesus, and they were all greatly respected. ³⁴ There was never anyone among them in need, because those who were the owners of lands or houses would sell them, bring the proceeds of the sale, [35] and lay them at the feet of the apostles, to be distributed to any who were in need.

Barnabas.* [36] One such instance involved Joseph, a Levite and a native of Cyprus, to whom the apostles gave the name Barnabas, meaning "son of encouragement." [37] He sold a field that belonged to him and then brought the money to the apostles and laid it at their feet.

5 The Fraud of Ananias and Sapphira.*

[1] There was a man named Ananias who with his wife Sapphira sold a piece of property. [2] With the approval of his wife, he held back some of the proceeds, and he brought the remainder to the apostles and laid it at their feet.

[3] Then Peter asked, "Ananias, why has Satan so gained control of your heart that you lied to the Holy Spirit and retained part of the sale price of the land? [4] While it remained unsold, did it not belong to you? And after it was sold, were not the proceeds yours? What caused you to contrive this scheme? You have lied not to men but to God."

[5] When Ananias heard these words, he collapsed and died, and a great sense of fear seized all who heard about it. [6] The young men came forward and wrapped up his body. Then they carried him out and buried him.

[7] After about three hours, his wife came in, unaware of what had happened. [8] Peter said to her, "Tell me whether you sold the land for this much." She replied, "Yes, that was the price." [9] Then Peter asked her, "Why did the two of you agree to put the Spirit of the Lord to the test? Listen! The footsteps of those who have buried your husband are at the door, and they will also carry you out."

[10] Instantly, she fell down at his feet and died. When the young men came in, they found her dead. And so they carried her out and buried her beside her husband. [11] And a great sense of fear seized the whole Church* and all those who heard of this.

Life of the First Community—III.* [12] Many signs and wonders were done among the people by the hands of the apostles. They all used to assemble in Solomon's Portico. [13] No one else dared to join them, but the people esteemed them highly. [14] More believers, men and women, were constantly being added to their ranks. [15] People brought those who were sick into the streets and placed them on cots and mats so that when Peter passed by, his shadow might fall on some of them. [16] A large number of people also came from the neighboring towns around Jerusalem, bringing with them the sick and those tormented by unclean spirits, and all of them were cured.

Conclusion of the Trial.* [17] Then the high priest and his colleagues from the party of the Sadducees rose up, filled with jealousy, [18] and they arrested the apostles and placed them in the public jail. [19] But during the night the angel of the Lord opened the prison doors, led them out, and said, [20] "Go, stand in the temple, and tell the people everything about this new life." [21] Accordingly, they entered the temple at daybreak and taught the people.

When the high priest and his colleagues arrived, they convened the Sanhedrin, the full assembly of the elders of Israel, and sent to the jail to have them brought in. [22] But when the temple police went to the prison, they did not find them there. So they returned and announced, [23] "We found the jail securely locked and the guards stationed outside the doors, but when we opened the doors we found no one inside."

[24] Now when the captain of the temple guard and the chief priests heard this report, they were at a loss to understand what this would come to. [25] Then someone arrived to report, "The men whom you imprisoned are standing in the temple and teaching the people." [26] The captain thereupon went with the temple officers and brought them in, although without force, for they were afraid of being stoned by the people.

[27] When they had brought them in, they had them stand before the Sanhedrin. The high priest questioned

them, saying, [28] "Did we not give you strict orders not to teach in this name? Yet, despite that, you have filled Jerusalem with your teaching, and you appear determined to hold us responsible for that man's death."

[29] Peter and the other apostles replied, "We must obey God rather than men. [30] The God of our ancestors raised up Jesus after you had put him to death by hanging him on a tree. [31] God exalted him at his right hand as leader and Savior so that he might grant repentance and forgiveness of sins to Israel. [32] And we are witnesses to these things, as is the Holy Spirit whom God has given to those who obey him."

[33] When they heard this, they became enraged, and they wanted to put them to death. [34] However, one member of the Sanhedrin, a Pharisee named Gamaliel who was a teacher of the law and respected by all the people, stood up and ordered that the apostles be sent outside for a little while.

[35] Then he addressed them, "Men of Israel, consider carefully what you intend to do to these men. [36] Some time ago Theudas * appeared. He claimed to be someone important, and about four hundred men decided to follow him. He was killed, and all of his followers disbanded, and everything came to naught. [37] After him, Judas the Galilean rose up at the time of the census. He also convinced people to follow him, but he too was killed and his followers were dispersed.

[38] "Therefore, I advise you to keep away from these men and let them go. If this movement is human in origin, it will fail. [39] If, however, it comes from God, you will never be able to overcome them, but may find yourselves fighting against God."

His words persuaded them. [40] After they summoned the apostles once again, they had them scourged. Then, ordering them not to speak in the name of Jesus, they released them. [41] They left the Sanhedrin, rejoicing that they had been considered worthy to suffer humiliation for the sake of the name.* [42] And every day, both in the temple and at home, they never stopped teaching and proclaiming Jesus as the Christ.

D: Jerusalem, First Center of Diffusion*

6 **Institution of the Seven Deacons.*** [1] In those days, as the number of disciples grew, the Hellenists made a complaint against the Hebrews,* asserting that their own widows were being neglected in the daily distribution of food. [2] And so the Twelve called together the entire community of disciples and said, "It is not right for us to neglect the word of God in order to wait on tables. [3] Therefore, brethren, we direct you to select from among you seven* men of good reputation, men filled with the Spirit and with wisdom, to whom we may assign this task. [4] We will then be able to devote ourselves to prayer and to the ministry of the word."

[5] The entire community found this proposal to be acceptable, and they chose Stephen, a man full of faith and the Holy Spirit, together with Philip, Prochorus, Nicanor, Timon, Parmenas, and Nicholas of Antioch who was a convert to Judaism. [6] They then presented these men to the apostles, who prayed and laid hands on them.*

[7] The word of God continued to spread ever more widely. The number of the disciples in Jerusalem increased greatly, and a large number of priests became obedient to the faith.

Accusation against Stephen. [8] * Stephen, a man filled with grace and power, began to work great wonders and signs among the people. [9] Then certain members of the so-called Synagogue of Freedmen, people from Cyrene and Alexandria, as well as others from Cilicia and Asia, came forward to debate with Stephen. [10] However, they were unable to refute him because of his wisdom and the Spirit who inspired his speech.

[11] So they bribed some men to say, "We heard this Stephen speak blasphemous words against Moses and against God." [12] After this, stirring up the people as well

as the elders and the scribes, they seized Stephen, placed him under arrest, and brought him before the Sanhedrin.

[13] Then they called forward false witnesses who claimed, "This man never stops speaking against this holy place and the Law. [14] For we have heard him assert that Jesus of Nazareth will destroy this place and change the traditions that Moses handed down to us." [15] All those who sat in the Sanhedrin looked intently at Stephen, and his face appeared like the face of an angel.

7 Stephen's Discourse.
[1] Then the high priest asked him, "Are these things true?" [2] He replied, "Brethren and fathers, listen to me. The God of glory appeared to our ancestor Abraham while he was in Mesopotamia, before he lived in Haran, [3] and said to him, 'Leave your country and your relatives and go to the land that I will show you.'

[4] "Therefore, he departed from the land of the Chaldeans and settled in Haran. And after his father died, God led him to the land where you now dwell. [5] He did not give him any of this land as a heritage, not even as little as a foot, but he promised to give it to him as his possession, and to his descendants after him, even though he was childless.

[6] "This is what God said: 'His descendants will reside in a country not their own, and they will be enslaved and oppressed for four hundred years. [7] But I will bring judgment on the nation that enslaved them,' God said, 'and after that they will come out and worship me in this place.' [8] Then he gave him the covenant of circumcision. And so, when he became the father of Isaac, he circumcised him on the eighth day, as Isaac did for Jacob, and Jacob did for the twelve patriarchs.

[9] "The patriarchs were jealous of Joseph and they sold him into Egypt, but God was with him [10] and rescued him from all his afflictions. He gave Joseph wisdom and the favor of Pharaoh, the king of Egypt, who appointed him governor of Egypt and his entire household.

[11] "Then a severe famine struck all of Egypt and Canaan, causing severe affliction, and our ancestors could find no food. [12] However, when Jacob learned that there was grain available in Egypt, he sent our ancestors there on their first visit. [13] During their second visit, Joseph made himself known to his brothers, and his ancestry became known to Pharaoh. [14] Then Joseph sent for his father Jacob and his entire family, seventy-five people in all.

[15] "Jacob migrated to Egypt, and after he and our ancestors had died there, [16] they were brought back to Shechem and placed in the tomb that Abraham had purchased from the sons of Hamor at Shechem for a sum of money.

[17] "When the time of the promise that God had pledged to Abraham drew near, our people in Egypt had greatly increased in number. [18] Then a new king came to power who had never heard of Joseph. [19] He dealt treacherously with our people and forced our ancestors to abandon their infants so that they could not survive.

[20] "It was at this time that Moses was born, who was pleasing to God. For three months he was nursed in his father's house, [21] but after he had been abandoned, the daughter of Pharaoh adopted him and brought him up as her own son. [22] Moses was trained in all the wisdom of the Egyptians, and he was powerful both in word and in deed.

[23] "When he was forty years old, he decided to visit his fellow countrymen, the children of Israel. [24] When he saw one of them being maltreated, he went to his aid and avenged the victim by slaying the Egyptian. [25] He thought that his brethren would realize that God was offering them deliverance through him, but they did not understand.

[26] "The next day, he came upon two of them fighting, and he tried to reconcile them, saying, 'Men, you are brethren! Why are you trying to hurt one another?' [27] But the man who had wronged his neighbor pushed him aside, saying, 'Who appointed you to be our ruler and judge?

[28] Do you intend to kill me as you killed the Egyptian yesterday?' [29] Moses fled when he heard this, and he dwelt as an alien in Midian and became the father of two sons.

[30] "After forty years had passed, an angel appeared to him in the desert near Mount Sinai in the flame of a burning bush. [31] When Moses saw it, he was amazed, and as he approached to examine it, the voice of the Lord said to him, [32] 'I am the God of your ancestors, the God of Abraham, Isaac, and Jacob.'

"Moses was terrified and did not dare to look. [33] Then the Lord said to him, 'Take off the sandals from your feet, for the place where you stand is holy ground. [34] I have seen the oppression of my people in Egypt and have heard their sighs, and I have come down to rescue them. Now come! I will send you to Egypt.'

[35] "This Moses whom they rejected by saying 'Who appointed you to be our ruler and judge?' God now sent forth as both ruler and liberator through the angel who appeared to him in the bush. [36] It was he who led them out, performing wonders and signs in Egypt, at the Red Sea, and for forty years in the desert. [37] It was this Moses who said to the children of Israel, 'God will raise up for you, from your own people, a prophet like me.' [38] It was he who was in the assembly in the desert with the angel who spoke to him on Mount Sinai and with our ancestors, and who received words of life to hand on to us.

[39] "This is the man whom our ancestors refused to obey. Instead they thrust him aside, and in their hearts they turned back to Egypt, [40] saying to Aaron, 'Make gods for us who will lead us on the way. As for this Moses, who led us out of the land of Egypt, we do not know what has happened to him.'

[41] "It was then that they made a calf, offered a sacrifice to the idol, and rejoiced over the work of their hands. [42] So God turned away from them and gave them up to worship the host of heaven, as it is written in the book of the Prophets:

'Did you bring me sacrifices and offerings
    during those forty years in the desert,
    O house of Israel?
43 No, you carried aloft the tent of Moloch
    and the star of your god Rephan,
    the images that you had made to worship.
And so I shall send you into exile beyond Babylon.'

44 "While they were in the desert, our ancestors had the Tent of Testimony, as God commanded when he directed Moses to make it according to the pattern he had been shown. 45 Our ancestors with Joshua brought it with them when they dispossessed the nations that God drove out before our ancestors. It remained there until the time of David, 46 who found favor with God and desired to provide a dwelling for the God of Jacob.

47 "However, it was Solomon who built a house for him. 48 Yet the Most High does not dwell in houses made with human hands. As the prophet says,

49 'Heaven is my throne,
    and the earth is my footstool.
What kind of house can you build for me? asks the Lord.
    Where shall my resting place be?
50 Did not my hand make all these things?'

51 "You stiff-necked people, with uncircumcised hearts and ears! You are always resisting the Holy Spirit, just as your ancestors used to do. 52 Was there ever a prophet whom your fathers did not persecute? They killed those who foretold the coming of the Righteous One, and now you have become his betrayers and murderers. 53 You received the Law through God's angels, and yet you have not observed it."

Stephen's Martyrdom. 54 When they heard this, they became enraged, and they ground their teeth at him. 55 But Stephen, filled with the Holy Spirit, looked up intently to heaven and saw the glory of God, and Jesus standing at God's right hand. 56 "Look!" he cried. "I see the heavens opened and the Son of Man standing at the right hand of God."

[57] On hearing these words, they covered their ears, cried out loudly, and rushed en masse against him. [58] Then they dragged him out of the city and began to stone him. The witnesses laid their coats at the feet of a young man named Saul. *

[59] While they were stoning Stephen, he prayed aloud, "Lord Jesus, receive my spirit." [60] Then he knelt down and cried out in a clear voice, "Lord, do not hold this sin against them." And with these words he fell asleep.

8 The Church Becomes Open to the Gentiles.* [1] Saul approved of his death. That day marked the beginning of a severe persecution of the Church in Jerusalem, and everyone except the apostles scattered to the country districts of Judea and Samaria. [2] Stephen was buried by devout men who made loud lamentations over him. [3] Saul, meanwhile, began to inflict great harm on the Church. He entered house after house, dragging off men and women and sending them to prison. [4] Now those who had been scattered went from place to place proclaiming the word.

E: The Mission in Judea and Samaria

Springtime in Samaria.* [5] Philip went down to a city in Samaria and began proclaiming the Christ to them. [6] The crowds welcomed the message proclaimed by Philip because they had heard and seen the signs he was doing. [7] For unclean spirits emerged with loud shrieks from many people who were possessed, and many others who were paralyzed or crippled were cured. [8] Thus, there was great joy in that city.

The Encounter with Magic. [9] * A man named Simon had been in that city for some time practicing magic and had astounded the people of Samaria, claiming to be someone great. [10] All of them, from the least to the greatest, believed in him, declaring, "This man is the power of

God that is called 'The Great One.'" * [11] And they listened to him because for a long time they had been captivated by his magic.

[12] However, when the people came to believe Philip as he preached about the kingdom of God and the name of Jesus Christ, they were baptized, both men and women. [13] Even Simon himself became a believer. After his baptism, he was constantly in Philip's company, and he was astonished when he saw the great signs and mighty deeds that were taking place.

The Holy Spirit. [14] When the apostles in Jerusalem heard that Samaria had accepted the word of God, they sent Peter and John to them. [15] When they arrived there, they prayed for them that they might receive the Holy Spirit, [16] for as yet he had not come upon any of them; they had only been baptized in the name of the Lord Jesus. [17] Then they laid hands on them, and they received the Holy Spirit.

Condemnation of Simony. [18] When Simon saw that the Spirit was bestowed by the laying on of the apostles' hands, he offered them money, [19] saying, "Give me this power too so that anyone on whom I lay my hands may receive the Holy Spirit." [20] But Peter said to him, "May your silver perish with you, because you thought that you could obtain God's gift with money. [21] You have no part or share in this, for your heart is not upright in the eyes of God. [22] Repent, therefore, of this wickedness of yours and beg the Lord that if possible you may be forgiven for devising your evil scheme. [23] I see that you are engulfed in the gall of bitterness and the chains of wickedness."

[24] Simon said in reply, "Pray for me to the Lord that nothing of what you have spoken about may befall me." [25] Then, after giving their testimony and proclaiming the word of the Lord, they returned to Jerusalem, preaching the good news to many Samaritan villages.

Baptism of a High Official.* [26] Then the angel of the Lord said to Philip, "Get up and head south along the road that

leads from Jerusalem down to Gaza, the desert road."
²⁷ Therefore, he got up and set out.

Now there was an Ethiopian eunuch, * an official at the
court of the Candace, that is, the queen of the Ethio-
pians, who was in charge of her entire treasury. He had
come to Jerusalem to worship ²⁸ and was now returning
home. As he sat in his chariot, he was reading the prophet
Isaiah.

²⁹ Then the Spirit said to Philip, "Go up and join that
chariot." ³⁰ When Philip ran up, he heard him reading
from the prophet Isaiah, and he asked, "Do you understand what you are reading?" ³¹ He replied, "How can I,
unless I have someone to instruct me?" Then he invited
Philip to get in and sit beside him.

³² This was the Scripture passage he had been reading:

"Like a sheep he was led to the slaughter;
    like a lamb that is silent before its shearer
    he did not open his mouth.
³³   In his humiliation justice was denied him.
    Who will be able to speak of his posterity?
    For his life on earth has been taken away."

³⁴ Then the eunuch said to Philip, "Please tell me,
about whom is the prophet speaking—about himself or
someone else?" ³⁵ And so Philip, starting with this text of
Scripture, proceeded to explain to him the good news of
Jesus.

³⁶ As they were traveling along the road, they came to
some water. The eunuch said, "Look, here is some water.
What is to prevent me from being baptized?" [³⁷ And
Philip said, "If you believe with all your heart, you may."
The eunuch said in reply, "I believe that Jesus Christ is
the Son of God."] * ³⁸ Then he ordered the chariot to
stop, and Philip and the eunuch both went down into the
water, and he baptized him.

³⁹ When they came up out of the water, the Spirit of the
Lord snatched Philip away, and the eunuch did not see
him again, but he went on his way rejoicing. ⁴⁰ Philip,
however, appeared in Azotus * and continued his journey,

proclaiming the good news in every town until he reached Caesarea.

9 Conversion of Saul on the Road to Damascus. [1]* Now, Saul,* still breathing threats and violence against the Lord's disciples, went to the high priest [2] and asked him for letters to the synagogues at Damascus,* authorizing him to arrest any men or women there who were followers of the Way and bring them back to Jerusalem.

[3] While he was drawing near Damascus on his journey, suddenly a light from the sky flashed around him. [4] He fell to the ground and heard a voice saying to him, "Saul, Saul, why are you persecuting me?" [5] He asked, "Who are you, Lord?" The reply came, "I am Jesus, whom you are persecuting. [6] Now get up and go into the city, and you will be told what you have to do."

[7] The men who were traveling with him stood there speechless, for they had heard the voice but had seen no one. [8] Saul got up from the ground, but when he opened his eyes he was unable to see. Therefore, they led him by the hand and brought him into Damascus. [9] For three days, he was without sight and neither ate nor drank.

Saul's Baptism. [10] There was a disciple in Damascus named Ananias. In a vision, the Lord said to him, "Ananias." He answered, "Here I am, Lord." [11] The Lord said to him, "Get up and go to the Street called Straight,* to the house of Judas, and ask for a man from Tarsus named Saul. He is praying, [12] and in a vision he has seen a man named Ananias come in and lay his hands on him so that he may regain his sight."

[13] Ananias answered, "Lord, I have heard from many people about this man and how much harm he has done to your saints* in Jerusalem. [14] Now he has come here with authority from the chief priests to imprison all who invoke your name."

[15] However, the Lord said to him, "Go, for this is the man I have chosen as a vessel to bring my name before

the Gentiles and their kings and before the people of Israel. [16] I myself will show him how much he will have to suffer for the sake of my name."

[17] And so Ananias went forth and entered the house. He laid his hands on Saul and said, "Brother Saul, the Lord Jesus who appeared to you on your way has sent me so that you may regain your sight and be filled with the Holy Spirit." * [18] Immediately, something like scales fell from his eyes, and he regained his sight. He got up and was baptized; [19] then, after taking some food, he regained his strength.

Saul Preaches in Damascus. For several days, Saul stayed with the disciples in Damascus, [20] and he began to preach in the synagogues that Jesus is the Son of God. [21] All those who heard him were astounded, and they said, "Is not this the man who in Jerusalem was persecuting those who invoked this name? And did he not come here for the specific purpose of arresting them so that they might be taken to the chief priests?" [22] But Saul's strength continued to increase, and he confounded the Jews who lived in Damascus by showing that Jesus is indeed the Christ.

[23] After some time had passed, the Jews devised a plan to kill him, [24] but their plot became known to Saul. They were keeping watch on the city gates day and night so that they might kill him, [25] but his disciples took him one night and let him down in a basket over the wall.

Saul in Jerusalem and Tarsus. [26] When he arrived in Jerusalem, he tried to join the disciples, but they were all afraid of him because they did not believe that he had become a disciple. [27] However, Barnabas took him and brought him to the apostles. He related to them how on his journey Saul had seen the Lord who had spoken to him, and how at Damascus he had preached boldly in the name of Jesus.

[28] Saul then moved about with them in Jerusalem, speaking boldly in the name of the Lord. [29] He also engaged in debate with the Hellenists * but they began

planning to kill him. [30] When the brethren learned of this, they brought him to Caesarea and sent him off to Tarsus. *

Period of Peace for the Church. [31] * Meanwhile, the Church throughout Judea, Galilee, and Samaria enjoyed peace, building up strength and living in the fear of the Lord. Encouraged by the Holy Spirit, * the Church grew in numbers.

Peter Heals Aeneas at Lydda. [32] As Peter traveled throughout the region, he went down to visit the saints living in Lydda. * [33] While there, he found a man named Aeneas who had been bedridden for eight years, for he was paralyzed. [34] Peter said to him, "Aeneas, Jesus Christ heals you. Get up and make your bed." He immediately stood up. [35] All the inhabitants of Lydda and Sharon saw him, and they turned to the Lord.

Peter Restores Tabitha to Life. [36] In Joppa, there was a disciple named Tabitha, or Dorcas in Greek, whose life was devoted to performing good works and giving to those in need. [37] In those days, she became ill and died. After they had washed her body, they laid her out in an upper room. * [38] Since Lydda was near Joppa, the disciples, on hearing that Peter was there, sent two men to him with the request, "Please come to us without delay."

[39] Peter immediately set out with them, and when he arrived, they escorted him to the upper room. All the widows stood around him, weeping and showing him the tunics and other clothes that Dorcas had made while she was with them.

[40] Peter sent them all out and knelt down and prayed. Then he turned to the body and said, "Tabitha, get up." She opened her eyes, saw Peter, and sat up. [41] He gave her his hand and helped her up. Then he called the saints and the widows, and he showed her to them alive. [42] It came to be known throughout Joppa, causing many to come to believe in the Lord. [43] Peter stayed on for many days in Joppa at the house of a tanner * named Simon.

F: Baptism of the Centurion Cornelius

10 **The Vision of Cornelius.** [1] * In Caesarea, there was a man named Cornelius who was a centurion of the so-called Italian cohort. * [2] He was a devout and God-fearing man, as were all the members of his household. He gave alms generously to the people and prayed constantly to God.

[3] One afternoon about three o'clock, * he had a vision in which he clearly saw an angel of God approaching him and calling to him, "Cornelius!" [4] He stared at him in terror and asked, "What is it, Lord?"

The angel said, "Your prayers and acts of charity have ascended as a memorial offering before God. [5] Now send some men to Joppa and summon a man named Simon, who is also called Peter. [6] He is lodging with another Simon, a tanner, whose house is by the sea." [7] When the angel who spoke to him had departed, he summoned two of his servants and a devout soldier on his staff. [8] He told them all that had happened and sent them to Joppa.

The Vision of Peter. [9] * About noon * the next day, as they were on their way and approaching the city, Peter went up on the roof to pray. [10] He became hungry and wanted something to eat, but while it was being prepared, he fell into a trance. [11] He then saw heaven opened and something that looked like a large sheet descending, being lowered to the ground by its four corners. [12] In it were all kinds of four-footed animals as well as reptiles and birds of the air.

[13] A voice then said to him, "Get up, Peter! Kill and eat!" [14] But Peter said, "Certainly not, Lord. For I have never eaten anything profane or unclean." [15] The voice spoke again to him, for a second time, "What God has made clean, you must not call profane." [16] This happened three times, and then immediately the object was taken up into heaven again.

[17] While Peter was wondering about the meaning of the vision he had seen, suddenly the men who were sent by

Cornelius appeared. They had asked for directions to Simon's house, and now they were standing at the entrance [18] and inquiring whether Simon known as Peter was lodging there.

[19] As Peter was still thinking about the vision, the Spirit said to him, "Some men have come to see you. [20] Hurry down and go with them without any hesitation, for I have sent them."

[21] Then Peter went down to the men and said, "I am the one you are looking for. What is the reason you have come?" [22] They replied, "A centurion named Cornelius, who is greatly respected by the entire Jewish nation as an upright and God-fearing man, was directed by a holy angel to summon you to his house and to hear what you have to say." [23] So he invited them in and gave them lodging.

The next day, he set out with them, accompanied by some of the brethren from Joppa. [24] On the following day, they reached Caesarea. Cornelius had been expecting them and had called together his relatives and close friends. [25] When Peter arrived, Cornelius came out to meet him and, falling at his feet, did him reverence. [26] But Peter helped him up, saying, "Stand up. I am only a man myself."

[27] While they conversed together, they went inside where a large crowd had gathered. [28] Peter said to them, "You are well aware that Jews are forbidden to associate with or visit a Gentile. However, God has shown me that I should not call anyone profane or unclean. [29] That is why I came without offering any objection when I was summoned. I would like to know exactly why you sent for me."

[30] Cornelius replied, "Four days ago, at this very hour, three o'clock in the afternoon, * I was in my house praying when suddenly I saw a man in shining robes standing before me. [31] He said, 'Cornelius, your prayer has been heard and your almsgiving has not been forgotten by God. [32] Therefore, send to Joppa and ask for Simon, who is also called Peter. He is lodging at the house of Simon

the tanner, by the sea.' ³³ And so I sent for you immediately, and you have been kind enough to come. Now all of us have assembled here in the presence of God to listen to everything that the Lord has commanded you to say."

Peter's Speech. ³⁴ Then Peter addressed them: "I now understand how true it is that God has no favorites, ³⁵ but that in every nation all those who fear God and do what is right are acceptable to him. ³⁶ He sent his word to the children of Israel and proclaimed the good news of peace through Jesus Christ, who is the Lord of all.

³⁷ "You are well aware of what was proclaimed all over Judea, beginning in Galilee after the baptism of John, ³⁸ how God anointed Jesus of Nazareth with the Holy Spirit and with power. He went around doing good and healing all those who were oppressed by the devil, for God was with him.

³⁹ "We are witnesses to everything he did in the Jewish countryside and in Jerusalem. They put him to death by hanging him on a tree, ⁴⁰ but God raised him to life on the third day and allowed him to be seen ⁴¹ not by all the people but by witnesses who were chosen by God in advance—by us who ate and drank with him * after he rose from the dead. ⁴² He commanded us to preach to the people and to bear witness that he is the one designated by God as Judge of the living and the dead. ⁴³ To him all the Prophets bear witness that everyone who believes in him will receive forgiveness of sins through his name."

The Baptism of Cornelius. ⁴⁴ While Peter was still speaking, the Holy Spirit descended upon all who were listening to his message. ⁴⁵ The circumcised believers who had accompanied Peter were astonished that the gift of the Holy Spirit should have been poured out on the Gentiles also. ⁴⁶ For they heard them speaking in tongues and proclaiming the greatness of God.

Peter said further, ⁴⁷ "Can anyone withhold the water of baptism from these people who have received the Holy

Spirit just as we have?" ⁴⁸ Then he ordered them to be baptized in the name of Jesus Christ. ⁴⁹ Afterward, they asked him to stay with them for a few days.

11 Peter's Explanation of Cornelius' Baptism.

¹ The apostles and the brethren in Judea heard that the Gentiles too had accepted the word of God. ² Therefore, when Peter went up to Jerusalem, the circumcised believers protested to him, ³ saying, "Why did you enter the house of uncircumcised men and eat with them?"

⁴ Peter replied by explaining the facts to them step by step, saying, ⁵ "While I was praying one day in the city of Joppa, I fell into a trance and had a vision. I saw something like a large sheet lowered down from heaven by its four corners, and it landed close to me.

⁶ "I looked into it carefully and observed four-footed animals, wild beasts, reptiles, and birds. ⁷ I also heard a voice saying to me, 'Get up, Peter! Kill and eat!' ⁸ But I said, 'Certainly not, Lord. For nothing profane or unclean has ever been in my mouth.' ⁹ But the voice spoke to me from heaven for a second time, 'What God has made clean, you must not call profane.' ¹⁰ This happened three times, and then everything was taken up into heaven again.

¹¹ "At that very moment, three men arrived at the house where we were staying. They had been sent to me from Caesarea. ¹² The Spirit instructed me to go with them without any hesitation. These six brethren also went with me, and we entered the man's house. ¹³ He told us how he had seen an angel standing in his house who said, 'Send to Joppa and ask for Simon who is also called Peter. ¹⁴ He will give you a message that will grant salvation to you and your entire household.'

¹⁵ "As I began to speak, the Holy Spirit descended upon them just as it had upon us at the beginning, ¹⁶ and I remembered the word of the Lord, how he had said, 'John baptized with water, but you will be baptized with the Holy Spirit.' ¹⁷ If then God gave them the same gift

that he gave to us when we came to believe in the Lord Jesus Christ, who was I to oppose God?"

[18] When they heard this, they held their peace, and they praised God, saying, "God has given even to the Gentiles the repentance that leads to life."

A Church at Antioch.* [19] Meanwhile, those who had scattered after the persecution that arose because of Stephen traveled as far as Phoenicia,* Cyprus, and Antioch, preaching the word only to Jews. [20] However, among them there were some natives of Cyprus and Cyrene who went to Antioch where they started preaching also to the Greeks, proclaiming to them the good news of the Lord Jesus. [21] The hand of the Lord was with them, and a great number of them became believers and turned to the Lord.

[22] News of this reached the ears of the Church in Jerusalem, and they sent Barnabas to Antioch. [23] When he arrived and perceived the grace of God, he rejoiced, and he encouraged them all to remain faithful to the Lord with resolute devotion, [24] for he was a good man, filled with the Holy Spirit and with faith. And a large number of people were added to the Lord.

[25] Barnabas then went to Tarsus* to look for Saul, [26] and when he had found him, he brought him to Antioch. For a whole year they met with the Church and taught a large number of people. It was in Antioch that the disciples were first called Christians.

G: Threats against the Church*

A Famine in the World.* [27] During these days, some prophets* came down from Jerusalem to Antioch. [28] One of them, named Agabus, stood up and predicted through the Spirit that a severe famine would afflict the entire world. This in fact occurred during the reign of Claudius. [29] The disciples decided to send relief to the brethren living in Judea, each according to his means. [30] This they did, delivering it to the elders* through Barnabas and Saul.

12 **Persecution, Death, and Imprisonment.*** [1] It was about this period of time that King Herod* persecuted certain members of the Church. [2] He had James, the brother of John, killed with the sword, [3] and when he noted that this pleased the Jews, he proceeded to arrest Peter as well. Since this happened during the feast of Unleavened Bread, [4] he imprisoned him and assigned four squads of four soldiers each to guard him, intending to subject him to a public trial after Passover. [5] While Peter was thus imprisoned, the Church prayed fervently to God for him.

[6] On the night before Herod was to bring him to trial, Peter, secured by two chains, was sleeping between two soldiers, while guards outside the door were keeping watch over the prison. [7] Suddenly, an angel of the Lord appeared, and a light flooded the building. He tapped Peter on the side and awakened him, saying, "Get up quickly!" And the chains fell away from his wrists. [8] Next, the angel said to him, "Fasten your belt and put on your sandals." After he did so, the angel instructed him, "Wrap your cloak around you and follow me."

[9] Accordingly, Peter followed him out. He did not realize that the intervention of the angel was real, thinking that he was seeing a vision. [10] After passing through the first guard post and then the second, they reached the iron gate that led out to the city. This opened for them of its own accord. They went outside and had walked the length of one street when suddenly the angel left him.

[11] Then Peter came to his senses and said, "Now I am positive that the Lord sent his angel and rescued me from Herod's clutches and from all that the Jewish people were expecting." [12] As soon as he realized this, he went to the house of Mary, the mother of John, also called Mark,* where many had assembled and were at prayer.

[13] When he knocked at the outer door, a maid named Rhoda came to answer it. [14] Recognizing Peter's voice, she was so overjoyed that, instead of opening the door, she ran in with the news that Peter was standing outside. [15] They

said to her, "You are out of your mind," but she insisted that it was true. Then they said, "It must be his angel."

¹⁶ Meanwhile, Peter continued to knock, and when they opened the door they saw him and were astounded. ¹⁷ He motioned to them with his hand to be silent. After he described to them how the Lord had brought him out of the prison, he said, "Report this to James * and the brethren." Then he left and went to another place.

¹⁸ At daybreak, there was a great deal of commotion among the soldiers about what had become of Peter. ¹⁹ After instituting a search for him and being unable to find him, Herod interrogated the guards and ordered their execution. Then he left Judea to reside for a while in Caesarea.

Death of Herod Agrippa I. * ²⁰ For a long time, Herod had been very angry with the people of Tyre and Sidon, who now came to him in a body. After gaining the support of Blastus, the king's chamberlain, they asked for peace because their country depended on the king's territory for their food supplies.

²¹ On the designated day, Herod donned his royal robes and, seated on a throne, delivered a public address to them. ²² They began to acclaim him, shouting, "This is the voice of a god, not a man!" ²³ Immediately, the angel of the Lord struck him down because he had not attributed the honor to God. He was eaten away by worms and died.

Return of Barnabas and Saul to Jerusalem. * ²⁴ Meanwhile, the word of God continued to spread and gain more followers. ²⁵ Then, after Barnabas and Saul had completed their mission, they returned to Jerusalem, bringing with them John, also called Mark. *

II: ANTIOCH*

A: Paul's First Missionary Journey*

13 **Barnabas and Paul Sent Out on Mission.** * ¹ In the Church at Antioch, there were prophets and teachers:

Barnabas, Simeon who was called Niger, Lucius of Cyrene, Manaen who had been brought up with Herod the tetrarch, and Saul. [2] On one occasion, while they were worshiping the Lord and fasting, the Holy Spirit said, "Set Barnabas and Saul apart for me to do the work to which I have called them." [3] Then, after completing their fasting and prayer, they laid their hands on them and sent them off.

[4] Having been sent on their mission by the Holy Spirit, they went down to Seleucia, * and from there they set sail for Cyprus. [5] When they arrived in Salamis, * they proclaimed the word of God in the Jewish synagogues, while John served as their assistant.

**At Cyprus Facing a Proconsul and a Magician.* ** [6] When they had traveled through the whole island as far as Paphos, * they encountered a magician named Bar-Jesus, who was a Jewish false prophet. [7] He was an attendant of the proconsul Sergius Paulus, a learned man who had summoned Barnabas and Saul because he wanted to hear the word of God. [8] However, the magician Elymas (for that is the translation of his name) opposed them in an attempt to prevent the proconsul's conversion to the faith.

[9] Then Saul, also known as Paul, * filled with the Holy Spirit, looked intently at Elymas [10] and said, "You offspring of the devil, you enemy of righteousness, filled with every kind of deceit and fraud, will you never cease to pervert the straight paths of the Lord? [11] Now take note of how the hand of the Lord will strike you. You will be blind, and for a period of time you will not be able to see the sun." Immediately, he was enveloped in a dark mist, and he groped about for someone to lead him by the hand. [12] When the proconsul saw what had happened, he became a believer, having been deeply impressed by the teaching of the Lord.

Paul's Arrival at Antioch in Pisidia. [13] * Paul and his companions set sail from Paphos and arrived at Perga* in Pamphylia. There, John left them and returned to

Jerusalem. [14] Then they went on from Perga and arrived at Antioch * in Pisidia.

On the Sabbath, they went into the synagogue and took their seats. [15] After the readings from the Law and the Prophets, the officials of the synagogue sent this message to them, "Brethren, if you have any words of exhortation to offer to the people, please do so."

Paul's Speech in the Synagogue. [16] Then Paul stood up, motioned with his hand, and began to speak, saying, "Listen, men of Israel and you others who fear God! * [17] The God of this people Israel chose our ancestors and made our people great while they were dwelling as foreigners in Egypt. With uplifted arm, he led them out, [18] and for about forty years he endured their conduct in the desert.

[19] "After he had destroyed seven nations in the land of Canaan, he gave their land to his people as their inheritance [20] at the end of about four hundred and fifty years. * After that, he appointed judges for them until the time of the prophet Samuel.

[21] "Then they asked for a king, and God gave them Saul, son of Kish, a man from the tribe of Benjamin. He reigned for forty years, [22] after which God removed him and raised up David as their king. In commending him, he said, 'I have found David, the son of Jesse, to be a man after my own heart. He will carry out my every wish.'

[23] "From this man's descendants, God has fulfilled his promise by raising up for Israel a savior, Jesus. [24] Prior to his coming, John had already proclaimed a baptism of repentance to all the people of Israel. [25] And as John was nearing the end of his work, he said, 'I am not the one you believe me to be. One is coming after me whose sandals I am not worthy to unfasten.'

[26] "Brethren, children of the family of Abraham, and those others among you who fear God, we are the ones to whom this message of salvation has been sent. [27] The people of Jerusalem and their leaders failed to recognize Jesus

or to understand the words of the Prophets that are read on every Sabbath, and they fulfilled those prophecies by condemning him. [28] Even though they found no basis to justify his execution, they asked Pilate to have him killed.

[29] "When they had carried out everything that was written about him, they took him down from the tree and placed him in a tomb. [30] However, God raised him from the dead, [31] and over a period of many days he appeared to those who had come up with him from Galilee to Jerusalem. These are now his witnesses before the people.

[32] "We have come here to proclaim to you the good news—what God promised to our ancestors [33] he has fulfilled for us, their children, by raising Jesus up as it is written in the second psalm:

'You are my Son;
　this day I have begotten you.'

[34] "God raised him from the dead, never to be subjected to corruption. He declares it in these words, 'To you I will give the blessings promised to David.' [35] And he also says in another psalm, 'You will not allow your Holy One to suffer corruption.' [36] When David had served God's purposes during his lifetime, he fell asleep, and he was buried with his ancestors, and he saw corruption. [37] However, the one whom God raised up did not see corruption.

[38] "You must understand, brethren, that it is through him that forgiveness of sins is being proclaimed to you. [39] All those who believe are justified from all the things from which they could not be justified by the Law of Moses. [40] Beware, then, lest what the Prophets have foretold will happen to you:

[41]　'Look carefully, you scoffers!
　　Be amazed and perish!
　For I am doing a work in your days
　　that you will never believe
　　even if someone tells you.'"

[42] As they were leaving the synagogue, the people urged them to speak further on these subjects on the following

Sabbath. [43] After the congregation had dispersed, many Jews and devout converts to Judaism followed Paul and Barnabas, who spoke to them and urged them to remain faithful to the grace of God.

Paul's Speech to the Gentiles. [44] On the next Sabbath, almost the entire city gathered to hear the word of the Lord. [45] When the Jews saw the crowds, they were filled with jealousy, and with blasphemy they contradicted whatever Paul said. [46] Then both Paul and Barnabas spoke out boldly, saying, "It was necessary that the word of God should be proclaimed to you first. However, since you have rejected it and judge yourselves to be unworthy of eternal life, we now turn to the Gentiles. [47] For so has the Lord commanded us to do, saying,

'I have made you a light for the Gentiles
  so that you may bring salvation
  to the farthest corners of the earth.'"

[48] When the Gentiles heard this, they were delighted, and they praised the word of the Lord. All those who were destined for eternal life became believers. [49] Thus, the word of the Lord continued to spread throughout the entire region.

[50] However, the Jews incited the devout women of the upper classes and the leading men of the city. As a result, a campaign of persecution was stirred up against Paul and Barnabas, and they were driven out of the territory. [51] And so they shook the dust from their feet in protest against them and went to Iconium. * [52] And the disciples were filled with joy and with the Holy Spirit.

14 **Jews and Gentiles at Iconium.*** [1] In Iconium, they went into the Jewish synagogue and spoke so effectively that a great number of both Jews and Greeks became believers. [2] However, the Jews who refused to believe stirred up the Gentiles and poisoned their minds against the brethren. [3] Therefore, they stayed there for a considerable period of time, speaking boldly on behalf of the Lord, who confirmed the message of his grace by enabling them to work signs and wonders.

⁴ However, the people in the city were divided, some siding with the Jews, others with the apostles. ⁵ Eventually, a plot was hatched by both the Gentiles and the Jews, together with their leaders, to attack and stone them. ⁶ When they became aware of this, they fled to the Lycaonian cities* of Lystra and Derbe and to the surrounding area. ⁷ There they preached the good news.

At Lystra Paul and Barnabas Are Taken for Gods.* ⁸ At Lystra, there was a man who was crippled. Lame from birth, he had never once been able to walk. ⁹ He listened to Paul speaking. Paul looked intently at him, and, seeing that he had the faith to be healed, ¹⁰ called out to him in a loud voice, "Stand up on your feet." The man sprang up and began to walk.

¹¹ * When the crowds saw what Paul had done, they shouted in Lycaonian, "The gods have come down to us in human form!" ¹² They called Barnabas Zeus, and since Paul was the chief speaker, they called him Hermes. ¹³ And the priest of Zeus, who was on the outskirts of the city, brought oxen and garlands to the gates, since he and the people intended to offer sacrifice.

¹⁴ However, when the apostles Barnabas and Paul learned about this, they tore their clothes* and rushed into the crowd, shouting, ¹⁵ "Men, why are you doing this? We are only human beings, just like you. We proclaim to you the good news so that you may turn from these idols to the living God who made heaven and earth and the sea and all that is in them.

¹⁶ "In the past, God allowed all the Gentiles to go their own way. ¹⁷ However, even then he did not leave you without a witness in doing good, for he sends you rain from heaven and crops in their seasons, and he provides you with food and fills your hearts with joy." ¹⁸ Yet, even with these words, they were barely able to prevent the crowds from offering sacrifice to them.

End of the First Mission.* ¹⁹ Shortly thereafter, some Jews arrived on the scene from Antioch and Iconium, and they won over the crowds. They stoned Paul and dragged him outside the town, believing that he was dead. ²⁰ But when the disciples gathered around him, he got up and entered the city. On the next day, he and Barnabas departed for Derbe.

²¹ After they had proclaimed the good news in that city and gained a considerable number of disciples, they returned to Lystra and then moved on to Iconium and Antioch. ²² They strengthened the disciples and encouraged them to persevere in the faith, saying, "It is necessary for us to undergo many hardships in order to enter the kingdom of God." ²³ In each Church, they appointed presbyters for them, and with prayer and fasting they commended them to the Lord in whom they had come to believe.

²⁴ Then they passed through Pisidia and came to Pamphylia. ²⁵ After proclaiming the word at Perga, they went down to Attalia,* ²⁶ and from there they sailed to Antioch,* where they had been commended to the grace of God for the work that they had completed. ²⁷ When they arrived, they called the Church together and related all that God had accomplished through them and how he had opened the door of faith to the Gentiles. ²⁸ And they stayed there with the disciples for some time.

B: The Council of Jerusalem*

15 **The Question of Circumcision.** ¹ Some men who had come down from Judea were teaching the brethren, "Unless you are circumcised in accordance with the tradition of Moses, you cannot be saved." ² As a result, Paul and Barnabas engaged in a lengthy and acrimonious debate with them, and finally it was decided that Paul and Barnabas and some of the others should go up to Jerusalem to discuss this question with the apostles and the elders.

³ So the Church sent them on their journey; and as they passed through Phoenicia and Samaria, they reported how the Gentiles had been converted, and this news was received with great joy by all the brethren. ⁴ When they arrived in Jerusalem, they were welcomed by the Church and by the apostles and the elders, and they gave a report of all that God had accomplished through them. ⁵ But some from the group of Pharisees who had become believers stood up and declared, "It is necessary for the Gentiles to be circumcised and ordered to observe the Law of Moses."

Salvation through the Grace of Christ. ⁶ The apostles and the elders convened to consider this matter. ⁷ After a long period of debate, Peter stood up to address them. "Brethren," he said, "you are well aware that in the early days God made his choice among you that it would be through my mouth that the Gentiles would hear the message of the gospel and become believers. ⁸ And God, who knows the heart, bore witness by giving to them the Holy Spirit just as he did to us. ⁹ He made no distinction between them and us, for he purified their hearts by faith.

¹⁰ "Therefore, why are you determined to try God's patience by laying a yoke on the neck of the disciples that neither we nor our ancestors have found easy to bear? ¹¹ On the contrary, we believe that we are saved in the same way as they are, through the grace of the Lord Jesus." ¹² On hearing this, the whole assembly fell silent, and they listened as Barnabas and Paul described all the signs and wonders that God had worked through them among the Gentiles.

James on Dietary Law. ¹³ After they had finished speaking, James responded, "Brethren, listen to me. ¹⁴ Simon * has related how God first looked favorably upon the Gentiles and took from among them a people for his name. ¹⁵ This agrees with the words of the Prophets, as it is written,

¹⁶   'After this I will return
          and rebuild the fallen tent of David.

From its ruins I will rebuild it
and raise it up again,

17   so that the rest of mankind may seek the Lord,
as well as all the Gentiles whom I have claimed as
my own.

Thus says the Lord who is doing this,

18   as he made known from long ago.'

¹⁹ "Therefore, I have come to this decision. We should
not make things more difficult for the Gentiles who are
turning to God. ²⁰ Rather, we should send a letter simply
instructing them to abstain from things that have been
polluted by idols, from unchastity, from the meat of animals that have been strangled, and from blood. ²¹ For in
every town for many generations, Moses has had those
who proclaim him, for he is read aloud in the synagogues
on every Sabbath."

The Letter of the Apostles. ²² Then the apostles and the
elders, with the approval of the whole Church, decided to
choose representatives from their number and to send
them with Paul and Barnabas to Antioch. They sent
Judas, who was called Barsabbas, * and Silas, leaders in
the community, ²³ to deliver the following letter:

The apostles and the elders, your brethren,

To the brethren in Antioch, Syria, and Cilicia:

Greetings.

²⁴ It has come to our attention that some of our
number, without having received any instructions
from us, have upset you with their teachings and disturbed your peace of mind. ²⁵ Therefore, we have
decided unanimously to choose representatives and
send them to you together with our beloved
Barnabas and Paul, ²⁶ men who have dedicated their
lives to the name of our Lord Jesus Christ. ²⁷ And so
we are sending Judas and Silas who will confirm
these things by word of mouth.

²⁸ It is the decision of the Holy Spirit and also our
decision not to lay any further burden upon you

beyond these essentials: [29] you are to abstain from food that has been sacrificed to idols, from blood, from the meat of animals that have been strangled, and from unchastity. If you avoid these, you will be doing what is right.

Farewell.

Delegates at Antioch. [30] So the men departed. When they reached Antioch, they summoned together the entire congregation and delivered the letter. [31] Upon reading it, the community rejoiced at its encouragement.

[32] Judas and Silas, who were themselves prophets, spoke at length to strengthen and encourage the brethren. [33] After they had spent some time there, they were sent off in peace by the brethren to return to those who had sent them. [34] [But Silas decided to remain there.] * [35] Meanwhile, Paul and Barnabas remained in Antioch, where, along with many others, they taught and proclaimed the word of God.

C: Paul's Second Missionary Journey*

Paul and Barnabas Separate. * [36] After some time had passed, Paul said to Barnabas, "Let us go back and visit the brethren in all the cities where we proclaimed the word of the Lord so that we can see how they are progressing." [37] Barnabas wanted to take John, also called Mark, with them, [38] but Paul was adamant about not taking with them a man who had deserted them in Pamphylia and had not continued to share in their work.

[39] As a result, there was such a sharp disagreement that they parted company, and Barnabas sailed to Cyprus with Mark. [40] However, Paul chose Silas and set out on his journey, as the brethren commended him to the grace of the Lord.

Pastoral Visit to Asia Minor. * [41] He traveled through Syria and Cilicia, bringing strength to the Churches.

16 [1] He then moved on to Derbe and Lystra where there was a disciple named Timothy,* the son of a Jewish

woman who had become a believer, but his father was a Greek. [2] The brethren of Lystra and Iconium regarded him highly, [3] and Paul decided to take him along. Therefore, he had him circumcised, because of the Jews in that region who all knew that his father was a Greek.

[4] As they traveled from town to town, they made known to the brethren there the decisions that had been reached by the apostles and the elders in Jerusalem for the people to obey. [5] Day by day, the Churches grew strong in the faith and increased in numbers.

[6] They traveled through the region of Phrygia * and Galatia because they had been told by the Holy Spirit not to preach the word in the province of Asia. [7] When they approached the border of Mysia, they tried to go into Bithynia, but since the Spirit of Jesus did not allow them to do so, [8] they passed through Mysia and came down to Troas. *

Paul at Philippi. * [9] During the night, Paul had a vision in which a man of Macedonia appeared to him and pleaded with him, saying, "Cross over to Macedonia and help us." [10] Once he had seen this vision, we immediately arranged for passage to Macedonia, convinced that God had summoned us to proclaim the good news to them.

[11] We set sail from Troas and made a straight run to Samothrace. * On the following day, we reached Neapolis, [12] and from there we sailed to Philippi, * a leading city in the district of Macedonia and a Roman colony. We spent some time in that city.

[13] On the Sabbath, we went outside the city gate alongside the river where we assumed there would be a place of prayer. We sat down and spoke to the women who had gathered there. [14] One of the women, whose name was Lydia, was a worshiper of God. She was from the city of Thyatira and a dealer in purple cloth. As she listened to us, the Lord opened her heart to accept what Paul was saying. [15] When she and her household had been baptized, she urged us insistently, "If you regard me as a

believer in the Lord, come and stay at my home." And she won us over.

Paul Imprisoned at Philippi. [16] * On one occasion, as we were on our way to the place of prayer, we were met by a slave girl who was possessed by a spirit of divination and brought large profits to her owners by fortune-telling. [17] She began to follow Paul and the rest of us, shouting, "These men are servants of the Most High God, and they have come to proclaim to you a way of salvation." [18] She kept doing this for many days, until Paul became very greatly troubled. He turned and said to the spirit, "I command you in the name of Jesus Christ to come out of her." And the spirit came out of her instantly.

[19] When her owners realized that their hope of making money from her was gone, they seized Paul and Silas and dragged them into the marketplace before the authorities. [20] They brought them before the magistrates and said, "These men are causing a disturbance in our city. They are Jews, [21] and they are advocating practices that it is illegal for us as Romans to adopt or follow."

[22] The crowd joined in the attack against them, and the magistrates had them stripped and ordered them to be beaten. [23] After they had inflicted a severe beating on them, they threw them into prison and instructed the jailer to guard them closely. [24] Following these instructions, he put them in the innermost cell and locked their feet in the stocks.

Paul Set Free. [25] About midnight, Paul and Silas were praying and singing hymns of praise to God, and the prisoners were listening to them. [26] Suddenly, there was such a huge earthquake that the very foundations of the prison were shaken. At once, all the doors flew open, and everyone's chains were loosened.

[27] When the jailer awakened and saw all the doors of the prison wide open, he drew his sword, intending to kill himself, since he assumed that the prisoners had escaped. [28] However, Paul shouted in a loud voice, "Do not harm yourself, for we are all here."

²⁹ The jailer called for lights and, rushing in, he threw himself before Paul and Silas, trembling with fear. ³⁰ Then he brought them outside and said, "Sirs, what must I do to be saved?" ³¹ They answered, "Believe in the Lord Jesus, and you will be saved, and so too will your household." ³² After this, they preached the word of the Lord to him and to everyone in his house.

³³ At that late hour of the night, the jailer took them and bathed their wounds. Then he and his entire family were baptized without delay. ³⁴ Afterward, he brought them into his house and set a meal before them, and he and his entire household rejoiced over their belief in God.

³⁵ When it was daylight, the magistrates sent police officers with the order, "Let those men go." ³⁶ The jailer reported the message to Paul, saying, "The magistrates sent word to let you go. Now you can come out and depart in peace." ³⁷ But Paul said to the officers, "We are Roman citizens. They gave us a public beating and threw us into prison without a trial. And now they are going to release us secretly. Absolutely not! Let them come in person and escort us out themselves."

³⁸ The officers reported Paul's words, and the magistrates became alarmed when they learned that those men were Roman citizens. ³⁹ So they came and apologized to them, then escorted them out and begged them to leave the city. ⁴⁰ After emerging from the prison, they went to Lydia's home, where they met the brethren and spoke words of encouragement to them. Then they departed.

17 **Paul in Thessalonica.** ¹ * After they had passed through Amphipolis and Apollonia, they reached Thessalonica * where there was a Jewish synagogue. ² Following his usual practice, Paul went in, and for three Sabbaths he argued with them from the Scriptures, ³ explaining and proving that it was necessary for the Christ to suffer and rise from the dead. "And the Christ," he said, "is this Jesus whom I am proclaiming to you." ⁴ Some of them were convinced and joined Paul and Silas, as did a great many God-fearing Greeks as well as not a few prominent women.

[5] However, the Jews became jealous, and they recruited some ruffians from the marketplace, formed a mob, and soon had the city in an uproar. They stormed Jason's house, intending to bring them out before the crowd. [6] And when they could not find them there, they dragged Jason and some of the brethren before the city magistrates, shouting, "These people who have been causing trouble all over the world have come here also, [7] and Jason has given them shelter. They are all acting in opposition to the decrees of Caesar, claiming that there is another king named Jesus." [8] Upon hearing this, the mob and the magistrates were greatly agitated. [9] They then took a bond from Jason and the others before releasing them.

Paul in Beroea. [10] As soon as it got dark, the brethren sent Paul and Silas away to Beroea. Upon their arrival, they immediately went to the Jewish synagogue. [11] The people there were more receptive than those in Thessalonica. They received the word with great eagerness, and they examined the Scriptures every day to check whether these things were so. [12] Many of them became believers, as did a considerable number of influential Greek women and men.

[13] However, when the Jews of Thessalonica learned that the word of God was being proclaimed by Paul in Beroea, they followed him there to cause trouble and stir up the crowds. [14] Therefore, the brethren immediately sent Paul on his way to the coast, while Silas and Timothy remained behind. [15] After Paul's escorts brought him as far as Athens, they returned with instructions for Silas and Timothy to join him as soon as possible.

Paul in Athens.* [16] While Paul was waiting for them in Athens, he was outraged to note that the city was full of idols. [17] Therefore, he debated in the synagogue with the Jews and God-fearing Gentiles, and also in the city square with whoever chanced to be there. [18] Even a few

Epicurean and Stoic philosophers * argued with him. Some asked, "What is this man babbling about?" Others said, "Apparently, he is here to promote foreign deities," because he was preaching about Jesus and the resurrection.

[19] Therefore, they took him and brought him to the Areopagus * and asked him, "Can you explain to us what this new doctrine is that you are teaching? [20] You are presenting strange ideas to us, and we would like to find out what they all mean." [21] The major pastime of the Athenians and the foreigners living there was to spend their time telling or listening to the latest ideas.

Paul's Speech at the Areopagus. [22] * Then Paul stood before them in the Areopagus and said: "Men of Athens, I have seen how religious you are. [23] For as I walked around, looking carefully at your shrines, I noticed among them an altar with the inscription, 'To an Unknown God.' What, therefore, you worship as unknown, I now proclaim to you.

[24] "The God who made the world and everything in it, the Lord of heaven and earth, does not dwell in shrines made by human hands. [25] Nor is he served by human hands as though he were in need of anything. Rather, it is he who gives to everyone life and breath and all other things. [26] From one ancestor, * he created all peoples to occupy the entire earth, and he decreed their appointed times and the boundaries of where they would live.

[27] "He did all this so that people might seek God in the hope that by groping for him they might find him, even though indeed he is not far from any one of us. [28] For 'In him we live and move and have our being.' * As even your own poets have said, 'We are all his offspring.'

[29] "Since we are God's offspring, we ought not to think that the deity is like an image of gold or silver or stone, fashioned by human art and imagination. [30] God has overlooked the times of human ignorance, but now he commands people everywhere to repent, [31] because he

has fixed a day on which he will judge the world with justice by a man whom he has appointed. He has given public confirmation of this to all by raising him from the dead."

³² When they heard about the resurrection of the dead, some scoffed, but others said, "We should like to hear you speak further on this subject at another time." ³³ After that, Paul left them. ³⁴ However, some of them joined him and became believers, including Dionysius * the Areopagite, and a woman named Damaris, as well as some others.

18 Paul in Corinth. ¹ * At that point, Paul departed from Athens and moved on to Corinth. ² There he met a Jew named Aquila, a native of Pontus, who had recently come from Italy with his wife Priscilla because Claudius * had ordered all Jews to leave Rome. He went to visit them, ³ and because they were tentmakers just as he was, he stayed with them and they worked together. * ⁴ Every Sabbath, he entered into discussions in the synagogue, attempting to convert both Jews and Greeks.

⁵ After Silas and Timothy arrived from Macedonia, Paul devoted all his efforts to preaching the word, testifying to the Jews that Jesus was the Christ. ⁶ When they opposed him and began to hurl insults, he shook out his garments in protest and said to them, "Your blood be on your own heads! I have a clear conscience. From now on, I will go to the Gentiles."

⁷ With that, he left and went to the house of a man named Titus Justus, a worshiper of God, who lived next door to the synagogue. ⁸ Crispus, the leader of the synagogue, became a believer in the Lord along with his entire household. Many Corinthians who heard Paul came to believe and were baptized.

⁹ One night, the Lord appeared to Paul in a vision * and said, "Do not be afraid. Continue with your preaching, and do not be silent, ¹⁰ for I am with you. No one will attack you or try to harm you, for there are many in this

city who are my people." [11] And so he remained there for eighteen months, teaching the word of God to them.

Accusations before Gallio. [12] However, when Gallio became proconsul of Achaia, the Jews made a concerted attack on Paul and brought him before the tribunal, [13] saying, "This man is persuading people to worship God in ways that are contrary to the Law."

[14] Just as Paul was about to refute them, Gallio said to the Jews, "If you were accusing this man of some crime or fraudulent act, O Jews, I would be more than willing to listen to your complaint. [15] But since your argument is about words and names and your own Law, settle it yourselves. I have no intention of making judgments about such matters." [16] With that, he dismissed them from the tribunal. [17] Then they all attacked Sosthenes, the leader of the synagogue, and beat him in front of the tribunal. But Gallio remained unconcerned about their action.

Return to Antioch in Pisidia. * [18] After he remained in Corinth for some considerable time, Paul took leave of the brethren and sailed for Syria, accompanied by Priscilla and Aquila. At Cenchreae, he had his hair cut because he had taken a vow.

[19] When they reached Ephesus, * he left them there. He himself went into the synagogue and had discussions with the Jews. [20] When they asked him to stay longer, he declined, [21] but on taking leave of them he promised, "I will return to you, if God wills." Then he set sail from Ephesus. [22] When he landed at Caesarea, he went up and greeted the Church, * and then he went down to Antioch.

III: EPHESUS*

A: Paul's Third Missionary Journey*

Paul Strengthens the Churches. [23] After spending some time there, he departed and traveled through the regions of Galatia and Phrygia, strengthening all the disciples.

Apollos.* [24] Meanwhile, a Jew named Apollos, a native of Alexandria and an eloquent speaker, came to Ephesus. He was well-versed in the Scriptures, [25] and he had been instructed in the Way of the Lord. Filled with spiritual fervor, he spoke and taught accurately about Jesus, although he had experienced only the baptism of God.

[26] He then began to speak boldly in the synagogue, but when Priscilla and Aquila heard him, they took him aside and explained to him more accurately the Way. [27] And when he expressed a wish to cross over to Achaia, the brethren encouraged him and wrote to the disciples there, asking that they make him welcome. From the time of his arrival, he was of great help to those who by the grace of God had become believers. [28] For he vigorously refuted the Jews in public, establishing from the Scriptures that Jesus is the Christ.

19 Paul in Ephesus.*

[1] While Apollos was in Corinth, Paul traveled through the interior regions and came to Ephesus, where he found some disciples. [2] He said to them, "Did you receive the Holy Spirit when you became believers?" They replied, "No. We have not even heard that there is a Holy Spirit." [3] He asked, "Then how were you baptized?" They answered, "With the baptism of John."

[4] Paul said, "John baptized with the baptism of repentance, telling the people to believe in the one who was to come after him, that is, Jesus." [5] On hearing this, they were baptized in the name of the Lord Jesus. [6] When Paul had laid his hands on them, the Holy Spirit came upon them, and they spoke in tongues and prophesied. [7] There were about twelve of them in all.

[8] He then entered the synagogue, and during the next three months he spoke out fearlessly and argued persuasively about the kingdom of God. [9] But some remained stubborn in their disbelief and began to malign the Way publicly. So he withdrew from them, taking the disciples with him, and began to hold daily discussions in the hall

of Tyrannus. [10] This continued for two years, with the result that all the residents of the province of Asia, both Jews and Greeks, heard the word of the Lord.

New Encounter of the Church with Magic.* [11] So extraordinary were the wonders God worked through Paul [12] that when handkerchiefs or aprons that had touched his skin were brought to the sick, they were cured of their diseases and the evil spirits came out of them.

[13] Then some itinerant Jewish exorcists used the name of the Lord Jesus over those possessed by evil spirits, saying, "I adjure you by the Jesus whom Paul proclaims." [14] Seven sons of a Jewish leading priest named Sceva were among those who were doing this. [15] But the evil spirit responded, "Jesus I know, and Paul I know, but who are you?" [16] Then the man with the evil spirit sprang at them, overpowered them, and prevailed over them so violently that they fled out of the house battered and naked.

[17] When this became known to all the residents of Ephesus, both Jews and Greeks, everyone was awestruck, and the name of the Lord Jesus came to be held in ever increasing honor. [18] Moreover, many of those who had become believers came forward and openly confessed their deeds, [19] while a great number of those who practiced magic collected their books and burned them publicly. When the value of these books was calculated, it was found to come to fifty thousand silver pieces. * [20] In such ways did the word of the Lord spread ever more widely and successfully.

Paul's Future Plans.* [21] After all this had been accomplished, Paul decided in the Spirit to visit Macedonia and Achaia and then return to Jerusalem. "And after I have been there," he said, "I must also visit Rome." [22] Then he sent two of his assistants, Timothy and Erastus, to Macedonia, while he himself stayed a while longer in the province of Asia.

The Riot of the Silversmiths. [23] About that time, a serious disturbance broke out concerning the Way. [24] A man named Demetrius was a silversmith who crafted silver shrines of Artemis * that provided considerable employment for the craftsmen. [25] He called a meeting of these craftsmen and of those in similar trades, and addressed them: "As you men know, our prosperity depends upon this business. [26] And as you can now see and hear, not only in Ephesus but also throughout most of the province of Asia this Paul has persuaded and turned away a considerable number of people by insisting that gods fashioned by human hands are not gods.

[27] "Therefore, we are facing a dangerous situation. Not only may our business be discredited, but it could also happen that the temple of the great goddess Artemis will become an object of scorn, and that she who is worshiped throughout the province of Asia and the entire world will be deprived of her greatness."

[28] When they heard this, they became enraged and began to shout, "Great is Artemis of the Ephesians!" [29] The entire city was in an uproar, and the people all rushed to the theater, dragging along with them Gaius and Aristarchus,* Macedonians who were Paul's traveling companions. [30] Paul wanted to appear before the crowd, but the disciples would not permit him to do so. [31] Even some officials of the province of Asia who were friendly to him sent him a message urging him not to venture into the theater.*

[32] Meanwhile, some were shouting one thing, some another, for the assembly was in an uproar, and most of the people had no idea why they had all come together. [33] Some of the crowd prompted Alexander, whom the Jews had pushed forward. Then Alexander motioned for silence and tried to offer some type of defense. [34] However, as soon as the crowd recognized him to be a Jew, all of them shouted in unison for about two hours, "Great is Artemis of the Ephesians!"

[35] Finally, the town clerk quieted the crowd and said, "Citizens of Ephesus, is there anyone who does not know that the city of the Ephesians is the guardian of the tem-

ple * of the great Artemis and of her statue that descended from heaven? ³⁶ Since these things cannot be denied, you ought to remain calm and do nothing rash. ³⁷ These men whom you have brought here are not temple robbers, nor have they uttered any blasphemy against our goddess.

³⁸ "Therefore, if Demetrius and his fellow artisans have a complaint against anyone, the courts are open, and proconsuls are available. Let them bring charges there against one another. ³⁹ If there are further charges to present, let these be settled in the lawful assembly. ⁴⁰ As it is, we are in danger of being charged with rioting today. There is no reason for it, and we will be unable to offer any justification for this commotion." ⁴¹ When he had said this, he dismissed the assembly.

20 Journey to Macedonia and Greece. ¹ * When the uproar was over, Paul sent for the disciples, and after encouraging them, he embraced them and set out on his journey to Macedonia. * ² As he traveled through those areas, he gave the believers much encouragement. Then he arrived in Greece, ³ where he stayed for three months.

Return to Troas. He was about to set sail for Syria when a plot against him was devised by the Jews, and so he decided to return by way of Macedonia. ⁴ He was accompanied by Sopater son of Pyrrhus from Beroea, by Aristarchus and Secundus from Thessalonica, by Gaius from Derbe, and by Timothy, as well as by Tychicus and Trophimus from Asia. * ⁵ They went ahead and were waiting for us in Troas. * ⁶ We sailed from Philippi after the feast of Unleavened Bread, and five days later we joined them in Troas, where we stayed for seven days.

B: Paul's Witness and Testament*

Paul Raises Eutychus to Life. ⁷ On the first day of the week, when we gathered for the breaking of the bread, Paul spoke to the people, and because he was going to leave on the next day, he continued speaking until midnight. [8] There were many lamps in the upper room where we were assembled, [9] and a young man named Eutychus, who was sitting on the window ledge, became ever more drowsy as Paul talked on and on. Finally, overcome by sleep, he fell to the ground three floors below, and when they picked him up, he was dead.

[10] Paul went down, threw himself upon him, and took him in his arms. "Do not be alarmed," he said. "He is still alive." * [11] Then he went back upstairs and broke bread and ate. He went on to converse with them until dawn, at which time he left. [12] Meanwhile, they had taken the boy home, greatly relieved that he was alive.

Journey to Miletus. [13] We went on ahead to the ship and set sail for Assos, where we were to take Paul aboard, since he intended to continue his journey by land. [14] When he met us in Assos, we took him aboard and went to Mitylene.

[15] We sailed from there, and on the following day we reached a point opposite Chios. A day later, we reached Samos; and the day after that, we came to Miletus. [16] For Paul had decided to sail past Ephesus in order to avoid spending time in the province of Asia. He was eager to be in Jerusalem, if possible, on the day of Pentecost.

Paul's Farewell Speech at Miletus.* [17] From Miletus, he sent a message to Ephesus, summoning the elders of the Church. [18] When they came to him, he addressed them as follows:

"You yourselves know how I lived among you the whole time from the first day that I set foot in the province of Asia. [19] I served the Lord with all humility and with tears, enduring the trials that befell me as a result of the intrigues of the Jews. [20] I did not hesitate to tell you what was for your benefit as I proclaimed the word to you and taught you publicly as well as from house to house. [21] I have attested to Jews and Gentiles alike about repentance before God and faith in our Lord Jesus.

[22] "And now, compelled by the Spirit, I am on my way to Jerusalem without knowing what will happen to me there, [23] except that in every city the Holy Spirit warns me that I will face imprisonment and hardships. [24] As for me, I do not regard my life as of any value, only that I finish the race and complete the mission that I received from the Lord Jesus—to bear witness to the gospel of God's grace.

[25] "I have gone among you proclaiming the kingdom, but now I realize that none of you will ever see my face again. [26] Therefore, I solemnly declare to you this day that I am innocent of the blood of all of you, [27] for I did not shrink from proclaiming to you the entire plan of God. [28] Keep watch over yourselves and over all the flock of which the Holy Spirit has made you overseers, and be shepherds of the Church of God that he purchased with the price of his own blood.

[29] "I know that after I have gone, savage wolves will come among you and will not spare the flock. [30] Even from your own ranks men will come distorting the truth in order to entice the disciples to follow them. [31] Therefore, be on your guard. Remember that for three years I never ceased night and day to warn every one of you with tears.

[32] "And now I commend you to God and to the word of his grace that is able to build you up and give you your inheritance among all who are sanctified. [33] I have never coveted anyone's silver or gold or clothing. [34] You are aware that I worked with my own hands to support myself and my companions. [35] In all this, I have shown you that by such hard work we must help the weak, keeping in mind the words of the Lord Jesus who himself said, 'It is more blessed to give than to receive.' " *

[36] When he had finished speaking, he knelt down and prayed with them. [37] They were all weeping loudly as they embraced Paul and kissed him, [38] for they were deeply distressed at his words that they would never see his face again. Then they escorted him to the ship.

IV: FROM JERUSALEM TO ROME*

A: Last Journey to Jerusalem*

21 **Arrival at Tyre.** [1] When we * had finally torn ourselves away from them and set sail, we traveled directly to Cos, and the next day to Rhodes, and from there to Patara. [2] There, we found a ship bound for Phoenicia, so we went on board and set sail. [3] After sighting Cyprus, we passed by it on our left and sailed to Syria, landing at Tyre where the ship was to unload her cargo.

[4] We sought out the disciples there and stayed with them for seven days. Through the Spirit, they advised Paul to abandon his plans to move on to Jerusalem. [5] However, when our time with them was ended, we left and continued on our journey. All of them, including women and children, escorted us outside the city. Kneeling down on the beach, we prayed [6] and then bid farewell to one another. Afterward, we boarded the ship and they returned home.

Arrival at Ptolemais and Caesarea. [7] We finished our voyage from Tyre and arrived at Ptolemais, where we greeted the brethren and stayed with them for one day. [8] On the next day, we left and came to Caesarea, where we went to the house of Philip the evangelist, who was one of the Seven, * and stayed with him. [9] He had four unmarried daughters who possessed the gift of prophecy.

[10] After we had been there for several days, a prophet named Agabus arrived from Judea. [11] He came up to us, took Paul's belt, bound his own feet and hands with it, and said, "Thus says the Holy Spirit: 'In this way the Jews in Jerusalem will bind the owner of this belt, and they will hand him over to the Gentiles.'"

[12] When we heard this, we joined with the people who lived there in begging Paul not to go up to Jerusalem. [13] Then Paul replied, "What are you doing, weeping and breaking my heart? For I am ready not only to be bound but even to die in Jerusalem for the name of the Lord

Jesus." ¹⁴ Since he would not be dissuaded, we finally gave up and said, "The Lord's will be done."

B: Various Events and Paul's Defenses at Jerusalem

Paul Is Welcomed by the Elders.* ¹⁵ At the end of our stay, we made preparations and went up to Jerusalem. ¹⁶ Some of the disciples from Caesarea accompanied us and brought us to the house of Mnason of Cyprus, one of the early disciples, with whom we were to stay.

¹⁷ When we arrived in Jerusalem, the brethren gave us a warm welcome. ¹⁸ On the next day, Paul paid a visit to James. We accompanied him, and all the elders were present. ¹⁹ After greeting them, he reported in detail what God had done among the Gentiles through his ministry.

²⁰ When they heard this, they gave praise to God. Then they said to Paul, "You can see, brother, how many thousands of believers there are among the Jews, and all of them are zealous upholders of the Law. ²¹ They have been informed in your regard that you teach all the Jews who live among the Gentiles to forsake Moses and that you tell them not to circumcise their children or to observe their custom. ²² What then is to be done? They are sure to hear that you have arrived.

²³ "This is what we suggest that you do. We have four men here who are under a vow. ²⁴ Take these men, go through the rite of purification with them, and pay the expenses involved with the shaving of their heads. In this way, all will know that there is nothing in these reports they have been given about you and that you observe the Law. ²⁵ As for the Gentiles who have become believers, we have informed them of our decision that they must abstain from meat that has been sacrificed to idols, from blood, from anything that has been strangled, and from unchastity."

²⁶ Therefore, on the next day Paul took the men and purified himself along with them. He then entered the

temple to give notice of the date when the period of purification would end and the offerings would be made for each of them.

Paul's Arrest in the Temple.* [27] When the seven days were nearly over, the Jews from the province of Asia saw him in the temple. Stirring up the whole crowd, they seized him, [28] shouting, "Men of Israel, help us! This is the man who is teaching everyone everywhere against our people, the Law, and this place. What is more, he has brought Greeks into the temple and defiled this holy place." [29] They had previously seen Trophimus the Ephesian with him in the city and assumed that Paul had brought him into the temple.

[30] Thus, the entire city was in turmoil, and people came running from all directions. They seized Paul and dragged him out of the temple, and the gates were then shut. [31] While they were trying to kill him, word reached the commander of the cohort that all Jerusalem was in an uproar. [32] Immediately, he took soldiers and centurions with him and charged down on them.

When the Jews saw the commander and the soldiers, they stopped beating Paul. [33] Then the commander came forward, arrested him, and ordered him to be bound with two chains. Next he asked who he was and what he had done. [34] Some in the crowd shouted one thing and some another; and since the commander could not arrive at the truth because of the uproar, he ordered that Paul be taken into the barracks. [35] When he came to the steps, the violence of the crowd was so intense that he had to be carried by the soldiers. [36] The crowd that followed kept shouting, "Away with him!"

[37] Just as he was about to be taken into the barracks, Paul said to the commander, "May I say something to you?" The commander replied, "So you speak Greek? [38] Then you are not the Egyptian * who recently started a revolt and led the four thousand assassins into the desert." [39] Paul asserted, "I am a Jew from Tarsus in Cilicia, a citizen of no mean city. May I have your per-

mission to speak to the people?" ⁴⁰When the permission
was granted, Paul stood on the steps and raised his hand
to the people for silence. As soon as quiet was restored,
he started speaking to them in Aramaic. *

22 Paul's Speech to the People of Jerusalem.* ¹ "Brethren
and fathers, listen to what I have to say to you in my
defense." ²When they heard him addressing them in
Aramaic, they became even more quiet than before.

Then he continued, ³ "I am a Jew, born at Tarsus in
Cilicia, but brought up in this city. As a pupil of Gamaliel,
I was thoroughly trained in the Law of our ancestors. I
have always been zealous toward God, just as all of you
are today. ⁴I even persecuted the followers of this Way to
their death, sending both men and women to prison in
chains, ⁵ as the high priest and the whole council of elders
can testify. From them I also received letters to our
brethren in Damascus, and I set out to bring prisoners
back from there to Jerusalem for punishment.

⁶ "While I was on my way and drawing near Damascus,
around midday a great light from the sky suddenly shone
all around me. ⁷ I fell to the ground and heard a voice saying, 'Saul, Saul, why are you persecuting me?' ⁸ I
answered, 'Who are you, Lord?' Then he said to me, 'I am
Jesus of Nazareth, whom you are persecuting.'

⁹ "Now those who were with me saw the light, but they
did not hear the voice of the one who was speaking to me.
¹⁰ I asked, 'What do you want me to do, Lord?' The Lord
said to me, 'Get up and go into Damascus. There you will
be told everything that you have been appointed to do.'
¹¹ I could not see because of the brilliance of that light,
and so my companions led me by the hand to Damascus.

¹² "A man named Ananias, who was a devout observer
of the Law and highly regarded by all the Jews who lived
there, ¹³ came to see me. Standing beside me, he said,
'Brother Saul, regain your sight.' Instantly, I saw him.

¹⁴ "Then he said, 'The God of our ancestors has chosen you to know his will, to see the Righteous One, and

to hear him speak. ¹⁵ For you will be his witness* to tell all what you have seen and heard. ¹⁶ And now, what are you waiting for? Get up, be baptized, and have your sins washed away, calling on his name.'

¹⁷ "After I had returned to Jerusalem, and while I was praying in the temple, I fell into a trance ¹⁸ and saw Jesus there. 'Hurry and leave Jerusalem at once,' he said, 'because they will not accept your testimony about me.' ¹⁹ But I replied, 'Lord, they themselves know that in every synagogue I used to imprison and scourge those who believe in you. ²⁰ And while the blood of your martyr Stephen was being shed, I myself stood by, giving my approval and guarding the coats of his murderers.' ²¹ Then he said to me, 'Go! I am sending you far away to the Gentiles.'"

Paul Claims His Roman Citizenship.* ²² Up to this point, the crowd had listened to him, but then they raised their voices and began to shout, "Rid the earth of this man! He should not be allowed to live." ²³ And as they were shouting and throwing off their cloaks and flinging dust into the air, ²⁴ the commander ordered that he be brought into the barracks and gave instructions that he be interrogated while being scourged to discover the reason for this outcry against him.

²⁵ But when they had stretched him out and bound him with thongs, Paul said to the centurion who was standing nearby, "Is it lawful for you to scourge a man who is a Roman citizen and who has not been condemned?" ²⁶ When the centurion heard this, he went to the commander and asked, "What are you going to do? This man is a Roman citizen."

²⁷ Then the commander came to him and inquired, "Tell me, are you a Roman citizen?" And he answered, "Yes." ²⁸ The commander responded, "It cost me a great deal of money to acquire this citizenship." Paul replied, "But I was born a citizen." ²⁹ Then those who were about to interrogate him withdrew hurriedly, and the commander himself was alarmed when he realized

that Paul was a Roman citizen and that he had put him in chains.

Paul's First Trial—before the Sanhedrin.* ³⁰ Since the commander wanted to learn with certitude what Paul was being accused of by the Jews, he released him on the following day and ordered the chief priests and the entire Sanhedrin to meet. Then he brought Paul down and had him stand before them.

23

¹ Paul looked intently at the Sanhedrin and said, "Brethren, to this very day, I have conducted myself before God with a perfectly clear conscience." ² At this, the high priest Ananias * ordered his attendants to strike him on the mouth.

³ Then Paul said to him, "God will strike you, you whitewashed wall! How can you sit there to judge me according to the Law and then in defiance of the Law order me to be struck?" ⁴ The attendants said, "Do you dare to insult God's high priest?" ⁵ Paul replied, "Brethren, I did not realize that he was the high priest. It is clearly written: 'You shall not curse the ruler of your people.'"

⁶ Well aware that some of them were Sadducees and the others were Pharisees, Paul called out in the Sanhedrin, "Brethren, I am a Pharisee and the son of Pharisees. I am on trial concerning our hope in the resurrection of the dead." ⁷ When he said this, a dispute ensued between the Pharisees and the Sadducees, and the assembly was divided. ⁸ For the Sadducees hold that there is no resurrection and that there are no angels or spirits, while the Pharisees believe in all three.

⁹ Then a great uproar arose, and some of the scribes belonging to the party of the Pharisees stood up and forcefully stated, "We find nothing wrong with this man. What if a spirit or an angel has really spoken to him?" ¹⁰ When a violent dissension arose, the commander was fearful that Paul would be torn to pieces. He ordered the

soldiers to go down, seize him from their midst, and bring him into the barracks.

[11] On the following night, the Lord appeared to Paul and said, "Keep up your courage! For just as you have borne witness to me in Jerusalem, so you must also bear witness in Rome."

A Plot To Kill Paul. * [12] When morning came, the Jews formed a conspiracy and bound themselves by an oath * not to eat or drink until they had killed Paul. [13] There were more than forty who entered this pact. [14] They went to the chief priests and elders and told them, "We have bound ourselves by a solemn oath not to consume any food until we have killed Paul. [15] You and the Sanhedrin should make an official request to the commander to bring him down to you on the pretext that you want to investigate his case more thoroughly. We on our part have arranged to kill him before he arrives."

[16] However, the son of Paul's sister learned of the plot. He thereupon went to the barracks and related the news to Paul. [17] Paul then summoned one of the centurions and said, "Take this young man to the commander, for he has something to report to him." [18] He brought him to the commander and said, "The prisoner Paul called me and requested that I bring this young man to you. He has something to tell you."

[19] The commander took him by the hand, drew him aside, and asked him in private, "What is it that you have to report to me?" [20] He replied, "The Jews have agreed to request you to bring Paul down to the Sanhedrin tomorrow on the pretext of inquiring more thoroughly into his case. [21] Do not believe them. More than forty of them are waiting for your consent to their request, for they have sworn an oath not to eat or drink until they have killed him. They are ready now and are waiting only for your consent." [22] The commander dismissed the young man, ordering him, "Tell no one that you have given me this information."

C: Paul's Imprisonment and Defenses at Caesarea

Paul Is Imprisoned at Caesarea. * [23] Then he summoned two of his centurions and said, "Have two hundred soldiers ready to leave for Caesarea by nine o'clock tonight, * along with seventy cavalrymen and two hundred auxiliaries. [24] Also provide mounts for Paul to ride, and deliver him to Felix the governor." [25] He then wrote a letter as follows:

[26] Claudius Lysias

To his Excellency the governor Felix: *

Greetings.

[27] This man was seized by the Jews and was about to be killed by them; but when I learned that he was a Roman citizen, I arrived on the scene with my troops and rescued him.

[28] Wanting to learn what charge they were making against him, I had him brought before their Sanhedrin. [29] I discovered that the accusation dealt with questions about their Law, but that there was no charge against him that merited death or imprisonment. [30] Now I have been informed of a plot to assassinate this man. I am sending him to you without delay, and I have instructed his accusers to present to you their case against him.

[31] Therefore, the soldiers, acting in accordance with their orders, took Paul and escorted him during the night to Antipatris. [32] On the next day, they returned to the barracks, leaving the cavalrymen to escort him the rest of the way. [33] When they arrived in Caesarea, they delivered the letter to the governor and handed over Paul to him.

[34] After reading the letter, the governor asked Paul what province he was from, and on learning that he was from Cilicia, [35] he said, "I will hear your case as soon as your accusers arrive." Then he ordered that he be held in custody in Herod's praetorium.

24 Paul's Second Trial—before Felix.* [1] Five days later, the high priest Ananias came down with some of the elders and an advocate named Tertullus, and they presented charges against Paul to the governor. [2] Then Paul was summoned, and Tertullus began the prosecution.

He said, "Because of you we have enjoyed an unbroken period of peace, and reforms have been made in this nation as a result of your caring concern. [3] We acknowledge this everywhere and in every way with the utmost gratitude, most noble Felix.

[4] "But in order not to detain you needlessly, I beg you to be kind enough to listen to a brief statement. [5] We have found this man to be a troublemaker. He is a fomenter of dissension among Jews all over the world and a ringleader of the sect of the Nazarenes. [6] When he even tried to profane the temple, we placed him under arrest. [[7] We would have judged him according to our own Law, but the commander Lysias came and forcibly removed him out of our hands, ordering his accusers to appear before you.] * [8] If you examine him yourself, you will be able to ascertain the validity of all the charges we bring against him." [9] The Jews supported the charge, asserting that these things were true.

[10] Then the governor motioned to Paul to speak, and he replied, "I know that you have administered justice to this nation for many years, and therefore I feel confident in presenting my defense. [11] As you can verify for yourself, no more than twelve days have elapsed since I went up to worship in Jerusalem. [12] They did not find me disputing with anyone in the temple or stirring up a crowd either in the synagogues or throughout the city. [13] Nor can they offer you any proof concerning their charges against me.

[14] "But this much I will admit to you: it is as a follower of the Way, which they call a sect, that I worship the God of my ancestors, believing everything that is in accordance with the Law or is written in the Prophets. [15] I hold

the same hope in God as they do that there will be a resurrection of the righteous and the wicked alike. [16] Accordingly, I strive at all times to have a clear conscience before God and man.

[17] "After several years, I came to bring charitable gifts to my people and to offer sacrifices. [18] They found me in the temple after I had completed the rite of purification. There was no crowd with me, nor was I involved in any disturbance.

"However, some Jews from the province of Asia were there, [19] and they are the ones who should have appeared before you to give such evidence if they had any charge against me. [20] At the very least, those who are present here should state what crime they discovered when I was brought before the Sanhedrin, [21] unless it has to do with this one declaration I made when I stood up among them, 'I am on trial on account of the resurrection of the dead.'"

In the Procurator's Hall. * [22] Then Felix, who was well informed about the Way, adjourned the hearing with the comment, "When Lysias the commander comes down, I shall issue a ruling on this case." [23] He also ordered the centurion to keep Paul in custody, but allow him some freedom, and not to prevent any of his friends from caring for his needs.

[24] Several days later, Felix came with his wife Drusilla, * who was a Jewess. He sent for Paul and listened to him speak about faith in Christ Jesus. [25] But as Paul discussed justice, self-control, and the coming judgment, Felix became frightened and exclaimed, "Go away for the present. When I have an opportunity, I will send for you." [26] At the same time, he hoped that Paul would offer him a bribe. Therefore he used to send for him quite often and converse with him.

[27] After two years had passed, Felix was succeeded by Porcius Festus, * and since he wanted to ingratiate himself with the Jews, Felix left Paul in custody.

25 Paul's Third Trial—before Festus.* [1] Three days after
his arrival in the province, Festus went up from Caesarea
to Jerusalem, [2] where the chief priests and the leaders of
the Jews informed him about Paul. They urged him [3] as a
favor to send for Paul to bring him to Jerusalem. They
were going to kill him in an ambush along the way.

[4] Festus replied that Paul was in custody in Caesarea,
and that he himself would be returning there shortly. [5] He
said, "Let your authorities come down with me, and if
this man has done something improper, they can bring a
charge against him."

[6] After staying with them for eight to ten days, Festus
went down to Caesarea. On the next day, he took his seat
on the tribunal and ordered Paul to be summoned.
[7] When he appeared, the Jews who had come down from
Jerusalem surrounded him, and they leveled many serious charges against him that they were unable to prove.

[8] Paul said in his defense, "I have committed no offense
against the Jewish Law, or against the temple, or against
the Emperor." [9] Festus, anxious to ingratiate himself with
the Jews, asked Paul, "Do you wish to go up to Jerusalem
and stand trial there before me on these charges?"

[10] Paul replied, "I am standing before the tribunal of
Caesar, and this is where I should be tried. I have committed no crime against the Jews, as you yourself well
know. [11] If I am guilty of any capital crime, I do not ask to
be spared death. However, if there is no substance to the
charges they are bringing against me, then no one has the
right to turn me over to them. I appeal to Caesar." *
[12] Then, after Festus had conferred with his advisors, he
said, "You have appealed to Caesar. To Caesar you shall
go."

Paul's Fourth Trial—before Agrippa. * [13] Some days later,
King Agrippa and Bernice arrived in Caesarea to pay
their respects to Festus. [14] Since they spent several days
there, Festus raised the subject of Paul's case before the
king, saying, "There is a man here who was left in cus-

tody by Felix. [15] When I was in Jerusalem, the chief priests and the elders of the Jews brought charges against him and requested his condemnation. [16] I told them that it was not the custom of the Romans to hand over anyone before he had met his accusers face to face and had had an opportunity to defend himself against their charges.

[17] "Therefore, when they had come here, I wasted no time; the very next day, I took my seat on the tribunal and ordered the man to be summoned. [18] When the accusers rose, they did not charge him with any of the crimes that I was expecting. [19] Instead, they had certain points of disagreement with him about their own religion and about someone named Jesus, a dead man who Paul asserted was alive.

[20] "Since I did not feel qualified to deal with such questions, I asked him if he would be willing to go to Jerusalem to stand trial on these charges. [21] But Paul appealed to be held in custody for the Emperor's decision, and I ordered him to be held until I could send him to Caesar." [22] Agrippa said to Festus, "I would like to hear this man for myself." He replied, "Tomorrow you will hear him."

[23] On the next day, Agrippa and Bernice arrived with great pomp and entered the audience hall, accompanied by officers of high rank and prominent men of the city. Festus ordered Paul to be brought in. [24] Then he said, "King Agrippa and all of you here present with us, you see this man about whom the entire Jewish community petitioned me, both in Jerusalem and here, shouting loudly that he should not be allowed to live any longer.

[25] "I have found nothing deserving of death, but when he made his appeal to the Emperor, I decided to send him. [26] However, I have nothing definite about him to put in writing for our sovereign. Therefore, I have brought him before all of you, and especially before you, King Agrippa, so that after this examination I may have something to write. [27] For it seems senseless to me to send on a prisoner without indicating the charges against him."

26 **Paul's Defense before Agrippa.** [1] Agrippa said to Paul, "You have permission to speak for yourself." Then Paul stretched out his hand and began to defend himself: [2] "I consider myself fortunate, King Agrippa, that it is before you that today I am to defend myself against all the accusations of the Jews, [3] particularly since you are well acquainted with all our Jewish customs and controversies. Therefore, I implore you to listen to me patiently.

[4] "The Jews all know my way of life from my youth, which I first lived among my own people and in Jerusalem. [5] They have known about me from my youth, and they could testify, if they were willing, that I belonged to the strictest sect of our religion and lived as a Pharisee. [6] But now I am on trial because of my hope in the promise made by God to our ancestors.

[7] "Our twelve tribes worship night and day with intense devotion in the hope of seeing its fulfillment. It is because of this hope that I am accused by the Jews, O king. [8] Why should it seem incredible to any of you that God raises the dead?

[9] "I myself once thought that I had to do everything possible against the name of Jesus of Nazareth. [10] And that is what I did in Jerusalem. With the authorization of the chief priests, I not only sent many of the saints * to prison, but when they were being condemned to death, I cast my vote against them. [11] In all the synagogues, I tried by inflicting repeated punishments to force them to blaspheme, and I was so enraged with fury against them that I even pursued them to foreign cities.

[12] "On one such occasion, I was traveling to Damascus with the authorization and commission of the chief priests. [13] At midday, as I was on my way, O king, I saw a light from the sky, brighter than the sun, shining all around me and my companions. [14] We all fell to the ground, and I heard a voice saying to me in Aramaic, 'Saul, Saul, why are you persecuting me? It is hard for you to kick against the goad.' *

¹⁵ "I asked, 'Who are you, Lord?' The Lord answered, 'I am Jesus, whom you are persecuting. ¹⁶ Get up now and stand on your feet, for I have appeared to you for this purpose, to appoint you as my servant and as a witness to what you have seen of me and what you will yet see. ¹⁷ I will rescue you from your own people and from the Gentiles to whom I am sending you. ¹⁸ You are to open their eyes so that they may turn from darkness to light * and from the power of Satan to God. Thus, they may obtain forgiveness of their sins and an inheritance among those who have been consecrated through faith in me.'

¹⁹ "And so, King Agrippa, I did not disobey the vision from heaven. ²⁰ Rather, I started to preach, first to the people in Damascus, and then in Jerusalem and throughout the countryside of Judea, and also to the Gentiles, calling on them to repent and turn to God and prove their repentance by their deeds. ²¹ That is why the Jews seized me in the temple and tried to kill me.

²² "But I have had help from God to this very day, and I stand here and testify to both the lowly and the great. I assert nothing more than what the Prophets and Moses said would occur: ²³ that the Christ must suffer, and that, by being the first to rise from the dead, he would proclaim light to the people and to the Gentiles."

Reactions to Paul's Speech. ²⁴ While Paul was still speaking in his own defense, Festus exclaimed, "You are out of your mind, Paul! Too much learning is driving you insane." ²⁵ But he replied, "I am not out of my mind, most excellent Festus. What I am asserting is true and reasonable. ²⁶ The king understands these matters, and to him I now speak freely. I am confident that none of this has escaped his notice, for all this was not done in a corner. * ²⁷ King Agrippa, do you believe the Prophets? * I know that you do."

²⁸ Then Agrippa said to Paul, "Do you think that in such a brief time you can persuade me to become a Christian?" ²⁹ Paul responded, "Whether in a short time

or longer, I pray to God that not only you but also all who are listening to me today may become what I am, except for these chains."

³⁰ Then the king rose, and with him the governor and Bernice and those who had been seated with them. ³¹ And as they were leaving, they said to one another, "This man is doing nothing that deserves death or imprisonment." ³² And Agrippa said to Festus, "This man could have been set free if he had not appealed to Caesar."

D: The Journey to Rome*

27 **Paul's Voyage toward Rome.** ¹ When it was decided that we* should sail for Italy, Paul and some other prisoners were handed over to Julius, a centurion of the Augustan cohort. ² We embarked on a ship from Adramyttium* that was about to sail to ports in the province of Asia, and we put out to sea, accompanied by Aristarchus, a Macedonian from Thessalonica.

³ On the next day, we landed at Sidon, * and Julius was considerate enough to allow Paul to visit his friends there and be cared for by them. ⁴ From there, we put out to sea again and sailed around the sheltered side of Cyprus because of the headwinds. ⁵ Then, crossing the open sea off the coast of Cilicia and Pamphylia, we reached Myra in Lycia. *

Storm and Shipwreck. ⁶ There the centurion found an Alexandrian ship* that was bound for Italy and put us on board. ⁷ For a good many days, we made little headway, and we experienced difficulty in reaching Cnidus. * Then, as the wind continued to pose difficulties, we sailed for the sheltered side of Crete off Salmone. ⁸ We moved along the coast with difficulty and reached a place called Fair Havens, * near the city of Lasea.

⁹ Much time had already been lost, and sailing had now become hazardous, since the time of the Fast* had already gone by. Therefore, Paul gave them this warning, ¹⁰ "Men, I can see that this voyage will be fraught with

danger and involve heavy losses, not only of the ship and the cargo but also of our lives."

[11] However, the centurion paid more attention to the advice of the captain and of the ship's owner than to what Paul said. [12] Since the harbor was unsuitable for spending the winter, the majority were in favor of putting out to sea from there, in the hope that they could reach Phoenix, * a harbor of Crete facing southwest and northwest, and spend the winter there.

[13] When a gentle southerly breeze began to blow, they thought that they would be able to achieve their objective. They weighed anchor and began to sail past Crete, hugging the shore. [14] But before long a violent wind, called a northeaster, swept down on them. [15] Since the ship was caught up in it, we had to give way to the wind and let ourselves be driven along.

[16] As we passed along the sheltered side of a small island called Cauda, * we managed with some difficulty to secure the ship's lifeboat. [17] After hoisting it up, they used cables to undergird the ship. Then, afraid of running aground on the shallows of Syrtis, * they lowered the sea anchor and so let themselves drift.

[18] We were being pounded so violently by the storm that on the next day they began to throw the cargo overboard. [19] Then on the third day, they threw the ship's gear overboard with their own hands. [20] For many days, neither the sun nor the stars could be seen, and the storm continued to rage until we finally abandoned all hope of being saved.

[21] When they all had gone without food for a long time, Paul stood up among them and said, "Men, you should have listened to me and not have set sail from Crete. Then you would have avoided all this damage and loss. [22] I urge you now to keep up your courage. There will be no loss of life among you. Only the ship will be lost.

[23] "Last night an angel of the God to whom I belong and whom I serve appeared to me, [24] and he said, 'Do not

be afraid, Paul. You shall appear before Caesar. Furthermore, for your sake God has granted safety to all those who are sailing with you.' ²⁵ Therefore, men, keep up your courage. I have complete trust in God that what he told me will be fulfilled. ²⁶ But we will run aground on some island."

²⁷ On the fourteenth night, we were still drifting across the Adriatic Sea. * About midnight, the sailors began to suspect that they were nearing land, ²⁸ so they took soundings and found that the water was twenty feet deep. A little farther on they again took soundings and found fifteen feet.

²⁹ Fearing that we might run aground on the rocks, they let down four anchors from the stern and prayed for daylight to come. ³⁰ The sailors then tried to abandon ship. They had already lowered the lifeboat into the sea, on the pretext that they were going to lower some anchors from the bow. ³¹ But Paul said to the centurion and the soldiers, "Unless these men stay * with the ship, you cannot be saved." ³² Then the soldiers cut the ropes of the lifeboat and set it adrift.

³³ Just before daybreak, Paul urged all of them to take some food, saying, "This is the fourteenth day that you have been in suspense, going hungry and eating nothing. ³⁴ Therefore, I beg you to take some food. You need it to survive. Not one of you will lose even a hair of his head."

³⁵ After he had said this, he took bread, gave thanks to God in front of them all, broke it, and began to eat. ³⁶ Then they were all encouraged and began to eat. ³⁷ Altogether, there were two hundred and seventy-six persons on board. ³⁸ After they had eaten as much as they wanted they lightened the ship by throwing the grain into the sea.

³⁹ In the morning, they did not recognize the land, but they sighted a bay with a sandy beach, and they decided to run the ship aground on this if they could. ⁴⁰ And so they cut loose the anchors and left them in the sea. At the

same time, they loosened the ropes that held the rudders.
Then, hoisting the foresail to the wind, they made for the
beach. ⁴¹ But they struck a reef, and the vessel ran
aground. The bow became stuck and remained unmov-
able, while the stern was broken to pieces by the pound-
ing of the waves.

⁴² The soldiers decided to kill the prisoners lest any of
them might swim away and escape. ⁴³ However, the centurion was determined to spare Paul's life, and he prevented them from carrying out their plan. He ordered
those who could swim to jump overboard first and make
for land, ⁴⁴ while the rest were to follow either on planks
or on pieces of wreckage from the ship. In this way, all
were brought safely to land.

28 Paul at Malta. ¹ Once we had made our way to safe-
ty, we learned that the island was called Malta. * ² The
natives * treated us with unusual kindness. Since it had
begun to rain and was cold, they lit a bonfire and welcomed all of us around it.

³ Paul had gathered an armful of sticks and put them
on the fire when a viper, driven out by the heat, attached
itself to his hand. ⁴ On seeing the snake hanging from his
hand, the natives said to one another, "This man must be
a murderer. Although he escaped from the sea, Justice *
has not allowed him to live."

⁵ However, he shook off the snake into the fire and suffered no harm. ⁶ They were expecting him to swell up or
drop dead, but after waiting for a long time and seeing
nothing unusual happen to him, they changed their
minds and began to say that he was a god.

⁷ In the vicinity of that place there were lands belonging to the leading man of the island, whose name was
Publius. * He received us and gave us his hospitality for
three days. ⁸ It so happened that this man's father was sick
with a fever and dysentery. Paul visited him and cured
him by praying and laying hands on him. ⁹ After this happened, the rest of the sick people on the island also came

and were cured. [10] They honored us with many marks of respect, and when we were about to set sail, they put on board all the supplies we needed.

From Malta to Rome. [11] Three months later, * we set sail on a ship that had wintered at the island. The ship was from Alexandria, with the Dioscuri as its figurehead. [12] We landed at Syracuse * and spent three days there. [13] Then we sailed along the coast and came to Rhegium. * After one day there, a south wind came up, and we reached Puteoli in two days.

[14] In Puteoli, we found some brethren, and we were invited to stay with them for seven days. And so we came to Rome. [15] When the brethren there learned of our arrival, they came out to meet us as far as the Forum of Appius * and the Three Taverns. On seeing them, Paul gave thanks to God, and his courage was strengthened.

E: Paul's Activity at Rome*

Meetings with the Jewish Leaders. [16] On his arrival in Rome, Paul was allowed to live by himself, with a soldier guarding him. * [17] Three days later, he called together the leaders of the Jews. When they had assembled, he said to them, "Brethren, although I have done nothing against our people or our ancestral customs, I was arrested in Jerusalem and handed over to the Romans. [18] After they had examined me, the Romans wanted to release me because they had found nothing against me that deserved the death penalty. [19] But the Jews objected, and I was compelled to appeal to Caesar, even though I had no accusation to make against my own nation. [20] This is the reason I have asked to see you and speak with you, for it is because of the hope of Israel that I wear these chains."

[21] They replied, "We have received no letters from Judea about you, nor have any of the brethren who arrived here reported or spoken anything evil about you. [22] But we would like to hear from you what you think, for all we know about this sect is that it is denounced everywhere."

[23] And so they agreed on a day to meet with him, and they came to his lodgings in great numbers. From early morning until evening, he presented his case to them, testifying to the kingdom of God and attempting to convince them about Jesus as he argued from both the Law of Moses and the Prophets. [24] Some were persuaded by what he had said, but others refused to believe.

[25] Having failed to reach an agreement among themselves, they began to leave. Then Paul made his final statement, "How right the Holy Spirit was when he spoke to your ancestors through the prophet Isaiah, saying,

[26]   'Go to the people and say
     You will indeed listen but never understand,
       and you will indeed look but never perceive.
[27]   For this people's heart has become dull,
       their ears have been stopped up,
       and they have shut their eyes,
   lest their eyes might see,
       their ears might hear,
       and their hearts might understand.
   Then they would be converted,
       and I would heal them.'

[28] "Therefore, let it be known to you that this salvation offered by God has been sent to the Gentiles, and they will listen." [[29] And when he had said this, the Jews departed, arguing vigorously among themselves.] *

Conclusion—But Not an End.* [30] Paul remained there in his lodgings for two full years at his own expense. He welcomed all who came to him, [31] and without hindrance he boldly proclaimed the kingdom of God and taught about the Lord Jesus Christ.

PAUL, APOSTLE OF CHRIST

The Gospel of the Gentiles

The Gospels are certainly the most important of the New Testament writings, but they were not the first to be composed. As early as the year A.D. 50, some young communities of former Gentiles were receiving Letters from an "apostle," namely, Paul, who had not belonged to the Twelve or to the circle around Jesus. Of the great figures of newborn Christianity, this "first Christian author" is the most remarkable one known to us, and he remains such through the testimony he has left us in his writings.

I. CHRONOLOGICAL ORDER OF THE LETTERS

Modern criticism has come to the following conclusions in this area.

A first series of Letters was written at intervals during the fifties and sixties; there is practically no one who doubts that Paul was their author.

—*1 and 2 Thessalonians:* The first two Christian writings that have come down to us. They were surely written in Corinth between A.D. 50 and 52, in order to encourage a recently founded community and to clarify some points of doctrine (although some scholars have questioned the authorship of 2 Thessalonians).

—*1 and 2 Corinthians:* Two Letters written in A.D. 56, during Paul's time in Ephesus. They contain rather spirited interventions occasioned by disorders and divisions in the community.

—*Philippians:* A Letter that is especially cordial in tone. It is the first Letter that Paul wrote from prison and can be dated to A.D. 56, although others place it with the Letters of Paul's Roman captivity between A.D. 61 and 63. We know that Paul was imprisoned more than once.

—*Galatians:* A fiery Letter to a Church in full crisis; probably written in A.D. 56 or 57.

—*Romans:* A lengthy theological writing, covering at greater length, and in a more serene tone, the same themes the writer had dealt with in the Letter to the Galatians. It may date from A.D. 57 or 58.

A second and later series of texts is known as the Captivity Letters (which may include the Letter to the Philippians, as noted a moment ago). They can be attributed to Paul, although a bit tentatively, and dated from A.D. 61 to 63, the period of his imprisonment in Rome.

—*Colossians:* A Letter that encourages authentic faith and authentic Christian life in face of the commingling of religions and new ideas.

—*Philemon:* A short note of recommendation for a fugitive slave.

—*Ephesians:* A circular Letter inspired by a profound theology and mysticism.

A third series of Letters is addressed no longer to communities but to individuals, pastors of souls, and is lavish with recommendations and guidelines for the exercise of their responsibilities. These are known as the Pastoral Letters and must be dated to A.D. 66 or 67 at the latest, if they are to be attributed to Paul. Some exegetes think the Letters may be the work of disciples and written around the eighties.

—*1 and 2 Timothy:* Two Letters.

—*Titus:* One Letter.

Toward the end of the 1st century a final writing supposedly by Paul was in circulation, but the attribution is most uncertain. It was written by someone else who remains anonymous.

—*Hebrews:* A lengthy piece of theology and exhortation, written either just before the destruction of Jerusalem in A.D. 70 or much later, between A.D. 80 and 90.

II. WHO WAS PAUL?

Until His Conversion

Saul was born around the beginning of the century, in Tarsus, the capital of Cilicia in Asia Minor, a little city but open to cultural influences and commercial exchanges between East and West. He was from a family of Diaspora Jews who belonged to the tribe of Benjamin and were intent on a strict observance of the religion of their fore-bears. They did not, however, reject all contact with the life and culture of the Empire; in fact, they had acquired Roman citizenship and thereby become the Paulus family.

In about A.D. 36/37 a mysterious event changed the course of Saul's life in an instant. The persecutor of Christians became the most ardent missionary of the Gospel.

On the road to Damascus, he had a vision that changed his life. He saw Christ, who revealed that he was totally one with all who believed in him: "Why are you perse-cuting me?" (Acts 9:4).

After His Conversion

Paul underwent a radical turnaround. From then on, he did nothing but put into practice the unshakable cer-titude that he received on that day. His Letters set forth this conviction: Christ is living and reconciles human beings in his Spirit; salvation is given by him to the Gentile world and indeed to all peoples. His entire exis-tence was henceforth seized by this mission. His life and thought were animated by an unconquerable love for Jesus.

Allowing Gentiles to become part of the Christian com-munities posed theoretical problems. Paul was present at the Council of Jerusalem in A.D. 48/49, which rendered liberating decisions on this point (Acts 15; Gal 2:1-10).

Thereupon Paul traveled to the great urban centers of the Mediterranean world, proclaiming the Gospel of Jesus Christ and establishing churches, i.e., small groups of men and women, free people and slaves, Jews and Greeks, who believed in Christ. His plan was to go to the ends of the known world, possibly as far as the Spanish coast, by way of Rome. All the while, he nurtured the young Churches by his Letters and delegates, recalling the main lines of the Gospel—Jesus Christ is the only Savior.

We have no sure information on the subsequent course and end of Paul's life. He would be executed at Rome on the Ostia Road (Via Ostiensis), probably in A.D. 66/67. Many, especially those who defend the attribution of the Captivity Letters to Paul, think that he had once again regained his freedom, had visited the Churches of Greece and Asia Minor, and perhaps had even gone to Spain. Arrested once again, he endured a harsh imprisonment.

Writings

The traditional order of the Letters, as seen in any Bible, is not based on chronology. Their order is primarily one of length, longest to shortest. In reading them, however, it is advantageous to follow the chronological order.

THE LETTER TO THE ROMANS

HUMAN BEINGS ARE JUSTIFIED THROUGH FAITH

Paul wanted to visit Rome—the center of the universe in his day—on more than one occasion, but he was prevented from doing so (see Rom 1:13). Now, in the winter of A.D. 56-57, his third missionary journey has been completed and he has established the Church in the principal Mediterranean urban centers, from Jerusalem to Illyricum (Rom 15:19). In addition, the great crises in Corinth and Galatia seem to have subsided.

Hence, Paul seeks new fields. The West calls to him, and he projects a missionary journey that will take him to the cities along the Spanish coastline. To get there he must pass through Rome (see Rom 15:22-24), and he looks for the welcome and assistance of the Christian community established in the capital.

He will not be a stranger there. The Jewish community at Rome has more than 40,000 members and some fifteen synagogues. Moreover, the seed of the Gospel has already taken root in its midst. We will probably never know who were the first missionaries of Christ there. It may be that pilgrims from Rome were among the witnesses and converts on the day of Pentecost in the year A.D. 30.

In any case, merchants and travelers could surely have encountered the Gospel and the Church on their travels and in their business dealings and could then have become the promoters of a new community at Rome. St. Peter himself was there for a time and eventually suffered martyrdom under the infamous Emperor Nero, but doubtless his coming took place later than the date of this Letter.

The Church of Rome seems to have developed rapidly. In the year A.D. 49 an edict of Emperor Claudius expelled the Jews. Jewish Christians like Priscilla and Aquila were also affected; they found refuge and work in Greece and Asia (see Acts 18:2, 18, 26; 1 Cor 16:19). As a result, converts from paganism became the majority of Christians in Rome. This brought new problems and some difficulties, especially when the exiles returned after two or three years.

In order to announce his coming, Paul dictated a Letter to his secretary, Tertius (Rom 16:22), and entrusted it, apparently, to Phoebe, "a deaconess of the Church at Cenchreae" (Rom 16:1), who was about to travel to Rome. But if he wanted simply to announce his arrival, why did he send so lengthy a Letter? It is probable that his person and ideas were sufficiently well known in Rome and that there was debate over the positions he had taken.

Writing thus to a community, Paul gave free expression to the main concerns that preoccupied him concerning the life of the Church and, above all, concerning faith. To facilitate the reading we can group its themes around three main centers: the necessity of faith, the riches of the faith, the demands of the faith.

We shall discover, contained in these central ideas, the most profound intuitions regarding the realism of the incarnation (Rom 1:3-4), justification and redemption (Rom 3:21-26; 8:2-4), the universality of sin and salvation (Rom 5:12-19), the Paschal Mystery present in Baptism (Rom 6:2-5), the hope of Christians and the future of the universe (Rom 8:19-23), the divine sonship (Rom 8:14-17), the certainty of salvation (Rom 8:28-39), the mystery of Israel and the theology of history (Rom 9—11), spiritual worship (Rom 12:12), and the new priesthood (Rom 15:15-16).

Paul sets forth on a theological level what Jesus himself signified and practiced when he mingled with tax collectors and sinners; he did not condone what they did but he affirmed that justice is a grace of the Father and that it is not acquired by a person's moral, legal, or cultural effort—no matter how scrupulous that might be.

God's love is offered to everyone by God; it is he who sets free, and it is up to each person to embrace this liberation as a source of life. The redemption and salvation of human beings is of another order than that of social, personal, and historical situations. It pertains to a human transformation inaugurated in Jesus.

Hence, if such liberation is given in the mystery of Christ, in Baptism that enables one to participate in it, and in faith in his Gospel, what is the value of the Law and the whole Old Testament and what is the destiny of Israel? This is a question that needs an answer to show the fundamental unity of revelation, of the promise of fulfillment in Christ. Such an answer is even more necessary since non-Jewish Christians ran the risk of ignoring the plan of God inaugurated in Creation and the time of preparation that constitutes the Old Testament and even looking down on Jewish Christians. It is an answer that Paul carefully provides in this Letter (Rom 9:1—11:36).

The Letter presents the essence of Paul's message and his mission. It is regarded as the first formulation of Christian theology. Yet its tranquil tone is far different from the stormy character of the Letter to the Galatians whose themes it amplifies. Nonetheless, we sense herein the stirrings of an impassioned soul, for example beneath some uncalled-for blow (Rom 2:17ff), in the trust of being in God's grace (ch. 8), in the convert's compassion for those of his race (Rom 9:1-15; 10:1; 11:14-16), and in the enthusiasm of the Apostle of Christ (Rom 11:33-36).

The Letter to the Romans also distinguishes itself by its literary variety. In its construction, Paul makes use of liturgical pieces and hymns; he follows the expository style of the rabbis or employs the methods of orators of his day. All of this adds up to an exceptional example of Paul's work.

Did Paul really reach Rome? Yes, but later than he had hoped. In the spring of A.D. 58, he arrived at Jerusalem with the funds collected for the poor Christians of the Mother Church (2 Cor 8–9). He was arrested in the temple and spent two years in custody at Caesarea before appealing to Caesar as a Roman citizen. In the spring of the year A.D. 60, Paul, apostle and prisoner of Jesus Christ, entered Rome (Acts 28:16) and was welcomed by the Christian community there.

The Letter to the Romans may be divided as follows:

Prologue: (1:1-17)
  I: Justification through Faith in Jesus (1:18—4:25)

PROLOGUE

1 **Set Apart for the Gospel.** [1] Paul,* a servant of Christ Jesus, called to be an apostle and set apart for the service of the gospel [2] that God promised beforehand through his Prophets* in the holy Scriptures, [3]* the gospel concerning his Son who according to the flesh was descended from David, [4] and who according to the Spirit of holiness was proclaimed to be the Son of God in power by his resurrection from the dead: Jesus Christ our Lord.

[5] Through him we have received grace and our apostolic commission to proclaim the obedience of faith among all the Gentiles for the sake of his name. [6] And you are among those who are called to belong to Jesus Christ.

[7] To all of you who are God's beloved in Rome and called to be saints:* grace to you and peace from God our Father and the Lord Jesus Christ.

Thanksgiving and Prayer.* [8] First of all, I give thanks to my God through Jesus Christ for all of you because your faith has been proclaimed throughout the world. [9] For God, whom I serve with my spirit in the gospel of his Son, is the witness on my behalf that I remember you constantly in my prayers, [10] always asking that by God's will I may somehow be granted my desire of coming to visit you. [11] For I am longing to see you so that I may bestow on you some spiritual gift to strengthen you— [12] or, rather, so that we may be mutually encouraged by each other's faith, both yours and mine.

[13] I want you to be aware, brethren,* that I have often planned to visit you (although until now I have been prevented from doing so) because it has been my desire to achieve some harvest among you as I have among other Gentiles. [14] I have an obligation to Greeks and non-

Greeks * alike, to both the educated and the ignorant.
[15] Thus, I am ready to preach the gospel also to you who
are in Rome.

The Gospel of God*

Power of Salvation for All Believers. [16] For I am not
ashamed of the gospel, since it is the power of God that
offers salvation to everyone who has faith—to Jews first,
and then to Gentiles as well. [17] In it the righteousness of
God is revealed, beginning in faith and established in
faith. * As it is written: "The one who is righteous will live
through faith."

I. JUSTIFICATION THROUGH FAITH IN JESUS*

A: The World in the Wrath of God*

Exchanging the Truth of God for a Lie. [18] The wrath of God
is being revealed from heaven against all the ungodliness
and wickedness of those who by their wickedness suppress the truth. [19] For that which can be known about
God is clearly evident to them because God has revealed
it plainly to them. [20] Ever since the creation of the world
the invisible attributes of God's eternal power and divine
nature have been clearly understood and perceived
through the things he has made.

Therefore, the conduct of these people is inexcusable.
[21] Despite knowing God, they refused to honor him as
God or give thanks to him. As a result, their speculations
became foolish and their uncomprehending hearts
became darkened. [22] Although they claimed to be wise, in
reality they became fools, [23] exchanging the glory of the
immortal God for images fashioned in the likeness of a
mortal man or birds or four-footed animals or reptiles.

[24] Therefore, God abandoned them in the sinful lusts
of their hearts to impurity and the mutual degradation of
their bodies. [25] They exchanged the truth of God for a lie
and offered worship and service to the creature rather
than to the Creator, who is blessed forever. Amen.

²⁶ * That is why God abandoned them to their shameful passions. Their women exchanged natural intercourse for unnatural practices. ²⁷ Likewise, men gave up natural relations with women and were consumed with passion for one another. Men committed shameful acts with men and received in their own persons the fitting penalty for their perversion.

²⁸ Furthermore, since these people did not see fit to acknowledge God, he abandoned them to their depraved way of thinking and to all types of vile behavior. ²⁹ As a result, they are filled with every kind of wickedness, evil, greed, and malice. Reveling in envy, murder, strife, deceit, and malice, they are gossips, ³⁰ slanderers, God-haters, insolent, arrogant, and boastful, as they devise new ways of doing evil and rebel against their parents. ³¹ They are senseless, faithless, heartless, and ruthless. ³² Although they are fully cognizant of God's decree that those who behave in this way deserve to die, they not only do these things themselves but also praise all those who engage in such conduct.

2 Judging Is Inexcusable.
¹ Therefore, you have no excuse, whoever you may be, when you pass judgment on others. For in judging others you condemn yourself, since you are doing the same things. ² We are all aware that God's judgment on those who commit such deeds is just. ³ How can you then suppose that you will escape the judgment of God for doing such things when you are condemning those who perform the same things?

⁴ How can you despise the riches of God's kindness and forbearance and patience? How can you fail to realize that his kindness is meant to lead you to repentance? ⁵ By your obstinate refusal to repent you are storing up retribution for yourself on the day of wrath when God's righteous judgment will be revealed.

⁶ For God will repay everyone in accordance with what his deeds deserve.* ⁷ To those who seek after glory and honor and immortality by persevering in good works, he

will grant eternal life. [8] But for those who are slaves to selfish ambition and follow the path of wickedness and not of truth, wrath and fury will be their lot.

[9] There will be affliction and distress for everyone who does evil—Jews first and then Gentiles. [10] However, glory, honor, and peace await everyone who does good—Jews first, and then Gentiles. [11] For God shows no partiality. *

The Law and Conscience.* [12] All those who have sinned outside the Law will perish outside the Law, and all who sinned under the Law will be judged by the Law. [13] For it is not those who hear the Law who are justified by God; rather, it is those who observe the Law who will be justified. [14] Therefore, when Gentiles, who do not have the Law, act by nature in conformity with the Law, they are a law for themselves, even though they have no Law. [15] They show that the requirements of the Law are inscribed in their hearts; and their own conscience will also bear witness for them, since their conflicting thoughts will accuse or even defend them *[16] on the day when, according to the gospel, God will judge the thoughts of all through Jesus Christ.

[17] * You call yourself a Jew and rely on the Law and are proud of your relationship to God, [18] and you know his will and are able to distinguish between right and wrong because you have been instructed in the Law, [19] and you are confident that you are a guide to the blind, a light for those in darkness, [20] an instructor of the foolish, and a teacher of the simple because in the Law you have the embodiment of knowledge and truth.

[21] You, then, who teach others, do you not teach yourself? You who preach against stealing, are you yourself a thief? [22] You who forbid adultery, are you yourself an adulterer? You who abhor idols, do you commit sacrilege? [23] You who boast of the Law, do you dishonor God by breaking it? [24] As it is written, "Because of you the name of God is reviled among the Gentiles."

Circumcision and the Heart.* ²⁵ Circumcision has value if you obey the Law. However, if you break the Law, you have become as if you had never been circumcised. ²⁶ In the same way, if one who is not circumcised keeps the precepts of the Law, will not his uncircumcision be regarded as circumcision? ²⁷ Then the man who is not physically circumcised but nevertheless observes the Law will condemn you who have the written code and circumcision but break the Law.

²⁸ A man is not a Jew who is only one outwardly, nor is true circumcision external and physical. ²⁹ Rather, the Jew is one who is a Jew inwardly, and true circumcision is of the heart—spiritual, not literal. He receives his praise not from human beings but from God.

3 **The Value of Judaism.** ¹ Is there any advantage, therefore, in being a Jew? Or what is the value of circumcision? ² A great deal in every respect. In the first place, they were entrusted with the words of God. ³ What if some were unfaithful? Will their lack of faith nullify the fidelity of God? ⁴ By no means! God must be true even if every human being is a liar,* as it is written,

"That you may be justified in your words,
and vindicated when you are judged."

⁵ But if our wickedness serves to confirm the righteousness of God, what are we to say? Is God unjust (I speak of him in human terms) to bring retribution upon us? ⁶ Of course not! For that would imply that God could not judge the world. ⁷ But if, as a result of my falsehood, God demonstrates his truthfulness, to his greater glory, why am I still being condemned as a sinner? ⁸ And why not say, as some people slanderously accuse us of proposing, "Let us do evil so that good may result"? Such people deserve their condemnation.

The Whole World Guilty before God.* ⁹ Well, then, are we any better? * No, not at all. For we have already charged that both Jews and Gentiles alike are all under the power of sin. ¹⁰ As it is written,

"There is no one who is righteous,
  not even one.

11 There is no one who has understanding,
  there is no one who seeks God.

12 All have turned away;
  together they have become worthless.
There is no one who shows kindness,
  not even one.

13 Their throats are open graves;
  they use their tongues to deceive.
The venom of vipers is on their lips;

14 their mouths are full of cursing and bitterness.

15 Their feet hasten to shed blood;

16 ruin and misery mark their paths.

17 The way of peace they do not know;

18 there is no fear of God before their eyes."

[19] Now we know that what the Law says is addressed to those who are under the Law, so that every mouth may be silenced and the entire world may be seen as guilty before God. [20] For no one can be regarded as justified in the sight of God by keeping the Law. The Law brings only the consciousness of sin.

B: The Redemption in Jesus Christ*

God's Righteousness through Faith in Jesus Christ.* [21] But now the righteousness of God that is attested by the Law and the Prophets has been manifested apart from law: [22] the righteousness of God through faith in Jesus Christ for all who believe. No distinction has been made. [23] For all have sinned and thereby are deprived of the glory of God, [24] and all are justified by the gift of his grace that is given freely through the redemption in Christ Jesus.

[25] God designated him to be a sacrifice of expiation of sin through faith by the shedding of his blood because in his divine forbearance he allowed to be unpunished the sins previously committed. [26] He thus demonstrated his righteousness in the present time so that he might show

himself to be just as the one who justifies anyone who has faith in Jesus.

Justification through Faith Apart from the Works of the Law.
[27] What reason then does one have to boast? It is excluded! By works of the Law? No, rather by the law of faith. [28] For we maintain that one is justified by faith apart from the works of the Law.

[29] Is God the God only of the Jews? Is he not also the God of the Gentiles? Yes, he is the God of the Gentiles too, [30] since there is only one God, and he will justify both the circumcised and the uncircumcised on the basis of their faith. [31] Are we thereby nullifying the Law by this faith? By no means! On the contrary, we are upholding the Law.

C: Abraham Justified through Faith*

4 **Justified through Faith, Not Works.*** [1] What then are we to say about Abraham, our ancestor according to the flesh? [2] If Abraham was justified by the works he did, he has good reason to boast, but not in the eyes of God. [3] For what does Scripture say? "Abraham placed his faith in God, and it was credited to him as righteousness." *

[4] Now when a man works, his wages are not regarded as a gift but as something that is due to him. [5] However, when someone who does not work places his faith in one who justifies the godless, such faith is reckoned as righteousness. [6] * In the same way, David speaks of the blessedness of the one to whom God attributes righteousness apart from works:

[7]   "Blessed are those whose iniquities are forgiven
        and whose sins are blotted out.
[8]   Blessed is the man
        to whom the Lord imputes no guilt."

Justified before Being Circumcised.* [9] Is this blessedness granted only to the circumcised, or does it apply to the uncircumcised as well? We have asserted that Abraham's faith "was credited to him as righteousness." [10] How was it credited? Was it when he was circumcised or uncircumcised? Not when he was circumcised, but when he was uncircumcised.

[11] Abraham received the sign of circumcision as a seal of the righteousness that he had by faith while he was still uncircumcised. In this way, he was the father of all who believe without being circumcised and who thus have righteousness credited to them. [12] Therefore, he is the father of the circumcised who have not only received circumcision but also follow that path of faith traversed by Abraham before he was circumcised.

Justified Apart from the Law.* [13] It was not through the Law that Abraham and his descendants received the promise that he would inherit the world, but through the righteousness of faith. [14] If those who live by the Law are the heirs, faith is null and the promise is void. [15] For the Law produces only wrath, and where no Law exists, there cannot be any violation.

[16] Therefore, the promise depends on faith, so that it may be a free gift and the promise may be guaranteed to all descendants, not only to the adherents of the Law but also to those who share the faith of Abraham. For he is the father of all of us, [17] as it is written, "I have made you the father of many nations," in the sight of God in whom he believed, the God who gives life to the dead and calls into being what does not exist.

The Power of Faith.* [18] Though he hoped against hope, he believed that he would become the father of many nations, in fulfillment of the promise, "So shall your descendants be." [19] His faith was not shaken when he considered his own body, which was as good as dead (for he was about one hundred years old), and the barren womb of Sarah. [20] Confident in the promise of God, he did not doubt in unbelief; rather, he was strengthened in his faith and gave glory to God, [21] remaining fully convinced that he was able to fulfill his pledge. [22] Therefore, his faith "was credited to him as righteousness."

[23] "It was credited to him" was not written with Abraham alone in mind. [24] This was also meant for us as well, to whom it will be credited as righteousness—for us who believe in him who raised from the dead Jesus our Lord [25] who was handed over to death for our sins and who was raised to life for our justification.

II: FAITH, THE RICHES OF LIFE*

A: At Peace with God

5 **Hope Does Not Disappoint.** [1] Therefore, now that we have been justified by faith, we are at peace* with God through our Lord Jesus Christ, [2] through whom by faith we have been given access to this grace in which we now live, and we rejoice in the hope of the glory of God. [3] And not only that, but we also glory in our sufferings, because we realize that suffering develops perseverance, [4] and perseverance produces character, and character produces hope. [5] Such hope will not be doomed to disappointment,* because the love of God has been poured into our hearts through the Holy Spirit that has been given to us.

Reconciliation Already Obtained. [6] At the appointed time, while we were still helpless, Christ died for the ungodly. [7] Indeed, it is seldom that anyone will die for a just person, although perhaps for a good person someone might be willing to die. [8] Thus, God proved his love for us in that while we were still sinners Christ died for us.

[9] And so, now that we have been justified by Christ's blood, how much more certainly will we be saved through him from divine retribution. * [10] For if, while we were enemies, we were reconciled to God through the death of his Son, how much more certain it is that, having been reconciled, we shall be saved by his life. [11] And not only that, but we now even trust exultantly in God through our Lord Jesus Christ, through whom we have already been granted reconciliation.

B: Adam and Christ—Sin and Grace*

Humanity's Sin through Adam. [12] Therefore, sin entered the world as the result of one man, and death* as a result of sin, and thus death has afflicted the entire human race inasmuch as everyone has sinned. [13] Sin was already in the world before there was any Law, even though sin is not reckoned when there is no Law. [14] Nevertheless, death reigned over all from Adam to Moses, even over those who had not sinned by disobeying a command, as did Adam who prefigured the one who was to come.

Grace and Life through Christ. [15] However, the gift is not like the transgression. For if the transgression of one man led to the death of the many,* how much greater was the overflowing effect of the grace of God and the gift of the one man Jesus Christ that has abounded for the many. [16] The gift of God cannot be compared with the sin of the one man. For the one sin resulted in the judgment that brought condemnation, but the gift freely given after many transgressions resulted in justification. [17] For if, because of one man's transgression, death reigned through that man, how much more shall those who receive the abundance of grace and the gift of righteousness come to reign in life through the one man Jesus Christ.

[18] Therefore, just as one man's transgression brought condemnation for all, so one man's righteous act resulted in justification and life for all. [19] For just as through the disobedience of one man the many were made sinners, so by the obedience of one man the many will be made righteous. *

Purpose of the Law. [20] When the Law was added, offenses multiplied; but the increase in sins was far exceeded by the increase in grace. [21] Hence, as sin's reign resulted in death, so the grace of God also might reign through righteousness resulting in eternal life through Jesus Christ our Lord.

C: Death and Life with Christ*

6 **Baptized in Christ Jesus.*** [1] What then shall we say? Should we persist in sin in order that grace may abound? [2] Of course not! We have died to sin. How can we live in it any longer? [3] Do you not know that all of us who have been baptized into Christ Jesus were baptized into his death? [4] Through that baptism into his death we were buried with him, so that, just as Christ was raised from the dead by the glory of the Father,* so we too might begin to live a new life.

[5] For if we have been united with him in a death like his, we shall also be united with him in his resurrection. [6] We know that our old* self was crucified with him, so that our sinful body might be destroyed and we might no longer be enslaved to sin. [7] For whoever has died has been freed from sin.

[8] However, if we have died with Christ, we believe that we shall also live with him.* [9] We know that Christ, once raised from the dead, will never die again. Death no longer has power over him. [10] When he died, he died to sin once and for all. However, the life he lives, he lives for God. [11] In the same way, you must regard yourselves as being dead to sin and alive for God in Christ Jesus.

[12] Therefore, do not allow sin to reign over your mortal body and make you obey its desires. [13] Nor should you present any part of your body as an instrument for wickedness leading to sin. Rather, present yourselves to God as having been raised from death to life and the parts of your body to God as instruments for righteousness. [14] For sin is no longer to have any power over you, since you are not under the Law but under grace.

A Slave of Righteousness. [15] What then? Should we sin because we are not under the Law but under grace? Of course not! [16] Do you not know that if you offer yourself as an obedient slave, you are the slave of the one you obey—either of sin, which leads to death, or of obedience, which leads to righteousness?

¹⁷ Once you were slaves of sin, but, thanks be to God, you have become obedient in your heart to that pattern of teaching to which you have been delivered. ¹⁸ Now, having been set free from sin, you have become slaves of righteousness.

¹⁹ I am speaking in human terms because you are still weak human beings. For just as you once offered your bodies as slaves to impurity and to lawlessness leading to greater iniquity, so now present them as slaves to righteousness for sanctification.

²⁰ When you were slaves of sin, you were free from the restraints of righteousness. ²¹ But what advantage did you get then from the things of which you are now ashamed? For the end of those things is death. ²² However, now that you have been freed from sin and bound to the service of God, the benefit you receive is sanctification, and the end is eternal life. ²³ For the wages of sin is death, but the gift freely given by God is eternal life in Christ Jesus our Lord.

D: Christ Has Freed Us from the Law*

7   The Time of the Law Has Passed.*

¹ Are you aware, brethren (for I am certain that you are people who have knowledge of the Law), that a person is bound by the Law only during that person's lifetime? ² For example, a woman is bound by the Law to her husband as long as he lives, but if her husband dies, she is released from her husband in regard to the Law. ³ Therefore, she will be judged to be an adulteress if she has relations with another man while her husband is still alive. However, if her husband dies, she is free from that provision of the Law, and if she then has relations with another man, she is not an adulteress.

⁴ In the same way, brethren, through the body of Christ you have died to the Law and have been set free to belong to another, that is, to the one who rose from the dead in order that we might bear fruit for God. ⁵ For when we

were in the flesh, our sinful passions were aroused by the Law and at work in our bodies, and they bore fruit for death. [6] But now, we are released from the Law, having died to that which held us captive, so that we may serve in the new life of the Spirit in contrast to the old written code. *

The Function of the Law. * [7] What then should we say? That the Law is sinful? Absolutely not! Yet if it had not been for the Law, I would not have known what sin was. I would not have known what covet is if the Law had not said, "You shall not covet." [8] But sin seized the opportunity offered by the commandment and produced in me all kinds of covetousness. Apart from the Law, sin is dead.

[9] I lived apart from the Law, but when the commandment came, sin came to life, [10] and I died. The commandment that was for life proved to be death for me. [11] For sin, seizing an opportunity offered by the commandment, deceived me, * and through it killed me. [12] And so the Law is holy, and the commandment is holy and just and good.

[13] Did what is good, then, cause my death? By no means! But in order that sin might be recognized as such, it brought about my death through what is good, and therefore through the commandment sin became completely sinful.

Sin and Death. [14] We clearly understand that the Law is spiritual, but I am unspiritual, sold into slavery to sin. [15] I do not understand my own actions. For I do not do what I want; rather, I do what I hate. [16] Now if I do what I do not want, then I agree that the Law is good. * [17] This indicates that it is no longer I who do it, but sin that dwells in me. [18] For I know that nothing good dwells in me, that is, in my flesh. I have the desire to do what is good, but I cannot do what is good. [19] For I do not do the good I desire; rather, it is the evil I do not desire that I end up doing. [20] Now if I do what I do not desire, it is no longer I who do it, but sin that dwells in me.

[21] I have thus discovered this principle: when I want to do what is good, evil lies close at hand. [22] In my innermost self, I delight in the Law of God, [23] but I perceive in the members of my body another law at war with the Law that I cherish in my mind. Thus, I am made captive to the law of sin that dwells in my members.

[24] What a wretched man I am! Who will rescue me from this body destined for death? [25] Thanks be to God through Jesus Christ our Lord. So then, with my mind I am a slave to the Law of God, but with my flesh to the law of sin.

E: The Spirit of God Dwells in Christians*

8 **There Is No Longer Any Condemnation.** [1] Hence, there is now no condemnation for those who are in Christ Jesus. [2] For the law of the Spirit of life in Christ Jesus has set you free from the law of sin and death. [3] That which the Law, weakened by the flesh, was unable to do, God has done. By sending his own Son in the likeness of our sinful nature as a sin offering, he condemned sin in the flesh [4] so that the righteous requirements of the Law* might be fulfilled in us who live not according to the flesh but according to the Spirit.

Animated by the Spirit and Rendered Children of God.* [5] Those who live according to the flesh fix their attention on the things of the flesh, while those who live according to the Spirit set their thoughts on spiritual things. [6] The desires of the flesh result in death, but the desires of the Spirit result in life and peace. [7] Indeed, the desires of the flesh will be hostile to God, for they do not submit to the Law of God, nor could they do so. [8] Those who live according to the flesh can never be pleasing to God.

[9] You, however, do not live according to the flesh but according to the Spirit, since the Spirit of God dwells in you. Anyone who does not possess the Spirit of Christ cannot belong to him. [10] But if Christ is in you, then even though the body is dead as a result of sin, the Spirit is alive

in you because of righteousness. [11] If the Spirit of him who raised Jesus from the dead dwells in you, then the one who raised Christ from the dead will also give life to your mortal bodies through his Spirit that dwells in you. *

[12] Consequently, brethren, we are not debtors to the flesh and obliged to live according to the flesh. [13] If you do live according to the flesh, you will die. However, if by the Spirit you put to death the deeds of the body, you will live.

[14] * Those who are led by the Spirit of God are children of God. [15] For you did not receive a spirit of slavery leading to fear; rather, you received the Spirit of adoption, enabling us to cry out, "*Abba!* Father!" [16] The Spirit himself bears witness with our Spirit that we are children of God. [17] And if we are children, then we are heirs—heirs of God and joint heirs with Christ, provided that we share his sufferings so that we may also share his glory.

The Future Glory That Shall Be Revealed. * [18] I consider that the sufferings we presently endure are not worth comparing with the glory to be revealed in us. [19] Indeed, creation itself eagerly awaits the revelation of the children of God. [20] For creation was subjected to frustration, not of its own choice but by the will of the one who subjected it, in the hope [21] that creation itself will be freed from its slavery to corruption and share in the glorious freedom of the children of God.

[22] As we know, the entire creation has been groaning in labor pains until now— [23] and not only creation, but we ourselves, who have the firstfruits of the Spirit, groan inwardly as we wait for our adoption as children, the redemption of our bodies. [24] For in hope we were saved. Now to see something does not involve hope. For why should we hope for what we have already seen? [25] But if we hope for what we do not yet see, then we wait for it with patience.

[26] In the same way, even the Spirit helps us in our weakness. For we do not know how to pray as we should, but the Spirit himself intercedes for us with sighs that cannot

be put into words. [27] And the one who searches hearts knows the mind of the Spirit, because the Spirit intercedes for the saints in accordance with God's will.

[28] We know that God makes all things work together for good for those who love him * and who are called according to his purpose. [29] For those whom he foreknew he also predestined to be conformed to the image of his Son so that he might be the firstborn among many brethren. [30] Those whom he predestined he also called, and those whom he called he also justified, and those whom he justified he also glorified.

Who Can Separate Us from the Love of Christ? [31] What then can we say in response to all this? If God is for us, who can be against us? [32] He did not spare his own Son but gave him up for all of us. How then can he fail also to give us everything else along with him?

[33] Who will bring any charge against those whom God has chosen? It is God who acquits. [34] Who will condemn? Christ Jesus, who died, or rather rose again, who is at God's right hand and intercedes for us? * [35] Who then can separate us from the love of Christ? Will hardship, or distress, or persecution, or famine, or nakedness, or danger, or the sword? [36] As it is written,

"For your sake we are being slain all day long;
    we are treated like sheep to be slaughtered."

[37] No, throughout all these things we are conquerors because of him who loved us. [38] For I am convinced that neither death, nor life, nor angels, nor principalities, nor present things, nor things to come, nor powers, [39] nor height, nor depth, * nor any other creature will be able to separate us from the love of God in Christ Jesus our Lord.

F: The Lot of the Jewish People*

9 **Paul's Love for Israel.** [1] I am speaking the truth in Christ—I am not lying, as my conscience bears witness for me through the Holy Spirit [2] that I have great sorrow and unending anguish in my heart. [3] I would even be willing to be accursed, cut off from Christ for the sake of my brethren who are my kinsmen according to the flesh. [4] They are Israelites * who have the adoption, the glory, the covenants, the Law, the worship, and the promises. [5] To them belong the patriarchs, and from them, according to the flesh, came the Christ, God forever, who is over all. * Amen.

The Word of God Has Not Proved False. [6] It is not as though the word of God has proved false. For not all who were Israelites truly belong to Israel, [7] and not all of Abraham's children are his true descendants. On the contrary, "It is through Isaac that descendants will bear your name."

[8] In other words, it is not through physical descent that people are regarded as children of God. Rather, the children of the promise are those who are counted as descendants. [9] For this is how the promise was worded: "About this time next year I shall return, and Sarah will have a son."

[10] And not only that, but Rebekah became pregnant by one man, her husband Isaac. [11] Yet even before her children had been born or done anything good or bad, in order that God's purpose of election might prevail, [12] dependent not on human works but on his call, she was told, "The older shall serve the younger." [13] As it is written,

> "I loved Jacob,
> but Esau I hated." *

Has God Been Unjust? [14] * What then are we to say to that? Has God been unjust? Of course not! [15] For he says to Moses,

> "I will have mercy
> on whomever I will have mercy,
> and I will have pity
> on whomever I will have pity."

[16] Therefore, it does not depend on anyone's will or exertion but on God's mercy. [17] For Scripture says to Pharaoh, "I have raised you up so that I may display my

power in you and that my name may be proclaimed throughout the earth." [18] Consequently, he shows mercy to whomever he wills, and he hardens the hearts of whomever he wills.

[19] In response, you will say to me, "Why then does he still find fault? Who can resist his will?" [20] But who indeed are you, a human being, to argue with God? Can something that is made say to its maker, "Why did you make me like this?" [21] Surely, the potter can mold the clay as he wishes. Does he not have the right to make out of the same lump of clay one vessel for a noble purpose and another for ordinary use?

[22] What if God, although wishing to show his wrath and to make known his power, nevertheless with great patience endured the objects of his wrath * destined for destruction? [23] He did so in order to make known the riches of his glory to the recipients of his mercy whom he prepared long ago for glory. [24] We are the ones whom he has called not only from the Jews but also from the Gentiles.

Witness of the Old Testament. [25] As indeed he says in Hosea,

"Those who were not my people
    I will call 'my people,'
and her who was not beloved
    I will call 'beloved.'
[26] And in the very place
        where it was said to them,
        'You are not my people,'
    there they shall be called
        children of the living God."

[27] And Isaiah cries out in regard to Israel:

"Though the number of the Israelites
    will be like the sand of the sea,
    only a remnant of them will be saved.
[28] For the sentence of the Lord on the earth
        will be executed quickly and with finality."

²⁹ Isaiah had foretold previously:

"If the Lord of hosts
    had not left us any descendants,
we would have become like Sodom
    and been made like Gomorrah."

A Misguided Zeal. ³⁰ What then shall we say? That the Gentiles who did not strive for righteousness have achieved it, that is, righteousness based on faith, ³¹ but that Israel, who did strive for righteousness based on the Law, did not succeed in attaining it? ³² Why did this happen? Because they did not pursue it by faith but on the basis of works. They tripped over the stone that causes one to stumble, ³³ as it is written:

"Behold, I am laying in Zion
    a stone that will make people stumble
    and a rock that will cause them to fall.
But the one who trusts in him
    will never be put to shame." *

10

¹ Brethren, my heart's desire and my prayer to God for them is that they may be saved. ² I can testify to the zeal that they have for God, but it is not based on knowledge. ³ For, being ignorant of the righteousness that comes from God, and thereby seeking to establish their own, they have not submitted themselves to God's righteousness. ⁴ For Christ is the fulfillment of the Law for the justification of all who believe.

The Word Is Near You. * ⁵ Concerning the righteousness that comes from the Law, Moses writes, "The person who does these things will attain life by them." ⁶ However, the righteousness that comes from faith says, "Do not say in your heart, 'Who will go up to heaven?' (that is, to bring Christ down), ⁷ or 'Who will descend into the abyss?' (that is, to bring Christ up from the dead)." * ⁸ But what does it say?

"The word is near you,
    on your lips and in your heart"

(that is, the word of faith that we proclaim).

⁹ If you confess with your lips, "Jesus is Lord," * and believe in your heart that God raised him from the dead, you will be saved. ¹⁰ For one believes in the heart and so is justified, and one confesses with the mouth and so is saved. ¹¹ As Scripture asserts, "No one who believes in him will be put to shame." ¹² For there is no distinction between Jew and Gentile. The same Lord is Lord of all, and his generosity is manifested to all who call upon him. ¹³ Indeed, "everyone who calls on the name of the Lord will be saved."

Not All Have Responded to the Good News. ¹⁴ But how can they call on him if they have not come to believe in him? And how can they believe in someone about whom they have never heard? And how can they hear without someone to preach to them? ¹⁵ And how will there be people to preach if they are not sent? As it is written, "How beautiful are the feet of those who proclaim the good news!"

¹⁶ However, not all have accepted the good news. As Isaiah says, "Lord, who has believed our message?" ¹⁷ So then, faith comes from what is heard, and what is heard comes through the word of Christ.

¹⁸ And so I ask: Have they not heard? Indeed, they have:

"Their voice has gone out all over the world,
    and their words to the ends of the earth."

¹⁹ Well then, I ask: Is it possible that Israel failed to understand? First Moses says:

"I will make you envious
    of those who are not a nation.
I will rouse your anger
    against a foolish nation."

²⁰ And Isaiah boldly states:

"I was found by those
    who were not looking for me.
I have revealed myself to those
    who never asked for me."

²¹ But regarding Israel, he says:

> "All day long I have stretched forth my hands
>   to a disobedient and rebellious people."

11 The Remnant of Israel.* ¹ I ask, then: Has God reject-
ed his people? Of course not! I too am an Israelite, a
descendant of Abraham, of the tribe of Benjamin. ² God
has not rejected his people whom he foreknew. You surely must know what Scripture asserts in the passage about
Elijah where he pleads with God against Israel: ³ "Lord,
they have killed your Prophets, they have torn down your
altars. I alone am left, and they are seeking my life."

⁴ What was God's response to him? "I have spared for
myself seven thousand men who have not knelt before
Baal." ⁵ So too, at the present time, there is a remnant,
chosen by grace. ⁶ But if it is by grace, then it is no longer
by works; otherwise grace would no longer be grace.

⁷ What follows, then? Israel was unable to attain what it
was seeking. The elect attained it, but the rest were hardened, ⁸ as it is written:

> "God gave them a spirit of lethargy:
>   eyes that could not see
>   and ears that could not hear,
> down to this very day."

⁹ And David says:

> "Let their table become a snare and a trap,
>   a stumbling block and a retribution for them.
> Let their eyes be darkened so that they cannot see,
>   and their backs be bent forever."

A Providential Misstep.* ¹¹ And so I ask: Have they stum-
bled so that they might fall? By no means! However,
through their transgression salvation has come to the
Gentiles, and this has stirred them to envy. ¹² Now if their
transgression results in riches for the world, and their loss
results in riches for the Gentiles, how much greater riches will their full participation bring!

[13] Now I am addressing you Gentiles. Inasmuch then as I am the apostle to the Gentiles, I glory in my ministry [14] in the hope that it will arouse the jealousy of those who are of my flesh so that some might be saved. [15] For if their rejection leads to the reconciliation of the world, what will their acceptance be but life from the dead?

The Gentiles' Salvation.* [16] If the firstfruits are holy, then so is the whole lump of dough. And if the root is holy, so are the branches. [17] But if some of the branches were broken off, and you, a wild olive shoot, have been grafted in their place to share in the rich root of the olive tree, [18] do not boast over against the branches! If you start to boast, remember that it is not you who support the root but the root that supports you.

[19] You will assert, "Branches were broken off so that I might be grafted in." [20] That is true. They were broken off because of their unbelief, but you hold your place only because of your faith. Therefore, do not rise up in pride but be filled with awe. [21] For if God did not spare the natural branches, he might not spare you either.

[22] Therefore, keep in mind the kindness and the severity of God: his severity toward those who fell, but his kindness to you provided that you remain deserving of that kindness. Otherwise, you also will be cut off, [23] while those who do not persist in their unbelief will be grafted in, since God has the power to do so again. [24] For if you have been cut from what is by nature a wild olive tree and grafted contrary to nature into a cultivated one, how much more easily will these natural branches be grafted back into their own olive tree.

All Israel Will Be Saved.* [25] I do not want you to be unaware of this mystery, brethren, lest you think yourselves too wise: this hardening that has afflicted Israel will continue only until the full number of the Gentiles has come in. [26] This is how all Israel will be saved, as it is written,

"The Deliverer will come out of Zion;
      he will banish godlessness from Jacob.

²⁷ And this will be my covenant with them
        when I take away their sins."

²⁸ As far as the gospel is concerned, they are enemies for your sake. However, as regards election, they are beloved for the sake of the patriarchs. ²⁹ For the gifts of God and his calling are irrevocable.

³⁰ Just as you who were at one time disobedient to God have now received mercy as a result of their disobedience, ³¹ so they too have now become disobedient in order that, through the mercy shown to you, they too may receive mercy. ³² For God has imprisoned all in disobedience so that he may show mercy to all.

The Judgments of God Are Unfathomable.* ³³ Oh, the depth of the riches and wisdom and knowledge of God! How inscrutable are his judgments and how unfathomable his ways!

³⁴   "For who has known the mind of the Lord,
        or who has been his counselor? *
³⁵   Or who has given him anything
        in order to receive something in return?" *

³⁶ For from him and through him and for him are all things. To him be glory forever. Amen.

III: THE NEED FOR FAITH IN DAILY LIFE*

12 **The New Life and the True Worship.** ¹ Therefore, brethren, I implore you by the mercies of God to offer your bodies as a living sacrifice that is holy and acceptable to God—a spiritual act of worship. ² Do not be conformed to the world, but be transformed by the renewal of your minds, so that you will be able to discern the will of God and to know what is good and acceptable and perfect.

Right Use of the Gifts of the One Body. ³ Through the grace that God has bestowed upon me, I advise every one of you not to think of yourself too highly, but to regard yourself objectively, based on the measure of faith that God has granted. [4] For just as in one body we have many parts, and the parts do not all have the same function, [5] so we, though many, make up one body in Christ, * and individually we are all parts of one another.

[6] We all have different gifts according to the grace given to us. If it is a gift of prophecy, we should exercise it in proportion to our faith. [7] If it is a gift of ministry, we should engage in serving others. If it is a gift of teaching, we should teach. [8] If it is a gift of exhortation, we should encourage. Whoever gives alms should do so generously; whoever leads should do so conscientiously; whoever performs acts of mercy should do so cheerfully.

A Truly Sincere Love. [9] Let your love be sincere. Loathe what is evil and hold fast to what is good. [10] Love one another with genuine affection. Esteem others more highly than yourself. [11] Do not be lacking in zeal, but serve the Lord with spiritual fervor. [12] Be joyful in your hope. Be patient in times of affliction. Persevere in prayer. [13] Contribute to the needs of the saints, and practice hospitality. [14] Bless those who persecute you; bless them and do not curse them. [15] Rejoice with those who rejoice; weep with those who weep. [16] Live in harmony with one another. Do not consider yourself to be better than others, but associate with the lowly, and never be conceited.

[17] Do not repay anyone evil for evil. Rather, be concerned about doing what is good in the eyes of all. [18] As much as possible, and to the extent of your ability, live in peace with everyone.

[19] Dearly beloved, never seek revenge. Leave that to the time of retribution. For it is written, "Vengeance is mine, says the Lord. I will repay." [20] On the contrary,

> "If your enemy is hungry, feed him;
>   if he is thirsty, give him something to drink.
> By doing this,
>   you will heap burning coals * on his head."

[21] Do not be conquered by evil, but conquer evil with good.

13 **Obedience to Authority.*** [1] Let everyone submit himself to the governing authorities, for there is no authority except that which derives from God, and whatever authorities exist have been instituted by God. [2] Consequently, anyone who resists authority is rebelling against what God has appointed, and those who so resist will bring judgment upon themselves.

[3] Rulers are a source of fear not to those who do good but rather to those who do evil. Do you wish to be free of fear from someone in authority? Then continue to do what is right and you will receive his approval. [4] For he is acting as God's representative for your welfare. But if you do what is evil, then be afraid for he does not wear a sword for nothing. People in authority are God's servants to mete out punishment to wrongdoers.

[5] Therefore, you are obliged to submit, not only because of fear of punishment but also because of conscience. [6] That is why you also pay taxes, for the authorities are God's servants, and they devote themselves to this service. [7] Pay to each person what is rightfully his—taxes to the one to whom taxes are due, tolls to the one to whom tolls are due, respect to the one to whom respect is due, honor to the one to whom honor is due.

Love Is the Fulfillment of the Law.* [8] Owe nothing to anyone except the debt of love you owe one another. The one who loves others has fulfilled the Law. [9] "You shall not commit adultery, You shall not kill, You shall not steal, You shall not covet," and every other commandment are all summed up in this: "You shall love your neighbor as yourself." [10] Love cannot result in any harm to the neighbor; therefore, love is the fulfillment of the Law.

Live Honestly As in the Light.* [11] Do this knowing that the hour has come. It is time for you to awaken from sleep. For our salvation is nearer to us now than it was when we first began to believe. [12] The night is nearly over, and the day is at hand.

Let us therefore cast aside the works of darkness and put on the armor of light. [13] Let us behave honorably as in the day: not in orgies and drunkenness, not in debauchery and licentiousness, not in quarreling and jealousy. [14] Rather, put on the Lord Jesus Christ and allow no opportunity for the flesh to gratify its sinful desires.

14 The Weak and the Strong in the Community.

[1] * Welcome anyone whose faith is weak, but do not get into arguments about doubts. [2] One person may have the faith to eat any kind of food, whereas a weak person may eat only vegetables. [3] The one who eats everything must not look contemptuously on the one who does not, and the one who abstains must not pass judgment on the one who eats, for God has welcomed both. [4] What right do you have to pass judgment on someone else's servant? The master will determine whether that servant will stand or fall. But the servant will be upheld, for the Lord has the power to enable him to stand.

[5] One person may consider one day to be more sacred than another, while another may judge all days to be alike. Let everyone be convinced in his own beliefs. [6] Whoever observes the day observes it for the Lord. Also, the one who eats, eats in honor of the Lord, since he gives thanks to God, while the one who abstains, abstains in honor of the Lord and thereby also gives thanks to God.

[7] None of us lives for himself, and none of us dies for himself. [8] If we live, we live for the Lord, and if we die, we die for the Lord. Therefore, whether we live or die, we are the Lord's. [9] It was for this reason that Christ died and came to life again: so that he might be Lord of both the dead and the living.

[10] Why then do you pass judgment on your brother? Or why do you despise your brother? All of us will have to stand before the judgment seat of God. [11] For it is written,

"As I live, says the Lord,
every knee shall bow before me,
and every tongue shall give praise to God."

Consideration for the Weak Conscience. [12] So, then, each one of us will have to give an account of himself to God. [13] Therefore, let us cease passing judgment on one another, but rather judge never to put a stumbling block or hindrance in the way of a brother. [14] I know, and am convinced in the Lord Jesus, that nothing is unclean in itself. However, it is unclean for someone who believes it to be unclean.

[15] If your brother is seriously offended by what you eat, then you are no longer being guided by love. Do not allow the food that you eat to destroy anyone for whom Christ died. [16] Do not let what you think is good to become what others say is evil. [17] For the kingdom of God is not a matter of food and drink but of righteousness, peace, and joy in the Holy Spirit. [18] The one who serves Christ in such things is pleasing to God and respected by others.

[19] Let us * then pursue the ways that lead to peace and mutual edification. [20] Do not destroy the work of God for the sake of food. All food is indeed clean, but it is wrong for you to cause others to fall by what you eat. [21] It is best not to eat meat or drink wine or do anything else that causes your brother to stumble.

[22] Whatever faith you have, keep it between yourself and God. Blessed is the one who has no reason to condemn himself because of what he approves. [23] But whoever has doubts is condemned if he eats, because he does not act from faith. Whatever does not proceed from faith is sin.

15 Patience and Self-Denial. [1] Those of us who are strong must resolve to put up with the failings of the weak and not please ourselves. [2] Each of us must consider his neighbor's good for the purpose of building him up. [3] Even Christ never sought to please himself, but, as it is written, "The insults of those who insult you have fallen upon me." [4] For everything that was written in the past was written for our instruction, so that by perseverance

and the encouragement of the Scriptures, we may continue to have hope.

[5] May the God of perseverance and encouragement grant that you may live in harmony with one another, following in the example of Jesus Christ, [6] so that with one mind and one voice you may glorify the God and Father of our Lord Jesus Christ.

God's Fidelity and Mercy.* [7] Therefore, accept one another for the glory of God, just as Christ has accepted you. [8] For I tell you that Christ became a servant of the circumcised to manifest God's truthfulness by confirming the promises given to the patriarchs [9] and so that the Gentiles might glorify God for his mercy, as it is written:

> "Therefore, I will praise you among the Gentiles
>   and sing praises to your name."

[10] And again it says:

> "Rejoice, O Gentiles, with his people." *

[11] Further it adds:

> "Praise the Lord, all you Gentiles,
>   and let all the peoples praise him."

[12] And again Isaiah asserts:

> "The root of Jesse shall come,
>   the one who will arise to rule the Gentiles;
>   the Gentiles will hope in him." *

[13] May the God of hope fill you with all joy and peace in believing, so that you may grow rich in hope by the power of the Holy Spirit.

EPILOGUE*

Apostle to the Gentiles.* [14] Brethren, I myself am convinced that you yourselves are immersed in goodness, filled with all knowledge, and able to instruct one another. [15] Nevertheless, I have written to you rather boldly to refresh your memory in some respects because of the grace given to me by God. [16] He has appointed me to be a minister of Christ Jesus to the Gentiles in the priestly service of the gospel of God, in order that the Gentiles might become an acceptable offering consecrated by the Holy Spirit.

[17] In Christ Jesus, then, I have reason to glory in my service of God. [18] I will not dare to speak of anything except what Christ has accomplished through me to lead the Gentiles to obedience to God by word and deed, [19] by the power of signs and wonders, through the power of the Spirit of God.

So from Jerusalem * and the surrounding area, even as far as Illyricum, I have completed the preaching of the gospel of Christ. [20] Moreover, I have always striven to preach the gospel of Christ where the name of Christ is not known, not wanting to build on someone else's foundation. [21] Rather, as it is written:

> "Those who have never been told of him shall see,
>   and those who have never heard of him shall understand."

Paul's Plans for Traveling—Even to Spain. * [22] That is why I have so often been prevented from coming to you. [23] But now, since there is nothing more to keep me in these regions, and since for a good many years I have desired to visit you, [24] I hope to see you when I am on my way to Spain. Then, after I have enjoyed your company for a while, you can send me on my way there.

[25] Presently, however, I am going to Jerusalem to minister to the saints. [26] For Macedonia and Achaia * have resolved to make a contribution for the benefit of the poor among the saints in Jerusalem. [27] They were pleased to do so, and indeed they are indebted to them, for if the Gentiles have come to share in their spiritual blessings, they owe it to them to share their material blessings with them.

[28] Therefore, when I have completed this task and have delivered the fruit of their generosity to them, I will set out for Spain and visit you along the way. [29] And I am sure

that when I come, I shall do so with the full measure of the blessing of Christ.

[30] Therefore, I exhort you, brethren, by our Lord Jesus Christ and by the love of the Spirit, to join me in my labors by praying to God for me [31] that I may be delivered from the unbelievers in Judea and that my service in Jerusalem may be acceptable to the saints there. [32] In that way, I can come to you in joy, if God so wills, and be refreshed together with you. [33] The God of peace be with you all. Amen.

16 Recommendation of Phoebe. [1] * I commend to you our sister Phoebe, who is a deaconess * of the Church at Cenchreae. [2] Welcome her in the Lord in a manner worthy of the saints, and help her with whatever she may need from you, for she has been a benefactor of many people, including myself.

List of Greetings. [3] Give my greetings to Prisca and Aquila, my fellow workers in Christ Jesus. [4] They risked their lives for me, and I as well as all the Churches of the Gentiles am grateful to them. [5] Greet also the Church that assembles in their house.

Give my greetings to my beloved friend Epaenetus, who was the first convert to Christ in the province of Asia. [6] Greet Mary, who has worked extremely hard for you. [7] Greet Andronicus and Junia, * my relatives who were in prison with me; they are eminent in the ranks of the apostles and were in Christ before I was.

[8] Greet Ampliatus, my beloved in the Lord. [9] Greet Urbanus, our fellow worker in Christ, and my dear friend Stachys. [10] Greet Apelles, * who has proved worthy in the service of Christ, and those who belong to the family of Aristobulus. *

[11] Greetings to my kinsman Herodion. Greet those in the Lord who belong to the household of Narcissus. * [12] Greet Tryphaena and Tryphosa * who labor diligently in the Lord's service. Greet my dear friend Persis, who also

works hard for the Lord. [13] Give my greetings to Rufus, *
one chosen by the Lord, as well as to his mother who has
also been a mother to me.

[14] Greet Asyncritus, Phlegon, Hermes, Patrobas, Hermas, and the brethren who are with them. [15] Greetings to
Philologus and Julia, Nereus and his sister, and Olympas,
as well as all the saints who are with them. [16] Greet one
another with a holy kiss. All the Churches of Christ send
you their greetings.

Beware of Dissenters. [17] I urge you, brethren, to watch out
for those who incite dissensions and obstacles in opposition to the teaching that you have learned. Take care to
avoid them. [18] For such people are not servants of our
Lord Jesus Christ but of their own appetites, and by
smooth words and flattery they deceive the minds of the
simple. [19] Your obedience has become known to all and
has caused me to rejoice greatly over you. However, I want
you to be wise in what is good and innocent in what is evil;
[20] then the God of peace will soon crush Satan under your
feet. The grace of our Lord Jesus Christ be with you.

Greetings from Paul's Companions at Corinth. [21] Timothy,
my coworker, sends greetings to you, as do Lucius and
Jason * and Sosipater, my kinsmen. [22] I, Tertius, who
am writing down this letter, greet you in the Lord.
[23] Greetings also from Gaius, * my host and the host to
the whole Church, and from Erastus, the city treasurer, and our brother Quartus. [[24] The grace of our Lord
Jesus Christ be with you all. Amen.] *

Glory to God through Jesus Christ *

25   Now to him who has the power to strengthen you
      in accordance with the gospel that I preach
      and the proclamation of Jesus Christ,
      according to the revelation of the mystery
      that was kept secret for long ages
26   but is now revealed,
      and through the prophetic writings is made known
      to all the nations

according to the command of the eternal God
to bring them to the obedience of faith—
27 to God who alone is wise,
through Jesus Christ
be glory forever! Amen.

THE FIRST LETTER TO THE CORINTHIANS

COMMUNITIES MAKING THEIR WAY IN THE GREAT CITIES

Once again, the Church is born in a large city. In the first century A.D., Corinth was the capital of central and southern Greece. In this important commercial center at the heart of the Mediterranean world, all possible ideas commingled, creating a cultural and religious ferment.

The city was known for its sporting life, but also for the moral corruption that gave it its reputation. "Live like a Corinthian" was a slogan suggesting an environment teeming with criminality and libertinism. Seamen coming ashore in this cosmopolitan port were certainly not the only ones to take advantage of that life. Sacred prostitution flourished in the temple of Aphrodite, the favorite goddess of the city.

"There are many in this city who are my people," the Lord had told Paul in a vision (Acts 18:10).

From the winter of A.D. 50–51 to the summer of A.D. 52, the Apostle laid the foundations of a vital community, whose members he recruited chiefly from among pagans of modest circumstances (Acts 18:1-18).

Two years later, while preaching the Gospel in Ephesus, Paul was informed of the divisions that were agitating his young Greek Church. In addition, two Christians came from Corinth to lay their problems before him. He then wrote the present Letter, which we know as the First Letter to the Corinthians; it had been preceded, however, by another that has been lost (see 1 Cor 5:9).

The outline is a simple one. Serious incidents have been brought to the Apostle's knowledge; these have also raised some concrete questions, of varying degrees of importance; Paul simply deals with the several points one after another.

As a result, this Letter is in no sense a systematic doctrinal treatise. The author follows the list of the situations experienced at Corinth, and this enables him to see the dynamic growth of a young Church, but also its crises.

Nonetheless, this Letter gives us a rather alarming portrait of the community. It shows that the Gospel does not transform a pagan mentality in one day. The newly baptized must review their behavior in the light of the message of Jesus and rectify their judgment, which is permeated by the thinking and morals of their environment.

These Greeks are characteristically prompt to embrace new ideas and can easily regard the Church as simply a philosophical group. Their love of freedom threatens to lead them back to libertinism and turn them into a cause of scandal for those who are weaker or more demanding. In order to exalt the life of the spirit, they look down on what comes from the body and they more easily become its slaves. Like all Christians, they are tempted to choose in the Gospel that which corresponds with their own likes and to neglect the rest.

This Letter is an exceptional document in the history of the early Church. In addition to the internal problems of a community, it also brings before us important issues that are debated: confronting a civilization's currents of ideas and ways of life; dissension in thought and disparity in fortune; discipline within the community; questions of sexuality in the face of an environment wherein eroticism seems to be the rage (Corinth is the capital of dissoluteness); and the problem of marriage and celibacy.

Other issues that it lays bare concern the social relations of Christians with pagans; the attitude toward other religious practices; the types of behavior in the Liturgy; and the demands of the spiritual initiative. Most of all, because of its birth in the midst of a culture, Christianity must question itself, in fact as well as in theory, about its originality and its differences with respect to the life of an age and an environment.

In this context, we are more interested in what inspires the reaction of Paul. Obviously, as a Jew, he would be mistrustful *of the cultural and religious agitation of Corinth; if he does not like the rigorist legalism of the scrupulous, he is also without pity for those who confuse freedom with disorder.*

Nonetheless, he does not respond simply according to his own religious tastes; in the face of questions posed and dangers encountered, he meditates on the essential points of faith: salvation in the Death and Resurrection of Christ, the mystery of the Church, the presence of the Spirit, the meaning of the Eucharist, the requirements of a faith that wishes to grow and its influence on the behavior of the baptized, and the hope that guides the Christians' existence and colors their view of the world in the light of Easter.

Paul reminds his correspondents that the Gospel is not a philosophical theory to be discussed. He brings them personally into the presence of the dead and risen Christ who gathers together and transforms human beings in the Church—which is his Body—and calls them to a radical renewal of life.

Despite the dangers he must point out and the sufferings they cause him (2 Cor), Paul will always be proud of this community that he has founded in such a pervasive pagan environment. He praises its sincere and active faith, as well as its generosity, which is not without some illusions and a dangerous feverishness; he admires the rich gifts that the Spirit is pouring out on this handful of men and women who live the Gospel and challenge all the cultural pressures brought to bear on them by their environment.

The First Letter to the Corinthians may be divided as follows:

I: Greetings and Thanksgiving (1:1-9)

II: Divisions in the Church of Corinth (1:10—4:21)

III: Deviant Behavior (5:1—6:20)

IV: Marriage and Celibacy among Christians (7:1-40)

V: Christians and Pagan Customs (8:1—11:1)

VI: Liturgical Assemblies and Their Problems (11:2—14:40)

VII: The Resurrection (15:1-58)

VIII: Final Recommendations and Greetings (16:1-24)

I: GREETINGS AND THANKSGIVING

1 **Address to a Church.*** [1] Paul, called by the will of God to be an apostle of Christ Jesus, and Sosthenes* our brother, [2] to the Church of God in Corinth,* to those who have been sanctified in Christ Jesus and called to be holy together with all those everywhere who call on the name of our Lord Jesus Christ, their Lord as well as ours. [3] Grace to you and peace from God our Father and the Lord Jesus Christ.

[4] I continually give thanks to my God for you because of his grace that has been granted to you in Christ Jesus. [5] For through him you have been enriched in every way in all facets of speech and knowledge, [6] as our testimony about Christ has been confirmed in you.

[7] Therefore, you do not lack any spiritual gift as you wait for the revelation of our Lord Jesus Christ. [8] He will keep you steadfast until the very end, so that you may be blameless on the day of our Lord Jesus Christ. [9] God is faithful, and it is by him that you have been called into fellowship with his Son, Jesus Christ our Lord.

II: DIVISIONS IN THE CHURCH OF CORINTH*

The Existence of Factions. [10] Brethren, I exhort you in the name of our Lord Jesus Christ to be in full agreement with one another and not permit any divisions to arise among you. Be perfectly united in mind and purpose. [11] For I have heard reports from Chloe's people, brethren, that there are quarrels among you. *

[12] What I mean is that each of you is asserting, "I belong to Paul," or "I belong to Apollos,"* or "I belong to Cephas," or "I belong to Christ." [13] Has Christ now been divided? Did Paul die on the cross for you? Was it in Paul's name that you were baptized?

[14] I am thankful that I never baptized any of you, aside from Crispus and Gaius, [15] so that no one can say you were baptized in my name. ([16] I also baptized the house-

hold of Stephanas. Aside from those I do not know if I baptized anyone else.)

The Message of the Cross and Human Wisdom.* ¹⁷ For Christ did not send me to baptize but to preach the gospel—and to do so without words of human wisdom lest the cross of Christ be devoid of its meaning. ¹⁸ Indeed, the message of the cross is foolishness to those who are perishing, but to us who are being saved it is the power of God. ¹⁹ For it is written,

> "I will destroy the wisdom of the wise,
>   and the understanding of the learned I will bring
>   to naught." *

²⁰ Where now are the wise ones? Where are the men of learning? Where are the debaters of this present age? Has God not shown the wisdom of the world to be foolish? ²¹ For since, in the wisdom of God, the world was unable to come to know him through wisdom, he chose, through the folly of preaching, to save those who have faith.

²² Jews demand signs, and Greeks look for wisdom, ²³ but we proclaim Christ crucified. This is a stumbling block to Jews and foolishness to Gentiles; * ²⁴ but to those who are called, both Jews and Greeks, Christ is the power of God and the wisdom of God. ²⁵ For the foolishness of God is wiser than human wisdom, and the weakness of God is stronger than human strength.

God Has Chosen Those Who Count for Nothing. ²⁶ Consider, brethren, your calling. Not many of you were wise by human standards, * not many were powerful, not many were of noble birth. ²⁷ Rather, God chose those who were regarded as foolish by the world to shame the wise; God chose those in the world who were weak to shame the strong. ²⁸ God chose those in the world who were lowly and despised, those who count for nothing, to reduce to nothing those who were regarded as worthy, ²⁹ * so that no one could boast in the presence of God.

³⁰ It is through him that you are in Christ Jesus, who became for us wisdom of God, as well as righteousness,

sanctification, and redemption. [31] Therefore, as it is written, "If anyone wishes to boast, let him boast in the Lord."

2 Jesus Christ—and Him Crucified. [1] When I came to you, brethren, I did not proclaim to you the mystery of God * with words of eloquence or wisdom. [2] For I resolved that, while I was with you, I would know nothing except Jesus Christ—and him crucified. [3] I came to you in weakness, in fear, and in great trepidation. [4] My message and my proclamation were not made with persuasive words of wisdom, but in a demonstration of the Spirit and of power, * [5] so that your faith might rest not on human wisdom but on the power of God.

A: The Mysterious Wisdom of God

The Plan of God, True Wisdom. [6] However, to those who are mature, we do speak of wisdom, although not a wisdom of this age or of the rulers of this age * whose end is not far distant. [7] Rather, we speak of the mysterious and hidden wisdom of God, which God decreed before the ages for our glory. [8] None of the rulers of this age comprehended it. If they had, they would not have crucified the Lord of glory. * [9] For as it is written,

"Eye has not seen, ear has not heard,
　　nor has the human heart imagined
　　what God has prepared for those who love him."

The Spirit Enables Faith To Mature. [10] However, God has revealed these things to us through the Spirit. For the Spirit explores everything, even the depths of God. [11] And just as no human being comprehends any person's innermost being except the person's own spirit within him, so also no one comprehends what pertains to God except the Spirit of God.

[12] We have not received the spirit of the world but the Spirit who is from God, so that we may understand the gifts bestowed upon us by God. [13] And we speak of these things in words taught to us not by human wisdom but

by the Spirit, expressing spiritual things in spiritual words. *

¹⁴ An unspiritual person refuses to accept what pertains to the Spirit of God, for to him such things are foolish. He is unable to understand them because they can be discerned only in a spiritual way. ¹⁵ A spiritual person* discerns all things, and he is himself subject to no one else's judgment:

¹⁶   "For who has ever known the mind of the Lord?
       Who has ever been his instructor?"

But we possess the mind of Christ.

3 You Are Still Infants in Christ.

¹ Brethren, I could not talk to you as spiritual people, but as worldly, as infants in Christ. ² I fed you with milk, rather than with solid food that you were not ready to digest. Indeed, even now you are still not ready to receive it, ³ for you are still of the flesh.

As long as jealousy and rivalry continue among you, are you not of the flesh and acting as mere mortals? ⁴ Whenever someone says, "I belong to Paul," and another asserts, "I belong to Apollos," are you not acting in a merely human fashion?

B: Missionaries and Servants of Christ*

God's Coworkers. ⁵ What then is Apollos? What is Paul? We are only servants through whom you have come to believe, as the Lord assigned each to accomplish. ⁶ I planted the seed, and Apollos watered it, but God caused it to grow.

⁷ Therefore, neither the one who plants nor the one who waters is of any importance but only God who causes the growth. ⁸ The one who plants and the one who waters have a common end, and each will be rewarded in accordance with his labor. ⁹ For we are God's coworkers; you are God's field, God's building.

¹⁰ By the grace that God has given to me, I laid a foundation like a skilled master builder, and someone else is

building on that foundation. But each one must be careful how he builds on it. [11] For no one can lay any foundation other than the one that has already been laid, namely, Jesus Christ.

[12] Now if anyone builds on that foundation with gold, silver, and precious stones, or with wood, hay, and straw, [13] the work of each person will come to light. For the Day * will disclose it, because it will be revealed with fire, and the fire itself will test the worth of each person's work. [14] If what has been built survives, the builder will be rewarded. [15] If it burns down, that person will suffer loss. The person will be saved, though only by passing through fire. *

You Belong to Christ. [16] Do you not realize that you are God's temple, and that the Spirit of God dwells in you? [17] If anyone destroys God's temple, God will destroy that person. For the temple of God is holy, and you are that temple.

[18] Let no one delude himself. If anyone among you considers himself to be wise by worldly standards, he must become a fool in order to be truly wise. [19] For the wisdom of this world is foolishness with God. It is written,

"He catches the wise in their own craftiness,"

[20] and again,

"The Lord knows the thoughts of the wise,
    that they are futile."

[21] And so, let no one boast about human beings. For everything belongs to you, [22] whether Paul or Apollos or Cephas, the world or life or death, the present or the future. All belong to you, [23] and you belong to Christ, and Christ belongs to God.

4 **Do Not Judge before the Appointed Time.** [1] People should regard us as servants of Christ and stewards of the mysteries of God. [2] Now it is required of stewards that they be found trustworthy. [3] It is of no importance to me if I am to be judged by you or by any human court. I do not even judge myself.

[4] I personally have nothing on my conscience, but that does not mean that I am innocent. It is the Lord who judges me. [5] Therefore, do not pronounce judgment before the appointed time, until the Lord comes. He will bring to light what is hidden in darkness and will disclose the motives of all hearts. Then each one will receive the proper praise from God.

Fools for Christ. [6] Brethren, I have applied all this to Apollos and myself for your benefit, so that you may learn from us the meaning of the saying, "Do not go beyond what has been written." * None of you should become inflated with pride against anyone else. [7] Who made you so important? What do you have that you did not receive? And if you have received it, why do you boast as though you had not received it?

[8] You already have everything! You have already become rich! You have become kings without our help! How I wish that you truly reigned so that we might reign with you! *

[9] It seems to me that God has designated us apostles as the last of all, like men sentenced to death, because we have become a spectacle to the world, to angels, and to men. [10] We are fools for the sake of Christ, but you are wise in Christ. We are weak, but you are strong. You are held in honor, but we are in disrepute.

[11] To this very hour, we endure hunger and thirst. We are poorly clad and beaten and homeless, [12] and we exhaust ourselves working with our hands. When we are cursed, we bless; when we suffer persecution, we endure it; [13] when we are slandered, we respond gently. We are regarded as the rubbish of the world, the dregs of humanity, to this very day.

The Authority of a Father in Christ. [14] I am writing all this not to make you ashamed but to admonish you as my beloved children. [15] Even though you have ten thousand tutors in Christ, you do not have many fathers, for I became your father in Christ Jesus through the gospel.

[16] I appeal to you then to be imitators of me. [17] For this reason I have sent you Timothy, who is my beloved and faithful son in the Lord. He will remind you of my ways in Christ, as I teach everywhere in every Church.

[18] Some of you have become arrogant, on the assumption that I am not coming to you. [19] However, I will come to you soon, if it is the Lord's will, and then I will ascertain the actual power of these arrogant people as opposed to their words. [20] For the kingdom of God * is not a matter of words but of power. [21] What would you prefer? Am I to come to you with a whip or with love and a spirit of gentleness?

III: DEVIANT BEHAVIOR*

5 **Reports of Sexual Immorality.** [1] There have been widely circulated reports of sexual immorality among you, immorality of such a nature that not even pagans practice—the union of a man with his father's wife. [2] How can you be proud of yourselves? You should rather have been overcome with grief and expelled from the community anyone who acted in such a manner.

[3] I for my part am with you in spirit, even though I am not physically present. I have already passed judgment on the man who did this, as if I were actually present. [4] In the name of our Lord Jesus Christ, when you have all assembled together and I am with you in spirit through the power of our Lord Jesus, [5] you are to hand over this man to Satan to be destroyed in the flesh, so that on the day of the Lord his spirit may be saved.

[6] Your boasting is not good. Do you not know that a small amount of yeast leavens the whole batch of dough? [7] * Throw out the old yeast so that you may become a fresh batch of unleavened dough. And truly you already are, because Christ, our paschal lamb, has been sacrificed. [8] Therefore, let us celebrate the feast, not with the

old yeast, the yeast of depravity and wickedness, but with the unleavened bread of sincerity and truth.

⁹ In my letter, I wrote to you not to associate with people who are leading immoral lives. * ¹⁰ Obviously, I was not referring to contact with people in the world who are immoral or with those who are greedy or thieves or worshipers of false gods, since to do this you would have to leave the world. ¹¹ What I really meant to get across was that you should not associate with any brother or sister who is sexually immoral, greedy, an idolater, a slanderer, a drunkard or a robber. You should not even eat with such a person.

¹² It is no concern of mine to judge those who are outside the fold. * It is your responsibility to judge those who are inside. ¹³ God will pass judgment on the outsiders. Banish the evil person from your midst.

6 Avoid Lawsuits against Each Other. * ¹ If any of you has a dispute with another, how can you seek judgment before those who are unrighteous * instead of before the saints? ² Do you not know that the saints will judge the world? And if the world is to be judged by you, how can you consider yourselves as incompetent to deal with smaller cases? ³ Do you not realize that we are to judge angels? * Why then should we not deal with matters of this life?

⁴ Therefore, if you have such matters to resolve, how can you seek judgment from those who have no standing in the Church? ⁵ I write this to make you ashamed. Is it really possible that there is no one among you who is wise enough to mediate a dispute between brethren? ⁶ Why should a brother go to court against another brother, seeking a decision from unbelievers?

⁷ In truth, the very fact that you engage in lawsuits with one another is a misfortune for you. Why not prefer to be wronged? Why not prefer to be defrauded? ⁸ Instead, you yourself are guilty of wronging and defrauding your own brethren.

⁹ Are you not aware that wrongdoers will never inherit the kingdom of God? Do not be deceived! Fornicators, idolaters, adulterers, male prostitutes, sodomites,* ¹⁰ thieves, extortioners, drunkards, slanderers, swindlers—none of these will inherit the kingdom of God. ¹¹ Some of you were once such as these. However, now you have been washed clean, you have been sanctified, you have been justified in the name of the Lord Jesus Christ and in the Spirit of our God.

All Things Are Lawful for Me!* ¹² "All things are lawful for me," but not all things are beneficial. "All things are lawful for me," but I will not allow myself to be dominated by anything. ¹³ "Food is meant for the stomach and the stomach is meant for food," but God will destroy them both. However, the body is not meant for immorality but for the Lord, and the Lord for the body. ¹⁴ God raised up the Lord, and he will raise us up also by his power.

¹⁵ Do you not know that your bodies are members of Christ? Should I then take Christ's members and make them members of a prostitute? Never! ¹⁶ Do you not know that anyone who joins himself to a prostitute becomes one body with her? For it is said, "The two shall become one flesh." ¹⁷ But anyone who joins himself to the Lord becomes one spirit with him.*

¹⁸ Flee from sexual immorality! Every other sin that a person commits is outside the body, but the fornicator sins against his own body. ¹⁹ Do you not know that your body is the temple of the Holy Spirit within you, whom you have received from God, and that you are not your own? ²⁰ You have been purchased at a price. Therefore, glorify God in your body.

IV: MARRIAGE AND CELIBACY AMONG CHRISTIANS*

7 **Christian Marriage.*** ¹ Now I will move on to the matters about which you wrote. Yes, it is a good thing for a man to refrain from touching a woman. ² However, to avoid the temptation to immorality, each man should have his own wife and each woman her own husband. [3] A husband should give to his wife her conjugal rights, and likewise a wife should fulfill her conjugal obligations to her husband. [4] For a wife does not have authority over her own body, but the husband does. Likewise, a husband does not have authority over his own body, but the wife does.

[5] Do not deprive one another, except perhaps by mutual consent for a specified time so as to devote yourselves to prayer. Then come together again so that Satan may not tempt you by taking advantage of your lack of self-control. [6] I suggest this not as a command but by way of concession. [7] I wish that all of you would be as I myself am. However, each person has a particular gift from God, one having one kind and another a different kind.

[8] To the unmarried and to widows, I say that it is a good thing for them to remain as they are, as I do. [9] However, if they are unable to exercise self-control, they should marry, for it is better to be married than to burn with passion.

[10] To those who are married, I give this command, which is not mine but the Lord's: a wife should not separate from her husband— [11] and if she does separate, she must either remain unmarried or become reconciled to her husband—and a husband should not divorce his wife.

Living at Peace with an Unbelieving Spouse.* [12] To the rest, I say this (I, not the Lord): If any brother has a wife who is an unbeliever, and she is willing to remain with him, he should not divorce her. [13] And if any woman has a husband who is an unbeliever, and he is willing to remain with her, she should not divorce him. [14] For the unbelieving husband is made holy through his wife, and the unbelieving wife is made holy through her husband. Otherwise, your children would be unclean, whereas in fact they are holy.

[15] However, if the unbelieving partner chooses to separate, let that person go. The brother or sister is no longer bound in this case. God has called you to live in peace.

¹⁶ As a wife, how can you be certain that you will save your husband? As a husband, how can you be certain that you will save your wife?

Living Where Christ Calls Us. ¹⁷ Everyone should accept the role in life assigned to each one by the Lord, continuing as he was when the Lord called him. This is the rule that I give to all the Churches. ¹⁸ Was a man called after he had been circumcised? Then he must remain circumcised. Was a man uncircumcised when he was called? He should remain uncircumcised. ¹⁹ To be circumcised is of no importance, and to be uncircumcised is of no importance. What matters is keeping God's commandments. ²⁰ Everyone should remain as he was when he was called.

²¹ Were you a slave when you were called? Do not let that concern you. But if you have an opportunity to gain your freedom, take it. ²² For whoever was called in the Lord as a slave is a freedman of the Lord, just as whoever was free when he was called is a slave of Christ. ²³ You were purchased at a price. Do not become slaves of men. ²⁴ Therefore, brethren, everyone should remain before God in the condition in which he was called.

Virginity—Total Consecration to Christ.* ²⁵ In regard to virgins, I have received no instructions from the Lord, but let me offer my own opinion as one who by the Lord's mercy can be considered trustworthy. ²⁶ I think that in this time of stress, a man should remain in his current state. ²⁷ Are you bound to a wife? Do not seek to be free. Are you free of a wife? Then do not look for a wife. ²⁸ However, if you do marry, you do not sin, nor does a virgin sin if she marries. But those who marry will experience hardships in this life, * and from these I would like to spare you.

²⁹ What I am saying, brethren, is that our time is short. From now on, those who have wives should live as though they had none, ³⁰ and those who mourn as though they were not mourning, and those who rejoice as though they were not rejoicing, and those who buy as though they had nothing, ³¹ and those who make use of

the world as though they had no dealings with it. For the world as we know it is passing away.

[32] It is my wish that you be free of all anxieties. An unmarried man devotes himself to the Lord's affairs and is concerned as to how he can please the Lord. [33] However, a man who is married devotes himself to worldly matters and is concerned about how he can please his wife, [34] and his interests are divided. In the same way, an unmarried woman or a virgin is concerned about the affairs of the Lord and strives to be holy in both body and spirit, whereas the married woman is concerned about worldly matters and how she may please her husband.

[35] I am speaking about this for your own good. I have no intention to impose any restraint upon you, but I wish you to be guided by a sense of propriety, to devote yourself to the Lord free from distraction.

Freedom To Marry.* [36] If a man feels that he is behaving improperly toward his virgin because a critical moment has come * and it seems that something should be done, let him do what he wills. He does not sin if there is a marriage. [37] However, if he stands firm in his resolve and is under no obligation and, being free to carry out his will, decides in his heart to keep his virgin, he also does well. [38] Therefore, the man who gives her in marriage does well, and the one who does not give her in marriage does better.

[39] A wife is bound to her husband as long as he lives. But should the husband die, she is free to marry anyone she wishes, only let it be in the Lord. [40] However, in my opinion she is happier if she remains as she is, and I believe that I too have the Spirit of God.

V: CHRISTIANS AND PAGAN CUSTOMS*

A: The Question of Meat Sacrificed to Idols

8 **An Idol Is Nothing.** [1] Now concerning the question of meat that has been sacrificed to idols, we are well aware that all of us possess knowledge. However, while knowledge puffs up, love builds up. [2] Anyone who believes that his knowledge about something is complete will soon discover that his knowledge is flawed, [3] but anyone who loves God is known by him.

[4] Now in regard to the eating of meat sacrificed to idols, we know that idols are nothing in the world and that there is only one God. [5] Indeed, even though there are so-called gods in heaven and on earth—and there are in fact many gods and many lords— [6] for us there is

one God, the Father,
　　from whom all things are
　　and for whom we exist,*
and one Lord, Jesus Christ,
　　through whom all things are
　　and through whom we exist.

Do Not Cause a Brother To Fall. [7] However, not everyone possesses this knowledge. There are some who have become so accustomed to idolatry up until now that when they consume meat that has been sacrificed to an idol, their conscience in its weakness is defiled.

[8] Obviously, food cannot bring us closer to God. We do not lack anything if we do not eat, and we have no advantage if we do. [9] Just take care that your freedom does not become a stumbling block to the weak. [10] If someone who regards you as knowledgeable observes you eating in an idol's temple, will he not, burdened by a weak conscience, be influenced to eat food that has been sacrificed to idols?

[11] Therefore, through your knowledge, this weak believer is brought to destruction, the brother for whom Christ died. [12] And when you sin against your brethren and wound their weak consciences, you sin against Christ. [13] Hence, if food can lead my brother to sin, I will never again eat meat lest I cause the downfall of one of my brethren.

B: The Example of Paul's Apostolate

9 **A Missionary's Rights.** [1] Am I not free? Am I not an apostle? Have I not seen Jesus our Lord? Are you not my work in the Lord? [2] Although others may not regard me as an apostle, at least I am to you, for you are the seal of my apostleship in the Lord.

[3] To those who seek to pass judgment on me, my defense is this. [4] Do we not have the right to eat and drink? [5] Do we not have the right to be accompanied by a believing wife like the other apostles, the brethren of the Lord, and Cephas? * [6] Are Barnabas * and I the only ones who do not have the right to refrain from working? [7] What soldier would ever serve in the army at his own expense? Who plants a vineyard without eating its fruit? Or who tends a flock without consuming some of its milk?

[8] I am not saying this based simply on human authority, for the Law says the very same thing. [9] In the Law of Moses it is written, "You shall not muzzle an ox while it is treading out the grain." Is it for oxen that God is concerned, [10] or does he not rather say this for our sake? Without question it was written for our sake, for whoever plows should plow in hope and whoever threshes should thresh in hope, both in expectation of a share in the crop. [11] If we have sown a spiritual crop for you, is it unreasonable for us to expect from you a material harvest? [12] If others have this claim on you, do not we?

Despite this, we have never availed ourselves of any such right. On the contrary, we put up with anything rather than place an obstacle to the gospel of Christ. [13] Do you not know that those who perform the temple service receive their food from the temple, and that those who officiate at the altar share in the offerings? [14] In the same way, the Lord ordered that those who preach the gospel should get their living from the gospel. *

I Have Become All Things to All. [15] However, I have never availed myself of any of these rights, and I have not written this to influence you to grant me such treatment; I would rather die first. No one shall deprive me of this boast! [16] If I proclaim the gospel, that is no reason for me to boast, for the obligation to do so has been given to me, and woe to me if I fail to fulfill it.

[17] If I proclaimed the gospel of my own volition, I would deserve a reward; but if I do not do so voluntarily, I am simply discharging the commission that has been given to me. [18] What then is my reward? It is simply that in my preaching I may offer the gospel free of charge and not make use of the rights that the gospel affords me.

[19] Although I am free and belong to no man, I have made myself a slave to all so as to win over as many as possible. [20] To the Jews, I became like a Jew in order to win the Jews. To those under the Law, I became like one under the Law—although I myself am not under the Law—in order to win over those under the Law. [21] To those outside the Law, I became like one outside the Law—although I am not outside the Law of God but am subject to the Law of Christ—in order to win over those outside the Law. [22] To the weak, I have become weak in order to win over the weak. I have become all things to all, so that by every possible means I might save some. [23] I do all this for the sake of the gospel so that I might share it with you.

C: Flee from Idolatry*

Discipline Yourself So As Not To Be Disqualified. [24] You are well aware that while all the runners in the stadium compete in the race, only one wins the prize. Run in such a way as to win the prize. [25] Everyone who seeks a prize submits himself to rigorous self-discipline in every respect. They do so to win a perishable crown, while we seek an imperishable one. [26] Therefore, I do not run without purpose, nor do I fight like a man beating the air. [27] Rather, I discipline my body and bring it under control, for fear that after preaching to others I myself may be disqualified.

10 The Lesson of Israel's Past.*

[1] Brethren, I do not want you to be unaware that our ancestors were all under the cloud and all passed through the sea, [2] and they were all baptized into Moses in the cloud and in the sea. [3] All ate the same spiritual food, [4] and all drank the same spiritual drink—for they drank from the spiritual rock that followed them, and that rock was Christ. [5] Yet God was not pleased with most of them, and they were struck down in the desert.

[6] These events occurred to offer examples for us so that we might not desire evil things as they did. [7] Do not become idolaters, as some of them did. It is written, "The people sat down to eat and drink, and they rose up to engage in revelry."

[8] Let us not indulge in sexual immorality as some of them did, and twenty-three thousand of them died in a single day. [9] Let us not put Christ to the test, as some of them did, and they were destroyed by serpents. [10] And do not complain, as some of them did, and they were slain by the Destroyer. * [11] All these things happened to them to serve as an example, and they have been written down as a warning to us upon whom the end of the ages has come.

[12] Therefore, if you think you are standing securely, take care that you do not fall. [13] No trial has confronted you except what a person can stand. God is faithful, and he will not allow you to be tried beyond your strength. But together with the trial he will also provide a way out and the strength to bear it.

The Eucharist Versus Pagan Sacrifices.*

[14] Therefore, my dear friends, avoid idolatry at all costs. * [15] I am talking to you as sensible people. Judge for yourselves what I say. [16] The cup of blessing that we bless, is it not a sharing in the blood of Christ? The bread that we break, is it not a sharing in the body of Christ? [17] Because there is one bread, we who are many are one body, for we all partake of the one bread.

¹⁸ Consider the people of Israel. * Are not those who eat the sacrifices participants in the altar? ¹⁹ What then am I implying? That meat sacrificed to idols is anything, or that an idol is anything?

²⁰ No, I simply mean that pagan sacrifices are offered to demons, not to God, and I do not want you to become partners with demons. ²¹ You cannot drink the cup of the Lord and the cup of demons. You cannot partake of the table of the Lord and the table of demons. ²² Do we truly wish to provoke the Lord to jealous anger? * Are we stronger than he is?

Concerning Idol Offerings. ²³ "All things are lawful," you may say—but not all things are beneficial. All things may be lawful—but not all things are constructive. ²⁴ No one should seek his own advantage in preference to that of his neighbor. ²⁵ You may eat whatever meat is sold in the market without raising questions on grounds of conscience, ²⁶ for "the earth and all it contains belong to the Lord."

²⁷ If an unbeliever invites you to a meal and you decide to accept, eat whatever is set before you without raising any questions on the grounds of conscience. ²⁸ However, if someone says to you, "This food was offered in sacrifice," then do not eat it, out of consideration for the one who informed you and for the sake of conscience— ²⁹ I mean the other person's conscience, not your own. For why should my freedom be governed by someone else's conscience? ³⁰ If I partake of the meal with thankfulness, why should I be criticized for eating food for which I give thanks?

Give No Offense. ³¹ Therefore, whether you eat or drink, or whatever you do, do everything for the glory of God. ³² Give no offense to Jews or to Greeks or to the Church of God, ³³ just as I try to please everyone in everything I do, not seeking my own good but that of the many, so that they may be saved.

11 [1] Be imitators of me, as I am of Christ.

VI: LITURGICAL ASSEMBLIES AND THEIR PROBLEMS*

A: Propriety in Worship*

The Question of Head Coverings. [2] I praise you because you remember me in everything and you maintain the traditions just as I handed them down to you.

[3] But I want you to understand that Christ is the head of every man, and the husband is the head of his wife, and God is the head of Christ. [4] Any man who prays or prophesies with his head covered brings disgrace on his head. [5] And any woman who prays or prophesies with her head unveiled brings disgrace upon her head, for it is just as though she had her head shaved. [6] Indeed, if a woman refuses to wear a veil, then she might as well have her hair cut off. If it is disgraceful for a woman to have her hair cut off or her head shaved, then she should wear a veil.

[7] It is not right for a man to have his head covered, since he is the image of God and the reflection of his glory, whereas woman is the reflection of the glory of man. [8] For man was not made from woman, but woman was made from man. [9] Nor was man created for the sake of woman, but woman was created for the sake of man.

[10] Therefore, a woman should have on her head a sign * of her dependence, because of the angels. [11] Nevertheless, in the Lord, woman is not independent of man, nor is man independent of woman. [12] Although woman came from man, so does every man come from a woman, and all things come from God.

The Question of Long Hair. [13] Judge for yourselves. Is it proper for a woman to pray to God with her head unveiled? [14] Does not nature itself teach you that if a man has long hair, he is disgraced, [15] whereas if a woman has long hair, it is her glory? For her hair was given to her as a covering. [16] However, if anyone wishes to argue further on this point, we have no such custom to do so, nor do any of the Churches of God.

B: The Lord's Supper, Sign of Unity*

Do You Despise the Church of God? [17] Now in giving you this instruction I cannot praise you, because your meetings tend to do more harm than good. [18] To begin with, when you come together in your assembly, I hear that there are divisions among you, and to some extent I am inclined to believe it. [19] There must be such factions among you so that it will become clear to you which groups should be trusted.

[20] * When you do assemble, it is not to eat the Lord's supper, [21] for each of you goes ahead with his own supper, and one goes hungry while another has too much to drink. [22] Do you not have homes in which you can eat and drink? Or do you have such contempt for the Church of God that you humiliate those who have nothing? What should I say to you? Should I praise you? In this matter, I cannot praise you.

You Proclaim the Death of the Lord. [23] * For what I received from the Lord I handed on to you: the Lord Jesus, on the night he was betrayed, took bread, [24] and after giving thanks he broke it and said, "This is my body that is for you. Do this in remembrance of me."

[25] In the same fashion, after the supper,* he also took the cup and said, "This cup is the new covenant in my blood. Whenever you drink it, do this in remembrance of me." [26] And so, whenever you eat this bread and drink this cup, you proclaim the death of the Lord until he comes.

God's Judgment on the Community.* [27] Therefore, anyone who eats the bread and drinks the cup of the Lord in an unworthy manner is guilty of an offense against the body and blood of the Lord. [28] Everyone should examine himself about eating the bread and drinking from the cup. [29] For a person who eats and drinks without discerning the body of the Lord is eating and drinking judgment on himself.

[30] That is why many of you are weak and ill, and a number of you have fallen asleep. [31] If we were to examine ourselves, we would not be condemned. [32] However, when we are judged by the Lord, he is disciplining us to save us from being condemned together with the world.

Practical Conclusion. [33] Therefore, brethren, when you come together for the meal, wait for one another. [34] If anyone is hungry, he should eat at home, so that in assembling you may not incur condemnation. As for the other matters, I will resolve them when I come.

C: The Gifts of the Spirit in the Service of the Church*

12 **Discerning the Gifts of the Spirit.** [1] Now in regard to the gifts of the Spirit, brethren, I do not want you to be uninformed. [2] You know that when you were still pagans you were constantly being enticed and led astray to the worship of mute idols. [3] Therefore, I wish you to understand that no one speaking under the influence of the Spirit of God says, "May Jesus be cursed." * Likewise, no one can say "Jesus is Lord," except under the influence of the Holy Spirit.

The Spirit Distributes the Gifts for the Common Good. [4] * There are different varieties of gifts, but the same Spirit. [5] There are different kinds of service, but the same Lord. [6] There are different forms of activity, but the same God who produces all of them in everyone.

[7] To each of us, the manifestation of the Spirit is given for the common good. [8] To one, is given through the Spirit the utterance of wisdom; and to another, the utterance of knowledge according to the same Spirit. [9] Another by the same Spirit is granted faith, while still another is granted the gift of healing by the same Spirit.

[10] To one, is granted the gift of mighty deeds;* to another, the gift of prophecy; and to yet another, the gift

to discern spirits. One receives the gift of tongues and another the ability to interpret them. ¹¹ One and the same Spirit works all these things, distributing them individually to each person as he wills.

You Are the Body of Christ.* ¹² The body is one, although it has many parts; and all the parts, though many, form one body. So it is with Christ. ¹³ For in the one Spirit we were all baptized into one body, Jews as well as Greeks, slaves as well as free men, and we were all given the same Spirit to drink.

¹⁴ Now the body is one, although it has many parts. ¹⁵ If the foot were to say, "Because I am not a hand, I do not belong to the body," it nevertheless still belongs to the body. ¹⁶ Or if an ear were to say, "Because I am not an eye, I do not belong to the body," it nevertheless still belongs to the body.

¹⁷ If the whole body were an eye, how would we be able to hear? If the whole body were an ear, how would we exercise a sense of smell? ¹⁸ But God arranged each part in the body as he intended. ¹⁹ If all the members were identical, where would the body be?

²⁰ As it is, there are many members, but one body. ²¹ The eye cannot say to the hand, "I do not need you," any more than the head can say to the feet, "I do not need you." ²² On the contrary, those parts of the body that seem to be weaker are in fact indispensable, ²³ and those parts of the body that we regard as less honorable we clothe with greater honor, and our less respectable parts are treated with greater propriety, ²⁴ whereas our more respectable members have no need of this.

But God has so designed the body as to give greater honor to the more humble parts, ²⁵ in order that there may be no dissension within the body and each part may have equal concern for all the others. ²⁶ If one member suffers, all suffer together with it. If one member is honored, all the members rejoice together with it.

²⁷ You therefore are the body of Christ, and each of you is a part of it. ²⁸ And those whom God has appointed in the Church are first apostles, second prophets, third teachers; then doers of mighty deeds, those who have the gifts of healing, helping others, administering, and various kinds of tongues. ²⁹ Are all apostles? Are all prophets? Are all teachers? Are all doers of mighty deeds? ³⁰ Do all possess gifts of healing? Do all speak in tongues? Do all interpret? ³¹ Set your hearts on the greater gifts.

Hymn to Love.* Now I will show you a more excellent way.

13 ¹ If in speaking I use human tongues
   and angelic as well,
   but do not have love,*
   I am nothing more than a noisy gong or a clanging
      cymbal.
² If I have the gift of prophecy
   and the ability to understand all mysteries and all
      knowledge,
   and have all the faith necessary to move mountains,
   but do not have love,
   I am nothing.
³ If I give away everything to feed the poor
   and hand over my body to be burned,
   but do not have love,
   I achieve nothing.

⁴ Love is patient;
   love is charitable.
   Love is not envious;
   it does not have an inflated opinion of itself;
   it is not filled with its own importance.
⁵ Love is never rude;
   it does not seek its own advantage.
   It is not prone to anger;
   neither does it brood over setbacks.
⁶ Love does not rejoice over wrongdoing
   but rejoices in the truth.

7   Love bears all things,
     believes all things,
     hopes all things,
     endures all things.

8   Love never fails.
     Prophecies will eventually cease,
     tongues will become silent,
     and knowledge will pass away,

9   for our knowledge is partial
     and our prophesying is partial;

10 but when we encounter what is perfect,
     that which is imperfect will pass away.

11 When I was a child,
     I used to talk like a child,
     think like a child,
     and reason like a child.
     However, when I became a man,
     I put all childish ways aside.

12 At the present time we see indistinctly, as in a mirror;
     then we shall see face to face.
     My knowledge is only partial now;
     then I shall know fully,
     even as I am fully known.

13 Thus there are three things that endure: faith, hope,
           and love,
     and the greatest of these is love.*

14 Seek the Gifts That Build Up the Community.* [1] Make
love your aim, but strive earnestly after the spiritual gifts,
especially for that of prophecy. [2] If anyone speaks in
tongues, he is speaking not to men but to God, and no
one understands him, for he is speaking mysteries in the
Spirit. [3] On the other hand, the one who prophesies
speaks to men for their building up, their encouragement,
and their consolation.

[4] Whoever speaks in a tongue builds himself up, but
whoever prophesies builds up the Church. [5] I wish that
all of you could speak in tongues, but I would much pre-

fer that you could prophesy. For the one who prophesies is greater than the one who speaks in tongues, unless the latter can interpret what he is saying so that the Church may be built up.

[6] Now suppose, brethren, that I should come to you and speak in tongues. Of what value would I be to you if you were unable to discern from my words any revelation or knowledge or prophecy or instruction? [7] Even inanimate things produce sound, such as a flute or a harp. If they do not produce distinct notes, how can anyone tell what tune is being played?

[8] Or again, if the bugle call is unclear, who will get ready for battle? [9] Similarly, if you speak in tongues and your speech is unintelligible, how will anyone be able to understand what you are saying? For you will be talking to empty air.

[10] There are many different languages that are used in the world, and none of them is without meaning. [11] But if I do not comprehend the meaning of the language, I will be a foreigner to the speaker and he will be a foreigner to me. [12] Since you are eager to acquire spiritual gifts, try to excel in those that build up the Church.

[13] Therefore, anyone who speaks in tongues should pray for the ability to interpret. [14] For if I pray in a tongue, my spirit is at prayer but my mind derives no benefit. [15] What then should I do? I will pray with my spirit, but I will also pray with my mind. I will sing with my spirit, but I will also sing with my mind.

[16] If you are praising only with the spirit, how will the uninstructed person who is present be able to answer "Amen" to your thanksgiving when he does not comprehend what you are saying? [17] Your thanksgiving may be inspiring, but the other person has not been edified.

[18] I thank God that I speak in tongues more than any of you, [19] but when I am in the church I would prefer to speak five intelligible words to instruct others rather than ten thousand words in a tongue.

²⁰ Brethren, do not be childish in your thinking. Be like infants in regard to evil, but in your thinking be mature. ²¹ In the Law * it is written,

> "By people speaking strange tongues
>   and by the lips of foreigners
> I will speak to this people,
>   and even so they will not listen to me,
> says the Lord."

²² Clearly, then, tongues are intended as a sign not for believers but for unbelievers, while prophecy is designed not for unbelievers but for believers.

²³ Therefore, if the whole Church has assembled and everyone is speaking in tongues, would not any uninstructed person or any unbeliever on entering conclude that you are all out of your minds? ²⁴ However, if everyone is prophesying and an unbeliever or uninstructed person should enter, he would be reproved by all and judged by all, ²⁵ and the secrets of his heart would be revealed. Then he would fall down and worship God, declaring, "God is truly in your midst."

Let Everything Be Done Properly and in an Orderly Fashion.
²⁶ And so, what then should be done, brethren? When you assemble, each of you should bring a psalm or some lesson or a revelation, or speak in a tongue, or offer an interpretation. Everything should be done with the goal in mind of building up. ²⁷ If any of you speak in a tongue, let only two or at most three come forward, one at a time, and someone must interpret. ²⁸ If no one is available to interpret, let those who speak in tongues be silent in the church and speak only to themselves and to God.

²⁹ As for the prophets, let two or three speak, and let the rest weigh their words. ³⁰ Should a revelation be made to someone else who is sitting there, let the one who is speaking stop. ³¹ You can all prophesy, but one at a time, so that all may receive instruction and encouragement. ³² Indeed, the spirits of the prophets are subject to their prophets' control, ³³ for God is not a God of disorder but of peace.

As in all the Churches of the saints, [34] * women are to keep silent at the assemblies. For they are not permitted to speak, since the Law asserts that they are to be subordinate. [35] If there is anything they wish to know, they should ask their husbands at home. It is improper for them to speak in the church.

[36] Did the word of God originate with you? Or are you the only ones to whom it has come? [37] Anyone who claims to be a prophet or to have spiritual powers must recognize that what I am writing to you is a commandment of the Lord. [38] Anyone who does not acknowledge this should be ignored.

[39] Therefore, brethren, be eager to prophesy and do not forbid speaking in tongues. [40] But ensure that everything is done properly and in an orderly fashion.

VII: THE RESURRECTION*

A: The Resurrection of Christ

15 **The Risen Christ, Foundation of Our Faith.** * [1] And now, brethren, I want to remind you of the gospel I proclaimed to you, which you received and in which you stand firm. [2] Through it you are also being saved, provided that you are holding fast to what I proclaimed to you. If not, then you have believed in vain.

[3] * For I handed on to you as of primary importance what I received: that Christ died for our sins, in accordance with the Scriptures, [4] that he was buried and that he was raised to life on the third day in accordance with the Scriptures, [5] and that he appeared to Cephas, and later to the Twelve. [6] Then he appeared to more than five hundred of the brethren at one time, most of whom are still alive, although some have fallen asleep. * [7] After that he appeared to James, * and then to all the apostles.

[8] Last of all, he appeared to me, as to one born abnormally. [9] For I am the least of the apostles. I am not worthy to be called an apostle, because I persecuted the

Church of God. ¹⁰ However, by the grace of God I am what I am, and the grace he has bestowed upon me has not proved to be fruitless. Indeed, I have worked harder than any of them—although that should not be credited to me but to the grace of God within me. ¹¹ But whether it was I or they, this is what we preach and what you have come to believe.

B: The Resurrection of the Dead

The Resurrection and Faith.* ¹² Now if Christ is proclaimed as raised from the dead, how can some of you say that there is no resurrection of the dead? ¹³ If there is no resurrection of the dead, then Christ has not been raised. ¹⁴ And if Christ has not been raised, then our preaching is useless, and so is your faith. ¹⁵ We are even false witnesses to God, for we testified that he raised Christ when he did not raise him up, assuming it is true that the dead are not raised.

¹⁶ For if the dead are not raised, then Christ has not been raised. ¹⁷ And if Christ has not been raised, your faith is without any foundation, and you are still in your sins. ¹⁸ Then those who have fallen asleep in Christ are utterly lost. ¹⁹ If it is for just this life that we have hoped in Christ, we are the most pitiable of all men.

Christ, the Firstfruits.* ²⁰ But Christ has been raised from the dead, the firstfruits of those who have fallen asleep. ²¹ For since death came into the world through a man, the resurrection of the dead has also come through a man.

²² Just as in Adam all die, so all will be brought to life in Christ, ²³ but each one in proper order: Christ the firstfruits; afterward, at his coming, those who belong to Christ. ²⁴ Then comes the end, when he hands over the kingdom to God the Father, after he has destroyed every sovereignty and authority and power. * ²⁵ For he is destined to reign until he has put all his enemies under his feet.

²⁶ The last enemy to be destroyed is death. ²⁷ For he has put all things under his feet. But when it says "all things

are put under," it is obvious that this excludes the one who subjected everything to him. [28] When all things are subjected to him, then the Son himself will also be subjected to the one who made all things subject to him, so that God may be all in all.

Practical Faith. [29] Otherwise, what will people accomplish when they have themselves baptized for the dead? * If the dead are not raised at all, why should anyone be baptized for them? [30] And why should we be placing ourselves in danger every hour? [31] I face death every day—that is as sure as the pride that I have in you, brethren, through Jesus Christ our Lord.

[32] With only human hopes, what would I have gained by fighting those wild beasts at Ephesus? If the dead are not raised,

> "Let us eat and drink,
>   for tomorrow we die."

[33] Do not let anyone lead you astray. "Bad company corrupts good morals." [34] Come to your senses and sin no more. For some of you have no knowledge of God. I say this to your shame.

C: The Mode of the Resurrection

The Resurrected Body. [35] Someone may ask, "How are the dead raised? What sort of body will they have when they come back?" [36] This is foolish. What you sow must die before it is given new life, [37] and what you sow is not the body that is to be but a bare grain of wheat or of something else. [38] God gives to it a body that he has chosen, and to each kind of seed its own particular body.

[39] Not all flesh is alike. There is one kind for human beings, another for animals, another for birds, and another for fish. [40] There are both heavenly bodies and earthly bodies. The splendor of heavenly bodies is of one kind, and that of earthly bodies is another. [41] The sun has a splendor of its own, the moon another splendor, and the

stars still another. Indeed, the stars differ among themselves in splendor.

[42] So it is with the resurrection of the dead. What is sown is perishable; what is raised is imperishable. [43] What is sown in dishonor is raised as glorious. What is sown in weakness is raised in power. [44] What is sown is a physical body; what is raised is a spiritual body.

The Natural and the Spiritual Body. If there is a natural body, there is also a spiritual body. [45] As it is written, the first man, Adam, became a living being; the last Adam has become a life-giving spirit. [46] But the spiritual body did not come first. Rather the natural body came first, and then the spiritual.

[47] The first man was formed from the dust of the earth; the second man is from heaven. [48] The man formed from dust is the pattern for earthly people; the heavenly man is the pattern for those who are of heaven. [49] Just as we have borne the image of the man formed from dust, so shall we also bear the likeness of the heavenly one.

Where, O Death, Is Your Victory?* [50] What I am asserting, brethren, is that flesh and blood cannot inherit the kingdom of God, nor can the perishable inherit what is imperishable.

[51] Listen while I tell you a mystery. We shall not all fall asleep, but we shall all be changed [52] in an instant, in the twinkling of an eye, at the sound of the last trumpet. For the trumpet will sound, and the dead will be raised imperishable, and we will be changed. * [53] For this perishable body must be clothed with the imperishable, and this mortal body must put on immortality.

[54] When this perishable body puts on imperishability, and this mortal body puts on immortality, then will the words that are written be fulfilled:

"Death has been swallowed up in victory.
[55]   Where, O death, is your victory?
    Where, O death, is your sting?"

[56] The sting of death is sin, and the power of sin is the Law. [57] But thanks be to God who gives us the victory through our Lord Jesus Christ.

[58] Therefore, my beloved brethren, stand firm and immovable, devoting yourselves completely to the work of the Lord, knowing that in the Lord your labor is not in vain.

VIII: FINAL RECOMMENDATIONS AND GREETINGS*

16 **The Collection.** [1] Now in regard to the collection for the saints, * you should follow the instructions I gave to the Churches of Galatia. [2] On the first day of every week, * each of you should set aside and save whatever you can spare, so that when I come to you, no collections will have to be taken. [3] And when I arrive, I shall send those who have been approved by you with letters of recommendation to deliver your gift to Jerusalem. [4] If it seems advisable that I should also go, they will accompany me.

Paul's Plans. [5] I shall come to visit you after passing through Macedonia—for I am going to pass through Macedonia. [6] I may stay for some time with you, perhaps even for the entire winter, and then you can send me forth on my journey, wherever I may be going. [7] I do not want to see you now in passing. If the Lord permits, I hope to spend some time with you. [8] However, I will remain in Ephesus until Pentecost, [9] because a wide door for productive work has been opened for me, although there are also many adversaries to face.

News of Other Missionaries. [10] If Timothy comes, put him at ease, for he is doing the work of the Lord just as I am. [11] Therefore, let no one treat him with disdain. Rather, send him on his way in peace when he leaves you to come to me, for the brethren and I are expecting him.

[12] As for our brother Apollos, I urged him strongly to visit you with the others, but he was determined not to go at this particular time. He will come to you when he has the opportunity.

¹³ Keep alert; stand firm in the faith; be courageous; be strong. ¹⁴ Everything that you do should be done in love.

¹⁵ As you know, brethren, the members of the household of Stephanas were the first converts in Achaia, and they have devoted themselves to the service of the saints. ¹⁶ I urge you to put yourselves at the service of such people and of all those who work and toil with them.

¹⁷ I was delighted at the arrival of Stephanas and Fortunatus and Achaicus, because they have made up for your absence. ¹⁸ For they have raised my spirits as well as yours. Such men deserve recognition.

Salutations and Best Wishes. ¹⁹ The Churches of Asia send you greetings. Aquila and Prisca greet you warmly in the Lord, together with the Church that meets in their house. ²⁰ All the brethren send their greetings. Greet one another with a holy kiss.

²¹ I, Paul, have written this greeting with my own hand. ²² If anyone does not love the Lord, let him be accursed. * O Lord, come! ²³ The grace of the Lord Jesus be with you. ²⁴ My love to you all in Christ Jesus.

THE SECOND LETTER TO THE CORINTHIANS

THE DRAMA OF THE APOSTOLATE

After the First Letter to the Corinthians, some serious distur-bances troubled the community of Corinth. Relations between Paul and those he considered his "children" went through a cri-sis caused by some radical challenges to him. His correspondents were, of course, only too familiar with the facts; therefore, there was no need to describe these to them. As a result, there is a dan-ger that we may not understand this highly emotional Letter. Fortunately, the rather numerous references in the text itself make it possible to sketch a picture of the dark situation.

In A.D. 56, Paul was in Ephesus (Acts 19). He learned that some Jewish Christian intriguers (men who were converts from Judaism) were rousing the Corinthian community against him. He made a lightning visit but was received with coldness; pressed for time, perhaps weary and too personally caught up in the conflict, he settled nothing, and his passage through the community rather increased the disorder. He promised to return later and take all the time needed.

The affair became worse. Passions mounted and intrigues and cabals multiplied. One part of the community categorical-ly rejected Paul's authority and vilified his person. Another part remained silent and let things ride. Some missionaries, claiming a recommendation from the communities of Palestine and boasting of having known Jesus himself, wanted to estab-lish themselves as leaders of the Corinthian community.

They cunningly sought to destroy Paul's reputation, mock-ing his supposedly authoritarian and jealous character, lack of eloquence, and timidity. They denied his vocation of apos-tle and went so far as to call into doubt the purity of his Gospel as well as his intentions. These were the people who would soon reproach him for not obliging the Gentile converts to practice the Jewish Law. They were united by a systemat-ic opposition to Paul, and for them all means were good. The Apostle unmasks these agitators in the last two chapters of this Letter.

While Paul waited in Ephesus, he was publicly insulted back in Corinth, probably by one of his closest fellow workers: he speaks of an offense and an offender (2 Cor 2:5; 7:12). Impelled by his feelings, he sent a Letter that would be judged to be too severe (2 Cor 2:3-4, 9-11), and in it he demanded that reparation be made for the offense. Some exegetes regard the last four chapters of Second Corinthians as a fragment of this lost Letter.

A bit later, Paul sent one of his coworkers, Titus, a firm and capable diplomat, to turn the situation around. The community was stabilized and the offender punished (1 Cor 2:6).

But Titus was slow in returning. Paul, who had been forced to leave Ephesus because of the riot of the silversmiths (Acts 19:23-40; 21:1), was unable to bear the waiting any longer and set out on his journey. He encountered Titus in Macedonia and received excellent news. He immediately sent Titus to Corinth to carry out the collection for the penniless mother Church of Jerusalem. A little later, around the year A.D. 56, he dictated this Second Letter to the Corinthians.

The complexity of the situation and Paul's emotions explain the tone of the Letter. Arising from a heart that is overflowing with love yet revolted at the same time, it defies all analysis. Indeed, certain exegetes believe they distinguish portions of at least three different Letters therein. In any case, it is the movements of thought that are important, and they will be brought out in the notes.

After making his point about the sorrowful affair, Paul is led to meditate on the drama of the Christian apostolate: a mystery of human weakness and divine greatness. Then he stresses the ecumenical aspect of the collection: a sign of unity between Christians of Gentile origin and those of Jewish origin.

Finally—resolved to drain the abscess—Paul lays the blame at the feet of those who have calumniated him. He initiates a strong counterattack in order to safeguard the Christian life of the Corinthians, whom he has evangelized at length. In no other place do we feel so concretely the link between the Apostle's faith and his authority.

The Second Letter to the Corinthians is less rich in doctrinal instruction than the first, but it has the great merit of introducing us to the interior life and mysticism of the Apostle. We must look to the psychology and passionate nature of Paul for the unity of these chapters. In order to understand the Apostle, we must continually go back to this ardent Letter, which can be regarded as his personal diary, his "confessions."

Nowhere else in his writings does his personality come through so clearly with its contrasting strength and weakness, its boldness and reserve, its impetuosity and tenderness. We find him to be an organizer and a missionary, a founder and a pastor, a mystic and a man of action. And what a profound awareness he shows of the apostolic mission and its originality! The First Letter to the Corinthians provided a first reflection on the meaning of the apostolate; here we find the experience, mysticism, spirituality, and, at the same time, theology of the apostolate.

The Second Letter to the Corinthians may be divided as follows:

I: ADDRESS

1 **Greeting to the Church.** [1] Paul, an apostle * of Christ Jesus by the will of God, and Timothy our brother, to the Church of God in Corinth, and to all the saints throughout Achaia: [2] grace to you and peace from God our Father and the Lord Jesus Christ.

Sufferings and Consolation.* [3] Blessed be the God and Father of our Lord Jesus Christ, the Father of mercy and the God of all consolation. * ⁴He consoles us in all our afflictions and thereby enables us to console others in their tribulations, offering them the consolation with which we ourselves are consoled by God.

⁵For just as we share abundantly in the sufferings of Christ, so too, through Christ, do we receive our consolation. ⁶If we are being afflicted, it is for your consolation and salvation. If we are being consoled, it is to help us to console you and give you the patience and the strength to endure the same sufferings that we endure. ⁷Our hope for you is unshaken, because we know that as you share in the sufferings, you also share in the consolations.

⁸Brethren, we do not want you to be unaware of the hardships we experienced* in Asia. The burden we endured was far too heavy for us to bear, to such an extent that we even despaired of life itself. ⁹Indeed, in our hearts we felt that we were under a sentence of death. This was so that we not put our trust in ourselves but in God who raises the dead.

¹⁰He delivered us from this deadly peril, and he will continue to so deliver us. He on whom we have set our hopes will deliver us again, ¹¹as you assist us with your prayers, so that thanks may be given by many to God on our behalf for the blessing granted to us through the prayers of so many.

II: APOSTLE BY THE POWER OF JESUS AND FOR JESUS*

A: A Visit Not Made*

You Are Our Boast. ¹²Indeed, this is our boast: the testimony of our conscience that in our dealings with the world, and especially with you, we have conducted ourselves with simplicity and godly sincerity, depending not on worldly wisdom but on the grace of God. ¹³For we write nothing to you that you cannot read and comprehend. It is my hope that you will come to understand fully, ¹⁴as you have already understood in part, that on the day of the Lord Jesus we will have as much reason to boast of you as you will have reason to boast of us.

Our Language Is Not "Yes" and "No."* [15] So certain am I of this that I had originally intended to come to you first of all and thereby reward you with a double benefit. [16] I planned to visit you on my way to Macedonia, and then to come to you again on my return from Macedonia and have you send me forth to Judea.

[17] Since that was my original intention, was I being impulsive, or do you believe that my plans are based on human considerations, ready to say "Yes, Yes" and "No, No" at the same time? [18] As surely as God is faithful, our word to you has not been "Yes" and "No." [19] The Son of God, Jesus Christ, who was proclaimed to you by us, that is, by Silvanus * and Timothy and me, was not a mixture of "Yes" and "No." He was never anything but "Yes."

[20] In him is the "Yes" to every one of the promises of God. Indeed, it is through him that we say "Amen" to give glory to God. [21] However, it is God who enables both us and you to stand firm in Christ. He has anointed us [22] and marked us with his seal and given us the Spirit in our hearts, as a down payment of what is to come.

The Delay Was Intended Merely To Spare Them.* [23] I call upon God as a witness that it was only to spare you that I did not come again to Corinth. [24] We do not wish to lord it over your faith, but to work together with you for your joy, because you are standing firm in your faith.

2 [1] Therefore, I made up my mind not to have you endure another painful visit. [2] For if I cause you pain, then who would be there to cheer me up aside from you whom I offended? [3] And I wrote as I did, so that when I came I would not suffer distress from those who should have made me rejoice. I know all of you well enough to be certain that we both share the same joy. [4] It was with great distress and anguish of heart and many tears that I wrote to you, not to grieve you but to let you know how abundant is the love I have for you.

Forgiveness for the Offender. [5] If anyone has caused distress, he has done so not only to me but to some extent—not to exaggerate —to all of you. [6] The punishment that was imposed by the majority was appropriate. [7] But now you should forgive and encourage him so that he may not be overwhelmed by the burden of his distress. [8] Therefore, I urge you to reassure him of your love.

[9] I wrote to you to test your obedience in all matters. [10] Anyone whom you forgive I forgive as well. Whatever I have forgiven, if I have forgiven anything, I have done for your sake in the presence of Christ, [11] so that we may avoid being outwitted by Satan, for we are not unaware of his schemes.

Paul's Anguish.* [12] When I came to Troas to proclaim the gospel of Christ, and a door of opportunity was opened for me in the Lord, [13] my mind knew no relief because I could not find my brother Titus in that place. And so I said farewell to them and moved on to Macedonia.

B: Greatness and Weakness of the Apostles*

Ambassadors of God. [14] But thanks be to God, for he brings us to victory in Christ and through us he manifests the fragrance of the knowledge of him throughout the world. [15] We are indeed the aroma of Christ to God both among those who are being saved and among those who are perishing: [16] to the latter, the odor of death that leads to death; to the former, a fragrance of life leading to life.

Who is truly qualified for such a task? [17] For we are not like so many others who adulterate the word of God for profit. When we speak, we do so in Christ and in all sincerity, as men sent from God and standing in God's presence.

3 **A Letter from God.*** [1] Are we beginning once again to commend ourselves to you? Surely, as is true in some cases, we do not need letters of recommendation to you or from you. [2] You yourselves are our letter, one that is written on our hearts, so that it may be known and read by all. [3] And you make it clear that you are a letter from Christ entrusted to our care, a letter written not with ink but with the Spirit of the living God, and written not on tablets of stone * but on tablets of the human heart.

[4] Such is the complete confidence in God that we have through Christ. [5] Obviously, we are not competent of ourselves to take credit for anything as coming from us. Our competence comes from God [6] who has empowered us to be the ministers of a new covenant, not written but of the Spirit. For the letter kills, but the Spirit gives life.

Ministers of a New Covenant.* [7] Now if the ministry of death, engraved with letters on stone, was so glorious that the Israelites could not fix their glance on the face of Moses because of its glory, a glory that would soon fade, [8] how much greater will be the glory of the ministry of the Spirit?

[9] For if the ministry of condemnation was glorious, how much richer in glory will be the ministry of righteousness! [10] Indeed, what was once glorious is now without any glory in comparison with the surpassing glory. [11] For if what was destined to fade away was glorious, how much greater will be the glory of that which endures!

The Lord Is the Spirit.* [12] Therefore, since we have such hope, we can act with complete confidence, [13] and not like Moses who put a veil over his face so that the Israelites could not observe the radiance that was fading away. [14] However, their minds were hardened. Even to this very day, the same veil remains unlifted during the reading of the old covenant, * since only in Christ is it set aside. [15] Indeed, to this very day, whenever Moses is read, a veil lies over their hearts.

[16] However, when one turns to the Lord, the veil is removed. [17] Now this Lord is the Spirit, * and where the Spirit of the Lord is, there is freedom. [18] And as we gaze upon the glory of the Lord with unveiled faces, all of us

are being transformed into that same image from glory to glory, which comes from the Lord, who is the Spirit.

4 The Gospel of the Glory of Christ.* [1] Therefore, since we are engaged in this ministry through the mercy of God, we do not lose heart. [2] Rather, we have renounced all shameful and hidden ways. We do not engage in deception or falsify the word of God. By stating the truth in an open manner, we commend ourselves to the conscience of everyone in the sight of God.

[3] If our gospel is veiled, it is veiled to those who are perishing, [4] those unbelievers whose minds have been blinded by the god of this world to prevent them from seeing the light of the gospel of the glory of Christ, who is the image of God.

[5] We do not proclaim ourselves. Rather we proclaim Jesus Christ as Lord and ourselves as your servants for the sake of Jesus. [6] For the God who said, "Let light shine out of darkness," has enabled his light to shine in our hearts in order to enlighten them with the knowledge of the glory of God in the face of Jesus Christ.

The State of an Apostle.* [7] However, we hold this treasure in earthen vessels so that it may be clear that this immense power belongs to God and does not derive from us. [8] We are afflicted on all sides but not crushed, bewildered but not sunk in despair, [9] persecuted but not abandoned, struck down but not destroyed.

[10] We always carry around in our body the death of Jesus, so that the life of Jesus may also be manifested in our body. [11] For in our lives we are constantly being given up to death for Jesus' sake, so that the life of Jesus may be revealed in our mortal flesh. [12] As a result, death is at work in us, but life in you.

[13] Therefore, since we have that spirit of faith about which it has been written: "I believed, and therefore I spoke," we also believe, and therefore speak. [14] For we know that the one who raised the Lord Jesus will raise us

also with Jesus and bring us side by side with you into his presence. [15] Indeed, everything is for your sake, so that the grace that is abundantly bestowed on more and more people may cause thanksgiving to superabound, to the glory of God.

An Eternal Dwelling in Heaven. [16] Therefore, we do not lose heart. Even though our outer self is continuing to decay, our inner self is being renewed day by day. [17] Our temporary light afflictions are preparing for us an incomparable weight of eternal glory, [18] for our eyes are fixed not on what is seen but rather on that which cannot be seen. What is visible is transitory; what is invisible is eternal.

5 [1] Now we know that if the earthly tent in which we live is destroyed, we have a dwelling prepared for us by God, a dwelling in the heavens, not made with human hands, that will be eternal. [2] While we are in this earthly tent, we groan, longing to be clothed with our heavenly dwelling; [3] for when we have put it on, we will not be naked. *

[4] While we are enclosed in this earthly tent we groan, burdened because we do not wish to be stripped naked but rather to be further clothed, so that our mortal state may be swallowed up by immortality. [5] God is the one who has prepared us for this destiny, and he has given us the Spirit as a pledge of this.

[6] Therefore, we are always confident, even though we realize that as long as we are at home in the body, we are exiles from the Lord, [7] for we walk by faith, not by sight. [8] Yet we are filled with confidence, even as we long to be exiled from the body and be at home with the Lord.

[9] For this reason, whether at home or away, we strive to please him. [10] For all of us must appear before the judgment seat of Christ, so that each one may receive suitable recompense for his conduct in the body, whether good or bad.

Well Known to God. ¹¹ And so, with this fear of the Lord always foremost in our thoughts, we try to persuade others. We ourselves are well known to God, and I hope we are also well known to your consciences. ¹² We are not once again commending ourselves to you, but we are rather affording you an opportunity to boast about us. Then you will have an answer to those who boast of external appearances and not the heart. ¹³ If, indeed, we are out of our minds, it is for God; if we are rational, it is for your sake.

The Ministry of Reconciliation. ¹⁴ For the love of Christ urges us forward, once we conclude that one has died for all, and therefore all have died. ¹⁵ And he died for all, so that those who live might no longer live for themselves, but for him who for their sakes died and was raised to life.

¹⁶ Therefore, from now on we will not regard anyone according to human standards. Even though we once judged Christ from a human point of view, * we no longer do so. ¹⁷ Consequently, anyone united to Christ is a new creation. The old order has passed away. Behold, all has become new.

¹⁸ All this has been done by God, who has reconciled us to himself through Christ and entrusted us with the ministry of reconciliation. ¹⁹ In other words, God was in Christ, reconciling the world to himself, and not holding people's transgressions against them, and he committed to us the message of reconciliation.

²⁰ Therefore, we are ambassadors for Christ, since God is appealing to you through us. We implore you through Christ to be reconciled to God. ²¹ He made him who did not know sin to be sin for our sake, so that through him we might become the righteousness of God.*

6 ¹ As his coworkers, we urge you not to receive the grace of God in vain. ² For he says,

"In an acceptable time I have listened to you,
and on the day of salvation I have helped you."

Behold, now is the acceptable time; behold, now is the day of salvation. *

Ministers of God. [3] We avoid placing obstacles in anyone's way, so that no fault may be found with our ministry. [4] On the contrary, in everything we do we present ourselves as ministers of God: in steadfast perseverance; in afflictions, hardships, and distress; [5] in floggings, imprisonments, and riots; in labors, sleepless nights, and fasts; [6] in purity, knowledge, patience, and kindness; in holiness of spirit, genuine love, [7] truthfulness, and the power of God.

We wield weapons of righteousness with right hand and left,* [8] in times of honor or dishonor, praise or insult. We are regarded as impostors, and yet we speak the truth; [9] as unknown men, and nevertheless we are well known; as dying, and behold we live on; as scourged, but we are not put to death; [10] as sorrowful, and yet we are always rejoicing; as poor, and yet we make many rich;* as having nothing, and yet we possess everything.

C: Relations Have Been Established*

Paul's Heart Is Wide Open. [11] O Corinthians, we have spoken frankly to you, and we have opened our heart to you. [12] We are not withholding our love from you, but you have withheld yours from us. [13] I speak to you as my children. In return, also open wide your hearts to us.

What Relation Can There Be between Righteousness and Iniquity? [14] Do not associate with unbelievers. * For what basis can there be for a partnership between righteousness and lawlessness? What do light and darkness have in common? [15] Can Christ ever be in accord with Beliar?* What does a believer have in common with an unbeliever? [16] Can there be an agreement between the temple of God and idols? For we are the temple of the living God, and for this we have God's word:

> "I will live in them and walk among them.
> I will be their God,
>   and they shall be my people.

¹⁷ Therefore, come out from their midst
    and separate yourselves from them,
        says the Lord.
Do not touch anything unclean,
    and I will welcome you.
¹⁸ I will be a father to you,
    and you shall be my sons and daughters,
        says the Lord Almighty.''

7 ¹ Since we have these promises, beloved, let us cleanse ourselves from anything that can defile flesh or spirit, and thereby make our holiness perfect in the fear of God.

Trust Reestablished. ² Make room in your hearts for us. We have wronged no one, we have corrupted no one, we have exploited no one. ³ I do not say this to condemn you, for I have already told you that your place in our hearts is secure, so that we will live together and we will die together. ⁴ I have great confidence in you, and I boast about you with intense pride. Despite all of our afflictions, I am greatly encouraged and overflowing with joy.

⁵ * Even when we arrived in Macedonia, we were unable to rest our bodies, for we were afflicted in every way: conflicts on the outside and fears on the inside. ⁶ But God, who comforts the downcast, encouraged us by the arrival of Titus—⁷ and not merely by his arrival but also by the encouragement he received from you. He told us of your longing for me, your deep regrets, and your zeal for me, all of which cause me even greater joy.

⁸ Even if I did cause you sorrow with my letter, I do not regret it. I did regret this letter briefly, but, having come to realize that you were sorrowful only for a short time, ⁹ I now am able to rejoice, not because you were grieved but because your sorrow led to repentance. For you were sorrowful in a godly way and so received no harm because of us. ¹⁰ Such godly sorrow results in repentance that leads to salvation and causes no regret, whereas worldly sorrow produces death.

[11] For see what earnestness this godly sorrow has produced for you, what eagerness to repent, what indignation, what fear, what yearning, what zeal, what desire to see justice done. In every way, you have proved your innocence in this matter.

[12] Therefore, even though I wrote to you, it was not on account of the one who committed the offense or on account of the one who was wronged, but rather that you should be fully aware of your zeal for us in the sight of God. [13] In this we have been greatly encouraged.

In addition to being encouraged ourselves, we rejoiced still more at the joy of Titus, because his mind has been completely refreshed by all of you. [14] Anything I may have said to him in boasting about you has not caused me to feel ashamed. But just as everything we said to you was true, so our boasting to Titus has proved equally true. [15] And his affection for you grows even more as he recalls the obedience of all of you and how you welcomed him in fear and trembling. [16] I rejoice because I can rely completely on you.

III: THE COLLECTION FOR THE CHRISTIANS OF JERUSALEM*

8 **Example of Christians of Macedonia.** [1] Now we want you to know, brethren, about the grace of God that has been bestowed on the Churches of Macedonia. [2] In a period of severe affliction, their abundant joy and their extreme poverty have overflowed in rich generosity on their part. [3] I can testify that they contributed to the limit of their resources, and even beyond, [4] begging us insistently for the privilege of sharing in this service to the saints.

[5] Far exceeding our expectations, they gave themselves first to the Lord, and then, by the will of God, to us. [6] As a result, we urged Titus that, inasmuch as he had already begun this work of charity, he should bring this enterprise to a successful completion among you.

The Example of Christ. [7] Now, inasmuch as you excel in everything—in your faith, your eloquence, your knowledge, your concern for others, and your love for us *—so we want you also to excel in this generous undertaking.

[8] I am not saying this to you as a command, but rather I am testing the genuine character of your love by the concern you show for others. [9] For you are well aware of the grace of our Lord Jesus Christ. Although he was rich, he became poor for your sake so that by his poverty you might become rich. *

[10] I will now give you my advice about what I believe is appropriate in this matter. Last year, you were the first not only to engage in this good work but also to do so willingly. [11] Now finish it, so that your eagerness may be matched by completing it according to your means. [12] As long as the goodwill is present, the gift will be acceptable according to what one has, not according to what one does not have.

[13] I am not suggesting that others should have relief while you are reduced to difficult straits. Rather, there should be an equitable balance. [14] Your surplus at the present time should relieve the needs of others, so that at another time their surplus may relieve your needs, and in this way there will be equality. [15] As it is written,

> "The one who gathered much did not have too much,
>   and the one who gathered less did not have too little."

Paul Recommends the Delegates. [16] Thanks be to God for putting into the heart of Titus a concern for you that is the equal of mine. [17] For he not only welcomed our request, but, because of his great concern, he is coming to you of his own accord. [18] Together with him, we are sending the brother who is praised by all the Churches for his proclamation of the gospel. * [19] In addition, he has also been appointed by the Churches to be our traveling companion as we engage in our charitable work for the glory of the Lord and to show our eagerness to be of service.

20 In this way, we want to ensure that no one will be able to criticize us for our handling of this generous collection. 21 For we intend to do what is honorable not only in the Lord's sight but also in the sight of others.

22 And with them, we are also sending our brother * whose dedication we have tested in many ways and found to be exemplary. Now he is even more dedicated than before because of his great confidence in you.

23 As for Titus, he is my partner and coworker in your service. And as for the others, they are the apostles of the Churches and the glory of Christ. 24 Therefore, show these men, and all the Churches, the proof of your love and the legitimacy of our boasting about you.

9 Let the Offering Be Ready.
1 In regard to the ministry toward the saints, there really is no necessity for me to write to you. 2 For I am fully aware of your eagerness to help, which has been the subject of my boasting about you to the Macedonians, telling them that Achaia has been ready since last year. Your ardor has excited most of them.

3 Nevertheless, I am sending the brethren to ensure that our boasts about you may not seem to have been offered in vain. I want you to be as prepared as I said you would be. 4 For if I bring some Macedonians with me and they come to the realization that you are not prepared, it would be a source of shame to us—to say nothing of you—because of our confidence in you. 5 Therefore, I thought it necessary to encourage the brethren to go on to you ahead of us and arrange in advance for the gift that you have promised, so that it may be ready as a genuine gift and not as something that has been granted grudgingly.

God Loves a Cheerful Giver. 6 Remember this: if you sow sparingly, you will reap sparingly, and if you sow generously, you will reap generously as well. 7 Each person should give as much as he has decided in his heart, not with reluctance or under compulsion, for God loves a cheerful giver. [8] And God is able to enrich you with an abundance of every grace, so that, with all of your needs provided for, you may be able to produce a surplus of good works. [9] As it is written,

"He scatters abroad his gifts to the poor;
    his righteousness lasts forever."

Generosity Will Prompt Thanksgiving. [10] The one who provides seed for sowing and bread for food will supply and multiply your seed and increase the harvest of your righteousness. [11] Enriched in every way, you will be able to practice all your acts of generosity, which, through our intervention, will result in thanksgiving to God.

[12] The administering of this public service not only helps to satisfy the needs of the saints but also overflows in countless acts of thanksgiving to God. [13] Through the evidence of such service, you are giving glory to God for your obedient profession of the gospel of Christ and the generosity of your contribution to them and to all others as well. [14] At the same time, their hearts will go out to you in their prayers for you, because of the surpassing grace that God has bestowed upon you. [15] Thanks be to God for his indescribable gift. *

IV: PAUL'S SELF-DEFENSE*

10 **Recommendation from Human Beings or from God?*** [1] I myself, Paul, exhort you by the gentleness and the mercy of Christ, I who am "timid" when I am face to face with you, but "bold" when I am at a distance! [2] I beg you that when I am in your presence I will not have to act with boldness and the self-assurance that I consider necessary when I oppose some of those who accuse us of acting according to human standards. *

[3] * Although we are human beings, we do not engage in battle according to human standards. [4] For the weapons of our warfare are not merely human, but they possess the divine power to destroy strongholds. We demolish arguments [5] and every proud pretension against the

knowledge of God, and we compel every thought to surrender in obedience to Christ. [6] What is more, once your obedience is complete, we are prepared to punish every disobedience.

[7] * Face the facts squarely. If anyone is confident that he belongs to Christ, he should reflect on the fact that we belong to Christ as much as he does. [8] It is possible that I tend to boast a bit too much about our authority, which the Lord has entrusted to us for building you up rather than for tearing you down, but I will not apologize for doing so.

[9] Therefore, I do not want to seem to be someone who frightens you with my letters. [10] Some may assert, "His letters are impressive and forceful, but his personal appearance is insignificant, and he cannot speak well." [11] Let them understand that what we are in our letters when we are absent will be the same as what we are in our deeds when we are present.

[12] We do not dare to rank ourselves or to compare ourselves with any of those who commend themselves. But when they measure themselves by one another and compare themselves with one another, they only demonstrate their ignorance. [13] In contrast, we will not boast beyond the proper limits. Rather, we will measure ourselves according to the standard that God laid down for us, which enabled us to reach out all the way to you.

[14] We are not overreaching ourselves as we would be if we had not come to you; indeed, we came to you with the gospel of Christ. [15] Neither are we boasting immoderately of the labors of others. Our hope is rather that, as your faith increases, our influence among you will be greater than ever, [16] so that we may preach the gospel to regions beyond you, rather than boasting about work already done in someone else's region.

[17] If anyone would boast, let him boast in the Lord.* [18] For it is not the one who commends himself who is really approved, but the one whom the Lord commends.

11 Promised to One Spouse.

[1] I hope that you will put up with a little of my foolishness. Please bear with me. [2] For I am jealous of you with a godly jealousy, since I promised all of you to one spouse, to present you as a chaste virgin to Christ.

[3] However, I am afraid that, just as the serpent deceived Eve by his cunning, your thoughts may be led astray from a single-hearted fidelity to Christ. [4] For if someone comes and proclaims another Jesus* than the one we proclaimed, or if you receive a different spirit from the one you received, or a different gospel from the one you accepted, you put up with that readily enough!

[5] I do not regard myself as being inferior to these "super-apostles." [6] I may be untrained in the art of speaking, but the same is not true of me in regard to knowledge. In every way and in all respects, we have made this evident to you.

Paul's Apostolate.

[7] Did I make a mistake by preaching the gospel of God without charge, humbling myself* so that you might be exalted? [8] I robbed other Churches, accepting support from them in order to serve you. [9] And when I was with you and in need, I did not burden anyone, for the brethren who came from Macedonia supplied my needs.

I refrained, and will continue to refrain, from burdening you in any way. [10] As surely as the truth of Christ is in me, this boast of mine will not be silenced in the regions of Achaia. [11] And why? Because I do not love you? God knows I do.

[12] And I shall continue to do just as I am doing at present in order to thwart the efforts of those who are seeking the opportunity to be regarded as my equals in the aspects they boast about. [13] Such people are false apostles, dishonest workers who masquerade as apostles of Christ. [14] And no wonder! Even Satan masquerades as an angel of light. [15] Therefore, it should not be considered unusual that his servants also disguise themselves as min-

isters of righteousness. Their end will be appropriate to their deeds.

Paul's Boast. [16] I repeat: let no one take me for a fool. However, if you do, then treat me like a fool and let me boast a little. [17] In saying this, I am not speaking according to the Lord but out of foolishness in the conviction that I have something to boast about. [18] Since many boast of their human accomplishments, I will do likewise.

[19] Since you are wise yourselves, you gladly put up with fools! [20] For you endure it if someone makes slaves of you, or robs you of all you possess, or takes advantage of you, or puts on airs, or slaps you in the face. [21] To my shame, I must admit that we have been too weak for that sort of thing!

But whatever anyone dares to boast of—I am speaking out of foolishness—I also dare to boast of. [22] Are they Hebrews? So am I. Are they Israelites? So am I. Are they descendants of Abraham? * So am I. [23] Are they ministers of Christ? * (I am talking now like a madman.) I am too, having endured far greater labors, far more imprisonments, far harsher scourgings, and far more brushes with death.

[24] Five times I received from the Jews forty lashes minus one. * [25] Three times I was beaten with rods; once I was stoned; three times I was shipwrecked; once I was adrift in the open sea for a night and a day. [26] I have traveled continually and faced dangers from rivers, dangers from robbers, dangers from my own people, dangers from Gentiles, dangers in the city, dangers in the desert, dangers at sea, and dangers from false brethren.

[27] I have endured toil and hardship, and sleepless nights. I have been hungry and thirsty, and I have often gone without food. I have been cold, and often all but naked.

[28] Apart from these external things, I am burdened each and every day with the anxiety of caring for all the Churches. [29] Who is weak, and I am not similarly afflicted? Who is led into sinfulness, and I am not filled with indignation?

[30] If I must boast, I will boast of the things that exhibit my weakness. [31] The God and Father of the Lord Jesus

knows—he who is blessed forever—that I am telling the truth. [32] When I was in Damascus, the governor under King Aretas* assigned guards around the city of Damascus in order to arrest me. [33] However, I was let down in a basket through a window in the wall, and I thereby escaped from his clutches.

12 Caught Up into Heaven.* [1] Although nothing is to be gained by doing so, I must continue to boast. So I will move on to the visions and revelations given me from the Lord.

[2] I know a man in Christ who fourteen years ago (whether in the body or out of the body I do not know—God knows) was caught up to the third heaven. [3] And I know that this man (whether in the body or out of the body I do not know—God knows) [4] was caught up into paradise and heard inexpressible things, things that no man may repeat.

[5] About this man I am willing to boast, but about myself I will not boast, except as it concerns my weaknesses. [6] Actually, if I were to boast, I would not be a fool, because I would be telling the truth. However, I refrain from doing so in order that no one may regard me more highly than would be evident from what he has seen in me and heard from me.

A Boast of One's Weakness.* [7] Therefore, to keep me from becoming unduly elated by the wondrous nature of these revelations, I was given a thorn in the flesh, a messenger of Satan, to beat me and prevent me from becoming unduly elated. [8] Three times I begged the Lord to have it leave me, [9] but he answered me, "My grace is sufficient for you, for power is made perfect in weakness."

Hence, I will boast most gladly of my weaknesses, in order that the power of Christ may dwell within me. [10] For this reason, I rejoice when I endure weaknesses, insults, hardships, persecutions, and distress for the sake of Christ. For it is when I am weak that I am strong.

Characteristic Traits of an Apostle. [11] I have been very foolish, but it was you who drove me to it. I should have been commended by you, for in no way did I prove to be inferior to those super-apostles, even though I am nothing. [12] The traits of a true apostle were evident in what I did in your presence: perseverance, signs, wonders, and mighty deeds. [13] How then have you been less privileged than the other Churches, except that I myself did not place a burden on you? Forgive me for being so unfair!

[14] Now I am getting ready to come to you for a third time, and I do not intend to be a burden to you. What I want is not your money, but you yourselves. Children are not expected to save up for their parents, but parents for their children. [15] I will be happy to spend and be spent for you. Are you going to love me less because I love you so much more?

[16] In any case, let it be assumed that I myself did not prove to be a burden to you. However, you may say that I was crafty and took you in by a trick. [17] Did I take advantage of you through any of those I sent to you? [18] I urged Titus to come to you, and I sent a brother with him. Did Titus take advantage of you? Did not he and I walk in the same Spirit, in the same footsteps?

There Will Be No More Forgiveness. [19] Have you been supposing all this time that we have been defending ourselves before you? Not at all! We have been speaking in Christ and in the presence of God, my dear ones, doing all things to build you up. [20] I fear that when I come I may find you different from what I wish you to be, and that you may find me different from what you wish me to be.

I am afraid that this will lead to quarreling, jealousy, anger, factions, slander, gossip, conceit, and disorder. [21] I fear that when I come back my God may humiliate me in your presence and that I may have to mourn over many who previously sinned and have not repented of the impurity, immorality, and licentiousness in which they have indulged.

13 [1] This will be the third visit I am making to you. Every charge must be established on the testimony of two or three witnesses. [2] I warned those who have sinned, as well as everyone else, and I warn them now in my absence as I did when present on my second visit: when I come again, I will spare no one.

[3] This will give you the proof you seek that Christ is speaking in me. He is not weak in dealing with you, but he is powerful among you. [4] For he was crucified in weakness, but he is now alive by the power of God. Similarly, we are weak in him, but in dealing with you we will live in the power of God.

Examine Yourselves. [5] Examine yourselves to see whether you are in the faith. Test yourselves. Do you not realize that Jesus Christ is in you? If he is not, then you have failed the test. [6] It is my hope that you will come to the realization that we have not failed. [7] But we pray to God that you may not do anything wrong—not so that we may appear to have passed the test, but so that you may do what is right, even though we may appear to have failed.

[8] We have no power to do anything against the truth but only for the truth. [9] We rejoice when we are weak, just as long as you are strong. This is what we desire—that you may become perfect.

[10] I am writing this letter prior to my arrival so that when I come I may not have to treat you harshly in exercising the authority that the Lord has given me to build up and not to tear down.

V: CONCLUSION*

Live in Peace. [11] And now, brethren, farewell. Mend your ways. Encourage one another. Be of one mind and live in peace. Then the God of love and peace will be with you. [12] Greet one another with a holy kiss. * All the saints send you greetings.

[13] The grace of the Lord Jesus Christ and the love of God and the fellowship of the Holy Spirit be with you all.

THE LETTER TO THE GALATIANS
CHRISTIAN FREEDOM

Paul did not impose on Gentile converts either the Law of Moses or circumcision; he did not teach the Law. But was it possible to conceive of humanity being saved apart from the laws God gave to Moses? For some, there was no doubt: apart from the Law and its practices there was no salvation.

These Jewish Christians have been dubbed Judaizers. They taught that Gentiles must first submit to at least part of the Mosaic Law, especially circumcision, before they could become Christians (see Gal 1:7; 4:17, 21; 5:2-12; 6:12-13). In order to better cancel the authority and revolutionary teaching of Paul, they hinted that he was not a true apostle. The Galatians were perturbed.

Learning of this, Paul wrote a passionate Letter (probably in A.D. 56–57) in which irony vied with logic, in order to reestablish the truth. The issue was not simply his apostolate but the very truth of Christianity. Jesus Christ is the only Savior: True or false? If true, then what connection still exists between the Galatians and a Law that has now been left behind?

The Apostle clearly realized that to bond the Church to the former traditions of Judaism was to make her hateful to Gentiles and to condemn the growth of the Church and her mission as well. Above all, it was to deny the Church's very being.

The Letter to the Galatians informs us of this crisis. The Galatians were probably the descendants of three Gallic tribes that had settled in Cappadocia and Pontus in the second half of the third century B.C. In 25 B.C. this little state, which had expanded through the acquisition of territories from Lycaonia, Phrygia, and Pisidia, had become the Roman province of Galatia. It continued, however, to call itself the "region of Galatia," the land occupied by descendants of the immigrants.

Luke followed this usage when he says that the second (A.D. 49–52) and third (A.D. 53–57) missions of Paul and his companions passed through "the region of Phrygia and Galatia" (Acts 16:6; 18:23). It seems, then, that the Letter sent "to the Churches of Galatia" (Gal 1:2) is addressed precisely to these former Gauls, especially since their character, as it emerges from this document, is strangely like that of the Gauls of whom Julius Caesar speaks: inconstancy and lightness of mind, desire of novelty, love of freedom, very great generosity (The Gallic War IV, 59).

This Letter to "foolish Galatians," who have allowed themselves to be "bewitched" (Gal 3:1), is a burning stream of lava, a torrent of feeling: Paul, with his tender paternal love, is bewildered by such a rapid turnabout in some; the clever deceits of his detractors disgust him; he is terribly upset because the Gospel is being falsified. Then he becomes a pitiless dialectician and a polemicist who uses steely irony and contempt.

In retrospect, this was a happy crisis that allowed Christianity to assert its autonomy and henceforth to travel its own road amid the peoples and for their salvation! It obliged the Church to become a People of God that acknowledges no borders, a people universal in time and space, with a changeless Gospel but at the same time with a life and activity that are continually renewed! Henceforth, the only thing that counts for the salvation of human beings is faith in Christ.

The Letter to the Galatians may be divided as follows:

I: Paul Defends His Apostolate (1:1—2:14)
II: Paul Defends the Freedom of Christians (2:15—6:10)
III: Conclusion (6:11-18)

I: PAUL DEFENDS HIS APOSTOLATE*

A: Address

1 **Paul Commissioned by Christ Himself.** [1] * Paul, an apostle *—commissioned not by human authority or by any human being, but by Jesus Christ and God the Father who raised him from the dead— [2] and all the brethren * who are with me, to the Churches of Galatia. [3] Grace to you and peace from God our Father and the Lord Jesus Christ, [4] who gave himself for our sins to deliver us from the present evil age * in accordance with the will of our God and Father, [5] to whom be glory forever and ever. Amen.*

B: One Gospel, One Revelation, One Apostolate*

Loyalty to the Gospel. [6] I am astonished that you are so quickly deserting the one who called you by the grace of Christ and are turning to a different gospel. [7] In reality, there is not another one, but there are some who are troubling you by perverting the gospel of Christ. [8] But even if we or an angel from heaven should preach a gospel to you other than the one we proclaimed to you, let him be accursed! [9] We have said this before, and now I repeat it: if anyone preaches to you a gospel other than the one you received, let him be accursed! *

[10] Does it now appear to you that I am trying to gain the approval of human beings rather than the approval of God? Am I seeking to please people? If I were still trying to please people, I would not be a servant of Christ.

Paul's Gospel Revealed to Him by Christ. [11] * Brethren, I want you to be assured that the gospel I preached to you is not human in its origin. [12] I did not receive it from a human being, nor was I taught it. Rather, I received it through a revelation of Jesus Christ.

[13] Undoubtedly you have heard about my former way of life in Judaism, * how I fiercely persecuted the Church of God and tried to destroy it. [14] I progressed in Judaism

far beyond many of my contemporaries, inasmuch as I was much more zealous in upholding the traditions of my ancestors.

Paul's Early Years as a Christian. [15] However, when God, who had set me apart even before my birth, called me through his grace and chose [16] to reveal his Son to me so that I might proclaim him to the Gentiles, I did not confer with flesh and blood, * [17] nor did I go up to Jerusalem to consult with those who were apostles before me. Rather, I went off to Arabia, and afterward I returned to Damascus.

Paul's First Meeting with Peter.* [18] Then after three years, I did go up to Jerusalem to become acquainted with Cephas, and I stayed with him for fifteen days. [19] However, I did not set eyes on any of the other apostles, except for James, the brother of the Lord. * [20] I declare before God that I am not lying in anything I have written.

[21] Afterward, I went into the regions of Syria and Cilicia. * [22] I was still unknown by sight to the Churches of Judea that are in Christ. [23] They had only heard it said, "The one who was formerly persecuting us is now preaching the faith that he had once tried to destroy." [24] As a result, they gave glory to God because of me.

C: The Council of Jerusalem*

2 Confirmation of Paul's Gospel and Mission. [1] Fourteen years later, I traveled up to Jerusalem again, this time with Barnabas, and I also took along Titus. [2] I went up in response to a revelation, and I set before them the gospel that I preach to the Gentiles—in a private meeting with the leaders—to ensure that I was not running, or had not run, in vain.

[3] Yet not even Titus, who was accompanying me, was compelled to be circumcised, even though he was a Greek. [4] Yet some false brethren were secretly brought in to spy on the freedom we have in Christ Jesus, so that

they might reduce us to slavery. [5] But not for a single moment did we submit to them, in order that the truth of the gospel might remain untouched for you.

[6] As for those who were regarded as men of importance—whether or not they actually were important makes no difference to me, nor does it matter to God—these men did not add anything further to my message. [7] On the contrary, they realized that I had been entrusted with preaching the gospel to the uncircumcised, just as Peter had been entrusted with preaching the gospel to the circumcised ([8] for the one who worked through Peter in his mission to the Jews was also at work in me in my mission to the Gentiles).

[9] Therefore, when James and Cephas and John, who were acknowledged as pillars of the community, recognized the grace that had been bestowed upon me, they gave to Barnabas and me the right hand of fellowship, agreeing that we should go to the Gentiles while they concentrated on the Jews. [10] They asked only one thing: that we remember the poor, which is the very thing I was eager to do.

D: Paul Rebukes Peter*

Peter's Inconsistency at Antioch. [11] However, when Cephas came to Antioch, I opposed him to his face, because he was in the wrong. [12] For until some people came from James,* he had been eating with the Gentiles; but when they arrived, he drew back and kept himself apart because he was afraid of the circumcised. [13] And the rest of the Jews* carried out the same pretense that he did, so that even Barnabas was led astray by their pretense.

Paul's Rebuke. [14] But when I saw that their conduct was not in accordance with the truth of the gospel, I said to Peter in front of all of them, "You are a Jew, yet you are living like a Gentile and not like a Jew. How then can you require the Gentiles to live like Jews?"

II: PAUL DEFENDS THE FREEDOM OF CHRISTIANS*

A: It Is Faith That Saves*

Justified by Faith in Christ.* [15] We ourselves are Jews by birth and not Gentile sinners, * [16] yet we know that a man is justified not by the works of the Law but through faith in Jesus Christ. So we too came to believe in Christ Jesus so that we might be justified by faith in him and not by the works of the Law, for no one will be justified by the works of the Law.

[17] But if, in seeking to be justified in Christ, we ourselves are found to be sinners, is Christ then a servant of sin? By no means! [18] However, if I am now rebuilding what I previously tore down, then I prove myself to be a transgressor. [19] For through the Law I died to the Law* so that I might live to God.

I have been crucified with Christ. [20] And now it is no longer I who live, but it is Christ who lives in me. The life I live now in the flesh I live by faith in the Son of God who loved me and gave himself up for me. [21] I do not set aside the grace of God, for if justification comes through the Law, then Christ died for nothing.

3 **The Christian Experience.** [1] You foolish Galatians! Who has bewitched you? Before your very eyes Jesus Christ was clearly presented as crucified. [2] I only wish you to tell me this: Did you receive the Spirit by observing the Law or by believing what you heard?

[3] How can you be so foolish? After having begun with the Spirit, are you now ending in the flesh? [4] Is everything you have suffered to result in absolutely nothing—if indeed it was for nothing? [5] Does God give you the Spirit and work mighty deeds among you because you have kept the Law or because you believed what you have heard?

The Blessing of Abraham. [6] * Thus Abraham believed in God, and it was credited to him as righteousness. [7] You can be assured that those who have faith are children of Abraham. [8] Because Scripture foresaw * that God would justify the Gentiles by faith, it declared the gospel beforehand to Abraham, saying, "In you all the nations will be blessed." [9] For this reason, those who have faith share the blessing with Abraham, the faithful one.

The Curse of the Law. [10] In contrast, those who rely on the works of the Law are under a curse, for it is written "Cursed is everyone who does not persevere in doing all the things that are written in the book of the Law." [11] Now it is evident that no one is justified before God by the Law, for the one who is righteous will live by faith. [12] However, the Law is not based on faith. On the contrary, whoever does these things shall live by them.

[13] Christ redeemed us from the curse of the Law by becoming a curse himself for us, as it is written, "Cursed is everyone who is hung upon a tree." [14] This is so that the blessing bestowed upon Abraham might be extended to the Gentiles through Jesus Christ so that we might receive the promise of the Spirit through faith.

The Promise of the Covenant. [15] Brethren, allow me to give you an everyday example. Once a human will has been ratified, no one can make further additions to it or set it aside. [16] Now the promises were made to Abraham and his descendant. It does not say "and to your descendants," as referring to many, but it says "and to your descendant," that is, to one person, who is Christ.

[17] This is what I am saying: the Law, which came four hundred and thirty years later, cannot invalidate a covenant that had been previously ratified by God, so as to nullify the promise. [18] Obviously, if the inheritance comes from the Law, it no longer comes from the promise. However, God bestowed it on Abraham through a promise.

The Purpose of the Law. [19] Why then? It was added because of transgressions * until the descendant appeared to whom the promise had been made, and it was promulgated by angels through an intermediary. [20] Now an intermediary is not necessary when there is only one party, and God is one.

[21] Is the Law then opposed to the promises of God? Absolutely not! If the Law that had been given had the power to bestow life, then righteousness would have come through the Law. [22] But according to Scripture all things have been confined under sin, so that through faith in Jesus Christ what was promised might be given to those who believe.

The Benefit of Faith. [23] * Now before faith came, we were prisoners of the Law, confined as we waited for the faith that would eventually be revealed. [24] Therefore, the Law was our tutor to bring us to Christ, so that we might be justified by faith. [25] However, now that faith has come, we are no longer under a tutor.

Children of God in Christ. [26] Through faith you are all children of God in Christ Jesus. [27] For all of you who were baptized into Christ have clothed yourselves in Christ. [28] There is no longer Jew or Greek, there is no longer slave or free man, there is no longer male or female. For all of you are one in Christ Jesus. [29] And if you are Christ's, then you are the offspring of Abraham and heirs according to the promise.

4 **Set Free by Christ.** [1] What I am saying is that as long as an heir is a minor, he is no different from a slave, even though he is the owner of it all. [2] He remains under the supervision of guardians and trustees until the date designated by the father. [3] This is also true of us. As long as we were children, we were enslaved to the forces of this world.

[4] However, when the fullness of time had come, God sent his Son, born of a woman, born under the Law, [5] in order to redeem those who were under the Law, so that we might receive adoption as sons.

[6] And because you are sons, God has sent into our hearts the Spirit of his Son, crying out "*Abba!* Father!"

[7] Therefore, you are no longer a slave but a son; and if you are a son, then through God you are also an heir.

No Return to Slavery.* [8] Previously, when you did not know God, you were slaves to forces who were not really gods at all. [9] But now that you have come to know God— or rather to be known by God—how can you turn back once again to those powerless and destitute forces? How can you consider becoming enslaved once again? [10] You even observe special days and months and seasons and years. [11] Now I am afraid for you, that I have labored among you in vain.

Appeal To Enter into Freedom from the Law. [12] I beg you, brethren, to be like me, just as I have become like you. You never did me any wrong. [13] As you remember, it was because of illness * that I originally preached the gospel to you. [14] And though my illness was a trial to you, it did not lead to any scorn or revulsion; rather, you welcomed me as an angel of God, as if I were Christ Jesus himself.

[15] What has become of your blessedness? For I can testify that, if it had been possible, you would have plucked out your eyes and given them to me. [16] Have I now become your enemy because I have told you the truth?

[17] Others are seeking to curry your favor, but they are not sincere. They are attempting to alienate you from us so that you may make them the sole object of your attention. [18] It is good to be made much of for a good purpose at all times, and not just when I am in your presence. [19] You are my children, and I am experiencing the pain of giving birth to you all over again, until Christ is formed in you. [20] I truly wish that I could be with you now and be able to alter my approach to you, because I do not know what to think about you.

Sarah and Hagar Foreshadow the Two Covenants.* [21] And so tell me, you who are so eager to be subject to the Law: why do you not listen to the Law? [22] For it is written that Abraham had two sons, one by a slave woman and one by a free woman. [23] The son by the slave woman was born through the flesh. The son by the free woman was born through a promise.

²⁴ Now this is an allegory. These women represent two covenants. One covenant is given on Mount Sinai and bears children who are born into slavery; this is Hagar. ²⁵ Hagar stands for Sinai, a mountain in Arabia, and corresponds to the present city of Jerusalem, for she is in slavery together with her children. ²⁶ However, the Jerusalem that is above is the free woman, and she is our mother. ²⁷ For it is written,

> "Rejoice, you barren woman
> who never bore a child;
> break forth in song and shout with joy,
> you who never were in labor.
> For more numerous are the children of the deserted wife
> than the children of the one who has a husband."

²⁸ Now you, brethren, are, like Isaac, the children of the promise. ²⁹ But just as in those days the child who was born through the flesh persecuted the child who was born through the Spirit, so is it now also. ³⁰ However, what does Scripture say?

> "Drive out the slave woman and her son!
> For the son of the slave woman shall not share the
> inheritance
> with the son of the free woman."

³¹ Therefore, brethren, we are the children not of the slave woman but of the free woman.

B: There Is No Freedom Except in Christ*

5 **Faith Expressing Itself through Love.** ¹ It was for freedom that Christ set us free. Therefore, stand firm and refuse to submit again to the yoke of slavery.

² Listen to me! I, Paul, tell you that if you allow yourselves to be circumcised, Christ will be of no value to you. ³ Once again, I testify that every man who accepts circumcision is under obligation to observe the entire Law.

⁴ Those of you who seek to be justified by the Law have cut yourselves off from Christ and have fallen away from grace. ⁵ For it is through the Spirit and by faith that we eagerly hope to attain righteousness, ⁶ since in Christ Jesus neither circumcision nor lack of circumcision is worth anything. All that matters is faith expressing itself through love.

Against Being Misled. ⁷ You were running a good race. Who kept you from obeying the truth? ⁸ This change did not come from the one who called you. ⁹ A little yeast leavens the entire batch of dough. ¹⁰ I am confident of you in the Lord that none of you will think differently, and that anyone who is trying to confuse you will be condemned, no matter who it is.

¹¹ As for me, brethren, if I were still advocating circumcision, * why would I continue to be persecuted? If I were doing that, the cross would no longer be a stumbling block. ¹² I wish that those who are confusing you would even castrate themselves!

Proper Use of Freedom. ¹³ Brethren, you were called to freedom. However, make sure that you do not use your freedom as an opportunity for the flesh. Instead, serve one another in love. ¹⁴ For the entire Law can be summed up * in a single commandment: "You shall love your neighbor as yourself." ¹⁵ But if you continue biting and tearing one another to pieces, at least be on your guard lest you be consumed by one another.

¹⁶ Hence, I advise you to be guided by the Spirit, so that you will not gratify the desires of the flesh. ¹⁷ For the desires of the flesh are opposed to the Spirit, and those of the Spirit are opposed to the flesh. They are in conflict with one another, so that you cannot do what you want. ¹⁸ But if you are guided by the Spirit, you are not subject to the Law.

¹⁹ * Now the works of the flesh are obvious: fornication, impurity, licentiousness, ²⁰ idolatry, sorcery, enmities, strife, jealousy, anger, quarrels, dissensions, factions,

²¹ envy, drunkenness, carousing, and the like. I warn you, as I warned you previously, that no one who does such things will inherit the kingdom of God.

²² * In contrast, the fruit of the Spirit is love, joy, peace, patience, kindness, generosity, faithfulness, ²³ gentleness, and self-control. There is no law against such things. ²⁴ And those who belong to Christ Jesus have crucified the flesh with its passions and desires. ²⁵ If we live by the Spirit, let us also be guided by the Spirit. ²⁶ We should not become conceited, or provoke one another, or be envious of one another.

6 The Law of Christ.*

¹ Brethren, if anyone is detected committing a transgression, you who are spiritual must set him right in a spirit of gentleness. Meanwhile, you should take care so that you yourselves are not tempted. ² Bear one another's burdens, and in this way you will fulfill the law of Christ.

³ If anyone thinks he is something when in fact he is nothing, he is only deceiving himself. ⁴ Each person must examine his own work. Then he will have reason to boast with regard to himself alone and not in comparison with someone else. ⁵ For everyone has his own burden to bear.

⁶ Anyone who is being taught should give his teacher a share in all his possessions. ⁷ Do not be deceived; God cannot be mocked. A person will reap only what he sows. ⁸ The one who sows in his flesh will reap a harvest of corruption, but the one who sows in the Spirit will reap from the Spirit the reward of eternal life.

⁹ Let us never grow weary in doing what is right, for if we do not give up, we will reap our harvest in due time. ¹⁰ Therefore, while we have the opportunity, let us labor for the good of all, but especially for those members of the household of the faith.

III: CONCLUSION*

The Cross of Christ, Our True Boast. ¹¹ Observe what large letters I make when I am writing to you in my own handwriting. [12] It is those who want to gain human approval who are trying to compel you to be circumcised, their sole purpose being to escape persecution for the cross of Christ. [13] Even the circumcised do not themselves obey the Law. They want you to be circumcised so that they may boast in your flesh.

[14] May I never boast of anything except the cross of our Lord Jesus Christ, through which the world is crucified to me and I to the world. [15] Neither circumcision nor uncircumcision is important, but only a new creation.

Blessing and a Plea. [16] May peace and mercy be given to all who follow this rule, and to the Israel of God. *

[17] In the future, let no one make trouble for me, for I bear the marks of Jesus branded on my body.

[18] May the grace of our Lord Jesus Christ be with your spirit, brethren. Amen.

THE LETTER TO THE EPHESIANS
THE MYSTERY AND LIFE OF THE CHURCH

The Letters to the Philippians, Philemon, and the Colossians, along with Ephesians, form the group known as the "Captivity Letters." Philippians undoubtedly goes back to an earlier period. The other three make up a well-defined group in the Pauline epistolary.

But are these Letters really Paul's? The style is elevated and almost liturgical. Grandiose themes are treated in a sustained way; it is certainly not easy to recognize in them the pen that wrote, for example, the Letters to the Corinthians and the Letter to the Romans. Some therefore prefer to attribute these Letters to a Pauline school that operated after the death of Paul and was influenced by new ideas coming especially from Essene Judaism. According to others, a secretary of Paul drafted the text in a rather free way, in accordance with a fixed image of the Apostle.

It is possible to go even further: at that time it was not regarded as a forgery to publish, under the name of a famous personage, a text written by someone else in order to promote the work and thought of the former. But these are only hypotheses. How is it possible to prove that Paul did not pass through very different periods in his life? And why cannot the Letter to the Ephesians have been a work of his maturity?

The Letters to the Colossians and the Ephesians have more than one trait in common; we might even say that the latter borrows entire verses from the former. Colossians is more lively and direct; it intervenes at a moment of crisis in a Church. Ephesians takes up the same ideas and perhaps even the same text as the subject of a more serene and elevated contemplation.

This is all the more true since it is very doubtful that the Letter is addressed to a particular Church, that of Ephesus. Paul had stayed for about three years in that very large metropolis, and, while there, had attended to the problems of the Corinthians; that was an important period for his work and his thinking (see Acts 19–20). The addressees of the present Letter seem, however, to be anonymous. This great dogmatic reflection is not linked to any concrete situation and involves no personal connections. It may be said that the writer does not know his correspondents. Furthermore, the mention of "Ephesus" is lacking in some very early manuscripts.

We are led, then, to think that what we have is rather a circular Letter intended for the Churches of the region. Some scholars even think that our Letter to the Ephesians may be the Letter to the Laodiceans mentioned in Col 4:16.

During all the vicissitudes of Paul's mission to the Gentiles, a singular idea has been germinating in his mind: Christ is the sole principle of salvation—and it is this that constitutes his Gospel!

When he is imprisoned at Jerusalem and then placed in house arrest at Rome from A.D. 61 to 63, the Apostle has the time to deepen his understanding of the Christ event, for the crisis that had flared up among the Colossians has been doused. Thus, at fifty-seven years of age, he sets forth in the Letter to the Ephesians the mature fruit of his thought and his life. It is a lengthy theological meditation, a great vision of Christianity.

Contemplating God's entire plan for the salvation of the human race, Paul fixes his gaze on Christ the Lord established in heaven: this is the key to the Letter. Although he is seated at the right hand of his Father, Christ has not distanced himself from the world and human beings. His sovereignty spans all creation. He enables the community of the saved, his Church, to live and grow.

Through and in the Church he pours out his grace and love to the world. Through and in her, the risen Christ gathers human beings together in peace and unity, eliminating all discrimination of race and religious origin. The call of Gentiles to salvation and reconciliation with Jesus in the heart of the new Christian communities was the most beautiful testimony of the universal action of Christ.

The very facts of the life of the Church manifest the unfathomable depths of the riches of the mystery of Christ and the unheard-of newness of God's saving love. Beneath this dynamism, a new world appears—the Church is the first cell of the humanity of the Spirit. Paul contemplates her in the dimensions of the universe. He also describes her with the aid of splendid images: the Church is God's spouse (Eph 5:22-33), body (Eph 1:23; 4:16), and building (Eph 2:19-22). He thus sets forth the intimate as well as the organic bonds by which Christ unites believers in a community with her and leads them to their expansion.

The Letter to the Ephesians is the Letter about the Church and her mystery; Vatican Council II in its treatment of the Church drew extensively upon it.

In section III of the Letter, the author gives the baptized a number of more concrete directives. Concern for unity, charity, and progress in the community is the first requirement of the new life that has been received in Baptism. In this part, there are well-known passages on the organization of the Church and on Christian marriage. The passage on this last-named subject is included among recommendations for personal conduct and family morality. It is also the occasion for a final thought about the Church, described as the spouse of Christ.

This splendid document does not possess the direct and spontaneous qualities of a letter. Its slow and solemn style stems from the majesty of the Liturgy and the fervor of contemplation. It expresses the believer's awe concerning the grace of God given in Christ and manifested in the liturgical and communitarian life of the Church as well as in the development of her mission among the Gentiles.

The Letter to the Ephesians may be divided as follows:

> *I: Introduction (1:1-2)*
> *II: The Risen Christ, Lord and Savior of the Whole Human Race (1:3—3:21)*
> *III: New Life in the Church (4:1—6:20)*
> *IV: Conclusion (6:21-24)*

I: INTRODUCTION

1 **Address and Greeting.** * ¹ Paul, by the will of God an apostle of Christ Jesus, to the saints who are in Ephesus * and are faithful in Christ Jesus. ² Grace to you and peace from God our Father and the Lord Jesus Christ.

II: THE RISEN CHRIST, LORD AND SAVIOR OF THE WHOLE HUMAN RACE*

A: God's Glorious Plan of Salvation*

Conceived by the Father

³ Blessed be the God,
and Father of our Lord Jesus Christ,
who has blessed us in Christ
with every spiritual blessing in the heavens.

⁴ Before the foundation of the world
he chose us in Christ
to be holy and blameless in his sight
and to be filled with love.

⁵ He predestined us
for adoption as his children

through Jesus Christ,
in accordance with his purpose and pleasure,

6   to the praise of the glory
of his grace
that he so freely bestowed on us
in the Beloved.

Realized by the Son

7   In Christ
and through his blood
we have redemption*
and the forgiveness of our sins.
In accord with the riches of his grace,

8   God lavished on us
all wisdom and insight.

9   He has made known to us
the mystery of his will
in accordance with his good pleasure
that he had predetermined in Christ

10   to be realized when
the fullness of time had been achieved:
namely, the plan to bring all things,
both in heaven and on earth,
together* in Christ
as the head.

Fulfilled by the Holy Spirit

11   In Christ we were also chosen,
having been predestined
by the one who accomplishes all things
in accordance with the design of his will,

12   so that we,
who were the first ones
to place our hopes in Christ,
would devote ourselves
to the praise of his glory.

13   In Christ
you also heard the message of truth
and the gospel of your salvation,

and you came to believe in him.
In him,
you were marked with the seal
of the Holy Spirit
who had been promised.
14 That Spirit is the down payment* of our inheritance,
which we shall share
when God has redeemed us
as his own possession,
to the praise of his glory.

B: The Church's Unity with Christ*

Christ, Head of the Church. [15] Having heard of your faith
in the Lord Jesus and of your love toward all the saints,
[16] I therefore never cease to give thanks to God for you
as I remember you in my prayers. [17] I pray that the God
of our Lord Jesus Christ, the Father of glory, may give
you a spirit of wisdom and revelation to know him.

[18] I further pray that the eyes of your heart may be
enlightened so that you may know the hope to which he
has called you, how rich and glorious is his inheritance *
in the saints, [19] and how immeasurably great is the
power that he has exercised toward those who have
faith.

Such was his mighty power [20] that he exhibited in
Christ
when he raised him from the dead
and enthroned him
at his right hand in heaven,
21 far above
every principality and authority,
power and dominion,
and every other title
that can be named,
not only in this age
but also in the age to come.

²²   He has put all things
        under Christ's feet
        and has made him
        the head of the Church,
²³   which is his body,
        the fullness of him
        who fills the universe
        in all its parts.

2 Christ Brought Us from Death to Life.

¹ * You formerly were dead as a result of your transgressions and sins, ² which were your way of life in this worldly era, * obeying the ruler of the kingdom of the air, the spirit that is now at work among the children of rebellion. ³ We too were all numbered among them at one time. We were ruled by our sinful nature, succumbing to the temptations of the flesh and desires. And like all others, we were by nature children of wrath.

⁴ But God is rich in his mercy, and because he had such great love for us, ⁵ he brought us to life with Christ when we were already dead through sin—it is by grace that you have been saved. ⁶ He raised us up in union with Christ Jesus and enthroned us with him in the heavens, ⁷ so that in the ages to come he might show the immeasurable riches of his grace evidenced by his mercy to us in Christ Jesus.

⁸ * For it is by grace that you have been saved through faith. This has not come from you but from the gift of God. ⁹ It does not come from works, so that no one can boast. ¹⁰ For we are God's handiwork, created in Christ Jesus for a life of good works that God had prepared for us to do.

Jews and Gentiles Reconciled in the Church.*

¹¹ Therefore, do not forget that at one time you were Gentiles in the flesh, called the uncircumcised by those who refer to themselves as the circumcised because of a physical rite. ¹² Remember that you were at that time separated from Christ, excluded from the community of Israel, and for-

eigners to the covenants * of promise. You were in the world without hope and without God.

[13] But now in Christ Jesus, you who once were far off have been brought near through the blood of Christ.

[14]   For he is our peace,
         who has made the two into one,
         by breaking down the barrier of hostility.
         In his flesh
[15]   he has abolished the Law
         with its commandments and ordinances,
         so that he might create in himself
         a single new person * out of the two,
         thereby making peace,
[16]   and that he might reconcile both groups
         to God in one body
         through the cross,
         thereby putting that enmity to death.
[17]   Therefore, Jesus came
         and proclaimed peace
         to you who were far away
         and peace to those who were near.
[18]   For through him
         we both have access to the Father
         in the one Spirit.

[19] As a result, you are no longer strangers and foreigners. Rather, you are fellow citizens of the saints and members of the household of God, [20] built upon the foundation of the apostles and prophets, with Christ Jesus himself as the cornerstone. [21] Through him the entire structure is joined together and grows into a holy temple in the Lord. [22] In him you are also being built together into a dwelling place for God in the Spirit.

C: Paul's Commission To Preach the Mystery*

3 **The Mystery Made Known.** [1] This is the reason why I, Paul, a prisoner of Christ Jesus for the sake of you

Gentiles— * [2] For you surely must have heard of the mystery of God's grace that was entrusted to me on your behalf, [3] and how the mystery was made known to me by a revelation, as I have briefly written. [4] Reading this, you will be able to perceive my understanding of the mystery of Christ.

[5] It was not disclosed to human beings in previous generations, but now it has been revealed to his holy apostles and prophets by the Spirit, [6] namely that the Gentiles have become coheirs, members of the same body, and sharers of the promise in Christ Jesus through the gospel.

Mission to the Gentiles. [7] I became its minister by God's grace bestowed on me through the working of his power. [8] Although I am the very least of all the saints, this grace was given me: to proclaim to the Gentiles the unfathomable riches of Christ [9] and to enlighten all concerning the administration of the mystery that had been kept hidden throughout the ages in God, the creator of all things.

[10] In this way, the wisdom of God in its infinite variety might be made known through the Church to the principalities and powers in the heavens. [11] This was in accordance with the eternal purpose that he has carried out in Christ Jesus our Lord, [12] in whom we have free access to God in boldness and confidence because of our faith in him. [13] Therefore, I beg you not to lose heart over my sufferings for you. Truly, they are your glory.

Prayer for a Deeper Faith. [14] This is the reason why I kneel in prayer before the Father, [15] from whom every family* in heaven and on earth takes its name. [16] I ask that from the riches of his glory he may grant through his Spirit that you be strengthened with power in your inner being [17] and that Christ may dwell in your hearts through faith.

And I pray that, rooted and grounded in love, [18] you may have the power to comprehend with all the saints its breadth and length and height and depth, [19] and know Christ's love even though it is beyond knowledge, so that you may be filled with all the fullness of God.

20 To him who in all things is able
through the power
that is at work within us
to accomplish abundantly far more
than all we can ask or imagine,
21 to him be glory in the Church
and in Christ Jesus
through all generations,
forever and ever. Amen.

III: NEW LIFE IN THE CHURCH

A: For Christians in General*

4 **Christian Unity and Maturity.*** [1] Therefore, as a prisoner for the Lord, I implore you to behave in a manner worthy of the calling you have received, [2] with all humility, gentleness, and patience, bearing with one another in a spirit of love. [3] Make every possible effort to preserve the unity of the Spirit through the bond of peace.

[4] There is one body and one Spirit, as well as one hope to which you have been called by your vocation, [5] one Lord, one faith, one baptism, [6] one God and Father of all, who is over all and through all and in all.

[7] But each of us was given grace according to the measure in which Christ allotted it. [8] Therefore, it is written,

"When he ascended to the heights,
he took prisoners into captivity
and gave gifts to men."

[9] Now the word "ascended" implies that he also descended into the lower regions of the earth. [10] The one who descended is also the one who ascended far above all the heavens, so that he might fill all things.

[11] It was he who established some as apostles, some as prophets, some as evangelists, and some as pastors and teachers,* [12] to equip the saints for the work of ministry

in building up the body of Christ, [13] until all of us attain to the unity of faith and the knowledge of the Son of God, to full maturity, as measured by the full stature of Christ.

[14] In this way, we will no longer be like children, tossed back and forth by the waves and swept along by every new wind of teaching, emanating from human cunning and craftiness and leading people into error. [15] Rather, professing truth and love, we will in all things grow into him who is the head, Christ. [16] From him, the entire body, joined and held together by every ligament, continues to grow and to build itself up in love, as each part performs its particular function.

The Newness of the Christian Life. [17] Therefore, I declare and attest in the Lord that you must no longer live as the Gentiles do, in the futility of their minds. [18] They are darkened in their understanding and alienated from the life of God because of their ignorance and their hardness of heart. [19] Having lost all sensitivity, they have abandoned themselves to vice, committing every kind of impurity in growing excess.

[20] That is not how you learned Christ. [21] Clearly, you were told about him and were taught what the truth is in Jesus. [22] You were taught to cast aside the old self of your former way of life that had been corrupted by its captivating desires. [23] You are to be renewed in the spirit of your minds, [24] and to clothe yourselves with the new self created in God's image, in the way of uprightness and holiness that belong to the truth.

A Life Based on Love. [25] Therefore, cease your lying and speak the truth to each other, for we are all members of one another. [26] If you are angry, do not sin. Do not let the sun set on your anger, [27] and do not give the devil an opening. [28] Anyone who has been stealing must no longer do so; rather, let him labor, performing some honest work with his own hands, so that he may have something to share with those in need.

²⁹ Let no foul word ever pass your lips. Say only what is useful for edification, so that your words may benefit your listeners. ³⁰ And do not grieve the Holy Spirit of God who has marked you with his seal for the day of redemption. ³¹ Remove all forms of bitterness and wrath and anger and shouting and slander, as well as all malice from your lives. ³² Rather, be kind to one another and compassionate, and forgive one another as God has forgiven you in Christ.

5 ¹ Hence, be imitators of God, as beloved children, ² and walk in love, as Christ loved us and gave himself up for us as a sacrificial offering whose fragrance is pleasing to God.

Sins To Avoid. ³ Indeed, fornication and impurity of any kind, as well as greed, should not even be mentioned among you. Such talk is not fitting for saints. ⁴ You should never engage in any obscene or foolish or suggestive conversation. All this is completely out of place. Instead, you should rather be engaged in offering thanks to God.

⁵ You can be absolutely certain that no immoral or impure person or one who is greedy—that is, an idolater—will have any inheritance in the kingdom of Christ and of God.

⁶ Let no one deceive you with worthless arguments. These are the very things that bring down the wrath of God on those who are disobedient. ⁷ Do not associate with them.

Christians Are Children of Light. ⁸ Once you were darkness, but now you are light in the Lord. Live as children of light, ⁹ for light produces all goodness and righteousness and truth. ¹⁰ Discern what the Lord finds pleasing. ¹¹ Take no part in the fruitless deeds of darkness, but rather seek to expose them.

¹² For it is shameful even to speak of what deeds people do in secret. ¹³ However, everything that is exposed by the light is made visible, ¹⁴ and whatever is made visible is light. Therefore, it is said, *

> "Awake, O sleeper!
>   Rise from the dead,
>   and Christ will shine on you."

[15] Therefore, take care to live as intelligent people, and do not be like those who are senseless. [16] Make the most of the present time, for this is a wicked age. [17] Do not be foolish, but recognize what is the will of the Lord. [18] Do not get drunk on wine, which can lead to debauchery.

Rather, be filled with the Spirit, [19] as you sing psalms and hymns and spiritual songs with one another. Sing and chant to the Lord in your hearts, [20] giving thanks to God the Father at all times and for everything in the name of our Lord Jesus Christ.

B: Christ and Christian Spouses*

Be Subject to One Another in Christ. [21] Be subject to one another out of reverence for Christ. [22] Wives, be subject to your husbands as you are to the Lord. [23] For the husband is the head of the wife, just as Christ is the head of the Church, the body of which he is the Savior. [24] Just as the Church is subject to Christ, so also wives must be subject to their husbands in everything.

Love One Another in Christ. [25] Husbands, love your wives, just as Christ loved the Church and gave himself up for her [26] in order to sanctify her by cleansing her with water and the word, * [27] in order to present the Church to himself in splendor, without spot or wrinkle or any such flaw, but holy and without the slightest blemish.

[28] In the same way, husbands should love their wives as they do their own bodies. The man who loves his wife loves himself. [29] For no one ever hates his own body; rather, he nourishes it and cares for it, even as Christ does for the Church, [30] because we are members of his body.

[31]   For this reason
            a man shall leave his father and mother
            and be joined to his wife,
          and the two shall become one flesh.

[32] This is a great mystery. Here I am applying it to Christ and the Church. [33] However, each one of you should love his wife as he loves himself, and the wife should respect her husband.

C: Christ and the Members of the Household*

6 **Children and Parents.** [1] Children, obey your parents in the Lord, for it is only right that you should do so. [2] "Honor your father and your mother." This is the first commandment that is connected with a promise: [3] "that it may go well with you and that you may have a long life on earth."

[4] Fathers, do not provoke your children to anger, but bring them up in the discipline and instruction of the Lord.

Slaves and Masters. [5] Slaves, be constant in your unwavering obedience to your earthly masters with fear and trembling and with the same heartfelt sincerity that you show to Christ. [6] Do this not just when they are watching you, as if you only had to please human beings, but as slaves of Christ, wholeheartedly carrying out the will of God. [7] Do your work willingly, as for the Lord and not for human beings, [8] knowing that whatever good we may do, whether as slaves or as free men, we will be repaid by the Lord.

[9] And masters, treat your slaves fairly. Stop threatening them. Remember that both of you have the same Master in heaven, and he shows no favoritism.

D: The Christian Warfare*

Put On the Armor of God. [10] Finally, find your strength in the Lord and in his mighty power. [11] Put on the armor of God so that you will be able to stand firm against the deceit of the devil. [12] For we are not struggling against flesh and blood, but against the principalities, the powers, and the cosmic rulers of this present darkness, and against the spirits of evil in the heavens.

[13] Therefore, put on the armor of God, so that you will be able to hold fast on the evil day and to hold your ground with all your strength. [14] Stand firm, then, with the belt of truth fastened around your waist, with the breastplate of righteousness clothing you, [15] and with your feet shod in zeal to proclaim the gospel of peace.

[16] In all circumstances, hold in your hand the shield of faith with which you will be able to quench all the flaming arrows of the evil one. [17] And take the helmet of salvation as well as the sword of the Spirit, which is the word of God.

Be Vigilant in Prayer. [18] In all of your prayers and entreaties, pray always in the Spirit. To that end, keep alert and always persevere in supplication for all the saints. [19] Pray also for me, so that whenever I open my mouth, I may be given the proper words to make known with boldness the mystery of the gospel, [20] for which I am an ambassador in chains. Pray that I may proclaim it fearlessly, as is my duty.

IV: CONCLUSION*

A Personal Message. [21] So that you may know how I am and what I am doing, Tychicus, my beloved brother and a faithful minister in the Lord, will keep you informed. [22] I am sending him to you for this specific purpose, so that you will know how we are and that your hearts may be encouraged.

Final Greeting. [23] May God the Father and the Lord Jesus Christ grant peace and love with faith to all the brethren.

[24] Grace be with all who love our Lord Jesus Christ with undying devotion.

THE LETTER TO THE PHILIPPIANS

CHRISTIAN JOY

Philippi was a well-known city, founded by Philip of Macedon, father of Alexander the Great, in 358/357 B.C. It was also the site where Marc Antony defeated Brutus and Cassius in 31 B.C. In Paul's time, the city was the capital of the region of Macedonia and a center of trade because of its location on the Egnatian Way that linked Rome with the East. It was also a colony of military people, whose citizens enjoyed the full rights of those living in Italy.

The time was A.D. 49–50 and Europe was waiting for the Gospel. The moment constituted a turning point in the life of Paul and in the missionary efforts of the young Church. Philippi was the first European city in which Paul proclaimed Jesus Christ and founded a community of Christians. The Acts of the Apostles (16:11-40) has preserved the memory of that mission and of a visit of Paul, who retained a special affection for that community, as he did for the nearby one of Thessalonica (see 1 Thes 1–2). It was perhaps the only community from which he accepted any financial aid.

Paul began his preaching in Philippi at a "place of prayer" by the riverside. His exorcism of a slave girl resulted in his arrest, scourging, and imprisonment. After an earthquake during the night, Paul refused to escape and revealed his Roman citizenship (Acts 16:12-40).

The community seems to have been made up predominantly of Gentiles and to have had leading roles for women right from the start, especially Lydia, a "worshiper of God" (Acts 16:14f, 40), Euodia, and Syntyche (Phil 4:2f).

In order to ease Paul's imprisonment, the Christians of Philippi had recently sent Epaphroditus with a generous offering (Phil 4:10-18). Paul was in fact a prisoner, perhaps in Rome (see the final greeting in Phil 4:22); we would then be in the years A.D. 62–63. However, Paul was imprisoned more than once, although the Book of Acts does not record this fact (see 2 Cor 11:23).

He may also have written this Letter from Ephesus, which was closer and where he spent difficult days (see 1 Cor 15:32; 2 Cor 1:8; 4:8-10; 6:9). If so, the Letter can be dated A.D. 56–57, and the tone of closeness becomes more intelligible. Trust, surrender, and cordiality are the characteristics of this Letter from prison. It is, above all, a letter of joy and of fellowship in joy.

The absence of any grave problems to be treated enables Paul to carry on this heart-to-heart discourse. He injects in it something about his lot as a prisoner but he does not forget his fundamental preoccupation with the unity of Christians in the internal relations of the community. He goes on to pass quickly from one idea to another—leading some scholars to consider this writing as an amalgam of several Letters.

The Apostle offers personal news and is also aware that internal or external influences lead to the temptation to establish antagonistic groups. However, the desire for unity brings with it the refusal of all personal pretense. He emphasizes this point by setting forth Christ as an example— which results in our having the wonderful hymn to the Lord Jesus (Phil 2:6-11).

In contrast to the temptation to follow the easy way of life, Paul depicts the Christian life as a journey and even as a course to run, as the project of a life united with Christ so that—with him and through him—one may ultimately enter the city of God.

The Letter to the Philippians may be divided as follows:

  I: Introduction (1:1-11)
 II: News and Instructions (1:12—3:1a)
III: Warning against False Teachers (3:1b—4:1)
IV: Counsels and Thanksgiving (4:2-9)
 V: Acknowledgment of the Community's Gift (4:10-20)
VI: Conclusion (4:21-23)

I: INTRODUCTION

1 **Address.*** ¹ Paul and Timothy, servants of Christ Jesus, to all the saints in Christ Jesus at Philippi, together with their bishops and deacons: ² grace to you and peace from God the Father and our Lord Jesus Christ.

Joyful Prayer for the Philippians.* ³ I give thanks to my God every time I think of you. ⁴ I always pray for you, interceding for you with joy ⁵ because of your sharing in the gospel from the first day until now. ⁶ I am confident of this: that the one who began a good work in you will bring it to completion on the day of Christ Jesus. *

⁷ It is only right for me to feel this way toward you, because I hold you in my heart, for you have all shared with me in God's grace, both during my imprisonment and in the defense and confirmation of the gospel. ⁸ Indeed, God is my witness how I long for all of you with the affection of Christ Jesus.

⁹ And for this I pray: that your love may increase ever more and more in knowledge and full insight ¹⁰ to enable you to discover what is really important, so that on the day of Christ you may be pure and blameless, ¹¹ filled with the fruits of righteousness that comes through Jesus Christ for the glory and praise of God.

II: NEWS AND INSTRUCTIONS

To Live Is Christ.* ¹² Brethren, I want you to know that what has happened to me has actually helped spread the gospel, ¹³ for my imprisonment has become known not only throughout the praetorium * but to everyone else as well. ¹⁴ And the majority of the brethren having taken encouragement in the Lord from my imprisonment, dare more than ever to proclaim the word without fear.

¹⁵ It is true that some are proclaiming Christ out of envy and rivalry, but others are doing so with goodwill. ¹⁶ These latter ones do so out of love, aware that I have been put here for the defense of the gospel. ¹⁷ The former proclaim Christ out of selfish ambition, not in sincerity, but in an effort to increase my suffering while I am in chains. ¹⁸ But what does it matter, as long as in every way, with false motives or true, that Christ is proclaimed. And in that I rejoice.

Yes, and I will continue to rejoice, ¹⁹ for I know that through your prayers and with the help of the Spirit of

Jesus Christ this will result in deliverance for me. [20] It is my firm expectation and hope that I will not be put to shame in any way, but will act with complete fearlessness, now as always, so that Christ will be exalted in my body, whether by my life or by my death.

[21] For to me, to live is Christ and to die is gain. * [22] But if I continue living in the body, that will mean fruitful work for me. Hence, I do not know which I should choose. [23] I am pulled in opposite directions. My desire is to depart and to be with Christ, for that is far better, [24] but, it is a more urgent need for you that I remain in the body.

[25] Since I am convinced of this, I know that I shall remain and continue with all of you to ensure your progress and joy in the faith. [26] Thus, you will rebound with joy in Christ Jesus when I return to be with you once again.

Striving and Suffering for Christ. * [27] Only live in a manner worthy of the gospel of Christ. Then, whether I come and see you or simply hear news of you from a distance, I will know that you are standing firm and united in spirit, striving together for the faith of the gospel, [28] and being in no way intimidated by those who oppose you.

This will be a clear sign to them of their forthcoming destruction as well as of your salvation. All of this is in accord with God's design. [29] For it has been granted you not only to believe in Christ but also to suffer for him. [30] You are taking part in the same struggle that you have seen in me and that you now hear I am experiencing.*

2 **Unity and Humility.** * [1] Therefore, if there is any consolation in Christ, any comfort in love, any fellowship in the Spirit, any compassion and sympathy, [2] make my joy complete by being of the same mind, having the same love for one another, and united in thought. [3] Do nothing out of selfish ambition or vanity, but humbly regard others as better than yourselves. [4] Be concerned not only with your own interests but also with those of others.

[5] Let your attitude be identical to that of Christ Jesus.

The Humbled and Exalted Christ*

6 Though he was in the form of God,
   he did not regard equality with God
   as something to be grasped.

7 Rather, he emptied himself,*
   taking the form of a slave,
   being born in human likeness.

   Being found in appearance as a man,
8 he humbled himself,
   and became obedient to death,
   even death on a cross.

9 Because of this, God greatly exalted him
   and bestowed on him the name
   that is above all other names,

10 so that at the name of Jesus
   every knee should bend
   of those in heaven and on earth and under the earth,
11 and every tongue should proclaim
   to the glory of God the Father:
   Jesus Christ is Lord.*

Innocence of the Children of God.* [12] Therefore, my beloved, just as you have always been obedient when I am present, you must be so all the more now when I am absent, as you work out your salvation in fear and trembling. * [13] For it is God who is at work in you, enabling you both to desire and to act for his chosen purpose.

[14] Do everything without grumbling or arguing, [15] so that you may show yourselves blameless and beyond reproach, children of God without spot in the midst of an evil and depraved generation, among which you shine like lights in the world [16] as you hold fast tenaciously to the word of life. Then I will have cause to boast of you on the day of Christ that I did not run in vain or labor to no purpose.

[17] But even if my blood is to be poured out as a libation upon the sacrifice and the offering of your faith, I rejoice,

and I share my joy with all of you. [18] In the same way, you too must rejoice and share your joy with me.

Timothy Commended. [19] * I hope, in the Lord Jesus, to send Timothy to you soon, so that I may be cheered by hearing news of you. [20] I have no one else like him in his genuine concern for your welfare. [21] All the others serve their own interests more than those of Jesus Christ.

[22] His reputation is well known to you. Like a son helping his father, he has worked with me in the service of the gospel. [23] I hope to send him to you as soon as I see how things will go with me. [24] And I am confident in the Lord that I myself shall also come before long.

Epaphroditus Praised. [25] I have also decided that it is necessary to send you Epaphroditus, my brother and coworker and fellow soldier, who was your messenger and ministered to my needs. [26] He has missed all of you and been greatly distressed because you heard that he was ill. [27] And indeed he was dangerously ill and close to death. However, God had mercy on him—and not merely on him but on me as well, so that I would not have to endure one sorrow on top of another.

[28] Therefore, I am all the more eager to send him in order that you may rejoice on seeing him again and I may thereby feel less anonymous. [29] Receive him joyfully in the Lord, and value people like him very highly. [30] For he came perilously close to death for the work of Christ, risking his life to render me those services that you were unable to provide.

3 [1] Finally, my brethren, rejoice in the Lord.

III: WARNING AGAINST FALSE TEACHERS

Worship by the Spirit. * I do not mind writing the same things to you again; it is for your safety.

[2] Beware of the dogs! * Beware of evildoers! Beware of those who mutilate the flesh! [3] For we are the circumcision, * we who worship by the Spirit of God and who

boast in Christ Jesus and do not place any confidence in the flesh— [4] even though I too have reason for confidence in the flesh.

Joyous Sacrifice of All Things for Christ.* If anyone thinks that he has reasons to be confident in the flesh, I have more! [5] I was circumcised on the eighth day of my life. I was one of the people of Israel, the tribe of Benjamin. * I am a Hebrew and the son of Hebrews. In regard to the Law, I was a Pharisee; [6] in regard to religious zeal, I was a persecutor of the Church; in regard to righteousness under the Law, I was without fault.

[7] All these I once regarded as assets, but now I have come to regard them as losses because of Christ. [8] Even more than that, I count everything as loss because of the supreme good of knowing Christ Jesus my Lord. For his sake, I have suffered the loss of all other things, and I regard them as so much rubbish, in order that I may gain Christ [9] and be found in him.

I do not wish to have any righteousness of my own based on the Law, but one that comes through faith in Christ, the righteousness given by God in response to faith. [10] All I want is to come to know Christ and the power of his resurrection and to share in his sufferings by becoming conformed to his death, [11] so that I may attain the resurrection from the dead.

Racing toward the Goal.* [12] It is not that I have already attained this or have yet reached perfection. But I press on to take hold of that for which Christ once took hold of me. [13] Brethren, I do not claim to have taken hold of it as yet. Only this one thing: forgetting what is behind and straining forward to what lies ahead, [14] I press on toward the finishing line to win the heavenly prize to which God has called me in Christ Jesus.

[15] Those of us who are mature should adopt this same attitude. If on any matter you have a different point of view, this too God will make clear to you. [16] Only let us hold fast in our conduct to what we have already attained.

Our Citizenship Is in Heaven.* [17] Brethren, join in imitating me, * and take note of those who conduct themselves in accord with the model you have in us. [18] As I have told you before, and now remind you with tears, many live as enemies of the cross of Christ. [19] Their end is destruction. Their god is their stomach. Their glory is in their shame. Their minds are set on earthly things.

[20] But our citizenship is in heaven, * and from there we await our Savior, the Lord Jesus Christ. [21] He will transform our lowly bodies so that they will be conformed to his glorified body by the power that also enables him to make all things subject to himself.

4 [1] Therefore, my brethren, whom I love and for whom I long, my joy and crown: stand firm in the Lord, beloved.

IV: COUNSELS AND THANKSGIVING

Christian Concord.* [2] I exhort both Euodia and Syntyche to come to a mutual understanding in the Lord. [3] I also ask you, my loyal companion Syzygus, to help these women, for they have struggled alongside me in the work of the gospel, together with Clement and the rest of my fellow workers, whose names are in the book of life.

Rejoice without Ceasing.* [4] Rejoice in the Lord always. Again I say: Rejoice! [5] Let your kindness be known to everyone. The Lord is near. [6] Do not worry about anything, but present your needs to God in prayer and petition, with thanksgiving. [7] Then the peace of God, which is beyond all understanding, will guard your hearts and your minds in Christ Jesus.

All That Is Truly Human Is Christian.* [8] Finally, brethren, let your minds be filled with whatever is true, whatever is honorable, whatever is just, whatever is pure, whatever is pleasing, whatever is commendable, whatever is excellent, whatever is worthy of praise. [9] Do the things that you have learned, received, and heard from me and that you saw me doing. Then the God of peace will be with you.

V: ACKNOWLEDGMENT OF THE COMMUNITY'S GIFT*

Contentment in Any Circumstances. [10] I rejoice greatly in the Lord that now at last you have renewed your concern for me. You were, of course, concerned about me, but you had no opportunity to show it. [11] I do not say this because I have been in need, for I have learned to be content with whatever I have.

[12] I know how to live with little, and I know how to live with plenty. In any and all circumstances, I have learned the secret of being well fed and of going hungry, of having plenty and of being in need. [13] I can do all things in him who strengthens me.

Philippian Generosity. [14] Even so, it was kind of you to share my difficulties. [15] You Philippians are aware that in the early days of the gospel* when I set out from Macedonia, not a single Church other than yours shared with me in giving and receiving. [16] Even when I was in Thessalonica, you sent me something for my needs on more than one occasion.

[17] Do not think that it is the gift that I value most. What I desire is for the interest to mount up in your account. [18] I have been paid in full and have more than enough. I am satisfied now that I have received from Epaphroditus the gifts you sent. They are a fragrant offering, an acceptable sacrifice pleasing to God. * [19] And my God will fully supply all your needs out of the riches of his glory in Christ Jesus.

Doxology. [20] To our God and Father be glory forever and ever. Amen.

VI: CONCLUSION

Final Greetings.* [21] Give my greetings to every one of the saints in Christ Jesus. The brethren who are with me send their greetings to you, [22] as do all the saints here, especially those in the emperor's service.

Benediction.* [23] The grace of our Lord Jesus Christ be with your spirit.

THE LETTER TO THE COLOSSIANS

THE MYSTERY OF CHRIST

The Letters to the Ephesians and the Colossians are like twin sisters. They were entrusted to the same messenger: Tychicus; the style is the same, as is the thought. Furthermore, half of the Letter to the Ephesians is to be found in the Letter to the Colossians, which was certainly written first. The Letter to the Ephesians thus seems to be a deeper reflection on the same subject after the crisis in the Colossian community.

Some exegetes are reluctant to ascribe these two Letters to Paul. The tone and the subject are new; a different vision inspires the author when he speaks of Christ, the Church, and Baptism. And at that time, when people were much less scrupulous than today about literary ownership, some disciples could have written these Letters, in their master's name, in order to further his apostolic work. This position is not impossible. But why could not Paul's ideas develop, due partly to deeper experience, partly to the influence of new problems that he may have met? It is therefore not unjustified to think that these Letters were written in Rome in A.D. 62–63, toward the end of Paul's imprisonment.

Colossae was at that time a little city in the interior of Asia Minor, about 80 miles northeast of Ephesus. Paul probably never went there in person, but some new converts and missionaries had scattered from Ephesus to the other cities of the province; among these was Epaphras, to whom Paul here gives his apostolic approval.

The Greeks were once enamored of the image of a harmonious cosmos, but that is no longer the idea of the universe possessed by Paul's contemporaries. They often feel that they are in the grip of an existence without purpose, prisoners of obscure forces working in the world. So they seek to master these forces by means of practices and cults. This religious ferment, stemming from a civilization's malaise, influences even certain Jewish circles. These current troubles lend fuel to the crisis at Colossae.

In fact, the error that threatens the youthful Church bears the earmarks of an intermingling of the Jewish religion with Eastern influences and recalls the concepts of the Essene sect of Qumran. In an atmosphere of religious fear, its adherents make salvation depend on a multitude of human practices, observances, and rites. At the same time, to explain the laws of the world and history, which do not cease to astonish and frighten, they contrive a clever system of spirits, intermediaries between God and creatures, that preside over the life of the cosmos and the destiny of the world.

They give the imagination free rein to speculate about the role and place of mythological forces. In every age, human beings find reasons to avoid their responsibilities by believing that they are the playthings of anonymous forces and offering sacrifice to them!

Made aware that such a situation is present at Colossae, Paul immediately sees the danger. It is the very sovereignty of Christ that is being attacked. In its place, futile powers, impotent lords, and vain ideologies are erected as masters of our destiny. Until now, Paul has contemplated the presence of Christ in the life of Christians; this time, he contemplates Christ's place in the destiny of the cosmos.

He clearly affirms that Christ dominates everything. He is the author and head of the universe—set over human beings and over the cosmic forces. He is the Risen One living in full glory—set over all the faithful. He rules over his earthly Church in which he acts in meaningful ways so that she may develop and gradually succeed in crossing to his side.

Christians believe in this total primacy of Christ; they do not seek to join their existence to other forces, but they know that their existence is profoundly united with Jesus through Baptism, and they strive to develop this aspect of personal union even here below. Thus, their existence unfolds in the light, power, and love of Easter.

The Letter to the Colossians is the Easter letter par excellence. But Paul is too much of a realist to separate mysticism from ethical requirements. The human beings with a new self are those who never cease to model themselves on Christ; new values transform their activity and their life situation.

The Apostle's insights are developed in an ample style with an almost liturgical rhythm. They are far removed from the sparkling but choppy style of the early Letters. The author of the Letters to the Colossians and Ephesians repeatedly contemplates the Paschal Mystery of Christ in order to reflect on the meaning of life and on the destiny of the universe.

In the process, he forges a more highly developed Christology than that of the major Letters, but it comes from themes developed in them. The teachings (1) that Christ has created everything (Col 1:16), (2) that in him all things hold together (Col 1:17), and (3) that everything in heaven and on earth has been reconciled by his death (Col 1:20) flow from developing the ideas of 1 Cor 8:6; 10:4; and 2 Cor 5:19. And when Paul states that by the work of the Redemption Christ has subdued the principalities and powers (Col 2:15), he is expanding on Rom 8:38ff; Gal 4:3, 9; and Phil 2:10ff.

The Letter to the Colossians may be divided as follows:

  I: Introduction (1:1-14)
  II: The Supremacy of Christ (1:15—2:5)
  III: Instruction about Errors That Are Circulating (2:6-23)
  IV: Exhortation To Live as Christians (3:1—4:6)
  V: Conclusion (4:7-18)

I: INTRODUCTION

1 **Address.** [1] Paul, an apostle of Christ Jesus by the will of God, and Timothy our brother, [2] to the saints * and faithful brethren in Christ in Colossae. May God our Father grant you grace and peace.

A Community Pervaded by the Gospel.* [3] In all our prayers for you we always give thanks to God, the Father of our Lord Jesus Christ, [4] because we have heard of your faith in Christ Jesus and of the love that you have for all the saints ^{5} because of the hope that is stored up for you in heaven. You had learned of this hope through the word of truth, the gospel, * ^{6} that has come down to you.

Just as it is bearing fruit and growing throughout the entire world, so it has been bearing fruit among you, ever since the day when you heard it and came to understand the grace of God in truth. ^{7} You learned this from Epaphras, * our beloved fellow servant and a faithful minister of Christ on your behalf. ^{8} He was also the one who made known to us your love in the Spirit.

^{9} That is why, ever since the day we first heard about it, we have not ceased to pray for you and to ask that you may be filled with the knowledge of God's will through all spiritual wisdom and understanding. ^{10} And we ask this so that you may live in a manner worthy of the Lord and become fully pleasing to him, bearing fruit in every good work and continuing to grow in the knowledge of God.

^{11} May you be fortified with the strength that comes from his glorious power, and may you be granted patience and endurance, while joyfully ^{12} giving thanks to the Father who has enabled you to share in the inheritance of the saints in light. * ^{13} He has rescued us from the power of darkness and brought us into the kingdom of his beloved Son, ^{14} in whom we have redemption, the forgiveness of sins.

II: THE SUPREMACY OF CHRIST

In Christ, through Him, and for Him*

^{15} He is the image of the invisible God,
the firstborn of all creation.

^{16} For in him were created all things
in heaven and on earth,
whether visible or invisible,
whether thrones or dominions or rulers or powers—
all things were created through him and for him.

^{17} He exists before all things,
and in him all things hold together.

18   He is the head of the body,
     that is, the Church.
     He is the beginning,
     the firstborn from the dead,
     so that in every way
     he should be supreme.
19   For in him
     it pleased God
     to make all fullness dwell,*
20   and through him
     to reconcile all things for him,
     whether on earth or in heaven,
     by making peace through his blood of the cross.

Christ among the Gentiles. 21 * You yourselves were once
alienated and hostile in your intent because of your evil
deeds. 22 But now, through Christ's death in his body of
flesh, God has reconciled you to himself so that you may
stand holy, blameless, and irreproachable in his presence.

23 However, you must persevere in the faith, firmly
grounded and steadfast in your belief, and never allowing
yourselves to drift away from the hope of the gospel that
you accepted and that has now been proclaimed to every
creature under heaven, the gospel of which I, Paul, have
become a servant.

Christ's Suffering in His People. 24 I find great joy at present in suffering for you, and in my own body I am completing the sufferings that still must be undergone by
Christ for the sake of his body, the Church. * 25 I was
made a minister of that Church, with the commission
given to me by God to make fully known to you the word
of God, 26 the mystery that has been hidden throughout
the ages and from past generations but that now has been
revealed to his saints.

27 To these God chose to make known how rich is the
priceless glory that this mystery brings to the Gentiles—
Christ in you, your hope of glory. * 28 It is he whom we
proclaim, admonishing and instructing everyone in all

wisdom so that we may present everyone to Christ in a state of perfection. [29] For this I labor and struggle with all his energy working within me mightily.

2   **Closely United in Love.*** [1] I want you to realize how greatly I am struggling for you as well as for those in Laodicea* and all the others who have never seen me face to face. [2] I want their hearts to be encouraged and united in love so that they may grow rich in their complete understanding as they come to the knowledge of the mystery of God, that is, Christ, [3] in whom are hidden all the treasures of wisdom and knowledge.

[4] I am telling you all this so that no one may deceive you with deceptive arguments. [5] Even if I am not physically present to you, I am with you in spirit, and I rejoice to see your unity and the resolute firmness of your faith in Christ.

III: INSTRUCTION ABOUT ERRORS THAT ARE CIRCULATING

Walk in Christ. [6] * Therefore, just as you received Christ Jesus the Lord, continue to walk in him. [7] Be rooted and built up in him, and remain established in the faith as you were taught, overflowing with thanksgiving. [8] Make sure that no one leads you astray with an empty and deceitful philosophy that depends on human tradition* and worldly principles, and not on Christ.

God Has Given You Life in Christ. [9] For it is in him that the entire fullness of deity dwells in bodily form, * [10] and you share this fullness in him who is the head of every ruler and power. [11] In him also you were circumcised, not with a physical circumcision but with a spiritual stripping away of the old nature with the circumcision of Christ.

[12] When you were buried with him in baptism, you were also raised with him through faith in the power of God who raised him from the dead. [13] And even when you were dead in your sins and your flesh was uncircumcised, God gave you new life along with him. He has for-

given us all our sins, [14] erasing the record against us * with its decrees that are hostile to us. He set this aside, nailing it to the cross. [15] Disarming the rulers and powers, he made a public spectacle of them, parading them in his triumphal procession.

The Reality Is Christ.* [16] Therefore, do not allow anyone to pass judgment on you in regard to what you eat or drink, or about the observance of Festivals, New Moons, or Sabbaths. * [17] These are only a shadow of what is to come. The reality is Christ.

[18] Do not allow yourself to be declared disqualified by those who revel in false humility and worship angels and visions, their vanity foolishly inflated by a human way of thinking. [19] They are not united with the head, from whom the whole body, supported and held together by its ligaments and sinews, achieves the growth that comes from God.

[20] Since you died with Christ to the elemental principles of this world, why are you living in the world as if you were subject to it? [21] "Do not handle!" "Do not taste!" "Do not touch!" [22] All this refers to things that perish as they are used. They are simply human commands and teachings. [23] Rules of this type indeed appear to be wise in promoting self-imposed piety, false humility, and harsh treatment of the body, but they are of no value in combating the flesh.

IV: EXHORTATION TO LIVE AS CHRISTIANS

3 **Seek the Things That Are Above.*** [1] Therefore, since you have been raised with Christ, seek the things that are above, where Christ is, sitting at God's right hand. [2] Fix your thoughts on things that are above, not on things that are on the earth, [3] for you have died, and your life is hidden with Christ in God. [4] When Christ, who is your life, appears, then you also will appear with him in glory.

A New Self.* [5] And so you should put to death everything in your nature that is earthly: sexual immorality, impurity, passion, evil desires, and greed (which is idolatry).* [6] Because of these practices, the wrath of God will fall on those who are disobedient. [7] In the life you formerly lived, you used to do these things. [8] But now you must cast them all aside—anger, rage, malice, slander, and foul language out of your lips.

[9] Do not lie to one another, since you have stripped off the old self with its practices [10] and have put on the new self that is being renewed in knowledge after the image of its creator. [11] Now there is no longer Greek and Jew, circumcised and uncircumcised, barbarian and Scythian,* slave and free man. Rather, Christ is all and in all.

Characteristics of Life in Common.* [12] As God's chosen ones, holy and beloved, put on compassion, kindness, humility, gentleness, and patience. [13] Bear with one another, and forgive one another if anyone has reason to be offended with another. You must forgive just as the Lord has forgiven you.

[14] Over all these put on love, which is the bond of perfection. [15] And let the peace of Christ reign in your hearts, because it was for this that you were called together in one body. Always be thankful.

[16] Let the word of Christ * with all its richness dwell in you. Teach and admonish one another in all wisdom, singing psalms, hymns, and spiritual songs to God with gratitude in your hearts. [17] And whatever you do in word or deed, do everything in the name of the Lord Jesus, giving thanks to God the Father through him.

The Christian Family. [18] * Wives, be subject to your husbands, as is fitting in the Lord. [19] Husbands, love your wives and do not treat them harshly. [20] Children, obey your parents in everything, for this is pleasing to the Lord. [21] Fathers, do not provoke your children lest they lose heart.

Slaves and Masters. [22] Slaves, obey your earthly masters in everything, not only when you are being observed or in order to please them, but wholeheartedly, out of rever-

ence for the Lord. ²³ Whatever you do, do it wholeheartedly, as if you were doing it for the Lord and not for others, ²⁴ since you know that you will receive from the Lord
an inheritance as your reward for you are serving the
Lord Christ. ²⁵ But anyone who does wrong will be repaid
for what he has done. There will not be any favoritism
shown.

4 ¹ Masters, be just and fair in your treatment of your
slaves, knowing that you too have a Master in heaven.

Assiduous Prayer.* ² Persevere in prayer, with alert
minds and thankful hearts. ³ At the same time, pray for us
too, so that God may open a door to us to proclaim the
word, the mystery of Christ, for which I am in prison.
⁴ Pray that I may proclaim it as clearly as I should.

Christian Behavior.* ⁵ Conduct yourselves wisely toward
outsiders, making the most of your opportunity. ⁶ Let
your speech always be gracious and seasoned with wisdom, so that you will know how to respond properly to
all.

V: CONCLUSION

Tychicus and Onesimus. ⁷ * Tychicus will tell you all the
news about me. He is a beloved brother, a faithful minister, and a fellow servant in the Lord. ⁸ I am sending him
to you for this very purpose, so that you will know how
we are and that he may cheer your hearts. ⁹ He will be
accompanied by Onesimus, our trustworthy and beloved
brother, who is one of you. They will tell you about everything that has happened here.

Paul's Coworkers. ¹⁰ Aristarchus, * my fellow prisoner,
sends you his greetings, as does Mark, the cousin of
Barnabas. (You have received instructions about him; if
he comes to you, make him welcome.) ¹¹ And Jesus who
is called Justus also greets you. Of all those who are of the
circumcision, these are the only ones who are working
with me for the kingdom of God, and they have been a
great comfort to me.

¹² Epaphras sends you greetings. He is one of you, a servant of Christ Jesus, and he is always pleading earnestly in his prayers on your behalf so that you may seek perfection and fulfill the will of God. ¹³ I can testify for him that he has worked tirelessly for you and those in Laodicea and Hierapolis. * ¹⁴ Luke, * the beloved physician, and Demas send you greetings.

Notes for the Laodiceans. ¹⁵ Give my greetings to the brethren in Laodicea, and to Nymphas * and the Church in her house. ¹⁶ Then when this letter has been read to you, see to it that it is also read to the Church at Laodicea; and I ask you in turn to read my letter that is coming from Laodicea. ¹⁷ Also tell Archippus: * "See that you carry out fully the ministry that you received in the Lord."

Paul's Signature.* ¹⁸ I, Paul, write this farewell in my own hand. Remember my chains. Grace be with you.

THE FIRST LETTER TO THE THESSALONIANS

THE GOSPEL OF HOPE

A few pages, dealing with a particular need of a young community, written in Corinth in the winter of A.D. 50–51, twenty years after Christ's Death and Resurrection: such is the first written document of Christianity.

During his Second Missionary Journey, Paul left Philippi in haste under the pressure of persecution (see Acts 16:19-40). He still showed the signs of this when he reached Thessalonica (today: Salonika), the first great European metropolis he encountered on his journey. The city was the capital of the Roman province of Macedonia and housed a great Mediterranean naval base.

The city was immense; commerce at the port was constant; ideas circulated; the teachers of thought and religion were in search of clients and their own prosperity. All this made it an important focus for missionary activity. Paul and his team spent only a short time there (from three weeks to three months—see Acts 17:2).

Paul could not but proclaim to many people the joyous message that inspired him; it was heard by a few dozen, perhaps a few hundred men and women, out of a countless population (estimated at 200,000). Persecution began (organized by a hostile Jewish population), and the Apostle's work was violently interrupted; there he was, a fugitive once again (see Acts 17:1-8). What was left of his hastily founded community? He was uneasy.

From Athens he had sent Timothy and Silas, his fellow workers, to gain information about this community now shaken by persecution. They rejoined him in Corinth, and their report was a good one. The community, which one would have thought to be so weak, was in fact growing; it was animated by an unexpected spirit of hope, faith, and love. Paul was surprised, even after fifteen years of missionary work, and gave utterance to his joy: the Gospel is God's work in the midst of a pagan world! This was the Apostle's constantly repeated experience.

In this first Letter of Paul, then, we will not look for a clear plan or lengthy trains of thought; what abound are marks of thoughtfulness and moving memories. The Letter is first of all a message of encouragement, gratitude, and affection. It is still a refreshing testimony to the birth of a community that is animated by the Gospel amid the turmoil of a great city.

Certainly, there are shadows. In a first preaching, Paul could not explain all aspects of the Christian message. And he regarded it as necessary to clarify some points that remained questionable or misunderstood.

One point especially holds his attention, for it preoccupies the new believers—the question of the parousia or Second Coming of Christ. Every one of the five chapters of the Letter ends with a reference to the Second Coming (1:9-10; 2:19-20; 3:13; 4:13-18; 5:23-24), with chapter 4 according it major consideration. Hence, the Second Coming of Christ may be regarded in some respect as the Letter's principal theme.

Among the Thessalonians, the Second Coming is thought to be imminent. Yet some believers have already died. Will they be absent from God's great convocation?

Paul's thought from this first writing is already firm. It is completely oriented toward the end of history when the dead and the living will be reunited with the risen Jesus, the universal victor, so as to live with him for eternity. The Christian hope, founded on the great event of Easter morning, will not prove deceptive. All believers will participate in Christ's triumph over evil and death.

In the Apostle's eyes, the Christian life is an active waiting for the Lord: a waiting that builds up the Church in love; a waiting that makes Christians turn their eyes to heaven, even while fully involving believers, along with all other human beings, in the realities of this world, such as marriage and work; finally, a waiting that ceaselessly strengthens fidelity to and union with the Lord. Why? Because heaven will be simply the marvelous flowering of the friendship entered into here below; we will be with the Lord forever.

Another characteristic of the Letter is Paul's affirmation of the divinity of Christ. First he links together Christ and God the Father as the common source of divine blessings and as the object of prayer (1:1; 3:11). Then he identifies Christ as "the Lord" in the Old Testament phrase "Day of the Lord" (5:2).

The First Letter to the Thessalonians may be divided as follows:

I: *Salutation (1:1)*
II: *Evangelization Is the Work of the Spirit (1:2—3:13)*
III: *God Wills Your Sanctification (4:1—5:11)*
IV: *Building Up the Community (5:12-22)*
V: *Conclusion (5:23-28)*

I: SALUTATION

1 **Address and Greeting.** [1] Paul, Silvanus, * and Timothy to the Church of Thessalonians in God the Father and the Lord Jesus Christ: grace to you and peace.

II: EVANGELIZATION IS THE WORK OF THE SPIRIT*

A Model for All Believers.* [2] We always give thanks to God for all of you and mention you in our prayers. [3] We constantly remember before our God and Father your work of faith and your labor of love and your perseverance in hope * in our Lord Jesus Christ.

[4] Brethren, beloved by God, we know that he has chosen you, [5] because our gospel * came to you not merely in words alone but also in power and in the Holy Spirit and with profound conviction. And you are fully aware what sort of people we proved to be when we were among you for your sake.

[6] And you in turn became imitators * of us and of the Lord, for despite great suffering you received the word with joy in the Holy Spirit, [7] so that you became a model for all the believers in Macedonia and Achaia. *

[8] Not only has the word of the Lord rung forth from you in Macedonia and Achaia, but also your faith in God has become known everywhere. Therefore, we do not have the need to speak about it. [9] For the people themselves report what kind of reception we had from you, and how you turned to God from idols to serve the living and true God [10] and await his Son from heaven whom he raised from the dead—Jesus, who will deliver us from the wrath that is to come.

2 **Paul's Loving Treatment of the Thessalonians.*** [1] You yourselves are well aware, brethren, that our visit to you has not been in vain. [2] Although we had suffered and been shamefully mistreated at Philippi, as you surely recall, God gave us the courage to declare the gospel of God to you despite great opposition.

[3] The exhortation we impart does not spring from deceit or impure motives or trickery. [4] God has judged us worthy to be entrusted with the gospel. Therefore, when we speak, our intention is not to please human beings but to please God who tests our hearts.

⁵ As you are also aware, and as God is our witness, we have never resorted to flattering words or to your sense of greed. ⁶ Neither did we seek praise from human beings, whether from you or from others.

⁷ As apostles of Christ, we could have imposed our will on you, * yet we were as gentle in our treatment of you as a mother nursing and caring for her own children. ⁸ Our affection for you was so great that we were determined to share with you not only the gospel of God but also our very lives, because you had become so dear to us.

⁹ You surely remember, brethren, our toil and drudgery as we worked night and day so that we would not be a burden to anyone while we proclaimed the gospel of God to you. ¹⁰ You are witnesses, as is God, that our treatment of you who believed has been devout, upright, and blameless.

¹¹ As you are well aware, we treated each one of you as a father treats his children, ¹² urging and encouraging you and pleading with you to lead lives worthy of God who calls you into his kingdom and glory.

The Word of God Is at Work.* ¹³ We also unceasingly give thanks to God because, when we handed on the word of God to you, you accepted it not as a human word but as what it truly is, the word of God, which is at work in you who believe. ¹⁴ Indeed, brethren, you have become imitators of the Churches of God that are in Judea in Christ Jesus. For you have suffered the same treatment from your own countrymen as they did from the Jews, ¹⁵ who killed both the Lord Jesus and the Prophets and also persecuted us.

They displease God and have become enemies of the entire human race ¹⁶ by trying to prevent us from speaking to the Gentiles so that they may be saved. In this way, they constantly reach the full measure of their sins. The wrath of God has begun to overtake them at last.

The Glory and Joy of the Apostles.* ¹⁷ Brethren, when we were separated from you for a brief time—in body but not in heart—we had an intense longing to see you again face to face. [18] Therefore, we were determined to come to visit you—I, Paul, on more than one occasion—but Satan thwarted us. * [19] For what is our hope or our joy or our crown of honor in the presence of our Lord Jesus upon his return? Is it not you yourselves? [20] You truly are our glory and our joy. *

3 **Standing Firm in the Lord.** [1] * Therefore, when we * could not stand it any longer, we decided to remain alone in Athens. [2] We sent Timothy, our brother and coworker for God * in the gospel of Christ, to confirm and encourage you in your faith, [3] so that no one might be troubled by these hardships.

You yourselves realize that we were destined to endure such afflictions. [4] In fact, when we were with you, we warned you beforehand that we could suffer persecution, and that is what has now come to pass, as you are well aware. [5] For this reason, when I could bear it no longer, I sent to learn of your faith, lest the tempter might have put you to the test and all our labor might have been for naught.

[6] But Timothy has just now returned to us from you and brought us the joyful news of your faith and love. He tells us that you always speak fondly of us and long to see us just as much as we long to see you. * [7] For this reason, brethren, in the midst of our distress and hardship we have been reassured by your faith. [8] For now we live inasmuch as you stand firm in the Lord.

Plea for Growth in Holiness. [9] How can we possibly give thanks to God for all the joy we feel in the presence of our God because of you? [10] We pray fervently day and night that we will be allowed to see you face to face once again and complete whatever may be lacking in your faith.

[11] May our God and Father himself and our Lord Jesus prepare the way to you. [12] May the Lord * cause your love to increase and overflow for one another and for everyone

else, just as our love does for you. [13] May he so strengthen your hearts in holiness that you may stand blameless before our God and Father at the coming of our Lord Jesus with all his holy ones. * [Amen.]

III: GOD WILLS YOUR SANCTIFICATION*

4 Respect for the Body.* [1] Finally, brethren, you learned from us how you ought to live so that you may be pleasing to God—and as you are indeed doing. Now we ask and exhort you in the Lord Jesus to do so even more. [2] For you know what instructions we gave you by the authority of the Lord Jesus.

[3] It is the will of God that you should lead a life of sanctity. You must refrain from sexual immorality. [4] Each of you must learn to acquire a wife from pure and honorable motives, [5] not to gratify passion * like the Gentiles who do not know God. [6] No one is ever to wrong or take advantage of a brother in this regard.

As we have previously instructed you and solemnly warned you, the Lord is the avenger in all this. [7] For God has called us to holiness, not to impurity. [8] Therefore, anyone who rejects these instructions * rejects not human authority but the God who also gives his Holy Spirit to you.

An Honorable Life.* [9] In respect to brotherly love, there is no necessity to write to you about that, for you yourselves have been taught by God to love one another. [10] And indeed you have shown your love to all the brethren throughout Macedonia. However, we urge you, brethren, to make even greater progress in this regard.

[11] Strive to live quietly, to attend to your own affairs, and to work with your hands, as we instructed you. * [12] In this way, you will earn the respect of outsiders and not have to be dependent on anyone.

The Dead and the Living at the Lord's Coming.* [13] We do not wish you to be uncertain, brethren, about those who have fallen asleep. * You should not grieve as do those who have no hope. ¹⁴ For we believe that Jesus died and rose again, and so too do we believe that God will bring forth with Jesus those who have fallen asleep in him.

¹⁵ Indeed, we can assure you, on the word of the Lord himself, that we who are still alive at the coming of the Lord will not have any advantage over those who have fallen asleep. * ¹⁶ When the command is given, at the sound of the archangel's voice and the call of God's trumpet, the Lord himself will descend from heaven, and those who have died in Christ will be the first to rise.

¹⁷ Then those of us who are still alive and are left will be caught up * together with them on clouds in the air to meet the Lord. And so, we will be with the Lord forever. ¹⁸ Therefore, comfort one another * with these words.

5 **The Christian Life Is One Long Vigil.** * ¹ In regard to specific dates and times, * brethren, it is not necessary to write you. ² For you yourselves are fully aware that the Day of the Lord * will come like a thief in the night. ³ When people are saying, "Everything is peaceful and secure," instant destruction * will overwhelm them, in the manner that labor pains suddenly come upon a pregnant woman, and there will be no means of escape.

⁴ However, brethren, you do not live in darkness, and therefore that Day will not catch you unawares like a thief. ⁵ For all of you are children of the light * and children of the day. We do not belong to the night or to the darkness. ⁶ So we must not fall asleep as the others do, but we must stay alert and sober.

⁷ Those who sleep do so at night, and those who get drunk do so at night. ⁸ But since we belong to the day, let us be sober, arming ourselves with faith and love as our breastplate and the hope of salvation as our helmet. * ⁹ * For God has not destined us to suffer wrath, but to achieve salvation through our Lord Jesus Christ. ¹⁰ He died for us so that, whether we are awake or asleep, we may live together with him. ¹¹ Therefore, encourage

one another and strengthen one another, as indeed you
are doing.

IV: BUILDING UP THE COMMUNITY*

Show Respect for Leaders. [12] * Brethren, we beg you to
respect those whose duty it is to labor among you as your
leaders in the Lord and to admonish you. [13] Show the
highest esteem for them in love because of their work. Be
at peace with one another.

[14] * We also exhort you, brethren, to admonish those
who are idle, encourage those who are afraid, support
those who are weak, and be patient with everybody.
[15] Make sure that no one pays back evil for evil. Rather,
always aim to achieve what is best for each other and for
everyone.

[16] * Rejoice always; [17] pray continually; [18] give thanks in
all circumstances; for this is the will of God for you in
Christ Jesus.

Do Not Extinguish the Spirit. * [19] Do not quench the Spirit.
[20] Do not despise prophecies. * [21] Test everything, and
hold fast to what is good. [22] Avoid every form of evil.

V: CONCLUSION*

Final Prayer. [23] May the God of peace himself grant you
the gift of perfect sanctity, and may you—spirit and soul
and body*—be preserved blameless for the coming of
our Lord Jesus Christ. [24] The one who calls you is faithful, and he will accomplish this.

Final Greeting. [25] Pray for us, brethren. [26] Greet all the
brethren with a holy kiss. [27] I charge you before the Lord
to have this letter read to all the brethren.

[28] The grace of our Lord Jesus Christ be with you.

THE SECOND LETTER TO THE THESSALONIANS

CHRISTIAN REALISM

Paul's First Letter to the Thessalonians was so clear and encouraging that it sufficed to reassure the community as a whole. However, persecution continued to afflict the new believers. Naturally, then, the thought arose in the minds of some of them: was this the necessary and immediate prelude to the end of time? Indeed, whatever the reason, the expectation of the Lord was passing through a serious crisis. Some, belonging perhaps to the lazy folk to whom Paul has alluded earlier (1 Thes 4:11; 5:14), claimed that the Day of the Lord was imminent. They caused a kind of panic or feverish expectation.

At the same time, they no longer engaged in work but roamed around as beggars and thus became an embarrassment to the community (2 Thes 3:6-15). They even seem to have circulated spurious letters for the purpose of authenticating their ideas, or at least Paul thinks that they did (2 Thes 2:2), and he attaches his genuine signature to the present Letter (2 Thes 3:17).

To counter their teaching and cut short any type of undisciplined straying, Paul dictated this Second Letter to the Thessalonians. He seems to have written it from Corinth in the year A.D. 51. He first had to correct the doctrinal error of those who were convinced of the imminence of the Second Coming (2 Thes 2:1-12), then the practical error to which these same believers were led: they were overly anxious to rid themselves of earthly things and to neglect their duties (2 Thes 2:13—3:15).

The Apostle shows that it is not by abandoning the world but by courageously facing up to it that Christians make their way to the Lord and are a sign to those who do not share their faith. They must put aside every type of bizarre speculation and evasion and instead pitch in to build the future in the journey toward God.

This Letter remains a lesson in realism for Christians at the very moment when the Church found herself buffeted by the crisis of a civilization, and it offers us a dramatic vision of human history.

531

Some scholars have questioned Paul's authorship of the Letter because of close similarities in subject matter and phrasing. Yet who but Paul could sound more like himself!

Others see contradictory ecclesiologies (teachings about the end time) in the two Letters. They claim the First Letter speaks of an imminent return of Christ while the Second indicates that before Christ comes there are certain events that must take place.

However, the First Letter does not rule out intervening events but merely mentions the unexpected character of the Second Coming. The intervening events mentioned in Second Thessalonians can fit nicely into the previous teaching, and at the same time they rebut the new misunderstanding at Thessalonica that the Day of the Lord had already come.

The Second Letter to the Thessalonians may be divided as follows:

I: Salutation (1:1-2)
II: Perseverance in Faith (1:3-12)
III: The Day of the Lord (2:1-12)
IV: Never Weary of Doing Good (2:13—3:15)
V: Conclusion (3:16-18)

I: SALUTATION*

1 **Address and Greeting.** [1] Paul, Silvanus, and Timothy to the Church of Thessalonians in God our Father and the Lord Jesus Christ: [2] Grace to you and peace from God our Father and the Lord Jesus Christ.

II: PERSEVERANCE IN FAITH*

A Word of Praise. [3] Brethren, we must always give thanks to God for you, and it is only right that we do so. For your faith grows ever more, and the love that all of you have for one another continues to increase. [4] Therefore, we boast incessantly of you to the Churches of God for your steadfastness and faith despite all the persecutions and tribulations that you have had to endure.

Judgment and the Coming of the Lord. [5] All this is proof of God's just judgment, and it shows that you are worthy of the kingdom of God, for the sake of which you are suffering. [6] It is only just that God will repay with suffering those who make you suffer [7] and grant relief to you who are suffering, and to us as well. This will take place when the Lord Jesus is revealed from heaven with his mighty angels.

[8] He will come in blazing fire to inflict punishment on those who do not know God and do not obey the gospel of our Lord Jesus. [9] They will suffer the penalty of eternal destruction, excluded from the presence of the Lord and from the majesty of his power [10] on that Day when he comes to be glorified by his holy ones and to be adored by all believers, among whom you will be present since you believed the testimony we offered to you.

Prayer for the Community. [11] Therefore, we always pray for you, asking that our God will make you worthy of his call and by his power bring to fulfillment every good resolve and every work of faith. [12] In this way, the name of our Lord Jesus may be glorified in you, and you in him, according to the grace of our God and Lord Jesus Christ.*

III: THE DAY OF THE LORD*

2 Has the Day of the Lord Already Come?* [1] As to the coming of our Lord Jesus Christ and our being gathered to him, we beg you, brethren: [2] do not become too easily thrown into confusion or alarmed, either by something spiritual or by a statement or by a letter claiming to come from us, alleging that the Day of the Lord is already here. * [3] Let no one deceive you in any way.

The Adversary and the Obstacle.* That Day cannot come * before the final rebellion occurs and the lawless one is revealed, the son of destruction. [4] He is the adversary who sets himself in opposition to, and exalts himself above, every so-called god or object of worship, and who even seats himself in the temple of God, declaring himself to be God.

⁵ Do you not remember that I told you these things when I was still with you? ⁶ And you also know what is now restraining him, * so that he may not be revealed before his time comes. ⁷ For the mystery of lawlessness is already at work, but the one who restrains it will continue to do so until he is removed.

The Two Comings.* ⁸ Then the lawless one will be revealed, and the Lord Jesus will slay him by the breath of his mouth and destroy him by the splendor of his coming.

⁹ His coming will be the work of Satan made manifest in all power and signs and wonders of falsehood, ¹⁰ and in every wicked deception designed for those who are perishing because they refused to accept the love of the truth * and thereby gain salvation.

¹¹ For this reason, God imposes on them a powerful delusion. They believe what is false, ¹² so that all who have not believed the truth but instead have taken pleasure in wickedness will be condemned.

IV: NEVER WEARY OF DOING GOOD*

Call To Remain Steadfast. ¹³ * However, we must always give thanks to God for you, brethren beloved by the Lord, because God chose you from the beginning to be saved through sanctification by the Spirit and through belief in the truth. * ¹⁴ It was for this purpose that he called you through our gospel so that you might come to share in the glory of our Lord Jesus Christ.

¹⁵ Therefore, stand firm, brethren, and hold fast to the traditions * that you have been taught, whether by word of mouth or by a letter of ours. ¹⁶ And may our Lord Jesus Christ himself and God our Father, who loved us and through his grace gave us unending encouragement and a sure hope, * ¹⁷ comfort your hearts and strengthen you in every good deed and word.

3 **Request for Prayers.** ¹ Finally, brethren, pray for us, so that the word of the Lord may spread rapidly and be glorified, as it was with you. ² Pray too that we may be rescued from wicked and evil people, for not all have faith.

³ However, the Lord is faithful. He will strengthen you and protect you from the evil one. ⁴ And we are confident in the Lord that you are doing and will continue to do all that we direct you to do. ⁵ May the Lord guide your hearts to the love of God and the steadfastness of Christ.

Christian Value of Work.* ⁶ In the name of our Lord Jesus Christ, brethren, we command you to keep your distance from any of the brethren who are living an idle existence and who disregard the tradition you received from us. ⁷ For you yourselves know how you should follow our example. We were not idle when we were with you. ⁸ We did not ever accept food from anyone, but with toil and drudgery we worked night and day so that we would not burden any of you. ⁹ We did so, not because we have no right to accept such help, but to present ourselves as a model for you to imitate.

¹⁰ In fact, even when we were with you, we charged that anyone who was unwilling to work should not eat. ¹¹ Now we have been told that some among you are living a life of idleness, not working but acting as busy-bodies. ¹² We command and urge such people in the name of the Lord Jesus Christ to do their work quietly and earn their own living.

¹³ Brethren, never grow weary of doing what is right. ¹⁴ If anyone refuses to obey our instructions in this letter, take note of him and have nothing to do with him so that he may be put to shame. ¹⁵ However, do not treat him as an enemy, but admonish him as a brother.

V: CONCLUSION*

Final Prayer. ¹⁶ May the Lord of peace himself give you peace at all times and in every way. The Lord be with all of you.

Final Blessing. ¹⁷ I, Paul, write this greeting in my own hand. It is the distinguishing mark of every letter of mine. ¹⁸ The grace of our Lord Jesus Christ be with you all.

THE FIRST LETTER TO TIMOTHY
GUIDELINES FOR PASTORS OF THE CHURCH

The Letters to Timothy and Titus form a group apart in the literature attributed to Paul. They are addressed not to communities but to individuals, Timothy and Titus, that is, men who were responsible for the government, instruction, and behavior of communities. Because the Letters give guidelines for pastors of the Church, they are called the Pastoral Letters.

A very ancient tradition has placed these Letters among those of Paul; today, however, there are doubts about this attribution, doubts stronger than in the case of the Letters to the Colossians and the Ephesians. In these Pastoral Letters we do not see the vehemence of the Letter to the Galatians or the sensitivity of those to the Corinthians. The tone is weightier, the style more opaque, the vocabulary very different.

Certainly, numerous ideas dear to Paul are presented in their pages, but they lack much of the mystical Pauline aspect. The newness of the faith appears less dazzling. They place a great deal of emphasis on piety, good conduct, and an honorable life, while listing lengthy moral recommendations. The life of communities is also different. We no longer find the previous animation stemming from countless charisms and ministries, such as prophecies; leaders appear to be invested with a regular and stable office, and the Letters speak primarily to them. Doctrine itself is no longer affirmed as such, in opposition to Judaism or paganism and in its fresh and vibrant newness. There is a tradition to maintain and to renew, a teaching to conserve and to deepen.

We thus have the image of a Church seeking to organize her life and functions. A very great crisis threatens her, possibly very much like the Church we encountered at Colossae. The new Christian doctrine is set forth in answer to a heretical movement that mixes together Jewish ideas and Eastern speculations. This movement was important at the end of the first century and the beginning of the second. In the face of these new currents, Christianity had to make precise its teaching and its identity.

Not a few critics are therefore inclined to date the Pastoral Letters toward the end of the first century. But without reaching that conclusion, regarding which various difficulties can be raised, it would be enough to imagine a Paul advanced in years, who makes use of secretaries and is writing in rather difficult practical circumstances. Since he is addressing individuals, it is not surprising that he no longer has the same enthusiasm as when he was writing to entire communities. On the other hand, the problems are new, and so too, therefore, are the answers.

It is of little importance, however, whether these Letters were from Paul himself or from the Pauline tradition. The directions they give are precious because of their reflections on fidelity, on Christian behavior, on the effort to live continually in faith, and on organizing the responsibilities and relationships in the Church. They provide us with important concerns for the thought and life of communities. We can, however, assign them to the last period of Paul's life, the years to which the Book of Acts makes no reference.

After the Apostle was set free in A.D. 63/64, there is reason to believe that he undertook a Fourth Missionary Journey (not recorded in Acts 28). This belief is based on (1) Paul's expressed intention to travel to Spain (see Rom 15:24, 28); (2) the implication by the early Church historian Eusebius that Paul was released after his first Roman imprisonment; and (3) early attestations by Clement of Rome and the Canon of Muratori that he preached the Gospel in Spain. The places Paul may have visited are indicated by statements of intent to do so in his earlier Letters and by their mention in the Pastoral Letters.

After this last visit, Paul left Titus in Crete and Timothy in Ephesus. This was the period that ended with a new arrest of Paul: he would be condemned to death and executed on the Via Ostiensis about the year A.D. 67.

Timothy was Paul's chief fellow worker; he was often with Paul when the latter wrote his Letters, so much so that more than one of them are described as written by Paul and Timothy. The Book of Acts (16:1-2) tells us of the calling of a man who was fervent and faithful, though in poor health (1 Tim 5:23). From that point on he was a traveling companion of Paul (see Acts 17:14-15; 18:5; 20:4; 2 Cor 1:19) and carried out rather difficult missions for him in Macedonia (see Acts 19:22) and in the tumultuous community of Corinth (see 1 Cor 4:17; 16:10).

If the Second Letter to Timothy was written in Rome, almost on the eve of Paul's martyrdom, the first may have been written some time earlier, around A.D. 64 or 65, after a mission in Macedonia. Paul, to whom God had entrusted the care of the Churches among the pagans, insists, in the First Letter, that Timothy exercise, firmly and courageously, the office he received from Christ in the rite of the laying on of hands, which entails the proclamation of the truth, the organization of worship, and the guidance of the People of God and their varied groups. This last is the starting point for a theological and spiritual reflection on ministry in the Church.

The Letter to Timothy may be divided as follows:

I: SALUTATION*

1 Address. [1] Paul, an apostle of Christ Jesus by command of God our Savior* and Christ Jesus our hope, [2] to Timothy, my loyal child in the faith: grace, mercy, and peace to you from God the Father and Christ Jesus our Lord.

II: TIMOTHY, CHAMPION OF THE TRUTH*

On Holding Fast to Sound Doctrine. [3] When I was setting out for Macedonia, * I urged you to stay on in Ephesus to instruct certain people that they are not to teach erroneous doctrines [4] and not to concern themselves with myths and endless genealogies. These promote controversies and do not produce godly edification in faith.

[5] The aim of this instruction is love that derives from a pure heart, a good conscience, and a sincere faith. [6] Some people have departed from these and turned to empty speculation, [7] desiring to be teachers of the Law; but they understand neither the words they are using nor the matters about which they make such confident assertions.

Purpose of the Law. [8] We are well aware that the Law is good, provided that one uses it properly, [9] recognizing that laws are not designed for the upright. They are for the lawless and insubordinate, for the godless and sinful, for the unholy and irreligious; they are for those who slay their fathers and mothers, for murderers, [10] for those who are fornicators, sodomites, * slave traders, liars, perjurers, and for whatever else is contrary to the sound teaching [11] that conforms to the glorious gospel of the blessed God, which has been entrusted to me.

Called To Preach the Gospel. [12] I am grateful to Christ Jesus our Lord who has given me strength, because he judged me trustworthy and appointed me to his service, [13] even though in the past I was a blasphemer, a persecutor, and an insolent man. However, I have been treated with mercy because I had acted out of ignorance and unbelief. [14] As a result, the grace of our Lord overflowed for me with the faith and the love that are in Christ Jesus.

[15] This saying can be trusted and merits complete acceptance: * Christ Jesus came into the world to save sinners. I myself am the greatest of these. [16] But for that very reason I was treated mercifully, so that in me Jesus Christ might exhibit his inexhaustible patience, making me an example for those who would come to believe in him for eternal life. [17] To the King of the ages, immortal, invisible, the only God, * be honor and glory forever and ever. Amen.

Never Falsify the Gospel. [18] To you, Timothy, my child, I am giving these instructions in accordance with those prophecies once made about you, * so that by following them you may fight the good fight [19] with faith and a good conscience. Some people have spurned their conscience and destroyed their faith. [20] Among them are Hymenaeus * and Alexander whom I have handed over to Satan so that they may learn not to blaspheme.

III: QUALITIES OF PUBLIC WORSHIP AND CHURCH LEADERS*

2 **Prayer for Those in Authority.** * [1] I urge then, first of all, that supplications, prayers, intercessions, and thanksgivings be offered for everyone, [2] for kings and for all those who hold positions of authority, so that we may be able to lead a tranquil and quiet life with all possible devotion and dignity. [3] To do so is right and acceptable to God our Savior, [4] who desires everyone to be saved and to come to full knowledge of the truth.

[5] * For there is one God,
    and there is one mediator between God and man,
    Christ Jesus, himself a man,
[6]   who gave himself as a ransom for all.

This was the testimony he offered at the appointed time. [7] And I was made a herald and an apostle of it (I am telling the truth; I am not lying), a teacher of the Gentiles in faith and truth.

Positions at Public Worship.* [8] I desire, then, that in every place the men should pray, lifting up their hands reverently in prayer without anger or argument. [9] I also ask that the women should dress themselves modestly and decently in suitable clothing. They should be adorned not with braided hair or with gold or pearls or expensive clothes,* [10] but with good works, as is fitting for women who profess their reverence for God.

[11] Women are to learn in silence with complete submission. [12] I do not allow a woman to teach or to hold authority over a man. She should keep silent. [13] For Adam was formed first, and Eve afterward. [14] Furthermore, Adam was not deceived; it was the woman who was deceived and fell into sin. [15] However, women will be saved through the bearing of children, provided that they continue to persevere in faith, love, and holiness, marked by modesty.

3* Qualifications of Bishops. [1] This saying can be trusted: Whoever wants to be a bishop desires a noble task. [2] Therefore, a bishop must be above reproach, the husband of only one wife, temperate, self-controlled, respectable, hospitable, and a good teacher. [3] He must not be a drunkard, not violent but gentle, not prone to quarreling, not greedy.

[4] He must manage his own household well and ensure that his children are submissive and respectful in every way. [5] For if someone does not know how to manage his own family, how can he take care of the Church of God? [6] He should not be a recent convert so that he will not become conceited and incur the same condemnation as the devil. [7] He must also enjoy a good reputation among outsiders so that he may not fall into disgrace and into the devil's snare.

Qualifications of Deacons. [8] Similarly, deacons must exhibit a sense of dignity, not indulging in double-talk or excessive consumption of wine, and not being greedy. [9] They must hold fast to the mystery of the faith with a clear conscience. [10] Let them first be tested. They can be appointed as deacons only if they are beyond reproach.

[11] Women * must likewise exhibit a sense of dignity and not be given to spreading slander. They must be temperate and faithful in all things.

[12] Deacons must have only one wife and be able to manage their children and their own households. [13] Those deacons whose work is exemplary will achieve a high standing and gain great assurance in their faith in Christ Jesus.

Greatness of the Divine Majesty. [14] While I am hoping to come to you soon, I am writing to you about these matters [15] so that if I am delayed, you will know how to regulate your conduct in God's household—that is, in the Church of the living God, the pillar and bulwark of the truth. [16] Without any doubt, the mystery of our religion is great:

> He was made visible in the flesh,
> vindicated by the Spirit,*
> seen by angels,
> proclaimed to the Gentiles,
> believed in throughout the world,
> taken up in glory.

IV: GENERAL REGULATIONS*

4 **False Asceticism.** [1] The Spirit clearly says that during the last times some will abandon the faith. They will run after deceitful spirits and demonic doctrines, [2] through the hypocrisy of liars whose consciences have been branded as with a burning iron. [3] They forbid marriage and require abstinence from foods * that God created to be accepted with thanksgiving by those who believe and who know the truth. [4] For everything created by God is good, and nothing is to be rejected, provided that it is received with thanksgiving, [5] for it is made holy by the word of God and by prayer.*

The Benefits of Godliness. [6] If you offer these instructions to the brethren, you will prove to be a good servant of Christ Jesus, nourished on the truths of the faith and of the good teaching that you have followed. [7] Have nothing to do with profane myths and old wives' tales; rather, train yourself in godliness.

[8] While physical training has some value, the benefits of godliness are unlimited, since it holds out promise not only for this life but also for the life to come. [9] This saying can be trusted and merits complete acceptance. [10] For this is why we toil and struggle, because we have placed our hope in the living God, who is the Savior of all, especially of all those who believe.

Pastoral Duties. [11] These are the things you must insist upon in your teaching. [12] Let no one regard you with contempt because of your youth, but serve as an example to the believers in your speech and conduct, in your love, your faith, and your purity.

[13] Until I arrive, devote yourself to reading, * to exhortation, and to teaching. [14] Do not neglect the gift that was bestowed upon you when, as a result of prophecy, the elders laid their hands on you. *

[15] Meditate on these things and put them into practice so that your progress may be evident to everyone. [16] Be conscientious about your life and your teaching. Persevere in both of these tasks, for by doing so you will save both yourself and your listeners.

V: SPECIFIC REGULATIONS FOR VARIOUS GROUPS*

5 **Different Age Groups.** * [1] Never speak harshly to an older man; rather, appeal to him as if he were your father. Treat younger men as brothers, [2] older women as mothers, and younger women as sisters, with the greatest purity.

Widows. * [3] Give proper consideration to those widows who are truly in need. [4] If a widow has children or grandchildren, these should learn first of all to carry out their

religious duty to their own family and repay their debt to
their parents, for this is pleasing in the eyes of God.

[5] However, a widow who is truly in need and is alone in
the world places all her trust in God and never ceases her
prayers and supplications night and day. [6] But the widow
who is interested solely in pleasure is dead even while she
lives.

[7] Insist upon these things, so that people may be
beyond reproach. [8] And whoever does not provide for relatives, especially for those who are living with him, has
disowned the faith and is worse than an unbeliever.

[9] A woman should not be enrolled as a widow if she is
not at least sixty years old. In addition, she must have
been married only once, [10] and have a reputation for good
works by bringing up her children, offering hospitality to
strangers, washing the feet of the saints, * helping those in
distress, and being active in all kinds of good work.

[11] However, refuse to enroll younger widows, for when
their passions distract them from the service of Christ,
they will want to marry again [12] and will incur condemnation for having broken their original vow. [13] In addition,
they fall into the habit of being idle, as they go around
from house to house, and also become gossips and busy-
bodies, saying things that would better be left unsaid.

[14] Therefore, I think younger widows should marry
again, bear children, and manage their households, so
as not to give our enemies any occasion to revile us.
[15] Indeed, some have already turned away to follow Satan.

[16] If any woman believer has relatives who are widows,
she must assist them herself. The Church should be free
of such burdens and consequently able to assist those
who are widows in the true sense.

Presbyters. * [17] Presbyters who do their duty well should
be considered deserving of a double honor, * especially
those who labor at preaching and teaching. [18] For Scripture
says, "You shall not muzzle an ox while it is treading out the
grain," and "A worker deserves his wages."*

[19] Never accept any accusation brought against a presbyter except on the evidence of two or three witnesses. [20] As for those who persist in sin, rebuke them publicly, so that the others may also be afraid.

[21] In the presence of God and Christ Jesus and the chosen angels, * I charge you to follow these rules impartially and without being influenced by any favoritism. [22] Do not lay hands on others too hastily or you may find yourself regarded as an accomplice in the sins of others. Keep yourself pure.

[23] Stop drinking nothing but water. Take a little wine for the sake of your stomach and your frequent ailments.

[24] The sins of some people are so flagrant that they are publicly known before judgment, while the sins of others will only become known later on. [25] In the same manner, good works are often easily recognized, but even if they are not, they cannot remain hidden forever.

6 Slaves.* [1] All those who are under the yoke of slavery must regard their masters as worthy of complete respect, so that the name of God and our teaching may not be brought into disrepute. [2] Those whose masters are believers must not despise them because they are brethren. On the contrary, they should serve them more, since those who receive the benefits of their services are believers and beloved brethren.

VI: FINAL CHARGE*

False Teaching about Wealth. These are the things you should teach and recommend. [3] Whoever teaches something different and does not agree with the wholesome instruction of our Lord Jesus Christ and with the godly teaching [4] is a conceited person who understands nothing and who has an unhealthy enthusiasm to engage in arguments and to dispute the meaning of words. From these come envy, dissension, slander, base suspicions, [5] and unending disputes among people whose minds are corrupted and who are deprived of truth, supposing that godliness is a means of gain.

[6] Godliness produces great gain, but only to those who are content. [7] For we brought nothing into this world, and we can take nothing out. [8] If we have food and clothing, let us be content with these.

[9] However, those who want riches fall into temptations and are trapped into many senseless and harmful desires that plunge them into ruin and destruction. [10] The love of money is the root of all evils, and in their desire for it some have wandered away from the faith and pierced themselves with many serious wounds. *

Fight the Good Fight. [11] But as for you, man of God, * you must shun all this. Rather, pursue righteousness, godliness, faith, love, fortitude, and gentleness. [12] Fight the good fight of faith. Take hold of the eternal life to which you were called when you made your noble confession * of faith in the presence of many witnesses.

[13] In the sight of God, who gave life to all things, and before Jesus Christ, who himself made that noble confession of faith in his testimony before Pontius Pilate, I charge you [14] to obey the commands of God without fault or failure until the appearance of our Lord Jesus Christ, [15] which he will make manifest at the proper time—he who is the blessed and only ruler of all, the King of kings and the Lord of lords. [16] He alone is immortal and dwells in unapproachable light. No one has seen him or is able to do so. To him be honor and everlasting power. Amen.

Right Use of Riches.* [17] Instruct those who are rich in this world's goods that they should not be proud, nor should they trust in the uncertainty of riches but rather in God who richly provides us with everything we need for our enjoyment. [18] Tell them to do good and to be rich in good works, to be generous in giving and ready to share. [19] In this way, they will acquire the treasure of a good foundation for the future so that they will be able to grasp the life that is true life.

VII: CONCLUSION*

Admonition to Timothy. [20] My brother Timothy, guard carefully what has been entrusted to you.* Avoid the profane chatter and the contradictions of what is wrongly considered to be knowledge. [21] By professing it some people have strayed far from the faith.

Farewell. Grace be with all of you.*

THE SECOND LETTER TO TIMOTHY

THE GOOD FIGHT

This document presents itself as a last testament. Is it a letter of Paul? We accept it as such based on the reasons given in the Introduction to the First Letter to Timothy.

The Apostle is again a prisoner in Rome in A.D. 67. Conditions in prison are harsh, quite different from those of his previous imprisonment, when he preached freely in the house of his internment (see Acts 28:16). Now he languishes in a cold dungeon and wears the chains of a common criminal.

He feels terribly alone. No one has defended him in court, and only Luke is with him. His days are numbered, and he is preparing for the supreme sacrifice.

Timothy was at Ephesus when Paul sent his First Letter to him (1 Tim 1:3), and he is still there at the writing of this Second Letter. Paul is disturbed by what is going on in the developing communities: every new and alien idea is finding supporters; everyone who makes claims or calls himself enlightened is successful, to the detriment of the Gospel, of unity, and of the Church's mission.

The Apostle is also worried about the welfare of the Churches during this time of persecution under Nero. He sees it as a time to strengthen the internal character of the Church, to seek out and confirm new leaders, to clarify the faith of the developing communities, and to remain rooted in the tradition.

Paul has had experience of fighting for Jesus, and he urges his correspondent to endure the struggle with the same courage. He calls for fidelity and boldness: fidelity to the Gospel that Christ has entrusted to his Church; boldness in trying to have people live in accordance with the Gospel.

Aware that Timothy is fully versed in the apostolic teaching, Paul does not instruct him further on doctrine. He makes allusion to several important doctrines, including salvation by God's grace, the person of Christ, and perseverance. Finally, he lays special stress on the divine inspiration of Sacred Scripture.

This is a letter of farewell, a testament, the testimony of a man who regrets nothing. Despite his abandonment, the misunderstandings, the torments, and his imminent execution, thanksgiving flows from his heart. He has trusted only in the Christ who rose from the dead, and he has not been deceived.

Before dying, however, Paul wants to see his "beloved child," Timothy, once again and at least to strengthen him in his mission. He urges Timothy to come before winter (2 Tim 4:21) and to bring the warm cloak Paul left at Troas. Timothy is also to bring the Apostle's scrolls and parchments, possibly to enable Paul to do some further reading and writing (2 Tim 4:13).

The Second Letter to Timothy may be divided as follows:

I: SALUTATION*

1 **Address.** [1] Paul, an apostle of Christ Jesus by the will of God, whose promise of life is fulfilled in Christ Jesus, [2] to Timothy, my beloved child: grace, mercy, and peace from God the Father and Christ Jesus our Lord.

Thanksgiving and Prayer. [3] I am grateful to God—whom I worship with a clean conscience as did my ancestors—when I remember you constantly in my prayers night and day. [4] As I recall your tears, * I long to see you again so that my joy may be complete. [5] I also remember your sincere faith, a faith that first came to life in your grandmother Lois and in your mother Eunice, and that I am convinced also dwells in you. *

II: THE ENDURANCE OF A MAN OF GOD*

Revive the Gift of God. [6] For this reason, I remind you to stir up the gift of God that is within you through the laying on of my hands. * [7] For God did not give us a spirit of timidity but rather a spirit of power and of love and of wisdom. [8] Therefore, you should never be ashamed of bearing witness to our Lord, nor of me because I am imprisoned for his sake. Rather, you should utilize the strength that comes from God to share in my hardships for the sake of the gospel.

[9] God saved us and called us to a life of holiness, not because of our works but according to his own purpose and the grace that has been bestowed upon us in Christ Jesus from all eternity. * [10] That grace has now been revealed by the appearance * of our Savior Jesus Christ. He has abolished death and brought life and immortality to light through the gospel, [11] for which I have been appointed a herald and an apostle and a teacher. *

Guard the Treasure Entrusted to Us. [12] That is the reason why I am undergoing my present sufferings. However, I am not ashamed, for I know the one in whom I have placed my trust, and I am confident that he is able to guard until that Day * what he has entrusted to me. [13] Follow the pattern of sound teaching that you heard from me, with faith and love that are in Christ Jesus. [14] With the help of the Holy Spirit who dwells in us, guard the treasure that has been entrusted to us.

Comfort Those in Suffering. [15] As you are well aware, everyone in Asia has deserted me, including Phygelus and

Hermogenes. * ¹⁶ May the Lord be merciful to the household of Onesiphorus, * because he has often been a comfort to me in my troubles, and he has never been ashamed of my chains. ¹⁷ When he arrived in Rome, he concentrated on searching for me until he found me. ¹⁸ May the Lord grant that he will find mercy from the Lord * on that Day. He also helped me in many ways at Ephesus, as you are well aware.

III: THE EXEMPLARS OF A MAN OF GOD*

2 **Accept Your Share of Sufferings.*** ¹ As for you, my child, take strength from the grace that is in Christ Jesus. ² And the things you learned from me in the presence of many witnesses you must pass on to trustworthy people who will be capable of teaching others.

³ Together with me, bear your share of sufferings like a good soldier of Christ Jesus. ⁴ A soldier does not become involved in everyday affairs, for his task is to obey his commanding officer. ⁵ In a similar vein, no athlete can receive the winner's crown unless he has competed according to the rules. ⁶ Again, the farmer who does the hard work should have the first claim on the crops. ⁷ Think about what I am saying, for the Lord will help you to understand it perfectly.

Remember That Jesus Christ Is Risen.* ⁸ Remember the gospel that I preach: Jesus Christ, a descendant of David, was raised from the dead. ⁹ It is because of this that I have endured great suffering, even to the point of being chained like a criminal. But the word of God cannot be chained. ¹⁰ Therefore, I endure everything for the sake of those who are chosen, so that they too may obtain the salvation that is in Christ Jesus, with eternal glory.

¹¹ This saying can be trusted:

If we have died with him,
  we shall also live with him.
¹² If we endure,
  we shall also reign with him.

> If we deny him,
>   he will also deny us.
> [13] If we are unfaithful,
>   he will remain faithful,
>   for he cannot deny himself.

A True Servant of the Lord. * [14] Remind people of these things, and warn them before God * that they must stop arguing over words. This does no good and only causes harm to those who are listening. [15] Make every effort to present yourself before God as one who is worthy of his approval, a worker who has no need to be ashamed, but who imparts the word of truth without any alteration.

[16] Avoid idle and worldly chatter, for those who indulge in it will become more and more ungodly, [17] and their teaching will spread like a plague. Included among these are Hymenaeus * and Philetus, [18] who have gone astray from the truth. They claim that the resurrection has already taken place, and they damage the faith of some. [19] However, the foundation that God has sealed * remains firm, and it bears this inscription: "The Lord knows those who are his own," and "Everyone who calls on the name of the Lord must turn away from wickedness."

[20] In every large house, there are utensils not only of gold and silver but also of wood and clay—some for noble purposes and some for ordinary purposes. [21] If someone avoids these things I have mentioned, he will be regarded as a vessel of special value, dedicated and useful for the master of the house, and ready to perform any good work.

[22] Turn away from youthful passions and pursue righteousness, faith, love, and peace, together with those who call on the Lord * with a pure heart. [23] Avoid foolish and stupid speculations, for you are well aware that they only result in quarrels.

[24] A servant of the Lord should not engage in quarrels but should be kind to everyone. He should be a good teacher and patient, [25] correcting with gentleness those

who oppose him. For God may grant them repentance so that they may come to recognize the truth ²⁶ and regain their senses, enabling them to escape the snare of the devil who had held them captive and subjected them to his will.

IV: THE TASKS OF A MAN OF GOD*

3 **Repulse the Onslaughts of False Teachers.** ¹ You must realize that there will be great distress in the last days. ² People will love nothing but themselves and money. They will be boastful, arrogant, abusive, disobedient to their parents, ungrateful, irreligious, ³ and devoid of natural affection. They will be implacable, slanderous, licentious, brutal, and haters of everything that is good. ⁴ They will be treacherous, reckless, conceited, and lovers of pleasure rather than lovers of God ⁵ as they maintain the appearance of godliness * but deny its power. Avoid persons like that!

⁶ They are the type who insinuate themselves into households and gain control of the women there who are burdened by their sins and obsessed with their desires, ⁷ and who are always seeking to be taught but unable to ever arrive at a knowledge of the truth.

⁸ Just as Jannes and Jambres opposed Moses, so these men, with their depraved minds and their deceitful pretense of faith, also oppose the truth. ⁹ But they will not succeed in their efforts. As was the case with those men, their folly will become obvious to everyone.

Remain Faithful in Persecution. ¹⁰ As for you, however, you have followed my teaching, my way of life, my aims, my faith, my patience, my love, my perseverance, ¹¹ my persecutions, my sufferings—the things that I faced in Antioch, Iconium, and Lystra and that I endured. Yet the Lord brought me out safely from all of them. *

¹² Indeed, persecution will afflict all who want to lead a godly life in Christ Jesus, ¹³ while wicked people and im-

postors will grow ever worse, deceiving others and being themselves deceived. [14] But as for you, stand by what you have learned and firmly believed, because you know from whom you have learned it. *

Gain Wisdom from the Inspired Scriptures. [15] Also remember that from the time you were a child you have known the sacred Scriptures. From these you can acquire the wisdom that will lead you to salvation through faith in Christ Jesus. [16] All Scripture is inspired by God and is useful for teaching, for refutation, for correction, and for training in uprightness, * [17] so that the man of God may be proficient and equipped for good work of every kind.

V: THE PREACHING OF A MAN OF GOD*

4 **The Charge To Preach.** [1] In the presence of God and of Christ Jesus, who is to judge the living and the dead, * and by his appearing and his kingdom, I charge you: [2] preach the message; be persistent in doing so, whether in season or out of season; convince, reprove, and encourage, but with great patience and instruction.

The Need for Preaching. [3] For the time is coming when people will not accept sound doctrine, but they will follow their own desires and accumulate teachers who will preach to their itching ears. [4] They will shut their ears to the truth and be captivated by myths. [5] As for you, always be sober. Endure hardships, do the work of preaching the gospel, and carry out your ministry to the fullest extent. *

VI: THE TRIUMPHS OF A MAN OF GOD*

Reward for Fidelity. [6] As for me, I am already being poured out as a libation, and the time has come for my departure. [7] I have fought the good fight; I have finished the race; I have kept the faith. [8] Now waiting for me is the crown * of righteousness, which the Lord, the righteous judge, will award to me on that Day—and not only to me, but to all those who have eagerly longed for his appearance.

Comfort in Trial. [9] Make every effort to come to me as soon as possible. [10] Because of his love of worldly pursuits, Demas * has deserted me and gone off to Thessalonica. Crescens has gone to Galatia, and Titus has left for Dalmatia. [11] No one but Luke * is with me. Get Mark and bring him with you, for he has been helpful to me in my ministry.

[12] I have sent Tychicus * to Ephesus. [13] When you come, bring along with you the cloak * that I left with Carpus in Troas, and also the scrolls, particularly the parchments.

[14] Alexander the coppersmith * has done me a great deal of harm. The Lord will repay him for his deeds. [15] Be on guard yourself against him, for he has been strongly opposed to our teaching.

[16] At the first hearing of my case, no one came to court to support me. Every one of them deserted me. May it not be held against them! [17] But the Lord stood at my side * and gave me strength so that through me the message might be fully proclaimed and all the Gentiles might hear it.

Thus was I rescued from the lion's jaws. [18] The Lord will rescue me from every evil attack and bring me safely into his heavenly kingdom. To him be glory forever and ever. Amen. *

VII: CONCLUSION*

Final Greetings. [19] Greet Prisca and Aquila, * and the household of Onesiphorus. [20] Erastus * remained in Corinth, while I left Trophimus ill in Miletus. [21] Do your best to get here before winter. Eubulus sends greetings to you, as do Pudens and Linus and Claudia and all the brethren. *

Farewell. [22] The Lord be with your spirit. Grace be with all of you. *

THE LETTER TO TITUS
LEAD AN UPRIGHT LIFE

The Gospel has been preached and communities established for several decades; it is now that the first real problems begin. Some Christians, doubtless of Jewish origin, are mingling with the Gospel some theories propagated by rather marginal Jewish groups. The relaxed morals of paganism are also infiltrating the communities. It has become necessary to remind people that Christian salvation has been brought by the coming of Christ. It has also become necessary to sketch the main lines of proper behavior in everyday private and social life. Finally, it has become necessary to provide the Churches with an organization.

The First Letter to Timothy and the Letter to Titus deal with the same problems. The tone is sometimes peremptory in reminding people that Christian convictions must be translated into practical behavior.

If we accept the attribution of this Letter to Paul, it would date from A.D. 64 or 65 and be addressed to Titus, Paul's personal delegate on the island of Crete. Paul relies on Titus to give the communities a solid organization and to combat those who are falsifying the word of God.

Titus was a Gentile Christian converted by Paul (see Tit 1:4) who became one of his most helpful coworkers. The Apostle took him along to Jerusalem when he went there to meet the leaders of the Church and discuss his Gospel (see 2 Tim 2:8). The leaders accepted Titus as a Christian without imposing circumcision on him, thereby vindicating Paul's teaching (see Gal 2:3-5).

There is no reference in Acts to Titus, but he is mentioned 13 times in the rest of the New Testament. Titus worked with Paul at Ephesus on his Third Missionary Journey and possibly his Fourth (see Introduction to First Timothy). From there the Apostle sent him to assist the Church at Corinth (see 2 Cor 2:12f; 7:5f; 8:6), where he courageously and tactfully carried out his mission of reconciliation (see 2 Cor 7:6-16).

Upon Paul's release from his first Roman imprisonment, he and Titus worked in Crete (see Tit 1:5). When Paul departed, he left Titus behind to continue the work (Tit 1:5; 2:15; 3:12f).

In the present Letter, Paul asks Titus to bring his ministry in Crete to a close. To do so, Titus must organize the churches (Tit 1:5-9), oppose the false teachers (Tit 1:10-14; 3:9-11), and instruct the churches on genuine Christian conduct (Tit 2:1—3:8). When his replacement arrives, Titus is to meet Paul at Nicopolis on the west coast of Greece (Tit 3:12).

The last we hear of Titus is that he went on mission to Dalmatia (see 2 Tim 4:10).

The Letter to Titus may be divided as follows:

I: Salutation (1:1-4)
II: Church Organization (1:5-16)
III: Proper Conduct for Christians (2:1—3:11)
IV: Conclusion (3:12-15)

I: SALUTATION*

1 **Address.** ¹ Paul, a servant of God * and an apostle of Jesus Christ, to further the faith of those whom God has chosen and their knowledge of religious truth, ² with its hope of eternal life that God, who does not lie, promised before the beginning of time, ³ and who now at his appointed time has revealed his word through the proclamation with which I was entrusted by the command of God our Savior, ⁴ to Titus, my loyal child in the faith we share: * grace and peace from God the Father and Christ Jesus our Savior. *

II: CHURCH ORGANIZATION

A Bishop Must Be Blameless. * ⁵ The reason I left you behind in Crete was so that you could finish up the work that remained to be done and appoint presbyters in every town as I directed you. ⁶ Each man must be blameless and the husband of only one wife, with children who are believers and free from any suspicion of licentious or rebellious behavior.

[7] For in his role as God's steward a bishop * must be blameless. He must not be arrogant or quick-tempered or prone to drunkenness or violent or avaricious. [8] Rather, he must be hospitable, a lover of goodness, prudent, upright, devout, and self-controlled. [9] In addition, he must hold firmly to the authentic message he has been taught, so that he may be able both to exhort with sound doctrine and to refute those who contradict it.

For the Pure All Things Are Pure.* [10] For there are also many rebellious people, especially among the Jewish converts, * who deceive others with their empty talk. [11] It is essential to silence them, since they are ruining whole households by teaching for dishonest gain what it is not right to teach. [12] It was one of their very own prophets, a man from Crete, who said,

> "Cretans have always been liars, vicious beasts, and
> lazy gluttons."

[13] This testimony is true. Therefore, rebuke them sharply so that they may be restored to a sound faith, [14] rather than paying attention to Jewish myths or to the commandments of those who turn away from the truth.

[15] To the pure all things are pure, but to those who are corrupt and without faith nothing is pure.* Their very minds and their consciences have been corrupted. [16] They profess to know God, but they deny him by their deeds. They are detestable and disobedient, totally unfit for any good work.

III: PROPER CONDUCT FOR CHRISTIANS

2 **Teach What Is Consistent with Sound Doctrine.*** [1] As for you, teach what is consistent with sound doctrine. [2] Exhort the older men to be temperate, dignified, self-controlled, and sound in faith, in love, and in perseverance.

³ Similarly, exhort the older women to be reverent in their behavior, not to be slanderous or slaves of drink, and eager to teach what is good. ⁴ They can then instruct the younger women to love their husbands and their children, ⁵ to be self-controlled and chaste, to be diligent homemakers, to be agreeable, and to respect the authority of their husbands so that the word of God may not be derided.

⁶ Likewise, exhort the younger men to exercise self-control. ⁷ Show yourself to them in all respects as a model of good works, while in your teaching exhibit integrity and dignity ⁸ and a soundness of speech that cannot be criticized. Then any opponent will be put to shame when he can find nothing evil to say about us.

⁹ Exhort slaves to be submissive to their masters and to give them satisfaction in every respect. They are not to talk back to them, ¹⁰ nor are they to steal from them. Rather, they should show themselves to be completely trustworthy so that in every way they may add luster to the doctrine of God our Savior.

The Grace of God Has Appeared.* ¹¹ For the grace of God has appeared bringing salvation to the entire human race. ¹² It teaches us to reject godless ways and worldly desires, and in the present age to lead lives that are temperate, just, and godly, ¹³ while we await our blessed hope, the appearance of the glory of our great God and Savior Jesus Christ. * ¹⁴ He gave himself for us in order to deliver us from all iniquity and to purify for himself a people as his own who are eager to do good.

The Goodness of God Our Savior.* ¹⁵ These are the things you should expound. Exhort and reprove with all authority. Let no one disregard you.

3 ¹ Remind everyone to be subject to rulers and authorities, to obey them, to be ready to perform any honorable task,* ² to slander no one, to avoid quarrels, to be gentle, and to be gracious to everyone.

³ For we ourselves were once foolish, disobedient, led astray, and enslaved by various passions and pleasures, passing our days in malice and envy. We ourselves were hateful, and we hated one another.

4   But when the goodness and loving kindness
          of God our Savior appeared,
5 *   not because of any righteous deeds on our part
          but because of his mercy,
       he saved us through the bath of rebirth
          and renewal by the Holy Spirit,
6   whom he lavished on us abundantly
          through Jesus Christ our Savior,
7   so that we might be justified by his grace
          and become heirs in hope of eternal life.

⁸ This saying can be trusted.

Be Devoted to Good Works.* I want you to stress these points, so that those who have come to believe in God will be determined to devote themselves to good works. All this is right and beneficial for people. ⁹ But avoid foolish arguments, genealogies, dissensions, and quarrels about the Law, for they are unprofitable and futile.

¹⁰ Warn a heretic once or twice, but afterward reject him. ¹¹ You may be sure that such a person is perverted and sinful and stands self-condemned.

IV: CONCLUSION*

Final Message. ¹² As soon as I have sent Artemas* or Tychicus to you, do your best to come to me at Nicopolis, where I intend to spend the winter. ¹³ Send Zenas the lawyer and Apollos* on their way, and see to it that they lack nothing. ¹⁴ Meanwhile, our people must be taught to devote themselves to good works in order to meet urgent needs* so that they will not be unfruitful.

Farewell. ¹⁵ All those with me send you greetings. Greetings to those who love us in the faith.

Grace be with all of you. *

THE LETTER TO PHILEMON
LET THE SLAVE BECOME A BROTHER

Paul entrusted his Letter to the Colossians to Tychicus and assigned him as a companion "Onesimus, our trustworthy and beloved brother" (Col 4:9). Onesimus was perhaps a lazy slave and a thief, who had run away from Colossae. He had reached one of the larger cities—Caesarea or Rome—where outlaws could hide. When did he meet Paul? We do not know. The Apostle accepted him, instructed him in the Gospel, and grew fond of him. But he also had to regulate the situation of this man whose owner could have hunted him down and even put him to death; in addition, Paul risked being accused of complicity, a serious crime during that age.

Since the slave belonged to a rich Christian of Colossae, named Philemon, whom the Apostle himself had converted to the faith, probably during his stay at Ephesus, Paul sends the slave back to his master with a letter of recommendation. He hopes that Philemon will free Onesimus and allow yesterday's slave to become his fellow worker in the apostolate. This subtle and skillful Letter gives us a glimpse of Paul's warmth and his boundless respect for a less circumspect human being but one redeemed by the blood of Jesus Christ.

Paul does not take a position on the social structures of his time that divided human beings into slave and free (see 1 Cor 7:20-24; Eph 6:5-9; Col 3:22—4:1). But for believers there is no division between Jew and Greek or between slave and free; they know that all are equal in God's sight, and they believe that all are brothers and sisters in the Church. Without directly attacking social structures, Paul does, in a concrete case, propose a new attitude for Christians. Slaves are no longer regarded as things; they are persons and, more than that, they are brothers and sisters in the Lord. The Apostle expects Philemon to give spontaneous and concrete witness to this new manner of conceiving the relationships among human beings and actually living them.

560

The present Letter is reminiscent of similar letters of recommendation written in the Greco-Roman world of the time. It begins with a salutation, is followed by expressions of thanksgiving and petition, discusses the principal subject matter, and ends with a conclusion and farewell. It stresses Christian love for others, which, if followed out to its rightful conclusion, will eliminate the scourge of slavery in the world. The Letter is also dominated by the theme of forgiveness, which is found throughout the New Testament (see, e.g., Mt 6:12-15; 18:21-35; Eph 4:32; Col 3:13). Although Paul does not use the word, he exemplifies the Biblical definition of forgiveness.

The Letter to Philemon may be divided as follows:

> *Salutation (1-3)*
> *Thanksgiving and Prayer (4-7)*
> *Plea for Onesimus (8-20)*
> *Conclusion (21-25)*

Salutation.* [1] Paul, a prisoner of Christ Jesus, and Timothy* our brother, to Philemon, our beloved friend and fellow worker, [2] to Apphia our sister, to Archippus* our fellow soldier, and to the Church that meets in your house: [3] grace to you and peace from God our Father and the Lord Jesus Christ.

Thanksgiving and Prayer.* [4] I always give thanks to my God when I remember you in my prayers, [5] because I hear of the love and faith that you have for the Lord Jesus and for all the saints.* [6] I pray that the sharing of your faith may become even more effective so that you may come to perceive all the blessings we have in Christ. [7] Your love has given me much joy and encouragement because the hearts* of the saints have been refreshed by you, my brother.

Plea for Onesimus.* [8] Therefore, although I am confident that in Christ I have the right to command you to do your duty, [9] I would rather appeal to you on the basis of love. I, Paul, an old man, and now also a prisoner for Christ Jesus, [10] am appealing to you on behalf of my child, * Onesimus, whom I have fathered during my imprisonment.

[11] He was formerly useless to you, but now he is indeed useful both to you and to me. [12] Therefore, I am sending him back to you, that is, I am sending my very own heart. * [13] I wanted to keep him with me so that he might be of service to me on your behalf during my imprisonment for the gospel, [14] but I did not want to do anything without your knowledge, so that your good deed might be voluntary and not compelled.

[15] Perhaps this is the reason he was separated from you for a while, so that you might have him back forever, * [16] no longer as a slave, but as more than a slave: as a brother. He is beloved especially to me, but even more so to you, both as a man * and in the Lord.

[17] * Therefore, if you consider me to be a friend, welcome him as you would welcome me. [18] If he has wronged you in any way or owes you anything, charge that to my account. [19] I, Paul, am writing this with my own hand: I will repay it. I say nothing about the fact that you owe me your very self. [20] Yes, my brother, grant me some benefit * in the Lord. Set my heart at rest in Christ.

Conclusion. * [21] I have written to you confident of your acceptance, and in fact I am certain that you will do even more than I ask. [22] At the same time, please prepare a guest room for me, for I am hoping through your prayers to be restored to you.

[23] Epaphras, * my fellow prisoner in Christ Jesus, sends you greetings, [24] and so do Mark, Aristarchus, Demas, and Luke, * my fellow workers.

[25] The grace of the Lord Jesus Christ be with your spirit. *

THE LETTER TO THE HEBREWS
CHRIST, THE ONE TRUE PRIEST

A tradition going back at least to the end of the second century describes this important writing as the Letter of St. Paul to the Hebrews. But the correctness of these data—genre of the work, author, addressees—is challenged by critics nowadays. Is it a letter? Only the last section is in the epistolary style. At the beginning there is no greeting to the readers nor is there subsequently any direct dialogue with a community, nor are there any references to concrete events. The pages seem rather to be a sermon throughout.

Is it by Paul? At more than one point the thought may recall that of the Apostle, but the tone, the choice of main themes, the atmosphere, and the manner of arguing force us to look for a different author. The author is certainly of Jewish origin, since he is completely at home with the Bible. In addition, he has quite a gift of eloquence. His faith is complete and deep, he is highly educated, he is devoted to teaching and familiar also with the work of Philo, a famous philosopher of Alexandria. Among the various possible authors that fit this picture the favorite is Apollos, of whom Luke speaks admiringly in the Acts of the Apostles (18:24-28), but this is, and will always remain, simply a guess.

As for the addressees—Jews—the author is seeking to revive the faith and courage of converts of long standing, who in all probability were of Jewish origin. In debating with them the author continually cites the Scriptures and ceaselessly recalls the most important ideas and realities of the Jewish religion. These individuals know Jewish tradition, its great personages, its worship, and its Law. Persecution has dispersed them, and they live in poverty, uprooted and excluded from their former religious activities. The modest and youthful Church of Christ crucified does not seem to them to bear comparison with Judaism, which benefits from a long and often glorious past and the splendor of its worship.

563

In response, the Letter begins by emphasizing the grandeur of the mystery of Christ's Death and Resurrection for all human beings. It stresses the superiority of Christ, who is the express image of God, superior to Moses, to Aaron, to the angels, and to any other thing. A brother to humans and a sharer in their misery and anguish, he is also the Son of God. Believers must not look with nostalgia to the past but press on toward heaven where the human condition will find its fulfillment in eternity. Secondly, the author states that the old dispensation has gone and a new dispensation is here—the New Covenant. Now people can come to Christ wherever they are, not by way of Jerusalem—except in a figurative way, through the heavenly Jerusalem. Thirdly, the author highlights the glorious priesthood of Christ in contrast to the superseded priesthood of Jerusalem. Jesus is now at God's right hand, pleading for us eternally. Since he knows what it is like to be human, he can plead with full understanding. Hence, we can go to the throne of grace with full confidence of being heard.

The author emphasizes the need for perseverance. His addressees must not quit and fall like their ancestors in the wilderness. And such a sorrowful event will never take place if they stand fast and do not become discouraged. To help them stand fast, the author sets before them the glories of faith and a series of personages who have possessed it in abundance. He preaches a wonderful sermon on those who used faith in God to endure even the greatest of trials.

Along the way, the author insists on the internal dynamism of God's Revelation. It has only one goal: the Redemption of the world in Christ. It is a movement toward a fullness and an accomplishment. And the Scriptures are what enable people to be gripped by its power and its teaching. The realities of the Old Testament are there like a sketch, figure, or shadow of a greater reality. They are of the terrestrial order in order to announce a heavenly and eternal order: the unique supremacy of the work of Christ. The Biblical meditation is developed and deepened in order to better express the mystery of Christ. Hence, this Letter introduces us to the Christian reading of the Old Testament. It utilizes some thirty-three citations from the Old

Testament as well as fifty-three reminiscences or allusions. All the citations are attributed to God himself, most often introduced by the anonymous formula "he said." The author then passes from theological reflection to moral exhortation. The appeals are multiplied: live in faith and hope for the things to come, and in constancy amid trials.

As far as the date in which this Letter was written, it was certainly completed by the year A.D. 90 since it is cited by Clement of Rome. One is tempted to situate it around A.D. 67, just before the destruction of the temple. For the cessation of the worship at Jerusalem would certainly have been echoed in this writing that speaks so much about sacrifices and sanctuaries; yet a reading gives the impression that these realities are still functioning. However, such a reasoning is not decisive, for in speaking of the temple, the author hardly describes what is taking place in the ostentatious sanctuary built by Herod. He is more acquainted with the ideal images, set forth in the Pentateuch, concerning the tabernacle of the desert at the time of Moses.

The Letter to the Hebrews may be divided as follows:

   I: *Prologue (1:1-4)*
  II: *The Son of God, Superior to the Angels (1:5—2:18)*
 III: *A High Priest for Humanity (3:1—5:10)*
 IV: *Christ, the One True Priest (5:11—10:18)*
  V: *Perseverance in Faith (10:19—12:29)*
 VI: *Conclusion (13:1-25)*

I: PROLOGUE*

1 ¹ In previous times, God spoke to our ancestors
      in many and various ways
        through the Prophets,*
² but in these last days he has spoken to us
      through his Son,
    whom he appointed heir of all things
      and through whom he created the universe.

³ He is the reflection of God's glory
      and the perfect expression of his very being,*
      sustaining all things by his powerful word.
    Achieving purification from sins,
      he took his seat at the right hand of the Majesty on
        high.
⁴ So he became as far superior to the angels
      as the name he has inherited is superior to theirs.

II: THE SON OF GOD, SUPERIOR TO THE ANGELS*

Messianic Enthronement.* ⁵ For to which of the angels
did God ever say,

    "You are my Son;
      this day I have begotten you"?

Or again,

    "I will be his Father,
      and he will be my Son"?*

⁶ And again, when he brings his firstborn into the
world, he says,

    "Let all the angels of God pay him homage."

⁷ Of the angels he says,

    "He makes his angels winds,
      and his servants flames of fire."

⁸ But of the Son he says,

    "Your throne, O God, is forever and ever,
      and a righteous scepter is the scepter of your king-
        dom.

9   You have loved righteousness and detested wickedness;
        therefore God, your God, has anointed you
        with the oil of gladness far above your companions."

[10] He also says,

   "In the beginning, O Lord, you laid the foundations
        of the earth,
   and the heavens are the work of your hands.
11   They will perish, but you remain;
        they will all wear out like a garment.
12   You will roll them up like a cloak;
        like a garment they will be changed.
   But you are ever the same,
        and your years will have no end."

   [13] But to which of the angels has he ever said,

   "Sit at my right hand
        until I make your enemies your footstool"?

   [14] Are not all angels ministering spirits sent forth to
serve for the sake of those who will inherit salvation?

2   The Oneness of Christian Salvation.* [1] Therefore, we
should pay much closer attention to what we have heard
so that we do not drift away. [2] For if the message delivered
by angels proved to be so valid that every transgression
and disobedience brought a proper punishment, [3] how
shall we escape if we ignore so great a salvation?

   It was first announced by the Lord and then confirmed for us by those who heard him. [4] God also testified to it by signs and wonders and various miracles,
and by gifts of the Holy Spirit distributed according to
his will.

Christ Our Brother.* [5] For it was not to angels that God
subjected the world to come, about which we are speaking. [6] But someone has offered this testimony somewhere:

   "What is man that you are mindful of him,
        or the son of man that you care for him?

> [7] You made him a little lower than the angels,
>> yet crowned him with glory and honor
>
> [8] and put everything under his feet."

Now in putting everything under his feet, he left nothing that is not subject to his control. Right now we do not yet see everything under his feet. [9] However, we do see Jesus, who was made a little lower than the angels, now crowned with glory and honor because he suffered death, so that by the grace of God he might taste death for everyone.

[10] In bringing many sons to glory, it was completely fitting that he, for whom and through whom everything exists, should make the author of their salvation perfect through sufferings. [11] Both the one who sanctifies and those who are sanctified all proceed from one Father. That is why Jesus is not ashamed to call them brethren, [12] saying,

> "I will proclaim your name to my brethren; *
>> in the midst of the assembly I will praise you."

[13] And again,

> "I will put my trust in him."

And again,

> "Here I am,
>> together with the children God has given me."

[14] Therefore, since the children are all made of flesh and blood,* Jesus likewise shared in the same flesh and blood, so that by his death he might destroy the one who has the power of death—that is, the devil— [15] and set free those who throughout their lives had been held in slavery by the fear of death.

[16] For clearly he did not come to help angels but rather he came to help the descendants of Abraham. [17] Therefore, he had to be made like his brethren in every way in order that he might become a compassionate and faithful high priest before God and expiate the sins of the people. [18] Because he himself was tested by suffering, he is able to help those who are being tested.

III: A HIGH PRIEST FOR HUMANITY*

3 **Christ's Fidelity Is Superior to That of Moses.*** [1] Therefore, holy brethren, who share in a heavenly calling, concentrate your thoughts on Jesus, the apostle and the high priest of our profession of faith. [2] He was faithful to the one who appointed him, just as Moses was faithful in God's household.

[3] However, he is deserving of a greater glory than Moses, just as the builder of a house is more honored than the house itself. [4] For every house is built by someone, but the builder of all is God.

[5] Now Moses was faithful as a servant in God's household, testifying to the things that would later be revealed, [6] whereas Christ was faithful as a son watching over his house. And we are that house if we hold firm to our confidence and take pride in our hope.

The "Today" of God. [7] * Therefore, as the Holy Spirit says,

"Today, if you hear his voice,
[8]   harden not your hearts as at the rebellion,
    in the day of testing in the desert,
[9] where your ancestors tried me and tested me
    though they had seen what I could do
    [10] for forty years.
As a result I became angered with that generation,
    and I said, 'Their hearts have always gone astray,
    and they do not know my ways.'
[11]   Therefore, I swore in my anger,
    'They will never enter into my rest.'"

[12] Take care, brethren, that none of you will ever have an evil and unbelieving heart that will cause you to forsake the living God. [13] Rather, encourage each other every day, as long as it is today, so that none of you will become hardened by the deceitfulness of sin.

[14] For we will become partners with Christ only if we maintain firmly until the end the confidence we originally had, [15] as it is said,

"Today, if you hear his voice,
    harden not your hearts as at the rebellion."

[16] Who were those who heard and yet rebelled? Were they not all those whom Moses had led out of Egypt? [17] And with whom was he angered for forty years? Was it not with those who had sinned and whose corpses lay in the wilderness? [18] And to whom did he swear that they would never enter into his rest, if not to those who disobeyed? [19] So we see clearly that they were unable to enter because of their refusal to believe.

4 **The Sabbath Rest of God's People.*** [1] Therefore, since the promise of entering into his rest endures, we must take care that none of you be judged to have fallen short. [2] For we too have received the good news just as they did, but the message they heard was of no benefit to them because those who listened did not combine it with faith. [3] For we who have faith enter into that rest, just as God has said:

"Therefore, I swore in my anger,
    'They will never enter into my rest.'"

Yet God's work had been finished at the beginning of the world. [4] For somewhere he says in reference to the seventh day, "And God rested on the seventh day from all his works." [5] And in this passage it says, "They will never enter into my rest."

[6] Seeing, therefore, that some will enter into that rest, and since those who first had received the good news failed to enter because of their refusal to believe, [7] God once more set a day—"today"—when long afterward he spoke through David, as already quoted:

"Today, if you hear his voice,
    harden not your hearts."

[8] Now if Joshua had given them rest, God would not have spoken afterward of another day. [9] Therefore, a Sabbath rest still remains for the people of God, [10] since those who enter into God's rest also cease from their own labors as God did from his. [11] Let us then make every

effort to enter into that rest, so that no one may fall by following that example of refusing to believe.

The Word of God Is Living.* [12] Indeed, the word of God is living and active. Sharper than any two-edged sword, it pierces to the point where it divides soul and spirit, joints and marrow; it judges the thoughts and the intentions of the heart. [13] Nothing in creation is hidden from his sight. Everything is uncovered and exposed to the eyes of the one to whom we must all render an account.

A Compassionate High Priest.* [14] Therefore, since we have a great high priest who has passed through the heavens, Jesus, the Son of God, let us hold fast to our profession of faith. [15] For we do not have a high priest who is unable to sympathize with our weaknesses, but one who has been tested in every respect as we are, but without sinning. [16] Let us then approach the throne of grace with confidence so that we may receive mercy and find grace when we are in need of help.

5 [1] Every high priest is taken from among men to represent them in their dealings with God, to offer gifts and sacrifices for sins. * [2] He is able to deal patiently with those who are ignorant and misguided, since he himself is subject to weakness. [3] And as a result of this, he must make sin offerings for himself as well as for the people. [4] Moreover, one does not assume this position of honor on his own initiative, but only when called by God, just as Aaron was.

[5] Even Christ did not confer upon himself the glory of becoming a high priest. Rather, he was appointed by the one who said to him:

> "You are my Son;
>   this day I have begotten you."

[6] And he says in another place:

> "You are a priest forever,
>   according to the order of Melchizedek."

[7] During the course of his earthly life, Jesus offered up prayers and petitions with loud cries and tears to the one who had the power to save him from death, and he was heard because of his godly fear. [8] Although he was a Son, he learned obedience through his sufferings, [9] and when he had been made perfect, he became the source of eternal salvation for all who obey him, [10] and he was designated a high priest by God according to the order of Melchizedek.

IV: CHRIST, THE ONE TRUE PRIEST*

Deepen the Christian Life. * [11] We have much to say about this subject, but it is difficult to explain because you have been slow in learning. [12] By this time you should have been teachers, yet you still need to have someone explain to you the basic elements of God's words.

You need milk, not solid food. [13] Anyone who lives on milk is still an infant and is ignorant of the word of righteousness. [14] But solid food is for adults whose faculties have been trained by practice to distinguish between good and evil.

6 [1] * Therefore, let us leave behind the basic teaching about Christ and advance toward maturity. We must not be forever laying the foundation: repentance for actions that lead to death, faith in God, [2] instruction about baptisms and the laying on of hands, the resurrection of the dead, and eternal judgment. [3] And we will do so, if God permits.

[4] * For when people have once been enlightened and have experienced the heavenly gift, and have shared in the Holy Spirit, [5] and have tasted the goodness of the word of God and the powers of the age to come, [6] and then in spite of all this have fallen away, it is impossible to restore them again to repentance. For they are crucifying the Son of God for themselves once again and are holding him up to contempt.

⁷ When the soil drinks in the rain that repeatedly falls on it and produces a crop that is useful to those for whom it was cultivated, it receives a blessing from God. ⁸ However, if it brings forth thorns and thistles, it is worthless, and a curse hangs over it. It will end by being burned.

⁹ But, beloved, in spite of what we have just said, we are convinced that your status is far superior as you proceed to salvation. ¹⁰ For God would not be so unjust as to ignore your work and the love that you have shown for his name by the services you have rendered to the saints and still continue to render.

¹¹ However, we desire that each one of you will show the same diligence until you have achieved the ultimate fulfillment of your hope. ¹² We do not want you to allow yourselves to become sluggish; rather, we want you to become imitators of those who through faith and patience are now heirs of the promises.

Cling Tightly to Hope.* ¹³ When God made his promise to Abraham, since he had no one greater by whom to swear, he swore by himself, ¹⁴ saying, "I will surely bless you and multiply your descendants." ¹⁵ And so, after waiting patiently, he obtained the promise.

¹⁶ Human beings swear by someone greater than themselves, and the oath given as confirmation puts an end to all argument. ¹⁷ Likewise, when God desired to show even more clearly to the heirs of his promise the unalterable nature of his purpose, he confirmed it by an oath.

¹⁸ Therefore, by these two unchangeable acts in which it was impossible for God to lie, we who have taken refuge in his protection have been strongly encouraged to grasp firmly the hope that has been held out to us. ¹⁹ We have this hope as the anchor of the soul, a hope that enters the sanctuary behind the veil,* ²⁰ where Jesus has entered as a forerunner on our behalf, having become a high priest forever according to the order of Melchizedek.

A: A Different Kind of High Priest*

7 **Melchizedek.*** [1] This Melchizedek, the king of Salem and a priest of God Most High, met Abraham as he was returning from his defeat of the kings, and he blessed him. [2] Abraham gave him a tenth of everything. His name first means "king of righteousness," and then "king of Salem," that is, "king of peace." [3] Without father, or mother, or genealogy, and without beginning of days or end of life, thus bearing a resemblance to the Son of God, he remains a priest forever.

[4] Just consider now how great this man must have been for the patriarch Abraham to give him a tenth of his spoils. [5] The descendants of Levi who succeed to the priestly office are required by the Law to collect tithes from the people, that is, from their fellow countrymen, although they too are descended from Abraham. [6] However, Melchizedek, who was not of the same ancestry, received tithes from Abraham and blessed him who had received the promises.

[7] It is indisputable that a lesser person is blessed by one who is greater. [8] In the one case, it is ordinary mortal men who receive tithes; in the other, the recipient is one of whom it is attested that he is alive. [9] One could even say that Levi himself, who receives tithes, actually paid tithes through Abraham, [10] inasmuch as he was still in his father's loins when Melchizedek met Abraham.

Another High Priest according to the Order of Melchizedek.* [11] If perfection was therefore achieved through the Levitical priesthood, on the basis of which the Law was given to the people, what need would there have been for another priest to arise according to the order of Melchizedek rather than one according to the order of Aaron? [12] For when there is any change in the priesthood, there must also be a change in the Law.

[13] Now the one about whom these things were said belonged to a different tribe, from which no one has ever

served at the altar. [14] For it is clear that our Lord was descended from Judah, a tribe about which Moses said nothing in regard to priests.

[15] This becomes even more obvious now that another priest has arisen, one like Melchizedek, [16] who was one not through a legal requirement concerning physical descent, but by the power of an indestructible life. [17] For it is attested of him:

"You are a priest forever,
    according to the order of Melchizedek."

[18] The earlier commandment is abrogated because of its weakness and ineffectiveness, [19] since the Law brought nothing to perfection. On the other hand, a better hope is introduced through which we draw nearer to God.

[20] This was confirmed by an oath. When others became priests, no oath was required, [21] but this one became a priest with the swearing of an oath by the one who said to him,

"The Lord has sworn, and he will not repent:
    'You are a priest forever.'"

[22] Accordingly, Jesus has also become the guarantee of a better covenant.

[23] Furthermore, the former priests were many in number, because they were prevented by death from remaining in office. [24] However, Jesus holds a perpetual priesthood because he remains forever. [25] Therefore, he has the full power to save those who approach God through him, since he lives forever to intercede for them.

The High Priest That We Needed.* [26] It was fitting that we should have such a high priest—holy, innocent, undefiled, separated from sinners, and raised high above the heavens. [27] Unlike the other high priests, he has no need to offer sacrifices day after day, first for his own sins and then for those of the people. He accomplished this once for all when he offered himself. [28] The Law appoints as high priests those who are subject to weakness, but the word of the oath, which came later than the Law, appointed the Son who has been made perfect forever.

B: A New Kind of Priesthood*

8 **Another Sanctuary.*** [1] The main point of what we have been saying is this: we have such a high priest. He has taken his seat at the right hand of the throne of the Majesty in heaven, [2] and he is a minister of the sanctuary and of the true tabernacle established by the Lord and not by human beings.

[3] Every high priest is appointed to offer gifts and sacrifices, and so it is necessary for this one also to have something to offer. [4] Actually, if he were on earth, he would not be a priest at all, since there are already others who offer gifts according to the Law, * [5] although the sanctuary in which they offer worship is only a shadow and a reflection of the heavenly one. This is the reason why, when Moses was about to erect the tabernacle, he was warned, "See to it that you make everything according to the pattern that was shown you on the mountain."

Another Covenant.* [6] But Jesus has now received a ministry that is far superior, for he is the mediator of a far better covenant that has been established on better promises. [7] For if that first covenant had been faultless, there would have been no necessity to establish a second one to replace it. [8] * However, God finds fault with his people, and he says,

"Behold, the days are coming, says the Lord,
    when I will establish a new covenant
with the house of Israel
and with the house of Judah.
[9]   It will not be like the covenant
    that I made with their ancestors
on the day when I took them by the hand
    to lead them out of the land of Egypt.
For they did not remain faithful to my covenant,
    and therefore I abandoned them, says the Lord.

10   This is the covenant that I will make
       with the house of Israel
       after those days, says the Lord.
   I will plant my laws in their minds
       and inscribe them on their hearts.
   I will be their God,
       and they will be my people.
11   And they shall not teach one another,
       each saying to his neighbor and his brother,
       'Know the Lord.'
   For they shall all know me,
       from the least of them to the greatest.
12   I shall forgive them for their wicked deeds,
       and I shall remember their sins no more."

[13] By calling this covenant "new," he has made the first one obsolete. And anything that is obsolete and aging will shortly disappear.

9   The Ancient Worship.* [1] Now the first covenant also had regulations for worship and an earthly sanctuary. [2] For a tabernacle was constructed. In the outer section, called the Holy Place, were located the lampstand, the table, and the consecrated bread.

[3] Behind the second veil was the tabernacle called the Holy of Holies [4] in which stood the gold altar of incense and the ark of the covenant overlaid on all sides with gold. In that ark were the gold jar containing the manna, and Aaron's staff that had sprouted buds, and the tablets of the covenant. [5] Above it were the cherubim of glory overshadowing the place of atonement (but we cannot discuss these things in detail now).

[6] With these arrangements for worship having been made, the priests continually enter the first tabernacle to carry out their ritual duties. [7] However, the high priest alone enters the second tabernacle, and he can do so only once a year, and not without the blood that he offers for himself and for the errors that the people had committed.

[8] By this the Holy Spirit reveals to us that as long as the first tabernacle remains standing, the way into the sanctuary has not been disclosed. [9] This is a symbol of the present time, during which the gifts and sacrifices that are offered are unable to cleanse the conscience of the worshiper. [10] They deal only with food and drink and various ceremonial washings, regulations in regard to the body that are imposed until the coming of the new order.

Christ Has Come.* [11] But now Christ has arrived as the high priest of the good things that have come. He has passed through the greater and more perfect tabernacle not made by human hands, that is, not a part of this creation, [12] and he has entered once for all into the sanctuary not with the blood of goats and calves but with his own blood, thus obtaining eternal redemption.

[13] The blood of goats and bulls and the sprinkling of ashes of a heifer sanctify those who have been defiled and restore bodily purity. [14] How much more, then, will the blood of Christ, who through the eternal Spirit offered himself without blemish to God, purify our conscience from acts that lead to death so that we may worship the living God.

A Covenant Sealed with the Blood of Christ.* [15] For this reason, he is the mediator of a new covenant, so that those who have been called may receive the promised eternal inheritance, since his death has served to redeem the sins that were committed under the first covenant.

[16] Now when a will is involved, it is obligatory to prove the death of the one who made it. [17] For a will takes effect only at death, since it has no force while the one who made it is still alive.

[18] Hence, not even the first covenant was inaugurated without blood. [19] For when all the commandments of the Law had been proclaimed by Moses to all the people, he took the blood of calves and goats, together with water and scarlet wool and hyssop, and sprinkled both the book

itself and all the people, [20] saying, "This is the blood of the covenant that God has commanded you to observe."

[21] And in the same way, he sprinkled with blood both the tabernacle and all the liturgical vessels. [22] Indeed, under the Law almost everything is purified by blood, and without the shedding of blood there is no forgiveness.

[23] Therefore, it was necessary for the copies of the heavenly things to be purified with these rites, but the heavenly things themselves required still greater sacrifices.

Once and for All.* [24] For Christ did not enter a sanctuary made by human hands, a mere copy of the true one, but he entered into heaven itself, so that he now appears in the presence of God on our behalf.

[25] Nor was it his purpose to offer himself again and again, as the high priest enters into the sanctuary year after year with the blood that is not his own. [26] For then he would have had to suffer over and over again since the creation of the world. But as it is, he has appeared once and for all at the end of the ages to abolish sin by sacrificing himself.

[27] And just as human beings are destined to die but once, and after that to face judgment, [28] so Christ, having been offered once to take away the sins of many, will appear a second time, not to deal with sin but to bring salvation to those who are eagerly waiting for him.

C: A Unique Sacrifice*

10 **The Law Was a Shadow.** [1] The Law contains little more than a shadow of the good things to come and not the true image of them. These sacrifices that are offered year after year can never bring the worshipers to perfection. [2] If they could, those sacrifices would no longer be offered, for the worshipers would have been cleansed once for all and would no longer feel guilty for sins.

³ However, in these sacrifices sins are brought to mind year after year, ⁴ because sins cannot be taken away by the blood of bulls and goats.

One Sacrifice for Sins. ⁵ That is why, when Christ came into the world, he said,

> "Sacrifice and offering you did not desire,
>> but a body you have prepared for me.
> ⁶ You took no delight
>> in holocausts and sin offerings.
> ⁷ Then I said, 'As it is written of me in the scroll,
>> behold, I have come to do your will, O God.'"

⁸ First he says, "Sacrifices and offerings, holocausts and sin offerings, you neither desired nor delighted in," even though they are offered according to the Law. ⁹ Then he adds, "Behold, I have come to do your will." He thus abolishes the first to establish the second. ¹⁰ And it was by this "will" that we have been consecrated through the offering of the body of Jesus Christ once for all.

¹¹ * Day after day every priest stands to perform his ministry, offering over and over again the same sacrifices that can never remove sins. ¹² But Jesus offered one sacrifice for sins for all time, and then took his seat at the right hand of God, ¹³ where he now waits until his enemies are made his footstool. ¹⁴ Therefore, by a single offering he has made perfect forever those who are being sanctified.

¹⁵ The Holy Spirit also testifies to us about this. For he first says,

> ¹⁶ "This is the covenant that I will make with them
>> after those days, says the Lord.
> I will place my laws in their hearts
>> and inscribe them on their minds."

¹⁷ Then he also asserts,

> "Their sins and their lawless acts
>> I will remember no more."

¹⁸ When these have been forgiven, there are no longer any offerings for sins.

V: PERSEVERANCE IN FAITH*

A: The Need To Stand Firm

Let Us Approach with Sincerity of Heart.* [19] Therefore, brethren, the blood of Jesus has given us confidence to enter the sanctuary [20] by the new and living way that he has opened for us through the veil, that is, through his flesh. [21] Since we have a great priest over the household of God, [22] let us approach with sincerity of heart and the full assurance of faith, with hearts sprinkled clean from an evil conscience and bodies washed in pure water.

[23] Let us remain firm in the confession of our hope without wavering, for the one who made the promise is trustworthy. [24] And let us consider how to spur one another to love and good works. [25] Do not neglect to attend your assemblies, as some do, but rather encourage one another, especially since you can see the Day* approaching.

Apostasy Remains Unforgiven.* [26] If we deliberately persist in sin after having received the knowledge of the truth, then there no longer remains any sacrifice for sins. [27] There is only a terrifying expectation of judgment and of a fierce fire that will consume the adversaries.

[28] Anyone who violates the Law of Moses is put to death without mercy on the testimony of two or three witnesses. [29] How much more punishment do you think is deserved by the one who has contempt for the Son of God, profanes the blood of the covenant by which he was sanctified, and insults the Spirit of grace? [30] For we know the one who said,

"Vengeance is mine; I will repay,"

and

"The Lord will judge his people."

[31] It is a dreadful thing to fall into the hands of the living God.

Do Not Abandon Your Assurance.* [32] Remember the days gone by when, after you had been enlightened,* you endured a difficult struggle filled with suffering. [33] Sometimes you were publicly exposed to abuse and persecution, and sometimes you were companions of those who were treated in the same way. [34] You not only had compassion upon those who were in prison but also cheerfully accepted the confiscation of your property, because you realized that you possessed something better and more lasting.

[35] Therefore, do not lose your confidence now, since your reward will be so great. [36] You need to be steadfast if you want to do the will of God and receive what he has promised.

[37]   "For, after a little while,
        he who is to come will do so,
        and he will not delay.
[38]   My righteous one shall live by faith,
        but if he shrinks back,
        I will not be pleased with him."

[39] But we are not among those who draw back and are lost. Rather, we are among those who have faith and are saved.

B: The People of Faith*

11 **What Faith Is.** [1] Faith is the assurance of what we hope for and the conviction about things that cannot be seen.* [2] Indeed, it was because of it that our ancestors were commended.

[3] By faith we understand that the universe was created by the word of God, so that what is seen came into being from the invisible.

The Faith of the Early Patriarchs. [4] * By faith Abel * offered to God a better sacrifice than that of Cain. Because of this he was attested as righteous, God himself bearing witness to his gifts. Although he is dead, he continues to speak through it.

[5] By faith Enoch * was taken up so that he did not see death. He was found no more, because God had taken

him, and before he was taken up he was attested to have pleased God. [6] But without faith it is impossible to please him, for whoever comes to God must believe that he exists and that he rewards those who seek him.

[7] By faith Noah,* having been warned by God about things not yet seen, took heed and built an ark to save his household. Through his faith he condemned the world and inherited the righteousness that derives from faith.

The Faith of Abraham and His Descendants. [8] By faith Abraham* obeyed when he was called to set out for a place that he was to receive as an inheritance. He went forth without knowing where he was going. [9] By faith he sojourned in the promised land as in a foreign country, dwelling in tents with Isaac and Jacob, who were heirs with him of the same promise. [10] For he was looking forward to a city with firm foundations, whose architect and builder is God.

[11] By faith Abraham also received the power of procreation, even though he was well past the age—and Sarah herself was barren*—because he believed that the one who had made the promise would be faithful in fulfilling it. [12] Therefore, from one man, himself as good as dead, came forth descendants as numerous as the stars of heaven and as innumerable as the grains of sand on the seashore.

[13] All these died in faith without having received what had been promised, but from a distance they saw far ahead how those promises would be fulfilled and welcomed them, and acknowledged themselves to be strangers and foreigners on the earth. [14] People who speak in this way make it clear that they are looking for a country of their own. [15] If they had been thinking of the land that they had left behind, they would have had the opportunity to return. [16] But in fact they were longing for a better country, a heavenly one. Therefore, God is not ashamed to be called their God, for he has prepared a city for them.

¹⁷ By faith Abraham, when put to the test, offered up Isaac. He who had received the promises was ready to offer up his only son, ¹⁸ of whom he had been told, "Through Isaac descendants shall bear your name." ¹⁹ For he reasoned that God was able even to raise someone from the dead, and in a sense he was given back Isaac from the dead. *

²⁰ By faith Isaac* gave his blessings to Jacob and Esau for the future.

²¹ By faith Jacob, * as he was dying, blessed each one of the sons of Joseph and bowed in worship, leaning on his staff.

²² By faith Joseph,* near the end of his life, mentioned the Exodus of the Israelites and gave instructions about his burial.

²³ By faith Moses* was hidden by his parents for three months after his birth, because they saw that he was a beautiful child, and they did not fear the king's edict.

²⁴ By faith Moses, when he had grown up, refused to be called a son of Pharaoh's daughter. ²⁵ He preferred to be ill-treated along with the people of God rather than to enjoy the fleeting pleasures of sin. ²⁶ He considered that abuse suffered for the sake of the Messiah was a more precious gift than all the treasures of Egypt, for he was looking ahead to the final reward.

²⁷ By faith Moses departed from Egypt, unafraid of the wrath of the king; he persevered as if he could see the one who is invisible.

²⁸ By faith he kept the Passover and sprinkled the blood so that the Destroyer would not harm the firstborn of Israel.

The Faith of the Israelites and Rahab. ²⁹ By faith the people crossed the Red Sea as though it were dry land. However, when the Egyptians attempted to do so, they were drowned.

³⁰ By faith the walls of Jericho * fell when the people had marched around them for seven days.

[31] By faith Rahab * the prostitute did not perish with those who were disobedient, for she had received the spies in peace.

The Faith of the Judges and Prophets. [32] What more shall I say? Time is too short for me to speak of Gideon, Barak, Samson, and Jephthah, of David and Samuel and the Prophets, * [33] who by faith conquered kingdoms, administered justice, and obtained the promises. They closed the mouths of lions, * [34] quenched raging fires, * and escaped the edge of the sword. Their weakness was turned into strength as they became mighty in battle and put foreign armies to flight.

[35] Women received their dead * back through resurrection. Others who were tortured refused to accept release in order to obtain a better resurrection. [36] Still others were mocked and scourged, even to the point of enduring chains and imprisonment.

[37] They were stoned,* or sawed in two, or put to death by the sword. They went about in skins of sheep or goats—destitute, persecuted, and tormented. [38] The world was not worthy of them. They wandered about in desert areas and on mountains, and they lived in dens and caves of the earth.

[39] Yet all these, even though they were commended for their faith, did not receive what was promised. [40] For God had made provision for us to have something better, and they were not to achieve perfection except with us. *

C: Let Us Run with Eyes Fixed on Jesus*

12 **You Have Not Yet Resisted to the Point of Bloodshed.**
[1] Therefore, since we are surrounded by such a great cloud of witnesses, * let us throw off everything that weighs us down and the sins that so easily distract us and with perseverance run the race that lies ahead of us, [2] with our eyes fixed on Jesus, the author and perfecter of our faith. For the sake of the joy that lay before him, he endured the cross, ignoring its shame, and is now seated at the right hand of the throne of God.

³ Reflect on how he endured such great hostility from sinners so that you may not grow weary and lose heart. ⁴ In your struggle against sin, you have not yet resisted to the point of shedding your blood.

God Is Treating You as His Children.* ⁵ You have forgotten the exhortation that addresses you as children:

"My son, do not scorn the discipline of the Lord
    or lose heart when you are punished by him.
⁶   For the Lord disciplines those whom he loves,
        and he chastises every son whom he acknowledges."

⁷ Endure the trials you receive as a form of discipline. God is treating you as sons. For what son is there who is not disciplined by his father? ⁸ If you have not received the discipline in which all share, then you are illegitimate and not true sons.

⁹ In addition, we have all received discipline from our earthly fathers, and we respected them. Should we not then be even more willing to submit to the Father of spirits and live? ¹⁰ They disciplined us for a short time as they thought best, but he does so for our benefit so that we may share his holiness.

¹¹ At the time that discipline is received, it always seems painful rather than pleasant, but afterward it yields a harvest of peace and uprightness to those who have been trained by it. ¹² Therefore, strengthen your drooping hands and your weak knees, ¹³ and make straight paths for your feet, so that your weakened limbs may not be disabled but rather may be healed.

Seek Peace and Sanctification.* ¹⁴ Seek peace with everyone, as well as the holiness without which no one will ever see the Lord. ¹⁵ See to it that no one is deprived of the grace of God, and that no root of bitterness may spring up and cause trouble, resulting in the defilement of many.

¹⁶ Do not be like Esau, an immoral and worldly-minded person who sold his birthright for a single meal. ¹⁷ Afterward, as you know, when he sought to inherit the

blessing, he was rejected. Even though he sought it with tears, he found no possibility for repentance.

Listen to the One Who Is Speaking.* [18] You have not come to something that can be touched: a blazing fire, or complete darkness, or gloom, or a storm, [19] or the sound of a trumpet, or a voice speaking words that made those who heard them beg that nothing more be said to them. [20] For they could not bear to hear the command that was given, "If even an animal touches the mountain, it must be stoned to death." [21] Indeed, so terrifying was the sight that Moses cried out, "I am terrified and trembling."

[22] But you have come to Mount Zion and to the city of the living God, the heavenly Jerusalem. You have come to myriads of angels in joyful gathering, [23] and to the assembly of the firstborn* whose names are written in heaven, and to God the judge of all, and to the spirits of the righteous who have been made perfect. [24] You have come to Jesus the mediator of a new covenant and to the sprinkled blood that speaks more powerfully than even the blood of Abel.

[25] See that you do not reject the one who is speaking. For if those did not escape when they rejected the one who warned them on earth, how much more is this true of us if we turn away from the one who is from heaven? [26] At that time, his voice shook the earth, but now he has promised, "Once more I will shake not only the earth but heaven as well."

[27] The words "once more" indicate the removal of what can be shaken—that is, all created things—so that what cannot be shaken may remain. [28] Therefore, since we are receiving a kingdom that cannot be shaken, let us give thanks, offering to God a worship that is pleasing to him. [29] For our God is a consuming fire.

VI: CONCLUSION

13 **Aspects of the Christian Life.*** [1] Let mutual love continue, [2] and do not forget to offer hospitality to strangers, for by doing this some have entertained angels without knowing it. * ³ Be mindful of those who are in prison, as though you were imprisoned with them, and of those who are being maltreated, since you too are in the body.

⁴ Let marriage be held in honor by all, and the marriage bed kept undefiled, for those who are immoral and adulterers will have to face God's judgment. ⁵ Do not succumb to the love of money, but be content with what you have, for God has said, "I will never forsake you or abandon you." ⁶ Therefore, we can say with confidence:

> "The Lord is my helper;
> I will not be afraid.
> What can anyone do to me?"

Let Us Seek the City That Is To Come.* ⁷ Remember your leaders who spoke the word of God to you. Keep in mind the outcome of their way of life and imitate their faith. ⁸ Jesus Christ is the same yesterday, today, and forever.

⁹ Do not be led astray by all kinds of strange doctrines. It is good for us to have our hearts strengthened by grace, and not by ceremonial foods, which have not benefited those who partake of them.

¹⁰ We have an altar * from which those who serve the tabernacle have no right to eat. ¹¹ For the bodies of those animals whose blood is brought into the sanctuary by the high priest as a sin offering are burned outside the camp. * ¹² Therefore, Jesus also suffered outside the city gate in order to sanctify the people by his own blood. *

¹³ Let us then go to him outside the camp * and bear the abuse he endured. ¹⁴ For here we have no lasting city, but we are seeking the one that is to come. ¹⁵ Through him let us continually offer up to God a sacrifice of praise, * that is, the fruit of lips that confess his name.

¹⁶ * Do not neglect to do good works and to share with others what you have, for these are the kind of sacrifices that please God. ¹⁷ Obey your leaders and submit to them, for they watch over your souls and will have to render an account in that regard. Make this a joy for them to

do rather than a grief, for that would be of no advantage to you.

[18] Pray for us. We are sure that our own conscience is clear, and our desire is to act honorably in everything we do. [19] I especially ask you to do this that I may be restored to you as soon as possible.

Final Doxology. [20] * May the God of peace—who brought back from the dead our Lord Jesus, the great shepherd of the sheep, by the blood of the eternal covenant— [21] make you perfect in every respect so that you may do his will. And may he enable us to achieve what is pleasing to him through Jesus Christ, to whom be glory forever and ever. Amen.

News and Farewell. [22] I urge you, brethren, to listen to my words of exhortation; that is why I have written to you only a short letter. [23] I want to let you know that our brother Timothy has been set free. * If he arrives in time, he will be with me when I see you.

[24] My greetings to all your leaders and to all the saints. * Those from Italy send you their greetings as well.

[25] Grace be with all of you.

THE CATHOLIC LETTERS

There are seven New Testament Letters that have this in common: they are in the form of letters, but no one has ever thought of attributing them to Paul. These are: The Letter of James, The First Letter of Peter, The Second Letter of Peter, The First Letter of John, The Second Letter of John, The Third Letter of John, and The Letter of Jude.

Most of these Letters are not addressed to specific communities but deal with general questions that are relevant to a very wide circle of readers. For this reason, they certainly deserved to be grouped together, as they have been since the fourth century, under the title of "Catholic Letters," i.e., General or Universal Letters, Letters intended for the Church as a whole. The particular destination of the brief Second and Third Letters of John could be a problem in this regard. However, it is very likely that their brevity caused them to be annexed to the First Letter of John as simple appendices that had little effect on the overall title.

These seven Letters gradually acquired authority throughout the Church, all the more so since they carried the signatures of important men: James, Peter, John, and Jude. However, critics disagree widely both as to these attributions and as to the dates of the Letters.

The Catholic Letters do not form a homogeneous group, but they do possess some common traits. We are no longer involved in the great struggles of Paul to affirm—against Jewish claims and pagan illusions—that salvation has been given in Christ Jesus and him alone. We find in these documents a Christianity that is no longer in the early years after its formation; the communities are already more firmly established and have acquired their habitual ways.

The problem the Letters deal with is perhaps that of keeping communities from yielding to wear and tear and becoming lax, of keeping them from losing their taste for essentials and returning to alien ideas.

We have the impression of entering a world that is less familiar to us and of hearing questions that are somewhat alien to us, if not downright bizarre.

These Letters deal with problems that occupied Christianity, or at least parts of it, at the time they were written: e.g., certain false doctrines—a form of Gnosis in Asia Minor (1 John); Gnostic-Antinomian tendencies (2 Peter; Jude); the non-occurrence of the Second Coming (2 Peter); severe sufferings and persecutions of the Christian communities (1 Peter).

At the same time, these Letters do not have a uniform literary form. James, Peter, and Jude have written real pastoral Letters, destined for an entire region of the Christian world. With the circle of addressees increasing, their message turns easily into an impersonal treatise and into the general considerations of a homily or of an episcopal mandate. On the other hand, the Third Letter of John is a private missive, addressed to a benefactor of Christian missionaries.

The first two Letters of John lend themselves to discussion: the First because of its lack of all epistolary structure, and the Second because of the ambiguous way in which it designates its addressees. However, scholars view them as real Letters addressed to a community or communities that the author knows intimately and precisely and that are within the radius of his customary apostolic solicitude. The First Letter of John thus fits the genre of the Letters of James, Peter, and Jude, while the Second is a more intimate communication.

The theology of these Letters is a faithful reproduction of the preaching of Jesus. The sacred authors repeat the teachings of their Master with complete fidelity. Hence, Christian love holds the greatest importance in them, especially in James and above all in John.

The Letters also endow their authors with well-defined personalities. James is a Christian well versed in the sapiential and prophetic schools who masterfully dispenses austere moral teaching. Peter is a pastor of souls who harmoniously unites doctrinal and moral teaching, exhortation and warning. John is the disciple of love who takes on a polemical ardor in the face of attempted deviations from Christianity. Jude is a disciple rooted in a rich apocalyptic foundation who writes as the implacable foe of error.

Comparing the contents of these Letters with the other writings of the New Testament, we find that they contain some doctrinal points that are exclusive to them: the Sacrament of the Anointing of the Sick (James), Christ's descent to the netherworld (1 Peter), and the final conflagration (2 Peter).

At the same time, these Letters are filled with incisive passages on authentic Christianity. They are replete with reminders to let the Gospel be the life-giving activity that it should be rather than something tasteless due to boastful theories.

THE LETTER OF JAMES

FAITH ACTIVE IN WORKS

Without the first verse, this writing would have no resemblance at all to a letter. In it we find moral exhortations, striking aphorisms, and finely etched portraits succeeding one another in no discernible order. We also find themes such as courage in trials, concern for true wisdom, and critique of social conditions, which make us think of the great sapiential writings of the Old Testament with their didactic bent. This type of thinking was thus still active in the first Christian generations.

We also find here all the vigor of prophetic invective to denounce abuses and injustice. Jewish, Greek, and Christian ideas all seem to meld together. And though the name of Christ is cited only in an occasional manner, this pressing sermon is an application of the Beatitudes. It is preoccupied with the authenticity of the Christian faith.

In these recommendations that follow one another in rapid succession, we can discern a few prophetic and evangelical concerns.

The Letter of James will always be cited for its concern for the weak and the afflicted, its understanding of poverty and distrust of wealth, its lively attack on social injustice, and its warnings to businessmen.

Apparently, for many Christians of that time, faith seems to have been an occasion for fine discourses or gratuitous considerations apart from any life commitment. James retaliated against such a way of thinking. This has led some to suppose that the author was opposed to the great Pauline teaching concerning salvation by faith alone in Jesus Christ (see Rom 3:28).

However, the reality is that Paul and James were speaking of the same thing from different viewpoints. For Paul, faith is an incontestable change and commitment of life; James knows people for whom faith is nothing more than discourses, discus-

sions, and doctrinal debates, without any impact on their existence. For Paul, works are the observances prescribed by the Law on which one would like to make salvation depend by attributing it to people's merits instead of God's grace. But it is not in this sense that James speaks of works; for him, they express the commitment to faith, a Christianity in action. In order to understand Paul and James, we must pinpoint the concrete problems that each of them is addressing; they are not the same for each.

The problems of the liturgical assembly hold a large place in the Letter of James. There are references to listening to the word of God, songs of praise, the confession of sins followed by prayer, and the Anointing of the Sick. The author goes even farther. He criticizes the assemblies of worship that follow the style of social gatherings and provide the wealthy with the occasion to pursue their ambition and their success. For him, as well as for the Prophets and for Christ, authentic worship commits one to a fraternal life, and it is above all the sum total of the Christian life that is the true spiritual worship. Outside of this, every Liturgy is only so much ornamentation. True religion is the care of widows, orphans, the sick, and the disenfranchised.

This piece of writing circulated under the name of "James." Christian tradition has identified this person with James, who, like Jude and Simon, was "a brother of the Lord" (Mt 13:55; Mk 6:3). He was perhaps the son of Alphaeus who is named in all the lists of the Twelve. He had a very important place in the mother community of Jerusalem. Paul mentions him among the witnesses of the Resurrection (see 1 Cor 15:7). He is also found at the Upper Room with the first group of Christians (see Acts 1:12-14).

When Peter left prison, he was concerned to get news of his deliverance to James immediately (see Acts 12:17). After his conversion, Paul got in touch with him (see Gal 1:18-19). James played a decisive role in the Council of Jerusalem; though his mentality was Jewish, he showed himself conciliatory toward and receptive to converts coming from paganism (see Acts 15:13-29).

Beginning with the first scattering of the Apostles in A.D. 36/37, James seems to have taken responsibility for the mother Church; the elders gathered around him; he welcomed Paul when the latter brought the collection taken up in the Churches (see Acts 21:18-26), shortly before Paul's arrest in the temple (Pentecost, A.D. 58). James died a martyr around A.D. 62. If the present Letter is from that James, it must be dated to around A.D. 60. But Hellenistic influences and an affinity with other Christian writings of a later date prevent too certain an attribution.

The Letter is addressed to "the twelve tribes of the Dispersion," which is another way of saying that it is addressed to the Church scattered throughout the world, to the true Israel (see Rom 2:29; 9:6; Gal 6:16; Phil 3:3). The term "Dispersion" (in Greek diaspora) signified all the Jews living outside of Palestine (see Jud 5:19; Ps 147:2; Jer 15:7). Here the reference is to Christians of Jewish origin, who are scattered throughout the Greco-Roman world.

Whatever be the case with the author, the date, and the addressees, this document—recognized as inspired—is a strong warning against a purely verbal Christianity and is a call to a faith that has the courage to change lives.

The Letter to James may be divided as follows:

I: Salutation (1:1)
II: Exhortation To Practice Patience (1:2-18)
III: Exhortation To Practice Faith (1:19—2:26)
IV: Exhortation To Practice Christian Living (3:1—5:18)
V: Conclusion (5:19-20)

I: SALUTATION

1 **Greeting.*** [1] James, a servant of God and of the Lord Jesus Christ, to the twelve tribes of the Dispersion: greetings.

II: EXHORTATION TO PRACTICE PATIENCE

Trials—the Test of a Faith in Progress.* [2] My brethren, consider it a cause of great joy whenever you endure various trials, [3] for you know that the testing of your faith will develop perseverance. [4] And let perseverance complete its work so that you may become perfect and complete, and not be deficient in any respect.

A Believer's Prayer.* [5] If someone among you lacks wisdom, he should ask God, who gives to all generously and without finding fault, and it will be given to him. [6] But he is to ask with faith, without doubting, for the one who doubts is like a wave of the sea that is driven and tossed about by the wind. [7] A man like that should not think that he will receive anything from the Lord, [8] since he is of two minds and inconsistent in everything he does.

Rich and Poor.* [9] The brother who is in modest circumstances should take pride in being raised up. [10] Likewise, the one who is rich should glory in being brought low, for he will disappear like a flower of the field. [11] Once the sun comes up with its scorching rays and withers the grass, its flower droops and its beauty vanishes. So too the rich man will fade away in the midst of his affairs.

Trials and Temptations. [12] Blessed is the man who perseveres when he is tempted, for when he has been proven, he will receive the crown of life that the Lord has promised to those who love him.*

[13] * While experiencing temptation, no one should say, "God is tempting me." For God cannot be tempted by evil, and he himself tempts no one. [14] Rather, temptation occurs when someone is attracted and seduced by his own desire. [15] Then the desire conceives and gives birth

to sin, and that sin, when it reaches full growth, gives birth to death.

Light and Life.* ¹⁶ Do not be deceived, my beloved brethren. ¹⁷ Every good act of giving and every perfect gift are from above, coming down from the Father of all light. With him there is no alteration or shadow caused by change. ¹⁸ By his own choice he gave us birth through the way of truth so that we may be a kind of firstfruits of all his creation.

III: EXHORTATION TO PRACTICE FAITH

Living by God's Word.* ¹⁹ Remember this, my beloved brethren: everyone should be quick to listen but slow to speak and slow to anger. ²⁰ For human anger does not bring about the righteousness of God. ²¹ Therefore, rid yourselves of everything sordid and of every wicked excess, and welcome in all humility the word that is implanted in you and is able to save your souls.

²² Be doers of the word and not just hearers who only deceive themselves. ²³ For anyone who listens to the word and fails to do it is like someone who looks at his face in a mirror. ²⁴ After seeing his reflection, he goes off and immediately forgets what he looked like. ²⁵ However, the one who looks intently at the perfect law of freedom and perseveres—not forgetting what he has heard but putting it into practice—will be blessed in everything he does.

²⁶ If anyone thinks that he is religious but does not restrain his tongue, he is deceiving himself, and his religion is worthless. ²⁷ Religion that God our Father accepts as pure and undefiled is this: to come to the aid of orphans and widows in their hardships and to keep oneself untarnished by the world.

2 **Rich and Poor in the Christian Assembly.*** ¹ My brethren, since you are believers in our glorious Lord Jesus Christ, you must never practice favoritism. ² Suppose a man wearing a gold ring and expensive clothes comes into your assembly as well as a poor man dressed in shabby clothes. [3] If you lavish special attention on the one wearing the expensive clothes and say, "Please sit in this good seat," while to the poor man you say, "Stand over there," or "Sit on the floor at my feet," [4] have you not shown favoritism among yourselves and judged by wrongful standards?

[5] Listen to me, my beloved brethren. Did not God choose those who are poor * in the world to be rich in faith and to be heirs of the kingdom that he promised to those who love him? [6] But you have humiliated the poor man. Furthermore, is it not the rich who oppress you? Are they not the ones who drag you into court? [7] Is it not they who blaspheme the noble name that was invoked over you?

[8] You will be doing well if you truly observe the sovereign law enjoined in Scripture, "You shall love your neighbor as yourself." [9] However, if you show partiality, you are committing a sin and stand convicted by the law as lawbreakers. [10] For whoever observes the whole Law but trips up on a single point is held guilty of breaking all of it.

[11] The one who said, "You shall not commit adultery," also said, "You shall not kill." Now if you do not commit adultery but you do kill, you have become a lawbreaker. [12] Therefore, always speak and act as those who will be judged by the law of freedom. [13] For judgment will be without mercy to the one who has not shown mercy, but mercy triumphs over judgment.

True Faith Is Proved by Works.* [14] What good is it, my brethren, if someone claims to have faith but does not have good works? Can such faith save him? [15] * Suppose a brother or sister is naked and lacks his or her daily food. [16] If one of you says to such a person, "Go in peace; keep warm and eat well," but does not take care of that person's physical needs, what is the good of that? [17] In the same way, faith by itself is dead if it does not have works.

[18] But perhaps someone will say, "You have faith and I have works." Show me your faith without works, and by

works I will show you my faith. [19] You believe that there is one God. You do well to assert that. But even the demons believe and tremble.

[20] You fool! Do you want proof that faith without works is futile? [21] Was not Abraham our father justified by works when he offered his son Isaac on the altar? [22] Thus, you can see that his faith and his works were active together; his faith was brought to completion by works.

[23] Thus, the words of Scripture were fulfilled that say, "Abraham believed God, and it was credited to him as righteousness," and he was called the friend of God. [24] You can see, then, that a man is justified by works and not by faith alone.

[25] Likewise, Rahab the prostitute,* was she not also justified by works when she welcomed the messengers and sent them away by a different road? [26] For just as the body is dead without a spirit, so faith without works is also dead.

IV: EXHORTATION TO PRACTICE CHRISTIAN LIVING

3 **Avoid Faults of the Tongue.*** [1] My brethren, not many of you should become teachers, for you know that we will face a more severe judgment. [2] For all of us fall short in many ways. Anyone who never makes a mistake in speech has reached perfection * and is able to control every part of his body.

[3] When we put a bit into a horse's mouth to make it obey us, we also guide its entire body. [4] Or think of ships. Even though they are large and are driven by strong winds, they are steered by a very small rudder on whatever course the helmsman chooses. [5] In the same way, the tongue is a small member but its pretensions are great.

Consider how a small fire can set ablaze a great forest. [6] And the tongue is also a fire, a world of evil that infects the entire body. It sets afire the entire course of our existence and is itself set on fire by Gehenna.

[7] For every species of beast and bird, of reptile and sea creature, can be tamed and has been tamed by man, [8] but no one can tame the tongue. It is a restless evil, full of deadly poison. [9] With it we bless the Lord and Father, and with it we curse people who are made in the likeness of God. *

[10] Out of the same mouth flow blessings and curses. This should not be so, my brethren. [11] Does a spring pour forth from the same opening both fresh and salt water? [12] Can a fig tree, my brethren, produce olives or can a grapevine produce figs? Neither can salt water yield fresh water.

True Wisdom and Its Opposite.* [13] Who among you is wise and understanding? Prove by your good life that your works are done with the humility that comes from wisdom. [14] But if your hearts are filled with bitter envy and selfish ambition, do not be boastful in defiance of the truth.

[15] Such wisdom does not come down from above, but is earthly, unspiritual, and demonic. [16] For where there is envy and selfish ambition, there will also be disharmony and every type of wickedness.

[17] However, the wisdom that comes from above is first of all pure, then peaceable, gentle, and considerate, full of mercy and good fruits, without any trace of partiality or hypocrisy. [18] And a harvest of righteousness is sown in peace by those who are peacemakers.

4 **The Need To Control Passions.*** [1] What is the source of these conflicts and quarrels among you? Are they not the result of your passions * that are at war within you? [2] You want something that you cannot have, so you commit murder. And you covet something but cannot obtain it, so you engage in quarrels and fights. You do not have because you do not ask. [3] When you ask, you do not get what you want because you do not ask for it with the proper motives, seeking rather to indulge your passions.

⁴ Adulterers! Do you not know that love of the world results in enmity with God? Therefore, whoever wishes to be a lover of the world makes himself an enemy of God. ⁵ Or do you suppose that it is without reason that Scripture says, "He yearns jealously for the Spirit that he sent to live in us"?* ⁶ But he has bestowed an even stronger grace. Therefore, it says,

> "God resists the proud,
>   but he gives grace to the humble."

⁷ Hence, be subject to God. Resist the devil, and he will flee from you. ⁸ Draw near to God, and he will draw near to you. Cleanse your hands, you sinners, and purify your hearts, you waverers. ⁹ Be sorrowful, lament, and weep. Let your laughter turn to mourning and your joy to gloom. ¹⁰ Humble yourselves before the Lord, and he will exalt you.

Do Not Judge Others.* ¹¹ Do not slander one another, my brethren. Whoever speaks ill of a brother or passes judgment on a brother speaks ill of the Law and passes judgment on the Law. But if you judge the Law, you are not keeping it but passing judgment upon it. ¹² There is only one Lawgiver and Judge, the one who is able to save or to destroy. Who then are you to pass judgment on a neighbor?

A Warning against Presumption.* ¹³ Come now, you who say, "Today or tomorrow we shall head off to this or that town and spend a year doing business there and making money." ¹⁴ Yet you do not know what tomorrow will bring.

What is your life, after all? For you are like a mist that appears for a brief time and then vanishes. ¹⁵ Instead, what you ought to say is, "If it is the Lord's will, we shall live to do this or that." ¹⁶ But instead you boast in your arrogance, and all such boasting is evil. ¹⁷ Anyone who knows the right thing to do and fails to do it commits a sin.

5 Woe to the Rich.*
¹ Come now, you who are rich. Lament and weep over the miseries that will soon over-

whelm you. [2] Your riches have rotted. Your clothes are all moth-eaten. [3] Your gold and silver have corroded. Their corrosion will serve as a witness against you and consume your flesh like a fire. You have hoarded wealth for the last days.

[4] Behold, the wages you fraudulently withheld from the laborers who harvested your fields are crying out, and the cries of those harvesters have reached the ears of the Lord of hosts. [5] You have lived on earth in luxury and self-indulgence. You have gorged yourselves as on the day of slaughter. [6] You have condemned the righteous man and murdered him, even though he offered you no resistance.

Patience, for the Lord's Coming Is Near.* [7] Therefore be patient, brethren, until the coming of the Lord. Think of how patiently a farmer awaits the precious crop from his fields until they have received the early and the late rains. [8] You too must be patient. Take courage, for the coming of the Lord is near. *

[9] Brethren, do not raise complaints against one another lest you yourselves be brought to judgment. Behold, the Judge is standing at the gates.

[10] As an example of patience in enduring hardship, brethren, consider the Prophets who spoke in the name of the Lord. [11] Indeed, those who had perseverance are the ones we call blessed. You have heard of the perseverance of Job and have come to understand the Lord's purpose in this respect, because the Lord is merciful and compassionate.

Do Not Swear. [12] Above all, my brethren, do not swear, either by heaven or by earth, or use any oaths at all. Let your "Yes" mean "Yes" and your "No" mean "No." Otherwise you may be condemned. *

Anointing of the Sick. [13] * Is anyone among you suffering? He should pray. Is anyone cheerful? He should sing songs of praise. [14] Is anyone among you sick? He should send for the presbyters of the Church so that they may pray over him and anoint him with oil in the name of the Lord.

[15] The prayer of faith will save the sick person, and the Lord will raise him up. And if he has committed any sins, he will be forgiven.

Confession and Intercession. [16] Therefore, confess your sins to one another and pray for one another, so that you may be healed. The prayer of a righteous man is powerful and effective.

[17] Elijah was a man like us. Yet when he prayed fervently that it might not rain for three and a half years, it did not rain on the earth. [18] Then he prayed again, and the heavens gave forth rain, and the earth once again brought forth its harvest.

V: CONCLUSION

The Peace of Fraternal Love. * [19] My brethren, if one of you should stray from the truth and another succeeds in bringing him back, [20] remember this: A person who brings back a sinner from erring ways will rescue his soul from death and cover a multitude of sins.

THE FIRST LETTER OF PETER

WITNESSES TO HOPE

Grave threats darken the horizon for the Churches located in Asia Minor. For the most part, these communities have been founded by Paul and his coworkers. They bring together in one assembly, one faith, and one conception of life Jews and Gentiles who have become Christian. Such a union could appear strange to people on the outside. In addition, these men and women have broken away from the ways of life and thought of those who surround them. Christians are thus suspected of subversive behavior and morals.

If persecution has not struck as yet, it is just around the corner. We can think of the Emperor Nero, who gave rise to the first persecutions in A.D. 64. We have the impression that for the moment Christians are being subjected mainly to pressures, vexations, scorn, and suspicions, and they are despised and ostracized from the social life of their area.

In such circumstances, could Christians forget that, according to the Old Testament and the Gospel, the onset of opposition announces the last times and that Christ has promised persecution as an advance sign of his return (see Mt 5:11f; 10:22; Lk 21:12-19)? Believers must not be frozen in fear. The moment must inspire a renewal of hope. They must remain filled with courage, joy, simplicity, and loyalty, keeping their eyes on the future, the great future of the encounter with Jesus (see 1 Pet 1:5, 13, 20; 2:12; 4:5, 13, 17; 5:1-4, 10). This is not a case of minimizing the judgment that is also coming, for Christians regard it with hope, not fear.

The First Letter of Peter seems to be an excellent example of catechesis as practiced around the sixties of the first century. Here and there, the author seems to have read Paul, the discourses in Acts, or passages of the Gospels; we have in this document part of the patrimony of Christian initiation and instruction.

In addition to giving us a theology of Baptism, a teaching about the baptismal life, this document is also one of the texts best suited for conveying an understanding of the mystery of the Church, the community that carries out God's plan in the midst of the world, the new human race that is maturing in Christ. The theology of the Church is in this case a spirituality of joy.

In this Christian milieu one places the Gospel into evidence when one speaks of salvation, hope, and the time of God for humanity. One must focus on the mystery of Christ: the innocent, humble, and suffering Christ, in whose footsteps believers must walk, exposed to all kinds of attacks (see 1 Pet 2:9, 21-23).

Appeal is always made to this Letter when the topic is Christ's descent to the netherworld (see 1 Pet 3:19f; 4:6). The theme can receive diverse interpretations, among which it is difficult to navigate. It certainly stresses Christ's sovereignty over all humanity from its origin as well as his sovereignty over the universe, and it demonstrates the universal efficacy of his redemptive work.

This Letter presents the Christian life as something simple and right, without any complicated rule of life but with the sense of love and loyalty. When they are threatened by persecution and when they live in a perspective of the end of the world, these Christians do not construct any new project for society. They accept the structures and conditions of life that form part of their world. However, in this real context, they want to bear witness to righteousness, loyalty, and the meaning of human duties. It is in this sense that we must read the passage concerning slaves, women, and public officials (see 1 Pet 2:13—3:7). In the face of persecution, they reflect on the meaning of suffering and on the Beatitudes. They must remember that the servant is not greater than the Master, as Christ declared (see Mt 10:24).

A very ancient tradition, the first attestations of which go back to the end of the first century, attributes this Letter to Peter, the head of the Apostles. Critical studies often cast doubt on the attribution because of the difficulties it raises, but good arguments for it are not lacking. The text is written in simple and correct Greek; Peter was linked with the family of Zebedee, which ran a fishing business in Galilee, and so would have known the language. Moreover, in its final redaction, the Letter may have been fine-tuned by the writer's secretary, Silvanus or Silas, a Greek by birth and found more than once in the company of Paul (see Acts 15:22; 17:4; 2 Cor 1:19).

Peter would have written this Letter from "Rome," which was the most current interpretation of "Babylon" (1 Pet 5:13). For in Judaism this name signified the power that from time to time oppressed the Jewish faith and scattered the people, and from the first century B.C. onward that power was Rome.

In a more dramatic context, the Book of Revelation (18:2, 10, 21) uses the same image for the public authority that persecutes. On the other hand, we also know that Peter was martyred in Rome, under Nero, in A.D. 64 or 67.

The First Letter of Peter may be divided as follows:

I: SALUTATION*

1 **To the Faithful in the Dispersion.** [1] Peter,* an apostle of Jesus Christ, to all the exiles of the Dispersion who are now living in Pontus, Galatia, Cappadocia, Asia, and Bithynia, [2] chosen* in the foreknowledge of God the Father, through sanctification by the Spirit, to be obedient to Jesus Christ and to be sprinkled with his blood: may grace and peace be yours in abundance.

II: THE PRIVILEGES AND RESPONSIBILITIES OF SALVATION*

The Song of the New Life.* [3] Blessed be the God and Father of our Lord Jesus Christ. In his great mercy he has given us a new birth to a living hope through the resurrection of Jesus Christ from the dead [4] and to an inheritance that is imperishable, undefiled, and unfading. It is reserved in heaven for you [5] who because of your faith are being protected by God's power until the salvation that is ready to be revealed at the end of time. *

[6] This is a reason for you to rejoice, even if now for a little while you must suffer trials of many kinds. [7] Thus, the genuine quality of your faith—which is more valuable than gold that is perishable even if it has been tested by fire—may be proved worthy of praise, glory, and honor when Jesus Christ is revealed.

⁸ Although you have not seen him, you love him; and even though you do not see him now, you believe in him and are filled with a joy that is indescribable and glorious. ⁹ For you are achieving the goal of your faith, that is, the salvation of your souls.

¹⁰ This salvation was the subject of intense scrutiny and investigation by the Prophets* who spoke about the grace that you were to receive. ¹¹ They were searching out the time and the circumstances to which the Spirit of Christ* within them was pointing when it testified in advance to the sufferings that Christ would endure and the glories that would then follow.

¹² It was revealed to them that they were serving not themselves but you when they spoke of the things that have now been announced to you through those who proclaimed the good news to you by the Holy Spirit sent from heaven. Even the angels long to catch a glimpse of such things.

Convictions for Living.* ¹³ Therefore, prepare your minds for action. Be calm and fix your hopes completely on the grace that you will be granted at the revelation of Jesus Christ. ¹⁴ Like obedient children, do not yield to the evil desires you had in your former ignorance. ¹⁵ He who called you is holy. Therefore, be holy yourselves in all your conduct. ¹⁶ For Scripture says, "Be holy, for I am holy."

¹⁷ If you address as Father the one who judges everyone impartially on the basis of each person's deeds, live in reverent fear during the time of your exile here. ¹⁸ For you are aware that you were ransomed from your futile way of life inherited from your ancestors not with perishable things like silver or gold, ¹⁹ but with the precious blood of Christ,* a lamb without blemish or defect.

²⁰ He was chosen before the foundation of the world, but in this final age he has been revealed for your sake. ²¹ Through him you have come to believe in God, who raised him from the dead and gave him glory, so that your faith and your hope are fixed on God.

²² Now that you have purified your souls by your obedience to truth so that you have genuine love for your brethren, love one another intensely with all your heart. ²³ You have been born anew, not of perishable but of imperishable seed, through the living and enduring word of God. * ²⁴ For:

All flesh is like grass,
  and all its glory like the flower of the field.
The grass withers, and the flower fades,
²⁵   but the word of the Lord endures forever.

It is this word that has been proclaimed to you.

2 ¹ Rid yourselves, therefore, of all malice, and all deceit, hypocrisy, and envy, and all slander. ² Like newborn infants, long for pure spiritual milk, so that by it you may advance on the path to salvation, ³ now that you have tasted that the Lord is good.

The Mystery of the Church. * ⁴ Come to him, a living stone, rejected by men but chosen by God and precious. ⁵ You, too, are like living stones, being built up into a spiritual temple and a holy priesthood * to offer spiritual sacrifices acceptable to God through Jesus Christ. ⁶ For it states in Scripture,

"See, I am laying a stone in Zion,
  a cornerstone chosen and precious.
Whoever believes in it
  will not be put to shame."

⁷ Therefore, it is precious to you who believe. However, for those who do not believe,

"The stone that the builders rejected
  has become the cornerstone,"

⁸ and

"A stone that makes them stumble,
  and a rock that makes them fall."

They stumble because they disobey the word—for this they were born. *

⁹ But you are "a chosen race, a royal priesthood, a holy nation, a people claimed by God as his own possession," so that you may proclaim the praise of him who called you out of darkness into his marvelous light.

10   Once you were not a people,
            but now you are God's people.
        Once you had not received mercy,
            but now you have received mercy.

III: GOD'S PEOPLE IN A HOSTILE WORLD*

Lead a Good Life amidst Pagans.* ¹¹ Beloved, I urge you as aliens and exiles not to succumb to the desires of the flesh that wage war against the soul. ¹² Conduct yourselves honorably among the Gentiles so that, although they now malign you as evildoers, they may observe your good works and glorify God on the day of visitation.

Christianity Is Not a Subversive Group.* ¹³ For the Lord's sake, submit to every human institution, whether of the emperor as supreme ¹⁴ or of governors as sent by him to punish those who do wrong and to commend those who do good works. ¹⁵ For it is the will of God that by doing right you should silence the ignorant talk of fools.

¹⁶ As servants of God, behave as free people, but do not use your freedom as a means to cover up wrongdoing. ¹⁷ Give due honor to everyone. Love your fellow believers. Fear God. Honor the emperor.

Recommendations for Slaves.* ¹⁸ Slaves, submit to your masters with due respect, not only to those who are kind and forbearing but also to those who are harsh. ¹⁹ It is a sign of grace if you endure the pain of unjust suffering because of your awareness of God.

²⁰ What credit do you deserve if you are patient when you are beaten for doing wrong? However, if you are patient when you do what is right and suffer for it, you have earned merit with God.

[21] * This, in fact, is what you have been called to do, because Christ himself suffered for you and left an example for you to follow in his footsteps.

[22]   He committed no sin,*
         and no deceit was found on his lips.

[23] When he was abused, he did not retaliate. When he suffered, he made no threats, but he placed his trust in the one who judges justly. [24] He himself bore our sins in his body on the cross, so that we might die to sin and live in righteousness.

By his wounds you have been healed. [25] For you were like sheep who had gone astray, but now you have returned to the shepherd and guardian of your souls.*

3 Recommendations for Spouses.*

[1] In the same way, you who are wives should accept the authority of your husbands. Then, even if they do not believe the word, they may be won over without words simply by the conduct of their wives [2] as they observe your reverence and your chaste behavior.

[3] * Do not seek to adorn yourself externally—by the braiding of your hair and the wearing of gold jewelry or fine clothing. [4] Rather, let your adornment be of your inner self, the imperishable beauty of a gentle and quiet spirit, which is precious in the sight of God.

[5] It was in this way that the holy women who placed their hope in God long ago used to adorn themselves and be submissive to their husbands. [6] Thus, Sarah obeyed Abraham and called him her "lord." You are now her daughters as long as you live good lives and never allow fears to alarm you.

[7] Likewise, you who are husbands must show consideration for your wives in your life together. Treat your wife with respect, for even though she is the weaker partner, she is also an equal heir of God's gift * of life. Thus, your prayers will not be hindered in any way.

Mutual Love.* [8] Finally, all of you should be united in spirit, sympathetic, filled with love for one another, compassionate, and humble. [9] Do not repay evil with evil or abuse with abuse. On the contrary, repay with a blessing. This is what you were called to do, so that you might inherit a blessing. [10] For:

"If anyone wishes to love life
　　and to experience good days,
he must restrain his tongue from evil
　　and his lips from deceitful speech.
[11]　He must turn away from evil and do good,
　　seek peace and pursue it.
[12]　For the eyes of the Lord are on the righteous
　　and his ears are attentive to their prayer.
However, the face of the Lord
　　is set against those who do evil."

IV: CHRISTIAN CONDUCT IN SUFFERING AND PERSECUTION

The Blessings of Suffering for Righteousness.* [13] Now who is going to harm you if you are eager to do what is right? [14] Yet even if you should suffer for doing what is right, you are thereby blessed. Have no fear of others, and refuse to be intimidated by them. [15] Rather, revere Christ as Lord in your hearts.

Always be prepared to offer an explanation to anyone who asks you to justify the hope that is in you. However, do so with gentleness and respect [16] and with a clean conscience so that those who slander you for your good behavior in Christ may be put to shame. [17] For it is better to suffer for doing what is right, if such is the will of God, than for doing what is wrong.

Christ's Victory and Descent to the Netherworld, and Christian Baptism.* [18] For Christ also suffered for our sins once for all, the righteous for the unrighteous, in order to bring you to God. He was put to death in the flesh but raised to life in the spirit.

[19] In the spirit * also he went to preach to the spirits in prison, [20] those who had refused to obey long ago while God waited patiently in the days of Noah during the building of the ark. In it only a few persons, eight in all, were saved through water.

[21] This water prefigured Baptism, which now saves you. It does so not by the washing away of dirt from the body but by the pledge of a good conscience given to God through the resurrection of Jesus Christ. [22] He has entered heaven and is at the right hand of God, with angels, authorities, and powers made subject to him.

4 [1] Therefore, since Christ suffered in the flesh, you should arm yourselves also with the same intention. For anyone who has suffered in the flesh has finished with sin [2] and for the remainder of life on earth must be ruled not by human passions but by the will of God.

[3] You have already spent enough time in doing what the Gentiles like to do, pursuing a life of debauchery, licentiousness, drunkenness, orgies, carousing, and sacrilegious idolatry. [4] They are surprised that you no longer join them in a life of dissipation, and they revile you as a result. [5] However, they will have to render an account to him who stands ready to judge * the living and the dead.

[6] And this is the reason why the gospel was preached even to the dead, so that, although they might be judged in the flesh like men, they might enjoy the life of God in the spirit.

Qualities of a Christian Community Waiting for Christ.*
[7] The end of all things is near. Therefore, lead disciplined lives and be watchful in prayer. [8] Above all, maintain the fervor of your love for one another, because love covers a multitude of sins.

[9] Be hospitable to one another without complaining. [10] Like good stewards of the varied graces of God, use whatever gift each one of you has received to serve one another.

[11] Whoever speaks should do so as one who is speaking the very words of God. Whoever serves should do so with the strength that God provides. In all things, let God be glorified through Jesus Christ, for to him belong all glory and power forever and ever. Amen.

Courage and Joy in Suffering.* [12] Beloved, do not be surprised that you are being tested by a fiery ordeal,* as though it were something extraordinary. [13] But rejoice insofar as you are sharing in the sufferings of Christ, so that your joy will be without limit when his glory is revealed.

[14] If you are reviled for the name of Christ, consider yourself blessed, for upon you rests the Spirit of glory* and of God. [15] * However, let none of you suffer as a murderer, a thief, or any other kind of criminal, or as one who meddles in another person's business. [16] Let it be because you are a Christian,* not considering it a disgrace, but glorifying God because you bear this name.

[17] The time has come for the judgment of the household of God to begin. If it begins with us, how will it end for those who refuse to obey the gospel of God?

[18] And:

> "If it is hard for the righteous to be saved,
>> what will become of the godless and those who are
>> sinners?"

[19] And so, those who suffer in accordance with God's will entrust their souls to a faithful Creator, while continuing to do good.

5 **Faithful and Humble Leadership.*** [1] I now exhort the presbyters* among you, as a fellow presbyter myself and a witness to the sufferings of Christ, and as one who has shared in the glory that is to be revealed. [2] Be shepherds of the flock of God that has been entrusted to your care. Watch over it, not as a duty, but willingly in accord with the will of God, not for sordid gain, but because you are eager to do so.

³ Do not lord it over those in your charge, but be examples to the flock. ⁴ Then, when the chief Shepherd appears, you will receive the crown of glory that never fades away.

Humility and Firm Faith. ⁵ * In the same way, you who are younger must be submissive to those who are older. And all of you should clothe yourselves with humility in your relationships with one another, for

"God opposes the proud,
   but he gives grace to the humble."

⁶ Therefore, humble yourselves under the mighty hand of God, so that at the proper time he may exalt you. ⁷ Cast all your anxiety on him, because he cares about you.

⁸ Remain sober and alert, for your enemy the devil is on the prowl like a roaring lion, looking for someone to devour. ⁹ Resist him and be firm in your faith, for you are well aware that your brethren throughout the world are undergoing the same kinds of suffering.

Promise of Strength and Vindication. ¹⁰ After you have suffered for a brief period, the God of all grace, who has called you to his eternal glory in Christ, will himself restore, confirm, strengthen, and support you. ¹¹ All power belongs to him forever and ever. Amen.

V: CONCLUSION

Final Greetings.* ¹² I have written this brief letter to you through Silvanus, whom I regard as a faithful brother, in order to exhort you and to testify that this is the true grace of God. Stand firm in it.

¹³ Your sister Church * in Babylon sends you greetings, as does my son Mark. ¹⁴ Greet one another with a loving kiss. *

Peace to all of you who are in Christ.

THE SECOND LETTER OF PETER
AWAITING THE DAY OF THE LORD

With this Letter we find ourselves already at the beginning of the second century. The Church is experiencing a difficult transition from the primitive stage to the post-apostolic stage. For several decades her members have lived the newness of the Christian Faith and, so to speak, sung its praises; the coming of Jesus remained near and his return was thought to be imminent.

Now these two poles are disappearing from view, the former in the past and the latter in a future that is more and more out of focus. A distance is being established with respect to the immediate experience of Christianity's beginnings. A new climate must be forged for remaining in the faith and practicing the Christian life in everyday existence.

Such a transformation is not achieved without crisis. It bears the visage of uncertainty as well as anxiety.

The first point that comes under attack is orthodoxy. The most diverse religious ideas and the most varied Gnostic currents are unfurled within the Empire, often accompanied by immorality. Will Christianity simply vanish in the wake of this maelstrom of competing ideas and morals?

The delay of the Parousia, or Return of Christ, has already disquieted spirits. Now there is danger that Christians will resign themselves to this delay to the detriment of a fundamental aspect of the Christian symmetry and conscience. Will the tension toward fulfillment and the perspective of being confronted with a judgment be lost in out-of-focus ideas that have no impact on life?

In order of time, this writing was probably the last of the New Testament and thus of the entire Bible. It is a spirited exhortation to discouraged spirits; even more vigorously it attacks the spreaders of dangerous doctrines that sow disorder. It does not lack power when it evokes the final devastation of the world, but it also teaches patience, the sense of living under the judgment of God, and progress in faith and in grace.

In defending the essentials of the faith, the Letter emphasizes the word of God as transmitted by the Prophets and the Apostles, and it already cites the Letters of Paul as forming a literary whole well known in the Church. This passage bears witness to the awareness of Biblical inspiration and also to the conviction that Scripture must be interpreted within the Church.

To get his meaning across, the author imitates a literary genre current in the Judaism of the time: the testament of the ancestors—in other words, the practice of placing one's own exhortations and advice in the mouths of Patriarchs who are about to die. Our author has thought of the man who took first place in the origins of Christianity, namely, Peter, who speaks in Jesus' name (see 1 Tim 1:14-15). St. Jerome tells us that many denied Peter was the author of the document.

This Letter seems strange to us by reason of its many expressions and its very style. But it contains an important lesson for Christianity, which must be able to accept ongoing history, even while refusing to settle down calmly in it. The Letter claims to be a continuation of the First Letter of Peter (see 2 Pet 3:1), but in fact it is to be connected rather with the Letter of Jude, from which it takes various themes and explains them more fully. (See Introduction to Jude.)

The Second Letter of Peter may be divided as follows:

  I: Salutation (1:1-2)
 II: Exhortation to Growth in Christian Virtues (1:3-21)
III: Warning against False Teachers (2:1-22)
IV: The Fact of Christ's Return (3:1-16)
 V: Conclusion (3:17-18)

I: SALUTATION

1 **Address.*** [1] Simon Peter,* a servant and apostle of Jesus Christ, to those who have received a faith as precious as ours through the righteousness of our God and Savior Jesus Christ: [2] may grace and peace be yours in abundance through the knowledge * of God and of Jesus our Lord.

II: EXHORTATION TO GROWTH IN CHRISTIAN VIRTUES

Strengthen Your Vocation.* [3] His divine power has bestowed on us everything that is necessary for life and for devotion through our knowledge of him who called us by his own glory and virtue. [4] By these he has given us his precious promises, great beyond all price, so that through them you may escape from the corruption with which evil desires have infected the world and thereby may come to share in the divine nature. *

[5] * In view of all this, you should make every effort to supplement your faith with virtue, and virtue with knowledge, [6] and knowledge with self-control, and self-control with endurance, and endurance with piety, [7] and piety with mutual affection, and mutual affection with love.

[8] If you possess these qualities and they increase in abundance, they will prevent your knowledge of our Lord Jesus Christ from being ineffective and unfruitful. [9] For anyone who lacks them is near-sighted or blind, since he has forgotten how his past sins were washed away.*

[10] Therefore, brethren, be diligent in providing a firm foundation for your call and election. If you do this, you will never stumble, [11] and you will receive a glorious welcome into the eternal kingdom of our Lord and Savior Jesus Christ. *

The Witness of an Apostle.* [12] Therefore, I will continue to emphasize these things repeatedly, even though you already know them and are well grounded in the truth you possess. [13] For I think it is right, to refresh your memory as long as I remain in this body, * [14] since I know that my death* will come soon, as our Lord Jesus Christ made clear to me. [15] And I shall also make every effort to ensure that you will always recall these things after my departure.

[16] We did not rely upon cleverly concocted myths when we made known to you the power and coming of our Lord Jesus Christ. Rather, we had beheld his majesty with our own eyes. [17] For he received honor and glory from God the Father when a voice came to him from the transcendent Majesty, saying, "This is my beloved Son in whom I am well pleased." [18] We ourselves heard this voice that came down from heaven, when we were with him on the sacred mountain.

Pay Close Attention to the Message of the Prophets.*
[19] This confirms the message of the Prophets more fully for us. You would do well to pay close attention to it, as to a lamp shining in a dark place, until the day dawns and the morning star rises in your hearts.

[20] First of all, however, you must understand that no prophecy of Scripture is a matter of private interpretation. [21] No prophecy ever came from human initiative. Rather, when people spoke as messengers of God, they did so under the inspiration of the Holy Spirit. *

III: WARNING AGAINST FALSE TEACHERS*

2   **False Teachers Will Arise.** [1] Just as there were false prophets who arose among the people, so there will be false teachers among you. They will introduce their disruptive views and even deny the very Master who redeemed them, thus bringing swift destruction on themselves.

[2] Many will be seduced by their licentious ways, and because of these teachers the way of truth will be brought into disrepute. [3] In their greed they will exploit you with concocted stories.

The Condemnation of False Teachers. However, their condemnation has been hanging over them for a long time, and the destruction awaiting them does not slumber. [4] For God did not spare the angels who sinned, but he cast them into the dark abyss to be chained, where they are being held until the judgment. * [5] Nor did he spare the ancient world, * even though he saved Noah, a herald of righteousness, one of eight, when he brought a flood upon the world with its godless people.

[6] God also reduced the cities of Sodom and Gomorrah to ashes, thereby condemning them to total ruin and making them an example of what awaited the ungodly. [7] However, he rescued Lot, an upright man who was sickened by the licentiousness of the lawless society in which he lived, [8] for that man was greatly tormented in his righteous soul by the crimes that he saw and about which he was told day after day.

[9] Therefore, the Lord knows how to rescue the godly from their trials and to hold the wicked for punishment until the Day of Judgment. [10] Above all, he will punish those who succumb to the desires of their corrupt human nature and show no respect for authority.

The Ways of False Teachers. Bold and headstrong, they are not afraid to insult celestial beings, [11] whereas angels, despite their superior strength and power, do not bring slanderous accusations against such men in the Lord's presence. * [12] These men are like wild beasts, mere creatures of instinct born to be caught and killed.

They pour abuse on things they do not understand, and in their corruption they also will be destroyed, [13] receiving the penalty * for doing wrong. They regard it as a pleasure to carouse in broad daylight. While they share your table, they are ugly blots and blemishes, reveling in their pleasures.

[14] They have eyes that are always on the trail of adultery, insatiable in their desire for sinful pursuits. They seduce unstable people, and their hearts are fixed on greed. Truly, they are an accursed brood. * [15] They have abandoned the straight path and have gone astray, fol-

lowing in the steps of Balaam, the son of Beor, * who loved to receive payment for wrongdoing. [16] However, he received a rebuke for his crime when a mute donkey spoke with a human voice and put a stop to the prophet's madness.

[17] Such people are waterless springs and mists driven by a storm. For them the gloom of darkness has been reserved. [18] They speak boastful words devoid of meaning, and by arousing licentious desires of the flesh they entice people who are just escaping from living in error.

[19] They promise them freedom, although they themselves are slaves of depravity. * For people are slaves of whatever has mastered them. [20] If they have escaped the world's defilements through coming to know our Lord and Savior Jesus Christ and then again become entangled and are overpowered, they are worse off in this latter state than they were before.

[21] It would have been better for them never to have known the way of righteousness than, having known it, to turn back and abandon the holy commandment that was handed on to them. [22] What happened to them manifests the truth of the proverbs:

"The dog returns to its own vomit," *

and

"The washed sow returns to wallowing in the mud."

IV: THE FACT OF CHRIST'S RETURN

3 **The Day of the Lord Will Come.** * [1] Beloved, this is now the second letter I have written to you. In both of them I have tried to stir up your memories for a clear understanding [2] so that you might remember the words spoken in the past by the holy Prophets and by the apostles at the command of our Lord and Savior.

[3] First of all, you must understand that in the last days scoffers will appear who have led lives of indulgence. [4] They will say, "Where is this 'coming' that was promised?

Ever since our ancestors * died, everything has remained just as it was from the beginning of creation."

⁵ * These people deliberately ignore the fact that by the word of God the heavens existed long ago, and that the earth stands out of water in water. ⁶ Furthermore, by these waters also the world of that time was deluged and destroyed. ⁷ By the same word, the present heavens and earth have been reserved for fire, being kept for the Day of Judgment and the destruction of sinners.

⁸ But do not ignore this one fact, beloved: with the Lord one day its like a thousand years, and a thousand years are like one day. ⁹ The Lord does not delay in keeping his promise, as some think in terms of delay, but he is patient with you. It is not his wish that any should perish but rather that all should be brought to repentance.

¹⁰ However, the Day of the Lord will come like a thief. The heavens will disappear with a mighty roar, * and the elements will be dissolved in flames, and the earth and all that it contains will be disclosed.

Wait for and Speed the Day of God.* ¹¹ Since everything is to be destroyed in this way, consider what sort of people you ought to be, living holy and saintly lives. ¹² Wait for and speed the coming of the Day of God, * on which the heavens will be set ablaze and all the elements will melt because of the intense heat. ¹³ We eagerly await the promised new heavens and a new earth * in which righteousness dwells.

¹⁴ Therefore, beloved, in expectation of all this, do everything possible to lead blameless lives that are above reproach so that he will find you at peace. ¹⁵ Think of our Lord's patience as your opportunity to be saved; * our beloved brother Paul told you this when he wrote to you with the wisdom that was given to him, ¹⁶ speaking of it * in all his letters. In them, there are some things that are difficult to understand, which the ignorant and the unstable distort in the same way that they distort the other Scriptures, to their own destruction.

V: CONCLUSION

Guard against Error and Grow in Grace. [17] Therefore, beloved, you have been forewarned about this. Take care that you are not led astray by the errors of unprincipled people and thus lose your secure position. [18] Rather, grow in the grace and the knowledge * of our Lord and Savior Jesus Christ.

Doxology. To him be glory both now and for all eternity. Amen.

THE FIRST LETTER OF JOHN

TO LIVE IN LOVE

At the end of the first century, several currents of religious thought described as "Gnostic" were beginning to circulate; their spokesmen emphasized a special religious "knowledge" (Greek: gnosis), from which they expected salvation. Among them certain themes were constantly repeated, but in a radically dualistic perspective: light and darkness, truth and falsehood, life and death.

Against these innovators, four ideas had to be developed: knowledge of God, the person of Jesus, the reality of sin, and fraternal love.

Knowledge of God, who is light and love, brings Christians their happiness. This knowledge comes not from an inspiration from on high nor from the searching of our minds; it is given in Jesus Christ, in whom we touch, as it were, the self-manifestation of God, a point that is emphasized at the beginning of the Letter. Christian faith goes back to the direct testimony of those who were with the Lord.

Jesus is the Son of God. But he had a real body, really gave his blood, suffered, and rose from the dead. If the coming of Christ in the flesh is rejected (see 1 Jn 4:2), Christianity in its entirety collapses. There is no longer any redemption or any knowledge of God.

Christ saves from sin. Therefore, sin exists. We must acknowledge this and accept our being saved from it. This realism does not open the way to discouragement, but on the contrary is a prerequisite for hope.

Finally, God is love, communion. He first loves, and Jesus bears witness to this love. To believe in God means to enter into this relationship of love.

Never has it been made so clear that fraternal love is so essential to faith. Faith is not a form of abstract speculation, but a participation with God in the victory over evil, which is here called "the world."

The way of entering into the themes, repeating them, enriching them, and advancing in a spiral fashion is characteristic of this document, as it already was of the Gospel of John. We cannot regard the work as an occasional Letter; rather it is a long-matured effort to respond to the crisis that was agitating the communities.

Let us think of it, therefore, as a circular Letter, a meditation rather than a treatise, a text for preaching and teaching.

Where did it come from?

So great is its affinity in thought and form with the fourth Gospel that it evidently came, if not directly from the author of that work, then at least from circles close to him. The document was probably written toward the end of the first century, in Asia Minor (perhaps at Ephesus), and for the Churches of that province.

The First Letter of John may be divided as follows:

Prologue: (1:1-4)
  I: Walk in the Light (1:5—2:28)
 II: Children of God (2:29—4:6)
III: Remain in Love (4:7-21)
IV: Believe in the Son of God (5:1-12)
Epilogue: (5:13-21)

PROLOGUE*

1
An Authentic Communion of Life

¹ This is what we proclaim to you:
    what existed from the beginning,
    what we have heard,
    what we have seen with our own eyes,
    what we have looked at
    and touched with our hands—
    we are speaking of the Word of life. *

² That life was made visible;
    we have seen it and bear witness,
    proclaiming to you the eternal life *
    that was with the Father
    and was revealed to us.

³ What we have seen and heard
    we declare to you
    so that you may have fellowship * with us.
    For our fellowship is with the Father
    and with his Son Jesus Christ.

⁴ We are writing this
    so that our joy may be complete.

I: WALK IN THE LIGHT
God Is Light*

⁵ This is the message
    that we have heard from him
    and that we declare to you:
    God is light,
    and there is no darkness * at all in him.

⁶ If we claim that we have fellowship with him
    while we continue to live in darkness,
    we are lying and do not live in the truth.

⁷ However, if we live in the light
    as he himself is in the light,
    then we have fellowship with one another,
    and the blood of Jesus his Son
    purifies us from all sin.

Deliverance from Sin*

8 If we claim that we are sinless,
   we are only deceiving ourselves,
   and the truth is not in us.
9 However, if we confess our sins,
   he who is faithful and just
   will forgive our sins
   and cleanse us from all wrongdoing.
10 If we say that we have never sinned,
   we make him out to be a liar,
   and his word is not in us.

2 ¹ My dear children,
   I am writing this to you
   so that you may avoid committing sin.
   However, if anyone does sin,
   we have an Advocate with the Father,
   Jesus Christ, the Righteous One.
2 He is himself the sacrifice for our sins—
   and not only for our sins
   but also for the sins of the whole world.

The Commandment of Love*

3 Now we may be certain that we know him
   if we obey his commandments.
4 Whoever says, "I know him,"
   but does not keep his commandments,
   is a liar,
   and the truth is not in him. *
5 However, the love of God is truly perfected
   in the one who obeys his word.
   This is how we can be certain
   that we are in union with him:
6 whoever claims to abide in him
   must live just as he himself lived.

7 Beloved,
   I am not writing a new commandment * for you,
   but an old commandment
   that you have had from the beginning.

The old commandment is the word
that you have heard.

8 And yet I am writing you a new commandment,
whose truth is in him and in you,
because the darkness is passing away
and the true light is already shining.

9 Whoever says, "I am in the light,"
yet hates his brother,
is still in the darkness.

10 Whoever loves his brother lives in the light,
and there is nothing in him
to make him stumble.

11 Whoever hates his brother is in the darkness,
and he walks about in darkness.
He does not know where he is going
because the darkness has blinded him.

The Concupiscences of the World*

12 I am writing to you, dear children,
because your sins have been forgiven
on account of his name.

13 I am writing to you, fathers,
because you have known him
who has existed from the beginning.
I am writing to you, young people,
because you have conquered the evil one.

14 I am writing to you, dear children,
because you have known the Father.
I am writing to you, fathers,
because you have known him
who has existed from the beginning.
I am writing to you, young people,
because you are strong,
and the word of God abides in you,
and you have overcome the evil one.

15 Do not love the world
or what is in the world.
If anyone does love the world,
the love of the Father is not in him.

16   For everything that is in the world—
      the concupiscence of the flesh,
      the concupiscence of the eyes,
      and the pride of life—
      comes not from the Father
      but from the world. *

17   And the world with all its enticements
      is passing away,
      but whoever does the will of God
      abides forever.

Behold the Antichrist*

18   Dear children,
      this is the last hour.
      You have heard that the Antichrist was coming,
      and now many antichrists have already come. *
      Thus, we know
      that it is the final hour.

19   They went out from us,
      but they never really belonged to us.
      If they had belonged to us,
      they would have remained with us.
      By departing from us,
      they made it clear
      that none of them belonged to us.

20   However, you have been anointed
      by the Holy One, *
      and you all have knowledge.

21   I write to you
      not because you do not know the truth
      but because you do know it,
      and because no lie can come from the truth.

22   Who is the liar
      but the one who denies that Jesus is the Christ?
      The antichrist is
      anyone who denies both the Father
      and the Son.

23   Whoever denies the Son
      does not have the Father,

but whoever acknowledges the Son
has the Father also.

24 Let what you heard from the beginning
remain in you.
If what you heard from the beginning
remains in you,
then you will remain in the Son
and in the Father.

25 And this is the promise he made to us:
eternal life.

26 I write these things to you
in reference to those
who seek to lead you astray.

27 But as for you,
the anointing you received from him
remains in you,
and therefore you do not need anyone
to teach you.
This same anointing
teaches you everything
and is true and not false,
so abide in him just as he taught you.

28 And now, dear children,
abide in him,
so that when he appears
we may have confidence
and not be put to shame by him
at his coming.

II: CHILDREN OF GOD

Everyone Whose Life Is Righteous Has Been Born of God*

29 If you know that he is righteous,
you also know that everyone whose life is righteous
is born of him.

3 ¹ See what love
the Father has bestowed on us,

enabling us to be called the children of God,
and that is what we are.
If the world does not recognize us,
that is because it did not know him.

2 Beloved,
we are God's children now.
What we shall be
has not yet been revealed.
However, we do know that when he appears
we shall be like him,
for we shall see him as he really is.

3 Everyone who has this hope in him
keeps himself pure,
just as he is pure.

The Rupture with Sin*

4 Everyone who sins breaks the law,
for sin is lawlessness.

5 You know that he appeared
in order to take away sins,
and that there is no sin in him.

6 Whoever remains in him does not sin, *
and whoever sins has not seen him
nor known him.

7 Dear children,
do not let anyone deceive you.
Everyone who does what is right is righteous,
just as he is righteous.

8 Everyone who sins comes from the devil,
for the devil has been a sinner
from the very beginning.
The Son of God appeared for this very purpose:
to destroy the work of the devil.

9 Whoever is born of God
does not sin,
because his seed * remains in him.
He cannot sin
because he is begotten by God.

10 This is what distinguishes
the children of God from the children of the devil:
anyone who fails to live righteously
does not belong to God;
neither does anyone who fails to love a brother.

The Message of Love*

11 For from the beginning
you have heard the message
that we should love one another,

12 unlike Cain who was from the evil one
and slew his brother.
And why did he slay him?
Because his own deeds were evil
while those of his brother were righteous.

13 Do not be surprised, my brethren,
if the world hates you.

14 We know that we have passed
from death to life
because we love our brethren.
Whoever does not love remains in death.

15 Anyone who hates his brother
is a murderer,
and you know that no murderer
has eternal life abiding in him.

16 This is how we know what love is:
he laid down his life for us,
and we in turn must be prepared
to lay down our lives for our brethren.

17 If anyone is rich in worldly possessions
and sees a brother in need
but refuses to open his heart,
how can the love of God abide in him?

18 Dear children,
let us love not in word or speech
but in deed and truth. *

19 This is how we know
that we belong to the truth

and reassure our hearts in his presence

20 even if our hearts experience a sense of guilt.
For God is greater than our hearts,
and he knows everything.

21 Beloved,
if our hearts do not condemn us,
we can approach God with confidence

22 and receive from him whatever we ask,
because we obey his commandments
and do whatever is pleasing to him. *

23 And this is his commandment:
that we should believe
in the name of his Son, Jesus Christ,
and love one another just as he commanded us. *

24 All those who keep his commandments abide in
    him,
and he abides in them.
And the proof that he abides in us
is the Spirit that he has given us.

4

The Spirit of the Antichrist in the World*

1 Beloved,
do not trust every spirit,
but test the spirits
to see whether they are from God.
For many false prophets
have gone out into the world.

2 This is how you can recognize the Spirit of God:
every spirit that acknowledges
that Jesus Christ has come in the flesh *
is from God,

3 and every spirit that does not acknowledge Jesus
is not from God.
This is the spirit of the Antichrist,
about whose coming you have been told,
and that it is already in the world.

4 Dear children,
you are from God *

and you have conquered them,
for the one who is in you is greater
than the one who is in the world.
5 They are from the world;
therefore, what they say is from the world,
and the world listens to them.
6 We are from God.
Anyone who knows God listens to us,
while anyone who is not from God
refuses to listen to us.
This is how we can distinguish
the spirit of truth from the spirit of falsehood. *

III: REMAIN IN LOVE*

What Love Is

7 Beloved,
let us love one another,
because love is from God. *
Everyone who loves is born of God
and knows God.
8 Whoever does not love
does not know God,
because God is love.
9 God's love was revealed to us
in this way:
God sent his only-begotten Son into the world
so that we might have life through him.
10 This is what love is:
not that we have loved God,
but that he loved us
and sent his Son as expiation for our sins. *
11 Beloved,
since God loved us so much,
we should love one another.
12 No one has ever seen God,
but if we love one another,
God abides in us,
and his love is made complete in us.

13 This is how we can be certain
that we abide in him
and that he abides in us:
he has given us a share in his Spirit. *

14 Moreover, we have seen for ourselves
and can testify
that the Father has sent the Son
as the Savior of the world.

15 God abides in anyone who acknowledges
that Jesus is the Son of God,
and that person abides in God.

16 We have come to know
and to believe in
the love that God has for us.
God is love,
and whoever abides in love
abides in God,
and God in him.

17 This is how love is made perfect in us,
enabling us to have confidence
on the Day of Judgment,
because even in this world
we have become like him.

18 In love there is no fear;
indeed, perfect love casts out fear,
because fear has to do with punishment,
and whoever fears
has not yet achieved perfection in love.

19 Therefore, we love because he first loved us.

20 If someone says, "I love God,"
but at the same time hates his brother,
he is a liar.
For whoever does not love the brother
whom he has seen
cannot love God
whom he has not seen.

21 This is the commandment
we have received from him:

whoever loves God
must also love his brother.

IV: BELIEVE IN THE SON OF GOD*

5

Faith Conquers the World

1 Everyone who believes
that Jesus is the Christ
is born of God,
and everyone who loves the parent
loves the one begotten of him as well.

2 This is how we know
that we love the children of God:
by loving God and obeying his commandments.

3 For the love of God is this:
that we keep his commandments.
And his commandments are not burdensome,

4 for everyone born of God
conquers the world.
And the victory that conquers the world
is our faith.

5 Who indeed conquers the world
except the one who believes
that Jesus is the Son of God?

6 This is the one
who came by water and blood,
Jesus Christ—
not by water alone,
but by water and blood.
And to this the Spirit bears witness,
for the Spirit is truth. *

7 Thus, there are three * witnesses,

8 the Spirit, the water, and the blood,
and these three are as one. *

9 If we accept human testimony,
the testimony of God is greater.
For it is the testimony of God,
the testimony that he has given about his Son.

10 Whoever believes in the Son of God
    has this testimony in himself,
    but those who do not believe in God
    have made him out to be a liar
    by refusing to believe the testimony
    that God has given about his Son.
11 And this is the testimony:
    God gave us eternal life,
    and this life is in his Son.
12 Whoever possesses the Son
    possesses life;
    whoever does not possess the Son of God
    does not possess life.

EPILOGUE*

So That You May Know*

13 I write these things to you
    who believe in the name of the Son of God
    so that you may know
    that you have eternal life.

Prayer for Sinners*

14 And thus we can have confidence in him
    that if we ask anything
    that is in accordance with his will,
    he hears us.
15 And if we know that he hears us
    in regard to whatever we ask him,
    we may be sure
    that all we ask of him will be ours.
16 If anyone sees a brother commit a sin
    that does not lead to death,
    he should intercede for him,
    and God will grant him life—
    provided that the sin is not deadly.
    There is a sin that leads to death,
    and I do not say
    that you should pray about it. *

17   All wrongdoing is sinful,
        but not all sins are deadly.

The Great Certitudes*

18   We know that one born of God does not continue to
             sin,
        because he who is born of God protects him,
        and the evil one has no power over him.

19   We know
        that we are from God
        and that the entire world
        lies under the power of the evil one.

20   We also know
        that the Son of God has come
        and given us understanding
        so that we can know the one who is true.
        And we are in the one who is true,
        since we are in his Son Jesus Christ.
        He is the true God and eternal life.

21   Dear children,
        keep away from idols.

THE SECOND LETTER OF JOHN
THE WAY OF TRUTH

New teachers have been preaching an alien type of knowledge (gnosis); they are enthusiasts for a profound spiritual knowledge that has no need of faith in Jesus or of his Gospel of love.

A community—the "chosen Lady and . . . her children," as it is called here—is exposed to the danger of losing what is the very heart of the faith and of Christian life. A "presbyter" (or elder) intervenes, whose authority is so great that the community must accept it, for he is a witness from the earliest time, a witness of Christ.

This person is certainly the one whose voice resounds in the fourth Gospel and in the First Letter of John.

This Second Letter is even older than the preceding one; the threat to the Churches has hardly shown its face; the response to it is as yet only sketched, but in a lively and direct way. The First Letter, on the other hand, will go more deeply into the threat and give a much fuller reply. We must refer to that Letter in order to understand the concern in the present document, which is from the same period (toward the end of the first century) and addressed to a Church of Asia Minor.

The Second Letter of John may be divided as follows:

Salutation (1-3)
The Commandment of Love (4-6)
Warning against False Teachers (7-11)
Conclusion (12-13)

Salutation. [1] The Presbyter* to the chosen Lady and to her children whom I love in the truth—and not I alone but also all who know the truth— [2] because of the truth that abides in us and will be with us forever. [3] Grace, mercy, and peace will be with us from God the Father and from Jesus Christ, the Son of the Father, in truth and love.

The Commandment of Love.* [4] It was a cause of great joy to me to discover that some of your children have been walking in the truth* just as we have been commanded by the Father. [5] But now, Lady, I am making this request of you, not as though I were writing you a new commandment but simply one that we have had from the beginning: let us love one another.* [6] And this is love: when we walk according to his commandments.* This is the commandment that you have heard from the beginning, and you must follow it.

Warning against False Teachers.* [7] Many deceivers have gone forth into the world, those who refuse to acknowledge that Jesus Christ has come in the flesh. Any such person is the Deceiver* and the Antichrist. [8] Be on your guard that you do not lose what we have worked to accomplish so that you will receive your reward in full. *

[9] Anyone who fails to remain faithful to the teaching of Christ but goes beyond* it does not have God. Only the one who remains faithful to the teaching possesses both the Father and the Son. [10] If anyone comes to you and does not impart this teaching, do not receive him into your house or welcome him.* [11] For anyone who welcomes him has a share in his evil deeds.

Conclusion. [12] I have much to write to you, but I do not think it prudent to do so with paper and ink.* Instead, I hope to visit you and to talk with you face to face so that our joy may be complete.

[13] The children of your sister, the chosen one,* send you greetings.

THE THIRD LETTER OF JOHN
PERSONAL AND DOCTRINAL PROBLEMS

This is a letter of encouragement that deals with the problems of individuals. Above all, it has to do with the life of a local Church in which communication has become difficult, probably because of the appearance there of the Gnostic initiates, of whom we have already spoken in the Introduction to the First Letter of John. They were spreading false teachings, agitating Churches, and destroying the true Gospel.

Let us review the situation. Diotrephes, head of a local Church and probably involved in the new Gnostic currents of thought, has refused to communicate with the "Presbyter," who is certainly a witness of Jesus and in charge of all the Churches of the region; in all likelihood, he is John the Apostle. The man locally in charge rejects the itinerant missionaries, whose task it was to proclaim the Gospel and establish and develop Churches.

However, in this community there is a steadfast man, Gaius, who must be supported in his behavior and his undertakings; he is a man who courageously receives and supports the missionaries.

A third person comes on the scene: Demetrius, who likewise deserves to be supported and encouraged.

This Letter was written about the same time as the other two Letters of John.

The Third Letter of John may be divided as follows:

Salutation (1-2)
Commendation of Gaius (3-8)
Condemnation of Diotrephes (9-10)
Exhortation to Gaius (11)
Example of Demetrius (12)
Conclusion (13-15)

Salutation. ¹ The Presbyter* to my beloved Gaius, whom I love in the truth. ² Beloved, I pray that everything is going well with you and that your bodily health is equal to that of your soul. *

Commendation of Gaius. ³ I rejoiced greatly when some of the brethren * arrived and related how faithful you are to the truth, and that you continue to walk in the truth. ⁴ Nothing gives me greater joy than to hear that my children are walking in the truth.

⁵ * Beloved, you have been faithful in everything you do for the brethren, especially to strangers. ⁶ They have testified before the Church to your love. Please continue to help them on their journey in a manner worthy of God. ⁷ For they began their journey for the sake of the Name, * and they have refused to accept any support from non-believers. ⁸ Therefore, we ought to show hospitality to such people so that we may be collaborators in the truth.

Condemnation of Diotrephes. ⁹ I have previously written something to the Church, but Diotrephes,* who enjoys being in a position of leadership, refuses to acknowledge our authority. ¹⁰ Therefore, if I come, I shall draw attention to what he is doing. He has circulated false charges against us. And not content with that, he not only refuses to welcome the brethren but interferes with those who want to do so and expels them from the Church.

Exhortation to Gaius. ¹¹ Beloved, do not imitate what is evil; rather, imitate what is good. Whoever does what is good is from God. Whoever does what is evil has never seen God. *

Example of Demetrius. ¹² Everyone has spoken favorably about Demetrius, * and so has the Truth itself. We also will vouch for him, and you are well aware that our testimony is true.

Conclusion. ¹³ * I have much to write to you, but I do not think it prudent to do so with pen and ink. ¹⁴ Instead, I hope to visit you in the very near future, when we can talk together face to face.

¹⁵ Peace be with you. The friends * send you their greetings. Greet each of our friends there by name.

THE LETTER OF JUDE
CONTENDING FOR THE FAITH

The Letter of Jude, which consists of only twenty-five verses, is a strange and surprising document, in which many of the
details escape us. One thing is clear, however: there was a need
to defend the essentials of the faith handed down by the
Apostles and to warn people against erroneous currents of
thought that combined immorality and mysticism in an odd
way.

Some groups were tearing the communities apart, right in
the midst of the community gatherings. These people, who
thought of themselves as spiritual, went on inventing classes
and hierarchies of celestial beings, to the point of dissolving the
lordship of Christ and of insulting the angels.

Although the Letter does not indicate for whom it was specifically intended, it was most likely aimed at the Jews of the
Dispersion (i.e., those living throughout the Roman empire)
who had accepted Christ as their Savior. If such were not the
case, it would be difficult to understand the reason for the use
of such obscure personages in Jude's Old Testament illustrations and for the citations from apocryphal books that would
have meant very little to a Gentile audience.

We are here in the final period of the apostolic age, toward
the end of the first century. The author, who speaks so vehemently in the name of truth, writes under the name of Jude, a
brother of James (the most representative person of the
Jerusalem Church: see Gal 1:19; 2:9; Acts 15:13-21; Jas:
Introduction) and therefore perhaps also a relative of Jesus
(see Mt 13:55; Mk 6:3).

It is possible, though not necessary, to identify this Jude with
the apostle of the same name: Jude Thaddeus (see Mt 10:3;
Mk 3:18; Lk 6:16; Jn 14:22; Acts 1:13). Perhaps this person
filled some office after the death of his brother James in A.D.
62. He may have exhorted the faithful to fight for the true faith
against a distortion of the Gospel.

Whoever the author was, he wrote in some of the best Greek of the New Testament. Furthermore, he shows great acquaintance with Jewish writings of his time, the texts of apocalypses that he cites and that he approximates in his writing. His energetic and picturesque style is also reminiscent of the early Prophets of the Old Testament.

His violent intervention must have had some success, for in fact it is picked up in the Second Letter of Peter, but with some revisions (see, for example, verses 17-18 cited almost verbatim in 2 Pet 3:3).

We should not be surprised that the author is not afraid to employ abusive formulas; these are formulas often already in use in the religious literature of the time. We should attend rather to the author's deeper concern: not to let the Christian mystery be enfeebled.

Indeed, the Letter opens with a salutation and a splendid expression of the awareness of being a Christian (1-4). It goes on to warn against false teachers (5-19). Then it provides a capsule program of the Christian life encompassing faith, prayer, love, mutual assistance, and avoidance of corruptors of the faith (20-23). It concludes with one of the most beautiful doxologies of the New Testament, noting that we must stand one day before the living God, who gives us strength to persevere and make progress (24-25).

The Letter of Jude may be divided as follows:

Salutation (1-2)
Benefits of Being a Christian (3-4)
Character and Doom of the False Teachers (5-16)
Appeal to the Faithful (17-19)
A Program of the Christian Life (20-23)
Doxology (24-25)

Salutation. ¹ Jude, a servant of Jesus Christ, and the brother of James, * to those who have been called, who are dear to God the Father and have been kept safe by Jesus Christ: ² may mercy, peace, and love be granted you in abundance.

Benefits of Being a Christian. [3] Beloved, I was just at the point of writing to you about the salvation we share, when it became necessary for me to write and urge you to fight earnestly for the faith that was once and for all entrusted to the saints.* [4] For certain men have infiltrated your ranks, people who long ago were designated for condemnation.* These godless persons pervert the grace of our God into an excuse for immorality and disown our only Master and Lord, Jesus Christ.

Character and Doom of the False Teachers.* [5] Although you already know all this, allow me to remind you that the Lord, who once delivered the people out of the land of Egypt, afterward destroyed those who refused to believe.* [6] Remember also that the angels, who were dissatisfied with the dominion that had been assigned to them and abandoned their proper dwelling place, have been kept bound by him in darkness with eternal chains until the judgment of the great Day. * [7] And do not fail to remember Sodom and Gomorrah and the neighboring cities, which in a similar way indulged in sexual immorality and perversion. They serve as an example of those who undergo the punishment of eternal fire.*

[8] In the same way, these dreamers defile their bodies, make light of authority, and insult celestial beings.* [9] Even the archangel Michael, when he engaged in an argument with the devil about the body of Moses, did not dare to bring a slanderous accusation against him, but instead said: "May the Lord rebuke you!" * [10] However, these people pour abuse on anything they do not understand, and the very things that they know by instinct, like irrational animals, lead to their destruction.

[11] Woe to them! They have followed in the footsteps of Cain; they have abandoned themselves to the error of Balaam for the sake of gain; and they have perished in the rebellion of Korah.* [12] * They are blemishes at your love feasts, eating with you without fear. They are shepherds who feed only themselves. They are like clouds blown about by winds without giving rain, or like trees in

autumn barren and uprooted and so twice dead. [13] They are like wild sea waves whose foam reflects their shameless deeds, or like wandering stars for whom the gloom of darkness is stored up forever.

[14] * Enoch, in the seventh generation from Adam, also prophesied against them when he said, "Behold, the Lord is coming with tens of thousands of his saints, [15] to pronounce judgment on humanity and to convict all the ungodly for all the godless deeds that each has impiously committed and for all the defiant words spoken against him by godless sinners." [16] These are grumblers and fault-finders. They indulge their own passions,* and their mouths are full of bombastic talk as they flatter others in order to achieve their own ends.

Appeal to the Faithful. [17] But you, dear friends, must remember the predictions made by the apostles of our Lord Jesus Christ.* [18] For they said to you, "In the final age there will be scoffers who will follow their own ungodly passions." * [19] It is these people who create divisions, who follow their natural instincts and do not possess the Spirit.

A Program of the Christian Life.* [20] However, you, dear friends, must build yourselves up in your most holy faith and pray in the Holy Spirit. [21] Keep yourselves in the love of God as you await our Lord Jesus Christ in his mercy, who will grant you eternal life.

[22] Have compassion for those who are wavering. [23] Save others by snatching them out of the fire. And for still others have compassion mixed with fear, hating even the tunic defiled by their bodies.

Doxology.* [24] Now to him who is able to keep you from falling and to bring you safely to his glorious presence, unblemished and rejoicing, [25] to the only God, our Savior, through Jesus Christ, our Lord, be glory, majesty, power, and authority, before all time, now, and forevermore. Amen.

VISIONS OF HOPE

"And behold, I am with you always, to the end of the world" (Mt 28:20). Each of the Gospels ends with a chapter that leads into the time of the Church. The Acts of the Apostles and the Letters, especially those of Paul, attest to the spread of the Good News, the presence of the Lord in the life of the communities, and the action of the Spirit. True enough, the Christian message ran into many difficulties and much opposition; but these enabled Christians to understand better the originality of their faith and the urgency of missionary work. Besides, had not Jesus often predicted persecution for his disciples?

At some moments, however, persecution took the form of a systematic political plan that was well organized and efficiently carried out throughout the vast empire subject to Rome. The aim was to exterminate the Christian movement everywhere and completely.

Would Christianity be able to weather the storm? How were people not to waver? What was to be thought of these events, and, above all, how were Christians to be steadfast in their faith in the face of oppression?

Here, in the Book of Revelation or the Apocalypse, we have a first effort to interpret the signs of a difficult time. In hours of crisis the need is to revive profound convictions; this Book sets forth these convictions in its own vigorous way, which takes the form of visions.

THE BOOK OF REVELATION

THE AGE OF THE MARTYRS

The resistance of Christians to worship of the emperor was a sure sign to the Roman authorities that they were trying to draw people away from it! The result was persecution: it had already occurred at the end of Nero's reign (the burning of Rome, A.D. 64), but now, and most especially, under Domitian (A.D. 81–96).

Was Christianity destined to disappear due to persecution by the public authorities? Or, at least, would not many Christians abandon the struggle? The time for protestations of loyalty to the Roman state was past (see Rom 13:1-7; Tit 3:1; 1 Pet 2:13-17); now it was necessary to resist, even to the acceptance of martyrdom.

A man, or group of people, experienced this anguish. Here he gives free rein to his protest against oppression and cries out a message of encouragement, and this on a grandiose stage: an enormous catastrophe strikes the earth, the present world disappears under the judgment of God, and a new world begins, the age of joy and God's salvation.

The author uses images we find bewildering, for in them the substance and the details change continually, and the most glaring colors are set in contrast; there are numerical sayings, each of which is thick with hidden meanings: everything is symbolical.

This is the kind of literature that is born in periods of disturbance. It is at such times that people speak of "apocalypses." The word means the act of revealing, of removing the veil. The author speaks on the basis of a vision that comes to him from above; the vision aims at unveiling the reality hidden in the future and the true meaning of what is coming, a meaning known only to God.

Understood in this way, an apocalypse is a special kind of prophecy. It is a reclusive literature because it is addressed to initiates and uses a mysterious language; it seeks to escape the surveillance of oppressors and of censors. It is a protest of conscience against intolerable pressures, a claim to a different vision of society and the world, a call to resistance in the midst of torment. The apocalyptic current entered the Bible beginning in the second century B.C.; at that time we find it especially in the Book of Daniel, in the Book of Joel, and in some passages of Isaiah (see chs. 24–27) and of Zechariah (chs. 9–11).

Furthermore, we must not forget the extraordinary descriptions given by Ezekiel. In the Jewish world all this material would be used in order to draw from it extremely subtle new constructs. We may recall the apocalypse in the Synoptic Gospels (Mk 13; Mt 24:10-36; Lk 17:22-37; 21:5-33) and certain passages of Paul (1 Thes 4:15-17; 2 Thes 2:1-12).

In this literary genre our Book of Revelation is a prime example. It was written at a difficult time, at the end of the first century, and aims, first, at quickening the life of the community in the face of internal crises (chs. 1–3).

Its primary purpose is to encourage these communities to stand up to the persecution that is inflicted on Christians when they refuse to offer sacrifice to the emperor (Rev 13:12-18; 14:9-13).

The author of this work calls himself "John" (Rev 1:1, 4, 9; 22:8) and describes himself to his readers as their "brother and partner in the suffering" (Rev 1:9), who has been exiled to the island of Patmos because of his faith.

He certainly belongs to the category of individuals whom the New Testament calls prophets (Rev 1:1-20; 22:9), and he enjoys great authority in the churches in the region of Asia Minor.

He does not, however, claim to be John the Apostle, son of Zebedee, with whom tradition has identified him; in fact, he never describes incidents of which he was an eyewitness, as the author of the fourth Gospel does.

There are undoubtedly many similarities with the Johannine writings, but the differences are even greater: the language is different; above all, the theological setting is different.

We do not, therefore, know anything specific about the author, whom the readers of his own time must have known. If we judge by the detailed knowledge and skill with which he handles the apocalyptic genre, he was, in all probability, of Jewish descent.

The Christian Apocalypse is not simply a song of God's power, but a splendid praise of Christ, who brings to fulfillment the destiny of the world through a breaking off of history.

It is also a book about the Church. In this new People of God, who are characterized by attachment to Christ, fidelity, and resistance, the most fascinating figures that emerge are the martyrs.

The Book of Revelation may be divided as follows:

Prologue: (1:1-20)

I: Letters to the Churches (2:1—3:22)

II: Celestial Visions about What Is To Come (4:1—22:5)

Epilogue: (22:6-21)

PROLOGUE

1 **The Revelation or Apocalypse of Jesus Christ.*** [1] The revelation of Jesus Christ, which God entrusted to him so that he might show his servants what must soon take place. He made it known by sending his angel to his servant John, [2] who has borne witness to the word of God and to the testimony of Jesus Christ by reporting everything that he has seen.

[3] Blessed * is the one who reads the words of this prophecy, and blessed are those who keep what is written in it, for the appointed time is near.

He Is, He Was, and He Will Return.* [4] John, to the seven Churches * in Asia: grace to you and peace from him who is, who was, and who is to come, and from the seven spirits before his throne, [5] and from Jesus Christ, the faithful witness, * the firstborn from the dead and the ruler of the kings of the earth. He loves us and has washed away our sins with his blood [6] and made us to be a kingdom and priests to serve his God and Father—to him be glory and power forever and ever. Amen.*

[7]   Behold, he is coming with the clouds;
       every eye will see him,
       even those who pierced him.
    All the peoples of the earth will mourn him.
       So shall it be. Amen.

⁸ "I am the Alpha and the Omega," says the Lord God, "the one who is, and who was, and who is to come, the Almighty."

"I Am the First and the Last."* ⁹ I, John—your brother and partner in the suffering and the kingdom and the patient endurance that are ours in Jesus—was on the island of Patmos * because I had proclaimed the word of God and given testimony to Jesus. ¹⁰ On the Lord's day, I was caught up in the spirit,* and I heard behind me a loud voice, like the sound of a trumpet, ¹¹ that said, "Write down on a scroll * what you see and send it to the seven Churches: to Ephesus, Smyrna, Pergamum, Thyatira, Sardis, Philadelphia, and Laodicea."

¹² Then I turned to see whose voice it was that had spoken to me, and when I turned I beheld seven gold lampstands. ¹³ * And in the midst of the lampstands I saw one like a son of man, * dressed in a robe that reached down to his feet and with a golden breastplate around his chest. ¹⁴ His head and his hair were white with the whiteness of wool, like snow, and his eyes were like a burning flame. ¹⁵ His feet were like burnished bronze refined in a furnace, and his voice was like the sound of rushing waters. ¹⁶ In his right hand he held seven stars. From his mouth there protruded a sharp, two-edged sword, and his face shone like the sun in all its brilliance.

¹⁷ When I saw him, I fell at his feet as though dead, but he laid his right hand on me and said, "Do not be afraid. I am the First and the Last. I am the Living One. ¹⁸ I was dead, but now I am alive forevermore, and I hold the keys to death and the netherworld.

¹⁹ "Now write down what you have seen, what is happening now, and what will take place afterward. ²⁰ The mystery of the seven stars that you saw in my right hand, and of the seven gold lampstands, is this: the seven stars are the angels of the seven Churches, and the seven lampstands are the seven Churches themselves.

I: LETTERS TO THE CHURCHES*

2 **To Ephesus.*** ¹ "To the angel of the Church in Ephesus,* write:

" 'These are the words of the one who holds the seven stars in his right hand and who walks in the midst of the seven lampstands:

² " ' "I know your deeds, your hard work, and your endurance. I know that you cannot tolerate wicked people, and how you have put to the test those who claim to be apostles but are not, and have found them to be impostors. ³ I am also aware of your perseverance and how you have toiled for my name without becoming weary.

⁴ " ' "However, I have this complaint against you: you have lost the love you had at first. ⁵ Remember from where you have fallen. Repent and do as you did originally. Otherwise, unless you repent, I will come to you and remove your lampstand from its place. ⁶ Nonetheless, this may be said in your favor: you detest the works of the Nicolaitans, which I also hate.

⁷ " ' "Whoever has ears should listen to what the Spirit says * to the Churches. To anyone who is victorious, I will give the right to eat from the tree of life that is in the paradise of God." ' '

To Smyrna.* ⁸ "To the angel of the Church in Smyrna,* write:

" 'These are the words of the First and the Last, who was dead and came to life again:

⁹ " ' "I know of your hardships and your poverty, but in reality you are rich. I am aware of the slander of those who claim to be Jews but are actually members of the synagogue of Satan. ¹⁰ Do not be frightened when thinking about the sufferings that you will have to endure. The devil will throw some of you into prison so that you may be tested, and you will endure affliction for ten days. Remain faithful until death, and I will give you the crown of life.

[11] " ' "Whoever has ears should listen to what the Spirit says to the Churches. Anyone who is victorious will not be harmed by the second death." '

To Pergamum.* [12] "To the angel of the Church in Pergamum, * write:

" 'These are the words of the one who has the sharp double-edged sword:

[13] " ' "I know that you live in the place where Satan is enthroned. Yet you have remained firm in support of my name, and you did not deny your faith in me even at the time when Antipas, * my faithful witness, was put to death among you, where Satan lives.

[14] " ' "Nevertheless, I have a few things against you. Some of you are holding to the teaching of Balaam, * who instructed Balak to place temptations in the path of the Israelites, encouraging them to eat food sacrificed to idols and to engage in fornication. [15] Likewise, there are some of you who follow the teaching of the Nicolaitans. [16] Therefore, repent. If you do not do so, I will come to you quickly and attack them with the sword of my mouth.

[17] " ' "Whoever has ears should listen to what the Spirit says to the Churches. To anyone who is victorious I will give some of the hidden manna. I will also give him a white stone, upon which will be inscribed a new name, known only to the person who receives it." '

To Thyatira.* [18] "To the angel of the Church in Thyatira, * write:

" 'These are the words of the Son of God who has eyes like a burning flame and feet like burnished bronze:

[19] " ' "I know your deeds—your love, your faithfulness, your service, and your endurance—and that you are doing greater works than you did at first. [20] Nevertheless, I have this against you, that you tolerate that woman Jezebel, who calls herself a prophetess and who by her teaching is luring my servants into acts of fornication and encouraging them to eat food that has been sacrificed to idols.

²¹ " ' "I have given her time to repent, but she refuses to repent of her fornication. ²² So I will cast her onto a bed of pain, and all those who commit adultery with her will suffer intensely unless they renounce her practices. ²³ I will also strike her children dead. Thereby all the Churches will be shown that I am the one who searches minds and hearts and I will give to each of you what your works deserve.

²⁴ " ' "And I say to the rest of you in Thyatira who have not accepted this teaching and who have no knowledge of what are designated as the deep secrets of Satan, * I shall not impose any further burden on you, ²⁵ but hold firmly to what you have until I come.

²⁶　　" ' "To anyone who is victorious
　　　　and perseveres in doing my works until the end,
　　　I will give authority over the nations,
²⁷　　the same authority that I received from my Father,
　　　　to rule them with an iron rod
　　　and shatter them like clay pots.

²⁸ And to such a person I will also give the morning star.

²⁹ " ' "Whoever has ears should listen to what the Spirit says to the Churches." '

3 To Sardis.* ¹ "To the angel of the Church in Sardis, * write:

" ' These are the words of the one who has the seven spirits of God and the seven stars:

" ' "I know your deeds. You have a reputation for being alive, but you are dead. ² Be on guard and strengthen what remains and is at the point of death. For I have not found any of your deeds perfect in the sight of my God. ³ Therefore, remember the teaching that you have received and heard. Hold on to it and repent. If you do not wake up, I will come like a thief, and you will never know at what hour I will come upon you.

⁴ " ' "However, there are still a few in Sardis who have not soiled their robes, and they will walk with me dressed

in white, for they are worthy. [5] Anyone who is victorious will be dressed like these in white robes, and I shall not blot his name from the book of life. * Rather, I shall acknowledge it in the presence of my Father and his angels.

[6] " ' "Whoever has ears should listen to what the Spirit says to the Churches." '

To Philadelphia.* [7] "To the angel of the Church in Philadelphia, * write:

" 'These are the words of the holy one,
    the true one,
    who has the key of David,
who opens the door,
    and no one can shut it;
who closes the door,
    and no one can open it:

[8] " ' "I know your deeds. I have set before you an open door * that no one will be able to close. I know that your strength is limited, yet you have kept my word and have not disowned my name. [9] Behold, I will make those of the synagogue of Satan who claim to be Jews but are not, for they are lying—I will make them come and fall down at your feet and recognize that I have loved you.

[10] " ' "Because you have kept my word to endure patiently, I will keep you safe during the time of trial that is going to come upon the whole world to put the inhabitants of the earth to the test. [11] I am coming soon. Hold fast to what you already have so that no one may rob you of your crown.

[12] " ' "Anyone who is victorious I will make into a pillar in the temple of my God, and never again will he depart from it. I will inscribe on him the name of my God and the name of the city of my God, the new Jerusalem, which is coming down out of heaven from my God, as well as my own new name. *

[13] " ' "Whoever has ears should listen to what the Spirit says to the Churches." '

To Laodicea.* ¹⁴ "To the angel of the Church in Laodicea, * write:

" 'These are the words of the Amen, the faithful and true witness, the source of God's creation:

¹⁵ " ' "I know your deeds, that you are neither cold nor hot. I wish you were either hot or cold. ¹⁶ As it is, since you are lukewarm, neither cold nor hot, * I will spit you out of my mouth. ¹⁷ For you say, 'I am rich; I have prospered; I have everything I want,' never realizing that you are wretched, pitiable, poor, blind, and naked. *

¹⁸ " ' "I advise you to buy from me gold that has been refined by fire so that you will be truly rich, and white robes to clothe you so that you may keep the shame of your nakedness from being seen, and ointment to smear on your eyes so that you may see. ¹⁹ I reprove and discipline all those whom I love. * Therefore, be sincere in your desire to repent.

²⁰ " ' "Behold, I am standing at the door, knocking. If one of you hears my voice and opens the door, I will come in and dine with that person and that person with me. ²¹ To anyone who is victorious, I will give the right to sit with me on my throne, as I myself overcame and sat with my Father on his throne.

²² " ' "Whoever has ears should listen to what the Spirit says to the Churches." ' "

II: CELESTIAL VISIONS ABOUT WHAT IS TO COME*

A: Christ, Lord of History*

4 **Vision of the Throne.*** ¹ Following this, I had a vision of heaven with an open door, and I heard the voice like a trumpet that I had heard speaking to me before, saying, "Come up here, and I will show you what must take place after this." ² At once I was caught up in the spirit, * and there in heaven I beheld a throne. ³ Seated upon the throne was one whose appearance was similar to that of jasper and carnelian, and surrounding it was a rainbow that looked like an emerald.

⁴ Encircling the throne were twenty-four thrones, and seated on them were twenty-four elders, * dressed in white with gold crowns on their heads. ⁵ Emanating from the throne were flashes of lightning and rumblings and peals of thunder. Burning in front of the throne were seven flaming lamps, the seven spirits of God, ⁶ and in front of the throne there was something like a sea of glass as transparent as crystal.

In the center of the throne and around it there were four living creatures,* and they were covered with eyes in front and in back. ⁷ The first living creature resembled a lion, the second resembled an ox, the third had a human face, and the fourth resembled an eagle in flight. ⁸ Each of the four living creatures had six wings, and all of them were covered with eyes all around and underneath their wings. Day and night they never stop saying:

"Holy, holy, holy
   is the Lord God, the Almighty,
who was, and who is, and who is to come."

⁹ And whenever the living creatures give glory and honor and thanks to the one who sits on the throne, who lives forever and ever, ¹⁰ the twenty-four elders prostrate themselves before him who is seated on the throne and worship the one who lives forever and ever. As they lay down their crowns in front of the throne, they cry out:

¹¹   "Worthy are you, O Lord our God,
        to receive glory and honor and power,
   for you created all things;
        by your will they were created
        and have their being."

5 Vision of the Lamb.* ¹ Then I saw in the right hand of the one who was seated on the throne a scroll with writing on both sides and sealed with seven seals. ² And I beheld a mighty angel who proclaimed in a loud voice, "Who is worthy to open the scroll and break its seals?" ³ But there was no one in heaven or on earth or under the earth who was able to open the scroll and examine it.

[4] I began to weep bitterly because no one was found worthy to open the scroll and examine it. [5] Then one of the elders said to me, "Do not weep. The Lion of the tribe of Judah, the Root of David, has triumphed, and thus has won the right to open the scroll and its seven seals."

[6] Then I saw, standing in the center of the throne, encircled by the four living creatures and the elders, a Lamb that had been slain. He had seven horns and seven eyes, which are the seven spirits of God sent forth into the entire world. [7] He came forward and took the scroll from the right hand of the one who was seated on the throne.

[8] When he had taken the scroll, the four living creatures and the twenty-four elders prostrated themselves before the Lamb. Each of the elders was holding a harp, and they had gold bowls filled with incense, which are the prayers of the saints. [9] They sang a new song: *

> "You are worthy to receive the scroll
>   and to open its seals,
> for you were slain,
>   and with your blood you purchased for God
>   people of every tribe and language, nation and
>   race.
> [10]   You have made them to be a kingdom and priests to
>   serve our God,
>   and they will reign on earth."

[11] In my vision, I heard the voices of a multitude of angels who surrounded the throne and the living creatures and the elders. These angels numbered thousands upon thousands and ten thousand times ten thousand of them. [12] And they cried out with a loud voice:

> "Worthy is the Lamb that was sacrificed
>   to receive power and riches, wisdom and strength,
>   honor and glory and praise."

[13] Then I heard every creature in heaven and on earth and under the earth and in the sea, and all that is in them, saying:

"To the one seated on the throne
and to the Lamb
be blessing and honor and glory and might
forever and ever."

[14] The four living creatures said, "Amen," and the elders prostrated themselves in worship.

B: Prelude to the End of Times: Israel and the Church*

6 **The First Four Seals and the Horsemen.*** [1] Then, in my vision, I saw the Lamb break open the first of the seven seals, and I heard one of the four living creatures shout in a voice like thunder, "Come!" [2] I looked, and before my eyes I saw a white horse, and its rider was holding a bow. He was given a crown, and he rode forth as a victor to amass still further conquests.

[3] When he broke open the second seal, I heard the second living creature shout, "Come!" [4] And another horse came forth; it was red. Its rider was empowered to take away peace from the earth so that people would slay each other. He was given a large sword. *

[5] When he broke open the third seal, I heard the third living creature shout, "Come!" I looked, and there was a black horse, and its rider was holding a pair of scales * in his hand. [6] Then I heard what sounded like a voice emanating from the midst of the four living creatures, saying, "A quart of wheat costs a day's wages, and three quarts of barley cost a day's wages. But do not damage the olive oil or the wine."

[7] When he broke open the fourth seal, I heard the voice of the fourth living creature shout, "Come!" [8] I looked, and there was a pale green horse. Its rider was named Death, and Hades * followed close behind. They were given authority over a fourth of the earth, to kill with sword, famine, and plague, and by means of wild beasts.

The Fifth Seal: Vision of the Martyrs.* [9] When he broke open the fifth seal, I saw underneath the altar the souls of those who had been slain on account of the word of God and for witnessing to it. [10] They shouted in a loud voice, "How long is it to be, holy and true Master, before you judge the inhabitants of the earth * and avenge our death?"

[11] Each of them was given a white robe, * and they were instructed to be patient for a little longer until the roll was completed of their fellow servants and brethren who were still to be killed as they themselves had been.

The Sixth Seal: the Universe Disturbed.* [12] In my vision, when he broke open the sixth seal, there was a violent earthquake. The sun turned as black as coarse sackcloth, the moon became as red as blood, [13] and the stars in the sky fell to earth like unripe figs dislodged from a tree when shaken by a strong wind. [14] The heavens were torn apart like a scroll being rolled up, and every mountain and island was dislodged from its place.

[15] Then the kings of the earth, the nobles, and the commanders, the rich and the powerful, and the whole population, both slaves and free, hid themselves in caves and among the rocks of the mountains. [16] They shouted to the mountains and the rocks, "Fall on us and hide us from the face of the one who sits on the throne, and from the wrath of the Lamb. [17] For the great day of their wrath has come, and who can endure it?"

7 An Immense Crowd before God's Throne.*

[1] After this I saw four angels standing at the four corners of the earth, holding back the four winds of the earth so that no wind could blow on land or on the sea or on any tree. [2] Then I saw another angel rising from the east, bearing the seal of the living God. He cried out in a loud voice to the four angels who had been given the power to ravage the land and the sea, [3] "Do not damage the land or the sea or the trees until we have set the seal on the foreheads of the servants of our God."

[4] Then I heard how many had been marked with the seal—one hundred and forty-four thousand from all the tribes of Israel:

5   From the tribe of Judah, * twelve thousand,
     from the tribe of Reuben, twelve thousand,
     from the tribe of Gad, twelve thousand,

6   from the tribe of Asher, twelve thousand,
     from the tribe of Naphtali, twelve thousand,
     from the tribe of Manasseh, twelve thousand,

7   from the tribe of Simeon, twelve thousand,
     from the tribe of Levi, twelve thousand,
     from the tribe of Issachar, twelve thousand,

8   from the tribe of Zebulun, twelve thousand,
     from the tribe of Joseph, twelve thousand,
     from the tribe of Benjamin, twelve thousand.

9 After this, in my vision, I witnessed a vast throng that no one could count, from every nation, race, people, and language. They were standing before the throne and before the Lamb, dressed in white robes and holding palm branches in their hands. 10 They cried out in a loud voice:

> "Salvation belongs to our God,
>   who sits on the throne,
>   and to the Lamb."

11 All the angels who were standing around the throne, and around the elders and the four living creatures, prostrated themselves before the throne and worshiped God, 12 saying:

> "Amen. Praise and glory,
>   wisdom and thanksgiving,
> honor and power and might,
>   be to our God forever and ever. Amen."

13 Then one of the elders spoke to me and inquired, "Who are these people, all dressed in white robes, and where have they come from?" 14 I replied, "My lord, you are the one who knows." Then he said to me, "These are the ones who have survived the great tribulation. They have washed their robes and made them white in the blood of the Lamb.

15 "That is why they stand before the throne of God
and worship him day and night in his temple,
and the one who sits on the throne will shelter
them.

16 They will never again experience hunger or thirst,
nor will the sun or any scorching heat cause them
discomfort.

17 For the Lamb who is at the center of the throne
will be their shepherd.
He will guide them to springs of living water,*
and God will wipe away every tear from their eyes."

8 The Seventh Seal.*

¹ When the Lamb broke open the seventh seal, there was silence in heaven for about half an hour. ² And I saw that seven trumpets were given to the seven angels who stand in the presence of God.

³ Another angel came forward with a gold censer and stood at the altar.* He was given a large quantity of incense to offer, with the prayers of all the saints, on the gold altar that stood before the throne.

⁴ The smoke of the incense together with the prayers of the saints rose before God from the hand of the angel. ⁵ Then the angel took the censer, filled it with fire from the altar, and emptied it upon the earth. Immediately, there came peals of thunder, rumblings, flashes of lightning, and an earthquake.

⁶ The seven angels who held the seven trumpets now made ready to blow them.

The First Four Trumpets.* ⁷ When the first angel blew his trumpet, there was a storm of hail and fire, mixed with blood, and it fell upon the earth.* A third of the earth was burned up, as well as a third of the trees and all the green grass.

⁸ * When the second angel blew his trumpet, something that looked like a huge mountain ablaze with fire was hurled into the sea. A third of the sea turned into blood, ⁹ a third of the creatures living in the sea died, and a third of the ships were destroyed.

¹⁰ When the third angel blew his trumpet, a great star fell from the sky, burning like a torch. It came down on a third of the rivers and on the springs of water. ¹¹ This star was called "Wormwood," and a third of the waters turned to wormwood. * Great numbers of people died from the waters that had become bitter.

¹² When the fourth angel blew his trumpet, a third of the sun was struck, a third of the moon, and a third of the stars. As a result, a third of their light was darkened, * and the day lost its illumination for a third of the time, and so did the night.

The Cry of the Eagle.* ¹³ In my vision, I heard an eagle cry out in a loud voice as it flew high overhead, "Woe! Woe! Woe to the inhabitants of the earth because of the other trumpet blasts that the three angels have not yet blown!"

9 The Fifth Trumpet: the First Woe.*

¹ Then the fifth angel blew his trumpet, and I saw a star that had fallen from the sky to the earth. He was given the key to the shaft leading down to the abyss. ² When he unlocked the shaft of the abyss, smoke rose up from the abyss like smoke from a huge furnace, so that the sun and the sky were darkened by the smoke from the abyss. ³ And out of the smoke locusts dropped down onto the earth, and they were given the same powers that scorpions have on the earth. ⁴ They were commanded not to damage the grass or the earth or any plant or tree, and they were told to attack only those people who did not have God's seal on their foreheads.

⁵ They were given permission to torture these people for five months, but they were not allowed to kill them, and the torment they were to inflict was to be like that of a scorpion when it stings someone. ⁶ During that time, these people will seek death but will not find it; they will long to die, but death will elude them.

⁷ In appearance the locusts were like horses equipped for battle. On their heads they wore what appeared to be gold crowns. Their faces were like human faces, ⁸ and

their hair was like women's hair. Their teeth were like lions' teeth, [9] and their chests were like iron breastplates. The sound of their wings was like the rumble of many horses and chariots rushing into battle.

[10] These locusts had tails and stings like those of scorpions, and in their tails they had the power to torment people for five months. [11] They had as their king the angel of the abyss, whose name in Hebrew is Abaddon, and in Greek, Apollyon.

[12] The first woe has passed, but two more are still to come.

The Sixth Trumpet: the Second Woe.* [13] Then the sixth angel blew his trumpet, and I heard a voice * emanating from the horns of the gold altar that stood in the presence of God. [14] It said to the sixth angel who was holding the trumpet, "Release the four angels who are bound at the great river Euphrates."

[15] And so the four angels, who had been held in readiness for this very hour, day, month, and year, were released to kill a third of mankind.* [16] The number of their cavalry troops was two hundred million. This was the number I heard.

[17] This is how I saw the horses and their riders in my vision. The riders wore breastplates in shades of red, blue, and yellow. The heads of the horses were like heads of lions, and issuing forth from their mouths were fire, smoke, and sulfur. [18] By these three plagues of fire, smoke, and sulfur that poured forth from their mouths, a third of mankind was killed. [19] The power of the horses was in their mouths and in their tails. Their tails were like serpents, with heads that inflicted harm.

[20] However, the rest of mankind who survived these plagues did not repent of the work of their hands or cease their worship of demons * and of idols of gold, silver, bronze, stone, and wood, which can neither see nor hear nor walk. [21] Nor did they repent of their murders, their sorcery, their sexual immorality, or their thefts.

10 **A Small Scroll: Sweet and Bitter.*** [1] Then I saw another mighty angel coming down from heaven. He was wrapped in a cloud, with a rainbow over his head. His face was like the sun, his legs were like pillars of fire, [2] and his hand held a small scroll that had been opened.

Placing his right foot on the sea and his left foot on the land, [3] the angel gave forth a great shout like the roar of a lion. And when he shouted, the seven thunders spoke. [4] After the seven thunders had spoken, I was preparing to write when I heard a voice from heaven say, "Seal up what the seven thunders have spoken, but do not write it down."

[5] Then the angel whom I had seen standing on the sea and on the land raised his right hand to heaven [6] and swore by him who lives forever and ever and who created heaven and earth and the sea and everything that is in them: "There will be no further delay. [7] When the time comes for the seventh angel to sound his trumpet, the mysterious purpose of God* will be fulfilled, just as he announced to his servants the Prophets."

[8] Then I again heard the voice that had spoken to me from heaven, and it said, "Go and take that open scroll from the hand of the angel who is standing on the sea and on the land." [9] Therefore, I went to the angel and asked him to give me the small scroll. He replied, "Take it and eat it. It will turn your stomach sour, but in your mouth it will taste as sweet as honey."

[10] I took the small scroll from the angel's hand and ate it. In my mouth it did taste as sweet as honey, but when I had eaten it my stomach turned sour. [11] Then I was told, "You must prophesy once again about many peoples, nations, languages, and kings."

11 **The Two Witnesses and the Fate of Jerusalem.*** [1] I was next given a staff to use as a measuring rod, and I was told, "Go forth and measure the temple of God and the altar, and count the people who are worshiping there. [2] However, exclude the outer court of the temple from your measurements, because it has been handed over to the Gentiles and they will trample on the holy city for forty-two months. * ³ I will grant my two witnesses authority to prophesy for those twelve hundred and sixty days, wearing sackcloth."

⁴ These are the two olive trees and the two lampstands that stand in the presence of the Lord of the earth. ⁵ If anyone tries to harm them, fire pours forth from their mouths and consumes their enemies. Anyone who attempts to harm them will surely be killed in this manner. ⁶ They have the power to shut up the sky so that it does not rain during the time they are prophesying. They also have the power to turn water into blood and to afflict the earth with every type of plague as often as they desire.

⁷ When they have completed their testimony, the beast that comes up from the abyss will wage war against them and overpower and kill them. ⁸ Their corpses will lie in the street of the great city, known by the symbolic names of Sodom and Egypt, where their Lord was crucified.

⁹ People of every race, tribe, nation, and language will gaze at their corpses for three and a half days and refuse to allow them to be buried. ¹⁰ The inhabitants of the earth will gloat over them as they celebrate and exchange gifts, because these two prophets had been a source of torment to them.

¹¹ However, after the three and a half days, the breath of life from God entered them, and when they rose to their feet, great terror filled those who saw them. ¹² Then I heard a loud voice from heaven say to them, "Come up here," and while their enemies were watching, they went up to heaven in a cloud.

¹³ At that very hour there was a violent earthquake, and a tenth of the city was destroyed. Seven thousand people were killed during the earthquake. Those who survived were overcome with fear and gave glory to the God of heaven.

¹⁴ The second woe has passed, but the third will come quickly.

The Seventh Trumpet: the Third Woe. * [15] The seventh angel blew his trumpet, and voices in heaven were heard crying loudly:

> "The kingdom of the world belongs
>> to our Lord and his Messiah,
>> and he will reign forever and ever."

[16] Then the twenty-four elders who sit on their thrones in the presence of God prostrated themselves and worshiped God, [17] saying:

> "We give you thanks, Lord God Almighty,
>> who are and who were.
> For you have taken your great power
>> and have begun to reign.
[18]
> The nations rose in rage,
>> but now your wrath has come.
> It is the time for judging the dead
>> and for rewarding your servants the Prophets,
> as well as the saints who revere your name,
>> both small and great,
> and for destroying those who destroy the earth."

[19] Then God's temple in heaven was opened, and the ark of his covenant * was seen within his temple. There followed flashes of lightning, rumblings, peals of thunder, an earthquake, and a violent hailstorm.

C: The Great Confrontation:
Pagan Rome and the Church*

12 **Two Signs in Heaven: the Woman and the Dragon.** * [1] A great sign appeared in heaven: a woman clothed with the sun, with the moon beneath her feet, and a crown of twelve stars on her head. [2] She was with child and about to give birth, crying aloud in the anguish of her labor.

[3] Then another sign appeared in heaven: a huge red dragon with seven heads and ten horns, and seven diadems crowning his heads. [4] His tail swept away a third of the stars in the sky and hurled them to the earth.

The dragon stood in front of the woman who was about to give birth, so that it might devour her child as soon as it was born. [5] She gave birth to a son, a male child who is destined to rule all the nations with an iron rod. And her child was taken up directly to God and to his throne. [6] The woman herself fled into the wilderness where she would be looked after for twelve hundred and sixty days * in a place prepared for her by God.

[7] Next, war broke out in heaven, with Michael * and his angels in combat against the dragon. The dragon and his angels fought back, [8] but they were defeated, and they lost their place in heaven. [9] The great dragon—the ancient serpent who is called the devil, or Satan, the deceiver of the whole world—was hurled down to earth, and his angels were cast down with him.

[10] Then I heard a loud voice in heaven say:

"Now have come the salvation and the power
    and the kingdom of our God
    and the authority of his Messiah.
For the accuser * of our brethren has been cast out,
    the one who accused them day and night before
        our God.
[11]   They have conquered him
    by the blood of the Lamb
    and by the word of their testimony;
even in the face of death
    they did not cling to life.
[12]   Therefore rejoice, you heavens,
    and you who dwell in them!
But woe to you, earth and sea,
    because the devil has come down to you.
He is filled with rage,
    for he knows that his time is short."

[13] When the dragon realized that he had been hurled down to earth, he pursued the woman who had given birth to the male child. [14] But the woman was given the two wings of the great eagle so that she could fly away

from the serpent into the wilderness, to the place where she was to be looked after for a year, two years, and a half year. *

¹⁵ Then from his mouth the serpent spewed out water like a river after the woman to sweep her away with the flood. ¹⁶ However, the earth came to the rescue of the woman: it opened its mouth and swallowed the river spewed from the dragon's mouth.

¹⁷ Then the dragon became enraged at the woman and went off to wage war on the rest of her offspring, those who keep God's commandments and bear witness to Jesus.

A Beast Rises from the Sea. * ¹⁸ Meanwhile, I took my position * on the seashore.

13 ¹ Then I saw a beast rising out of the sea. It had ten horns and seven heads. On its horns were ten diadems, and on its heads were blasphemous names. ² The beast that I saw resembled a leopard, but it had feet like those of a bear, and its mouth was like the mouth of a lion. The dragon conferred on the beast his own power and his throne, as well as great authority.

³ One of his heads appeared to me to have been mortally wounded, but its mortal wound had been healed. The whole world then became fascinated with the beast, ⁴ and they worshiped the dragon because he had conferred authority on the beast. They also worshiped the beast, saying, "Who can compare with the beast? Who can fight against it?"

⁵ It was allowed to mouth its haughty and blasphemous words, and it was granted permission to exercise its authority for forty-two months. * ⁶ It opened its mouth to utter blasphemies against God, as well as against his name and his dwelling and all those who live in heaven.

⁷ The beast was also allowed to wage war on the saints and conquer them, and it was given authority over every tribe, people, language, and nation. ⁸ All the inhabitants of the earth will worship it, all those whose names have

not been written from the creation of the world * in the book of life belonging to the Lamb who was slain.

⁹ Whoever has ears should listen to these words:

10   "If anyone is to go into captivity,
             into captivity he will go.
        If anyone is destined to be slain by the sword,
             by the sword he must be slain."

This demands patient endurance and faithfulness on the part of the saints.

A Beast Rises from the Earth.* ¹¹ Then I saw another beast, this one rising up out of the earth. It had two horns like those of a lamb, but it spoke like a dragon. ¹² It wielded all the authority of the first beast on its behalf, and it forced the earth and all its inhabitants to worship the first beast, whose mortal wound had been healed. ¹³ It performed great signs, even making fire come down from heaven to earth in the sight of all.

¹⁴ By the signs it was allowed to perform on behalf of the beast, it deceived the inhabitants of the earth, persuading them to erect an image for the beast that had been wounded by the sword and yet lived. ¹⁵ It was permitted to give life to the beast's image so that it could even speak and cause all those to be put to death who would not worship the image of the beast.

¹⁶ It also forced all the people, both small and great, both rich and poor, both free and slave, to be branded on the right hand or on the forehead. ¹⁷ No one could buy or sell anything except one who has been branded with the name of the beast or with the number of its name.

¹⁸ There is wisdom here. Let anyone who has understanding calculate the number of the beast, for it is the number of a person. The number is six hundred and sixty-six.

14 The Song of the Martyrs.*

¹ Next in my vision, I saw the Lamb standing on Mount Zion, and with him were one hundred and forty-four thousand * people who had his

name and his Father's name written on their foreheads.
[2] I heard a sound from heaven like that of a mighty torrent or a loud peal of thunder. It was like the sound of harpists playing their harps.

[3] They were singing a new song * before the throne and before the four living creatures and the elders. No one could learn this song except the one hundred and forty-four thousand who had been redeemed from the earth.
[4] These are the ones who have not defiled themselves with women. * They are virgins, and they follow the Lamb wherever he goes. They have been redeemed as the firstfruits of mankind for God and for the Lamb. [5] No lie was found on their lips. They are irreproachable.

The Nearness of the Judgment.* [6] Then I saw another angel flying in midair, with an eternal gospel to proclaim to all those who live on the earth, to every nation, race, language, and people. [7] He said in a loud voice, "Fear God and give him glory, for the time has come for his judgment. Worship him who made heaven and earth, the sea and the springs of water."

[8] A second angel followed him, saying:

"Fallen, fallen is Babylon the great.
    She has made all the nations drink
        the wine of the wrath of her immorality."

[9] A third angel followed them, crying out in a loud voice, "Anyone who worships the beast or its image and receives its mark on his forehead or hand [10] will also drink the wine of God's wrath, poured undiluted into the cup of his wrath. * Such people will be tormented in burning sulfur in the presence of the holy angels and of the Lamb. [11] The smoke of their torment will rise forever and ever. There will be no respite day or night for those who worship the beast or its image or for those who receive the mark of its name."

[12] This demands patient endurance on the part of the saints who keep the commandments of God and remain faithful to Jesus.

¹³ Then I heard a voice from heaven say, "Write: Blessed * are those who die in the Lord from now on."

"Yes," says the Spirit, "they will find rest from their labors, for their deeds go with them."

One Like a Son of Man.* ¹⁴ Now in my vision, I saw a white cloud, and seated on the cloud was one "like a son of man," * with a gold crown on his head and a sharp sickle in his hand. ¹⁵ Another angel then came out of the temple and called out in a loud voice to the one seated on the cloud, "Use your sickle and reap, for the time to reap has come, because the harvest of the earth is fully ripe." ¹⁶ So the one who was seated on the cloud swept over the earth with his sickle, and the earth was harvested.

¹⁷ Another angel came out of the temple in heaven, and he too had a sharp sickle. ¹⁸ Then from the altar came forth still another angel who was in charge of the fire, and he cried out in a loud voice to the one who had the sharp sickle, "Take your sharp sickle and gather the clusters from the vines of the earth, for her grapes are ripe."

¹⁹ So the angel swung his sickle over the earth and gathered in its vintage, which he then cast into the great winepress of God's wrath. ²⁰ The winepress was trodden outside the city, and blood flowed from the winepress to the height of a horse's bridle for a distance of two hundred miles.

15 The Seven Angels and the Seven Plagues.* ¹ Then I saw in heaven another great and wondrous sign: seven angels with the seven plagues, the last plagues of all, for through them the wrath of God is completed.

The Song of Moses and the Song of the Lamb.* ² I saw something that looked like a sea of glass mixed with fire. Standing beside the sea of glass and holding the harps that God had given them were those who had been victorious over the beast and its image and over the number of its name. They were holding harps given them by God ³ and singing the song of Moses, the servant of God, and the song of the Lamb:

"How great and wonderful are your works,
    Lord God Almighty!
Just and true are your ways,
    O King of the nations!
4   Who shall not fear you, O Lord,
        and bring glory to your name?
        For you alone are holy.
All nations will come
    and worship before you,
    for your acts of justice have been revealed."

D: The Justice and Triumph of God*

Vision of the Temple. ⁵ After this, in my vision, the temple, that is, the tabernacle of the Testimony, * was opened in heaven, ⁶ and from the temple emerged the seven angels with the seven plagues. They were robed in clean, shining linen, and breastplates of gold were fastened around their chests.

⁷ Then one of the four living creatures gave to the seven angels seven gold bowls full of the wrath of God, who lives forever and ever. ⁸ The temple was filled with the smoke from the glory of God and from his power, so that no one could enter the temple until the seven plagues of the seven angels were completed.

16 The Seven Bowls of the Wrath of God.* ¹ Then I heard a loud voice from the temple say to the seven angels, "Go forth and pour out on the earth the seven bowls of the wrath of God."

² The first angel went forth and poured out his bowl on the earth. Immediately, foul and malignant sores broke out on those who had the mark of the beast and who worshiped its image. *

³ * The second angel poured out his bowl on the sea. It turned to blood, like the blood of a dead person, and every living thing in the sea died.

⁴ The third angel poured out his bowl on the rivers and the springs of water, and they turned to blood. ⁵ Then I heard the angel in charge of the waters say:

> "You are just, O Holy One,
> > who are and who were,
> > in these your judgments.
⁶ > For they have shed the blood
> > of the saints and the Prophets,
> and you have given them blood to drink,
> > as they deserve."

⁷ And I heard the altar respond:

> "Yes, Lord God Almighty,
> > true and just are your judgments."

⁸ The fourth angel poured out his bowl on the sun, and the sun was allowed to burn people with its flames. ⁹ They were scorched by the fierce heat, and they cursed the name of God who had the power to inflict those plagues, but they refused to repent and pay him homage.

¹⁰ The fifth angel poured out his bowl on the throne of the beast, and its kingdom was plunged into darkness. * People gnawed their tongues in agony ¹¹ and cursed the God of heaven because of their pains and sores, instead of repenting for what they had done.

¹² The sixth angel poured out his bowl on the great river Euphrates, and its water was dried up to prepare the way for the kings from the East. ¹³ I saw three unclean spirits like frogs * come forth from the mouth of the dragon, from the mouth of the beast, and from the mouth of the false prophet.

¹⁴ These are demonic spirits with the power to work miracles. They were sent to the kings of the entire world to assemble them for battle on the great day of God the Almighty.

¹⁵ * "Behold, I am coming like a thief! Blessed is the one who stays awake and keeps his clothes close by so that he will not have to go naked and be exposed to

shame." [16] These spirits then assembled the kings at the place that in Hebrew is called Armageddon. *

[17] The seventh angel poured out his bowl into the air, and a loud voice came out of the temple from the throne, saying, "It is done!" [18] Then there followed flashes of lightning, rumblings, peals of thunder, and a violent earthquake—so violent that there has never been one like it since the human race has inhabited the earth.

[19] The great city was split into three parts, and the cities of the nations collapsed in ruin. Babylon the Great was also remembered by God, as he made her drink the cup filled with the wine of his fury and wrath. [20] Every island vanished, and no mountains were to be found. [21] Huge hailstones, each weighing about one hundred pounds, fell from the sky on the people, and they cursed God on account of the plague of hail that turned out to be so terrible.

17 Babylon the Great, the Infamous Harlot.* [1] One of the seven angels who held the seven bowls approached me and said, "Come here and I will show you the judgment on the great harlot who is enthroned over many waters. [2] The kings of the earth have committed fornication with her, and the inhabitants of the earth have become drunk on the wine of her harlotry."

[3] Then he carried me away in the spirit * into the wilderness, and I saw a woman seated on a scarlet beast that had seven heads and ten horns and was covered with blasphemous names. [4] The woman was clothed in purple and scarlet and adorned with gold and jewels and pearls. In her hand she held a gold cup filled with accursed things and the impurities of her harlotry.

[5] On her forehead was written a mysterious name: "Babylon the Great, the mother of harlots and of every abomination on the earth." [6] And I noticed that the woman was drunk with the blood of the saints and the blood of those who had borne witness to Jesus.

When I saw her, I was utterly astounded. [7] But the angel said to me, "Why are you astounded? I will explain to you the mystery of the woman and of the beast with the seven heads and the ten horns that carries her. [8] The beast that you saw was once alive but is now alive no longer. It is about to ascend from the abyss and go to its destruction. All the inhabitants of the earth whose names have not been written in the book of life since the foundation of the world will be astonished when they see the beast, because it was once alive but is now alive no longer, and yet it is still to come.

[9] "This calls for a mind with wisdom. The seven heads represent seven hills upon which the woman is seated. They also represent seven kings. [10] Five have already fallen, one is still living, and the other has not yet come. When he does come, he must remain only for a short while. [11] As for the beast that was alive but is now alive no longer, it is at the same time the eighth and one of the seven, and it is headed for destruction.

[12] "The ten horns that you saw are ten kings who have not yet begun to reign. They will have royal authority for only a single hour together with the beast. [13] They are all of the same mind and will confer their power and authority on the beast. [14] They will wage war against the Lamb, but because the Lamb is Lord of lords and King of kings,* he will overcome them—he and those who are with him, the called, the chosen, and the faithful."

[15] The angel continued, "The waters that you saw, where the harlot sits, represent peoples, multitudes, nations, and languages. [16] The ten horns that you saw and the beast will hate the harlot. They will render her desolate and naked; after they devour her flesh, they will burn her up with fire.

[17] "For God has influenced their hearts to carry out his purpose by agreeing to confer their royal powers upon the beast until the words of God will be fulfilled. [18] The woman you saw is the great city that has authority over the kings of the earth."

18 The Fall of Babylon the Great.* [1] After this I saw another angel coming down from heaven. He had great author-

ity, and his splendor illumined the earth. [2] He cried out in a mighty voice:

> "Fallen, fallen is Babylon the Great!
>   She has become a dwelling place for demons,
> a haunt for every unclean spirit
>   and for every filthy and loathsome bird.
> [3] For all the nations have drunk
>   the wine of the wrath of her harlotry.
> The kings of the earth have committed fornication with her,
>   and the merchants of the earth have grown rich
>   from her wealth and luxury."

[4] Then I heard another voice from heaven saying:

> "Depart from her, my people,
>   so that you will not take part in her sins
>   and share in her plagues.
> [5] For her sins are piled up as high as the heavens,
>   and God has remembered her crimes.
> [6] Pay her back as she has done to others,
>   and repay her double for her deeds;
>   mix her a double portion of her own poison.
> [7] Give her torment and grief
>   to equal the measure of her glory and luxury.
> In her heart she says,
>   'I rule as a queen.
> I am not a widow,
>   and I will never experience grief.'
> [8] Therefore, in a single day
>   her plagues will come upon her:
>   pestilence and mourning and famine.
> And she will be consumed by fire,
>   for mighty is the Lord God who judges her.

Funereal Ode over Rome.* [9] "The kings of the earth who committed fornication with her and shared in her luxury will weep and mourn over her when they behold the smoke of her immolation. [10] In terror at her torment, they will keep their distance and say:

" 'Woe, woe, O great city,
  mighty city of Babylon.
  In one hour your judgment has come.'

¹¹ "The merchants of the earth will weep and mourn over her, since no one buys their cargo anymore: ¹² their cargo of gold, silver, precious stones, and pearls; purple and scarlet cloth, silks, and fine linens; all sorts of fragrant wood and all kinds of objects of ivory, all kinds of objects of expensive wood, bronze, iron, and marble; ¹³ cinnamon and spices; incense, myrrh, and frankincense; wine and olive oil; fine flour and wheat; cattle and sheep; horses and chariots; and slaves, that is, human lives. They will say:

¹⁴   " 'The fruit you longed for
       is no longer available to you.
     All your riches and splendor are gone,
       and you will never find them again.'

¹⁵ "The merchants of these things who made a fortune from her will stand far off, weeping and mourning aloud, and terrified as they behold her torment:

¹⁶   " 'Woe, woe, O great city,
       clothed in fine linen and purple and scarlet,
       adorned with gold, jewels, and precious stones!
¹⁷   Within one hour
       all this wealth has been destroyed.'

"All the ship captains and voyagers, all the sailors and those who make their living by trading upon the sea, will stand far off ¹⁸ and exclaim as they see the smoke caused by her immolation, 'Has there ever been a city to compare with this great city?' ¹⁹ Then they will throw dust on their heads and with mourning and weeping cry out:

     " 'Woe, woe, O great city,
       where all who had ships at sea
       became rich through her wealth!
     Within one hour
       she has been brought to ruin.
²⁰   Rejoice over her, O heaven,

you holy ones, apostles, and prophets!
For God has passed judgment on her for you.' "

21 Then a mighty angel picked up a stone the size of a large millstone and threw it into the sea, saying:

"This is how
the great city of Babylon will be thrown down,
never to be found again.
22 The sound of harpists and minstrels,
flute players and trumpeters,
will never be heard in you again.
Craftsmen of every trade
never will be found in you again.
The sound of a millstone
will never be heard in you again.
23 The light from a lamp
will never be seen in you again.
The voices of a bridegroom and bride
will never be heard in you again.
Since your merchants were the world's great men,
all the nations were led astray by your enticements.
24 In you * was found the blood of the Prophets,
of the saints,
and of all who have been slain on the earth."

19 Song of Victory and Wedding Day of the Lamb.* 1 After
this I heard what sounded like the roar of a great multitude in heaven, shouting:

"Alleluia! *
Salvation and glory and power belong to our God,
2 for true and just are his judgments.
He has condemned the great harlot
who corrupted the earth with her harlotry.
And he has paid her back
for the blood of his servants."

3 Once again they shouted:

"Alleluia!
Her smoke will rise
forever and ever."

⁴ The twenty-four elders and the four living creatures threw themselves to the ground and worshiped God who was seated on the throne, and they cried:

"Amen. Alleluia!"

⁵ Then a voice came from the throne, saying:

"Praise our God,
　all you his servants,
and all who fear him,
　small and great alike."

⁶ And I heard what seemed to be the sound of a vast multitude, like the sound of a torrential stream or of great peals of thunder, crying out:

"Alleluia.
The reign of the Lord our God,
　the Almighty, has begun.
⁷ Let us rejoice and be glad
　and give him glory.
For the wedding day of the Lamb has come,
　and the bride has made herself ready.
⁸ She has been permitted to wear
　a bright and clean garment of fine linen."

(The fine linen represents the righteous deeds of the saints.)

⁹ Then the angel said to me, "Write: 'Blessed * are those who are invited to the wedding banquet of the Lamb.' " And he added, "These are the true words of God."

¹⁰ I fell at his feet to worship him, but he said to me, "You must not do that! I am a fellow servant with you and with your brethren who have given witness to Jesus. * Worship God! For the witness to Jesus is the spirit of prophecy."

E: Recapitulative Visions of the History of Salvation*

The White Horse and the King of Kings.* ¹¹ Now I saw heaven opened, and a white horse appeared. Its rider was called "Faithful and True," for with righteousness he judges and wages war. [12] His eyes were like fiery flames, and on his head were many crowns. The name inscribed on him was known to no one but himself.

[13] He was clothed in a robe dipped in blood, and he was known by the name The Word of God. [14] The armies of heaven were following him, riding on white horses and dressed in fine linen, white and clean.

[15] Coming out of his mouth was a sharp sword with which to strike down the nations. He will rule them with an iron scepter, and he will tread the winepress * of the fury of the wrath of God the Almighty. [16] On his robe and on his thigh * he had a name inscribed: "King of kings and Lord of lords."

The Great Booty. * [17] Then I saw an angel standing in the sun, and with a loud voice he cried out to all the birds flying in midair, "Come here! Gather together for the great supper of God, [18] to eat the flesh of kings, the flesh of commanders, and the flesh of warriors, the flesh of horses and their riders, the flesh of all, both free and slave, both small and great."

The Beast and the False Prophet. * [19] Next I saw the beast and the kings of the earth and their armies gathered together to wage war against the one upon the horse and against his army. [20] The beast was captured, and with it the false prophet who in its presence had performed the signs by which he had deluded those who had received the mark of the beast and those who had worshiped its image.

These two were thrown alive into the fiery lake of burning sulfur. [21] The rest were killed by the sword that came forth from the mouth of the rider on the horse, and all the birds gorged themselves on their flesh.

20 The Dragon.* [1] Then I saw an angel coming down from heaven, with the key to the abyss and a great chain in his hand. [2] He seized the dragon, that ancient serpent, who is the devil, or Satan, and chained him up for a thou-

sand years. ³ He threw him into the abyss and locked and sealed it over him, so that he would not again deceive the nations until the thousand years were ended. After that he must be released, but only for a short time.

The Reign of the Martyrs: Return and Destruction of Satan.*
⁴ Next, I saw thrones on which were seated those who had been given the authority to judge. I also saw the souls of those who had been beheaded for bearing witness to Jesus and the word of God. They had not worshiped the beast or its image and had not received its mark on their foreheads or their hands. They lived and reigned with Christ for a thousand years. *

⁵ The rest of the dead did not come to life until the thousand years were ended. This is the first resurrection. ⁶ Blessed * and holy are those who share in the first resurrection. The second death has no power over them. They will be priests of God and of Christ, and they will reign with him for a thousand years.

⁷ When the thousand years are ended, Satan will be released from his prison ⁸ and will emerge to lead astray the nations in the four corners of the earth—Gog and Magog—in order to gather them for battle. They are as numerous as the sands of the sea. *

⁹ They marched across the breadth of the earth * and laid siege to the camp of the saints and the beloved city. However, fire came down from heaven and devoured them. ¹⁰ The devil who had led them astray was thrown into the fiery lake of burning sulfur, where the beast and the false prophet had been flung to be tormented day and night forever and ever.

Preparation for the Judgment.* ¹¹ Then I saw a great white throne, and the one who was seated upon it. The earth and the sky fled so far from his presence that they could no longer be found.

The Resurrection and Judgment.* ¹² And I saw the dead, great and small, standing before the throne, and the scrolls were opened. Then another scroll was opened, the book of life, and the dead were judged according to their deeds, as were recorded in the scrolls.

¹³ The sea gave up all the dead who were in it, and Death and Hades gave up the dead that were in them. The dead were judged according to their deeds. ¹⁴ Then Death and Hades were hurled into the fiery lake. This fiery lake is the second death. * ¹⁵ Anyone who was not found written in the book of life was thrown into the fiery lake.

F: The New Jerusalem: A New World and a New People*

21 **The New Heaven and the New Earth.** ¹ Then I saw a new heaven and a new earth. For the first heaven and the first earth had passed away, and there was no longer any sea. * ² And I saw the holy city, the new Jerusalem, coming down out of heaven from God, like a bride adorned and ready for her husband. ³ And I heard a loud voice proclaim from the throne:

"Behold, God's dwelling is with mankind;
   he will dwell with them.
They will be his people,
   and he will be their God,
   God-with-them. *
⁴ He will wipe every tear from their eyes,
   and there will no longer be death.
Neither will there be any mourning or crying or pain,
   for the old order has passed away."

⁵ The one seated on the throne then said, "Behold, I am making all things new." He also said, "Write this down, for these words are trustworthy and true." ⁶ Then he said to me, "It is done. I am the Alpha and the Omega, the Beginning and the End. * To those who are thirsty I will give to drink without cost from the spring of life-giving water.

⁷ "The one who is victorious will inherit these things, and I will be his God and he will be my son. * ⁸ But as for the cowardly, the faithless, the depraved, the murderers, the sexually immoral, the sorcerers, the idolaters, and

liars of every kind, their place is the fiery lake of burning sulfur, which is the second death." *

The New Jerusalem. ⁹ One of the seven angels who had the seven bowls filled with the seven final plagues came forward and said to me, "Come, and I will show you the bride, the wife of the Lamb." ¹⁰ Then he carried me away in the spirit * to the top of a very high mountain and showed me the holy city Jerusalem coming down out of heaven from God. ¹¹ It possessed the glory of God and had the radiance of some priceless jewel, like jasper, clear as crystal.

¹² Its wall was of a great height, with twelve gates, * and at the gates there were twelve angels. On the gates were written the names of the twelve tribes of Israel. ¹³ There were three gates to the east, three to the north, three to the south, and three to the west. ¹⁴ The city wall had twelve foundation stones, and on them were the names of the twelve apostles of the Lamb.

¹⁵ The angel who was speaking to me was carrying a gold measuring rod to measure the city, * its gates, and its wall. ¹⁶ The city was laid out like a square, with its length and its width identical. He measured the city with his measuring rod: it was fifteen hundred miles * in length and width, and equal in height.

¹⁷ Then he measured its wall, and it was one hundred and forty-four cubits * high by human measurements, which the angel employed. ¹⁸ * The wall was built of jasper, while the city itself was of pure gold, as bright as clear glass.

¹⁹ The foundations of the city wall were adorned with precious stones of every kind. The first of the foundation stones was jasper, the second sapphire, the third turquoise, the fourth emerald, ²⁰ the fifth onyx, the sixth carnelian, the seventh chrysolite, the eighth beryl, the ninth topaz, the tenth chrysoprase, the eleventh jacinth, and the twelfth amethyst. ²¹ The twelve gates were twelve pearls, each of the gates fashioned from a single pearl, and the street of the city was pure gold, like transparent glass.

²² I did not see any temple there, for the Lord God Almighty and the Lamb are its temple. ²³ And the city had no need for the sun or the moon to shine on it, for it was lit by the glory of God, and its lamp was the Lamb. ²⁴ * The nations will walk by its light, and to it the kings of the earth will bring their treasures.

²⁵ The gates of the city will never be shut during the day—and there will be no night there. ²⁶ The nations will come into it bringing their treasures and wealth. ²⁷ However, nothing unclean will ever enter it, nor will anyone who does abominable or deceitful things, but only those who are written in the Lamb's book of life. *

22

¹ Then the angel showed me the river of the water of life, bright as crystal, flowing from the throne of God and of the Lamb * ² down the middle of the street. On either side of the river was the tree of life * with its twelve crops of fruit, yielding fruit each month. The leaves of the trees are for the healing of the nations.

³ Nothing accursed will be found there anymore. The throne of God and of the Lamb will be in it, and his servants will worship him. ⁴ They will see his face, * and his name will be on their foreheads. ⁵ And there will be no more night. They will have no need for light from a lamp or from the sun, for the Lord God will give them light, and they will reign * forever and ever.

EPILOGUE: MY RETURN IS NEAR *

Worship God Alone. ⁶ The angel said to me, "These words are trustworthy and true, for the Lord God who inspires the prophets has sent his angel to show his servants what soon must take place.

⁷ " 'Behold, I am coming soon!' * Blessed is the one who observes the words of prophecy contained in this book."

⁸ I, John, am the one who heard and saw these things. And when I had heard and seen them, I knelt at the feet

of the angel who had shown them to me to worship him.
⁹ However, he said to me, "You must not do that. I am a
fellow servant of you and of your brethren the prophets
and of those who observe the words of this book. Worship
God!"

The Great Separation. * ¹⁰ Then he said to me, "Do not
seal up the words of prophecy that are in this book, for
the time is near. ¹¹ Let the wicked persist in acting
wickedly, and let the vile continue in their vileness, but let
the righteous persevere in righteousness, and let the
holy continue to be holy."

¹² " 'Behold, I am coming soon, and I will bring with
me my reward to repay everyone as his deeds deserve. ¹³ I
am the Alpha and the Omega, the First and the Last, the
Beginning and the End.'

¹⁴ "Blessed * are those who wash their robes clean so
that they will be free to eat from the tree of life and may
enter the city by the gates. ¹⁵ Others must remain outside:
the dogs, * the sorcerers, the sexually immoral, the murderers, the idolaters, and everyone who loves and practices deceit.

"Come, Lord Jesus!" * ¹⁶ " 'I, Jesus, sent my angel to you
with this testimony for the churches. I am the Root and
the Offspring of David, * the bright Morning Star.' "

¹⁷ The Spirit and the bride say, "Come!" Let each lis-
tener say, "Come!" Let everyone who thirsts come forward, and let the one who desires it receive the gift of life-
giving water.

¹⁸ I warn everyone who hears the words of prophecy in
this book: if anyone adds to them, God will add to him
the plagues written about in this book; ¹⁹ if anyone takes
away from the words in this book of prophecy, God will
take away his share in the tree of life and in the holy city,
which are written about in this book.

²⁰ The one who gives this testimony says, "Yes, I am
coming soon."

Amen. Come, Lord Jesus! *

²¹ The grace of the Lord Jesus be with you all.

NOTES

THE GOSPEL ACCORDING TO MATTHEW

1:1—2:23 Who was Jesus? Where did he come from? The prologue of Matthew's Gospel immediately confronts us with this question. The author has not simply gathered up some scattered recollections to complete his album on the life of Christ; rather, from the very first moment he is transmitting the Church's testimony of faith.

1:1-17 To the ancients a genealogical tree was not only a set of data on one's civil status but also a manifestation of one's membership in a community and the importance of ancestry (Gen 5:1-11; Ex 6:14-24; 1 Chr 1—9; Ezr 2:59-63). The genealogy of Jesus is drawn up with special care; it is perhaps somewhat artificial, but it is quite solemn. In bringing Jesus on the scene, the entire history of the nation is recapitulated. He is the son of Abraham, in whom all the nations shall be blessed (Gen 18:18); he is the son of David, to whom the future of the people was entrusted (2 Sam 7:13-14); in other words, he is the one who will carry out God's plan for Israel and the entire human race; he is the One Sent, the consecrated of God (Messiah, Christ).

The opening sentences of the Gospel are thus a "Book of Genesis," an account of the new beginning of humanity and the world (Gen 2:4; 5:1). Luke will carry the genealogy of Jesus back to Adam himself (Lk 3:23-38). In Matthew's list Joseph plays a well-defined part: it is by means of him that Jesus is given a *de jure* place in history. But at this point the Gospel unexpectedly avoids the phrase "the father of" ("begot"), and Joseph is simply the husband of Mary. The entire mystery of Jesus' origin is already stated in these few words.

1:1 *Christ:* is the Greek translation of the Hebrew "Messiah," which means "anointed," that is, consecrated. Priests were anointed (Lev 4:3, 5; 16:15); so were kings (1 Sam 10:1 [Saul]; 16:11 [David], etc.), so much so that the reigning monarch was sometimes given the title of "Messiah," or "Anointed One" (see Pss 2:2; 89:38; etc.). The name "Jesus Christ," which at this point was still an alternative for or associated with "Jesus of Nazareth," is already to be found in the initial preaching of the apostles (see Acts 3:6).

1:3 The genealogy names four women: Tamar (see Gen 38; 1 Chr 2:4), Rahab (see Jos 2; 6:17), the wife of Uriah, i.e., Bathshcba (see 2 Sam 11; 12:24), and Ruth (see Book of Ruth). These four women were foreigners who in some way became part of the history of Israel. They symbolize the salvation that God intends for all peoples.

1:16 It is important to note that in the case of Christ's birth, the text uses a formula that is far different from the one used for the other persons in the genealogy. In doing so, the evangelist is paving the way for the teaching of Christ's virginal conception, which took place without the intervention of any man.

1:18-25 At the beginning of creation the Spirit made the waters fruitful (Gen 1:2; Ps 33:6-7); the Spirit restored life to a people who had been destroyed and were in exile (Ezek 37:1-14; Isa 44:2-4). Now the Spirit creates the new human being, the new Israel, in the womb of the Virgin. How mysterious the interventions of God that turn upside down the course of events and the ways of human beings! Joseph, who is irrevocably bound to Mary because at that time an espousal was a definitive act, is witness to the incomprehensible; he has too much trust in his wife to abandon her to the sentence imposed by the Law if she were to be thought an adulteress. But who will show him the way out of this impossible situation? A revelation of heaven makes his mission known to him in a dream, as the announcement of angels and messengers had to the patriarchs. Joseph obeys, and through him Jesus finds a place publicly in the dynasty of David.

What will this son become, whose name "Jesus" is already a program, since it means "God saves"? The prophecy of Isaiah, which had remained mysterious to the minds of believers, is now fulfilled. Such is the main message of this text that was originally addressed to Jews, namely, that God is in our midst to give us victory and to live the covenant to the full. "Emmanuel" means "God is with us" (Lk 1:31; Jn 1:14). That is the ultimate message.

1:21 *Jesus:* is a transcription of the Greek *Iêsous,* which in turn is a transcription of the Hebrew *Jehoshuah* ("Joshua" in translations) or *Jeshua* in its later form. It means "God saves."

1:23 See Isa 7:14. God's promise of salvation to Judah in the time of Isaiah is seen to be fulfilled in the birth of Jesus. This is the first of some 60 citations, most of them Messianic, that Matthew takes from the Old Testament.

1:25 *Engaged in no marital relations:* literally, "did not know," "know" being the usual word for conjugal relations (see Gen 4:1). The meaning of "he engaged in no marital relations with her . . ." is: "without his knowing her, she bore a son." The Hebrew word "until" neither implies nor excludes marital conduct after Jesus' birth.

2:1-12 We shall never be able to identify with certainty these men of study and prayer, who may also have been astrologers (called by a Persian name, "Magi"). Orientals thought that a new star appeared at the birth of great persons (Num 24:17). In any case, the hour has come for pagans to share in the joy of encounter with God. This Gospel also confirms the expectation of Israel and cites the Prophets (Mic 5:1; 2 Sam 5:1-3): the new future of the People of God originates in the dynasty of David and in his native place, Bethlehem (1 Sam 16), but the mission of the Messiah goes beyond religious and national frontiers. The Messianic age is beginning (see Ps 72:10-11; Isa 9:1, 5; 49:23; 60:1-5; Lk 2:30-34).

2:1 *Bethlehem:* about five miles south of Jerusalem.

2:4 *Chief priests:* in the plural signifies the high priest now in office and his predecessors and members of their respective families. Herod's act of consulting with the chief priests and teachers of the Law has some affinity with a Jewish legend about the child Moses in which Pharaoh is warned by sacred scribes about the coming birth of a deliverer of Israel from Egypt and plots to destroy the deliverer.

2:6 This prophecy of Micah (5:2) had been pronounced seven centuries earlier.

2:11 Because of the Old Testament texts of Ps 72:11; Isa 60:6, the wise men were thought to be kings. *House:* indicates that the wise men did not visit Jesus on the night of his birth as did the shepherds. Although there are three gifts, this does not mean there were three wise men.

2:15 The citation from Hos 11:1, which originally referred to God's calling Israel (God's son) out of Egypt, is here applied to Jesus. Just as Israel was called out of Egypt at the time of the Exodus, so Jesus, the Son of God, will be called out of Egypt at the New Exodus.

2:17-18 The citation of Jer 31:15 originally referred to Rachel, the wife of Jacob, weeping for her children taken into exile in 721 B.C. Matthew applies it to the mourning for the Holy Innocents.

2:19-23 Herod died in 4 B.C. We do not know for sure to which prophecies (note the plural "Prophets") v. 23 is alluding. Some believe Matthew is here thinking of the Old Testament declarations that the Messiah would be despised (e.g., Ps 22:6; Isa 53:3), for "Nazorean" was a synonym for "despised" (see Jn 1:45f). Or he may be saying that according to the plan of God Jesus was to live his childhood and youth in Nazareth and begin his ministry there. Some think "Nazorean" fulfills the prophecy of Isaiah (11:1): Jesus is the "shoot" (*nezer* in Hebrew) of the race of Abraham and David.

2:20 *For those who sought to kill the child are dead:* another subtle reference to the Moses-Christ parallel. After fleeing from Egypt because the Pharaoh sought to kill him, Moses was told to return in similar words: "for all the men who wanted to kill you are dead" (Ex 4:19).

2:22 *Archelaus:* son of Herod who ruled Judea and Samaria for ten years (4 B.C. to A.D. 6) and was deposed because of his cruelty. After him Judea became a Roman province administered by "procurators" appointed by the Emperor. *Galilee:* the northern part of Palestine, whose principal cities were: Capernaum, Cana, Nazareth, and Tiberias. Its people were not very highly esteemed by the Jews of Jerusalem and Judea (see Jn 1:46; 7:52) probably because of the strong Hellenization of the region and the mixed (Jew-Gentile) population there. It was the primary region of Jesus' public ministry and is viewed as a providential indicator of his Messianic mission to the Gentiles (see Isa 66:18f; Am 9:11f).

2:23 *Nazareth:* a town that stands on the last spurs of the Galilean hills, some 87 miles north of Jerusalem.

3:1-17 This account is concerned with the person and prophetic message of John (1-6), his baptism (6), his criticism of the Pharisees and Sadducees (7-10), his teaching about Jesus (11-12), and his baptism of Jesus (15-17).

3:1 *John the Baptist:* the cousin and precursor of Jesus (see Lk 1:5-80). *Desert of Judea:* a twenty-mile barren region from the Jerusalem-Bethlehem plateau to the Jordan River and the Dead Sea.

3:2 *Repent:* a change of heart and conduct—a return to keeping the Mosaic Law. *Kingdom of heaven:* a phrase found only in Matthew (33 times); in Mark and Luke it is "kingdom of God." The kingdom of heaven is the rule of God, both as present reality and as future hope. The kingdom is a central part of Jesus' message.

3:3 All four Gospels quote Isa 40:3 and apply it to John the Baptist. *Make his paths straight:* a phrase that is equivalent to "Prepare the way for the Lord" in Lk 3:4. In ancient times, when the king was to travel to a distant land, the roads were improved. Similarly, the spiritual preparation for the coming of the Messiah was made by John in calling for repentance and the remission of sins and announcing the need for a Savior.

3:4 John's simple food, clothing, and life-style were reminiscent of Elijah (see 2 Ki 17), and Jesus later declares that John was the Elijah who had already come (see Mt 17:10ff; see also Mal 4:5).

3:7-10 John heavily criticizes members of two religious sects of the Jews who come to receive his baptism. The Pharisees were a legalistic and separatist group who strictly kept the Law of Moses as well as the unwritten "tradition of the elders" (Mt 15:2). The Sadducees were more worldly and politically-minded, closely connected with the high priests, and they accepted only the first five Books of the Old Testament as their Scriptures. They also rejected belief in the resurrection after death.

3:11-12 *I am not worthy to carry his sandals:* bearing sandals was one of the duties of a slave. The baptism of John prepares for the purifying action *with the Holy Spirit and fire* that Jesus will effect (see Isa 1:25; Zec 13:9; Mal 3:2) and that was seen very dramatically at Pentecost (Acts 1:5, 8; 2:1-16). Refusal of this Baptism instituted by Christ leads to final condemnation in imperishable fire (see Isa 34:8ff; Jer 7:20).

3:12 The separation of the good and the bad that will take place at Christ's Second Coming is compared to the way farmers separated *wheat* from *chaff.* After trampling out the grain, they used a large fork to pitch the grain and the chaff into the air. The kernels of wheat fell to the ground while the light chaff was borne away by the wind, then gathered up and burned.

3:13-17 The theophanies of the Old Testament were meant to convey something of the ineffable transcendence of God (Ex 3); the theophany that here begins the New Testament reveals something of the inner life of God: God is three persons. The dove perhaps suggests the Creator Spirit (Gen 1:2), but may also symbolize the divine goodwill that was restored after the flood (Gen 8:8-12), or the very People of God (Hos 7:11; 11:11; Isa 60:8), the formation of which is the work of the Spirit.

3:15 *All that righteousness demands:* i.e., all observances, everything that is part of God's plan. Jesus obeys the Father's will in everything (Phil 2:8).

3:17 This heavenly pronouncement intermingles language from Ps 2:7 and Isa 42:1, prophetic terminology that was well known to those with Messianic expectations (see Mt 17:5; Mk 1:11; 9:7; Lk 3:22; 9:35).

4:1-11 This important passage is again filled with echoes and citations of the Old Testament. The intention is to show the experience and struggles of the Messiah, the new head of the People of God. Just as Moses remained forty days on Sinai, so the Messiah remains forty days in the wilderness (Ex 34:28), forty days being symbolic of a time of preparation for divinely planned activities. Jesus refuses to make use of his miraculous power simply to relieve human need (3f), or to satisfy requests of unbelievers (5ff), or to embrace a Messianic role that would be purely political. The basic theme is the obedience of Jesus to God as he is known through the Old Testament. He rebuffs all three temptations with Scriptural truth from Deuteronomy.

4:3 *If you are the Son of God:* in the sense of the Messianic King of Ps 2.

4:4 A citation of Deut 8:3, indicating that the miracles of the Exodus were signs of God's religious care for Israel.

4:5 *Summit of the temple:* the southeast corner of the wall of the Jerusalem temple, projecting over a ravine.

4:6-7 The devil applies Ps 91:11-12 to the Messiah since it deals with God's protection of the righteous. Jesus declares (through the words of Deut 6:16) that we should not demand miracles from God as evidence of his care for us.

4:10 The citation (Deut 6:13) used by Jesus calls for the basic attitude of worship that everyone should have toward God.

4:12-25 By action and word Jesus inaugurates the kingdom of heaven. The phrase means the kingdom of God, but, like the Jews of his time, Matthew avoids naming God and says, instead, "heaven." This kingdom or reign is a power that will continue to make its way into the world from now on. Jesus begins his activity in Galilee, a northern province, which some, thinking of Isa 8:23 and 9:1, regarded as the Messiah's land. It was a region in which different populations and religions lived side by side. The faithful followers of Yahweh, who were pretty much cut off from Jerusalem and its temple, gathered in the synagogues. Different populations, even in the pagan Decapolis (a confederation of ten inde pendent Greek cities, beyond the Jordan), acknowledge the Messiah.

4:12-17 *John had been arrested:* After John's arrest (v. 12), Jesus makes Capernaum the center of his activity (v. 13) and preaching (v. 17). The citation from Isa 9:1-2 identifies the ministry of Jesus as fulfilling the prophecy of the restoration of the northern kingdom defeated by the Assyrians in 721 B.C. See notes on Mk 1:14 and Lk 3:20.

4:13 *Capernaum:* on the shore of the Lake (in Hebrew: Sea) of Galilee (v. 18), also known as the Lake of Tiberias or Gennesaret, in territory that had belonged to the tribes of Zebulun and Naphtali.

4:18-22 We see the first Church being born; disciples follow the Lord not only to share intimacy with him but to be *fishers of men,* to be witnesses to him and gather together people in his name —for he is the Messiah. Three of the four (Simon, James, and John) will go on to hold a closer relationship with Jesus (see Mt 17:1; 26:37; Lk 8:51).

4:23-25 As a conclusion to the first part of his Gospel, Matthew gives a summary of Jesus' ministry, which consisted in teaching, preaching, and healing (v. 23; see also Mt 9:35).

4:24 *Syria:* the area north of Galilee, between Damascus and the Mediterranean Sea.

4:25 *Decapolis* (i.e., the Ten Cities): a league of Greek cities; all were east of the Sea of Galilee and the Jordan River except Sythcopolis (Beth Shan).

5:1—7:28 The Sermon on the Mount is the first of five great discourses in this Gospel (chs. 5–7; 10; 13; 18; 24–25). The Lucan parallel is the "Sermon on the Plain" (Lk 6:20-49), although some of the sayings in the "Sermon on the Mount" have parallels in other parts of Luke. Matthew's Sermon contains beatitudes or declarations of blessedness (5:1-12), admonitions (5:13-20; 6:1-7, 23), and contrasts between Jesus' moral teaching and Jewish legislative traditions (5:21-48).

Matthew here presents a catechism of Christian initiation and opposes it to the Jewish religious ideal. The ensemble of moral, social, religious, cultural, general, and collective requirements that holds good for the whole People of God was received by Moses on Mount Sinai. Jesus presents a new charter that he gives "on the Mount" (5:1) as if on a new Sinai. It does not take anything away from the Law but goes to the root of human conduct. Good intentions are not to replace act and obedience, but all that take place in the heart and spirit of persons, their plans and their intentions, are already acts.

5:1-12 The Beatitudes have been rightly termed "Eight Words for Eternity." If we read them carefully, we will realize that the happiness proclaimed by Jesus is poles apart from what we habitually think, say, and do. In the first three Beatitudes are listed the faults that must be corrected if human beings are to be perfect—spiritual arrogance, pride, and desire for pleasure. In the next three Beatitudes are found the virtues that must regulate our relations with God, our neighbor, and ourselves—justice, mercy, and purity. In the last two Beatitudes, Christ urges his followers to be zealous in spreading the Gospel and peace, and he promises that they will be rewarded with honor and power in the kingdom of God for all that they have had to suffer for him.

5:13-16 Only the certitude that God comes into our very midst can open up a horizon to our human condition. But where can we read the testimony of such a coming if not in the experience of the disciples? We cannot receive Jesus or discern the Father unless we strive to lead better lives.

5:17-48 The Gospel of Matthew wants to stress the point that Jesus has no contempt for "the Law or the Prophets" (= the Old Testament); on the contrary, he takes them very seriously. But throughout his life he felt free to proclaim the true meaning of the Law by placing himself above even Moses. In his view, the Law is good, and there is nothing to discuss. In contrast to the commonly accepted rules, Jesus does not deal with secondary details; the essentials, on the other hand, cause no problem; therefore he does not discuss the Law. Instead, he goes farther and deeper, down into the human heart.

5:18 *Single letter:* literally, *iota* (Greek) = Hebrew *yod,* the smallest letter of the Hebrew alphabet. *Tiny portion of a letter:* literally, the *apex* or tip of a letter, the bit that distinguishes similar letters.

5:21-26 Murderers must appear before the highest Jewish judicial body, the Sanhedrin, and they deserve death and the fire, symbolized by Gehenna, the valley southwest of Jerusalem that was the center for an idolatrous cult during the monarchy in which children were offered in sacrifice (see 2 Ki 23:10; Jer 7:31). To embrace the kingdom of God is to become a person of reconciliation, to free oneself of all murderous desires. Indeed, even when they suffer offenses but are innocent, the disciples of Jesus must have the courage to take the first step toward establishing peace.

5:22 *Gehenna:* a little valley southwest of Jerusalem and a popular image of hell because of the refuse that burned there continually.

5:26 *Penny:* the smallest Roman copper coin.

5:27-32 At this period, the laws on divorce were tolerant for husbands, intransigent for wives. Jesus rejects this inequality and confronts husbands with their responsibilities by radically condemning divorce. Matthew's text contains the clause, "except if the marriage was unlawful," which is lacking in the parallel passages of Luke and Mark, but occurs again in Mt 19:9. The Greek word *porneia,* "unchastity," is generic and so has given rise to much discussion. The widely accepted opinion among scholars today is that it was a technical term used by the Jewish Christian community to signify a degree of relationship that constituted an impediment to marriage according to the Law (Lev 18:6-18; Acts 15:29).

5:33-37 What good is multiplying oaths between God and human beings? Is this not a sign that lying and unbelief have perverted human realities? In the kingdom of God, the dialogue between persons will rediscover its truth and its loyalty.

5:38-42 The Old Testament commandment of an eye for an eye (see Lev 24.20) was intended to moderate vengeance—seeking to ensure that the punishment not exceed the injury done. Jesus calls for further moderation and liberality by giving suggestions for breaking the infernal circle of hatred and disputation.

5:43-47 Just as God invites the unrighteous to respond to him through the evidence of his love, so the disciples of Jesus must bear the same love toward their enemies.

5:46 *Tax collectors:* those who collected taxes on behalf of the occupying authorities; for this reason, and also because they engaged in fraud, they were regarded as public sinners.

5:48 The life of the kingdom is that of children of God; therein lies its secret and its demands (see Lev 11:43; Deut 18:13).

6:1—7:29 Almsgiving (vv. 2-4), prayer (vv. 5-15), and fasting (vv. 16-18) are characteristics of the Jewish religion, or of the "righteous." Jesus does not teach other practices but is concerned with the spirit of our religious acts so that they may lead to God's presence and bring the joy of being children of God. Believers do not vaunt themselves or make a show of their religion; they listen to God. True religion is authentic spiritual life rather than spectacle and confusion or human respect.

6:7-15 In response to a request from his disciples to teach them to pray (see Lk 11:1), Jesus entrusts them with the fundamental Christian prayer, the Our Father. It is also called the Lord's Prayer because it comes to us from the Lord Jesus, the master and model of prayer. The Lord's Prayer constitutes the summary of the whole Gospel, lies at the center of the Scriptures, and is the most perfect of prayers. The object of the first three petitions is the glory of the Father: the sanctification of his name, the coming of the kingdom, and the fulfillment of his will. The four others present our wants to him: they ask that our lives be nourished, healed of sin, and made victorious in the struggle of good over evil.

6:13 *Temptation:* In the New Testament, temptation is a test in which Satan tries to destroy the believer. Consequently, it cannot be attributed to God. God, however, can give the strength and means of overcoming it: this is the meaning of the petition. The Semitic expression "do not lead us into" is therefore to be understood as meaning "do not allow us to enter into or succumb to temptation" (see Mt 26:41; 1 Tim 6:9).

6:16-18 Fasting is an action that evinces a desire to live more closely in the disinterested service of God; this produces profound joy. The sole fast prescribed by the Mosaic Law was that of the Day of Atonement (see Lev 16:31), but in later Judaism fasting became a regular practice (see *Didache* 9:1).

6:19-21 In this and the two following texts Jesus is responding to the faulty side of our way of thinking and acting. In order to affirm the primacy of God so simply and surely, we must live unceasingly in the presence of the Father. Those who guard their inner freedom, the desire for light, understand Jesus. But it is impossible to be open to God when desire for possessions has become the motivating force of one's life.

6:22-23 Those with good vision can readily direct their bodily movements. Similarly, those who utilize the prophetic vision of Christ can direct their way to God.

6:24 *Money:* literally, "Mammon" (an Aramaic word), a personification of wealth.

6:25-34 Jesus warns us against making real human needs the object of overly anxious cares and thus becoming enslaved by them. The remedy for such an attitude is to seek first God's kingdom and to show confidence in God's providence.

7:1-5 Those who judge others separate themselves from their neighbors; those who love them are completely present to their neighbors. God has not given us consciences to judge others but to judge ourselves.

7:6 Jesus stresses the point that teaching should be given in accordance with the spiritual capacity of the learners. *Dogs:* unclean dogs of the street were held in low esteem.

7:7-11 To acknowledge God as Father one must have the audacity to pray and the certitude that this appeal is not in vain, for the disciple seeks the One whom he knows as Love.

7:12 Here in a word is what one must retain of the Law and the Prophets, i.e., the Old Testament: to have for others the same concern one has for oneself, out of love for God. This so-called Golden Rule is found in negative form in rabbinic Judaism as well as Hinduism, Buddhism, and Confucianism.

7:13-14 In Jewish literature, we often encounter this doctrine of the "two ways"; it is also found in the *Didache* and the *Epistle to Barnabas.* It is a way of enabling the reader to choose for God. It means that one does not enter the kingdom except by a conversion of life—the choice to follow Jesus.

7:15-23 There will always be impostors to exploit religious sentiments and the Gospel itself for advancement of their own ideas, their own persons, and their own circle. Jesus offers a criterion to discern true disciples: do their lives, attitudes, and comportment bear witness to the spirit of Jesus?

7:22 *On that day:* i.e., on the day of judgment; Jesus speaks of himself as the final judge of human beings (see Mt 25:32-46).

7:24-27 Jesus calls for obedience to his Word: those who build their lives on the Gospel are united with Christ, and nothing else can provide meaning and force to a human life in the always unforeseen elaboration of problems and events.

7:28-29 These two verses constitute the formula with which the evangelist concludes each of the five great discourses of Jesus. Verse 29 expresses the newness of the Gospel teaching. The scribes based their teaching on the Scriptures and on the instructions of their teachers. Jesus, on the other hand, speaks as a supreme legislator who has power to modify even the Scriptures.

Jesus' astounding authority is not that of religious tradition; it radiates from his person. He himself incarnates this "new justice," this new mode of living and thinking that he teaches and establishes among human beings. Jesus' listeners could easily see the great difference between the kind of teaching of the scribes and Pharisees and that of Jesus with its total confidence and power.

8:1—10:42 This section gathers together ten accounts of miracles of Jesus. Interspersed among them are sayings of Jesus about discipleship. This has led some authors to speak of a portrayal of Jesus as "Messiah of the Word" in chs. 5—7 and "Messiah of the Deed" in 8—9. By his sayings and actions Jesus bears witness that evil and sickness are no longer the last word for people, for human beings are not slaves of fate since the goodness of God is manifested in the goodness of Jesus.

8:1—9:34 The ten miracle stories found herein are a third of the miracle stories that are told in detail in all the Gospels together. But the New Testament contains repeated references to a thaumaturgic activity that was continual (see Mt 4:23; Lk 4:41; Acts 2:22).

8:1-4 Leprosy made a person ceremonially unclean as well as physically afflicted. The man with leprosy in this passage technically breaks the Law as he comes to prostrate himself at the feet of Jesus. The Master also breaks the Law when he touches the man and sovereignly decides to heal him. The sick man welcomes Christ's word, and the kingdom is opened to him. He becomes a model and sign of the Christian made clean by Christ.

8:5-13 Jesus commends a Roman centurion (leader of a hundred soldiers) for having greater faith than any Israelite and prophesies the ingathering of the Gentiles before healing his servant from afar. This passage shows that the great pilgrimage of peoples toward the kingdom has begun and evokes the beautiful image of the feast wherein all believers are definitively gathered together. Outside of this communion and joy there is only darkness; the "weeping and gnashing of teeth" (a phrase found outside Matthew only in Lk 13:28) describes the anguish of those who have remained insensitive to the call that has been welcomed by the very people they have denigrated.

8:8 *Lord, I am not worthy . . . will be healed:* these words of the centurion have become those of believers who go to encounter the Lord in Holy Communion.

8:16-17 Jesus is the Servant announced by Isa 53:4 who will expiate the sins of humankind. By the power of his Word he triumphs over the evil that keeps human beings in bondage symbolized by sickness.

8:18-22 Jesus has subordinated family ties to the needs of his mission of salvation and requires the same sacrifice of those called to share that mission, while other members of the family can perform the deeds of filial piety. These are "dead" only in the sense that they have not received the same call to separate themselves from family responsibility in order to preach the Gospel of the kingdom. They can nonetheless be his disciples in another sense.

Hence, following Jesus means Christians should be ready to make whatever sacrifice he asks of them. In the final analysis, they are followers of Christ, people who believe in him. They received faith in Christ at Baptism and are bound to serve him. By recourse to frequent prayer and true friendship with the Lord, they should strive to discover what Jesus asks of them in their service of him.

8:20 *Son of Man:* the most common and enigmatic title of Christ used in the Gospels (81 times) and in Acts 7:56—frequently by Christ himself. It was well suited to his purpose of both veiling and revealing his person and mission. On the one hand, it meant simply "man" (see Ezek 2:1) and emphasized the lowliness of the human condition (Mt 8:20; 11:19; 20:28), especially in Christ's humiliation and death (Mt 17:22). On the other hand, it expressed the triumph of Christ's Resurrection (Mt 17:9), his return to glory (Mt 24:30; Dan 7:13), and his Second Coming as judge of the world (Mt 25:31).

Christ made use of this title at his trial before the Sanhedrin (Mt 26:64) when he prophesied that he would be vindicated and be seated in future glory at the right hand of God not merely as man but as Lord (see Dan 7:13; Mk 14:62).

This title was employed by Jewish apocalyptic literature (1 Enoch, 2 Ezra, 2 Baruch) to describe a unique religious personage endowed with extraordinary spiritual power who would receive the kingdom from God at the end of the ages. Early Christians revered this title as a reminder of Christ's twofold destiny of humiliation and joy, which was also their own (Mt 24:30f).

8:23-27 This passage attests to Jesus' power over nature and its frightful forces. This fact is preserved as a sign, for the Church resembles a boat buffeted by so many storms. She is invited to place herself in Christ's hands with great trust.

8:28-34 The sense of the anecdote about the pigs who serve as refuge for the demons and perish by drowning is that the Messiah has come; he triumphs over the evil powers that keep human beings in bondage and oppose the kingdom of God. The deliverance of the mentally ill signified that the "time" of the devil had come to an end. Thus, this is another account calling for confidence and courage in the struggle against evil. It must have especially delighted the Jews for whom pigs were unclean animals according to the Law (Lev 11:7) and who saw the pagan owners of the accursed flock suffering a loss.

8:28 *Gadarenes:* the city of Gadara was eight miles south of the lake.

8:29 *Son of God:* on the lips of the demons, this phrase is tantamount to "Messiah," for they would scarcely set themselves in opposition to him if they knew his full divinity. The same title is given to Jesus in Mk 3:12. *To torment us before the appointed time:* to confine us to hell (see Lk 8:31) before the Last Judgment. Until then, the demons have a certain freedom to roam about the world (see 2 Pet 2:4 with 1 Pet 5:8).

9:1-8 The two preceding accounts have attested Jesus' power over the frightful forces of nature and the unchained powers of hell. Here Christ delivers human beings from sin itself. For the first time he proclaims the forgiveness of sins—which is an act of God.

9:1 *His hometown:* Capernaum, which Jesus had made his headquarters.

9:3 *Blaspheming:* i.e., usurping God's prerogative to forgive sins.

9:5-6 Christ indicates that it is easier to heal a person physically than to heal him spiritually. It is easier to heal a broken leg than a broken heart. As Son of Man, in his human nature, Christ has the power to forgive sins. Therefore, he could also bestow it on his apostles (see Mt 18:18; Jn 20:22); and just as they worked miracles only in his name (see Acts 3:6), they and their successors can forgive sins only in his name and by his authority.

9:9-13 Jesus calls Matthew the tax collector to follow him, then eats at Matthew's house together with "many tax collectors" and "sinners." The Jews are shocked, but Jesus reminds them that it is the sick who need a doctor and God desires mercy rather than sacrifice.

9:10 *Tax collectors:* see note on Mt 5:46.

9:14-17 The time when Jesus lived on earth was one of joy and grace. Later there would be a time for Jesus' disciples to fast, for the Bridegroom would be taken from them. In ancient times, goatskins were used to hold wine. As the wine fermented, it would expand and the new wineskins would stretch. But a used wineskin could not expand any more and would break. In the same way, the teaching that Jesus brings cannot be kept in the old forms.

9:18-26 Jesus rewards the faith of a father in distress and the trust of a sick and timid woman. He does not deceive those who believe him to be Master of the impossible. Human beings organize ceremonies of sorrow that are important in the East (v. 23); Jesus brings life, for this twofold gesture announces that in the kingdom of God sickness and death no longer have a place (see Jn 5:26-29): this is the message that the Church must proclaim.

9:18 *Official:* literally, "ruler" or "leader." See note on Mk 5:22.

9:23 *Flute players:* musicians who were hired to play at mourning ceremonies. *Crowd:* mourners who were hired to wail and lament.

9:24 *Asleep:* sleep is a metaphor for death (see Ps 87.6 LXX; Dan 12:2; 1 Thes 5:10). Jesus does not deny the child's death but indicates that she will arise from it as from a sleep.

9:27 *Son of David:* a popular Jewish title for the Messiah who was to come (e.g., Mt 12:23; 20:30; 21:9; 22:41-45; see note on Mt 1:1).

9:34 The debate with the Pharisees on this claim will continue in Mt 12:25ff.

9:35-38 As in Mt 4.23 25, the evangelist concludes this part of his book with an action of Christ that shows compassion for the distress of the crowds and inculcates confidence in his followers. Jesus insistently works to impart the mercy of God upon all who come to him. He calls upon all who have the privilege of believing in him and benefiting from his salvation to share his concern for the misery of their neighbors. He seeks people who, like him and after him, will apply themselves to this task.

10:1-42 This section of Matthew is called the Instructions to the Apostles; collected in it are the texts describing the mission of the disciples, applicable to the early Church and for all future time. The disciples begin the great enterprise; through them Christ's authority and power continue among human beings—so long as they act truly in his Spirit and share his lot. Thus is born a new People of God.

10:1-15 Israel was made up of twelve tribes; the kingdom of Jesus was to have twelve founders (see Mt 19:28; Rev 21:12-14): the "Twelve" or the "apostles." The latter is a Greek word (plural) meaning "those who are sent"; Jesus himself chose the term (Lk 6:13).

10:4 *Iscariot:* i.e., "Man from Kerioth," a place in the southernmost part of Palestine.

10:5 *Do not travel:* the Good News about the kingdom was to be proclaimed first to Jews alone. After his Death and Resurrection, Jesus commanded the disciples to take the message to all nations (Mt 28:19; see Mt 21:43). *Samaritans:* a race of mixed blood resulting from the intermarriage of Israelites left behind when the people of the northern kingdom were exiled and Gentiles were brought into the land by the Assyrians (2 Ki 17:24). In the time of Jesus, Jews and Samaritans were bitterly opposed to one another (see Jn 4:9).

10:14 *Shake the dust from your feet:* a symbolic act practiced by the Pharisees when they left an unclean Gentile area. Here it represents a solemn warning to those who reject God's message.

10:15 *Sodom and Gomorrah:* see Gen 19:23-29.

10:16-25 The disciples are prolongations of Christ, so to speak. Whatever happened to him will also happen to them. But if they persevere they will be saved.

10:17 *Courts:* the lower courts, connected with local synagogues, that tried less serious cases and scourged those found guilty.

10:23 *You will not have finished . . . before the Son of Man comes:* this may be interpreted in two ways: (1) the disciples will not have converted all of Israel before the Second Coming of Christ; (2) the disciples will not have preached the Gospel in all the towns of Palestine before the destruction of Jerusalem occurs in A.D. 70, which is a portent of the end of the world.

10:25 *Beelzebul:* "Baal the Prince," or Beelzebub, "Lord of the Flies." The former is the name of an ancient pagan divinity (see 2 Ki 1:1-14), the latter a contemptuous distortion of the name.

10:26-36 In the face of fierce opposition and trials of all kinds, the apostles must not lose heart, for they will be given the courage to bear true witness to Jesus and his message.

10:28 *Gehenna:* see note on Mt 5:22.

10:34 As Simeon predicted (Lk 2:34), Jesus will be a sign of contradiction even within families. Those who accept the Gospel will be at peace with God, but they will have to bear persecution at the hands of those who do not.

10:38 *Take up his cross:* this is the first time Matthew mentions the cross, which was an instrument of death. The picture is of a man, already condemned, required to carry the beam of his own cross to the place of execution (see Jn 19:17). Here it symbolizes the necessity of total commitment—even unto death—on the part of Jesus' disciples.

10:39 Those who renounce their earthly life in order to confess Jesus will obtain the happiness of eternal life.

10:41 *Prophet:* the last prophet of the old covenant was John the Baptist.

11:1—13:51 To be committed to Christ means to acknowledge him as the expected Messiah. By his words and his actions, he takes a clear position toward John and toward the Pharisees. To decide for Christ means to discover the inner life of Jesus. It is not right to proclaim the coming of the kingdom; we are invited to experience it, to experience the power of God. The following passages enable us to question ourselves about our faith.

11:1-30 In striking images John had proclaimed the time of wrath and the purification by God. Jesus himself had joined in this movement of renewal. Now the prophet is in prison, the victim of his mission. All around Jesus the enthusiasm of the crowds concerning John begins to falter. How then can they be made to acknowledge the awaited Messianic revolution consisting in the decisive judgment of the wicked and the liberation of the righteous (Mt 3:12)? But then who is the Messiah and what is the kingdom of God? One must pass from questioning to decision, to the act of faith in Jesus.

11:1-6 By letting John know that the announcement of the Prophets is being fulfilled (Isa 26:19; 29:18; 35:5f; 61:1), Jesus reassures him and places him on guard against an overly human idea of the Messiah; he encourages the Baptist to persevere in faith until the end. The kingdom of God is not to be confused with the accomplishment of our projects and our human victories; it is a gift of God.

11:3 *The one who is to come:* i.e., the Messiah. *Wait for another:* it is not clear whether John is uncertain about Jesus or is simply sending his disciples to Jesus.

11:6 *Takes no offense at me:* literally, "is not scandalized," that is, for whom I am not a hindrance or stumbling block (Greek: *skandalon*). It is from the idea of a stumbling block on the way of goodness that "scandal" derives its moral meaning, in both the active sense of giving scandal and the passive sense of taking scandal. In current idiom, a bad example is called "scandalous" when it causes a stir.

11:7-15 Jesus eulogizes the strength of John the Baptist's religious convictions, the austerity of his life (7f), and his unique prophetic role as precursor of the kingdom of God, which for Jesus is the salvation of human beings (4-5), not political revolution or the acquisition of power.

11:11 John's greatness consists primarily in his task of announcing the imminence of the kingdom of God (Mt 3:1). Yet to be a member of the kingdom is so sublime a privilege that even the least member is greater than the Baptist!

11:16-19 Indecisive children do not want to play either at a wedding when a flute is sounded or at a funeral when a dirge is sung; such are the Jews who reject the salvation that God offers them: the severity of John frightens them and the goodness of Jesus shocks them. People often hesitate as much before joy as before repentance! But the kingdom of God does not wait; God realizes here below his plan—his "Wisdom"—as the acts of John and Jesus bear witness.

11:20-24 The fate of the privileged cities of Chorazin (about two miles from Capernaum) and Bethsaida (on the northeast shore of the Sea of Galilee) will be worse than that of cities traditionally regarded as godless (Tyre and Sidon: Am 1:9f; 1 Sam 23; Ezek 26—28; Zec 9:2-4) or wicked (Sodom: Gen 18:16-19; Ezek 16:46-56), which did not have the opportunity to witness Jesus' miracles and hear his preaching as had the people in most of Galilee. The people of Chorazin and Bethsaida have failed to recognize the presence of God in Jesus because they wanted to avoid penance. The same is true for the people of Capernaum, Jesus' headquarters on the north shore of Galilee (see Mt 4:13).

11:25-27 The self-revelation of Jesus reached one of its high points in this moving prayer. It enables us to enter into the most hidden core of his life, into his innermost experiences. Between him and the Father there is an exchange of life, a profound and unique bond, a mutual commitment of their entire being—in short, an inexpressibly mysterious oneness. In the Bible, all this is summed up in the verb "know." This is why Jesus alone can reveal to other human beings who the Father is for them.

11:28-30 *Yoke* and *burden* evoke the Mosaic Law. The law of Christ is sweet, for it is not a list of customs, obligations, and conventions but primarily the sharing of a life, an apprenticeship of love.

12:1-50 The Good News of the kingdom spreads from town to town; a new law of salvation is announced and runs up against the refusal of those in authority. The conflict between Jesus and Judaism now appears inevitable. The newness of the Gospel totally upsets recognized habits of thinking and ways of acting. The more Jesus bypasses the Law for the service and salvation of human beings, the more he enters into conflict with his religious environment. Those who are close to Jesus are those who believe in him.

12:1-14 Jesus reminds the Pharisees, who are attached to the letter of the Law, that a religion without love is worthless (Hos 6:6), and in order to make them face up to their blindness he cites an incident of the Old Testament (David and his companions: 1 Sam 21:2-7), a practical aspect of worship (the priests do not abstain from work in the temple on the Sabbath: Lev 24:8; Num 28:9), and a requirement of good sense (the sheep in the pit). Jesus utters his decision with authority: he claims to be Lord of the Sabbath, and he is more than the Sabbath, that is, the very place of God's presence.

12:2 The Pharisees had set down 39 categories of actions forbidden on the Sabbath, based on interpretations of the Law and Jewish customs. One of these was harvesting. By picking wheat and rubbing it in their hands, the disciples were technically harvesting according to the religious leaders. But the disciples were picking grain because they were hungry, not because they wanted to harvest the grain for profit. Hence, they were not working on the Sabbath.

12:3-4 Each Sabbath 12 fresh loaves of bread (the bread of the Presence) were to be set on a table in the Holy Place (Ex 25:30; Lev 24:5-9). The old loaves were eaten by priests. The loaves given to David (1 Sam 21:1-6) were the old loaves that had just been replaced by fresh ones. Although the priests were the only ones allowed to eat this bread, David and his men were allowed to eat it because of their need for food, showing that laws should be enforced with discernment and compassion.

12:5-6 The Sabbath-work is related to worshiping God, changing the shewbread (Lev 24:8), and doubling the usual daily burnt offerings (Num 28:9f). Hence, the Law itself requires works that break the Sabbath rest (*violate the Sabbath*) because of the higher duty of God's service. If temple duties outweigh the Law, how much more does the presence of Jesus with his proclamation of the kingdom (*one greater than the temple*) justify the conduct of his disciples. If people become more concerned with the means of worship than with the God they worship, they will miss God even while they think they are worshiping him.

12:8 *Lord of the Sabbath:* the ultimate justification for the disciples' violation of the Sabbath rest is that Jesus is the Son of Man, the Messiah, who has supreme authority over the Law.

12:9-14 By healing the man with a withered hand, Jesus corroborates his teaching: it is licit to do good on the Sabbath; no law can oppose the doing of good. He thus rejects the false interpretation put forth by the Pharisees who are attached to the letter of the Law to the detriment of the glory of God and the good of human beings. The very persons who are scandalized by Christ's miracle are in no way held back from plotting his death even though it is the Sabbath.

12:14 *Pharisees . . . began to plot how they might put him to death:* even though Matthew does not mention them here, the Herodians were also involved in the plot (see Mk 3:6).

12:15-21 Evidently, at least for a while, Jesus gave up preaching in the synagogues (*he departed*). The prohibition against making known his miracles was in this case probably due to the wish to avoid conflict with the Pharisees. If we want to understand Jesus' purpose and way of life, we will find the appropriate images in the Servant Songs of Isaiah; here the second of these (Isa 42:1-4) is cited. Jesus recalled these passages, which are the most profound in the Old Testament, when he thought about and spoke of his mission.

12:22-32 On certain days, Jesus confronts physically, so to speak, the forces of evil that keep human beings enslaved, as in the case of a possessed man rendered deaf and mute. By healing him Jesus shows that he frees people from every type of alienation and possession; he sets back the incursion of evil. How could the Pharisees suspect that Jesus belongs to this world of darkness? Moreover, they admit that their own "children," i.e., disciples, also fight to free human beings from the powers of evil! When Jesus acts, the Spirit is at work, the kingdom of God is at hand, and everyone must take part in it. The *blasphemy against the Spirit* consists in ascribing to the devil the work of the Holy Spirit and is the result of becoming hardened in an attitude of refusal, which may one day be irremediable. This warning is given to the Pharisees and, through them, to every reader.

12:23 *Son of David:* see note on Mt 9:27-31.

12:24 *Beelzebul:* see note on Mt 10:25.

12:32 God desires the salvation of all human beings (1 Tim 2:4) and calls everyone to repentance (2 Pet 3:9). Christ's Redemption is superabundant satisfaction for all sin and reaches every person (Rom 5:12-31). Christ gave his Church the power to forgive sins through the Sacraments of Baptism and Penance. This power is unlimited; she can forgive every sin of the baptized as often as they confess with the necessary dispositions.

12:33-37 Jesus denounces hypocrites whose words are vanity and calumny. Every spoken word reflects the heart's overflow and is known to God. Hence words are critically important (see Eph 5:3f, 12; Col 3:17; Jas 1:19; 3:1-12).

12:38-42 An opinion current among circles of apocalyptic thought at the time looked for the Messiah to perform a unique sign. Jesus offers only the sign of his Death and Resurrection typified by the story of Jonah in the belly of the whale (Jon 1:17).

12:39 *Adulterous:* i.e., in the spiritual sense of being unfaithful to the generation's spiritual husband (God).

12:40 *Three days and three nights:* this manner of speaking denotes a common Jewish way of reckoning time and includes at least part of the first and part of the third day. Any part of the whole was counted as if it were the whole. Thus, even the time from Jesus' Death till sunset on Good Friday is counted as a day. (The Old Testament depicted the Messiah as one who would suffer [Ps 22; Isa 53] and rise from the dead on the third day [Ps 16:9-11; Isa 53:10f].)

12:41-42 The people of Nineveh who repented (see Jon 3:1-10) and the *queen of the south* (i.e., of Sheba—see 1 Ki 10:1-3—a country in southwest Arabia now called Yemen) were pagans who responded to lesser opportunities than the one that had been presented to Israel in the person of Jesus, *one greater* than Jonah *or* Solomon.

12:43-45 A person's religious history is a repeated exchange of good and evil. The option for evil can reach the point of taking full possession of the person. The same is true for the religious leaders of Israel. Just cleaning up one's life without filling it with God leaves plenty of room for Satan to return.

12:46-50 Belonging to Jesus has nothing to do with the bonds of blood relations. The Church is never based on attachments of race, class, or culture. She is the family of God. Only one who does the will of Jesus' *heavenly Father* belongs to his true family.

12:46 *His mother and his brethren:* "brethren" here is used in the sense of "cousins" or "relatives." If they were true brothers of Jesus, sons of Mary, the Gospel would say: "his mother and the sons of his mother," which was the normal manner of speaking in Israel of that time. The Church has never wavered in her teaching that Mary was a Virgin and that Jesus was her *only* son, just as he is the *only* Son of the Father (Lk 1:26).

In the ancient tongues of Hebrew, Arabic, and Aramaic, there were no concrete words to indicate the different types of relatives that exist in modern languages. In general, all who belonged to the same family clan, including tribes, were called "brethren" or "sisters." (See, for example, Jn 19:25, which mentions a certain Mary, sister of Mary the Mother of Jesus. If they were really sisters, they would not bear the same name. Also note that in Mt 27:56, the second Mary is called "the mother of James and Joses" [i.e., Joseph], two personages who are called "brethren" of the Lord in Mt 13:55.)

In addition, in the first Christian community when the Gospels were written, there existed a very influential group composed of Jesus' relatives and his countrymen of Nazareth, called the "brethren of the Lord." The leader seemed to be James, who became bishop of the Judean community. This group were late in believing in Jesus even though they had lived with him for several years (Mk 3:21; Jn 7:3-5). When speaking of them, the evangelists use the name the community gave them: "brethren of the Lord" or "N. brother of Jesus."

12:47 This verse is omitted in some mss.

13:1-52 This is the beginning of the Third Discourse in Matthew's Gospel, which includes seven parables of Jesus about the kingdom of heaven, a plan hidden in God and only incompletely manifested to us (13:10-17, 34f; see Eph 3:4ff). Each parable presents a different aspect of the kingdom and helps us to perceive the multifaceted reality that is growing among us throughout history. However, there is no point in looking for a meaning in every detail of a parable; it is more profitable to look for the essential message.

13:3a *Parables:* stories that are illustrative comparisons between religious truths and events of everyday life. Those told by Jesus are so living, direct, and natural as to be unforgettable. They bear witness to a true poetic and pedagogical genius. The Synoptic Gospels contain some 30 parables. John's Gospel contains no parables but makes good use of other figures of speech.

13:3b-9 At this period, seed was scattered everywhere on as yet uncultivated ground, before any plowing was done and without the sower having a clear idea of whether it would take root. Some seed was wasted, but the sower was not discouraged, knowing that the harvest would come and this was all that counted. In the Old Testament, the harvest was a symbol of the Messianic age (see Ps 126:5-6; Am 9:13).

13:10-15 The parables make use of a language that is clear and rich for those whose heart is open but obscure and deceptive for those whose heart is closed. Already Jesus sees the new community, where his message is richness of life, separating itself from official Judaism, which will lose even that which it has, i.e., its role as custodian of God's Covenant. The Word of Christ always works in a twofold way; it fills those who accept it but leads to the hardening up of those who refuse it.

13:11 *Mysteries:* also translated as "secrets." The word is used in Dan 2:18, 19, 27 and in the Dead Sea Scrolls to designate a divine plan or decree affecting the course of history that can be known only when revealed. In this case, the secret or mystery is that the kingdom is already present in the ministry of Jesus.

13:16-17 The disciples, unlike the unbelieving crowds, have seen and heard what *many prophets and righteous people* of the Old Testament *longed to see . . . and to hear* without having their longing filled.

13:18-23 It is not enough for us to hear the word; we must accept it with all its demands so that it may transform our existence. The four types of persons described in the parable are: (1) those who never accept the *word of the kingdom* (19); (2) those who believe for a while but fall away because of *persecution* (20-21); (3) those who believe, but in whom the word is choked by *worldly cares* and *the lure of riches* (27); and (4) those who hear *the word* and produce an abundant crop (23).

13:24-30 The parable of the weeds is proper to Matthew. Through it Jesus teaches that the Last Judgment (of which the "harvest" is a common metaphor), i.e., the separation of the good from the wicked, is to be awaited with patience. The explanation is given in Mt 13:37-43.

13:25 *Weeds:* probably darnel, which looks very much like wheat while it is young, but can later be distinguished.

13:31-32 The mustard seed is the smallest one used by the Palestinian farmers and gardeners of that day, but it could reach a height of some ten or twelve feet. Thus, the kingdom of heaven, notwithstanding the humble ministry of Jesus, is already dawning and in the end will be shown in all its magnificence.

13:32 *Tree . . . its branches:* an allusion to Dan 4:21, indicating that the kingdom of heaven will become worldwide and people from all nations will find refuge therein (see also Ezek 17:23; 31:6; Dan 2:35, 44f; 7:27; Rev 11:15).

13:33 The parable of the yeast is an invitation to faith in the efficacy of the ministry of Jesus. Despite its modest and unspectacular character, it constitutes a stage in the eschatological coming of the kingdom of God. The greatness of the kingdom is shown by the enormous amount of flour, enough to feed well over a hundred people.

13:34-35 Matthew stresses that Jesus speaks in parables to reveal God and his kingdom; in this way he shows that the Messiah fulfills the Scriptures. The "prophet" is, in this case, the psalmist (see Ps 78:2).

13:36-43 The explanation of the parable of the weeds stresses the Last Judgment in which Christ and those who have believed in him will triumph over the forces of evil. It thus teaches one to be converted without delay and to remain steadfast in faith till the end.

13:44-46 The parables of the hidden treasure and the pearl reveal the hidden character of the kingdom of heaven and its great worth. It represents the supreme value to which human beings must aspire.

13:47-50 The parable of the net repeats the teaching of the parable of the weeds, with its emphasis upon the final exclusion of the wicked from the kingdom. It thus calls for an authentic conversion on the part of the listeners.

13:51-52 To those who believe, the parables reveal God's mysterious plan for human beings. Thus, the teacher of the law, the scribe, once he has become a disciple, knows how to see the link between the Old and the New Testaments and is enriched by their basic harmony.

13:53—18:35 A new and tragic phase in the life of Jesus, and therefore also in the life of the kingdom, begins here and illustrates the accounts and words of this fourth part of the Gospel. The drama is infused with a growing intensity. Christ hides himself from the enthusiasm of the crowds who want him to embrace their hope for national freedom. This stirs up hostility and leads to defection. The kingdom that he proclaims is suspect in the eyes of the defenders of legalism and traditions; not even his disciples have a good understanding of the life that he teaches. Powerless, they live under this tension, which prepares for the Passion, and their incredulity will even contribute to it; but they still remain the core of the new community of believers.

13:53—17:27 The main purpose of this section is to place the Person of Jesus at the center of the mystery of the kingdom of God. The evangelist shows Jesus receiving a mixed reception, beginning with his rejection at Nazareth and the execution of the Baptist (Mt 13:53—14:12). He then alludes to the Eucharistic mystery in the accounts of the multiplication of the loaves (Mt 14:19; 15:36), and the walking on the water (Mt 14:22-33). Finally, he reports the doctrinal conflict between Jesus and the religious authorities (Mt 15:1-20) and raises anew the question of the sign of Jonah (Mt 16:1-4; see note on Mt 12:38ff). This sign will later be explained as referring to the Passion, Death, and Resurrection of Jesus (Mt 16:21ff), which must occur before the kingdom of God reaches a new stage (Mt 16:28). This is the message of the Scriptures (Mt 17:5).

13:53-58 At Nazareth, everyone knows the mother of Jesus and his brothers and sisters, i.e., his closest relatives, as it was customary to say in those days (see note on Mt 12:46-50). He thus has his place in this little village. But how can the villagers be expected to acknowledge the Messiah in one of their compatriots? God's action and word manifested among men is the mystery of the Incarnation; this seems too human. Even the believer might hesitate in believing in the Lord present among us, in the places and times in which daily life unfolds.

14:1-12 At the ominous banquet in the fortress of Machaerus we find various members of the family of Herod. Antipas was the second-born of Herod the Great and ruled over Galilee and Perea. We come upon him several times in the New Testament (Lk 9:7; 23:7; Acts 4:27); Caligula will exile him to Gaul in A.D. 39. His half-brother Philip died in Rome without ever attaining political power. Herodias, niece of both men and wife of Philip, was ambitious and desired to be the wife of a ruler.

14:1 *Tetrarch:* ruler of one quarter of the kingdom of his father, Herod the Great.

14:6 *The daughter of Herodias:* her name was Salome, as we are told by the Jewish historian Flavius Josephus.

14:10 The beheading of the Baptist probably occurred in A.D. 29 in the fortress of Machaerus, east of the Dead Sea, as is attested by Flavius Josephus.

14:13—16:12 Exegetes have named this the "Section of the Loaves" because of the frequency with which the word "bread" is used therein. It seems to symbolize the teaching and salvific acts of Jesus, with a particular reference to the founding of the Church.

14:13-21 At the time of the temptation in the desert, Jesus had refused to renew the miracle of the manna either for himself or to attain his own success. Moreover, six times in the Gospels (two of which are in Matthew) we read an account like this one. Thus, the first generation of Christians attached a particular importance to the deed. It is first of all an act of mercy, a sign of the goodness of God, who satisfies material and spiritual hunger at the last days. It is also the manifestation of Jesus as the new Moses, as the new founder of the people—he too feeds the crowd in the desert (Ex 16); he acts like the great men of God such as Elisha (2 Ki 4:42-44). In addition, something even more mysterious is part of this extraordinary moment. How can one not discern in this account a climate of Liturgy? For Christians the giving of bread announces the joy of the Eucharist: the Lord present in the assembly, satisfying every hunger with the Bread of Life that is himself (see Jn 6).

14:19 Note the resemblance of this verse to that of the institution of the Eucharist (Mt 26:26). Obviously in the eyes of the primitive Church this meal was a prelude and prefiguration of the Eucharistic banquet, which in its turn recalls the Messianic banquet. Particularly allusive are the breaking of the bread and the action of the disciples in distributing the bread.

14:21 *In addition to women and children:* women and children were not permitted to eat with men in public. Hence they were in a place by themselves and would greatly increase the number given for the men: 5000!

14:22-33 For people of the Bible, raging waves and the dead of night evoke the forces hostile to God and his faithful. In calming the storm, Jesus has manifested himself as the master of the powers of evil. To follow him means to escape from their clutches. This is a dangerous path at times in which we must risk everything for him because it is he. "It is I," he says, and in these words any Christian, after the Ascension and Resurrection, would detect echoes of "I am," the decisive self-disclosure of God (Ex 3:14; Isa 43:10; 51:12). In Peter himself, the first among the disciples, we discern the drama of every believer: strong when he entrusts himself totally to the Lord, yet threatened and uncertain when he does not take refuge in him alone.

14:25 *Fourth watch:* 3:00–6:00 A.M. The Romans divided the night into *four watches:* (1) 6:00–9:00 P.M., (2) 9:00–midnight, (3) midnight–3:00 A.M., (4) 3:00–6:00 A.M. The Jews divided the night into three watches: (1) sunset–10:00 P.M., (2) 10:00 P.M.–2:00 A.M., (3) 2:00–sunrise. Apparently, the apostles labored for several hours against the storm waves. Their enthusiasm of the previous evening for an overly earthly Messianism had greatly evaporated in the face of hard labor and the fear of being shipwrecked.

14:33 *Son of God:* the apostles probably used this title in a Messianic way (see Mt 3:17; 11:25-30) but with superficial understanding. Since Jesus' divine nature was hidden during his life on earth, the disciples did not yet grasp his divinity at this time (Phil 2:5-8). But they were beginning to realize that he was the Messiah.

14:34 *Gennesaret:* the plain northwest of the lake of the same name.

15:2ff The "oral" tradition consisted of practices and regulations meant to fill out the written Law of Moses; many Pharisaic Jews did not hesitate to claim that this tradition, like the Torah, had been revealed on Sinai. The oral tradition allowed for a vow by which a man could free himself from his obligations to his own parents: the material goods meant for them were promised to God and thus declared "sacred offerings."

15:10-20 Every ancient religion attempted to distinguish clearly the two notions of clean and unclean as regards objects and affairs of life. The Book of Leviticus proposes a developed code of ritual purity, which was above all a way of expressing the grandeur of God and of establishing laws of respect in the behavior of human beings. However, as time went on, this great inspiration was lost in a soulless formalism. In the tightly regulated life of the Jews of the first century A.D., the dispositions of the heart held such a small place that even the apostles have trouble understanding the teaching of Jesus. He unmasks hypocrisy. How can one not be shocked by his words, which overturn even the religious assurance of humans!

15:21-28 The Israelites regarded themselves as *children* of God because they were heirs of the promises made to the patriarchs and depositaries of the divine revelation. On the contrary, they called the Gentiles *dogs* out of contempt for their idolatrous and immoral practices. Jesus makes use of these two terms but softens the second, which in the Greek is "little dogs," i.e., pet dogs in the home. His point was that the Gospel was to be offered first to the Jews. The woman understood his implication and was willing to settle for the "crumbs." Jesus rewarded her faith.

15:21-22 *Tyre* and *Sidon:* these were Phoenician cities; *Canaanite* was the ancient name of their populations.

15:29-39 This second miracle of the loaves has many analogies with the first multiplication of the loaves. Therefore, some exegetes speak of a duplication, i.e., a different reporting of the same episode. However, there are so many diverse circumstances in the two episodes that Matthew and Mark believe in two distinct miracles.

16:1-4 The preaching, works, and extraordinary miracles of Jesus constituted a convincing proof of his Messiahship. The Pharisees and Sadducees demand *a sign from heaven,* like the stopping of the sun. Jesus flatly refuses to do so. He offers only *the sign of Jonah,* which foreshadows the mystery of his Death and Resurrection (see Mt 12:38-42).

16:4 *Adulterous:* i.e., unfaithful to the Lord.

16:5-12 The disciples at first misunderstand their Master, for whom the nourishment of humans is not reduced to bread alone. Jesus wishes to preserve his own from legalism. The yeast of the Pharisees and Sadducees is the rigid teaching of specialists of religion who snuff out freedom, joy, spontaneity, and commitment.

16:13ff Following the section of the bread (Mt 14:13—16:12), the evangelist appends a series of episodes that have to do with the revelation of the mystery of Christ. In addition to the text taken from Mark, which sets forth the theology of the Messianic secret and the suffering Servant, he presents the passages that speak of the primacy of Peter (Mt 16:17-19) and the payment of the temple tax (Mt 17:24-27), thus highlighting the theme of the foundation of the Church. The new People of God will then rise not from a Messianic triumphalism but from the mysterious drama of the Messiah's Passion and Resurrection.

16:13 *Caesarea Philippi* had been built by Herod Philip near the springs of the Jordan, at the foot of Mount Hermon. The name "Caesarea" was given as an act of homage to the Roman Emperor; since so many cities had the name, some further qualifier had to be added ("Philip's Caesarea"). "Caesarea in Palestine," to take one example, was the ordinary residence of the governor (see Acts 23).

16:16 *The Son of the living God:* in addition to the Messiahship of Jesus found in the other Synoptics at this point, Matthew also has an acknowledgment by Peter of Jesus' divinity. Many exegetes believe this is an addition based on Peter's later understanding of the mystery of Christ after the risen Lord appeared to him (see 1 Cor 15:5; Lk 24:34). In any case, Matthew has already mentioned that all the disciples had recognized the divinity of Christ (Mt 14:33).

16:17 *Flesh and blood:* a Scriptural expression that designates human beings in their weak and fragile condition. *Has not revealed this to you but my heavenly Father:* the source of Peter's confession of Christ's divinity is the heavenly Father.

16:18 *You are Peter, and on this rock I will build my Church:* the Aramaic word for "rock" (*kepa*) is transliterated into Greek as *Cephas,* the name used for Peter in the Pauline letters (1 Cor 1:12; Gal 1:18), and is translated as "Peter" in Jn 1:42. *Church:* a word that occurs only here and in Mt 18:17 (twice) in the New Testament. The Church will have Peter as her foundation stone. But of course her real foundation is faith in Jesus, the Son of God. Peter will have the primacy among all the apostles and be the visible head of the Church, as will his successors, the Popes. *The gates of the netherworld* designate the powers of death. The Church will resist all the vicissitudes of time because of her foundation on a rock.

16:19 Receiving the power of the *keys,* symbol of authority, Peter becomes Christ's representative on earth. He is given the power to *bind* and *loose,* i.e., to condemn or absolve, to prohibit or allow. Peter is the *doorkeeper* (Mk 13:34) but not the *Teacher* or the *Father* (Mt 23:9-10).

16:20 *Not to tell:* since the Jews were looking for a national and political Messiah, Jesus urged his disciples not to tell anyone that he was the Messiah.

16:21 The apostles now knew that Jesus was the Messiah, but their idea of it was inexact. They thought of a political Messiah, the glorious dominator of peoples. Jesus offers a triple prediction that spells out the last stages of his ministry. He thus prepares them for the scandal of the cross (see Mt 17:22f; 20:17f) and enlightens them concerning the true Messianism, which is spiritual, humble, and suffering.

16:22-23 Peter unknowingly offers Jesus the facile and worldly Messianism that would put him in opposition to the will of the Father. He unwittingly repeats the temptation of Satan at the beginning of Christ's ministry (Mt 4:1-11).

16:25 In order to receive eternal life, one must be ready to bear any sacrifice—even the renunciation of earthly life. The Greek word for "life" means either *life* or *soul*; also in v. 26.

16:28 Coming after v. 27, which alludes to the Second Coming of Christ, i.e., as Judge at the end of the world, this verse may refer to the destruction of Jerusalem in A.D. 70, which came to be regarded as a punishment from God for the refusal of the Jews to accept Jesus as the Messiah. The verse may also refer to Christ's Resurrection and his appearances thereafter as well as to the Transfiguration, which is a manifestation of his glory.

17:1-8 At the Transfiguration, the same voice that at the moment of his Baptism had indicated to Jesus the way of a suffering Messianism now manifests him as the true Messiah to the three apostles who would witness his agony in the garden. For a few seconds Jesus' humanity is resplendent with the divine glory of which he had divested himself during his earthly life.

17:1 *A high mountain:* since the 4th century, this has been identified with Tabor (1843 feet high) on the Plain of Esdraelon.

17:9-13 According to an ancient story, Elijah was assumed into heaven, while a prophecy claimed that he would return to prepare the people for the Messianic Age (see Mal 3:23-24; Sir 48:1-11).

17:14-21 This miracle has the purpose of highlighting the power of Jesus against the power of Satan, thus erasing all doubts that Jesus is the Messiah. Jesus states with some disappointment that not even his disciples have attained true faith.

17:21 This verse is missing in the most important manuscripts and seems to be taken from Mk 9:29.

17:22-23 This is the second of Christ's three predictions of his Passion (see Mt 16:21-23) and the least detailed. The disciples are *overwhelmed with grief*.

17:24-27 On reaching the age of twenty, every Jew had to pay two drachmas each year (Ex 30:13; 2 Chr 24:9; Neh 10:32). It was approximately two days' wages and was used for the upkeep of the temple. The two drachmas had to be paid in Jewish money; this explains the presence of money changers in the entrance halls of the temple (Mt 21:12; Jn 2:15). *Silver coin:* literally, a "stater," which was worth four drachmas, or twice the amount of the tax.

Jesus submits to the law out of respect for others, but he affirms that as Son of Man he is not bound by it. Christians who obey the law remain free with respect to all authority and are subject to God alone.

18:1-35 In this fourth collection of the sayings of Jesus, there are a good number that we have already met, and we recognize here, at times, the tone of the "Sermon on the Mount" (chs. 5—7). Everything is focused on the coming of the kingdom, but the words of Jesus now apply to the community life of the disciples. Chapter 18 is known as the "ecclesiastical discourse" because it describes the demands made by brotherhood in the Church of Jesus, which is a community of love, prayer, and forgiveness.

18:1-4 The true disciple of Jesus must renounce all ambition and become as simple and humble as a child.

18:5-11 Woe to those who give scandal to the *little ones,* i.e., the disciples of the Gospel, so as to make them fall. The Lord identifies himself with them and issues severe threats for those who wish to pervert them. Indeed, they have angels who always see the face of the Father in heaven—the guardian angels — thus showing their great worth in God's eyes.

18:8-9 These verses are already to be found substantially in Mt 5:29-30; the evangelist repeats them because they have to do with "scandal." The point is that no one can be saved who does not break completely with evil.

18:11 This verse is missing from the most important manuscripts and seems to have been transferred to this point from Lk 19:10.

18:12-14 In this parable, Jesus suggests what price the Father attaches to the salvation of sinners. The evangelist uses it as an appeal to the community that it may never become inhospitable to the least of believers, no matter how lost they may appear.

18:15-22 When believers live with trust in God and in communion with one another, Christ is in their midst. Doubtless, judgment is to be passed upon those who "sin," i.e., who gravely and publicly injure the unity; but all must remain ready to forgive without measure.

18:22 *Seventy times seven:* the Greek word may also be translated "seventy-seven times."

18:23-35 The law of pardon must ceaselessly renew the fraternal relationships in the Church. It is founded on the goodness of God who gratuitously forgives the immense sin of human beings.

18:24 *Ten thousand talents:* an enormous sum, equivalent to about 250,000 kg of silver. The Attic talent in circulation at that time was worth 6000 drachmas, and a drachma weighed about 4 gr.

18:28 *One hundred denarii:* the denarius was a Roman silver coin with the image and name of the emperor on it; it weighed about 4 gr and was the salary for a day's work. A hundred denarii were therefore a sum 600,000 times less than the ten thousand talents.

19:1—25:46 A new series of incidents, followed by a great discourse on the end of the world, make up the fifth part of the Gospel of Matthew. Jesus now goes to Judea, location of the official religion.

19:1-12 The interpreters of the Law thought up many subtle ways of making divorce easy; they lacked understanding of the essential point. Jesus' purpose is to recover the purity of the original state and the will of the Creator himself for the human race. He could not allow the unity of the couple to be at the mercy of circumstances, since this unity had been asserted by God as a call inherent in the very condition of man and woman (see Gen 2:24).

Did the rule admit exceptions? The phrase in v. 9: "except if the marriage was unlawful," has been the subject of much debate (on this point see what was said at Mt 5:32). In the Judaism of that age, not to marry seemed something repugnant and almost a crime; not to have a posterity seemed a punishment; however, some religious sects did practice voluntary continence. John and Jesus had renounced marriage in order to live solely for their mission of proclaiming the kingdom of God.

19:12 The virginity recommended by Jesus manifests the new creation of the New Covenant and is the prelude to the kingdom (see Mt 22:30). However, the renunciation of marriage out of love for the kingdom is possible only through the medium of a charism, a special gift of God (see 1 Cor 7:7).

19:13-15 The Gospel has retained this spontaneous and true gesture because it is also a sign. To enter into the kingdom, i.e., into intimacy with God, one must be free of all pretense and become poor and little. For humans are always weak and needy before God.

19:16-26 To follow Jesus means to be as poor and free as he is. But how can people detach themselves from what they are? Nothing would seem more impossible. Yet to be a Christian is to believe in the impossible things that God can accomplish in human beings.

19:27-30 Communion of life with Jesus is worth far more than all the things of the earth abandoned by the disciples, for they will reign with him in his eschatological kingdom.

20:1-16 The parable of the workers in the vineyard teaches that the promised kingdom is a gift of grace and not a wage. For salvation is not the fruit of a commercial contract but consists in a communion of love, a filial response on the part of humans to the initiative of God, who offers them his friendship. Christians who do good cannot boast of rights before God. They should merely do all they can to correspond with God's call and render themselves ever less unworthy of his friendship.

20:2 *Denarius:* a Roman coin that was the normal daily wage at the time— what a Roman soldier also received.

20:3 *Nine o'clock:* literally, "third hour."

20:5 *Noon . . . three in the afternoon:* literally, "sixth hour . . . ninth hour."

20:6 *Five o'clock:* literally, "eleventh hour."

20:17-19 At the moment when he starts out for Jerusalem, Jesus clearly confronts the drama of his sacrifice. This third prediction of the Passion is much more detailed than the first two.

20:20-28 The apostles were still dreaming of an earthly Messianic kingdom and seeking an important role in it. However, their recompense would be a gift from the heavenly Father, not a right of their own. Jesus' mission in the world was to save human beings and not to assign them their prize.

20:22 *Drink the cup:* in the idiom of the Bible, this meant to meet suffering (see Isa 51:17; Jer 25:15; Ps 75:9).

20:28 As the suffering Servant (Isa 53), Jesus has come to expiate the sins of all, offering the Father his own life as the price of the ransom, i.e., as the supreme expression of love.

20:29-34 Until the very end Jesus is the one who hears the cry of the distressed, the one who gives human beings light and calls them to follow him.

21:1-11 One of the key events in the life of Jesus. He seemed to be fulfilling what was most attractive in the Old Testament prophecies: here is the Messiah in the midst of his people, God's messenger in the midst of the human race, and joyous shouts of acclamation arise on every side. *Hosanna* means "Grant salvation!" but it is above all a shout of applause. Jesus allows himself to be acclaimed as the "Son of David," the Savior from the royal line, the figure that the believing people had, generation after generation, tried to picture for themselves in light of the promise made to David (2 Sam 7). But the sumptuous display in the courts of princes was of quite a different nature. Once again, Jesus rejects all dreams of prestige; here he is, in the midst of the people, riding the beast of the poor, the donkey, and linking himself in this manner with the Davidic tradition.

21:5 *Daughter of Zion:* i.e., Jerusalem, which rises on Mount Zion; the citation is from Isaiah 62:11. There follows the prophecy of Zechariah 9:9, which describes the Messiah, a humble and meek king taking peaceful possession of his kingdom.

21:7 *He sat on them* [the cloaks]: from Mark (11:2) and Luke (19:30), we know that Jesus rode on the colt. It was customary for a mother donkey to follow her offspring closely. Hence Matthew mentions two animals.

21:9 *Blessed is he who comes in the name of the Lord:* taken from Ps 118:26f, this phrase does not express the customary greeting directed at the pilgrim who had reached the Holy City. Like the *Hosanna* mentioned above, it is an acclamation to the Messiah who is taking possession of his kingdom.

21:12-17 As if to stress the authority of the Messiah, the evangelist follows up the entry into Jerusalem with Jesus' cleansing of the temple. He then adds the acclamation of the children, in whom he sees the fulfillment of another prophecy. John, on the other hand, places the cleansing of the temple at the beginning of Christ's public ministry. While not ruling out two distinct cleansings, scholars usually prefer the chronology of John, since the Synoptics have chosen to assign the whole of Christ's activity in Judea to the last period of his life.

21:13 Jesus combines two Old Testament prophecies: Isa 56:7 ("My house shall be called a house of prayer") and Jer 7:11 ("Has this house, which bears my name become in your eyes a den of thieves?").

21:18-22 The cursing of the fig tree is a symbolic act, a kind of parable in action. It signifies the condemnation of Israel, which has now become a sterile plant. The ancient Prophets often had recourse to this type of teaching.

21:23-27 This is the first of five controversies between Jesus and the religious authorities of Judaism in Matthew 21:23—22:46. They are in a question-and-answer form and are interrupted after the first by three parables on the judgment of Israel (Mt 21:28-32; 21:33-46; 22:1-14).

21:27 The religious authorities claim ignorance of the origin of John's baptism and thereby demonstrate that they cannot speak with authority. Therefore, Jesus refuses to tell them by what authority he acts.

21:28-32 The parable of the two sons denounces a religion that is content with words and appearances. The facile "Yes" on the lips is a poor disguise for the refusal of the heart. To the hypocrisy of the recognized teachers, Jesus opposes the true faith of the poor. The evangelist utilizes this parable to indicate the end of Israel's privileges and the entrance of Gentiles into the growing Church.

21:33-46 The parable repeats, almost word for word, passages from the beautiful, sad song of the vineyard in Isaiah 5; Jesus is speaking of God and his people. How can we forget the tragic history of the Prophets, who were rejected, tormented, and stoned to death (2 Chr 24:21; Heb 11:37; Lk 13:34)? Is not the son here Jesus himself?

Scholars believe that some allegorical elements have been added herein to a basic parable originally spoken by Christ. One reason for their belief is the newly found apocryphal Gospel of Thomas, which contains (#65) a more primitive form of the parable.

21:44 Some manuscripts do not have this verse, which indicates that both hostility and apathy are wrong responses to Christ. It may be an early addition to this Gospel based on Luke 20:18.

22:1-14 The meaning of this parable is similar to that of the preceding one. The Messianic Kingdom is likened to a nuptial banquet. The king is God; the servants are the Prophets; the invited guests are the Israelites; the punishment of the city refers to the destruction of Jerusalem in A.D. 70; the new invitees are the Gentiles. Some retouches have made the parable a warning to the Church of Matthew as well as a statement of God's judgment on Israel.

22:11-13 Scholars speak of these verses almost as another parable, that of the wedding garment. In this world the good and the wicked are mixed together, for it is the time of patience and mercy. During this time Christians must cooperate with God's grace, which is tantamount to wearing the wedding garment.

22:14 *Many . . . chosen:* this does not seem to allude to the number of the elect, since that is a secret that the Father had reserved to himself. It means that all the Israelites have been invited, but only few of them have accepted the Gospel.

22:15-22 Here the series of controversies between Jesus and the religious authorities is resumed, beginning with the question of paying taxes to the Roman emperor. For over twenty years, the Roman emperor had been levying a tax on Palestine; the Jewish people regarded it as a sign of unjust oppression. To pay it was regarded as a denial of Jewish hopes; to challenge it meant taking the side of revolutionary agitators. Only the elderly and children were exempt; the Zealots forbade their members to pay it.

22:16 *Herodians:* partisans and courtiers of the reigning dynasty of the Herods. Though they were Jews in religion, their spirit was Gentile. They conspired with their enemies the Pharisees against Christ.

22:19 *Denarius:* the daily wage of a laborer.

22:21 Jesus emphasizes that it is not enough to give to Caesar what is due to Caesar; people must also give to God what is due to God, i.e., worship and good works (see Mt 21:41, 43).

22:23-33 Faith in a resurrection became common only toward the end of the Old Testament period. Not all shared the certainty; the Sadducees, the aristocrats of the priestly class and men concerned more with politics than with religion, considered it a rather debatable theological novelty. They debate it with Jesus, using arguments that emerge as caricature and prevent access to the heart of the question. Jesus answers in the name of the Jewish faith in God: God stands on the side of life.

22:24 *If a man dies . . . his brother:* this custom is known as the "law of the levirate," from the Latin word for brother-in-law (*levir*). It was intended to continue the family line of the deceased brother (see Deut 25:6).

22:34-40 Instead of dividing the Law into a string of precepts (the Rabbis counted 248) and prohibitions (365), Jesus unifies it in two essential commandments: love of God (Deut 6:5) and neighbor (Lev 19:18). These form the basis of every precept.

22:41-46 For centuries people had been awaiting a Christ, or Messiah, who would be a son of David; they saw him pictured in an ancient royal psalm that became a song of Messianic expectation (Ps 110). But Christ is more than the heir to David's throne; he possesses the authority of God. Only during his Passion will Jesus expressly claim to be the Messiah (26:63-64).

23:1-7 It was considered a fine thing to show off Jewish piety even in the way one dressed: men wore phylacteries (see note on v. 5, below), and made extra long the tassels with which, according to the Law, their prayer shawls should be adorned.

23:5 *Phylacteries:* little boxes containing tiny parchment scrolls that had texts of Scripture on them (Ex 13:1-10; 13:11-16; Deut 6:4-9; 11:13-21) and were placed in little tubes; the boxes were attached to the forehead and the left fore arm, in keeping with a literal interpretation of Deut 6:8; 11.18. The tassels had a blue thread running through them as a symbol of heaven; they were to remind the wearer of the commandments of God (Num 15:38).

23:8-12 Here Jesus obviously does not abolish the words "Rabbi," "father," and "teacher." He condemns ambition and despotism on the one hand and blind servility on the other. The true Father of Christians is God, and the true Master is Christ, the Son of God. In others, paternal and magistral authority is never absolute, but relative and subordinate to the divine authority.

23:13-28 At that period, Jews tried to win Gentiles over to their religion; those who came were called proselytes. There were also Gentiles who sympathized with Jewish ways and were called "God-fearers." There must have been rivalries between Jews and Christians in this area.

23:14 This verse is identical with Mark 12:40 and seems to have been interpolated from that text.

23:15 *Convert:* a proselyte, that is, a Gentile who had accepted the faith of Israel. *Worthy of Gehenna:* worthy of damnation.

23:16-22 Jesus shows that the Pharisees were wrong in saying that swearing by the gold of the temple and by the offering that lies on the altar is more binding than swearing by the temple or by the altar.

23:23-24 The Law prescribed a tithe on the most important products. However, the Pharisees had extended it to even the most insignificant herbs, and yet they neglected the duties toward one's neighbor, such as justice, compassion, and fidelity. Thus, they strained their liquids so as not to involuntarily swallow an insect and render themselves unclean yet gave no thought to observing the more grave commandments of the moral law.

23:27 *You are like whitewashed tombs:* an allusion to the custom of white-washing tombs so that no one might inadvertently touch them and contract a legal uncleanness (see Num 19:16).

23:29-36 The final curse becomes a prophecy of judgment. It sketches the long history of the opposition between the Israel of human beings and the Israel of God, from the first murder of which the Bible speaks to the last (in the order in which the books of the Bible were placed at that period), that is, from Abel (Gen 4:8) to Zechariah (2 Chr 24:20-22).

23:37-39 Jesus offers a lament over Jerusalem, which by failing to accept him opened herself to catastrophe. However, at the end time the Israelites will be con-verted and acclaim Jesus in his Second Coming (Ps 118:26; see Rom 11:25-33).

24:1—25:46 Five discourses give the Gospel of Matthew its characteristic struc-ture. Here is the last discourse, which brings together prophecies and parables that speak of the last times of humanity and distinguish its phases. At the center of the scenario is the return of Christ. This great passage is known as the "eschatological discourse," because it deals with the end, the last times (Greek: *eschaton*).

24:1-31 The prophetic sayings about the last "days" abound in descriptions of panic, wars, earthquakes, and cosmic upheavals; these descriptions are called "apocalypses," that is, "revelations." They defy the imagination in order better to bring out the greatness of God's manifestation in the history of humanity (see Isa 13:10-13; Jer 21:9; Ezek 5:12; Am 8:8-9; Joel 2:10; 3:3; 4:17-21). Jesus makes use of this entire scenario in order to warn believers about the trials and conflicts in which their fidelity will be tested, and in order to encourage the missionaries of the Gospel.

24:1-2 Jesus announces the destruction of the temple, which is the sign of God's presence among his people. Hence, one must envisage a radical change in the religious life.

24:3-14 There are many indications of Christ's coming at the end of the world. However, no one should be mistaken. Neither the explosion of religious move-ments, nor the confusion of human societies, nor the catastrophes that pervade human history are signs of the end. The believer must stand fast under trials, which may appear to be excessive at times.

24:15-22 *The abomination of desolation* was a pagan idol placed in the midst of the Jerusalem temple (see Dan 9:27; 11:31; 12:11; 1 Mac 1:54). The destruc-tion of Jerusalem in A.D. 70 is described here in order to convey a lesson about the future.

24:28 A popular proverb cited also in Luke 17:37. In this context it signifies both the uncertain time of the Lord's coming and his universal presence.

24:29-31 The coming of the Son of Man is described in the words of the Old Testament (see Isa 13:9-10; 34:4; Am 5:18; Zec 12:10) in order to express the glory and power of God and the confusion of humanity. Christ dead and risen: this is the sign that converts human beings.

24:32—25:46 The perspective of the end of the world must keep the commu-nity on its guard. But it also concerns each disciple, for it has an effect on the end of each individual too. Let everyone be vigilant and active so as not to find oneself barred from the kingdom.

24:32-35 This parable is intended to revive the hope of the first Christians, who are under persecution, with the perspective of the proximity of the glorious kingdom, in accord with the schema of the apocalyptic tradition. Indeed, every Christian lives in this expectation, for with Christ the last period of history has begun.

24:36-42 The early Church is exhorted not to fall into indifference because judgment comes less quickly than expected. The life of humans cannot be exhausted in the gloomy flow of hours and days; it has another horizon: the coming of God, which is unforeseeable but completely certain. It hovers like a threat over the uncaring who seclude themselves in their securities. But it is a power and a source of strength for believers.

24:43-44 This very brief parable of the owner of the house and the thief reinforces the theme of vigilance, for one does not know when the Son of Man will come.

24:45-51 Jesus addresses the religious leaders of his time to place them on guard: the time to render accounts has arrived. But the coming of God is still to take place, and the disciples will be tempted to no longer believe in it. The parable of the faithful servant remains a wake-up call for them. The religious leaders and Christians must not neglect to work for the kingdom as if the Master were always present—God is in their midst.

25:1-13 The parable of the ten virgins illustrates a fundamental thought: we must wait with watchful perseverance for the coming of Christ glorified, likened to the arrival of a bridegroom. In the dazzling nuptial ceremony of Palestine, the bride awaited the bridegroom while merrymaking with friends. Around midnight the bridegroom would come accompanied by lamps. After an initial explosion of joy, the cortège would return to the house of the bridegroom, where the banquet would be celebrated.

25:1 *Then:* at the time of the Second Coming.

25:14-30 The parable of the talents completes the preceding one. The Christian religion is not a simple passive expectation. It demands a complete commitment. One must make fruitful the gifts given by God while awaiting the Lord's glorious return.

25:15 *Talents:* a talent was equivalent to 6000 denarii, that is, to the salary for 6000 days of work.

25:31-46 This passage constitutes the conclusion of the eschatological discourse with the description of the Last Judgment. In the second part of the great discourse (Mt 24:37), the individual judgment was repeatedly indicated. Now there comes before us the supreme Judge, Jesus Christ in glory, who at the end of time will judge all peoples, without distinction between Jew and Gentile, and will separate the good from the wicked in accord with everyone's works.

26:1—28:20 One person dominates this account: Jesus. He submits to the death that hangs over sinful humanity, but he comes forth from the tomb as conqueror of death and evil. Matthew constantly cites Scripture in order to convince the intended readers of his work, Christians converted from Judaism, that the seeming failure of Jesus was in reality the fulfillment of God's plan.

26:1-5 Matthew emphasizes Jesus' awareness to carry out his Father's saving plan. Probably the plot was hatched on Wednesday.

26:3 Joseph, surnamed Caiaphas, son-in-law of Annas, was high priest, that is, supreme head of the Jewish priesthood and president of the Sanhedrin, from A.D. 18 to 36.

26:6-13 The anointing at Bethany anticipates the burial rites for the Savior after his death. Providing for burial was in the eyes of the Jews a more important good work than almsgiving itself. In John 12:1-8, the woman is called Mary, and Judas is the apostle who becomes indignant. Luke (7:36-50) reports another anointing.

26:11 *The poor you will always have with you:* with these words Jesus does not intend to sanction poverty as if to condemn efforts to eradicate misery. He makes a simple observation: his disciples will have many occasions to aid the poor who, as Deuteronomy 15:11 states, will never be wanting in Israel.

26:14-16 For the early Christians, if there is a dark deed it is the ever incomprehensible deed of Judas, who comes to the fore here. Matthew is thinking of the prophecy of the righteous man sold for thirty pieces of silver (see Zec 11:12). That amount is also the compensation paid to one whose slave has been gored by an ox (see Ex 21:32).

26:17-19 In the history of Israel one event dominates all others, the Passover (Ex 12–13), and in the worship of Israel one feast summarizes the whole faith, the Passover. It celebrates the passage of God in the midst of his people and is the hour of liberation, salvation, and the covenant. Jesus' Death and Resurrection constitute the true Passover, definitive for all humankind. The Last Supper of Jesus will be its inauguration.

26:17 *The first day of the feast of Unleavened Bread:* this date corresponds with Thursday, the 14th of Nisan. The feast really began on the 15th of Nisan and lasted until the 21st. However, since the leavened bread was eliminated from all the houses before midday on the 14th, the morning of this date was improperly regarded as the first day of the feast, which in reality began only with the setting of the sun, when according to Jewish custom the 15th began. Passover here refers to the paschal lamb, which was immolated around three o'clock on the 14th of Nisan.

26:20-25 The Passover supper began around six o'clock on Thursday. This passage focuses on the divine foreknowledge of Jesus, who is not overcome by the course of events and regards them as ordinary. He sees them as the putting in motion of the will of his Father.

26:26-30 This is the beginning of the new Covenant promised in Jer 31:31-33, the new sacrifice. For Jesus this meal is more than a final farewell; his entire work is summed up in this sign. He shares his life and love with sinners; he acts as the Servant of God whose sacrifice of himself ransoms his fellow human beings from sin and reconciles them with the Father (see Isa 42:6; 49:6; 53:11-12). Jesus anticipates his sacrifice; he anticipates his gift of himself. By offering his body and blood on the cross he saves humankind. A Covenant is established in which all the saved will share in the same love (see Jer 31:31-34). The Eucharist replaces Sinai (see Ex 24:6-8).

26:31-35 During the Passover meal, some psalms were sung, i.e., the so-called Hallel (113—118). Two followed the account of the origin of Passover. The others were recited after the meal. On the way to the Mount of Olives, Jesus predicts to the disciples their crisis of faith. They have indeed acknowledged him as Messiah and have a deep love for him, as shown by Peter's words. However, they have not yet understood the scandal of the cross, and so their fidelity will be shaken, at least momentarily.

26:34 The cock would begin crowing at 3:00 A.M. (see Mk 13:35).

26:36-46 The first Christian community never succumbed to the temptation to make Jesus into a hero. Never did he appear more human and more pitiable than in this passage. His inner turmoil in the face of his approaching suffering and death could not be more profound than in this hour of the agony. Three times the prayer of the Our Father rises on the lips of Christ; it is a prayer of complete abandonment into God's hand. And Jesus bears this "temptation," this trial, alone as perhaps no other human could have done. He utters no word of resentment or pride at the moment when he accepts and confronts the ultimate and sorrowful stage of his mission.

26:47-56 Jesus practices what he had taught (Mt 5:39). He regards himself as the suffering Servant (see Isa 53) who accepts his sacrifice in silence so as to accomplish his mission. It is love that reestablishes order, for in the face of hypocritical force violence remains powerless.

26:47-48 Judas was well aware of the customs of his Master, and that he was wont to retire to the garden of Gethsemane. *Kiss:* this was the customary greeting of a disciple for his teacher.

26:53 *Do you suppose that I cannot appeal to my Father for help . . .?*: by these words Jesus emphasizes the voluntary character of his Passion. Jesus freely accepts the will of God, expressed in Scripture. The same reason is repeated in v. 56. *Twelve legions:* a Roman legion consisted of 6000 men.

26:57-68 According to Matthew and Mark, immediately after his arrest Jesus was led before the Sanhedrin for a session that very night. Another session was held in the morning; then Jesus was consigned to Pilate. The religious trial has two phases: the first centers upon the false testimony of witnesses, the second upon the question put to Jesus by the high priest. The Law (Deut 17:6) required that two witnesses agree in their testimony against an accused person. Jesus supposedly had said that he had power over the temple, which was the house of God. But had he not said that his body was the true dwelling of the Father (Jn 2:21)? Now that every political and nationalist interpretation of his words seems excluded, since he is alone, rejected, helpless, he dares to say that he is the Messiah and not only the son but the lord of David (Ps 110:1; Dan 7:13).

26:69-75 At the very moment when the Master openly proclaims himself to be the Messiah, no one acknowledges it. In the opinion of all, he is lost. Even Peter, the leader of Jesus' followers, denies any link with him.

27:1-2 According to Matthew and Mark, the members of the Sanhedrin came together officially for a second time in the morning to pronounce the sentence of condemnation. In the light of a different scenario found in Luke and John, scholars believe it is more probable that during the night Jesus appeared before Annas for a private interrogation and then was brought to Caiaphas. In the morning he appeared before the Sanhedrin, where he was declared deserving of death. The

Jewish tribunal did not have the power over life and death. Therefore, Jesus was led before Pontius Pilate, who from A.D. 26 to 36 was the governor (procurator) in Judea, which passed into the direct dominion of Rome in A.D.6.

27:3-10 This story is typical of Matthew's style; the sad incident suggests to him various references to the Scriptures (Zec 11:12-13; Jer 18:2-3; 32:6-15). The memory of Judas was a burden to the early Christians (see Acts 1:16-20).

27:9 *Spoken through the prophet Jeremiah:* the statement actually comes from Zechariah 11:12, 13. However, the Hebrew canon of Scripture was divided into three sections: The Law, The Writings, and The Prophets (see Lk 24:44). Since Jeremiah came first in the order of the Prophetic Books, the Prophets were at times collectively referred to by his name.

27:11-26 For a second time (the wise men were the first to use the title, Mt 2:1-12), Jesus is called "King of the Jews," and once again it is a pagan who gives him the title. The governor says he is convinced of the innocence of Jesus (see Deut 21:6), but he yields to the insistence of the Jewish authorities.

27:11 The members of the Sanhedrin had condemned Jesus because of his claim to be a transcendent and superhuman Messiah. Now before Pilate, they cleverly laicize the accusation, portraying Jesus as a dangerous political instigator opposed to the Roman domination. The whole trial is begun on the alleged kingship of Jesus.

27:14 The silence of Jesus recalls the attitude of the Servant of the Lord, who like a lamb does not open his mouth in the face of those who shear him (Isa 53:7).

27:19 A Gentile woman declares Jesus' innocence. *By a dream:* for Matthew, dreams are the means of communication from God (1:20; 2:12, 13, 19, 22).

27:24 *Washed his hands:* this gesture of Pilate was in use among the Jews (see Deut 21:6) and among other peoples. However, this symbolic action does not exempt the Roman procurator of his responsibility. He has acknowledged the innocence of the accused yet has condemned him.

27:25 The nation accepts the responsibility for Jesus' death. The Second Vatican Council has declared that the guilt for Jesus' death is not attributable to all the Jews of his day or to any Jews of later times. We are responsible for Jesus' death. He died for our sins.

27:27-31 Jesus is delivered up to suffering, misunderstanding, ridicule. "He was despised and shunned by others, a man of sorrows who was no stranger to suffering"; "I did not shield my face from insults and spitting" (Isa 53:3; 50:6). The praetorium was the residence of the Roman governor.

27:32 *Cyrene:* a Greek colony on the Libyan coast; a large Jewish community lived there. See note on Mk 15:21.

27:33 *Skull* (Latin: *calvaria*): a rounded, rocky elevation, about fifteen feet high. It was a used out quarry that functioned as a garbage dump.

27:34 The wine mixed with gall was meant to alleviate suffering.

27:35 *Crucified him:* crucifixion was an excruciating means of execution that the Romans had borrowed from Persians, Phoenicians, and Carthaginians. The victims were nailed to a cross by means of heavy wrought-iron nails driven through their wrists and heels. Most hung on the cross for days before dying of suffocation (when the legs were no longer able to support the body, the diaphragm was constricted and breathing became impossible). Although the pain would be unbearable as the hours dragged on, some did linger and had to have their legs broken to hasten death (see Jn 19:33). The recent discovery of the bones of a crucified man, near Jerusalem, dating between A.D. 7 and 66, sheds light on the position of those nailed to the cross. *Lots:* a few late manuscripts add here: "lots, so that the word spoken by the Prophet might be fulfilled: 'They divide my garments among them, and for my clothing they cast lots'" (Ps 22:19).

27:38 The crucifixion between two thieves recalls the prophecy of Isaiah 53:12: He "was counted among the transgressors."

27:45-56 Everything proclaims that the Son of God, dying on the cross, is triumphant over the forces of the world and of death; the old covenant is finished, and the time is coming when the kingdom will be open to all human beings (see Heb 9:12; 10:20; Ezek 37; Dan 12:2; Rev 21).

27:45-46 *Midday . . . three o'clock:* literally, "sixth hour" . . . "ninth hour." Psalm 22, whose first verse is here invoked by Jesus, recapitulates all the sufferings of the just people in the Old Testament. It clearly expresses their extreme anguish but also their certainty of final vindication.

27:53 The phenomena that accompany the death of Jesus evoke the apocalyptic literary genre of the Day of the Lord. In fact, according to the evangelists, that day corresponds with the day of the death of Jesus, which signals the beginning of the new era. Because of the obscurity of this language it is difficult to determine the historicity of the resurrection of some dead people mentioned here. Some Fathers of the Church and exegetes believe this passage refers to the liberation from limbo of the just of the Old Testament, who then enter with Jesus into the glory of the heavenly Jerusalem.

27:56 *Magdalene:* "Of Magdala," a place on the west side of Lake Tiberias, near Capernaum.

27:57-61 The story of the burial provided by a rich man certainly recalls Isaiah's prophecy of the Servant (53:9 LXX). See also note on Mk 15:42-47.

27:62 *Preparation day:* This was Friday, the day on which the meal was prepared for the Sabbath, which was a day of complete rest.

28:1-10 The Resurrection of Christ is a mystery of faith; it was not accessible to the senses, as other events are. Our faith in it is based on the word of those who witnessed the risen Christ.

28:10 It is difficult to harmonize the accounts of the appearances of the risen Jesus set forth by the four evangelists and St. Paul (1 Cor 15:3-7). There are no authentic divergences, only independent narratives. Every sacred author gives one episode or other and stresses one phrase or other of the Lord in accord with some unknown criteria or particular theology.

Scripture describes at least ten appearances of Jesus to his apostles and disciples between his Resurrection and his Ascension forty days later. He appeared to: (1) Mary Magdalene at the tomb (Mk 16:9; Jn 20:11-18); (2) the women on the road (Mt 28:9, 10); (3) the two disciples on the road to Emmaus (Lk 24:13-35); (4) Peter (Lk 24:34; 1 Cor 15:5); (5) ten of the eleven apostles, with Thomas absent (Lk 24:36-43; Mk 16:14; Jn 20:19-25); (6) all eleven apostles, with

Thomas present (eight days later) (Jn 20:26-31); (7) seven disciples by the shore of the Sea of Galilee (Jn 21:1-25); (8) more than 500 disciples, most likely on a mountain in Galilee (1 Cor 15:6); (9) James (1 Cor 15:7); and (10) the apostles at his Ascension (Acts 1:3-11). After his Ascension he also appeared to Paul (1 Cor 15:8).

28:11-15 Matthew is here combating the fables that were circulated in Jewish circles to ridicule the testimony of the early Church.

28:16-20 The last passage of the Gospel is not a conclusion but a new beginning, a new departure. From a mountain whose vantage point embraces the ends of the earth and the limits of history, we see the destiny of humankind. Now Jesus is established in his lordship in dazzling glory, and his hands hold the fate of the world. Now his faithful spread his message and his mystery; now there is one Baptism for all humanity and one communion with God for all persons. It is the time of the universal mission: God is with us; such is the very name of Jesus: "Emmanuel" (Mt 1:23; see Isa 7:14). On the face of Christ we read the mystery of the Church.

28:19 The evangelist places on the Lord's lips the trinitarian formula that was in use in the baptismal Liturgy of the time (A.D. 70–80).

THE GOSPEL ACCORDING TO MARK

1:1-13 Around the year 30, after centuries of silence, a prophet named John appears and unsettles his contemporaries. They are captivated by the force of his personality and the vehemence of his message. Then Jesus comes on the scene. Mark uses this story as a kind of prologue for his book, a kind of key for understanding the pages that follow: the Gospel, the "good news," is here bursting out in the midst of humanity; the action of Jesus inaugurates the kingdom of God, the time of salvation.

1:1-8 The Gospel is not primarily a book but rather God's action for the salvation of humankind. The entire Book of Mark depicts Jesus as the promised and awaited one (the Messiah) and as the Son of God (see Mk 8:35; 10:29).

1:2 *The prophet Isaiah:* the quotation that follows is a combination of Malachi (3:1) and Isaiah (40:3). See note on Mt 27:9.

1:8 *Baptize you with the Holy Spirit:* see note on Mt 3:11.

1:9-11 Mark retains only the essential elements of the divine manifestation, which here is given only to Jesus, whose mission is announced.

1:9 *At that time:* Jesus probably began his public ministry about A.D. 27 at approximately 30 years of age (see Lk 3:23). *Nazareth:* see note on Mt 2:23. *Baptized by John:* see note on Mt 3:15 for the meaning of Jesus' baptism.

1:10-11 This passage has the involvement of all three persons of the Trinity: (1) the Father speaks; (2) the Son is baptized; and (3) the Holy Spirit descends on the Son.

1:12-13 Jesus is already committed to his mission of combating Satan, the representative of all the forces of evil that batter humanity.

1:14—8:30 People had a simple idea of the Messiah as a glorious figure: they were expecting a national hero, a political liberator, a restorer of their independence and their public worship, a leader who would bring Israel to world domination. But the reason why Jesus comes before the nation is quite different. This first part of Mark's Gospel describes three periods. Three times the author gives a general summary of the activity of Jesus and describes a mission of the disciples; each period ends with a scene of hostility and lack of understanding. At the end of this first half of the book, the confession of Peter at Caesarea recognizes the Messiah without any misunderstanding. From that point on, the road will lead to the Passion; that development occupies the second half of the Gospel.

1:14 *After John had been arrested:* the ministry of Jesus begins under the sign of his precursor's martyrdom. This simple chronological marker is a veiled prefiguration of the suffering and death that await the Messiah. See note on Lk 3:20.

1:16-20 See note on Mt 4:18-22.

1:21-28 See note on Lk 4:31-41.

1:24 *The Holy One of God:* this title is used only here and in Lk 4:34 and Jn 6:69. It refers more to Jesus' divinity than to his Messiahship (see Lk 1:35).

1:30 *Simon's mother-in-law:* Paul (in 1 Cor 9:5) speaks of Peter being married.

1:32 At sunset, the strictly enjoined Sabbath rest came to an end.

1:40 *Leprosy:* see Lev 13–14.

1:41 *Touched him:* an act that caused defilement according to the Law (see Lev 13:45-46). Jesus' compassion superseded any consideration of defilement.

1:44 For this ritual cleansing, see Lev 14:1-32.

2:1—3:6 In the five controversy stories that are combined here, the plot to put Jesus to death, which is the key to Mark's Gospel, is already made clear.

2:6 *Scribes:* men trained in the oral traditions that flowed from the written Law. In this Gospel, they are adversaries of Jesus except in one incident (Mk 12:28-34).

2:10 *Son of Man:* see note on Mt 8:20.

2:13 *Lake:* Tiberias.

2:14 *Levi:* another name of Matthew (Jews often had two names). The taxes in question were collected on goods that entered or left the city. The system was established by the Romans, but the collection of taxes and duties was handed over to private organizations whose employees were not infrequently corrupt. See also note on Mt 5:46.

2:15 *His:* i.e., Levi's (see Lk 5:29). *Sinners:* those who were ostentatiously wicked and those who did not follow the Law as interpreted by the scribes. The term was customarily applied to collaborators, robbers, adulterers, and the like.

2:18-22 See notes on Mt 9:14-17 and Lk 5:33-39.

2:20 The Jews were obliged to fast only on the Day of Atonement. However, devout persons fasted two times a week (on Monday and Thursday). Jesus does not disapprove of such acts. He merely points out that his coming has inaugurated the time of joy foretold by the Prophets, in which it was legitimate for his disciples to benefit from the presence of the Bridegroom, i.e., the Messiah. He then alludes to his violent death after which his disciples would fast while awaiting the glorious and definitive coming of the heavenly Bridegroom.

2:22 *New wine:* the Gospel; the old wine is the practices of Judaism.

2:23-28 See notes on Mt 12:2; 12:3-4; 12:5-6; and 12:8.

2:26 *Abiathar:* high priest in the time of David. In 1 Sam 21:2-3 his father, Ahimelech, is named.

2:27 Mark alone has preserved this saying of Jesus.

3:1-6 See note on Mt 12:9-14.

3:7-35 This is the second period in the first half of the Gospel. A group of disciples has been formed; to these men who are really listening to him Jesus explains his message of the coming kingdom.

3:7-12 Mark begins this second section with a summary of the activity of Jesus.

3:8 This verse demonstrates Jesus' great popularity with people from all of Israel as well as its surrounding neighbors. Mark recounts Jesus' work in all the regions mentioned except Idumea: Galilee (1:14), the region beyond the Jordan (5:1; 10:1), Tyre and Sidon (7:24, 31), Judea (10:1), and Jerusalem (11:11). *Idumea:* the Greek form of the Hebrew "Edom"; but here it refers to an area in western Palestine south of Judea rather than the earlier Edomite territory.

3:13-19 Among those who listened to Jesus there was a group that included women and 72 men who were later sent on mission (see Lk 10:17). Following the Ascension, the group had swelled to 120 believers who waited in Jerusalem (Acts 1:15). From such followers, Jesus here chooses 12 to be apostles (those given a special commission).

3:14-16 Lists of the apostles are also found in Mt 1:2-4; Lk 6:12-16; and Acts 1:13. The order in which the names are given varies, but Peter always comes first and Judas is always placed at the end.

3:14 *Whom he also named apostles:* missing in some manuscripts.

3:17 *Sons of Thunder:* the Aramaic nickname emphasizes the fiery character of the two brothers.

3:20-35 In these verses, which are peculiar to Mark's Gospel, the author highlights contrasting reactions to the person of Jesus. The crowds search him out. His relatives think he is out of his mind and understand nothing about his mission; they want to take him by force and bring him back to his own town.

3:20-21 The foundation of the eschatological community is followed by this passage, which recounts the failure to comprehend even on the part of relatives and above all the hostile refusal of the leaders of Judaism to accept him.

3:20 *Home:* i.e., Matthew's house (see Mt 2:15).

3:22-30 See notes on Mt 12:22-32 and 12:32.

3:31-35 See notes on Mt 12:46-50 and 12:47.

4:1-34 Mark has, so to speak, his own "theory of parables," which he here places on the lips of Jesus. In his view, parables were and remained enigmatic: their meaning was clear only to the disciples, those who really "heard" Jesus ("hear" is the key word in these texts) and believed in him. See notes on Mt 13:1-51; 13:3a; 13:3b-9; 13:10-15.

4:11 *Mysteries:* see note on Mt 13:11.

4:12 The citation is from Isaiah 6:9-10. Acts (28:26-27) and Romans (11:7-16, 29-32) cite the same passage of Isaiah to show that the rejection by the people of the Covenant had been foretold and that God's plan cannot be checkmated by the defection of human beings. It is not that God wants them to reject the word. They do that on their own because they do not want to receive God's forgiveness.

4:13-20 See note on Mt 13:18-23.

4:21-23 Just as a lamp is placed to provide light, not to hide it, so Jesus, the light of the world, is destined to be revealed.

4:24-25 As an example of the way in which the sayings of Jesus were handed on, we may observe that the parable about measure is applied here to the reception of the "word," but is used in Matthew (7:2) and Luke (6:38) with reference to judgment of one's brother or sister.

4:25 *To the one who has, more will be given . . . :* one of the meanings of this text is that those who appropriate the truth more will receive more truth in the future; however, those who do not respond to what little truth they may know already will not profit even from that amount.

4:26-29 This parable, the only one peculiar to Mark, illustrates his idea of the power of the Gospel. The term *harvest* is an image of the judgment (see Joel 4:13; Rev 14:15).

4:30-32 See notes on Mt 13:31-32 and 13:32.

4:33-34 These words mitigate and partly explain the warning in v. 12. Jesus with his parables adapted himself to the imaginative eastern mentality, without running afoul of the susceptibility of that people who were still stubbornly attached to the idea of a triumphal Messiah. He offered the possibility of reflections and further elucidations.

4:35— 5:43 The so-called "Parables of the Lake" are followed by a characteristic grouping of four miracles, which demonstrate the evangelist's Christological intention. With his merciful power, Jesus appears as the Master of natural elements, demons, sickness, and death itself. The section gives a very accurate selection of prodigies worked by the Savior. The accounts are possibly pre-Marcan, and they have been endowed by the evangelist with a particularly vivid narrative taken from the preaching of Peter. These are the so-called "Miracles of the Lake."

4:35-40 See note on Mt 8:23-27.

5:1-20 The scene shifts to the Decapolis, a group of ten more or less autonomous cities east of the Jordan; it is as if in a pagan land the forces of evil could enslave and destroy human beings. The demons are condemned to take refuge in the pigs, impure animals par excellence in Jewish eyes. See also note on Mt 8:28-34.

5:1 *The region of the Gerasenes* was southeast of Lake Tiberias.

5:2 Caves were used for tombs.

5:9 *My name is Legion . . . there are many of us:* a Roman legion was made up of 6,000 men. The word "legion" gives the idea that the man was possessed by many demons and also provides an inkling of the numerous powers opposed to Jesus, who incorporates the divine power.

5:20 See note on Mt 4:25.

5:21-43 A woman, who according to the ideas of the time was unclean and would contaminate by her touch, touches Jesus in a hidden gesture of hope; he frees her from her disease with kind words.

When Jesus restores the girl to life, he does it privately, because he does not want the Messiah to be thought of as a magician; only three witnesses are there, those present at the Transfiguration (Mk 9:2) and the agony (Mk 14:33). These men would bear witness to the mystery of Jesus who dies and rises in order to save humanity from evil and death, and thus to Jesus as the authentic Messiah. See note on Mt 9:18-26.

5:22 *Leaders of the synagogue:* laymen who held administrative responsibilities such as taking care of the building and supervising the worship. Most synagogues had only one ruler, but there were exceptions (see Acts 13:15). There were also cases of honorary leaders.

5:37 *Peter, James, and John:* while Matthew focuses his attention mainly on Peter, Mark stresses this privileged group of three disciples. They will be witnesses of the raising of Jairus's daughter (Mk 5:37-43), the Transfiguration of Jesus (Mk 9:2-13), and the agony in the garden (Mk 14:32-42). Obviously Mark depends on the preaching of Peter, yet Peter rarely emphasized his privilege.

6:1-6a This story of a breach completes the second section of the first part. See note on Mt 13:53-58.

6:3 *Brother:* see note on Mt 12:46.

6:6b—8:30 The very term *Messiah* is charged with too many facile hopes and misunderstandings, and Jesus avoids using it. If he reveals himself, it is through words and actions in the midst of events and encounters. The tragic end of John the Baptist prefigures his own destiny. Jesus bears witness to the goodness of God, shepherd of his people, and nourishes human beings with his word and his bread. His relationship with the disciples becomes closer and closer. Despite their failure to attain a full understanding of who he is, they are given the grace to recognize him as the Messiah.

6:6b-13 Jesus impresses on the disciples that the preaching of the Gospel demands a genuine and unconditional detachment from earthly things.

6:13 At the time of Jesus, *oil* was frequently used to heal sickness. The anointing by the apostles set forth the healing power conferred on them by Jesus and prefigured the Sacrament of the Anointing of the Sick.

6:14-16 Jesus' name is known even in the palace of the tetrarch of Galilee: Antipas, a son of Herod the Great; out of habit, the people continue to call this Herod "king."

6:17-29 See note on Mt 14:1-12.

6:30 *Apostles:* this word occurs in Mark only here; it is also found in some manuscripts in Mk 3:14. The apostles were authorized representatives of Jesus, and in this sense it is used in the New Testament of the Twelve (Mk 3:14) and also of Paul (Rom 1:1). In a broader sense it is applied to a larger group including Barnabas (Acts 14:14), James, "brother of the Lord" (Gal 1:19), and possibly Andronicus and Junia (Rom 16:7). See also note on Mk 3:13-19.

6:35-44 See notes on Mt 14:13-21; 14:19; and 14:21.

6:37 *Two hundred denarii:* two hundred days' wages, for a day's wage was one denarius (see Mt 20:2).

6:43 The Jews regarded bread as a gift of God. Accordingly, the scraps that fell during a meal were to be picked up and placed in small wicker baskets that people carried about. The disciples each filled a basket.

6:45-52 See notes on Mt 14:22-33 and 14:25.

6:50 *It is I:* literally, "I am," the formula that reveals the name of the Lord in the Old Testament (see Ex 3:14; Isa 41:4, 10, 14; 43:1-3, 10, 13). Hence, the evangelist is alluding to Jesus as the Son of God.

6:53-56 The verses describe the responses of Jesus to the crowd's interest in him; they believe in his power to alleviate their sufferings.

7:1-13 Jesus reproaches the teachers, who insist upon "traditions" that they themselves have sometimes invented, with a legalism that allows them to have a good conscience, even as they disregard the essential demands of the Law (Ex 20:12; 21:17; Lev 20:9; Isa 29:13). See also note on Mt 15:2ff.

7:4 Moses had prescribed a few ablutions for priests when they prepared for service at the altar (Ex 30:17-21). However, Rabbinic tradition had gone beyond the spirit of this prescription and arbitrarily extended it. Jesus condemns this Pharisaic formalism and censures his opponents who out of love for their traditions had nullified the more important commandments of the Law. His disciples—like the great majority of the common people—paid little attention to these prescriptions of the Pharisees. *And tables:* found only in some early manuscripts.

7:8 *The commandment of God . . . the traditions of men:* Jesus makes a clear contrast between the two. The commandment of God is found in Scripture and is binding; the traditions of men (also known as the tradition of the elders: v. 3) are not found in Scripture and are not binding.

7:11 *Corban:* an Aramaic word meaning "offered to God."

7:14-23 Jesus settles the question of clean and unclean foods that was erecting a barrier between Jews and pagans and was troubling Jews who had converted to Christianity (see Acts 10:11, 15; Rom 14:14-23; 1 Tim 4:3-4; Tit 1:15). See also note on Mt 15:10-20.

7:16 This verse is lacking in some of the most ancient manuscripts; it was probably added here from Mk 4:9 or 4:23.

7:24-30 See notes on Mt 15:21-28 and 15:21-22.

7:31-37 The miracle of the deaf mute is omitted by the other evangelists. This man may also have been a pagan, for the population of the Decapolis was mostly pagan. The various gestures that Jesus performs on the man had the sole purpose of strengthening his faith. Mark might have recounted them in detail to foreshadow the future Christian Sacraments.

8:1-10 See note on Mt 15:29-39.

8:10 *Dalmanutha:* location unknown.

8:11-13 See note on Mt 16:1-4.

8:14-21 See note on Mt 16:5-12.

8:22-26 Jesus' actions and the healing of the blind man seem to have the same purpose as his actions and the healing of the deaf mute (see Mk 7:3-37). Some scholars regard both healings as a means of expressing the gradual enlightenment of the disciples about Jesus' Messiahship.

8:27-30 Many scholars believe that Peter's confession of Jesus' Messiahship constitutes the central point of this Gospel. It is the decisive doctrinal turning point in which we have the end of the Messianic Secret. Up to this point Jesus demanded the greatest secrecy about the mystery of his person. Henceforth, Jesus utters repeated exhortations concerning the following of the Messiah.

The apostles had recognized the Messiah through Peter's confession in spite of the humble and insignificant appearances of their Master's public activity. Now they must cling with faith to the suffering Messiah and accept the scandal of the cross.

8:31—16:8 Where are we to find the revelation that God wants to communicate to humanity? We must look to the cross, understand and share the condition of Jesus, and answer the call that he gives us to follow him. It is a suffering and humiliated Christ who saves the human race. Of this Mark is certain.

8:31—10:52 It is with full awareness and deliberation that Jesus sets out toward the fulfillment of his mission. He speaks on three occasions of the way of suffering and humiliation that he sees opening before him, and on all three occasions he encounters closed minds.

8:31-33 See notes on Mt 16:21 and 16:22-23.

8:31 *The elders, the chief priests, and the scribes:* the members of the Sanhedrin.

8:34—9:1 See note on Mt 16:25.

8:35-37 The Greek word for "life" can also mean "soul." "Life" is used in a double sense—earthly life and eternal life.

9:1 *Come with power:* the reference is to the new age of humanity that begins with the death of Jesus.

9:2-8 See notes on Mt 17:1-8 and 17:1.

9:9-13 See note on Mt 17:9-13.

9:14-29 See note on Mt 17:14-21.

9:29 Other ancient manuscripts omit: "and by fasting."

9:30-32 Mark very effectively alternates the glorious and suffering aspects of the Messiah, following up the most spectacular exorcism in the Gospel with Jesus' second prediction of his Passion. He also implies that the initiative for the death of the Servant (see Isa 53) belongs to God.

9:31 *Son of Man:* see note on Mt 8:20.

9:33-37 This incident and the sayings that follow it are most likely intended to be a commentary on the lack of understanding exhibited by the disciples. They are to serve the poor and lowly. Jesus used children as the symbol for the *anawim*, the poor in spirit, i.e., the lowly in the Christian community.

9:38-41 *Not one of us:* though the man was not one of the Twelve, he was a believer in Jesus and acted in his name. Therefore, Jesus counsels the Twelve that they should not oppose him.

9:42-47 See note on Mt 18:5-11.

9:43 *Cut it off:* Jesus is here using hyperbole, a figure of speech that exaggerates to make a point. He means that sometimes sin can be overcome only by taking drastic action. *Gehenna:* the name, from the Hebrew *Ge Hinnon,* of a small valley southwest of Jerusalem; it was a popular image for hell because of the refuse that was continually burned there.

9:44, 46 These verses are omitted in the best manuscripts; they are repetitions of v. 48 (see Isa 66:24).

9:49 This somewhat obscure verse was perhaps introduced because of the reference to fire in v. 48. Fire signifies the testing that precedes God's judgment (see 1 Cor 3:13-15). Salt, a symbol of fidelity, was sprinkled on sacrificial victims so that they might be pleasing to God (Lev 2:13). When the testing is endured with fidelity, it makes the believer acceptable to God.

10:1-12 Divorce was practiced by permission of the Mosaic Law (Deut 24:1). But a permission supposes a weakness; it does not represent the law that gives life. From the beginning, God willed the unity of the couple in marriage (see Gen 1:27 and 2:24). Jesus recalls this requirement and shows, too, that the Scriptures ought to be interpreted in light of the fundamental perspectives of God's plan and not on the basis of the changeable desires and needs of human beings.

10:1 *Region of Judea beyond the Jordan:* Judea was the southern part of Palestine, which had formerly been the southern kingdom. Jesus went south from Capernaum over the mountains of Samaria into Judea and then east across the Jordan to Perea, the territory of Herod Antipas.

10:13-16 This episode is common to the Synoptics, but Mark alone recounts the human traits of the divine Master, such as his indignation at the disciples' hindering action and his affectionate attitude in embracing the children.

10:17-27 See note on Mt 19:16-26.

10:28-31 See note on Mt 19:27-30.

10:32-34 See note on Mt 20:17-19. *Gentiles, who will . . . put him to death:* the predictions of the Passion in Mark's Gospel do not mention the word "crucified." However, crucifixion is implied by the fact that he was to be handed over to the Gentiles to be killed, since this was the customary Roman means of executing non-Romans.

10:35-45 What was Christ's own understanding of his life, of the kingdom, of what it meant to be a disciple? An answer is given in this decisive passage (see vv. 42-45). So important are these verses that Luke points up their essential context by placing them in the account of the Supper (Lk 22:24-27) and John in the explanation of the washing of the feet (Jn 13:12-17). The kingdom of God has nothing to do with ambitions for political or social power; true greatness is found not in prestige or rule but only in service.

10:38 *Drink the cup that I drink:* a Hebraism for sharing someone's fate. In the Old Testament, the "cup of wine" was a metaphor for God's wrath against sin and rebellion (Ps 75:9; Isa 51:17-23; Jer 25:15-28; 49:12; 51:7). Thus, the cup Jesus had to drink refers to the punishment of sins that he bore in place of all human beings (see Mk 10:45; 14:36). *Baptism:* an image of Jesus' suffering and death.

10:46-52 This healing is the last miracle of Jesus in Mark's Gospel.

10:46 *Son of Timaeus* is the meaning of *Bartimaeus* in Aramaic.

10:51 *Rabbi:* means "master" (see Jn 20:16; Mt 23:7).

11:1—12:16 We are at Jerusalem, where the decisive action takes place. Jesus' confrontation with the established religion takes on an irremediable character. Mark groups together in three days the events that consummate the break and thus open the way of faith in Christ to the whole world. The time of Israel is ended. The presence of Jesus in the Holy City and in the temple is like a visit from God, a fulfillment, and a judgment.

11:1-11 The simplicity of the event and the modest mount ridden by Jesus (see Zec 9:9) suggest that "the coming kingdom" (v. 10) will not bring a political restoration and that the Messiah was not to be a national hero. See also note on Mt 21:1-11.

11:9 *Hosanna:* an acclamation meaning "Grant salvation!" The citation is from Ps 118:25.

11:12-14 The Prophets used the image of a fig tree with respect to Israel (see Jer 8:13; 29:17; Joel 1:7; Hos 9:10, 16). Jesus' cursing of the fig tree is regarded as a parable in action representing a judgment on Israel's barrenness and Jerusalem's rejection of Jesus' teaching (see Isa 34:4; Hos 2:14; Lk 13:6-9).

11:15-19 During his trial Jesus will be accused of having tried to set up a new temple (Mk 14:58; 15:29).

11:17 The first part of the citation is from Isa 56:7. Only Mark has reported to us the expression *for all the nations.* Thus, the gesture of Jesus takes on a Messianic meaning, alluding to the conversion of the Gentiles. *Den of thieves:* see Jer 7:11.

11:20-26 See note on Mt 21:18-22.

11:26 This verse is found only in some manuscripts; it was probably added from Mt 6:15.

11:27-33 The increasing hostility toward Jesus arose from the chief priests, scribes, and elders (v. 27) as well as the Herodians and Pharisees (Mk 12:13) and the Sadducees (Mk 12:18). They rejected the messengers sent by God—John the Baptist and Jesus—and so incurred the judgment alluded to in these verses and confirmed by the parable of the tenants (Mk 12:1-12).

12:1-12 This parable was probably inspired by the peasant rebellions of the period. The parable would have an immediate impact on Jewish hearers, who were well acquainted with the "Song of the Vineyard" in Isa 5:1ff. See also note on Mt 21:33-46.

12:13-44 The discussions continue. His opponents seek to have Jesus contradict himself so as to accede to their demands. But the questioners are caught in their own trap. And the masks of their false religion fall away. Who among us has not in some way acted like these scribes, Pharisees, and Sadducees when a decision of faith had to be made!

12:13-17 See note on Mt 22:15-22.

12:15 *Denarius:* the daily wage of a laborer.

12:18-27 To the conservative Sadducees, the resurrection of the dead—asserted toward the end of the Old Testament (see Isa 26:19; 2 Mac 7:9-14,

23-26; 12:43-46; Wis 2:23-24; 3:1-9; Dan 12:2-3)—was an idea to be eliminated by ridicule. They postulate an unlikely application of the law of the levirate, according to which a man must provide a posterity for the widow of his brother, if the latter has died childless. See also note on Mt 22:23-33.

12:28-34 This friendly dialogue between Jesus and a scribe is unique in the Synoptic Gospels. See also note on Mt 22:34-40.

12:28 *First of all the commandments:* among the 613 precepts listed by the teachers of the Law; of these, 365 (as many as the days of the year) were negative, that is, contained prohibitions, and 248 (as many as the parts of the human body were thought to be) were positive.

12:35-37 Every king was an "Anointed" (Messiah or Christ), and Ps 110, which is cited here, is an acclamation addressed to a king. The Israelite tradition was utterly convinced that the Anointed One par excellence would belong to the dynasty of David (2 Sam 7:1-17). Then, too, many psalms, including 110, were attributed to David. Against this background Jesus asks a question based on this psalm, with the intention of carrying the thought a step further: he suggests that the Messiah's origin is mysterious and that his kingship differs from that which his contemporaries await. The early Church will use the same psalm to show that the Resurrection of Jesus is his authentic enthronement as Messiah (see Heb 1:3; 5:6; 6:20; 7:11, 21; 10:12-13).

12:35 The audience of Jesus is not specified here; in Matthew he is speaking to the Pharisees, and in Luke to the scribes.

12:38-40 See notes on Mt 23:1-39.

12:41-44 Jesus praises the offering of the poor widow because she gave more than all the others, although her gift was by far the smallest. She willingly gave out of her poverty (*all that she had to live on*), while the others gave *out of their abundance*. Therefore, she provides a striking contrast to the pride and pretentiousness of the scribes, who were denounced in the previous section.

12:41 *Treasury:* a room with thirteen boxes, near the inner court of the temple, into which women could enter.

12:42 *[She] put in two copper coins, that is, about a penny:* literally, "She put in two *lepta,* which is a fourth of an *as.*" The fact that the poor widow gives two *lepta* shows that she could have given less. A *lepton* was the smallest Greek coin. For his readers' sake, Mark explains the amount in Roman terms ("fourth of an *as,*" a penny).

13:1-37 For over two centuries the Jewish world had been familiar with these strange visions that were meant to explain in advance the events that would occur at the end of the world. The series of pictures describes the unfolding of a catastrophe. These literary pieces were known as "apocalypses," that is, revelations (see Isa 24—27; Ezek 34—36; Dan 7—12; Zec 14:1-20; etc.).

In the present discourse, the longest in Mark's Gospel, Jesus, too, speaks of the final destiny of the human race and borrows from the Jewish apocalypses the somewhat terrifying images that became part of the literary genre of apocalypse as found in the first three Gospels. The discourse is therefore known as "the Synoptic apocalypse." And because it bids us reflect on the ultimate lot of humankind and the world, it is also known as the "eschatological discourse," that is, a discourse about the end.

13:1-2 See note on Mt 24:1-2.

13:3-8 See note on Mt 24:3-14.

13:3 *Peter:* the disciples named were the first to be called (see Mk 1:16-20). In Mark, all of Jesus' teaching is given privately to these four disciples.

13:9-20 See note on Mt 24:15-22.

13:14 *The abomination of desolation* refers, in Dan 11:31; 12:11, and 1 Mac 1:54; 6:7, to the statue of the pagan emperor that was set up in the temple as a symbol of his divinity. Jesus is thus foretelling that this scandalous event will be repeated.

13:21-23 False messiahs who try to lead Christians astray can be resisted by clinging to revealed Truth taught by Christ's Church.

13:24-27 The discourse now takes on clearly cosmic proportions. The upheaval in the elements is described in the customary expressions derived from apocalyptic language. However, the whole passage is centered upon the glorious appearance of the Messiah in his Second Coming. The emphasis is on the joy of the elect at the coming of the Son of Man rather than on their terror over the destruction of the world. See note on Mt 24:29-31.

13:28-31 See note on Mt 23:32-35.

13:30 It was typical of apocalypses that they announced events as if they had to do with the present generation. It was a way of involving the reader, of saying: "This passage has to do with you."

13:32-37 See note on Mt 24:36-42.

14:1—16:8 The Passion Narrative that makes the deepest impression is perhaps that of Mark's Gospel. The writer does not aim to move the reader, still less to satisfy our curiosity with edifying anecdotes and points of information. The description is vivid, unpolished, clear-cut. Mark piles up concrete, detailed incidents in order to highlight the tragic character of the struggle that Jesus is carrying on alone, isolated in his silence and humiliation. It is precisely in his abasement that Jesus shows himself to be the Messiah, the King of Israel, Son of God, and Savior of the world.

14:1-2 We are at the religious high point of the year, the time of Passover, which is followed by the feast of Unleavened Bread, that is, an eight-day celebration during which only unleavened bread was eaten (see Deut 16:1-8; Ex 12:5-20).

14:3-9 At this period the burial of the dead was regarded as an indispensable work of charity and of greater merit than almsgiving. In the present circumstances of Jesus, the woman's gesture of respect becomes a sign of his imminent death. In addition, in Mark's Gospel the ointment is poured on the head of Jesus, suggesting an act of consecration.

14:5 *Three hundred denarii:* a year's wages, a denarius being a day's wages for a laborer.

14:10-11 See note on Mt 26:14-16.

14:12-16 See notes on Mt 26:17-19 and 26:17.

14:17-21 See note on Mt 26:20-25.

14:22-25 Four accounts of the Lord's Supper are found in the New Testament (Mt 26:26-28; Mk 14:22-24; Lk 22:19-20; and 1 Cor 11:23-25). Matthew and Mark are similar to one another while Luke and Paul are also similar to each other. All four accounts include (1) the taking of the bread; (2) the thanksgiving or blessing; (3) the breaking of the bread; (4) the saying, "This is my body"; (5) the taking of the cup; and (6) the explanation of the relation of blood to the Covenant. Only Luke and Paul record the command to continue to celebrate the Supper, "Do this in memory of me" (Lk 22:19; 1 Cor 11:24).

In giving his body and blood Jesus anticipates the action of his enemies, and his death becomes an offering to God, the sacrifice of the Servant who expiates the sin of the entire people (Isa 53). By this act he establishes the New Covenant; it inaugurates a new relationship between God and humanity.

14:27-31 Despite the protestations of the Twelve that they will never abandon him, Jesus predicts that they will do so. But he also reassures them that after his Resurrection he will see them again in Galilee (Mk 16:7; see Mt 26:32; 28:7, 10, 16; Jn 21) where he first called them (Mk 1:14-20).

14:32-42 See note on Mt 26:36-46.

14:43-52 See notes on Mt 26:47-56 and 26:47-48.

14:51-52 This detail is only in Mark. Many commentators have considered the young man to be Mark himself.

14:53-65 See note on Mt 26:57-68.

14:55 *Sanhedrin:* the highest tribunal of the Jews. In New Testament times, it numbered 71 members: chief priests, elders, and scribes, plus the high priest who presided over the proceedings. The Romans gave the tribunal much authority but not over capital punishment (see Jn 18:31). See also note on Mt 27:1-2.

14:61-65 Just when he is being judged and abased, Jesus for the first time openly declares himself to be the Messiah, of royal descent and divine rank (Ps 110:1; Dan 7:13).

The Jewish authorities are scandalized and condemn him. He then suffers the harsh lot of the Servant prophet.

14:61 *Son of the Blessed One:* in late Judaism people avoided uttering the name of God, as a sign of respect; they preferred other expressions such as "the Blessed One" or "the Power" (v. 62).

14:66-72 See note on Mt 26:69-75.

14:68 *Then the cock crowed:* these words are found in most manuscripts but omitted in some.

15:1-5 See notes on Mt 27:11-26 and 27:11.

15:6 Outside the Gospels no such Passover privilege is explicitly found in other sources. However, this does not mean it didn't exist.

15:9 According to Mark, Barabbas had been arrested in a rebellion, possibly in a political rebellion against the Romans. Thus, he was a hero with the people and fed their national pride. When Herod brings forth Jesus as the King of the Jews, the same people will have none of it—a Messiah reduced to a pitiful state, chained, and despised!

15:16-20 See note on Mt 27:27-31.

15:21 Those condemned to death were usually forced to carry the crossbeam of the cross, often 30 to 40 pounds, to the place of crucifixion. Jesus starts out by doing the same (see Jn 19:7), but he is so weak as a result of his scourging and overall ill-treatment that the soldiers decide to have someone else take over that task. The man chosen is Simon, a man from Cyrene, an important city of Libya, North Africa, with a large Jewish population, who is probably in Jerusalem for the Passover celebration. *Alexander and Rufus:* the sons are named probably because they were known to the early Christians to whom Mark's Gospel is addressed.

15:24 See note on Mt 27:35.

15:25 Mark sketches the Passion in a quasi-liturgical fashion and as it were in thirds: the coming together of the Sanhedrin at the first hour (6 A.M.); cruci-fixion at the third hour (9 A.M.); darkness at the sixth hour (12 P.M.); and death at the ninth hour (3 P.M.). The "third hour," however, must be taken in a wide sense, between 9 A.M. and 12 P.M., for Jesus was crucified at 12 P.M. (see Jn 19:14). See also note on Mt 27:35.

15:28 This verse is omitted by the best manuscripts.

15:33-41 After hours on the cross, there comes a final humiliation (v. 36). While God remains silent, the crucified Jesus cries out his aloneness in the words of Ps 22:2, and breathes his last. But the work of Jesus has been completed. The end of Judaism has come, signified by the tearing of the curtain of the temple. Even now a pagan recognizes Jesus as the Son of God; this is the first time in Mark's Gospel that a human being is allowed to give him this title.

15:40 *James the younger:* this James is known as "the Lesser," to distinguish him from the other apostle of the same name, the son of Zebedee and brother of John. From Mt 27:56 we know that Salome was the wife of Zebedee.

15:42-47 The burial of Jesus is arranged by Joseph of Arimathea, a respected member of the Sanhedrin who had not consented to the decision of that body con-cerning Jesus (see Lk 23:51). Matthew calls Joseph a "rich man" (Mt 27:57), which recalls the text of Isaiah's prophecy about the Suffering Servant (53:9: "They assigned him a grave with the wicked and a burial place with evil doers").

16:1-8 What has happened so surprises the women that they do not take the trouble to spread the message of joy. The Gospel of Mark ends on this fascinat-ing note of mystery.

The scene at the tomb is not meant as a proof of the resurrection but as a proclamation of it; we are told that Jesus' destiny has been accomplished; the reality of his person is now fully revealed, and the order is given to announce that the crucified one is risen. See also the note on Mt 28:1-10.

16:1 The Sabbath is over; the time therefore is after sunset. The duty of the Sabbath rest ended at sunset.

16:9-20 *The Longer Ending:* this passage is found in the great majority of manuscripts. It has traditionally been accepted as a canonical part of the Gospel and was defined as such by the Council of Trent. Although it is cited by the Fathers of the Church as early as the 2nd century, its vocabulary and style point to someone other than Mark as the author. It is a summary of the material con-cerning the appearances of the risen Lord and reflects traditions found in Luke (ch. 24) and John (ch. 20).

It is probable that first-generation Christians wanted to complete Mark's work with a summary of the Resurrection stories and a summary view of the Church's mission. The Lord, who has been restored to his divine glory with the Father, is present and at work in the missionary activity of his disciples; this fact is highlighted in a wonderful sentence that is found only here in the New Testament.

The Shorter Ending: this passage is found in four late Greek manuscripts after v. 8 before the Longer Ending. It is thought to have originated to provide an ending in itself or to give a smoother transition between v. 8 and v. 9.

The Freer Logion: this passage is found in one manuscript, preserved in the Freer Gallery of Art in Washington, DC, and was known to St. Jerome in the 4th century. It is regarded as an interpolation to soften the condemnation of the disciples in v. 14.

THE GOSPEL ACCORDING TO LUKE

1:1-4 Like the Greek historians of his time, Luke begins his book with a prologue. He dedicates the work to a distinguished person, Theophilus (otherwise unknown to us), who has already been taught the good news. Some scholars believe that the name is symbolic for it means "lover of God," hence all Christians.

1:5—2:52 The Gospel is first and foremost a proclamation of what Jesus did and taught and, above all, of his Death and Resurrection for the salvation of humankind; everything that the preachers of the mission and message of Jesus proclaimed led toward the mystery of Easter. But, like Matthew, Luke decided to preface all that with a description of the period preceding the public appearance of Jesus, because the Church wanted to know the mystery of Jesus back to its very beginnings.

The events described by Matthew, however, are not focused on the birth, which is recounted for us through the experiences of Joseph; Luke speaks directly of the birth through the experience of Mary. Regarding Mary, the opening pages of the third Gospel have provided the Church down the centuries with an abundant, and still flowing, wellspring for its faith (Marian teachings), its devotion (the "Hail, Mary"), and its art.

Some points emerge with utter clarity: Mary is the Mother of Jesus; the birth took place at Bethlehem; and the newborn child was placed in a manger. The primary statement made is undoubtedly this: that Jesus was born not by the will of human beings but by the initiative of God, and that he was born of a virgin mother.

1:5-25 The time is toward the end of the reign of Herod the Great (37–4 B.C.). A faithful and devout couple have been praying for the salvation of the people (v. 13). The husband belonged to the eighth class of priests (1 Chr 24:10) and had the joy of entering every so often into the sanctuary. In the midst of the service, an angel—Gabriel, the messenger of the time of salvation (Dan 9:21-27)—appears to him and tells him of an unexpected birth. Like Isaac (Gen 21:2), Samson (Jdg 13:3-7), and Samuel (1 Sam 1), this child will be the result of a miracle, and, even before his birth, he is destined for the service of God; he will live as an ascetic, a "Nazirite" (see Num 6:3-4; Jdg 13:4-5); he will be the mysterious forerunner of the last times, the new Elijah whom the people expected in accordance with an old tradition (Mal 3:23-24). His name will be John, which means: "The Lord is gracious."

1:5 *Judea:* meant here is the entire territory of Palestine.

1:9 Incense was offered in the Holy Place, the room in front of the Holy of Holies or innermost part of the temple. The rite of incense was performed morning and evening at the time of sacrifice.

1:25 *The humiliation I have endured among my people:* lack of children deprived the parents of personal happiness but also brought about social reproach (see Gen 16:2—Sarai; 25:21—Rebekah; 30:23—Rachel; 1 Sam 1:1-18—Hannah; see also Lev 20:20-21; Ps 128:3; Jer 22:30).

1:26-38 Mary, a young girl, is betrothed, despite the fact that she has the unusual intention of remaining a virgin; "betrothed": that is, according to the custom of the time, she was legally married but did not yet live with her husband. Confronted with this surprising message, she gives no sign of fear or doubt: she reflects, meditates, believes. This woman has the "grace," that is, the favor of God; she is greeted as if Messianic joy were being proclaimed to the Daughter of Zion, the new Jerusalem (see Zep 3:14; Zec 9:9).

The Bible has often spoken of promised sons; but this Jesus is the very Messiah of Israel, according to the mysterious prophecy of Isaiah on which Israel constantly and hopefully meditated (vv. 32-33; see Isa 7:14; 9:6); he is even far more: the Son of God (v. 35). The body of Jesus was to take form in the flesh of Mary, and this was to come about not through human planning but through the presence and action of God himself (see Ex 40:34-35; Num 9:15; 10:34), of the Spirit who creates and gives life (Gen 1:2; Ps 104:30; Isa 11:1-6).

1:26 *In the sixth month:* i.e., after the time of John's conception.

1:27 *Virgin:* i.e., one who had not yet had sexual relations. Mary's question in v. 34 and the reference in v. 27 that she was "betrothed" (pledged to be married) clearly make this point. Mary had just entered her teens, for betrothal usually took place after puberty, but intercourse was not allowed until marriage. The betrothal could be severed only by divorce or death.

1:28 *Hail, full of grace:* this phrase may also be translated as "Hail, O highly favored one." *The Lord is with you:* other ancient manuscripts add: "Blessed are you among women" (as in Lk 1:42).

1:34 *I am a virgin:* literally, "I do not know man," "know" referring to the conjugal relationship.

1:36-37 In confirmation of what the angel has said to her, Mary is given word of the pregnancy of her aged relative Elizabeth. God has effected a pregnancy for a woman past childbearing years. Thus, he can effect a pregnancy for Mary also, because nothing is impossible for him.

1:39-45 By the account of the Visitation, Luke establishes the connection between the traditions about John and those about Jesus. At first commonplace, this meeting of two expectant mothers goes beyond the ordinary. As conscious believers, enlightened by the Holy Spirit, they understand that the time of salvation is inaugurated by the young lives they bear within themselves. We are already made aware that John bears witness to Jesus. And the first Christian generations place on the lips of Elizabeth the praise of Mary the believer.

1:39 *A town of Judah:* according to tradition, this was Ain Karim, 100 miles south of Nazareth and four miles west of Jerusalem.

1:46-55 Mary's splendid canticle, the *Magnificat,* proclaims a new course for history, the end of injustice, and the birth of a new world, that of the kingdom, in which everything is different from our habitual experience. Every people gives thanks to God; the joy of the poor bursts forth; hope is born for the salvation of the despised of this world.

The *Magnificat,* which is very similar to the canticle of Hannah (see 1 Sam 2:1-10) and has become the Christian song of thanksgiving, lends itself to be the prayer of those who have suffered but have never lost their hope in God. The entire prayer of the Old Testament converges upon this one, but with a wholly renewed power; it is easy to see why the Church never tires of reciting it. It is one of the gems of the Church's daily office of Evening Prayer (Vespers).

1:67-79 The hour of light has come, and the Messiah is the star that rises (v. 78; see Num 24:17; Isa 60:1; Mal 3:20) or, again, the branch that springs from David (Jer 23:5; 33:15; Zec 3:8; 6:12). The Canticle of Zechariah, the Benedictus, rings out daily in the liturgical office of Morning Prayer (Lauds). The whole faith of the Old Testament is woven into its proclamation of peace, that is, fulfillment and joy for humanity, as a gift from God.

2:1-21 The Gospel of Jesus' birth is perhaps the best known passage of the Bible.

The birth of Jesus is described both as parallel to and in contrast with the birth of John. For lack of room in the inn, the young mother looks to a stable for an unobtrusive retreat in which to give birth to her son. Beginning in the 2nd century, the place was said to be a cave close to Bethlehem. She had a manger in which to lay the child.

Apart from Mary and Joseph, there were no relatives or friends present to welcome this child: only a few shepherds, people who lived on the margins of society and whose trade was at that time severely criticized and despised by the teachers of the Law.

The passage is full of grand ideas about faith; we may say also that it is rich in theology. The birth is described as the coming of the Messianic child. We are in Bethlehem, the native city of David who founded a royal and Messianic dynasty and who marked, as it were, a new beginning (1 Sam 16:1f; Mic 5:1). God bursts into the midst of the poor, proclaiming joy and peace for the whole world.

The event went unnoticed by the chroniclers of the age, and yet it changed the destiny of the human race. In order to bring out its universal significance, Luke locates it in relation to the history of the world: Herod the Great (37-4 B.C.) is still in power; Augustus (29 B.C.–A.D.14) has imposed Roman rule on the entire Mediterranean world, "the entire world" (Greek: *oikumenē*) known at the time (v. 1). But the general census that Augustus has ordered is the instrument of providence for fulfilling the prophecies, since it leads to Mary's journey from Nazareth to Bethlehem (v. 4).

A 6th-century monk, Dionysius Exiguus ("Little Denis"), wanted to mark the beginning of the Christian year, but he miscalculated and dated the birth of Jesus as occurring in the year A.D. 754 from the foundation of Rome (instead of 6–7 years earlier). But the mistake is of little importance, for Dionysius' insight was correct: this event, more than any other, deserves to date the history of humanity, for it is the hinge on which all of history turns.

2:2 *Quirinius:* Publius Quirinius, legate of Syria, conducted a census of Palestine in A.D. 6, ten years after the death of Herod the Great. The information we have does not allow us to decide whether Luke is referring to this census or to another.

2:7 *Manger:* the legend of the ass and the cattle at the manger was perhaps suggested by Isa 1:3.

2:14 *On whom his favor rests:* some read "to men of goodwill," but it seems better not to contrast God's peace and human goodwill.

2:21-40 This section describes the Jewish rites associated with a birth. In addition to circumcision, forty days after the birth Jewish parents celebrated the rites of purification and ransoming, which in the context of the ancient religion represented a respect for life and a sense of the sacred (see Ex 13:2; Lev 12:2-8; Num 18:15-16). This child, who is bought back with the offering of the poor, is the Messiah and has come to carry out the mission entrusted to the Servant as foretold in the great prophetic songs of Isaiah (42:6; 49:6; 52:10): to save all of humankind, to bring light to all peoples.

Some hearts are already drawn by the joyous conviction that the prophecies are fulfilled, and the hymn of the elderly prophet Simeon is, despite its brevity, among the richest of Christian canticles. But who can recognize the mission of the Messiah unless they accept the light of God? That mission elicits hostility; and Mary will experience the repercussions of the Savior's painful lot, because faith in the Savior will bring to light the deep religion of hearts and put an end to the legalism of Judaism.

2:41-50 In the village where Jesus spends his apprenticeship as a human being and grows "in wisdom and in age and in grace with God and men" (v. 52), this favor of God did not prevent him from sharing the life lived by everyone else. Then a significant event interrupted the course of everyday life.

Jesus had reached the age when a Jewish boy had completed his religious instruction and was beginning to observe the precepts of the Law; he was recognized as religiously mature. Therefore, he joined his parents in the pilgrimage to Jerusalem.

In this passage we find him in the temple in open discussion with those charged with teaching the Law. What he has to say reveals an extraordinary religious vision. In acting as he does, he claims a freedom that surprises his parents.

Thus, at his first encounter with Judaism and its religious center, at the moment when he speaks for the first time, Jesus declares himself Son of God and is aware of his own mystery and of his mission. That is what Luke wants to bring out in this story.

Mary and Joseph are now informed of the boy's uncommon destiny, but the unexpected thunderbolt of Jesus' statement confuses them; it utters a mystery that is beyond them.

The Lord is not done with surprising even believers, indeed believers first of all! There are days when we must draw inspiration from the attitude of Mary as she meditates on what God has done.

3:1—4:13 The word of God finds expression in the history of humankind. By listing the many temporal rulers and religious authorities, Luke enables us to date John's activity as occurring between the fall of A.D. 27 and Passover of 28. But he also wants to contrast these earthly rulers and religious authorities with the sovereignty and authority of Jesus. The deeper movement of history does not take place at the level of official appearances; in fact, it is Jesus who is fulfilling the destiny of the world by giving history its true meaning.

Luke sums up in a single passage all the information that he intends to offer on the work of John. More than the other evangelists, he stresses the point that salvation is offered to everyone; in his citation of Isaiah he highlights the final verse, thereby underscoring the thought that the new age is meant for the authentic children of Abraham and not solely for the chosen people. At the end of the passage he immediately jumps ahead to the imprisonment of John, of which Mark and Matthew speak at a later point and at greater length (Mt 14:1-12; Mk 6:14-29). His intention is to make a clear distinction between the Jesus movement and the Johannine movement: when the time of Christ begins, that of John, the forerunner, is finished.

3:1 *Lysanias:* an unknown governor. *Abilene:* a region northeast of Damascus.

3:2 *Caiaphas* was the current high priest (A.D. 18–36). Annas, that is, Ananiah, had preceded him from 5 B.C. to A.D. 15. He is named here because he still exercised considerable influence.

3:20 John's imprisonment occurred sometime after the beginning of Jesus' ministry (see Jn 3.22-24). Luke mentions it here to bring his section on John's ministry to a conclusion before starting his account of that of Jesus (see also Mt 4:12; Mk 1:14). Later he alludes to John's death (Lk 9:7-9). See also note on Mk 1:14.

3:21-22 Jesus here shows himself to be in solidarity with sinners by receiving the bath of repentance. But a unique event also takes place: The Messiah receives his investiture from heaven. The Holy Spirit will be present in him (see Isa 11:2); over him are pronounced the words used in consecrating kings (Ps 2:7), but here they attest that he is the Son of God in a sense hitherto unsuspected (see Lk 1:35).

3:23-38 Luke gives a genealogy that is meant not as a historical document but as the assertion of a legal status. Jesus is linked to Joseph, even though it was known that the link was not one of blood; the reason for doing so is that at that time only men and not women had rights. The genealogy then moves back to David, without following the line of kings. From that point it continues again, not only as far as Abraham, but—and this is the chief novelty of the passage—as far as Adam, who comes from the hand of God. Luke's intention is to stress the point that Jesus belongs not only to the chosen people but to the entire human race, which he has come to save.

Whereas Matthew specifically mentions three groups of 14 generations, Luke lists 77 names, according to a scheme of sevens. From the beginning of the human race until Jesus there are eleven series of seven (11 x 7). Jesus comes as Messiah in the eschatological stage of history (see 4 Esdras 14:11).

3:23ff. It may be helpful to record another interpretation of the difference between this genealogy and that of Matthew: in virtue of the law of the levirate, Joseph (it is said) had two fathers, one biological (Jacob), the other legal (Heli); thus two different lists are used as far back as Shealtiel.

4:1-13 By means of images, we are shown the drama Jesus experienced in his conscience, his struggle to follow with determination the great options of his existence. He knows the temptations for immediate success, domination, and prestige, the temptations to which Israel succumbed during its sojourn in the desert and that remain the lot of the Church, every believer, and every person. Jesus refuses to use his powers for his own benefit but accepts poverty and destitution; he does not seek the glory of a political Messiah and does not yield to the idols of power. He turns away from the seduction of prestige; when he goes to Jerusalem it will not be to mount the pinnacle of the temple but to carry the supreme trial of the cross.

There is, in this choice without compromise, a radical recognition of God and the true values he is forever giving us to reflect upon. The victory of Christ over the forces of evil foreshadows the power of his mission (see Lk 10:18; 11:22; 12:16), which is achieved through patience on the cross and the triumph of the Resurrection after the final attacks of the spirit of evil (see Lk 22:3, 53). To live with Christ is to accept this struggle humbly and resolutely.

4:14—9:50 The Gospel does not try to reconstitute an exact chronology and geography of the life of Christ. Its intention is to present to us the sayings and actions of the Lord, to arouse and renew our faith in him, and to make us grasp the essential requirements of our existence. As in Matthew and Mark, the first stage of Jesus' mission, which takes place in Galilee, leads to the recognition of Jesus as it moves from the first question about him to the profession of faith.

4:16-21 By reading his own vocation and mission in the great passage from Isaiah (61:1), Jesus will direct the thinking of the Church and every apostle: God's work is to proclaim salvation to the poor and the oppressed.

4:23 *Hometown:* i.e., Nazareth, where Jesus was brought up. *Capernaum:* see notes on Mt 4:12-17; 4:12; and 4:13.

4:25-27 These verses illustrate the theme of universal salvation, so dear to Luke, with allusions to the miracles of Elijah and Elisha (1 Ki 17; 2 Ki 5).

4:28 The words of Jesus hinted at the rejection of the people of Israel and the election of the Gentiles. The people of Nazareth become infuriated, but Jesus escapes their fury in a mysterious manner.

4:31-41 In the Gospel, the accounts of miracles are intended to attest, first of all, that God the Savior is present for people in Jesus Christ. There is a sensible and visible evil in the sickness, wherein we see hostile forces at work. Christ brings healing; he changes the condition of human beings and saves them from alienation. Demons are sharper than humans in penetrating the divine powers of him who frees humans from the grip of death. However, Jesus reduces them to silence, because he does not want people to regard him as a triumphant liberator but to discover, in his words and actions as man amidst his human brothers and sisters, the true visage of the Messiah, Son of God.

4:34 See note on Mk 1:24.

4:42-44 The good news of the kingdom, this announcement of the coming of God (Lk 4:18; 6:20-28), must reach all human beings.

5:1-11 This passage demonstrates the art of the writer. Luke inserts the call of the first disciples into a context of preaching and performing mighty deeds. He slightly weakens the abrupt character that the event retains in Mark (1:16-18) and gives a greater human plausibility to the response of these men. But he stresses just as much the demands of the apostolic task. Trying to draw people away from the evils that assail them entails many difficulties. God requires humans to participate in this endeavor and to carry out their missionary work as a team in which all must share the pain. In this passage, Peter already occupies a representative place. Nonetheless, upon meeting Christ he discovers how much he himself is the victim of evil and sin. Jesus expects those who are his to be totally committed to the Word and, if necessary, to renounce their profession, their situation, and their security.

5:12-16 When duly confirmed as the Law requires (see Lev 14:2-3), the cure of a leper will attest to the priests the power of Jesus over an evil that destroys humans.

5:17-26 The description of the miracle worked for the paralyzed man is vivid, as in Matthew and Mark, even if, in order to make it more intelligible to his readers, Luke speaks simply of a roof instead of a Palestinian roof-terrace.

5:27-32 No one could be regarded as more of a sinner in the time of Jesus than the tax collectors (also translated as "publicans") sitting at their customs post. Christ, more than once, created a scandal in the eyes of right-thinking people, who were quick to distinguish between the righteous and sinners. The Church recalls these occasions to keep herself from becoming a closed sect. The lesson is still valid today: to refuse to associate with others because we have catalogued them as sinners and because we consider ourselves to be in the ranks of the righteous is opposed to the Gospel. We must all regard ourselves as sinners and rejoice over the salvation that Jesus offers everyone. Moreover, only those receive salvation who loyally acknowledge the need of being saved.

5:27-28 See notes on Mt 5:46 and Mk 2:14.

5:30 *Sinners:* see note on Mk 2:15.

5:33-39 For the moment, Jesus refuses to impose on his disciples the ascetic and devout practices of Judaism. (See note on Mk 2:20.) The Messiah is here—it is a time of joy. God, so to speak, becomes the Spouse of all people. The three Synoptic Gospels add other sentences, which underline the newness of the Gospel. It is not a rearrangement of ancient law and doctrines; the New Covenant requires a new mentality and a new openness.

The last verse, proper to Luke, alludes to the refusal to accept the Gospel on the part of the teachers of the law. They rejected the wonderful newness of the Gospel and were content with the teachings to which they were accustomed.

6:1-11 In resisting servitude to traditions, Jesus gives the example of the freedom David showed in face of the Law (see 1 Sam 21:2-7); in his act of healing

Jesus recalls the true meaning of the Sabbath. See notes on Mt 12:1-14; 12:2; 12:3-4; 12:5-6; 12:8; 12:9-14.

6:5 *Son of Man:* see note on Mt 8:20.

6:12-16 This is an important moment in Luke's eyes, as shown by the fact that Jesus prepares himself through prayer. The apostles are twelve in number in order to make clear their future work, which is comparable to that of the twelve tribes of Israel: that is, they are the builders of the new People of God (see Acts 1:25). The word "apostle" is derived from a Greek word meaning "sent," "missionary."

6:17-19 The picture of the crowds pressing upon Jesus shows the hope raised by Jesus from the very beginning of his public ministry. People came to him from everywhere, even from the nearby pagan towns, to obtain healing. Jesus came among us as the sign of salvation and the act by which God delivered it to us. When giving the Beatitudes in the Sermon on the Plain, he will announce the true salvation.

6:20-49 The remainder of ch. 6 corresponds to the "Sermon on the Mount," which the Gospel of Matthew places at the beginning of Jesus' activity (Mt 5–7). Luke offers a more concise and less solemn text. His readers have little knowledge of Jewish life; it was therefore pointless to contrast the old Law with the demands of the Gospel. The latter are stated in a more absolute manner. Matthew describes the interior attitude, the disposition of heart, without which no one can enter the kingdom of God. Luke prefers to evoke a more concrete and living tone. He underlines with special insistence the deportment in regard to riches; this is the test of entrance into the kingdom.

6:20-26 The Beatitudes of the Gospel of Matthew bring forth an unexpected message (Mt 5:3-12). The short sentences in which Luke opposes the blessedness and woe of people reach us in an even more powerful manner. The Old Testament loved such contrasting formulas, but here the reader is directly challenged: "you." In announcing the kingdom Jesus overturns the system of values on which we base our lives, relations, judgments, and actions. He denounces as false our more recurrent ideas. More than once, Luke underlines God's predilection for the most deprived, who do not let themselves be deceived by pretension or by riches. Here we touch upon an essential point of a Christian conception of existence.

6:27-36 *Love your enemies*—here is one of the most revolutionary slogans of the Gospel for each age and each existence. It is quite common to recommend solidarity with those who are near to us through family, religion, homeland, or political affiliation. Judaism, for example, insisted on love of neighbor inside the community. Jesus shatters all limits and sweeps away all objections that restrict charity. For him, the call to love others is not guided by our preferences but by the need and distress of others. The correlation of conflicts and hatred must be broken. A love that is gratuitous and without boundaries—like the love of God taught to us by Jesus—is the mark of a true disciple. The Lord himself gave us an example of such love on the cross (see Lk 23:34).

6:37-42 These varied sentences have to do with the relations of people to one another. Developed is the meaning of mercy (v. 37)—a characteristic trait of Luke's work—generosity (v. 38), and clear-sightedness regarding self that prevents one from judging others (v. 37). In Matthew's Gospel, the parable of the blind leading the blind is used to denounce the false teachers of Judaism (Mt 15:13-14). In Luke, it has become a recommendation of clear-sightedness addressed to the disciples. This varied usage of the same theme demonstrates the liberty of the evangelists—or of tradition—in the working out of a theme.

6:43-49 An authentic life does not deceive; it is by someone's acts that we discern what truly fills the heart. True disciples are not satisfied with talk and appearances. For them, listening to the Word of God means transforming their whole existence.

7:1-50 The first 17 verses in this section recount two miracles of Christ, which highlight his mission both to the Jews and to the Gentiles. The next 33 verses then have to do with Jesus and the Baptist. The first Christian generations no doubt encountered groups who were followers of John the Baptist. Hence, it was most necessary to comprehend well the destiny of this prophet. Several times Luke sketches a parallel between John and Jesus (see Lk 1:5-56; 3:1-20; 9:7-9). Each time the Baptist impresses us by his courage, and each time Christ's mission seems so different from his. Between these two destinies there is a kind of rupture, the difference of the two Testaments.

7:1-10 Every miracle testifies to Christ's power to save people. But this miracle is reported above all to teach the cost of faith in Jesus and to astound us with the faith of a pagan. Luke describes the deep religious attitude of this man. At that time, it was only at great cost that a Roman official would invite a Jew or show consideration for the one God worshiped by a conquered people. This miracle, granted to a pagan who trusted solely in the power of Jesus, discreetly announces the call of non-Jews to salvation (see Acts 10:34-35).

7:11-17 Luke is the only one who reports this incident, which takes place in a village in the area of Nazareth. God manifests himself once again as he did in the time of the prophets Elijah and Elisha (see 1 Ki 17:17-24; 2 Ki 4:18-37).

7:18-23 Jesus answers John by telling him of the signs which he, Jesus, is performing: those foreseen by the Prophets (Ps 72:2, 12-13; Isa 61:1-2). He is not the liberator of a nation but someone who takes the side of the wretched and marginalized of this world (see Lk 4:16-19).

7:24-35 John the Baptist, messenger of the Savior, surpasses the Prophets because he precedes and announces the coming of the Lord (Lk 1:17, 76; Mal 3:1), but Jesus alone inaugurates this new time of the kingdom. The austere preaching of John moved the people and the tax collectors, those who were despised, whereas the officials of the religion rejected him in the same way they disdained the call to joy addressed to them by Jesus. This shows the narrow-mindedness of those who believe themselves wise in the face of the unexpected accomplished by God. But the true believers welcome the plan of the Lord who saves, i.e., his "wisdom."

7:36-50 The other three evangelists place this incident just before the Passion. Luke, however, keeps it here to show that his primary concern is with the mercy and forgiveness of God. He is the only evangelist to hand down the memory of good relations between Jesus and the Pharisees who invite him to dine (see also Lk 11:37; 14:1): these men, too, are children of Israel and will be given the instruction that they really need.

7:37 The woman is certainly not Mary Magdalene (see Lk 8:2) nor Mary the sister of Lazarus (Lk 10:39; Jn 11:5). The immense popularity of Mary Magdalene was due to a confusion, which occurred as far back as Christian antiquity, between the sinful woman who is forgiven here and the real Mary Magdalene, who was one of the main figures on Calvary and at the tomb.

8:2-3 Some women belong to the group of disciples; this was an occurrence quite rare at that period. As for Mary of Magdala (Mary Magdalene), the expression "seven demons" suggests some violent illness with symptoms that were disconcerting for a woman.

8:4-8 Since the time of the Prophets, harvesting was a current image of the Judgment (Joel 4:13). Sowing evokes the activity of Jesus. Jesus knows from experience that preaching the Gospel converts only hearts that are well disposed. Nevertheless, he underlines with optimism the growth of the seed: despite all risks and obstacles, the Word of God will make progress among human beings.

8:9-10 At the moment, only the disciples are sensitive to the riches of the Gospel; the others do not yet have a free heart. See also note on Mt 13:11.

8:11-15 In the meditation of the early communities, the parable of the sower becomes a lesson for the believer. In daily life, in trials, in the pleasures of life, the work of the demon is an obstacle to the Gospel. Jesus knows this. He also knows the generosity of which humans are capable. He puts us on guard but also calls us to make a persevering effort to let our life be transformed by his teachings.

8:16-18 Are the mysteries of the kingdom definitively denied to others (v. 10)? No. The secret is not forever. Soon the disciples will bring the message to all people (see Lk 12:1-12). How will they receive it? We will be judged on the yield of the Word in our life (see Lk 19:25-26).

8:19-21 The true family of Jesus is made up of those who hearken to the Word. Luke places this episode as a conclusion to the texts on receiving the Gospel. Belonging to Jesus is the joy of the believer.

8:20 *Brethren:* i.e., according to Hebrew idiom, close relatives. See note on Mt 12:46.

8:22-25 God alone is master of the sea (see Pss 65:7; 89:10; 107:25-28). The authority of Jesus over the unleashed elements shows his power divine.

8:26-39 The incident is meant to show that Jesus is stronger than all the forces of evil lumped together, the forces of Satan himself. Jesus goes to face these forces in a pagan region east of the Lake of Tiberias, where, it was thought, Satan must be reigning supreme. There is a herd of pigs there, animals unclean in Jewish eyes; the herd dashes over the cliff, signifying the return of the demons to their hell.

8:40-56 This episode places before us two distressed people. The first is a father on the verge of losing his young daughter, with the rites of mourning under the specter of death already organized. The second is a woman humiliated by a sickness that carries the stigma of legal impurity, preventing her from participating in religious services and from approaching the Prophet (see Lev 15:19-27). Jesus intervenes in their distress and manifests his power and goodness, both of which are those of God. Nevertheless, he refuses to give his intervention a dramatic character; the only witnesses of the girl's raising from the dead—described in the same way as the action of Elijah (see 1 Ki 17:17, 22)—will be apostles, who are no longer seeking miracles. Here then is the portrait of Jesus: he brings life to those who approach him with faith.

9:1-6 The Twelve are to share the mission of Jesus, to announce and attest the coming of salvation. Like their Lord, the apostles of the kingdom must be disinterested and conscious of the grave importance of the Gospel. They will accept hospitality simply and without consideration of personal interest. It is by clearly dissociating themselves from incredulity that they will announce the judgment that is coming (see Acts 13:51; 18:5).

9:7-9 People speak of the return of Elijah as a precursor of the day of the Lord (Mal 3:23). They have known John. Now Jesus' renown reaches the palace of the prince whom he will encounter in the course of his Passion (see Lk 23:7-12). The murderer of John evinces an idle curiosity. The action of Jesus compels each of us to ask ourselves: What do we say of Jesus?

9:10-17 The preaching of Jesus so excites the crowd that they go so far as to disturb him in his retreat. He receives them and speaks to them about the kingdom of God. The miracle of the loaves is like a renewal of the prodigy of the manna expected at the time of the Messiah. In this account, Christians already discern the signs of the Eucharist: God nourishes his people. See also notes on Mt 14:13-21; 14:19; and 14:21; and Mk 6:43.

9:18-36 At the opening of this passage, Jesus is found in prayer—thus Luke underlines the importance of the moment. Christ invites the Twelve to declare themselves concerning who he is. Peter precedes the others—in the Gospel, Peter's faith has a large role (see Lk 22:31-33)—in acknowledging Christ as God, that is, as the expected Messiah whose unity with God is astonishing. In order to avoid all ambiguity about himself, Jesus recommends secrecy and for the first time announces his Passion. Contrary to what people expect, the Messiah will not save his people by a popular or political uprising but by his Death and Resurrection. The title "Son of Man" suggests the Passion and announces a glorious coming on the last day.

9:23-27 To believe in Christ is to strive to share the mystery of his Death and Resurrection. To do so it is necessary for each of us to go beyond ourselves and our egoism in the ordinary conditions of life. *See the kingdom of God:* this expression evokes the appearances of the risen Lord or the work of the Spirit in the primitive Church.

9:28-36 In a vision on a mountain, three disciples behold, for one instant, the divine splendor of Jesus. Moses and Elijah, who announced God's plan in the Law and the Prophets, attest that it will now be accomplished by the Passion, that "passage" of Jesus, which is the new '"Exodus." As formerly in the Exodus God manifested himself in the cloud, now through the one he designates as his Son, his Chosen One (see Isa 42:1; 49:7), he will give to all people the definitive liberation. The evangelist hardly explains the unfolding of this mysterious event. He gives us the shattering experience of Jesus' inner life to prompt our faith in Christ: to hear this man is to hear God.

9:35 *My Chosen One:* this is similar to a Palestinian Jewish title found in the literature of the Dead Sea Scrolls and to Isa 42:1.

9:37-43a Returning to the people, Jesus resumes the struggle. In contrast with the lapse of the disciples, the Messiah manifests his sovereign power against all the forces that enchain us, of which the person afflicted with a demon is a striking example.

9:43b-45 Amid popular success, Jesus keeps his eyes fixed on his Passion, the decisive act of salvation. For the believers, as for the disciples, it remains difficult to accept the necessity of the cross.

9:46-48 As a result of their lack of pretense, children are the beloved of God and become models for the believer (see Lk 18:15-17). We must share this regard of Christ for the little ones, even in the way of thinking and living.

9:49-50 It is necessary to accept the initiative of all those who make use of the name of Christ.

9:51—19:27 We are at a crossroads in the life of Christ: Jesus begins to go to Jerusalem where his mystery is to be accomplished. This journey will take him from Galilee to the Holy City. In this section, Luke brings together a part of the teaching of Jesus that the other evangelists do not have or that they give in very different contexts. In these ten chapters, we find some of the most moving words of Christ about the mercy of God.

9:51-56 The Samaritans refused passage to Jewish pilgrims on their way to the temple in Jerusalem, because they did not give recognition to that sanctuary. The critical text says simply that Jesus "rebuked" the disciples (v. 55); some manuscripts have: "And he said, 'You do not know what kind of spirit you are of, for the Son of Man did not come to destroy lives, but to save them.' "

9:54 An allusion to 2 Ki 1:10-12.

9:57-62 Jesus demands an unconditional commitment from those who hesitate. The preaching of the kingdom is of primary urgency. On its account, we are to renounce every possession and free ourselves from even the most sacred human attachments.

10:1-16 The number of those sent suggests universality, since the ancient leaders of Israel traditionally numbered seventy-two (see Num 11:24-29), and seventy-two pagan nations were listed (see Gen 10). In this passage, Luke brings together various recommendations of Jesus in order to draw up a program for the missionaries.

10:12 *That day:* the day of judgment.

10:13-15 See note on Mt 11:20-24.

10:15 *The netherworld:* the place of the dead, i.e., the underworld (as in Acts 2:27, 31).

10:17-20 In the joy of the disciples, Jesus sees the beginning of the defeat of the forces of evil inflamed against human beings, and of their leader Satan (see Lk 11:20). Jesus shares their joy; but he invites them to rejoice most of all that they are the elect of the Father, a happiness that radically surpasses all missionary success.

10:21-24 In this inspired prayer, Jesus lays bare the profound movement of his heart and the very mystery of his person. He is gripped by the revelation made to the poor (i.e., *children*); he lives, in an inexpressible fashion, in unity with the Father in the Spirit. The expectation of kings and prophets, i.e., of the Old Testament, is now accomplished, for Jesus is here and shares with human beings God's mysterious presence. The Church knows that by herself she is nothing in this world, but she is astounded to bring forth for all people this great revelation of God. This text constantly brings her back home to the heart of the Gospel.

10:25-37 Jesus gives pride of place in his teaching to the commandment of love, which sums up the entire Law (see Mt 22:40); but love of God and love of neighbor are henceforth joined inseparably.

10:30 *Going down:* Jericho lies in the deepest depression on earth, at 800 feet below sea level.

10:32 *Levite:* a minister of the temple.

10:35 *Denarii:* plural for *denarius,* a laborer's daily wage.

10:37 The scribe had asked who was his neighbor. Jesus responds with the example of the Samaritan who, without regard for national rancors and religious disputes, recognizes the neighbor in an unknown person who is in need of help. Hence, the person who loves will know immediately how to individualize who his neighbor is. It is not necessarily—as the Jews thought—a person of the same nation, race, or religion.

10:38-42 The incident is intended to teach that the disciples of Jesus must not allow secondary things to take precedence over essentials, namely, the hearing of the Word of God in order to feed on it and put it into practice (see Lk 6:47; 8:21; 11:28; Acts 6:2). The village in which the two sisters lived was Bethany. Like the preceding parable, this thoughtful incident is told only in Luke.

11:1-4 In the eyes of Luke, the prayer of the disciples is connected to the prayer of Jesus himself. It is a profession of faith in which the community says the essence of what it requests: the kingdom of God, daily sustenance, forgiveness, and strength in time of trial. The form of the Our Father given here is shorter than the one handed down in the Gospel of Matthew.

11:5-13 In the Palestine of that time, people went to bed early; moreover, the entire family slept in a single room, and the door was secured from inside with a heavy bar. Thus, awakening a neighbor caused a great deal of inconvenience, but the latter would be ashamed to remain insensitive. And since God is mercy itself, could he refuse the request of believers when it concerns essentials (see Lk 18:1-8; 22:44)?

11:14—12:12 The suspicion with which his adversaries regard Jesus becomes accusation and snare; they treat him as an agent of Satan and demand signs of him. In this confrontation that is more and more manifest, Jesus does not soften his message in any way; rather he demands that one choose for or against him. The time of waiting is over; the time of decision is at hand.

11:14-22 There are groups who claim to cast out demons—the word "children" designates the members or disciples of a group. Why then should his opponents be suspicious of Jesus, especially since he actually heals sicknesses? The miracles that he works manifest the power of God, for in order to conquer Satan who is reputedly at work in sicknesses one must be stronger than he is.

11:27-28 The happiness of the kingdom of God is open to those who accept the Word of Jesus. This is a warning to adversaries who reject it. Thus, the true grandeur of Mary is not in having given Jesus his body but in having welcomed the message (see Lk 1:38; 8:21).

11:29-32 Many long for prodigies that would forcibly remove the need for faith. Their desire is vain. The true sign that attests the mission of Jesus is the totality of his work and the force of his person as well as his call to conversion. Thus, past generations had seen messages for them in the wisdom of Solomon (see 1 Ki 10:1-11) and the word of Jonah (Jon 3).

11:33-36 Luke here brings together two sentences that have a theme of the lamp. It is a call to throw off blindness and be open to the light that is Jesus (see Lk 8:16). The light of faith transforms one's life.

11:37-54 In Luke these strong rebukes seem to have been given by Jesus in private conversations with Pharisees and scribes, whereas in Matthew (23:13ff) the charges are uttered publicly in the presence of outsiders. This is a further aspect of the "gentleness of Christ," which Luke means to communicate.

11:38 *Had not first washed:* this referred to the ceremonial washing, which was part of the "oral" traditions of the Pharisees, i.e., practices and regulations meant to fill out the written Law of Moses (see Mt 15:9; Mk 7:3, and note on Mk 7:4).

11:42 *Tithes:* see note on Mt 23:23-24.

11:44 *Like unmarked graves:* as Passover drew near, Jews used to whitewash tombs in order to avoid touching them inadvertently, which would have caused a legal uncleanness (see Num 19:16).

11:51 *Abel . . . Zechariah:* these two names recall the first and the last slayings recounted in the Hebrew Bible (see Gen 4:1-16; 2 Chr 24:17-22). What is being recalled is therefore the entire history of murders committed against men of God in the course of the Old Testament.

12:1-12 True disciples do not let the message become altered and are not afraid to bear clear witness to the Gospel, to confess their faith in Jesus. Persecutions should not intimidate them; indeed, it is better to be condemned by opinion than to lose God. Believers are certain that the Lord will never abandon them; they rely on the help of the Spirit to proclaim simply and without alteration the essence of the message (see Acts 4:8; 5:12; 7:55).

12:10 *Everyone who speaks . . . against the Holy Spirit will not be forgiven:* the meaning of this verse is obscure. Perhaps the meaning is that when Jesus was alive, people could be excused from failing to recognize him as the Savior, but such an excuse will no longer be possible once his mission has been confirmed by the power of the Spirit at Pentecost.

12:13-14 The Law of Moses dealt with temporal questions (see Ex 2:14; Acts 7:27), and the rabbis willingly offered their opinions. Jesus has not come to sustain us in our personal interests but to save us. The Gospel does not foster greed in any form; it demands detachment from earthly goods. This episode serves as an introduction to a series of teachings concerning money, an important theme for the Gospel of Luke.

12:15-21 The desire for and the satisfaction in accumulating riches closes one to God and deprives one of lucidity. The goods of earth do not have a vocation for eternity. The spiritual future of human beings is more important. The Word and Life of Jesus are sustained by this conviction.

12:22-31 When the concern for earthly goods rules one's whole life, and even one's prayer, we have become enslaved to them. Christ's disciples remain free: they trust in God. Jesus does not preach unconcern but concern for what is essential: to accept the kingdom and to live the Gospel.

12:32-34 This recommendation to be detached from one's goods and to give them to those in need is more pressing in Luke. The true treasure of the kingdom is to be detached from money.

12:35-48 The Jews were wont to ask: "When will the kingdom come?" Christians asked: "When will the Lord return?" When forced to be vigilant, attention inevitably wanes. But the Lord is near, and our life is with him; we must not be sleeping when he returns.

12:35-38 Vigilant servants are bound to work and to be ready even into the night. The disciples are to be focused on meeting their Lord, who will be their joy.

12:38 *Second watch:* i.e., between 9:00 P.M. and midnight. *Third:* i.e., between midnight and 3:00 A.M. See note on Mt 14:25.

12:39-40 See note on Mt 24:45-51.

12:41-48 When Peter poses this question, he is answered by a parable summoning all leaders of the community to faithful vigilance.

12:49-50 The allusion is to the baptism in fire and the Spirit that begins on Pentecost (see Lk 3:16; Acts 2:3, 19) and also to the Passion that is to cleanse the people of their sins (see Mk 10:38).

12:51-53 The Gospel brings not security but the division (see Lk 2:34-35) that, according to Micah (7:6), is a prelude to the last times.

12:54-56 Understanding the signs of the times means recognizing the time of salvation, the time of Jesus. No concern is more important than this, for one's very salvation is in question.

12:57-59 One must put one's life in order before the judgment, for afterward it will be too late. We are urged to settle disputes quickly in accord with Gospel values. Matthew will turn this text into an inducement to fraternal charity (Mt 5:25-26).

13:1-5 Jesus is told of a bloody repression that had just occurred in Galilee. He indicates that it is useless to fix the blame upon its victims (see Jn 9:3). Such events remind us that the judgment is only suspended and that death can surprise us at any time. Hence, they are a call to repent.

13:6-9 In the other Synoptic Gospels (Mt 21:18-22; Mk 11:12-14, 20-25) the incident of the barren fig tree stresses the strictness of the judgment. In Luke's parable, the threat of judgment is replaced by a lesson on God's patience.

13:10-17 The cure of a crippled woman on the Sabbath is in the eyes of the ancients a direct victory over Satan; it is an act of God who sets human beings free. The religious leaders are prevented by their conformist attitude from recognizing the cure as an obvious sign from God. In the face of such absurd legalism Jesus calls for simple common sense.

13:18-21 The work of Jesus will have a future of infinite proportions although it had such seemingly insignificant beginnings. See notes on Mt 13:31-32; 13:32; and 13:33.

13:22-30 This passage brings together scattered quotations of Jesus. After recalling that salvation demands effort and is not given by acquired privilege, the words open up frightful perspectives on the refusal of Israel while showing the Gentiles abounding in the kingdom. The religious conception is reversed here. People must not presume upon the certainty of their salvation. Salvation is a grace that needs their cooperation.

13:31-33 Some Pharisees who are friends of Jesus alert him to the danger, but he does not fear the ruler of Galilee. In his eyes, Herod is nothing more than a sly fox, and no longer the lion, symbol of mortal danger. Despite any threats, Christ is resolved to pursue his mission till the very end with its tragic result in Jerusalem.

13:34-35 Like the Prophets, Jesus foretells the destruction of the Holy City, but he also evokes a day when all peoples will acknowledge the Lord (see Lk 21:24; Rom 11:25-27). See also note on Mt 23:37-39.

14:1-24 Luke is an artful composer of Gospel scenes. Here he brings together different themes in the unfolding of a repast. The Jews thought of the kingdom of God as a gathering of people at a banquet in heaven. And, for Luke, this repast doubtless has the value of an announcement and a symbol. Jesus has the honor of being invited on the Sabbath to dine with a group of Pharisees, the representatives of Jewish thought. His hosts follow solid principles of thought and congratulate themselves on their good education. They closely watch Jesus' behavior out of curiosity mingled with apprehension. And one might say that Jesus goes out of his way to shock them.

14:1-6 Jesus does not lose himself in compliments and conversation but posits an act, a sign of the salvation that he brings to human beings. This is a new miracle, again performed on a Sabbath. Religion is for the liberation of persons, not their enslavement. To keep the Sabbath is to bear witness to it (see Lk 6:6-11; 13:10-17). See note on Mt 12:9-14.

14:7-11 These reflections on the choice of places at a banquet could be nothing more than simple counsels of worldly wisdom. But Jesus wishes to stress that humility holds first place in the values of the kingdom, contrary to the values of the world (see Lk 1:51-52; 18:14).

14:12-14 A repast should not be a worldly affair. Luke calls for humility (see Lk 1:53; 6:20; 7:22) and disinterest.

14:15-24 The kingdom of God is portrayed as a banquet in which God gathers together the Elect. People can refuse the call, but one day the gathering of joy will take place—this is one of Jesus' principal certitudes. The parable goes farther; the officials, the habitués of religion, cheat themselves. Their affairs come before the joy of the kingdom, which opens itself to those who are regarded as ordinary and are often excluded: the marginalized of society or of religion. This proposal is shocking for official Judaism. And it should also be for any society that is closed in upon itself, and especially if it calls itself the Church of Jesus. See note on Mt 22:1-14.

14:23 *Compel people to come:* they must be emphatic on the need to enter, but the Gospel excludes any coercion.

14:25-35 This section is tantamount to a short catechism on discipleship. The phrase "cannot be my disciple" runs through it like a refrain (vv. 26, 27, 33).

14:25-33 This passage indicates that one must renounce everything to follow Jesus, even the most legitimate values and attachments, for the Gospel relegates all other considerations to a secondary level. That is the point of the word "hate" in the Old Testament (see Lk 16:13; Gen 29:31, 33; Deut 21:15-16; Isa 60:15). This renunciation is not some passing fancy but a radical demand: the two parables of the builder and the warrior could have been nothing more than simple invitations to reflect before deciding anything; Luke turns them into a call to make a serious commitment.

14:26 *Hate his father and mother:* Jesus does not intend to abolish the fourth commandment about honoring and taking care of one's parents. He simply sets forth the supreme conditions to be his disciple. In order to follow him, one must be disposed to sacrifice the most tender affections and even to renounce one's life (see Jn 12:25). The expression is softened and explained in Mt 10:37.

14:28-30 Whoever wishes to follow Jesus must weigh his own strengths so as not to launch out into a spiritual adventure thoughtlessly and rashly. Jesus illustrates this thought with two comparisons.

14:34-35 If the energy and conviction of disciples who have made a commitment begin to weaken, they become like salt that has lost its taste or its value.

15:1-32 These three joyous parables of Luke's Gospel disclose the sentiments that the Father and Jesus have toward human beings. God is untiringly concerned for those who are far off, the sinners or unbelievers. His joy is to seek out and find those who are lost. This desire and this joy of God are revealed to us in the comportment of Christ himself toward sinners. In turn, the Church must trust in the mercy of God and must seek out and welcome those who seem far away. May she always bear witness to the value that human beings have in the eyes of God.

15:1-2 In the name of God's love for sinners, Jesus overthrows several customs of his day. He refuses to accept the attitudes held by well-regarded religious figures: scorn toward others and smugness in their own self-sufficiency.

15:3-7 The parable of the lost sheep pushes antithesis to the extreme so that persons may never doubt God's tenderness for them.

15:8-10 The parable of the lost coin demonstrates what a great contrast there is between the joy of heaven and the disdain of the Pharisees and the so-called clean!

15:8 *Coins:* literally, "drachmas," a drachma being the Greek coin corresponding to the Roman denarius, a laborer's daily wage.

15:11-32 The parable of the prodigal son, one of the most enchanting stories of Jesus, completes the two preceding parables. It is God who awaits sinners, and it is humanity that is encouraged to seek God. We recognize in it all the misery of sin: abandonment, solitude, and distress. The parable describes the path to conversion and finally the great certitude of the believer: beyond all human hope, God harbors for every person the unfailing affection of a father for his child. He awaits the child and welcomes it joyously. It is easy to see in the discontent of the elder son the anger of the Pharisees at the welcome Jesus gives to sinners.

15:15 *Pigs:* unclean animals for the Jews.

16:1-13 From the very origins of the Gospel tradition, the parable of the crafty steward has created difficulty. People could evolve abusive applications from it: e.g., does it promote fraud? In order to avoid any false interpretation, different sentences of Jesus concerning money have been joined to the parable.

16:1-8 It is a fact that people bring a great deal of initiative and intelligence to their affairs even when these are worthy of criticism or unjust. Alas, believers put forth little effort for the kingdom! This is the lesson to be retained from the parable. It is a call for lucidity and creative intelligence. Jesus is suggesting the *skill* of a swindler, not fraud or theft.

16:8 *Children of light:* a Hebrew expression signifying those enlightened by a superterrestrial faith as opposed to the *children of this world,* who are focused solely on their earthly interests.

16:9-13 Money dominates all of life and society. The attitude toward money is a test of the fidelity of Christians. Those who seek imperishable goods are detached from perishable ones. They know how to give alms (v. 9), and they earn and manage their goods with honesty (vv. 10-11). Yet money means little in reality; the true good is the gift of God (v. 12). Hence, the quest for gain and fortune must not be first in the life of Christians, for then money would become a false god for them (v. 13).

16:14-15 More than once Jesus denounces the pretense of those who pass themselves off as religious people (see Lk 11:39-40; 18:9; 20:47).

16:16 The Law and the Prophets designates the Old Testament as it was read in the synagogues. We must make an effort in order to enter the kingdom of God.

16:17 The Law will not pass away, for it includes the whole revelation given to the chosen people, with its prophetic character (see Lk 24:27, 44).

16:18 Divorce was allowed and regulated by Old Testament law (see Deut 24:1-4). The position of Jesus is a radical one, as numerous New Testament passages attest (see Mt 5:31-32; 19:1-12; Mk 10:1-12; 1 Cor 7:10-11).

16:19-31 The rich man cannot avoid the message of this passage; indeed, this is for him a sufficient sign and a more persuasive one than the most amazing miracle. *Abraham's side:* literally, "Abraham's bosom"; in the language of the day this suggested the post of honor at the heavenly banquet (see Mt 8:11).

16:23 *Netherworld:* see note on Lk 10:15.

17:1-3a Scandal is the snare that one extends to others in order to lead them into evil. It is especially grave when it is placed along the way of the "little ones."

17:3b-4 Fraternal pardon is one of the best signs of the presence of the Gospel. Faults among brothers and sisters are continual; hence, openness to reconciliation must be constant.

17:5-6 See note on Mt 21:18-22.

17:7-10 The Pharisees and many religious people are more concerned about their reward than about what they can do for God. The disciple is subservient to his master in a work that is far greater than himself. That is his happiness and his recompense even here below.

17:11-19 The episode of the ten people afflicted with leprosy illustrates first of all the ingratitude of Israel—which believes that the gifts of God are owed to it—and the faith of the Gentiles. For a Jewish author, it is odious to give an example containing a Samaritan, a heretic regarded as more disgraceful than a pagan. However, a stranger more open to the Lord's call than the average believer would provide an example capable of inculcating admiration forever.

17:20-21 As for when the kingdom will come, it is useless to wait for mysterious signs. The kingdom is already at work in the personal action of Jesus.

17:22-37 This description of events must be read in light of the particular literary genre being used, but this does not lessen its urgency. The other two Synoptic Gospels place these exhortations in the "eschatological discourse."

17:36 Some manuscripts add this verse, probably taken from Mt 24:40.

18:1-8 We might ask whether prayer is useless or whether it is unfitting to remain insistent in God's presence. This parable recommends a tenacious persistence. If the Lord is tardy in coming or in responding, it is to allow time for conversion and for faith. But the prayer of believers is not a cry in the wind. It is especially necessary during the end times, which will be a great trial for the faith and for trust in the Lord.

18:9-14 What Jesus criticizes is not the Pharisee's ascetical effort but his sense of self-sufficiency before God, himself, and other human beings, and his harshness toward others. On the other hand, Jesus does not approve of the everyday behavior of the tax collector, but offers his sincerity, humility, and repentance as an example. God's goodness bewilders us: from it sinners can expect compassion and grace; salvation is an unmerited and unexpected gift.

18:15-17 One must receive the kingdom as a little child, that is, as a poor person who is regarded as insignificant in society and who awaits everything from its father. One can never stop being struck by this insistence of Jesus concerning the spirit of childhood. It is a reversal of the daily norms of our lives (see Lk 9:46-48).

18:18-30 A rich young man is animated by the desire for a more personal commitment, going beyond the simple observance of the ten commandments. However, he cannot resolve himself to the first radical gesture—giving up his possessions. The Christian community retained this example as a warning. Riches, as Luke often stresses, are an obstacle to salvation. In a life encumbered by riches, there is no place for the Lord. Yet the Lord fills to the brim whoever has the courage to prefer him to everything else. Such courage is the gift of God (see Lk 12:33).

18:31-34 Six times in Luke's Gospel Jesus refers to his tragic end, so deeply does this affect his entire work. The Prophets had borne witness to it beforehand.

18:35-43 The community retains this episode as an example of faith and witness to Jesus, Son of David, that is, the people's Messiah and Savior.

19:1-10 The lesson is obvious: it is God who saves the rich (see Lk 18:27), because he alone can change the human heart. Zacchaeus's generosity in atoning for the wrongs he has done goes beyond anything the Jewish or the Roman law could require of a judged and condemned thief.

19:11-27 This parable is unusual in that its chief personage is an aspirant to the throne, for it seems to be inspired by the story of Archelaus, who went to Rome in 4 B.C. to obtain the succession to Herod the Great in Judea, and whose return was marked by a slaughter not yet forgotten in the memory of the people.

19:13 *Gold coins:* literally, *minas; a mina,* was a Greek coin equal to a hundred drachmas or Roman denarii, that is, a hundred times the daily wage of a laborer. In the time of Jesus, it weighed about 350 grams of silver.

19:28—21:38 The Messiah reaches Jerusalem, where he is to complete God's plan. His encounter with the city is a powerful one, but will end in his rejection. The plan of God will nonetheless be carried out in a way different from human expectations: in suffering, death, and resurrection, in the Paschal Mystery.

19:28-40 By accepting the acclamations of his many disciples, Jesus proclaims himself to be the Messiah, the king, the son of David, whom Israel has awaited. The scene seems to be a repetition of the ceremony of Solomon's proclamation and consecration (see 1 Ki 1:33-40). The surprising thing is the modest circumstances: the colt is the mount of the poor, the mount of the ancient period of nomadism. The Old Testament imagined various scenarios for the coming of the Messiah; they were all glorious, except for one, that of Zechariah (9:9).

19:41-44 Luke alone records the incident of Jesus weeping over Jerusalem— here and in Lk 13:34, although Mt 23:21 does show Jesus grieving over it. The method mentioned by which Israel's enemies will conquer and level Jerusalem is precisely the one used by the Romans in A.D. 70.

19:45-48 Jesus demands respect for the temple and installs himself in it to proclaim the message of God. It is thus that he conceives and exercises the royal authority of the Messiah. Like the Prophets, he refuses to allow religion to deteriorate into a business affair.

20:1—21:4 "Who gave you this authority?" Sooner or later, such a question was bound to be asked of Jesus. However, coming from the members of the Jewish high tribunal, it is nothing more than a snare. Jesus places himself in solidarity with John the Baptist, the envoy of God. If they do not have the courage to speak about the dead prophet, how can they be ready to loyally confront the response of Christ? He reduces them to silence, debate being useless.

20:1-8 See note on Mk 11:27-33.

20:9-19 When we read ch. 5 of Isaiah, we understand that it is God who puts the authorities of this people on trial. The parable sums up in a few words the entire history of conflict between the leaders and God's messengers; is not the last messenger, that is, the heir, Jesus himself? See also note on Mt 21:33-46.

20:20-26 The tribute was a tax collected by the Roman occupiers. To justify its payment meant collaborating with the enemy of the people; to disallow its payment meant labeling oneself as rebellious in the eyes of the Romans. The snare seems to be inescapable, but Jesus foils the plan by loudly proclaiming the absolute primacy of God (see Lk 12:31). See also note on Mt 22:15-22.

20:24 *Coin:* i.e., a *denarius,* the normal day's wage for a laborer at that time.

20:27-40 The party of the Jewish high priests had not yet accepted the belief in the resurrection that had been proclaimed for two or three centuries (Dan 12:2-3) and that the Pharisees had accepted (see Acts 23:8). When the present life is taken as a model of the future life, the reality of the resurrection is misunderstood, since the resurrection radically transforms the human condition.

20:41-44 Most Jews expected the Messiah to be simply an heir of God's chosen king (see 2 Sam 7:1-17). Citing an ancient royal psalm, Jesus conveys that the Messiah is of divine origin and that he will bring a kingdom that transcends anything we might ordinarily imagine.

20:45-47 Jesus reproaches the teachers of religious thought for their vanity (Lk 11:43), greed (Lk 16:14), and artificial and ostentatious piety (Lk 18:11-12).

21:1-4 See note on Mk 12:41-44.

21:5-38 Scenes of terror and visions of hope alternate in this great discourse. If we are to understand its tone and vocabulary, we must put ourselves in the atmosphere created by various terrifying and magnificent pages of the Old Testament. On the eve of the catastrophe that destroyed both Jerusalem, for the first time, and the state of Israel in 587 B.C., some prophets had a presentiment of the spiritual ruin of the people and had warned them, with harsh invectives, of future punishments. Later on, people began to ask about the ultimate destiny of the world and humanity; this created a restlessness that was eschatological, that is, concerned with the ultimate end, the last times.

In the "apocalypses" or "revelations," some authors imagined awe-inspiring scenes of wars, disasters, and judgment, which would usher in the coming of God and the salvation of the people. These accounts, which are to be read in accordance with their particular literary genre, always remain bewildering.

21:5-6 Around the year 19 B.C., Herod the Great undertook a splendid reconstruction of the temple. The very magnificence of the restored temple caused a sense of self-reliance and presumption (see Lk 13:34-35; 19:46; Jer 7:1-15; 26; Ezek 8:11; Mic 3:9-12).

21:7-19 For a Jew, the destruction of the temple inaugurates the great tribulation of the end times. We understand that the disciples are worried. Jesus gives them signs: those more distant (vv. 10-11) will be taken up again even later on (vv. 25-26), those closer describe the events of the troubled years A.D. 66–70: appearances of false messiahs, civil wars and struggles, persecution of Christians. This persecution is a privileged sign of the coming of the kingdom of God, and it is seen to be severe. But let those who bear witness to Christ take courage, for they will not be abandoned. The Passion is the way to glory for the Christian community as it is for the Lord. Courage will be given to them to announce the essence of the message: Jesus Christ dead, risen, and to come.

21:20-24 The evils that overtake the holy city are like a judgment of God upon it. But the tragic fate of Jerusalem and its temple inaugurates the laborious period in which is born the new world until all the pagans have heard the Good News of salvation and Israel itself is converted (see Rom 11:25-27).

21:25-33 At the end of the final crisis, which is described in the violent images dear to the Prophets and the authors of the apocalypses (see Isa 13:10; 24:23; 34:4; Ezek 32:7-8; Joel 4:15), Jesus, the victorious Christ, will come to judge the world and deliver those who have remained faithful and are ready to welcome him (see Dan 7:13). The signs, especially persecutions, are pledges of hope and deliverance (see Rom 8:23; Eph 1:14; 4:30).

21:32 In the apocalyptic genre, a "generation" signifies an age of the world, a stage in God's plan.

21:34-36 Since in Luke's perspective the end of the world is not considered to be imminent, the exhortation to be vigilant voiced here is more pressing so that the delay may not numb the heart of the Christian. At the same time, there is an invitation to pray that the day of the Lord may not come unexpectedly and find us unprepared to appear before the divine Judge.

21:37-38 During the final week of his life (Sunday to Thursday), Jesus taught in the temple in the morning, and all the people came to hear him.

22:1—24:53 The salvation of human beings is accomplished in a unique event: Christ's Death and Resurrection. This is the Paschal mystery. The account that follows is fashioned by this principal testimony; hence it must be read as a unified whole. From the beginnings of the Church, this is the Gospel, the essence of the Christian announcement.

22:1-2 Before the episodes of the Passion unfold, the plot thickens with the adversaries of Jesus. The leaders of the people take the initiative in the plot, and the traitor serves them as an instrument, but it is the spirit of evil who initiates the last combat.

22:3-6 See note on Mt 26:14-16.

22:7-38 Now we see the initiative of Jesus, which appears so clearly in this last supper. The account is an integral part of the Passion, i.e., the Death and Resurrection of Jesus, for the Church that announces the Gospel of Christ the Savior is also the Christian community that celebrates the Eucharist, the memorial of salvation. Jesus enters the decisive event; this last act is, as it were, the summary of his every act and word: sharing, offering, gift, presence, and covenant of God in the midst of his followers.

Luke has placed actions and words of Jesus here that the other evangelists report in other contexts. This is so the community can meditate on them each time it assembles to break the bread of the Lord? He thus leaves us a liturgical rule (the text of the Eucharistic institution) and, connected with it, communitary and missionary directives.

22:7-13 Jesus takes the initiative, freely and fully, for this last Passover of the old covenant, this repast that inaugurates a new covenant.

22:14-18 For the Jews, the Passover is the memorial of the liberation of the people (see Ex 12); for Jesus, it prefigures the Messianic Banquet in which all human beings are reunited in the presence of God. All his hope for happiness becomes a promise for believers.

22:19-20 In a prophetic gesture Jesus proclaims and establishes the new covenant between God and humanity (see Ex 24:8; Jer 31:31), which he is preparing to seal by his freely accepted sacrifice. In this action, by changing the bread and wine into his body and blood (see 1 Cor 10:6; 11:23-27), he institutes the Eucharist, which calls to mind and renders present to the gathered community his act of love for humanity (see Acts 2:42, 46). Along with Paul, Luke has preserved for us what is perhaps one of the earliest texts of the first Christian Eucharists.

22:21-23 The announcement of Judas's plan stresses the initiative of Jesus, who does not deviate from his sacrifice. Celebrating the Eucharist, believers and the leaders of the community must question themselves concerning their loyalty toward the Lord.

22:24-27 To celebrate the Eucharist means to abandon one's search for honor and to discover that all authority in the Christian community has no other title except that of service.

22:25 *Benefactor:* a term often used for leaders of pagan nations.

22:28-30 See note on Mt 19:27-30.

22:30 The image, drawn from the Jewish tradition, signifies a privileged share in the glory of the Messiah.

22:31-34 It is not in the quality of her human leaders but in the prayer of Jesus that the Church finds the assurance of perseverance in the faith.

22:35-38 A time of happiness is ending. Henceforth, the Church must confront trials. And she must not think of defending herself with the weapons employed by societies to achieve their freedom or ensure their interests.

22:39-46 Tempted to refuse the terrible and humiliating trial of the cross, Jesus struggles in prayer to accept the will of the Father. The divine aid that he receives, as once Elijah did (see 1 Ki 19:7-8), does not mitigate the tragedy of the moment. This passage remains one of the great texts on the distress of human beings in the face of their death. It is intended to be a lesson, as is emphasized, from its beginning to its end, by the repeated invitation to pray so as not to be the prey of a temptation that seems to be all-consuming.

22:43-44 These two verses are not found in some early mss.

22:47-53 Immediately cutting short any resistance on the part of his disciples, Jesus heals the servant wounded by one of them—this is the single miracle in the account of the Passion. It is typical of Luke that the servant be healed (for tradition holds that Luke was a physician).

22:53 All the events happen under the sign of Satan, who has stirred up the powers of darkness against Jesus.

22:54-65 Luke seems to report the true chronology of the events more exactly than Matthew and Mark. After his arrest, Jesus is quickly brought to the house of the high priest, where Annas his predecessor most likely also dwelled. Annas interrogates him but in a private manner (Jn 18:12-24). While Jesus is waiting for the trial, which according to Luke took place only in the morning, the guards pass time by insulting him and making fun of him.

Peter finds himself in the same courtyard and, recognized by the bystanders, denies his Master. Jesus, who has probably heard everything from where he stood, looks at him (a point mentioned only by Luke), strengthening him in his faith that had been profoundly shaken (v. 61). Note how Luke does not emphasize the crescendo of the denials. Rather, he attenuates them, and moreover does not speak of curses and oaths.

22:66-71 In contrast to Matthew and Mark, Luke does not mention the false testimonies brought against Jesus. In any case, the authorities have resolved to put him to death and seek only to have their decision confirmed. Jesus speaks solemnly about his mission and his person. He is the Envoy of God, united with him in a very particular way, and his kingdom will be inaugurated henceforth, from his Resurrection (v. 69; Ps 110:1; Dan 7:13).

22:66 *Sanhedrin:* see note on Mk 14:55.

23:1-7 The Roman governor, who usually resided at Caesarea in Palestine, was in the religious capital at the time when the Passover was being celebrated. The religious leaders accuse Jesus before him as the civil power. Twisting the reality (see Lk 21:20-26), they invent political wrongs so as to have Jesus put to death. From the beginning the Roman governor is convinced of Jesus' innocence, and he would prefer to extricate himself from this case and give it to others, for it could create nothing but trouble for him with the people and the leaders.

23:8-12 Also present in Jerusalem was Herod Antipas, ruler of Galilee, a man interested in extraordinary phenomena, ready to be scornful of them, and unwilling to accept any responsibility (see Lk 9:9; Acts 4:27).

23:13-25 Pilate is convinced that the accused is innocent. But he proposes to punish him so that the authorities might have the impression of having been heard. Finally, he yields to violence. Luke emphasizes above all the decisive responsibility of the leaders of the people. See notes on Mt 27:11-26; 27:11; 27:14; 27:24; 27:25.

23:17 Many manuscripts add this verse, probably taken from Mt 27:15 or Mk 15:6.

23:26-31 In place of solitude, Luke speaks of numerous people who take pity on Jesus; the people are already distancing themselves from the ignoble decision of their leaders. This recalls the conversion announced by the prophet Zechariah (Zec 12:10-14). But Jesus is haunted by a sorrowful vision: the ruin of Jerusalem and the official religion in which the Word of God has no effect. See also note on Mk 15:21.

23:32-43 Jesus is placed in the ranks of evildoers. He is stripped of his clothes and vinegar is presented to him, fulfilling Psalms 22:19 and 69:22 before our very eyes. The people are silent. The leaders make fun of a Messiah who wishes to save human beings. The soldiers deride his royal title, the reason for his condemnation well affixed to the wood of the cross. This apparently humiliated king testifies to a true royalty by the unheard-of love that he gives: he asks for pardon of his killers and welcomes into his kingdom the thief who repents. See also note on Mt 27:35.

23:33 *Crucified:* see note on Mt 27:35.

23:34 This is the first word uttered by Jesus from the cross, reported only by Luke, the evangelist of mercy and meekness. Its authenticity is seemingly not open to doubt even though it is omitted in numerous codices written in an anti-Semitic age.

23:35 *Stood there watching:* Luke, the friend of the crowds, does not include the people with those leaders who insulted the Crucified. They are there to watch.

23:43 This is the second word of the crucified Jesus, also reported only by Luke, and it concludes with the pardon of the good thief. Thus, salvation flows from the cross.

23:44-49 The crucified Just One expires and everything bears testimony in his behalf: a prayer of complete trust rises to his lips, a pagan acknowledges his innocence, the people already manifest their repentance (see Zec 12:10), and his dear ones are nearby. Is this a tableau of desolation? Yet a mysterious expectation grips us.

23:46 Luke omits the word of abandonment found in Matthew and Mark. Instead, Jesus dies as the prototypical good person, who at the end of his life commends his spirit into the hands of the Father. Luke leaves aside the citation from Psalm 22 and reports verse 6 of Psalm 31, the prayer that the rabbis were wont to recite in the evening and that is still recited today at Night Prayer in the Liturgy of the Hours.

23:48 To the confession of the centurion, Luke adds that of the crowds, who had assisted in silence at the drama of the crucifixion. The centurion symbolizes the Roman world that recognizes the innocence and transcendental dignity of Christ, while the crowds indicate the rejection on the part of the chosen people.

23:50-56 The burial of Jesus, a human gesture, must be accomplished before the rise of the evening star or before the lights are lit for the evening, for then the Sabbath will have arrived—when all work is prohibited.

23:50 *Man named Joseph:* Luke shows the goodness of Joseph of Arimathea. At the same time, he shows that not every member of the Sanhedrin voted to condemn Jesus.

24:1-12 The man who was thought to have been buried forever receives the important title "the Living One," a title that the Old Testament reserves to the Lord (see Jos 3:10; Jdg 8:19; Rev 1:18), and the hearts of the witnesses are opened to the Word of God. This is the first Christian Sunday, the Lord's Day, the new day (v. 1). Luke does not mention the order given to the disciples to wait for Jesus in Galilee; in his view, the mystery finds its completion in Jerusalem, and it is from Jerusalem that the Christian mission will make its way throughout the entire world.

24:13-35 Since Friday nothing has taken place; God has not intervened. These two followers of Jesus are overwhelmed by the catastrophe and wounded in their hopes. A stranger overtakes them and seems indifferent to what has taken place. Indeed, he even knows how to explain its meaning. But a shared meal suffices for them to recognize Jesus in the breaking of the bread.

This is an astonishing lesson about the design of God and the meaning of the cross. The entire history of the people of God teaches us that suffering is a source of life and death is a passage to a resurrection. Christ, in whom the whole history of humanity is recapitulated, could follow no other road in order to open the entrance to the kingdom of his Father. This wonderful account of the disciples at Emmaus always teaches us the paths of faith and how everything is decided in the encounter with Christ, in the acceptance of his Word, in the acknowledgment of his presence. He no longer sojourns among us under earthly conditions: the essential thing is to live his Word and partake in his Eucharist.

24:34 In this verse Luke has included one of the earliest testimonies to the appearance of the Risen Lord to Peter (see Lk 22:21-32; 1 Cor 15:5).

24:36-49 It is truly the Lord who is present, the one whom they have known and seen die. He therefore has truly risen! But nothing is as it was before: his presence is not explained; it merely attests, by its reality, that salvation was given, that death and sin are vanquished. Now the disciples realize that the salvation announced in a mysterious fashion by the Old Testament is accomplished in Jesus. And the Risen Lord charges them to proclaim it everywhere, to teach people about it by their testimony and by the power of the Spirit of Pentecost. This passage contains, in summary form, an entire model for Christian preaching: the fulfillment of the Scriptures and of God's plan, the proclamation of forgiveness and conversion, the call to faith and holiness. The Book of Acts will tell how the Church carried out this mission.

24:50-53 Recognized and worshiped as Lord by his disciples, Jesus is taken away from our world. The Gospel of Luke ends with this vision, which the Acts of the Apostles situates forty days later (Acts 1:2-3, 9-11). Regardless of the date and the unfolding, the event surpasses history and time; after his resurrection, Jesus is established in his dignity of the Son of God. Henceforth, we live on earth in the time of praise and bearing witness.

THE GOSPEL ACCORDING TO JOHN

1:1—2:12 As believers contemplate Christ, they cannot but reflect on the fate of the universe and the destiny of the human race. They believe that creation is the work of God. In Jesus they see the Word who is of God and has come to renew creation. In the view of the evangelist, both the testimony of John the Baptist and the changing of water into wine at the wedding feast of Cana attest to this renewal.

These first texts seem to comprise a week in the life of Jesus, as if the author wanted to establish a parallel between the first week of creation and the new work of God in Jesus.

1:1-18 Rather than being an introduction, this well-known "Prologue of John" resembles an "overture." The entire Gospel is summed up in a few lines and all its essential themes are brought together. The great conviction of faith is immediately proclaimed: Jesus is God who has entered into the world and history to save us. With this key in hand, it is possible to understand all that Jesus says and does. This majestic prelude, written in rhythmic prose, unfolds in three stages (1:1-5; 1:6-14; 1:15-18).

1:1-5 In the first stage of the Prologue, we wonder at Jesus, the Word, whose person and existence infinitely transcend the world and history. We also call to mind creation, which is from the very outset an action of the Word, that is, of the creative Word of God, the divine Wisdom and source of life that makes the world exist (see Gen 1:1; Prov 8:22f.). At the same time, we proclaim the new creation, for the Word offers human beings a new life that comes from God and illumines their entire existence.

This Prologue is a hymn to the *Word* (in Latin, *Verbum*; in Greek, *Logos*). The term "Word" sums up and goes beyond everything that the Old Testament had glimpsed of the presence of God amid humanity by means of his Word; it includes and is superior to everything that the philosophy of the age could imagine regarding God's reflection in the universe.

1:6-14 The second stage of the Prologue calls to mind the struggle of human beings against the light. John came, a man sent to announce the coming of the light to God's own, that is, the people of Israel. But he was not the Messiah! In Jesus, and in Jesus alone, the very Word of God became flesh, in order that the gift of the Lord might be present among us, in our human existence.

1:6 *John,* i.e., the Baptist.

1:15-18 The third stage of the Prologue expresses our conviction. Human beings may await various messiahs and various revelations, but Jesus is the only true Christ foretold by the Law, that is, by the Old Testament. He is more than a new Moses, because in him the former covenant yields place to the new and definitive covenant. He is not only the extraordinary and only One Sent, but he is the Son, equal in every way to the Father (John gives us here the perfect formulation of the mystery of the incarnation).

1:19-51 Right from the Prologue, Jesus Christ is present in this Gospel as the Word and the only-begotten Son of God. Jesus communicates his life to us and makes known to us his glory. We are present at a great trial. In this trial, Jesus appears as witness of the truth, he alone. John's whole Gospel draws the reader, page after page, into this drama.

1:19-28 At that time, there was lively expectation in Israel that the great personages of the past would reappear in order to prepare for the coming of the Messiah (in Greek: Christ) (see Deut 18:15; Sir 48:10-11; Mal 3:23).

The sudden popularity of John the Baptist alarms "the Jews," i.e., all those who have authority. In the political circles of the priesthood, there is fear of uprisings; among the "pure," i.e., the Pharisees, there is concern for the good observance of the practices of the Law. The response comes—public and confirmed by the prophet Isaiah (40:3): John is not the Messiah, but the Precursor who announces him. By contrast, here is a testimony to the unique role of Jesus.

1:19 *The Jews:* this phrase occurs more than 70 times in the fourth Gospel—sometimes in a favorable sense (Jn 4:20), others in a neutral sense, but most often in a pejorative sense referring to the leaders of the Jews who were hostile to Jesus (Jn 8:48, etc.). Here it means the delegation sent by the Sanhedrin to assess the activities of an unauthorized teacher.

1:20 *Christ:* the Messiah, the anointed vicegerent of the Lord, usually regarded as the heir of David.

1:21 *Elijah:* this prophet who had been carried away to heaven in a fiery chariot was expected to return to earth to announce the end time. *The Prophet:* i.e., the Prophet mentioned in Deut 18:15, 18, the one like Moses (see Acts 3:22), who was expected to be the Messiah and repeat the prodigies of the Exodus.

1:29-34 John knows that he acts as a prophet gripped by the mission of God. And at the threshold of the Gospel, he presents the image of the lamb who will be evoked again at the end of the Passion. It is connected with the Jewish Passover and symbolizes the deliverance from Egypt (Ex 12:1-28); it also fits in with the portrait of the mysterious Servant of God, foretold by a prophet as an innocent victim led like a lamb to the slaughter, who was not only to atone for the sins of humanity but also to justify sinners (Isa 53:7, 11-12). It further recalls the great apocalyptic Lamb who would destroy evil in the world (Rev 5—7; 17:14).

1:31 *I myself did not know him:* this may refer to the fact that John lived in the desert until he appeared publicly to Israel (see Lk 1:80) and thus did not know Jesus very well. It may also indicate that John did not know that Jesus was the Messiah until he saw the sign mentioned in vv. 32-33.

1:32 For Jesus' Baptism, see notes on Mt 3:13-17; 3:15; 3:17.

1:33 *The one who is to baptize with the Holy Spirit:* John baptized with water, but Jesus would baptize with the Holy Spirit. We can see in this a reference to the sending of the Holy Spirit. In this Gospel that occurs on Easter Sunday (Jn 20:22).

1:35-51 The movement of Jesus is separated from the movement of the Baptist. In the very first encounter, Jesus wins over Andrew, and perhaps the disciple who is not named was the beloved disciple, sufficiently interested in Andrew's call to still remember the hour (v. 39). Jesus gives Simon a new name indicative of his future mission (see Mt 16:18); with authority he calls Philip, and he reads the heart of Nathanael.

In this man so unexpected because of his lowly origin (v. 46), the disciples recognize the Messiah Israel expected. And Jesus unveils to them his mystery: Messiah of Israel, he is also the Son of Man who reunites heaven and earth in his kingdom. He is the sole mediator who gives access to the Father, as indicated in v. 51, an allusion to the dream of Jacob (see Gen 28:12).

The Gospel then offers us a meditation on the free gift and the happiness of being called by Jesus, a charter of the spiritual life. The dialogue with the first disciples lets us understand where Jesus leads those who follow him: there where he dwells at the side of the Father (see Jn 1:18). Intimacy with Christ, shared knowledge, and faith are the principal traits that describe the life of disciples. The Church must be the community where people share the certainty and the joy of having encountered Christ.

1:39 *Four o'clock in the afternoon:* literally, "the tenth hour" (from sunrise: 6:00 A.M.) in the Roman method of telling time.

1:41 *Messiah:* Greek transliteration of the Hebrew word for "Anointed One," which is used only here and in Jn 4:25 in this Gospel. The Greek translation *Christos* ("Christ") appears everywhere else.

1:42 *Cephas* in Aramaic signifies "stone, rock" (see Mt 16:18). It was not used at that time as a personal name. *Peter:* i.e., *Petros,* the Greek equivalent of *Cephas.*

1:43 *Jesus:* literally, "he," which could also refer to Peter.

1:44 *Bethsaida:* on the northern shore of Lake Tiberias.

1:45 *Nathanael* was certainly the apostle Bartholomew; see Mt 10:3.

1:47 *A true Israelite, in whom there is no deception:* this phrase recalls the fact that Jacob was the first to bear the name "Israel" (Gen 32:29), but he was an "Israelite" in whom there *was* deception (Gen 27:35-36).

1:48 *Under the fig tree:* a phrase signifying Messianic peace (see Mic 4:4; Zec 3:10).

1:51 *Son of Man:* see note on Mt 8:20 for the use of this term in the New Testament. In John, it occurs 13 times and is commonly associated with themes of crucifixion and suffering (Jn 3:14; 8:28) and revelation (Jn 6:27, 53) as well as eschatological authority (Jn 5:27; 9:39).

2:1-12 The evangelist calls special attention to the presence of the Mother of Jesus. Her role is to call Jesus to the cross and then stand by him in his Passion (Jn 19:25-26).

2:1 *Cana* was five miles northeast of Nazareth.

2:4 *Woman:* a universal address from son to mother; it is used again in Jn 19:26, where its meaning becomes evident: Mary is the new Eve, mother of the living (Gen 3:15, 20). *My hour has not yet come:* the hour is that of Jesus' glorification and return to the Father (see Jn 7:30; 8:20; 12:23, 27; 13:1; 17:1; 19:27). It is determined by the Father and cannot be anticipated. The miracle worked at Mary's intercession is a prophetic symbol of it.

2:10 The first wine represents the first Covenant, the second better wine represents the New Covenant. Jesus is prefiguring the Messianic banquet.

2:11 *Signs:* a term used by John to indicate Jesus' miracles, emphasizing the significance rather than the marvelous character of the event (see Jn 4:54; 6:14; 9:16; 11:47). These signs reveal Jesus' glory (Jn 1:14; Isa 35:1-2; Joel 3:18; Am 9:13).

2:12 *Brethren:* that is, his close relatives. See notes on Mt 12:46-50 and 12:47.

2:13—4:54 The author of the fourth Gospel brings us from one Jewish feast to another; he seems to want to make them the points of reference with which to link the discourses of Jesus.

The incidents that follow are therefore connected with the feast of Passover. They attest that Jesus has come to establish a new and spiritual worship that is no longer reserved to a single people or to a place.

2:13-22 Passover is the feast of Unleavened Bread, a sign of renewal (see Ex 12:15). Jesus knows, better than the Prophets (Isa 1:11; Jer 7:4; Am 5:21), that his Father has nothing to do with this traffic in sacrifices and offerings, if the interior gift of the heart is lacking.

In fact, in the evangelist's view, this temple of stone has already lost its function, and the true dwelling of the Father among human beings will be the humanity of the risen Jesus, who is the focal point of all worship. The construction of the new temple in Jerusalem had been begun by Herod the Great in 20–19 B.C. According to v. 20, then, we are in the year A.D. 27–28.

2:23—3:12 To be filled with wonder at what Jesus can do, as was Nicodemus, is not yet faith. Faith is acceptance of the testimony of Jesus about God and about the plan of Jesus. Faith is another life, a transformed existence. The flesh—i.e., we with our material and intellectual possibilities—does not have the power to transform our life.

This transformation comes like the wind—mysterious and surprising—the same word in Hebrew and Greek expressing spirit and wind. The idea here is to bring to mind an event (rebirth) in which God alone has the initiative. Only those who open themselves to the Spirit, those who want to be reborn in Baptism and transformed as children of God, can believe in the new life that Jesus reveals and whose source is the Spirit—for they live it as by a gift.

3:1 *Nicodemus:* a member of the Sanhedrin or ruling council in virtue of his being a teacher of the Law.

3:3 *Kingdom of God:* this is the basic theme of the preaching of Jesus in the Synoptic Gospels. In John, it appears explicitly only in this verse. However, in the Synoptics it almost disappears in the Passion Narrative, whereas in John it is given particular emphasis there. John identifies the kingdom of God with the very person of Jesus. During the public ministry, the splendor of Jesus' kingship was somewhat veiled by his fragile humanity, but in the Passion it comes shining through in his exaltation on the cross, which, for John, is intrinsically connected with Jesus' glorification in heaven. *From above:* the Greek word *anothen* could be translated "from above" or "again." Jesus means "from above," but Nicodemus understands "again."

3:5 *Born of water and the Spirit:* this phrase refers to Christian Baptism, the necessary vehicle for our spiritual rebirth, wrought by the Holy Spirit. It may be that here the evangelist is clarifying the words of the Lord according to a later and more mature understanding of Christian teaching, as lived in the primitive community.

3:13-21 The evangelist prolongs the conversation with Nicodemus in meditation on Jesus. What, then, is the mystery of Jesus and what does he bring to the human condition? The evangelist meditates on the Son of God, the divine messenger now glorified at his Father's side.

From Jesus, life came through the cross—as is suggested by the allusion to the bronze serpent intended to cure dying Hebrews (see Num 21:9). The cross was a testimony of God's love for the world and for each one of us. The cross was also the light given to us. This light enables us to recognize our conduct in truth and compels us to make a decisive choice: either to submit to Jesus and be saved, or to flee and be condemned.

3:14 *So must the Son of Man be lifted up:* the reference is to the lifting up on the cross, which in John's view is identical with the glorification of Jesus.

3:22-30 Using an image familiar to the Jews (see Deut 31:16; Jer 2:2; Hos 2:18f; Mt 9:15), John attests that Jesus is the true Bridegroom, that is, the one in whose person God enters into the new and definitive covenant with his own.

The witness, moreover, sets himself aside: he is only the friend of the Bridegroom, whose role is to ask for the hand of the bride and, when the wedding feast is prepared, to introduce her to the Bridegroom.

3:23 *Aenon:* the place has not been identified with certainty.

3:31-36 The evangelist continues his reflection on the mystery of Christ. Jesus is the Son who receives from his Father the fullness of life. He has the mission to reveal it and communicate it to those who believe in him, by giving them the Spirit with whom he himself is filled (v. 34). In rich and symbolic words, he is to show how much the believer's life is a gift of God and a newness of existence beyond anything that is in the earthly power of people.

3:34 *For God gives him the Spirit without measure:* another translation is: "And he gives the Spirit without measure."

4:1-3 Jesus is forced to leave Judea in order to distance himself from the hostility of the Pharisees who are jealous of his growing popularity. The journey through Samaria affords him an opportunity to proclaim the Gospel in a mission land, so to speak, for the Samaritans were tantamount to Gentiles in the eyes of the Jews.

4:4-30 Jesus converses with a woman, a daughter of Samaria, and therefore belonging to what the Jews considered to be a heretical breed and as accursed as the Gentiles; in addition, she is well known as a sinner. But God's gift is for everyone. Jesus is the living water, and for peoples dwelling on the edge of the wilderness, living water symbolizes life, hope, renewal, and spiritual riches.

Jesus urges the new worship of God as Father "in Spirit and truth." This means to pray to the Father in the Holy Spirit and in Jesus who is the truth. Such worship springs up from the heart; it comes from the Spirit.

4:4 The inhabitants of Samaria were a mixed race, descended from the intermarriage of Israelites and Assyrian colonists. Although they worshiped the same God as the Jews and believed in the Pentateuch, they disowned the Jerusalem temple and priesthood and erected a rival sanctuary on Mount Gerizim in the 4th century B.C. (see 2 Mac 6:2).

4:5 *Sychar* was in the neighborhood of ancient Shechem. See Gen 33:18-20; 40:21f.

4:6 *Noon:* literally, "the sixth hour." See note on Mk 15:25.

4:9 *Samaritan woman:* characterized as ritually unclean by the Jews, who were therefore forbidden to drink from any vessel handled by them.

4:11 *Well is deep:* the depth of the well, which still exists, has not been determined. The estimates given over the centuries range from 240 feet to 150 feet to 75 feet (the most recent).

4:20 *This mountain:* Gerizim (2,849 feet high, south of Sychar).

4:23 *In Spirit and truth:* the *Spirit* is the Holy Spirit and the *truth* is Jesus. For he is the true Son of God.

4:25 The Samaritan Messiah was called the *Ta'eb*. He revealed the secrets of God to his people. Jesus reveals to us how much God loves us.

4:26 *I am he:* this phrase may also be translated as "I AM," the name Yahweh used for himself in the Old Testament (see note on Mk 6:50). The phrase "I am" is used in the text of this Gospel 23 times (4:26; 6:20, 35, 41, 48, 51; 8:12, 18, 24, 28, 58; 10:7, 9, 11, 14; 11:25; 13:19; 14:6; 15:1, 5; 18:5, 6, 8). In several of these passages, Jesus joins the phrase with seven significant metaphors that express his saving relationship toward the world: "I am the bread of life" (Jn 6:35, 41, 48, 51). "I am the light of the world" (Jn 8:12). "I am the gate of the sheepfold" (Jn 10:7, 9). "I am the good shepherd" (Jn 10:11, 14). "I am the resurrection and the life" (Jn 11:25). "I am the way, and the truth, and the life" (Jn 14:6). "I am the true vine" (Jn 15:1, 5).

4:31-38 Jesus is not thinking of an ordinary harvest. The arrival of the Samaritans announces the crops of the end time, the harvest in which all will be gathered together by the coming of God. Samaritans wore white robes: they are the harvest.

4:39-42 The personal and prolonged encounter with Jesus allows believers to measure the magnitude of their mission. This Jewish teacher is not only a prophet who announces salvation. He is the Messiah who brings about salvation for the whole world, for all human beings.

4:43-45 Jesus' stay in Galilee and his ministry in his own town will not be crowned by a more satisfactory success than the one in Judea, the heart of Judaism. With this sad reflection, the fourth evangelist confirms a saying of the Lord found in Mt 13:57 and parallels.

4:46-54 Jesus shows the price of faith (believing in the Word) to his unbelieving companions (v. 44) even though they had already seen him at work. Faith, and it alone, is necessary to be saved. To believe is to welcome in Jesus the salvation that God gives. The miracle is first of all a response to faith. Then it sheds light on the man's faith and makes it strong. The cure is reported less to bring a demonstration of faith than to call upon us to believe. This account may be a third version of the cure of the centurion's son (Mt 8:5-13) or servant (Lk 7:1-10).

4:52 *One o'clock in the afternoon:* literally, "the seventh hour." See note on Mk 15:25.

5:1-47 Every Jewish feast is a memorial of what God has done for his people in deeds that manifest his power to create and restore. It is in this setting that the evangelist places an important action of Jesus, which leads to a debate over the meaning of the action: Is God himself at work here?

5:1-18 Jesus, the Son of God, claims a power that belongs to God alone. In addition, by breaking the Sabbath precept, Jesus proclaims the end of the old covenant. The incident is perhaps to be connected with the feast of Pentecost, which, according to Jewish tradition, commemorates the promulgation of the Law on Sinai. This would make Jesus' action even more eloquent.

5:2 *Bethesda,* also called Bethsaida or Bethzatha.

5:3 *Waiting for the movement of the water:* these words appear only in the Caesarean and Western recensions.

5:4 This verse is lacking in many important manuscripts, including the oldest.

5:19-30 The action of Jesus creates scandal and anger among the religious authorities. He has to explain his activity and especially his claim that he and the Father are one. The evangelist deepens this affirmation of Jesus' divinity. What would be seen as blasphemous in anyone else is here a profound reality.

Jesus is one with his Father. All the work of Jesus is God's action among us. Jesus has the power to give or restore life to those who welcome his word as that of God, even if they are victims of sin. To encounter Jesus is to face judgment and to experience eternal life even now. To accept or refuse his work: no decision is more important for us.

5:31-47 The claim made by Jesus has to be confirmed. People cannot testify on their own behalf. There was, of course, John the Baptist's testimony in favor of Christ, but it had already become no more than a remembrance. It is in the works of Jesus that believers recognize the attestation of the Father.

But how could other people accept this recognition, those who are only preoccupied with their rank in the world, with their person, or with their religious role? Victimized by such an attitude, they falsify even the testimony of Scripture to protect themselves. Only those people can come to Jesus who rid themselves of their pretensions, human and even religious, those who are truly inflamed with love for God.

6:1-71 The Jewish Passover is near at hand, and with it the days on which unleavened bread is eaten as a sign of renewal; the action also recalls the manna that fed the Hebrews in the wilderness. It is in this context that the evangelist places Jesus' act of feeding the hungry crowd. The whole action is a sign and foreshadowing of a new Passover and a true life-giving food. Jesus himself, in his person, is the bread of life that God offers to humanity. In order to receive this bread that makes a person live forever, one must believe in the Word.

6:1-15 This is one of the rare passages in which all four Gospels are clearly parallel. At this point, John introduces the discourse on the bread of life. The sign of the loaves is seen as a symbol of the food given to mankind in the Word of God and especially in the Eucharist.

6:7 *Two hundred days' wages:* literally: two hundred denarii. A denarius was the average wage for a day's work (see Mt 20:2).

6:16-21 This account is connected with the preceding passage in the oldest tradition. Like the miracle of the loaves, it shows the absolute mastery Jesus exercises over creatures. For the disciples it is an invitation to believe without reserve: with Jesus present, they will lack nothing, and nothing can put them in peril.

6:20 *It is I:* literally, "I AM," the formula that reveals the name of the Lord in the Old Testament (see Ex 3:14; Isa 41:4, 10, 14; 43:1-3, 10, 13). Hence, the evangelist is alluding to Jesus as the Son of God. See note on Jn 4:26.

6:22-71 Jesus' gestures and actions are always signs of God; in them is expressed something of the mystery of Christ. Thus, the fourth evangelist places on the lips of Jesus a discourse that unveils the mystery. Here, then, is the deep meaning of the miracle of the loaves: Jesus is the Messenger of God, the true Bread handed over to gain life with God for the whole world.

Thus, it is announced that the words of Jesus are food for people, and that the life of Jesus is given on the cross for the salvation of all. But the Christian addressees of the fourth Gospel could not read this discourse without interpreting it as already announcing the rite inaugurated at the Last Supper (Mt 26:26), the Eucharist, memorial of the body handed over, of the blood shed, of the sacrifice of the cross.

Therefore, this discourse can be read on two levels. The author of the Gospel certainly wanted it so read: the word of God instructs one in the ways of God and the word of God is the bread of life that nourishes the spiritual hunger of God's people.

6:22-33 There is a hunger for everlasting life, a hunger for God! And there is a bread of God, a food that gives everlasting life to those who believe in Jesus. The miracle of the manna was a symbol of this food (Ex 16:4, 13-15).

6:31 *Bread from heaven:* see Ex 14:4, 15, 32-34; Ps 78:24. There was a belief that the manna had been hidden by Jeremiah (see 2 Mac 2:5-8) and would reappear at Passover in Messianic times.

6:34-40 Jesus makes an astonishing affirmation: there is a Bread of God for us, and it is a person. Jesus himself fulfills his Father's plan for us; in Jesus God is present so that we may have true life. To receive God's Bread is to believe in Jesus and accept him as the Son of God to receive through him the life his Father intends for us. What an astonishing gift! Jesus does not allow himself to be worshiped as a god or a hero; he says of himself that he came to satisfy the hunger of people and to fulfill our life. Every other food is only a diversion for our essential hunger. Jesus is the Bread that satisfies this hunger.

6:35 *I am . . . :* this is the first of seven self-descriptions of Jesus introduced by "I am" (see Jn 8:12; and 9:5; 10:7, 9; 10:11, 14; 11:25; 14:6; 15:1, 5). These echo Ex 3:14 (see notes on Jn 4:26 and 6:20).

6:41-47 During the period in the wilderness, the Hebrews doubted the Lord and "grumbled" against him; the memory of this had remained as a warning for all time (see Ex 16; Num 11; Ps 106:25).

When the fourth Gospel speaks of "the Jews," the reference is to this mentality, this attitude of rejection, rather than to people as a whole or even to their leaders.

6:48-58 In what sense does Jesus do the Father's will? By giving his life. He does not use the word "sacrifice," but the terms "flesh" and "blood" express that idea in a very realistic way. In this gift, the life of the Father is given to human beings and becomes their everlasting life. That is a strong statement, and yet the objection of the Jews, who take it in the most material sense, does not lead to any toning down of it. On the contrary!

6:59-71 After the success of the multiplication of loaves, scandal arises. The "flesh" (v. 63)—that is, people with their petty desires and thoughts—could not but be shocked by a revelation as absolute as the one they have just heard (that Jesus is the living Bread come down from heaven). Many of his disciples as well as some other people stopped following him, and Judas was already thinking of handing him over.

Only the Spirit gives people the will to believe that the Father speaks in Jesus. It is the Spirit who inspires Peter's profession of faith (see Mt 16:16; Mk 8:29; Lk 9:20). But the Spirit would not be given in fullness until after Jesus' Resurrection (see Jn 7:39).

In regard to Jesus, there is a division among the people. This division and Peter's profession of faith mark a parting of the ways in the life of Jesus. The time of revelation to the disciples has begun and from now on the conflict with the official religion will develop irreconcilably.

6:63 *Flesh:* the human being with its desires and thoughts.

7:1—9:41 The feast of Tabernacles, one of the most important Jewish solemnities, was a harvest festival. There was also a commemoration of the miraculous deeds that God had done for his people in the wilderness, with a joyous feast of lamps, a festival of lights. The feast was the ideal setting in which to present Christ as the Word of God who had come to enlighten and save everyone.

7:1-13 From now on the threat of death hangs over Jesus and creates tension for him. The tension has to be relieved as quickly as possible. A gathering of people in Jerusalem would be a good occasion for rallying them and neutralizing the adversaries. An impressive public manifestation by Jesus would also be helpful; people would at least know what to make of him. So reason the "brethren" of Jesus—that is, the relatives if not the disciples.

But these perspectives of glory have no hold on Jesus. He has come to fulfill God's plan; this is not the same as looking for a temporary success. He also has come to turn back the course of evil, falsehood, and hatred in the world. Jesus overcame the hatred of the world by handing himself over to it.

7:3 *Brethren:* i.e., according to Hebrew idiom, close relatives. See note on Mt 12:46.

7:14-24 Personal success is never the motive for an action of Jesus. His words and his miracles testify that he is the messenger of the Father. Jesus lives by this testimony, of which he is convinced, and does not defend any doctrine of a school or group; one care alone impels him: that the Father's plan for us be recognized and fulfilled.

Only those will understand Jesus who take the Law seriously in its deep inspiration and know the price of fidelity to God. But those who accuse Jesus of violating the Law and take upon themselves the authority to condemn him fail to recognize him.

7:15 The people want to know how Jesus can teach like a rabbi, when he was never trained by one and never quotes his teacher.

7:21 *A single work:* the work of which Jesus speaks may be the cure of the paralytic that is recounted in Jn 5:1-15.

7:25-36 The new prophet intrigues the people. He is one of theirs, yet claims an origin that does not cease to be mysterious. Some of the people are tempted to recognize him as the Messiah. The official authorities rebel against this temptation and want him arrested. In veiled words, Jesus announces his return to the Father (vv. 33-34). The authorities see this as an attempt to flee Palestine.

In all these contrasts there is perhaps some irony. Jesus escapes the people who want to place him in their preconceived ideas, just as he escapes the people who want to lay hands on him. Jesus can be talked about endlessly; it is quite another thing to accept his mystery.

7:37-39 The last day was for the pilgrims a festival of water. How many symbolic meanings water evokes! Water had flowed miraculously from the rock in the midst of the wilderness to slake the thirst of the Hebrews (Ex 17:1-7). The Prophets had foretold a spring that would some day open in the midst of the people (Ezek 47.1, Zec 14.8). In all areas affected by drought, water is a sign of life and joy; it is a gift of God. Christians think of Pentecost and Baptism.

7:37-38 An alternative reading and translation is: "If anyone is thirsty, let him come to me, and let him who believes in me drink. As Scripture has said. . . . " In this second reading, the Scripture passage refers to Jesus and not to the believer. See Ps 105:41; Isa 44:3; 48:21; Ezek 36:25; Joel 3:1; etc.

7:40-52 The upper class felt only contempt for the ordinary people. How could one accept a Messiah who came from distant Galilee, where Jews mingled with Gentiles and were cut off from the heart of Jewish life? Some justified their rejection by citing passages of the Law, but there were others who appealed to the spirit of the Law.

7:53—8:11 This story is missing in a number of ancient manuscripts and is inserted at other points in others; it does not seem to be from the author of the fourth Gospel, for it is written in quite a different style. However, it has been accepted by the Church as the work of an inspired author.

We are struck by the portrait of Jesus found herein: his silence, his sober gesture, his refusal to use religion as a pretext to spy on and judge others, and his courage to proclaim his own truth. It is pointless to ask what he wrote on the ground. Let us dwell on what he considered the Law to be: it condemns sin not so that people may judge one another but so that they may feel the need to be saved by God. And it is to this salvation that he bears witness.

8:4 *Caught in the very act of adultery:* Jewish law required witnesses to have seen the act.

8:5 *Stone such women:* stoning was required only if the woman was a betrothed virgin (Deut 22:23-24). The Law also demanded the execution of *both* parties (Lev 20:10; Deut 22:22).

8:7 The Law stipulated that the first stones were to be cast by the witnesses (Deut 17:7).

8:12-20 Here is another symbol, which has the feast of Lights for its setting and enables us to understand more fully the part Jesus intends to play in the life of human beings: he is light. We may think of the luminous cloud during the journey in the wilderness (see Ex 13:21; Wis 18:3), the form in which God was leading his people.

8:12 *I am:* see notes on Jn 6:20 and 6:35.

8:20 *The treasury of the temple:* not the place where the offerings were stored, since this was closed to the public, but the adjacent room where the boxes for the offerings stood (see Mk 12:41; Lk 21:1).

8:21-30 The discussion is continued so that the reader may come into direct contact with the mystery of Jesus. Who then is he? He does not belong to the world of sin but gathers around himself those who believe in him. Without this faith in him, people remain shut up in death, cast off from God. A sudden word is uttered: *I am,* the name by which God revealed himself to Moses (Ex 3:14). Jesus is so closely united to his Father that he can claim the title "Lord" for himself. Jesus will appear as Judge and Lord when he is lifted up on the cross (Jn 3:14; 19:37).

8:31-59 The Jews can rightly protest that they are not illegitimate children, that is, using the imagery of the time, they have not grown up in idolatry but in faith in the true God. But that is not enough. To oppose Jesus and reject the truth means entering into an agreement with the devil. Jesus says that he is superior even to Abraham, the father of the people.

8:56 Abraham rejoiced at the promise given to him by the Lord that the future Messiah would come from his descendants (Gen 12:7; 15:2f; 17:15f; see Gal 3:16). *My day:* that is, the presence of the Messiah, whom Abraham saw and greeted "from a distance" (Heb 11:13).

8:58 *I AM:* see notes on Jn 6:20 and 6:35.

9:1-41 The preceding chapters have made grand statements about Jesus, e.g., that he is the light of the world; in those chapters, however, the evangelist was guiding us through sometimes difficult reasonings. Here, on the other hand, is a lively story that illustrates the teaching that has been given. The man born blind is an image of the catechumen and of Christians, who allow themselves to be enlightened by Jesus. Not only their eyes but their hearts open to the light.

9:1-7 In the view of the ancients, every illness had its origin in some sin, perhaps a secret one. Jesus firmly condemns this mentality. The blind man must take himself to the Pool of "Siloam" (= "Sent"); the evangelist emphasizes the word. Jesus is the one sent by the Father to bring light; it is he who opens the eyes of faith in those who go down into the pool of Baptism.

9:7 *The Pool of Siloam:* it was at the foot of the southern spur of the temple mount.

9:8-23 Who, then, is Jesus? Again there is questioning. Again also Jesus upsets the Pharisees, who have lost the essence of religion in the complexities of their traditions. The care for observances makes them forget that the Sabbath is first of all a testimony of liberty. In the presence of these teachers, the blind man who has been cured declares that Jesus is a prophet. They challenge his attestation and denounce it as a fraud. Thus an inquiry is made to give themselves basis for their treatment of the man. A climate of fear ensues and no one feels free to speak.

9:24-34 The miraculously cured individual is interrogated a second time. His questioners bring up Moses to show that Jesus is in contradiction with him. This, they think, cannot be refuted. But it is necessary to recognize here the presence of the same God who spoke to Moses! The man born blind recognizes that Jesus came from God with a special mission. That is too much for them. They throw him out bodily.

9:35-38 This is an encounter with Jesus, who identifies himself as the Son of Man—that is, as a being with a divine prerogative who has come to bring people to the presence of and communion with God. The profession of faith comes to the lips of the man born blind when he encounters Jesus, who is our light.

9:39-41 Human beings cannot remain indifferent or neutral in the presence of Jesus: we must opt either for light or for darkness. In this choice, the divine judgment comes into play with a sentence of life or death—which foretells the division between synagogue and Church. The lot of each person depends on one's attitude of faith or unbelief toward Jesus. Those who realize they are walking along the way of error and open themselves to the light of the Gospel revelation will be saved. Those who delude themselves that they possess the truth and voluntarily close their eyes to the light will be lost.

While the man born blind receives not only his physical sight but also the light of faith, the Jews who claim that they have sight are blind in a spiritual sense, because they refuse the light of revelation brought by Christ. True blindness is not the physical blindness of the blind man but the lack of belief. The Pharisees are convinced that they possess the truth and oppose themselves to the Envoy of God. They deprive themselves of the way to salvation. For they remain slaves of the sin of unbelief.

10:1—11:54 The parable of the good shepherd, the feast of the Dedication, and the raising of Lazarus are three passages that describe who Christ is and what he wants to be for us. The ideas of life and unity dominate in these pages. The desire of Jesus is that we have access to the full reality of life. He gives life to the point of giving up his own; he is the life.

Another preoccupation impels him: to gather into one all who believe in him. So the work of God is to overcome the forces of death, destruction, and dispersion, forces that disfigure the world and our existence.

10:1-21 The image of the flock and the shepherd occurs frequently in the Bible to describe the relationship of Israel with God, or simply the relations of the people with their leader (this language came spontaneously to any civilization of antiquity). More than once the Prophets denounced as wicked shepherds those in authority who exploited the people or led them astray: kings, princes, priests, prophets of comfort (see Jer 23; Ezek 34; Zec 11:4-17). In the final analysis (they said), God alone is the shepherd to whom the flock belongs and who can properly lead and feed it. They were longing for a devoted shepherd who would act solely in God's name.

Jesus now dares to describe himself as this Messiah-shepherd, who comes to deliver human beings from those who enslave them for their own profit or to impose upon them their own convictions. There are no other ways of reaching life and the knowledge of God: Jesus is the "gate"; he is the Shepherd who knows and gathers believers into a single flock. The word "know" signifies a mutual exchange, a reciprocal and radical belonging. This is the main assertion of the passage.

10:21 This is a reference to the incident of the man born blind (in the preceding chapter).

10:22-39 In the fourth Gospel, the trial of Jesus takes place throughout the book, and on each occasion the Lord asserts his oneness with the Father in unequivocal terms. Here we have a new disagreement, connected with the feast of the Dedication of the temple, which was celebrated toward the end of December. It commemorated the historical fact that in 165 B.C. Judas Maccabeus wrested the temple from the pagan king who had profaned it by installing an idol in it. It was thus a celebration of the liberation, purification, and restoration of the holy place and of its worship (see 1 Mac 4:36-39; 2 Mac 1:9-18; 10:1-8).

10:23 *Portico of Solomon:* located on the east side of the temple, and thus sheltered against the winds from the wilderness.

10:30 *I and the Father are one:* this is the most solemn declaration of the passage. Jesus expresses his perfect unity with the Father (literally, "one thing"), so that his power is identified with that of the Father. Trinitarian theology takes its start from this verse. For here Jesus affirms in peremptory fashion his identity of operation and will with the Father. This is clear from the violent reaction of the Jews, who seek to stone him because he is guilty of blasphemy.

10:34 *Your Law:* the term *Law* usually meant the Pentateuch, but it was also used in the sense of the whole Old Testament—as it is in this case. *You are gods:* these words from Ps 82:6 referred to the judges (as well as other leaders or rulers) of Israel whose tasks were appointed by God (see Ex 22:28; Deut 1:17; 16:18; 2 Chr 19:6).

10:40-42 The testimony of John the Baptist is recalled: the Prophet announced a Messiah whose dignity and power were superhuman (see Jn 1:26-34).

11:1-54 Unceasingly, Jesus attests that he has come to give life. The Resurrection is the sign that shows he came to give life. Death is no longer the last word on the human condition, and life now assumes an unusual stability; it is filled with endless hope.

11:1-16 Death spares no one, not even friends of the Son of God. But unhurriedly and without fear, Jesus confronts it in order to liberate from it those he loves. Death can no longer be the final destination; henceforth, it is simply a passage for which sleep is like a first image.

The Gospel of Luke also speaks of the two sisters, Martha and Mary, but without naming their village (Lk 10:38-42); we know from this passage that it was Bethany, and we also learn that they had a brother. Bethany was on the eastern slope of the Mount of Olives, about two miles from Jerusalem.

One notes the decision of Jesus to accomplish his work without hesitation even to the destiny established by his Father (v. 9); and his light must instill courage into those who follow him (vv. 10-11).

11:16 *Twin,* i.e., *Didymus,* is the Greek translation of the Aramaic *Toma,* which means "twin."

11:17-44 Faced with the death of a friend and the sufferings of the man's relatives, Jesus responds with true humanity and a compassionate heart; by restoring life to Lazarus, he shows himself to be the Son of God, to whom the Father has given everything he asks for. The hope of a resurrection on the last day was shared by many believers, such as Martha; this conviction had been growing for about a century or two in fervent Jewish circles, such as that of the Pharisees (2 Mac 7:9-14, 22f; 12:43-45; Dan 12:1-3; see Wis 2:3—3:9). In the time of Jesus, however, the priestly caste in Jerusalem opposed the belief (Acts 23:6-9) and tried to ridicule it (Mt 22:23-33). Here Jesus not only confirms the hope but also reveals that he is the one who fulfills it.

11:17 *Four days:* the Jews believed that the soul remained near the body for three days after death, giving hope for a return to the body. By the fourth day there was no hope of coming back.

11:19 *To console them:* according to Jewish custom, there were thirty days of mourning: three days of very great mourning, four days of great mourning, and 23 days of lighter mourning.

11:45-54 There is peril for the city and its religion unless they accept the unimaginable: that God no longer needs his temple and henceforth is present through Jesus Christ alone. Because of civic and religious considerations it is necessary to decide the fate of this man, who unsettles the certainties and confronts the institutions and the established power.

Without realizing it, Caiaphas, the high priest who had held this office since A.D. 18 and would continue to hold it until A.D. 36, makes a statement that is at the heart of the Christian Faith: Christ will die for all, so that the entire human family may have life. The temple and Jewish tradition are now transcended by a worship and a salvation that are universal.

11:49 *That year:* i.e., at that time. The Jews believed that the high priest possessed a gift of prophecy, which was at times unknowingly carried out (see v. 51).

11:53 Jesus is placed under a death sentence, which the careful reader with suspect to be illegal because of Nicodemus' question to the authorities in Jn 7:51: "Does our Law allow us to pass judgment on someone without first giving him a hearing to ascertain what he is doing?"

11:54 *Ephraim:* on the edge of the wilderness of Judea, 16 miles north of Jerusalem.

11:55—21:25 It is the feast of Passover in Jerusalem, a time when faith and hope are reborn in the minds of the people, as they commemorate their deliverance from slavery, the formation of the people, the Covenant, the journey to the mountain of God, and the promised land. Lambs are sacrificed, reproducing the shedding of the blood that had preserved the life of Israel long ago. The feast is full of memories, which are at the same time a promise of a different future. This future is now becoming a reality.

There is now a new Passover, the once-for-all Passover that is accomplished not in a ritual but in an action: Jesus fulfills the former Covenant by bringing to pass that which it had announced and prefigured (Ex 12:1-13, 16); he is the true Lamb who gives his life and whose blood poured out delivers the people from enslavement to evil and sin and opens the way to the true promised land, to the Father, in a communion of life with him.

The last section of the Gospel of John is centered on this mystery of the Passion of Christ.

The fate awaiting Jesus from the first pages of this Gospel is fulfilled; his adversaries have decided to put him to death and are waiting to have the sentence executed. It is the reign of darkness. But the hour of Jesus' death and defeat is another reality, that of triumph and glory; and it will be confirmed by the Resurrection of the Crucified.

The time of the Church will be inaugurated. She will receive the Spirit promised by Jesus and—as is indicated by the last signs (the miraculous catch of fish and the investiture of Peter)—will be established and sent forth to preach everywhere. She is to proclaim salvation and life so as to gather together all believers until the day when Christ will return in his glory as Son of God and Savior of the world.

11:55—12:50 The time for signs has ended. The glory that the signs announced is going to appear. How? It will not be through the deceitful glory of human triumphs; it will be through the presence of God in the action of Jesus and in the transformation of the human condition. Jesus' hour of glory is above all the hour of his death.

11:55—12:11 According to the tradition followed by the fourth Gospel, the woman who pours the perfume on the feet of Jesus is Mary, the sister of Lazarus. With the prodigality of love she expresses her gratitude for the raising of her brother from the dead; but Jesus evokes his own death, and Mary's gesture points ahead to this, anticipating by her anointing the rite of burial: it is an act of veneration.

Wasteful squandering? Only Judas, whose shadow already darkens the picture, thinks so. It is not such veneration of Christ that turns his attention to the poor; it is avarice—at the same time that Jesus is being glorified at Bethany, the plot against him is being laid for civic reasons, as we saw earlier.

11:55-57 This is probably the Passover of the year 30, which was to be Jesus' last. The devout Jews journeyed to Jerusalem to complete the ritual purifications necessary for Passover celebrations (see Ex 19:10-11, 15; Num 9:6-14; 2 Chr 30:1-3, 15-18). Since Jesus had been present in Jerusalem at the feasts of Tabernacles and Dedication, the populace expected him to be there again. A warrant had been issued for his arrest, and anyone who knew his whereabouts had to declare it under penalty of complicity.

12:3 *Pint:* Greek: *litra,* i.e., about a half-liter.

12:5 *Three hundred denarii:* a year's wages, a denarius being a day's wages for a laborer.

12:12-19 To a greater degree than the Synoptics, the fourth Gospel describes this entry as a triumph and stresses above all the theme of the glory of Christ.

The raising of Lazarus has provoked the enthusiasm of the crowd, and for the first time Jesus allows himself to be acclaimed "King of Israel"; he lets himself be known as the King-Messiah announced by Zechariah (9:9).

12:13 *Branches of palm:* customarily used in victory celebrations (see 1 Mac 13:51; 2 Mac 10:7). *Hosanna:* an acclamation meaning "Grant salvation!" The citation is from Ps 118:25. *He who comes in the name of the Lord:* see note on Mt 21:9. *The King of Israel:* a reference to the coming king mentioned by Zep 3:14-15 and Zec 9:9. See also note on Mt 21:9.

12:15 *Daughter of Zion:* see note on Mt 21:5.

12:17 Another reading for this verse is given in some manuscripts: "Then the crowd that was with him began to bear witness that he had called Lazarus out of the tomb and raised him from the dead."

12:20-36 Jesus' single-day success does not divert him from his hour, nor that of his adversaries, and it is his deciding moment. This page with so many themes gives us a glimpse into his thinking.

To the crowd, among whom are sympathetic Gentiles, he proposes the image of a grain of wheat that must die. Conscious of the necessity for his death, he realizes the fruitfulness of his approaching sacrifice for the whole world.

Paradoxically, that death is elevation and glorification: it will show who Jesus is and be the reversal in the fate of human beings. As in the account of the agony in the garden related by the Synoptics (Mt 26:36-46; Mk 14:32-42; Lk 22:39-46), he overcomes his fear in the face of what humans regard as ruin; he dominates the cruel paradox.

His death transforms the fate of the world: it is defeat for the forces of evil and opens up hope for those called to the communion of Jesus, to life.

Here is an unexpected Messiah who completes God's work by his own death; as here, so elsewhere we read constantly of Christ's invitation to his disciples to share his lot (see Mt 16:25; Mk 8:35; Lk 9:24). Believers may fear death but not lose hope, since for Jesus, in whom they believe, the hour of death was the hour in which he conquered the devil, was glorified by the Father, and showed himself to be the light of the world. This beautiful text leaves us the meditation of the ancient Church on the cross of Christ; it has become the glorious cross.

12:20 *Greeks:* not Jews, but adherents of Judaism, although without embracing its practices.

12:31 *Prince of this world:* Satan, who has the ability to control human beings by drawing them away from God (see Jn 14:30; 16:11; 2 Cor 4:4; Eph 2:2; 6:12).

12:34 *Law:* taken here as the entire Old Testament (see Jn 10:34), and referring specifically to Pss 89:37; 110:4; Isa 9:7; Dan 7:14. *Son of Man:* see notes on Jn 1:51 and Mt 8:20.

12:37-43 The early Christian generations always remained astonished at Israel's refusal of the light, and they meditated on the text of Isaiah on the blindness of people when faced with an unexpected work of God. To recognize the light is to choose to accept its demands: such a choice turns a life upside down; it is necessary to accept the risk of being marginalized from the usual social and religious milieu.

12:40 This text, like others in the Old Testament, appears to say that hardened hearts and blinded eyes are God's doing. However, the evangelist is simply assuring Christian readers that even though God would give people every opportunity to convert, many would still choose to stay in their sin.

12:42 John is indicating that in the Israel of his time there is, as always, a remnant that believes. But they are not a true People of God because of their fear of being excommunicated by the authorities.

12:44-50 But who is the light? It is Jesus himself, sent by the Father to make known the Father's love and to save believers. All through the Gospel, Christ has testified how deeply aware he is of this mission because of the unity in which he lives with his Father. What Jesus says in these few verses sums up his entire teaching concerning his mission.

12:47-48 This parallels the statement found at the end of the Sermon on the Mount (Mt 7:24-27). Everything hangs upon a person's acceptance or rejection of what Jesus has said.

13:1—14:31 This is the first of three parts that can clearly be distinguished in Jn 13:1—17:26. These pages constitute the best known section of the fourth Gospel, which at this point becomes the great book of meditation for Christians. The author develops a lengthy farewell address in the setting of the final meal. On the eve of his death, Christ lets his disciples know the deepest secrets of his love for God.

The other two parts in this lengthy piece are: the community of the witnesses to Christ (15:1—16:33) and the priestly prayer of Jesus (17:1-26). Scholars believe that the three parts probably reflect three redactional stages.

13:1-17 The story of the Last Supper is not told in John, and we shall never know exactly why, but the farewell meal here is described in the same spirit. By washing the feet of his disciples, Jesus performs the action of a slave; love has indeed made him the servant of his friends.

13:18-32 The announcement of the betrayal of Jesus comes in the discourse that follows the washing of the feet. Jesus brings the crisis to a head. The traitor can no longer remain in the intimacy of the Lord, sharing his table and his confidences. The darkness must one day be separated from the light (see v. 30).

Now the drama of the Passion begins; Jesus considers it the hour of his glory. He acts with a knowledge of the events that is the knowledge of God. Jesus is the Lord, as indicated by his title "I AM." This attestation serves to make the faith of the disciples stronger.

For the first time we meet "the disciple whom Jesus loved"; we shall find this unusual "name" three more times: once beneath the cross (Jn 19:26f), and the other two times in connection, once again, with Peter (Jn 20:2-10; 21:20-22). The tradition has always identified this disciple with John.

13:19 See note on Jn 4:26.

13:33-35 Jesus is not the first to recommend friendship, mutual service, and brotherly affection. But to love as he loved goes so much further as to become an absolute. It is no doubt for the purpose of underlining this that the fourth Gospel puts the commandment to love in the context of farewells; it likewise makes evident that this law of life is the most original sign of the community's faithfulness to Christ.

To love, to serve to the point of taking the last place and giving one's life, goes beyond human strength. Perhaps the dialogue with Peter is there to say that good feelings are not enough and that it takes the grace given by the death of Christ to have such strength.

13:36-38 Peter's denial is predicted in all four Gospels (Mt 26:33-35; Mk 14:29-31; Lk 22:31-34 and here).

14:1-31 Facing the death of Jesus, or facing our death, we might be shaken by fear. After all, without God is not existence for us a flight from the useless to nothingness? We have, then, to meditate on this chapter 14, where the themes are intermingled too numerously to discern the whole universe of meaning each verse opens to us. Yes, there is fulfillment, but it comes from God; it is abiding in God, truth in God, life from God. The symbols tell us that the fulfillment comes about in the communication of life from the Father, from Jesus, and from the Spirit.

14:1-5 The departure of Jesus ought not to become a time of discouragement amid hostility or uncertainty. The departure opens to all people the possibility of being in communion with God. Jesus gives the disciples the light and the life to enter this communion: he is the way not only through his teaching but also through his presence and his being—but what do we call the way and the goal of life for us?

14:1 *You place your trust in God:* this could also be translated as an imperative: "Place your trust in God!"

14:6-11 We can reflect upon the mystery of God to struggle to develop a better understanding of our life and the meaning of the world. But our power to discern cannot establish any certainties on our own. To know the Father, to discover what he wants for us, and to enter into his communion, we first have to look on Jesus, on his work, and on his love. Only the gift of the Son reveals the love of the Father in its fullness.

14:12-26 Here is a beautiful hymn on what it means to be Christians. They are not nostalgic survivors of a great experience that is past. In daily life, with its insults and interrogations, they remain in true communion with Christ and continue his work—i.e., they bear in his name the testimony of salvation and the testimony of truth. This communion, unceasingly renewed, gives them strength to cope with attacks of despair, falsehood, incomprehension, and nothingness— what John often calls "the world."

In this effort, which is never finished, they are uplifted by a new and constant presence of God: the Spirit. It is the Spirit who gives Christians the power to experience the divine presence in their inmost being, because the Spirit makes them live in the participation of God. It is the Spirit who gives Christians the courage to obey, as Christ did, the will of God, who is love, truth, testimony. It is the Spirit who makes them penetrate the heart of the words and acts of Jesus in the questions and debates of life.

The Spirit is the consoler of Jn 16:5-13. The Greek word *Parakletos* means an advocate, one who aids by his power and advice. In the situations and struggles of living as a Christian, the Spirit supports us so that we may remain united with God and bear witness to him before the world.

14:22 *Judas (not Judas Iscariot):* Jude Thaddeus (see Mt 13:15).

14:27-31 Christ's departure is imminent. Is the triumph over evil that the Passion effects merely a spectacle? No, this departure expresses Christ's free decision to do the will of the Father and to be at the Father's side, which is his true state of being. Such is God's peace, whose way and meaning are opened for believers. Yes, there is a fulfillment and a happiness for us—it is this that the word "peace" evokes in the Bible. It is not found in the satisfaction of the passions. True peace is a divine gift, to which Christ gives us access in our communion with God.

14:28 *The Father is greater than I:* this does not refer to the trinitarian relation between the Father and the Son. It probably refers to the fact that Jesus was sent by the Father and that the messenger (in the Hebrew mentality) is inferior to the one who sends him.

15:1—16:23 To the Lord's testament (farewell discourse) were added new instructions, as though to complete it. No doubt people did not want to lose other words of the Master, often meditated on, to explain the condition of the Christian community.

It is the life of the community on which these chapters throw light. In this group of texts, chs. 13 to 17, none of our usual words are pronounced: People of God, Body of Christ, Church, congregation. The words preferred are: to abide in, to love, to testify. In ch. 16, an image is used that suggests this mystery: the image of the vine and the branches. In these texts, love is above all a characteristic of the community itself. It is the Spirit who gives these groups the strength to exist as people of love and as witnesses of Christ.

15:1-11 Every reader of the Bible knows that the image of the vine suggests not only the union but also the tragic relationship between God and Israel. The Prophets rebuked the people of the Old Testament for not producing the fruit God expected of them, for being a spouse often unfaithful to her calling to bear witness to God among the nations (see Isa 5:1-7; Jer 2:21; Ezek 19:10-14; Hos 10:1). Jesus is the new Israel, the only vine that the Father has planted. This means that the radical, constitutive reality of the Church is her inclusion in Christ through Baptism, grace, and close attachment, and that any fruitfulness the disciple may have depends on this union with Christ.

15:12-17 There are many reasons for people to regroup: affinity, interest, defense. But the Christian community has only one reason: Christ and his choice of us. It also has only one way of life: to love like Christ, who went so far as to give his life. To have Christ's love is a gift. Then prayer is not a delusion; then the Christian community's mission can bear fruit. The fruit has already been given, God's love for us. In Christianity all is a gift.

15:18—16:4 The trial of Jesus, which the fourth Gospel unveils all through its pages, will not cease until the Father, to whom he is going, will have rendered justice to him in glorifying him. This drama, which people sometimes would like to conceal through reassuring words and sentiments, will not cease until the end of time. Persecution awaits Jesus, not because of some fatal error but because Christianity is different from what we want and claim it to be.

The early Christians were excluded from the synagogue; hatred and violence were stirred up against them under the guise of religion. Blindness and stubbornness: this is the world in the Johannine sense, the world of the persecutors. The Spirit is the strength and the light that assists the persecuted to hold fast in this affront, which no doubt also comes to pass in the heart of every believer.

16:4b-15 The disciples have to overcome sadness at the departure and absence of Jesus so that they may understand the meaning of the event: passage to glory, gift of the Spirit, and the beginning of a new era in the world. But until the end of history the trial of Jesus will not stop, and the disciples will have to testify to him in a world where unbelief appears unceasingly.

The testimony of Christians can never stop; such testimony does not depend on the intelligence and the strength of people but on the action of the Spirit, who unveils to Christians, in faith, the glory of Christ and the view that history takes of this light (Christ). It is not a matter of a new revelation but of a discovery of what the words, actions, Death, and Resurrection of Jesus mean for each era: the truth of God that denounces the falsehood of sin, the goodness of God that denounces evil, and the condemnation of the forces that enslave people. The Spirit is the Paraclete: defender of Jesus in the heart of believers, defender of believers facing unbelief and refusal of the light—that is, the world in the sense the world is taken here (Jn 15:5-15). The Spirit is strength, support, light (see Jn 14:16).

16:16-33 The departure of Jesus will be a moment of disarray for the disciples; his absence will more than once be a moment of disarray for believers. But that is not the last word. The sufferings, like the pains of giving birth, make a testimony fruitful. Let us rather look at the Death and Resurrection of Christ; they are the definitive events in history. From the cross and Easter a new light is given to believers; a new confidence with God is offered to them. Christ will be the mediator; with him believers will be one with God. This intimacy will be a time of endless joy and peace for people who have believed they are children of God.

What is the return of Christ? Is it the glorious coming at the end of time or the Resurrection manifested in the appearances? The two things go together. The Resurrection will inaugurate a new era, the last times; and the end of time will manifest the glory of the Risen One.

17:1-26 The hour has come for Jesus to do the final action that shows how far his union with the Father reaches and how great is the gift he makes of himself to human beings for their salvation. This sublime prayer reveals the ultimate meaning of his sacrifice; the title that has been given to the chapter, the "priestly prayer," is well deserved. But it is also a "missionary" prayer, since at the moment when there seems to be nothing but failure and isolation, Jesus adheres to God's plan. He is entirely the One Sent, who completes the mission given to him by the Father. He thinks only of this mission that his disciples must continue.

17:1-5 The word "glory" speaks of the greatness of God, of his final intervention, of his presence that gives strength, meaning, and fulfillment to people. Paradoxically, this glory is revealed in the destiny of Jesus, glory that is manifested during the Passion. One observes the love that was given to Christ for all eternity, love that became eternal life, shared by believers.

17:6-19 People who have accepted his word and recognized his truth live in close union with Jesus, which is a wonderful gift from the Father. Jesus calls for their fidelity.

People who have accepted the words of Jesus are no longer trapped in worthlessness, emptiness, and falsehood—in everything that is a denial of God and what is here called "the world." Their future is not in running away but in being insulted and giving testimony. The trial of Jesus continues in these people. May they remain in truth and faith; may they not become a prey of the falsehood, worthlessness, and unbelief that are the face of the Evil One or of Evil.

17:12 *The one destined to be lost* (literally, "The son of perdition"): Judas the traitor (see Jn 13:18). The literal translation reflects a Hebraism, meaning one who is destined for destruction, and this by his own free action. It is by this free choice that the Scripture is fulfilled.

17:20-26 The prayer of Jesus indicates the destiny of his followers for all times and places. He asks what is essential for them: that they live in the bonds of peace and unity that express their union with Christ. Here is the mystery of the Church in the light of the sacrifice of Christ: the Church is anchored in the inexpressible love of the Son and the Father; this is the mystery of communion. Christians testify to this communion when they live in it. Hence, they will discover more and more, in terms of experience, who Christ is and who the Father is: the glory of Christ and the name of the Father will be unveiled to their eyes as the highest realities.

18:1—19:42 Jesus does not submit passively to what happens; he controls his life and his sufferings; he even wills them and defines their meaning. The fourth Gospel, more than the others, emphasizes his sovereign freedom. Jesus is not, however, only pretending to share the human condition: he is a human being who suffers hostility, violence, and death, and the Passion Narrative demonstrates this. John, no less than the Synoptics, emphasizes the realistic character of the events; in fact, some details are even peculiar to him. In the fourth Gospel, the Passion and cross are an exaltation or uplifting of Jesus, a glorification by the Father, and a manifestation of all his love for humanity. By traveling the way of the cross with full awareness and on his own initiative, Jesus makes the truth of God shine forth.

18:1-11 Fear and disgust have no place in this account of the arrest. From the beginning, Jesus manifests his sovereign liberty to enter upon the Passion; it is his initiative and his destiny. The betrayal by Judas and his wicked cohorts cannot take away the liberty of Jesus, any more than the violence of Peter can defend it. Jesus depends only on his Father; he gives his life willingly.

18:1 *Kidron:* a brook fed by the rains, divided the hill of Jerusalem from the Mount of Olives.

18:3 *Detachment of soldiers:* this refers to a complement of Roman troops—either 600 (a cohort) or 200 men, hinting at Roman complicity in the plot against Jesus even prior to his trial before Pilate. *Lanterns and torches:* these may stress that the hour of darkness has come.

18:5 *Nazorean:* this is the form found in Mt (2:23 and 26:71) and Acts (e.g., 2:22), not the *Nazarene* of Mark. *I am:* probably intended by John as an expression of divinity (see note on Jn 4:26).

18:9 The citation may refer to Jn 6:39; 10:28; or 17:12.

18:11 *Cup:* symbol of a person's calling and, above all, of his tragic destiny ("lots" were shaken in a cup); here it signifies the bitter hour of the Passion (see Mt 22:39).

18:12-27 In the fourth Gospel, the trial before the Jewish authorities is told in a few swift strokes; throughout his public ministry Jesus has spoken about his ministry and the mission he has undertaken; the trial is already over. Annas, who appears here, was a high priest removed from office by the Romans, but by his influence he controlled Jewish life. *Another disciple* (v. 15): John, the one "whom Jesus loved."

18:19-24 It is not very probable that this nighttime inquiry before Annas, mentioned only by John, is the same as the trial before Caiaphas mentioned by the Synoptics (at night by Mt and Mk and in the morning by Lk).

18:22-23 Jesus remains calm and self-restrained throughout the entire Passion. He responds to the guard's aggressiveness with meekness, but he does not fail to defend the legitimacy of his behavior and to point out the injustice done to him. Hence, Christians' defense of their rights is compatible with meekness and humility (see Acts 22:25).

18:28—19:22 We should try to imagine the scene. A Roman official, Pontius Pilate, had been governor of restless Judea since A.D. 26 (we are now in the year 30). He had two guiding principles: to keep public order at any cost, and not to compromise his own reputation with Emperor Tiberius. The Jewish authorities wanted to rid themselves of Jesus in a legal way, thereby saving their own good name. Jesus himself did not want to disappear in an uprising, but had decided to go forward even to torture and execution on the cross (see Jn 18:32). In seven successive steps, dealing now with the Jews, now with Jesus, the governor is led to seek, find, and proclaim the truth. Jesus is in fact innocent; he claims the title of king, not in order to dominate but in order to give. This man, whose innocence the governor asserts three times and whom he wishes to set free, says that he is Son of God, and explains his present subordination to an earthly authority as a phase in a divinely willed plan over which the imperial official has no power (Jn 19:10-11).

The Gospel notes that this event took place around midday on the day of Preparation for the Passover; it was the hour when they began to slaughter the lambs for the feast. The new Passover, marking God's deliverance of humanity, is at hand; the new Passover Lamb is about to offer the true and final sacrifice.

18:28 *Praetorium:* the residence of the Roman procurator. *Passover meal:* unlike the members of the Sanhedrin, Jesus has already celebrated the Passover supper (Mt 26:20-29).

18:40 *Barabbas . . . thief:* the word for *thief* can also mean *revolutionary* (see note on Mk 15:9).

19:1 Pilate was obviously hoping that a scourging would suffice for the Jews and he could then release Jesus.

19:12 *Friend of Caesar:* an honorific Roman title given to high officials for merit.

19:13 *Stone Pavement:* Greek, *lithostrotos;* it has been identified with the great courtyard of the fortress Antonia, northeast of the temple, and therefore with the praetorium, the place or headquarters mentioned in Jn 18:28.

19:14 *Noon:* literally, the sixth hour. See note on Mk 15:25.

19:17 *Carrying the cross:* see note on Mk 15:21.

19:18 *Crucified him:* see note on Mt 27:35.

19:19 The *inscription* is found in all four Gospels under a slightly different form. John gives the most complete form, corresponding to the Latin of the three forms: INRI = *IESU NAZARENUS REX IUDAEORUM* ("Jesus the Nazorean, King of the Jews"). See also note on Jn 18:5.

19:22 *What I have written, I have written:* by this statement, Pilate affirms the truth of Jesus' divinity, which is rejected by his opponents. At the same time, Pilate stresses the inscription's public and universal character—for it can be read by Jews (*Hebrew*, i.e., Aramaic), Greeks (*Greek*), and Romans (*Latin*).

19:23-37 To the last moment, Jesus retains a keen awareness that he is completing God's work for the world, the will of God that all of the Scriptures (so frequently cited) proclaim. We see how Jesus' final gestures are symbols of the gifts given to humankind.

In dividing the garments of the crucified man, the soldiers are careful not to tear the seamless tunic. By calling attention to this, John perhaps wishes to signify the unity that Christ leaves as a heritage to those whom he wills to save.

Tradition identifies John with the beloved disciple (see Jn 13:23; 20:2-10; 21:7-20; and compare Jn 1:35-39; 18:15) to whom Jesus entrusts his mother. As she did with the servants at Cana (Jn 2:5), Mary will teach the disciple how to follow the example and teaching of her Son. The passage suggests the maternal vocation of the Mother of Jesus in relation to all believers.

The author bears witness to the fulfillment of the Scriptures. The words "I thirst" recall Ps 69:22: "In my thirst they gave me vinegar to drink." By drinking the sour wine offered to him, Jesus finishes the cup of his suffering (Jn 18:11).

Jesus is pierced by a lance, immolated like the Passover lamb, the bones of which are not broken. From his opened breast spurt blood, the sign of life surrendered, and water, the sign of the Spirit that he gives to believers (see Jn 7:38-39). Spiritual meditation has taken these symbols further; the blood and water are seen as prefigurations of the Eucharist and Baptism, the two Sacraments that form and feed the Church, this new Eve that has come forth from the opened side of the new Adam, Jesus Christ.

All are called to the heart of the Redeemer where they can joyfully draw water from the fountain of salvation (see Isa 12:3). A privileged disciple, doubtless the beloved disciple once again, offers a special guarantee of the truth of the events and the richness of their meaning: in his mind it is a case not of the sad death of a human being but of the fulfillment of God's plan, the shining forth of his love and his glory.

19:30 *It is finished:* this may correspond to the loud cry mentioned in Mt 27:50 and Mk 15:37. Jesus died as a victor, completing what he came to accomplish. *Gave up his spirit:* a description of death that is out of the ordinary—it may suggest an act of will.

19:38-42 Some disciples, who until now were afraid to declare themselves, proceed to the burial of Jesus. According to Jewish custom, an executed criminal could not be put in a tomb where other people had already been buried; to do so would have brought dishonor on them. But the sepulcher where Jesus is put is new in another sense perhaps—in it lies concealed the source of new life.

19:39 One hundred pounds: literally, "a hundred litrai." Myrrh and aloes: possibly a fulfillment of Ps 45:9.

20:1—21:25 Here, as in the rest of his work, John is pleased to dwell on some incidents not set down, or at least barely noticed, by the Synoptics; more than once, these are episodes involving the very person who is passing them on to his brethren in the faith. We owe to John the most extensive part of the Easter Gospel. By speaking of the empty tomb, he emphasizes the victory of life over death. When he describes one or other of the appearances, he wants to show how Jesus was recognized by his followers, what his new presence in their midst is like, how we are to believe in Christ, the mission to be carried out in the world in order to bear witness to him, and the gift of the Spirit to all believers. The last chapter, which has every appearance of having been added by disciples to the first edition of John's Gospel, emphasizes and expands the ecclesial perspective: The Resurrection, which ends the earthly career of Jesus, begins the earthly career of the Church.

20:1-10 Why is the body no longer there and why are the linen cloths still there? The beloved disciple, who had come with Peter, becomes the witness of the event and its meaning. Because he looks at the linen cloths with faith, he understands them as belonging to God's plan: the linen cloths mean that Jesus is alive.

The tomb is the symbol of death, but in the presence of this tomb the sign of death is changed. We are here at the beginning of a new life. Death is overcome.

20:11-18 To Mary Magdalene everything has been taken away, even the mortal remains of the One who has just died. But the appearance of the living Christ stands out in bold relief before her. And nothing is as it was before. The time of privileged encounters and sensible presence is past. The joy of Mary will be to announce to the disciples this new Covenant: Jesus lives with the Father, who is our Father too. Believers are brothers and sisters of Jesus. Here lies the mystery of the Church—that is, in the communion with Jesus.

20:16 Rabbouni is more solemn than "Rabbi"; it means "My Teacher."

20:17 Jesus tells Mary Magdalene not to delay. She must immediately go and announce his Resurrection to the disciples, while he will ascend to the Father before returning to manifest himself to them in full possession of all his prerogatives as the firstborn among many brothers. He had foretold that his glorification was necessary in order for the Holy Spirit to be sent. Hence, for John, the Ascension takes place on the same day as the Resurrection. The external and more demonstrative Ascension described in the Acts of the Apostles (1:6-11), forty days after the Resurrection, was only Jesus' sensible and definitive departure from the disciples after the various appearances to sustain and confirm their faith.

20:19-23 This is the first "Sunday" of the Church, the day on which the risen Lord meets his disciples. The season of joy has come (see Jn 15:11; 16:20-24; 17:13). He who comes, alive, into the midst of his followers is the same one who took on himself the suffering of the cross. He will now make them preachers of his mystery and ministers of his forgiveness. He sends the Spirit upon them as the Spirit had been sent on him by the Father at his Baptism, when he was beginning his mission (see also Ezek 37:9; Jn 15:26-27); this marks the beginning of the apostolic mission, which is a continuation of the work of Jesus Christ.

20:24-29 The true happiness of the disciples was not to have seen the Lord but to have understood the meaning of his Passion. The Passion makes known God's love. Blessed are they who believe in this love. Christian generations who have not known the visible Christ will meet him in faith.

20:30-31 The purpose of John's Gospel was to bring people to belief in Jesus: there is life only in communion with him.

These verses undoubtedly constituted the first conclusion of the fourth Gospel.

21:1-14 This miraculous catch is the final "sign" given by Jesus. He does not reveal himself; he remains mysterious, but the true disciple is able to recognize him (see Jn 21:20).

21:15-19 In this touching dialogue, Christ makes Peter a sign of his own perennial presence with his followers as their Good Shepherd (see ch. 10). Catholic tradition has seen in this passage the fulfillment of the promise made at Caesarea Philippi: "I will give you the keys of the kingdom of heaven" (Mt 16:17-19; see also Lk 22:31-32). The First Vatican Council made reference to vv. 15-17 in its definition that Jesus appointed Peter supreme shepherd and ruler over the whole flock.

21:20-23 Peter will ultimately make the supreme sacrifice, but what will become of the beloved disciple of whom the fourth Gospel often speaks (Jn 13:23; 19:26-27; 20:2-10; see Jn 1:35-39; 18:15)? The first Christian generations still believed in the imminent return of Christ in glory (2 Thes 2), although they had not begun to experience the time of the Church. We no longer have the same preoccupation. However, the response made by Jesus still holds: what is important is to follow Christ faithfully.

21:24-25 The faith of believers is a grace, but it goes back in history to those who were witnesses: those who saw the deeds and understood their meaning. Nonetheless, the life of Jesus goes beyond everything that can be written or said about him, even in a Gospel. Opening or closing the sacred writing, we are brought back to the encounter with Christ himself.

THE ACTS OF THE APOSTLES

1:1—12:25 In the Gospel of Luke, the life of Jesus takes the form of an ascent to Jerusalem, where through him God will decisively intervene in the destiny of humanity. The Book of Acts allows us to be present at the spread of the Gospel from that center to the ends of the earth. The Holy City is very important as the starting point of evangelization.

The experience of the young Christian community becomes exemplary, as in stories of foundations. Thus in chs. 1–7 everything takes place in Jerusalem, while in chs. 8–12 the city serves as the starting point and point of return of the stories. The Church of Jerusalem, then, is the source of Christianity: it is the mother Church and the inspiration for every other Church and for the whole Church.

1:1-26 The first two chapters of Acts serve a special purpose. In them we move from the risen Jesus to the community that is founded and established in the midst of the Jewish people—the community that is the starting point of the main routes along which the life of the Church develops. For readers of that period, the language used constantly recalls the great traditions of the Old Testament: the entire plan of God is recapitulated in these passages that in turn establish the perspective for what follows.

1:1-2 One author conceived the third Gospel and the Book of Acts as a single whole; the combination is not the result of chance. The first work tells the story of the actions and teachings of Jesus, "beginning from [John's] baptism" (see Acts 1:22; 10:37); the second shows us the life and activity of the risen Lord, which is likewise made visible in the deeds and acts of the various communities.

1:1 *Theophilus:* perhaps a rich and distinguished person who has paid for the publication of the work. He is the same person as in Lk 1:3.

1:3-8 This is the important theme that characterizes the period of the Lord's appearances (the period lasts forty days, between Easter and Pentecost; the number 40, which recurs so often in the Bible, is a symbol of fullness). The story highlights what it means to experience the risen Lord.

It is the Spirit who links the past phase of the life of Jesus with its present phase. This Spirit, often promised by Jesus (Lk 11:13; 24:49), brings to fulfillment all the blessings that the Messiah was to bring (see Joel 4:9; Am 9:11). The day of national restoration is no longer something to be awaited; the decisive moment has already arrived, and the Spirit is beginning to unite the peoples.

1:9-11 The Ascension is not the final act, but the beginning of the time to come. The cloud that hides Jesus from the eyes of the disciples recalls the cloud that covered the people in the wilderness, accompanying them night and day on their journey (Ex 40:36-38); it is a sign of God's presence, of his glory (Lk 9:34f). The risen Jesus reunites earth with heaven, i.e., the world of human beings with the world of God.

1:12 *Sabbath day's journey:* about two-thirds of a mile.

1:14 This is the only place in which the mother of Jesus is mentioned in Acts; the collateral relatives of Jesus, *his brethren,* will later on have an important place in the Jerusalem community (Acts 12:20; 15:13; 21:18; see note on Mt 12:46).

1:15-26 The ministry (*diakonia:* service) of the apostle ("one who is sent") appears from the outset as a solidly established institution, and one that is indispensable for the people of God. The apostles are twelve in number, as though to preside over the twelve tribes, i.e., the true Israel (see Acts 26:7), and it is around them that this community of one hundred and twenty (or ten for each apostle) has formed.

1:19 The language spoken is Aramaic.

2:1-47 For the first time, the witnesses come in contact with the crowd, which is made up of persons from all the nations. We are at the center of the world that is the starting point for a universal future.

2:1-13 The gift of the Spirit founds the Church as a living reality; Christ has prepared the way for the Church; the Spirit comes to take possession of her, to animate her, to help her with his charisms. Thus, for every community of believers, Pentecost is the feast of its own birth. The Spirit is "poured out" (see Acts 2:17) like rain, which is the source of life in an arid land; as Jesus had promised, there is a "baptism with the Spirit" (Acts 1:5).

The phenomena that accompany the event are rich in symbolism and also have a biblical meaning: they call to mind the theophanies, i.e., the manifestations of God to his people in order to change their anonymous destiny into a life-giving covenant (see Ex 19:18; Deut 4:9-24, 36; Ps 68).

Pentecost, which occurred fifty days after Passover, was the feast on which the firstfruits of the harvest were offered to God, but it was above all the feast of the covenant and of the gift of the Law.

2:4 *Different languages:* i.e., different from their usual language. The reference may also be to ecstatic language (see Mk 16:17; 1 Cor 14:2-23).

2:10 *Proselytes:* those who had accepted circumcision and the Jewish Law.

2:14-39 The author of Acts does not make up his discourses like the historians of antiquity, who liked to place their own thoughts and reactions on the lips of their subjects. In Luke's view, the Word is decisive for the life of the community.

This sermon is the first; therefore, it has programmatic value in addition to its function in the immediate context. It proclaims the paschal event to all of Israel and even to distant peoples. The same fundamental pattern will recur in the other addresses of the apostles to the Jews.

2:15 *Nine o'clock in the morning:* literally, "the third hour." See notes on Mt 27:35 and Mk 15:25.

2:40-47 Luke offers us three general descriptions of the first community, each depicting their manner of life: here, and in Acts 4:32-35 and 5:12-16.

3:1-10 Peter's action, as he takes the initiative in the first miracle that Acts ascribes to the disciples of the wonderworker of Nazareth, has special significance: it is done "in the name of Jesus Christ of Nazareth" and aims to show the presence of Christ and his divine activity.

3:1 *Three o'clock in the afternoon:* literally, "the ninth hour." See notes on Mt 27:35 and Mk 15:25.

3:2 The *Beautiful Gate:* it was made of Corinthian bronze and led from the court of the Gentiles to the court of the women, on the side where Solomon's Portico was (v. 11).

3:11-26 The discourse that follows embodies the *kerygma* (i.e., the essentials of Christian preaching) as intended for a Jewish audience.

3:13 *Servant:* the Greek word can also be translated as "son" or "child" (see Acts 3:26; 4:25, 27, 30). However, scholars believe that the word "servant" fits in better with the underlying idea of Jesus as the suffering Servant of the Lord (Isa 52:13—53:12).

3:15 *Author of life:* this may also be rendered as the "prince of life" or the "pioneer of life"—indicating Jesus as the originator of salvation.

4:1-22 The religious authorities understand very well the main points of Peter's discourse: Jesus has been raised; therefore, he has entered the sphere of God. Christians are not healers possessed of some secret or magical art; they act and teach with an authority that does not belong to a group of people. They do it in the name of Jesus Christ. When the Jewish authorities ask Peter and John why they are still preaching in the name of Jesus even though they have been told not to do so anymore, Peter and John answer, "You be the judges about whether it is right in the sight of God to listen to you rather than to God. We cannot possibly refrain from speaking about what We have seen and heard."

Concerning the name of Jesus, Peter says, "There is no salvation in anyone else, nor is there any other name under heaven given to men by which we can be saved." This is a call to salvation. To act in the name of Jesus, or to invoke him, means that every action of God is done through Jesus. God's role in the last times announced by Joel (3.5) is fulfilled through Jesus alone. If the Jewish authorities accept the fact that the movement of the History of Salvation lies in this new initiative of Jesus, they would signal the failure of their mandate and their institutions. As it is, they seek to escape embarrassment by cutting short the interrogation. But they cannot withstand the assurance of the apostles.

4:1 *Captain of the temple guard:* a priest who oversaw the activities of the police within the temple. *Sadducees:* a religious sect of the Jews that insisted upon human free will but denied immortality, the resurrection, and the existence of angels.

4:6 *John* and *Alexander:* not otherwise known.

4:23-31 The prayer begins with an invocation of the Creator, embracing the horizon of the world: heaven, earth, and sea. It follows the traditional practice of calling for God's protection of his people. This community is the new people compelled to make a new Exodus; and this people needs strength from God for this departure and this journey. It is rejected by the Jews who act like the pagan nations as these are characterized by the Old Testament. The future of the people is going to be bleak if its authorities refuse to recognize the name of God's holy Servant.

The invocation of the prayer for the apostles is made in the name of Jesus, and all the new people receive the gift of the word as at the first Pentecost, but in a situation of defense and interrogation. Such a prayer is the type of Christian prayer for times of crisis, for a community that must face an uncertain future and an unexpected road.

4:23 *Went back:* probably to the same Upper Room where the apostles had met (Acts 1:13) and where the community may have continued to meet (Acts 12:12).

4:32-35 These verses present a view of the early Church. Luke stresses the internal bonds of the community at the moment of persecution. The picture he paints shows the voluntary sharing of material possessions, an activity connected with Jesus' teaching on detachment and fraternal love (see Lk 8:3; 12:33; 16:9-13). The text does not say that all sold their property—only that they were prepared to do so if a member of the community was in need. The comportment of Barnabas and then that of Ananias and Sapphira demonstrate the right use of property in the Church.

4:33 *Bore witness to the resurrection:* although the death of Christ was a significant event, his Resurrection was the most compelling event of his life, and the apostles could not but proclaim it.

4:36-37 Barnabas is given as an example of the new understanding of property. He will soon play a chief role in the life of the Church (Acts 9:27; 11:22-30; 12:25; 13:1-15, 46; see 1 Cor 9:6; Gal 2; Col 4:10).

5:1-11 The sharing of goods is voluntary, but gold has a fascinating power. A couple lies to the community, contrary to the life of the Spirit. They violate the life of the community and undermine it. In the Old Testament (Jos 7:1), such people were to be put to death. Paul would have harsh words on the problem of riches and neglect of the poor when the Christians of Corinth later failed to respect the assembly, the Body of Christ.

5:11 The word *Church* (Greek: *ekklesia,* "assembly called together"), already heard on the lips of Jesus (Mt 16:18), appears for the first time in Acts at the end of this story. In the Greek world, the word denoted an assembly convoked for deliberation; in the Jewish tradition, the *ekklesia* was the assembly of God's people, which God had called together in the wilderness.

5:12-16 These verses show the components of a believing community: its unity, its internal communication, and its worship. Luke emphasizes the difference between this community and the rest of society. In the miracles worked by the apostles, the Spirit of Pentecost shines forth, continuing the work of Jesus, which is so significant of a change in the human condition.

5:17-42 The apostles continue their activity without letting themselves be intimidated. A time in prison is ended with deliverance, described in Old Testament terminology—with angels personifying God's providential intervention as in the Exodus. Luke stresses the positive conclusion of the matter: the Word of God cannot be chained.

Standing in the midst of the Sanhedrin and the party of the Sadducees (who desire to crush the new movement), Peter repeats the message about Jesus. His discourse has the same structure as the previous ones, and the name of Jesus remains at the center of the discussion. Of the life of Jesus, only the trial and death are recalled, but Peter stresses that the God of their ancestors has raised the one who was hung on a gibbet and has exalted him as head of a people capable of introducing them to repentance. The apostles are to bear witness to the Resurrection under the power of the Spirit, and nothing can stifle their testimony.

The suppression of the leaders of this new movement is decreed. They are saved by the intervention of Gamaliel, who was a teacher of Paul (Acts 22:3). He speaks in the manner of a sage of the Old Testament and points out that there have been other uprisings that have come to naught and only time will tell if this enterprise of the followers of Christ is a more serious thing. For their part, the apostles express their joy at suffering everything for Christ. The community has a provisional freedom but looks to the future to bring the good news of the risen Christ to the world.

5:36 *Theudas:* one of the many agitators of the period. Another agitator was *Judas the Galilean,* who rebelled around the year A.D. 6 and was the leader of the most terrible uprising prior to that of 70. He had a following in the Zealot party. The movements of Theudas and Judas were probably associated—and both occurred in the time of Quirinius.

5:41 *The name:* some manuscripts add "of Jesus." In Judaism, "the Name" signified God himself. Christians immediately took over the term and applied it to Jesus who had been given "the name that is above all other names" (Phil 2:9).

6:1—8:4 The community at Jerusalem lived in the impetus of the Resurrection and of the Spirit. It could not stay by itself and remain sheltered from the threats of religious authorities. Its energy made it go out into the world and tell the good news.

6:1-7 The Church decides on the ministers needed in order to maintain her freedom to pray and preach. The "deacons," all of whom have Greek names, are not limited to an economic function; we also see them in the service of the Gospel, as in the case of Stephen (Acts 6:8) and Philip (Acts 8:6; 21:8), who also baptizes (Acts 8:12-13). The laying on of hands is a sign of the official investiture of those who have been appointed by the choice of the assembly.

6:1 *Hellenists . . . Hebrews:* although the Church at this time was composed of Jews, these were of two types. Hellenists and Hebrews. The Hellenists were Greek-speaking Jews born outside Palestine who followed a Grecian philosophy. Hebrews spoke Aramaic and followed Jewish customs.

6:2-3 *Twelve . . . seven:* the Twelve are representative of the twelve tribes of Israel; the Seven represent the Gentiles dwelling in Canaan (see Acts 13:19; Deut 7:1).

6:6 *Laid hands on them:* the Jewish practice of assigning someone for a task and calling down God's blessing on that person to carry it out (Num 27:18, 23; Deut 34:9).

6:8—7:60 The first Christian martyr has his gaze fixed on Christ in profound attachment to his person (Acts 7:55) and in an interior imitation of Christ's suffering and death. Unlike the Passion of Jesus, however, that of Stephen is accompanied by a lengthy discourse that has as its basic theme God present in the midst of humanity in Jesus Christ. The lengthy interpretation of the history of Israel, made up of citations from the Old Testament, is less a demonstration than an indictment of a religion that is locked into its past.

7:58 *Saul:* i.e., Paul, the future apostle, who is here mentioned for the first time; see Acts 22:20.

8:1-4 The Hellenist Christians are driven out of Jerusalem. Their dispersion proceeds in an underground manner throughout the narrative until the moment when we will encounter a list of people who emigrate to Cyprus and Antioch. There, for the first time, the Church is opened to Gentiles (Acts 11:9ff). During this period, Luke shows the Gospel spreading to Samaria, Gaza, and the coast as far as Caesarea, Damascus in Syria, and Tarsus. The Gospel is received by many different cultures and people: the Pharisean persecutor, the functionary, the peasant of the plain of Sharon, the notable rich of Joppa, the artisan, the army, and the non-Jewish Greeks of Antioch.

Luke presents Paul under the somber traits of persecutor; once he becomes an apostle, Paul will remain marked by the memory of the time when he wanted to obstruct the path of the infant Gospel (see Acts 22:20; 26:10; 1 Cor 15:9; Gal 1:13, 23; Phil 3:6).

8:5-8 Another deacon brings about an opening of the Church to the world. Since their separation, their installation of a worship of their own, and their intermingling with other peoples, the Samaritans who were once brethren in religion with the Jews have come to be regarded by the latter as heretics every bit as evil as the Gentiles. The Gospel is a powerful means of salvation for all human beings, surpassing the ancient religions and political frontiers. Presented here is the first step. The ministry of Philip the deacon is described in the spirit of the Gospels, and Luke stresses the climate of joy that follows in the wake of the good news.

8:9-25 The proclamation of the Gospel is faced with an important problem as in our day. Can human beings own spiritual forces? Under an Eastern influence, personages endowed with the power of performing prodigies circulated throughout the Empire. There were itinerant exorcists or healers (Acts 9:11, 18). Simon has an outstanding reputation in this sphere. Now the magician has come to believe in the word of the Gospel. The community at Jerusalem is troubled to hear of prodigies and conversions in Samaria, a rejected land; an apostolic inspection can only confirm the facts and give them the authentication of the Spirit.

Simon the magician is attracted by the prestige that would be given him by the Spirit, and he wants to have the Spirit at his disposal, as do the apostles. He is even ready to pay well for it (whence the word "simony"). But he receives a stern refusal. Luke wants to set aside the forgeries that one could ascribe to Christ and the Spirit. We have here an example of a faith that becomes deeper, for the author stresses the importance of intercessory prayer for one another in matters of conversion.

8:10 *The Great One:* perhaps a divine title, which Simon has given himself.

8:26-40 In this passage, Luke shows us the encounter of the Church with a new cultural environment. The official in charge of the treasury of the queen of Ethiopia (Candace, like Pharaoh, is a title of a ruler) is interested in a passage of the Old Testament that speaks of a mysterious personage who is overwhelmed by suffering for the salvation of all; the passage is Isa 53, often used by the first community to express the mystery of Christ. The marvelous elements in this story of Philip recall God's freedom of action in the time of the ancient Prophets: angel, Spirit, instantaneous transportation (see 1 Ki 18:12; 2 Ki 2:16; Ezek 3:12, 14; Dan 14:36). We will come across Philip the deacon again later on as the father of four daughters (Acts 21:9).

8:27 *Eunuch:* may be simply a court title; for eunuch in the literal sense, see the prophecy of Isa 56:3-7.

8:37 This verse is added by some ancient manuscripts.

8:40 *Azotus* (called Ashdod in the Old Testament as one of the five Philistine cities) was about 25 miles north of Gaza. *Caesarea,* on the coast, was 33 miles north of the modern Tel Aviv, and served as the headquarters for the Roman governors.

9:1-30 The story of Paul's conversion is repeated twice more in this Book, with some variations in details (Acts 22:4-21; 26:9-18).

The heart of the story is the identification of Jesus with the persecuted community of believers: The Lord can no longer be separated from his Church. Saul is given the mission of carrying the name of Jesus to Israel and the rulers of the nations.

9:1 *Saul:* present at the stoning of Stephen (Acts 7:58), he was born in Tarsus and had studied under Gamaliel (Acts 22:3).

9:2 *Damascus:* an important city of the Roman province of Syria with a large Jewish population; it was some 150 miles from Jerusalem and a four-to-six-day journey. *Way:* behavior, a concept of life, the teaching of the Lord, teaching about salvation; in short, Christianity (see Acts 16:17; 18:25-26). The Romans granted the high priest authority in religious matters, even over Jews outside of Palestine.

9:11 *Street called Straight:* one of the oldest streets in the world. In Paul's time, Damascus was laid out in the form of a rectangle intersected by "straight" streets. The longest of them all was the "Street called Straight."

9:13 *Saints:* so named because Christians are consecrated to Christ, the Holy One (Acts 3:14). The word recurs in verses 32 and 41. See also note on Rom 1:7.

9:17 It was the resurrected Christ who appeared to Paul. Paul insisted on this point and based his qualifications as an apostle on it (see 1 Cor 9:1; 15:8).

9:29 *Hellenists:* see note on Acts 6:1.

9:30 *Tarsus,* the capital of Cilicia (in Asia Minor), was Paul's native place (Acts 22:3); it is there that Barnabas will go looking for him (Acts 11:25).

9:31-43 Luke gives us a new panoramic picture in which the themes of fervor and growth are stressed. A precarious peace is established, providing the time to contemplate the Church living and animated by the Spirit and planted in the whole land of ancient Israel. In verse 31, Church refers, not to a single Church, as it usually does in Scripture, but to all the communities. Peter visits the various centers, especially those in the area of the present-day Tel Aviv. His miracles are recounted in the manner of pages in the Gospels.

9:31 *Encouraged by the Holy Spirit:* this Book stresses the work of the Holy Spirit (see Acts 13:2). Hence, it is sometimes called "The Acts of the Holy Spirit."

9:32 *Lydda:* a town about 12 miles from Joppa.

9:37 The body was washed in preparation for burial.

9:43 *A tanner:* one who tans hides of animals and hence is considered unclean by the Law. Peter's stay with him prepares the way for his mission to the Gentiles who were considered to be unclean by the Jews.

10:1—11:18 The moment in which the Christian movement entered into the Gentile world was a major event for the Church. Luke speaks of God's initiative that captures the world through the Resurrection and the Spirit and expresses itself in the dynamism with which the Lord animates the first community. To illustrate it, he elevates an account of conversion to the rank of an historic event and an irreversible theological fact. Indeed, it is the longest account in the Acts of the Apostles.

Cornelius, a Roman official in Caesarea—the city that is the seat of government—is, along with his entire family, a "God-fearing" man, i.e., one who has accepted the beliefs and principal practices of Judaism, though not going so far as to share the Jewish way of life and become part of the people through circumcision.

In his inner righteousness and generosity, Cornelius is recognized by God as suitable to enter into communication with him. However, to find the truth that he desires he must hear the announcement of the facts concerning Jesus from the mouth of eyewitnesses and thus must meet Peter—who is living some 30 miles away. Only then will these Gentiles master the word of Christ and make it their own through the inspiration of the Spirit (Acts 10:40).

Thus, Cornelius is no longer the central figure of our account. Luke wishes to stress a fact: the initiative of God to liberate the Gospel from being shut up in the Jewish world. The community of Jerusalem, still bound by its Jewish ties, opens itself to the outside world by a series of encounters, but it is blocked from doing so by a redoubtable problem. The Jewishness of the first disciples prevents them from frequenting the Gentiles' houses of prayer and from sharing their tables without incurring a legal uncleanness and violating the Law. How then can they live in community and partake in the Eucharist, for example?

Must not the Gentiles first be made part of Israel through circumcision? In the face of the gift given by God to the Gentiles "as . . . upon us at the beginning" (Acts 11:15), in the face of this Pentecost of the Gentile nations (Acts 10:45), the community of Jerusalem must also be converted and realize that the religious and ritual appurtenances can no longer provide superiority or priority, that these are no longer to be regarded as a wall of separation—finally, that no person can be declared unclean (Acts 10:27).

The text is carefully constructed. Each personage has a vision that presents itself as an enigma. Then it becomes clear in the concrete action, the encounter, and the mutual hospitality. Peter's discourse is the pivotal point of the account. Like its predecessors (Acts 2:14-41; 3:11-26), it relates the major themes of the announcement of Jesus. The Spirit authenticates the word concerning Jesus and inspires Gentiles to become witnesses of the Resurrection.

The concrete problems of the entry of Gentiles into the Church and of contacts between Jews and Gentiles will be definitively regulated at the Council of Jerusalem (Acts 15:10, 19-21), but Paul will struggle all his life against the Judaizing practices and theories that tempt certain communities of Israelite origin (see Gal 2; 5). The encounter of Peter and Cornelius leads to the formation of the first Christian community made up of the two most difficult milieux: the Christian and the Gentile. Henceforth, the Church will no longer be able to shut herself up within her own confines.

10:1 *Italian cohort:* an auxiliary unit of soldiers.

10:3 *Three o'clock:* literally, "about the ninth hour." This time period was a Jewish hour of prayer (see Acts 3:1).

10:9-16 The vision that now occurs makes it possible for Peter to sit down at table and eat with Gentiles without feeling any guilt. Hence, it is clear that at first not even the apostles fully understood the Lord's teaching about the Law. However, with the aid of this vision and the inspiration of the Holy Spirit the apostles ultimately arrive at a fuller understanding.

10:9 *Noon:* literally, "about the sixth hour."

10:30 *Three o'clock in the afternoon:* literally, "about the ninth hour."

10:41 *Ate and drank with him:* those who shared a table with Jesus after he rose from the dead were given unmistakable evidence of the Lord's bodily Resurrection (see Lk 24:42f; Jn 21:12-15).

11:19-26 The narrative picks up the story of persecution (see Acts 8:14). But we leave the coast of Palestine for a region some 300 miles further north. A new Church enters the picture, that of Antioch, where Barnabas is encouraging the converts from paganism.

In Antioch, the name *Christian* is used for the first time (v. 26), and it will henceforth be used by all the disciples of the Lord for the community in the service of the Lord.

11:19 *Phoenicia:* a land 15 miles wide and 120 miles long on the northeastern coast of the Mediterranean Sea, with Tyre and Sidon as its principal cities. *Cyprus:* the island home of Barnabas (see Acts 4:36), located in the northeastern Mediterranean, 60 miles from Syria. *Antioch:* the third most important city (after Rome and Alexandria) of the Roman Empire, located in Syria, in the northeast corner of the Mediterranean. It was from the Church of Antioch that Paul's three missionary journeys were launched (see Acts 13:1-4; 15:40; 18:23).

11:25 *Tarsus:* see note on Acts 9:30.

11:27—12:25 Calamities strike the Church—famine, persecution, political conflicts. This corresponds to the description of the signs of the last times in Luke (21:9-13). As the Gospel says, it is not the time of the end but the time of perseverance. When the signs of crisis are manifested in the world, believers testify to the hope and the effort for a change. The Church emerges from these threats with tranquil joy and humility. This account brings to a close the first twelve chapters of Acts.

11:27-30 A collection is organized in the Church. The action is an application of one of the essential elements of the community: the sharing of goods, which gives a new meaning to economic property. Paul will regard this kind of mutual help as very important (see Rom 15:31; 1 Cor 16:15; 2 Cor 8:4; 9:1, 12, 13; Gal 2:10).

11:27 *Prophets:* the first mention of the gift of prophecy in this Book. Prophets are to preach, exhort, explain, or predict (see Acts 13:1; 15:32; 19:6; 21:9f; Rom 12:6; 1 Cor 12:10; 13:2-8).

11:30 *Elders:* collaborators of the apostles, or substitutes for them (see Acts 20:17f).

12:1-19 Death and imprisonment are the fate of the disciple. Jesus has foretold it emphatically. Herod puts James ("the Greater"), the brother of John, to death by the sword. Since this pleases some of the Jews, he intends to put Peter to death, too, and takes him into custody. But Peter is freed from prison by an angel and goes back to the community, which rejoices that he is freed. Peter now departs from Acts without any indication of his further activity and his fate— martyrdom. Luke also leaves us in suspense regarding the end of Paul, on the last page of Acts.

12:1-2 *Herod:* i.e., Herod Agrippa I, ruler of Judea and Samaria from A.D. 41 to 44; he was a nephew of the Herod Antipas whom we meet in the Passion of Jesus.

James ("the Greater") was the first of the apostles to drink the Lord's cup (Mk 10:39) and give his life for the Master; his brother, *John,* will be the last of the apostles to leave the scene.

12:12 *Mark:* cousin of Barnabas (see Col 4:10); we find Mark in Acts 12:25; 13:5, 13; 15:37-39, and in the service of Paul the prisoner (Col 4:10; Philem 24; 2 Tim 4:11). He was a disciple of Peter (1 Pet 5:13), and tradition considers him to be the author of the second Gospel.

12:17 *James:* this is James the Lesser, a brother of the Lord, i.e., one of Jesus' collateral relatives; we will find him presiding over the Church of Jerusalem (Acts 15; 17). Peter is said, in words surely carefully weighed, to have gone "to another place"; Acts will not speak of him again.

12:20-23 This time again, in the manner of the Old Testament, the intervention of the hand of God is emphasized. The account poses the problem of war: it is a scourge in which the economy is tied to the will for power. Here the war against Tyre and Sidon is put off thanks to a compromise. But the political pride of a leader who takes himself for God is dissipated by a mortal sickness, which popular tradition interprets as a punishment.

The episode accords with the chronology of the time. It inserts Acts into universal history. Herod died, after a great feast, eaten by worms, in A.D. 44.

12:24-25 As in a refrain, Luke again refers to the vital power of the Gospel. With the return of Barnabas and Saul from Antioch, a new page begins.

12:25 *Mark:* see note on Acts 12:12.

13:1—18:22 Under the impulse of the Spirit and the call of events, the community of Jerusalem finds the main points of its internal fire; it has broken out of the Jewish world to spread the Gospel into the Gentile world. New communities have been founded in which the Spirit stirs up the same internal fire and strong missionary initiative. The cycle of Jerusalem ends with the establishment of the Church at Antioch (Acts 11:19-26). In the second cycle in Acts, this young Church is the point of departure and return for all the stories, replacing Jerusalem as the center for the spread of the Gospel. Henceforth, the action takes place outside of Palestine; the Church now exists independently of the temple and of Jewish life in the Holy Land.

According to the historians of the period, Antioch, a main communications center of the Mediterranean world, was a "hotbed of falsehood." Two missionary journeys take off from it: the first to Asia Minor (Acts 13:1—14:28), the second as far as Greece (Acts 15:36—18:23). We shall witness the encounter with quite different environments, from Oriental magic to Greek philosophy.

Paul will soon take the initiative in this missionary activity by means of the first two voyages ordinarily called missionary journeys of the Apostle. The Council of Jerusalem is called upon to officially resolve the problem in the community between converts from the Gentiles and converts from Judaism.

13:1—14:28 A missionary undertaking begins that will reach into the heart of Asia Minor. The story dwells at length on the outward journey; the return is told in a few verses, but makes clear that in the interim some Churches have been born that have their own life and personality. The Gospel will be addressed first of all to Jews and then directly to the Gentiles. Is Christianity a complete novelty or Judaism with a new face?

13:1-5 Events suggest the vitality of the community of Antioch, whose importance is also underlined by the list of people available. Paul and Barnabas are chosen to go on mission. The laying on of hands by the community here is not a communication of powers (as in Acts 6:6) but a confirmation of the inspiration of the Spirit.

13:4 *Seleucia:* this was Antioch's seaport, 16 miles to the west. *Cyprus:* the Gospel had already been preached there (see Acts 11:19f).

13:5 *Salamis:* a town on the east coast of Cyprus.

13:6-12 The problem preoccupying some spiritual authorities once again comes to the fore: What is Christianity's relation to magic? Luke once again dissociates the Church from the magical arts practiced at the time (see Acts 8:18-24).

13:6 *Paphos:* a town 100 miles west of Salamis.

13:9 *Known as Paul:* Saul drops his Hebrew name and uses his Roman name, Paul, to show that he has entered fully into his mission to the world of the "nations." Henceforth, he will also be mentioned before Barnabas, his companion in missionary activity.

13:13-52 Christianity came into being within Judaism and brought the history of Israel to its conclusion. Therefore, the proclamation of the word must follow that same order: it is to be addressed first to the Jews, then to the Gentiles (see Acts 11:19-20). Only at the end of Acts will the mission be aimed directly at the Gentiles without first passing through the synagogue (see Acts 28:28). This sermon of Paul is delivered to Jews and follows the pattern of early Christian preaching that has already characterized the discourses of Peter.

13:13 *Perga:* the capital of Pamphylia, which was a province of Asia Minor, 80 miles long and 20 miles wide, between the provinces of Lycia and Cilicia on the southern coast of Asia Minor.

13:14 *Antioch:* a city 110 miles from Perga strategically situated for commerce, which was a Roman colony and had a large Jewish population. *Pisidia:* a district north of Pamphylia that was 120 miles long and 50 miles wide.

13:16 *Others who fear God:* Gentiles who accept the beliefs and moral principles of Judaism without becoming members of the Jewish people by circumcision.

13:20 *Four hundred and fifty years:* this could also refer to the period of the Judges until the time of the prophet Samuel.

13:51 *Iconium:* an important crossroads and center of agriculture in the province of Galatia.

14:1-7 A good number of both Jews and Gentiles accept the Gospel. But the crucial question is this: Since the Gospel is so anchored in the movement of the history of Israel, is it not a perversion to open the Church to the Gentiles? And the answer is: No. It is a new message: that the word of God is for everyone.

14:6 *Lycaonian cities:* Lycaonia was a district east of Pisidia, north of the Taurus Mountains, and part of the Roman province of Galatia. *Lystra:* a Roman colony about 20 miles from Iconium and 130 miles from Antioch. *Derbe:* a town about 60 miles from Lystra.

14:8-18 A new problem arises for the Church: the kind of reaction shown here by a crowd of rural Gentiles, who regard the two apostles as divinities. Peter had already raised up Cornelius when the latter knelt before him (Acts 10:25). The sermon here, the first one on the Gospel to Gentiles, is a fragment. It is to be completed in light of the more fully developed discourse in Acts 17:22-31.

When addressed to Gentiles, the *kerygma* was profoundly different than when addressed to Jews. It urged the abandonment of dead idols in order to turn to the living God. Proofs were not taken from Scripture; rather the emphasis was on God manifesting himself to all human beings through the cycles of life and of the world.

14:11-13 The strange reaction of the people of Lystra to the cure performed by Paul is a result of local folklore that told tales of the gods coming to earth without being recognized. Struck by the deed performed, the people believe that the gods—in the guise of Zeus and Hermes—have visited again in the form of these two wonderworkers. Zeus was the chief of the gods and patron of the city, and Hermes was a son of Zeus and messenger of the gods (like the Roman Mercury).

14:14 *Tore their clothes:* an expression of horror and revulsion at someone's blasphemy (see Mt 26:65).

14:19-28 The Gospel of Jesus has been planted in Asia Minor as a force of life. On the return of Paul and Barnabas to Antioch, the first movement of the community is to gather to hear what God has helped them to accomplish, and to give thanks, as was done on Peter's return to Jerusalem (Acts 11:18). The Christian community in Antioch lives the good news of Jesus.

14:25 *Attalia:* the finest harbor on the coast of Pamphylia (see note on Acts 13:13).

14:26 *Antioch:* see note on Acts 11:19.

15:1-35 Christian communities have sprung up everywhere and include converts from both Jews and Gentiles. Radical problems have also arisen. The Church is clearly aware that she exists thanks only to the union of the two very contrasting portions of humanity of that time: Jews and Gentiles (Acts 15:14-17); this union should express the true reality of salvation in Jesus Christ. What we see here is an authentically theological inquiry, which consists in interpreting the experience of the apostles' encounters with the Gentiles and shedding light on them from the Scriptures.

As they reflect on the words of the Prophets, the members of the Council realize that the People of God, with which all the prophecies are concerned, exists in its full reality only at the moment when Gentile inquiry meets the original nucleus of Jewish testimonies. However, the practical decisions made are more cautious than the great theological statements. The Council asks for the observance of some elementary precepts that no Jew can abandon and that people know almost everywhere.

They are not to eat meat that has been sacrificed, because this would signify a fellowship with the divinities of the Gentiles (see 1 Cor 10:18-20). They are to avoid illegitimate unions ("unchastity"). They are not to eat flesh with blood in it ("[abstain] from the meat of animals that have been strangled, and from blood" [v. 20]), since according to the mind of the time blood was the sacred principle of life. The last two concern dietary laws (see Gen 9:14; Lev 3:17; Deut 12:16, 23; 1 Sam 14:34; Ezek 33:25).

All agree on these theological principles and their practical consequences. What a staggering sentence we read here for the first time, one that has passed from the Council to our own day: "It is the decision of the Holy Spirit and also our decision"!

15:14 *Simon:* the Greek text has "Simeon." "Simon," the Semitic name of Peter, is unusual but fits well on the lips of James, who was very attached to Jewish culture.

15:22 *Barsabbas:* otherwise unknown. *Silas* is perhaps Paul's coworker (from Acts 15:40 on).

15:34 This verse is lacking in the better manuscripts.

15:36—18:22 The planned visit to the communities already established turns into the "second missionary journey," during which the Gospel enters into the daily life and culture of the Greco-Roman world.

15:36-40 The choice of members of the team is not without difficult but nor mal confrontations. Attitudes toward John Mark lie at the origin of the tension (see Acts 13:5; 13:13). Finally, two teams are formed for two different projects. Barnabas takes John with him, and Paul takes Silas.

15:41—16:8 Paul is opposed in principle to the circumcision of Christians of non-Jewish origin, but Timothy is a special case. If he were not circumcised, he could not speak in a synagogue and, in addition, he would have been regarded as an apostate, since his mother was Jewish; in the present missionary program, the first contacts were still taking place in the synagogues. The Spirit mysteriously intervenes to decide which direction the mission is to take. The whole Book of Acts is written in this perspective: the entire spread of the Gospel has been guided by the Spirit (see 1 Pet 1:12).

16:1 *Timothy:* a fellow worker of Paul, to whom the latter will address two Letters.

16:6 *Phrygia:* originally, this was the Hellenistic country of Phrygia, but it had now become part of the Roman provinces of Asia (which was only one-third of Asia Minor) and *Galatia.* Galatian Phrygia contained both Iconium and Antioch. *Asia* included Mysia, Lydia, and Caria in addition to parts of Phrygia.

16:8 *Troas:* a Roman colony and an important seaport 10 miles from the ancient city of Troy. Paul returned to it after his third missionary journey (Acts 20:5-12).

16:9-15 The account shifts to the first person, "we" (v. 10),as Luke will do three more times (Acts 20:5-15; 21:1-18; 27:1—28:16); these passages probably represent personal notes of Luke about events that he himself witnessed (see Lk 1:1). The listeners and different social groups are always addressed according to the same order. One tries at first to make the Jewish community change its mind and accept the fulfillment of the history of its people; then one turns to the Gentiles. At Philippi, Paul encounters some Jews who are influenced by Hellenism and devoted to commerce. The home of Lydia becomes the center of a community.

16:11 *Samothrace:* an island in the northeastern Aegean Sea. *Neapolis:* the seaport for Philippi, ten miles away.

16:12 *Philippi:* a city in eastern Macedonia. Some of its members establish a flourishing Christian community to which one of Paul's Letters will later be addressed.

16:16-40 Even when it is not stirred up by the reaction of the Jews, opposition to the Gospel arises out of a desire for ill-gotten gain. Some Jews at Ephesus claim Christianity advocates customs that as Roman citizens they cannot legally tolerate in the cities of the Empire.

The account of Paul's deliverance is centered above all on the transformation that takes place in the jailer. It is an account of conversion. Paul makes good use of his Roman citizenship to keep the field open for his future missionary activity (see Acts 22:19).

17:1-15 Jewish groups resent the rise of Christian communities as a rival enterprise and a risk for their peaceful establishment in the cities of the Empire—something that is always precarious. Unless the Jews accept Jesus as the fulfillment of the Scriptures, they can do nothing but be opposed to such communities.

The community of the Thessalonians will later receive the first two Letters written by Paul, which enable us to glimpse the fervor and anxieties of a young Church. The substance of Paul's preaching at Thessalonica is summed up in verse 3: there we find the general structure of the discourses of Acts. A woman once again appears in a new role (Acts 17:12; 18:2) and is even named for her own sake, with no reference to a man (Acts 17:34). Christian lay people suffer in the name of the apostles. The opposition they encounter is on the juridical level. The confrontation with the Roman world will take place on a political level, where Roman culture and civilization are better expressed.

17:1 *Amphipolis . . . Thessalonica:* cities on the so-called Egnatian Way, which ran east and west through Greece and also included Philippi. Thessalonica was the capital of Macedonia with a population of more than 200,000, and it lay about 100 miles from Philippi.

17:16-21 Paul reaches Athens, which some 500 years before had been at the height of its glory in philosophy, literature, and art. In the twilight of its fame, it still housed a highly regarded university and was a force in philosophical thinking, as evidenced by the Epicureans and Stoics who engage Paul in discussion. He is led to the Areopagus, before a body that functioned in matters pertaining to religion, culture, and education. They evaluate him as the promoter of a new religion.

17:18 *Epicurean and Stoic philosophers:* followers of the two prevailing philosophical systems. The Epicureans follow Epicurus (342–271 B.C.) in abandoning the search for pure truth by reason as hopeless and giving themselves over to present pleasures. The Stoics follow Zeno and Chrysippius (3rd century B.C.) and embrace a philosophy of self-repression because of human self-sufficiency. *What is this man babbling about?:* it seems to be a way of saying that the speaker is an eclectic, gathering ideas from all sources. *Jesus and the resurrection:* the Athenians misconstrue Paul's words, thinking that he is speaking about Jesus and the goddess Anastasis, which means resurrection.

17:19 *Areopagus:* this may refer either to a hill of Ares west of the Acropolis or to the Council of Athens that once met on it.

17:22-31 Paul's speech is a masterpiece of judicious adaptability to the Greek mentality. Yet he and his hearers are on different wave lengths. He preaches a way of life and calls for a faith while the cultured Greeks seek only a truth that satisfies the mind. A crucified and resurrected God can make no impact on them, and they take Paul for a buffoon (v. 14). Others think of him as a fanatic worshiper of new gods: "Jesus" and "Resurrection," his spouse (v. 18). Paul first sets forth his theodicy: there is one God, who is spiritual, personal, and provident (vv. 22-26). Then he cites their poets, interpreting them in a monotheistic fashion (vv. 27-30). Finally, his Christology is very brief (v. 31), because of the uproar provoked by the subject of the resurrection, which was openly rejected by all the Hellenistic schools of philosophy.

17:26 *From one ancestor:* or "from one blood." *Decreed their appointed times:* or "decreed limits to their existence."

17:28 *In him we live and move and have our being:* a citation from the writings of the Cretan poet Epimenides (6th century B.C.). *We are all his offspring:* a citation from the Cilician poet Aratus (c. 315—240) as well as from Cleanthes (331—233 B.C.). Paul also quotes Greek poets in 1 Cor 15:33 and Tit 1:12.

17:34 *Dionysius:* the passage suggests that this individual should be known to the readers. A theologian of the 5th or 6th century published mystical writings under this name. Some claim that this Pseudo-Dionysius (Denis) was the first bishop of Paris in the 3rd century.

18:1-17 These passages deal with one of Paul's most important activities. The great city of Corinth was at that time a cosmopolitan place and had a rather bad reputation due to the erotic cult of the goddess Aphrodite.

With its reference to Gallio in verse 12, the account provides us with a sure chronological clue to the events reported, since an inscription enables us to pinpoint the proconsulate of Gallio, a brother of Seneca, to the years A.D. 51—52 or 52—53.

18:2 *Claudius:* Emperor of Rome from A.D. 41 to 54. He expelled the Jews from Rome because of "their continuous tumults instigated by *Chrestus*," a common misspelling for "Christ." Needless to say, the tumults were instigated not *by* Christ but by the differing opinions people held *about* him.

18:3 Paul was probably taught the trade of tentmaker in his youth, in accord with the Jewish custom of giving manual training to sons.

18:9 *In a vision:* Paul now glimpses in a vision (see Acts 23:11) the Lord whom he has already seen in a resurrected body at his conversion (see Acts 9:4-6; 1 Cor 15:8) and in the temple in ecstasy (see Acts 22:17-18).

18:18-22 After more than two and a half years of labor in Corinth, Paul embarks for Antioch. The Nazirite vow was a special consecration to God, usually lasting 30 days and taking the form of a special way of life (see Num 6:1-21).

Instead of reaching Antioch Paul lands at Ephesus, which will soon become the center of the following cycle of the Book. He leaves Priscilla and Aquila there, who will become the nucleus of a Christian community.

18:19 *Ephesus:* a leading city of Asia Minor and the capital of the province of Asia, where the temple of Artemis (Diana) was located.

18:22 *He went up and greeted the Church:* although this could refer to a congregation in Caesarea, the words "he went up" indicate that it was the Church at Jerusalem, which was about 2500 feet above sea level.

18:23—20:38 According to the author of Acts, Ephesus is the third center for the spread of God's word. The city was a great center of commerce, and in it the cultural and religious currents of the Greco-Roman world and the East came together. Paul remains there for more than two years, and it is thought that he there wrote the Letters to the Corinthians, the Philippians, and perhaps the Galatians. Later on, the Letter to the Ephesians, one of the imprisonment letters, would be addressed to this community.

The early Church was now encountering other religious currents (besides the Judaic), and non-Jewish life was coming to the fore. And the essence of the faith had to be brought out in the face of multiple cultural influences.

18:23—20:6 Paul remains at Syrian Antioch for some time, probably through the spring of A.D. 53, and then starts his third missionary journey. Setting out for Ephesus, some 1500 miles to the west, he revisits the Churches around Pisidian Antioch, Iconium, Lystra, and Derbe. The account of this third journey focuses on his work at Ephesus (Acts 19:1—20:1).

18:24-28 Apollos is a talented preacher who knows the Scriptures and instructs in the new Way of the Lord. He speaks and teaches accurately about Jesus, although he knows only of John's baptism. He too begins to express himself fearlessly in the synagogue. When Priscilla and Aquila hear him, they take him home and explain to him God's new Way in greater detail. Some scholars believe that he was the author of the Letter to the Hebrews.

19:1-10 The foundation of the Church of Ephesus takes place in the house of a Greek professor. In all likelihood, during this same period Paul's group established the nearby Churches, such as those of Colossae, Laodicea, and Hierapolis.

19:11-20 Here we have a new account of miracles analogous to those of Peter (Acts 5:15); the Gospel changes one's life. Then the account becomes picturesque in reporting a new encounter with a milieu influenced by magic. From the Gospels, we know that there were Jewish exorcists (Mt 12:27) and that some even acted in the very name of Jesus (Mk 9:38; Lk 9:49). Those at Ephesus must have moved with ease in this city of superstition where books of magic proliferated. And the feeling is that since there is a new name circulating—that of Paul's Jesus—why not profit from that name so as to be up-to-date! However, once again we see the affirmation of the incompatibility between the magic enterprise and the Christian life. The Gospel will never be a secret act in the hands of sorcerers.

19:19 *Fifty thousand silver pieces* was an enormous sum, representing the wages for 50,000 days of work.

19:21-22 Luke announces the two stages that comprise the last part of Acts (21–28). He presents beforehand each cycle of new events in the course of the one that precedes.

19:24 *Artemis:* the Greek name for the Roman goddess Diana. However, Artemis also had the characteristics of Cybele, the mother goddess of fertility worshiped in Asia Minor. She was one of the most widely worshiped female deities in the Hellenistic world (see Acts 19:27), and her temple at Ephesus was known as one of the seven wonders of the ancient world.

19:29 *Aristarchus:* later he traveled with Paul from Corinth to Jerusalem (Acts 20:3f) and again from Jerusalem to Rome (Acts 27:1f; Col 4:10).

19:31 The story mentions the sympathy Paul won from some officials of the province ("asiarchs," "heads of Asia"). It also underscores the participation of lay believers in the struggle (vv. 29-30).

19:35 *Guardian of the temple:* a title given by Rome to cities that provided a temple for the cult of the Emperor. Ephesus was recognized as the provider of the temple of Artemis and of the cult of the Emperor. The statue of the goddess (425 feet long and 220 feet wide, with 127 marble columns 62 feet high and less than four feet apart) was thought of as having descended from heaven.

20:1-16 This departure constitutes an important moment as indicated by the fact that Luke inserts a list of Paul's companions. Then he describes three brief journeys: one to Greece, to revisit the communities, especially that of Corinth, which had caused some trouble; the second to Troas; and the third to Miletus, on the return route to Jerusalem.

In connection with these journeys we discover new aspects of the life of the communities. The Eucharist, which had been mentioned at the beginning of Acts (2:46), is clearly referred to here: Christians come together on Sunday ("the first day of the week") in order to "break bread," after a lengthy hearing of the Gospel and a communal reflection on it. The raising of the boy is a sign of the presence of the Lord; through his Resurrection, life is possible in its fullness.

20:1 Paul had apparently been seeking to preach in Troas on his way to Macedonia, meet Titus at Troas with a report from Corinth (see 2 Cor 2:12f), and continue collecting the offering for Judea (see Rom 15:25-28; 1 Cor 16:1-4; 2 Cor 8:1—9:15).

20:4 These men have no doubt been assigned to accompany Paul and the collection for the needy in Judea (see 2 Cor 8:23).

20:5 Here begins the second so-called "we-section" of Acts (see note on Acts 16:9-15).

20:7-38 In this chapter, it is no longer a case of proclaiming the word or creating a Church; it is a moment of respite and retreat that clears up Paul's personal destiny and expresses the principal concerns for the development and perseverance of a Church. Paul is aware that he will never return (see Acts 21:14), and he envisages undergoing the same suffering as Christ. The Book of Acts will not recount his martyrdom any more than it will enlighten us about Peter's martyrdom, for this Book is not intended to be a biography of the apostles. Its purpose is to make known the life of the Churches and the power of the Spirit who animates them, the great realities that ensure their development, their relationships, and their unity. The communities are to find themselves devoted to one another, but with the Spirit (v. 28) and the living tradition that carries them along. The atmosphere recalls Christ's discourse after the Last Supper (Jn 14—16). Paul gives his testament.

20:10 Paul's action of throwing himself upon a boy thought to be dead recalls that of Elijah in raising the son of the widow of Zarephath (1 Ki 17:21) and that of Elisha in raising the son of the Shunammite (2 Ki 4:34). Thus, as Peter had raised Tabitha (Acts 9:40), so now Paul raises Eutychus.

20:17-38 This farewell scene is especially important for the history of the Church as an institution. Those whom Paul summons are the "elders" (in Greek: *presbyteroi,* whence our "priests"), whom he describes (v. 28) as "shepherds" and "overseers" (Greek: *episkopoi,* whence our "bishops"; see 1 Pet 2:25), i.e., as responsible for the spiritual nourishment, guidance, and protection of the People of God. This authority they receive not from the assembly of the faithful but from the Spirit.

Here, in substance, is the ecclesial structure in which we live today (although only later would a distinction be made between "presbyters" and "bishops").

20:35 *It is more blessed to give than to receive:* a saying of Jesus that is not found in the canonical Gospels.

21:1—28:31 The period of missionary journeys is over. The new series of events begins in Jerusalem with an address of the elders of the community to Paul (Acts 21:20-26), followed by an address of Paul to the people (Acts 22:1-21). Then follows a series of four trials, of increasing importance, in Jerusalem and in Caesarea (Acts 23:1ff; 24:1ff; 25:1ff; 26:1ff). In this suffering of Paul, which makes him, like every martyr, a sharer in the suffering of Jesus, the basic theme of the discourses, almost their very reason for being, is the resurrection. Finally, there is the journey to Rome. In the capital of the Empire, the decisive turning point comes. Paul henceforth addresses himself to the Gentiles without any longer taking account of the privilege of the Jews to be the first to receive the message (Acts 28:28).

21:1-18 This is the third "we-section" (see note on Acts 16:9-15).

21:1-14 Right from the beginning, the presence of the Spirit is apparent. It is he who urges Paul toward his destiny, and his presence is signified by the prophets who discuss the hour from which all want to save Paul. The assembly takes up the words of our Lord in the Garden of Olives: "The Lord's will be done" (v. 14).

21:8 *Seven:* see Acts 6:2-4.

21:15-26 The elders extend a cordial but anxious welcome. Paul gives the community of Jerusalem an account of his mission, and the Church offers thanks. In this Jewish city, in a community presided over by James, a relative of Jesus deeply attached to Judaism, Paul accepts to live in the Jewish manner—in accord with his dictum: "I became all things to all" (1 Cor 9:22). He must also give proof of his good faith: if he does not impose the practices of Judaism on Gentiles, he does not on the other hand wish to turn away those of Jewish origin from those practices.

In fact, Paul does not blame Jewish practices but those who insist on making them the condition of salvation. As a Jew himself, he loyally consents to perform a typically Jewish act of devotion: he joins a group of pilgrims who have taken a Nazirite vow (see Acts 18:18); at the appointed time he will come to be purified in the temple in accord with the prescriptions of the Law (Num 6:1-21) and will even pay the expenses. The Book of Acts does not say anything about Paul bringing the collection of the Churches to this mother community that has fallen in need.

21:27-40 Now the time for imprisonment and captivity has arrived, sparked by a misunderstanding. The Jews come to believe that Paul is bringing into the temple a non-Jew—someone who is forbidden under penalty of death from entering the inner courts. Hence, a cry of sacrilege rings out. In reality, hatred is about to explode. Judaism has felt the jolt of a nascent Christianity and has reacted defensively to it. This reflexive sentiment has already been at work against Stephen (see Acts 6:11-14), and the same accusations were formulated against Jesus (Mt 26:61; 27:40; Mk 14:58; 15:29).

The defensive reaction is a violent, irrational, and almost visceral one. It has to be such in order that the Christian originality may be manifest and that one may know what to hold on to. The commander of the cohort, who watches the temple from the fortress installed at the northwest corner, intervenes to prevent a riot. The soldiers believe they are arresting a nationalist extremist. Luke stresses once more that neither Paul nor Christians have ever been involved in a subversive plot against the Empire.

21:38 *The Egyptian:* in A.D. 54, an Egyptian agitator, Ben Stada, had stirred up the Jewish nationalists to whom reference is made here, as we know from the historian Flavius Josephus. The Roman authorities were forced to put down the riot, and thousands were killed. *Assassins:* literally, *sicarii,* violent nationalists who carried a short dagger, called *sica* in Latin, and did not hesitate to use it.

21:40 *Aramaic:* the language spoken by Jews at this time; Hebrew was no longer spoken or understood by the people after the Babylonian exile (587 B.C.).

22:1-21 Paul refers chiefly to his conversion and explains it. That event dominated his life: the story is told three times in Acts (9:1-19; 22:1-21; 26:9-18). In speaking to Jews, as he does here, Paul mentions a detail that is omitted in the other two accounts: he received his mission in the temple (vv. 17-21).

22:15 *His witness:* Paul is to be a witness to Jesus' Resurrection in the same way that the apostles have been, since he too has seen the risen Lord (see Acts 1:8; 10:39-41; Lk 24:48).

22:22-29 Luke doubtless recalls this fact to emphasize that the Empire has no reason to suspect Christianity of any subversive intent.

22:30—23:11 In the last cycle of Acts, each discourse is inserted into a very colorful account. The episode of the affront to the high priest, a man with a poor reputation, is not lacking in irony. In addition, each time there is a "suspense" created that becomes ever more intense. In the present case, the subject of the resurrection stirs discord among the hearers, because it was a matter of dispute within Jewish theology. In fact, belief in the resurrection, with the resultant different fates of the good and the bad, came into existence late in Judaism (2 Mac 7:9, 11, 14, 23, 29, 36; 12:38-46; Dan 12:2f; see Wis 3:1-5, 16). It was accepted by the Pharisees, but the Sadducees tried to combat it, even by ridiculing it (see Mt 22:23-33; Mk 12:18-27; Lk 20:27-38).

As is the case with the other discourses, this one also wishes to make clear that Paul and the Churches are innocent of the accusations of the Jews and the suspicions of the Romans. Then the debate, which at first was carried out on the juridical level, is raised to the level of theological realities.

23:2 *Ananias* was high priest from A.D. 47 to 59.

23:12-22 Luke contrasts the correct behavior of the Roman authorities with the blind fanaticism of the Jews: from the outset the Romans realized that there was nothing subversive about Christianity. This is proof of the loyalty of Christians. Note the reference to Paul's sister and nephew; this is the only information we have about his family.

23:12 *Oath:* they call God's curse upon themselves if they fail to carry out the commitment they have assumed.

23:23-35 The commander cannot risk having a Roman citizen assassinated while in his custody, so he seeks to transfer Paul to the jurisdiction of Felix, the governor of the province of Judea. He also sends a letter to Felix summarizing the events, from the riot in the temple to the commander's discovery of a plot against Paul's life. The most important thing he says is that there is no charge against Paul deserving of death or punishment. Felix then agrees to hear the case himself.

23:23 *Nine o'clock tonight:* literally, "the third hour of the night."

23:26 *Felix:* M. Antonius Felix was governor (procurator) of Judea from A.D. 52 to 60, and he ruled with an iron hand.

24:1-21 The language is that of grave accusations and fine speeches. Once again, Paul dispels the Jewish accusations and the Roman suspicions. He is given a trial, but those who are directly opposed to him, and should be there, are missing, i.e., the Jews of Asia who stirred up more than one riot against him during his missionary journeys. Accusations leveled at him are not backed up by the facts. More profoundly—and herein lies the problem—the first Christians are convinced that their faith is not a perversion of, a secession from, or an opposition to Judaism but the fulfillment of its historical hope. The resurrection is their most ineradicable certitude. But this belief also exists among some people in Israel. More and more in the course of the trial, stress is placed on the subject of the hope of the resurrection.

24:7 This verse is lacking in the better manuscripts.

24:22-27 Felix is willing to listen to Christian teaching, but not to take the risk of converting his ways. He governs with complacencies, cruelties, and briberies, and he doubtless will have contributed to stirring up discontent, the precursor of the rebellion that would lead to the destruction of the Jewish State in A.D. 70. He seems to have been sympathetic to Paul, while keeping him in detention beyond the time provided by the Law.

24:24 *Drusilla:* at the age of fifteen, this daughter of Herod Agrippa I had abandoned her first husband, the king of Emesa, in order to become Felix's third wife.

24:27 *Porcius Festus* was an excellent governor and remained in office from A.D. 59 to 62. The "two years" to which reference is made here ran from A.D. 57 to 59.

25:1-12 The governors change, but at Jerusalem the Jewish authorities do not forget Paul. They seek once again to suppress the Apostle by a criminal act, but they appeal to the governor in vain. Since the dispute is religious in theme, why not entrust it to the jurisdiction of the Sanhedrin, while continuing the debates? Paul cannot consent to this for he realizes that he would never receive justice.

25:11 A Roman citizen could not be transferred from one jurisdiction to another without his consent. Paul had an unassailable right to appeal to Caesar.

25:13-27 Paul has already appeared in the presence of Drusilla (Acts 24:24); this time, he meets Agrippa and Bernice. The three children of Herod Agrippa I (Acts 12:1) have made his acquaintance. Bernice has also become famous because of her ties to Titus. The meeting takes place in a formal setting. The Roman governor probably thinks that his guests who are Jewish in origin can shed light on the dispute. Before giving a kind of curriculum of life, Paul places into evidence the Christian belief in the resurrection and shows Christianity as the fulfillment of the Jewish hope for the betterment of all human beings.

We now read the third account of Paul's conversion (see Acts 9:1-19; 22:1-21), which puts more emphasis on Paul's mission being in accord with prophetic callings in the Old Testament. It is a splendid Christian biography of Paul, a vision of Christianity as the fulfillment of the destiny of Israel, and a profession of faith in the Resurrection of Jesus being for the salvation of all human beings.

26:10 *Saints:* see note on Acts 9:13.

26:14 *It is hard for you to kick against the goad:* a well-known expression in the Greek world to express the futility of opposing the gods.

26:18 *From darkness to light:* a figure used often by Paul (see Rom 13:12; 2 Cor 4:6; Eph 5:8-14; Col 1:13; 1 Thes 5:5).

26:26 *Not done in a corner:* a phrase stressing the fact that the Gospel is based on real events lived out in history. The king is bound to confirm the truth of the things Paul says.

26:27 *Do you believe the Prophets?:* this question by Paul puts King Agrippa in a no-win situation. If he says "Yes," Paul will insist that he recognize Jesus as the fulfillment of the Prophets. If he says "No," he will earn the wrath of the devout Jews, who accept the Prophets as God's spokespersons. So Agrippa skirts the question.

27:1—28:15 A journey full of vicissitudes. For 15 days, the ship will drift from the coast of Crete to the Island of Malta, without any planned direction because the mariners cannot rely on the stars or the sun, which supplied the only way of determining direction at that time (Acts 27:20). Paul very calmly takes control of the situation; he is used to the sea and has already experienced three shipwrecks (see 2 Cor 11:25).

Paul evidently cannot think of founding a community on Malta, since it is a mere stopover, but he does effect cures. There are three more stopovers: Syracuse, Rhegium, and Puteoli. In the last-named place Paul has the joy of finding some brothers (Acts 28:13-14). In Rome, he finds a community of Christians of whose origin we know nothing, but which has already received from him the great Letter on salvation in Jesus Christ; the members of this community go to meet Paul at a place over 30 miles from the City (at the Forum of Appius and the Three Taverns, north of Terracina: Acts 28:15-16). He was, therefore, known and expected.

27:1 This begins the final "we-section" in Acts (see note on Acts 16:9-15). *Augustan cohort:* a name identifying the Roman legion to which the centurion belonged.

27:2 *Adramyttium:* a harbor on the west coast of the province of Asia.

27:3 *Sidon:* a city 70 miles north of Caesarea.

27:5 *Myra in Lycia:* an important harbor on the journey from Egypt to Rome as well as a prominent place for storing grain.

27:6 *Alexandrian ship:* a ship traveling from Egypt to Rome with a cargo of grain.

27:7 *Cnidus:* a city at the southeastern part of Asia Minor. A journey from Myra to Cnidus was 170 miles and required 10 to 15 days. *Crete:* an island 160 miles in length. *Salmone:* a promontory on the northeast tip of Crete.

27:8 *Fair Havens:* a city midway on the southern coast of Crete. *Lasea:* a city about five miles from Fair Havens.

27:9 *The Fast:* the fast that was called for on the Day of Atonement, i.e., either late September or early October. The season for sailing lasted from Pentecost (May–June) to Tabernacles (five days after the Fast). Sailing was regarded as hazardous after September 15 and as catastrophic after November 11.

27:12 *Phoenix:* a city with a harbor that provided protection from storms.

27:16 *Cauda:* a city about 23 miles from Crete.

27:17 *Syrtis:* a sandy stretch of land off the coast of Tunis and Tripoli in North Africa.

27:27 *Adriatic Sea:* the name was used generally for the seas between Italy, Greece, and Africa.

27:31 *Unless these men stay:* Paul points out that if the sailors jump ship, the passengers will be unable to bring the vessel to shore by themselves and will perish.

28:1 *Malta:* a port of the province of Sicily, though located 58 miles away from the island itself.

28:2 *Natives:* literally, "barbarians"—which was the name the Greeks attached to all non-Greek speaking people.

28:4 *Justice:* a personification of divine avenging justice.

28:7 *Publius:* this local magistrate was the representative of the praetor of Sicily.

28:11 *Three months later:* the time was probably February of the year A.D. 60. *Dioscuri:* i.e., Castor and Pollux, pagan divinities who protected seafarers.

28:12 *Syracuse:* the most important city of Sicily, located on its east coast.

28:13 *Rhegium:* a town of Italy located opposite Messina and close to the narrowest part of the strait that lies between Italy and Sicily. *Puteoli:* the chief port of Rome, located almost 200 miles from Rhegium in the northern part of Naples.

28:15 *Forum of Appius:* a town 43 miles from Rome and known for its uncivilized behavior. *Three Taverns:* a town 33 miles from Rome.

28:16-29 As he has done throughout the Book, Paul first contacts the Jews established in the city. He must clarify his situation with regard to this colony. And he must first of all proclaim the Gospel as the fulfillment of Israel's Scriptures and its hope. The Jews see and hear, as the apostles did, but they choose not to understand because they do not make the connection from the past to the future. Henceforth, the Word will be directly addressed to the Gentiles without passing through the synagogue. Paul's speech is a last appeal and a conclusion.

We conclude from Acts that the movement of the Resurrection and Pentecost now enters freely into the whole universe. The limits of the old Israel have crumbled; the People of God gathers together all humanity.

28:16 Though he lived in a house of his own choice, he was under house arrest during his stay in Rome.

28:29 This verse is lacking in the oldest manuscripts.

28:30-31 Luke knows that Paul died a martyr in Rome, but he does not speak of it, just as he says nothing of Peter's activity after his deliverance from the hands of Herod. His purpose is not to give us a history of the Church but to show the spread of the Gospel down to the point of its tree entry among all the peoples.

According to the most popular view, Paul wrote the Captivity Letters (Ephesians, Colossians, Philippians, and Philemon) during this first Roman imprisonment. One tradition of the early Church also presupposes that Paul was set free after two years. Clement of Rome in his Epistle to the Corinthians (5:5-7) says that Paul went "to the end of the West," i.e., that he carried out the missionary journey to Spain that he had planned (see Rom 15:24). This point is also attested by the Muratorian Fragment (lines 37-38) and by the apocryphal Acts of Peter (chs. 1 and 3).

THE LETTER TO THE ROMANS

1:1 *Paul:* in accord with ancient custom, Paul puts his name at the beginning of the Letter; for information about Paul, see Acts 9:1ff; Phil 3:4-14; and the Introduction to his Letters, pp. 369-370. *Servant:* literally, (1) a "slave," who belongs wholly to his master and is not free to leave, or (2) a "servant," who chooses to serve his master (see Ex 14:31; Ps 18; Isa 41:8-9; 42:1). *Apostle:* one especially commissioned by Christ (see note on Mk 6:30). *Gospel:* see note on Mk 1:1-8. The word Gospel occurs with special frequency in the collection of Paul's Letters (40 times).

1:2 *Prophets:* not just the writers of the Prophetic Books of the Bible but the whole Old Testament, which prophesied about Jesus (see Lk 24:27, 44). *Holy Scriptures:* the Old Testament.

1:3-4 An early Christian profession of faith that proclaims Jesus' sonship as the Messianic descendant of David (see Mt 22:42; 2 Tim 2:8; Rev 22:16) and as the Son of God, as indicated by the Resurrection. Since Jesus is a "life-giving spirit" (1 Cor 15:45), he is able to give the Spirit to those who believe in him.

1:7 *Saints:* the Greek meaning of the word accentuates the idea of "holiness." All Christians are saints insofar as they are "set apart" for God and are being made increasingly "holy" by the Holy Spirit (see 1 Cor 1:2; 1 Thes 4:7). The Christian community regarded its members as made holy through Baptism (Rom 6:22; 15:16; 1 Cor 6:11; Eph 5:26f).

1:8-15 Paul acknowledges that he has no authority over the Church of Rome, which he did not found; he presents himself as a simple Christian who wants to be one in faith with his brothers and sisters through mutual instruction and edification. The word *non-Greeks* (literally, "barbarians") (v. 14) signifies here that the pagans had not received Greek culture.

1:13 *Brethren:* all those (both men and women) who believe in the Gospel are kin of Paul (see Rom 4:3).

1:14 *Greeks and non-Greeks:* literally, "Greeks and barbarians." The "Greeks" were all who spoke Greek or followed the Greek way of life; the "non-Greeks" were all the other Gentiles to whom Paul preached.

1:16-17 This extremely dense paragraph sums up the entire Letter. When we hear the word "gospel" we should not think of a book, but of the proclamation of salvation through faith. The citation in v. 17 from the prophet Habakkuk (2:4), each word of which here takes on a Christian value, constitutes the theological pivot of the entire Letter.

1:17 *Beginning in faith and established in faith:* literally, "from faith to faith," i.e., by an ever more perfect faith. But other interpretations have been given.

1:18—4:25 In comparison with the liberation brought by the Gospel, humanity apart from Christ and without grace seems to be filled with sin and alienation. Paul begins by sketching a grim picture of the world as a prison and of the darkness in which human beings walk, whether Jews or Gentiles, who have abandoned themselves to their passions and to their own vain efforts (Rom 1:18—3:20). But into this world that is without vitality or a future, the love of God bursts forth and brings liberation. This conviction is central to the section. And this justification is given to whoever believes in Christ (Rom 3:20-31). What does "believe" mean? Paul explains it at length, using what he regards as the magnificent example of Abraham (Rom 4:1-25).

1:18—3:20 Without Christ the world goes astray and cannot reach its goal, which is God. It is under "the wrath of God," an Old Testament phrase that indicates the ineradicable opposition between God and evil (see Isa 9:11-20; 10:4; 30:27). Thus, the world is a victim of corruption, of its useless efforts, of its lack of a sense of sin. Paul is especially sensitive to this situation and paints the dark scene on two panels: an indictment against paganism and a statement on the failure of Judaism. Neither paganism nor Judaism can save human beings.

1:26-27 See note on 1 Tim 1:10.

2:6 *Will repay everyone in accordance with what his deeds deserve:* a combination of Ps 62:12 and Prov 24:12 from the Septuagint (the Greek translation of the Old Testament).

2:11 *God shows no partiality:* a basic teaching of both the Old and the New Testament (see Deut 10:17).

2:12-24 This passage is an important one for theology: God speaks to all human beings through the law of conscience; the authentic virtues and the interior resistances of the Gentiles bear witness to this fact.

2:15 Paul takes up and develops the teaching of Jer 31:33 and Wis 17:11.

2:17-20 In the original, the sentence is left incomplete; it has been translated in a way that makes it complete.

2:25-29 For Israel, circumcision was the sign of its covenant with God; to receive it was to belong to the People of God, and the Jews were proud of it. But was the rite enough, when the person did not live the reality that the rite signified? The Prophets had long been criticizing formalism and calling for a religion of the heart (see Jer 4:4; 9:24-25; Lev 26:41; Deut 10:16; 30:6; Sir 35:1-10; Dan 3:36-40; Phil 3:3-7).

3:4 *Every human being is a liar:* these words are taken from Ps 116:11 LXX; the rest of the verse comes from Ps 51:6 LXX.

3:9-20 To ensure the solidity of his inquiry concerning the universal reign of sin, Paul applies the Biblical proof to it. In the manner of the rabbis, he offers several citations on human corruption from the Psalms and the Book of Isaiah (the references are—in the order of the citations—Pss 14:1-3; 5:9; 140:4; 10:7; Isa 59:7-8; Pss 36:1; 143:21). Paul has led us in this descent into the hell of sin, in which humankind lies impotent, in order to enable us to appreciate the greatness of redemption and the necessity of faith.

3:9 *Are we any better?:* i.e., are Jews better than Gentiles in God's sight?

3:21-31 By dying on the cross, Jesus Christ publicly manifested the justice of God, that is, the faithful fulfillment of what God had promised for the salvation of every human being.

3:21-26 *Sacrifice of expiation* alludes to the cover of the ark, known as the "propitiatory," which played an important role in the Jewish ritual of the Day of Atonement (Lev 16). It was sprinkled with the blood of animals, as though to atone for collective sin. By giving his life, Christ really freed the people from sin and brought them God's forgiveness.

4:1-25 There is but one dispensation, that of grace and faith, which excludes all human pride and allows us to receive everything from God with thanksgiving. The story of Abraham is the purest illustration of this truth. Christian faith is present germinally in the faith of the father of believers (see Gal 3:6-8).

4:1-8 The father of believers can do nothing that is of value before God. He is regarded as just, i.e., holy and close to God, because he acknowledges that he is poor and entrusts himself wholly to the Lord. To forgive sins constitutes the gratuitous act par excellence, the act of God (vv. 7-8).

4:3 At first glance, it seems that the Letter of James (2:24) goes against this statement of Paul. However, it is clear from the context in James that the phrase "by works and not by faith alone" does not mean that *genuine* faith is not sufficient for justification but rather that *faith* unaccompanied by works is not *genuine*. Thus, the teaching of James does not conflict with that of Paul.

4:6-8 When a sinner repents, God takes away his unrighteousness by forgiving him when he confesses his sins (see Ps 32:3-5; Ezek 18:23, 27f, 32; 33:14-16.

4:9-12 Abraham became the friend of God (see Gen 15:6) before being circumcised (see Gen 17:19). This means that circumcision is neither the source of nor the condition for being justified; it is simply given as a sign of the promise that God made to Abraham because he believed (Gen 17). Circumcision is the external mark of the Covenant—not the source of righteousness. It is faith that links Christ to the chosen people, who are neither Jews nor Gentiles.

4:13-17 Abraham owes nothing to the Law, for this came into force a long time after him (see Gal 3:17). Moreover, no law can do anything but "lay bare" sin and condemn the sinner (see Gal 3:10). Now, the promise of salvation is something else—it is a grace of God. In Abraham, it is assured to all who believe. Thus, all believers have access to the historic plan of God, and Paul loves to celebrate the universality of faith.

4:18-25 God is the "Master of the Impossible"; he is even powerful enough to bring about the raising of a dead person. It is in such certitude that believers live. Abraham believed in the word of the Lord who announced that two "dead" bodies, i.e., sterile people, himself and Sarah, would give life to Isaac (Gen 15:5). Moreover, circumstances called into question the fulfillment of the promise; yet Abraham—ever the father of believers—never doubted. Thus, he shared the condition of Christians who steadfastly believe in Life because they believe in the risen Jesus, the Son of the Living God. The object of faith is the Passover of Christ.

5:1—11:36 Without faith human beings remain in the night of sin. When they have been justified through Christ and believe in the redemption he gives, they enter into a new life, that of salvation. Paul confronts the believer with a living reality.

First, he speaks of peace and reconciliation (Rom 5:1-11); he must then show how Christ opens for us the way of deliverance from sin (Rom 5:12-21), from death (Rom 6:1-23), and from the Law (Rom 7:1-25); the song of Christian life is a song of the Spirit and of hope. But Paul cannot forget the lot of the Israel that rejects the Gospel; he enters upon a lengthy discussion and asserts again that the love of God is stronger than any human rejection (chs. 9–11).

5:1 *We are at peace:* some manuscripts and Fathers of the Church give: "Let us have peace."

5:5 *Such hope will not be doomed to disappointment:* the hope of believers is more than just an earthly optimism. It is the assurance of our future destiny based on the love of God for us—revealed to us by the Holy Spirit and demonstrated for us by Christ's Death.

5:9 *Saved . . . from divine retribution:* the image expresses the tragic situation of humanity without God, that is, without hope and without an authentic future (see Rom 1:18; 1 Thes 1:10).

5:12-21 The religious history of humanity is here summarized in an incisive synthesis. We should keep our gaze fixed on the luminous heights to which Paul wants to lead us: his vision points to life, grace, and the salvation given in Christ Jesus. The vision is all the more fascinating in that it stands out against the dark background of sin and death.

5:12 *Death:* physical death is the penalty for sin as well as the symbol of spiritual death, the ultimate separation of a human being from God. *Inasmuch as everyone has sinned:* we start life with a sinful nature (see Gen 8:21; Pss 51:7; 58:4; Eph 2:3).

5:15 *The many:* this has the same meaning as "everyone" in verse 12 (see Isa 53:11; Mk 10:45).

5:19 *Disobedience* is the refusal to acknowledge the primacy of God when it comes to giving life meaning. *Obedience* is the commitment of one's life to the plan and call of God.

6:1-23 Salvation is grace that transcends sin and the power of human beings or even of the Law. This passage urges us to reflect on the meaning of Baptism in the life of a Christian.

6:1-14 In the History of Salvation, there is a unique event: the Death and Resurrection of Jesus; it is the departure for a new life. Through Baptism, the believer enters into this experience of Christ and shares its power. Baptism inaugurates a newness of life that will be brought to completion in the future.

6:4 *Glory of the Father:* God who reveals his power and holiness.

6:6 The adjective *old* has a precise meaning for Paul: it describes the reality of a sinful world that is closed against the new life that has its source in Christ (see 1 Cor 5:7-8; 2 Cor 3:14); the *old self* and the *sinful body* signify the human being as marked by sin (Gal 3:26-29).

6:8 In the experience of Christ, resurrection followed upon death; hence, believers who die with Christ are raised to a new quality of moral life. This resurrection is already a fact, and it exerts itself more and more in the life of believers.

7:1-25 Human alienation finds expression in three main forms: sin, death, and law. Salvation delivers human beings from this threefold enslavement. The law here is, of course, the Law of Moses, but it is also the command given by God to the first couple and, in the last analysis, every law that is imposed from outside.

7:1-6 Christians have been freed from the Law. This is a way of saying that a new regime, that of the Spirit, henceforth energizes their life.

7:6 *Written code* or "letter" is here the written Law of Moses.

7:7-12 Christ was put to death because he affirmed the priority of the spirit over legalism. In fact, it is sin that falsifies the human condition. Without having the power to neutralize it, the Law unmasks it and then buries human beings under the weight of guilt (see Gal 3:10-14, 19-22).

7:11 *Deceived me:* an allusion to the temptation by the serpent in Gen 3:13.

7:16 *I agree that the Law is good:* the Holy Spirit reveals to Paul the essential goodness of the Law even when Paul is inclined to rebel against it and disobey it.

8:1-39 In the experience of the love of God there are three dominant elements: the life of the Spirit (vv. 5-13), the sure realization of being children of God (vv. 14-17), and the certainty of future glory (vv. 18-30). This ascending description ends with a triumphant hymn to the unfailing love of the Lord (vv. 31-39).

8:4 *Righteous requirements of the Law:* although the Law is not a means of salvation, it still plays a role in the life of a believer as a moral guide, obeyed out of love for God and by the power of the Holy Spirit. This marks the fulfillment of Jeremiah's prophecy of the New Covenant (Jer 31:33ff).

8:5-17 What is the Christian life in its deepest reality? Paul thinks of all that the Holy Spirit inaugurates in the existence of the believer. He is the Spirit of the Father and of Christ, dwells in every Christian, and is a source of spiritual life for each. We can look upon him as the soul of the Church. He is the power of a progressive transformation, which culminates in the resurrection of the body. In a privileged moment—that of prayer—believers grasp their new state as children of God. Thus, believers escape from the flesh, i.e., an orientation to and a realization of a life without future and without accomplishment (see Gal 5:16-25).

8:11 For the connection between the Resurrection of Christ and that of believers, see 1 Cor 6:14; 15:20, 23; 2 Cor 4:14; Phil 3:21; 1 Thes 4:14.

8:14-17 Because of the Holy Spirit's presence in them, Christians possess a new life as well as a new relationship with God. They have become adopted children of God and heirs through Christ, sharing both in his sufferings and in his glory.

8:18-30 The exalting perspective of salvation is expanded to the dimensions of the universe. Paul takes up a Biblical idea: the cosmos is linked with the fate of humankind, cursed then redeemed. All creation prepares for the new world (v. 22). Paul beautifully sketches the proofs of this movement that is nearing its fulfillment: (1) the presentiment of the universe whose Creator and Lord is Christ (vv. 19-22); (2) the firm hope of believers transformed through Baptism and urged to seize fully that which—even here below—the Spirit inaugurates in them (vv. 23-25); (3) the very prayer by which the Spirit inspires this grand aspiration (vv. 26-27); and finally (4) the will of God, whose love embraces believers in order to associate them with the risen and glorified Christ, so that they may be in the image of his Son, who is himself the perfect image of the Father (see Col 1:15) (vv. 28-30).

8:28 *We know that God makes all things work together for good for those who love him:* some manuscripts have: "We know that all things work together for good to those who love God."

8:34 The reasons why no one can condemn us who are God's elect are three: (1) Christ died for us; (2) Christ is alive and seated at God's right hand, a position of awesome power; and (3) Christ himself makes intercession for us.

8:39 In the terms *angels . . . principalities . . . height . . . depth* Paul is perhaps speaking of spiritual entities that were considered to be intermediaries between God and humanity.

9:1—11:36 Paul was born a Jew. In his eyes, Christianity was the historical fulfillment of the destiny and hope of Israel, the authentic conclusion of the Old Covenant, which was destined to shine out brightly in the New Covenant that was inaugurated by the Passover of Christ. But reality confronts him with agonizing problems. It had been necessary to make Jewish Christians understand that the salvation given by Jesus Christ caused a break from the Jewish religious system (see 2 Cor 3; Gal; Rom 7). An even more serious problem: Israel had officially rejected Jesus and now rejected the Gospel and the young Church. Paul's reflections are organized in three stages: first, he stresses the fidelity of God (Rom 9:6-29); he then points out Israel's responsibility (Rom 9:31—10:21); finally, with the entire plan of God in view, he insists that the infidelity of Israel is only provisional and partial (Rom 11:1-32). A hymn to the wisdom of God (Rom 11:33-36) ends these difficult pages.

9:4 *Israelites:* descendants of Jacob, who was named Israel by God (see Gen 32:28). The name originally designated the whole nation of Israel (see Jdg 5:7), but after the division into two kingdoms it was given to the northern kingdom alone. In New Testament times, Palestinian Jews used the term "Israelites" to indicate that they were God's chosen people.

Paul shows that God's promises to them are still in effect: *adoption,* i.e., as God's children (see Ex 4:22f; Jer 31:9; Hos 1:1); *glory,* i.e., God's presence among them (see Ex 16:7, 10; Lev 9:6, 23; Num 16:19); *covenants,* e.g., the Abrahamic (see Gen 15:17-21; 17:1-8), the Mosaic (see Ex 19:5; 24:1-10); the Levitical (Num 25:12f; Jer 33:21; Mal 2:4f), the Davidic (see 2 Sam 7; 23:5; Pss 89:4f, 29f; 132:11f), and the New Covenant (prophesied in Jer 31:31-40); and the *promises,* especially those made to Abraham (see Gen 12:7; 13:14-17; 17:48; 22:16-18) and the Messianic promises (e.g., 2 Sam 7:12, 16; Isa 9:6f; Jer 23:5; 31:31-34; Ezek 34:23f; 37:24-28).

9:5 *Came the Christ, God forever, who is over all:* another possible translation is: "came the Christ. God who is over all be praised."

9:13 *Hated:* in the Biblical sense of the word, that is, "I preferred Jacob."

9:14-29 Paul thinks with astonishment of the unforeseeable calls of God, who chooses individuals and people from the midst of a sinful world. The image of the potter signifies in the Bible the sovereign freedom of God that defies all expectations. The texts from Hosea (2:25 and 1:10) spoke of the conversion of Israel; Paul interprets them as proclamations of an unprecedented initiative of God: the call of the Gentiles.

9:22 *Objects of his wrath:* human beings who by sinning incur God's anger.

9:33 This verse uses a combination of two texts from Isaiah that was apparently in common use by the early Christians to defend Christ's Messiahship (see 1 Pet 2:4, 6-8; see also Ps 118:22; Lk 20:17f).

10:5-13 In Jesus God has placed himself at our disposal; we need only acknowledge the risen Christ. This is one of the earliest formulas with which candidates for Baptism professed their faith.

10:7 Paul here combines Deut 30:13 and Ps 107:26.

10:9 *Jesus is Lord:* the word "Lord" occurs some 6,000 times in the Septuagint (the Greek translation of the Old Testament) for "Yahweh," the name of the God of Israel. Here it is applied to Jesus by an early baptismal profession of faith to indicate Christ's divinity.

11:1-10 The threat to "harden" human beings (Isa 29:10) is often cited in the New Testament in censuring seemingly irremediable human blindness (see Mt 13:14; Jn 12:40; Acts 28:26). God is not indifferent to human rejection.

11:11-15 Everything works together to carry out God's plan, which is to save all human beings. The Gospel, poorly accepted by a large part of Israel, has now been announced to the Gentile world. This fact should stir up the envy of the Israelites and make them take more careful notice of Christ. Paul hopes for their conversion and already foresees it as a passage from death to life, like the great resurrection of the people about which Ezekiel speaks in ch. 37.

11:16-24 As for the Gentile converts who may be tempted to look down on their Jewish brothers, the Apostle recalls their own spiritual origins: the Church was born from the Jewish people; she is the fulfillment of the Remnant of Israel. The Gentiles were grafted like a wild olive shoot onto this olive tree. Each one of them must remember that God has called them out of love and mercy. Even in their rejection of Jesus, the Jews do not lose their quality of belonging to the chosen people.

The lesson is always valid: no one can boast about being saved. Anti-Semitism can be nothing but a scandal in the Christian world: "We are spiritual Semites"

(Pope Pius XI). The originality of the Church of Jesus consists in bringing about the unity of humankind, and first of all of the two opposed groups that are the Jews and the Gentiles (Eph 2:14-16).

11:25-32 Prolonging the vision of the Prophets, Paul declares that the chosen people have not been definitively rejected; God does not go back on his choice. The coming of salvation remains open to the People of the Promise. The fate of Israel is not closed off from the salvation that it contributes to bring about for the profit of the Gentiles. In spite of detours of an often tragic history, the Lord continues to guide his people toward a glorious destiny in order to show that he saves his people because he loves them. The entry of the Gentiles cannot signify the exclusion of Israel; God's mercy is for all.

11:33-36 Having arrived at this summit where all humankind is reunited in the salvation of God, Paul cannot refrain from crying out in adoration and admiration.

11:34 This citation is from the Septuagint of Isa 40:13.

11:35 This citation is from an old Greek version of Job 41:3a and does not coincide with the Hebrew text of Job 41:11a.

12:1—15:13 Following his custom, Paul ends his Letter (before the Epilogue) with a number of ideas and counsels for Christian life in the midst of everyday reality.

12:5 *One body in Christ:* see 1 Cor 12:12-27.

12:20 *Burning coals:* this means that the responsibility of the other is increased, or else that he is given a stimulus to repentance. In any case, the doing of good must not depend on its acknowledgment by the other.

13:1-7 Christians do not keep themselves apart from the city in which they live and normally carry out their duties in the civic community. Society is willed by God as an organized entity. Authority comes from God and is supposed to serve the common good. Paul here gives a practical rule of conduct for Christians. In the face of power, Christians choose neither disinterest nor subversion.

13:8-10 The fact that love fulfills the whole Law is an essential tenet of Christianity, and Paul shows how it is true in the concrete.

13:11-14 Paul does not say that the end time is near. Rather he affirms that those who have been baptized, and delivered from the grasp of evil, of Satan who is the prince of darkness (Col 1:13), live in a new era. This new state also requires a new way of conduct. As Paul contrasted flesh and spirit, now he contrasts light and darkness—an image that is current to his epoch and self-explanatory. To put on Jesus Christ is to act in accord with the Holy Spirit and his inspirations—in short, to carry out the very meaning of Baptism.

14:1—15:6 Two groups or tendencies are already manifested in the early Christian communities. Some cling, though not without some scruples, to the religious practices in which they have been reared: refusal of sacrificed meats or abstentions from foods on certain days—and these may be termed "the weak." Others, in the same freedom of the Gospel, criticize the former—and these may be termed "the strong." The text evokes a situation like that in Corinth (1 Cor 8:4-13).

Paul has always been categorically opposed to confusing grace with the Law; he has refused to impose either Jewish or Gentile practices on new converts and has declared that all ancient religious practices are excluded as a way to gain justification. He is undoubtedly also aware of the teaching of Jesus concerning what is clean and unclean (Mk 7:1-23). Moreover, he has never refused to allow Christians of Jewish origin to esteem attachment to their religious tradition. He has put clamps on the new freedom only when such freedom turns into provocative pretense and an attitude of superiority.

Freedom is not given to enable someone to criticize others; it does not consist in remonstrating with others about theory or comportment. No principle of freedom can lead to an attitude of scorn or incomprehension. Christians maintain a desire for the salvation of all, and regard everyone as a brother or sister for whom Christ died. They are open to safeguard the relations and exchanges of a varied and pluralist community. Profound respect for the conscience of each person is required, as is the refusal to judge one another. Most important, all must have the freedom to act according to their consciences before God (see Acts 15).

14:19 *Let us:* some manuscripts and Fathers of the Church have: "We."

15:7-13 It is the unity of believers that glorifies God (Rom 15:6). That is why, despite the fact that Christ himself preached only to the Jews—to the circumcised—he willed that the Gentiles should also be called to salvation and thereby attest that they too are loved by God. In that same love, all Christians should embrace their neighbors.

15:10 The citation from Deut 32:43 is given in the Septuagint version.

15:12 The citation is based on Isa 11:10 and Rev 5:5; 22:16. *Root of Jesse:* Jesse was the father of David (see 1 Sam 16:5; Mt 1:6), and the Messiah was the "Son of David" (Mt 21:9). *The Gentiles will hope in him:* this prophecy is fulfilled in the evangelization of the Gentiles.

15:14—16:27 Paul has set forth his main ideas on Christian faith in Christ dead and risen. He now briefly explains his plans and in this context tells his readers in what his ministry consists. The letter ends with a liturgical hymn that is also a profession of faith.

15:14-21 Paul regards his apostolic work as a sacred service, as a Liturgy of God in the world of human beings; in fact, it is in the name of God and under the inspiration of the Holy Spirit that the Apostle intervenes to prompt people to belief and to lead the human family to be committed to God. He looks upon this action as the true sacrifice, one that expresses a gift and a love for life itself. It is understood that a community that proclaims the Gospel is also a community that celebrates the Eucharist (see Rom 1:9; 12:1; Phil 2:17).

Paul is conscious that, aided by the power of Christ and the Holy Spirit, he is carrying out a proper task. He makes the Gospel present in the human groups of the Gentile world and rejoices in having accomplished a foundational work.

15:19 *Jerusalem* and *Illyricum,* which borders on Macedonia in the northwest, are the two extremes of Paul's apostolate at this time.

15:22-33 Rome is not to be anything more than a stopover on Paul's journey to Spain. For he plans to travel to the very ends of the West to continue his mission to make the Gospel present where it has not yet been announced. Apparently, he intends to go to Jerusalem to bring to indigent Christians ("saints") of that mother community the fruits of the collection organized by Christians converted from paganism. This will be not only a gesture of mutual aid but a test of unity among Christians of both Gentile and Jewish origin (see 1 Cor 16:14; 2 Cor 8—9; Gal 2:10). A genuine fraternal communion requires a new practice of exchanging goods with one another.

In the wake of the Galatian crisis, the Apostle is justified in thinking that he risks being badly received in Judea. The prayer of the Romans will be a comfort to him. The Book of Acts tells the story of his arrest in Jerusalem (ch. 21) and his journey to Rome (chs. 27—28).

15:26 *Achaia:* the Roman province of southern Greece.

16:1-24 Relations between the Churches became closer thanks to the fraternal relations among their members. Many of the persons named here remain unknown to us. *Phoebe,* who exercises a ministry of assistance among poor and sick women in Cenchreae, the port of Corinth, is possibly the bearer of the Letter. *Prisca and Aquila:* since "Prisca" is a variant of "Priscilla," it is obvious that these are the same two people who are placed at Rome, Corinth, and Ephesus by the Book of Acts and Paul's Letters (see Acts 18:2, 18-19, 26; 1 Cor 16:19; 2 Tim 4:19). In the Greek, Roman, and Jewish names, we can assume differences of social condition. Thus, this list testifies to the internal diversity of communities assembled together in the Church of Christ and, at the same time, to the responsibilities held by members of each group, made up of lay people, men or women, celibate or married.

In the midst of these salutations, a severe condemnation is lodged against all those who sow division and scandal. Paul is probably thinking of Judaizing preachers (see Gal 5:7-12; Phil 3:18f) or teachers of religion preoccupied with their profit.

16:1 *Phoebe, who is a deaconess:* this verse seems to allow an office of a woman deacon although Scripture does not define the specific responsibilities of a woman deacon. See also 1 Tim 4:14.

16:7 *Junia:* this name is usually taken to be masculine; others see it as feminine. In fact, some manuscripts have "Julia" in place of "Junia."

16:8-10 *Ampliatus . . . Urbanus . . . Stachys . . . Apelles:* these are all common names of slaves found in the imperial household.

16:10 *Aristobulus:* some think this name refers to the grandson of Herod the Great and the brother of Herod Agrippa I.

16:11 *Narcissus:* sometimes identified with Tiberius Claudius Narcissus, a wealthy freedman of the Roman Emperor Tiberius.

16:12 *Tryphaena and Tryphosa:* may refer to twin sisters who were wont to bear names based on the same root. *Persis:* i.e., a Persian woman.

16:13 *Rufus:* possibly the Rufus mentioned in Mk 15:21 as the son of Simon the Cyrenian, who helped Jesus carry his cross.

16:21 *Jason:* possibly the person mentioned in Acts 17:5-9. *Sosipater:* some think this is the son of Pyrrhus from Beroea who is called Sopater in Acts 20:4.

16:23 *Gaius:* some think this is the Titus Justus in whose house Paul lodged while in Corinth (see Acts 18:7 and 1 Cor 1:14). *Erastus, the city treasurer:* this may be the same person referred to in Acts 19:22 and 2 Tim 4:20. He may also be the person mentioned in the following Latin inscription recently found on a block of stone at Corinth: "Erastus, commissioner of public works, bore no expense of this pavement."

16:24 This verse is found in some manuscripts (see v. 20).

16:25-27 This fine liturgical hymn expresses the Church's joy at living in a time when the mystery of salvation is being fulfilled. *Mystery:* Paul uses this word to set forth: (1) the Incarnation (see 1 Tim 3:16); (2) Christ's saving Death on the Cross (see 1 Cor 2:1, 7); (3) the restoration of all things in Christ (see Eph 1:9); (4) the change wrought by Christ's Resurrection (see 1 Cor 15:51); and (5) the inclusion of both Jew and Gentile in the Kingdom of God (see v. 25).

THE FIRST LETTER TO THE CORINTHIANS

1:1-9 From the outset Paul emphasizes his calling as an apostle, because if throughout the Letter he teaches, reproaches, and corrects, he does so in the name of the mission he has received from Christ. See note on Mk 6:30.

1:1 *Sosthenes:* perhaps the same person as in Acts 18:17.

1:2 *Church of God in Corinth:* see note on 2 Cor 1:1.

1:10—4:21 The divisions in the Church cannot be regarded simply as a phenomenon inevitable in any form of communal life. The divisions here bear on essentials; they show that the Gospel has not been understood and that people had an erroneous idea of the role of the apostles.

1:11 The name *Chloe* probably identifies a Christian woman of Corinth, some members of whose household have brought the news to Paul.

1:12 *Apollos:* one of the important figures in the beginnings of Christianity, and Paul speaks more than once of his sincerity (see Acts 18:24-29; 1 Cor 3:4-5, 22; 16:12). Some scholars think he may be the author of the Letter to the Hebrews. *Cephas:* the apostle Peter (see Jn 1:42), who may have paid a visit to Corinth.

1:17-25 The most beautiful construction of the human spirit cannot by itself bring salvation to the human race. This section does not oppose faith and philosophy to one another. It affirms above all that people are saved not by an intellectual theory but by God's intervention in Jesus Christ. Faith does not consist in an ideology.

1:19 The citation is from Isa 29:14, where the Lord denounces the "wise" for their policy of seeking an alliance with Egypt against King Sennacherib of Assyria. *The wise:* the 6th-century B.C. Athenian statesman Aristedes remarked that every street in Corinth had its own so-called wise man, who claimed to have a solution to all the problems of the world.

1:23 Jesus was a stumbling block for the Jews, because they were expecting a Messiah who would perform sensational wonders (see Mt 12:38; Jn 4:48); he was foolishness to Gentiles, because he did not act in accordance with human wisdom.

1:26 *Wise by human standards:* literally, "wise according to the flesh," that is, in the eyes of human beings.

1:29-31 "Boasting" refers to a person's sin in thinking that one is saved by oneself. The truth is that we live only from God and for God. Hence, the only "boasting" possible is "boasting in the Lord."

2:1 *Mystery of God:* God's plan of salvation, which involves Jesus and the cross (see 1 Cor 1:18-25; 2:2, 8-10). Some manuscripts have "testimony" in place of "mystery."

2:4 Paul is not downgrading study and preparation for preachers. He is simply stressing that in addition to such things they also need the Holy Spirit working in their hearts in order for their words to bear fruit.

2:6 *Rulers of this age:* not only the Jewish and Roman leaders under whom Jesus was crucified (see Acts 4:25-28) but also the cosmic powers that were in league with them (see Eph 1:20-23; 3:10).

2:8 Here *the Lord of glory* is Jesus Christ. In the Old Testament, it is a title of God (see Ex 24:16; Pss 24:7; 29:9); Paul is therefore asserting here the divinity of Jesus.

2:13 *Expressing spiritual things in spiritual words:* another possible translation is: "expressing spiritual realities to spiritual people."

2:14-15 *Unspiritual person . . . spiritual person:* an *unspiritual person* is one who follows mere natural human instincts (see Rom 8:9; Jude 19); a *spiritual person* is one who follows the Spirit of God. The former lives according to the "natural" order and the latter according to the "supernatural" order.

3:5—4:21 The apostles are not inventors of foreign mysteries and strange secrets. They are sent to build up the community of God, and are therefore subject to the Lord's judgment. This is one of the main texts in which Paul gives a glimpse of how he understood his personal mission.

3:13 *The Day:* the day of judgment—to the joy of the righteous and the gloom of the wicked. *Fire:* an element that destroys but also purifies.

3:15 Many theologians see in this verse an implicit reference to purgatory.

4:6 *Do not go beyond what has been written:* this proverbial saying was perhaps current in Corinth; there are those, however, who think that this was originally a marginal note and was later inserted into the text. In any case, the meaning seems to be: Do not exaggerate, do not make things complicated.

4:8 Although the Corinthians are only beginners in faith, they act as if they have already reached the level of mature Christians. Paul shows how ludicrous this attitude is in the face of the hardships that the very preachers of the faith encounter and endure day after day.

4:20 *Kingdom of God:* the reign of God in the lives of his people, consisting of a new birth (Jn 3:3-8) and new life in Christ (2 Cor 5:17), which is evinced by dedicated membership in the Church and service to others (Mt 25:40ff).

5:1—6:20 Paul here denounces some behaviors as real scandals. He has confidence, nonetheless, that the power of Christ will transform the lives of the baptized.

5:7-8 These verses have been described as the earliest Easter homily in Christian literature. Paul urges the Corinthians to keep the feast of Unleavened Bread (which followed Passover) by living the Christian life in total dedication to God (see Rom

12:1-2; 1 Pet 2:5). The true Passover is the Death of Christ, which should give rise to a life of newness, purity, and integrity in the same way that during the feast of Unleavened Bread the old bread gave way to unleavened bread.

5:9 This earlier Letter has been lost, although some scholars suggest that a fragment of the original Letter can be found in 2 Cor 6:14—7:1.

5:12 *Those who are outside the fold:* non-Christians. A Jewish expression. See Mk 6:11.

6:1-11 Paul condemns the litigiousness of some members of the Church.

6:1 *Unrighteous:* describes simply those who have not yet been justified by faith, that is, non-Christians, as contrasted with the *saints,* that is, Christians sanctified by God.

6:3 *Angels:* here the fallen angels (see Letter of Jude 6).

6:9 *Sodomites:* see note on 1 Tim 1:10.

6:12-20 In this city of Corinth, with its reputation for corruption, some Christians claim that they have the right to free love: "All things are lawful for me!" Paul's response gives us the first intuitions of a Christian reflection concerning what the body is for—a reflection that is totally new in this Greek environment in which the spirit is exalted while the body is denigrated almost to the point of being a slave. The Christian ethic is not locked in on disputes about what is permitted and what is prohibited. Indeed, in its eyes, all the realities of life have a meaning.

A person's behavior cannot be reduced to a physical way of acting (v. 13). It expresses and sheds light on human and spiritual values. And since in this case one must strive to deregulate established pagan customs, Paul stresses this point especially with regard to sexuality. A new conception of the body and sexual life imposes itself on those who live in union with Christ. It concerns their whole being, which has the indwelling of the Holy Spirit and is destined for the resurrection. Freedom does not authorize the corruption of life.

6:17 *One spirit with him:* the spiritual union of believers with Christ is a higher one than the marriage bond and the model of the union that should exist in the marriage relationship.

7:1-40 The Apostle here expounds some basic ideas about marriage; elsewhere he will develop some deeper aspects of it (Eph 5:4-33). His reply is formulated in response to concrete situations. When he speaks of celibacy, he manifests something of his personal conviction resulting from his experience of a life devoted entirely to Christ. This chapter remains one of the major Christian documents for understanding consecrated virginity, but also for keeping alive in the Church the discussion of marriage and celibacy as choices of ways of life.

7:1-11 The call to celibacy is an excellent gift, but conjugal life is also a gift of the Lord and continues to be the normal condition. In speaking of couples, Paul emphasizes their life in common, their mutual belonging, and the reciprocal gift of self. He reminds his readers of the clear Gospel message: the conjugal community is an indissoluble one (see Mt 5:32; 19:9; Mk 10:11-12; Lk 16:18). Spouses may follow calls to a more intense spiritual life, but let them first safeguard the essential realities of their union.

7:12-16 What is to be done if one of the spouses is a pagan? The pagan spouse has the right to be free, and if he or she wants to leave the household, the Christian spouse ("the believing partner": v. 15) regains his or her own freedom. This is the so-called Pauline Privilege.

7:25-35 Paul looks for words and ideas to render intelligible the entirely new experience of virginity as the gift of one's life to the Lord. Man and woman are made for one another, but when Christ came into the world, he threw a new light on the realities of the present world: these do not say the final word about the human condition, but represent only a stage (this includes even marriage; see Mt 22:30) on the way to the final fulfillment. We must judge everything in the light of the coming kingdom and give first place to love of the Lord.

Jesus had already stressed the grandeur of celibacy as a radical consecration to God and to the kingdom, but he did not impose it (Mt 19:10-12). Paul gives the same counsel to those Christians of Corinth who are not bound by the state of matrimony.

7:28 *Hardships in this life:* literally, "tribulations of the flesh," which refer not so much to the difficulties of spouses as to the trials proper to the last times. Those who possess material goods or family in this world will feel more deeply the trial of having to leave them (see Lk 17:26-37). Christians ought to be already living, at least spiritually, in that eschatological era.

7:36-40 It is not clear whether Paul is speaking of a father who has a daughter of marriage age, or of the guardian of an orphan, or simply of fiancés (a Jewish espousal was a real marriage, but not yet consummated). Paul is keeping to his general principle: Answer God's call in the life situation in which we find ourselves.

Another translation could read as follows:

" [36] If a man feels that he is behaving improperly toward his fiancée and he believes that something should be done because he is having difficulty restraining his passions, they should marry as he wishes. There is nothing sinful in that. [37] However, if he stands firm in his resolve and is under no obligation, and, being free to carry out his own will, he decides to respect her virginity, he will do well. [38] Therefore, the man who marries his fiancée does well, and the man who refrains from marriage does better still."

7:36 *A critical moment has come:* this probably refers to the fact that the woman or virgin may soon be beyond the usual age to marry and bear children or the fact that passions are becoming uncontrollable (see 1 Cor 7:9).

8:1—11:1 Paul is clearly convinced that as we do not allow any value to idols, neither do we allow it to meats sacrificed in honor of idols. Christians are therefore free to eat them. But this principle holds only for a firm and enlightened faith that rises above every danger of contamination by superstition.

8:6 *For whom we exist:* another possible translation is: "toward whom we return." *Through whom all things are:* this is the earliest mention in the New Testament of the role of Jesus in creation.

9:5 *The other apostles, the brethren of the Lord, and Cephas:* i.e., the missionaries or the heads of communities who were related to Jesus. It may be assumed that the married apostles, such as Peter, were accompanied by their wives.

9:6 *Barnabas:* see Acts 4:36-37; 11:25-26; chs. 13—14; 15:36-39.

9:14 *Those who preach the gospel should get their living from the gospel:* see Mt 10:10; Lk 10:7-8. This is one of the rare instances in which Paul expressly cites a saying of the Lord.

9:24—11:1 To take part in a sacred meal in the temples of idols is to run the risk of being seduced by idolatry. The reader should not play down this danger, which is connected with the danger of scandalizing the weak.

10:1-13 Paul calls to mind the story of the Hebrews in the wilderness, where the people were given all the gifts needed for life: the water and the manna, which symbolize Baptism and the Eucharist.

According to a tradition dear to the rabbis, the rock that Moses struck followed the Hebrews so that they might always have water; Paul uses this interpretation in order to make the point that since the time of the Exodus Christ has been leading the people (see Num 20:8).

If the events in the life of the desert community foreshadow the reality of the Church, the behavior of the Israelites at that time must also serve as a warning that is ever actual: in order to please God, it is not enough to belong to the Church and to receive the Sacraments; Christians must also be committed to an unwavering effort to be faithful, relying on the help of the Spirit.

In this section, Paul is teaching us how to read the Old Testament in a Christian perspective.

10:10 *The Destroyer:* the angel charged with inflicting divine punishments (see Ex 12:21-28).

10:14-22 Taking part in a form of worship means entering into communion with the divinity to which it is offered. Christians, who participate in the Body and Blood of Christ in the Eucharist, are well aware of this. By emphasizing the radical opposition between the Eucharist and pagan cults, Paul makes clear the place that the Eucharistic celebration had in the early Church. This participation gives rise to the Body of Christ that is the Church, but it also requires a serious commitment to live according to the Gospel.

10:14 *Avoid idolatry at all costs:* the Christians of Corinth must do their utmost to avoid idolatry especially since they are surrounded by temples of other gods. They daily come into contact with temples for the worship of Apollo, Asclepius, Demeter, Aphrodite, and other pagan gods and goddesses. The most common temptation was that of the worship of Aphrodite with its many sacred prostitutes (which at one time numbered 1000).

10:18 *The people of Israel:* literally, "Israel according to the flesh," that is, Jews by birth, as distinct from "the Israel of God," to which persons belong by faith (see Rom 2:28-29).

10:22 *Provoke the Lord to jealous anger:* in the Old Testament, this points to the incompatibility of adoring God and worshiping idols.

11:2—14:40 Gatherings of Christians are liturgical assemblies. The members listen to the Word of God, give thanks, break bread, the Lord is present and the Spirit enters their hearts. On more than one point, Christians readily imitated the mode of acting of the Jews, who came together in their synagogues on the Sabbath, but they were more distrustful of the religious customs of the pagans. In any case, through the celebration of the Eucharist and the inspiration of the Holy Spirit, the Christian Liturgy is profoundly original. Paul does not wish to impose laws upon it but insists that it be genuine worship.

11:2-16 In ancient times men went with heads uncovered, while women wore a veil as a sign of modesty and also of dependence on their husbands.

11:10 *Sign:* of the presence of the Lord, who demands holiness and propriety (see Deut 23:15).

11:17-34 From the very beginning, the Church has celebrated the Eucharist. She does so by renewing the actions and words of Jesus on the night of the Last Supper, and here we have the most ancient document written about it. The document evokes the celebration itself and expresses its most profound meaning. Nevertheless, Paul does not intend to give an explanation of the subject. He is simply intervening in the face of abuses. He stresses that the Eucharist is not to be celebrated in the same way as one organizes a sacred meal in a temple with one's friends. We are not going to partake passingly in some magical or symbolic food of immortality. Celebrating the Eucharist is a serious action that engages the whole community in the highest reality of its faith: the union with Christ in his Passion, the unity that he imparts to human beings, and the expectation of his coming and its accomplishment for all. Such an action entails exigencies for Liturgy and life.

11:20-22 Before the Eucharist, the Corinthians apparently held an ordinary meal, an early form of the *agape* (see 2 Pet 2:13; Jude 12). Paul condemns the abuses that occurred in it.

11:23-25 This is the earliest written New Testament account of the institution of the Eucharist. The words over the bread and the cup stress the Lord's self-giving, and the words "Do this in remembrance of me" command Christians to repeat his action.

11:25 *After the supper:* i.e., after the Passover supper. The Lord's Supper was first celebrated by Jesus in connection with the Passover meal (see Mt 26:18-30). *The cup:* a symbol of the New Covenant in the blood of Jesus (Lk 22:20; see Jer 31:31-34). The Old Covenant was the Mosaic Covenant (see Ex 24:3-8).

11:27-34 In this passage Paul presents a profound teaching: The reception of Christ's Body is a source of life and unity; it also has an effect on the relationships of human beings and on their salvation. But if the fraternal bond created by communion loosens, as at Corinth, the community becomes disunited in spirit and in body.

12:1—14:40 These pages have new relevance today. Such words as "charism" and "prophet" have once again become common in the Church. We are deeply interested in the relationships, undertakings, and inspirations that characterize the life and vitality of communities. God does indeed grant the grace of renewal for the sake of the authentic development of the Christian community. Nevertheless, we should not stop at the visible gifts, but should seek initiatives that help to unite the community and promote true love and the knowledge of the mystery of Christ. Christian experience is not a spectacle but a lived reality. This is a principle for discernment.

12:3 *Cursed:* to say this is to fail to recognize Jesus as the messenger of God (see Jn 8:48f; 9:24).

12:4-6 Note that these verses speak of the intervention of the three divine Persons. The charismatic movement cannot become a competition of visions nor a conflict of claims and a quest for prestige.

12:10 *Mighty deeds:* this phrase refers to actions that cannot be explained by natural means—hence, actions of God intended to show his power and purpose.

12:12-31a The Church, united and in harmony like a physical body, really forms the Body of Christ (1 Cor 10:17; Col 1:8-24; Eph 1:22-23; 5:23), brought into being by participation in his Eucharistic Body and given life by the life of the Spirit. This is one of Paul's major ideas regarding the mystery of the Church.

12:31b—13:13 This may be termed a passage for the ages. The word "love" summarizes for Paul all the newness that Jesus brings to the world. Wherever love exists, something of the eternal and the divine enters into the life and communication of human beings. In comparison to love, every other value is relative and transitory; love is the ultimate meaning.

We should leave aside all the cloying sentiments with which the words "love" and "charity" are often burdened and read these few strophes to rediscover this supreme reality that is so simple, so demanding, and so sublime. What a reversal this emphasis on genuine love is for the Corinthians! All the gifts that they like permit pretense, vanity, and ostentation even in the religious sphere; love is the direct opposite of all that.

Where love is lacking, all the charisms lose their power and meaning, even those that are the most needed and the most fruitful for the mission of the Church. The gifts are all provisional. When humankind attains its completion in the love of God, it will be genuinely and definitively fulfilled. In the fullness of this communion and in the complete vision of the Lord, faith and hope themselves will be left behind. But love alone will remain; it is eternal, for God is love (1 Jn 4:8). Even on earth, love is the reality and the power by which Christians must live.

13:1 *Love:* the Greek term for this word means selfless concern for the welfare of others regardless of whether they are lovable or not. It arises from a willingness to love in obedience to the command of God and a desire to follow Christ's love manifested on the cross (see Jn 13:34f; 1 Jn 3:16).

13:13 *The greatest of these is love:* this conclusion follows from the fact that God is love (1 Jn 4:8) and has communicated his love to us (1 Jn 4:10) and commands us to love one another (Jn 13:34f).

14:1-25 The Corinthians aimed especially at a spectacular gift that Paul calls the gift of tongues. The reference is to a type of ecstatic prayer: the inspired person speaks in the midst of the assembly, using incomprehensible words, in a kind of religious rapture; he or she sings the praises of God, either in foreign languages that an inspired interpreter can translate, or by repeating litanies of hardly articulated words, without any order, in a state of ecstasy.

In v. 14, Paul contrasts "spirit" and "mind": the spirit is the innermost part of the soul, where the Holy Spirit acts in mysterious ways; the mind is the soul insofar as it reflects and analyzes itself; it is the level, that is, of self-consciousness and the communication of thought.

When inspiration disregards the mind, the way is opened to enthusiasm and disorder, instead of fraternal exchanges and communion.

14:21 *In the Law:* i.e., the Old Testament; see Rom 3:10-19 where Paul cites a number of passages from the Old Testament and then calls them "the Law" in v. 19.

14:34-35 Paul is not against women speaking in church (see 1 Cor 11:5). He is against women speaking in a disorderly manner in church.

15:1-58 According to Greek thought, the soul is imprisoned in the body; it alone is destined for immortality, and death comes to set it free. As heirs of this mentality, the Corinthians are unable to understand why there should be a resurrection of the body. Does Christianity perhaps desire that the soul again become a prisoner? Paul corrects this notion, which is not in accord with the Christian faith.

The biblical tradition holds that the human being is one, created by God in body and soul. Death does not constitute the deliverance of the soul, but the unraveling of this unity. It is a violent state produced by sin. In atoning for sin, Christ has conquered death. It is the whole person that is saved and the whole person that is involved in the resurrection. But Paul takes account of the objection that the Greeks can bring up: the resurrection is not a simple return to the earthly condition; the risen body does not limit the aspirations of the spirit. It will be "spiritual," a new creation in the risen Christ.

15:1-11 Paul takes as his starting point a fact: the resurrection of Christ. This is the primordial certainty of the Christian faith. He recalls this teaching of the Church and confirms it by listing the witnesses who had seen the risen Christ. In this passage, we find the main elements of the Christian creed and, at the same time, the earliest written witness to the handing on of the original teaching of the Church and to the appearances of Jesus Christ.

15:3-5 Paul offers two lines of testimony for Christ's Passion and Resurrection: (1) the testimony of the Old Testament (e.g., Ps 16:8-11; Isa 53:5f, 11) and (2) the testimony of eyewitnesses (Acts 1:21f). He lists only six appearances of the risen Christ; the Gospels and Acts offer ten (see note on Mt 28:10).

15:6 *Have fallen asleep:* an image of death. The same expression is used in vv. 18, 20, and 51, and is the usual one in the New Testament. In it, Christians indirectly expressed their faith in the resurrection (in Greek the same verb means both "to awaken" and "to bring back to life"). From this phrase, we also derive our word "cemetery," i.e., literally, a place of sleepers.

15:7 *Appeared to James:* Paul inserts the risen Lord's appearance to James as a kind of transition to his own experience of seeing Christ. Like Paul, James, "the brother of the Lord" (Gal 1:19), had not been a disciple of Jesus (see Acts 1:12f). An account of such an appearance to James is found in the *Gospel of the Hebrews,* an apocryphal Jewish-Christian gospel.

15:12-19 The Resurrection of Jesus, to which the apostles are witnesses, is the basic proof that there is a resurrection of the dead; the Old Testament initially voiced a hope of this (Ps 16:10; Job 19:25; Ezek 37:10) and later taught it explicitly (2 Mac 7:9). The Resurrection of Jesus is thus the very foundation of our faith; Christ is the firstborn of the dead, who will rise in their turn.

15:20-28 Paul contrasts two states of the human race: on the one side, the fallen state of sin, symbolized by Adam; on the other, the state of life and salvation brought about by Christ (see Rom 5:17-21).

15:24 *Sovereignty and authority and power:* these words signify all the forces, angelic and human, that are opposed to the Kingdom of God (see 1 Cor 2:6; Col 2:15).

15:29-34 *Baptized for the dead* (v. 29) refers to a rite, unknown to us, a type of baptism by proxy. Paul uses the image of *wild beasts* (v. 32) to express the hostility he encountered at Ephesus. In v. 33 he is citing Menander, a Greek comic poet, although by this time the saying may already have become a popular proverb.

15:50-58 Using images traditional in the Bible, Paul describes in a few lines the great day of universal salvation, when humanity reaches its destiny.

15:52 The *trumpet* was part of apocalyptic choreography (see Mt 24:31; 1 Thes 4:16); it symbolized the solemn proclamation of the divine plan (see the seven trumpets of the Book of Revelation: 8:6-11, 19).

16:1-23 The collection for the Church of Jerusalem—the "saints"—had an important place in Paul's outlook, because it was a sign of communion between the Churches that originated in the Gentile world and the mother Church that had grown up at the heart of Judaism (see Acts 24:17; Rom 15:25-26; 2 Cor 8—9; Gal 2:10).

16:1 The *saints* in Jerusalem were obviously in dire need—possibly as a result of the famine recorded in Acts 11:28 (about A.D. 44 or 46) or the persecution to which they were subjected (Acts 8:1).

16:2 *On the first day of every week:* i.e., Sunday, the Lord's Day (see Acts 20:7; Rev 1:10). *Each of you should set aside:* each Sunday Christians were to bring what they had set aside for the Lord's work. It was then probably collected at the worship service. Justin Martyr indicates in his *Apology* (1:67-68) that during his day (c. A.D. 150) offerings were brought to the altar on Sundays.

16:22 *Accursed.* = "anathema," separated from the community. *O Lord, come!:* in Aramaic *Marana tha:* a liturgical acclamation in the Aramaic-speaking communities of Palestine.

THE SECOND LETTER TO THE CORINTHIANS

1:1 *Apostle:* a person specially commissioned by Christ (see notes on Mk 6:30; 1 Cor 1:1-9; Heb 3:1). *Timothy:* a fellow worker of Paul (see Acts 18:5) and his companion on the second and third missionary journeys. *Brother:* a fellow believer, a brother in Christ (see Acts 9:17; Heb 2:11). *Church of God in Corinth:* the community of believers at Corinth, the local representative of the universal Church. "Church of God" is an expression used only by Paul and solely in Acts 20:28, 1 Cor 1:2, and here. It corresponds to the Old Testament expression "assembly (or community) of the LORD" (see Deut 23:2; see also Num 16:3; 20:4; 1 Chr 28:8). *Saints:* another term for God's people, those who have been set apart as holy to the Lord (see note on Rom 1:7). *Achaia:* Greece as distinct from Macedonia. Although the Letter was written specifically for the situation in Corinth, it was also intended for Christians elsewhere in Greece. Copies would doubtless be made and circulated to them.

1:3-11 The Gospel is the power of liberation not only in time of exaltation when the gifts of the Spirit carry the whole community along but also in the most difficult trials of an apostle's life. Paul has known sickness and the fear of an approaching death, he has suffered persecution, and he has experienced misunderstanding and rejection at the hands of his own communities. Discouraged and weighed down, he discovers the weakness of an apostle, whose evidence is inscribed forever in his life. However, another certitude—one even more profound—imposes itself upon him: the joy of being in the hand of the Lord and imitating Jesus himself!

The word "consolation" occurs in some form ten times in these lines, not as a facile formula but as a term that expresses inner freedom, strength renewed, the reversal of a situation, the experience of being blessed by God who triumphs over evil and death. In addition, the solidarity of Christians is deepened in trials and in joy, for they all belong to the one Body of Christ. Paul's safety serves as a source of comfort for his followers, and their prayer is a means of sustenance for him.

1:3 *Consolation:* i.e., comfort and encouragement.

1:8 *We experienced:* throughout the Letter, Paul uses the editorial plural (*we, us, our, ourselves*). These terms should be taken as referring to Paul alone—except where the context demonstrates otherwise. *Asia:* Asia Minor, with its capital at Ephesus, which was a Roman province.

1:12—7:16 Paul recalls recent events. There must be a full understanding between himself and the Corinthians; let them no longer have any doubt of his sincerity and intentions. The preaching of Christ is not a teaching that can be accommodated to each person's taste. The apostle exists only by the power of Jesus and for Jesus, who calls every human being to salvation. To take sides for or against the apostle is to take a position on the Gospel and on Jesus himself. At the same time, Paul describes the way he thinks of his own life: an apostle not only comes in the name of Jesus but is so bound to his Master and his message that he shares the lot and imitates the Death and Resurrection of Jesus.

1:12—2:13 Paul had promised to come to Corinth twice: once from Ephesus before going on to Macedonia in the north and then on his return from Macedonia when going on to Ephesus. However, because of a situation that had arisen, he had canceled one or both of these visits. He has been criticized for this and here gives his explanation.

1:15-22 Paul insists that his dialogue with the Corinthians is not one of "Yes" and "No" at the same time—just as Jesus, the Son of God, did not simultaneously say "Yes" and "No." Indeed, God fulfilled his promises by sending his Son among us, and Christ also did what his Father wanted. Thus, Christ is a "Yes," consenting to the Father's plan. Similarly, we say "Yes" to Christ, first at our Baptism when we receive the first outpouring of the Spirit and then at every Eucharist when we say "Amen" (which means, "Yes, it is true"). When we sin, on the other hand, we say "No" to Christ.

1:19 *Silvanus:* another fellow worker of Paul. The Hebrew name was Silas, but this was romanized to Silvanus (see Acts 18:5).

1:23—2:4 Paul explains why he has substituted a severe Letter for the announced visit. The details of the incidents escape us, but we know that Paul was attacked by an agitator who was opposed to the Apostle's coworkers. Paul estimated that an immediate visit would inflame the situation whereas a letter would foster reflection, an examination of conscience, and ultimately peace and harmony. The Letter of which he speaks has been lost; according to some, however, it is to be found in the last chapters of the present Letter.

2:12-13 What Paul is saying about Macedonia is interrupted by what follows, and is picked up again in 2 Cor 7:5.

2:14—6:10 The Corinthian incident seems to have been resolved and good relations to have been established. Difficult as the trial was, it served to clarify and deepen the meaning of the apostolic ministry for Paul, who now has a better grasp of the dimensions of his mission. What force this life attains under the direction of Christ! The power of God is manifested in a person who is weak, ill, and under attack!

3:1-6 Preachers are circulating, exhibiting and collecting their letters of credibility from one Church to another. But how futile are merely human recommendations and written documents! The apostolate is attested by one's life. The existence of the community of Corinth and the Spirit's action in it certify that Paul and his coworkers have been chosen by God. This is the new covenant announced by the Prophets that inserts itself into the lives of individuals and peoples (see Jer 31:31-33; Ezek 11:19; 36:26).

For the first time in Christian literature, the idea of a "New Covenant" and the term itself make their appearance, and a clear distinction is drawn between the two Testaments. Paul has understood that there has been a radical change: from the letter to the Spirit, from the written book to the live hearts of human beings.

3:3 *Tablets of stone:* a reference to the Law given on Sinai (see Ex 24:12).

3:7-11 Proceeding in the manner of the rabbis, Paul freely interprets an episode in the life of Moses (see Ezek 34:29-35) in order to assert the superiority of the New Testament. Set down by Moses, the Law denounces sin without giving the power to conquer sin; it thus condemns people without glorifying or saving them. It is not God's definitive gift.

Indeed, Paul dares to compare the ministry of the apostles to that of Moses, which was the most prestigious in the Old Testament. He dares to state that the apostolic ministry is greater than that of the founder of the Jewish people. And he invites everyone to enter fully into this New Covenant so as to surpass definitively the universe of the Old Testament. The Letter to the Romans will later offer a lengthy development of this singularly new vision in that age.

3:12-18 Paul continues to comment in rabbinical fashion on the veil of Moses. The veil is now over the faces of the Jews. He makes clear that they refuse to accept the provisional character of the Old Covenant—they do not truly understand either Moses or the Old Testament, for Christ is the key to both. It is he who established a new and definitive Covenant, which leads to life and is the power of liberation, the source of freedom. The light of the risen Christ is reflected in the life of believers by their transformation in an ever more profound manner.

3:14 *Old covenant,* i.e., "Old Testament": this is the first time that this expression, referring to a collection of Scriptures, appears in a Christian text.

3:17-18 *This Lord is the Spirit:* the "Lord" to whom the Christian turns (v. 16) is the life-giving Spirit of the living God (vv. 6, 8), who is also the Spirit of Christ. This Spirit is the inaugurator of the New Covenant and the ministry.

4:1-6 Paul has been defamed as one who does not impart the authentic teaching of Christ. He responds that, on the contrary, everything he preaches is nothing but authentically Christ's. For Paul, the Gospel is not a narrative of the past but the action of God today. The apostle, qualified for the ministry of this New Covenant, cannot falsify the Gospel in order to seek his own glory. His entire existence is illumined by the light and glory of Christ, the image of God, and the sole image that can take profound hold of a person's life. Illuminated by Christ, the apostle himself becomes a light to irradiate every conscience that refuses to be seduced by the god of this world, i.e., Satan, who personifies the traits of perversion capable of undermining a human existence.

4:7-15 In his life, Paul shows the "mystique" of the apostle. He knows that his existence must be identified with that of Christ, that he must enter into Christ's struggle and his agony. Thus, he reproduces in his person and his action the Paschal Mystery, the mystery of death and life, suffering and victory, until the day when he will share fully, with all the saved, in the life of the risen Lord.

5:3 *Naked:* without an earthly tent (body), which is the condition of those who have died.

5:16 *We once judged Christ from a human point of view:* literally: "we knew Christ according to the flesh." The literal translation does not mean that Paul met Jesus during the latter's mortal life; it means, rather, that before Paul was converted he had human prejudices regarding Jesus, but now no longer does so.

5:21 This is a splendid summary of the redemption. God made the penalty for sins to fall on Jesus (see Isa 53:6; Gal 3:13). Christ, the only one who is entirely righteous, took our sins upon himself at Calvary and endured the punishment reserved for us, i.e., death and separation from God. He made it possible for us to receive his righteousness and be recommended to God. Yet all this stems from the love of the Father, who prompted Christ by his plan and enabled him to bring it about by his grace.

6:2 This verse does not exclude from grace and salvation those people who lived before Christ's coming. For they received the promises that were later fulfilled in Christ (2 Cor 1:20) and saw and welcomed their fulfillment from a distance (see Jn 8:56; Heb 11:13).

6:7 *Weapons . . . with right hand and left:* with the right hand, offensive weapons (the sword); with the left, defensive weapons (the shield).

6:10 *We make many rich:* i.e., rich toward God, for true wealth does not consist in worldly possessions (see Lk 12:15, 21). Even if believers have none of the world's goods, they possess everything in him who is Lord of all (see 1 Cor 1:4f; 3:21-23; Eph 2:7; 3:8; Phil 4:19; Col 2:3).

6:11—7:16 After the gripping testimony concerning the apostolate and its mystery, the Letter returns to concrete situations of the community of Corinth. Moving appeals, pastoral concern, and profound attachment come to the fore in these lines.

6:14 *Do not associate with unbelievers:* Paul is here thinking of the Old Testament prohibition on intermingling (Deut 22:10ff). The false teachers among the Corinthians are servants of Satan; hence, believers should not associate with them, for such association will destroy the harmony and fellowship that unite them in Christ.

6:15 *Beliar:* (= nothingness, uselessness) is a Greek variant of the Hebrew "Belial," which designates idols and Satan, a title used for Satan in the writings of Qumran. This passage may have been taken from another Letter of Paul to the Corinthians. The passage interweaves several citations from the Old Testament (which are in order: Lev 26:11-12; Ezek 37:27; Isa 52:11; Jer 51:45; 2 Sam 7:14; Jer 31:9; Isa 43:6).

7:5ff Paul picks up, after an interruption, the account of events that he had been giving earlier (2 Cor 2:13). *Titus* (v. 6) is not mentioned in the Book of Acts, but he is mentioned in other Letters of Paul (Gal 2:1-3; 2 Tim 4:10), and is the addressee of another.

8:1—9:15 In the Churches that he establishes among the Gentiles, Paul inculcates a sense of generosity on behalf of the mother Church of Jerusalem, which finds herself in great material distress (see Acts 24:17; Rom 15:25-27; Gal 2:10). For him, this initiative is not something secondary but a sign of the authenticity of his mission. He wishes to attest in deeds, for Jews and Gentiles, that the love of Christ brings down the wall of separation so long standing between them (see Eph 2:13-17).

The Corinthians had already decided some time ago that they would take up a collection (see 1 Cor 16:1), but the project had been abandoned because of the disputes that raged among them. Paul relaunches the project.

8:7 *Your love for us:* some manuscripts read: "our love for you."

8:9 Paul now returns to the point, expressed earlier, about Jesus' experience. Instead of using life and death (2 Cor 5:15) or sin and righteousness (2 Cor 5:21), he uses poverty and wealth. This passage has been interpreted by many scholars as referring to Jesus' preexistence with God ("wealth") (see Jn 1:1) and to his Incarnation and Death ("poverty") (see Phil 2:6-8). Others take it to refer to phases of Jesus' earthly existence, i.e., his sense of intimacy with the Father (Jn 10:15, 30; 11:42) and his feeling of estrangement from him in his Death (Mk 15:34).

8:18 *The brother who is praised . . . gospel:* the reference is very likely to Luke.

8:22 *Our brother:* not identified.

9:15 *Indescribable gift:* i.e., his own Son (Jn 3:16). It is God who has first given himself to us in the person of his Son; thus, all genuine Christian giving is our response for such a gift (see 2 Cor 8:9; 1 Jn 4:9-11).

10:1—13:10 All at once, the tone of the Letter changes. The text becomes harsh and unyielding. It indicates that some missionaries have slipped into the Corinthian community, probably Jewish Christian in origin, who wish to take over this new Church. Their human and religious pretensions go beyond all measure. They strive to discredit Paul, and many Christians lend a complacent ear to their calumnies and caricatures. Paul rebukes both his attackers and those who failed to defend him, for the Christian life itself is at stake and the authenticity of the Gospel of Jesus is threatened. The Letter is no longer a paternal address to children but a strong indictment.

Some exegetes think that these chapters were part of a stern Letter mentioned earlier (2 Cor 2:3); if so, the text predates the rest of the present Letter.

10:1-18 In order to be accepted and applauded, the false apostles seek their human prestige. They have nothing more than that, for they usurp the work of others. In contrast, Paul and his coworkers are missionaries of the Gospel in the midst of Gentiles and it was they who founded the community of Corinth—that is their recommendation. The work of God has become a reality through their efforts.

10:2 *Human standards:* literally, "according to the flesh."

10:3-4 Paul is ready to wage war, but his weapons are not those prized by this world and forged by human pride and arrogance. They have "the power of God" (e.g., the Word of God and the Spirit) and can demolish arguments and every pretension put forth against "the knowledge of God" (see Rom 1:18-23). Among the latter are the reasonings by which the false apostles strive to shake the faith of the Corinthian Christians (see 1 Cor 2:13f).

10:7-8 Paul makes use of Jeremiah's description of the purpose of the prophetic power given him by God (see Jer 1:9-10; 12:16f; 24:6). The Apostle's intention is to build up, not to tear down.

10:17 *Let him boast in the Lord:* boasting is not wrong when it is done "in the Lord." Paul boasts of God's work accomplished through him in the community (2 Cor 10:13-16; see 2 Cor 1:12-14). This is his recommendation (2 Cor 3:1-3). See note on 1 Cor 1:29-31.

11:4 *Another Jesus:* the false apostles present Jesus cast in the mold of Judaistic teachings (see 2 Cor 11:22). *Different spirit:* e.g., a spirit of bondage, fear, and worldliness (see Rom 8:15; 1 Cor 2:12; Gal 2:4; 4:24; Col 2:20-23) instead of a Spirit of freedom, love, joy, praise, and power (see 2 Cor 3:17; Rom 14:17; Gal 2:4; 5:1, 22; Eph 3:20; Col 1:11; 2 Tim 1:7). *Different gospel:* i.e., a gospel that is really no gospel at all (see Gal 1:6-9).

11:7 *Humbling myself:* apparently Paul's opponents took issue with the fact that he failed to accept payment for his services. This went counter to the practice of first-century traveling philosophers and religious teachers, who exacted payment in proportion to the worth of their performance.

11:22 *Hebrews . . . Israelites . . . descendants of Abraham:* apparently, the false apostles are Jewish Christians who feel superior to Gentile Christians. They want to impose distinctly Jewish practices on Gentile converts. Paul is completely opposed to such a thing (see Rom 2:28f; 1 Cor 12:13; Gal 3:28f; Eph 2:11-18; Col 3:11) and emphasizes that he is everything they are—a Hebrew, an Israelite, and a descendant of Abraham.

11:23 *Ministers of Christ:* Paul states that though the false apostles can claim the title, he can claim it with far greater force because of his unremitting labor and ceaseless endurance of trials. *Far more brushes with death:* a biographical fragment about a dramatic series of sufferings of which Acts says nothing, perhaps because they had been endured in the first decade of Paul's apostolate.

11:24 *Forty lashes minus one:* see Deut 25:3; thirty-nine, in order not to risk going beyond the forty allowed by the Law.

11:32 *King Aretas:* Aretas IV, father-in-law of Herod Antipas, who ruled over the Nabatean Arabs from c. 9 B.C. to A.D. 40.

12:1-6 Paul here provides an exceptional testimony. His spirit was elevated to the highest contemplation of the divine mysteries, which no human words can describe. He was caught up to the third heaven, that is, beyond the created world, to the point of losing all awareness of his own bodily life, so greatly was his spirit overwhelmed by this experience. This event occurred around the year 42, five years after his conversion; at that time, Paul was in Syria or Cilicia, some years still before the beginning of his great missions.

12:7-10 Paul refers to a mysterious trial, possibly an illness, of which Christ did not will to cure him and which increased the difficulties of his apostolic life.

13:11-13 The final greeting includes the most carefully worded and the richest of the formulas that name the Trinity (v. 13); it has now deservedly found a place in the Liturgy as a greeting to the faithful.

13:12 *Kiss:* a symbol of mutual affection and trust still used in the Near East. It corresponds to the handshake in the West.

THE LETTER TO THE GALATIANS

1:1—2:14 Without preliminary, Paul gets right to the point. He distinguishes two problems that his detractors, in order to inflame the conflict, cleverly intermingle: a question of persons and a question of ideas. First of all, Paul furnishes proofs of the authenticity of his apostolate. He specifies that his call comes directly from Christ and the Father. He received his Gospel by an immediate revelation from Christ, began at once to proclaim it without asking for the authorization of any human person, and on coming to Jerusalem interacted on an equal plane with the apostles, who approved his evangelization of the Gentiles. Finally, in the incident at Antioch, he showed his independence of Peter.

This first part of the Letter is one of our best sources of information about the history of the newborn Church and the life of Paul.

1:1-10 Without taking the time for another introduction, Paul tells us how he sees his apostolate in Christ's work of salvation. One must read these lines in order to understand what constitutes a mission of the Church. This Letter will be the "Gospel of the Cross."

In his address, Paul sets forth his name, his mission as apostle, and the name of those to whom he is writing as well as the central teaching of the Christian faith—the Resurrection of Jesus (see Acts 17:18; Rom 1:4; 1 Cor 15:20; 1 Pet 1:3).

1:1 *Apostle:* see note on 1 Cor 1:1-9.

1:2 *Brethren:* i.e., fellow Christians (see Gal 3:15; 4:12; 5:11; 6:18). *Galatia:* probably the Roman province of Galatia and an extended area southward, through which Paul traveled on his first missionary journey (Acts 13:14—14:23).

1:4 *The present evil age:* that is, the age in which sin reigns and Jesus Christ has not been accepted.

1:5 For similar doxologies, see Rom 9:5; 11:36; 16:27; Eph 3:21; 1 Tim 1:17.

1:6-24 Paul stresses that there is only one Gospel, one revelation, and one apostolate—all of which he shares with the original apostles. He discussed this apostolate and what it means first at Jerusalem with Peter (Cephas) and James and then at Antioch with Peter.

1:9 *Accursed:* "anathema," a term signifying condemnation.

1:11-17 For Paul, everything begins with the event that took place on the road to Damascus. He does not describe it here but expresses its meaning. It was for him the revelation of the risen Lord in all his glory as well as the investiture that established Paul as the prophet of the last times, charged by divine authority to proclaim the mystery of salvation and to introduce the Gentiles into the new world where the Spirit is at work (see Is 49:1; Jer 1:5). This mission is clear; Paul has no need of consulting with "flesh and blood," i.e., to embrace other human considerations or instructions. His destiny is laid out by the Lord himself.

1:13 *Judaism:* i.e., the Jewish faith and way of life that developed during the intertestamental period. The word comes from "Judah," the name of the southern kingdom that existed from the tenth to the sixth century B.C. and ended with the Babylonian Exile.

1:16 *Flesh and blood:* a phrase that in the New Testament always connotes human weakness or ignorance (see Mt 16:17; 1 Cor 15:50; Eph 6:12). Paul's teaching came not from any human person but directly from God.

1:18-24 Paul visited Jerusalem to become acquainted with the head of the apostles (see Acts 9:23-31), whom he calls "Cephas" (Aramaic for "Rock"), the name given to Peter by Jesus himself (see Mt 16:18). He then went to Syria and Cilicia (including his hometown Tarsus) and probably did some evangelizing there. He was known to Christians in Judea only by reputation.

1:19 *James, the brother of the Lord:* i.e., the cousin of Jesus, who was head of the Church of Jerusalem after the scattering of the apostles; see Acts 12:17; 15:13; 21:18.

1:21 For Paul's time in Syria (Antioch) and Cilicia (Tarsus) see Acts 9:30; 11:25-26.

2:1-10 Despite slight differences of detail, the passage speaks of the same assembly in Jerusalem that Acts 15 narrates: the same apostles, the same opponents, the same discussions, the same results in essentials. Paul was with Barnabas, who had an important place in the early stages of his mission (Acts 9:27; 11:25; 13:2; 15:2). When Paul wrote this Letter, about seven years after the events, he was completing the collection for the poor Christians of Jerusalem; this collection was for him a sign of unity (see 1 Cor 16:1; 2 Cor 8—9).

2:11-14 The Council of Jerusalem had acknowledged the freedom of Gentile Christians from the Jewish Law, but the question of table fellowship between Jewish Christians and Gentile believers was not yet settled. When Peter came to Antioch, he at first ate with non-Jews, since faith in Christ brings all people together. But when Jewish Christians arrived from Jerusalem, he gave up doing so. Paul rebuked Peter's inconsistency in an important religious matter. Peter's behavior was clearly wrong, and even grievously wrong if the table fellowship in question involved the meal at the Lord's Supper (see 1 Cor 11:17-25). The reason why Jews would not eat with Gentiles was that they were considered to be unclean. If Peter was refusing to eat with Gentile-Christians, he was implicitly saying that they were still in sin, which would mean that their Baptism had no effect, which meant that their cross did not redeem them.

2:12 *Some people came from James:* i.e., Jewish Christians who still believed in the Law and in circumcision (Acts 15:1, 5; 21:20f) and either came from James or claimed to be from him. *Circumcised:* i.e., Jewish Christians.

2:13 *Jews:* i.e., Jewish Christians.

2:15—6:10 Paul has explained his view of the apostolate; almost by degrees he now passes on to the defense of freedom for the new converts. He reverses the accusation brought against him. Indeed, one can falsify the Gospel by making the practices of the Jewish Law a prerequisite for becoming Christian. Faith in Christ, and it alone, saves believers and sets them free. Paul sketches his thinking about Baptism and about the indissoluble bond that must exist between faith and the Sacrament.

2:15—4:31 Law or faith: the famous antithesis. Two religious outlooks are opposed: to accept the one is to reject the other. Christianity's purpose is not to produce a better Law but to offer faith. On one side, there is an objective, external norm of good and evil, and even a slavery; on the other side, there is a principle of internal action, a spiritual dynamism, a call, even more the very life of God in the heart of human beings, a freedom.

Christianity cannot shut itself up in a code, no matter how noble; it is a Person, and Christians are those in whom Christ lives (Gal 2:20) and the Spirit acts (Gal 4:6). If there is a moral for Christians, a "law of Christ" (Gal 6:2), it can only be the living and free expression of the love that God inspires in the human heart: "You shall love!"

2:15-21 The baptized must not look elsewhere: Christ has become their very self, and faith lays hold of and permeates their entire life. This statement of Paul is at the same time a self-revelation of a highly mystical nature.

2:15 *Gentile sinners:* a usual formula for describing pagans as opposed to the chosen people. In this passage it has no pejorative meaning; Paul will in fact say that Jews and Gentiles alike are sinners and in need of redemption (see Rom 3:23f)

2:19 *I died to the Law:* the formula is obscure because it is overly concise. Christians have died to the Law because it left them frustrated since it helped them recognize their brokenness but did not liberate them from that brokenness. Only the love of Jesus can do that.

3:6-22 God has a blessing for humankind; it is reserved to faith. The promise made to Abraham was a personal, free, and direct commitment of God, and such it remained and still remains for all human beings; it is this promise that Christ fulfills.

3:8 *Scripture foresaw:* Paul personifies Scripture, thus stressing its divine origin (see 1 Tim 5:18).

3:19 *Because of transgressions:* i.e., in order that transgressions might be brought to light. Where there is no Law, there is no transgression (see Rom 5:13; 7:7).

3:23—4:7 In a few words, Paul provides great affirmations about faith and Baptism. He gives praise to the Person and work of Christ and to the action of the

Holy Spirit. He sets forth the new meaning of the condition of human beings, their divine filiation, and their unity. The mystery of Christianity is found in these few lines.

4:8-11 The baptized have suddenly become concerned with the calendar of Jewish feasts or of pagan cults; do they, then, believe themselves to be slaves of the forces that they think rule the world and do they therefore desire to conciliate those forces by rites? God is not to be confused with any force, known or unknown, of this world.

4:13 *Illness:* a sickness, of what kind we do not know, that afflicted Paul during his second missionary journey (see Acts 16:6).

4:21-31 A famous allegory, but one that is obscure and subtle for the modern reader. Paul wants to show by means of the Old Testament itself that we must go beyond the Law. In this perspective, he gives a free interpretation of an incident in the life of Abraham (see Gen 16:15; 21:2-14). The text explains the meaning of the enmity between two women, two descendants, two cities, two covenants.

5:1—6:10 After an involved argumentation, Paul turns to a more direct style, using shorter sentences, and he becomes more pressing. He calls upon the Galatians to measure the gravity of their about-face. Any compromise is out of the question; they must choose between the Law and Christ.

5:11 *Advocating circumcision:* probably an accusation by Paul's opponents that he also had advocated circumcision since he had allowed Timothy (whose mother was Jewish) to be circumcised (Acts 16:1-3). *Cross . . . stumbling block:* see 1 Cor 1:13.

5:14 *Entire Law can be summed up:* the whole spirit and intention of "the Law and the Prophets" is expressed by doing to others what you would want them to do to you (see Mt 7:12).

5:19-21 For other lists of vices, see 1 Cor 6:9f; Eph 5:5; Rev 22:15.

5:22-23 For other lists of virtues, see 2 Cor 6:6; Eph 4:2; 5:9; Col 3:12-15. Paul stresses that justification by faith does not mean advocating libertinism. He stresses that the Holy Spirit brings forth in believers Christian virtues and he lists nine of them. These have come to be known as "the fruits of the Holy Spirit."

The text of the Vulgate originally listed three other fruits, making a total of twelve. This formed the basis for the twelve fruits of the Holy Spirit listed in older catechisms, e.g., the *Baltimore Catechism:* charity, joy, peace, patience, benignity, goodness, long-suffering, mildness, faith, modesty, continence, and chastity. In truth, the three fruits not named in the original Greek are contained in one or other of the nine named: "long-suffering" in *patience,* and "modesty" and "continence" in *self-control.*

6:1-10 To the spiritual urge that leads the believer to live in solidarity with others and in service to them, Paul gives the name *law of Christ* (6:2), *law of faith* (Rom 3:27), and *law of the Spirit of life* (Rom 8:2).

6:11-18 Paul himself underlines the importance of the Letter (v. 11) and for one last time situates the problem of the Galatians before the mystery of the cross. There is an old world, that of circumcisions and human successes, and a new world, in which God calls the new Israel, i.e., all Christians, true children of Abraham. Christians belong to this world. For them, the cross is something to be shared. They agree to suffer for Christ and with him. It involves more suffering than being circumcised, but they have become "new" people (2 Cor 5:17), delivered from the world, i.e., sin. There is no other way of salvation except the cross of Christ, nor any other assurance before God. Paul knows this from experience, for he bears in his body the traces of the blows received in the exercise of his missionary work (2 Cor 6:5; 11:23-27).

6:16 *The Israel of God:* i.e., the Church (see Rom 9:6f) as opposed to Israel according to the flesh (see 1 Cor 10:18).

THE LETTER TO THE EPHESIANS

1:1-2 For the form used at the beginning of each of Paul's Letters, see note on Rom 1:1.

1:1 *In Ephesus:* omitted in many manuscripts.

1:3—3:21 The style here becomes solemn and liturgical in the manner of the great Jewish blessings, for the Church is celebrating the plan of God. The stages of the divine plan are set forth in a great movement. To God the Father belongs all the initiative to make human beings his children. Everything is realized "in Christ": indeed, the whole movement of the universe is oriented toward Christ as an edifice is built on its cornerstone and held up by it. Christ is at the same time the heart and summit, the movement and purpose of history.

He gathers together the whole of humankind, reuniting in the Church both Gentiles (v. 13) and Jews (vv. 11-12), the two groups whose irreconcilable antagonism is the sign of the broken unity of the human family. And all the forces of the universe—notably the "heavenly forces": i.e., angels or demons, secret powers of fatality or fecundity to whom religions customarily give names—are carried along in this élan of rebirth and accomplishment. The universe is led to peace under the authority of Christ. There is thus a grand meaning to the world and to history!

Henceforth, the gift of the Spirit enables Christians to live by it. Indeed, there is a fulfillment of human beings, an "inheritance," as the Bible says when it wishes to sum up in a word the blessings promised to believers. The Spirit, who is presently at work in the Church, is the pledge of this inheritance. Since the Resurrection of Jesus, this redeemed universe, i.e., a universe delivered from sin and the Law and placed under God's plan, is being built up by the life of the Church, by the dynamism of the Gospel.

However, no one can say that any person is predestined either for salvation or for condemnation. When Paul speaks of choosing and placing apart in advance (vv. 5, 11), he simply wishes to indicate that salvation is a grace for all the People of God, that it is the fulfillment of God's plan.

1:3-14 These verses form a single sentence in the Greek. In it Paul sets forth the blessings that we have from the Father, then those from the Son, and finally those from the Holy Spirit.

1:7 *Redemption:* Paul uses the Greco-Roman practice of redeeming slaves by the payment of ransom to show what Christian redemption means. Christ's death ("his blood") constitutes the ransom necessary to free sinners from the bondage of sin and the curse of the Law (see Gal 3:13).

1:10 *Bring . . . together:* i.e., "recapitulate." The Greek verb contains two ideas: to gather together or unite and to place under a rule or head.

1:14 *Down payment:* for "if the Spirit of him who raised Jesus from the dead dwells in you, then the one who raised Christ from the dead will also give life to your mortal bodies through his Spirit that dwells in you" (Rom 8:11).

1:15—2:22 Our spirit is gripped with admiration before the diverse aspects of the mystery of Christ: Resurrection, Ascension, universal Kingship, mysterious and activating presence in the Church. The power of God is present in this mystery and sweeps away every other force. And with Christ rises the Church, the community of those called.

Paul clearly distinguishes the glorified Christ reigning in heaven and his mystical body developing on earth. We cannot confuse the Church and the Lord. But they are intimately connected. The community of those called is realized and grows under the impulsion of the life that Christ gives it. This community is the "fullness" of God, for in it everything must be reunited to be filled with God's presence and love. The Church is the mystery of grace and charisms, of unity and growth (see Rom 12:4f; 1 Cor 12:12; Col 1:18).

The Apostle then goes on to describe the sinful state of humankind, in the grip of the power of evil (Eph 2:1-10), and the new state of humankind in which Gentiles and Jews now form a single new person, created in Christ and reconciled to one another and to God (Eph 2:11-22).

1:18 *Inheritance:* a Biblical word signifying what God promised to the chosen people. This was initially identified with the land and the blessings connected with it. But as revelation progressed, the true meaning of the "inheritance" was increasingly understood, until its definitive content was revealed in the New Testament: the inheritance is the state of the risen Jesus himself, communicated to those who believe in him.

2:1-7 In Greek, these verses comprise a single sentence.

2:2 *This worldly era:* i.e., synonymous with "rulers of this world." It may also refer to the first of the two ages of the world—the present evil age and the age to come (see 1 Cor 3:19; 5:10; 7:31; Gal 1:4; Tit 2:12).

2:8-9 We are saved by God's gift, not by the works of the Law (see note on Rom 3:20-21).

2:11-22 On the esplanade of the Jewish temple a wall separated Gentiles from Jews, symbolizing the deep division within humanity. Gentiles seemed definitively excluded from any call of God. The death of Jesus radically alters the situation: Jews and Gentiles alike have access to God; God's plan embraces the entire human race.

2:12 *The covenants:* i.e., those made with Abraham, with Moses, and with David (see note on Rom 9:4).

2:15 *A single new person:* i.e., a new humanity made up of Jews and Gentiles in the Christian community.

3:1-21 No one could have foreseen the call and reconciliation of the Gentiles. It is now a fact in the fraternal life of communities and in the spread of the

Gospel, announcing the joy of salvation to all peoples. It shows that the mystery of God is being revealed, for in Christ all human beings can now approach God. Since his conversion on the road to Damascus, Paul has had no other desire but to proclaim and manifest this mystery.

The Apostle finally completes the prayer that he started several times previously. He asks that God himself may enable believers to comprehend the inexpressible riches of the mystery. This is true not only for the initiated but also for all the "saints," i.e., all those who have been baptized and called.

3:1 The sentence breaks off and is continued in v. 14.

3:15 *Every family:* in this case, the family of the human race.

4:1—5:20 Christians must conduct themselves in a manner that befits their calling. First of all, they must have unity in the one body of the Church. Unity requires humility as a preliminary condition and meekness and loving patience in bearing with one another. The chief gifts that Paul has in mind are those that Christ communicates to us after the Ascension.

The Spirit of Christ allots to each Christian the measure of Christ needed to fulfill the function of each. This entails a change from one's old self to a new self in Christ. In this connection, six vices are specified to be avoided: lying, anger, stealing, bad language, uncurbed temper, and lust. Although Paul singles out lying to be described as unbecoming for fellow-members of the body of Christ, the same could be said of all vices.

4:1-16 The plan of God, which Paul has just revealed, is a vision of unity. To explain this, Paul follows rabbinical practice in taking a passage from Ps 18 and commenting on the two words that strike him: "ascended" and "gave." In his interpretation, the text announces the Ascension of Christ, who had first descended in the Incarnation on earth and even down to the subterranean regions, the place of the shadowy survival of the dead (see 1 Pet 3:9); the text then proclaims the sovereignty of Christ over all powers; finally, it speaks of the outpouring of the Spirit on Pentecost.

4:11 Other lists of ministers in the Church are found in Rom 12:6-8 and 1 Cor 12:28. *Apostles:* mentioned here because of their role in establishing the Church (see Eph 2:20). In a broader sense, the term "apostle" is also applied to Paul (see Eph 1:1). *Prophets:* those who brought a message from God appropriate to their people's situation. *Evangelists:* missionary preachers (see Acts 2:8 and 2 Tim 4:5), not the writers of the Gospels. *Pastors and teachers:* those who have pastoral care of the people and feed them with the food of the Scriptures.

5:14 *It is said:* the text cited was probably taken from an early Christian liturgical hymn (see also Isa 26:19; 60:1).

5:21—6:9 Christianity promotes, in community and in family, a new kind of relationship that is marked by humility and mutual submission. Here is a practical essay on the subject. The Old Testament had a lofty idea of marriage and liked to use the image of spouses to suggest God's faithful love for his people (Ps 45; Song 1:3; Isa 54:4, 8; 62:4-5; Ezek 16; Hos 1:3).

In the same tradition, Christians compare the relationship of Christ and the Church with a marriage (Mt 9:15; 22:2-4; 25:1-13; Jn 3:29; 2 Cor 11:2; Rev 19:7; 21:2-9). Here Paul goes even further: marriage as such is related to the mystery of Christ and the Church; the reciprocal love of Christ and the Church becomes the foundation and model for the life of spouses, who ought to be a sign and manifestation of that reciprocal love. There is a profound connection between the oneness of marriage and the oneness of Christ with the Church; the former reveals the ultimate intention of the creator when he created the human couple: an intention that the first generation of Christians saw in the text of Gen 2:24 (see Mt 19:5; Mk 10:8; 1 Cor 6:16-17). Chapter 5 of the Letter to the Ephesians, following the same theological line of thought, gives us one of the finest passages on the mystery of the Church and the spirituality of marriage. Paul's ideas on marriage may be completed by a reading of 1 Cor 7:1-14 and Col 3:18-19.

5:26 *Cleansing her with water and the word:* a reference to Baptism (pouring of water and sacramental formula). Perhaps Paul had in mind the Oriental practice in the purification of a wife.

6:1-9 Christian life also gives a new meaning to relations between children and parents. In an age less attentive than ours to the lot of little children, Paul was already emphasizing the responsibility of parents, without denying the duties of the young. The atmosphere he suggests is one of dialogue.

As for slavery, Paul does not pass judgment on the social structure of his age (see 1 Cor 7:21-22; Col 3:22-25; 1 Tim 6:1-2; Tit 2:9-10; Philem), but he does foretell new relations between master and slave, since all are equal before God, whatever the differences in their roles and social obligations.

6:10-20 Christ's triumph over evil and the devil must be appropriated by individual Christians in the human sphere through a kind of spiritual warfare against the malevolent spirits in the heavens. For this, Christians need to be clothed with the armor of God (see Isa 11:5; 59:17; see also Wis 5:17-20)—a spiritual armor. They must strive to counter the forces of evil by relying on the Gospel and prayer.

6:21-24 Paul issues a personal message and a final blessing. He sends Tychicus, his coworker, to carry the Letter personally to the addressees and to be his surrogate. He then offers final greetings. The fact that he does not give any personal references such as can be found in his Letters seems to indicate that the Letter was a circular one, not sent to the Ephesians alone.

THE LETTER TO THE PHILIPPIANS

1:1-2 While writing to all of the baptized—"the saints"—the author thinks in particular of the responsibility of the "bishops" (literally, "overseers"), that is, of those who, under the higher authority of the apostles and with the help of deacons (literally, "assistants"), lead and encourage the community (see 1 Tim 3:1; 5:17; Tit 1:5-9).

1:3-11 This prayer, filled with confidence and thanksgiving, gives us a glimpse of the deep attachment held by Paul, the prisoner, for the living community of Philippi that shares his concerns and his initiatives. He regards the action and life of Christians as a project that must be ceaselessly developed until the encounter with Christ at his Second Coming. Hence, he prays that believers might have the spiritual sense that will enable them to take hold of the essential, i.e., the very will of the Lord, in any situation: faith and love will help discern what is the best thing for them to do.

1:6 *The day of Christ Jesus:* the Second Coming of the Lord in all his glory, when the faithful will be with him and will share in eternal glory (see 1 Cor 1:8; Phil 1:10; 2:16; 3:20f; 1 Thes 4:17; 5:10; 2 Thes 1:10).

1:12-26 Little concerned for his own fate, the prisoner is interested only in the progress of the Good News of Christ. Certain missionaries, jealous of his success among the Gentiles, profit from his captivity to gain influence at his expense (see 1 Cor 1). Far from taking offense, Paul is able to rejoice in this: for it means that Christ is better known and loved.

Never before has he let his readers discern the profound bond that unites him to Jesus, a bond inaugurated by Baptism and sealed by the Eucharist but a bond that is lived in the whole initiative of his existence. He has already attained his spiritual maturity, and all his desire is fixed on Christ. As in the Second Letter to the Corinthians (5:6-8), he lets us glimpse his eager longing for an immediate meeting with the Savior. There is a part of him that can no longer wait for the day of the resurrection. This striking text constitutes one of the highest points of Christian mysticism.

1:13 *Praetorium:* this may refer to the praetorian guard in the city of Paul's imprisonment or to the governor's residence in a Roman province (see Mk 15:16; Acts 23:35).

1:21 Paul has reached the highest level of spiritual growth.

1:27-30 At Philippi itself, Paul quickly encountered persecution (see Acts 16:19-40; 1 Thes 2:2). His mission was plagued by unceasing threats and perils (see 2 Cor 11:24—12:10). The life and activity of Christians partakes of the Lord's Passion (see Mt 5:12; Acts 5:41).

1:30 This verse refers to the Apostle's earlier imprisonment in Philippi (Acts 16:29-34; 1 Thes 2:2) and to his present situation in chains.

2:1-5 For those who live by faith, united to Christ and the Holy Spirit, communion is the most precious of goods. It demands a complete turnaround extending to true humility. This means a generous abnegation that makes one prefer the interests of others rather than one's own. Paul presses ahead on this subject and suddenly, gripped by the shining example of Christ, he then chants the hymn of the incredible abasements of God.

2:6-11 The full breadth of the mystery of Christ is expressed in this hymn, which was either written by Paul himself or perhaps taken from the Liturgy of another community. The mystery is celebrated in two of its major aspects: descent and return, which form a curve whose two ends meet.

During his stay on earth, Jesus was deprived of the glory that belonged to him, so that he might receive it again from the Father as a reward for his supreme sacrifice. He descended into the ultimate depths of abasement; then the movement was reversed: the Father glorified him, made the universe subject to him, and gave him the supreme prerogative, the regal and Divine title of "Lord."

In the background here, Paul was thinking of the pride shown by created beings who want to be equal to God (the desire of Adam); he contrasts with this the self-giving and self-denial of Christ. But the hymn reminds us even more clearly of the songs of the Servant of God (especially Isa 53), which echoed strongly in the preaching of Jesus and in the teaching and Liturgy of the very early Church.

It is the whole mystery of the incarnate Son of God that Paul here chants with such clarity and depth: his preexistence, his abasement, and his exaltation. And the Apostle does so in order to exhort some Christians to live the demands of their Baptism!

2:7 *He emptied himself:* this means, not that Jesus ceased to be equal to God, but rather that in his humanity he stripped himself of the Divine glory, manifesting this only at the Transfiguration (Mt 17:1-8), and subsequently received it again from the Father (v. 8).

2:11 *Jesus Christ is Lord:* a common acclamation used by the early Christians (see Rom 10:9; 1 Cor 12:3).

2:12-18 Christians are touched by the Lord to the very depths of their being. Their conduct, their plans, and their testimony are the authentic expression of this in their life. Using the religious language of the time, Paul regards his role as apostle and the surrender of his life as an offering and sacrifice, a true worship of God (see Rom 1:9; 15:16).

2:12 *Fear and trembling:* an expression common in the Old Testament to indicate awe and devotion in God's service (see Ex 15:16; Jud 2:28; Ps 2:11; Isa 19:16).

2:19—3:1a Paul announces to the Philippians that he is sending them his most trusted coworker—Timothy, whom they already know (see Acts 16:1-15). He also hopes to visit them himself upon being released. And he will send Epaphroditus back to them when he is well. The last line (v. 1a) seems to be the beginning of a conclusion to the Letter.

3:1b-3 In a Letter that seemed to be coming to an end, a new subject is introduced. Paul is opposing the Jews or Jewish Christians who regard the practice of certain rites as indispensable, notably circumcision, even for those who believe in Christ. Christianity is total union with Christ in the greatest spiritual freedom. It cannot consist—like Judaism—in meticulous practices that lead to formalism. There is no salvation except in Jesus Christ, as the Letters to the Romans and to the Galatians demonstrate at length. Anything else is a human practice that pertains to the order of the flesh.

If the word "circumcision" must be used, it can refer only to the circumcision of the heart; if there is need to speak of worship, it can only be a spiritual worship. Christ has now become the sole focus of Paul's interest; his entire life will be dedicated to knowing Christ, the Lord and Savior of the world, and making him known to others.

3:2 *Dogs:* this is the name given to Gentiles by Jews (see Mt 15:26); here it is applied ironically to the Judaizers (see Gal 5:12). *Those who mutilate the flesh:* i.e., the Judaizers who insist that the Gentile Christians must agree to submit to circumcision (see Gal 5:12).

3:3 *We are the circumcision:* Christians are the true People of God and offspring of Abraham (see Gal 3:7, 29; 6:15).

3:4b-11 Paul had everything needed to forge for himself a brilliant career in Judaism, and he dreamed about it. He was a Jew of the most elite tribe and the most rigorous sect as well as a zealous advocate and defender of his religion. His encounter with Jesus on the road to Damascus—a Jesus who identified himself totally with his followers and who loved him unconditionally—turned everything upside down for Paul.

Henceforth, Christ becomes his sole interest. His very existence will be the knowledge of the Lord Jesus, that is, communion in his Paschal Mystery of dying and rising to new life, and participation in his work for the salvation of the world. One thing is evident for Paul: human beings can become fully realized only by giving themselves to Christ without reservation.

3:5 *The tribe of Benjamin* was descended from the one son of Jacob who was born in Palestine (Gen 35:16f), and it had always been faithful to the Davidic dynasty. The Jerusalem temple was in the territory of Benjamin.

3:12-16 Grasped by Christ on the road to Damascus, Paul strains toward him with his whole being, and this aim of his life energizes all his forces. The Christian life is inner growth, deepening, and development, and Paul loves to describe it as a course to be run. Once anyone has begun the race, there cannot be any stopping: "If you say 'Enough,' you are already dead" (St. Augustine). Those who have already "reached perfection" are Christians whose faith has matured and can be termed "mature."

3:17—4:1 Paul stresses that the Christian life is carried along by a profound hope. We turn that hope away from its goal when we fix its fulfillment in the realities of earth and even more when we polarize it on failed religious practices. Paul was probably thinking of the Jewish dietary customs and the circumcision that some Jewish-Christian preachers wanted to impose on new communities.

3:17 *Join in imitating me:* since Paul's wholehearted imitation of Christ is well known to his readers (1 Cor 4:6; 11:1; Phil 4:9; 1 Thes 1:6; 2 Thes 3:7, 9), he encourages them to follow his example in that respect.

3:20 *Our citizenship is in heaven:* Christians are, as it were, aliens in this world, for their real home is heaven. They are not of the world but fully involved in it (see Jn 17:14-16; 1 Cor 7:29-31; 1 Pet 2:11).

4:2-3 Lines of communication are established in all the new communities, and women play an important role in their life and apostolate. Doubtless, members at times experience the difficulty of living and working together, as is the case between *Euodia* and *Syntyche*. Paul is confident that these two good women will be reconciled to one another. *Clement:* it is possible, but not certain, that this is Clement, the first Roman Pope. *Book of life:* an image current at the time to evoke the collectivity of the saved (see Ex 32:32; Ps 69:29; Isa 4:3; Dan 12:1; Rev 3:5).

4:4-7 Joy is the great secret of Christians, the sign that faith has triumphed over all fears, the normal fruit of a spiritual life that progresses. The peace of God is more profound than any kind of peace that the human spirit can attain solely by its own effort.

4:8-9 Radically detached from earthly goods, a purified heart is able to recognize the gifts of Christ through all human values. In these verses, Etienne Gilson saw "the eternal charter of Christian humanism."

4:10-20 Even when in need, Paul did not want to depend on the communities for material help (see 1 Cor 9:14, 18; 2 Cor 11:7-10; 12:13-18; 1 Thes 2:5-9; 2 Thes 3:7-9), and he made no exception except for the Christians of Philippi with whom he had especially cordial ties. Like a true poor person, he remains free in any situation, enriched or deprived, ready to accept whatever will come—for the important thing is to serve the Gospel.

4:15 *Early days of the gospel:* during Paul's second missionary journey, when he first preached the Gospel in Europe at Philippi (Acts 16:9ff).

4:18 *A fragrant offering, an acceptable sacrifice pleasing to God:* Paul sees the Philippians' gift to him in terms of the Old Testament sacrifice of thanksgiving and praise (see Lev 7:12-15; Rom 12:1; Eph 5:2; Heb 13:15f).

4:21-22 Paul mentions especially those who in some way ensure the service of the emperor: dignitaries and soldiers, freedmen or slaves. Hence, Christians are also part of these circles.

4:23 Paul adds a typical closing benediction. *Your spirit:* i.e., the whole person viewed from his inner side (see Gal 6:18; 2 Tim 4:22; Philem 25).

THE LETTER TO THE COLOSSIANS

1:2 *Saints:* Christians are called *saints* because through Baptism they have been consecrated to God and are called to live accordingly.

1:3-14 The power of the Gospel to live and spread is extraordinary; it is God's grace and action among human beings. In the vitality of a young Church, Paul recognizes this work of the Lord, and he prays that it will develop in all its richness. Thanksgiving and prayer succeed each other in this introduction and indicate the principal features of an authentic Christian life: to accept the truth of the Gospel; to grow in faith, love, and hope; and to know God more in order to be more faithful in the concrete.

Nonetheless, the initiative comes from the Lord. It is he who changes our life; it is he who frees us from the bondage of sin and leads us into a new world, the kingdom of Christ. Now he is extending to all the Gentiles the salvation formerly reserved for Israel—"the inheritance of the saints." Such a text gives us the echo of what might have been the mystique of Baptism and the joy of the Christian in the early Church.

1:5 This verse refers to the three theological virtues of faith, hope, and love, which also appear in Rom 5:2-5; 1 Cor 13:13; Gal 5:5f; 1 Thes 1:3; 5:8; Heb 10:22-24. For the special nuance mentioned here, that hope gives rise to faith and love, see Tit 1:2.

1:7 *Epaphras:* a Colossian and founder of the Church of Colossae, who is now with Paul.

1:12 *Light:* this term is used to symbolize glory (Isa 60:1-3; 1 Tim 6:16), life (Jn 1:4), holiness (Mt 5:14; 6:23; Acts 26:18; 1 Jn 1:5), love (Jas 1:17; 1 Jn 2:9f), and truth (Pss 36:9; 119:105, 130; 2 Cor 4:6). Thus, the character of light is found in God (1 Jn 1:5), Christ (Jn 8:12), and Christians (Eph 5:8).

1:15-20 This great hymn to Christ and his universal primacy was probably a baptismal hymn. It draws upon the most beautiful motifs of the Old Testament on Divine wisdom (see Prov 8:1-9, 12; Wis 7:21—8:12; Sir 24). In the perspective Paul adopts here, he contemplates Christ as the image of the invisible God and clearly asserts his Divine preexistence (see 2 Cor 4:4; Phil 2:6; Heb 1:3).

Christ is before all and above all; whether we consider the universe or the History of Salvation, he is both the reason for being and the explanation of everything in them. If we seek the origin of, the rationale for, or the end of creation, he is the one we must name. All the heavenly forces and hierarchies so prized in certain Jewish or Christian circles in Colossae—in a word, everything that claims to rule the universe—are subject to him as the Creator.

He alone is Lord of the world. He alone is the power giving life to the Church, that is, his Body. He alone is the Mediator who reconciles all beings with one another and with God. We experience a universe disordered by sin; it is re-created and transformed in him. Hence, for the Christian, history has a movement and a meaning: it is oriented toward Christ, directed by him, and consummated in him.

Paul wants to enunciate a hope that is infinitely more than merely human, a hope founded in faith (see Rom 8:19-22; 1 Cor 15:22-28; Phil 3:21): the risen Christ is the center in whom two worlds are united, the Divine and the created.

1:19 *All fullness (plêrôma):* the fullness of deity (see Col 2:9) or, better, the universe full of the creative and redemptive presence of God. According to Paul, the risen Christ rules the whole of creation, what has been raised from sinfulness to salvation.

1:21-29 By dying on the cross, Christ has accomplished the reconciliation of all human beings. The Gospel changes their condition before God, provided that they accept it with faith. Paul rejoices in suffering to announce such a message, for he knows that the ordeal of a missionary is united with the Passion of Christ and contributes to the life and growth of the Church. He is captivated by the "mystery" of God. This term frequently means, depending on the context, Christ as prophesied, Christ who has come into this world, Christ continuing his work in the Church, Christ in his triumphal return.

Here, in this grand perspective of unity, Paul focuses his attention on the present aspect of the mystery. Today, Jews and Gentiles are admitted into the same inheritance, they are members of the same body, and they benefit from the same promise; today, even the multitudes of the Gentiles whom Israel regarded as excluded from the Covenant are called to the embrace of the Church. This is the wonderful mystery that the Apostle is charged to reveal.

1:24 *For the sake of his body, the Church:* nothing is lacking in the sufferings of Christ, but believers who form a single reality with him (his body) prolong and complete his Paschal Mystery of Death and Resurrection by their trials and sufferings.

1:27 Christ dwells in us when we are regenerated (see Eph 3:17). We partake of the divine nature by feeding on him (Jn 6:56) and by having his word abide in us, and we grow in grace and bear fruit as we abide in him (Jn 15:5f).

2:1-5 The Apostle draws his strength from faith, and believers draw their unity from that same faith: i.e., knowledge of the mystery of God, whose riches love will never cease uncovering. It is not a case of speculating about abstract ideas or empty words, but of recognizing the action of God in history and in the hearts of human beings—today as yesterday—so as to save them.

2:1 *Laodicea:* a town about 11 miles away from Colossae; the Letter was to be read there too (Col 4:16).

2:6-15 Paul states that human laws, even the Law of Moses, could forbid sin but not overcome it; they drive human beings to sin and are like a sentence of death. We could imagine all sorts of hidden forces that might rule the world, but they can only add to the alienation of humans. Christ has liberated believers from this tyranny of observances and myths. In his Resurrection, he is the sole master through whom human beings are raised, and all the imaginable forces are subjected to him. For Christians, the conception of the world and life has changed; having been baptized, they share in the very life of God. This is a much more profound turnaround than the ancient circumcision. Why then do the Colossians insist on seeking salvation in material observances, human theories, and myths?

2:8 *Human tradition:* literally, "philosophy," a word that occurs only here in the New Testament. In this context, it refers not to systematic thought but to religious speculations.

2:9 *The entire fullness of deity dwells in bodily form:* i.e., in the risen and glorified body of Christ.

2:14 *Record against us:* the reference is perhaps to the Mosaic Law. The latter pointed out the way of the commandments but did not give the power to observe; as a result, it became the source of indictment.

2:16-23 Certain Colossian Christians of Jewish extraction minutely observed the customs of the Jewish religion, others were partial to visions and revelations, and still others gave themselves over to ascetical practices. All of them acted as if their method was necessary for salvation. But wasn't it Christ who saved them and who enabled his Church to live as a new seed in the world? To believe is to be set free and to dedicate oneself entirely to the Lord. What can human rites, exercises, usages, and theories do in this respect?

2:16 *Observance of Festivals, New Moons, or Sabbaths:* observances that were in vogue on a yearly, monthly, or weekly basis. These were usually reckoned according to heavenly bodies, sun, moon, and stars (see Col 2:8).

3:1-4 It is not a question here of having contempt for earthly realities but of a new movement by which Christians must let themselves be grasped. Seemingly, Baptism has changed nothing for them, but in reality they live henceforth united to Christ in an even more mysterious manner. They have entered the world of the Resurrection. It is a certitude that transforms the idea that they have of their existence. At the same time, it is an impatient longing for the return of the Lord, when this change in their lives will be made complete.

3:5-11 This is a Christian endeavor, something that expresses the reality of life and the transformation of Baptism, and something that enables believers to become each day a bit more what they in fact are, i.e., living members of the risen Christ. Morality is then no longer a list of recommended reactions but a thrust that opposes sin and degradation, a growth in an ever more profound affinity with the Lord. United with Christ, Christians are new persons who no longer identify themselves by cultural references or by ethical and religious differences. Union with Christ basically destroys all divisions (see Gal 3:28).

3:5, 8 See Rom 1:29-31 and Gal 5:19-21 for other lists of vices.

3:11 *Scythian:* the Scythians lived on the steppes of Asia and were regarded as barbarians par excellence.

3:12-17 The Church is a community of persons bound together by love to give testimony to love. Without ceasing, models must be invented to express this truth. As a community united with the Lord, the Church lives in peace and joy. She lives in faith and mutual pardon, and she puts forth her deepest sentiments in prayer and thanksgiving.

3:16 *Word of Christ:* principally Christ's teaching, which was transmitted orally at that time but which also includes the Old Testament and the New. *Hymns:* these set forth some of the most important doctrines and have been preserved for us only in Paul's Letters (e.g., Col 1:15-20; Eph 5:14; Phil 2:6-11; 1 Tim 3:16).

3:18—4:1 Husbands and wives, parents and children, masters and slaves were accustomed in ancient society to live in accord with links of superiority and submission. Paul does not reverse this social structure. However, neither is he content simply to enumerate the rights of husbands, parents, and masters so as to oppose them with the duties of wives, children, and slaves. He stresses a reciprocity of duties and preaches a Christian attachment—"in the Lord"—an appeal to conscience. He does not call upon slaves to revolt but gives them another way to look upon themselves—the fact that they belong to the Lord takes precedence over their dependence on their human masters. And in a near contradiction of terms, slaves are regarded as heirs of the Lord.

This short list of precepts of family morality was developed at length in the Letter to the Ephesians (5:21—6:9).

4:2-4 Prayer keeps the conscience watchful and revives the concern for the apostolate.

4:5-6 The behavior of Christians must serve as a sign to those who do not share their faith. The present period is the time of the Church, which must be regarded as a final time of grace, both short (see 1 Cor 7:29) and perilous (see Eph 5:16), in which human beings can open themselves to salvation while waiting for Christ's Second Coming (see Gal 6:10).

4:7-17 *Tychicus* is assigned to carry the Letter to the Colossians. *Onesimus,* his companion, is the slave whom Paul has converted and is now sending back to Colossae, while recommending him to his former owner (Letter to Philemon). Also named are *Mark,* who was for a short time Paul's associate in the apostolate and is generally regarded as the author of the Second Gospel; then *Luke,* to whom we owe the Third Gospel and the Book of Acts; and finally *Epaphras,* founder of the Church of Colossae. The Letter to the Laodiceans (v. 16) may be the Letter to the Ephesians, which probably circulated in the communities of the region.

4:10 *Aristarchus:* a native of Thessalonica and companion of Paul at Ephesus and on the journey to Macedonia (see Acts 19:29; 20:4).

4:13 *Hierapolis:* a town six miles from Laodicea and 14 miles from Colossae. Its Church may have been founded during Paul's stay at Ephesus (Acts 19) but probably not by Paul himself (see Col 2:1).

4:14 *Luke:* this is the only place where the author of the Third Gospel is described as a medical doctor; see Philem 24 and 2 Tim 4:11. *Demas:* a Christian who later deserted Paul (2 Tim 4:10).

4:15 *Nymphas:* probably a Laodicean in whose house Christians met for church services. The early Church had no buildings of its own and so Christians were accustomed to meeting at the homes of individuals for instruction and services, e.g., Prisca and Aquila (Rom 16:5; 1 Cor 16:19), Philemon (Philem 2), and Mary the mother of John Mark (Acts 12:12).

4:17 *Archippus:* perhaps the son of Philemon (Philem 2); he was to take care of the Church of Colossae in the absence of Epaphras.

4:18 Paul ordinarily dictated his Letters, but added to them a few words in his own hand (1 Cor 16:21; Gal 6:11; 2 Thes 3:17).

THE FIRST LETTER TO THE THESSALONIANS

1:1 *Silvanus:* the Roman form of the Hebrew name "Silas"; this man, along with Timothy, was a fellow worker with Paul in the Macedonian apostolate (see Acts 16–18). *Church: ekklesia* in Greek, it was originally used of the People of God in the Old Testament; it designates here the Messianic gathering convoked by Jesus. The term Church is further defined as those who are "in God the Father and the Lord Jesus Christ." Being *in union* with these two persons of the Deity means a new sphere of life, on an infinitely higher plane. *Grace* and *peace:* i.e., Messianic blessings that find their basis in both persons, the Father and Jesus Christ, Lord, as the basis for the community's existence.

1:2—3:13 This is a magnificent passage in which Paul describes his experience as a missionary in an important pagan city. He has had faith in the efficacy of the Gospel and its universal power. He has not hesitated to seek out pagans, those who were once thought to be excluded from God's kingdom. The Spirit of Pentecost breathes everywhere.

1:2-10 In the announcement of the Gospel and the success of his preaching, Paul recognizes the work of the Spirit. He rejoices at the vitality of this young Church. It is God who gives her the power to break away from the pagan life. What a radical change of life conversion entails for the converts! It means turning away from idols, i.e., from all that deceives, and toward the true God to serve him and to await the coming of Jesus Christ. In this very first passage of Christian literature the three divine Persons are named; also listed are the three characteristic virtues of the Christian life: faith, hope, and love.

Behind the term *wrath* in v. 10 there is a whole theology of history (see Rom 1:18—4:25): all human beings are sinners; sin degrades and destroys the person who rejects love and justice. Punishment is a manifestation of God who judges. But by redeeming humanity from sin, Jesus has delivered it from the wrath; he takes away sin and death and gives life—this is the Christian certainty.

1:3 *Faith . . . love . . . hope:* together with 1 Thes 5:8, this is the earliest mention of the three so-called theological virtues (see 1 Cor 13:13). The accent here is on eschatological hope in accord with the Letter's emphasis on the Second Coming of Christ (see 1 Thes 1:10; 2:12, 19; 3:13; 4:13—5:11; 5:23).

1:5 *Our gospel:* this is the Gospel of God the Father (1 Thes 2:8) who originated it and of Christ (1 Thes 3:2) who brought it forth by his atoning death. Paul, Silas, and Timothy had received it through faith and preached it to others. *Power:* a power residing in the Gospel itself (see Rom 1:16) and also coming from the Holy Spirit (see Rom 15:13, 18f; 1 Cor 2:4f), which delivered the Thessalonians from spiritual bondage.

1:6 *Imitators:* all Christians are to imitate God (see Eph 5:1) and Christ (see 1 Cor 11:1) as well as their spiritual leaders (see 2 Thes 3:7, 9; 1 Tim 4:12; Tit 2:7; 1 Pet 5:3) and their fellow Christians (see 1 Thes 2:14; 1 Cor 4:6; 11:1), for all believers are one in Christ.

1:7 *In Macedonia and Achaia:* the two Roman provinces in Greece. The phrase amounts to saying "in all Greece."

2:1-12 In the quest for disciples, fame, and profit, the teachers of thought and of religion seek to found schools in this city where all currents came together at the time. Paul sketches for himself another portrait, that of messenger of Christ. Fearlessness, openness, and authenticity are the mark of the apostle seized by the Gospel. The missionary fervor takes root in God and in Jesus Christ and transforms human hearts. It then creates ties that are as strong as those of parenthood.

Paul always wanted to combine evangelization with manual work; this was doubtless to earn his own living and not be a burden on anyone, but also to reach out to human beings where they were living their lives (see Acts 20:33-35; 2 Cor 11:7-20; 12:13-18; 2 Thes 3:7-9). But he was also able to devote himself entirely to preaching (see Acts 18:3-5).

2:7 *We could have imposed our will on you:* another possible translation is: "we could have been a burden to you." It was accepted among the early Christians that apostles are entitled to the support of the Churches (see 1 Cor 9:3-14; 2 Cor 11:7-11). Paul insisted on this right although he did not always make use of it.

2:13-16 It is the Word of God that is at work in the preaching of the apostles. Heard and accepted, then recognized as coming from God, it deploys its energy in the life of human beings. It prompts pagan converts to imitate Christ with the same ardor possessed by Christians of the mother Church of Jerusalem. Hence, the converts are not second-class believers. The beautiful title "you who believe" immediately designated those who accepted the Gospel.

We are amazed by the violent indictment leveled by Paul at his compatriots, for on several occasions he states his pride in belonging to the Jewish people (see 2 Cor 11:22; Phil 3:4-6) and proclaims his love for his racial brothers and sisters (see Rom 9:3-5; 10:2—11:2). His reaction here flows from the persecution that the Jewish colony carried out against him at each stage of his mission, whereas in his view the people of the Promise should discover in the Gospel the fulfillment of their historic mission.

Paul reprises the vehement diatribe of the Prophets against the blindness of the chosen people and calls down the wrath of God and his judgment (see 1 Thes

1:10). This threat is addressed against all who oppose the call of salvation that awaits them (see Rom 2:8) and especially against those who hinder others from responding to that call. When Paul paints a picture of the pagan life, he gives hardly more than a nuance of it. Hence, this passage cannot be used to justify any anti-Semitism (see Rom 1:18-22).

2:17-20 Paul perceives the hand of Satan—i.e., the forces hostile to God and to the fulfillment of human beings—behind everything that paralyzes his missionary action.

2:18 *But Satan thwarted us:* we do not know how this occurred. Concerning Satan as enemy of the Gospel, see Rom 16:20; 1 Cor 7:5; 2 Cor 11:14; Eph 6:11-13; 1 Tim 3:6). Hence, he has already been defeated (see Col 2:15), and Christians should not feel overwhelmed by him (see Eph 6:16). His final overthrow is certain (Rev 20:10).

2:20 *You truly are our glory and our joy:* this is true now (see Phil 4:1) as well as at the Second Coming of the Lord.

3:1-13 Persecution has ravaged the small community. Sent to these new Christians, Timothy reassures Paul. In the Apostle's thanksgiving and in his prayer for the continual progress of the community, we divine his deep attachment for Christians that he has evangelized. The missionary's action must be pervaded by prayer—both private and liturgical.

3:1 *We:* in this First Letter Paul uses the first person plural extensively. That is not true of the later letters.

3:2 *Coworker for God:* see also 1 Cor 3:9. *Gospel of Christ:* see notes on 1 Thes 1:5 and Mk 1:1. *Confirm:* literally, "build you up."

3:6 Paul is rendered joyful because of their "faith" (i.e., their right attitude toward God), their "love" (i.e., their right attitude toward others), and their longing "to see" him (i.e., their right attitude toward the Apostle).

3:12 *Lord:* in Paul's usage this word is usually applied to Jesus, not the Father (see, e.g., Rom 10:9; 1 Cor 1:2; Phil 2:11).

3:13 *Holy ones:* usually translated as "saints," referring to all Christians.

4:1—5:11 Conversion to Christ involves a total rejection of the values and the way of life that one previously led. Speaking of sanctification and holiness in Biblical language, we are conscious of being in the presence of the Lord. This gives new value to the destiny, action, and relationships of human beings—nothing is any longer lost in insignificance. In his correspondence, Paul always underlines some important traits for one's way of life, in keeping with the needs of the community. He does so usually by way of a warm exhortation, but sometimes also by way of a warning. The Christian life is a journey toward a goal: union with God in Christ.

4:1-8 In the language of the period, two interpretations are possible: that each person should take a spouse in order to live honorably (see 1 Cor 7:2); or that each should exercise self-control and self-respect. In either case, and in light of the dissolute morals of the period, the affirmation of marriage and of sexual morality was a rejection of a meaningless and sordid existence. Paul has a high idea of human beings, for he views them in the call of God addressed to him. The effort of Christians arises from living ties with the divine Persons.

4:5 *Acquire a wife . . . gratify passion:* another possible translation is: "control your own body in a way that is holy and honorable and not to succumb to lustful passion."

4:8 *Instructions:* this word does not necessarily refer to the sayings of Jesus but rather to guidelines set forth in the Holy Spirit.

4:9-12 God pours the Spirit into the hearts of believers and that Spirit guides them in God's ways. However, other questions remain: certain Christians, awaiting the imminent coming of the Lord, experience a crisis of laziness (see 2 Thes 3:6-12); they must be seriously reminded of the personal and social life, without which love is but a futile word.

4:11 The early Church strongly believed in the need of Christians to earn their living. However, some of the converts—possibly as a result of their belief in Christ's imminent return (see 2 Thes 3:11)—were not working and so were letting others support them.

4:13-18 We are now at the heart of the Letter. Some Christians of Thessalonica have a few difficulties. One or other believer has died, and they cannot shake the image of those beautiful cemeteries built at the edge of cities like "high places" of despair. Christ must appear; this definitive coming mobilizes the hope of all; but will not Christians who have died be deprived of this grand and triumphant coming?

In speaking of this resurrection, Paul uses the images and symbols of the Jewish apocalypses, just as in describing the return of Christ he compares it to the "parousias" or official visits of the emperors to the great cities, where the people escorted them in a lengthy procession. The scene has its grandeur, but the essential is to be found elsewhere: the solid conviction of believers that they are with Christ forever. These words sum up the final message of Christian hope.

4:13 *Those who have fallen asleep:* sleep was an especially apt metaphor for death, since the finality and horror of death disappear in the assurance of the resurrection.

4:15 Here Paul seems to be hoping that the parousia would take place within his own lifetime. We can say that while entertaining the possibility of his own death (see 2 Tim 4:6-8) and not wanting to go against Christ's teaching about the date of the parousia (see Mt 24:48; 25:5; Lk 19:11-27), Paul (and all the first Christians) reckoned on the prospect of remaining alive until Christ's return (Rom 13:11; 1 Cor 7:26, 29; 10:11; 15:51-52; 16:22; Phil 4:5). *The word of the Lord:* this may refer to a special revelation or simply be a general reference to the teachings of Jesus.

4:17 *Will be caught up:* literally, "will be carried away," which in the Vulgate is translated by *rapiemur.* This Latin word has given birth to the idea of the "Rapture," i.e., that believers will be carried away from the troubles of this world. It simply means that those who are alive on the Last Day will not have to die; they will be transformed.

4:18 *Comfort one another:* vv. 13-18 are not primarily intended to provide a chronology of future events but rather to urge the Thessalonians to comfort one another.

5:1-11 The Old Testament announced unceasingly the Day of Yahweh, which would be one of judgment, liberation, gathering of the people, and sometimes of all humankind (see Am 5:18-20). The image is taken over by Christians. In this framework, Paul reprises the teaching of Christ. God alone is the master of time, but human beings must keep vigil in the expectation of God (see Mt 24:36-44; Lk 17:26-37; 21:34-36; Acts 1:7).

Indeed, there is a greater difference between being a Christian and not being one than between day and night. Christians are those who can see clearly, even in the daily conduct of their existence. The Gospel of Jesus, light of the world, becomes in the very practice of life a new way of seeing that goes to the heart of the real and of human destiny.

5:1 *Dates and times:* a well-known phrase describing the end time (see Acts 1:16f). Apparently, the Thessalonians had already been instructed about the basic features of the Second Coming when Paul had visited them.

5:2 *Day of the Lord:* the Old Testament uses this phrase as a time of God's judgment (see Isa 2:12-21; Joel 2:1, 31; Am 5:18; Zep 1:7, 14; Mal 3:23-24) but also of his blessing (see Am 5:18ff; Isa 13; Joel 3:5; 4:16-20). The New Testament uses the phrase in the same sense (see Rom 2:5; 2 Pet 2:9) but also utilizes it in other ways: e.g., the "day of redemption" (Eph 4:30); the "Day of God" (2 Pet 3:12) or "of Christ" (1 Cor 1:8; Phil 1:6); and "that day" (2 Thes 1:10). That *Day* is the culmination of all things prefigured by signs (see 2 Thes 2:3), but its coming will be like a thief in the night (see Mt 24:43f; Lk 12:39f; 2 Pet 3:10; Rev 3:3; 16:15).

5:3 *Destruction:* this does not mean annihilation but exclusion from the presence of the Lord (see 2 Thes 1:9), i.e., ruination of one's life and accomplishments. And it will be a ruin that occurs in an instant. *Labor pains:* the stress here is not on the pains so much as their suddenness and inevitability. *No means of escape:* literally, "They will not escape."

5:5 *Children of the light:* in Semitic languages, to be "children of [something]" meant to be characterized by it. Christians not only live in the light but are characterized by light.

5:8 Paul makes use of a metaphor of armor that he also utilizes in Rom 13:12; 2 Cor 6:7; 10:4; and Eph 6:13-17. However, he does not affix a particular virtue to the same piece of armor.

5:9-10 These verses provide a summary of the primitive preaching, which was wholly focused on the deliverance of humanity in Jesus Christ and on a life in union with him. *Whether we are awake or asleep:* i.e., whether we are alive or dead.

5:12-22 In this section Paul gives brief but cogent instructions in building a community. He especially lists the responsibilities of Christians toward leaders (vv. 12-13), toward all (vv. 14-15), toward themselves (vv. 16-18), and toward public worship (vv. 19-22).

5:12-13 Christians must show respect for their leaders, just as those same leaders must show caring leadership for their people. The leaders were undoubtedly the "bishops" and "presbyters" of 1 Tim 3:1-2; 5:17; Tit 1:5. Christians must hold these leaders in the highest esteem and render them wholehearted support in a spirit of love.

5:14-15 Christians must warn the recalcitrant, such as those who are lazy and do not pull their weight at Thessalonica. They must also encourage the fainthearted, like those troubled about their friends who had died before the Second Coming of Christ (1 Thes 4:13) and confused about what that event meant for themselves (1 Thes 5:1-11). They must also help those afflicted with moral or spiritual weakness in the face of persecution (1 Thes 3:3-5) or temptation (1 Thes 4:3-8) or the like. Finally, they should show patience with everyone. Above all, they should never pay back evil for evil in accord with the words of Christ (see Mt 5:38-42).

5:16-18 In order to carry out the regulations given in vv. 12-15, Christians need personal communion with God. They are to be joyful always (see Mt 5:11-12; Acts 5:41; 16:25; Phil 1:18; 4:4). Indeed, they are to be "sorrowful, and yet always rejoicing" (2 Cor 6:10). However, this Christian joy does not depend on earthly circumstances or feelings. It stems from what Jesus has done for us supernaturally, which never goes away.

At the same time, Christians are to be constant in prayer. It is vital for them to lift the heart to God while being occupied with their duties. Concerning prayer, see 1 Thes 1:3; 2:13; Rom 1:9-10; Eph 6:18; Col 1:3; 2 Tim 1:3.

Finally, Christians are to give thanks in all circumstances. Regardless of their human situation, they know that God has called them to eternal salvation and gives them the grace to attain it. Therefore, no matter what the circumstances may be, they can remain in a state of thankfulness (see Eph 5:20).

5:19-22 Paul now speaks about the responsibilities in communal worship. Christians must never extinguish the Spirit (v. 19). He is probably referring to curbing the charisms in any way. Guiding the charisms is necessary, but overcontrol is detrimental. In particular, the gift of prophecy must be esteemed properly and all charismatic manifestations must be duly tested. Any evil that tries to mask itself as a genuine representation of the Spirit must be discarded. Only then can worship be true.

5:20 *Prophecies:* the reference is not to the Old Testament Prophets but to those who exhorted the Christian communities (see 1 Cor 12:10-29; 13:2; 14:3).

5:23-28 This Letter concludes like a liturgy: blessing, kiss of peace, request to have the apostolic Letter read publicly, and final wish.

5:23 *Spirit and soul and body:* i.e., the whole Christian person. The spirit is that which is open to the influence of grace; it is also the source of divine life with the Christian (see Rom 5:5). This is the only place in Paul that refers to this tripartite division.

THE SECOND LETTER TO THE THESSALONIANS

1:1-2 The salutation is identical to that of First Thessalonians (1:1) except for two additions: (1) God is called "our" Father (v. 1), the Father of Christians—his Fatherhood of Jesus is expressed in other Letters (e.g., 2 Cor 1:3; Eph 1:3; 1 Pet 1:3). (2) The phrase "from God our Father and the Lord Jesus Christ" is added to v. 2 to identify the sources of "grace and peace." Paul regards Jesus as the Deity *in the fullest sense* since he names him on a par with the Father as coauthor of the favor and the relationship promised in the blessing.

1:3-12 Paul thanks God for the progress made by his valiant community in their faith, love, courage, and good name. All this will be manifested and judged at the Lord's Coming, which Paul describes once more by utilizing the dramatic scenario current among the Jews of his day. Woe to those who oppose God, for they will be immediately distanced from the Lord. But what glory there will be for those who believe!

The concept of revelation, or apocalypse, that emerges in this passage represents an essential idea of the Old and New Testaments: our religion is, above all else, something that precedes and transcends time. In history God is constantly manifesting himself as the Savior of humanity. To illustrate it, one can have recourse to the grand imaginative visions of the judgments set forth in Isa 24—27; Dan 7—12; Mt 24—25; Mk 13; and Lk 17:22-37; 19:11-27; see also introduction to the Book of Revelation.

1:12 *The grace of our God and Lord Jesus Christ:* another translation possible is: "The grace of our God and of the Lord Jesus Christ."

2:1-12 Paul uses the style and manner of apocalypses, but he speaks first and foremost as an apostle. He employs images and symbols to express where he is going and where he is leading the faithful. From the very beginning of Biblical history, God and Satan (i.e., the forces of evil) are involved in an implacable combat in which human beings are at the same time the terrain and the stakes. Christ is the conqueror of these evil forces. His victory, obtained on the cross, will be manifested on the great Day of his majestic return. We must prepare for this Coming.

2:1-3a Paul indicates that a problem has arisen concerning the circumstances surrounding the Day of the Lord. In times of crisis, there are always falsehood-mongers to whom the faithful give willing ear—but whom they should avoid altogether. So the Apostle intends to set forth certain features of the Day in order to correct what is being falsely claimed.

2:2 *Is already here:* Paul insists that the Day of the Lord has not already come, for the final days have not begun and their completion is not imminent.

2:3b-12 Making use of images borrowed from the Prophets and from the authors of apocalypses, Paul brings on stage the forces of evil and the true witnesses of God: they constitute respectively the adversary and the obstacle. The portrait of the adversary gathers together in one personage all the doers of evil who are based on the historical enemies of God's people in the Old Testament—especially Antiochus IV Epiphanes (see Dan 11:36) who in his supreme folly wanted to make himself a god.

The obstacle, which was doubtlessly well known to the Thessalonians, stands for a more obscure reality for us; it could refer to the ensemble of believers who work to bring about the Kingdom of God (see also note on 2:6 below). Even though their victory is to be awaited, it is no less assured. This victory is based upon the Paschal Mystery with its twofold aspect of Death and Resurrection. Throughout the centuries, the forces of death and the People of God never cease to confront one another in the life of the world, in the heart of each person.

2:3b-4 *That Day cannot come:* these words have been supplied in the text in order to bring out more clearly Paul's meaning; the original sentence is incomplete. *The lawless one . . . the son of destruction . . . the adversary:* the leader of the rebellion, who will also come to be called "the Antichrist" (1 Jn 2:18; 4:3; 2 Jn 7).

2:6 *What is now restraining him:* some suggestions about the identity of this obstacle (in addition to the one mentioned in note 2:3b-12 above) are: the Roman State and its emperor; the principle of law embodied in the state; the Holy Spirit through the Church; and the preaching of the Gospel (possibly by Paul himself), for the end could not come until the Gospel was preached to all nations (see Mk 13:10).

2:8-12 Paul describes what will precede the Lord's coming. He glimpses, toward the end of human history, a spectacular offensive launched by the forces of evil under the instigation of Satan. A great apostasy will follow (see Mt 24:10-12; Lk 18:8; 21:12-19; 1 Tim 4:1). *The lawless one* is both anti-God and anti-Christ, but he will not have the last word. On the day, when he thinks he has conquered, he will be confronted with the dazzling manifestation of Christ and completely overcome.

2:10 *Love of the truth:* one of Paul's most felicitous expressions, it refers to love of the Gospel, the acceptance of this unprecedented gift that comes from the Father, Christ, and the Spirit. To refuse it is to exclude oneself from love forever.

2:13 — 3:15 Paul is thankful that he and his coworkers can look forward to salvation for themselves and for their converts. The beneficiaries of God's saving work cannot rest on their laurels, however. They must be ever active in good works and keep the teachings (traditions) of the Church. The Apostle goes on to ask the converts to pray for him and his coworkers and calls down God's grace on them.

He also sets forth the proper solution for idlers. The Thessalonians must admonish idlers yet deal charitably with their mistakes. Such persons are not to be cast out of the community, but to be given frequent warnings.

2:13—3:5 Here we find the same advice as was given in the First Letter. Christian life unfolds in the love of the three divine Persons; fidelity to the authentic tradition that the apostles have transmitted in writing or by living word; prayer; and constancy of effort.

2:13-14 These two verses show the harmonious working of all three Persons of the Trinity in the divine plan of salvation: God the Father chooses and calls his people; God the Son shares his glory with his own; and God the Holy Spirit imparts his sanctifying grace. *From the beginning:* another translation possible is: "as the firstfruits."

2:15 *Traditions:* i.e., the teachings contained in tradition; they are both oral and written (see 2 Thes 2:5; 3:6; 1 Cor 11:2), just as was the case with rabbinic law (see note on Mt 15:2ff).

2:16 Jesus is here named before the Father; despite the double subject, the verbs in the Greek text are in the singular number. Could the unity of Father and Son be better expressed?

3:6-15 In putting work at the service of the community, Paul places it under the sign of love for God, for one's brothers and sisters, and for the Church. To eat one's own bread constitutes the primary dignity of a person (v. 10). By demanding exemplary conduct from Christians, Paul remains in line with Jesus and the primitive Church (see Mt 18:15-18; 1 Cor 5:1-13).

3:16-18 In order to discourage forgeries of his letters (see 2 Thes 2:2), Paul takes care to authenticate the letters that he dictates and causes to be set down—he writes out a few words with his own hand (see also 1 Cor 16:21 and Col 4:18). In the cases of Galatians and Philemon, it appears that Paul wrote more than just the concluding phrases (see Gal 6:11 and Philem 19).

THE FIRST LETTER TO TIMOTHY

1:1-2 The majority of Paul's Letters were sent to Churches, but four were addressed to individuals: Timothy (two Letters), Titus, and Philemon. Titus and Timothy were not apostles but evangelists (see 2 Tim 4:5). Timothy (whose father was Greek and his mother a Jewish Christian) had been converted by Paul's preaching (see Acts 16:1-3) and so was Paul's "loyal child in the faith."

1:1 *Savior:* this title, given to both the Father and Jesus, is characteristic of the later Letters of Paul, perhaps in reaction to the pagan environment in which the gods were "saviors" and the emperor was worshiped as a god. *Jesus our hope* is one of Paul's finest descriptions.

1:3-20 In writing to the Colossians, Paul had already denounced the infatuation with hazardous theories that characterized some Christians of Jewish origins in the region of Ephesus. Once again, fanciful theologies, hollow ideas, and obscure mythologies are being given free rein in Ephesus. Some converts from Judaism—who are familiar with the new Greek mythological currents as well as the play of Biblical genealogies—give themselves up to speculations without end or purpose and they abandon the essence of faith and love.

They claim to be teachers of the Law, but they preach nonsense. Hence, they must be reminded that the Law is primarily a discipline of life rather than an object of speculation (see Rom 7:12-16; Gal 3:19); above all, the importance of a sane doctrine that fixes one's thoughts and guides one's life must be inculcated in them. In the midst of an anarchic agitation, Christians must always come back to the profound meaning of the Gospel, exemplified by Paul's life and vocation.

1:3 *When I was setting out for Macedonia:* an event not mentioned in Acts; hence, it probably occurred after Acts 28 between Paul's first and second Roman imprisonment. He had founded the Church at Ephesus on the Third Missionary Journey some eight years earlier (see Acts 19:1—20:1).

1:10 *Sodomites:* adult males who have relations with boy prostitutes. The latter are also known as *catamites* after the Latin name *(Catamitus)* of Ganymede, the cupbearer of the gods in Greek mythology. See also Rom 1:26f and 1 Cor 6:9. *Slave traders:* literally, "dealers in men," who included slaves but also men destined to be thrown into the arena or to serve unmentionable vices.

1:15 *This saying can be trusted and merits complete acceptance:* a formula that corresponds to the Aramaic expression in the Gospels: "Amen, I say to you." It is found only in the Pastoral Letters—here and in four other places: 1 Tim 3:1; 4:9; 2 Tim 2:11; Tit 3:8. (In the first, third, and fourth of these it is abbreviated.)

1:17 *Immortal, invisible, the only God:* here again Paul gives the true God titles used in pagan worship; see vv. 1 and 11.

1:18 *Prophecies...about you:* Timothy received his investiture as an apostle in the presence of prophets, that is, charismatic individuals who had the gift of guiding the faithful along their way to God or of calling men to the missionary apostolate (see 1 Cor 12:28-29; Acts 13:1-3; Eph 3:5).

Fight the good fight: the Christian life is one long struggle against (1) Satan (see 2 Cor 2:11; Eph 6:11-12); (2) the flesh (see Rom 7:23; Gal 5:17; 1 Pet 2:11); (3) the world (see Jn 16:33; 1 Jn 5:4f); and (4) death (see 1 Cor 15:26; Heb 2:14f). Christians are called upon to be filled with faith and to use the armaments of faith (see Eph 6:14-18), and to be vigilant (see 1 Pet 5:8). Through Christ, they will attain the final victory with its eternal rewards (see Rom 16:20; 2 Tim 4:8; Rev 2:17; 3:5; 21:7).

1:20 *Hymenaeus:* see 2 Tim 2:17f. *Alexander:* possibly the same person as in 2 Tim 4:14. *Handed over to Satan:* these individuals were probably excluded from the community and abandoned "to Satan." This excommunication was inflicted for the purpose of correcting them and making them come to their senses as they rediscovered their desire for salvation and the Gospel (see 1 Cor 5:5).

2:1—3:16 This section instructs Timothy about the public worship of the community and lists some qualifications that bishops and deacons must possess. In the process, it bestows on the Church two time-hallowed titles: "the Church of the living God" and "the pillar and bulwark of the truth."

It then concludes by stressing the universality of Jesus' role in his Resurrection visitation to angels as well as humans and in his enthronement as Lord of the Church. Hence, the belief in Christ's Paschal Mystery is shown to be one of the basic aspects of the faith of the Church.

2:1-7 Nero was in power, and Paul perhaps had a presentiment of a dark future for Christians. He therefore urges them to include all human beings in their intercession. Liturgical prayer must be universal prayer, for it is carried along by a conviction: God has sent his Son to bear witness that the Father wills the salvation of the whole world. It is the mission of Paul and ultimately of the Church to make this truth well known.

2:5-6a This text was probably part of a very early creed. Some scholars regard it as a Christian version of the Jewish *shema:* "Hear, O Israel, the LORD, our God, is LORD alone . . . " (Deut 6:4f). The Letter to the Hebrews gives a lengthy development of this central affirmation of the Christian faith.

2:8-15 First of all, Paul describes the attitude of prayer, stressing that it must arise from a heart filled with love (see Mt 6:14; Mk 11:25). Then he issues recommendations for different groups and states of life. In keeping with the custom of the time, women were excluded from official roles in worship (see 1 Cor 14:34-35).

We see a teaching already in existence concerning style of dress, a teaching that has often been renewed in the Church: Christians should endeavor *to be* rather than *to appear.* The New Testament several times recognizes the value of virginity (see 1 Cor 7:8, 25); but here, in opposition to heretics who forbade marriage (1 Tim 4:3), Paul emphasizes the point that the vocation of women is to give life.

2:9 This verse does not place a total ban on wearing jewelry or expensive clothes or braiding one's hair. These things are singled out here because in the society of Paul's day they were signs of unconscionable extravagance and self-importance.

3:1-16 Christian communities have multiplied and grown; the Church needs organization. Bishops ("overseers") or presbyters ("elders") preach, lead liturgical meetings, and govern the local Churches under the more or less close supervision of the Apostle or his delegates (Timothy at Ephesus, Titus in Crete). These authorities, who are carefully chosen, are aided by deacons, who are appointed to help the apostles in material matters (see Acts 6:1-6) and also in their missionary work (see Acts 8:5-13, 38): to take upon themselves the management of the organization and to bring help to the poor and the sick. It seems that some women, too, may have had similar tasks (v. 11; see Rom 16:1).

Thus, Paul sketches a hierarchy of the Church. To serve the Church, Paul demands solid human qualities on the part of candidates. People cannot proclaim the mystery of faith, i.e., announce that God saves the world through Jesus Christ, unless they live that faith. A fragment from a hymn of the time is used to celebrate this mystery: Incarnation, Resurrection, Mission, Ascension.

3:11 *Women:* this word could refer either to women deacons or to women who were the wives of deacons. Scholars usually opt for the first reference since there is no possessive (e.g., "their") and since they are introduced by the same word as in v. 8 ("similarly . . . likewise"), indicating that women too could possess the ministry of deacon. See note on Rom 16:1, in which verse Paul sends greetings to "our sister Phoebe, who is a deaconess of the Church at Cenchreae."

3:16 *He was . . . vindicated by the Spirit:* the holiness and divinity of Christ were made known in the Resurrection (see Rom 1:4). These six lines are regarded as a fragment of a hymn of the time.

4:1-16 The time left to announce salvation to the whole world is limited; it is the end time, an age of crisis. In fact, troubled spirits jumble religious ideas together, seeking salvation in a pseudo-asceticism. But true Christians know how to celebrate creation and its realities in a positive way. Such an outlook in matters of doctrine rejects anything that is disordered and inconsistent; it endorses godliness, i.e., the worship of God and the desire to seek his will; attentiveness to the great virtues; love for the public reading of Sacred Scripture (v. 13); and teaching. An apostle finds the strength to persevere in this line of thought by ceaselessly renewing the gift that was given to him through the laying on of hands, i.e., when the community consecrated him for his office, in the name of the Lord.

4:3 *They forbid marriage and require abstinence from foods:* this asceticism was not from the Bible but from the erroneous belief that the material world was evil, which was a principal tenet of Gnosticism.

4:5 *It is made holy by the word of God and by prayer:* another possible translation is: "it is made holy by the invocation of God in prayer."

4:13 *Reading:* i.e., the public reading of Scripture.

4:14 *Laid their hands on you:* an action that had various meanings in the Old Testament, among which was the transmission of authority (e.g., from Moses to Joshua: see Num 27:18-23; Deut 34:9). In the New Testament it symbolizes (1) the bestowal of blessings and benediction (see Mt 19:13, 15; Lk 24:50); (2) the restoration of health (see Mt 9:18; Acts 9:12, 17); (3) the imparting of the Holy Spirit (see Acts 8:17, 19; 19:6); and (4) the gifts and rights of an office (as in this verse and in Acts 6:6; 13:3; 2 Tim 1:6).

5:1—6:2a Paul sets forth the attitude that Timothy should have toward various groups in his Church: the old and the young, widows, presbyters, and slaves. With reference to slavery, one should note that the New Testament does not attack the institution directly but attacks the principle of slavery. For Christian slaves are freedmen of the Lord and their owners are slaves of the Lord (1 Cor 7:21-23). In Christ Jesus there is no distinction between slave and free; all are baptized in one Spirit and form one body (see 1 Cor 12:13; Gal 3:28, Col 3:11). Ultimately, the principle of Christian love prevented Christians from regarding other human beings as slaves.

5:1-2 The apostle must have an attitude of respect and closeness for the different categories of the faithful.

5:3-16 In reading this passage, the circumstances of the period and concrete conditions in the community must be taken into account. Different types of widows are discussed. Some have a family; in their case, the accent is placed upon a true exchange on the family level. Other widows are all alone; they can serve the Church and are taken into her care.

When he speaks of young widows, the author cannot resist injecting a caricatural trait; he refuses to let them engage in the exclusive service of Christ and the Church out of fear that later events in their existence may take away their initial enthusiasm. It seems that some communities had the bad experience of premature vows. (1 Corinthians 7:9, 40 exhibited much less distrust in such cases.) It is interesting to note the existence of organized groups of widows in the community.

5:10 *Washing the feet of the saints,* i.e., the faithful, was a ritual of hospitality (see Lk 7:44; Jn 13:1ff). It was necessary because the roads were dusty and the footwear consisted of sandals.

5:17-25 Presbyters do not seem to be on the same level as the bishops (i.e., "overseers") mentioned earlier (1 Tim 3:1-7), although they preside at the Liturgy and explain the Scriptures. This fact seems to pave the way for the monarchical episcopate that developed in the Church during the second and third centuries. The poverty required of his ministers by Christ does not prevent the Gospel workers from earning a living by their labor, even though Paul himself has always refused to accept any assistance. But anyone who has the desire to serve the Church must have shown to be a serious Christian. The responsibility for the community must not be conferred lightly on anyone.

Paul then places his full attention on his favorite disciple (v. 23).

5:17 *Double honor:* i.e., respect and an honorarium for their labor.

5:18 Both citations (Deut 25:4 and Lk 10:7) are called "Scripture." This shows that whatever portions of the New Testament were available at the time were already regarded as equal to the Old Testament in authority.

5:21 *The chosen angels:* in contrast to the fallen angels (see 2 Pet 2:4; Jude 6).

6:1-2b Paul speaks on more than one occasion of the lot of slaves (see 1 Cor 7:21-24; Gal 3:28; Eph 6:5-9; Col 3:22-25; Tit 2:9-10; Philem 10-17; see 1 Pet

2:18-20). What he speaks of here is not about the social institution of the time but about fidelity and relationships within a de facto institution.

6:2c-19 The final instruction to Timothy concerns combating false teaching about wealth, fighting the good fight of the faith, and amassing true riches in place of earthly wealth. In order to understand the kind of disastrous teaching we are dealing with here, it suffices to examine the portrait of a false teacher. He is a man who gives in to every snare, chasing after reputation, emotional satisfaction, and money without paying any real attention to the faith. The true teacher, on the other hand, knows how to embrace suffering and live according to the truth. He is a man who professes the faith and fights for it while totally enveloped by the mystery of Christ that is evoked in the beautiful final hymn in 1 Tim 6:14-16.

6:10 Money in itself is neither good nor bad. It is *the love of money* that is evil, and indeed the root of all types of evil. Therefore, it is not wrong for believers to be well off—so long as they do not take pride in their riches but use them "to do good."

6:11 *Man of God:* a well-known title that had been applied to Moses and the Prophets in the Old Testament (see Deut 33:1; 1 Sam 2:27). It highlights the spiritual power possessed by leaders of the Church.

6:12 *Confession:* perhaps the profession of faith that Timothy made when consecrated to the ministry.

6:17-19 This passage calls for Christians to cast off the quest for riches that permeated their society and to change their attitude toward them.

6:20-21 Once again one of the major themes of the Letter is highlighted in this Conclusion: guard the deposit of faith that has been entrusted to you.

6:20 *What has been entrusted to you:* literally, "the deposit," that is, sacred doctrine, the authentic Gospel (see 1 Tim 1:10-11; 2 Tim 1:13-14). *Wrongly considered to be knowledge:* the ensemble of doctrines that were taught by heretics and that on many points foreshadowed the Gnosticism of the second century.

6:21 *All of you:* the plural indicates that this Letter was intended to be read to the whole community.

THE SECOND LETTER TO TIMOTHY

1:1-5 Paul begins his Letter with a salutation that is similar to the one found in 1 Timothy, adding to it the words "whose promise of life is fulfilled in Christ Jesus." He calls Timothy his "beloved child," and the actual greeting is the same as that of 1 Timothy, showing that everything we have comes to us from God through Christ. As in most of his Letters (the exceptions are Gal, 1 Tim, and Tit), Paul then follows his salutation with a section thanking God for the recipients of the Letter. He focuses on his relationship with Timothy and his confidence in Timothy's faith.

1:4 *Your tears:* those shed by Timothy when Paul was leaving Ephesus (see 1 Tim 1:3).

1:5 According to Acts 16:1, Timothy's mother (Eunice) was a Jewish Christian while his father was a Greek and apparently an unbeliever. Here we learn that his grandmother (Lois) was also a Christian.

1:6-18 Paul warns that self-interest and discouragement must not get the best of the apostle's ardor and determination. Rather, he must rely upon the graces that were given him when he received the ministry and was gripped by the Spirit at his missionary sending forth (see 1 Tim 4:14). He must once again place himself at the service of the Gospel, which is the announcement of the coming of Christ and the salvation that he gives. There is no missionary life without spiritual renewal.

The last seven verses go on to give examples of men of God who have endured: Paul and Onesiphorus.

1:6 *Laying on of . . . hands:* see note on 1 Tim 4:14.

1:9 Paul insists that redemption from sin and the call to holiness are freely given to human beings in accord with God's plan (see Eph 1:4).

1:10 *Appearance:* the reference here is to the Incarnation.

1:11 *Teacher:* most manuscripts read: "teacher of the nations," which scholars regard as a gloss based on 1 Tim 2:7.

1:12 *That Day:* the day of judgment and crowning. *What he has entrusted to me:* i.e., the deposit of faith (see 1 Tim 6:20). Another possible translation is: "what I have entrusted to him," i.e., the fruits of his ministry.

1:15 Paul is deeply disappointed that he has been deserted by Christians from Asia, including two upon whom he was counting—Phygelus and Hermogenes. Some scholars believe that Phygelus was the leader of lapsed Christians in Rome (see Phil 1:15f).

1:16 *Onesiphorus:* a helper of Paul— probably during his first Roman imprisonment (see v. 8)—whose household was in Ephesus and who is not mentioned elsewhere (see 2 Tim 4:19 below).

1:18 *Lord . . . Lord:* the first "Lord" doubtless refers to Christ and the second to the Father.

2:1-26 The author then goes on to enumerate eight exemplars that a man of God can follow in some way: Paul (vv. 1-2), a soldier (vv. 3-4), an athlete (v. 5), a farmer (vv. 6-7), Jesus (vv. 8-13), a worker (vv. 14-19), a vessel (vv. 20-23), and a servant (vv. 24-26).

2:1-7 The apostolate requires a person's complete commitment. He bears and transmits the message entrusted by God to the Christian community.

2:8-13 Another heading for this section would read "Be a memorial of Jesus Christ," i.e., be a person whose whole being and action recalls the Resurrection of Christ and renders it present to those he meets, while announcing to them that its fullness will take place at the time of the Lord's return. This is the finest picture one could give of the life of Paul.

Verses 11b-13 are probably from a baptismal hymn; to be baptized meant that one should live out, throughout one's days, the mystery of Christ's Death and Resurrection (see Rom 6:8; 1 Cor 15:31; Gal 6:14; Phil 3:10; Col 3:3-5).

2:14-26 In the portrait of a true missionary, a certain number of virtues must be present: honesty, respect for and acceptance of everyone, courage in persecution, truthfulness without alteration, and rejection of faddish witticisms. The author once more condemns the errors being propagated in the region of Ephesus; they have the look not of a new religion but of a feverish and babbling emotionalism. The Greek mind had difficulty in accepting the resurrection of the body (see Acts 17:32; 1 Cor 15:22), and some avoid the problem by saying that the resurrection has already taken place at Baptism but that it is solely a case of a spiritual resurrection.

They forget above all that the faith is founded on the word of God, which provides the initiative and that believers have merely to respond. It is the quality of their faith that classifies believers in the Church, not the abundance of their opinions. Yet leaders must be very kind and not condemn any of the members of the community.

2:14 *Before God:* many manuscripts read: "before the Lord."

2:17 *Hymenaeus:* see 1 Tim 1:20. His punishment has not helped him.

2:19 *Foundation . . . sealed:* the foundations of buildings in antiquity were sealed and adorned with inscriptions. As inscriptions Paul uses Scripture texts that complement one another: Num 16:5 (God cares for those he loves) and Num 16:26; Isa 26:13; 52:11 (these must lead upright lives).

2:22 *Those who call on the Lord:* i.e., Christians (see Acts 19:14ff; Rom 10:12f).

3:1-17 For the last times, Jesus had already announced somber perspectives: false messiahs would be preached to mislead people into doctrines of perversion (see Mt 24:4-5, 24). For his part, Paul too has evoked this revival of evil for the end of history (see 2 Thes 2:3-12; see also 1 Jn 2:18-24; 4:3; 2 Jn 7). Undoubtedly, magicians practiced their wiles at Ephesus; in fact, according to Jewish legend, *Jannes* and *Jambres* were leading sorcerers who opposed Moses before Pharaoh (see Ex 7:8ff). Like Paul, everyone who announces the Gospel must accept persecution (see Mt 5:10-11; 10:22; Jn 15:19-20; Acts 13:1—14:28). It is a call for strength and firmness.

The important thing for the envoy of God and the Church is to remain faithful to the word of God as reported in Scripture. He is assured of finding therein nourishment for his faith and help for his ministry. This text is often referred to as bearing witness to the inspiration of Scripture.

3:5 *Godliness:* i.e., true religion (see 1 Tim 4:7).

3:11 Lystra was Timothy's native place; for the persecutions, see Acts 13:50; 14:5-19.

3:14 *From whom you have learned it:* Timothy had been instructed by his Jewish grandmother and mother (see 1 Tim 1:5).

3:16 The verse gives clear witness to the inspiration of Scripture. The Jews of that day believed in the inspiration of the three parts of the Old Testament. However, they ascribed the highest type of inspiration to the *Pentateuch* or Five Books attributed to Moses (also known as the "Torah" or Law), a lower type to the *Prophets,* and an even lower one to the *Writings.*

The sacred writers of the New Testament cited the Old Testament about 350 times in such a way as to show that Christians shared the belief of the Jews in the divine origin of the sacred books. In addition, the New Testament speaks of inspiration in the Old Testament Scriptures explicitly here and in 2 Pet 1:19-21, and of the New Testament writings implicitly in 2 Pet 3:14-16.

In the *Constitution on Divine Revelation,* Vatican II says: "Holy Mother Church, relying on the belief of the apostles, holds that the Books of both the Old and the New Testament in their entirety, with all their parts, are sacred and canonical because, written under the inspiration of the Holy Spirit, they have God as their Author" (no. 11).

However, this does not mean that God used the sacred author as a secretary to whom he dictated. Nor did he simply reveal to the human author the contents of the Book and the way in which this should be expressed. Rather, the human author is a living instrument endowed with reason who under the divine impulse brings his faculties and powers into play in such a way that all can easily gather from the Book produced by his work his distinctive genius and his individual characteristics and features. In other words, the sacred author, like every author, makes use of all his faculties—intellect, imagination, and will—to consign to writing whatever God wanted written, and no more.

By virtue of the *divine condescension,* things are presented to us in the Bible in a manner that is in common use among human beings. For as the substantial Word of God made himself like human beings in all things except sin (see Heb 4:15), so God's words, spoken by human tongues, have taken on all the qualities of human language except error.

4:1-5 Apostles, missionaries, and pastors are first of all men of the Gospel and evangelization. The project that animates their existence is to awaken human beings to the true worship of the living God. This is a much more pressing task when a swarm of vain ideas sows confusion. Such a time has come, says Paul.

4:1 *living and the dead:* Christ will return to judge both the living and the dead (see Mt 25:31; Jn 5:26-29; 1 Thes 4:15-17). This was doubtless an early teaching (see Acts 10:42; 1 Pet 4:5) and it became part of the Creed.

4:5 At the end of this verse, the Vulgate adds the words "Be sober."

4:6-18 In these last moments Paul affirms that his blood is about to be shed as a sacrifice to God (it was Jewish practice to pour oil or wine on a burnt offering: see Ex 29:40; Phil 2:17). He then uses images from sports to express his certainty of having remained steadfast in the faith. Although his fate had recently been a sad one and he was abandoned and betrayed, his gaze remains fixed on the Lord to announce the Gospel of salvation to the very end and to enter into his Kingdom.

4:8 *Crown:* probably a reference taken from the laurel wreath that was accustomed to be placed on the head of a winning athlete or a victorious soldier (see 2 Tim 2:5; 1 Cor 9:25).

4:10 *Demas* had been with Paul during the latter's first imprisonment in Rome (see Col 4:14; Philem 24). *Crescens* is mentioned only here in the New Testament. *Galatia* here means Gaul, according to the terminology used at that time by writers of Greek. *Dalmatia* is equivalent to present-day Albania and part of the former Yugoslavia; it is also called Illyricum in the New Testament (see Rom 15:19).

4:11 *Luke:* the "beloved physician," mentioned in Col 4:14 and Philem 24, who accompanied Paul throughout much of his Second and Third Missionary Journeys (see note on Acts 16:9-15). *Mark:* the same person who had left Paul and Barnabas in the midst of the First Missionary Journey (see Acts 13:13). Paul's refusal to take him along on the Second Missionary Journey caused Barnabas to separate himself from the Apostle and take Mark with him on a mission to Cyprus (see Acts 15:36-41). However, Mark later proved himself to Paul and was present with him during the first Roman imprisonment (see Col 4:10; Philem 24).

4:12 *Tychicus:* a fellow worker of Paul (see Acts 20:3-5; Eph 6:21; Col 4:7).

4:13 *Cloak:* probably a long-sleeved traveling garment that Paul could use to keep warm during his imprisonment. *Carpus:* possibly the Apostle's host at Troas, but nothing is known for certain about him. *Scrolls:* undoubtedly some type of printed documents. *Parchments:* perhaps leather scrolls of Old Testament Books.

4:14 *Alexander the coppersmith:* this seems to be the same Alexander mentioned in 1 Tim 1:20; he may have testified against Paul in court. *The Lord will repay:* citation from Pss 28:4; 62:13; and Prov 24:12.

4:17 *The Lord stood at my side:* Paul's ultimate strength lay in his total dependence on the one who commissioned him (see 2 Cor 12:9-10; Phil 4:11-13).

4:18 It is noteworthy that this doxology is centered on Christ the Savior and Redeemer (see Rom 16:25; Gal 1:5).

4:19-22 This conclusion gives a series of short requests, instructions, and greetings.

4:19 *Prisca and Aquila:* Prisca (see Rom 16:3; 1 Cor 16:19) is the diminutive form of Priscilla (see Acts 16:2, 18f, 26). She and her husband Aquila were Jewish Christians who had met Paul on his first visit to Corinth during the Second Missionary Journey. They had come to Corinth from Rome, and like Paul they were tentmakers (see Acts 16:2f). Later they went with Paul to Ephesus (see Acts 18:18f), where their house became a Christian meeting place for several years before they returned to Rome (Rom 16:3f; 1 Cor 16:19). They had now gone back to Ephesus (see 1 Tim 1:3). *Onesiphorus:* see note on 2 Tim 1:16.

4:20 *Erastus:* see note on Rom 16:23. *Trophimus:* a Christian from Ephesus (see Acts 21:29), who accompanied Paul to Jerusalem (see Acts 20:4) and was thought by the Jews to have entered the temple, thus leading to the riot that resulted in Paul's arrest (see Acts 21:29ff) and first imprisonment at Rome. *Miletus:* a seaport on the coast of Asia Minor about 50 miles from Ephesus.

4:21 Nothing is known for certain about *Eubulus* and *Pudens.* There is a western tradition that *Linus* was the successor of Peter as Bishop of Rome, and that *Claudia* was his mother.

4:22 Some manuscripts add the words "Jesus Christ" after "Lord" and "Amen" at the end of the verse. The first "you" in the Greek (translated as "your") is singular, indicating that the Letter was addressed to Timothy alone; the second is plural ("all of you"), indicating that it was intended to be read aloud to the community.

THE LETTER TO TITUS

1:1-4 In this beautiful salutation the author highlights the centrality of the Letter's salvation theme in two ways. (1) He defines the role of an apostle—to tell all people of God's plan to lead them to eternal life. (2) He specifically mentions Christ's role as Savior, which he does in no other salutation.

1:1 *Servant of God:* this is the only place Paul applies the phrase to himself; elsewhere he calls himself "servant of Christ" (see Rom 1:1; Gal 1:10; Phil 1:1). *Apostle:* see note on Mk 6:30.

1:3-4 *God our Savior . . . Christ Jesus our Savior:* the term "Savior" is applied three times to God the Father (here and Tit 2:10; 3:4; see also 1 Tim 1:1; 2:3; 4:10) and three times to Jesus (Tit 1:4; 2:13; 3:6; see also 2 Tim 1:10).

1:4 *My loyal child in the faith we share:* Titus is Paul's true child because he accepts and will proclaim the faith that Paul preaches. This links Titus with the developing chain of tradition.

1:5-9 The young communities remain under the direct supervision of the Apostle or his delegate. But the latter establishes a group of people entrusted with its day-to-day operation and regular instruction. Such delegates are given various names in the New Testament: *presbyters, bishops, and pastors.* Each one seems to be responsible for the community.

After the disappearance of the Apostles and their immediate delegates, the situation will evolve; the community will be led by a *bishop,* who presides over the college of *priests* and the group of *deacons.* At the time of this Letter, the leaders possess an authority linked to that of the Apostle. They must truly imitate his manner of life and also fulfill the primary task of preaching the word of God.

1:7 *Bishop:* (i.e., "overseer") this term could replace *presbyter* (i.e., "elder": vv. 5-6) because the two were equivalent at that time (see Acts 20:17, 28).

1:10-16 There will always be troublemakers who profit from fables and practices that they propagate; they monopolize religion instead of entering into the Gospel. The important thing, Jesus had declared (see Mk 7:1-23), was not to wash one's hands or to forbid foods but to give oneself to God with an upright and sincere heart (see Mt 5:8). The author sternly reminds the Cretans of their now firm reputation as liars, and he does not miss the opportunity to cite (in v. 12) a saying (which had become a veritable proverb) of one of their poets, Epimenides of Cnossos, who lived in the sixth century B.C.

1:10 *Jewish converts:* literally, "those of the circumcision." These individuals (who have come to be called "Judaizers") had two basic characteristics: (1) the belief that Christians had to be circumcised and also keep the Jewish ceremonial law (see notes on Gal, ch. 2); (2) a fondness for unscriptural Jewish myths and genealogies (see note on 1 Tim 1:3-20).

1:15 This is a proverb that takes on a Christian meaning (see Mt 15:10-20; Rom 14:14-23). Christians have been purified by the sacrificial Death of Christ. Hence, to them "everything created by God is good, and nothing is to be rejected, provided that it is received with thanksgiving" (1 Tim 4:4). On the other hand, to those who are corrupt and without faith, nothing is pure. They set up man-made prohibitions against certain foods, marriage, and the like (see Mt 15:10-11, 16-20; Mk 7:14-19; Acts 10:9-16; Rom 14:20).

2:1-10 The moral rules set forth here could also have been voiced by a Stoic philosopher of the time. The author does not criticize the social climate of his day, but he wants the Christian communities to be models of honesty and dignity. He describes a new spirit: charity. Christians of all ages and all conditions who form the Church must show by their most ordinary actions that they live for God. On these matters, see Eph 5:21—6:9; Col 3:18-21.

2:11-14 Here, at the center of the Letter, is a beautiful passage for Christmastime. The manifestation (or epiphany) of God must change our way of knowing and living. Christians are on the way to an event; they are hastening toward the final manifestation of Christ in glory. Hence, this text is also a valuable testimony to the faith of the early Christians in the divinity of Christ (v. 14).

2:13 *Of our great God and Savior Jesus Christ:* this is a clear statement of the divinity of Christ (see also Rom 9:5). Some, however, offer another translation that does not possess that same clarity: "of the great God and of our Savior Jesus Christ."

2:15—3:8a The fact that someone's life is no longer ruled by passion, egoism, and wickedness is always surprising. It is the sign that such a person is marked by the idea of God's goodness. With these practical recommendations, the author knows how to evoke in a few words the major aspects of the Christian mystery: love of God; salvation through grace; Baptism; the gift of the Spirit; and the expectation of fulfillment in the end time.

3:1 *To be ready to perform any honorable task:* another possible translation is: "to be open to every good enterprise."

3:5-7 The effects of Baptism are delineated: rebirth, forgiveness of sins by Christ, reception of the Holy Spirit, and the right to eternal life (of which the indwelling Spirit is a pledge—see 2 Cor 1:22).

3:8b-11 The act of believing is not something pertaining only to one's spirit; it engages one's whole life. The author shows himself to be severe toward those who spend their time and their understanding on idle discussions and on speculations whose object is no longer the sincere search for truth. Here, for the first time, is enunciated the idea of the seditious person, the "heretic," a word borrowed from the philosophical schools of the time. In a Christian setting, he is a person who chooses the elements of the faith that suit him and is ready to deny essentials and divide the community.

3:12-15 Paul takes the opportunity to stress one more time that Christians should do what is good (see Tit 3:1, 8, 14). This will ensure that their lives will not be "unfruitful." The practice of doing good is above all the concrete mutual help among those who are disenfranchised.

3:12 *Artemas:* apparently one of Paul's coworkers, who is mentioned nowhere else. *Tychicus:* a trusted coworker of Paul who on several occasions seems to be traveling with the Apostle or for him (see Acts 20:4; Eph 6:21f; Col 4:7f; 2 Tim 4:12). *Nicopolis:* a city in the Roman province of Epirus on the west coast of Greece.

3:13 *Zenas . . . Apollos:* almost certainly the bearers of this Letter. Zenas is a coworker of Paul mentioned nowhere else. Apollos is the well-known Alexandrian

Jewish convert who was fully instructed at Ephesus and worked effectively in the Church of Corinth (see Acts 18:24-28; 19:1; 1 Cor 1:12; 3:4-6; 16:12).

3:14 *Urgent needs:* another possible translation is: "practical needs."

3:15 *Grace be with all of you:* some manuscripts have: "The grace of the Lord [or 'of God'] be with all of you. Amen." *All of you:* the plural form indicates that Paul intended the Letter to be read to the whole Church (see 1 Tim 6:21; 2 Tim 4:22).

THE LETTER TO PHILEMON

1-3 The salutation indicates that a group of Christians meets together in Philemon's house and should aid him to decide Onesimus' fate. These include Apphia, thought to be his wife, and Archippus, thought to be his son, who is also a pastor like Paul ("fellow soldier [of Christ]"). Under the circumstances, Philemon would have had to be an extremely strong-minded individual to resist the eloquent plea of Paul and his protégé Timothy.

1 *Timothy:* see Introduction to First Timothy.

2 *Archippus:* the apostolic worker mentioned in Col 4:17. *Fellow soldier:* the only other use of this phrase in the New Testament is in Phil 2:25 concerning Epaphroditus. It exemplifies Paul's use of military terms to symbolize the service of a Christian (see Rom 6:13; 13:12; 2 Cor 10:3f; Eph 6:10).

4-7 Recalling his friend's love and faith, Paul prays that Philemon's active participation in the Christian faith will be increased as a result of the latter's perception of God's great goodness to both of them. He is implying what he makes specific elsewhere—that good works are the result of a mature knowledge of the faith (see Col 1:9f). In this case, Philemon's Christian maturity will lead to the beneficial treatment of Onesimus at his hands.

5 *Saints:* all the faithful are "saints" in virtue of their consecration to Christ.

7 *Hearts:* literally, "intestines," the part of the body that was considered to house the emotions of pity and love (see vv. 12, 20).

8-20 With a touch of humor, Paul utilizes a double play on words. He plays with the meaning of the name "Onesimus," which is "useful," and with the meaning of another Greek word, *chrestos,* which is part of *achrestos,* the word for "useless," and *euchrestos,* the word for "useful." In the background is the point that *chrestos* sounds like *Chrestos,* which means "Christ."

Paul also takes the responsibility to relieve any financial burden that Philemon may have incurred in the affair, but he ends up saying that it is Philemon who is more indebted to the Apostle himself! Indeed, the slave's flight may turn out to be a grace—it offers Philemon the chance to acknowledge him as a "brother" in Christ.

10 *My child:* Paul became a father to Onesimus by converting him (see 1 Cor 4:15; Gal 4:19).

12 *My very own heart:* a wonderful description at a time when slaves were regarded as things.

15 Paul reasons that since he has found Christ, Onesimus is returning to Philemon as a beloved brother in Christ rather than as just a slave. Master and slave are now both brothers in Christ. Hence, for Philemon to treat Onesimus solely as a runaway slave would be entirely unfitting with his Christian witness.

16 *As a man:* literally "in the flesh."

17-19 Paul is doing the same thing for Onesimus with Philemon that Christ did for us with God the Father.

20 *Benefit:* the Greek for this word is another play on the name Onesimus: what Paul wishes to get out of the master is Onesimus himself; he wants to be able to make use of the Useful One.

21-25 The Apostle is confident not only that his request will be more than fully granted but also that he will soon have the joy of being reunited with Philemon. He thus sees hope for a quick release from imprisonment.

23 *Epaphras:* founder of the Church at Colossae, who may have been a tenant in the house in which Paul lived as a prisoner (see Acts 28:30).

24 *Mark, Aristarchus, Demas, and Luke:* see notes on Col 4:7-17; 4:10; and 4:14; also notes on 2 Tim 4:10; 4:11.

25 See note on Phil 4:23.

THE LETTER TO THE HEBREWS

1:1-4 From the opening words to the final "Amen" (Heb 13:21), readers are to keep their gaze fixed on Christ. In this magisterial sentence, "God . . . has spoken to us through his Son" (Heb 1:2), which is one of the most tightly packed and beautiful of the entire New Testament, the essence of the Letter is expressed.

God has spoken definitively in Christ, who is his real, living Word. Everything that can be said about the plan of God is made fully real in Christ. Using expressions taken from Alexandrian thought, the author says that the Son, born of the Father, is in every respect equal to him; the glorified Christ is far superior to the world of the angels, and he gives existence and salvation to every creature.

Thus, seven great theological themes are set forth: (1) *Theism:* God exists; (2) *Revelation:* God has revealed himself through the Prophets and through his Son; (3) *Incarnation:* God became man in Jesus Christ; (4) *Creation:* God created all things through Christ; (5) *Providence:* God upholds all things by his almighty word; (6) *Redemption:* by his mediatorship and his suffering Christ made salvation possible; and (7) *Ascension:* the Lord Jesus has ascended into heaven and sits at the right hand of the Father.

1:1 *Through the Prophets:* this refers not only to the Prophets but to all the writers of the Old Testament, for they constituted the preparation for the coming of Christ.

1:3 *Perfect expression of his very being:* that is, there is an identity of nature (see Wis 7:25-26).

1:5—2:18 How can God, who is inaccessible and transcendent, communicate with human beings? Are not intermediaries needed to establish the link between the heavenly world and the terrestrial one? This was a question that preoccupied many Jewish circles after the Exile. In reply they insisted on the role and importance of beings who were neither human nor divine: angels. They even imagined that the intervention of the angels was needed to bring the Law to Moses (see Heb 2:2; Gal 3:19). However, if it is necessary to multiply intermediaries between God and humans, does not this mean that humanity remains decisively distant from the Lord? The perspective is completely reversed when one speaks of Christ.

No one is like him in intimacy with God, neither is anyone like him in proximity to humans. The link between heaven and earth is established in his very Person. It is the principal aim of the Letter to the Hebrews to hold to these two aspects of Christ: he is united through and through with God, and he is completely one with human beings. In this first part of the Letter, he is presented as Son of God and brother to human beings.

1:5-14 In Christ God has spoken in a definitive way (Heb 1:2), and the author sees this truth already proclaimed in the Old Testament. He cites a series of passages, almost all of which were regarded in the Jewish tradition as announcements of the Messiah. What are angels? Merely subordinates, mediators, and messengers ever being replaced. But the Son is the Firstborn. This is the title of honor reserved for Christ that includes a priority over creatures (see Col 1:15). He receives adoration, is enthroned, and partakes unceasingly in the status of God.

1:5 *I will be his Father, / and he will be my Son:* before the coming of Christ, this text from 2 Sam 7:14 and the text of Ps 2 were acknowledged to be Messianic.

2:1-4 The Law of Sinai, which according to rabbinic tradition was communicated by angels, binds humanity to live in a certain way. Much greater is the authority of the voice of Christ transmitted to the Church by the Apostles with the evident guarantee of the Spirit (see Mt 10:1; Mk 16:20; Acts 1:8). This is the first of five warnings scattered throughout the Letter (the other four are: Heb 3:7—4:13; 5:11—6:12; 10:19-39; and 12:4-29).

2:5-18 The Son of God, who became a human being and was crucified, is Lord of the universe (see Phil 2:6-11); all human beings have been brought into solidarity with him. To throw light on this destiny of Christ, the author gives a free interpretation of Ps 8:5-7. Angels and institutions are incapable of establishing a bond between God and humanity; in Christ humanity is given one of its own, but one who is the true high priest (v. 17) and capable of being its guarantor in heaven. The principal theme of the Letter is here announced.

2:12 *I will proclaim your name to my brethren:* a quotation from Ps 22:23, a psalm that describes the sufferings of the Servant of God. The key phrase is "my brethren" (i.e., the Septuagint text; the Hebrew has "the community"), which is spoken by the triumphant Messiah.

2:14 *Flesh and blood:* i.e., the human condition.

3:1—5:10 The Covenant with Israel was entered into in the wilderness. Two great figures stood out: Moses and Aaron—the two mediators of the Law and sacrifice, of authority and worship. But when the work of Christ becomes known, all of that proves to have been provisional. And to speak of Christ the author develops two ideas: fidelity to God and solidarity or sympathy with humans. In between these two developments he inserts a long exhortation to serious Christians.

3:1-6 The fidelity of Jesus is greater than that of Moses. Both were "apostles," sent by God to the people, and "priests," i.e., representatives of the people before God. But Moses acted in the world as a servant who carries out a limited mandate. Christ accomplishes his work personally, in his own name, like a Son. This work belongs to him; and it is the community of believers that he establishes in the world of God.

3:7—4:11 Like Israel of the Exodus, the Church is on the march, on earth, certain of the promise of God but exposed to temptation. Since the Jewish people love to cling to the great epoch in the wilderness, the author invites them to profit from the lesson of that time—which is one of fidelity—offering them a commentary on Ps 95. His argument, which follows the exegetical methods of the time, may seem somewhat complicated. The generation of Hebrews delivered from Egypt did not enter the promised land because it rebelled against God (see Ex 17:1-7; Num 14:28-35). The memory of that rebellion remained alive in the Jewish tradition (see 1 Cor 10:1-11). Ps 95, which at that period was attributed to David, was written long after the Exile, when the perspective was no longer the conquest of Canaan. The promise to enter into the rest of God has not become something distant: it is deeply involved with the fulfillment of creation, with sharing today in the divine life by following Christ along the way he has opened up (Heb 4:14).

4:1-11 The first "rest" in Scripture was the one that God took on the seventh day of creation (see Gen 2:3). The second "rest" was the one God promised to the Israelites in Canaan, but which they were not allowed to enter because of their lack of faith (see v. 2 and Ps 95:11). The third "rest" was the one Jesus took upon entering the eternal sphere after completing the work of Redemption (see Eph 1:20; 2:6; 4:8). These "rests" foreshadow the ultimate "rest" that awaits all Christians (v. 11), provided they have a living faith in the person and work of Jesus.

4:12-13 The word of God is living and effective. It pierces into the most inner part of believers who open themselves completely to it. This dynamic word of God appears in both the Old and the New Testament (see Pss 107:20; 147:18; Isa 40:8; 55:11; Gal 3:8; Eph 5:26; Jas 1:18; 1 Pet 1:23).

4:14—5:10 Trait by trait, the portrait of the high priest is developed. It is fully verified only in Christ; moreover, we are now beyond the priesthood of Aaron and the earthly liturgy. Christ has set free his own; the Risen One who now lives forever expresses that compassion for humans to which he bore witness in his Passion. This priest is more one with human beings than Aaron was. He is established by God to perform more than a passing service for them. As Son and according to the order of Melchizedek (who will be spoken about later) he is engaged with all his person in his supplication and his sacrifice. The Passion is the most solemn prayer of intercession, the greatest act of obedience at the heart of humanity.

5:1 *To offer gifts and sacrifices for sins:* on the Day of Atonement (which the author is here envisioning), atonement was made for the sins of the Israelites (see Lev 16:34).

5:11—10:18 This is the central part of the letter. Its themes center around a single great idea: Christ, "high priest of all the good things that have come" (Heb 9:11), or "that are to come." The vision starts with the past and with a reflection on all the religious situations already experienced, then leaves them and focuses on their fulfillment: the future of humanity with God, in and with Christ. Proofs are piled up to show that this new priesthood transcends all the ancient institutions, brings them to fulfillment, and renders them things of the past.

The word "priest" is taken here in the sense used by the Old Testament and by religions of the time: the man of worship, the man who represents his brothers and sisters in ritual actions that will enable them to be purified and have access to the divinity. Jesus Christ appears as the only one who is the presence of the forgiveness of sin, the one who gives access to God, the representative of all that humanity expects from God. Every other priesthood and all other sacrifices are only a sketch, sign, shadow, prefiguration, and expectation. They are now surpassed. The ancient words and hopes are evoked to say more than they could have suggested without the faith in Christ.

5:11—6:12 The author warns his readers against regressing spiritually and morally. They must become "perfect"—what we would call "adults" or "mature." That is, they must not be content with the rudiments of faith but must deepen their faith by reflection. Six basic teachings are enumerated and apostasy is condemned. Finally, a note of hope is given. A life marked by love cannot be insignificant; and this love has a concrete expression: the service of the saints (Heb 6:10), i.e., the sustenance of the poor of the Jerusalem community (see Rom 15:25-31; 2 Cor 8:4; 9:1-15).

6:1-2 Six basic teachings are mentioned. (1) *Repentance:* turning away from the darkness of sin and useless rituals. (2) *Faith in God:* i.e., turning to the light of God. (3) *Instruction about baptisms:* e.g., Jewish initiation rites for proselytes, John the Baptist's baptism, and the Baptism commanded by Jesus. (4) *Laying on of hands:* a rite connected with ordaining or commissioning (see Acts 6:6; 13:3; 1 Tim 5:22; 2 Tim 1:6), with healing the sick (see Mk 6:5; 16:18; Lk 4:40; Acts 28:8), and with bestowal of blessings (see Mt 19:13-15). (5) *Resurrection of the dead:* the resurrection of all people in the end time (see Jn 5.25-29). (6) *Eternal judgment:* the lot of those who reject God.

6:4-8 The author asserts that repentance for apostates is impossible. However, he may be using hyperbole to impress on his readers that abandoning Christ is most serious.

6:13-20 In the beginning, before any law and any institution of worship, there were two immutable realities: God's promise and his oath. There were also two figures: Abraham and Melchizedek. The author wishes to stress one solid point: God committed himself radically to the future and salvation of human beings, a future and a salvation that become realities forever through Christ—as the following chapters will explain.

6:19 The veil separated the two most sacred parts of the Jewish temple.

7:1-28 A mysterious figure made his appearance in the story of Abraham: Melchizedek (see Gen 14:17-20), and Ps 110—which held a special place in Israel's meditation on the Messiah—speaks of a mysterious priesthood of the kind exercised by Melchizedek (v. 4). The Letter to the Hebrews says that those passages foretell the priesthood of Christ. Yet the priesthood of Christ cannot be measured by the same standard as the Jewish priesthood, because it renders the latter obsolete.

7:1-10 The figure of Melchizedek is full of symbols. His name means "king of righteousness"; his reign was one of "peace." Most unusually, the Bible gives us no chronological or genealogical information about him, naming neither his ancestors nor his descendants. His priesthood does not seem to be connected in any way with a hereditary line of priests, but only with his own person, as though it were something everlasting. And Abraham, to whom is given all the power to bless and the promises for Israel, receives a blessing from Melchizedek and offers him a tithe. All the more, then, does this priest stand above all the descendants of the Patriarch, and especially Levi, from whom descends all the Jewish priests whose standing the people acknowledge by paying them a tithe (see Lev 27:30-33; Num 18:21f). In the person of Abraham, they all bowed down to the mysterious priesthood of Melchizedek, who prefigured Jesus.

7:11-25 Jesus Christ, foretold by the person of Melchizedek, does not have a place in the priestly genealogies that were set up after Moses; his priesthood is based on the commitment of God himself, on the divine oath (vv. 20-22). He is the definitive mediator between God and humanity.

7:26-28 A first conclusion rises as a chant of freedom and a beautiful hymn to Christ. Perishable offerings are no longer anything but a symbol of self-giving already completed in reality: Christ alone can commit himself completely to God, become an offering, and in his very person be the representative of human beings before God. *The Son who has been made perfect forever:* Jesus, the Son, is God, and he shares the divine attributes, e.g., holiness (see v. 26; Jn 8:46; 2 Cor 5:21); eternity (see Mic 5:2; Jn 1:1; 8:58; 17:5, 24; Col 1:17); omnipotence (see Heb 1:3; Mt 28:18; Rev 1:8); omniscience (see Mt 9:4; Jn 6:64; 16:30; Col 2:3); immutability (see Heb 1:11f; 13:8); omnipresence (see Mt 28:20; Jn 3:13; Eph 1:23); creative power (see Heb 1:8, 10; Jn 1:3; 1 Cor 8:6; Col 1:16f); power to forgive sins (see Mk 2:5, 7-10; Lk 24:47; Jn 1:29; Acts 10:43; 1 Jn 1:7); the right to be worshiped (see Mt 8:2; Phil 2:10).

8:1—10:18 Speaking about a high priest means speaking about worship, the Covenant, the sanctuary, and sacrifices. Point by point, the author describes the practices of Jewish worship; in doing so his aim is to draw a radical contrast between them and the immense newness of Christ. Jesus not only excelled the Levitical priests in dignity; he also accomplished the true worship that surpasses all prestige from the ceremonial codified in the Law of Moses.

8:1-5 The author recalls some passages of the Bible (Ps 110:1-4; Num 24:6; Ex 25:40) to show that both the sanctuary in the wilderness and the sanctuary in Jerusalem were signs pointing to true worship, which consists in having access to God. As priest, Jesus acts at that level of reality and not at the level of signs.

8:4 By his human birth Jesus belonged to the tribe of Judah (see Heb 7:12-14), whereas priests were taken from the tribe of Levi (see Deut 18:1). Some scholars take the present tense of the verb "offer" as an indication that the temple was still standing in Jerusalem and so the Letter must have been written before A.D. 70 when the temple was destroyed by the Romans.

8:6-13 Israel was known as the people of the Covenant, the Covenant that was expressed in the Law and in worship. A text had been in circulation since the time of Jeremiah that was critical of the past and full of hope for a new future: it was the prophecy of the New Covenant, with which everyone was familiar (see Jer 31:31-34). The author cites it in its entirety (vv. 8-12). In this New Covenant the relationship between God and human beings will no longer be based on laws and institutions, but will have as its basis the person of Jesus Christ, mediator of a life-giving relationship with God (see 1 Tim 2:5).

The priesthood of Christ has given rise to the ministerial or hierarchical priesthood and the common priesthood of the faithful, which differ from one another in essence and not only in degree and each of which is a participation in the royal priesthood of Christ: "The ministerial priest, by the sacred power he enjoys, teaches and rules the priestly people; acting in the person of Christ, he makes present the Eucharistic Sacrifice, and offers it to God in the name of all the people. But the faithful, in virtue of their royal priesthood, join in the offering of the Eucharist. They likewise exercise that priesthood in receiving the Sacraments, in prayer and thanksgiving, in the witness of a holy life, and in self-denial and active charity" (Vatican II: *The Church,* no. 10).

8:8-12 The New Covenant is superior to the old because of the following: (1) God's laws are inner principles (v. 10a) enabling his people to carry out his will (see Ezek 36:26f, Rom 8:2-4). (2) God and his people enjoy an intimate fellowship (v. 10b). (3) There will nevermore be sinful ignorance of God (v. 11). (4) Forgiveness of sins will last forever (v. 12).

9:1-10 Once a year, on the Day of Atonement (see Lev 16:2-19; Ex 30:10), the high priest entered alone into the innermost part of the temple, the Holy of Holies. He poured blood on the altar to obtain forgiveness of sins. (For more details on the worship in the temple, see Ex 25—31 and 35—40.)

9:11-14 The whole of Jewish hope, which was revived on the Day of Atonement, now finds its definitive fulfillment in the Passover of Christ. His is the true sacrifice. This time, a human being sheds his own blood, i.e., willingly gives his life to God for the benefit of his brothers and sisters; this time, a human being purifies the human conscience from within by his obedience; this time, a human being has access to God. The risen Christ remains in this relationship of giving and presence, once and for all, definitively and eternally. There is no longer any other sacrifice to perform. This is the future, filled with "the good things that have come" (v. 11).

9:15-23 In the Jewish mind sacrifice and blood were reminders of atonement and Covenant (see Ex 24). The New Covenant is accomplished by the Paschal Mystery of Christ. In Greek, the word *diathêkê* signified both "covenant" and "testament"; it was easy to move from the one meaning to the other, as the author does in vv. 15 and 16.

9:24-28 Everything that could envisage priesthood, rites, and cults, without in fact obtaining them, is now a reality in Christ: sin is forgiven, access to God is available, reconciliation is realized, and the Paschal event is living, efficacious, and eternal. Christ, who offered himself, is at God's right hand for the benefit of human beings. There is no need of new sacrifices, and so he will not return for that but for the complete fulfillment of his promise of life and love.

10:1-18 The great, endless act of self-giving that extends through the entire existence of Christ is the authentic priestly act, the authentic sacrifice of Christ.

He takes away sin and restores the bond with God in his own person, in his own living experience. He founds the New Covenant, the new people who have access to God.

10:11-12 *Every priest stands to perform his ministry . . . Jesus . . . took his seat:* members of the Levitical priesthood always "stood" because their work was never finished; Jesus "took his seat" because his work was completed.

10:19—12:29 A definitive event has been realized for the world: the Death and Resurrection of Christ. The Letter to the Hebrews makes us aware of this by presenting it as the act of the authentic priesthood, the authentic sacrifice, while at the same time downgrading the status of the preceding religious regime, although that too had been established by God. So too faith in Christ is a decisive step forward in the life of a human being. The believer is henceforth engaged in a march toward the full encounter with the Lord. In the midst of temptations, fears, and risks, the Christian life is not a simple fidelity to a past but a thrust forward toward the future, toward God. These chapters are a pressing invitation not to let such perspectives be obscured.

10:19-25 The path that leads to God is a person, Christ recognized under the characteristics of a high priest. Once baptized, Christians are associated with the Son of God. They must strengthen their conviction and the links of mutual love. May the signs of crises be a call for them to prepare for the return of the Lord.

10:25 *The Day:* this refers to the Day of the Lord at the end of time.

10:26-31 Once again the author repeats this somber warning (see Heb 6:1-8; Mt 12:31). Those who rebel against Christ exclude themselves from Christ's forgiveness, from his life, and from his grace. Let them, therefore, meditate on the threats of God's vengeance about which the Bible speaks, and especially the texts cited here (see Ex 24:8; Deut 17:6; 32:35f; Isa 26:11).

10:32-39 As soon as they were baptized and enlightened, believers sacrificed everything for Christ and confronted all difficulties. Now is not the time for them to be discouraged. The Lord will come and he is the recompense for all who do not weaken. Faith is the courageous commitment to Christ.

10:32 *Been enlightened:* an ancient phrase for "been baptized"; "enlightenment" or "illumination" was an ancient term for Baptism (see Heb 6:4; Eph 5:14).

11:1-40 Before exhorting his readers to serve Christ, the author shows the importance and power of faith throughout sacred history. This is a magnificent chapter of Biblical theology that should inspire the courage of believers and urge them to read the Old Testament in order to give new vigor to the impulse of faith.

11:1 Theologians have often cited this sentence. Faith establishes human beings in the invisible and orients them toward the future, toward the fulfillment. The spiritual writer Charles Péguy affirmed: "The faith that I love most, says God, is hope."

11:4-40 Christian faith has firm roots in the Old Testament. Note v. 6, in which theologians have seen an assertion of the irreplaceable necessity of faith for salvation: the belief that God exists and has a personal relationship with human beings. The references to Biblical personages and the Old Testament citations are mainly from the Book of Genesis, from Exodus when speaking of Moses, and from Joshua and the following Books when speaking of the others. But the author adds non-Biblical details, such as the fate that legend attributed to Isaiah (v. 37). A similar list of heroes is found in Sirach (44:1—50:21).

11:4 *Abel:* see Gen 4:1-15. Christ himself referred to the righteousness of Abel (see Mt 23:35).

11:5 *Enoch:* see note on Gen 4:25—5:32 (last paragraph).

11:7 *Noah:* see Gen 5:28—9:29; Ezek 14:14.

11:8 *Abraham:* see Gen 11:27—25:11. The New Testament refers to this Patriarch as the exemplar of those who live by faith and as the father of all believers (see Rom 4:11f, 16; Gal 3:7, 9, 29).

11:11 *Sarah herself was barren:* probably refers to the fact that she was past the age of childbearing (see Gen 18:11f).

11:19 Isaac, who was to be sacrificed, was saved and came back from the dead, so to speak (see Gen 22); in this respect, he prefigured Jesus crucified and risen.

11:20 *Isaac:* see Gen 27:1—28:5.

11:21 *Jacob:* see Gen 47:28—49:33. *Each one of the sons:* both of Joseph's sons, Ephraim and Manasseh, received a blessing from Jacob; hence two tribes descended from Joseph whereas only one tribe descended from each of his brothers.

11:22 *Joseph:* see Gen 37:1—50:26.

11:23-28 *Moses:* see Ex 1—15; Acts 7:17-36.

11:30 *Jericho:* see Jos 6. The Israelites did not conquer the city through military action but merely followed God's instructions in faith (see 2 Cor 10:4).

11:31 *Rahab:* see Jos 2:1-24; 6:22-25; Mt 1:5; Jas 2:25.

11:32 All those mentioned in this verse held positions of power (Judges, Prophets, and one King) but none praised for anything but faith in God. They are given in pairs and out of chronological order, with the more important person mentioned first. *Gideon:* see Jdg 6—9; *Barak:* see Jdg 4—5. *Samson:* see Jdg 13–16; *Jephthah:* see Jdg 11—12. *David.* King (see 1 Sam 13:14; 16:1, 12; Acts 13:22) and Prophet (see Heb 4:7; 2 Sam 23:1-3; Mk 12:36); *Samuel and the Prophets:* Samuel was the last of the Judges and the first of the Prophets (see 1 Sam 7:15; Acts 3:24; 13:20); he anointed David as King (see 1 Sam 16:13) and was renowned as a man of intercessory prayer (see 1 Sam 12:19, 23; Jer 15:1).

11:33 *Mouths of lions:* e.g., Daniel in the lions' den (see Dan 6).

11:34 *Quenched raging fires:* e.g., Daniel's friends, Shadrach, Meshach, and Abednego, in the fiery furnace (see Dan 3).

11:35 *Their dead:* allusion to the two miracles worked by Elijah and Elisha (1 Ki 17:23; 2 Ki 4:36). *Tortured:* e.g., the Maccabean patriots of the second century B.C. (see 2 Mac 7).

11:37 *They were stoned:* e.g., Zechariah, the son of Jehoiada the priest, who was put to death for stating the truth (see 2 Chr 24:20-22; Lk 11:51). *Sawed in two:* an ancient Jewish tradition said that Isaiah was killed in this way by order of King Manasseh.

11:40 The saints of the Old Testament were able to reach the perfection of life with God only through Christ, who is "the resurrection and the life" (Jn 11:25f).

12:1-29 Christians have only one person on whom to keep their eyes as the object of faith and salvation: Christ (see Heb 11:26f; Acts 7:55f; Phil 3:8). They look to the Crucified Lord to understand how to behave at all times, and especially in difficulties and persecution.

12:1 *Surrounded by such a great cloud of witnesses:* the author may be thinking of an athletic contest in a large amphitheater wherein the heroes just mentioned are inspiring examples for us, urging us on to stand firm in the faith and even to martyrdom if need be.

12:5-13 God treats us as his sons and daughters. And the trials that we must withstand in order to make progress in the faith is another sign of this point for us. Hence, we must take heart.

12:14-17 Once again the author places their responsibilities before his hearers. They must not revert to the past by returning to Judaism. This would be tantamount to dishonoring the gift of salvation and perverting the atmosphere of the community.

12:18-29 The author alludes to the Covenant of Sinai, which was a fascinating and terrifying spectacle in the history of Israel (see Ex 19—20; Deut 4:11; 9:19). The New Covenant is a celebration of peace and festivity. Israel's way of life was only a figure for the conduct of the Church. Once people are gripped by the Covenant of grace, they cannot turn back toward an insufficient religion of yesteryear—that would be to show disdain for God. The Lord is "a consuming fire": the image evokes all at once his holiness, his demands, his judgment to the very depths of a being, and his hold that burns one's existence.

12:23 *Assembly of the firstborn:* either all the elect or the angels as the first creatures.

13:1-6 The Letter's conclusion opens with a series of recommendations concerning the conduct and attitude of Christians.

13:2 *Some have entertained angels without knowing it:* e.g., Abraham (see Gen 18), Gideon (see Jdg 6), and Manoah (see Jdg 13).

13:7-15 The remembrance of leaders, who perhaps confronted martyrdom, is a call to fidelity. It provides the author with the opportunity to insert a new development in the Letter. Christians must cling to the teaching received from their leaders and not to the doctrines of Judaism. They should, therefore, look to Christ; only in him and nowhere else will believers find what can evoke the altar or the sacrifice. If Christ suffered outside of Jerusalem and not in the temple, was that not perhaps a sign that the worship of Mosaic times must be replaced by the definitive worship, which is spiritual? Note three important verses in this section: v. 8, a splendid profession of faith in Christ; v. 14, the thrust toward the future and the realities that endure; and v. 15, life as praise of God (see Ps 50:14, 23; Hos 14:3).

13:10 *Have an altar:* an allusion to Eucharistic worship and sacrifice, compared with the Levitical worship and sacrifices of the Old Testament ("the tabernacle").

13:11 *Camp:* here, as in v. 9, the author uses the great Jewish rite of atonement as a point of comparison (see Lev 16:27).

13:12 Christ's death outside Jerusalem symbolized the removal of sin in the same way that the removal of the bodies of sacrificed animals outside the camp of Israel had done.

13:13 *Let us then go to him outside the camp:* this is a call to separate from Judaism. Just as Christ died in disgrace outside the city, so Christians should be willing to face scorn by leaving Judaism for Christ.

13:15 *Sacrifice of praise:* "sacrifice" here means an offering to God (see Rom 12:1; Phil 4:18). There is no longer need for animal sacrifices.

13:16-19 Christians will have to facilitate the task of the leaders of the community and to put their preoccupations in prayer, even when these leaders believe themselves obliged to remind them of the difficult demands of fidelity.

13:20-25 The author artfully summarizes his ideas and his concerns. The news that he gives seems to indicate that he is waiting for Timothy in order to visit Palestine with him. The mention of "those from Italy" can indicate that he is in a port in Italy or simply that he is surrounded by Italians in some city of the Empire.

13:23 *Timothy has been set free:* the event to which the author is referring is unknown to us

13:24 *Saints:* a term in use among the early Church for God's people, those who have been set apart as holy to the Lord (see note on Rom 1:7).

THE LETTER OF JAMES

1:1 Only this verse gives the writing the form of a letter. Concerning the author and the addressees, see the Introduction. *Servant:* see note on Rom 1:1. *Twelve tribes:* they prefigured the new People of God (see Acts 26:7; Rev 7:4).

1:2-4 The Christian is exposed to the opposition of society. *Joy . . . various trials:* a teaching based on the words of Jesus (see Mt 5:10-12; Jn 10:11).

1:5-8 A believer's prayer requires lucidity and courage to pursue a Christian way of life—that is, wisdom.

1:9-11 In becoming Christians, the rich lose their privileged position in society and the poor wait to be enriched by God. Both of them must live in the spirit of the poor of the Bible (see Ps 72:4, 12; Mt 5:3; Lk 1:52).

1:12 Those who bear trials patiently will go from distress to sharing the joy and life of the Lord.

1:13-15 The passage from trials to temptations reveals the depths of a person—and is one more reason to be vigilant.

1:16-18 Light and life are opposed to sin and death. They are the grace of the new birth through the Gospel and Baptism.

1:19-27 It costs nothing to place oneself among the distracted listeners and let oneself go to the demon of words for the sake of words. Hearing the Gospel for the sake of putting it into practice obliges one to notice the sufferings of others, to be concerned with truth, to cling to the Christian originality in the face of current mentalities and morals.

2:1-13 Remaining impartial is the most difficult as well as the most significant demand of the Bible and the Gospel. But even in the liturgical assembly notables are often honored because of their fortune and their culture, while the poor are sometimes put down. The Gospel cannot stand for such discrimination. On the contrary, it calls for all to be poor.

2:5 *Poor:* the poor of the Lord, who relied on God alone and were in turn loved by God and under his protection (see Ps 35:10; Isa 61:1; Mt 5:3; 11:5; Lk 6:20; 1 Cor 1:17-20).

2:14-26 The main concern of the Letter is expressed in this passage. The author attacks a faith that is satisfied with words and ideas that do not lay hold of one's existence and do not find expression in charity and prayer. Paul had said that salvation comes only through faith in Jesus Christ, but this is a faith that unsettles and transforms one's life (see Rom 3:28; Gal 2:16). Like him, James too gives Abraham, the model for believers, as an example, and at first sight the two writers seem to draw contrary conclusions. In fact, however, James regards Abraham's action as a gesture and expression of his faith; in this context, Paul speaks rather of the fruits of the Spirit (see Rom 12—14; 1 Cor 13:1; 4:20; Gal 5:13; 6:10). The two writers both cite Rahab, of whom the Book of Joshua speaks. The Letter of James by no means minimizes faith; rather it demands an authentic life.

2:15-16 These verses illustrate a faith that is faulty similar to the way 1 Jn 3:17 illustrates a love that is faulty. What is needed is a faith that is genuine, i.e., operative.

2:25 *Rahab the prostitute:* the author of the Letter is not intending to approve Rahab's occupation but simply to commend the faith she showed in helping the spies (see Jos 2; see also Heb 11:31).

3:1-12 What is more beautiful and what more ugly than the tongue? All the wisdoms of the world repeat it, and the sages of the Old Testament more than once issued denunciations against inconsiderate words (see Prov 10:9; 13:3; 15:1-4; 18:21; 21:23; Sir 5:11—6:1). Christ had spoken of the evil that comes forth from the mouth of man (see Mk 7:21-23). There is a kind of passionate outburst of words that disfigures society; with a word one can disrupt an assembly, with a lie break a friendship or unleash a rivalry—in short, destroy the world's harmony. We might say that an infernal power is at work; "Gehenna" was the cursed spot around Jerusalem that became a symbol for hell. The author is speaking especially to those who have the responsibility to teach in the assemblies. What a perversion it is to announce God's praise yet do harm to one's neighbor.

3:2 *Perfection:* so difficult is the tongue to control that those who are successful gain control of themselves in all other areas of life as well.

3:9 *In the likeness of God:* human beings are made in the likeness of God (see Gen 1:26f); hence, to curse them is tantamount to cursing God (see Gen 9:6).

3:13-18 There is a way of life and a concept of relationships that are inspired by a sense of God. There is another that is nothing more than the uncontrolled expression of passions. The Old Testament thus opposed wisdom and folly (see Prov 2:6; 8:22-31; Wis 7:22—8:1; Sir 1:1-4; 24:3-22). Paul distinguished between the fruits of the flesh and the fruits of the Spirit (see Gal 5:22-25). The Christian faith is transmitted by mildness, conciliation, goodness, and peace.

4:1-10 Troubles, unjust and murderous confrontations, and wars are the scourges of social life, and Christians share in them. Murderous passions are given free rein even in the community, creating antagonisms and divisions. The desire to possess and to monopolize things seems to be without limits and takes over the human heart. Hence, let all Christians question themselves about their innermost affiliation and choice. Do they really opt for God or do they live under the weight of their evil passions? When someone became unfaithful to God in the concrete, the Old Testament as well as Christ designated it as adultery (see Hos 3:1; Mt 12:39; 16:4). All these evils are the result of a failure to pray. True prayer is a drawing near to God, and it requires a reversal of mentality.

4:1 *Passions:* literally, "pleasures." The author is not saying that pleasures are evil in themselves; the evil consists only in the way they are used.

4:5 *He yearns jealously for the Spirit that he sent to live in us:* two other translations are possible (because James is citing a passage that does not appear in any extant Bible manuscript): "The Spirit he caused to live in us envies intensely" and "The Spirit he caused to live in us longs jealously." The meaning of the translation in the text is that God jealously longs for our fidelity and love (see Jn 4:4). The meaning of the first alternative translation is that because of the fall the spirit of man that was put in us at the Creation (see Gen 2:7) envies intensely—however, God's grace is able to overcome that envy (see Ex 20:5). The meaning of the second alternative translation is that it is the Holy Spirit who longs jealously for our full devotion.

4:11-12 Nothing is more current in the thoughts and conversations of human beings than passing judgment on others and slandering them. This is a usurpation. Only God can pass judgment, and it is he who has established a law—the law of love (see Lev 19:16-18; Mt 7:1-5).

4:13-17 This is a warning to those people who live only for the glory of their projects, the exploitation of others, and the lure of gain (see Mk 8:36). It reproduces the theme of human weakness (see Pss 39:5-7, 11; 102:3; Wis 2:4; 5:9-14), which obliges people to put their trust solely in God and not in self.

5:1-6 Here, we hear again the cries of the Prophets denouncing the injustice and inhumanity of riches (see Isa 5:8-10; Jer 5:26-30; Am 8:4-8); we also hear the voice of Christ placing us on guard against the danger of riches (see Lk 6:24; 18:24-27). The Bible has always seen the accumulation of goods as tarnished by some injustice. It instinctively feels how riches give birth to a type of person whose sense of his own human condition becomes warped and who loses sight of the proper relationship of fraternity and justice in regard to others.

5:7-11 For the Old Testament as well as for the New, the life of believers tends toward the final encounter with the Lord. The future of human beings does not rest in any terrestrial value in an absolute manner. It rests in God.

5:8 The expectation of the Lord's Second Coming (see 1 Cor 15:23) is the ultimate basis for Christian patience (see Jas 1:2—4:12; 1 Thes 3:13; 1 Pet 4:7; 5:10).

5:12 The Sermon on the Mount gives us the same recommendation in the same terms (see Mt 5:34-37).

5:13-18 The Church was to pay special attention to the sick. Catholic tradition sees in this passage a testimony to the Sacrament of the Anointing of the Sick. It was with an appeal to it that Pope Innocent I (in his Letter of March 19, 416, to Decentius, Bishop of Gubbio) justified the rite used in the Church and declared it to be a "Sacrament"; this doctrine was later solemnly defined by the Council of Trent despite the opposition of the Protestants (Session 14, November 25, 1551).

The reference to prayer ends with the example of Elijah. The Jewish tradition was familiar with several examples of Prophets who had interceded for the people (see Gen 18:22-32; Ex 32:11-14, 30-32). Elijah was a very popular figure both in Jewish tradition and in the early Christian tradition (which identified the coming Elijah with John the Baptist).

5:19-20 James regards the return of a straying brother to the truth as a real rescue from death (see Mt 18:12-13; 1 Jn 5:16). It would seem that the sins "covered," i.e., forgiven, are those of the brother who had gone astray (see 1 Pet 4:8) rather than those of the brother who brings him back to the truth (see Ezek 3:20-21; 1 Tim 4:16). In speaking of a "multitude of sins" James is perhaps including the sins of both (see Jas 2:13).

THE FIRST LETTER OF PETER

1:1-2 Christians regarded themselves as the true Israel and made use of the term Dispersion, which designated the Jews who had been dispersed and awaited the reunion of their people (see Jas 1:1). By divine choice, they are the New Covenant, evoked by the mention of the Blood of Christ (see Ex 24:3-8; Heb 9:12-14). Related to the three divine Persons, the Church is born of the Trinity. This is an extremely dense salutation.

1:1 *Peter:* see notes on Mt 16:18; 16:19; Jn 1:42. *Apostle:* see notes on Mk 6:30; Rom 1:1; Heb 3:1-6. *Exiles:* literally, "strangers" or "pilgrims," because the homeland and inheritance of the children of God are in heaven (see 1 Chr 29:15; Ps 39:13; Heb 13:14). *Living in Pontus . . . Bithynia:* Jewish and Gentile Christians living in Asia Minor.

1:2 *Chosen:* see note on Eph 1:3—3:21. *Father . . . Spirit . . . Jesus Christ:* all three persons of the Trinity are involved in the redemption of the Elect. *To be sprinkled with his blood:* in the Old Testament, the blood of a sacrificial animal was sprinkled on the altar and the benefit of the sacrifice descended on the offerer. The sprinkled blood of Christ brings us these benefits: (1) justification (see Rom 5:19); (2) sealing with God's Covenant promise represented for us in the Eucharist (see Lk 22:20); (3) cleansing of all sin (see 1 Jn 1:7); and (4) empowerment to become citizens of the Kingdom of heaven (see Heb 10:19).

1:3—2:10 The author stresses the privileges and responsibilities that come with salvation (the Greek word means "deliverance" or "preservation"). Salvation was prophesied in the past and achieved by God in Christ, and it calls for a life of holiness and love on the part of Christians, including the true worship of God, for they are a "nation of priests."

1:3-12 Adversity can do nothing in the face of the joyous certitude of believers. May they relive the fundamental experience of faith described in this grand praise. In Christ, the mercy of God gives human beings an inviolable faith that has no common measure with all human projects. The rebirth of Baptism opens another life and another history; a promise of salvation is on the way to being fulfilled. How then can Christ's personal love fail to take hold of hearts? The plan of God is not a theory but a reality in the life of each person. Today, the goal toward which all the expectations of the Prophets were directed, has become a reality and it brings about the joy of angels.

In this great passage of praise the fundamental experience of faith is described.

1:5 *The end of time:* i.e., the time of salvation, which is close at hand in the sense that it is certain; the glorious coming of Christ is the only really new thing to be awaited.

1:10 *This salvation was the subject of intense scrutiny and investigation by the Prophets:* the inspiration of the Prophets is attributed to the universal effectiveness of Christ, which works retroactively. The unity of the two Testaments is here highlighted.

1:11 *The Spirit of Christ:* the Holy Spirit is called thus because Christ sent him (see Jn 16:7) and ministered through him (see Lk 4:14, 18). *The sufferings that Christ would endure and the glories:* this is a theme found throughout the Bible (see Ps 22; Isa 52:13—53:12; Zec 9:9f; 13:7; Mt 16:21-23; 17:22; 20:19; Lk 24:26, 46; Jn 2:19; Acts 3:17-22; 4:12-16; 5:1, 4, 9f). Those who are united with Christ in everything, including suffering, will also be united with him in glory. And in the midst of their present sufferings they will benefit from the fact that he has already entered into his glory (see 1 Pet 2:3, 8, 21; 3:21f).

1:13—2:3 An existence given over to passions and inclinations is without meaning or real purpose. But Christians are delivered from insignificance; it is God who becomes their reason for living and its accomplishment. This is translated by a profound reversal of sentiments and behavior. Believers have a sense of God and his holiness, and they bear something of God's absoluteness in their existence. A life saved by the gift of Christ is an Easter. From then on, fraternal love becomes the goal. Thus, the Christian life is something new, a new birth, and a new destiny. It is developed by coming to maturity in one's reflection upon the word of God.

1:18-19 *Ransomed . . . with the precious blood of Christ:* i.e., bought back or redeemed in the way laid out in the Scriptures (see Ex 13:13; 21:30). Our need for being ransomed comes from our bondage to Satan and sin (see Jn 8:34; Rom 6:17, 23). Jesus has bought our freedom by paying not silver or gold but his own blood (see Eph 1:7; Rev 5:9), i.e., his Death (see Mt 20:28; Mk 10:45; Heb 9:15) or Christ himself (see Gal 3:13).

1:23 *Born anew . . . through the . . . word of God:* the Christian's new birth results from the action of the Holy Spirit (see Tit 3:5), but the word of God also plays an important part therein (see Jas 1:18). The latter presents the Gospel to us and summons us to repent and believe in Christ (see v. 25). *The living and enduring word of God:* another possible translation is: "the word of the living and enduring God."

2:4-10 The following terms—*spiritual temple, chosen race, royal priesthood, holy nation, a people claimed by God as his own possession*—were coined by the Old Testament to express Israel's awareness of itself as a people called upon to carry out God's plan. The Church regards herself as chosen by God and called to act in such a way that human life itself becomes a worship of God. This passage can be more profoundly understood by reflecting upon 1 Cor 3:16; Eph 2:20-22. In verses 9 and 10 citations from the Old Testament occur in this order: Isa 43:20-21; Ex 19:5-6; Hos 1:6-9; 2:23-24. These are reminiscences more than citations.

2:5 *Holy priesthood:* all who are united with Christ by faith share in the priesthood of Christ (see note on Heb 8:6-13).

2:8 *For this they were born:* the author states that by rejecting the Gospel, the people of the former Covenant have lost their prerogatives, which have now been given to the people of the New Covenant, i.e., Christians. The Scripture references in vv. 6-10 reflect the concern of early Christianity to explain Israel's unbelief in light of the Old Testament itself.

2:11—3:12 The author sets forth a few practical implications of what it means to be God's people in a hostile world. Christians are to be submissive to others—to civil authority, to masters, and to spouses in imitation of Christ's submissiveness. He ends up citing five virtues from Christ's life that should be of help to all.

2:11-12 Christians are to be on their best behavior in the midst of pagans even if for a time they are greeted with criticism and hostility because they do not accept the morals of the age. On the day of the Lord's arrival, everything will be made clear. While they wait for that day, Christians are on earth as a pilgrim people, i.e., they do not put their stamp of approval on any society and any culture.

2:13-17 Christianity is not subversive and does not oppose the organization of society on principle. The first persecutions were based on such accusations, and it is one more reason to stress their loyalty but also their sense of freedom. Political power has its ultimate foundation in God the Creator of human society, and not in the personality of those who govern (see Rom 13:1-7; Tit 3:1). In the Book of Revelation, the Christian attitude toward the imperial power will be less serene.

2:18-25 The first generations of Christians have above all the concern to spread the Gospel as the response to desire for salvation on the part of all people. The believers are only a handful. It would be a mistake to attribute to them the plan to develop a critique of the structures of society. But they themselves model new human and social relations. Many of them are slaves; in the Church, they are recognized as full Christians. This is one more reason not to lay oneself open to the accusation of insubordination that is leveled at these new communities. Hence, for the present moment, here is a way of living with service, even in conditions of injustice. The example of Christ imposes itself; it is interpreted here in magnificent terms by means of one of the great texts about the Servant of God (Isa 53:5-12). We should not interpret this text as presenting a doctrine of resignation. It calls for an attitude that refuses to respond to injustice with hatred or duplicity (see Eph 6:5-9; Col 3:22-25; 1 Tim 6:1-2; Tit 2:9-10).

2:21-25 The example of Christ is obvious; it is here interpreted in grandiose terms by means of the great text on the Servant of God in Isa 53:5-12.

2:22 *He committed no sin . . .:* Christ was absolutely sinless (see Acts 3:14; 2 Cor 5:21; Heb 4:15; 7:26; 1 Jn 3:5).

2:25 *The shepherd and guardian of your souls:* the sheep had wandered from their shepherd (Christ), but now they have returned to him. Thus, the Suffering

Servant, vindicated in the Resurrection (see Isa 52:13; 53:11), becomes the Good Shepherd (see Jn 10:11; 13:10). For "shepherd" in the Old Testament, see Ps 23; Isa 40:11; Ezek 37:24.

3:1-7 How does one's Christianity affect the way that one lives family life? The main problem is the difficult one of the wife who converts but is not followed by her husband. Let her not seek to put pressure on him, but let her give him the witness of a Christian wife whose gentleness and silence are in contrast to agitation and vanity.

A Christian husband is asked to regard his wife as a believing Christian in all respects, to understand feminine psychology, and to show great sensitivity of heart (see 1 Cor 7:12-15; Eph 5:32-33; Col 3:19).

3:3-5 The author does not prohibit the use of jewelry and other adornments but stresses the fact that the greatest adornments are spiritual ones.

3:7 *An equal heir of God's gift:* both spouses in a marriage have received the same gift from God. Hence, there should be mutual respect and love between them (see Eph 5:33; Col 3:19).

3:8-12 Mutual love of Christians is expressed in a new type of social relations and inner attitudes that lead up to evangelical behavior (see Lk 6:28; Rom 12:9-20).

3:13-17 Persecution must not come as a surprise to believers; it is their lot according to one of the Beatitudes of the Gospel (see Mt 5:10), almost repeated here word for word. Thus, Christians follow the example of Christ, ready to justify their hope but refusing to retaliate with hatred and violence. They are not enemies of society or other people, a crime that has apparently already been leveled at them.

3:18—4:6 The author presents the vision of a new world. Christ's Death and Resurrection have been victorious over sin; the risen Lord dominates the universe and all the good or evil forces in it, e.g., angels, dominations, and powers. Christ truly died and was in the sojourn of the dead, as the New Testament more than once attests (see Mt 12:40; Acts 2:31; Rom 10:7; Eph 4:8-10).

The intent of this passage is probably to say that nothing human or cosmic can be excluded from the Redemption that Christ effected. It is in this sense that we are to understand the article of the Creed that speaks of Christ "descending into hell." The story of Noah (see Gen 6:1—7:4) is interpreted as a saving of the righteous and a destruction of sin; it seems to be taken as a symbolic anticipation of Baptism, which at the time was received by immersion.

3:18-19 *In the spirit. . . . In the spirit:* another translation possible is: "by the Spirit . . . through which."

4:5 *Him who stands ready to judge:* the New Testament assigns judgment to both the Father and the Son on the last day (see Jn 5:27; Acts 17:31). *The living and the dead:* i.e., those who are alive as well as those who have died when the last day arrives.

4:7-11 Living in expectation of the Lord's Second Coming, Christian communities are characterized by a serious atmosphere, by relationships of responsibility and fraternity, and by concern for prayer and the Liturgy.

4:12-19 Hostility seems to be unleashed against the communities. We will always be astounded by the conviction of the first Christian generations in the face of persecution. They do not regard it as a strange fate but as something that indicates the arrival of a new age, that of the last times of history. It announces a change in the course of the things of the world. The destiny of Christ is not only an example to consider but a mystery to share in these conditions. However, the persecution in question must be a real one against the faith and not a reaction against the abuses committed by Christians themselves. Concerning the necessity of persecution and the meaning of the announcement of a change, see Mt 5:11-12; Lk 6:22-23; 21:12-19.

4:12 *Fiery ordeal:* literally, "fire for testing." Suffering is a source of purification.

4:14 *Spirit of glory:* because the Spirit bestows glory after trials.

4:15ff There is suffering that believers bring down upon themselves by their own sins and weaknesses and suffering that God allows to afflict them. In both instances, they should entrust themselves to God and offer their sufferings to him.

4:16 *Christian:* this word occurs only here and in Acts 11:26 in the New Testament.

5:1-4 The presbyters (or elders) exercise responsibilities in the life of communities (see 1 Tim 5:17; Tit 1:5-9). However, authority always experiences the temptation to exercise power for its own profit. This should not be the case in a Christian group. We might recall the word of Jesus: "I am in your midst as one who serves" (Lk 22:27). On this subject, we could also read Paul's reflection to the elders of the region of Ephesus (see Acts 20:28-35).

5:1 *Presbyters:* the official teachers of the Christian community (see 1 Tim 5:17f; Tit 1:5-8; Jas 5:14). *Witness to the sufferings of Christ:* Peter had been a witness of all the phases and aspects of Christ's ministry, including his suffering (see Mt 26:58; Mk 14:54; Lk 22:60-62; Jn 18:10-11, 15-16).

5:5-11 Nothing is more opposed to the Gospel than pretense and pride; hence this Letter insists on attitudes of submissiveness. It also recommends that Christians remain steadfast in the spiritual combat—which is more difficult to do in this context of threats—in order to achieve true victory. It is from God himself that believers await the courage. *You who are younger:* these may simply be the faithful distinguished from their leaders.

5:12-14 The Letter is doubtless written at Rome, the "Babylon" of the age (see Introduction). *Silvanus:* one of Paul's coworkers (see 1 Thes 1:1; 2 Thes 1:1; 2 Cor 1:19) also known by the name of "Silas" (see Acts 15:22; 17:4).

5:13 *Your sister Church:* literally, "Your chosen sister." *Mark:* an occasional companion of Paul (see Acts 12:25; 2 Tim 4:11) and probably the author of the second Gospel.

5:14 *Kiss:* on the liturgical kiss, see 1 Cor 16:20. *Peace to all of you who are in Christ:* in concluding, the author stresses a basic theme of the Letter—the union of believers with Christ.

THE SECOND LETTER OF PETER

1:1-2 From the very first words, the author addresses believers, those who have received salvation or righteousness. He insists on faith and on knowledge of the Lord, the Christ.

1:1 *Simon Peter:* see notes on Mt 16:18; 16:19; Jn 1:42. *Servant:* see note on Rom 1:1. *Apostle:* see notes on Mk 6:30; Rom 1:1; Heb 3:1-6. *To those:* probably the same addressees as in 1 Pet 1:1.

1:2 *Knowledge:* a key theme of the Letter (see 2 Pet 1:3, 5, 8; 2:20; 3:18), probably to combat the claims of the Gnostics.

1:3-11 Christianity is not just another religious theory among those that are actually in vogue. To believe is to place oneself personally under the very action of God and to know that the destiny of human beings is accomplished in his eternal Kingdom. Christians live in communion with God; the earthly dimension does not suffice for them. And these great realities are not mere words; they demand a radical change in the manner of conceiving one's destiny and conducting one's existence. Thus, regardless of the historical distance from the time of its foundation, the Christian life constitutes a new state of existence.

1:4 *Share in the divine nature:* an expression found only here in the Bible. The author uses it to express the fullness of divine life in Christ (see Jn 1:12; 14:20; 15:4f; Rom 6:5; 1 Cor 1:9f; 1 Jn 1:3b).

1:5-9 The author lists the virtues that are needed for a genuine Christian life.

1:9 This is similar to the warning in the Johannine Letters against the Gnostics (see 1 Jn 1:8f), who claimed to know God without keeping the commandments.

1:11 *Kingdom of . . . Christ:* it is also the Kingdom of the Father (see Eph 5:5; 2 Tim 4:1; Rev 11:15).

1:12-18 The testimony of an Apostle has a greater value than any arbitrary Gnostic speculation.

To emphasize this point, the author presents his work as a testament of Peter, who reminds the readers that the Lord had told him of his proximate death (see Jn 21:18-19) and insists above all on the fact that he had been a witness of the Transfiguration (see Mt 17:1-13; Mk 9:2-13; Lk 9:28-36), an event that bore witness to the glory of Christ and thereby guaranteed his glorious Return, which was being challenged at this time.

1:13 *Body:* literally, "tent."

1:14 *My death:* literally, "the time for laying aside this tent."

1:19-21 While awaiting the great Day of fulfillment, Scripture constitutes the light on the human journey. It cannot be handed over to the arbitrary interpretations of teachers of fortune who construe it in their own peculiar way; the inspiration of the Spirit must be respected.

1:21 *Under the inspiration of the Holy Spirit:* see note on 2 Tim 3:16. Both God and the authors were active in producing Scripture: God was the source of the content, but the writers used all their talents to set that message down.

2:1-22 The portrait of the false teachers is drawn in living colors. They deny Christ and his salvation, disfigure the Gospel's grand ideas about life, and seek their own profit and personal success. They "are not afraid to insult celestial beings" (v. 10)—either the angels or the evil powers whom they claim the right to judge although this right belongs to the Lord. The teachings of the Gnostics multiply theories about the heavenly beings. But these lofty speculations do not prevent them from being propagators of immorality; the author likens them to Balaam, who at this time had become the prototype of the false, venal, and corrupting teacher (see Num 22:2—24:25; Deut 23:5; Rev 2:14-15); all of their preaching focuses only on false freedom, enslavement, and degeneracy. Despite all this, these teachers of falsehood call themselves Christians.

The notice of their fate is severe. The author recalls the great chastisements of the past, the fall of the heavenly beings, the Flood, the unforgettable cursed cities of Sodom and Gomorrah, and the story of Balaam. These illustrations are taken from ancient Biblical accounts (see Gen 6:1-2; 6:5—8:22; 19:1-29; Num 22:2—24:25). Above all, the author wishes to exhort the believers to stand firm in their faith so that they will be spared on the day of judgment, as were Noah and Lot. Once in a while people have need of such efficacious admonition in order to take stock of their spiritual life.

2:4 The Bible gives no details on the sin of the angels. *The dark abyss* or Tartus: the term used by the Greeks for the place where the most wicked spirits were imprisoned.

2:5 *The ancient world:* the world before the Flood.

2:11 *In the Lord's presence:* some manuscripts have: "from the Lord."

2:13 *Receiving the penalty:* some manuscripts have: "receiving a reward." *In their pleasures:* some manuscripts have: "in their love feasts."

2:14 *Accursed brood:* literally, "children of a curse."

2:15 *Balaam, the son of Beor:* see Num 22—24. Even though God had forbidden Balaam to curse Israel, Balaam was intent on doing it because he wanted the money he had been promised by Balak. In the same way, the false teachers wanted to extract money from those who listened to them.

2:19 *Freedom . . . depravity:* the "scoffers" use "freedom" to divest themselves of the moral law. But it is faith in Christ that leads to good behavior and true freedom (see Rom 6:15; Jas 1:25; 1 Pet 2:16).

2:22 *The dog . . . vomit:* see Prov 26:11. *The washed . . . mud:* its source is unknown. The dog that returns to its own vomit and the sow that is washed portray people who have made a religious profession or outward change without an inner change that affects their nature. They soon return to their true nature.

3:1-10 We know the spectacle of an immutable universe; the days fly by and the seasons return. Could the fate of the world change someday? Christians of that day are loath to think of it and quick to deny it. To eliminate this uncertainty, the author first of all recalls the teaching of the Prophets, the Apostles, and Christ himself about the end of the world. Furthermore, in the Bible there are two or three passages that make us reflect: the manner in which the cosmos rises in the midst of the initial disorder as well as the drowning of everything at the Flood; hence, our world does not have the promises for eternity.

What then is the reason for the long delay. There are two reasons: first, the Lord does not count time as we do; above all, his mercy is immense and he awaits the conversion of everyone. But the announcement of the end remains such as was taught by the Gospels (see Mt 24:43; Lk 12:39-40; 1 Thes 5:2). In the face of the unforeseeable character of history and the unforeseeable plan of God, there is the temptation to take refuge in the name of the perpetuity of the cosmos.

3:4 *Our ancestors:* the faithful of the first Christian generation.

3:5-7 God created the world by his word, and that word will be just as active in the final conflagration.

3:10 *The Day of the Lord . . . a mighty roar:* this "Day" is also mentioned in Acts 2:20, 1 Cor 5:5, and 1 Thes 5:2 and refers to Christ's Second Coming, repeating the sayings of the Prophets (e.g., Joel 2:1; Zeph 1:7). This coming is certain, but the time is known only to the Father (see Mk 13:32). It will arrive suddenly, unexpectedly, and without warning (see 1 Thes 5:1-3), ushering in the solemn judgment (see Acts 17:31). *The heavens will disappear with a mighty roar:* this is apocalyptic, figurative language like that of the Books of Daniel and Revelation.

3:11-16 What is it that is delaying the coming of the Messiah? The sins of human beings. This is what many thought among the Jewish circles, and our author shared that conviction. He wishes above all to encourage Christians to stand fast and make progress in the faith. Their eyes are not fixed on a hazy horizon; rather, they live from the promise of an unimaginable renewal of humankind and the world through the Christ who comes.

3:12 *Day of God:* synonymous with "Day of the Lord." The idea of a final conflagration, found only here in the New Testament, was common in apocalyptic writings and in Greco-Roman thought.

3:13 *New heavens and a new earth:* promised by Isaiah (65:17; 66:22) and confirmed by Revelation (21:1).

3:15 *Your opportunity to be saved:* literally, "salvation."

3:16 *Speaking of it:* the teaching just set forth in this Letter, which is also found in Paul: God's saving will (see Rom 2:4; 9:22f; 1 Cor 1:7f); Christ's return (see 1 Thes 4:16f; 1 Cor 15:23-52); getting ready for the judgment (see Col 1:22f; Eph 1:4-14; 4:30, 5.5-14); God's just judgment (see Rom 2:5-9); and God's forbearance as time to repent (see Rom 2:4). *Other Scriptures:* this comparison of Paul's Letters with the rest of Scripture indicates that Christian writings are on a par with the Old Testament Books (see 2 Pet 1:21; 2 Tim 3:16).

3:18 *Grow in . . . knowledge:* the author closes by stressing knowledge once more (see note on 2 Pet 1:2). *To him be glory:* this doxology corresponds to the one in 1 Pet 5:11.

THE FIRST LETTER OF JOHN

1:1-4 An identical movement of life is transmitted from the Father to the Son, from the Son to his witnesses, and from his witnesses to believers. And the authenticity of this sharing is guaranteed by the real contact of the witnesses with the Son of God, the Word of Life (see Jn 1:1), the Messiah who is truly man. The Christian faith starts from a fact, an event, an experience. Thus, everything appears as a movement from God and a striving toward him, a fellowship of life. Without such an insertion in the bonds of the Church and this link with a real testimony, it would be vain speculation.

This Prologue deals with the same themes and makes use of the same words as the Prologue to John's Gospel (*beginning, Word, life*).

1:1 The Word of God was the source of life (see Deut 4:1; 32:47; Mt 4:4; Phil 2:16). John gives the title "Word" to the Son of God become man with whom the Apostles lived. Thus, they became eyewitnesses of his glory. They touched him and knew he was real. They heard him with their ears as he spoke the words of life. Everything they preached and wrote about him was based on fact.

1:2 *That life . . . the eternal life:* i.e., Christ. He is called "life" because he is the living one who has life in himself (see Jn 11:25; 14:6). He is also the source of life and sovereign over life (1 Jn 5:11). This Letter begins and concludes (1 Jn 5:11) with the theme of eternal life.

1:3 *Fellowship* (or communion): the word expresses one of the most important themes in Johannine mysticism: the unity of the Christian community, based on the oneness of each believer with God in Christ. This unity is described in the figures of the vine and the branches (see Jn 15:1-5) and the body and the head (see 1 Cor 12:12; Col 1:18). It also finds expression in various formulations: Christians "abide in God and God in them"; "they are born of God"; "they belong to God"; "they know God." Such a union with God is manifested in faith and fraternal love.

1:5-7 There is no fellowship with God in the absence of faith or love. Christians do not achieve fellowship with God the Light (see Jn 8:12) by giving themselves over to Illuminism or by some magical rite; they do so by believing in the Redemption brought about by Christ's Passion and by living in the truth (see Jn 3:31), i.e., by entering into a life experience that keeps the commandments of the Gospel in a concrete manner.

1:5 *Light . . . darkness:* light represents all that is good, true, and holy, whereas darkness stands for all that is evil and false (see Jn 3:19-21).

1:8—2:2 Christians do not live in some superior spiritual sphere far removed from our daily lives on earth. We must in all honesty acknowledge that sin is present in our lives with all its weight. If we do not do so, we oppose the whole experience attested by Scripture and render insignificant the voluntary sacrifice that Christ made of himself so that human beings might have life. Deliverance from sin is obtained not by evasion but by the act of God who forgives and justifies us in the very depths of our being.

2:3-11 Gnostics claimed to possess a special revealed "knowledge." But John stresses that there is a real and living knowledge of God, a true light, an authentic truth, and it is expressed in a life that is lived in accord with the commandments of God. Its great characteristic is love. New doctrines are being put forth. Christian teaching is a commandment of Jesus, which in this sense is old. Yet it is also new because it is revealed in Jesus as a fact as well as in the life of believers. In the face of everything that is without purpose or sense, faith is a ray of light, a victory over darkness, a bright dawn for the world.

2:4 John reiterates the testimony of Paul and James about faith and works. James said that faith without works is dead (see note on Jas 2:14-26). Paul indicated that rewards would be based on good and bad deeds (see 2 Cor 5:10; see also note on Rom 4:3). John says that Christians who do not keep the commandments of Jesus are liars and the truth is not in them. For faith in Christ without good deeds, i.e., keeping the commandments, is not authentic.

2:7-8 *New commandment:* see Jn 13:34f. The Biblical commandment to love was old (see Lev 19:18; also Mt 22:39-40). However, its newness is seen in (1) the new illustration of love on the Cross, (2) Christ's exposition of the Old Testament law (see Mt 5), which appeared to be new to those who heard it; and (3) the everyday experience on the part of believers as they grow in mutual love.

2:12-17 The author addresses all with affection: "Dear children," as he says. He wants to answer every one of them—the old as well as the young. He recalls that Christians are set free from sin, that they are the vanquishers of the power of evil, personified in the Bible as the devil, "the evil one." This victory is attained by the action of God and not by adhering to the speculations that are being spread about. Adhering therein is the "world"—a term that refers to all that is opposed to God. The fourth Gospel had already accustomed us to this language that opposes God to the world and light to darkness. The author wishes to speak thereby of all the limitations of the human, e.g., unregulated desires, the need to possess, and the satisfaction of extravagance. In the face of this seduction that troubles every existence, believers can stand fast only by a life marked profoundly by the word of God.

2:16 The author here defines three great sins of worldliness: *the concupiscence of the flesh, the concupiscence of the eyes, and the pride of life.* The first has to do with inordinate desire for sensuality (see Eph 2:3; 1 Pet 2:11; 2 Pet 2:10, 18). The second has to do with covetousness, which springs from the eyes and has to do with the desire for things (see Job 31:1; Ezek 23:12-17; Mt 5:27ff). The third has to do with worldly ambition, ostentation, pride and arrogance, independence of God (see Ps 10:4; Prov 16:5; Isa 13:11; Lk 1:51, 52; Jas 4:6, 10; 1 Pet 3:8; 5:5).

2:18-28 New teachers have arisen proclaiming a message different from that of the Gospel of Jesus. Is this not a sign that the end is near? The circumstances that Jesus had described in this respect (see Mk 13:22; see also 2 Thes 3:4; Rev 13:12-15) suddenly appear to be present. It is at least a time of crisis. The false teachers refuse to acknowledge either Christ or the Father, and they do away with the Gospel. The author is quick to set these teachers straight: those who do not accept the Gospel are no longer in the Church in spite of all appearances. Believers should cling to the teaching they originally received, i.e., to the great ideas of Christian initiation, for what is at issue is the Word of Jesus. They have been *anointed by the Holy One,* that is, they are penetrated by the word and the grace of Jesus. Let them not be concerned with new words and new teachings but be alert to await the Lord's coming.

2:18 Scripture distinguishes the *Antichrist* from many *antichrists* and from *the spirit of the Antichrist* (1 Jn 4:3). Here John is speaking of all who follow the Antichrist and imitate his evil spirit. He assumes that his readers know that a great enemy of his people will arise before Christ's return. This enemy is the *Antichrist,* "the man of lawlessness" (see notes on 2 Thes 2:3b-12 and 2:3b-4) and "the beast" (Rev 13:1-10). But before his coming there will be many antichrists characterized by (1) denial of Christ's Incarnation (see 1 Jn 4:2; 2 Jn 7) and Divinity (see 1 Jn 2:22); (2) denial of the Father (see 1 Jn 2:22); (3) non-possession of the Father (see 1 Jn 2:23); (4) falsehoods (see 1 Jn 2:22), deceptions (see 2 Jn 7); (5) many in number (see 1 Jn 2:18); (6) nothing in common with believers (see 1 Jn 2:19).

2:20 *Anointed by the Holy One:* reference to the Spirit who has been given to the Messiah (see Isa 11:2; 61:1), and then conferred by the Messiah on believers (see 1 Jn 3:24; 4:13; 2 Cor 1:21) so as to teach them about all things (see 1 Jn 2:27; Jn 16:13f; 1 Cor 2:10, 15). As a result, the words of Jesus are "spirit and life" (Jn 6:63).

2:29—3:3 The author takes ideas already expressed and develops them in new ways. In ch. 1:5-7 he used the phrase "God is light"; now he expresses the new theme that "God is righteous." God forgives human beings, bestowing upon them a condition in which they can stand before him. Here, too, it is not a question of abstract ideas but of life practices. What a bold affirmation about the Divine Sonship, what a dizzying perspective of a faith that must one day go beyond itself in the full vision of God!

3:4-10 Breaking away from sin does not take place by delighting in sublime thoughts but by the action of God in Jesus Christ. For it is Christ alone who is without sin (see Jn 8:26). And it is not words but deeds that bear witness to this liberation. To what options or influences does our life cling? Is it in the grip of the devil or does it cling to the word of God? Certainly, sin is part of the daily life of believers (1 Jn 1:8-10), but we are speaking about the fundamental and general choice between sin and righteousness. Which do we choose?

3:6 *Whoever remains in him does not sin:* the author is not speaking about sinless perfection (see 1 Jn 1:8—2:1). He is simply asserting that the life of believers is dominated not by sin but by doing the right thing.

3:9 *His seed:* a reference to Christ (see 1 Jn 5:18; Gal 3:16) or to the Holy Spirit (see 1 Jn 2:20-27) or to the seed of Divine life that God introduced into us.

3:11-24 There are two attitudes toward life—hate and love, murder and the offering of one's life. Cain is the Biblical prototype of all the homicidal impulses that arise in the human heart (see Gen 4; Heb 11:4); these come together in what the author's language terms "the world." This symbolizes death. Christian behavior—which is life, love, and offering of self—draws us away from the world. Christ gives us both the power to do so and the example to follow in the concrete reality of his Passion. Believers must do likewise. They can count on God's mercy. Verse 23, which expresses the whole intent of the Letter, brings out clearly the mind of the author in regard to the growing Gnosticism.

3:18 Like James, John insists on the value of good works. Love is not a mere matter of lip service; it must be seen and known in actions. Beautiful words are meaningless if they are not accompanied by good deeds.

3:22 Believers who have a good conscience desire nothing that is contrary to God's honor and glory. They will trust in God, who will give them the good things they request (see Ps 84:12).

3:23 This commandment has two parts: (1) belief in Christ (see Jn 6:29) and (2) love for one another (see Jn 13:34f). The Letter develops part one in 4:1-6 and the second part in 4:7-12.

4:1-6 We must learn to discern the thoughts of human beings—the "spirits." Among the teachers and theorists that had appeared at this time there were those who did not acknowledge Jesus as the Lord and Savior and wished to impose their views on the Christian communities. John says that this is perversion, the appearance of false christs of the end times (see 1 Jn 2:18-22). He strengthens believers by telling them that they do not belong to the world, i.e., this universe that delights in its limitations and its own insignificances. They must believe in the Gospel of God proclaimed by the witnesses who have been sent, among whom he places himself by saying "We are from God" (v. 6).

4:2 *Jesus Christ has come in the flesh:* see note on 1 Jn 1:1. John excludes the Gnostics, especially those known as Cerinthians, who taught that the Divine Christ came upon the human Christ at his Baptism and left him at the Cross—thus claiming that only the man Jesus died.

4:4 *From God:* another expression for "born of God" (1 Jn 2:29; 3:9). *The one who is in the world:* the devil (see Jn 12:31; 16:11).

4:6 *Spirit of truth . . . spirit of falsehood:* this refers to the theme of the two spirits, which is similar to the theme of the two ways (see Deut 11:26; Mt 7:13-14). Confronted by two worlds, those who live on earth choose one or the other by partaking of the spirit of either one (see 1 Jn 3:8, 19). However, those who choose the right one (*the spirit of truth*) will attain certain victory (see 1 Jn 2:13f; 4:4; 5:4f).

4:7-21 There are splendid pages in the Bible that speak of what love is—for example, Paul's hymn on love (1 Cor 13) and this text. The whole theology of love is developed in these verses, which give us the deepest understanding of Christianity as a great movement of life and experience, and not an abstract speculation. Love is reality: i.e., in God; it is witnessed to in an experience: i.e., in Christ; and it is expressed in the reality of fraternal love: i.e., among believers.

God and love: the two words go together, just as do knowledge of God and fraternal love. The living discovery of God does not take place in plumbing the most compelling ideas but in becoming like Christ, in the experience of fraternal love. Without this, no fellowship with God is possible. Fraternal love and faith in Christ go together; and this experience enables us to verify the value of every religion and every spirituality. Nothing else can deliver human beings from the fear of judgment.

4:7-8 *Love is from God:* hence, those who love God show that they are born of God. *God is love:* i.e., he is loving in his essential nature and in all his actions. The Gospel of John also affirms that God is spirit (see Jn 4:24) and light (see Jn 1:5) as well as true and just, powerful, holy, and faithful.

4:10 It was God who first loved us when we had no love for him or even for ourselves (see Rom 5:6-10). He showed his love by sending his Son to atone for our sins (see 1 Jn 2:2). This is the motive for our love for one another.

4:13 *A share in his Spirit:* this is the Spirit promised for the Messianic Age (see Acts 2:17-21, 33); he has been poured out into our hearts (see Rom 5:5; 1 Thes 4:8) and brings forth in us the inner certainty that the Apostles proclaimed outwardly (see 1 Jn 5:6f; Acts 5:32)—in this case about the Divine adoption of Christians (see Rom 8:15f; Gal 4:6).

5:1-12 In opposition to the fantasies spread about by the false teachers, John insists that there is no knowledge of God without an acknowledgment of his Son and acceptance of his commandments and his Gospel. There is no victory over the world (the forces of evil and human limitations) without adherence to Christ. There is no finding God except through the testimony in which he makes himself present: in Jesus Christ who offers his life for the world. Baptism and the Spirit are nothing if the blood is forgotten, for Redemption, the Paschal Mystery, and the Eucharist are the heart of faith. God's self-revelation includes the entire life of Jesus from his Baptism to his Cross: the water and the blood (see Jn 19:34). Hence, there is no knowledge of God that does not transform itself into faith in his Son and in the acknowledgment of other human beings as brothers and sisters because they are God's children.

5:6 John is answering the false teachers who claimed that Jesus was born only a man, then at his Baptism the Son of God descended on him, but he left Jesus before the latter's death on the Cross; therefore, it was only the man Jesus who died. In keeping with his teaching throughout the Letter that Jesus is God as well as man (1 Jn 1:1-4; 4:2; 5:5), John emphasizes that Jesus was Son of God all the time. This is a key point because if Jesus had died only as a man, his atonement would not have been enough to take away the sins of human beings.

5:7 *Three:* the Scriptures required three witnesses (see Deut 17:6; 19:15; 1 Tim 5:19). In many manuscripts the text has been amplified; thus the post-Tridentine Vulgate has: "There are three witnesses *in heaven: the Father, the Word, and the Spirit, and these three are as one: there are three witnesses on earth:* the Spirit, the water, and the blood, and these three are as one." The words in *italics* are not found in any of the early Greek manuscripts or translations, or in the best manuscripts of the Vulgate. They are almost universally regarded as a gloss.

5:8 The three witnesses converge; blood and water join the Spirit (see 1 Jn 2:20, 27; Jn 3:5; 4:14) in testifying (see Jn 3:11f) to the mission of the Son who gives life (v. 11; Jn 3:15).

5:13-21 Believers can be certain of partaking of the life of God; this whole Letter has given them the criteria that allow them to be sure of it.

5:13 This summary of the Letter is reminiscent of the Epilogue of John's Gospel (20:30f).

5:14-17 Believers are not perfect, they all have their weaknesses. However, these failures are not to be confused with refusal of Christ, which is refusal of fellowship with God. The Bible speaks to us about Abraham and Moses, who could intervene for the sins of human beings. In the Church, all members can intercede for their brethren. The author does not include in his prayer those who pervert the faith.

5:16 In general, the words *There is a sin that leads to death* refer not to just any sin that causes the loss of sanctifying grace (the "life of the soul"), but to an especially serious sin, such as apostasy, that causes the loss not only of grace but of faith as well. The distinction is intended to underscore the danger in which those who abandon the Christian fellowship ("are excommunicated") place themselves, and to instill a salutary fear into them.

5:18-21 The great certitudes that the speculations of the false teachers would like to shake are affirmed one last time, like a cry of victory. The community of God's children, adhering to Christ, overcomes the forces of evil, truly knows God, and shares his life. To seek anything else is idolatry. The *idols* to be avoided are either paganism or the false gods of the heart that can turn believers away from faith and love.

THE SECOND LETTER OF JOHN

1 *Presbyter:* i.e., a term (which may also be translated as "elder") used to designate a leader in the early Church (see notes on Titus 1:5-9 and 1:7). *Chosen Lady* (or "Sovereign Lady"): reference to one of the local churches of the time, which was under the leadership of the Presbyter and was confused by the advent of false teachers among her members.

4-6 For more details, see 1 Jn 2:3-11; 3:11-14; 4:7-21.

4 *Walking in the truth:* i.e., leading a specifically Christian way of life (see 1 Jn 1:6f; 2:6, 11; 3 Jn 3).

5-6 John stresses the truth that words and deeds go together. Love means keeping the commandments of Jesus. And when Christians keep them, they are leading a life of faith.

6 *His commandments:* see 1 Jn 2:7f; 3:23; 4:21.

7-11 The false teachers are under the sign of the Antichrist (see 1 Jn 2:18-26; 4:1-3). They want to "go beyond" the teaching of Christ, thus adulterating Christ, the Gospel, and Love. This seems to be the Gnostic teaching attacked in the First Letter of John—that the Son of God did not become flesh (see Jn 1:14) but came upon the man Jesus temporarily at his Baptism and left before the crucifixion (see note on 1 Jn 5:6).

7 *Deceiver:* another title of the Antichrist or of those associated with him (see 1 Jn 2:18f, 22; 4:2f). *Antichrist:* see note on 1 Jn 2:18.

8 The author stresses that a future reward awaits those who work faithfully on earth (see Mk 9:41; 10:29f; Lk 19:16-19; Heb 11:26). *We:* some manuscripts have "you."

9 *Goes beyond:* a reference to the Gnostics' claim that they had advanced far beyond the teaching of the Apostles; they were, in effect, teaching pure speculation as apostolic doctrine (see 2 Tim 2:16; Tit 3:9).

10-11 The author warns against feeding and housing the false teachers, for that would be sharing in their evil deeds and tantamount to public approval.

12 The Presbyter is well aware that some things are better spoken face to face than written. So he hopes to visit the Church soon. *Paper and ink:* paper came from papyrus reeds, which were easily acquired. Ink was made by mixing carbon, water, and gum. *Our joy:* or "your joy."

13 *Your sister, the chosen one:* most likely, another local church (perhaps that of Ephesus), which was also under the leadership of the Presbyter. Just as Christians are "brothers [and sisters]," the churches are "sisters."

THE THIRD LETTER OF JOHN

1 *Presbyter:* see note on 2 Jn 1. *Gaius:* a loyal member of one of the churches in the province of Asia, who bears a common Roman name—one mentioned in four other places in the New Testament (Acts 19:29; 20:4; Rom 16:23; 1 Cor 1:14).

2 John wishes Gaius well both spiritually and physically, for he knows that grace and health are two of the greatest gifts of God.

3 *Brethren:* most likely itinerant missionaries to whom Gaius showed Christian hospitality. *Walk in the truth:* i.e., practice true Christian living.

5-6 Apparently, the early church provided hospitality and support for missionaries because they had given up their means of livelihood in order to preach the faith to others and deserved some kind of compensation (see 1 Cor 9:3-12).

7 *Name:* of Jesus Christ (see note on Acts 5:41), which expresses the mystery of his divinity (see Phil 2:9; Jas 2:7; 1 Jn 2:12; 3:23; 5:13).

9 *Diotrephes:* a leader of the local church who overstepped his boundaries. He not only failed to give allegiance to the Presbyter but also refused to offer hospitality and support to the missionaries who came to his church.

11 John exhorts Gaius to keep on doing good and not be swayed by the un-Christian behavior of Diotrephes.

12 *Demetrius:* possibly the bearer of the Letter. He may have been an important member of the community or one of the missionaries. *Spoken favorably . . . and so has the Truth itself:* most likely, John is referring to the Truth of the Gospel in Demetrius' life. Like Gaius, Demetrius is "walking in the truth." He lives the life of love.

13-14 See 2 Jn 12-13 for a similar conclusion.

15 *Friends:* probably those who oppose Diotrephes and are loyal to the Presbyter.

THE LETTER OF JUDE

1 *Jude . . . the brother of James:* see Introduction. *Servant:* see note on Rom 1:1. *Kept safe by Jesus Christ:* he holds the universe together (see Col 1:17; Heb 1:3) and will ensure that Christians persevere in the faith and reach their eternal inheritance (see Jn 6:37-40; 17:11f; 1 Pet 1:3-5).

3 Those who possess the true faith must defend it zealously against all error. But this defense of the truth must always be carried out in a lawful manner. *Saints:* see note on Rom 1:7.

4 *Long ago were designated for condemnation:* the author may be referring to Old Testament denunciations of godless men or to Enoch's prophecy (see vv. 14-15) or he may mean that condemnation has long ago been ready to overtake them because of their sin (see 2 Pet 2:3).

5-16 The fate of those who pervert faith in Christ and the Christian life is sketched out, in the eyes of the author, in that which overtook the most infamous evildoers of the Bible and which the Jewish literature of the period readily recounts. Thus, a few Biblical scenes are strung together: the people rebelling in the wilderness (Num 14:26-35; see 1 Cor 10:5); the fall of the mysterious heavenly beings that are likened to angels (Gen 6:1-3); the chastisement of the wicked cities (Gen 19:1-29); the punishment of Cain (Gen 4:1-24); the error of Balaam (Num 22:2—24:25; 31:16); the revolt of Korah (Num 16:1-35). Upon those whom he regards as liars, the author calls down the prophecy of judgment that is placed on the lips of Enoch, that ancestor whose mysterious destiny is scrutinized in Jewish literature (see Gen 5:18-24; Wis 4:10f; Lk 3:32-38; Heb 11:5).

Who, then, are these men who pervert the Gospel? They are people who delight in bizarre speculations, who go so far as to deny the lordship of Christ and forget his Person, his role, and his unique work. They insult celestial beings; they doubtless misunderstand the angels or want to judge their merits and their respective roles. Even the archangel Michael,—according to the apocryphal book entitled *The Assumption of Moses*—left to God alone the task of condemning the devil (see Zec 3:2). They are spiritual in discourse but lax in morals and corruptors.

5 The first of three examples of divine punishment formerly meted out is that which befell those who had been saved but failed to keep the faith (see Num 14:28f).

6 The second example is taken from Gen 6:1-4 as elaborated in the apocryphal *Book of Enoch* (see Jude 14). Enoch says that the celestial beings let themselves be seduced by the "daughters of men." But in Jude as in 2 Pet 2:4, the statement that the angels sinned is not accompanied by any details.

7 The third example is taken from Gen 19:1-25. The townsmen of Sodom lusted not after human beings but after the strangers who were angels. The apocryphal *Testament of the Twelve Patriarchs,* like Jude 6-7, also compares the sin of the angels with that of the Sodomites.

8 The false teachers are undeterred by the punishment of the fallen angels (vv. 6-7). Yet they themselves, by their crime and punishment, are like those who were chastised in the Old Testament.

9 This is a reference to an incident recorded in the apocryphal *Assumption of Moses,* in which Michael the archangel has a dispute with the devil concerning who can claim Moses' body after his death. Jude argues that if an archangel refrained from reviling even the devil, mere human beings are certainly wrong to revile angels (*celestial beings*—v. 8).

11 The author gives three Old Testament personalities who each in some way illustrate the character of the false teachers: (1) *footsteps of Cain:* selfishness and hatred for a brother (see Gen 4:3f); (2) *error of Balaam:* surrendering integrity as a spiritual leader because of consuming greed (see note on 2 Pet 2:15); *rebellion of Korah:* rebelling against God's appointed leadership (see Num 16). Thus, the false teachers are loveless, greedy, and insubordinate—and destruction is sure to overtake them.

12-13 Jude now characterizes the false teachers by the use of six graphic metaphors: (1) *blemishes at your love feasts:* see notes on 1 Cor 11:17-24; 11:27-34; and 2 Pet 2:13; (2) *shepherds who feed only themselves:* instead of caring for their sheep (see Ezek 34:8-10; Jn 10:12f); (3) *clouds blown about by winds without giving rain:* the false teachers promise much but give nothing; (4) *trees in autumn barren and uprooted and so twice dead:* once again, a figure of empty promises; (5) *wild sea waves whose foam reflects their shameless deeds:* their product is like the foam or scum at the seashore; (6) *wandering stars:* as these provide no guidance for navigation, neither do the false teachers give any reliable guide to the Christian life.

14-15 Cited from the noncanonical *Book of Enoch* 1:9, probably from memory. *Enoch, in the seventh generation from Adam:* cited from Enoch 60:8; this refers to the Enoch in the line of Seth (Gen 5:18-24; 1 Chr 1:1-3), not the one in the line of Cain (Gen 4:17). The *Book of Enoch* was highly respected by many Jews and Christians of that time.

16 *These are . . . passions:* suggested by Enoch 5:5.

17 This is a reference to the apostolic preaching received through tradition, to which Jude alluded in v. 3.

18 Right from the start, the apostolic catechesis had announced that Christians should not be astonished at the appearance of men full of delirium (see Acts 20:29-30). *In the final age . . . ungodly passions:* this does not seem to be an exact Scripture citation, but see Acts 20:29-31; 1 Tim 4:1; 2 Tim 3:1-5; 4:3; 2 Pet 3:3; see also Mt 24:24; Mk 13:22.

20-23 Jude now tells Christians how to contend for the faith. (1) They must build themselves up in their faith, which is the orthodox body of truth and practice received from the Apostles (see Acts 2:42; Rom 6:17; Gal 1:23); they do so by having fellowship with the Lord and his people, by continuing in the Gospel and in the Word of God, and by worshiping in spirit and truth—especially the Eucharist. (2) They must be a praying people (see Lk 18:1), praying in the Holy Spirit (see Rom 8:26-27; Gal 4:6; Eph 6:18) that God's Kingdom may come and his will may be done (see Mt 6:10-11). (3) They are to remain in God's love by imitating Jesus (Mt 16:24) and by mutual love and support (see 1 Jn 5:1-4). (4) They are to wait expectantly for the Second Coming and to keep their eyes on the mercy of Jesus that leads to eternal life (see v. 3). (5) They are to tend to those who waver, snatching others from the judgment, and maintain an attitude of pity and concern but keep their distance from the corruptors.

24-25 One of the greatest doxologies of the New Testament concludes this brief Letter. Remaining in the presence of the living God gives Christians the power to persevere and make progress. All this is due to Jesus Christ, who sums up in himself the majesty, the power, and the authority of God.

THE BOOK OF REVELATION

1:1-3 Christians are living in the last period of history. They are facing difficult times, and God's plan is questioned. More than ever, faithfulness to his plan is required. Here then is a vision of faith concerning what is happening. The one who attests to it, in the Name of Christ, is prepared to give testimony for it even by shedding his blood.

1:3 *Blessed:* this is the first of seven beatitudes that appear in the book (see Rev 14:13; 16:15; 19:9; 20:6; 22:7; 22:14). The word "blessed" is more all-encompassing than "happy"; it indicates the favorable conditions in which God has placed a person (see Ps 1:1; Mt 5:3). *Prophecy:* i.e., any word from God, whether it foretells the future, commands, instructs, or sets forth history.

1:4-8 The greeting and the address introduce the work as a letter. *[He] who is:* this is how God revealed himself to Moses at the burning bush (Ex 3:14); this time, the divine name embraces the past, present, and future of humankind and is turned to the future, to the immediate fulfillment of all things: God, he *who is to come.* God is also described with the first and last letters of the Greek alphabet, *Alpha and Omega;* he is *the Beginning and the End,* the origin and the completion (a proper name of God according to Isa 44:6; 48:12). In addition, he is the master of all historical events, including the present ones, which, according to the author, are decisive. And Christ will appear in all the glory of his Resurrection and in the grandeur of the work accomplished to save humankind, comprising the body of the Church (see 1 Pet 2:5, 9), in the imminence of his coming to judge the world.

In order to speak of him, the author here multiplies Biblical reminiscences (Ex 19:6; Ps 89:28, 38, Isa 55:3). The seven spirits before the throne (v. 4) represent the Holy Spirit in the many ways that the Spirit manifests himself in the world (e.g., Isa 11:2, 5).

1:4 *Seven Churches:* the Churches (named in v. 11) formed a circle in the province of Asia and were separated from one another by some fifty miles.

1:5 *Faithful witness:* the Messiah is the witness to the promise the Lord made to David (2 Sam 7:1; Ps 89; Isa 55:3-4; Zec 12:8) in his person as well as in his work. He also fulfills this promise and is thus the efficacious Word, God's Yes (see Rev 3:14; 19:11, 13; 2 Cor 1:20). He is the heir of David (see Rev 5:5; 22:16) but also the firstborn from the dead because of his Resurrection (see Col 1:18) who will rule the universe after his enemies have been overcome (see Rev 19:6; Dan 7:14).

1:6 Those who follow Christ will be part of a kingdom, because they will rule over all the nations (see Isa 54:11-17; Dan 7:22, 27; Zec 12:1-3; see Rev 2:26; 5:10; 20:6; 22:5). They will also be priests because like Jesus the Priest they offer up the sacrifice of their own lives as a burnt offering of love.

1:9-20 The author describes himself as a Christian who has been exiled to a little island that lay off the coast of Miletus and Ephesus and was known as a prison island. Before his eyes the risen Christ appears. The majestic description derives its images from the portrait of the Son of Man in chs. 7 and 10 of the Book of Daniel. The description of his stance and clothing suggests majesty and power; this being who is master of life possesses the secret of all things and holds even the realm of death subject to him (v. 18).

The netherworld, or the lower world (Hebrew: *Sheol;* not to be confused with hell, the place of eternal damnation), is a localization of the realm of death, where, it is imagined, the dead dwell, deprived of the ability to perform any existential act. Another term for it is *Hades.* Christ has the power to release souls from the netherworld (see Jn 5:26-28).

The very figure of Christ shows the judgment to be imminent. But he is also present in the life of the Churches, and the author lists seven of them (seven is the number symbolizing universality).

The text speaks of the angels of the Churches; according to the religious vision of the world at that time, some heavenly representatives presided over the destinies of cities, peoples, and Churches. The seer might be speaking of the earthly persons in charge of the Churches. However, the Churches are also in the power of Christ and under his protection.

What is happening now and what will take place afterward (v. 19): these words anticipate the two main parts of the work.

1:9 *Patmos:* a small island in the Aegean Sea about 50 miles from Ephesus. According to the third-century Church historian Eusebius, John the Apostle was released from Patmos under the emperor Nerva (A.D. 96—98).

1:10 *In the spirit:* i.e., in a state of spiritual ecstasy (see also Rev 4:2; 17:3; and 21:10). *The Lord's day:* Sunday. In the Old Testament the expression "Day of the Lord" signifies some special intervention of God in history. For Christians, the eschatological age is the last times that have begun with the Resurrection of Christ; to celebrate the Lord's Day means therefore to commemorate his Paschal victory and to hasten his return (see Acts 20:7; 1 Cor 11:26; 2 Pet 3:12; see also the present-day liturgical acclamations after the consecration of the Eucharist).

1:11 *Scroll:* pieces of papyrus or parchment sewn together and rolled up. The book form came into use some time in the second century.

1:13-15 Jesus appears in garments that are priestly (the habit or long tunic) and royal (the golden breastplate). The white hair is a symbol of eternity; the flaming eyes signify omniscience, and the bronze feet, immutability. He is also a Judge, prepared to sentence those who are unfaithful (see Rev 2:16; 19:15; Isa 49:2; Eph 6:17; Heb 4:12). One or other of his attributes as Judge is used by the author at the beginning of each of the seven letters to indicate the circumstances of the Church addressed.

1:13 *Son of man:* see note on Mt 8:20.

2:1—3:21 Christian communities at the end of the first century found themselves faced with difficulties that were substantially the same as those faced by the Church in every age, from the Passover of Christ to the end of history. The real struggle was and would be that of fidelity in the midst of constant renewal. The letters here are addressed to seven Churches of Asia Minor; the number seven is symbolic, in the sense that these communities represent all the Churches with their difficulties and problems, their efforts to be faithful, and their undertakings.

Each letter follows the same pattern: Christ comes on the scene bearing one of the symbols listed in the great vision of Rev 1:9-20; he judges the communities according to their deficiencies, their fidelity, and their constancy; then he concludes with the promise of final victory.

In every age each community and each believer will read these letters in order to submit to the Lord's judgment and to hear once again his call. Addressed as they are to angels who, according to the religious thinking of the time, were regarded as presiding over the destiny of a community, they envisage first of all the leaders of the communities.

2:1-7 Under the pretext of Christian spirituality and freedom, a sect that, certainly without justification, claims reliance on one of the first deacons, Nicholas (see Acts 6:5), allows itself the most serious moral deviations and takes part very freely in pagan worship. (A similar group at Pergamum holds the teaching of Balaam [vv. 14-15], and a third at Thyatira follows the woman Jezebel [v. 20]. All three groups are usually termed Nicolaitans.)

The community of Ephesus does resist the danger that threatens it, but unfortunately in its effort to be faithful it has become judgmental. It has lost its charity. The time has come for it to be renewed. Otherwise, the community will lose its place. What a perspective is thus opened for fidelity! A new access to the tree of life militates against succumbing to sin (see Gen 2:9; 3:22-24); expressed in Jewish language, it is the hope of an unending life.

2:1 *Ephesus:* see introduction to the Letter to the Ephesians.

2:7 *Whoever has ears should listen to what the Spirit says . . . . :* this formula concludes each of the seven letters and stresses the role of the Spirit in Christ's relation with his Church. *Anyone who is victorious:* i.e., anyone who clings to the faith in the face of persecution. *Right to eat from the tree of life:* a right lost by our first parents but now restored by Christ who abrogated the decree that excluded human beings from the tree of life. God and humans are restored to the perfect fellowship that existed before the advent of sin.

2:8-11 Those Jews who did not acknowledge Christ as the one who fulfilled their hope, nor the Church as the true Israel, slandered the Christian community. They were regarded as partisans of the forces of opposition represented by Satan. However, the Christians must take courage, for the trial will last only for ten days, i.e., it will be of short duration—the reward for a life in God is near. Believers will escape the second death, i.e., defeat and definitive perdition at the judgment of God.

2:8 *Smyrna:* a city closely aligned with Rome that housed a large Jewish population hostile to Christians (see Acts 14:2, 19; 17:5, 13). One of the most famous early martyrs, Polycarp, was bishop of Smyrna.

2:12-17 In this city, a main center of emperor worship, the presence of Satan is visible. Deviant heresies, like that of the Nicolaitans, glorify participation in pagan forms of worship and in the moral disorders they represent, which in the eyes of the Old Testament is tantamount to prostitution. The episode of Balaam is evoked to stigmatize these wanderings of the conscience of believers (see Num 25:3; 31:16). The reward is illustrated by two symbols: the *manna,* i.e., the food of life (see Ps 78:24f), evokes all the blessings God bestows on those who remain faithful to him, blessings of which the Eucharist is the sign (see Ex 16:32-34; 2 Mac 2:4-8; Heb 9:4); the *white stone* probably recalls the stones upon which Greeks wrote the names of the candidates for whom they were voting in elections. God chooses us.

2:12 *Pergamum:* the ancient capital of Asia, built on a hill. Its name means "citadel" in Greek and is the origin of the word "parchment." It was the center of emperor worship in Asia.

2:13 *Antipas:* the first martyr of Asia, who was put to death under the emperor Domitian.

2:14 *Teaching of Balaam:* Balaam counseled the Midianite women on how to lead the Israelites astray (see Num 25:1-2; 31:16; see also Jude 11); thus he is the exemplar of teachers who lead the faithful into becoming completely worldly-minded.

2:18-29 A prophetess, who is compared to Jezebel of sad memory in the Books of the Kings of Israel (see 1 Ki 16:31; 2 Ki 9:22), is inciting Christians to take part in idolatrous worship. Some, who are doubtless Nicolaitans, believed that they could obtain a deeper religious knowledge through a mysterious initiation. Believers cling to Christ. He will be at their side on the Day of judgment, according to the classic images of Psalm 2. The *morning star* is the symbol of the Resurrection and its power —for Jesus rose from the dead just before dawn, the time when the morning star is visible.

2:18 *Thyatira:* a military outpost noted for its trade guilds.

2:24 *The deep secrets of Satan:* perhaps the esoteric teaching of the Nicolaitans.

3:1-6 This community seems to be dead! Hence, it is urged to change and become spiritually alive. From now on people must align themselves with Christ (see Mt 10:32). Those who truly follow Jesus will one day be clad in a white garment, which recalls the white garment worn by Jesus at the Transfiguration and Resurrection. It was the garment already being given at Baptism.

3:1 *Sardis:* capital of the ancient kingdom of Lydia, it was a wealthy and famous city.

3:5 Those who are victorious are promised three things: (1) they will receive white garments like those Christ will give to the faithful Sardinians; (2) their names will never be blotted out of the book of life; and (3) their names will be acknowledged by Christ in the presence of the Father and his angels.

White garments symbolize God's righteousness, victory, and glory (see Rev 3:18; 6:11; 7:9, 13f; 19:14). The *book of life* is a reference to the divine register in which the names of the redeemed are written (see Rev 13:8; 17:8; 20:12, 15; 21:27; Dan 12:1; Phil 4:3). Christians who were loyal to Christ were continually threatened with being stripped of their citizenship in cities they inhabited, i.e., having their names blotted out of the city's register. Christ's acknowledgment of them in heaven offers an eternal, safe citizenship in his eternal Kingdom (see Mt 10:32; Lk 12:8).

3:7-13 The Messiah, Son of David—who holds all power over the lot of the People of God, according to the image of Isa 22:22—addresses himself to the community of Philadelphia. Like the Church of Smyrna, it was suffering persecution, but it remained faithful. The reward of those who are faithful is evoked in symbolic terms: they will live in God's dwelling and meet God; they will be members of Christ's Body, bearing his name and sharing his lot.

3:7 *Philadelphia:* the gateway to the central plateau in the province of Asia. *The holy one, the true one:* see Rev 6:10 and Isa 40:25; Hab 3:2-3; Mk 1:24. *Key of David:* Christ is the Davidic Messiah empowered to control entrance into the Kingdom (see Isa 22:22; Mt 16:19).

3:8 The open door may refer to the missionary apostolate.

3:12 *Inscribe on him . . . my own new name:* this may be a name that characterizes his redemptive work and will not be known until the Second Coming or the name "the Word" (see Rev 19:13).

3:14-22 Christ cannot bear lukewarmness, since he is the "Amen," the one who commits himself completely (see 2 Cor 1:19-20). By his love he urges people to change their lives. He stands at the door and knocks, i.e., his coming is imminent (see Mk 13:29; Lk 12:35; 22:16). This may seem to be a threat, but it is above all a wonderful invitation—the invitation to share the most lovable intimacy with Christ, of which the Eucharistic Banquet is the inauguration. He invites us to be at his side when the Judgment and the destiny of the world are fulfilled.

3:14 *Laodicea:* a very wealthy city known for its banks, medical school, and textile industry as well as its lack of sufficient water, to each of which the letter alludes. *Amen:* a divine title (see Isa 65:16) applied to Christ (see 2 Cor 1:20). *Source of God's creation:* a concept that is found in Jn 1:3; Col 1:16f; Heb 1:2; see also Prov 8:22-31; Wis 9:1f.

3:16 *Lukewarm, neither cold nor hot:* i.e., complacent, self-satisfied, and indifferent to the real issues of faith in Christ—hence, lacking in zeal and useless.

3:17 *Never realizing that you are . . . naked:* the spiritual wretchedness of the community of Laodicea in contrast to its material prosperity. The Laodiceans may have interpreted their material wealth as a blessing from God and were thus deceived into thinking that their spiritual state was better than it truly was.

3:19 *I . . . discipline all those whom I love:* see Job 5:17; Ps 94:12; Prov 3:11f; 1 Cor 11:32; Heb 12:5-11.

4:1—22:5 In antiquity, books took the form of large scrolls. Thus, the most important and difficult part of the Book of Revelation is presented to us as a well-sealed scroll; the seals must be broken and, as they are, the visions unfold one after the other. In their main lines these visions intersect according to the classic plan of an apocalypse. After a grandiose inaugural vision (chs. 4 and 5), there is the prelude of events to come (Rev 6:1—11:9): it is the history of Israel, whose fall under the blows of the Roman armies is regarded as a judgment of God on his people. Then follow the trials and confrontations of the decisive moment (Rev 12:1—20:15): the nations come before us, slaves to the powers of evil that oppose the plan of God, who wants to save human beings. The Roman empire is certainly in the forefront. The Judgment will be even more terrible than that of Jerusalem if they remain hostile to Christ the Lord, to his Gospel, and to his Church. In any case, the great battle between God and the wicked powers will end with the extermination of these powers. Then, the drama can be resolved in the final accomplishment (Rev 21:1—22:15): God creates a new world reserved for his Elect.

But must we read, in this succession of numberless visions, the sketches of a mysterious calendar, a succession of events to come? The whole would then appear terribly supercharged, badly ordered, and—in a nutshell—incoherent. Doubtless, one can imagine that the elements of two different apocalypses—each redacted according to a similar movement—have been poorly coordinated, in a single book. But the author multiplies images and explanations to such an extent as to disconcert and baffle us. Yet, these events are described in such an ambiguous manner that they could be applied to all times. These things are always happening; we should always be ready for the end.

4:1—5:14 This is a view of history imparted by faith. The Book suggests it by immediately transporting us to the throne of God where the destinies of the universe are decided. Images are multiplied to suggest in advance and to represent the hidden meaning of history. This inaugural vision places the readers in the worship of God; it confirms the role of Christ as Master of the history of the world.

4:1-11 Emperors are entertained like gods and are thought to have power over the world's destiny. The truth is far different. Who indeed can open the door of the true God's dwelling and express the greatness of his life and plan? Here are innumerable symbols orchestrated like a brilliant symphony. Everything is inaccessible greatness: the peace of the light, the dread of the All-powerful, the power that dominates the universe, the perfect knowledge of all things. All this is what is proclaimed in these images.

Already present around God are the fathers, those great ancestors whose sacred history faith proclaims (see Sir 44—50; Heb 10—12); for he is the God of the living and not of the dead, the God of Abraham, Isaac, and Jacob, as Jesus attests in the Gospel (see Mk 12:26-27). The great manifestations (or epiphanies) of God depicted in the Old Testament are an invitation to adore God, and the author was inspired by them. We recognize the themes of Isaiah in the temple (see Isa 6) and especially the images of Ezekiel (see Ezek 1 and 10). In this way, the Jews were wont to express God's domination over the universe.

Thus, the sea, always felt to be a savage and hostile power, was itself tamed by the all-powerful God. All the forces of heaven that can be imagined—for example, those to which are attributed the government of the seasons and the rhythm of time, the four living creatures that represent the best of creation—are at the service of God. All these symbols form a great hymn to the Creator.

4:2 *In the spirit:* see note on Rev 1:10.

4:4 The *elders* exercise a priestly and royal role: they praise and adore God, offer him the prayers of the faithful, assist him in governing the world, and share in his power. The number twenty-four corresponds perhaps to the twenty-four classes or divisions of priests in 1 Chr 24:1-9, or to the twelve patriarchs plus the twelve apostles. They thus represent salvation history.

4:6 The *four living creatures* represent the created world that reveals God's goodness and power. Their many eyes symbolize the universal knowledge and providence of God. They continue to give glory to God through their work in creation. Their forms (*lion, ox, human, eagle*) represent what is noblest, strongest, wisest, and most agile in the created world. Ever since St. Irenaeus, Christian tradition had seen in them symbols of the evangelists Mark, Luke, Matthew, and John, respectively.

5:1-14 As we have seen, the whole universe sings of the limitless power of the Creator. But he is also the Master of the universe, and the book he holds in his hand represents the destiny of the world. The book is held closed by seven seals, i.e., it contains the totality of the events of history, though in a hidden fashion, which no one can unveil.

However, a mediator of the Revelation does exist. He is the Messiah, who is designated here by the titles foretold of him in the Old Testament: the lion of Judah (see Gen 49:9) to whom victory is promised (see Isa 11:1, 10; see also 2 Sam 7), the Messiah King, shoot of the stock from which David was descended.

It is Christ in the power of his Resurrection who receives the mastery over the destinies of the entire universe. He is represented in his glory after the manner of a Lamb slain but standing (the figure of the Paschal Lamb is the main title for Christ in this Book, used twenty-eight times). This unusual expression is intended to recall Passover, the passover lamb, and the sacrificial Death of Christ for the redemption of the human race, but also to assert that he is ever living and the conqueror of death. The seven horns symbolize an infinite power.

The one with infinite power is the Redeemer who has acquired the people by his Blood. The Creator ratifies this and places in Christ's hands the succession of events until their fulfillment. Then the angels, the elders, and all the great figures in heaven that can be imagined will each come in turn to render the worship due to the Master of time, and the entire universe unites to acclaim the risen one. Indeed, the coming of Christ is a capital turning point, and a new song is required to celebrate it (see Phil 2).

5:9 *New song:* a song that celebrates a new act of divine deliverance (see Rev 14:3; Pss 33:3; 96:1; 144:9; Isa 42:10). *With your blood you purchased for God people:* the theme of Christ's sacrificial Death (see Mk 10:45; 1 Cor 6:20).

6:1—11:19 The book of destiny is probably not a scroll in the classical sense. It is a document that is folded and then sealed, folded and sealed, etc., seven times. It resembles a Roman legal document. Thus, as each seal is broken, part of the document becomes legible. When the seventh seal is broken (Rev 8:1), the hour is going to sound; but we are still living in suspense: trumpets will sound, one after another until the seventh one; then the great act will be played out (Rev 11:15).

Nonetheless, the unfurling of the wrath is not described to frighten believers; the author wants to strengthen them, to announce to them that the destiny of the world has been turned around and God's plan is on the way to being fulfilled. In accord with the perspectives of the prophecies and the Gospel, a Remnant will be saved, the community of Christ and the true People of God (Rev 7). All the chapters that follow seem to interpret the history of the world in the perspective of the destiny reserved for the Jewish people. Yet the end of Jerusalem and its destruction are not the end of history; they are only a turning point (Rev 10:1—11:13)—then the time of the nations can truly begin (Rev 12:1—19:10).

6:1-8 The first secrets are unveiled. Already the images are terrifying. The colors of the horses suffice to create fright. Three horsemen sow war, famine, and pestilence, those great scourges in which the ancients see God's judgment on proud and indifferent ages and on unjust people (see, e.g., Lev 26:21-26; Deut 32:34; Ezek 5:17; 6:11f; 7:14f; 12:16; 14:13-21; 33:27; Jer 15:2-4; Mt 24:6f). Hades follows in the wake of the last horseman to swallow the victims into its gloomy abode.

There is some doubt about the figure of the first horseman, crowned and mounted on a white horse. Is it Christ, or a false Messiah, or simply another scourge, the well-known scourge of the voracious beasts who decimate travelers? The allegory of the four horses and horsemen who ride out into the four quarters of the world is taken from Zechariah (1:8-10; 6:1-8).

6:4 *A large sword:* symbol of war.

6:5-6 *Scales:* symbol of hunger: food is rationed and sold at very high prices. The rider with the scales probably represents social injustice. *A day's wages:* literally, "a denarius."

6:8 *Hades:* personification of the abode of the dead, i.e., the netherworld (see notes on Rev 1:9-20 and Mt 16:18).

6:9-11 Persecution is unleashed. The victims, as though immolated in sacrifice, are all reunited around God and already clothed in the garment of joy. This presence of the victims attests that oppression has been lifted on earth. For the people of the Bible possess too great a sense of justice to imagine that such violent injustices as persecutions constitute an indifferent thing in the eyes of God and that they can go unpunished forever. They are like a challenge to God (see Lk 18:7). God must intervene, and bloody persecutions are among the signs of the end (see Mk 13:9-13).

6:10 *Inhabitants of the earth:* i.e., humankind in its hostility to God (see Rev 3:10; 8:13; 11:10; 13:8, 12; 17:2, 8).

6:11 *White robe:* symbol of the joy and triumph of the Resurrection (see Rev 3:5, 18; 11:10; 13:8, 12; 17:2, 8). *Until the roll was completed of their fellow servants and brethren who were still to be killed:* there was an apocalyptic idea in the air—sparked by noncanonical literature—that God rules the world according to a predetermined time schedule (see 2 Esdras 4:35-37) and that the death of a certain number of the righteous must occur before the end takes place (see 1 Enoch 47:4).

6:12-17 The cosmic destruction announces the Day of the Lord (see Isa 34:4; Mk 13:6, 24f). It is an astonishing spectacle that this firmament will be rolled up like a large scroll. The cosmos enters a phase of distortion and convulsion. The threat hangs over everyone; no one escapes the paralyzing fear. The author uses to great advantage many of the images of the Old Testament (see Isa 2:10, 19; 34:4; Hos 10:8; Joel 2:11; 3:4).

7:1-17 In 587 B.C., on the eve of the destruction of Jerusalem, the survivors were, so to speak, marked to be preserved from the catastrophe (see Ezek 9). The great fear is not for the community of the persecuted. The calamities that will overtake the world will not touch them. Thus, God gathers together his Elect. They may go through the trial of the years 66 to 70 and finally the history of the world, which is that of the sufferings of the Church. But they will not fall prey to condemnation. This people that is gathered together is first of all the Remnant of Israel. From each of the twelve tribes there will be twelve thousand survivors: this is a symbolic number meaning fullness and perfection. Then the vision is enlarged: the Remnant becomes a multitude without number, gathered together from amid all the nations of the earth. From all sides come forth the martyrs and all those who endured trials: the whole Church. This is a grandiose celebration of happiness and triumph. In a striking foreshortening, the author sketches a tableau of the Church in the grip of tribulations and persecutions, assisted by Christ, her Shepherd, and led toward her heavenly victory, which anticipates the splendid final vision of the new Jerusalem (Rev 21:1—22:5).

7:5-6 Judah is placed first because of Christ, who is "the Lion of the tribe of Judah" (Rev 5:5). *Manasseh:* one of the two halves of the tribe of Joseph that are both cited (the other being Ephraim but called "Joseph" in v. 8)—doubtless in order to make up twelve tribes. Daniel is omitted probably because of a late tradition that the Antichrist was to arise from that tribe.

7:17 *Springs of living water:* i.e., the grace of God, which flows from Christ (see Rev 21:6; 22:1, 17; Jn 4:10, 14).

8:1-6 We are now at the great Day of God's Coming. Everything is unmoving in a solemn silence. It is the hour when the prayer of those persecuted—which is symbolized by the incense—is going to be heard (see Rev 6:9-11). Calamities arise to jostle the earth. At the sound of the trumpets, which are part of the scene for the Coming of God (see 1 Thes 4:16), seven tableaus will pass before our eyes in a dramatization without let-up.

8:3 The *altar* is the altar of incense in the Jewish sanctuary; the *gold censer* is the thurible or fire-shovel used to carry the burning coals from the altar of holocausts to the altar of incense.

8:7-12 The earth, sea, streams, sources, and stars—everything is disfigured. The universe becomes chaos and lays itself waste. The author amplifies images taken from the Book of Exodus (chs. 7—10).

8:7 See the seventh plague of Egypt (Ex 9:23f) and Joel 3:3.

8:8-11 See the first plague of Egypt (Ex 7:20f).

8:11 *Wormwood:* a bitter-tasting plant that is a metaphor for calamity, sorrow, and death (see Prov 5:3f; Jer 9:15; Lam 3:19).

8:12 See the darkness that occurred for three days during the ninth plague of Egypt (Ex 10:21-23).

8:13 After the universe, the human race will itself be struck. The eagle announces the three calamities.

9:1-12 A fallen star, doubtless Satan himself, opens the door of the abyss, which is regarded as the prison in which the evil spirits are held while awaiting their final punishment. An army of strange locusts escapes (see the eighth and ninth plagues of Egypt—Ex 10:12-15, 21-23—as well as the invasion of locusts in Joel 1:4—2:10). These do not devour the harvest, as one would expect, but attack humans. It is an invasion of a fierce army, led by a satanic being, whose name in Hebrew is *Abaddon,* meaning perdition or ruin, and in Greek *Apollyon,* meaning destroyer. The writer has not resisted the enticing pleasure of giving this being a name that is a caricature of the great Greek god Apollo. Job 3:21 is cited in v. 6.

9:13-21 These ancient monsters seem to have had an appointment to meet on the banks of the Euphrates, to be then unleashed as a savage horde on the people. The visionary is undoubtedly thinking of the four corps of the military that invaded Judea from Syria for the second phase of the Jewish War in an expedition that was particularly destructive and murderous. The event was always supposed to be a sign that jump-started consciences. Alas, it merely leads to bewilderment and decomposition!

9:13 *I heard a voice:* to show that the punishment inflicted on the pagans was the result of the prayer of the martyrs, described in Rev 6:9-10.

9:15 For the day of the divine wrath, see Rev 6:17.

9:20 *Demons:* spiritual beings allied with Satan and wielding an evil influence on human beings (see Deut 4:28; Ps 115:5-7; 1 Cor 10:20).

10:1-11 The large scroll, whose seven seals are being broken one after another, is said to contain the entire History of Salvation, which unfolds from Christ's Death and Resurrection to the day of the final judgment. This history is brought to mind from the viewpoint of the destiny of the Jewish people, but the last episode in this history includes the judgment and salvation of the nations, which are here set forth.

An angel brings forth and unrolls another text; the messenger dominates heaven and the sea, i.e., his announcement concerns the whole universe. The scroll that the angel is holding here contains the story of clashes between the Church and the forces that control the pagan world. It is a small scroll, because the events told in it are connected with the history of Israel, in which the end of Jerusalem introduces the era of the nations.

There will be no more delay. Everything remains secret, yet everything will be played out between the sixth and the seventh trumpet. The scene of the scroll that is eaten was inspired by an account of Ezekiel (2:8—3:3). The revelation is sweet and bitter: sweet because it is a word of salvation and makes known the final triumph of Christ and his faithful; bitter because it announces the trials and tribulations that in so many texts of the Bible precede the judgment of God. The Gospel speaks of the joy of the woman giving birth in sorrow (Jn 16:21).

10:7 *The mysterious purpose of God:* literally, "the mystery of God," i.e., the end of the present age when the power of evil will be overcome (see Rev 17:1—19:4, 11-21; 20:7-10; Rom 16:25f; 2 Thes 2:6-12) and the Kingdom of God is established and all creation is renewed (see Rev 21:1—22:5).

11:1-13 The holy city is crushed under the blows of Titus, but in the Church, the new Israel, everything that the temple, the altar, and the worshipers represent will not cease; true worship will continue. In a hostile world, the witnesses of Christ will continue to spread the Word of God, despite persecutions, until the Second Coming.

Let us try to see a bit more clearly into the details of the symbols used by the author to impart this certitude to believers subjected to torture. Measuring Jerusalem calls to mind—since Ezekiel (40:3) and Zechariah (2:5-6)—protection and reconstruction. But only the reserved part of the temple is spared, i.e., while the Church will be persecuted and even give forth martyrs, the saints will never be harmed. While the bodies of the holy ones (represented by the exterior of the temple) are crushed, their souls (represented by the interior of the temple) are safe in God's hands.

The two witnesses—perhaps Peter and Paul—combine the traits of several persons, especially Moses and Elijah (of whom Judaism of that time mentions the ascension: v. 11) and one of whom changed water into blood (Ex 7:17; 10:11), while the other predicted a drought (1 Kgs 17:1). The Gospel places both at the side of Christ during the Transfiguration (Mk 9:2-8).

Next come two mysterious personalities who, according to Zechariah (4:3, 14) cited in v. 4 of our text, represent the priesthood and the Kingdom uniting their efforts to guide the people of God. These are also Christian figures, of Christ first and then of the apostles—tradition names Peter and Paul, the two champions of the early Church, who died at Rome under Nero in A.D. 64 or 67.

Finally, these mysterious figures stand for the whole Church bearing witness to her faith and suffering for the sake of the Gospel even until martyrdom. It is not permitted to put their bones in the grave (v. 9), i.e., the testimony of the martyr Church cannot disappear into oblivion.

Just as the dry bones of the people of the Old Testament came to life in the eyes of the Prophet Ezekiel (37:5, 10), so the Christian martyrs are destined for resurrection and glorification.

The great city is symbolic of the high places of infidelity according to the Bible. In Rev 16:19; 17:18; 18:10, it is Rome; here, it is Rome or Jerusalem or any other city that makes itself omnipotent.

The beast cited in v. 7 (see Dan 7:21) represents the imperial power, destructive power, that claimed to be divine. Speaking of survivors (v. 13), the author thinks, perhaps, as did Paul (Rom 11:13-27), of a conversion of the Jewish people preceding Christ's Return.

11:2-3, 11 *Forty-two months . . . twelve hundred and sixty days . . . three and a half days . . . a year, two years, and a half year* (12:14): symbolic durations, designating typical periods of persecution according to Dan 7:25.

11:15-19 The seventh trumpet sounds to announce the definitive restoration of the Kingdom of God and Christ. With the resurrection of the dead, Israel sees the completion of its promises of salvation: there will be reward for true worshipers and condemnation for rebels. The thanksgiving of the elders can rise before the throne of God.

According to a Jewish tradition, allusions to which are found in the Second Book of Maccabees (2:5-8), the Ark of the Covenant, which was destroyed by the fire in the temple in 587 B.C., was to reappear in the last times; the hour for this has come.

A new Sinai arises in heaven forever. The hour of judgment is, in the final analysis, the judgment of the definitive and perfect Covenant. Certainly, the earthly temple is destroyed, but the true and complete worship takes place in heaven.

11:19 *Ark of his covenant:* the ark of the Old Testament was a chest of acacia wood (see Deut 10:1f) that symbolized God's throne and his presence among his people. It was probably destroyed during Nebuzaradan's destruction of the temple in Jerusalem (see 2 Ki 25:8-10). The New Testament writers use it to symbolize God's faithfulness to the Covenant made with his people.

12:1—15:4 The animosity exhibited by the public authorities against Christian communities has become persecution. Now the grand declarations of loyalty toward the power are ended (see Rom 13:1-7; Tit 3:1; 1 Pet 2:13-17). The time has come, not to organize some armed defense or subversion but to resist every pressure and to stand fast in fidelity to Christ even to the shedding of blood. At this point, the Roman empire comes on the scene as the instrument used by all the forces hostile to Christ, his Kingdom, and his faithful. The Roman empire is a symbol of all earthly empires with their claim to impose their own ideas and purposes as a religion. The struggle will end with the victory of the risen Christ and those who have put their trust in him.

Here then is the time of the nations or the pagans. In the previous chapters, which envisaged the last times from the viewpoint of Israel's destiny, its place had already been marked out in anticipation (Rev 10:1—11:13). This is the scene itself. The structure of the chapters that follow is less clear; however, we find once again the same procedure as in the seven visions and the seven bowls.

12:1-17 Two types play a role in this inaugural vision. The ancient prophecy of Genesis (3:15) is fulfilled: a struggle in which there is no truce opposes the posterity of the chosen people and the forces of evil. The woman who gives birth personifies first of all the chosen people, from which the Messiah is to be born; there is certainly a reference to him in v. 5, which cites some classic Messianic texts: Isa 66:7 and Ps 2:9.

A long-standing Christian tradition also identifies the woman with the Virgin Mary, an exemplar of the chosen people. Modern exegetes rarely support so explicit an interpretation, but do not deny that the role of the one called "woman" in the fourth Gospel (Jn 2:4; 19:26) may have indirectly inspired, at least partially, this description in the Book of Revelation.

The dragon (see Dan 7; 8:10) has all the characteristics of the power that rises up against God: seven heads, ten horns, behavior capable of destroying the order of the universe (v. 4, citing Dan 8:10). The dragon is Satan, the eternal accuser of human beings before God (see Job 1:6-11; 2:1-17). After this "the rest of her [the woman's] offspring" (v. 17)—i.e., the faithful followers of Christ—suffer a period of struggles and trials in "the wilderness" (v. 6), i.e., on the earthly journey of the Church. In these trials the Church will not lack the strength given by the manna (see v. 6), an evident reference to the Eucharist.

Hell can launch against the Church all the forces unleashed by the Roman political authorities. In this scene there is also a struggle between Michael and the dragon (v. 7), which illustrates the victory of Christ; the description draws its inspiration from the Book of Daniel.

12:6 *Twelve hundred and sixty days:* see note on Rev 11:2-3, 11.

12:7 *Michael:* i.e., God's champion according to Jewish tradition (see Dan 10:12-21; 12:1); his name means "Who can compare with God?"

12:10 *Accuser:* the translation for the Hebrew word "Satan" (see 1 Chr 21:1; Job 1–2; Zec 3:1). In Hebrew scripture, Satan is a type of district attorney who accuses people of their sins at the Last Judgment.

12:14 *A year, two years, and a half year:* see note on Rev 11:2.

12:18—13:10 This beast that is possessed of extraordinary power (seven heads and ten horns) personifies the Roman empire. Its historical success is a blasphemous parody of the Christian mystery; the emperors have themselves acclaimed with divine titles, while for Christians only God and the Lamb have a right to the title "Lord" (*Kyrios*). The head that was wounded and then healed probably refers to Nero who was forced to commit suicide (by pushing a sword into his head) and was said to have risen from the dead (again, a blasphemous parody of Jesus' Death and Resurrection).

12:18 *I took my position . . . . :* another translation is: "he took his position . . ."—which would join v. 18 to the preceding paragraph.

13:5 *Forty-two months:* see note on Rev 11:2-3, 11.

13:8 *Written from the creation of the world:* some place these words at the very end of the sentence (after the word "slain"). *Book of life belonging to the Lamb:* see note on Rev 3:5.

13:11-18 The beast comes probably from Asia, because it was the East that gave rise to so many religious currents of thought that promoted emperor worship. The time has come when pressures are brought to bear and people are seduced. This picture fits in very well with the reign of Domitian, who banished Christians from the empire for refusing to practice emperor worship, the new sign of civic submission. The majority of believers resist, despite pressures and seductions of every kind.

The number of the beast has always been a snare for those who seek, by way of abstruse calculations, to identify the Antichrist with some figure of their own time. The number probably conceals the name of some personage known to readers of that time; the letters of the Greek alphabet and those of the Hebrew alphabet also stood for numbers, as is still the case with the Roman alphabet to some extent. Using gematria, a procedure for interpreting numbers, it was certainly possible to discern in the number 666 the words "Emperor Nero" in Hebrew. If we read "616" instead of "666," as some manuscripts do, it could be "Emperor Nero" in Greek.

14:1-5 The great hopes of the Prophets (e.g., Isa 2:1-5) are here realized; the new chosen people, in a full and perfect number, gather at Zion, the mount of definitive encounter with God. The martyrs sing the new song of deliverance and victory (see Ex 15:1-18; Pss 33:1-3; 98:1). It expresses the virginal joy of those who have remained faithful to God, those who have not committed falsehood, adultery, and fornication—i.e., in the language of the Bible, those who have not succumbed to the worship of false gods. They have not followed the emperor but only Christ. They have been, as it were, espoused to Christ (see Rev 19:9; 21:2; 2 Cor 11:2).

14:1 *One hundred and forty-four thousand:* that is, twelve thousand from each tribe.

14:3 *New song:* see note on Rev 5:9.

14:4 *The ones who have not defiled themselves with women:* this probably refers to those who avoided defiling relationships with the pagan world. *Follow the Lamb:* as disciples (see Mt 19:21; Mk 8:34). *Firstfruits:* a word used to refer to the first converts in a region (see Rom 16:5) and the first to rise from the dead (see 1 Cor 15:20). The author of this Book regards believers as choice offerings to God and the Lamb.

14:6-13 In the Old Testament, Babylon had become a symbol of every empire that was hostile to the People of God.

14:10 *Cup of his wrath:* the Old Testament commonly portrays the wrath of God by a cup of wine to be drunk (see Ps 75:9; Isa 51:17; Jer 25:15). *Burning sulfur:* this figured prominently in the destruction of Sodom and Gomorrah (see Gen 19:24), and Ps 11:6 speaks of a similar fate awaiting the wicked. The figure is also found elsewhere in the Old Testament and in the final chapters of Revelation (19:20; 20:10; 21:8).

14:13 *Blessed:* the second beatitude (see note on Rev 1:3).

14:14-20 "You will see the Son of Man seated at the right hand of the Power and coming with the clouds of heaven," Jesus had declared in the presence of the high priest who condemned him (Mk 14:62, inspired by Dan 7:13). The Judgment is near; the time of vintage and harvest is its classic image in the Bible, evoking the reaping or storing of fruits as well as the harsh plundering of the terrain and the relentless gathering of the produce.

The winepress, in which the grapes are crushed, is an image of a battle aimed at savage extermination (see Isa 63:23); as such, it yields blood and not juice. Here the entire earth is involved; the *two hundred miles,* literally, "1600 stadia" (4 x 4 x 100), indicate this universality. The Judgment takes place outside Jerusalem—the author wants to indicate that those condemned are excluded from the assembly united around God.

14:14 *Son of man:* see note on Mt 8:20.

15:1 These constitute the decisive sign of the Judgment, whose execution will be set forth later.

15:2-4 Those who have resisted are like the Hebrews after their crossing of the Red Sea. Here the mass of water, so terrifying to the ancients, seems marvelously tamed. It is the turn of the martyrs to chant the song of liberation (see Ex 15:1-8), playing on instruments far superior to any earthly musical instruments.

15:5—19:10 Will heaven be mute in the presence of oppression by political authorities or by a civilization that turns human beings into slaves and claims to pass as God? Are the sufferings and martyrdom of victims a cry that is perhaps useless and fades away in the history of the world? The conscience of believers protests against this possibility. But it is necessary to determine in what God's Judgment consists: it will unmask the imposture and recognize the courage of those who have resisted this perversion. Here some scenes of this Judgment flash before our eyes.

15:5 *The temple, that is, the tabernacle of the Testimony:* i.e., the heavenly sanctuary. The phrase conflates the tabernacle of Moses and the temple of Solomon. The Old Testament had described in blazing images the God who mysteriously took possession of the temple. In the same images (see 1 Ki 8:10) we here contemplate the true temple of heaven, the manifestation of God. It is a description of the Judgment.

16:1-21 The story of the plagues in Egypt (Ex 7—12) remained deeply inscribed in the imagination of the Jews; once again, as in chapters 8–10 (vision of the trumpets), that story here inspires the description of the final cataclysm of the universe and of the lives of its peoples and nations. The desolating picture shows all the hostile forces united at Armageddon (the Megiddo of the Bible, where King Josiah died with his troops); it became a place of sinister memory, and an omen and symbol of military defeat and even annihilation (see 2 Ki 23:29-30; Zec 12:11). The great city Babylon, i.e., Rome, is collapsing.

16:2 Similar to the sixth plague of Egypt (see Ex 9:8-11).

16:3-4 Similar to the first plague of Egypt (see Ex 7:20f).

16:10 Similar to the ninth plague of Egypt (see Ex 10:21-23).

16:13 *Frogs:* an allusion to the second plague of Egypt (see Ex 7:26—8:11).

16:15 This verse interrupts the text. It fits in better in the literary atmosphere of the letters to the Churches, especially Rev 3:3, 4, 18. *Blessed:* the third beatitude (see note on Rev 1:3).

16:16 *Armageddon:* i.e., the "mountain of Megiddo," the site of many battles in antiquity (see Jdg 5:19f; 2 Ki 9:27; 2 Chr 35:20-24); it symbolized the final defeat of the powers of evil.

17:1-18 *Harlot and mother of harlots.* Such is Babylon because it is the wellspring of idolatry, especially by imposing emperor worship; and for the people of the Bible an idol is an abomination, and idolatry is prostitution (Ezek, chs. 16 and 23). The woman on the beast is named Babylon, a name that stands for all oppressions and all sufferings; the real reference is to imperial Rome, the famous city on the seven hills (v. 9), the center of the great empire that has enslaved the peoples of the Mediterranean basin (vv. 1, 15). She will drink the blood of Christians, especially during the terrible persecutions of Nero and Domitian.

The beast that once was and now is not, but is returning—a parody of God who is described as "he who is, who was, and who is to come" (Rev 1:4)—is probably Nero (A.D. 54–68), whose resurrection was predicted in some popular legends. And if the seven kings need to be identified (vv. 9-11), the list is as follows: Augustus, Tiberius, Caligula, Claudius, Nero, Vespasian, and Titus (omitting Galba, Otho, and Vitellius, interim emperors, who ruled in quick succession in A.D. 68-69, after the death of Nero). The eighth emperor acts as people would expect Nero to act if he returned to life, i.e., as a beast; we can give him a name: Domitian (A.D. 81-96), during whose reign the Book of Revelation was probably composed. The other ten kings (v. 12) lead peoples subject to the empire. Empires and governors waste the political and cultural patrimony of Rome (v. 16): tyranny and bullying will be the cause of its destruction.

17:3 *In the spirit:* see note on Rev 1:10.

17:14 *Lord of lords and King of kings:* a title that stresses the Lamb's supreme sovereignty (see Deut 10:17; Ps 136:2-3; Dan 2:47; 1 Tim 6:15).

18:1-8 The fall of Rome is described as if the empire were already collapsing.

18:9-24 Drawing upon the laments of Ezekiel over the fall of Tyre (Ezek 26–28), the author greets the fall of Rome as already complete. This satire on the ruins of the empire also harbors, in its final lines, a tone of poignant complaint. The tableau nicely sketches the maritime grandeur of Rome, the development of commercial exchanges—without forgetting the traffic in slaves and prostitutes (v. 13)—and the extraordinary accumulation of riches.

18:24 *You:* the Greek has "her."

19:1-10 No other image could better evoke the fulfillment of all the expectations of believers than this vast heavenly liturgy and the vision of the wedding feast (see Mt 22:1-14; 25:1-13).

The plea of the martyrs (see Rev 6:9) has been heard; the immense throng, along with the twenty-four elders and the four living beings, makes up the entire Church, reunited at last. The Kingdom of God reveals itself in all its reality. It is described as Christ's marriage to the Church and as the complete manifestation of the Covenant, which is God's ardent, jealous love for his people (see Isa 54:1-8; Hos 2:16-18) and Christ's nuptial love for his Church (see Eph 5:23, 25, 32; see also Jn 3:29).

19:1, 3, 4, 6 *Alleluia:* an important exclamation of praise in the Psalms that is found only here in the New Testament. It is derived from two Hebrew words meaning "Praise the Lord."

19:9 *Blessed:* the fourth beatitude (see note on Rev 1:3).

19:10 *Witness to Jesus:* the proclamation that the predictions of the Prophets have been truly fulfilled.

19:11—20:15 There now follows a new series of six tableaus, which the imagination projects onto the destiny of the world. Is it necessary then to foresee a new series of events in an ever more distant future? And is the history of God's judgments something that is forever beginning again? The author has no intention of setting forth an indefinite series of calendars of the future. But before sketching the tableau of the new heaven and the new earth, he wishes one last time to interpret the drama of the world; for he has at hand other materials, some of which greatly resemble those that he has already used. He organizes them to compose this rapid sequence: a powerful summary of the whole History of Salvation. It begins with Jesus and takes us well beyond the fall of Rome to the resurrection of the dead and the last judgment—a kind of tragic prelude whose contrast heightens the dazzling joy that will later inform the grand symphony of the heavenly Jerusalem.

19:11-16 To describe the victory of Christ, the author uses the classic images of the warrior Messiah who establishes justice (Isa 11:4), annihilates hostile powers (Isa 63:3), subjects the nations (Ps 2:9), and traverses the world as the efficacious Word of God (see Wis 18:14-18). Through him justice reigns upon the world. He is the truthful and faithful one who fulfills God's promise and makes his justice a reality.

19:15 *Will tread the winepress:* the image was commonplace in the Prophets for symbolizing God's destruction of the enemies of his people on the great day of his wrath (see Gen 49:9-12; Isa 63:1-6; Jer 25:30; Joel 4:13); the wine is the blood of the enemies.

19:16 *Thigh:* this should probably be "standard"; the two words are quite similar in Hebrew and can be confused. *King of kings and Lord of lords:* see note on Rev 17:14.

19:17-18 In a final, gigantic combat, the forces of destruction will be annihilated (see Rev 14:6-13). This is the terrible sacrifice of which Ezekiel speaks (39:2, 17-20).

19:19-21 The beast and the false prophet are thrown into the fiery lake and destroyed. The vision sums up in a single scene all the tableaus of the fall of Rome, and corresponds to that in Rev 14:14-20. The beast, the false prophet, and the entire campaign aimed at imposing emperor worship are described in ch. 13.

20:1-3 The dragon is enchained for a thousand years in the abyss, the dwelling of the powers of evil (see Rev 9:2). This refers to Satan's defeat when Jesus died and rose from the dead. The thousand year period means "for a long time." Satan's power is limited (as if he is imprisoned for a long time). Yet he still tempts the holy ones on the earth during this period.

20:4-10 While waiting for the History of Salvation to be completed, the witnesses to Christ's love already reign with Jesus when they take up their crosses and follow Jesus. However, before the final triumph arrives—the great Judgment that one imagines must complete history—evil unleashes a last terrible assault on the Church, as envisaged by Ezekiel (chs. 36–39) and Paul (2 Thes 2). Then will be fulfilled the prophecy of Genesis (3:15) that in advance sketched the profound link of the drama of history and its end: the annihilation of the serpent, the personification of evil.

A reign of a thousand years? This passage has served as the basis of all the millenniarist interpretations, which await the coming of a political kingdom of Christ on earth. Must we at least imagine a first earthly accomplishment of the Kingdom of God before the final and eternal transformation? But the author does not speak of a return of Christ in earthly conditions. He wants to affirm above all that those who have died as witnesses of Jesus are not separated from him while awaiting the full resurrection (vv. 11-13); he also wishes to suggest that from now on believers have access to the tree of life in heaven—of which the figure "one thousand" may be a symbol—hence that they partake in the communion of God. In any case, the thousand-year reign is a symbolic representation, which thus prohibits all speculation. At best it evokes a length of time and a life of the Church beyond persecutions. But we must not forget that for God a thousand years are like one day (see Ps 90:4).

20:4 *A thousand years:* early tradition took this verse literally: after a first real resurrection, that of the martyrs, Christ would return to earth and reign there for a thousand years. The Church has rejected this literal millenniarism.

20:6 *Blessed:* the fifth beatitude (see note on Rev 1:3). *The second death:* eternal death, or damnation, which cannot be followed by a resurrection.

20:8 Ezekiel speaks of "Gog, king of Magog." Here the two names symbolize the pagan nations gathered together against the Church at the end of the world.

20:9 The *earth* is Palestine; the *beloved city* is Jerusalem, a symbol of the Church.

20:11 The earth and the sky disappear; the first creation is abolished. Human beings alone remain, responsible toward God.

20:12-15 This is a grandiose final sequence. As in Daniel (12:1-7) and Matthew (25:31-36), all human beings appear before the tribunal of God and are judged according to their choices and life commitments. (This principle of judgment according to one's works is also found in Ps 62:12; Jer 17:10; Rom 2:6; 1 Pet 1:17 and elsewhere.) Everything is laid bare before the Lord—the same idea expressed in the symbol of books in Daniel (7:10). There is another book—that of Life; it contains the names of those who have resolutely chosen Christ in the face of idolatry and are now destined for glory (see Rev 13:8; 17:8). When one knows all that is represented by the concept of the netherworld, the sojourn of death and the power of death personified in the Bible, verse 14 announces the end of the anguish and fear that have weighed heavily on humankind throughout history.

20:14 *The second death,* in which death itself is swallowed up, is the definitive failure, the condemnation from which no resurrection can rescue (Rev 2:11; 20:6; 21:8).

21:1—22:5 A new city for human beings descends from heaven, as beautiful as a new bride; a new universe replaces the old; life gushes up in floods, and an endless feast begins. How can we interpret these marvelous images? We must let ourselves be captivated by the poetic evocation, by the incantation of this exciting symphony. We must project all the attention of people and the Church toward this meeting and this reconciliation, which we regard as the sole definitive condition for humankind—creating a mystical impetus toward Christ, a hope without frontiers.

Let us then strive to highlight some themes that this vision overlaps on one another. At the end of the work of salvation, it is a new creation that God accomplishes (v. 1), surpassing all the images of paradise. Gone are all things that constrained, all limits, imperfections, implacable necessities, evil: the sea, the sun and moon, and the night. Streams spring forth more attractive than those of Eden, for they are a share in the unfathomable life of God; the tree of life finds its power multiplied to infinity (Rev 22:2).

For human beings, this work of salvation is essentially the gathering of the People of God for a definitive Covenant with the Lord. It is presented as a wedding feast in which is realized—in unimaginable fullness—the love of God and human beings, of Christ and the Church, which in keeping with beautiful Biblical texts is expressed as a wedding (see Isa 54:5; 62:4; Mt 9:15; Jn 3:29; 2 Cor 11:2; Rev 19:1-10).

Dreams of the restoration of Jerusalem haunted the Jewish people, and the Prophets wrote about its spectacular resurrection like an image of the coming of God and the salvation of the people (see Ezek 40–48; Isa 65–66; Zec 14); the chant of Jerusalem is a crown-jewel in the Bible (see Pss 87; 122; 137; Isa 33:17-23). One day this movement finds its accomplishment far beyond all warrior or political images. We can think of inexpressible repatriation of human beings in the friendship of God, joy, and happiness. The future city of God's elect is no longer built up by force of arms—it is a gift and grace coming from on high; it is nothing less than splendor (Rev 21:15-21).

There is no more need of institutions and signs for worship—the temple itself is surpassed: the risen Jesus is the sole place where may be found the joy of really and directly encountering God (see Heb 9:11; Jn 2:21). What extraordinary and joyous celebration in the eternal face-to-face vision of the Lord!

21:1 The sea, the usual dwelling of the dragon and a symbol of evil, will disappear before the victorious march of the new Israel, as it did in the days of the Exodus, but this time for good.

21:3 This verse contains a combination of the classic formula of the Covenant ("You will be my people, and I will be your God") and the name Immanuel ("God-with-us"), which was regarded as a name of the Messiah (Mt 1:28)—a fine assertion of the divinity of Christ, who is God and man. The complete and definitive Covenant between God and humankind will be accomplished at the end of time (see Isa 12:6; Joel 4:17, 21; Zep 3:15-17; Zec 2:14).

21:6 *Alpha, Omega, Beginning, End:* on these divine titles see note on Rev 1:4-8. *Spring of life-giving water:* see note on Rev 7:17.

21:7 *He will be my son:* this expression is reserved in the Old Testament for the King Messiah (2 Sam 7:14). Jesus reveals its full meaning by proclaiming his own divine sonship. Believers now share in this state of Christ.

21:8 *Second death:* see note on Rev 20:6.

21:10 *In the spirit:* see note on Rev 1:10.

21:12 *Twelve gates:* see Ezek 48:30-35. The number twelve here most likely stresses that the Church of the New Testament is a continuation of the People of God of the Old Testament. See v. 14, in which the twelve foundation stones bear the names of the twelve apostles.

21:15 *Measure the city:* see Ezek 40—41. The measuring in Rev 11 was to ensure protection; here it is done to indicate the size and symmetry of the eternal dwelling place of God's people.

21:16 *Fifteen hundred miles:* literally, "twelve hundred stadia," about twelve thousand furlongs. In the mind of the ancients the square was the perfect form. When the number twelve, which symbolizes the new Israel, is multiplied by 1000, it signifies supreme perfection. The city possesses the symmetrical dimensions of a perfect cube, which is akin to its earthly counterpart, the inner sanctuary in the tabernacle and temple (see 1 Ki 6:20).

21:17 *One hundred and forty-four cubits:* a cubit measured about eighteen inches in length.

21:18-20 The materials used show that this is not an earthly city. The twelve foundation stones of the wall are decorated with twelve precious stones, which correspond to the twelve stones on the high priest's breastplate (see Ex 28:39). The gems form a magnificent kaleidoscope of colors symbolizing the ineffable glory of God.

21:24ff The author is alluding to Isa 60:1-20, which foretells the entrance of the nations into the People of God. The open gates are a sign of an everlasting feast.

21:27 *Book of life:* see notes on Rev 3:5 and 20:12-15.

22:1 An allusion to the Trinity, since "the river of the water of life" symbolizes the Spirit (see Jn 7:37-39). See also note on Rev 7:17.

22:2 *Tree of life:* see Gen 2:9; 3:22; Ezek 47:12.

22:4 *See his face:* no human could see God's face and live (Ex 33:20-23). This was in keeping with the custom in ancient times whereby criminals were banished from the king's presence (see Est 7:8; see also 2 Sam 14:24). However, the residents of heaven will look on God without harm because they are now holy (see Mt 5:8; Jn 1:18; 1 Cor 13:12; 1 Tim 6:16; 1 Jn 3:2).

22:5 *They will reign:* see Rev 5:10; 20:6; Dan 7:18, 27.

22:6-21 The Epilogue is a series of disparate propositions in which we find: statements of Christ and John that authenticate the Book (vv. 6-9, 16); a notification from Christ about the coming fulfillment of the prophecy (vv. 10-15); a warning from Christ to falsifiers of the Scripture (vv. 18-19); the word of Christ's promise and the word of the Christians' faith (v. 20); and the epistolary greeting (v. 21).

These serve to exhort the readers to take this whole revelation seriously. They should realize that they are living at the decisive moment and so fix their attention on the Lord who is coming!

22:7 *I am coming soon:* the speaker is Christ. *Blessing:* the sixth beatitude (see note on Rev 1:3).

22:10-15 The history of humankind continues up to the return of Christ. We must take his part and be polarized by the idea of a definitive lot, by the expectation of Life and Light, by the joyous certitude of the Elect. The author draws here on Ps 62:13 and Isa 40:10; 41:4; 44:6.

22:14 *Blessed:* the seventh beatitude (see note on Rev 1:3).

22:15 *Dogs:* they were regarded as despicable creatures; when the term was applied to people it referred to all types of ceremonially unclean persons and also to people of low moral character: e.g., male prostitutes (Deut 23:18) and unfaithful leaders (Isa 56:10).

22:16-21 At its beginning, the Book of Revelation took the form of a letter (Rev 1:4). Now it ends with the classic salutation of a letter—but a salutation preceded by a threat to forgers, who would otherwise be at ease in the exploitation of apocalyptic writings.

22:16 *The Root and the Offspring of David:* see note on Rev 5:5; see also Isa 11:1, 10; Rom 1:3. *The bright Morning Star:* a beautiful title for Christ, already used in Rev 2:28 to signify his power.

22:20 *Come, Lord Jesus!:* this is the ardent plea of those who, in the midst of persecutions and trials, await the return of Christ (see note on 1 Cor 16:22). The Church should ceaselessly strive to recover this fervent expectation for the one in whom she has placed her faith, her hope, and her love, the one from whom she awaits all things.

The New Testament is not a book that one can close upon itself. It is the charter of the Covenant, the Good News from which one must live. It remains open toward its fulfillment: on the last page we have the beautiful and ancient liturgical prayer of Christians: "Come, Lord Jesus!"

ANALYTICAL INDEX

Abandonment to God: Mt 2:11; 4:10; 28:17; Lk 4:8.

Absolution: the power promised and given to the pastors of the Church, Mt 16:19; 18:18; Jn 20:22f.

Affliction: benefits of, Jn 15:2; Acts 14:22; Rom 5:3; 2 Cor 4:8; 12:7; Phil 1:12; Heb 12:11; 1 Pet 2:20; comfort under, Mt 5:4ff; 11:28; Jn 16:20, 33; 2 Cor 1:4; 7:6; Heb 2:18; 1 Pet 4:13; Rev 3:10; joy in, Mt 5:12; Acts 5:41; Rom 5:3; 2 Cor 7:4.

Almsgiving: Mt 6:3; 10:42; 19:21; 25:35, 42; Lk 3:11; 6:35; 11:41; 12:33; 14:13.

Anger: Mt 5:22; Eph 4:26; Jas 1:19f.

Anxiety: to cast it upon God, Mt 6:25; Lk 12:22ff; Phil 4:6; 1 Pet 5:7.

Apostles: Mt 10:18, 19; Mk 16:15; Lk 6:13; 24:46; Jn 15:16, 27; 20:21; Acts 1:8; 10:42.

Apostolical Traditions: 1 Cor 11:2; 2 Thes 2:15; 3:6; 2 Tim 1:13; 2:2.

Armor of God: Rom 13:12; 2 Cor 6:7; Eph 6:10-17; 1 Thes 5:8.

Avarice: Lk 12:15-21; 1 Cor 5:11; 6:9f; Eph 5:3, 5; Col 3:5; 1 Tim 6:9; Heb 13:5; 2 Pet 2:3.

Beatitudes: Mt 5:3-11; Lk 6:20-23.

Brotherly Correction: Mt 18:15-17; Lk 17:3; 1 Tim 5:20; Jas 5:19f.

Brotherly Love: Jn 13:33-35; 15:9-14; Rom 13:8-10; Gal 5:13-15; Eph 5:1f; 1 Jn 3:14 16; 4:7-21.

Charity: the greatest of gifts, Mt 22:34ff; 1 Cor 13; Phil 1:9; 2 Jn 4.

Chastity: Mt 5:8, 27-32; Rom 12:1; 1 Cor 3:16f; 6:15-20; 7:7f, 25f; Gal 5:16f, 23f; 1 Thes 4:3-8; Tit 1:15; 1 Pet 2:11; Rev 14:1-5.

Christ: Son of God, Mt 3:17; 4:3; 14:33; 16:16; Mk 1:1; Lk 1:32; Jn 1:34; 10:36; Rom 1:3; equal to the Father, Jn 5:18f, 23; 10:30; 14:1, 9; 16:14f; 17:10; Phil 2:5f, died for all, Jn 3:16f; Rom 5:18; 2 Cor 5:14f; 1 Tim 2:3-6; rose from the dead, Mt 12:39f; 28:6; Acts 1:22; 2:24;

1 Cor 15:4, 14; will come to judge all people, Mt 19:28; 24:30-51; 25:31-46; Jn 5:22; eternal priest, Heb 7:24; mediator of new covenant, Heb 9:15; head of Church, Col 1:18.

Church: of God, 1 Cor 1:2, 10, 32; 11:22; 1 Thes 1:4; 1 Tim 3:5, 15; and of Christ, Mt 16:18; Acts 20:28; body of Christ, 1 Cor 12:12f, 27; Rom 12:5; Eph 1:22f; pillar of truth, Mt 16:10; 28:20; Jn 14; 16; membership in, Mt 4:17; 18:3; Mk 12:28; Lk 13:24; 18:17; Jn 3:3.

Commandments: Mt 22:36-40; Mk 12:28-31; Lk 10:27; must be obeyed, Mt 5:21f; 19:17-19; Mk 10:19; Lk 18:20; Jn 15:10.

Confession of Sins: Mt 3:6; Acts 19:18; Jas 5:16.

Confidence in God: Mt 10:29-33; Lk 12:32; Jn 14:1; 16:33.

Contrition: Mt 3:2; 4:17; Lk 13:3; 24:47; Acts 2:38; 3:19.

Conversion: Lk 15:11-32; 23:40-43; Jas 5:19f; 1 Pet 2:25.

Despair: remedy for, Lk 18:1; 2 Cor 4:8f; Gal 6:9; Heb 12:2f.

Detraction: Rom 1:30; 2 Cor 12:20; 1 Pet 2:1; Jas 4:11.

Envy: Mt 27:18; Phil 1:15.

Eucharist: real presence of the body and blood of Christ, Mt 26:26-28; Mk 14:22-24; Lk 22:19f; Jn 6:51f; 1 Cor 10:16; 11:24f; 27:29.

Faith: necessary to salvation, Mk 16:16; Acts 2:44-47; 4:12; Heb 11:6; efficacy, Mt 17:20, 21:21; Mk 16:17f; Jn 7:38; 14:12; Rom 1:16; Eph 6:16; profession, Mt 10:32; Mk 8:38; Lk 9:26; Rom 10:19ff.

Fear of God: Mt 10:28; Lk 1:50; 12:5; Rom 11:20; 2 Cor 7:1; Eph 6:5; Phil 2:12; Col 3:22; Heb 4:1.

Fidelity to God: Mt 24:45f; 25:21, 23; Lk 12:42-46; 1 Cor 4:2.

Fraud: condemned: Mk 7:21f; Acts 5:2; Rom 1:29.

911

Freedom: in Christ, Gal 4:31; 5:1; Jas 1:25; 2:12; 1 Pet 2:16.

Glory: of God, to be sought in all things, Mt 6:9; Jn 17:4; Acts 3:13; 1 Cor 6:20; Phil 1:20; Col 3:17.

Gluttony: Heb 12:16f.

God: almighty power of, Mt 19:26; Mk 10:27; 14:36; Lk 1:37; fidelity, justice, and mercy of, Jn 3:16; knowledge of, natural, Rom 1:19ff; 1 Cor 1:21; supernatural, 1 Cor 13:12; 1 Tim 2:4f; Heb 6:4ff; 1 Jn 2:13ff; love of—toward people, Mt 5:45; Jn 3:16; Rom 5:8; 1 Jn 3:16; 4:19ff; providence of, Mt 5:45; Lk 12:6f; Jn 5:17; Acts 17:26-28; 1 Cor 9:9; Col 1:17; 1 Tim 6:13; Heb 1:3; worship of, Mt 4:10; Lk 4:8; Jn 4:22-24; Rev 4:10; 5:14.

Good Works: Mt 5:11f; 10:42; 16:27; 1 Cor 3:8; 2 Tim 4:8.

Grace: Lk 1:28; 2:40; Jn 1:16; Rom 1:7; 1 Cor 16:23; 2 Cor 1:12; Gal 5:4f; Heb 13:9; Jas 4:6.

Gratitude: Acts 4:21; Eph 5:19f; Phil 4:6; Col 2:7; 3:15.

Happiness: condition for, Mt 5:1-12; Lk 11:28; Jn 13:17; Rom 4:7f.

Hatred: condemned, Mt 5:23ff, 43; Tit 3:3; 1 Jn 2:9-11; 3:14f; 4:20.

Heaven: Mt 5:12; 13:43; Jn 12:26; 14:3; 1 Cor 13:12; Rev 7:16.

Hell: Mt 8:12; 25:41; Lk 13:28.

Holy Scripture: Mt 4:4; 2 Tim 3:16f; 2 Pet 1:21.

Holy Spirit: his divinity, Acts 5:3f; 28:25f; 1 Cor 2:10f; 6:11, 19f; his works, Jn 3:3-8; 6:63; 14:16f, 26; 16:12-14; Acts 13:2, 4; Rom 5:5; 8:14, 26; Gal 5:18; Eph 6:18.

Hope: Acts 24:15; Rom 5:5; 15:13; 2 Cor 3:12; 1 Tim 4:10; Heb 3:6.

Hospitality: Rom 12:13; Tit 1:8; Heb 13:2; 1 Pet 4:9.

Humility: agreeable to God, Mt 3:11; Mk 9:34; Jn 13:4f; Acts 10:25; Rom 11:20; 12:16; 1 Cor 4:6; Phil 2:3; Col 3:12; Heb 11:24-26; 1 Pet 5:5; Jas 1:9; 4:10; Rev 4:10f; 19:10.

Hypocrisy: Mt 6:5; 7:5; 23:28; 24:51; Mk 12:15; Lk 12:1-3; 1 Tim 4:2; 1 Pet 2:1; Rev 3:1.

Ingratitude: Lk 17:17ff; Rom 1:21.

Inheritance: in Christ, Eph 1:11, 14; Col 1:12; 3:24; 1 Pet 1:4.

Injustice: Mt 23:14; Lk 16:11ff; 1 Cor 6:9; 2 Pet 2:9, 16.

Joy: Mt 2:10; Lk 15:7, 10; Jn 15:11; 16:20ff; Acts 2:46; Rom 14:17; 2 Cor 8:2; Jas 1:2ff.

Kingdom of God: Mt 6:10; Lk 11:2; Acts 1:3.

Life: value of, Mt 6:25-34; Lk 12:19-31; Jas 1:10; 4:15; 1 Pet 1:24; purpose of, Mt 5:48; Eph 1:4; 1 Thes 4:3ff; Tit 2:11ff; eternal, Mt 5:12; 19:29; 25:46; Jn 3:16; 5:24; 10:28; 17:3; Rom 2:7; 6:23; 1 Tim 1:16; Heb 13:14; Jas 1:12; 1 Jn 1:2; 2:25; Jude 21; Rev 2:7; 21:6; spiritual, Rom 6:4, 8; Gal 2:20; Eph 2:1ff; Col 3:3; 1 Jn 1:1-4; 1 Pet 4:1-6.

Love of God: motive for, Mt 22:37; Mk 12:30; Lk 10:27; Jn 3:16; 15:12ff; Rom 5:8f; 8:32-35; Gal 2:20; 1 Jn 3:16; 4:7ff; characteristic of, Jn 14:15-21, 24; 21:14-17; Rom 8:35-39; 1 Cor 16:22; Eph 5:2; 1 Jn 2:5; 3:16; 4:20; 2 Jn 6.

Lying: Jn 8:44; Acts 5:2ff; Eph 4:25; Col 3:9; Jas 3:14; Rev 21:8, 27.

Mary: Mt 1:18-25; Lk 1:26-38; mother of Jesus, Lk 2:6f; in the temple, Lk 2:22f; in Egypt, Mt 2:13-15; at Nazareth, Mt 2:23; Lk 2:39; loses Jesus, Lk 2:41-52; at Cana, Jn 2:1ff; during the public ministry, Mt 12:46-50; Mk 3:31-35; 6:3; Lk 8:19-21; at the foot of the cross, Jn 19:25-27; remains with apostles, Acts 1:14.

Meekness: exhortation to, Mt 11:29; Gal 6:1; Eph 4:2; Col 3:12; 1 Tim 6:11; Tit 3:2; Jas 1:21; 1 Pet 3:15ff; reward for, Mt 5:4; 11:29.

Morals: Rom 12; 13; 14; 15; Col 3; 4:1-6; 1 Thes 4:1-12.

Mortification of Flesh: Rom 6:12ff; 13:14; 2 Cor 4:10; Gal 5:24; Col 3:5; 1 Pet 4:1ff.

Murmuring against God: Phil 2:14; Jude 16.

Obedience: to God, Mt 7:24ff; Jn 4:34; 5:30; 6:38; 14:31; Acts 4:18ff; 5:29; Rom 1:5; 15:18ff; Phil 2:8ff; Heb 5:8ff; 11:8; 1 Pet 1:22; 1 Jn 3:24; to the Church, Mt 18:17; Heb 13:17; to the State, Mt 22:21; Rom 13:1-7; Tit 3:1; 1 Pet 2:13-17.

Patience: Rom 12:12; Eph 4:2; Col 3:12; Jas 3:17; 5:7, 8, 10.

Peace: of God, Rom 1:7; 2 Cor 1:2; Phil 4:7; of Christ, Lk 7:50; 8:48; Jn 14:27; Rom 5:1; 1 Cor 1:3; Gal 1:3; 2 Thes 3:16; peace with God, Acts 10:34-36; Rom 5:1; 2 Cor 5:18-20; Eph 2:12-18.

Perfection: striving for, Mt 5:48; 19:21; Rom 12:2; 1 Cor 15:58; 2 Cor 7:1; 13:11; Eph 4:15, 23ff; Phil 1:9-11; 3:12; 1 Thes 4:1-7; 5:23; 2 Tim 3:16; Heb 12:14; 1 Pet 1:13-16.

Persecution: Mt 5:10-12; Rom 8:35; 1 Cor 4:12; 2 Cor 4:9; 12:10; foretold, Mt 10:17; 23:34; 24:9; Mk 10:30; Lk 11:49; Jn 15:20.

Perseverance: exhortations to, Mt 10:22; 24:13; Lk 9:62; Acts 13:43; 1 Cor 15:58; Eph 6:18; Heb 3:6, 13; 10:23, 28; 2 Pet 3:17; rewarded, Lk 8:15; Rom 2:7; Heb 6:15; Jas 1:25.

Piety: 1 Tim 4:7ff; 6:5ff; 2 Tim 3:12; Jas 1:26f.

Poor: care of, Acts 6:1-3; 2 Cor 8:2-15; Gal 2:10; 1 Tim 5:16.

Prayer: Mt 6:5-13; 7:7-11; 18:19f; Mk 14:24-26; Lk 11:2-13; 18:1; Jn 14:13f; 15:7; 16:23f; Rom 8:26f; Eph 6:18; Phil 4:6; Col 4:2; 1 Thes 5:17; 1 Tim 2:1-3; Jas 4:3; 5:16-18; 1 Jn 3:22; 5:14f; the Lord's, Mt 6:9, 13; Lk 11:24.

Presumption: Jas 4:13, 16.

Pride: Mt 23:12; Lk 1:51f; 18:9-14; Gal 6:3; Jas 4:6, 16; 1 Pet 5:5.

Prudence: Mt 24:45; 25:13; 26:41; Lk 12:35; 21:36; 1 Cor 10:12; 1 Thes 5:6; 2 Tim 4:5; 1 Pet 4:7; 5:8.

Repentance: exhortations to, Mt 3:3; 4:17; Rev 2:5, 16, 21; 3:3, 19.

Resurrection of the Dead: Mt 22:30-32; Mk 12:26ff; Lk 20:37ff; Jn 5:28ff; 6:39; 11:24; Acts 17:18, 31f; 23:6; 24:15; 26:8; Rom 8:11; 1 Cor 6:14; 15:12-22; 2 Cor 1:9; 4:14.

Riches: perils of, Mt 6:24; 19:23-26; Mk 10:23-27; Lk 6:24; 12:16-21; 16:13; 18:24-27; 1 Tim 6:9ff; Jas 5:16; duties of, 1 Tim 6:17; Jas 1:10.

Sacraments (Institution and Administration): Anointing of the Sick, Jas 5:14f; Baptism, Mt 28:19; Mk 16:16; Confirmation, Acts 8:14-17; 19:1-6; Eph 1:13f; Heb 6:2-4; Penance, Mt 16:19; 18:18, Jn 20:22f; Holy Eucharist, Mt 26:17-29; Mk 14:12-25; Lk 22:7-23; 1 Cor 11:23-26; Holy Orders, Lk 22:19; Jn 20:22; Acts 6:6; 1 Cor 11:24f; Col 4:17; 1 Tim 5:22; 2 Tim 1:6f; 1 Pet 2:9; Matrimony, Mt 19:4-6; Eph 5:22-33; Col 3:18; 1 Pet 3:1.

Self-denial: Mt 16:24; Mk 8:34; Lk 9:23; 14:26; Jn 12:25; 1 Cor 9:25-27; Gal 5:24.

Sinner: prayer of, for pardon, Mt 8:2; Lk 15:17-19; 18:13.

Temptation: origin of, Mt 4:1-11; Lk 22:31ff; Jn 13:2; Acts 5:3; Rom 7:22ff; 2 Cor 12:7-9; Eph 6:11-17; 1 Thes 3:5; Jas 1:13ff; 1 Pet 5:8ff; value of, Jas 1; 2; 4; 1 Pet 1:6.

Unbelief: Lk 16:27-31; Jn 3:19ff; 5:44-47; 8:42-47; 10:24-26; 12:37-40; Acts 13:45ff; 1 Tim 1:13.

Watchfulness: Mt 24:42-44; 25:1-13; Mk 13:33-37; Lk 12:35-40; 21:34-36; 1 Cor 16:13; 1 Thes 5:6; 2 Tim 4:5; 1 Pet 4:7; 5:8.

Worship: to be offered to God alone, Mt 4:10; Lk 4:8; Acts 10:26; manner of offering, Jn 4:23f; Eph 5:19; Col 3:16.

THE SUNDAY GOSPELS (3-Year Cycle)

Year A

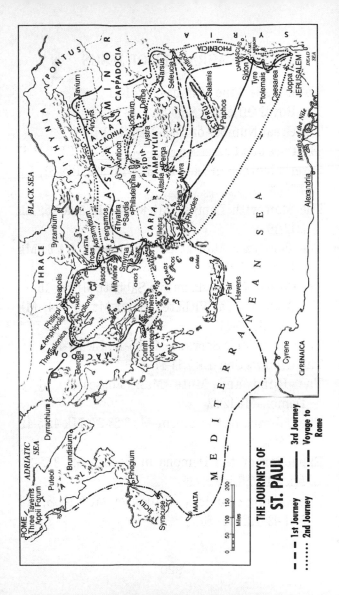

THE JOURNEYS OF
ST. PAUL

- - - 1st Journey
.... 2nd Journey
———— 3rd Journey
–··– Voyage to
       Rome

THE MIRACLES OF JESUS

Water Made Wine at Cana–Jn 2:1-11

The Royal Official's Son–Jn 4:46-54

The Great Number of Fish–Lk 5:1-11

The Cure of a Possessed Man–Mk 1:23-28; Lk 4:33-37

Peter's Mother-in-Law–Mt 8:14-15; Mk 1:29-31; Lk 4:38-39

The Man with Leprosy–Mt 8:1-4; Mk 1:40-45; Lk 5:12-16

The Paralyzed Man at Capernaum–Mt 9:1-8; Mk 2:1-12; Lk 5:18-26

The Cure at Bethesda on the Sabbath–Jn 5:1-15

The Man with a Withered Hand–Mt 12:9-14; Mk 3:1-6; Lk 6:6-11

The Centurion's Servant–Mt 8:5-13; Lk 7:1-10

The Widow's Son–Lk 7:11-17

The Blind and Mute Man Possessed by a Demon–Mt 12:22

The Calming of the Storm–Mt 8:23-27; Mk 4:35-41; Lk 8:22-25

Expulsion of the Demons in Gadara–Mt 8:29-34; Mk 5:1-20; Lk 8:26-39

The Raising of Jairus's Daughter–Mt 9:18-26; Mk 5:21-43; Lk 8:40-56

The Woman Suffering from Bleeding–Mt 9:20-22; Mk 5:25-34; Lk 8:43-48

Two Blind Men–Mt 9:27-31

The Mute Demoniac–Mt 9:32-34

Five Thousand Fed–Mt 14:13-21; Mk 6:35-44; Lk 9:12-17; Jn 6:1-15

Jesus Walks on the Water–Mt 14:22-33; Mk 6:45-52; Jn 6:16-21

The Faith of a Gentile Woman–Mt 15:21-28; Mk 7:24-30

Healing of a Deaf Man with a Speech Impediment–Mk 7:31-37

Four Thousand Fed–Mt 15:32-38; Mk 8:1-9

The Blind Man at Bethsaida–Mk 8:22

A Possessed Boy–Mt 17:14-21; Mk 9:14-29; Lk 9:37-43

Jesus Pays the Temple Tax–Mt 17:24-27

The Man Born Blind Jn 9:1-38

The Lame, Blind, Deformed, and Mute–Mt 15:29-31

A Woman Healed on the Sabbath–Lk 13:10-17

The Raising of Lazarus–Jn 11:1-44

The Man with the Dropsy–Lk 14:1-6

Ten Men with Leprosy–Lk 17:11-19

The Blind at Jericho–Mt 20:29-34; Mk 10:46-52; Lk 18:35-43

Jesus Curses a Fig Tree–Mt 21:18-22; Mk 11:12-14

Jesus Heals the Servant's Ear–Lk 22:49-51

The Great Catch of Fish–Jn 21:1-14

THE PRINCIPAL PARABLES OF JESUS

The Indecisive Children–Mt 11:16-19; Lk 7:31-35

The Two Debtors–Lk 7:41-42

The Fig Tree–Mt 24:32-35; Mk 13:28f; Lk 21:29-31

The Barren Fig Tree–Lk 13:6-9

The Importunate Widow–Lk 18:1-8

A Divided Kingdom–Mt 12:25-27; Mk 3:23-26; Lk 11:17f

The Workers in the Vineyard–Mt 20:1-16

The Unmerciful Servant–Mt: 18:21-35

The Mustard Seed and the Yeast–Mt 13:31f; Mk 4:30-32; Lk 13:18f

The Net–Mt 13:47-50

The Pharisee and the Tax Collector–Lk 18:9-14

The Rich Man and Lazarus–Lk 16:19-31

The Rich Fool–Lk 12:16-21

The Good Samaritan–Lk 10:29-37

The Ambitious Guest–Lk 14:7-14

The Sower–Mt 13:3-23; Mk 4:3-20; Lk 8:4-15

The Secretly Growing Seed–Mk 4:26-29

The Faithful Servant–Mt 24:45-51; Lk 12:42-48

The Unprofitable Servants–Lk 17:7-10

The Lost Sheep–Mt 18:12-14; Lk 15:3-7

The Good Shepherd–Jn 10:1-21

The Talents–Mt 25:14-30

The Lost (or Prodigal) Son–Lk 15:11-32

The Two Sons–Mt 21:28-32

The Ten Gold Coins–Lk 19:11-27

The Tenants–Mt 21:33-46; Mk 12:1-12; Lk 20:9-19

The Hidden Treasure and the Pearl–Mt 13:44-46

The Owner of the House–Mt 24:43f; Lk 12:39f

Union with Jesus–Jn 15:1-17

The Wedding Banquet/The Great Supper–Mt 22:1-14;
   Lk 14:16-24

The Weeds–Mt 13:24-30

The Crafty Steward–Lk 16:1-13

ST. JOSEPH ATLAS OF THE BIBLE

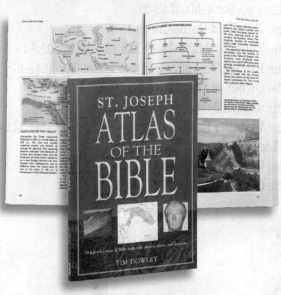

A completely new Bible Atlas for the Bible reader and student, with 79 full-color computer-generated original maps of Bible lands. The maps are carefully annotated to show the routes of the great travelers such as Abraham, Moses, and Paul, major battles, migrations, and invasions.

Richly illustrated throughout with full-color photographs, charts, and diagrams, with the text retelling clearly the story of God's people from the call of Abraham to the early spread of the Christian Church. 96 pages. Size 6¹/₂ x 9.

655/04—ISBN 978-0-89942-655-6

ST. JOSEPH BIBLE RESOURCES

In a concise and accessible format, this series provides essential Bible information for use in schools, in Bible study groups, or for the individual inquirer. 32 pages each. Size 6½ x 9.

BIBLE ATLAS—654/04 ISBN 978-0-89942-654-9

BIBLE FACTS AND FIGURES—653/04
ISBN 978-0-89942-653-2

NEW TESTAMENT INTRODUCTION—652/04
ISBN 978-0-89942-652-5

OLD TESTAMENT INTRODUCTION—651/04
ISBN 978-0-89942-656-3

THE WORLD OF THE BIBLE—662/04
ISBN 978-1-937913-76-2

PEOPLE OF THE BIBLE—663/04
ISBN 978-1-937913-77-9

BIBLE MEDITATIONS FOR EVERY DAY

This book gives a Bible passage for every day of the year. Each passage is introduced by an introduction which conditions the reader's mind and heart for accepting the Divine message. 384 pages. Size 5½ x 8¼.

277/04—Flexible cover ISBN 978-0-89942-277-0

THE GOSPELS SIMPLY EXPLAINED

Rev. Jude Winkler, OFM Conv.

Energize and enhance your personal or group Bible study as you learn the cultural and theological underpinnings of Matthew, Mark, Luke, and John. 208 pages. Size 5½ x 8¼.

668/04—Flexible cover ISBN 978-0-89942-714-0

ST. JOSEPH GUIDE TO THE BIBLE

Karl A. Schultz

This small volume will help readers select a Bible, develop a reading plan, practice *Lectio Divina* and begin to interpret the Bible with competence and confidence. 144 pages. Size 5 x 7.

656/04—Flexible cover ISBN 978-0-89942-657-0

ST. JOSEPH CONCISE BIBLE HISTORY

The ideal way for all Catholics to become acquainted with the history of God's Chosen People. It offers an excellent summary of Bible history from Creation to our Lord's life, death, and resurrection and on to the birth of the Church. Illustrated. 160 pages. Size 5½ x 8.

770/04—Flexible cover ISBN 978-0-89942-770-6

BIBLE DAY BY DAY

Rev. John C. Kersten, S.V.D.

Minute Bible meditations including a short Scripture text and brief reflection. Printed in two colors with 300 illustrations. 192 pages. Size 4 x 6¼.

150/19—Dura-Lux cover ISBN 978-1-937913-46-5